THE OXFORD HANDBOOK OF

DEVELOPMENTAL AND LIFE-COURSE CRIMINOLOGY

THE OXFORD HANDBOOKS IN CRIMINOLOGY AND CRIMINAL JUSTICE

GENERAL EDITOR: MICHAEL TONRY

The Oxford Handbooks in Criminology and Criminal Justice offer authoritative, comprehensive, and critical overviews of the state of the art of criminology and criminal justice. Each volume focuses on a major area of each discipline, is edited by a distinguished group of specialists, and contains specially commissioned, original essays from leading international scholars in their respective fields. Guided by the general editorship of Michael Tonry, the series will provide an invaluable reference for scholars, students, and policy makers seeking to understand a wide range of research and policies in criminology and criminal justice.

OTHER TITLES IN THIS SERIES

THE OXFORD HANDBOOK OF PRISONS AND IMPRISONMENT
John Wooldredge and Paula Smith

THE OXFORD HANDBOOK OF ENVIRONMENTAL CRIMINOLOGY
Gerben J.N. Bruinsma and Shane D. Johnson

OFFENDER DECISION MAKING
Wim Bernasco, Jean-Louis van Gelder, and Henk Elffers

SEX OFFENCES AND SEX OFFENDERS
Teela Sanders

THE HISTORY OF CRIME AND CRIMINAL JUSTICE
Paul Knepper and Anja Johansen

WHITE-COLLAR CRIME
Shanna R. Van Slyke, Michael L. Benson, and Francis T. Cullen

ORGANIZED CRIME
Letizia Paoli

CRIMINOLOGICAL THEORY
Francis T. Cullen and Pamela Wilcox

THE OXFORD HANDBOOK OF

DEVELOPMENTAL AND LIFE-COURSE CRIMINOLOGY

Edited by

DAVID P. FARRINGTON
LILA KAZEMIAN
ALEX R. PIQUERO

OXFORD
UNIVERSITY PRESS

Library of Congress Cataloging-in-Publication Data
Names: Farrington, David P., editor. | Kazemian, Lila, 1978– editor. | Piquero, Alexis Russell, editor.
Title: The Oxford handbook of developmental and life-course criminology /
edited by David P. Farrington, Lila Kazemian, Alex R. Piquero.
Description: New York : Oxford University Press, [2019] |
Includes bibliographical references and index.
Identifiers: LCCN 2017054211 | ISBN 9780190201371 (bb : alk. paper) |
ISBN9780190214388 (updf) | ISBN 9780190884895 (epub) |
ISBN 9780190201388 (online component)
Subjects: LCSH: Criminal psychology. | Developmental psychology.
Classification: LCC HV6080.O98 2018 | DDC 364.3—dc23
LC record available at https://lccn.loc.gov/2017054211

Contents

SECTION I INTRODUCTION

SECTION II THE DEVELOPMENT OF OFFENDING

SECTION III DEVELOPMENTAL AND LIFE-COURSE THEORIES

SECTION IV DEVELOPMENTAL CORRELATES AND RISK/PROTECTIVE FACTORS

SECTION V LIFE TRANSITIONS AND TURNING POINTS

SECTION VI DEVELOPMENTAL INTERVENTIONS

SECTION VII CONCLUSIONS

FOREWORD

THE Oxford Handbook series, under the general and able editorship of Michael Tonry, consists of one impressive volume after another. The individual works in the series differ in their substantive content, but they are special because they fulfill three core functions of the scholarly form of "the handbook": they serve as a comprehensive resource, allow for the organization of knowledge, and establish the existence of a coherent field within criminology. The current contribution is no exception in addressing these concerns.

First, I am fortunate to have several *Oxford Handbooks*, which I keep close at hand in my home office. I find myself reaching often to pull them off the shelf and consult them. They are a ready and important resource as I write, prepare lectures, or wish to clarify my thinking on a point either forgotten or never quite learned. In this regard, David Farrington, Lila Kazemian, and Alex Piquero have used their wisdom to create an invaluable resource. They have done a masterful job in recruiting a roster of knowledgeable scholars to write chapters on virtually every aspect of developmental and life-course criminology. As I commented previously about another of David's works, this volume is a "criminological Walmart," containing under one cover almost everything anyone might need to know about crime across the life course! Indeed, I have been given advance copies of the chapters, and I am already plotting how I will put many of them to use.

Second, recent years have seen the proliferation of criminological handbooks and encyclopedias—a clear sign that they are profitable for publishing houses. In this instance, capitalism is working in a good direction by financing the organization of knowledge. Admittedly, some of these enterprises are of uneven quality. But this is a small price to pay for the production of volumes that bring together knowledge into a form that is accessible to all scholars—from the specialist writing an article to the generalist seeking to learn a new area or perhaps make up a lecture.

As with other scientific fields, criminology is designed to reward with status and employment the publication of the peer-reviewed research article. This reward structure is beneficial in that the creation of new knowledge is essential to the growth of our discipline. But the embrace of the research article should not be pushed too far and become a fetish. Too often, unless accomplished in the form of a meta-analysis, efforts to organize knowledge, such as in handbooks, are seen as the "mere" summary of "the literature," only a half step above the devalued task of writing of a textbook. This scholarly arrogance is a mistake—for two reasons.

One reason is that individual articles, even those published in so-called tier-one journals, are just that—individual studies. As the replication crisis across scientific disciplines is unmasked, it is becoming increasingly clear that many individual studies are idiosyncratic and that their findings do not replicate. Reading any one study inevitably provides a selective understanding of reality. Only when knowledge is organized—when all studies are assessed analytically in one place—is it likely that the best evaluation of the extant evidence is possible. Quality handbooks, such as the current contribution, serve that purpose.

The other reason is that, as criminology has grown and spread into diverse social science disciplines, the sheer number of individual articles produced has become too numerous for any single scholar to find and master. It is possible, of course, to read "everything" on narrow topics in a few months' time and on many things over a career. Still, short of such intense specialization, the growth of knowledge means that scholars must rely on handbooks and similar high-quality reviews of research to gain a balanced understanding of the existing empirical and theoretical literature across topics. Again, the current volume fulfills this function of organizing knowledge by presenting 35 chapters in one location.

Third, a thick handbook containing tens of chapters cannot be compiled unless an area of study within a discipline has produced a large body of scholarship. The publication of the current volume thus serves another function: it confirms that developmental and life-course criminology is now a mature and vibrant area within the discipline. DLC criminology—and here I am using its now-standard acronym—has diverse roots. These include classic life histories (e.g., Shaw's *The Jack-Roller*), the career criminal paradigm, the tracking of birth cohorts (e.g., Wolfgang, Figlio, and Sellin's Philadelphia research), celebrated longitudinal studies (e.g., the Cambridge Study in Delinquent Development), and early integrated theories (e.g., Thornberry's interactional theory). But the turning point in criminology truly occurred in the early 1990s when, in a stroke of serendipity, three titles were published in close proximity: Gottfredson and Hirschi's (1990) *A General Theory of Crime*, Terrie Moffitt's (1993) "Adolescence-Limited and Life-Course–Persistent Antisocial Behavior," and Robert Sampson and John Laub's (1993) *Crime in the Making*. These spectacular works made it impossible for scholars to ignore the reality that crime was a life-long process, extending from womb to tomb. A new criminological paradigm—DLC—thus emerged and came to dominate theoretical and empirical work. DLC criminology's rising popularity is demonstrated empirically by entering the term "life-course criminology" into Google Books Ngram Viewer, which charts the frequency with which a term is used over time. Starting in the latter part of the 1990s, the Ngram graph for life-course criminology is nearly straight upward (a note of appreciation to Teresa Kulig for computing this graph for me).

In my 2010 Edwin H. Sutherland Address to the American Society of Criminology, I made the bold assertion that scholars should "accept that life-course criminology is criminology." I did not mean that all other types of inquiry were irrelevant, but only that the DLC perspective would be the prism through which such work would now be interpreted. It was no longer defensible to ignore that humans have a life that unfolds over time. Behavioral trajectories have a beginning, a duration, and an end. To be general theories, perspectives could not furnish a still snapshot of an offender at a given time but rather needed to keep the criminological camera rolling. Life is ongoing and dynamic—patterned but also prone to unexpected twists and turns.

In this context, the current volume teaches us three important lessons. The first lesson is that all stages in life matter. In my formative years in criminology starting four decades ago, my academic cohort's attention was affixed to the teenage years and to ideas such as social bonds to parents, drift and maturational reform, and delinquent subcultures rooted in blocked opportunity. By contrast, the DLC paradigm has taught us the importance not only of adolescence but also of childhood and adulthood. It is clear that, for many youths, the roots of a criminal career start in a biosocial process at or before birth. And for many adults, it is clear that desisting from offending is tied to events confined to this age period (e.g., marriage, jobs) and to cognitions that arise only after years of offending (e.g., "redemption scripts," the "feared self").

The second lesson is that the line between crime and antisocial conduct is fuzzy. Certainly, it matters if conduct is proscribed by law, and the choice to offend differs from the choice to engage in a so-called "analogous" or deviant behavior that does not carry state-imposed penalties. Still, the DLC perspective illuminates that the individuals who have early conduct problems are the same individuals who experience the early onset of delinquency, and that offenders are marked by the generality of deviance throughout their lives. The subject matter of criminology thus has broadened from a narrow focus on criminal acts per se to a broader focus on the complex of behaviors—of which crime is but one—that are interrelated across time and at any one time.

The third lesson is that because crime is developmental, the most rational and cost-effective means of preventing offending lie outside the criminal justice system. Indeed, DLC criminology is a potent antidote to the embrace of imprisonment as the lynchpin for crime control. A prison sentence represents a failure to act when the opportunity to do so presented itself. The DLC approach reminds us that most adult offenders show signs of misconduct as youngsters and are prime candidates for early intervention. Failing to act consigns these youths to a future of crime, harming others, and ultimately incarceration. Further, the DLC perspective teaches that the sources of offending are complex and vary over time, and hence they are unlikely to be changed by a punitive sanction aimed at scaring an "LCP" straight. Effective intervention needs to be guided not by crass political impulses but by the best criminological knowledge available.

In closing, to be a literate scholar, it is essential to possess a working knowledge of developmental and life-course criminology. The current handbook offers the opportunity to gain such an understanding. The volume is crafted so that readers are provided empirical knowledge pertaining to different life stages and contexts, key theoretical ideas, and insights on developmental prevention strategies. The result is a work of criminological consequence that promises to be the premier resource in the DLC area for years to come. I trust that readers will benefit from this special book as much as I have. An exciting criminological adventure awaits!

Francis T. Cullen
University of Cincinnati

PREFACE

DEVELOPMENTAL and life-course criminology is concerned with development from the womb to the tomb. More specifically, it is concerned with the development of offending and antisocial behavior, risk and protective factors for offending, explanations of the onset, persistence, and desistance of offending, the effects of life events on the course of development of offending, and the transmission of offending from one generation to the next. Research on developmental and life-course criminology spans not only the field of criminology but also psychology, sociology, and public health. As Frank Cullen points out in his Foreword, this area of research has become enormously influential in recent years, as evidenced by the founding of the American Society of Criminology's Division of Developmental and Life-Course Criminology and the new *Journal of Developmental and Life-Course Criminology*.

With contributions from the leading scholars of developmental and life-course criminology, the main goal of this volume is to provide a comprehensive, up-to-date, and authoritative review of the current state of knowledge. Specifically, this *Handbook* includes extensive reviews of the development of offending, the most influential theories, correlates of and risk/protective factors for offending, the effects of life transitions and turning points, and the effectiveness of developmental interventions.

Many people made this *Handbook* possible. We are especially grateful to all the contributors, who stuck with us during the long process of assembling the volume and through various drafts and revised drafts. Sadly, two of our contributors (Chester Britt and Rolf Loeber) died during this process, and we are very grateful to Michael Rocque and Lia Ahonen for helping to edit their chapters. Last but not least, Michael Tonry, the Oxford Handbooks series editor, and James Cook, our editor at Oxford University Press, have been brilliant, and it has been an honor to work with them.

David P. Farrington
Lila Kazemian
Alex R. Piquero

CONTRIBUTORS

Mikko Aaltonen is a Senior Researcher in the Institute of Criminology and Legal Policy at the University of Helsinki, Finland.

Sarah Anderson is a Doctoral Researcher at the University of Glasgow, Scotland.

Sarah Bacon is a Behavioral Scientist at the Centers for Disease Control.

Kristen M. Benedini is an Assistant Professor of Criminal Justice, Department of Political Science, University of Wisconsin-Eau Claire.

Leana A. Bouffard is Chair of the Department of Sociology at Iowa State University.

Chester L. Britt (deceased) was Chair of the Department of Sociology at Iowa State University.

Lisa M. Broidy is Professor of Sociology at the University of New Mexico.

Shawn D. Bushway is Professor of Public Administration and Policy at the University at Albany.

Christopher Cambron is a Postdoctoral Research Associate in the Center for Health Outcomes and Population Equity at the University of Utah, Salt Lake City.

Peter J. Carrington is Professor of Sociology and Legal Studies at the University of Waterloo, Canada.

Richard F. Catalano is the Bartley Dobb Professor for the Study and Prevention of Violence and Co-founder of the Social Development Research Group at the University of Washington School of Social Work.

Kristina K. Childs is an Assistant Professor in the Department of Criminal Justice at the University of Central Florida.

Kyungseok Choo is an Associate Professor of Criminal Justice and Economic Crime at Utica College, New York.

Olivia Choy is an Assistant Professor of Psychology at Nanyang Technological University, Singapore.

Elaine Eggleston Doherty is an Associate Professor in Criminology and Criminal Justice at the University of Missouri, St. Louis.

Abigail A. Fagan is an Associate Professor in the Department of Sociology, Criminology and Law at the University of Florida.

David P. Farrington is Emeritus Professor of Psychological Criminology in the Institute of Criminology at the University of Cambridge, England.

Bryanna Hahn Fox is an Assistant Professor in the Department of Criminology at the University of South Florida.

Trevor A. Fronius is a Senior Research Associate in the WestEd Justice and Prevention Research Center, in Woburn, Massachusetts.

Shaun Gann is an Assistant Professor in the Department of Criminal Justice at Boise State University.

Sarah Guckenburg is a Senior Research Associate in the WestEd Justice and Prevention Research Center, in Woburn, Massachusetts.

J. David Hawkins is the Endowed Professor of Prevention, and Founding Director of the Social Development Research Group, at the University of Washington School of Social Work.

Wesley G. Jennings is a Professor in the School of Criminal Justice at Texas State University, San Marcos.

Hae Rim Jin is an Assistant Professor of Criminology in the Department of Social and Cultural Sciences at the University of Houston–Clear Lake.

Darrick Jolliffe is Professor of Criminology at the University of Greenwich, England.

Lila Kazemian is an Associate Professor in the Department of Sociology at John Jay College of Criminal Justice, City University of New York.

David S. Kirk is Professor of Sociology and Professorial Fellow of Nuffield College at the University of Oxford, England.

Marvin D. Krohn is Professor of Criminology in the Department of Sociology, Criminology, and Law at the University of Florida.

John H. Laub is Distinguished University Professor in the Department of Criminology and Criminal Justice at the University of Maryland, College Park.

Marc Le Blanc is Emeritus Professor of Criminology and Psychoeducation at the University of Montreal, Quebec, Canada.

Jobina Li is a Policy Analyst with the Government of Canada, in Ottawa, Canada.

Siyu Liu is an Assistant Professor of Criminal Justice at Penn State University, Harrisburg.

Rolf Loeber is Distinguished Professor of Psychiatry, and Professor of Psychology and Epidemiology, at the University of Pittsburgh.

Paul Mazerolle is Pro Vice Chancellor in Arts, Education and Law and Director of the Violence Research and Prevention Program at Griffith University, Australia.

Tara Renae Mcgee is an Associate Professor in the School of Criminology and Criminal Justice at Griffith University, Australia.

Cameron McIntosh is a Senior Advisor in the Research Division of Public Safety Canada, in Ottawa, Canada.

Fergus McNeill is Professor of Criminology and Social Work at the University of Glasgow, Scotland.

Samara Mcphedran is a Senior Research Fellow in the Violence Research and Prevention Program at Griffith University, Australia.

Terrie E. Moffitt is the Knut Schmidt Nielsen Professor of Psychology and Neuroscience at Duke University and a Professor of Social Behaviour and Development in the Medical Research Council Social, Genetic, and Developmental Psychiatry Centre in the Institute of Psychiatry at Kings College London, England.

Julien Morizot is an Associate Professor in the School of Psychoeducation at the University of Montreal, Quebec, Canada.

Debra J. Pepler is Distinguished Research Professor of Psychology in the LaMarsh Centre for Child and Youth Research at York University, Canada.

Anthony Petrosino is Director of the WestEd Justice and Prevention Research Center, in Woburn, Massachusetts.

Carolyn Petrosino is Professor of Criminal Justice at Bridgewater University.

Alex R. Piquero is Ashbel Smith Professor of Criminology and Associate Dean for Graduate Programs in the School of Economic, Political, and Policy Sciences at the University of Texas at Dallas and Adjunct Professor in the Key Centre for Ethics, Law, Justice, and Governance at Griffith University, Australia.

Jill Portnoy is an Assistant Professor in the School of Criminology and Justice Studies at the University of Massachusetts, Lowell.

Adrian Raine is the Richard Perry University Professor in the Departments of Criminology, Psychiatry, and Psychology at the University of Pennsylvania.

Rheanna J. Remmel is a graduate student in the Clinical Psychology and Law program at the University of Alabama.

Zachary R. Rowan is an Assistant Professor in the School of Criminology at Simon Fraser University.

Robert J. Sampson is the Henry Ford II Professor of the Social Sciences at Harvard University.

Jukka Savolainen is a Research Professor in the Institute for Social Research at the University of Michigan.

Robert Schug is an Associate Professor of Criminology, Criminal Justice, and Forensic Psychology at California State University, Long Beach.

Torbjørn Skardhamar is a Professor in the Department of Sociology and Human Geography at the University of Oslo, Norway.

Christopher J. Sullivan is an Associate Professor in the School of Criminal Justice at the University of Cincinnati.

Jenna Terrell is a Research Associate in the WestEd Learning Innovations Program, in Atlanta, Georgia.

Delphine Theobald is an Associate Professor in Forensic Psychology at Kingston University London, England.

Carleen M. Thompson is a Lecturer in the School of Criminology and Criminal Justice at Griffith University, Australia.

Terence P. Thornberry is Distinguished Professor Emeritus in the School of Criminal Justice at the University at Albany and Research Professor in the Department of Criminology and Criminal Justice at the University of Maryland, College Park.

Kyle Treiber is University Lecturer in Neurocriminology in the Institute of Criminology at the University of Cambridge, England.

Carolyn Turpin-Petrosino is a Professor in the Criminal Justice Department at Bridgewater State University.

Catherine Tuvblad is an Assistant Professor of Criminology at Örebro University, Sweden.

Sarah B. Van Mastrigt is Associate Professor of Criminology and Legal Psychology in the Department of Psychology and Behavioural Sciences at Aarhus University, Denmark.

Allyson Walker is an Assistant Professor of Administration of Justice at Penn State University, Wilkes-Barre.

Brandon C. Welsh is a Professor of Criminology at Northeastern University, and the Royal Netherlands Academy of Arts and Sciences Visiting Professor and Senior Research Fellow at the Netherlands Institute for the Study of Crime and Law Enforcement in Amsterdam, Netherlands.

Helene Raskin White is Distinguished Professor of Sociology in the Center of Alcohol Studies and the Department of Sociology at Rutgers, the State University of New Jersey.

Per-Olof H. Wikström is Professor of Ecological and Developmental Criminology in the Institute of Criminology at the University of Cambridge, England.

Yaling Yang is an Assistant Professor of Pediatrics at Children's Hospital Los Angeles, University of Southern California.

Steven N. Zane is a Ph.D. candidate in the School of Criminology and Criminal Justice at Northeastern University.

Georgia Zara is an Associate Professor of Psychology at the University of Turin, Italy.

Izabela Zych is an Associate Professor in Educational and Developmental Psychology at the University of Cordoba, Spain.

SECTION I

INTRODUCTION

CHAPTER 1

....

DEVELOPMENTAL AND LIFE-COURSE CRIMINOLOGY

....

LILA KAZEMIAN, DAVID P. FARRINGTON, AND ALEX R. PIQUERO

DEVELOPMENTAL and life-course criminology is concerned with the study of the development of offending over the course of one's life, from onset to persistence and, eventually, desistance. Although these two theoretical approaches share many common features, they have distinctive focal concerns. Stemming from the field of sociology, the life-course perspective focuses attention on social structure and life events, whereas the developmental approach, stemming from the field of psychology, generally emphasizes the role of individual and psychological factors in the explanation of developmental processes. While the developmental approach investigates the onset of offending as well as the role of early risk and protective factors in the explanation of future offending, the life-course framework examines the influence of turning points in offending trajectories and in the process of desistance from crime. Developmental research examines effective processes for early prevention and intervention efforts, whereas life-course studies explore mechanisms to curb offending after onset. In many instances in the field of criminology, these two approaches have been integrated. Both approaches are necessary in order to build up a complete picture of offending careers.

At least up to the 1970s, criminologists carried out cross-sectional surveys and attempted to draw conclusions about the causes of offending from comparisons between individuals. One common feature of the emerging developmental and life-course approaches is their reliance on longitudinal data, particularly prospective rather than retrospective studies. Prospective longitudinal data are preferred for three main reasons: (1) they minimize retrospective bias; (2) they allow the researcher to establish causal ordering with more certainty; and (3) they enable the study of within-individual changes across different periods of the life course. Le Blanc and Loeber (1998, p. 116) explained that a major strength of the within-individual approach "... is that individuals serve as their own controls." Past research has mainly focused on contrasting offending patterns between individuals who possess particular risk factors and those who do not. Predictably, these between-individual comparisons have shown that individuals characterized by a greater number of risk factors are likely to have more active criminal careers when compared with those with fewer risk factors. For instance, it is expected (and unsurprising) that individuals who are married (versus single) or employed (versus unemployed) are less likely to engage in offending or to persist in offending over extended periods of time. In contrast, in order to develop effective post-onset intervention efforts, it is more valuable to determine whether offending declines for individuals after the turning points have occurred (Farrington 2007). For example, offending during unemployment periods is compared with offending during employment periods for the same individual (see, e.g., Farrington et al. 1986). In this comparison, each person acts as his or her own control, so all individual factors (e.g., impulsiveness, intelligence) are held constant. These types of within-individual comparisons yield much more convincing evidence about causal effects, compared with between-individual comparisons where there are inevitably many uncontrolled variables. From a theoretical viewpoint, the emphasis on within-individual change speaks directly to debates about stability and change.

Developmental criminology began with the classic American longitudinal studies of Sheldon and Eleanor Glueck and William and Joan McCord, as well as the famous Philadelphia Birth Cohort Studies by Wolfgang and colleagues and the Racine Cohort Studies by Shannon. These were soon followed by longitudinal studies in the United Kingdom (by Israel Kolvin, and Donald West and David Farrington), Scandinavia (by David Magnusson and Lea Pulkkinen), Canada (by Marc Le Blanc and Richard Tremblay), and New Zealand (by Phil Silva and David Fergusson). The 1980s proved to be the golden age for the initiation of American longitudinal studies (Farrington 2013). Three companion projects in Denver, Colorado; Rochester, New York; and Pittsburgh, Pennsylvania—known as the Causes and Correlates of Delinquency studies—were launched with funding from the Office of Juvenile Justice and Delinquency Prevention, as well as other major longitudinal studies such as the Oregon Youth Study and the Seattle Social Development Project (see, e.g., Thornberry and Krohn 2003). In the longitudinal surveys with the strongest designs, information is obtained repeatedly from different sources, including the participants themselves, their parents, their teachers, their peers, and official (criminal and health) records. Many findings from longitudinal studies are presented in this *Handbook*.

Since convictions are only the "tip of the iceberg" of offending, it is important to compare official records with self-reports of offending not only to assess convergence and divergence but also to estimate the "scaling-up factor." For example, in the Pittsburgh Youth Study there were over 20 self-reported offenses for every conviction (Theobald et al. 2014). Most longitudinal researchers focus on statistical analyses, but some present detailed case histories from childhood to adulthood (see, e.g., Zara and Farrington 2016).

Not all criminologists saw inherent value in studying the life course and especially in the use of longitudinal designs. Nearly three decades ago, Gottfredson and Hirschi

(1990) argued that since criminal propensity remains relatively stable across time, it was not very illuminating or informative to follow up individuals over long periods; they also maintained that the correlates of crime were the same at all ages. Sampson and Laub (1993, p. 16) responded to this by arguing that "the continuity to which they [Gottfredson and Hirschi 1990] refer is relative stability, which does not mean that individuals remain constant in their behavior over time." Most researchers agree that there is both stability and change in offending patterns across the life course (e.g., Piquero, Farrington, and Blumstein 2003; Kazemian 2007). Also, as mentioned, within-individual analyses in longitudinal studies provide more compelling evidence about causes of offending than between-individual comparisons in cross-sectional studies (Farrington 1988).

Whatever their background, most longitudinal researchers investigate not only violence and property crime but many other problem areas, including drug use, alcohol use, drunk driving, reckless driving, smoking, gambling, sexual behavior, relationship problems, employment problems, educational problems, and mental and physical health. Many researchers have concluded that offending is only one element of a larger syndrome of antisocial behavior that tends to persist from childhood to adulthood and from one generation to the next. The challenge is how to prevent and interrupt this persistence, and a number of longitudinal studies (e.g., the Montreal project of Richard Tremblay; see Vitaro et al. 2013) have tested the effectiveness of an experimental intervention designed to achieve this.

Many longitudinal researchers have proposed developmental and life-course (DLC) theories to explain their findings (Farrington 2005), many of which are presented in this *Handbook*. In most cases, their theories were highly influenced by their data. For example, Terrie Moffitt analyzed the Dunedin study of over 1,000 3-year-old children who were followed into their thirties (see, e.g., Caspi et al. 2016). Her more psychologically based theory distinguished between two specific types of offenders: one that offends early—and throughout—the life course (termed life-course–persistent offenders) and a second that restricts the offending to the adolescent period and desists by early adulthood (termed adolescence-limited offenders). Her framework emphasized childhood risk factors for life-course–persistent offending. In contrast, Robert Sampson and John Laub (1993; Laub and Sampson 2003) reanalyzed the Gluecks' study of 500 delinquent males and focused on their adult years, roughly from ages 30 to 70. Their more sociologically based theory emphasized informal social control by adult social institutions, such as marriages and jobs, and aimed to explain desistance.

In studying the development of offending, the most important phenomenon is the age-crime curve. In most times and places, the aggregate rate of offending increases up to a peak in the late teenage years (usually) and then decreases more gradually in the 20s and beyond. In general, the age-crime curve for males is more sharply peaked than the curve for females, which is flatter and has a higher average age of offending. The age-crime curve for individuals, however, may be very different from the aggregate curve. In recent years, inspired by the work of Daniel Nagin (2005), there has been a great deal of interest in identifying different offending trajectories.

Relatedly, following the work of Alfred Blumstein and his colleagues, as detailed in the influential National Academy of Sciences report on criminal careers (see Blumstein et al. 1986), developmental criminology also contributes to the advancement of knowledge about criminal careers (Piquero, Farrington, and Blumstein 2007). Criminal careers are typically characterized by several parameters, including age of onset, frequency, versatility, seriousness, duration, and desistance. Knowledge about all of these topics is renewed in this *Handbook*. Le Blanc and Fréchette (1989) and Le Blanc and Loeber (1998) discussed three processes underlying the development of offending behavior: activation, aggravation, and desistance. During their careers, offenders commit a variety of crimes with a particular frequency per year. Most offenders are versatile, with only a very small minority exhibiting specialization in certain offenses. There is little evidence of escalation in the seriousness of offending during criminal careers.

Developmental researchers have devoted substantial attention to the identification of early risk factors for persistent offending as well as to interventions that prevent the development of offending and antisocial behavior. The major risk factors for male offending are well known and highly replicable in longitudinal studies (Farrington 2015). They include individual factors (e.g., high impulsiveness, low achievement), parental factors (e.g., young or criminal parents), child-rearing factors (e.g., poor parental supervision, physical punishment), socio-economic factors (e.g., low family income, large family size, broken families), peer factors (e.g., associating with delinquent peers), school factors (e.g., attending a high–delinquency-rate school), and neighborhood factors (e.g., living in a high-crime neighborhood). Many risk factors and correlates of offending are reviewed in this *Handbook*. While a great deal is known about risk factors that predict the onset of offending, less is known about risk factors for other criminal career dimensions, such as persistence after onset, frequency, duration, specialization, or escalation.

The extent to which risk factors have causal effects is not entirely clear. For example, in the Pittsburgh Youth Study, peer delinquency was the strongest correlate and predictor of delinquency (between individuals), but it did not predict within-individual change. In other words, changes in peer delinquency did not predict changes in delinquency for the same individual from one wave to the next. In contrast, parental factors such as poor parental supervision and low involvement of the boy in family activities predicted the boy's delinquency both between and within individuals (Farrington et al. 2002). Because the concept of a cause requires that a change in an individual factor predicts a change in delinquency within individuals, it was concluded that parental factors might be causes of delinquency, but that peer delinquency was not. Because most offenses by young people are committed with other young people, peer delinquency is probably an indicator rather than a cause of delinquency.

The interest in protective factors against delinquency is growing, but much less is known about these factors (Ttofi et al. 2016). Protective factors are defined either as factors that predict a low rate of offending or as factors that predict a low rate of offending among people in a risk category. The first type of protective factor is not necessarily the "other side of the coin" to a risk factor. For example, in the Pittsburgh Youth Study, high achievement predicted a low probability of delinquency but low achievement did not predict a high probability of delinquency (compared with average achievement; see Farrington, Ttofi, and Piquero 2016). The second type of protective factor has important implications for intervention. For example, in the Cambridge Study in Delinquent Development, living in poor housing was a risk factor for delinquency, but boys who were living in poor housing and receiving good child-rearing had the same probability of delinquency as boys who were living in good housing (Farrington and Ttofi 2011). Therefore, the protective factor of good child-rearing nullified the risk factor of poor housing, suggesting that parent training to improve child-rearing might be effective in reducing the delinquency of boys living in poor housing. Results from the Pittsburgh and Cambridge studies, along with numerous other longitudinal projects, are described in this *Handbook*.

There has been a great deal of research on the influence of later life events on the course of development of offending, and the life event that has been studied most is getting married. Longitudinal research shows that offending by males decreases after they get married (compared with matched males who did not get married) and, conversely, that offending increases after males become separated or divorced (Theobald and Farrington 2009, 2013). Other important turning points that have been studied include cohabiting with a romantic partner, having a first child, moving house, obtaining a steady job, joining the military forces, and religion. This *Handbook* will discuss the influence of these kinds of turning points on offending patterns across the life course.

This volume offers a thorough overview of the issues relevant to contemporary developmental and life-course criminology. It is organized in five main thematic sections: (1) the development of offending, (2) developmental and life-course theories, (3) developmental correlates and risk/protective factors, (4) life transitions and turning points, and (5) developmental interventions.

Section II examines factors associated with the development of offending, with an exploration of various criminal career parameters. In Chapter 2, Britt provides a discussion of the age-crime link and reviews classic and contemporary research that has examined this question. Doherty and Bacon then present evidence on the association between age of onset and later offending (Chapter 3), followed by Mazerolle and McPhedran's investigation of changes in versatility and specialization across the life course (Chapter 4). In Chapter 5, Jennings and Fox assess the state of knowledge on patterns of acceleration, deceleration, escalation, and de-escalation over the course of criminal careers. Relatedly, Chapter 6 by Liu and Bushway offers an overview of the factors underlying the processes of persistence and desistance from crime. In Chapter 7, Morizot draws on existing longitudinal studies to examine how offending trajectories vary across various periods of the life course. This section concludes with an analysis of changes in co-offending patterns over the course of criminal careers (Chapter 8, by van Mastrigt and Carrington).

Section III of this *Handbook* summarizes the most influential developmental and life-course theories in the field of criminology and addresses controversies and points of contention between the different frameworks. In Chapter 9, McGee and Moffitt summarize Moffitt's dual taxonomy, which seeks to explain variations in life-course offending patterns across different types of offenders. Loeber (Chapter 10) provides an overview of his developmental model of pathways leading to problem behavior and delinquency. Farrington's Integrated Cognitive Antisocial Potential (ICAP) theory is laid out in Chapter 11, followed by Le Blanc's theory of the Interconnected Development of Personal Controls and Antisocial Behavior (Chapter 12). Chapter 13 presents Hawkins and Catalano's Social Development Model, and Thornberry and Krohn describe the concepts underlying Interactional Theory, as well as the empirical investigations of this theoretical framework, in Chapter 14. Wikström and Treiber (Chapter 15) then discuss the dynamics of change, as explained by Situational Action Theory (SAT) and the Development Ecological Action (DEA) model. This section concludes with a summary of Sampson and Laub's age-graded theory of informal social control, which seeks to explain variations in crime across different periods of life (Chapter 16).

Section IV of this volume investigates the developmental correlates of offending and also important risk and protective factors associated with criminal behavior. Choy and collaborators summarize the state of knowledge on the role of biosocial indicators in the explanation of offending behavior across the life course (Chapter 17). In Chapter 18, Jolliffe and Farrington discuss the influence of personality traits and other individual factors in the development of offending behavior. The following three chapters focus on various dimensions of the social environment. Fagan and Benedini assess the relationship between family influences and youth offending (Chapter 19). Chapter 20 (by Sullivan, Childs, and Gann) discusses the role of deviant friends, and this is followed by an overview of research on schools and crime (by Pepler, Chapter 21). White (Chapter 22) concludes this section with a review of longitudinal research exploring the connections between criminal behavior and substance use over time.

Section V presents an overview of the empirical evidence on the role of various life transitions and turning points in the explanation of offending behavior. In Chapter 23, Theobald, Farrington, and Piquero examine the impact of changes in family situations on persistence and desistance from crime. Savolainen, Aaltonen, and Skardhamar (Chapter 24) review research on the link between employment and crime over the life course and address recent controversies in this area of research. In Chapter 25, Kirk tackles an important but understudied topic, namely the impact of neighborhood context and residential mobility on persistence and desistance from crime. Bouffard and Jin (Chapter 26) provide a summary of empirical evidence on the influence of two often-neglected turning points in life-course research: religion and the military. The following two chapters examine the effects of contacts with the juvenile and criminal justice systems. Petrosino and colleagues (Chapter 27) assess the impact of juvenile system processing on subsequent delinquency outcomes, while Kazemian and Walker (Chapter 28) discuss the various individual and social consequences of incarceration. In Chapter 29, Anderson and McNeill expand on the cognitive indicators that may promote the desistance process. Broidy and Thompson (Chapter 30) close this section with a discussion of developmental and life-course findings on girls and women.

Section VI focuses on effective developmental interventions, which have been inspired by research on the development of criminal and antisocial behavior. Welsh and Zane (Chapter 31) highlight the features of effective family-based programs for the prevention of offending behavior. In Chapter 32, Zych and Farrington summarize the evidence on the effectiveness of developmental preschool and school programs against violence and offending. Zara then discusses some of the most effective cognitive-behavioral interventions to prevent offending behavior (Chapter 33), and Li and McIntosh offer a valuable assessment of the monetary costs and benefits associated with developmental prevention initiatives (Chapter 34).

The volume concludes with a summary of key findings from research reviewed in the various chapters, some reflections on the state of knowledge of developmental and life-course criminology, and a discussion of what we need to know and how we can find out.

REFERENCES

Blumstein, Alfred, Jacqueline Cohen, Jeffrey A. Roth, and Christy A. Visher. 1986. *Criminal Careers and "Career Criminals."* Washington, DC: National Academy Press.

Caspi, Avshalom, Renate M. Houts, Daniel W. Belsky, Honalee Harrington, Sean Hogan, Sandhya Ramrakha, Richie Poulton, and Terrie E. Moffitt. 2016. "Childhood Forecasting of a Small Segment of the Population with Large Economic Burden." *Nature Human Behaviour* 1: 0005.

Farrington, David P. 1988. "Studying Changes Within Individuals: The Causes of Offending." In *Studies of Psychosocial Risk: The Power of Longitudinal Data,* edited by Michael Rutter, 158–183. Cambridge, UK: Cambridge University Press.

Farrington, David P., ed. 2005. *Integrated Developmental and Life-Course Theories of Offending* (Advances in Criminological Theory, Vol. 14.). New Brunswick, NJ: Transaction.

Farrington, David P. 2007. "Advancing Knowledge About Desistance." *Journal of Contemporary Criminal Justice* 23(1): 125–134.

Farrington, David P. 2013. "Longitudinal and Experimental Research in Criminology." In *Crime and Justice in America 1975–2025,* edited by Michael Tonry. Chicago: University of Chicago Press.

Farrington, David P. 2015. "The Developmental Evidence Base: Psychosocial Research." In *Forensic Psychology* (2nd ed.), edited by David A. Crighton and Graham J. Towl. Chichester, UK: Wiley.

Farrington, David P., Bernard Gallagher, Lynda Morley, Raymond J. Ledger, and Donald J. West. 1986. "Unemployment, School Leaving and Crime." *British Journal of Criminology* 26: 335–356.

Farrington, David P., Rolf Loeber, Yanming Yin, and Stewart J. Anderson. 2002. "Are Within-Individual Causes of Delinquency the Same as Between-Individual Causes?" *Criminal Behaviour and Mental Health* 12: 53–68.

Farrington, David P., and Maria M. Ttofi. 2011. "Protective and Promotive Factors in the Development of Offending." In *Antisocial Behavior and Crime: Contributions of Developmental and Evaluation Research to Prevention and Intervention,* edited by Thomas Bliesener, Andreas Beelman, and Mark Stemmler. Cambridge, MA: Hogrefe.

Farrington, David P., Maria Ttofi, and Alex R. Piquero. 2016. "Risk, Promotive, and Protective Factors in Youth Offending: Results from the Cambridge Study in Delinquent Development." *Journal of Criminal Justice* 45: 63–70.

Gottfredson, Michael R., and Travis Hirschi. 1990. *A General Theory of Crime*. Stanford, CA: Stanford University Press.

Kazemian, Lila. 2007. "Desistance from Crime: Theoretical, Empirical, Methodological, and Policy Considerations." *Journal of Contemporary Criminal Justice* 23(1): 5–27.

Laub, John H., and Robert J. Sampson. 2001. *Shared Beginnings, Divergent Lives: Delinquent Boys to Age 70*. Cambridge, MA: Harvard University Press.

Le Blanc, Marc, and Marcel Fréchette. 1989. *Male Criminal Activity from Childhood Through Youth: Multilevel and Developmental Perspectives*. New York: Springer-Verlag.

Le Blanc, Marc, and Rolf Loeber. 1998. "Developmental Criminology Updated." In *Crime and Justice*, Vol. 23, edited by Michael Tonry. Chicago: University of Chicago Press.

Nagin, Daniel S. 2005. *Group-Based Modeling of Development*. Cambridge, MA: Harvard University Press.

Piquero, Alex R., David P. Farrington, and Alfred Blumstein. 2003. "The Criminal Career Paradigm." In *Crime and Justice*, Vol. 30, edited by Michael Tonry. Chicago: University of Chicago Press.

Piquero, Alex R., David P. Farrington, and Alfred Blumstein. 2007. *Key Issues in Criminal Career Research: New Analyses of the Cambridge Study in Delinquent Development*. Cambridge, UK: Cambridge University Press.

Sampson, Robert J., and John H. Laub. 1993. *Crime in the Making: Pathways and Turning Points through Life*. Cambridge, MA: Harvard University Press.

Theobald, Delphine, and David P. Farrington. 2009. "Effects of Getting Married on Offending: Results from a Prospective Longitudinal Survey of Males." *European Journal of Criminology* 6: 496–516.

Theobald, Delphine, and David P. Farrington. 2013. "The Effects of Marital Breakdown on Offending: Results from a Prospective Longitudinal Survey of Males." *Psychology, Crime and Law* 19: 391–408.

Theobald, Delphine, David P. Farrington, Rolf Loeber, Dustin A. Pardini, and Alex R. Piquero. 2014. "Scaling Up from Convictions to Self-Reported Offending." *Criminal Behaviour and Mental Health* 24: 265–276.

Thornberry, Terence P., and Marvin D. Krohn, eds. 2003. *Taking Stock of Delinquency: An Overview of Findings from Contemporary Longitudinal Studies*. New York: Kluwer/Plenum.

Ttofi, Maria M., David P. Farrington, Alex R. Piquero, and Matt DeLisi. 2016. "Protective Factors Against Offending and Violence: Results from Prospective Longitudinal Studies." *Journal of Criminal Justice* 45: 1–3.

Vitaro, Frank, Mara Brendgen, Charles-Edouard Giguere, and Richard E. Tremblay. 2013. "Early Prevention of Life-Course Personal and Property Violence: A 19-Year Follow-Up of the Montreal Longitudinal Experimental Study (MLES)." *Journal of Experimental Criminology* 9: 411–427.

Zara, Georgia, and David P. Farrington. 2016. *Criminal Recidivism: Explanation, Prediction and Prevention*. Abingdon, UK: Routledge.

SECTION II

THE DEVELOPMENT OF OFFENDING

CHAPTER 2

....

AGE AND CRIME

....

CHESTER L. BRITT

In the past decade, the United States Supreme Court has directly considered the age relationship with crime in reaching decisions about the appropriateness of sentencing juvenile offenders to death (*Roper v. Simmons* 543 U.S. 551 [2005]) as well as to life imprisonment without the opportunity for parole (*Miller v. Alabama*, 132 S. Ct. 2455, 2460 [2012]). These two rulings focused, in part, on the cognitive abilities of juvenile offenders and the effect of brain development on thinking through the long-term consequences of behavior. In light of research showing that brain development is often not complete until a person is in their mid-twenties, the Supreme Court determined that holding juveniles younger than 18 years to the same punishment standard as adults was not constitutional. Underlying the rationale of the Court's majority opinion was a causal explanation of crime—that brain development was a factor in crime commission—and a recognition of extensive social and behavioral science research on the causes of crime and other risky behaviors.

Debate over the meaning of, and how to explain, the relationship between age and crime has animated much research in criminology for at least the past 30 years. While there tends to be little disagreement about the aggregate relationship between age and crime, there has been much more debate, discussion, and research focused on variations in individual, age-specific patterns of criminal behavior. Some of the questions motivating this work have tried to assess: Do individual age-specific patterns of crime mirror the aggregate age relationship with crime? If not, then how do the individual patterns of crime vary by age? To what extent are changes in the crime patterns of individuals reflected in the overall age pattern of crime? For example, what happens if a greater percentage of the population commits just one crime? Alternatively, what happens if the percentage of the population committing crimes is stable, but these individuals increase the number of crimes they commit?

The following discussion provides an alternative framework for thinking about the research on age and crime, regardless of whether the study used aggregate or individual-level data. Contrary to a popular view in the research literature that emphasizes differences, there is considerable commonality of findings on age and crime, regardless of the approach taken to its study. The rest of this chapter is structured as follows: First, it provides an overview of what is meant by the age–crime curve and distinguishes that from the age distribution of crime. Second, basic facts of the age and crime relationship are discussed, followed by explanations of that relationship. Following is a discussion of whether individual age–crime curves fit the aggregate pattern and, finally, a final section providing an illustration of how varying assumptions of the age–crime curve affect aggregate patterns using simulations. Conclusions are then offered.

I. Age–Crime Curves and the Age Distribution of Crime

Prior to discussing the research on age and crime, an important distinction needs to be made between age–crime curves and the age distribution of crime—something that is often confused in the research literature but likely has its roots in Hirschi and Gottfredson's (1983) seminal paper on age and crime. An "age–crime curve" is a graphical representation of a crime rate or count by age. At the aggregate level, these kinds of curves may present age-specific arrest rates by year, gender, race, and crime type. At the individual level, there are many more variations that all focus on presenting individual patterns of criminal behavior over some designated period of time. For example, in a longitudinal study that follows several hundred individuals for some number of years, there will be a unique age–crime curve for each person included in the study. Individual age–crime curves can be further distinguished by looking at the frequency (rate) of criminal behavior or the participation (yes-no) in criminal behavior. Individual crime rates would typically measure the number of crimes an individual commits in a year, while individual participation measures whether the individual committed at least one crime in a year.

The age distribution of crime is fundamentally a histogram of crimes committed by age and so only includes those individuals with at least one crime during the measurement period. Similar to age–crime curves, age distributions of crime can be further distinguished by frequency and participation—each tells us something different. The age distribution of frequency of offenses would indicate the distribution of *all* crimes committed by each age category among offenders but would not be able to distinguish how many crimes an individual had committed. The age distribution of participation would indicate the proportion of active offenders at each age. When this histogram of crimes by age is smoothed, as in a probability density function or line graph, it generates a type of age–crime curve, but one that may have a different meaning from what most researchers mean when they reference an age–crime curve.

Why does this distinction matter? In large part, the difference between an age–crime curve and the age distribution of crime has implications for our attempts to explain the age relationship with crime. If our focus is on age–crime curves, whether individual or

aggregate, then our explanations should try to describe why frequency and/or participation rates change by age and possibly vary by some other characteristic. If our focus
is instead on the age distribution of crime, then our explanations should try to describe
why the distribution takes on a particular location and shape (e.g., measures of central
tendency, spread, and skew).

II. Age and Crime

Hirschi and Gottfredson's (1983) paper on age and crime helped to clarify age as one
of the known facts in the study of criminal behavior, which led them to argue that it
should not be used to test the validity of any theoretical explanation of crime. Their rationale was based on using a variety of empirical examples from the United States and
the United Kingdom that led them to conclude that the age–crime relationship was
invariant. Regardless of the type of data they analyzed—arrest, conviction, victimization, etc.—the same basic age relationship with crime appeared in data aggregated by
race, gender, historical period, or culture. The basic shape to the age–crime relationship
observed in aggregate data is now well known for most crime: A rapid increase in crime
occurs in the mid- to late teens, followed by a rapid decline in the early to mid-20s and
then gradually declining over increasingly older age groups. This is not to say that the
age-specific rates of crime were identical in their comparisons. For example, they noted
that property crimes (e.g., burglary and larceny) tended to peak at earlier ages than violent crimes (e.g., homicide and assault), while other offenses, such as white-collar and
family violence, may peak at much older ages (see also Steffensmeier et al. 1989; Britt
1992). The differences in the specific age of peak offending notwithstanding, Hirschi and
Gottfredson (1983, 2008; Gottfredson and Hirschi 1990) argued that the basic form of
the relationship was the same, regardless of where the specific peak age of offending
occurred or how slowly crime decreased with age. Hirschi and Gottfredson (1983)
then extended their claim of invariance to individual patterns of offending, where they
argued that individuals would exhibit the same age–crime curve over the life course that
was observed in aggregate data.

In light of the overall consistency in the observed relationship between age and crime,
Hirschi and Gottfredson (1983) concluded that no theory of crime could explain the
age–crime relationship. From their perspective, the same basic pattern was observed
in different demographic groups, in different historical eras, and in different countries,
which implied there was no single theoretical explanation that could realistically tie together all of the possible variations in a way that would explain the consistency in the
pattern they found across time and space. Sweeten, Piquero, and Steinberg (2013) have
referred to this claim as the "inexplicability hypothesis"—that criminological theory is
unable to explain the age–crime relationship.

As noted above, one of the problems that Hirschi and Gottfredson (1983) set in motion with their paper was confusion over the "age–crime curve" and the "age distribution

of crime." While their text emphasized the age *distribution* of crime, many of the figures on which their claims rested were *age–crime curves* that presented age-specific rates of crime. Their lack of clarity resulted in a wide range of responses and reactions to their "invariance hypothesis." The two primary approaches to assessing the validity of their claim to invariance took either a macro-level or a micro-level line of reasoning and analysis.

The macro-level approaches to testing the invariance hypothesis focused on using aggregate arrest data in the United States (e.g., Steffensmeier et al. 1989; Steffensmeier and Striefel 1991; Britt 1992) to test for differences and similarities across a range of age–crime distributions—a more direct set of tests of the invariance hypothesis. Steffensmeier et al. (1989), for example, used summary measures of discrepancy to assess the similarity–difference in any pair of age-specific distributions of crime. Their key findings showed that age-specific distributions of crime were statistically different over time and across offense type. Steffensmeier and Striefel (1991) used a similar analytical approach to show that age distributions of crime also varied significantly by gender. In an attempt to synthesize different approaches to analyzing multiple age distributions of crime, Britt (1992) suggested there were at least two different ways of thinking about invariance: parametric invariance and functional form invariance. Parametric invariance refers to whether the statistical parameters describing a distribution are the same, while functional form invariance refers to whether the same underlying mathematical function could describe a set of distributions that may differ only in the specific parameter estimates that would result in location shifts (i.e., measure of central tendency) or alter the shape (i.e., spread) of cases. He fit a series of age-specific distributions of crime with both a gamma distribution and a log-normal distribution, showing that either probability function offered a reasonably good fit, suggesting that the same age-generating process of criminal behavior was at work, but the parameters varied significantly over time and across offense type that were likely a consequence of other economic, social, psychological, historical, and cultural factors. More recently, MacLeod Grove, and Farrington's (2012) analysis of individual-level crime data in the United Kingdom illustrated how a gamma distribution fit the aggregated data quite well.

Micro-level approaches to addressing the invariance hypothesis focused more on the age-specific crime rates used in the Hirschi and Gottfredson (1983) paper and argued that aggregate arrest (or conviction) data could represent any number of different factors at work. For example, police could differentially enforce laws that targeted one age group over another, which would then alter age-specific crime rates (Blumstein et al. 1986). Another line of reasoning suggested that different levels of participation, as well as frequency of criminal offending, among different cohorts would also have important consequences for apparent peak ages of offending and the overall shape of the age–crime curve (see, e.g., Blumstein et al. 1986; Farrington 1986). Farrington (1986) also set out to show how individual patterns of offending did not follow the pattern as the aggregate age–crime curve—some individuals started committing crimes earlier, some later, some not at all. The extensive variation in individual patterns of crime by age was viewed as invalidating the invariance hypothesis, insofar as it was applied to individual-level data.

Since the mid-1990s, much of the research on the age–crime relationship has focused on individual-level data, which has been made easier with the increased accessibility of several large-scale prospective longitudinal studies that are capable of tracking one or more samples of youth through adulthood. This work has examined issues related to age of onset, length of time a person actively commits crimes, frequency of offending, as well as desisting from crime. Motivating much of this work has been the use of group-based trajectory models—a form of latent class analysis—to identify subpopulations in a sample of data with similar patterns of criminal behavior over time, but which lead to different age–crime curves. It is common for studies using this technique to identify anywhere from two to six subpopulations within a sample, each with a different age–crime curve profile. Consistent with Farrington (1986) and others (e.g., Moffitt 1993), these subpopulations of criminal offenders reveal varying age of onset and desistance, varying lengths of time of actively committing crime, varying individual crime rates, and varying degrees of participation in crime that also vary by time, location, and socio-demographic characteristics. Piquero (2008) and Jennings and Reingle (2012) have reviewed dozens of studies using group-based trajectory models and concluded that offenders do not all follow the same age–crime curve, since most studies found three or four distinct offending groups in the data analyzed.

III. Explaining the Age–Crime Relationship

Hirschi and Gottfredson (1983, 2008; Gottfredson and Hirschi, 1990) have been stead-fast in arguing that the age distribution of crime cannot be explained by any current theory. Implied by this claim is the idea that no set of covariates suggested by a theory (or even a group of theories) would be able to explain the age distribution of crime. The confusion noted above about whether Hirschi and Gottfredson (1983) meant age–crime curves or the age distribution of crime has been compounded by confusion over what it means to "explain" any age relationship with crime. By explanation, it seems clear that Hirschi and Gottfredson (1983) were referring to the *theoretical explanation* of the age–crime relationship rather than the *statistical explanation* of the age–crime relation-ship. Much of the research on age and crime since the publication of their paper has focused nearly exclusively on the statistical explanation of the relationship: Are there age-specific covariates that correlate with criminal behavior over the life course? (The short answer is yes.) What has not been the focus of much work is the theoretical ex-planation for the age–crime relationship. The theoretical explanation of the age–crime relationship would try to say *why* the covariates had the effects they did across the life course—there are few examples of this in criminology (see also Walsh 2009).

To date, there have been no comprehensive theoretical explanations of the age distribution of crime, although there have been attempts at explaining how or why the distribution may differ by cultural, geographic, or historical location (see, e.g., Greenberg 1985, 2001). The key challenge, and part of the basis of Hirschi and Gottfredson's (1983) claim, is the age distribution of crime has a pattern that is remarkably similar to the age distributions of motor vehicle accidents, of accidental deaths, of criminal victimization generally, and other forms of risky behavior that appear to be similar, though not identical, in many different cultures. Thus far, the combination of developmental, biosocial, psychological, and social factors that give rise to similar patterns of the age distribution of risky behavior have not been integrated into any kind of theoretical statement.

The key difficulty in explaining *why* the age distribution of crime takes on the shape it does would be akin to trying to explain why the heights of individuals are normally distributed. Across populations, the heights of individuals follow a normal distribution, but not with exactly the same mean or spread of cases—in some countries, individuals are taller, in others, shorter. In some countries, heights are more tightly grouped—there is less variation—while in others, there is greater variability. Nevertheless, the distribution of heights takes on a bell-shaped curve, indicative of a normal distribution. Why? There may be hundreds of factors that might explain individual heights—genetics, nutrition, etc.—but there is no theoretical explanation for why they are distributed normally. Hirschi and Gottfredson (1983) were trying to make a similar point about the age distribution of crime.

In contrast to the lack of theoretical explanation for the age distribution of crime, there have been limited attempts to explain age-specific patterns of criminal behavior. Two of the most frequently cited theories have emerged from developmental psychology and life course sociology. Moffitt's (1993) developmental theory focused on describing the onset of offending in adolescence, especially why it increases or decreases at specific points in time, and then why most adolescents stop committing crimes in a very short time. Sampson and Laub's (1993) life course explanation focused on explaining how informal social control—attachments to family, friends, school, and workplace—changed over the life course and was then key to understanding why individuals would be at greater (lesser) risk of criminal behavior at different points in the life course.

Attempts at the statistical explanation of the age–crime relationship have been much more common, although relatively little of this work has analyzed macro-level data. Britt (1997) looked at patterns of age-specific unemployment rates on the effects of age-specific arrest rates, while O'Brien and Stockard (2006) analyzed age-specific patterns of homicide and suicide. While both papers found evidence of age-specific variation in patterns of offending that correlated with unemployment (Britt, 1997) and non-marital birth rates and relative cohort size (O'Brien and Stockard 2006), these patterns did not explain the age distribution of crime.

At the individual level, the emergence of the criminal career paradigm (Blumstein et al. 1986)—a largely atheoretical, but data-driven, approach to the study of crime—focused on the many different statistical associations that helped to identify risk and protective factors of criminal behavior. To the extent that theory was relevant for much of the early work on criminal careers, it was used as a screening device to sift through prior research to locate some of the strongest correlates of crime and include them in future statistical models. Somewhat later, the growth of developmental and life course criminology tried to make sense of the statistical relationships with new theoretical approaches to the causes of crime (e.g., Le Blanc and Loeber 1998; Loeber and Le Blanc 1990; Moffitt 1993; Sampson and Laub 1993). The increased accessibility of longitudinal data sets allowed for the analysis of individual patterns of criminal behavior over increasingly longer periods of time, which opened up the possibility for researchers to start to look for age-specific correlates of crime that would statistically explain individual age–crime curves. For example, Osgood et al. (1996) analyzed data from the Monitoring the Future Study to examine the effects of routine activities over time to show that age-specific behaviors that placed youth in unsupervised situations statistically explained between about one-quarter and one-half of criminal behavior and drug use. Stolzenberg and D'Alessio's (2008) analysis of data from the National Incident-Based Reporting System found that age-specific offending correlated with patterns of co-offending. Shulman, Steinberg, and Piquero (2014) tested claims (e.g., Brown and Males 2011) that economic status could explain the age–crime relationship but found no support in their analysis of data from the National Longitudinal Survey of Youth. More recently, Sweeten, Piquero, and Steinberg (2013) analyzed data from the Pathways to Desistance study in what is likely one of the most systematic attempts to sort out whether the age relationship with crime can be explained statistically by a wide range of covariates. They showed how measures representing several different theories of crime have statistically significant effects on age-specific offending, resulting in their model statistically explaining about two-thirds of the decline in age-specific patterns of offending in their sample of offenders between the ages of 15 and 25.

Biosocial research on age and crime has made increasingly significant contributions to the statistical explanation of individual age–crime curves. Loeber et al. (2012), for example, analyzed IQ and cognitive impulsivity data from the Pittsburgh Youth Study. They found that cognitive impulsivity predicted criminal behavior among high-IQ youth but had no relationship with crime among low-IQ youth. Other researchers have also found links between neurotransmitter systems (e.g., dopamine and serotonin; Collins, 2004), hormonal and neurological changes (Walsh 2009), and personality traits (e.g., Blonigen 2010) with individual age–crime curves. This general and growing body of work appears to be key to understanding the U.S. Supreme Court's decisions in *Roper v. Simmons* (2005) and *Miller v. Alabama* (2012).

What does this work mean for the explanation of the age–crime relationship? To date, there are no theoretical explanations for the age distribution of crime, consistent with Hirschi and Gottfredson's (1983) claim more than three decades ago. At the same time, however, there are widely respected theories that attempt to offer age-specific explanations for why different characteristics of individuals and their life circumstances may affect their likelihood of committing crimes at any given point in the life course. Researchers have had much greater success at the statistical explanation of individual patterns of criminal behavior over time but have not been able to integrate these various findings—some biosocial/biopsychological, some psychological, some sociological—into a theoretical framework that could be applied to a wide variety of populations across time and place.

One of the challenges of integrating age-specific statistical analyses into a theoretical perspective is well illustrated with the Sweeten et al. (2013) paper noted above. Their analysis relies on age-specific covariates that are reflective of and relevant to at least five different theoretical perspectives in criminology. Not surprisingly, they identify a number of age-specific covariates that correlate with criminal behavior from age 15 to 25 and appear to explain (statistically) much of the age relationship with crime in this sample. The range of covariates used in their analysis does not fit well within any existing theoretical perspective but is consistent with the criminal career approach that tries to identify risk and protective factors rather than to develop a theoretical explanation for the statistical findings.

Another challenge to explaining the age–crime relationship has its roots in a longstanding weakness in criminological theory: the assumption that causal forces are symmetric, where the presence or the absence of a "cause" has the same effect on the outcome of interest. For example, the factors that caused a person to commit a first crime, when removed, should result in the person returning to a non-criminal status. An asymmetric cause would imply that how the current level of the cause was obtained—whether it moved to the current level through an increase or a decrease, for example—is important for understanding the kind of effect it would have on the outcome of interest (Lieberson 1985). This is not to say that the same factors are not still important but may not affect behavior in exactly the same way—a feature that many theories tend to gloss over—but they may be key to understanding the age relationship with crime (see, e.g., Ulmer and Steffensmeier 2014).

In thinking about the age–crime relationship and whether it can be explained, an assumption of symmetric causation would imply that the factors responsible for the increase in criminal behavior in the teen years are also the factors responsible for the decline in crime that starts in the late teens and early twenties. For example, many social learning–based approaches to explaining crime over time note that exposure to and involvement with criminal peers in the teen years helps to explain the increase in criminal behavior (see, e.g., Warr 2002). Yet the decline in criminal behavior often starts earlier than the separation from delinquent and criminal peers, suggesting that the causal effect of delinquent peers is not symmetrical—it may give rise to increased criminal offending but is less effective at capturing the decline in crime, even as young adults start to disengage from criminal peers (e.g., Warr 2002; Laub and Sampson 2003). This is typically viewed as a weakness in the theoretical approach—it is unable to explain both the increase and then the decrease in crime. While Hirschi and Gottfredson (1983) would disavow any utility to social learning approaches to the explanation of crime, they would be sympathetic to the theory's inability to explain the age–crime relationship, which reflects their viewpoint that a theory's ability to explain the age relationship with crime is not a useful test of the theory's validity.

IV. Reconciling Individual Age–Crime Curves and the Distribution of Crime

One of the key points of contention in trying to explain—both statistically and theoretically—the age-crime relationship has been the challenge of reconciling individual age–crime curves with the aggregate age distribution of crime. As noted above, there are two primary arguments for claiming that individual and aggregate age and crime patterns are so inconsistent that claims about one type of age–crime relationship cannot be applied to another type of age–crime relationship. The first, and most direct, example of this argument is the overwhelming evidence showing that individual age–crime curves do not all follow the same pattern as the aggregate age distribution of crime (e.g., Blumstein, Cohen, and Farrington, 1988a, 1988b). The second set of claims argues that aggregate patterns are simply a reflection of overall levels of age-specific participation in crime, especially when cross-sectional official statistics (e.g., arrest statistics) are analyzed. Consequently, should overall patterns of participation change, the argument goes, then the aggregate age distribution of crime will also change in ways to reflect varying degrees of participation in criminal behavior across the population (Farrington 1986; Blumstein et al. 1988a, 1988b; Loeber 2012).

Despite the scores of studies published on age and crime, there have been no obvious attempts to assess whether the patterns observed in individual-level data are truly inconsistent with what might be viewed in an aggregate age distribution of crime. Farrington's (1986) analysis of the Cambridge data comes closest to this type of analysis but is limited to a few hundred males, and MacLeod et al.'s (2012) analysis of a large criminal offender database in the United Kingdom provides an alternative example but, again, is based on a unique sample. The discussion now turns to a relatively simple simulation to examine the effects of individual age-specific offending patterns on the overall age distribution of crime that consider variations in both participation in and frequency of crime.

V. The Simulation

The focus of the simulation was a test for how different assumptions about age–crime curves in a population would affect the overall age distribution of crime committed. The different ways of configuring the data-generation process allow for an examination of the degree to which changes in the population's participation in crime—higher or lower—and the frequency with which individuals commit crime affect the aggregate age distribution of crime.

A. Data Generation

The data generated for this simulation rely on prior research using both group-based trajectory models and random coefficient growth curve models. The simulations based on group-based trajectory models assume four different trajectory groups in the population: high rate, adolescent limited, low rate, and non-criminal. The basis for such an assumption seems well grounded given the reviews by Piquero (2008) and Jennings and Reingle (2012). The data-generation process was kept relatively simple by assuming a Poisson process to generate counts of crime for each "individual" in each "time period." Based on a composite of prior research, the following quadratic growth curves use only "age" to generate the count data for the different groups of offenders:

- High rate: $-.1 + .3^*Age - .02^*Age^2$
- Adolescent limited: $-1.0 + .3^*Age - .03^*Age^2$
- Low rate: $-0.8 + .5^*Age - .05^*Age^2$
- Non-criminal: $-4.6 + .0^*Age - .00^*Age^2$

Figure 2.1 plots the four functions to illustrate the four characteristic age–crime curves for these groups. Note that the general shapes of these age–crime curves are similar to those that have appeared in numerous studies using the group-based trajectory modeling approach but are also constructed in such a way that they exhibit greater differences and slightly higher rates of criminal offending than are found in most papers relying on group-based trajectory approach.

Data for the fourth sample were generated by assuming a random coefficient growth curve model (RCM; e.g., Sweeten et al. 2013), rather than discrete groups in the population, again based on a quadratic growth curve:

- RCM: $(-3.0 + z_0) + (1.1 + z_1)^*Age - (.09 + z_2)^*Age^2$

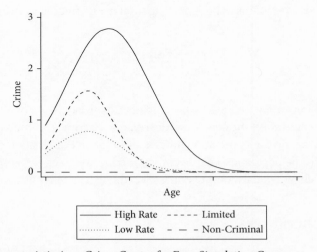

FIGURE 2.1 Characteristic Age–Crime Curves for Four Simulation Groups

Note that a small, random error (z_0, z_1, and z_2) has been added to each coefficient. Substantively, this allows each simulated individual to have a unique age–crime curve, as each case can hypothetically have three uniquely different coefficients.

For all simulations, a Poisson random number generator used the individual's estimated crime rate in each year based on one of the functions above to estimate the "number of crimes" at each point in time. This ensures a probabilistic element into estimating individual "frequency of offending," so that individuals within the same group will have different trajectories over time. Figure 2.2 presents the counts of crime for three of the simulated individual cases over a hypothetical 30-year period to illustrate what these data look like. The data generation for the simulations described below was done in both R and Stata. Other than random variation in the specific values generated in each program, there were no differences in the findings reported below.

The results of the simulation reported below reflect samples of 10,000 individuals for a time period of 30 years. A number of other simulations were run for samples ranging from 1,000 to 100,000 individuals and for time periods ranging from 10 to 30 years. The only differences that appear in the change in sample size are the smoothness of the various curves—there is greater volatility in the smaller samples, revealing greater statistical noise, but the underlying pattern doesn't change. The effect of varying the time period is the longer time period allows for convergence of all the age–crime curves toward zero—a feature that has been observed in some of the longitudinal research relying on long follow-up periods (e.g., Laub and Sampson 2003; Eggleston, Laub, and Sampson, 2004).

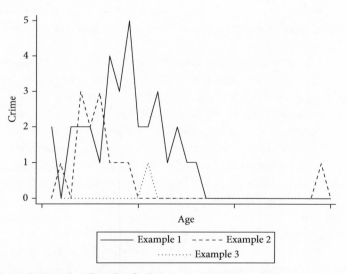

FIGURE 2.2 Sample (Simulated) Individual Age–Crime Trajectories

B. Simulation Conditions

Four different simulation conditions provide the basis for the comparisons below. Three of the simulations are based on different "mixtures" of the four trajectory groups, while the fourth is based on the random coefficient model:

- Condition 1: Equally sized groups—each at 25 percent
- Condition 2: High rate offenders set at 55 percent and each of the other three groups set at 15 percent each
- Condition 3: Non-offenders set at 55 percent and each of the other three set at 15 percent
- Condition 4: A single group (sample) but with random variation in individual coefficients

Prior research using group-based trajectory models on general population samples typically finds that about one-half of the sample would fall into the non-criminal group, similar to Condition 3. This suggests that the first two conditions represent fairly extreme and unlikely mixtures of offending groups to be found in the population. For example, Condition 1 suggests that 75 percent of the population was engaged in some kind of crime, 25 percent at a much higher rate. Condition 2 puts the criminally active at 85 percent, but with more than half of the population falling into the high rate group. Although the simulated populations represented by Conditions 1 and 2 are unlikely to be found in any study of a general population, they help to illustrate whether varying levels of participation in crime and frequency of offending affect the aggregate age distribution of crime. It is also worth noting that even in Condition 3, the frequency of criminal behavior is higher than we would expect to find—rather than an even distribution across the three offending groups, general population samples find very small high-rate groups (about 5 percent) and most individuals falling into the limited or low-rate groups.

For each of the four simulation conditions, there are two major components to the analysis. First, to establish that the results of the simulations reflect prior research, there is an analysis of the frequency of offending and participation in offending by age. These are similar to the individual age–crime curves that are the basis for much of the developmental and life course research published in the past two decades. Second, using the individual crime data generated for each of the four simulation conditions, two different sets of age distributions of crime are generated. In the first set, the age distribution of crime is based on participation in crime, while the second set uses frequency of crime to generate the age distributions.

Keep in mind that prior research critical of looking at the aggregate age distribution of crime has often claimed that it reflects patterns of participation in crime, rather than frequency of criminal behavior. These simulations provide a way of teasing out the extent to which that may be the case.

C. Findings

Figure 2.3 presents characteristic age–crime curves for average frequency of offending (i.e., individual crime rate) for the four simulation conditions. Panels A thru C present the results for the trajectory groups. Note that the overall crime rate by age for the four groups changes across the three different mixtures, as would be expected. The overall crime rate is indicated by the solid line in each plot and shifts up from Panel A to Panel B, when the

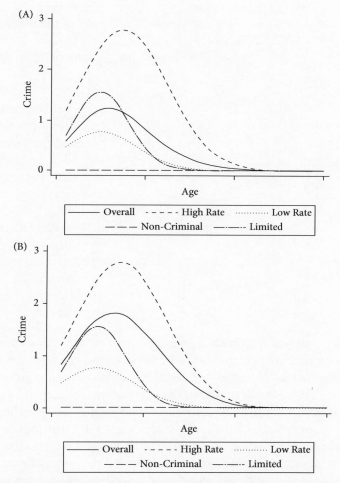

FIGURE 2.3 Characteristic Age–Crime Curves for Four Simulation Conditions: Frequency of Offending

Panel A: Condition 1 (Equally Sized Groups)
Panel B: Condition 2 (55% in High-Rate Group)
Panel C: Condition 3 (55% in Non-Criminal Group)
Panel D: Condition 4 (Random Coefficient Model)

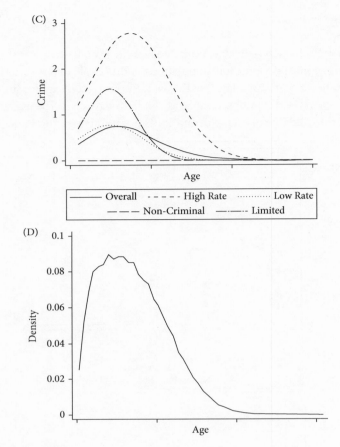

FIGURE 2.3 Continued

mixture changes from four equally sized groups to a mixture where more than half of the individuals are located in the high rate group. The overall crime rate then decreases in Panel C, where more than half of individuals are in the non-criminal group. The single age–crime curve in Panel D reflects the fact that the random coefficient model is based on a single growth curve, but with many individual variations (not shown in the plot).

Figure 2.4 presents characteristic age–crime curves for participation levels of offending for the four simulation conditions. The shapes of the curves in all four plots have changed to reflect the change in measurement, but the same patterns are observable across the four simulation conditions and consistent with previously published research using either group-based trajectory models (Panels A thru C) or random coefficient growth curve models (Panel D).

The age distributions of crime are based on the ages of each simulated individual who had one or more crimes at some age—the distribution is then the density plot (i.e., a smoothed histogram) of the ages of the individuals who had committed a crime. The age distributions of participation for the four simulation conditions appear in Figure 2.5 and reflect the ages of any criminal activity. There is a striking similarity of the distributions

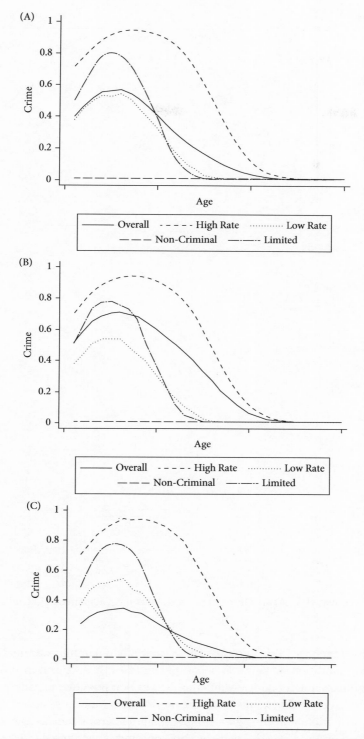

FIGURE 2.4 Characteristic Age–Crime Curves for Four Simulation Conditions: Participation in Offending

Panel A: Condition 1 (Equally Sized Groups)
Panel B: Condition 2 (55% in High-Rate Group)
Panel C: Condition 3 (55% in Non-Criminal Group)
Panel D: Condition 4 (Random Coefficient Model)

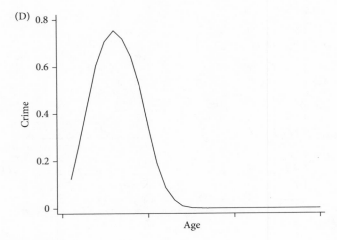

FIGURE 2.4 Continued

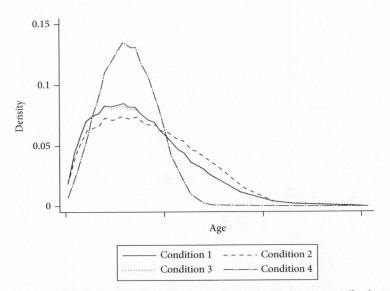

FIGURE 2.5 Simulated Age Distribution of Crime Based on Participation in Offending

for Conditions 1 (equally sized groups) and 3 (more than half non-criminal). The distribution for Condition 2, where over half of the cases were placed in the high-rate offending group, is not dramatically different—its peak is not quite as sharp as the other two group-based conditions, since there are more observations pushed out to the right tail of the distribution, reflecting greater participation in crime at older ages. The distribution for Condition 4 (RCM) is more heavily concentrated in the left tail (i.e., younger ages). The difference between the age distribution of crime for Condition 4 and the first three conditions is the proportion of the sample designated as high-rate offending in

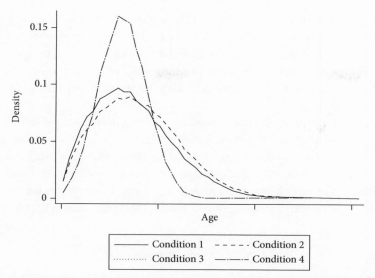

FIGURE 2.6 Simulated Age Distribution of Crime Based on Frequency of Offending

each condition. By allocating a substantial proportion of cases to the high-rate group, it had the effect of lowering the peak and thickening the right tail of the three group-based conditions.

The age distributions for frequency of offending appear in Figure 2.6. What makes the age distributions of frequency of offending different from participation in offending is that each individual's age will appear the same number of times as their number of offenses. In these distributions, then, individuals contribute all of their offenses, similar to what we might find in the UCR arrest data, where, for example, a 20-year-old arrested for two counts of robbery would appear in the arrest statistics as two 20-year-old offenders. Much like the age distributions for participation in offending, there is remarkable similarity across the three group-based simulation conditions, especially for Conditions 1 and 3, which are nearly impossible to distinguish in the plot. Interestingly, the aggregate age distributions of crime based on frequency of offending show a greater concentration of cases in the left tail of the distribution—even more like what we observe in official statistics.

D. Summary

The four simulation conditions reflect different age–crime curves at both the individual and the group level, as well as different hypothetical mixtures in some larger population. Yet when these individual age–crime curves are aggregated—think of these data as the simulated life course crime trajectories of 10,000 individuals—we can build an age distribution of crime that mirrors most of the current examples in published research and official publications. The aggregation of individual-level crime data result in age distributions of crime that are nearly indistinguishable from each other, even when over half of the sample is designated as high-rate offending. Importantly, the results of this simulation suggest that there is no inherent conflict in finding unique individual age–crime curves, as much research has, but then observing that the aggregate pattern is largely constant and not affected much by changes in participation and frequency of offending.

The simulations presented above were based on a fairly simple data-generating process that relied only on age. Additional covariates—both time-stable and time-varying—could have been added to the data-generation process. While the addition of covariates may have made the simulations more realistic, it is unlikely that their inclusion would have altered consequences of individual age–crime curves for the aggregate age distribution of crime, since an age effect would still be included as part of the model.

VI. CONCLUSION

Age is perhaps one of the strongest indicators of risk of committing a crime, but it is not something that lends itself to easy theoretical explanation. The many studies that have taken a developmental or life course approach to understanding the link between age and crime have well documented a number of age-specific covariates that correlate with crime. Similarly, biosocial research has also shown there to be several strong age-specific correlates of crime and other risky behavior. At the same time, these studies are typically limited to a modest sample size in one nation, sometimes a single or small number of cities within a nation. Despite all of the careful attention given to measuring age-specific correlates of crime, the work to date has been unable to explain how or why the aggregate age distribution of crime looks so similar cross-nationally, even though the covariates of age-specific criminal behavior may work in very different ways.

Where does this leave us? First, future research on age and crime should discard the false notion that many unique individual age–crime curves are incompatible with an invariant age effect on crime. In the same way that Hirschi and Gottfredson (1983) erred in claiming that individual age–crime curves would mimic the aggregate age distribution of crime, others have erred in inferring that the endless variability found in individual age–crime curves and similar aggregate distributions was an artifact of the legal system (e.g., Blumstein et al., 1986). In what seems to be overlooked in much of the developmental and life course research on age and crime, the application of growth curve models assumes a common statistical model—typically a quadratic equation that varies in the parameters. Thus, research showing significant variability in individual-level data relying on group-based trajectory models and random coefficient growth curve models tends to follow a similar basic functional form—what some have called a type of invariance (Britt 1992).

Second, the theoretical explanation for the age relationship with crime should use the relatively large and robust body of research on age-specific risk and protective factors.

There are many biosocial/biopsychological, psychological, and sociological character-istics that affect the likelihood of crime commission at different ages. Theoretical de-velopment needs to include the broad swath of these findings and link them together in ways that help to explain why changes in these factors affect criminal behavior. A useful starting point could be Sampson and Laub's (1993) age-graded informal social control theory. How could evidence on the effects of biosocial covariates, for example, be in-tegrated into the theory in a way that maintained the integrity of it? Alternatively, one could start with the available body of evidence—the facts about age and crime—and inductively build the explanation (Bernard and Snipes 1996). What are the common patterns and links of these age-specific correlates of crime? Ongoing biosocial research is pushing hard to understand and explain these links (see, e.g., Beaver, Barnes, and Boutwell, 2014).

Finally, rather than focus on whether Hirschi and Gottfredson (1983) were wrong (or right) about whether the age distribution of crime can be explained—statistically or theoretically—future efforts might focus more directly on what accounts for variation in distributions. We know that within the United States, age distributions of crime vary over time and by offense type and gender. Cross-national comparisons have yet to be done in any systematic fashion. What accounts for the differences? For example, when a time series comparison shows a location shift—the mean or median is increasing or decreasing—an important question would be why it is shifting. What are the other eco-nomic, cultural, and social forces at work in shifting a distribution? Examples of this type of work in economic sociology have tried to understand and to explain the changing distributions of income and wealth in the United States (e.g., Morris, Bernhardt, and Handcock, 1994; Handcock and Morris 1998).

Rolf Loeber (2012) posed the question: Does the study of the age–crime curve have a future? He concluded that it did—there are many things we do not know about the age–crime relationship. The age relationship with crime continues to be a tremendous puzzle for criminology. Age is a key indicator of the likelihood of committing a crime and has been for about as long as researchers have been collecting crime data (see, e.g., Quetelet 1984). At both the micro-level and the macro-level, the links between age and crime are complex, multifaceted, and bound to motivate researchers for years to come.

REFERENCES

Beaver, Kevin M., J. C. Barnes, and Brian B. Boutwell, eds. 2014. *The Nurture Versus Biosocial Debate in Criminology: On the Origins of Criminal Behavior and Criminality.* Los Angeles: Sage.

Bernard, Thomas J., and Jeffrey B. Snipes. 1996. "Theoretical Integration in Criminology." *Crime and Justice* 20: 301–348.

Blonigen, Daniel M. 2010. "Explaining the Relationship Between Age and Crime: Contributions from the Developmental Literature on Personality." *Clinical Psychology Review* 30(1): 89–100.

Blumstein, Alfred, Jacqueline Cohen, Jeffrey A. Roth, and Christy Visher, eds. 1986. *Criminal Careers and "Career Criminals,"* Vol. 1. Washington, DC: National Academy Press.

Blumstein, Alfred, Jacqueline Cohen, and David P. Farrington. 1988a. "Criminal Career Research: Its Value for Criminology." *Criminology* 26(1): 1–35.

Blumstein, Alfred, Jacqueline Cohen, and David P. Farrington. 1988b. "Longitudinal and Criminal Career Research: Further Clarifications." *Criminology* 26(1): 57–74.

Britt, Chester L. 1992. "Constancy and Change in the U.S. Age Distribution of Crime." *Journal of Quantitative Criminology* 8(2): 175–187.

Britt, Chester L. 1997. "Reconsidering the Unemployment and Crime Relationship: Variation by Age Group and Historical Period." *Journal of Quantitative Criminology* 13(4): 405–428.

Brown, Elizabeth, and Mike Males. (2011). "Does Age or Poverty Level Best Predict Criminal Arrest and Homicide Rates? A Preliminary Investigation." *Justice Policy Journal* 8(1): 1–30.

Collins, Randall E. 2004. Onset and Desistance in Criminal Careers: Neurobiology and the Age-Crime Relationship." *Journal of Offender Rehabilitation* 39(3): 1–19.

Eggleston, Elaine P., John H. Laub, and Robert J. Sampson. 2004. "Methodological Sensitivities to Latent Class Analysis of Long-Term Criminal Trajectories." *Journal of Quantitative Criminology* 20(1): 1–26.

Farrington, David P. 1986. "Age and Crime." *Crime and Justice* 7: 189–250.

Gottfredson, Michael R., and Travis Hirschi. 1990. *A General Theory of Crime.* Stanford, CA: Stanford University Press.

Greenberg, David F. 1985. "Age, Crime, and Social Explanation." *American Journal of Sociology* 91(1): 1–21.

Greenberg, David F. 2001. "Time Series Analysis of Crime Rates." *Journal of Quantitative Criminology* 17(4): 291–327.

Handcock, Mark S., and Martina Morris. 1998. "Relative Distribution Methods." *Sociological Methodology* 28(1):53–97.

Hirschi, Travis, and Michael R. Gottfredson. 1983. "Age and the Explanation of Crime." *American Journal of Sociology* 89(3): 552–584.

Hirschi, Travis, and Michael R. Gottfredson. 2008. "Critiquing the Critics: The Authors Respond." In *Out of Control: Assessing the General Theory of Crime,* edited by Erich Goode, 217–231. Stanford, CA: Stanford University Press.

Jennings, Wesley G., and Jennifer M. Reingle. 2012. "On the Number and Shape of Developmental/Life-Course Violence, Aggression, and Delinquency Trajectories: A State-of-the-Art Review." *Journal of Criminal Justice* 40(6): 472–489.

Laub, John H., and Robert J. Sampson. 2003. *Shared Beginnings, Divergent Lives: Delinquent Boys to Age 70.* Cambridge, MA: Harvard University Press.

Le Blanc, Marc, and Rolf Loeber. 1998. "Developmental Criminology Updated." *Crime and Justice* 23: 115–198.

Lieberson, Stanley. 1985. *Making It Count: The Improvement of Social Theory and Research.* Berkeley, CA: University of California Press.

Loeber, Rolf. 2012. "Does the Study of the Age-Crime Curve Have a Future?" In *The Future of Criminology,* edited by Rolf Loeber and Brandon C. Welsh, 11–19. New York: Oxford University Press.

Loeber, Rolf, and Marc Le Blanc. 1990. "Toward a Developmental Criminology." *Crime and Justice* 12: 375–473.

Loeber, Rolf, Barbara Menting, Donald R. Lynam, Terri E. Moffitt, Magda Stouthamer-Loeber, Rebecca Stallings, David P. Farrington, and Dustin Pardini. 2012. "Findings From the Pittsburgh Youth Study: Cognitive Impulsivity and Intelligence as Predictors of the Age–Crime Curve." *Journal of the American Academy of Child & Adolescent Psychiatry* 51(11): 1136–1149.

MacLeod, John F., Peter G. Grove, and David P. Farrington. 2012. *Explaining Criminal Careers: Implications for Justice Policy*. Oxford, UK: Oxford University Press.

Moffitt, Terrie E. 1993. "'Life-Course-Persistent' and 'Adolescence-Limited' Antisocial Behavior: A Developmental Taxonomy." *Psychological Review* 100(4): 674–701.

Morris, Martina, Annette D. Bernhardt, and Mark S. Handcock. 1994. "Economic Inequality: New Methods for New Trends." *American Sociological Review* 59: 205–219.

O'Brien, Robert M., and Jean Stockard. 2006. "A Common Explanation for the Changing Age Distributions of Suicide and Homicide in the United States, 1930 to 2000." *Social Forces* 84(3): 1539–1557.

Osgood, D. Wayne, Janet K. Wilson, Patrick M. O'Malley, Jerald G. Bachman, and Lloyd D. Johnston. 1996. "Routine Activities and Individual Deviant Behavior." *American Sociological Review* 61(4): 635–655.

Piquero, Alex R. 2008. "Taking Stock of Developmental Trajectories of Criminal Activity over the Life Course." In *The Long View of Crime: A Synthesis of Longitudinal Research*, edited by Akiva M. Liberman, 23–78. New York: Springer.

Quetelet, Adolfe. 1984. *Adolphe Quetelet's Research on the Propensity for Crime at Different Ages*. Cincinnati: Anderson.

Sampson, Robert J., and John H. Laub. 1993. *Crime in the Making: Pathways and Turning Points Through Life*. Cambridge, MA: Harvard University Press.

Shulman, Elizabeth P., Laurence D. Steinberg, and Alex R. Piquero. (2014). "The Age-Crime Curve in Adolescence and Early Adulthood Is Not Due to Age Differences in Economic Status." *Journal of Youth and Adolescence* 42(6): 848–860.

Steffensmeier, Darrell J., Emilie Andersen Allan, Miles D. Harer, and Cathy Streifel. 1989. "Age and the Distribution of Crime." *American Journal of Sociology* 94(4): 803–831.

Steffensmeier, Darrell J., and Cathy Streifel. 1991. "Age, Gender, and Crime Across Three Historical Periods: 1935, 1960, and 1985." *Social Forces* 69(3): 869–894.

Steffensmeier, Darrell, and Cathy Streifel. 2008. "Co-Offending and the Age-Crime Curve." *Journal of Research in Crime and Delinquency* 45(1): 65–86.

Sweeten, Gary, Alex R. Piquero, and Laurence Steinberg. 2013. "Age and the Explanation of Crime, Revisited." *Journal of Youth and Adolescence* 42(6): 921–938.

Ulmer, Jeffrey T., and Darrell J. Steffensmeier. 2014. "The Age and Crime Relationship: Social Variation, Social Explanations." In *The Nurture Versus Biosocial Debate in Criminology: On the Origins of Criminal Behavior and Criminality*, edited by Kevin M. Beaver, J. C. Barnes, and Brian B. Boutwell, 377–396. Los Angeles: Sage.

Walsh, Anthony. 2009. "Crazy by Design: A Biosocial Approach to the Age-Crime Curve." In *Biosocial Criminology: New Directions in Theory and Research*, edited by Anthony Walsh and Kevin M. Beaver. New York: Routledge.

Warr, Mark. 2002. *Companions in Crime: The Social Aspects of Criminal Conduct*. New York: Cambridge University Press.

CHAPTER 3

··

AGE OF ONSET
OF OFFENDING BEHAVIOR

··

ELAINE EGGLESTON DOHERTY
AND SARAH BACON*

AGE-OF-ONSET research is grounded in the criminal career framework, which posits that different aspects of an individual's criminal career (e.g., onset, desistance, seriousness, duration) should be evaluated separately (Blumstein et al. 1986). The criminal career framework, in turn, is rooted in the longstanding debate about the relationship between age and crime. As mentioned in the previous chapter, the age–crime curve, an aggregate measure of offending for all ages, maps the common patterns of the onset of offending, peak ages, and desistance from offending. Although there is a strong historical and contextual consistency of the age–crime curve (Hirschi and Gottfredson 1983), it conceals several patterns of offending behavior, some of which diverge sharply from the aggregated pattern reflected in the curve (Blumstein et al. 1986). Thus, while many researchers remain interested in comparing offenders with non-offenders, criminal career proponents focus on the differences within and among offenders (Hagan and Palloni 1988), with the age of onset of criminal behavior being one essential dimension of these differences.

In this chapter we first provide an overview of the empirical observations that have shaped the research (Section I). We view these empirical observations as the central "facts" regarding age of onset that must be taken into account in any discussion of the criminal career. We then discuss these empirical observations in their relation to the definitions and measurement of age of onset (Section II) and to the theoretical approaches to understanding and explaining age of onset (Section III) before discussing the importance and implications of age of onset research for prevention and intervention purposes (Section IV). For each of these areas of consideration we provide an

---

* The findings and conclusions of this chapter are those of the authors and do not necessarily represent the official position of the Centers for Disease Control and Prevention.

overview and a critical analysis of extant research followed by critical unanswered questions.

I. EMPIRICAL "FACTS" OF ONSET AND THE CRIMINAL CAREER

The age of onset of antisocial and delinquent behavior is among the most studied of all the developmental parameters of antisocial behavior (Moffitt, Caspi, Rutter, and Silva 2001). This is due, in part, to the fact that the age at which an individual commits his or her first criminal offense is highly indicative of the seriousness, frequency, and variety of offenses to follow (Loeber and LeBlanc 1990). A consistent finding from this research is that early onset of offending is correlated with a longer and more serious offending career (Farrington et al. 1990). In fact, some have gone so far as to say that "the demarcation of a childhood-onset of conduct problems is *central* to the psychiatric diagnosis of behavioral disorders, theorization in the social and behavioral sciences, and the scholarly study of individual crime patterns" (DeLisi and Piquero 2011, p. 290, emphasis added). In contrast, later-onset delinquents have been characterized as temporary offenders whose offending is limited to adolescence and to more trivial crimes (Tolan 1987; Tolan and Thomas 1995; Moffitt et al. 1996).

The notion that early onset of offending is associated with a longer and more serious offending career began to take hold beginning in the 1950s with the Gluecks, who were the first to assert that age of onset is an important dimension of the criminal career and that career criminals are more likely to have an early onset (Glueck and Glueck 1950). Research in the 1980s and 1990s provided ample evidence that those who begin offending at the earliest ages (1) continue to offend at the highest rates over the longest periods of time, (2) exhibit more diverse and serious delinquency, and (3) are at an increased risk of serious, violent, and chronic offending (e.g., Farrington et al. 1990; Piquero et al. 1999; Loeber and LeBlanc 1990; Farrington 1992; Patterson and Yoerger 1993; Tolan 1987; Tolan and Thomas 1995).

Thus, the essential and consistent point offered regarding the age of onset of criminal behavior is that an early onset is widely accepted as a harbinger of a more serious, persistent offending career. In fact, some have gone as far as to say that early onset is the *best* predictor of long-term repeat offending (Farrington et al. 1990; Hanson et al. 1984; Loeber, Stouthamer-Loeber, and Green 1991; Loeber and LeBlanc 1998; Moffitt et al. 2001; Moffitt 1993; Nagin and Farrington 1992a; Tolan 1987; West 1982; for reviews see Piquero, Farrington, and Blumstein, 2003; DeLisi and Piquero 2011). Yet there are several nuances surrounding this "fact" that add complexity and warrant further elaboration: How is early onset defined and measured? What is the theoretical explanation for this relationship between onset and offending? and What are the key policy and prevention implications of this "fact"?

II. Definitions and Measurement

An informed discussion of the meaning and significance of age of onset requires an understanding of what, exactly, is meant by the term. Conceptually, onset is broadly defined as the first occurrence of criminal behavior (Farrington et al. 1990; Loeber and LeBlanc 1990; Nagin and Farrington 1992a) or the age at which the delinquent career begins (Farrington 1992; Hamparian et al. 1978; Tracy 1990). Hirschi and Gottfredson (1983) define age of onset as the age at which criminality first appears, but how that is marked in time remains under question. Overall, a review of the literature reveals little consensus as to the exact operational definition of age of onset.

A. Defining "Early" and "Late" Onset

Much of the onset of delinquency research of the late 1980s and 1990s defines early onset as that which occurs from ages 10 to 12, or before puberty (Tolan 1987; Patterson and Yoerger 1993; Moffitt 1993). These "early"-onset offenders constitute a small percentage of offenders, while the adolescent-onset offenders constitute the vast majority. "Late"-onset offenders were defined as those having a first offense during ages 12 through 15, depending on the study (Tolan 1987; Patterson and Yoerger 1993; Moffitt 1993). Yet these studies restricted the focus to the juvenile years.

Research from the past 15 years has extended the time frame to include adulthood and argues that in order to determine what is meant by *early* and *late* onset, one must first determine what is meant by "on-time" or "expected" onset (e.g., Eggleston and Laub 2002). The age–crime curve tells us that the bulk of offending is committed by offenders in their teen years (Blumstein et al. 1986; Farrington 1986; Wolfgang, Figlio, and Selin 1972). Moffitt and colleagues (1996) find that the "vast majority of juvenile delinquent offenders whose participation in antisocial behavior is primarily limited to the teen years" (i.e., adolescence-limited offenders) has a self-reported onset of age 13 to 15 (p. 401). Using police contact data, Wolfgang and colleagues (1972) reported a mean age of onset of 14.4 years, a modal age of onset of 16, and a peak in the probability of onset between ages 16 to 17. Wolfgang and colleagues (1972) give us further insight into the proportion of boys at each age who have their first official police contact, with just 0.72 percent at age 7 having official contact with police, 5.9 percent before age 10, 11.9 percent at ages 10–11, and most boys (72.3 percent) having their first contact with police between the ages of 12 and 16. Shannon (1982) also provides information on "the normalcy of juvenile misbehavior" (p. 9). In each of the three birth cohorts sampled in Racine, Wisconsin (1942, 1949, 1955), 60 percent of the subjects had at least one or two police contacts by age 16 or 17, and a combination of self-report and official contacts shows that over 90 percent of the males and 60 percent to 70 percent of the females in each cohort committed an offense by age 18, with few continuing into adulthood.

As a result, the definitions of early and late onset have changed from the definitions used in the 1980s and 1990s research. Once the full life course is taken into account, and acknowledging that age 13 to 17 is the "normative" age of onset of delinquency, researchers have argued that early onset definitions need to begin even earlier than 10 to 12 (potentially even in very young childhood) (Nagin and Tremblay 2005). Aggression in preschool-age children may be simply a different manifestation of violence seen in early adulthood (Loeber and Hay 1997), and thus, the toddler years might be the true "onset" of deviance. Similarly, the definition of "late" onset has changed in more recent years. For instance, Eggleston and Laub (2002) define late onset as "adult" onset (i.e., age 18 or older), using the rationale that once the typical years of onset are incorporated into the timeline, the two atypical onset periods appear to be in early childhood and in early adulthood. More recently, Sohoni and colleagues (2014) have argued that late onset should be defined as age 25 or older given that this is the average age of achieving adult social roles and when perceptions of adult status begin to strengthen. To date, there is no consensus on these definitions. Moreover, the definitional challenges are further complicated by the question of which type of data is best to measure "onset" of criminal behavior.

B. Type of Data Source: Official Versus Self-Report Data

Because age of onset marks the discrete transition of an individual from non-delinquent to delinquent status, an examination of the age of onset of criminal behavior is particularly sensitive to issues of measurement. Official data, in the form of arrest and adjudication statistics, are relatively easy to obtain and serve as the basis for much criminological research. Use of official records eliminates concerns of recall and truthfulness in reporting, which are problematic with self-report data. Official data also generally include a record of the dates, and therefore the sequence, of offenses, which is useful in some research endeavors (Jackson 1990; Weis 1986). However, official records can be problematic when studying onset in several ways. Most importantly, official data do not measure the first occurrence of actual offending but rather the first occurrence of offending that results in official contact (Loeber and LeBlanc 1990).

As Farrington (1983) states explicitly, official data cannot reveal when a criminal career actually begins. In their pioneering work *Delinquency in a Birth Cohort* (1972), Wolfgang, Figlio, and Sellin indicate that exclusive use of court-determined delinquency would result in a biased view of the problem of delinquency. The probability of detection and processing by the juvenile justice system is low (Weis 1986), and the probability of a first occurrence of criminal behavior (i.e., onset) coming to the attention of the police or juvenile justice officials is even more remote. This results in a censoring of the left-hand side of the age-crime curve (Moffitt 1993), to the extent that Moffitt and colleagues (2001) report estimates of age of onset from official data a full three to five years after estimates from self-reports (see also Loeber et al. 2003). Similarly, in a discussion of the data obtained in the original Cambridge Study in Delinquent Development, West (1982) reports that 52.6 percent of those who had self-reported delinquency still had no official charges by age 16. This finding is continually reinforced as researchers with both official and self-reported data sources find that officially defined offenders have self-reported prior offending (e.g., Kazemian and Farrington 2005; Kirk 2006; McGee and Farrington 2010; Payne and Piquero 2018). However, it could be argued that official data provide a more valid source to measure criminal behavior than self-reports because, although not capturing *all* offending, this data source is a reliable assessment *across* individuals (i.e., one person's involvement in crime *in relation* to others').

Self-report data may offer some alternatives for addressing the concerns presented by the exclusive use of official data. Self-report data provide good measures of prevalence and individual offending rates and have shown "impressive reliability" (Weis 1986, p. 11). Given the low likelihood of ascertaining the true age of onset of criminal behavior with official data, it is intuitive that self-report data, especially prospective data, may be better suited to provide this information (see Kazemian and Farrington 2005). However, as in the case with official data, there are areas of concern with using self-report data. Of utmost concern is the feasibility of obtaining accurate reports of offending behavior. Recall of specific incidents is not likely to be accurate, and some individuals may purposefully misrepresent their involvement in criminal behavior (Farrington 1983). Of particular relevance to the present discussion is the possibility that chronic and persistent offenders are among the least likely to be included in survey research and/or to fully and accurately recall the extent of their criminal involvement (see, e.g., Kazemian and Farrigton 2005; Weis 1986). This possibility is especially problematic for an examination of early onset and the continuity of criminal behavior, in that those offenders who display the most extreme antisocial behavior are also those who began at the youngest ages and are the most likely to persist in it (Loeber 1982). It may also be the case that self-report data do not adequately address the domain of serious offending (Hindelang, Hirschi, and Weis 1979), which may be a better reflection of true "onset" rather than onset of trivial delinquent acts. In fact, Kazemian and Farrington (2005) find that self-reported prospective, retrospective, and official data on age of onset begin to increase in their rates of agreement as offenses move from minor to more serious in nature (see also Payne and Piquero 2018).

Despite the problems attendant to both official and self-report data, both have been put forth as valid and reliable measures of distinct domains of behavior (Hindelang, Hirschi, and Weis 1979; Weis 1986). However, recent empirical research shows that the type of data (self-reports versus police contact versus court referral) to define onset has implications in its relationship with future antisocial behavior (DeLisi et al. 2013). Thus, debates as to the value of official data versus self-report data are not easily resolved (Weis 1986). There is evidence to suggest that the use of official and self-report data, in concert with third-party reports and other forms of verification, may offer the most accurate and complete picture of an offending career. Citing the Cambridge Study in Delinquent Development as an exemplar, Farrington (1983) posits that the most valid information on the development of criminal behavior would be generated by the combination of a longitudinal survey employing official data and self-report interviews.

We would add that the self-reports, ideally, would be prospectively collected with relative frequency (e.g., every 6 months to a year) beginning in young childhood and extending into adulthood, which would be a costly and time-consuming endeavor. Barring that initiative, the question remains as to which definition of early and late age of onset from which data source would be the best reflection of the "onset" of one's criminal career.

C. Critical Questions

The definition and measurement of early versus normative versus late onset is still an open question, yet these definitions are central to several common research questions such as whether late offenders "truly" exist and the theoretical or policy importance of age of onset. Given that age is a continuous level variable, one concern is whether the delineation of "early" versus "late" is more of a red herring than a useful debate as the cut-offs continue to seem arbitrary. For instance, the search for a clear definition of the "late"-onset or "adult"-onset offender has proven to be elusive although not for lack of continued effort in the search. A similar line of inquiry could be directed at finding the "early"-onset offender in early childhood, but to what end? These definitional debates may be distracting researchers from further unpacking the development of the criminal career. A potentially more useful direction for future research may be to abandon the debates of how to define early versus late and focus on age as a continuous variable essential to the underlying structure of the full criminal career. Another direction of research might follow Burt and colleagues (2011), who contend that age of onset is merely a proxy for different types of behaviors (childhood aggression versus adolescent rule breaking) that have distinct influences on later criminal career trajectories. A focus on age-graded behavioral subtypes as predictive of future behavior reduces the importance of age in and of itself. These reconceptualizations would then have theoretical implications, a topic we address next.

III. Theoretical Explanations of the Relationship Between Age of Onset and the Criminal Career

Tolan (1987) conducted a cross-sectional study of volunteer 11- to 18-year-olds using self-report data to establish whether age of onset is an important discriminator when investigating criminal activity. Age of onset overshadowed other psychosocial variables in predicting involvement in delinquency. Among a number of individual, family, school, and demographic characteristics, the most informative discriminators of age of onset were family functioning and academic achievement and plans. However, in a later study, which used a longitudinal research design with a nationally representative sample, the influence of age of onset was found to be relatively small in magnitude, yet it did explain involvement in delinquency to some degree (Tolan and Thomas 1995). These results suggest that age of onset itself is an important predictor that cannot be ignored when investigating the causes and nature of offending.

Moreover, while there is some evidence that the covariates of offending are similar for adult-onset and juvenile-onset offenders (Eggleston and Laub 2002), and for childhood and adolescent offending (Beckley et al. 2016), others have found distinct predictors that distinguish adult-onset male offenders (Zara and Farrington 2009) and adult-onset female offenders (Simpson et al. 2016) from their childhood- or adolescent-onset counterparts. Based on the established fact that age of onset is an important predictor of future offending along with evidence that covariates of onset potentially change with age, many have placed age of onset as a central theoretical factor.

A. Theoretical Explanations of Age and Crime

The central fact that early onset is empirically associated with a more serious, persistent offending career has motivated a significant theoretical literature intended to explain it. At the core of developmental and life-course theories is the explanation of the relationship between age and crime and the assumptions surrounding the causal impact of onset age and one's criminal career. Specifically, two dominant assumptions have emerged by way of explanation: persistent heterogeneity and state dependence. According to a persistent heterogeneity argument, those with high levels of criminal propensity (e.g., low self-control) will be more likely to start offending at an early age and be more likely to have a long criminal career. Therefore, early onset has no causal influence on one's future offending but is simply a marker or flag indicating that someone possesses a high criminal propensity. A state-dependence argument, on the other hand, proposes that if adolescent onset is normative, an early onset is, by definition, "off time" (Elder 1998), leading to a disruption of social development and further risk of anti-social behavior—thus, a causal explanation.

This section describes each paradigm briefly and identifies three contrasting dominant theories that account for the relationship between age and offending (see Paternoster et al. 1997): one general and static theory (Gottfredson and Hirschi 1990), one typological and dynamic theory (Moffitt 1993), and one general and dynamic theory (Sampson and Laub 1993).

1. *Population Heterogeneity and State Dependence*

A population heterogeneity explanation of the continuity of criminal behavior assumes that an individual's propensity to commit crime is an antisocial characteristic that is established early in life and remains relatively stable thereafter (Nagin and Farrington 1992a; Nagin and Paternoster 2000). The association between past and future offending, then, is a reflection of these time-stable individual differences in criminal potential

(Nagin and Farrington 1992b). Pure population heterogeneity theories do not allow for any causal effect of prior offending (Paternoster et al. 1997), and the observed association between past and future offending (i.e., early onset and a longer criminal career), therefore, is due to self-selection. Thus, the higher an individual's propensity to engage in criminal behavior, the earlier they will begin such behavior, rendering the relationship between an early age of onset and the subsequent serious criminal career spurious as the underlying criminal propensity drives them both (Nagin and Paternoster 1991, 2000; Sampson and Laub 1997).

The second possible explanation for the robust relationship between onset of offending and the subsequent duration and severity of offending behavior is state dependence. The assumption of state dependence posits that the act of committing a crime has a genuine behavioral impact on and increases the probability of future offending (Nagin and Farrington 1992a; Nagin and Paternoster 1991, 2000; Sampson and Laub 1992). With specific regard to criminal behavior, past criminal involvement is thought to increase the likelihood of future criminal involvement by reducing internal inhibitions and external restraints to crime, while simultaneously strengthening incentives to crime (Nagin and Farrington 1992b; Nagin and Paternoster 2000). Nagin and Paternoster (2000) describe this as a "process of contagion" (p. 117) and suggest that this process contributes to the stability of criminal behavior. Theories of state dependence are consistent with the developmental and criminal career perspectives in that they recognize that changes and experiences in the life course can influence an individual's offending behavior (Paternoster et al. 1997).

Three prominent theories that overtly incorporate age and offending as well as an explanation for the relationship between age of onset and criminal career dimensions are Gottfredson and Hirschi's (1990), Moffitt's (1993), and Sampson and Laub's (1993). Gottfredson and Hirschi's theory is strictly a population heterogeneity theory, while both of the dynamic theories of Moffitt and Sampson and Laub are considered "mixed" theories with respect to the assumption that age of onset is an indicator of underlying propensity (population heterogeneity) *and* initiates a causal sequence (state dependence) of criminal behavior.

2. *Gottfredson and Hirschi's General Theory of Crime*

In their *General Theory of Crime* (1990), Gottfredson and Hirschi outline what is perhaps the best known theory of population heterogeneity. In short, these theorists argue that individuals who are low in self-control (and thus high in criminal propensity) will begin offending early in life, will continue to do so at higher rates, and will desist later in life than individuals with higher degrees of self-control (and thus lower in criminal propensity) (Farrington 1992; Piquero et al. 1999). Their position, then, is that there is no need to look at early or late onset of offending since it is simply a by-product of level of self-control rendering onset research redundant since it simply reiterates the difference in offending rates (Hirschi and Gottfredson 1983). Thus, after the first decade of the life course, dynamic factors can have only negligible effects on propensity (Paternoster and Brame 1997).

However, if there are different correlates of offending for individuals with an early versus a later age of onset, a developmental approach will be necessary. Nagin and Farrington (1992b) found that the determinants of early onset are different from those of late onset; thus, based on this finding, developmental research that investigates individual criminal offending longitudinally to allow the separation of offenders according to age of onset is needed.

3. *Moffitt's Dual Taxonomy*

Several theories posit that individuals follow different pathways of delinquency based on their age of onset and that at least two theories regarding delinquency are necessary to accommodate all individuals (Moffitt 1993; Moffitt et al. 1996; Tolan 1987; Tolan and Thomas 1995; Simons et al. 1994; Patterson and Yoerger 1993, 1997). The most widely cited typological approach is Moffitt's dual taxonomy (1993), which uses age of onset to retrospectively identify two distinct groups of offenders. The life-course–persistent (LCP) offender begins offending at an early age and continues his or her offending behavior throughout the life span. Neurological deficits and family/environment–person interactions characterize these life-course persisters who display difficult behavior as early as age 3 and have long and serious criminal careers. Moffitt's theory, as it explains the LCP offender, is reflective of a population heterogeneity process in that the continuity of behavior stems from antisocial tendencies that emerge early in life and persist thereafter. The second type of offender is the more common adolescence-limited offender (AL), whose offending behavior is limited to the adolescent years. The adolescence-limited individual mimics the life-course–persistent adolescent who appears to be achieving a level of independence that is unattainable through prosocial means. Once the adolescent-limited offender reaches adulthood, prosocial behavior is preferred to the now potentially detrimental antisocial behavior. The adolescence-limited criminal pattern, then, is restricted to the teenage years, and desistance after adolescence is a defining characteristic of this group.

Thus, according to Moffitt, it appears that at least two developmental pathways based on age of onset are needed to accurately depict criminal offending in the life course: one that is characterized by persistent heterogeneity (LCP) and one that is characterized by state dependence (AL). However, as Paternoster and colleagues (1997) state, "the jury may still be out on the importance of unique pathways to criminal offending" (p. 264), suggesting that a general but dynamic theory might best explain the relationship between age of onset and crime.

4. *Sampson and Laub's Age-Graded Theory of Informal Social Control*

Like Moffitt (1993), Sampson and Laub (1995) assert that the stability of criminal behavior is a result of both persistent heterogeneity and state-dependence effects. However, they posit a general approach as opposed to a typological one. In their age-graded theory of informal social control (1993), they acknowledge that the continuity of behavior, so widely documented in criminological research, dictates the inclusion of some degree of self-selection processes in explaining criminal behavior (Nagin and Paternoster 2000) while acknowledging state-dependence processes. Most related to onset research, Sampson and Laub (1993) acknowledge and explain the great deal of continuity in both offending and other life domains not only through childhood propensity (persistent heterogeneity) but also through a process they call cumulative disadvantage (state dependence).

Specifically, they explain continuity through a "cumulative, developmental model whereby delinquent behavior has a systematic attenuating effect on the social and institutional bonds linking adults to society (for example, labor force attachment, marital cohesion)" (Sampson and Laub 1993, p. 138). Thus, Sampson and Laub theorize that relatively stable levels of childhood differences (persistent heterogeneity) are influential in determining continuity in criminal involvement. Yet these individual differences are not sufficient; along with these individual differences, criminal involvement sets off a chain reaction of negative consequences where bonds to conventional society are continually weakened and criminal behavior is increasingly likely. Thus, those with childhood propensities are more likely to offend, and offend early, but the continuity in behavior is explained by both these individual differences as well as this "chain of adversity" (Sampson and Laub 1993, p. 147) as part of a state-dependent process of cumulative continuity of disadvantage.

B. Critical Questions

There is little to no question that the early-onset offender is at high risk for chronic offending. The question that remains is whether the continuity of antisocial behavior is due to a causal link between past and future offending (state dependence), or to a basic trait that is stable and is therefore the cause of each offense (population heterogeneity), or to both. Bacon, Paternoster, and Brame (2009) find preliminary evidence for a causal (i.e., state-dependent) impact of police contact on future offending, controlling for unobserved population heterogeneity; yet an extension of this study, while consistent with Bacon and colleagues in many ways, does not find evidence of a state-dependence process (El Sayed, Pacheco, and Morris 2016). In further contrast, Gann and colleagues (2015) find evidence that a series of social factors mediate the relationship between age of onset and criminal career patterns among serious juvenile offenders, suggesting evidence for a state-dependence process. This debate is far from resolved, and a continuation of research is needed as the answers have a direct impact on policy decisions for intervention strategies.

IV. POLICY AND PREVENTION IMPLICATIONS

As previously discussed, the most persistent offenders—those who exhibit the highest levels of continuity—also tend to experience earlier onset of offending, commit more serious offenses, and inflict the most harm. A goal of criminological inquiry, therefore, needs to be furthering our understanding of the mechanisms that drive this continuity so that we may then disrupt it. The fact that an early age of onset is such a powerful predictor of chronic and serious offending for long periods of time provides an important opportunity for juvenile justice or social services, or both, to intervene (Farrington et al. 1990; Piquero et al. 1999). The most effective interventions will be those based on a comprehensive understanding of the processes that drive the continuity of criminal behavior over time. For instance, prevention may be attainable for the early-onset offender if the intervention is administered very early in life and focuses on family and effective parenting (Moffitt 1993; Patterson and Yoeger 1997), while therapeutic programs, which focus on independence and education, may be best for the adolescent-onset offenders (Moffitt et al. 1996; Tolan 1987).

Ideally, we would be able to prospectively identify those youth most at risk for an early onset and long criminal career so that prevention efforts may be undertaken before any offending occurs. With respect to policy, a focus on the early-onset offender is consistent with the notion of criminal justice epidemiology and the efforts to strengthen "research connections between the fields of criminal justice and public health to inform evidence-based criminal justice practice" (Vaughn et al. 2012, p. 165). If possible, resources might be best utilized if targeted to these early onset persisters through both criminal justice and public health interventions (see Vaughn et al. 2014) and focus on key mediators, such as drug use in adolescence (Gann, Sullivan, and Ilchi 2015). Of course, the success of these efforts hinges on the challenge in accurately (and prospectively) predicting the long-term trajectories of continuity and change (Sampson and Laub 2003).

One implication of onset research that would not require prediction points to prevention strategies that attempt to delay onset (Farrington et al. 1990; Tolan and Thomas 1995). It seems logical that delaying onset would decrease both juvenile delinquency and adult offending if earlier onset is related to a more serious and longer criminal career. However, delaying onset would only be effective in reducing crime if it could redirect a criminal career as opposed to postponing a predetermined trajectory. Thus, the causes of criminal offending would need to be rooted in social factors as opposed to biological determinants, bringing us back to the importance of theoretical research and our understanding of the process of offending. For example, according to Moffitt (1993), the life-course persister may not benefit from a delayed onset since more stable neurological traits are prominent in causing the antisocial behavior. These policy and prevention implications reiterate the importance of research examining the relationship between onset and continuity in behavior (i.e., the debate between population heterogeneity and state dependence), highlighting the interdependencies between definitions, measurement, theory, and policy with regard to age of onset research.

References

Bacon, Sarah, Ray Paternoster, and Robert Brame. 2009. "Understanding the Relationship Between Onset Age and Subsequent Offending During Adolescence." *Journal of Youth and Adolescence* 38: 301–311.

Beckley, Amber L., Avshalom Caspi, Honalee Harrington, Renate M. Houts, Tara Renae McGee, Nick Morgan, Felix Schroeder, Sandhya Rarakha, Richie Poulton, and Terrie Moffitt. 2016. "Adult-Onset Offenders: Is a Tailored Theory Warranted?" *Journal of Criminal Justice* 46: 64–81.

Blumstein, A., Jacqueline Cohen, Jeffrey A. Roth, and Christy Visher. 1986. *Criminal Careers and "Career Criminals."* Washington, DC: National Academy Press.

Burt, S. Alexandra, M. Brent Donnellan, William G. Iacono, and Matt McGue. 2011. "Age-of-Onset or Behavioral Sub-Types? A Prospective Comparison of Two Approaches to Characterizing the Heterogeneity Within Antisocial Behavior." *Journal of Abnormal Child Psychology* 39: 633–644.

DeLisi, Matt, and Alex R. Piquero. 2011. "New Frontiers in Criminal Careers Research 2000–2011: A State-of-the-Art Review." *Journal of Criminal Justice* 39: 289–301.

DeLisi, Matt, Tricia K. Neppl, Brenda J. Lohman, Michael G. Vaughn, and Jeffrey J. Shook. 2013. "Early Starters: Which Type of Criminal Onset Matters Most for Delinquent Careers?" *Journal of Criminal Justice* 41: 12–17.

Eggleston, Elaine P. and John H. Laub. 2002. "The Onset of Adult Offending: A Neglected Dimension of the Criminal Career." *Journal of Criminal Justice* 30: 603–622.

El Sayed, Sarah A., Daniel F. Pacheco, and Robert G. Morris. 2016. "The Link Between Onset Age and Adult Offending: The Role of Developmental Profiles." *Deviant Behavior* 37: 989–1002.

Elder, Glen H. 1998. "The Life Course as Developmental Theory." *Child Development* 69: 1–12.

Farrington, David P. 1983. "Offending from 10 to 25 Years of Age." In *Prospective Studies of Crime and Delinquency*, edited by K. T. Van Dusen and S. A. Mednick, 17–37. Boston: Kluwar-Nijhoff.

Farrington, David P. 1986. "Age and Crime." In *Crime and Justice: An Annual Review of Research*, Vol. 7, edited by M. Tonry and N. Morris, 189–250. Chicago: University of Chicago Press.

Farrington, David P. 1992. "Criminal Career Research in the United Kingdom." *British Journal of Criminology* 32: 521–536.

Farrington, David P., Rolf Loeber, Delbert S. Elliott, J. David Hawkins, D. B. Kandel, M. W. Klein, Joan McCord, D. C. Rowe, and Richard E. Tremblay. 1990. "Advancing Knowledge about the Onset of Delinquency and Crime." In *Advances in Clinical Child Psychology*, Vol. 13, edited by B. B. Lahey and A. E. Kazdin, 283–342. New York: Plenum.

Gann, Shaun M., Christopher J. Sullivan, and Omeed S. Ilchi. 2015. "Elaborating on the Effects of Early Offending: A Study of Factors That Mediate the Impact of Onset Age on Long-Term Trajectories of Criminal Behavior." *Journal of Developmental and Life Course Criminology* 1: 63–86.

Glueck, Sheldon, and Eleanor Glueck. 1950. *Unraveling Juvenile Delinquency*. New York: The Commonwealth Fund.

Gottfredson, Michael and Travis Hirschi. 1990. *A General Theory of Crime*. Stanford: Stanford University Press.

Hagan, John, and Alberto Palloni. 1988. "Crimes as Social Events in the Life Course: Reconceiving a Criminological Controversy." *Criminology* 26: 87–100.

Hamparian, Donna M., Richard Schuster, Simon Dinitz, and John P. Conrad. 1978. *The Violent Few: A Study of Dangerous Juvenile Offenders*. Lexington, MA: Lexington Books.

Hanson, Cindy L., Scott W. Henggeler, William F. Haefele, and J. Douglas Rodick. 1984. "Demographic, Individual, and Family Relationship Correlates of Serious and Repeated Crime Among Adolescents and Their Siblings." *Journal of Consulting and Clinical Psychology* 4: 528–538.

Hindelang, Michael J., Travis Hirschi, and Joseph G. Weis (1979). "Correlates of Delinquency: The Illusion of Discrepancy Between Self-Report and Official Measures." *American Sociological Review* 44: 995–1014.

Hirschi, Travis, and Michael R. Gottfredson. 1983. "Age and the Explanation of Crime." *American Journal of Sociology* 89: 552–584.

Jackson, Patrick G. 1990. "Sources of Data." In *Measurement Issues in Criminology*, edited by Kimberley L. Kempf, 21–50. New York: Springer-Verlag.

Kazemian, Lila, and David P. Farrington. 2005. "Comparing the Validity of Prospective, Retrospective, and Official Onset for Different Offending Categories." *Journal of Quantitative Criminology* 21: 127–147.

Kirk, David S. 2006. "Examining the Divergence Across Self-Report and Official Data Sources on Inferences about the Adolescent Life-Course of Crime." *Journal of Quantitative Criminology* 22: 107–129.

Loeber, Rolf. 1982. "The Stability of Antisocial and Delinquent Child Behavior: A Review." *Child Development* 53: 1431–1446.

Loeber, Rolf, David P. Farrington, Magda Stouthamer-Loeber, Terrie E. Moffitt, Avshalom Caspi, Helene R. White, Evelyn H. Wei, and Jennifer M. Beyers. 2003. "The Development of Male Offending." In *Taking Stock of Delinquency,* edited by Terence Thornberry and Marvin Krohn, 93–136. New York: Springer.

Loeber, Rolf, and Dale Hay. 1997. "Key Issues in the Development of Aggression and Violence from Childhood to Early Adulthood." *Annual Review of Psychology* 48: 371–410.

Loeber, Rolf, and Marc LeBlanc. 1990. "Toward a Developmental Criminology." *Crime and Justice: A Review of Research* 12: 375–473.

Loeber, Rolf, and Marc LeBlanc. 1998. "Developmental Criminology Updated." *Crime and Justice: A Review of Research* 23: 115–198.

Loeber, Rolf, Magda Stouthamer-Loeber, and Stephanie M. Green. 1991. "Age at Onset of Problem Behavior in Boys, and Later Disruptive and Delinquent Behavior." *Criminal Behaviour and Mental Health* 1: 229–246.

McGee, Tara Renae, and David P. Farrington. 2010. "Are There Any True Adult Onset Offenders?" *British Journal of Criminology* 50: 530–549.

Moffitt, Terrie E. 1993. "Adolescent-Limited and Life-Course Persistent Antisocial Behavior: A Developmental Taxonomy." *Psychological Review* 100: 674–701.

Moffitt, Terrie E., Avshalom Caspi, N. Dickson, Phil A. Silva, and W. Stanton. 1996. "Childhood-Onset Versus Adolescent-Onset Antisocial Conduct Problems in Males: Natural History from Ages 3 to 18 Years." *Development and Psychopathology* 8: 399–424.

Moffitt, Terrie E., Avshalom Caspi, Michael Rutter, and Phil A. Silva. 2001. *Sex Differences in Antisocial Behavior: Conduct Disorder, Delinquency and Violence in the Dunedin Longitudinal Study.* Cambridge, UK: Cambridge University Press.

Nagin, Daniel S., and David P. Farrington. 1992a. "The Stability of Criminal Potential from Childhood to Adulthood." *Criminology* 30: 235–260.

Nagin, Daniel S., and David P. Farrington. 1992b. "The Onset and Persistence of Offending." *Criminology* 30: 501–523.

Nagin, Daniel S., and Raymond Paternoster. 1991. "On the Relationship of Past to Future Participation in Delinquency." *Criminology* 29: 163–187.

Nagin, Daniel S., and Raymond Paternoster. 2000. "Population Heterogeneity and State Dependence: State of the Evidence and Directions for Future Research." *Journal of Quantitative Criminology* 16: 117–145.

Nagin, Daniel S., and Richard E. Tremblay. 2005. "What Has Been Learned from Group-Based Trajectory Modeling? Examples from Physical Aggression and Other Problem Behaviors." *The Annals of the American Academy of Political and Social Science* 602: 82–117.

Paternoster, Raymond, and Robert Brame. 1997. "Multiple Routes to Delinquency? A Test of Developmental and General Theories of Crime." *Criminology* 35: 49–80.

Paternoster, Raymond, Charles W. Dean, Alex Piquero, Paul Mazerolle, and Robert Brame. 1997. "Generality, Continuity, and Change in Offending." *Journal of Quantitative Criminology* 13: 231–266.

Patterson, Gerald R., and Karen Yoerger. 1993. "Developmental Models for Delinquent Behavior." In *Mental Disorder and Crime*, edited by S. Hodgins, 140–172. Newbury Park, CA: Sage.

Patterson, Gerald R., and Karen Yoerger. 1997. "A Developmental Model for Late-Onset Delinquency." In *Motivation and* Delinquency, edited by D. W. Osgood, 119–177. Lincoln: University of Nebraska Press.

Payne, Jason L., and Alex R. Piquero. 2018. "The Concordance of Self-Reported and Officially Recorded Criminal Onset: Results from a Sample of Australian Prisoners." *Crime and Delinquency* 64: 448–471.

Piquero, Alex R., David P. Farrington, and Alfred Blumstein. 2003. "The Criminal Career Paradigm." In *Crime and Justice: A Review of Research*, edited by M. Tonry, 359–506. Chicago: University of Chicago Press.

Piquero, Alex, Raymond Paternoster, Paul Mazerolle, Robert Brame, and Charles W. Dean. 1999. "Onset Age and Offense Specialization." *Journal of Research in Crime and Delinquency* 36: 275–299.

Sampson, Robert J., and John H. Laub. 1992. "Crime and Deviance in the Life Course." *Annual Review of Sociology* 18: 63–84.

Sampson, Robert J., and John H. Laub. 1993. *Crime in the Making: Pathways and Turning Points through Life*. Cambridge, MA: Harvard University Press.

Sampson, Robert J., and John H. Laub. 1995. "Understanding Variability in Lives through Time." *Studies on Crime and Crime Prevention* 4(2): 143–158.

Sampson, Robert J., and John H. Laub. 1997. "A Life-Course Theory of Cumulative Disadvantage and the Stability of Delinquency." In *Developmental Theories of Crime and Delinquency: Advances in Criminological Theory*, edited by Terence Thornberry, 133–161. New Brunswick, NJ: Transaction Press.

Sampson, Robert J., and John H. Laub. 2003. "Life-Course Desisters? Trajectories of Crime Among Delinquent Boys Followed to Age 70." *Criminology* 41: 555–592.

Shannon, Lyle W. 1982. *Assessing the Relationship of Adult Criminal Careers to Juvenile Careers: A Summary*. Washington, DC: U.S. Government Printing Office.

Simpson, Sally S., Mariel Alper, Laura Dugan, Julie Horney, Candace Kruuttschnitt, and Rosemary Gartner. 2016. "Age-Graded Pathways into Crime: Evidence from a Multi-Site Retrospective Study of Incarcerated Women." *Journal of Developmental and Life Course Criminology* 2: 296–320.

Simons, R. L., Wu, C-I., Conger, R. D., and Lorenz, F. O. 1994. "Two Routes to Delinquency: Differences Between Early and Late Starters in the Impact of Parenting and Deviant Peers." *Criminology* 32: 247–276.

Sohoni, Tracy, Ray Paternoster, Jean Marie McGloin, and Ronet Bachman. 2014. "'Hen's Teeth and Horse's Toes': The Adult Onset Offender in Criminology." *Journal of Crime and Justice* 37: 155–172.

Tolan, Patrick H. 1987. "Implications of Age of Onset for Delinquency Risk." *Journal of Abnormal Child Psychology* 15: 47–65.

Tolan, Patrick H., and P. Thomas. 1995. "The Implications of Age of Onset for Delinquency Risk II: Longitudinal Data." *Journal of Abnormal Child Psychology* 23: 157–181.

Tracy, Paul E., Jr. 1990. "Prevalence, Incidence, Rates, and Other Descriptive Measures." In *Measurement Issues in Criminology*, edited by Kimberley L. Kempf, 51–77. New York: Springer-Verlag.

Vaughn, Michael G., Matt DeLisi, Kevin M. Beaver, Brian E. Perron, and Arnelyn Abdon. 2012. "Toward a Criminal Justice Epidemiology: Behavioral and Physical Health of Probationers and Parolees in the United States." *Journal of Criminal Justice* 40: 165–173.

Vaughn, Michael G., Christopher P. Salas-Wright, Matt DeLisi, and Brandy R. Maynard. 2014. "Violence and Externalizing Behavior among Youth in the United States: Is There a Severe 5 Percent?" *Youth Violence and Juvenile Justice* 12: 3–21.

Weis, J. G. 1986. "Issues in the Measurement of Criminal Careers." In *Criminal Careers and "Career Criminals,"* Vol. 2, edited by A. Blumstein, J. Cohen, J. A. Roth, and C. Visher, 1–51. Washington, DC: National Academy Press.

West, Donald J. 1982. *Delinquency: Its Roots, Careers and Prospects*. Cambridge, MA: Harvard University Press.

Wolfgang, Marvin E., Robert M. Figlio, and Thorsten Sellin. 1972. *Delinquency in a Birth Cohort*. Chicago: The University of Chicago Press.

Zara, Georgia, and David P. Farrington. 2009. "Childhood and Adolescent Predictors of Late Onset Criminal Careers." *Journal of Youth and Adolescence* 38: 287–300.

CHAPTER 4

·······································

SPECIALIZATION AND VERSATILITY IN OFFENDING

·······································

PAUL MAZEROLLE AND SAMARA MCPHEDRAN

EFFORT to classify criminals into "types" has a lengthy history within the field of Criminology (Lombroso, 1876; Wolfgang, Figlio, and Sellin, 1972). Indeed, a key part of enduring debates in the field relates to the merits and validity of general theories of offending behavior and whether they capture specific types of offenders or pathways to offending behavior across the life course (see Blumstein, Cohen, and Farrington 1988a; Hirschi and Gottfredson 1995; Sampson and Laub 1995). Against this background, debate continues over whether criminal careers tend to be characterized by "specialization" and, if so, to what extent (Britt, 1996). Indeed, efforts at understanding or conceptualizing offenders as specializing in specific types of offending (e.g., illicit drug trafficker, bank robber, domestic violence perpetrator) are a logical extension of theories that conceptualize offenders into specific types or pathways.

In the current context we use the term "specialization" to refer to the repeat commission by an individual of similar types of offenses over the course of their criminal career, and we contrast this with "versatility" (used interchangeably with "generalization"), meaning engaging in a wide variety of different types or forms of crimes. However, it should be noted that various definitions of specialization have been used in extant literature, and we return to this at a later juncture. Indeed, efforts to examine and understand specialization in offending are influenced by many dimensions, including the age of the sample employed (e.g., juvenile vs. adult), the types of data examined (e.g., self-reported offending data, official data), the time window considered (e.g., months and years vs. decades), and the procedures and definitions used to measure specialization.

The purpose of this chapter is not to undertake a detailed analysis and critique of every contribution to the specialization or versatility literature. Rather, we seek to present key elements of the specialization/versatility debate, from the theoretical to the methodological, with the aim of capturing the contested, evolving, and dynamic nature of this important topic. In Section I we discuss theoretical underpinnings of the specialization/versatility debate. In Section II, we consider the practical implications of this debate for policy and program development. Section III gives an overview of key empirical findings. Challenges and confounds within existing research are considered in Section IV. In Section V we present different ways in which specialization/versatility is operationalized. Finally, Section VI examines a range of data and measurement issues.

I. WHY SPECIALIZATION MATTERS: THEORETICAL AND PRACTICAL CONSIDERATIONS

From a theoretical perspective, efforts to understand offending specialization (and versatility) reflect two key, although somewhat overlapping, debates within the ongoing search for theoretical-explanatory frameworks of relationships between past and future criminal offending behavior (e.g., Paternoster et al. 1997; Nieuwbeerta et al. 2011). Indeed, to understand specialization or versatile offending patterns requires appreciation of the fact that they apply to offenders who repeat their offending over time. This in turn requires appreciation of the relationship between past and future offending behavior. The first of these debates centers around heterogeneity versus state-dependence conceptions or theories of the relationship between past and future offending. The second draws on debate regarding general versus typological theories of offending behavior.

Heterogeneity theories of offending attribute repeat offending among certain individuals to stable, underlying processes which are relatively time-invariant (e.g., Nagin and Paternoster 1991). Heterogeneity theories also attribute differences between individuals who do, and do not, offend (or who do, and do not, continue to offend) to underlying differences between those individuals in terms of, for example, their propensity toward criminal activity. In other words, stable underlying differences between individuals may relate to their levels of low self-control, impulsivity, or some other form of stable trait difference (e.g., temperament). It is important to note that while heterogeneity theories allow for change in offending behaviors and patterns over time, they do not allow for causal relationships between life changes and desistance from offending, instead attributing desistance to self-selection out of offending among those with a lesser underlying propensity toward criminal activity (Paternoster et al. 1997). According to this view, controlling for "stable criminal propensity" should mitigate relationships between past and future offending (Paternoster et al. 1997).

In contrast, state-dependent theoretical explanations of offending allow for causal relationships between past and future offending behaviors by suggesting that the commission of criminal acts can reduce inhibition and/or strengthen the motivation to engage in further criminal acts (Paternoster et al. 1997) through varying processes. State-dependence theories also allow that changes in life circumstances can causally affect the relationship between past and future behavior, for example, through shifts in interpersonal relationships increasing or decreasing the perceived "rewards" associated with criminal activities. For instance, Spelman's (1994) learning hypothesis entails that offenders will, over time, repeat acts that they have previously engaged in without being sanctioned and desist from acts that are likely to be detected and/or lead to punishment. In turn, this is speculated to lead to increasing "specialization" in a particular type of offending behavior (subject to consideration of the relative risks and rewards associated with that behavior). In short, state-dependence explanations of offending behavior over time allow for, and indeed enable through processes of learning and adaption, offending behavior to potentially become more specialized over time.

It has been noted that persistent heterogeneity and state-dependent theories are both "general" theories of crime, in that they typically argue that a common explanation of offending applies to all members of a given population (Paternoster et al. 1997). This leads to the next key theoretical debate in understanding offender specialization/versatility: the general versus typological debate. As there is a substantial literature already detailing the contrasting positions advanced by different contributors to this debate, we provide only a broad summary. Briefly, Gottfredson and Hirschi (1990), and others such as Sampson and Laub (1993), propose that a single theoretical explanation of offending, which draws on a central construct (or set of constructs; see Wilson and Herrnstein 1985) such as "low self-control" or "informal social control," is sufficient to explain all types of offending behavior, irrespective of variation in types of offending. According to this perspective, the underlying construct gives rise to offending, which, although driven by one "process," is able to manifest in a range of different ways (or different "types" of offending behavior) according to situational factors and opportunity considerations. As such, this theory is consistent with manifestations of generalized criminal behavior. However, it should be noted that there are some exceptions whereby general theories can allow for offending specific processes or pathways, such as toward retreatist offending (e.g., illicit drug use), expressive responses (e.g., violence), or instrumental (e.g., theft) responses to strain (see Agnew 1992). In summary, most general theories of criminal offending provide explanations of common paths or common precursors to crime and a tendency toward generalized or versatile criminal behavior.

In contrast, theories that invoke different "offender typologies" or suggest that different constructs underlie different types of crime (e.g., Moffitt 1993; Patterson and Yoerger 1993) lend themselves to the prediction that offending should be less versatile. These theories have been summarized as suggesting that generalized offending may reflect the presence of a single underlying construct or dimension associated with criminal behavior (such as "delinquency potential" or "antisocial potential"), while specialized offending may indicate the presence of multiple different underlying constructs or dimensions predictive of criminal behavior (e.g., "violence potential" and "theft potential,") (Farrington, Snyder, and Finnegan 1988).

Some theorists have developed taxonomic frameworks that predict specialization or generalization based on factors such as age of offending onset. For example, according to Moffitt (1993), "life-course–persistent" offenders are likely to begin involvement in criminal acts at an early age and continue engaging in criminal activities throughout their lifespan, whereas "adolescence-limited" offenders are unlikely to engage in offending early in life and likely to desist once they reach early adulthood. Moffitt (1993) predicts that the former group is likely to exhibit versatile offending patterns, whereas the latter group is more likely to display specialization (particularly in offending behavior associated with autonomy and status). It is useful to keep in mind Moffitt's (1993) framework, as well as Patterson and colleagues' (1989, 1993) contributions around early and late starters, as these theories demonstrate the close connections between the study of specialization/generalization and other characteristics of the criminal career such as onset age and persistence/desistance. In short, many of these criminal career dimensions appear substantively linked.

A crucial aspect of developmental theories of offending is that they allow for offending to be conceptualized as something that changes or evolves over time and that is driven by various underlying causes or constructs that differ between different individuals and/or "types" of offender (for examples, see Loeber and LeBlanc 1990; Osgood and Rowe 1994). Developmental theories allow for the possibility that some offenders may shift from specialization to generalization or vice versa at different stages of life (as well as offering frameworks within which processes such as persistence and desistance can be understood). Developmental theories of offending behavior are closely aligned with typological theories of offending but are not entirely incompatible with general theories of offending. In a general offending context, the processes of how informal social control changes across the age-graded life course recognize developmental influences (Sampson and Laub 1993), as do the processes of interactive or reciprocal influences on offending behavior over time (Thornberry 1987; Thornberry and Krohn 2005).

In summary, the issue of offending specialization or generality has many differing theoretical contexts—from general explanatory frameworks to typological, from static to dynamic processes, and from state-dependent to heterogeneity relationships. While it is not possible to provide definitive conclusions, most general theories foster conceptualizations of versatility offending patterns and most typological approaches allow for, and indeed depict, specialized types of offenders. Beyond the theoretical conceptions, how relevant is understanding specialized or generalized offending in more practical terms? Why is specialization or versatility in offending important for practitioners and policymakers charged with responding to crime across the community?

II. PRACTICAL RELEVANCE

Information about specialized relative to versatile participation in criminal activity has implications not only for criminological theory testing but also for crime and justice policy and program development as well as more front-line criminal justice responses. The key questions are how—and to what extent—can specialized or generalized patterns of offending affect and inform practical response to crime?

In the context of juvenile justice, for example, Piquero and colleagues (1999) note that if offending were specialized, this could allow better prediction of subsequent forms of offense types and in turn improve decision-making around how the justice system can best respond to earlier offenses. In contrast, those authors also highlight that a more generalized pattern of juvenile offending would suggest responses such as decriminalizing "status" offenses or incarcerating serious violent offenders would be unlikely to prevent further contact with the justice system or serious violent crimes, respectively (Piquero et al. 1999).

Identifying specialized or generalized offending has further relevance for front-line police responses. For example, if some offenders specialize, police authorities can target resources to known criminals when responding to or investigating certain forms of crime (e.g., bank robberies, rape). However, if offenders are generally versatile, it makes little sense to develop institutional responses aimed at specialized offenders. While this does not mean that police responses should not develop specialized team responses (e.g., drug squads, fraud squads, tactical response squads), it does mean that their focus is on offenses, not offenders, given their more generalized offending repertoires.

A generalized pattern of offending, if reflective of a single or unidimensional cause of criminal behavior, may also suggest that a general intervention or programmatic approach (if properly targeted) may be useful in reducing or preventing a broad range of different forms of offending (Piquero 2000). In other words, an effective correctional treatment program that addresses generalized criminogenic risks through, for example, cognitive behavioral change may well be effective in preventing different or multiple forms of crime in future.

Interestingly, how practical responses to crime relate to general versus specialized forms of offending is well illustrated in the domestic violence male perpetrator literature. A number of studies provide theoretical and empirical support for there being multiple types of domestically violent males (see Gondolf 1988; Saunders 1992; Holtzworth-Monroe and Stuart 1994; Bouffard and Zedaker 2016; Hilton and Eke 2016). However, criminal justice responses—including batterer treatment programs—appear conceived, designed, and structured with a homogeneous view of domestically violent men. This has given rise to weak program effects (Feder and Dugan 2002).

The key challenge for prevention and treatment program responses is in ensuring that the rationale and design of a program is matched to the causal context for offending. If a program is designed for a generalist offender, there should be little surprise that it will be ineffective at preventing future offending for more specialized offenders. Ultimately, the challenge for practitioners is in knowing who is, or is not, on a specialized or versatile offending pathway.

III. EMPIRICAL CONSIDERATIONS

With a handful of notable and pioneering exceptions (e.g., Shaw 1930/1966; Shaw and Moore 1931; Wolfgang, Figlio, and Sellin 1972), the majority of empirical study into specialization and generalization has taken place since the 1980s (see DeLisi and Piquero 2011, for identification of recent studies). Most studies are based on data from samples in the United States,[1] with a small selection of work emerging from other countries. Typically, research in this field has considered whether, in terms of statistical probability, specialized patterns of offending exist at levels greater than that expected based on chance alone (Osgood and Schreck 2007). It is fair to say that results obtained over the past decades of study have been mixed and inconsistent. This section provides an overview of key results and uncertainties, while the following sections explore different contributors to the variety of findings obtained.

Early studies in the field typically demonstrated considerable variation in offending. In Klein's (1984) review of over 30 studies existing at the time, for example, generalized offending was found to be more typical than specialized offending. Those early findings have since been augmented by a growing body of research which suggests that offenders typically exhibit considerable versatility in offending but that this versatility is often accompanied by a minor degree of specialization (e.g., Kempf 1987; Blumstein et al. 1988a and b; Farrington, Snyder, and Finnegan 1988; Osgood et al. 1988; Lattimore, Visher, and Linster 1994; Paternoster et al. 1998; Piquero et al. 1999; Mazerolle et al. 2000; Piquero, Farrington, and Blumstein 2003; Lynam, Piquero, and Moffitt 2004). Indeed, a literature review undertaken almost two decades after Klein's (1984) study concluded that while there is some evidence for specialization, criminal careers are generally characterized by versatile offending patterns (Piquero, Farrington, and Blumstein 2003). Alongside such findings, however, it has been noted that there is a tendency for perceptions of clear specialization by offenders to persist, which has been attributed in part to the political appeal of being able to devise policies and programs aimed at a certain type of offender (Harris, Mazerolle, and Knight 2009).

Notable variation in the strength of evidence for specialization has occurred across different studies, which has also prompted debate as to how the strength of evidence for specialization can be meaningfully interpreted. It has been acknowledged that caution must be applied when attempting to draw together findings about specialization and generalization from different studies due to sizable interstudy variations in conceptualization and measurement (Nieuwbeerta et al. 2011). Further cautions apply due to interstudy variations in sample size and composition, time period/s examined, and types of offending considered. These issues are discussed further below.

Insofar as any consensus of results exists, that consensus is weighted toward the finding that juvenile offenders tend to exhibit greater versatility of offending, while older offenders typically show a greater tendency toward specialization (e.g., Farrington 1986; Farrington, Snyder, and Finnegan 1988; Piquero et al. 1999). Exceptions have been noted, though, with a handful of observations suggesting that some juvenile offenders may display limited specialization in property, theft, and status offenses (Kempf 1987; Farrington, Snyder, and Finnegan 1988; Stander et al. 1989; Tracy, Wolfgang and Figlio 1990; Lattimore et al. 1994; Paternoster et al. 1998). These findings suggest that different patterns of specialization are likely to emerge among different types of juvenile offenders and that the heterogeneity of young offenders should be taken into account when considering specialization.

Among older offenders, there is evidence that specialization may occur across a variety of different types of offending behavior. Violent offending is the most intensively studied type of offending, with a range of studies finding specialized violent offending among adult samples (e.g., Blumstein et al. 1988a, 1988b; Brennan, Mednick, and John 1989; Britt 1996). Examples of types of offending where evidence of specialization has been found among adult samples include fraud offending (Blumstein et al. 1988b), property and drug offenses (Britt 1996), certain sexual offenses (Harris, Mazerolle, and Knight 2009; although see also Smallbone and Wortley 2004), robbery (Schwaner 2000), and arson (Soothill, Francis, and Liu 2008).

It does not follow from such findings that most or all adult offenders will specialize in a particular type of offending or show strong specialization. Rather, the findings to date are best viewed as an indicator that among adult offenders in general, the tendency toward repeating a particular type of crime is more likely to be observed relative to younger offenders in general and that specialization often occurs alongside notable versatility. The degree to which specialization is likely to be observed, in what particular crime types, and among what proportion of a given sample of offenders, remains unresolved.

IV. CORRELATES AND CONFOUNDS

The apparent relationship between age and specialization, while frequently observed, is not straightforward. Rather, the degree to which specialization is found in a given population or sample appears to interact with other characteristics of the criminal career—such as commencement of involvement in criminal activity, frequency of offending, and persistence of offending—which themselves may be associated with age-related/life-course factors. Regarding correlates of specialization/versatility, age of onset of criminal activity has received particular attention. This reflects, in part, the body of literature demonstrating that early-onset offenders tend to commit large numbers of offenses, over long periods of time, at high rates, leading to the prediction that early-onset offending should be associated with greater versatility of offending (Moffitt, 1994). While some studies support this prediction (e.g., Rojek and Erickson 1982; Mazerolle et al. 2000; DeLisi 2006), others have found little apparent relationship between onset age and later offending patterns and/or have observed that controlling for age ameliorates observed relationships (e.g., Tolan 1987; Piquero et al. 1999). Others highlight that over a period of decades, specialization appears to become somewhat more pronounced among younger-age-of-onset offenders relative to older-age-of-onset offenders (Yonai et al. 2013) or, alternatively, that any effects of early-onset offending on specialization are short-lived rather than long-term (Tzoumakis et al. 2013)[2].

Other characteristics of criminal activity, such as frequency of offending, represent a potential confound in studies of specialization/versatility. There is evidence suggesting, for example, that frequency of offending, rather than specialization, is what drives violent offending (Piquero 2000; Piquero, Jennings, and Barnes, 2012). However, frequency of offending has been taken into account in only a handful of specialization/versatility studies. For example, McGloin and others (2007) found that associations between age and specialization among a sample of convicted male offenders were mitigated by controlling for age-graded frequency of offending. Those authors also highlight that while specialization over long periods of time (such as several years or an entire criminal career) may be uncommon, specialization across short periods of time (months or a couple of years) may be relatively more common (McGloin et al. 2007). Other findings suggest that frequency of offending and specialization/versatility may be largely independent of one another (e.g., Brame, Paternoster, and Bushway 2004).

Research incorporating both age and offending persistence/desistance offers additional insights into specialization/versatility. Armstrong (2008a), for instance, found (among a sample of offenders aged up to 35 years) that age did not account for observed specialization trends across all offending types but did appear to influence trends in specialization for property and violent offenses. Taking into account differences in offender desistance behavior, Armstrong (2008a) also noted that specialization in drug offenses was less common among offenders who desisted from offending relative to offenders who persisted in criminal activity over time. Yonai et al. (2013) made similar observations, suggesting that "specialization trends may be attributed to offenders who persist in crime rather than those who desist from it" (p. 963).

Factors such as race and gender remain comparatively understudied, and it is difficult to draw out points of agreement and contention with any confidence or consistency. However, there are suggestive findings that female offenders may be more likely to display specialization in certain types of offending than males (e.g., Bouffard et al. 2008; Farrington, Snyder, and Finnegan 1988; Tumminello et al. 2013; for a contrasting perspective see Mazerolle et al. 2000). Other individual offender characteristics, such as personality factors, childhood experiences and family background, parental characteristics, peer relationships (but see Thomas 2015), and social factors, have not been well incorporated into specialization studies to date. This is in part due to methodological issues around the use of aggregate data, which is common in specialization research (discussed further below). The relative absence of studies taking into account individual factors is a notable oversight in current literature, given the well-established correlates between particular individual characteristics and criminal offending more broadly (Armstrong and Britt 2004). Illustrating this shortcoming in existing knowledge, Armstrong and Britt (2004) provide evidence that controlling for individual background characteristics of offenders can account for patterns of specialization that were apparent prior to those background factors being taken into account.

V. Operationalization

Extant literature has adopted a range of different operational definitions of what specialization entails. Although there is a general understanding among scholars that specialization refers to the tendency to engage in one particular type of offending, this has been operationalized as, variously, the tendency to repeat a certain type of offense on successive occasions (Farrington, Snyder, and Finnegan 1988), or the tendency to repeatedly offend in one particular domain of behavior (such as violence or drug offenses) over the course of a criminal career irrespective of temporal ordering of offenses (Bouffard et al. 2008). These different approaches to operationalization—one emphasizing a temporal dimension and one emphasizing a diversity element—are in turn complemented by different methodological approaches, which are discussed further below. While it is important to select a definition and methodological approach that matches the particular theory being tested or question of interest in a given piece of study (Sampson and Laub 2005), this variation nevertheless contributes to the inconsistent findings that have emerged to date.

Extending the variations in operationalization, different studies that fall under the general banner of "specialization research" have interrogated two separate aspects of specialization. One aspect addresses the question of offenders who specialize (and the types of offenses), while another branch deals with specialized types of offending (such as violent offending or sexual offenses) and seeks to understand what differentiates offenders who, for example, are, and are not, violent (see Osgood and Shreck 2007). Although related, these are not synonymous questions. As Osgood and Shreck (2007) note, the first question is useful in testing predictions such as whether offenders become more specialized with age, while the second line of enquiry is useful in the context of improving understanding about contributors to, and correlates of, types of crimes that may have significant social impact and relevance within specific policy contexts (such as preventing violence).

How different offense types are operationalized also varies across literature, with some research adopting a relatively broad approach to operationalizing different offenses and others taking a more fine-grained approach. It is common for studies of specialization to use very broad offense groupings such as "person, property, and other" or "violent, non-violent, and miscellaneous." While methodologically useful in terms of producing larger sample sizes per category, the broader the categories used, the more likely those studies are to observe a concentration of offenses within one category and to describe that as evidence of specialization (e.g., Piquero et al. 1999; Sullivan et al. 2006; Armstrong 2008a, 2008b). However, this approach may have insufficiently fine resolution to detect generalization across different subtypes of offending under that broad category (Farrington,

Snyder, and Finnegan 1988; Yonai, Levine, and Glicksohn 2010), and studies using more detailed categories of offending typically find relatively less evidence for specialization or different degrees of specialization within different subcategories of offense type (e.g., Lussier, LeBlanc, and Proulx 2005).

Importantly, these different approaches to operationalization also raise questions about how the term specialization is used within criminological theory and precisely what various different authors intend the term to denote. Does it mean, for example, a tendency toward one particular subtype of property crime, such as theft, or does it mean a tendency toward engaging in any type of property crime? What threshold should be applied when determining whether specialization is present (Sullivan et al. 2009)? To date, there has been little consensus on these issues, thus adding to the degree of inconsistency across existing studies.

VI. DATA AND MEASUREMENT

Aside from correlates and confounds associated with specialization research, and the varied operationalization of central concepts, historical lack of clarity over the extent to which offenders specialize in particular crime types can be attributed to data and measurement issues. In terms of data, it is pertinent to note that sample sizes, sample composition, and time periods examined vary substantially across different studies. However, a more fundamental difference lies in the use of self-report versus official data sources and the corresponding variations those sources may introduce into research findings. For example, studies drawing on official statistics (such as police or court records) capture only those behaviors that come to the notice of authorities, and even then may only include the most serious of a variety of simultaneous offenses, while self-report data may lack temporal information and/or be subject to recall and/or desirability bias. It is important to be aware that comparisons of self-report data and official data drawn from the same sample may produce conflicting results. For instance, using a New Zealand birth cohort, Lynam, Piquero, and Moffitt (2004) found little evidence of specialization when analyzing official records, whereas evidence of specialization emerged from analyses of self-report data. Unfortunately, studies of this nature are not widespread, as suitably detailed longitudinal datasets remain relatively scarce.

In terms of methodological differences, as the study of specialization has expanded, so too has the range of methodologies increased. Each of these methods has its own strengths and limitations, which are explored below. However, putting aside these strengths and limitations, each methodological approach also provides its own distinctive metrics, which are not readily comparable with one another. Collectively, the range of different methods used to study specialization (in conjunction with variations in operationalization and data sources) challenges the ability to integrate and synthesize findings across multiple different studies.

A. Transition Matrices

Many of the studies of specialization highlighted already—including those that found early evidence for weak specialization and/or differences in specialization across different ages, for example—were based on transition matrices, which indicate the degree to which different offenses are consistent with one another. Transition matrices are based on the probability that an individual who commits a particular offense will commit the same offense on subsequent occasions (e.g., Bursik 1980). The most well known among the transition matrix approaches is the forward specialization coefficient (FSC), proposed by Farrington (1986; see also Farrington et al. 1988). The FSC provides a value from 0 to 1, where 0 indicates "perfect versatility" (no relationship between successive offenses) and 1 indicates "perfect specialization" (successive are of the same type).

Briefly, the FSC takes the form:

$$\text{FSC}_{jk} = O_{jk} - E_{jk} / R_j - E_{jk}$$

where FSC_{jk} is the FSC for the cell occupying row j and column k, O_{jk} is the observed number of cases occupying cell jk, E_{jk} is the number of cases that would be expected in cell jk by chance, and R_j is the total number of cases in row j (Farrington et al. 1988; Paternoster et al. 1997).

Although the FSC is a useful and widely used measure, the FSC and transition matrices more broadly have been criticized on a number of grounds. Britt (1996), in particular, highlights the difficulties associated with meaningful interpretation of the FSC and particularly the challenge of assigning clear meaning to any given coefficient. Using Farrington and colleagues' (1988) interpretation of a coefficient of 0.107 as being around one-tenth of the way toward perfect specialization, Britt (1996) notes that the same coefficient could be interpreted as being "nine-tenths of the distance to complete versatility" (p. 196). The inability to assign a clear meaning to any given coefficient, in Britt's (1996) view, restricts the generality of the FSC. In contrast, however, it has been argued that while the language is "not precise, it is intuitive and eminently understandable" (Paternoster et al. 1998, p. 138), in much the same way that correlation coefficients are understood.

In addition, Britt (1996) raised questions about testing for significant differences between groups, based on the FSC. Specifically, Britt (1996) argued that the sampling distribution of the FSC was unknown, meaning that conventional statistical procedures for testing between-group differences were inapplicable. While this is a valid methodological concern, studies testing sampling distribution have since provided evidence that the FSC is approximately normally distributed, suggesting that conventional statistical testing may be usefully applied, albeit with due caution (Paternoster et al. 1998).

Two further criticisms of the FSC (and transition matrices in general), which have notable implications for the specialization debate, concern reliance on aggregated data and adjacent (temporally successive) offenses. Regarding aggregation, the FSC examines an entire sample or population rather than a specific individual (Mazerolle et al. 2000; Sullivan et al. 2006). As such, this limits the ability to apply techniques such as regression analysis to control for individual differences. Also, it cannot be established through aggregated data whether trends in specialization reflect individual tendencies toward greater specialization or are driven by changes in the offender population (Nieuwbeerta et al. 2011). For example, Armstrong (2008b) found evidence that changes in specialization in property relative to violence offenses were attributable to changes in offender populations studied (persisters vs. desisters), which suggests that the use of the FSC may not be suitable for detecting fine-level variations in specialization and versatility of offending. As Sullivan and colleagues (2006) note: "This is problematic because the criminal career framework . . . which prompted interest in specialization, and life-course criminology in particular . . . generally focuses on individual patterns of offending . . . ." (p. 205).

Transition matrices typically relate to sequential specialization; as such, they examine "adjacent" offenses and do not consider other offenses that may occur (Osgood and Schreck 2007). However, using the FSC as an example, if an offender alternates between two particular types of offenses, this approach would generate a FSC of 0 (perfect versatility), even though that value does not reflect the "actual" degree of specialization present (e.g., Piquero et al. 1999; DeLisi 2003; Sullivan et al. 2006; Nieuwbeerta et al. 2011). Similarly, this approach does not take into account the time between offenses, which may vary greatly between individuals and—given potential overlap between specialization and offending frequency—act as a confound in studies of criminal offending over a life course (Nieuwbeerta et al. 2011). In addition, heavy reliance on temporal information typically limits use of transition matrices to official data, rather than self-report data, which may result in undercounting of offenses and an incomplete or biased picture of offending behavior and potential specialization or versatility (Osgood and Schreck 2007).

B. Diversity Index

The diversity index considers an individual's history of offending and provides an estimate of the probability that any two offenses selected from that pool will differ from one another. Adapted from Agresti and Agresti (1978), the diversity index examines individual-level offending and (in contrast to the FSC) examines the overall amount of versatility shown by each individual offender (Mazerolle et al. 2000). The index provides a value ranging from 0 (representing the most specialization or least diversity) to a maximum of $(k-1)/k$, representing the most diversity or least specialization, that is spread equally across k categories (Agresti and Agresti 1978; see also Baker, Metcalfe, and Jennings 2013). Sullivan et al. (2006) suggest that a diversity index approach to the study of specialization is particularly suited to criminal career research and life-course criminology, given its focus on individual offending.

The diversity index has overcome some of the limitations of the FSC, particularly those associated with the use of aggregated data and reliance on temporal information; the diversity index has been applied to both official (e.g., Bouffard et al. 2008; Mazerolle et al. 2000) and self-report data (e.g., Sullivan et al. 2006). Studies using the diversity index have produced findings that suggest that greater offending versatility is found among younger offenders (both males and females) with an early onset age and as the number of offenses increases (Piquero et al. 1999; Mazerolle et al. 2000; McGloin et al. 2007). In addition, Nieuwbeerta et al. (2011), using the diversity index to examine a Dutch sample of offenders aged 12 to 72 years, found evidence for considerable overall diversity in offending, increasing diversity between early adolescence and young adulthood, and increasing specialization during adulthood. When focusing on frequent offenders and disaggregating the age–diversity curve, it emerged that high diversity was the most common general pattern of offending in adulthood, followed by a pattern of specialization (Nieuwbeerta et al. 2011). The authors concluded that "[w]hen offenders specialize during adulthood, they tend to specialize toward property crimes" (Nieuwbeerta et al. 2011, p. 21). Using a 36-month time period of data, Sullivan and colleagues (2006) found considerable variation in offending, but with a pattern of increasing specialization as the time period studied was narrowed. Those authors comment that, like the FSC, studies using the diversity index have typically used long time periods of data, which may not reveal short-term specialization (Sullivan et al. 2006).

The diversity index has also been subject to criticism. As Sullivan and others (2009) argue, the diversity index "is somewhat confounded with offending frequency, in that if offenders do not commit a number of crimes that is at least equivalent to the number of crime categories, they cannot obtain the maximum possible diversity score, even if all of their offenses are of distinct types" (p. 423). Osgood and Schreck (2007) made similar observations and also suggested that attempts to address the issue of frequency by imposing a minimum offense threshold or using control variables in a regression model have the limitation of reducing sample size and statistical power. A further criticism of the diversity index (and other methods studying individual-level offending patterns) is that overall (or "base") rates of a particular type of offense within a population are typically not accounted for. Without the ability to contrast individual-level offending patterns with population-level offending patterns, it may be problematic to make judgements about whether a particular individual is in fact specializing in a certain type of offense, or whether their offending pattern (although potentially including a high proportion of a certain type of offense) simply reflects the population-level proportions of offending in each different type of offense (Osgood and Schreck 2007). Finally, the diversity index has been criticized for being an indicator that can identify the presence or "extent" of specialization but (unless dichotomized, for example) not the type/s of crime in which offenders specialize, which may in turn limit its use within particular contexts (Sullivan et al. 2009).

C. Latent Class Analysis

An emerging set of methods testing specialization are based around latent class or latent transition models. Broadly, the latent class approach is a probabilistic technique which identifies clusters of items that group together (that is, share certain characteristics) on some underlying construct of theoretical interest, such as "offense specialization" (e.g., Osgood and Schreck 2007). To account for the possibility of offenders switching between different patterns or types of offending over time, latent transition models, which extend latent class analysis, have also been proposed as a useful methodological advance. This approach is described by McGloin, Sullivan, and Piquero (2009) as "a type of autoregressive model that examines change and stability in latent groups over time . . . [it] allows the analyst to obtain a probability of transition across latent categories, which can aid in inferring whether individuals show change in qualitative states and, if so, what form this change takes" (p. 249). As Francis and colleagues (2004) note, latent class methods differ from traditional cluster analysis methods because they are underpinned by statistical models, and provide "allocation formulae" which enable an offender to be allocated to a cluster by choosing the cluster with the highest probability of that individual belonging to it. McGloin and others (2009) argue that latent class methods have the benefit of enabling classes to be inferred from patterns in the data of interest, rather than being driven (or constrained) by researcher assumptions.

Relatively few studies to date have used latent class (or related) analyses, although those studies that have adopted this approach have produced useful insights. For example, Francis, Soothill, and Fligelstone (2004) provide suggestive evidence of a degree of specialization in shoplifting (for females), as well as non-violent property offending, fraud and general theft, and general violence (among males), among a sample of over 11,000 U.K. offenders from one birth cohort. McGloin and colleagues (2009) found a modest degree of specialization in drug and burglary/theft offenses among 658 male offenders but note that rather than indicating specialization in those types of crimes to the exclusion of any other offending, latent transition analyses instead revealed that some offenders tended to "favor" certain crimes over others (p. 253). Also, Baker, Metcalfe, and Jennings (2013), using a random sample drawn from the Philadelphia Birth Cohort Study, showed a degree of specialization among drug and violent offenses in particular, both within and between particular offending trajectory types (e.g., high-rate chronic offenders and high-rate adolescent offenders). In contrast, in an early application of latent class methodology, Britt (1994) found suggestive evidence of two classes based around delinquent versus non-delinquent youths, rather than specialization.

D. Item Response Theory and Related Approaches

Methods based around item response theory view data on each available item as having a probabilistic relationship to a latent construct of interest (Osgood and

Schreck 2007) and are a class of statistical models to describe the response behaviors of individuals to a set of categorically scored items. The most common item response theory models can be classified as generalized linear fixed- and/or mixed-effect models (Johnson 2007). While the use of such models in specialization/versatility research is not widespread, a growing body of research is adopting this type of approach.

Osgood and Schreck (2007), using multilevel regression modeling (drawing on item response theory), found specialization in violence among youths (although note that a portion of their findings may be due to their large sample size), while Bouffard and colleagues (2008), applying both the diversity index and Osgood and Shreck's (2007) method, found greater overall diversity among male partner violence perpetrators (n = 138) relative to female partner violence perpetrators (n = 79) and less specialization in intimate partner violence offending, specifically among males relative to females. In an earlier study using marginal logit modeling, Deane and others (2005) also found evidence for specialization, particularly among violent offenders.

It has been proposed that those studies using a latent class/transition or item response approach support the possibility of offending specialization being "more apparent than the early research suggests" (Baker, Metcalfe, and Jennings 2013, p. 915). However, it must also be noted that those studies have often considered relatively short data spans (e.g., five years: Francis, Soothill, and Fligelstone 2004; three years: McGloin et al. 2009; three years of cross-sectional data and two "waves" of longitudinal self-report data collection: Osgood and Schreck 2007), have found inconsistent and conflicting evidence of transition between specialization and versatility during those time periods rather than clear evidence of a stable specialized offending type, and have also—in keeping with a great deal of earlier study—found considerable evidence of generalized offending patterns alongside modest tendencies toward specialization among some offenders, along with corresponding age and gender effects (such as greater specialization with increasing age).

Latent class and item response methods, given their infrequent use to date in studies of specialization, have not yet been subject to extensive criticism. However, two important limitations have been noted. First, latent class methods may confound offense frequency with specialization, given that classes of offending may be based on the number of offenses as well as the type of offenses (Sullivan et al. 2009). Also, given the probabilistic creation of latent classes, these should not be viewed as pure indicators of specialization, and researcher subjectivity is required in assessing whether the classes obtained should be seen as evidence of specialization (Sullivan et al. 2009; see also Nagin and Tremblay 2005).

E. Comparing Methodologies

An appealing means of resolving inconsistencies that arise from use of different methods is to apply multiple different methods to the same dataset and compare the results produced by each different measurement technique (e.g., Fox and Farrington

2016). However, this approach is data dependent to a strong degree. As discussed above, not all commonly used methods of studying specialization/versatility can be applied to the same data; for example, the FSC may be not useful in instances where temporal information about offending sequence is unavailable. However, noting this limitation, in those instances where data can support a multi-method approach, the findings are likely to prove beneficial in improving the knowledge base. Arguably, the most encompassing study to date using a multi-method approach is that of Sullivan and colleagues (2009). In that study, the FSC, diversity index, latent class analysis, and item response modeling were applied to the same sets of data. The study found that all methods revealed some degree of specialization among offending, with greater specialization apparent when using the latent class and item response methods. However, the authors also highlighted that none of the methods produced particularly strong evidence for specialization (Sullivan et al. 2009).

VII. Summary and Conclusions

Despite the voluminous research devoted to the issue of offending specialization and versatility, and the emerging convergence that a small degree of specialization can exist within a criminal career demonstrating a high degree of generality, popular and indeed practical responses to offending appear biased toward the specialist offender. Such a bias disproportionality informs not only front-line policing responses but also a large number of treatment and prevention programs. Perhaps such approaches are influenced by popular, indeed unidimensional conceptions of criminality across the community.

To date, the weight of evidence about specialization/versatility remains in keeping with Klein's (1984) and Piquero, Farrington, and Blumstein's (2003) observations about versatile offending being a far more common characteristic of criminal careers than specialized offending. However, emerging evidence and the development of new techniques have offered important and novel insights into offender behavior across the life course. The accumulated body of literature invites the conclusion that offender specialization, while less common than versatility, is a far more nuanced concept than has often been thought. Findings are subject to influence not only by operationalization, methodology, and data selection but also by the heterogeneity of offenders, the many different correlates and predictors of participation in criminal activity, and other parameters of the criminal career.

Indeed, based on recent findings, it seems reasonable to argue that while versatility remains by far the most common offending pattern over a criminal career, periods of short- as well as long-term specialization can be expected to emerge among particular offenders. However, the details of what exactly this may look like, how those offenders may in turn differ from one another, and on which parameters remain uncertain. In terms of enabling robust tests of criminological theories, or informing practical interventions aimed at reducing or preventing criminal offending, it is clear that this field of study requires significant future development. In short, the science regarding offending specialization and versatility is far from settled.

Notes

1. The Philadelphia Birth Cohort Study merits particular acknowledgment; see DeLisi and Piquero (2011).
2. This study also raises important questions about how "early onset" is defined (see p. 157).

References

Agnew, Robert. 1992. "Foundation for a General Strain Theory of Crime and Delinquency." *Criminology*, 30(1): 47–88.

Agresti, Alan, and Barbara F. Agresti .1978. "Statistical Analysis of Qualitative Variation." In *Sociological Methodology*, edited by Karl F. Schuessler, 204–237. San Francisco: Jossey-Bass.

Armstrong, Todd A. 2008a. "Are Trends in Specialization Across Arrests Explained by Changes in Specialization Occurring With Age?" *Justice Quarterly* 25(1): 201–222.

Armstrong, Todd A. 2008b. "Exploring the Impact of Changes in Group Composition on Trends in Specialization." *Crime & Delinquency* 54(3): 366–389.

Armstrong, Todd A., and Chester L. Britt. 2004. "The Effect of Offender Characteristics on Offense Specialization and Escalation." *Justice Quarterly* 21(4): 843–876.

Baker, Thomas, Christi Falco Metcalfe and Wesley G. Jennings. 2013. "What Are the Odds? Predicting Specialization in Offending Over the Life Course." *Criminal Justice and Behavior* 40(8): 909–932.

Blumstein, Alfred, Jacqueline Cohen, and David Farrington. 1988a. "Criminal Career Research: Its Value for Criminology." *Journal of Criminology* 26(1): 1–35.

Blumstein, Alfred, Jacqueline Cohen, Somnath Das, and Soumyo D. Moitra. 1988b. "Specialization and Seriousness During Adult Criminal Careers." *Journal of Quantitative Criminology* 4(4): 303–345.

Bouffard, Leana A., Kevin A. Wright, Lisa R. Muftić, and Jeffrey A. Bouffard. 2008. "Gender Differences in Specialization in Intimate Partner Violence: Comparing the Gender Symmetry and Violent Resistance Perspectives." *Justice Quarterly* 25(3): 570–594.

Bouffard, Leana A., and Sara B. Zedaker. 2016. "Are Domestic Violence Offenders Specialists? Answers from Multiple Analytic Approaches." *Journal of Research in Crime and Delinquency* 53(6): 788–813.

Brame, Robert, Raymond Paternoster, and Shawn D. Bushway. 2004. "Criminal Offending Frequency and Offense Switching." *Journal of Contemporary Criminal Justice* 20(2): 201–214.

Brennan, Patricia, Sarnoff Mednick, and Richard John. 1989. "Specialization in Violence: Evidence of a Criminal Subgroup." *Criminology* 27(3): 437–453.

Britt, Chester A. 1996. "The Measurement of Specialization and Escalation in the Criminal Career: An Alternative Modeling Strategy." *Journal of Quantitative Criminology* 12(2): 193–222.

Bursik, Robert J. 1980. "The Dynamics of Specialization in Juvenile Offenses." *Social Forces* 58(3): 851–864.

Deane, Glenn, David P. Armstrong, and Richard B. Felson. 2005. "An Examination of Offense Specialization Using Marginal Logit Models." *Criminology* 43(4): 955–988.

DeLisi, Matt. 2003. "The Imprisoned Nonviolent Drug Offender: Specialized Martyr or Versatile Career Criminal?" *American Journal of Criminal Justice* 27(2): 167–182.

DeLisi, Matt. 2006. "Zeroing In on Early Arrest: Results from a Population of Extreme Career Criminals." *Journal of Criminal Justice* 34: 17–26.

DeLisi, Matt, and Alex R. Piquero. 2011. "New Frontiers in Criminal Careers Research, 2001–2011: A State-of-the-Art Review." *Journal of Criminal Justice* 39: 289–301.

Farrington, David P. 1986. "Age and Crime." In *Crime and Justice: A Review of Research,* Vol. 7, edited by Michael Tonry and Norval Morris, 189–250. Chicago: University of Chicago Press.

Farrington, David P., Howard N. Snyder, and Terrence A. Finnegan. 1988. "Specialization in Juvenile Court Careers." *Criminology* 26(3): 461–487.

Feder, Lynette, and Laura Dugan. 2002. "A Test of the Efficacy of Court-Mandated Counseling for Domestic Violence Offenders: The Broward Experiment." *Justice Quarterly* 19: 343–375.

Fox, Bryanna Hahn, and David P. Farrington. 2016. "Behavioral Consistency Among Serial Burglars: Evaluating Offense Style Specialization Using Three Analytical Approaches." *Crime and Delinquency* 62(9): 1123–1158.

Francis, Brian, Keith Soothill, and Rachel Fligelstone. 2004. "Identifying Patterns and Pathways to Offending Behavior: A New Approach to Typologies of Crime." *European Journal of Criminology* 1(1): 47–87.

Gondolf, E. W. 1988. "Who Are Those Guys? Toward a Behavioral Typology of Batterers." *Violence and Victims* 3: 187–203.

Gottfredson, Michael R., and Travis Hirschi. 1990. *A General Theory of Crime.* Stanford, CA: Stanford University Press.

Harris, Danielle A., Paul Mazerolle, and Raymond A. Knight. 2009. "Understanding Male Sexual Offending: A Comparison of General and Specialist Theories." *Criminal Justice and Behavior* 36(10): 1051–1069.

Hilton, N. Zoe, and Angela Wyatt Eke. 2016. "Non-Specialization of Criminal Careers Among Intimate Partner Violence Offenders." *Criminal Justice and Behavior* 43(10): 1347–1363.

Hirschi, Travis, and Michael Gottfredson. 1995. "Control Theory and the Life-Course Perspective." *Studies on Crime and Crime Prevention* 4(2):131–142.

Holtzworth-Munroe, Amy, and Gregory L. Stuart. 1994. "Typologies of Male Batterers: Three Subtypes and the Differences Among Them." *Psychological Bulletin* 16(3): 476–497.

Johnson, Matthew S. 2007. "Marginal Maximum Likelihood Estimation of Item Response Models in R." *Journal of Statistical Software* 20(10): 1–24.

Kempf, Kimberly L. 1987. "Specialization and the Criminal Career." *Criminology* 25(2): 399–420.

Klein, Malcolm W. 1984. "Offense Specialization and Versatility Among Juveniles." *British Journal of Criminology* 24(2): 185–194.

Lattimore, Pamela K., Christy A. Visher, and Richard L. Linster. 1994. "Specialization in Juvenile Careers: Markov Results for a California Cohort." *Journal of Quantitative Criminology* 10(4): 291–316.

Loeber, Rolf, and Marc LeBlanc. (1990). "Towards a Developmental Criminology." In *Crime and Justice: A Review of Research,* Vol. 12, edited by Michael Tonry and Norval Morris. Chicago: University of Chicago Press.

Lombroso C. 1876. *L'uomo Delinquente Studiato in Rapporto alla Antropologia, alla Medicina Legale, ed alle Discipline Carcerarie.* Milan: Hoepli.

Lussier, Patrick, Marc LeBlanc, and Jean Proulx. 2005. "The Generality of Criminal Behavior: A Confirmatory Factor Analysis of the Criminal Activity of Sex Offenders in Adulthood." *Journal of Criminal Justice* 33: 177–189.

Lynam, Donald R., Alex R. Piquero, and Terrie E. Moffitt. 2004. "Specialization and the Propensity to Violence: Support from Self-Reports but Not Official Records." *Journal of Contemporary Criminal Justice* 20(2): 215–228.

Mazerolle, Paul, Robert Brame, Ray Paternoster, Alex Piquero and Charles Dean. 2000. Onset Age, Persistence, and Offending Versatility: Comparisons Across Gender." *Criminology* 38(4): 1143–1172.

McGloin, Jean M., Christopher J. Sullivan, Alex R. Piquero, and Travis C. Pratt. 2007. "Local Life Circumstances and Offending Specialization/Versatility: Comparing Opportunity and Propensity Models." *Journal of Research in Crime and Delinquency* 44(3): 321–346.

McGloin, Jean M., Christopher J. Sullivan, and Alex R. Piquero. 2009. "Aggregating to Versatility? Transitions Among Offender Types in the Short Term." *British Journal of Criminology* 49: 243–264.

Moffitt, Terrie E. 1993. "Adolescence-Limited and Life-Course-Persistent Antisocial Behavior: A Developmental Taxonomy." *Psychological Review* 100(4): 674–701.

Moffitt, Terrie E. 1994. "Natural Histories of Delinquency." In *Cross-National Longitudinal Research on Human Development and Criminal Behaviour*, edited by Elmar G. M. Weitekamp and Hans-Jürgen Kerner. Dordrecht, The Netherlands: Kluwer.

Nagin, Daniel S., and Richard E. Tremblay. 2005. "Developmental Trajectory Groups: Fact or a Useful Statistical Fiction?" *Criminology* 43(4): 873–904.

Nagin, Daniel S., and Raymond Paternoster. 1991. "On the Relationship of Past to Future Participation in Crime." *Criminology* 29(2): 163–189.

Nieuwbeerta, Paul, Arjan A. J. Blokland, Alex R. Piquero, and Gary Sweeten. 2011. "A Life-Course Analysis of Offense Specialization Across Age: Introducing a New Method for Studying Individual Specialization Over the Life Course." *Crime & Delinquency* 57(3): 3–28.

Osgood, D. Wayne, Lloyd D. Johnston, Patrick M. O'Malley, and Jerald G. Bachman. 1988. "The Generality of Deviance in Late Adolescence and Early Adulthood." *American Sociological Review* 53: 81–93.

Osgood, D. Wayne, and David C. Rowe. 1994. "Bridging Criminal Careers, Theory, and Policy Through Latent Variable Models of Individual Offending." *Criminology* 32(4): 517–554.

Osgood, D. Wayne, and Christopher J. Shreck. 2007. "A New Method for Studying the Extent, Stability, and Predictors of Individual Specialization in Violence." *Criminology* 45(2): 273–312.

Paternoster, Raymond, Robert Brame, Alex Piquero, Paul Mazerolle, and Charles W. Dean. 1998. "The Forward Specialization Coefficient: Distributional Properties and Subgroup Differences." *Journal of Quantitative Criminology* 14(2): 133–154.

Paternoster, Raymond, Charles W. Dean, Alex Piquero, Paul Mazerolle, and Robert Brame. 1997. "Generality, Continuity, and Change in Offending." *Journal of Quantitative Criminology* 13(3): 231–266.

Patterson, Gerald R., Barbara D. DeBaryshe, and Elizabeth Ramsey. 1989. "A Developmental Perspective on Antisocial Behavior." *American Psychologist* 44(2): 329–335.

Patterson, Gerald R., and Yoerger, Karen. 1993. "Developmental Models for Delinquent Behavior." In *Mental Disorder and Crime*, edited by Sheilagh Hodgins, 140–172. Beverly Hills, CA: Sage.

Piquero, Alex R. 2000. "Frequency, Specialization, and Violence in Offending Careers." *Journal of Research in Crime and Delinquency* 37(4): 392–418.

Piquero, Alex R., David P. Farrington, and Alfred Blumstein. 2003. "The Criminal Career Paradigm." *Crime and Justice* 30: 359–506.

Piquero, Alex R., Wesley G. Jennings, and J. C. Barnes. 2012. "Violence in Criminal Careers: A Review of Literature from a Developmental Life-Course Perspective." *Aggression and Violent Behavior* 17: 171–179.

Piquero, Alex, Raymond Paternoster, Paul Mazerolle, Robert Brame, and Charles W. Dean. 1999. "Onset Age and Offense Specialization." *Journal of Research in Crime and Delinquency* 36(3): 275–299.

Rojek, Dean G., and Maynard L. Erickson. 1982. "Delinquent Careers: A Test of the Career Escalation Model." *Criminology* 20(1): 5–28.

Sampson, Robert J., and John H. Laub. 1993. *Crime in the Making: Pathways and Turning Points Through Life*. Cambridge, MA: Harvard University Press.

Sampson, Robert, J. and John H. Laub. 1995. "Understanding Variability in Lives Through Time: Contributions of Life-Course Criminology." *Studies on Crime and Crime Prevention* 4(2):143–158.

Sampson, Robert J., and John H. Laub. 2005. "Seductions of Method: Rejoinder to Nagin and Tremblay's "Developmental Trajectory Groups: Fact or Fiction?" *Criminology* 43(4): 905–913.

Saunders, D. G. 1992. "A Typology of Men Who Batter Women: Three Types Derived from Cluster Analysis." *American Orthopsychiatry*, 62:264–275.

Schwaner, Shawn L. 2000. "'Stick 'Em Up, Buddy': Robbery, Lifestyle, and Specialization Within a Cohort of Parolees." *Journal of Criminal Justice* 28: 371–384.

Shaw, Clifford R. 1930/1966. *The Jack-Roller: A Delinquent Boy's Own Story*. Chicago: University of Chicago Press.

Shaw, Clifford R., and Maurice E. Moore. 1931. *The Natural History of a Delinquent Career*. Chicago: University of Chicago Press.

Smallbone, Stephen W., and Richard K. Wortley. 2004. Onset, Persistence and Versatility of Offending Among Adult Males Convicted of Sexual Offenses Against Children. *Sexual Abuse: A Journal of Research and Treatment* 16: 285–298.

Soothill, Keith, Brian Francis, and Jiayi Liu. 2008. "Does Serious Offending Lead to Homicide? Exploring the Interrelationships and Sequencing of Serious Crime." *British Journal of Criminology* 48: 522–537.

Spelman, William. 1994. *Criminal Incapacitation*. New York: Plenum.

Stander, Julian, David P. Farrington, Gillian Hill, and Patricia M. E. Altham. 1989. "Markov Chain Analysis and Specialization in Criminal Careers." *British Journal of Criminology* 29(4): 317–335.

Sullivan, Christopher J., Jean M. McGloin, Travis C. Pratt, and Alex R. Piquero. 2006. "Rethinking the "Norm" of Offender Generality: Investigating Specialization in the Short-Term." *Criminology* 44(1): 199–226.

Sullivan, Christopher J., Jean M. McGloin, James V. Ray, and Michael S. Caudy. 2009. "Detecting Specialization in Offending: Comparing Analytic Approaches." *Journal of Quantitative Criminology* 25: 419–441.

Thomas, Kyle J. 2015. "Delinquent Peer Influence on Offending Versatility: Can Peers Promote Specialized Delinquency?" *Criminology* 53(2):280–308.

Thornberry, Terence. 1987. "Toward an Interactional Theory of Delinquency." *Criminology* 25:863–891.

Thornberry, Terence, and Marvin Krohn. 2005 "Applying Interactional Theory to the Explanation of Continuity and Change in Antisocial Behaviour." In *Integrated Developmental and Life-Course Theories of Offending. Advances in Criminological Theory*, Vol. 14, edited by David P. Farrington. New Brunswick, NJ: Transaction.

Tracy, Paul E., Marvin E. Wolfgang, and Robert M. Figlio. 1990. *Delinquency in Two Birth Cohorts*. New York: Plenum.

Tolan, Patrick H. 1987. "Implications of Age of Onset for Delinquency Risk." *Journal of Abnormal Child Psychology* 15(1): 47–65.

Tumminello, Michele, Christofer Edling, Fredrik Liljeros, Rosario N. Mantegna, and Jerzy Sarnecki. 2013. "The Phenomenology of Specialization of Criminal Suspects." *PLOS One* 8(5): 1–8 (e64703).

Tzoumakis, Stacy, Patrick Lussier, Mark Le Blanc, and Garth Davies. 2013. "Onset, Offending Trajectories, and Crime Specialization in Violence." *Youth Violence and Juvenile Justice* 11(2): 143–164.

Wilson, James Q., and Richard J. Herrnstein. 1985. *Crime and Human Nature*. New York: Simon & Schuster.

Wolfgang, Marvin E., Robert M. Figlio, and Thorsten Sellin. 1972. *Delinquency in a Birth Cohort*. Chicago: University of Chicago Press.

Yonai, Shachar, Stephen Z. Levine, and Joseph Glicksohn. 2010. "A National Population Based Examination of the Association Between Age-Versatility Trajectories and Recidivism Rates." *Journal of Criminal Justice* 41: 467–476.

Yonai, Shachar, Stephen Z. Levine, and Joseph Glicksohn. 2013. "Elaboration on Specialization in Crime: Disaggregating Age Cohort Effects." *Crime & Delinquency* 59(6): 951–970.

CHAPTER 5

....

ACCELERATION, DECELERATION, ESCALATION, AND DE-ESCALATION

....

WESLEY G. JENNINGS AND BRYANNA HAHN FOX

THE relationship between age and crime has been one of the most studied issues in criminology, with the vast majority of studies showing that aggregate crime rates are highest for individuals during adolescence and quickly decline to very low levels by adulthood (Britt 1992; Greenberg 1977; Rowe and Tittle 1977; Steffensmeier et al. 1989; Tittle and Grasmick 1997).

While the age–crime curve is in fact just a compilation of individual offending rates over time, many questions have been raised regarding the age–crime curve and its applicability to the criminal careers of specific individuals (Jennings et al. 2016; Lauritsen 1998; Piquero, Farrington, and Blumstein 2003). For instance, is the peak in crime rates during adolescence due to an increase in crimes committed by certain individual offenders, or is it the result of more individuals engaging in criminal behavior at those peak ages, or is it a result of both explanations?

In order to answer these questions, the prevalence of offending in the population and the frequency of offending within individual criminal careers must be examined. In both cases, researchers are concerned with patterns of changes seen in individual offending behaviors at certain times and ages and the causes of these behavioral changes. Addressing these and related issues requires knowledge about individual criminal careers, including how they start, why they end, and the cause of any changes in criminal activity seen along the way (Piquero, Farrington, and Blumstein 2003).

Two of these changes in criminal behavior, acceleration or deceleration and escalation or de-escalation, will be defined and discussed in this chapter, along with a brief review of relevant research on criminal careers and the developmental and life-course theories used to understand and explain these offending changes and etiology of their occurrence (Fox, Jennings, and Farrington 2015; LeBlanc and Loeber 1998; Lussier and Blokland 2014; Piquero, Farrington, and Blumstein 2003).

Section I begins with a brief review of the origin of the criminal career paradigm and a description of its various parameters. Section II includes a discussion of both static and dynamic developmental and life-course theories of crime. The next two sections provide a more in-depth discussion of acceleration/deceleration (Section III) and escalation/de-escalation (Section IV) as it relates to a criminal career, respectively. Section V concludes with suggestions for future research on these topics.

I. Criminal Careers

A criminal career is the longitudinal sequence of crimes committed by offenders of any type, frequency, and specialization (Blumstein, Cohen, et al. 1986). This conceptual framework and research paradigm is not to be confused with "career criminals," which are exclusively high-rate versatile offenders that persist over the life-course. And, in contrast, criminal careers of individuals may be long or short, begin early in life or during adolescence or adulthood, may reflect significant versatility or specialization in offenses, and may accelerate or decelerate in frequency and/or escalate or de-escalate in severity over time.

It is the recognition of this variation in criminal careers that has led criminologists to investigate issues related to why some people commit crime and some do not (prevalence), when people start offending (age of onset), the rate of crimes committed per year (frequency), why offending may become more or less frequent (acceleration/deceleration), why it may become more or less serious (escalation/de-escalation), or why it may become more or less specialized (specialization/versatility). Finally, criminal career researchers also examine why and how individuals continue offending (persistence) and why and when they eventually stop offending (desistance) (DeLisi and Piquero 2011; Piquero, Farrington, and Blumstein 2003).

A great deal of research in criminology has focused on the understanding of criminal careers since its inception in the mid-1980s (for summaries, see Blokland 2005; DeLisi 2005; DeLisi and Piquero 2011; Jennings et al. 2016; Piquero, Farrington, and Blumstein 2003, 2007; Piquero, Hawkins, and Kazemian 2011; Steffensmeier and Ulmer 2005). Most of this research has examined the within- and between-individual differences that help explain the dimensions of crime participation, age of onset, offending frequency, acceleration, escalation, specialization, persistence, and desistance from criminal behavior.

While there has been some variability reported in the findings, in general, most studies suggest that the best predictor of future offending behavior is an individual's past offending behavior (Blokland and Nieuwbeerta 2010; Farrington 2007). This means that people who commit violent crimes in adolescence will likely commit violence in adulthood, and high-rate offenders will likely continue offending at high rates in the future.

Criminal career research also suggests that a small fraction of the population, often called the "chronic offenders," commit the vast majority of all crimes (Farrington and West 1993; Wolfgang, Figlio, and Sellin 1972). Furthermore, results consistently show that, by and large, offenders are generalists, not specialists, though there is evidence of some short-term specialization in the midst of a great deal of criminal versatility (DeLisi and Piquero 2011). Finally, it is also clear that the prevalence of offending peaks in the late teenage years, with the peak age of onset of offending generally being observed in early adolescence, and that most offenders desist sometime in their twenties. These observations have been colloquially referred to as "facts" in criminology and extend from investigations of the "age–crime curve" and its aggregate patterns and trends over time (Farrington 2003; Jennings et al. 2016; Wolfgang, Thornberry, and Figlio 1987).

Despite these rather consistent findings on the static nature of criminal careers, many developmental and situational factors have also been identified as key influences on criminal activity over the life-course (DeLisi and Piquero 2011; Farrington 2003). For instance, life circumstances or "turning points," community and structural factors, parents, peers, genetics, biology, psychophysiology, personality, and individual traits have all been linked to the various dimensions of the criminal career (Farrington 2003; Moffitt 1993; Sampson and Laub 1995; Thornberry 1997). These factors generally fall under the broader realm of developmental and life-course criminological theories (DLC), which focus on specific contextual and developmental factors to explain criminal and antisocial behavior (Fox, Jennings, and Farrington 2015). Acknowledging the relevance of DLC theories in the investigations of criminal career dimensions including acceleration or deceleration and escalation or de-escalation, the major DLC theories related to criminal career research will be discussed in the section to follow.

II. Developmental and Life-Course Theories

DLC theories aim to identify and understand the various risk and protective factors for criminal behavior and the effects of situational and developmental factors on the commission of crime throughout the life-course (Farrington, 2003; Fox, Jennings, and Farrington 2015). DLC theories are therefore just a natural extension of the criminal career paradigm, including a variety of risk factors and life events in order to better predict how an individual's criminal career will unfold in terms of onset, persistence, frequency, specialization, and desistance from criminal activity (Farrington 2003; Fox, Jennings, and Farrington 2015; Piquero 2011).

Due to the long-term evaluation needed to assess these developmental and situational risk factors for offending and the follow-up time required to properly evaluate a criminal career, DLC research, by definition, requires the use of longitudinal, not cross-sectional designs to study the etiology and unfolding of criminal behavior over the life-course.

In this regard, DLC research can be far more difficult and time-consuming to properly conduct, but the benefits of utilizing more comprehensive theories and research designs to understand and evaluate criminal careers well outweigh the costs.

A. Static Theories

A prominent example of a static DLC theory is Gottfredson and Hirschi's (1990) self-control theory. This theory focuses on stable traits in individuals that are generally established early in life and lead to an increased propensity to commit criminal or anti-social behavior, regardless of events that take place throughout the life-course (Blokland and Niewbeerta 2010; Hirschi and Gottfredson 1995). In other words, static theories are generally "kinds-of-people" explanations for continuity and participation in crime (Sampson and Laub 2003, p. 24).

Specifically, self-control theory focuses on the level of self-control (or its inverse—impulsivity) as a static predictor for criminality, as individuals with low self-control tend to be highly impulsive, risk-taking, action-oriented, and irresponsible and therefore have negative outcomes in terms of school, work, family, and criminal behavior (DeLisi and Vaughn 2008; Gottfredson and Hirschi 1990). Hundreds of studies have empirically tested self-control theory and its premises, and the majority find some degree of support for low self-control as being a consistent and significant predictor of criminal behavior regardless of gender, race, location, measurements, data source, and even the degree and type of crimes committed over the life-course (see DeLisi 2005). However, self-control theory does not explain why people start, continue, or stop offending, as it is believed that life events such as getting married or gaining maturity and employment have no effect on offending as self-control is stable and continuous over the life-course and no changes in offending behaviors should occur (Farrington 2003).

B. Dynamic Theories

In comparison, dynamic theories stress the importance of individual development and situational context in predicting criminal behavior and state that changes in life circumstances or even specific situations are critical to explaining an individual's criminal career (Sampson and Laub, 2003). For instance, environmental opportunities, mental state, or changes in biology may alter an individual's motivation or inhibition to commit crime in a given situation, while broader community factors or life events may also modify the likelihood of criminal behavior depending on the social bonds to the community, spouse, family, school, or employment that come and go throughout life (Blokland and Nieuwbeerta 2010).

Among the most popular DLC theories are Sampson and Laub's (1993) age-graded theory of informal social control and Moffitt's (1993) developmental taxonomy of offending. The former postulates that weakened bonds with society due to specific events (e.g., getting arrested and labeled a criminal) or cumulative disadvantage (e.g., feeling estranged from "well-to-do" society) leads an individual at any moment to choose to commit or desist from crime (Sampson and Laub 1995). In other words, changes in circumstances or surroundings may encourage or prevent an individual from altering their behavior at various points throughout their criminal career.

Moffitt's (1993) developmental taxonomy identifies two types of offenders, adolescent-limited (AL) and life-course–persistent (LCP) offenders, which are characterized by distinct offending patterns and developmental factors leading to their unique criminal careers (for reviews see Moffitt 2006; Piquero and Moffitt 2005). AL offenders are generally well-adapted individuals whose criminal careers are confined to adolescence. It is at this point in time where teenagers commit crime in order to overcome the "maturity gap" by mimicking older peers or committing offenses to feel more "adult-like" such as underage drinking, drug use, and theft but not violent crime (Piquero, Jennings, and Barnes 2012).

In contrast, LCP offenders begin their antisocial or even criminal behavior early in childhood, commit a wide variety of crimes including violence, and their criminal careers tend to last the majority of their life span (Moffitt 1993). LCP offenders, believed to make up to 10 percent of all offenders, tend to have neurological and/or developmental impairments that lead to a lack of self-control (Piquero, Jennings, and Barnes 2012). But, unlike self-control theory, Moffitt's explanation suggests that self-control is the product of other dynamic factors such as biology, genetics, diminished cognitive capacities, poor environmental circumstances, and familial factors that may change over time but, when present, set the stage for adverse behavior throughout the life-course (Piquero, Jennings, and Barnes, 2012).

In short, it is increasingly clear that in order to understand the changes in offending behavior across the age–crime curve the relationship between developmental and life-course factors and individual criminal careers must be examined. Whether the contextual and/or developmental explanatory factors for criminality are static, or unchanging, in nature or whether they are dynamic and varying across the life-course is less apparent. However, a growing body of DLC research assessing these issues suggests that there are certain changes in criminal behavior, including acceleration and deceleration and escalation and de-escalation, that take place during a criminal career. The definitions and research on these changes in criminal behavior are described in the sections to follow.

III. Acceleration/Deceleration

According to LeBlanc and Loeber (1998), acceleration is an increase in the frequency of offending over time. Deceleration is just the opposite—a decrease in the rate of offending. In order to evaluate acceleration and deceleration in criminal activity over the life-course, it is first necessary to determine the individual crime rate, or lambda (λ), for each offender of interest. Unlike the age–crime curve, which shows the average offending rate for an aggregated population (Farrington 1986; Hirschi and Gottfredson 1983), lambda represents the frequency with which a specific offender commits crimes in a given year (Blumstein, Cohen, and Farrington 1988).

While DLC researchers have long examined the prevalence, frequency, and origins of criminal behavior, few studies have examined the variations in lambda across an individual criminal career (Piquero, Farrington, and Blumstein 2003). In fact, LeBlanc and Fréchette (1989) were among the first, and only, researchers to assess how individual crime rates vary with age. Using criminal history data on offenders from early adolescence to their mid-twenties, LeBlanc and Fréchette found that there were periods of acceleration and deceleration in offending even in that relatively short time frame of the criminal career. Additional studies have found that, like the age–crime curve, individual offending rates tend to accelerate during adolescence and reach their peak in the late teenage years, before decelerating in the early twenties (Farrington 1986; LeBlanc 2002).

However, other research has suggested that individual change in offending frequency is not highly correlated with age but may actually be a reflection of changes in life circumstances and contextual factors (Piquero, Farrington, and Blumstein 2003). For instance, one study found that increases in individual offending rates were significantly related to the increase of stressful events in the person's life, even when controlling for the offender's gender, socioeconomic status, and level of self-control (Hoffman and Cerbone 1999). Similarly, additional studies show that acceleration in an individual's criminal career is correlated with the increased presence and support of friends or family members who are engaged in considerable criminal behavior themselves (Gadd and Farrall 2004). Clearly, these findings on the timing and causes of acceleration in individual crime rates have implications both for criminological theory, in terms of the causes and changes in criminal behavior over the life-course, and for public policy on how to effectively address and prevent offenders at different stages of their criminal careers.

With respect to deceleration, there is considerably more research available from which to draw upon. In general, studies on deceleration and desistance have found that individual offending rates tend to decrease with age, particularly after adolescence and during the thirties and forties (Blumstein et al. 1986; Farrington 1986; LeBlanc and Frechette 1989; Piquero et al. 2001). Specifically, Farrington (1986) found that deceleration is most prevalent between ages 15 to 17 and 20 to 24, while the rate of deceleration was slower but far more constant from age 26 onward. Among these decelerators, the frequency of their offending generally plateaus a few years before decelerating, and ultimately, stopping altogether (LeBlanc 2002). For instance, among those who stop offending at age 20, they are most likely to have peaked at age 17 with nine crimes per year, decrease to six crimes per year at age 18, and drop to three crimes at age 19 before desisting at age 20 (LeBlanc 2002). Still, additional research shows that some offenders decelerate when they "drop" minor offenses over the course of their career and continue only the more serious crimes, while others quickly decelerate to the point of desistance even in early adolescence (LeBlanc 1993). Consequently, LeBlanc and Loeber (1998) stated that deceleration typically occurs in one of three ways: (1) early desistance from offending during adolescence, (2) desistance from specific offense types in the middle of a criminal career, and (3) slower aging out of the criminal career in adulthood (p. 162). In other words, like acceleration, deceleration may occur at different rates, for different reasons, and at different periods of the life-course for different offenders (LeBlanc 2002).

IV. Escalation/De-escalation

In general, the terms of escalation and de-escalation refer to patterns of increasing and/ or decreasing in crime seriousness. While some scholars have suggested that it is difficult to identify and predict violent offenders specifically based solely on early life-course risk (Laub and Sampson 2003), other researchers have demonstrated that once identified later in life, violent offenders typically have an early age of onset for criminal activity and commit a large number of offenses and a variety of offense types (Farrington 1991). In other words, violent offenders have periods of escalation and de-escalation throughout their offending career.

In this vein, Moffitt and colleagues' (1989) analysis of data from the Copenhagen Study suggested that first-time violent offenders were nearly two times as likely to subsequently commit a violent act relative to those offenders whose first offense was a property offense. This evidence tends to indicate that violent offenders may not necessarily have a tendency to de-escalate immediately following or in some point of time soon after committing a violent offense. Comparatively, Farrington and colleagues (1996) relied on data from the Pittsburgh Youth Study and revealed that the seriousness of self-reported delinquency was a robust predictor of court referrals for violence. Therefore, these latter results corroborate those of Moffitt and colleagues (1989) by indicating that patterns of offense escalation and patterns of stability of involvement in violence may be observed in adolescence as well.

Though evidence does exist pointing toward escalation and against de-escalation at least for involvement in violence, it is important to comment on the fact that more of the recent literature on the topic conversely reports that violent offending in general is a statistically rare event (Elliot 1994). Furthermore, researchers have also argued that when a violent offense is observed on any particular offender's criminal history, it is more than likely to be their one and only violent offense and that their criminal history is more of a garden variety. In fact, Zimring, Piquero, and Jennings (2007) have best summarized this in arguing that violent offenders cannot necessarily or even remotely be classified as violent specialists, rather they are just more frequent offenders with bouts of escalation and de-escalation, and they just simply roll the dice more often.

In addition, and most recently, Baker, Metcalfe, and Jennings (2013) utilized random logistic effects models disaggregated by trajectories and data from the Second Philadelphia Birth Cohort to demonstrate that the odds of coming into contact with the police for any particular offense are increased if the prior offense is of the same offense type. These results were maintained even after controlling for age of onset, age, offending trajectory group membership, and intermittency. As such, this more recent and robust analysis illustrates that offending careers may be easily characterized as versatile or escalating and de-escalating *within* the same type of offenses, but not necessarily versatile or escalating or de-escalating *across* different offense types (at least in the short term).

V. Directions for Future Research

Taken together, prior investigations into the criminal career dimensions of acceleration or deceleration and escalation or de-escalation have identified a number of relevant findings. For example, there are periods of the life-course (adolescence, early adulthood) where acceleration can be noted just as there are periods of the life-course such as late middle adulthood and beyond where deceleration can be observed. Comparatively, it appears that offenders are generally confined to committing offenses within a same or similar offense type category when crime switching is detected and that violence or de-escalation from violence is even more statistically rare.

In light of this evidence, we conclude with a series of recommendations for future acceleration/deceleration and escalation/de-escalation research to consider moving forward. First, future research should make an effort to further unpack the elements of acceleration and deceleration across different developmental periods of the life-course as well as across the entire life-course more generally. In this regard, researchers may want to consider taking various developmental periods of the life-course or age bands (ages 10–15, 15–20, 20–25, etc.) and then evaluate within-individual and potentially between-individual changes in terms of patterns of escalation and de-escalation in order to determine if acceleration and deceleration trends are age-graded. Second, research should continue to investigate and identify factors that promote deceleration and/or impede acceleration. Third, future research should utilize more advanced statistical models and research designs for examining escalation and de-escalation such as bivariate probit models, diversity index scores, and random effects logistic regression models, which provide the opportunity to more robustly assess specialization/versatility as it relates to escalation and de-escalation. Fourth, acceleration/deceleration and escalation/de-escalation research needs to be conducted across different cultures and international contexts. Finally, informed by continued research to identify the factors associated with acceleration/deceleration and escalation/de-escalation, evidence-based programs should be designed, implemented, and evaluated for their ability to affect acceleration/deceleration and/or escalation/de-escalation with a critical emphasis on the cost-effectiveness of these interventions. Ultimately, these are indeed important components of the criminal career paradigm that have yet to receive their rightful amount of attention, and future research should acknowledge this deficiency and make strides to address these gaps in the literature.

REFERENCES

Baker, Thomas, Cristi F. Metcalfe, and Wesley G. Jennings. 2013. "What Are the Odds? Predicting Specialization in Offending Over the Life-Course." *Criminal Justice and Behavior* 40: 909–932.

Blokland, Arjan. 2005. *Crime Over the Life Span: Trajectories of Criminal Behavior in Dutch Offenders*. Leiden, The Netherlands: Netherlands Institute for the Study of Crime and Law Enforcement.

Blokland, Arjan, and Phil Nieuwbeerta. 2010. "Considering Criminal Continuity: Testing for Heterogeneity and State Dependence in the Association of Past to Future Offending." *The Australian and New Zealand Journal of Criminology* 43: 526–556.

Blumstein, Alfred, Jacqueline Cohen, and David P. Farrington. 1988. "Criminal Career Research: Its Value for Criminology." *Criminology* 26: 1–35.

Blumstein, Alfred, Jacqueline Cohen, Jeffrey A. Roth, and Christy Visher. 1986. *Criminal Careers and "Career Criminals."* Washington, DC: National Academy Press.

Britt, Chester L. 1992. "Constancy and Change in the US Age Distribution of Crime: A Test of the 'Invariance Hypothesis'." *Journal of Quantitative Criminology* 8: 175–187.

DeLisi, Matt. 2005. *Career Criminals in Society*. Thousand Oaks, CA: Sage.

DeLisi, Matt, and Alex R. Piquero. 2011. "New Frontiers in Criminal Careers Research, 2000–2011: A State-of-the-Art Review." *Journal of Criminal Justice* 39: 289–301.

DeLisi, Matt, and Michael G. Vaughn. 2008. "The Gottfredson-Hirschi Critiques Revisited: Reconciling Self-Control Theory, Criminal Careers, and Career Criminals." *International Journal of Offender Therapy and Comparative Criminology* 52: 520–537.

Elliott, Delbert S. 1994. "Serious Violent Offenders: Onset, Developmental Course, and Termination." *Criminology* 32: 1–21.

Farrington, David P. 1991. "Childhood Aggression and Adult Violence: Early Precursors and Later Life Outcomes." In *The Development and Treatment of Childhood Aggression*, edited by Debra J. Pepler and Kenneth H. Rubin, 5–29. Hillsdale, NJ: Erlbaum.

Farrington, David P., and Donald J. West. 1993. "Criminal, Penal, and Life Histories of Chronic Offenders: Risk and Protective Factors and Early Identification." *Criminal Behavior and Mental Health* 3: 492–523.

Farrington, David P., Rolf Loeber, Magda Stouthamer-Loeber, Welmoet van Kammen, and Laura Schmidt. 1996. "Self-Reported Delinquency and a Combined Delinquency Seriousness Scale Based on Boys, Mothers and Teachers: Concurrent and Predictive Validity for African Americans and Caucasians." *Criminology* 34: 493–517.

Farrington, David P. 1986. "Age and Crime." In *Crime and Justice: An Annual Review of Research*, Vol. 4, edited by Michael Tonry and Norval Morris. Chicago: University of Chicago Press.

Farrington, David P. 2003. "Developmental and Life-Course Criminology: Key Theoretical and Empirical Issues." *Criminology* 41: 221–256.

Farrington, David P. 2007. "Advancing Knowledge About Desistance." *Journal of Contemporary Criminal Justice* 23: 125–134.

Fox, Bryanna B., Wesley G. Jennings, and David P. Farrington. 2015. "Bringing Psychopathy into Developmental and Life-course Criminology Theories and Research." *Journal of Criminal Justice* 43: 274–289.

Gadd, David, and Stephen Farral. 2004. "Criminal Careers, Desistance, and Subjectivity: Interpreting Men's Narratives of Change." *Theoretical Criminology* 8: 123–156.

Gottfredson, Michael R., and Travis Hirschi. 1990. *A General Theory of Crime*. Stanford, CA: Stanford University Press.

Greenberg, David F. 1977. "Delinquency and the Age Structure of Society." *Contemporary Crisis* 1: 189–223.

Hirschi, Travis, and Michael R. Gottfredson. 1983. "Age and the Explanation of Crime." *American Journal of Sociology* 89: 552–584.

Hirschi, Travis, and Michael R. Gottfredson. 1995. "Control Theory and the Life-Course Perspective." *Studies on Crime and Crime Prevention* 4: 131–142.

Hoffman, John P., and Felicia G. Cerbone. 1999. "Stressful Life Events and Delinquency Escalation in Early Adolescence." *Criminology* 37: 343–374.

Jennings, Wesley G., Rolf Loeber, Dustin Pardini, Alex Piquero, and David P. Farrington. 2016. *Offending from Childhood to Young Adulthood: Recent Results from the Pittsburgh Youth Study*. New York: Springer.

Laub, John H., and Robert J. Sampson. 2003. *Shared Beginnings, Divergent Lives: Delinquent Boys to Age 70*. Cambridge, MA: Harvard University Press.

Lauritsen, Janet. 1998. "The Age-Crime Debate: Assessing the Limits of Longitudinal Self-Report Data." *Social Forces* 77: 127–155.

Le Blanc, Marc. 2002. "The Offending Cycle, Escalation and De-escalation in Delinquent Behavior: A Challenge for Criminology." *International Journal of Comparative and Applied Criminal Justice* 26: 53–83.

Le Blanc, Marc, and Marcel Frechette. 1989. *Male Criminal Activity from Childhood Through Youth: Multilevel and Developmental Perspectives*. New York: Springer-Verlag.

Le Blanc, Marc, and Rolf Loeber. 1998. "Developmental Criminology Updated." In *Crime and Justice: An Annual Review of Research*, Vol. 23, edited by Michael Tonry. Chicago: University of Chicago Press.

LeBlanc, Marc. 1993. "Late Adolescence Deceleration of Criminal Activity and Development of Self- and Social Control: Concomitant Changes for Normative and Delinquent Samples." *Studies on Crime and Crime Prevention* 2: 51–68.

Lussier, Patrick, and Arjan Blokland. 2014. "The Adolescence-Adulthood Transition and Robins's Continuity Paradox: Criminal Career Patterns of Juvenile and Adult Sex Offenders in a Prospective Longitudinal Birth Cohort Study." *Journal of Criminal Justice* 42: 153–163.

Moffitt, Terrie E., Steve A. Mednick, and William F. Gabrielli. 1989. "Predicting Criminal Violence: Descriptive Data and Dispositional Factors." In *Current Approaches to the Prediction of Violence,* edited by David A. Brizer and Martha Crowner. New York: American Psychiatric Association Press.

Moffitt, Terrie E. 2006. "Life-Course Persistent Versus Adolescence-limited Antisocial Behavior." In *Developmental Psychopathology,* 2nd ed., edited by Dante Cicchetti and Donald Cohen. New York, Wiley.

Moffitt, Terrie E. 1993. "'Life-Course-Persistent' and 'Adolescence-Limited' Antisocial Behavior: A Developmental Taxonomy." *Psychological Review* 100: 674–701.

Piquero, Alex R., Alfred Blumstein, Robert Brame, Rudy Haapanen, Ed P. Mulvey, and Daniel S. Nagin. 2001. "Assessing the Impact of Exposure Time and Incapacitation on Longitudinal Trajectories of Criminal Offending." *Journal of Adolescent Research* 16: 54–74.

Piquero, Alex R. 2011. "Invited Address: James Joyce, Alice in Wonderland, the Rolling Stones, and Criminal Careers." *Journal of Youth and Adolescence* 40: 761–775.

Piquero, Alex R., and Terrie E. Moffitt. 2005. "Explaining the Facts of Crime: How the Developmental Taxonomy Replies to Farrington's Invitation. In *Integrated Developmental and Life-Course Theories of Offending: Advances in Criminological Theory*, edited by David P. Farrington. New Brunswick, NJ: Transaction.

Piquero, Alex R., David P. Farrington, and Alfred Blumstein. 2003. "The Criminal Career Paradigm." In *Crime and Justice: An Annual Review of Research*, Vol. 30, edited by Michael Tonry. Chicago: University of Chicago Press.

Piquero, Alex R., David P. Farrington, and Alfred Blumstein. 2007. *Key Issues in Criminal Career Research: New Analyses of the Cambridge Study in Delinquent Development*. New York: Cambridge University Press.

Piquero, Alex R., J. David Hawkins, and Lila Kazemian. 2011. "Criminal Career Patterns Between Adolescence and Emerging Adulthood. In *Offending Transitions from Adolescence to Adulthood*, edited by Rolf Loeber and David P. Farrington. New York: Oxford University Press.

Piquero, Alex R., Wesley G. Jennings, and J.C. Barnes. 2012. "Violence in Criminal Careers: A Review of the Literature from a Developmental Life-Course Perspective." *Aggression and Violent Behavior* 17: 171–179.

Rowe, Alan R., and Charles R. Tittle. 1977. "Life Cycle Changes and Criminal Propensity." *Sociological Quarterly* 18: 223–236.

Sampson, Robert J., and John H. Laub. 1995. "Understanding Variability in Lives Through Time: Contributions of Life-Course Criminology." *Studies on Crime and Crime Prevention* 4: 143–158.

Sampson, Robert J., and John H. Laub. 2003. "Desistance from Crime Over the Life Course." In *Handbook on the Life Course*, edited by Jeylan T. Mortimer and Michael J. Shanaban. New York: Kluwer Academic/Plenum.

Steffensmeier, Darrell J., and Jeffrey T. Ulmer. 2005. *Confessions of a Dying Thief: Understanding Criminal Careers and Illegal Enterprise*. New Brunswick, NJ: Transaction.

Steffensmeier, Darrell J., Emilie A. Allan, Miles D. Harer, and Cathy Streifel. 1989. "Age and the Distribution of Crime." *American Journal of Sociology* 94: 803–831.

Thornberry, Terence. P. 1997. "Introduction: Some Advantages of Developmental and Life-Course Perspectives for the Study of Crime and Delinquency." In *Developmental Theories of Crime and Delinquency*, Vol. 7, *Advances in Criminological Theory*, edited by Terence P. Thornberry. New Brunswick, NJ: Transaction.

Tittle, Charles R., and Harold G. Grasmick. 1997. "Criminal Behavior and Age: A Test of Three Provocative Hypotheses." *Journal of Criminal Law and Criminology* 88: 309–342.

Wolfgang, Marvin E., Terence P. Thornberry, and Robert M. Figlio. 1987. *From Boy to Man, from Delinquency to Crime*. Chicago: University of Chicago Press.

Wolfgang, Marvin E., Robert M. Figlio, and Thorsten Sellin. 1972. *Delinquency in a Birth Cohort*. Chicago: University of Chicago Press.

Zimring, Franklin, Alex R. Piquero, and Wesley G. Jennings. 2007. "Sexual Delinquency in Racine: Does Early Sex Offending Predict Later Sex Offending in Youth and Adulthood? *Criminology and Public Policy* 6: 507–534.

CHAPTER 6

....

PERSISTENCE AND
DESISTANCE

....

SIYU LIU AND SHAWN D. BUSHWAY

THE study of behavioral change is at the heart of life-course scholarship. Generally, the scholarship can be divided into two types: descriptive and explanatory. Descriptive research focuses on describing the criminal career path or the developmental process of criminal offending over the life-course using different approaches, including the criminal career paradigm (Blumstein et al. 1986), the developmental paradigm (Thornberry 1987; Gottfredson and Hirschi 1990; Moffitt 1993) or the life-course paradigm (Sampson and Laub 1993). Researchers also sometimes focus on describing a specific part of the offending career such as the desistance process (e.g., Bushway et al. 2001; Bushway, Thornberry, and Krohn 2003; Brame, Bushway, and Paternoster 2003; Kurlychek, Bushway, and Brame 2012). Explanatory research focuses on identifying factors or processes that can explain both short-term and long-term changes in offending, including long-term changes that look like desistance. These studies can be quantitative (e.g., Farrington and West 1995; Blokland and Nieuwbeerta 2005; Kreager et al. 2010; Yule, Paré, and Gartner 2015) or qualitative (Maruna 2001; Edin, Nelson, and Paranal 2001; Giordano, Cernkovich, and Rudolph 2002; Edin and Kefalas 2005; Edin and Nelson 2013).

Descriptively, there is little debate that offending in the aggregate increases during adolescence, peaks in the late teens, and then descends more gradually during the twenties and thirties. The debate during the 1980s and 1990s centered on the bold claims of Gottfredson and Hirschi (1990), who asserted that all individuals followed this basic pattern, with individual variation limited to differences in stable criminal propensity. Theorists quickly developed competing approaches that emphasized different pathways for individuals or groups of individuals. One early example of a theory that challenged Gottfredson and Hirschi's claim is Moffitt's (1993) offender typology. Moffitt (1993) identified three groups of individuals with distinctive offending paths: non-offenders, life-course–persistent offenders (LCP), and adolescence-limited

(AL) offenders. The two offending groups are identified by the age of onset and the age of desistance.

The late 1990s was also an exciting period for methodological advances such as group-based trajectory modeling (Nagin and Land 1993) and latent growth curve modeling (Bushway, Sweeten, and Nieuwbeerta 2009), which facilitated empirical tests of these ideas. While there is no consensus about the number of groups or the exact nature of the distinct groups, it is well supported that different patterns exist (Nagin, Farrington, and Moffitt 1995; Laub, Nagin, and Sampson 1998; Kratzer and Hodgins 1999; D'Unger, Land, and McCall 2002; Bushway, Thornberry, and Krohn 2003; Blokland et al. 2005; Block et al. 2010; Blokland and Os 2010; Jennings et al. 2010; Andersson et al. 2012; Liu 2015).

Current work in this area involves trying to better describe and then explain both persistence and desistance among individuals. Persistence in criminal offending may be observed when subjects are followed for sufficiently long period and found to have maintained a certain level of offending[1] (e.g., see Bushway, Sweeten, and Nieuwbeerta 2009). Desistance is discussed when offending declines to a zero or close-to-zero level, with other parameters also clearly defined, such as the crime indicators used (self-report or official detection), observation frequency (length of each follow-up period), and time period (number of years followed). Frequently, life-course researchers define persistence and desistance very specifically in a sample that is not followed over the entire life course (Bushway 2013).

However, operational challenges still exist in the identification of both persistence and desistance. For example, consistent exposure to the conventional social environment can be disrupted by non-random incapacitation. It is therefore difficult to disentangle criminal careers from criminal justice careers. Offenders might have been identified as persisters—or desisters for that matter—if only they have not been incapacitated by the system for a period of time. The counterfactual of an offender not subject to the sanction of the system for criminal behaviors cannot be naturally observed. Similarly, death also masks natural offending patterns. Both sources of incapacitation are not random events for offenders (Blokland, Nagin, and Nieuwbeerta 2005; Nieuwbeerta and Piquero 2008). Even in models that control for death and incarceration, the true offending rate might still be underestimated for those who were censored by death and incarceration (Bushway 2013). It is important to keep those challenges in mind when discussing desistance. Notwithstanding these challenges, the field of criminology continues to make progress in the study of desistance.

This chapter is organized into five sections. In Section I we discuss the challenges in the identification of persistent offenders. Section II provides a review of evidence on age–crime relationship and the heterogeneous patterns of desistance. In Section III we examine the controversy surrounding desistance as a process or a discrete point. Section IV summarizes the theoretical underpinnings of desistance. The chapter will conclude in Section V with a discussion on the future of research on desistance.

I. The Identification of Life-Course–Persistent Offenders

Moffitt (1993, p. 676) argues that only a small proportion of offenders (5 to 6 percent) should be characterized as persistent offenders. Yet the identification of this small group has been a challenge in the field of life-course criminology since its inception. Moffitt (1993) argued that this group can be observed and distinguished when they maintain similar levels of offending beyond the age of 40 (p. 677, Fig. 3). In a later publication (2006), Moffitt argued that the taxonomy was supported by data from the Gluecks, where life-course–persistent offenders on average have an extended criminal career of about 25.6 years (p. 587). Sampson and Laub (2003) used the Gluecks' data but regarded this extended criminal career, which petered out by age 70, as evidence of life-course desistance, rather than persistence. Essentially, Sampson and Laub (2003) came to a different conclusion because they adopted a very stringent definition of persistence. A group of researchers using the same definition and the Criminal Career and Life-Course Study (CCLS) in the Netherlands, which followed people into their seventies (Blokland, Nagin, and Nieuwbeerta 2005), reached a different conclusion, showing evidence of a small sample of people who maintained a stable offending rate until age 72.

Part of the challenge is that current methodologies in life-course criminology face considerable difficulty in accurately describing life-course persisters, who represent a very distinct but unusual group. Group-based trajectory modeling may force the persisters into a group with high probability simply because there is no other better alternative among the group memberships. This method, which is widely used in life-course studies, is not accommodating to outliers. Indeed, most life-course methods do a better job at describing individuals who follow the overall pattern of offending, rather than patterns that deviate from it (Bushway, Sweeten, and Nieuwbeerta 2009).

Certainly, the discussion on life-course persistence is still conditioned on the observation of individual life course. But very few datasets follow people to age 70. And, according to Sampson and Laub (2003), people who die before age 70 cannot be life-course persisters. Clearly, some allowance for death that interrupts a life before age 70 must be taken into account in the definition of life-course persistence (Bushway 2013). A recent review of longitudinal studies by Jolliffe and his colleagues (2017) emphasized the importance of the duration of criminal careers and the urgent need to have consistent definitions of offender groups (AL, LCP, and late-onset [LO]) to identify reliable explanatory factors.

Perhaps due to the challenges in identifying life-course persisters, more studies have focused on desistance. In the next section we will discuss the different patterns of desistance.

II. The Age–Crime Relationship and the Heterogeneity of Desistance Patterns

The general relationship between age and crime may be one of the most agreed-upon concepts in the study of life-course criminology. Yet the heterogeneity hidden behind the age–crime curve has fascinated criminologists for decades. Hirschi and Gottfredson (1983) argued that age is a causal factor of crime and that no other factors that change with age could explain this relationship. In other words, the relationship between age and crime is invariant. Farrington (1986) challenged the "invariant" hypothesis and delineated the characteristics of age–crime relationship to compare different populations descriptively, using peak age, median age, mean age, skewness, and kurtosis of the age–crime curve. Laub, Nagin, and Sampson (1998) used group-based trajectory modeling to show that two out of four groups of offenders do not follow the shape of a conventional age–crime curve.

Farrington (1986) also raised important questions relevant to the underlying mechanisms of the peak and post-peak patterns: What exactly does the peak of the curve mean, and how do we interpret the decline? One of the most basic but helpful inquiries into the age–crime relationship is whether sex differentiates the patterns, a step further into the heterogeneity behind the curve hinting at the potentially distinct social experiences each sex represents. Recent evidence exists to support the differential patterns of desistance by sex.

D'Unger and colleagues (2002) found a much less pronounced persistent category of female offenders and an earlier desistance pattern for low-rate female offenders when compared to their male counterparts. Liu (2015) identified statistically significant sex differences in the shape of the age–crime curves using the National Longitudinal Survey of Youth (1997). She found that female offending, measured by self-reported arrest and criminal behavior, starts declining about two years before that of males. Breaking the aggregate arrest curves down using group-based trajectory modeling, Liu (2015) indicated that male offenders in the sample who are estimated to have one or more arrests per year have a higher level of heterogeneity than female counterparts, with two delayed peaking groups among four. Females who have one or more arrests per year, on the other hand, fall into a single trajectory group and mostly desisted by age 20 (see Figure 6.1). This provides evidence that offenders follow distinctive desistance patterns, indicating possible differential desistance mechanisms.

Methodologically, Liu (2015) finds that assuming that everyone follows the same basic pattern with differences in level could obscure meaningful differences in desistance processes. Substantively, Liu (2015) lends supports to qualitative research on male and female desistance processes that have concluded that males and females have different desistance experiences (Laub and Sampson 2001; Edin, Nelson, and Paranal 2001; Edin

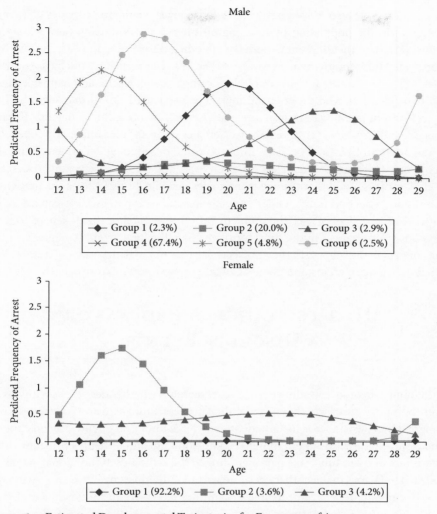

FIGURE 6.1 Estimated Developmental Trajectories for Frequency of Arrest

Source: Figure 2.3B in Liu (2015)

and Kefalas 2005; Skardhamar and Lyngstad 2009; Kreager, Matsueda, and Erosheva 2010; Kerr et al. 2011; Edin and Nelson 2013).

Using sex as a proxy to examine the heterogeneous composition of offenders, or their life experiences, is only one way to understand the post-peak age–crime relationship. Another way is to look backwards, rather than forwards. Tahamont et al. (2015) used New York State data to track offenders 10 years *before* their first prison term. Using group-based trajectory modeling, they found considerable heterogeneity in this group by presenting both an average curve and a disaggregated six-group graph. Despite the fact that most of the offenders maintained frequent contact with the criminal justice system, they present quite different pathways leading to their first prison spell.

Researchers have also moved beyond the debate over the different shapes of the age–crime curve in the population by focusing on the causal connection between significant life events and the different patterns of offending observed in the data. Results have demonstrated that employment, marriage, or becoming a parent does not have a uniform impact, nor is the impact age-invariant. For example, Laub, Nagin, and Sampson (1998) found that offenders who experienced marriage, particularly good marriages built on social cohesiveness, enjoy long-term preventive effects on offending behaviors. Kreager, Matsueda, and Erosheva (2010) examined females in an urban sample and found that teen and adult motherhood plays an important role in reducing delinquency and substance abuse. Compared to females, males embrace the role of parent quite differently. Kerr et al. (2011) argued that the age when males become fathers affects the magnitude of parenthood effect on crime. Older fathers appeared to experience a greater decrease in both crime and alcohol use. The problem with this research is that it is hard to know if these observed changes in the short term are related to longer-term changes captured by the concept of desistance. In the next section we summarize the ongoing debate about whether desistance is an instantaneous change, a process, or a mixture of both.

III. Desistance: A Process or a Discrete Event?

One ongoing debate surrounding desistance research is whether desistance happens at a discrete point in time or whether it is a gradual process. Blumstein and colleagues (1986) maintained that desistance is instantaneous: criminal offenders offend at a constant rate when active and desist from offending at some point, meaning that they instantly drop to a zero rate of offending. This paradigm linked the estimates of individual crime rate lambda (λ) to factors that vary between and within individuals over time (i.e., with age). Qualitative researchers have been able to capture this type of instantaneous desistance where subjects reported termination of a criminal career (Maltz 1996; Baskin and Sommers 1998; Maruna 1999; Harris 2014). However, it is not clear from these studies whether the rate of offending has been constant before the defining moment. Further, the apparent termination may not be permanent for some of the offenders as observation of offender behavior is often right-censored; the conclusion of an observation period occurs before the apparent desisters restart.

Criminal career scholars describe this "restarting" as "intermittency," where offenders continue with their criminal careers with periods of inactive intervals in between (Barnett, Blumstein, and Farrington 1989; Bushway and Tahamont 2015). Farrington (1986) also identified the pitfall that "even a five-year or ten-year crime-free period is no guarantee that offending has terminated" (p. 201).

Restarting, perhaps at a lower rate of offending, is also consistent with a more gradual desistance process, presented by the reduction of the frequency and severity of individual offending to zero or a near-zero level (Leblanc and Loeber 1998; Bushway et al. 2001; Laub and Sampson 2001). Many researchers have chosen the word "process" to describe desistance, perhaps for the reason that the individual agentic transformation, widely theorized to be the trigger of behavioral change, usually takes time to swing into full effect. According to this definition, the "process," or the glide path, could have been initiated by a particular life event such as employment, marriage to a prosocial partner (or break-up), the birth of a child, or other events (Laub and Sampson 2003), rendering the desistance process similar to a random walk in a time series (Bushway and Paternoster 2013).

As noted above, it is not hard to find compelling evidence showing a connection between life events and short-term changes in offending behavior that might be part of longer-term processes of decline (e.g., Farrington and West 1995; Edin, Nelson, and Paranal 2001; Paternoster et al. 2003; Edin and Kefalas 2005; King, Massoglia, and MacMillan 2007; Larson and Sweeten 2012; van Schellen, Apel, and Nieuwbeerta 2012; Bersani and Doherty 2013; Edin and Nelson 2013). Other studies using special populations such as drug-involved offenders, sex offenders, and intimate-partner violent offenders also examined the process these offenders followed to desistance (Martin et al. 2011; Harris 2014; Walker et al. 2014).

Culture is also discussed as part of the context for the life events that affect individuals. Savolainen (2009) cautioned that culture often frames the relevance of life events and also creates variation within a society in the acceptance of certain social practices such as premarital cohabitation, welfare receipt, and incarceration. Cultural factors differ across places, and over time, and therefore might drive variations in findings regarding the role of different life events on desistance.

Some newer evidence may support a comeback of instantaneous desistance (e.g., Kurlychek, Bushway, and Brame 2012). One possible explanation is that the apparent gradualness of desistance may be a modeling artifact from approaches that smooth over patterns of offending (Bushway and Tahamont 2015). Kurlychek and colleagues (2012) modeled recidivism using a sample of felony convicts with 18 years of follow-up data. Instead of estimating the age–crime curve, the authors approached the question by using competing hazard models that pair up well with competing models of desistance. For example, split-population hazards, which divide the sample into those who became inactive at the beginning of the observation and those who are still active at the beginning of the observation, captures the idea of instantaneous desistance. By contrast, a Weibull hazard model matches well with a slowly declining risk of offending (gradual desistance). Their results show that the split-population exponential model that assumes an instantaneous desistance process with a stable risk of recidivism over time (i.e., the criminal career model) fits the data better than models that assume a declining risk. Future work should focus on finding other ways to empirically differentiate between instantaneous desistance and desistance as a gradual process of decline.

It is interesting to note that theories that are consistent with instantaneous desistance have also begun to appear to compete more directly with life-course theories of gradual change. In the next section we discuss several major theories that frame the desistance discussion.

IV. THEORIES OF INDIVIDUAL CHANGE—EXTERNAL OR INTERNAL FORCES

The point of departure that distinguishes different theories relates to what drives the occurrence of desistance: external force (i.e., age, informal social control generated from the environment or a turning-point life event) or more internal, proactive force (identity shift or cognitive transformation). This, in turn, helps us contextualize the "process vs. discrete event" debate. Relevant theories on this debate are intertwined with each other in many ways but carry distinctive characteristics, all of which have significant implications in the empirical design of desistance studies.

Hirschi and Gottfredson (1983) highlighted the close relationship between age and crime, arguing that it is uniformly true that age has invariant effect on crime over time. Individuals who offend seem to go through a natural course as they age: onset in early adolescence, most active (peak) in late adolescence, and then desist in adulthood. This pattern forms the classic bell-shaped curve. Individuals whom Harris (2014) referred to as "natural desisters" in a sex offender sample reported that they simply desisted due to age, as they were "tired" or "too old" to be leading the former lifestyle (p. 13). They did not characterize any social event as having turned their lives around—they simply stopped. This "instantaneous desistance" is not inconsistent with a smooth aggregate bell curve, since people may exit at different ages.

However, many criminologists disagree with the notion that age is a causal factor for offending. For example, Sweeten and colleagues (2013) found that three-fourths of the age–crime relationship could be explained by a variety of time-varying factors in sociological, psychological, and biological realms based on multiple criminological theories. At the very least, it is impossible to include age as an explanatory variable if it is also part of the phenomenon under study.

Sampson and Laub solve this problem by advancing an age-graded theory of informal social control (1993; Laub and Sampson 2003). They emphasized that age may interact with different causal factors to produce different effects over time. These forces come from social bonds formed in offender's network, such as friends, family, colleagues, or others. Each social role offers the possibility of establishing certain bonds that in turn can put constraints on decisions toward crime. However, this theory highlights particularly the surrounding environment of the offenders. In this sense, Harris's (2014) natural desisters would not fit into Sampson and Laub's (2003) framework: they did not have any of the pretext of informal social control required by their theory.

To fill the void of individual agency in the earliest forms of life-course theories, Giordano and colleagues (2002) argued that cognitive transformation needs to occur before what they called "hooks for change," such as marriage or a job, can play the role of curbing crime (p. 992). The cognitive transformation calls for a perception of need to change, the perception of importance to do so because of the importance of the "hooks" in their lives, a change in the perceived appeal of crime, or a need to seek a "replacement self" to move into the new future (p. 1001). Later emotional transformation was added to the original theory to underscore the importance of prosocial significant others in offenders' lives (Giordano, Schroeder, and Cernkovich 2007). These new thinking patterns may work together to shape the decision-making process, filtering out unfavorable life choices such as crime. Massoglia and Uggen (2010) confirmed that individuals with persistent offending are fundamentally characterized by a delayed entrance into the self-recognized functional adult role. Once offenders realize the value of being mature and adopt an adult role, desistance may ensue.

Maruna and colleagues (2004) approached the change of behaviors from a different perspective: the change for good that we observe among offenders may not be a change of a self-image, but a change in how they interpret the past or the label they attach to themselves through a "looking glass" (p. 273). The change in behaviors may be a manifestation of a new understanding of life experience, stemming from a continuum of personality that precedes the occurrence of any social event. In other words, instead of a change in identity, Maruna (2001) argued for a new ability to take responsibility for one's own behaviors, an improvement upon the "it wasn't my fault" type of excuse (p. 147). The agency in taking control of one's own life is a key factor in a transformative future (Liem and Richardson 2014).

The identity theory of desistance (IDT) advanced by Paternoster and Bushway (2009) emphasized exactly this agentic power of self. From a cost-benefit analysis standpoint, the transition occurs when an offender realizes that crime is more costly than the gain from it and that failures from multiple life domains are interrelated. Fear of what kind of person one is becoming (the "feared self") motivates the adoption of a more prosocial identity. In this theory, the human agency involved, rather than an external push in the form of family bond or employment opportunity, is salient. This is somewhat congruent with Giordano, Cernkovich, and Rudolph (2002), who proposed the theory of cognitive transformation. However, IDT more explicitly links the arrival of opportunities with the adoption of the prosocial identity. Both theories reflect a strong movement away from theories that see individuals as passive responders to social context. This description of agent-driven change is consistent with instantaneous desistance, as opposed to models of gradual change.

Despite these differences, most theories recognize the role of opportunities to offend (and to not offend) in desistance. Lack of education and/or skills, and the perpetual circle of disadvantage exacerbated by the systematic prejudice toward the social stratum in which ex-offenders occupy in the society, contribute to the difficulty in achieving long-term desistance beyond the point of "aging-out." This may be part of the cause for "intermittency" that has been revitalized in recent literature. A failed or disheartened attempt at "getting out" could trigger offending relapse(s) and then a return to the old ways, even when the offender possesses the willpower to change.

There is a great deal more work to be done. For instance, we have only alluded to the kinds of changes in preferences that are integral to changes in identity. Part of the identity change to a non-offender, we think, is a change in the preference one has for crime—in essence, crime has much less appeal. Further, Giordano, Schroeder, and Cernkovich (2007) have argued that one's preferences for peers and the "party life" greatly diminishes among those seeking or maintaining a way out of crime.

Researchers have left the specific content of these changes in preferences for the moment unspecified, and much work needs to be done in understanding the link between changes in identity and behavioral attempts to support that new identity. Future work needs to further explicate and test the role of identity and social events in the transition to non-offending.

V. Discussions and Conclusions

It is a criminological fact that while some people persist in offending for long periods of time, a sizable subset—between 20 percent and 30 percent—of recently convicted offenders will never be arrested again (Schmidt and Witte 1988; Brame, Bushway, and Paternoster 2003; Kurlychek, Bushway, and Brame 2012). Comparisons of hazard models have repeatedly shown that split-population models, which allow for "instantaneous desistance," substantially outperform models that assume that individuals with a criminal history will continue to offend at a constant rate (Schmidt and Witte 1988; Kurlychek, Bushway, and Brame 2012). Ethnographic work similarly shows that even serious serial offenders will choose to exit offending (Baskin and Sommers 1998; Maruna 1999).

Although there is no debate about the existence of desisters, there is a considerable amount of debate about the ability to distinguish prospectively between desisters and persisters. For example, John Laub stated in his Sutherland address to the American Society of Criminology that "human agency induces an apparent instability or random component into life-course turning points making neat prediction—even from adult factors—inherently a difficult if not impossible endeavor" (Laub 2006, p. 244). Recent empirical research on long-term recidivism hazards has begun to test the limits of this claim (Kurlychek, Brame, and Bushway 2006, 2007; Blumstein and Nakamura 2009; Soothill and Francis 2009; Bushway, Nieuwbeerta, and Blokland 2011). Using hazard models, this research has shown definitively that individuals who have not offended for a very long time—between 7 and 10 years—have a very small probability of being arrested in the next year. In fact, they often seem to have the same level of risk as individuals without a criminal history at all. This line of research has thus established that it is possible to distinguish risk levels among individuals with criminal histories, although in this case it takes at least 7 years of waiting before the desisters reveal themselves.

Some scholars in criminology are very comfortable with the idea of prospectively identifying risk levels and of using these predictions in policy (see Andrews, Bonta, and Wormith 2006). However, as Rhodes (2011) warned, these more contemporaneous risk tools have a limited ability to make risk distinctions. An individual's criminal propensity can only be known within fairly wide confidence limits (Bushway et al. 2009), and any risk-prediction exercise will necessarily involve considerable error (Gottfredson and Moriarity 2006). If, as the evidence seems to be suggesting in ever louder ways, individuals are making choices to desist, the difficulty in being able to predict who among an active group of offenders will desist at any given point is hardly surprising. Moreover, the nature of this identity transformation does not lend itself to easy manipulation by outsiders.

In this chapter we have explored opportunities for new research to shed light on the issue of desistance. Researchers can begin by doing a better job of identifying those who have desisted once they have indeed stopped offending. Waiting for extremely long periods of time to be sure someone has "truly" stopped offending despite the fact that we know that their level of criminal propensity is very low seems wasteful. Another option is to utilize information from other domains in addition to information about the absence of offending in order to provide a richer picture of desistance. Those who change their identity necessarily engage in a number of other behaviors that structure and support their decision to desist (move, get jobs, alter their social networks, get their children back, start attending church or AA). These behaviors are observable and can shed light on the probability that an individual has desisted. Bushway and Apel (2012) develop this idea more fully in an essay on signaling.

We have also discussed using hazard models on panel data to explain short-term changes in behavior. In particular, hazard models can be used to compare instantaneous desistance with gradual declines in behavior over time. This approach, presented more fully in Kurlychek, Bushway, and Brame (2012), appears to show strong support for sudden, sharp changes in behavior consistent with a time series model of structural breaks. These empirical models fit well with new theories of agentic change that are also consistent with sharp, rather than gradual, changes. It is exciting to see theoretical and empirical work on desistance converging in important ways. Future work needs to concentrate on demonstrating whether this convergence is real or simply an illusion.

NOTE

1. While in a broad sense, persistence is observed when offending lasts well beyond age 40 (Moffitt 2006), a much more stringent definition of persistence is offered by Sampson and Laub (2003). They argued that to persist is to offend at a constant rate over the life course, which lasts until age 70, and this is contested by Bushway (2013). However, longitudinal data that do not suffer from right censorship due to incarceration, death, or conclusion of study observation are quite rare, making a long-term desistance difficult to observe.

REFERENCES

Andersson, Frida, Sten Levander, Robert Svensson, and Marie Torstensson Levander. 2012. "Sex Differences in Offending Trajectories in a Swedish Cohort." *Criminal Behaviour and Mental Health* 22: 108–121.

Andrews, Don A., James Bonta, and J. Stephen Wormith. 2006. "The Recent Past and Near Future of Risk and/or Need Assessment." *Crime and Delinquency* 52: 7–27.

Baskin, Deborah, and Ira Sommers. 1998. *Casualties of Community Disorder: Women's Careers in Violent Crime.* Boulder, CO: Westview Press.

Barnett, Arnold, Alfred Blumstein, and David P. Farrington. 1989. "A Prospective Test of a Criminal Career Model." *Criminology* 27: 373–388.

Bersani, Bianca E., and Elaine Eggleston Doherty. 2013. "When the Ties That Bind Unwind: Examining the Enduring and Situational Processes of Change Behind the Marriage Effect." *Criminology* 51: 399–433.

Block, Carolyn Rebecca, Arjan A. Blokland, Cornelia van der Werff, Rianne van Os, and Paul Nieuwbeerta. 2010. "Long-Term Patterns of Offending in Women." *Feminist Criminology* 5: 73–107.

Blokland, Arjan J., and Paul Nieuwbeerta. 2005. "The Effects of Life Circumstances on Longitudinal Trajectories of Offending." *Criminology* 43: 1203–1240.

Blokland, Arjan J., Daniel S. Nagin, and Paul Nieuwbeerta. 2005. "Life Span Offending Trajectories of a Dutch Conviction Cohort." *Criminology* 43: 919–954.

Blokland, Arjan J., and Rianne van Os. 2010. "Life Span Offending Trajectories of Convicted Dutch Women." *International Criminal Justice Review* 20: 169–187.

Blumstein, Alfred, and Kiminori Nakamura. 2009. "Redemption in the Presence of Widespread Criminal Background Checks." *Criminology* 47: 327–359.

Blumstein, Alfred, Jacqueline Cohen, Jeffrey A. Roth, and Christy A. Visher, eds. 1986. *Criminal Careers and "Career Criminals,"* Vol. 1. Washington, DC: National Academy Press.

Brame, Robert, Shawn D. Bushway, and Raymond Paternoster. 2003. "Examining the Prevalence of Criminal Desistance." *Criminology* 41:423–448.

Bushway, Shawn. 2013. "Life-Course-Persistent Offenders." In *The Oxford Handbook of Criminological Theory*, edited by Francis T. Cullen and Pamela Wilcox, 189–204. New York: Oxford University Press.

Bushway, Shawn D., and Robert Apel. 2012. "A Signaling Perspective on Employment-Based Reentry Programming." *Criminology and Public Policy* 11(1): 21–50.

Bushway, Shawn D., and Raymond Paternoster. 2013. "Desistance from Crime: A Review and Ideas for Moving Forward." In *Handbook of Life-Course Criminology*, edited by Chris L. Gibson and Marvin D. Krohn. Springer: New York.

Bushway, Shawn. D., Alex R. Piquero, Lisa M. Broidy, Elizabeth Cauffman, and Paul Mazerolle. 2001. "An Empirical Framework for Studying Desistance as a Process." *Criminology* 39: 491–516.

Bushway, Shawn D., Terence P. Thornberry, and Marvin D. Krohn. 2003. "Desistance as a Developmental Process: A Comparison of Static and Dynamic Approaches." *Journal of Quantitative Criminology* 19: 129–153.

Bushway, Shawn D., Gary Sweeten, and Paul Nieuwbeerta. 2009. "Measuring Long Term Individual Trajectories of Offending Using Multiple Methods." *Journal of Quantitative Criminology* 25: 259–286.

Bushway, Shawn, Paul Nieuwbeerta, and Arjan Blokland. 2011. "The Predictive Value of Criminal Background Checks: Do Age and Criminal History Affect Time to Redemption?" *Criminology* 49: 27–60.

Bushway, Shawn and Sarah Tahamont. 2015. "Modeling Long Term Criminal Careers: What Happened to the Variability?" *Journal of Research in Crime and Delinquency* 53: 372–391.

D'Unger, Amy V., Kenneth C. Land, and Patricia L. McCall. 2002. "Sex Differences in Age Patterns of Delinquent/Criminal Careers: Results from Poisson Latent Class Analyses of the Philadelphia Cohort Study." *Journal of Quantitative Criminology* 18: 349–375.

Edin, Kathryn, and Maria Kefalas. 2005. *Promises I Can Keep: Why Poor Women Put Motherhood Before Marriage*. Berkeley: University of California Press.

Edin, Kathryn, and Timothy Jon Nelson. 2013. *Doing the Best I Can: Fatherhood in the Inner City*. London: University of California Press.

Edin, Kathryn, Timothy J. Nelson, and Rechelle Paranal. 2001. *Fatherhood and Incarceration as Potential Turning Points in the Criminal Careers of Unskilled Men*. Evanston, IL: Institute for Policy Research, Northwestern University.

Farrington, David. P. 1986. "Age and Crime." In *Crime and Justice*, Vol. 7, edited by Norval Morris and Michael Tonry. Chicago: University of Chicago Press.

Farrington, David P. 1987. "Predicting Individual Crime Rates." In *Prediction and Classification: Criminal Justice Decision Making*, Vol. 9: *Crime and Justice*, edited by Don M. Gottfredson and Michael Tonry. Chicago: University of Chicago Press.

Farrington, David P., and Donald J. West. 1995. "Effects of Marriage, Separation, and Children on Offending by Adult Males." *Current Perspectives on Aging and the Life Cycle*, Vol. 4: *Delinquency and Disrepute in the Life Course*, edited by John Hagan. Greenwich, CT: JAI Press.

Giordano, Peggy C., Stephen A. Cernkovich, and Jennifer L. Rudolph. 2002. "Gender, Crime, and Desistance: Toward a Theory of Cognitive Transformation." *American Journal of Sociology* 107: 990–1064.

Giordano, Peggy C., Ryan D. Schroeder, and Stephen A. Cernkovich. 2007. "Emotions and Crime over the Life Course: A Neo-Meadian Perspective on Criminal Continuity and Change." *American Journal of Sociology* 112: 1603–1661.

Gottfredson, Michael R., and Travis Hirschi. 1990. *A General Theory of Crime*. Stanford, CA: Stanford University Press.

Gottfredson, Stephen D., and Laura J. Moriarty. 2006. "Statistical Risk Assessment: Old Problems and New Applications." *Crime and Delinquency* 52: 178–200.

Harris, Danielle Arlanda. 2014. "Desistance from Sexual Offending: Findings from 21 Life History Narratives." *Journal of Interpersonal Violence* 29: 1554–1578.

Hirschi, Travis, and Michael Gottfredson. 1983. "Age and the Explanation of Crime." *American Journal of Sociology* 89: 552–584.

Jennings, Wesley G., Mildred M. Maldonado-Molina, Alex R. Piquero, Candice L. Odgers, Hector Bird, and Glorisa Canino. 2010. "Sex Differences in Trajectories of Offending Among Puerto Rican Youth." *Crime and Delinquency* 56: 327–357.

Jolliffe, Darrick, David P. Farrington, Alex R. Piquero, John F. MacLeod, and Steve van de Weijer. 2017. "Prevalence of Life-Course-Persistent, Adolescence-Limited, and Late-Onset Offenders: A Systematic Review of Prospective Longitudinal Studies." *Aggression and Violent Behavior* 33: 4–14.

Kerr, David C.R., Deborah M. Capaldi, Lee D. Owen, Margit Wiesner, and Katherine C. Pears. 2011. "Changes in At-Risk American Men's Crime and Substance Use Trajectories Following Fatherhood." *Journal of Marriage and Family* 73: 1101–1116.

King, Ryan D., Michael Massoglia, and Ross MacMillan. 2007. "The Context of Marriage and Crime: Gender, the Propensity to Marry, and Offending in Early Adulthood." *Criminology* 45: 33–65.

Kratzer, Lynn, and Sheilagh Hodgins. 1999. "A Typology of Offenders: A Test of Moffitt's Theory Among Males and Females From Childhood to Age 30." *Criminal Behaviour and Mental Health* 9: 57–73.

Kreager, Derek A., Ross L. Matsueda, and Elena A. Erosheva. 2010. "Motherhood and Criminal Desistance in Disadvantaged Neighborhoods." *Criminology* 48: 221–258.

Kurlychek, Megan C., Robert Brame, and Shawn D. Bushway. 2006. "Scarlet Letters and Recidivism: Does an Old Criminal Record Predict Future Offending?" *Criminology and Public Policy* 5: 483–504.

Kurlychek, Megan C., Robert Brame, and Shawn D. Bushway. 2007. "Enduring Risk? Old Criminal Records and Predictions of Future Criminal Involvement." *Crime and Delinquency* 53: 64–83.

Kurlychek, Megan, Shawn D. Bushway, and Robert Brame. 2012. "Long-Term Crime Desistance and Recidivism Patterns: Evidence from the Essex County Convicted Felon Study." *Criminology* 50: 71–103.

Larson, Matthew, and Gary Sweeten. 2012. "Breaking Up is Hard to Do: Romantic Dissolution, Offending, and Substance Use During the Transition to Adulthood." *Criminology* 50: 605–636.

Laub, John H. 2006. "Edwin H. Sutherland and the Michael-Adler Report: Searching for the Soul of Criminology Seventy Years Later." *Criminology* 44: 235–257.

Laub, John H., Daniel S. Nagin, and Robert J. Sampson. 1998. "Trajectories of Change in Criminal Offending: Good Marriages and the Desistance Process." *American Sociological Review* 63: 225–238.

Laub, John H., and Robert J. Sampson. 2001. "Understanding Desistance from Crime." In *Crime and Justice*, Vol. 28, edited by Michael Tonry. Chicago: University of Chicago Press.

Laub, John H., and Robert J. Sampson. 2003. *Shared Beginnings, Divergent Lives: Delinquent Boys to Age 70*. Cambridge, MA: Harvard University Press.

Le Blanc, Marc, and Rolf Loeber. 1998. "Developmental Criminology Updated." In *Crime and Justice*, Vol. 23, edited by Michael Tonry. Chicago: University of Chicago Press.

Liem, Marieke, and Nicholas J. Richardson. 2014. "The Role of Transformation Narratives in Desistance Among Released Lifers." *Criminal Justice and Behavior* 41: 692–712.

Liu, Siyu. 2015. "Is the Shape of the Age-Crime Curve Invariant by Sex? Evidence from a National Sample with Flexible Non-parametric Modeling." *Journal of Quantitative Criminology* 31: 93–123.

Maltz, Michael D. 1996. "Criminality in Space and Time: Life Course Analysis and the Micro-ecology of Crime." In *Crime and Place*, edited by John E. Eck and David Weisburd. Monsey, NY: Criminal Justice Press.

Martin, Steven S., Daniel J. O'Connell, Raymond Paternoster, and Ronet D. Bachman. 2011. "The Long and Winding Road to Desistance from Crime for Drug-Involved Offenders: The Long-Term Influence of TC Treatment on Re-arrest." *Journal of Drug Issues* 41: 179–196.

Maruna, Shadd. 1999. "Desistance and Development: The Psychosocial Process of Going Straight." In *The British Criminology Conference: Selected Proceedings*, Vol. 2. Queens University, Belfast.

Maruna, Shadd. 2001. *Making Good: How Ex-convicts Reform and Rebuild Their Lives*. Washington, DC: American Psychological Association.

Maruna, Shadd, Thomas P. Lebel, Nick Mitchell, and Michelle Naples. 2004. "Pygmalion in the Reintegration Process: Desistance from Crime Through the Looking Glass." *Psychology, Crime and Law* 10: 271–281.

Massoglia, Michael, and Christopher Uggen. 2010. "Settling Down and Aging Out: Toward an Interactionist Theory of Desistance and the Transition to Adulthood." *American Journal of Sociology* 116: 543–582.

Moffitt, Terrie E. 1993. "Adolescence-Limited and Life-Course Persistent Antisocial Behavior: A Developmental Taxonomy." *Psychological Review* 100: 674–701.

Moffitt, Terrie E. 2006. "Life-Course Persistent Versus Adolescence-Limited Antisocial Behavior." In *Developmental Psychopathology*, Vol. 3: *Risk, Disorder, and Adaptation*, edited by Dante Cicchetti and Donald J. Cohen. New York: John Wiley.

Nagin, Daniel S., David P. Farrington, and Terrie E. Moffitt, 1995. "Life Course Trajectories of Different Types of Offenders." *Criminology* 33:111–139.

Nagin, Daniel S., and Kenneth C. Land. 1993. "Age, Criminal Careers, and Population Heterogeneity: Specification and Estimation of a Nonparametric, Mixed Poisson Model." *Criminology* 31: 327–362.

Nieuwbeerta, Paul, and Alex R. Piquero. 2008. "Mortality Rates and Causes of Death of Convicted Dutch Criminals 25 Years Later." *Journal of Research on Crime and Delinquency* 45: 256–286.

Paternoster, Ray, and Shawn Bushway. 2009. "Desistance and the 'Feared Self': Toward an Identity Theory of Criminal Desistance." *Journal of Criminal Law and Criminology* 99: 1103–1156.

Paternoster, Raymond, Shawn Bushway, Robert Apel, and Robert Brame. 2003. "The Effect of Teenage Employment on Delinquency and Problem Behaviors." *Social Forces* 82: 297–335.

Rhodes, William. 2011. "Predicting Criminal Recidivism: A Research Note." *Journal of Experimental Criminology* 7: 57–71.

Savolainen, Jukka. 2009. "Work, Family and Criminal Desistance Adult Social Bonds in a Nordic Welfare State." *British Journal of Criminology* 49: 285–304.

Sampson Robert J., and John H. Laub 1993. *Crime in the Making: Pathways and Turning Points Through Life*. Cambridge, MA: Harvard University Press.

Sampson, Robert J., and John H. Laub. 2003. "Life-Course Desisters? Trajectories of Crime Among Delinquent Boys Followed to Age 70." *Criminology* 41: 319–339.

Schmidt, Peter, and Ann D. Witte. 1988. *Predicting Recidivism Using Survival Models*. New York: Springer-Verlag.

Skardhamar, Torbjørn, and Torkild Hovde Lyngstad. 2009. "Family Formation, Fatherhood and Crime: An Invitation to a Broader Perspectives on Crime and Family Transitions." *Discussion Papers No. 579, Statistics Norway, Research Department*: 1–27.

Soothill, Keith, and Brian Francis. 2009. "When Do Ex-Offenders Become Like Non-Offenders?" *Howard Journal of Criminal Justice* 48: 373–387.

Sweeten, Gary, Alex R. Piquero, and Laurence Steinberg. 2013. "Age and the Explanation of Crime, Revisited." *Journal of Youth and Adolescence* 42: 921–938.

Tahamont, Sarah, Shi Yan, Shawn D. Bushway, and Jing Liu. 2015. "Pathways to Prison in New York State." *Criminology and Public Policy* 14(3): 1–23.

Thornberry, Terence P. 1987. "Toward an Interactional Theory of Delinquency." *Criminology* 25: 863–891.

van Schellen, Marieke, Robert Apel, and Paul Nieuwbeerta. 2012. "'Because You're Mine, I Walk the Line'? Marriage, Spousal Criminality, and Criminal Offending over the Life Course." *Journal of Quantitative Criminology* 28: 701–723.

Walker, Kate, Erica Bowen, Sarah Brown, and Emma Sleath. 2014. "Desistance from Intimate Partner Violence: A Conceptual Model and Framework for Practitioners for Managing the Process of Change." *Journal of Interpersonal Violence* 30: 2726–2750.

Yule, Carolyn, Paul-Philippe Paré, and Rosemary Gartner. 2015. "An Examination of the Local Life Circumstances of Female Offenders: Mothering, Illegal Earnings and Drug Use." *British Journal of Criminology* 55: 248–269.

CHAPTER 7

....

TRAJECTORIES OF CRIMINAL BEHAVIOR ACROSS THE LIFE COURSE

....

JULIEN MORIZOT

OVER 50 years ago, Robins (1966) showed that not all adolescents displaying delinquent and antisocial behavior would become adult criminals. In her classic longitudinal study, she observed that only a small group of individuals become criminals and develop an antisocial personality disorder. Others develop other forms of antisocial behavior without getting involved in criminal activity, and most actually became law-abiding, well-adjusted individuals. It was one of the first studies pointing to heterogeneity in criminal and antisocial behavior across the life course. Research surrounding the criminal career paradigm also points to meaningful heterogeneity in offending across the life course (Piquero, Farrington, and Blumstein 2003; DeLisi and Piquero 2011). At the aggregate level, longitudinal studies consistently showed that criminal behavior typically starts by early adolescence (between age 9 and 14 years), reaches a peak in prevalence by the end of adolescence (between age 16 and 19 years), and then rapidly decreases during emerging adulthood (between age 17 and 29 years). Since Wolfgang, Figlio, and Sellin's (1972) landmark study which proposed four distinct criminal careers or trajectories, there has been a great deal of debate about whether the aggregate age-crime trends reflect the trajectories of active offenders (Gottfredson and Hirschi 1986; Blumstein, Cohen, and Farrington 1988a, 1988b). A number of criminologists argued that offenders mainly differ in degree, not in kind (Gottfredson and Hirschi 1986; Rowe, Osgood, and Nicewander 1990). In contrast, it has been argued that the relationship between age and crime reveals changes in prevalence (participation) rather than in incidence (frequency) of offending. In other words, the number of active offenders peaks in late adolescence and declines rapidly thereafter, but individuals who remain active in offending tend to do so at a relatively stable rate across various periods of the life course (Blumstein, Farrington, and Moitra 1985; Farrington 1986; Piquero et al. 2003).

Thus, age–crime curve research also points to meaningful heterogeneity in criminal activity across the life course. As a result of these observations, a number of scholars have proposed developmental-typological theories laying out the argument that the aggregate age–crime curve is composed of distinct groups of individuals following distinct developmental trajectories.

This chapter is organized into four sections. Section I provides an overview of developmental-typological theories of criminal behavior best known by criminologists. These theories aim to explain heterogeneity in intra-individual change in criminal behavior across the life course by postulating developmental trajectories differing in terms of onset, variety and frequency of offending, criminal career duration, and period of desistance. The most popular statistical methods for modeling developmental trajectories are outlined in Section II, while Section III summarizes the empirical findings from available developmental trajectory research. Overall, available longitudinal studies tend to support only some postulates of developmental-typological theories. A number of directions for future research are proposed in Section IV, while Section V recaps some major conclusions of this chapter.

I. DEVELOPMENTAL-TYPOLOGICAL THEORIES OF CRIMINAL BEHAVIOR

The quantitative and qualitative changes in criminal behavior across the life course create an individual trajectory (Le Banc and Loeber 1998). A developmental trajectory refers to the course of criminal activity over time for a particular individual (or a group of individuals with similar course). These individual trajectories can vary in timing (onset, duration, offset), degree (frequency, seriousness), and nature (variety, behavioral sequence, etc.). If there are conceptually as many distinct developmental trajectories as there are individuals, many tend to be similar, and thus, individuals can potentially be clustered into a limited number of groups (Nagin and Land 1993; Nagin 2005). This is the basic idea of a typology (Block 1971).

A typology, or taxonomy, represents a classification system designed to help categorize individuals into qualitatively and quantitatively distinct profiles (Bailey 1994; Magnusson 1998; for an epistemological discussion, see Meehl 1992). A developmental typology of criminal behavior is thus a classification of individuals into homogeneous groups—or developmental types—so that those within a group tend to follow a similar trajectory. A typology can assist in the three major objectives of science: description, explanation, and prediction of natural phenomena (Skinner 1981; Bailey 1994). For decades, criminologists have been interested in and debated about whether individual offenders are best classified into categories reflecting different kinds of people or whether individual differences in offending reflect difference in degree (Brennan 1987; Gottfredson 1987; Gottfredson and Hirschi 1990), and these debates are still active (Gottfredson 2005; Sampson and Laub 2005; Skardhamar 2009; Greenberg 2016).

To account for the evidence of heterogeneity in the course of criminal behavior across the life course, a number of researchers proposed developmental-typological theories. The two major postulates of these theories are that each group or type has a distinctive developmental trajectory of criminal activity and etiological processes and factors.

Arguably, the best known developmental-typological theory is that of Moffitt (1993, 1994, 2006), who argued for the existence of two broad developmental types of offenders, in addition to a group of abstainers. First, life-course–persistent (LCP) offenders are characterized by early onset of conduct problems and delinquent behavior, generally during childhood but potentially even during infancy, which tends to persist through adolescence and adulthood. Their criminal activity is generally characterized by high level of variety, frequency, and seriousness. Even though some of these individuals will desist from more serious criminal activity during adulthood, they can engage in other antisocial behaviors such alcohol and substance use, marital and work problems, which can persist well into late adulthood. Etiologically, this type of offender is characterized by early constitutional risk factors (potentially explained in part by genetic factors) that set off a chain of several risk factors that unfolds across their childhood. Their neurodevelopmental deficits (e.g., impulsivity, inattention, irritability, and anger) often lead to a hard-to-manage temperament, which in turn interacts with exposure to lower parental warmth, harsh and erratic parenting styles, and so on. These risks then increase the probability that during late childhood and adolescence they will experience significant difficulties adjusting in other key life domains such as school engagement and achievement, employment, and so on. During childhood and adolescence, through a selection effect, LCP offenders affiliate with other delinquents who reinforce their antisocial tendencies. Moffitt (1994, 2006) suggested this group is mainly composed of males and that racial/ethnic minorities are at higher risk to become persistent offenders because they tend to live in the most disadvantaged environment (low socioeconomic status, family dysfunctions, etc.). LCP offenders represent about 5 percent of the general population.

In contrast, adolescence-limited (AL) offenders are characterized by a late onset of conduct problems and delinquent behavior during adolescence that tends to rapidly decrease by the end of adolescence. Their delinquent activity represents an ephemeral phenomenon, limited to adolescence. In comparison to LCP offenders, their criminal activity is generally characterized by significantly lower levels of variety, frequency, and seriousness. Etiologically, this offender type is mainly explained by a "maturity gap" and social mimicry of antisocial models. In other words, these youths are biologically and socially mature but cannot legally be independent individuals and freely engaged in adult-like activities. In order to circumvent this perceived maturity gap, they turn to their adolescent peer network. In particular, they tend to affiliate with and mimic deviant peers who appear more autonomous and who are involved in many adult-like activities that provide excitement, money, and social status. These deviant peers are typically LCP offenders. As AL offenders enter adulthood, however, they are rapidly granted the adult roles and status they were coveting and thus desist from antisocial activity. In contrast to LCP offenders, Moffitt (1994, 2006) suggested this group is equally open to males or females as well as to all racial/ethnic minorities. If one considers all youth who committed at least one antisocial or delinquent act during adolescence, this group could potentially constitute up to 85 percent in the general population.

Moffitt's (1993) description of abstainers (ABS) is less developed, but since her theory argues that antisocial activity during adolescence is the norm rather than the exception, this group represents a small number of individuals— as low as approximately 10 percent of the general population. The main etiological hypotheses for this group is that, during adolescence, these individuals either have no maturity gap because of early access to adult roles or, in some cases, they manifest an overcontrolled, timid, socially inept personality style during childhood and adolescence, which impedes affiliation with deviant peers.

Since the original statement of the theory, Moffitt (2006) has suggested that an additional small subgroup of persistent offenders was uncovered in a number of longitudinal studies. These individuals show early onset of conduct problems and delinquent behavior during childhood. Their criminal and antisocial activity also tends to persist during adolescence and adulthood, but at a significantly lower level than was expected by the original statement of the theory. It is unclear, however, if these low-level persistent offenders should be considered a distinctive developmental type with its own etiology (Moffitt, 2006). Low-level persistent offenders may simply be involved in other forms of antisocial behavior during their adulthood.

Patterson and Yoerger (1993, 1997, 2002) proposed two broad developmental types of offenders quite similar to those of Moffitt. They distinguished the two groups in terms of the onset of criminal activity at different ages. A small number of individuals, early starters, are arrested before age 14, while a larger number, late starters, are arrested after that age. According to Patterson, in addition to the timing of onset, the forms of delinquent and antisocial behavior manifested differ markedly between the two groups. During adolescence, early starters tend to show both covert and overt antisocial behaviors while late starters tend to show more covert behavior. Etiologically, while Moffitt suggested that constitutional/individual risk factors are involved for LCP offenders, Patterson's theory suggests that social learning is the most important explanatory factor for both types. For early starters, the training for antisocial behavior begins during the preschool years and cumulates throughout childhood. It is provided by parents using inadequate parenting practices. Later during adolescence, they select deviant peers because these relations maximize the payoffs for antisocial behavior. For late starters, the training for antisocial behavior is provided primarily by deviant peers and secondarily by family members. Based on the long-term, cumulative learning of antisocial behavior, the delinquent activity of early starters will tend to become more chronic and persist into adulthood. In contrast, late starters will desist more rapidly from delinquent and antisocial behavior as they would find the payoffs for prosocial activities higher than the payoffs for continued offending.

Other scholars proposed developmental-typological theories with more than two types. Le Blanc (Fréchette and Le Blanc 1987; Le Blanc and Fréchette 1989; Le Blanc 2005, 2015) proposed a typology of criminal activity with three types of offenders, in addition to a group of abstainers, which counts for approximately 10 percent of the general population. Le Blanc proposed a persistent offending trajectory that is very similar to Moffitt's LCP. Le Blanc argued that these individuals represent around 5 percent of the general population and 45 percent of the adolescents adjudicated by the juvenile court and placed in residential institutions or on probation. Their offending starts during childhood; the growth in their offending is rapid and important during the first half of adolescence; their offending peaks at the end of adolescence, but they maintain a high level of offending until the middle of their twenties; their offending declines and ends, on average, around their mid-thirties or early forties. This trajectory is characterized by high variety, frequency, and seriousness in offending. Le Blanc also argued that persistent offenders tend to follow a similar trajectory in many other forms of antisocial behavior (e.g., drug and alcohol abuse, spousal abuse). Thus, even though some of these individuals will gradually manifest significantly less criminal activity during adulthood, they will still be involved in other antisocial behaviors.

Le Blanc argued that Moffitt's AL group is too general and seems to include two distinct developmental trajectories (Fréchette and Le Blanc 1987; Le Blanc and Fréchette 1989). Individuals from the transitory offending trajectory represent approximately 40 percent of the general population. They start offending during adolescence; the growth in offending is rapid and significant during the middle of adolescence; their offending peaks around age 16; its decline is also rapid at the end of adolescence; they sometimes display an episode of relatively minor offending in their early twenties. This trajectory is characterized by variety, frequency, and some serious crimes against property. In addition, the transitory offenders tend to follow a similar trajectory for other forms of antisocial behavior, particularly during adolescence.

Finally, Le Blanc proposed the common offending trajectory, which represents around 45 percent of the general population. The antisocial and criminal activity of these individuals is occasional in an otherwise law-abiding development. Their offending occurs mainly around the middle of adolescence. It is manifested by minor acts such as vandalism, shoplifting, minor theft, or public mischief. Their average annual frequency for each of these types of crime is typically on average less than one. This trajectory of offending is an epiphenomenon of adolescence and in many respects, they could be referred to as "experimenters."

With regard to the etiology of the different developmental trajectories, even though Le Blanc's (2005, 2015) theory is not as explicit as that of Moffitt, he suggested that persistent offending is primarily caused by early and stable antisocial propensity (i.e., temperament traits or low self-control) rather than opportunities. Transitory offending, on the other end, is the result of weak propensity and opportunities, while common offending is mainly the result of opportunities.

In line with previous developmental typologies of criminal behavior, very similar types have been suggested for other antisocial behavior such alcohol and drug use. For instance, Zucker (1987, 2006) proposed a developmental typology of four courses of alcoholism, which also include a role for antisocial behavior. First, Zucker proposed an antisocial alcoholism type, which is very similar to Moffitt's LCP and Le Blanc's persistent offenders. This group is characterized by early onset of alcohol use, which tends to remain stable throughout adulthood. It is termed antisocial because the alcohol use is accompanied by early onset of delinquent behavior that progresses from minor offenses during childhood or early adolescence to potentially serious criminality during adulthood. There is also developmentally cumulative alcoholism, which is similar to Moffitt's AL and Le Blanc's transitory offending. Alcohol use of these individuals is characterized by either isolated or episodic episodes of abuse, which eventually have a cumulative effect, favoring the continuity of use into adulthood. This group is not characterized by comorbid antisocial behavior during adolescence. Zucker also proposed developmentally limited alcoholism, which is also similar to Moffitt's AL and perhaps more closely similar to Le Blanc's common offending. This group is also characterized by antisocial behavior, but only during adolescence. Finally, Zucker proposed a type called negative affect alcoholism. This group is characterized by severe and sustained alcohol use and alcohol-related problems (sometimes antisocial behavior), which emerges only during adulthood. This group is characterized by internalizing problems (anxiety, depression, etc.) during childhood and adolescence that tend to become more serious in early adulthood. Interestingly, Zucker argued that, contrary to the other three types, which are more common in males, this last type is more common in females.

A number of scholars argued that conceptually and empirically, it is possible to postulate the existence of a group of adulthood-limited offenders (e.g., Eggleston and Laub 2002; Gomez-Smith and Piquero 2005; Zara and Farrington 2010, 2013). This group is characterized by late onset of antisocial and criminal activity only during adulthood. It is much less studied, but it has been argued that individuals who start offending during adulthood and have never committed any offense during adolescence are rare. It is estimated that this group represents approximately 5 percent of the general population. The etiological factors related to this group of offenders are not well known, but it has been hypothesized that the increase in social freedom and status characteristic of emerging adulthood provide opportunities for engaging in risky and antisocial behavior (Arnett 2000). It has also been hypothesized that unemployment as well as the emergence of internalizing mental health problems or change in the personality profile characterized by increasing negative emotionality and alienation may be related to the surfacing of their criminal activity (Zara and Farrington 2010, 2013). As such, this group may share some similarities with Zucker's negative affect alcoholism.

Others theories conceptualize the heterogeneity in the development of criminal behavior in different ways. For example, distinctive developmental pathways in different forms of antisocial and delinquent behaviors have been proposed. A developmental pathway is the "orderly behavioral development between more than two problem behaviors with individuals differing in their propensity to progress along the successive problem behavior represented by the pathway" (Loeber and Burke 2011, p. 34). Loeber and colleagues (Loeber et al. 1993; Loeber and Hay 1994) proposed the existence of three pathways: authority conflict and overt and covert pathways. Yet other researchers use the term developmental pathway in a different way, but still relevant for conceptualizing heterogeneity in criminal behavior development. For instance, Frick (2012) refers to distinctive developmental pathways to conduct disorder or delinquent behavior as different manifestation and etiological factors. He proposed three pathways, namely the early- versus late-onset conduct disorder, conduct disorder with and without callous-unemotional (or psychopathic) traits, and conduct disorder with and without severe anger dysregulation.

In summary, even though this brief overview does not do justice to the complexity of the above-mentioned developmental-typological theories, overall they suggest the possibility that in a large representative sample of the general population with a longitudinal follow-up from late childhood or early adolescence to at least middle adulthood, up to six developmental trajectories of criminal behavior could be expected: abstainers (~10 percent), adolescence-limited/low-level offenders (~40 percent), adolescence-limited/high-level offenders (~35 percent), early-onset/low-level persistent offenders (~5 percent), early-onset/high-level persistent offenders (~5 percent), and adulthood-limited offenders (~5 percent). Note that these prevalence estimates are not meant to represent reality but rather to provide a rough idea of the plausible size of the different groups.

II. GROUP-BASED TRAJECTORY MODELING

Searching for distinct developmental trajectories consists in person-centered analyses (Magnusson, 1998). In contrast to the more common variable-centered approach that aims to explain relations between time and offending assuming a single population, the person-centered approach involves the identification of homogeneous subgroups of individuals with different developmental trajectories of criminal behavior. As such, person-centered analyses are also frequently referred to as classification methods (Sterba and Bauer, 2010).

Many classification methods have been used by criminologists to empirically identify developmental trajectories (Le Blanc 2002). The simplest method is to use "hard coding" of individuals as either offenders or non-offenders at each time point and then identify different groups who are abstainers, chronic offenders, temporary offenders, and so on. Another method is to define groups based on the age of offending onset (e.g., before age 14, between age 14 and 20, age 21 and older). Yet another method would be to classify individuals based on how many criminal offenses they committed across multiple years of their life course. The classic example of this is the offender classification of Wolfgang et al. (1972), which proposed four criminal careers (or trajectories) in a birth cohort of males: non-delinquent, one-time, non-chronic (one to four offenses), and chronic delinquents (five or more offenses). These researchers observed that almost two-thirds of the population never had any criminal record. They also found that 6 percent of the population can be characterized as chronic offenders. This group of individuals is small, but they commit two-fifths of the crimes known to police and two-thirds of the violent crimes according to Wolfgang et al. (1972). Hard coding of offending data can thus certainly prove useful. However, most of the typically used hard coding cut-off criteria are somewhat arbitrary (e.g., selecting particular age of onset), and other non-trivial limitations are associated with these methods (Piquero, Reingle-Gonzalez, and Jennings 2015).

In the last two decades, developmental criminologists have increasingly been using newly developed statistical methods to identify groups of offenders. These new methods avoid some of the biases of hard coding and are more (but not completely) objective for finding subgroups of individuals in the data. There have been rapid advances in the statistical methods for modeling longitudinal data (e.g., Harring and Hancock 2012) and longitudinal mixture modeling in particular (e.g., Nagin 1999, 2005; Nagin and Tremblay 2001; Muthén 2008; Feldman, Masyn, and Conger 2009; Muthén and Asparouhov 2009). It is beyond the scope of this chapter to discuss all of these methods. The focus will be on two variants in a set of analyses that has come to be known in criminology as group-based trajectory modeling (GBTM; Nagin 2005; Brame, Paternoster, and Piquero 2012).

GBTM is part of the family of models know in statistics as mixture modeling (McLachlan and Peel 2000). Conventional longitudinal models such as latent growth curve (LGC; Bollen and Curran 2006) or hierarchical linear modeling (HLM; Raudenbush and Bryk 2002) account for the associations among repeated measures of offending using a single population-level trajectory, which can vary only quantitatively across individuals. In contrast, GBTM uses different latent classes (trajectories) to account for the same association between offending over time (Nagin 2005; Muthén 2008). Even though there are multiple such models, only the two most commonly used in developmental criminology are presented. The first is latent class growth analysis (LCGA; Nagin and Land 1993; Nagin 2005; Muthén 2008). It is also known as semiparametric group-based modeling (Nagin 1999). LCGA accounts for the associations among repeated measures of offending using multiple latent classes that differ qualitatively between classes (between-class mean differences) but do not differ quantitatively within class (no within class variability). In other words, this model assumes that all individuals within a trajectory group follow the exact same developmental trajectory. Thus, LCGA is used to model qualitative differences in continuous changes in offending (Bauer and Curran 2003; Sterba and Bauer 2010).

The second model is growth mixture modeling (GMM; Muthén 2004, 2008). Essentially, GMM is a more general statistical model that accounts for the associations among repeated measures of offending also using multiple latent classes that differ qualitatively between classes but also differ quantitatively within class. In other words, a GMM model can be thought of as an LCGA model for which within class variation of the growth factors (intercept and slope) is allowed (Muthén 2004, 2008). GMM can be thought of as a combination of traditional LGC and latent class analysis. Thus, GMM is used to model both qualitative and quantitative differences in continuous changes in offending (Bauer and Curran 2003; Sterba and Bauer 2010).

LCGA has arguably been the most widely used form of GBTM in criminology (Piquero 2008; Nagin and Odgers 2010; Brame et al. 2012). It should be noted, however, that LCGA and GMM are essentially the same analysis, but with models of different parameterizations. It has been shown that in some circumstances, LCGA yield more classes than are needed, some of which differ only quantitatively (i.e., in level) and are combined into the same class when GMM is applied (e.g., Muthén and Muthén 2000; Kreuter and Muthén 2008). Whether within-class variability is necessary to model developmental trajectories of criminal behavior is simply an empirical question that should be more routinely tested by researchers (Petras and Masyn 2010).

As the latent classes are unknown a priori but estimated from the data, GBTM estimates a probability of membership in each trajectory group for all individuals. These posterior probabilities add up to one for each individual across all trajectory groups. In the final step of the analysis, individuals can be assigned to the latent class for which they have the highest probability of belonging. A discrete categorical variable representing trajectory group membership can then be saved and used in other analyses.

Determining the optimal solution (e.g., number of classes, shape of the trajectories) is an iterative process in which the researcher estimates multiple models with increasing number of trajectory groups. Statistical indices and tests have been developed to help determine the number of trajectory groups in the data, but this process can be challenging (Tofighi and Enders 2008). In most published work to date, the number of groups was determined using only the Bayesian Information Criterion (BIC), but due to its limitations, like any statistical tests or indices, it is recommended to use a combination of different information criteria and statistical tests (Marsh, Hau, and Grayson 2005; West, Taylor, and Wu 2012). Often information criteria will not lead to any clear decision for researchers (Nagin 2005). For instance, because information criteria are dependent on sample size, in sufficiently large samples, as the number of extracted trajectory groups increases, their value continues to decrease (see Marsh et al. 2005; West et al. 2012). Petras and Masyn (2010) thus suggested graphically presenting information criteria through "elbow plots" in order to visualize the gains associated with the addition of trajectory groups. Moreover, simulation studies suggested that likelihood ratio tests based on resampling methods will sometimes outperform information criteria and should thus be used routinely (e.g., Bootstrap Likelihood Ratio Test [BLRT]; McLachlan and Peel 2000). The entropy may also be calculated for each model in order to indicate the precision with which the cases are classified into the trajectory groups. Even though entropy should not be used to determine the number of classes, it provides a useful summary of the classification accuracy of different solutions. A final but essential criterion used to guide the selection of the optimal model is related to the substantive meaning and theoretical conformity of the extracted latent classes (Bauer and Curran 2003; Muthén 2003; Nagin 2005; Bauer 2007). The best GBTM solution should never be blindly chosen based only on statistical tests or criteria. For instance, it has been argued that GBTM analyses should result in qualitatively distinct trajectories, otherwise they would be of little heuristic value. Indeed, trajectories differing only in level of criminal behavior over time (i.e., quantitative differences) would arguably be better represented by analyses postulating a single population with variance (random effect) around growth parameters (Bauer 2007; Skardhamar 2009, 2010; Greenberg 2016). Moreover, for each estimated model, the researcher needs to look at the shape of the different trajectory groups and judge whether each group appears conceptually or theoretically meaningful.

Depending on the software program used, these models allow the inclusion of predictors of class membership (Muthén 2004, 2008; Nagin 2005; Petras and Masyn 2010). Even though the strategy of saving group membership as a discrete categorical variable is often used by researchers, it should be noted that this method does not take into account classification errors. Though posterior probabilities can be controlled for in post hoc analyses, there are methods to include predictors and outcomes directly in the model (Asparouhov and Muthén 2014). The analysis of predictors and consequences of trajectory groups can also inform the selection of the optimal solution (Muthén 2003, 2004; Nagin 2005). After all, developmental trajectories of criminal behavior that cannot be predicted by any risk factors or that are not associated to any consequential outcomes will appear to be of limited heuristic value.

It is important to note some additional challenges in GBTM, which are often overlooked. First, GBTM is essentially exploratory in nature and will always extract latent classes in almost any data set. Thus precautions should be taken to avoid working with a substantively meaningless or statistically improper model. For instance, it is well known that a mixture model can be a way to essentially approximate a non-normal distribution, which is not composed of substantively meaningful groups or subpopulations (Bauer and Curran 2003; Nagin 2005; Bauer 2007; Skardhamar 2010). Second, GBTM is prone to the problem of converging on a local solution (i.e., false maximum likelihood), that is, a model with no convergence issues but that is not the best in the data. This problem may stem from inadequate start values. It is thus recommended to use multiple random sets of start values (McLachlan and Peel 2000; Hipp and Bauer 2006). Third, whenever relevant, it is important to derive trajectories by adjusting for confounding factors such as incarceration time and mortality (D'Unger et al. 1998; Piquero et al. 2001; Eggleston, Laub, and Sampson 2004).

In closing this section, it is important to keep in mind that the latent classes identified with GBTM are not meant to represent "true types" in nature (Meehl 1992) but can be thought of as useful heuristics (Nagin and Tremblay, 2005). In fact, this is true of any statistical model, GBTM or other (MacCallum 2003). These models actually take into account uncertainty (posterior probabilities), so the trajectory groups can fairly be considered as statistical heuristics, in line with the concept of ideal types. Take the simple example of individuals who show a rapid increase in offending from adolescence to early adulthood, while others show an important decrease during the same period. It is fair to argue that considering these quite opposite courses of offending using a model assuming a single population can also be problematic, if only for the interpretation of the resulting average trajectory (Osgood

2005). GBTM can help uncover such latent subgroups without assuming true discrete types. Regardless of its limitations, GBTM appears to be useful for testing some aspects of developmental-typological theories (Nagin 2005; Nagin and Tremblay 2005; Sterba and Bauer 2010).

III. Empirical Findings from Developmental Trajectory Research

The popularity of developmental-typological theories, particularly Moffitt's taxonomy, paired with the progress of different prospective longitudinal studies as well as the availability of new statistical methods has led to the rapid growth of empirical studies searching for developmental trajectories of criminal behavior. Despite the usefulness of different hard coding cut-off criteria of longitudinal data to identify groups of offenders, this chapter is limited to studies using GBTM analyses (for a review on the prevalence, age of onset, and criminal career duration of different offending trajectory groups identified with various criteria [i.e., hard coding and statistical analyses combined], see Jolliffe et al. 2017a). Rather than some a priori cut-off criteria, these studies consider trajectory group membership as unobserved heterogeneity that can be inferred from the data, while explicitly taking into account classification uncertainty (i.e., posterior probabilities). It is also beyond the scope of this chapter to review the correlates and consequences of different offending trajectory groups (for a review, see Jolliffe et al. 2017b).

There is a plethora of published studies on this topic from various scientific disciplines using different measures of criminal and antisocial behavior. For example, there are trajectories of arrests (Wiesner, Capaldi, and Kim 2007), convictions (Blokland, Nagin, and Nieuwbeerta 2005; Piquero, Farrington, and Blumstein 2007), self-reported offending (Fergusson, Horwood, and Nagin 2000; Weisner and Capaldi 2003), offense seriousness (Chung et al. 2002), and violence (Loeber, Lacourse, and Homish 2006). There are also studies searching for trajectories in other forms of antisocial behavior such as physical aggression (Nagin and Tremblay 1999), reactive and proactive aggression (Barker et al. 2010), conduct problems (Odgers et al. 2007), externalizing behaviors (Bongers et al. 2004), sexual offending (Lussier et al. 2012), drug use (Flory et al. 2004; Guo et al. 2002), and deviant peer group affiliation (Lacourse et al. 2003).

Four narrative reviews of these studies have been published (Piquero 2008; Van Dulmen et al. 2009; Jennings and Reingle 2012; Piquero et al. 2015). In his extensive review, Piquero (2008) identified 90 published articles that searched for developmental trajectories in various outcomes related to criminal behavior and across different developmental periods. More recently, Jennings and Reingle (2012) reviewed 105 studies searching for trajectories of aggression, violence, and delinquency. This section draws heavily on these reviews, and interested readers should consult the original publications.

It is difficult to summarize the findings of existing studies because they differ markedly in (1) the nature of the outcome (parental ratings of aggression, self-reported delinquent behavior, official records of arrests or convictions, etc.), (2) the composition of the sample (representative sample versus justice system samples such as adjudicated youths, arrestees, parolees), (3) the developmental periods targeted (childhood only, adolescence only, from adolescence to adulthood, etc.), (4) the length of the longitudinal follow-up (from 2 or 3 years up to more than 50 years), and (e) the geographical and cultural context. Still, a number of consistencies across studies suggest that summary observations can be made based on the number and the shape of extracted trajectory groups (Piquero 2008; Jennings and Reingle 2012; Piquero et al. 2015).

Studies have generally identified between two and seven trajectories. However, the large majority of studies identified four trajectory groups, followed by those identifying three and then five groups (Jennings and Reingle 2012). Among studies identifying four trajectory groups, the most common outcomes are aggression (particularly for childhood studies), self-reported delinquent behavior, and official records of convictions or arrests. Among studies finding three groups, the most common outcome is aggression (again, particularly for childhood studies). In contrast, for studies identifying five trajectory groups, the most common outcomes are self-reported delinquency, official convictions, and aggression. Studies based on self-report tend to identify more trajectory groups than those based on official records, arguably because self-reports provide more variance in outcome scores. Moreover, studies using conceptually broader outcome measures (e.g., externalizing or antisocial behavior scales compared to offending variety measures that considered a limited number of offenses) tend to extract more groups, again because broader measures will tend to provide more variance in outcome scores. Furthermore, studies with longer follow-up length tend to identify more trajectory groups.

With regard to the shape of the trajectories, several of the studies that found four groups report a similar model: stable-low, stable-high, increasing, and decreasing trajectories (e.g., White, Bates, and Buyske 2001; Odgers et al. 2008; Campbell et al. 2010; Maldonado-Molina, Jennings, and Komro 2010; Miller et al. 2010; Lynne-Landsman et al. 2011; Mata and van Dulmen 2012; Krohn et al. 2014). This so-called "cat's cradle" model has also been consistently found for substance use outcomes (Sher, Jackson, and Steinly 2011). A number of studies identifying four groups report a slightly different, alternative model: stable-low, stable-high, and two kinds of decreasing trajectories (e.g., Nagin and Tremblay 1999; Shaw, Lacourse, and Nagin 2005; Di Giunta et al. 2010; van de Rakt, Murray, and Nieuwbeerta 2012).

Trajectory groups similar to the two developmental types of offenders proposed by Moffitt (1993) as well as the abstainers appear to be consistently identified in studies with longitudinal follow-up spanning adolescence and early adulthood or later (e.g., Nagin, Farrington, and Moffitt 1995; Chung et al. 2002; Fergusson and Horwood 2002; Bushway, Thornberry, and Krohn 2003; Sampson and Laub 2003; Blokland and Nieuwbeerta 2005; van der Geest, Blokland, and Bijleveld 2009; Andersson et al. 2012; Farrington, Piquero, and Jennings 2013; Besemer, Axelsson, and Sarnecki 2016; for more studies, see Piquero 2008; Jennings and Reingle 2012). First, even though the labels used to describe this group vary as a function of the length of follow-up, available studies tend to observe a group similar to the AL offenders (sometimes called "desistors") showing high levels of delinquent behavior during adolescence that decreased toward the end of adolescence or early adulthood. Second, available studies also consistently revealed a group similar to the LCP offenders (sometimes called "chronic," "persistent," or "high-level") showing high levels of delinquent behavior during adolescence, which remained high or decreased only slightly during adulthood. Third, nearly all studies (with the exception of adjudicated samples) identified a large group of abstainers (sometimes called "non-offenders"), who show essentially no delinquent activity during adolescence or early adulthood. In many studies, individuals from this group have an extremely low probability of offending that they can be considered abstainers. Fourth, different long-term longitudinal studies identified more than one group of persistent offending, namely high-level and low-level persistent offenders (e.g., Nagin et al. 1995; D'Unger et al. 1998; Piquero et al. 2001; Sampson and Laub 2003; Eggleston et al. 2004; van der Geest et al. 2009; Piquero et al. 2010; Besemer et al. 2016). Fifth, several studies also support the notion that there are different trajectories of offending limited to adolescence (e.g., Chung et al. 2002; Fergusson and Horwood 2002; Bushway et al. 2003; Wiesner and Capaldi 2003; Hoeve et al. 2008; van der Geest et al. 2009; Boers et al. 2010; Monahan et al. 2010; Pepler et al. 2010; Connell, Klostermann, and Dishion 2011; Jennings 2011; Andersson et al. 2012). Sixth, a few longitudinal studies spanning adolescence and at least a part of adulthood revealed a late-onset group (sometimes called "increasers" or "late-onsetters") (e.g., Chung et al. 2002; Bushway et al. 2003; Sampson and Laub 2003; van der Geest et al. 2009; Boers et al. 2010; Mata and van Dulmen 2012; Besemer et al. 2016). The onset typically observed in this group is during late adolescence rather than during adulthood.

Overall, as discussed in a previous section, developmental-typological theories point to the possibility of up to six developmental trajectories of criminal behavior from adolescence to adulthood in the general population. Most available studies did not cover such a long developmental period. The available studies tend to support the hypothesis that trajectory groups similar to the AL, LCP, and abstainers proposed by Moffitt (1993) can be observed in various longitudinal studies (Piquero 2008; Van Dulmen et al. 2009; Jennings and Reingle 2012; Piquero et al. 2015). However, a majority of studies identified more than these three trajectory groups. There is good evidence suggesting that there is more than one persistent or chronic offending trajectory. There is even stronger evidence suggesting different trajectories limited to adolescence. These findings clearly challenge the theories postulating the existence of only two developmental types of offenders (Moffitt 1993, 1994; Patterson and Yoerger 1993, 1997). Moreover, many studies did not have a follow-up long enough to adequately test the validity of Moffitt's theory. For instance, studies limited to adolescence cannot be used to test the validity of the LCP. These studies are also unable to rigorously test the validity of the AL because they cannot track desistance during emerging adulthood (i.e., a group that shows a decrease in offending during late adolescence cannot automatically be inferred as an AL, as it could very well be a low-level persistent). Taking trajectory groups similar to Moffitt's LCP offenders as an example, Skardhamar (2009) also pointed out that there are substantial discrepancies in criminal career parameters across studies purported to support the developmental type (e.g., period of activation and peak of offending at very different ages, different offending variety, different rates of desistance). Finally, as argued by Sampson and Laub (2003), while groups of persistent or chronic offenders are identified in different longitudinal studies, long-term studies suggest that eventually all individuals desist from crime. This is another challenge to any theory postulating the existence of life-course persistent offenders.

IV. DIRECTIONS FOR FUTURE RESEARCH

Typological or GBTM research can be helpful for testing various aspects of developmental-typological theories, and it has been popular in recent years. This research, however, is characterized by a number of conceptual/theoretical and methodological issues that should be addressed in future research.

First, more prospective longitudinal studies are needed. With developmental-typological theories and GBTM research in mind, studies should include a large enough sample to detect small trajectory groups. For instance, if a theory suggests that a type of persistent offender with a psychopathic personality constitutes 1 percent of the population, one would need a sample of several hundreds, if not thousands, to estimate stable mixture models detecting this latent group. If not a complete birth cohort, these studies should be truly representative of the population (i.e., nationally stratified samples) since only these samples can provide true prevalence estimates of developmental trajectory groups. Moreover, additional multi-site studies should be started for confirmatory research purposes (e.g., D'Unger et al. 1998; Broidy et al. 2003). These studies should rest on multiple sources of information (parental ratings, peer reports, self-reports, official records of arrests and convictions, etc.) in order to model developmental trajectories that are not based on characteristics of a specific method or on some measurement artifacts. In addition, if developmental criminologists are interested in the long-term trajectories of antisocial behavior and crime, they should begin their longitudinal studies during infancy or the preschool years in order to identify developmental trajectories of behaviors that are conceptually similar to offending (i.e., heterotypic continuity), such as physical aggression, lying, or theft, all of which can be observed very early in life (Tremblay et al. 1999; Tremblay 2010).

Second, developmental criminologists should investigate the trajectories of all categories of antisocial behavior (e.g., vandalism, theft, fraud, violence, sexual offenses, substance use) and systematically compare them (Le Blanc 2015). Several studies using adolescents' and adults' samples confirmed that criminal behaviors co-occur with various analogous behaviors such as alcohol and drug abuse, spousal violence, work absenteeism, and so on (e.g., Jessor and Jessor 1977; Krueger et al. 2007). Using distinct forms of antisocial behavior is important because they may have distinct etiological factors (Tackett et al. 2005) and their co-development may be entwined across the life course (Morizot and Le Blanc 2007; Le Blanc 2015). For instance, Piquero et al. (2002) and MacDonald et al. (2009) modeled joint trajectories of violent and non-violent offending, while Trim et al. (2015) modeled joint trajectories of antisocial behavior and substance use. Chen and Jaffee (2015) also showed that in GBTM analyses, including other forms of antisocial behavior (which they called heterotypic antisocial behaviors) in addition to offending, allowed for a better understanding of the offender groups. For instance, these authors demonstrated that the group characterized by offending onset during late adolescence or early adulthood was in fact already showing other antisocial behaviors during their adolescence. Moreover, they showed that for persistent offenders, even if their offending tends to decrease during adulthood, they still display the highest levels of all groups in other forms of antisocial behavior. Additional studies like these are needed in order to better understand the co-development and complex interplay between trajectories of various antisocial behaviors. Multiple-process GBTM studies may help to better understand developmental processes such as activation, aggravation, and desistance (Le Blanc and Loeber 1998).

Third, perhaps due to the early prospective longitudinal studies focused on male samples, there are considerably more developmental trajectory studies on males (particularly the long-term studies). Further research is needed on the developmental trajectories of females (Piquero 2008; Fontaine et al. 2009; Piquero et al. 2015). This is important because of the known "gender gap" in criminal and antisocial behavior, i.e., the prevalence and seriousness of male offending is significantly more important. Cauffman, Monahan, and Thomas (2015) showed that male and female trajectories of offending may have a similar shape, but the correlates and consequences distinguishing the trajectories may be different across gender. Rather than focusing solely on quantitative measures (i.e., prevalence and number of trajectories), Lanctôt (2015) argued that it might be helpful to compare male and female trajectories using qualitative measures of adjustment. Since early prospective longitudinal studies also focused on white/Caucasians, more research on the role of racial/ethnical background in trajectory group membership is also needed. This research should go beyond documenting the proportions of individuals from different racial/ethnic backgrounds within the different trajectory groups (for a research agenda, see Piquero 2015). It should also examine whether ethnic-specific developmental trajectories are needed, possibly using multiple-group models to systematically test differences in conceptually similar trajectory groups across ethnic groups (Schaeffer et al. 2006). A recent study by Broidy et al. (2015) showed that gender and race/ethnicity may actually have an interactive effect in influencing trajectories of offending, which shed new light on the role of these important factors.

Fourth, further research is needed on the predictors (risk and protective factors) of developmental trajectory groups. Sampson and Laub (2005) showed that it is difficult to make long-term predictions or differentiate the trajectory groups using a number of known childhood risk factors. In a recent review, Jolliffe et al. (2017b) showed that, contrary to the postulates of most developmental-typological theories, there is currently little evidence that specific risk factors are associated with specific developmental types of offending. It may be that researchers need to test more complex predictive models that are proposed by theory. Loeber, Slot, and Stouthamer-Loeber (2006) argued that exposure to risk factors is generally gradual and increases over many years. This may explain the difficulty of making long-term predictions of trajectory group membership. Likewise, Patterson and Yoerger (1993, 1997, 2002) argued that there are developmental shifts in cascade effects among risk factors. Thus, another reason for the difficulty to make long-term predictions of trajectory group membership with simple predictive models may be because the risk factors that start the developmental sequence of risk are partially or fully mediated by other proximal factors (e.g., Dodge et al. 2009; Martel et al. 2009). Criminologists need to test such mediated and cascade models of risk for the different developmental trajectories.

Some additional variables could be used to predict trajectory group membership or make intergroup comparisons despite not being formally suggested by current developmental-typological theories. For example, it would be useful to document further the economic, mental, and physical health correlates or consequences of the different trajectory groups (Odgers et al. 2008; Piquero et al. 2010). Moreover, it would be helpful to link life narratives and other qualitative data to trajectory groups membership (McAdams and McLean 2013), which may prove useful to better understand why individuals persist or desist from criminal activity (Maruna 2001). Moreover, as argued by different scholars, it would be interesting to compare the trajectory groups on different variables related to human agency (Sampson and Laub 2005; Paternoster et al. 2015). Different sociocognitive constructs related to agency could be used, for instance, motivations and life goals (Deci and Ryan 2000). These may help us understand why some known turning points or life events can change or modify a developmental trajectory toward desistance for some individuals but not others.

Furthermore, given the central role of self-control in contemporary criminology (Piquero 2009; DeLisi 2011) and the number of recent longitudinal studies that suggest that self-control and personality traits appear to mirror the development and desistance of antisocial behavior (Morizot 2015), more research is needed to better understand the role of early temperament and personality traits in predicting trajectory groups. Particularly, the interactive effect of self-control and major turning points (e.g., marriage) on changing or inflecting developmental trajectories of offending should also be evaluated. Finally, given the growing recognition of the role of genetics and other biological factors (Beaver 2013; Raine 2013), it would be interesting for researchers to test whether these factors may differentiate among the trajectory groups. For example, after deriving trajectories of criminal behavior in a genetically informative study (e.g., twin study), it would be interesting to evaluate whether the different trajectory groups identified through GBTM are characterized by different heritability estimates (e.g., Barnes, Beaver, and Boutwell 2011). Recent studies suggest that well-defined trajectory groups could show different heritability estimates (Viding et al. 2005).

Fifth, there needs to be more explicit research on the possible policy implications of GBTM research. Even though some scholars warned criminologists of the dangers of reifying trajectory groups for practice (Skardhamar 2009), the accumulation of results from GBTM research could, in the long run, potentially inform criminal justice policy and practice. For instance, knowledge on specific age of onset, critical periods of offending activation (increase in variety, frequency or seriousness), or specific patterns of risk factors in developmental trajectories may eventually help in screening for indicated prevention programs (Le Blanc 1998). A number of evidenced-based prevention programs appear to be effective in preventing crime, but they generally show small to moderate effect sizes (Farrington and Welsh 2007). This suggests that these may be helpful for only some youth, perhaps those from particular developmental trajectories. In line with a differential approach to prevention and treatment, Le Blanc (2015) proposed a number of specific intervention targets at different developmental periods according to different trajectories of criminal behavior. A better understanding of the potential differential effects may help improve future prevention and treatment programs.

Sixth, as previously mentioned, GBTM research needs to be guided by theory. This of course implies that criminologists should have at their disposal formal developmental-typological theories. Arguably the best formulated such theory is that of Moffitt (1993, 1994, 2006). Many researchers using GBTM argued that they conducted a test of the validity of Moffitt's typology. The results of available GBTM studies suggest that modifications or perhaps alternative developmental-typological theories are needed. For instance, taken together, existing developmental-typological theories suggest there may be up to six conceptually coherent trajectories of criminal behavior across the life course. Whether some or even all of these trajectories are truly theoretically meaningful and valid constructs that need their own etiological theory is certainly debatable. Le Blanc (2015) suggested there are only three meta-trajectories, which can be subdivided into more specific trajectories likely representing differences in degrees, rather than kind. New theories should also not be restricted to criminal behavior, but should rather make explicit postulates about its complex interplay with other forms of antisocial behavior. For example, Zucker's (2006) theory focuses on alcohol use but includes other antisocial behaviors.

Finally, a pressing need for developmental criminologists involved in GBTM research is arguably to systematically undertake more rigorous tests of the validity of developmental-typological theories. To do so, criminologists should adopt a construct validation approach (Loevinger 1957; Skinner 1981). There have been calls to strengthen the theoretical bases of GBTM research and more systematically demonstrate its validity and usefulness (Sampson and Laub 2005; Skardhamar 2009, 2010). Adopting a construct validation approach is arguably one of the best ways to respond to these needs. This approach emphasizes a sequential interplay between new theoretical developments and empirical research. For a classification (a typology or taxonomy) of developmental trajectories of criminal behavior to be methodologically defensible, theoretically sound, and useful, researchers must consider three important and interrelated stages to evaluate its construct validity: theory formulation, internal validition, and external validition. At the first stage, theory formulation, researchers must have a precise definition of each type and an explanation of their etiology (risk factors and their interaction, promotive and protective factors, hypothesized mediated or cascading effects among risk factors, etc.), their developmental trajectory, and their consequences in different life domains (i.e., prognosis). Ideally, such a theory should describe the treatment implications of the typology. At the heart of the typological approach is the use of "ideal types," or "mental constructs that may be used to summarize observed characteristics among relatively homogeneous groups of individuals" (Skinner 1981, p. 72). The point is important because even though they are hypothetical constructs, ideal types have important functions in scientific knowledge development. They can stimulate theoretical speculation, point to aspects of a theory that is open to falsification, encourage comparisons of alternative theories, and provide a basis for empirically classifying individuals (Wood 1969).

At the second stage, internal validation, the researcher must propose an operational definition of the developmental typology and examine its internal properties (Skinner 1981). This part of the construct validation is arguably the one that has been most neglected in previous GBTM research. The point here is to ensure that the classification is robust and not merely a measurement or statistical artefact. To give just one example, it is actually challenging to determine whether trajectory groups extracted with GBTM are truly discrete constructs. Currently, psychological or achievement tests must meet stringent requirements before being used in different practical contexts (see AERA, APA, and NCME 2014). As argued by Skinner (1981), a developmental typology of criminal behavior should meet the same requirements.

Finally, the third stage of the construct validation approach is external validation. At this stage, researchers should demonstrate the descriptive and predictive validity of the typology (Skinner 1981). There are a number of studies that test whether variables can predict trajectory group membership or if the trajectory groups can be distinguished in consequential outcomes (Piquero et al. 2015; Jolliffe et al. 2017b). However, these are often (but not always) atheoretical, ex post facto analyses, rather than carefully planned at the theory formulation stage. Exploratory research is still important when a construct or theory is not clearly formulated or if there is a paucity of knowledge available. In addition to descriptive and predictive validity, researchers must demonstrate the generalizability of the typology. Taking Moffitt's (1993) theory as an example, it was noted that there is sound empirical evidence that two trajectory groups similar to the AL and LCP types are identified in different samples. However, GBTM research tends to find more groups than is predicted by the theory; many are hardly generalizable across studies (Skardhamar 2009). Finally, external validation also involves demonstrating the clinical validity of the typology. However, much research needs to be done before even thinking about the potential clinical or practical utility of a developmental typology of criminal behavior.

V. Conclusion

Over the past 20 years, theory and research on developmental trajectories of criminal behavior across the life course have been increasingly popular among criminologists. To paraphrase Block (1971), even though studying the "typical trajectory of criminal behavior" (i.e., analyses postulating a single population) is important and useful, searching for "types of criminal behavior trajectories" (i.e., GBTM analyses) can potentially be highly valuable for developmental and life-course criminology. This review suggests that developmental-typological research can be helpful for testing theory. For instance, current GBTM research tends to identify a larger number of offending trajectories than is postulated by most developmental-typological theories. It should be recognized, however, that GBTM has non-trivial limitations. Thus, researchers involved in this kind of research should use great caution when interpreting results from GBTM analyses. Perhaps more fundamentally, to date, despite the large number of published GBTM studies, there has been no convincing research demonstrating that the different trajectories proposed in developmental-typological theories are actually non-arbitrary categories truly existing in nature. In other words, it is hard to argue that they are real "types" or "taxa" (see Meehl 1992). They are, however, very useful heuristics that help interpret the complex reality of individuals' trajectories of criminal behavior. There is a need for upgraded or new developmental-typological theories that take into account recent empirical research findings.

Even though there have been an increasing number of studies searching for developmental trajectories of criminal behavior over the last 20 years or so, there is still much left to do. In recent years, this kind of research has been criticized by some criminologists. Open dialogue is welcome and beneficial, as it can potentially lead to improvement of theory and research in this discipline. Despite these calls for caution, it is hoped that this kind of research will continue to flourish as it can provide important and useful knowledge to further developmental and life-course criminology.

References

American Educational Research Association (AERA), American Psychological Association (APA), and National Council on Measurement in Education (NCME) (2014). *Standards for Educational and Psychological Testing*, 3rd ed. Washington, DC: AERA, APA, and NCME.

Andersson, Frida, Sten Levander, Robert Svensson, and Marie T. Levander. 2012. "Sex Differences in Offending Trajectories in a Swedish Cohort." *Criminal Behavior and Mental Health* 22: 108–121.

Arnett, Jeffrey J. 2000. "Emerging Adulthood: A Theory of Development from the Late Teens Through the Twenties." *American Psychologist* 55: 469–480.

Asparouhov, Tihomir, and Bengt O. Muthén. 2014. "Auxiliary Variables in Mixture Modeling: Three-Step Approaches Using Mplus." *Structural Equation Modeling* 21: 329–341.

Bailey, Kenneth D. 1994. *Typologies and Taxonomies: An Introduction to Classification Techniques*. Thousand Oaks, CA: Sage.

Barker, Edward D., Frank Vitaro, Éric Lacourse, Nathalie M. G. Fontaine, René Carbonneau, and Richard E. Tremblay. 2010. "Testing the Developmental Distinctiveness of Male Proactive and Reactive Aggression with a Nested Longitudinal Experimental Intervention." *Aggressive Behavior* 36: 127–140.

Barnes, J. C., Beaver, Kevin M., and Brian B. Boutwell. 2011. "Examining the Genetic Underpinnings to Moffitt's Developmental Taxonomy: A Behavioral Genetic Analysis." *Criminology* 49: 923–954.

Bauer, Daniel J. 2007. "Observations on the Use of Growth Mixture Models in Psychological Research." *Multivariate Behavioral Research* 42: 757–786.

Bauer, Daniel J., and Patrick J. Curran. 2003. "Distributional Assumptions of Growth Mixture Models: Implications for Overextraction of Latent Trajectory Classes." *Psychological Methods* 8: 338–363.

Beaver, Kevin M. 2013. *Biosocial Criminology: A Primer*. 2nd ed. Dubuque, IA: Kendall/Hunt.

Besemer, Sytske, Johan Axelsson, and Jerzy Sarnecki. 2016. "Intergenerational Transmission of Trajectories of Offending over Three Generations." *Journal of Developmental and Life Course Criminology* 2: 417–441.

Block, Jack. 1971. *Lives Through Time*. Berkeley, CA: Bancroft.

Blokland, Arjan A. J., Daniel S. Nagin, and Paul Nieuwbeerta. 2005. "Life Span Offending Trajectories of a Dutch Conviction Cohort." *Criminology* 43: 919–954.

Blokland, Arjan A. J., and Paul Nieuwbeerta. 2005. "The Effects of Life Circumstances on Longitudinal Trajectories of Offending." *Criminology* 43: 1203–1240.

Blumstein, Alfred, Jacqueline Cohen, and David P. Farrington. 1988a. "Criminal Career Research: Its Value for Criminology." *Criminology* 26: 1–35.

Blumstein, Alfred, Jacqueline Cohen, and David P. Farrington. 1988b. "Longitudinal and Criminal Career Research: Further Clarifications." *Criminology* 26: 57–74.

Blumstein, Alfred., David P. Farrington, and Soumyo Moitra. 1985. "Delinquency Careers: Innocents, Desisters, and Persisters." *Crime and Justice: An Annual Review of Research* 6: 187–219.

Boers, Klaus, Jost Reinecke, Daniel Seddig, and Luca Mariotti. 2010. "Explaining the Development of Adolescent Violent Delinquency." *European Journal of Criminology* 7: 499–520.

Bollen, Kenneth A., and Patrick J. Curran. 2006. *Latent Curve Models: A Structural Equations Perspective*. New York: Wiley.

Bongers, Iija L., Hans M. Koot, Jan van der Ende, and Frank C. Verhulst. 2004. "Developmental Trajectories of Externalizing Behaviors in Childhood and Adolescence." *Child Development* 75: 1523–1537.

Brame, Robert, Raymond Paternoster, and Alex R. Piquero. 2012. "Thoughts on the Analysis of Group-Based Developmental Trajectories in Criminology." *Justice Quarterly* 29: 469–490.

Brennan, Tim. 1987. "Classification: An Overview of Selected Methodological Issues." *Crime and Justice: A Review of Research* 9: 201–248.

Broidy, Lisa M., Daniel S. Nagin, Richard E. Tremblay, John E Bates, Bobby Brame, Kenneth A. Dodge, David Fergusson, John L. Horwood, Rolf Loeber, Robert Laird, Donald R. Lynam, Terrie E. Moffitt, Gregory S. Pettit, and Frank Vitaro. 2003. "Developmental Trajectories of Childhood Disruptive Behaviors and Adolescent Delinquency: A Six-Site, Cross-National Study." *Developmental Psychology* 39: 222–245.

Broidy, Lisa M., Anne L. Stewart, Carleen M. Thompson, April Chrzanowski, Troy Allard, and Susan M. Dennison. 2015. "Life Course Offending Pathways Across Gender and Race/Ethnicity." *Journal of Developmental and Life Course Criminology* 1: 118–149.

Bushway, Shawn D., Terence P. Thornberry, and Marvin D. Krohn. 2003. "Desistance as a Developmental Process: A Comparison of Static and Dynamic Approaches." *Journal of Quantitative Criminology* 19: 129–153.

Campbell, Susan B., Susan Spieker, Nathan Vandergrift, Jay Belsky, Margaret Burchinal, and the NICHD Early Child Care Research Network (2010). "Predictors and Sequelae of Trajectories of Physical Aggression in School-Age Boys and Girls." *Development and Psychopathology* 22: 133–150.

Cauffman, Elizabeth, Kathryn C. Monahan, and April G. Thomas. 2015. "Pathways to Persistence: Female Offending from 14 to 25." *Journal of Developmental and Life Course Criminology* 1: 236–268.

Chen, Frances R., and Sara R. Jaffee. 2015. "The Heterogeneity in the Development of Homotypic and Heterotypic Antisocial Behavior." *Journal of Developmental and Life Course Criminology* 1: 269–288.

Chung, Ick-Joong, Karl G. Hill, J. David Hawkins, Lewayned D. Gilchrist, and Daniel S. Nagin. 2002. "Childhood Predictors of Offense Trajectories." *Journal of Research in Crime and Delinquency* 39: 60–90.

Connell, Arin M., Susan Klostermann, and Thomas J. Dishion. 2011. "Family Check-Up Effects on Adolescent Arrest Trajectories: Variation by Developmental Subtype." *Journal of Research on Adolescence* 22: 367–380.

Deci, Edward L., and Richard M. Ryan. 2000. "The 'What' and 'Why' of Goal Pursuits: Human Needs and the Self-Determination of Behavior." *Psychological Inquiry* 11: 227–268.

DeLisi, Matt. 2011. "Self-Control Theory: The Tyrannosaurus Rex of Criminology Is Poised to Devour Criminal Justice." *Journal of Criminal Justice* 39: 103–105.

DeLisi, Matt, and Alex R. Piquero. 2011. "New Frontiers in Criminal Careers Research, 2000–2011: A State-of-the-Art Review." *Journal of Criminal Justice* 39: 289–301.

Di Giunta, Laura, Concetta Pastorelli, Nancy Eisenberg, Maria Gerbino, Valeria Castellani, and Anna S. Bombi. 2010. "Developmental Trajectories of Physical Aggression: Prediction of Overt and Covert Antisocial Behaviors from Self- and Mothers' Reports." *European Child and Adolescent Psychiatry* 19: 873–882.

Dodge, Kenneth A., Patrick S. Malone, Jennifer E. Lansford, Shari Miller, Gregory S. Pettit, and John E. Bates. 2009. "A Dynamic Cascade Model of the Development of Substance-Use Onset." *Monographs of the Society for Research in Child Development* 74(3): Serial No. 294.

D'Unger, Amy V., Kenneth C. Land, Patricia L. McCall, and Daniel S. Nagin. 1998. "How Many Latent Classes of Delinquent/Criminal Careers? Results from Mixed Poisson Regression Analyses of the London, Philadelphia, and Racine Cohort Studies." *American Journal of Sociology* 103: 1593–1630.

Eggleston, Elaine P., and John H. Laub. 2002. "The Onset of Adult Offending: A Neglected Dimension of the Criminal Career." *Journal of Criminal Justice* 30: 603–622.

Eggleston, Elaine P., John H. Laub, and Robert J. Sampson. 2004. "Methodological Sensitivities to Latent Class Analysis of Long-Term Criminal Trajectories." *Journal of Quantitative Criminology* 20: 11–26.

Farrington, David P. 1986. "Age and Crime." *Crime and Justice: A Review of Research* 7: 189–250.

Farrington, David P., Alex R. Piquero, and Wesley G. Jennings. 2013. *Offending from Childhood to Late Middle Age: Recent Results from the Cambridge Study in Delinquent Development*. New York: Springer.

Farrington, David P., and Brandon C. Welsh. 2007. *Saving Children from a Life of Crime: Early Risk Factors and Effective Interventions*. New York: Oxford University Press.

Feldman, Betsy J., Katherine E. Masyn, and Rand D. Conger. 2009. "New Approaches to Studying Problem Behaviors: A Comparison of Methods for Modeling Longitudinal, Categorical Adolescent Drinking Data." *Developmental Psychology* 45: 652–676.

Fergusson, David M., and L. John Horwood. 2002. "Male and Female Offending Trajectories." *Development and Psychopathology* 14: 159–177.

Fergusson, David M., L. John Horwood, and Daniel S. Nagin. 2000. "Offending Trajectories in a New Zealand Cohort." *Criminology* 38: 525–552.

Flory, Kate, Donald R. Lynam., Richard Milich, Carl Leukefeld, and Richard Clayton. 2004. "Early Adolescent Through Young Adult Alcohol and Marijuana Use Trajectories: Early Predictors, Young Adult Outcomes, and Predictive Utility." *Development and Psychopathology* 16: 193–213.

Fontaine, Nathalie M. G., René Carbonneau, Frank Vitaro, Edward D. Barker, and Richard E. Tremblay. 2009. "A Critical Review of Studies on the Developmental Trajectories of Antisocial Behavior in Females." *Journal of Child Psychology and Psychiatry* 50: 363–385.

Fréchette, Marcel, and Marc Le Blanc. 1987. *Délinquances et Délinquants* [Delinquents and Delinquencies]. Boucherville, Québec: Gaëtan Morin Éditeur.

Frick, Paul J. 2012. "Developmental Pathways to Conduct Disorder: Implications for Future Directions in Research, Assessment, and Treatment." *Journal of Clinical Child and Adolescent Psychology* 41: 378–389.

Gomez-Smith, Zenta, and Alex R. Piquero. 2005. "An Examination of Adult Onset Offending." *Journal of Criminal Justice* 33: 515–525.

Gottfredson, Don M. 1987. "Prediction and Classification in Criminal Justice Decision Making." *Crime and Justice: A Review of Research* 9: 1–20.

Gottfredson, Michael R. 2005. "Offender Classifications and Treatment Effects in Developmental Criminology: A Propensity/Event Consideration." *Annals of the American Academy of Political and Social Science* 602: 46–56.

Gottfredson, Michael R., and Travis Hirschi. 1986. "The True Value of Lambda Would Appear to be Zero: An Essay on Career Criminals, Criminal Careers, Selective Incapacitation, Cohort Studies, and Related Topics." *Criminology* 24: 213–233.

Gottfredson, Michael R., and Travis Hirschi. 1990. *A General Theory of Crime*. Stanford, CA: Stanford University Press.

Greenberg, David F. 2016. "Criminal Careers: Discrete or Continuous?" *Journal of Developmental and Life Course Criminology* 2: 5–44.

Guo, Jie, Chung, Ick-Joong, Karl G. Hill, J. David Hawkins, Richard F. Catalano, and Robert D. Abbott. 2002. "Developmental Relationships Between Adolescent Substance Use and Risky Sexual Behavior in Young Adulthood." *Journal of Adolescent Health* 31: 354–362.

Harring, Jeffrey R., and Gregory R. Hancock. 2012. *Advances in Longitudinal Methods in the Social and Behavioral Sciences*. Charlotte, NC: Information Age.

Hipp, John R., and Daniel J. Bauer. 2006. "Local Solutions in the Estimation of Growth Mixture Models." *Psychological Methods* 11: 36–53.

Hoeve, Machteld, Arjan Blokland, Judith Semon Dubas, Rolf Loeber, Jan R. M. Gerris, and Peter H. van der Laan. 2008. "Trajectories of Delinquency and Parenting Styles." *Journal of Abnormal Child Psychology* 36: 223–235.

Jennings, Wesley G. 2011. "Sex Disaggregated Trajectories of Status Offenders: Does CINS/FINS Status Prevent Male and Female Youth from Becoming Labeled Delinquent?" *American Journal of Criminal Justice* 36: 177–187.

Jennings, Wesley G., and Jennifer M. Reingle. 2012. "On the Number and Shape of Developmental/Life Course Violence, Aggression, and Delinquency Trajectories: A State-of-the-Art Review." *Journal of Criminal Justice* 40: 472–489.

Jessor, Richard, and Shirley L. Jessor. 1977. *Problem Behavior and Psychosocial Development: A Longitudinal Study of Youth*. New York: Academic Press.

Jolliffe, Darrick, David P. Farrington, Alex R. Piquero, John F. Macleod, and Steve van de Weijer. 2017a. "Prevalence of Life-Course Persistent, Adolescence-Limited, and Late-Onset Offenders: A Systematic Review of Prospective Longitudinal Studies." *Aggression and Violent Behavior* 33: 4–14.

Jolliffe, Darrick, David P. Farrington, Alex R. Piquero, Rolf Loeber, and Karl G. Hill. 2017b. "Systematic Review of Early Risk Factors for Life-Course Persistent, Adolescence-Limited, and Late-Onset Offenders in Prospective Longitudinal Studies." *Aggression and Violent Behavior* 33: 15–23.

Kreuter, Frauke, and Bengt O. Muthén. 2008. "Analyzing Criminal Trajectory Profiles: Bridging Multilevel and Group-Based Approaches Using Growth Mixture Modeling." *Journal of Quantitative Criminology* 24: 1–31.

Krohn, Marvin D., Alan J. Lizotte, Shawn D. Bushway, Nicole M. Schmidt, and Matthew D. Phillips. 2014. "Shelter During the Storm: A Search for Factors That Protect At-Risk Adolescents from Violence." *Crime and Delinquency* 60: 379–401.

Krueger, Robert F., Kristian E. Markon, Christopher J. Patrick, Stephen D. Benning, and Mark D. Kramer. 2007. "Linking Antisocial Behavior, Substance Use, and Personality: An Integrative Quantitative Model of the Adult Externalizing Spectrum." *Journal of Abnormal Psychology* 116: 645–666.

Lacourse, Éric., Daniel S. Nagin, Richard E. Tremblay, Frank Vitaro, F., and Michel Claes. 2003. "Developmental Trajectories of Boys' Delinquent Group Membership and Facilitation of Violent Behaviors During Adolescence." *Development and Psychopathology* 15: 183–197.

Lanctôt, Nadine. 2015. "Development of Antisocial Behavior in Adolescent Girls." In *The Development of Criminal and Antisocial Behavior: Theory, Research and Practical Applications*, edited by Julien Morizot and Lila Kazemian, 399–411. New York: Springer.

Le Blanc, Marc. 1998. "Screening of Serious and Violent Juvenile Offenders: Identification, Classification, and Prediction." In *Serious and Violent Juvenile Offenders: Risk Factors and Successful Interventions*, edited by Rolf Loeber and David P. Farrington, 167–193. Thousand Oaks, CA: Sage.

Le Blanc, Marc. 2002. "The Offending Cycle—Escalation and De-Escalation in Delinquent Behavior: A Challenge for Criminology." *International Journal of Comparative and Applied Criminal Justice* 26: 53–83.

Le Blanc, Marc. 2005. "An Integrative Self-Control Theory of Deviant Behavior: Answers to Contemporary Empirical and Theoretical Developmental Criminology Issues." In *Integrated Developmental and Life Course Theories of Offending: Advances in Criminological Theory*, Vol. 14, edited by David P. Farrington, 125–163. Piscataway, NJ: Transaction.

Le Blanc, Marc. 2015. "Developmental Criminology: Thoughts on the Past and Insights for the Future." In *The Development of Criminal and Antisocial Behavior: Theory, Research and Practical Applications*, edited by Julien Morizot and Lila Kazemian, 507–537. New York: Springer.

Le Blanc, Marc, and Marcel Fréchette. 1989. *Male Criminal Activity from Childhood Through Youth: Multilevel and Developmental Perspectives.* New York: Springer-Verlag.

Le Blanc, Marc, and Rolf Loeber. 1998. "Developmental Criminology Updated." *Crime and Justice: An Annual Review of Research* 23: 115–198.

Loeber, Rolf, and Jeffrey D. Burke. 2011. "Developmental Pathways in Juvenile Externalizing and Internalizing Problems." *Journal of Research on Adolescence* 21: 34–46.

Loeber, Rolf, and Dale F. Hay. 1994. "Developmental Approaches to Aggression and Conduct Problems." In *Development Through Life: A Handbook for Clinicians*, edited by Michael Rutter and Dale F. Hay, 488–516. Oxford: Blackwell Scientific.

Loeber, Rolf, Éric Lacourse, and D. Lynn Homish. 2006. "Homicide, Violence and Developmental Trajectories." In *Developmental Origins of Aggression*, edited by Richard E. Tremblay, Willard W. Hartup, and John Archer, 202–219. New York: Guilford.

Loeber, Rolf, N. Wim Slot, and Magda Stouthamer-Loeber. 2006. "A Three-Dimensional, Cumulative Developmental Model of Serious Delinquency." In *The Explanation of Crime: Contexts and Mechanisms*, edited by Per-Olof H. Wikström and Robert J. Sampson, 153–194. New York: Cambridge University Press.

Loeber, Rolf, Phen Wung, Kate Keenan, Bruce Giroux, Magda Stouthamer-Loeber, Welmoet B. Van Kammen, and Barbara Maughan. 1993. "Developmental Pathways in Disruptive Child Behavior." *Development and Psychopathology* 5: 103–133.

Loevinger, Jane. 1957. "Objective Tests as Instruments of Psychological Theory." *Psychological Reports* 3: 635–694.

Lussier, Patrick, Chantal van den Berg, Catrien Bijleveld, and Jan Hendriks. 2012. "A Developmental Taxonomy of Juvenile Sex Offenders for Theory, Research, and Prevention." *Criminal Justice and Behavior* 39: 1559–1581.

Lynne-Landsman, Sarah D., Julia A. Graber, Tracy R. Nichols, and Gilbert J. Botvin. 2011. "Trajectories of Aggression, Delinquency, and Substance Use Across Middle School Among Urban, Minority Adolescents." *Aggressive Behavior* 37: 161–176.

MacCallum, Robert C. 2003. "Working with Imperfect Models." *Multivariate Behavioral Research* 38: 113–139.

MacDonald, John M., Amelia Haviland, and Andrew R. Morral. 2009. "Assessing the Relationship Between Violent and Nonviolent Criminal Activity Among Serious Adolescent Offenders." *Journal of Research in Crime and Delinquency* 46: 553–580.

Magnusson, David. 1998. "The Logic and Implications of a Person-Oriented Approach." In *Methods and Models for Studying the Individual*, edited by Robert B. Cairns, Lars R. Bergman, and Jerome Kagan, 33–64. Thousand Oaks, CA: Sage.

Maldonado-Molina, Mildred M., Wesley G. Jennings, and Kelli A. Komro. 2010. "Effects of Alcohol on Trajectories of Physical Aggression Among Urban Youth: An Application of Latent Trajectory Modeling." *Journal of Youth and Adolescence* 39: 1012–1026.

Marsh, Herbert W., Kit-Tai Hau, and David Grayson. 2005. "Goodness of Fit Evaluation in Structural Equation Modeling." In *Contemporary Psychometrics. A Festschrift for Roderick P. McDonald*, edited by Albert Maydeu-Olivares and John J. McArdle, 275–340. Mahwah, NJ: Erlbaum.

Martel, Michelle M., Laura Pierce, Joel T. Nigg, Jennifer M. Jester, J., Kenneth Adams, Leon I. Puttler, Ann Buu, Hiram Fitzgerald, and Robert A. Zucker. 2009. "Temperament Pathways to Childhood Disruptive Behavior and Adolescent Substance Abuse: Testing a Cascade Model." *Journal of Abnormal Child Psychology* 37: 363–373.

Maruna, Shadd. 2001. *Making Good: How Ex-Convicts Reform and Rebuild Their Lives.* Washington, DC: American Psychological Association.

Mata, Andrea D., and Manfred H. M. van Dulmen. 2012. "Adult-Onset Antisocial Behavior Trajectories: Associations with Adolescent Family Processes and Emerging Adulthood Functioning." *Journal of Interpersonal Violence* 27: 177–193.

McAdams, Dan P., and Kate C. McLean. 2013. "Narrative Identity." *Current Directions in Psychological Science* 22: 233–238.

McLachlan, Geoffrey, and David Peel. 2000. *Finite Mixture Models.* New York: Wiley.

Meehl, Paul E. 1992. "Factors and Taxa, Traits and Types, Differences of Degree and Differences in Kind." *Journal of Personality* 60: 117–174.

Miller, Shari, Patrick S. Malone, Kenneth A. Dodge, and Conduct Problems Prevention Research Group. 2010. "Developmental Trajectories of Boys' and Girls' Delinquency: Sex Differences and Links to Later Adolescent Outcomes." *Journal of Abnormal Child Psychology* 38: 1021–1032.

Moffitt, Terrie E. 1993. "Adolescence-Limited and Life-Course Persistent Antisocial Behavior: A Developmental Taxonomy." *Psychological Review* 100: 674–701.

Moffitt, Terrie E. 1994. "Natural Histories of Delinquency." In *Cross-National Longitudinal Research on Human Development and Criminal Behavior*, edited by Elmar G. M. Weitekamp and Hans-Jurgen Kerner, 3–61. Dordrecht, The Netherlands: Kluwer.

Moffitt, Terrie E. 2006. "Life-Course Persistent Versus Adolescence-Limited Antisocial Behavior." In *Developmental Psychopathology*, Vol. 3: *Risk, Disorder, and Adaptation*, 2nd ed., edited by Dante Cicchetti and Donald J. Cohen, 570–598. New York: Wiley.

Monahan, Kathryn C., Laurence Steinberg, Elizabeth Cauffman, and Edward P. Mulvey. 2010. "Trajectories of Antisocial Behavior and Psychosocial Maturity from Adolescence to Young Adulthood." *Developmental Psychology* 45: 1654–1668.

Morizot, Julien. 2015. "The Contribution of Temperament and Personality Traits to Antisocial Behavior Development and Desistance." In *The Development of Criminal and Antisocial Behavior: Theory, Research and Practical Applications*, edited by Julien Morizot and Lila Kazemian, 137–165. New York: Springer.

Morizot, Julien, and Marc Le Blanc. 2007. "Behavioral, Self, and Social Control Predictors of Desistance from Crime: A Test of Launch- and Contemporaneous-Effect Models." *Journal of Contemporary Criminal Justice* 23: 50–71.

Muthén, Bengt O. 2003. "Statistical and Substantive Checking in Growth Mixture Modeling: Comment on Bauer and Curran (2003)." *Psychological Methods* 8: 369–377.

Muthén, Bengt O. 2004. "Latent Variable Analysis: Growth Mixture Modeling and Related Techniques for Longitudinal Data." In *Handbook of Quantitative Methodology for the Social Sciences*, edited by David Kaplan, 345–368. Newbury Park, CA: Sage.

Muthén, Bengt O. 2008. "Latent Variable Hybrids: Overview of Old and New Models." In *Advances in Latent Variable Mixture Models*, edited by Gregory R. Hancock and Karen R. Samuelsen, 1–24. Charlotte, NC: Information Age.

Muthén, Bengt O., and Tihomir Asparouhov. 2009. "Growth Mixture Modeling: Analysis with Non-Gaussian Random Effects." In *Longitudinal Data Analysis*, edited by Garrett Fitzmaurice, Marie Davidian, Geert Verbeke, and Geert Molenberghs, 143–165. Boca Raton, FL: Chapman and Hall/CRC Press.

Muthén, Bengt O., and Linda K. Muthén. 2000. "Integrating Person-Centered and Variable-Centered Analysis: Growth Mixture Modeling with Latent Trajectory Classes." *Alcoholism: Clinical and Experimental Research* 24: 882–891.

Nagin, Daniel S. 1999. "Analyzing Developmental Trajectories: A Semi-Parametric, Group-Based Approach." *Psychological Methods* 4: 139–177.

Nagin, Daniel S. 2005. *Group-Based Modeling of Development*. Cambridge, MA: Harvard University Press.

Nagin, Daniel S., David P. Farrington, and Terrie E. Moffitt. 1995. "Life-Course Trajectories of Different Types of Offenders." *Criminology* 33: 111–140.

Nagin, Daniel S., and Kenneth C. Land. 1993. "Age, Criminal Careers, and Population Heterogeneity: Specification and Estimation of a Nonparametric, Mixed Poisson Model." *Criminology* 31: 327–362.

Nagin, Daniel S., and Candice L. Odgers. 2010. "Group-Based Trajectory Modeling (Nearly) Two Decades Later." *Journal of Quantitative Criminology* 26: 445–453.

Nagin, Daniel S., and Richard E. Tremblay. 1999. "Trajectories of Boys' Physical Aggression, Opposition, and Hyperactivity on the Path to Physically Violent and Non-Violent Juvenile Delinquency." *Child Development* 70: 1181–1196.

Nagin, Daniel S., and Richard E. Tremblay. 2001. "Analyzing Developmental Trajectories of Distinct but Related Behaviors: A Group-Based Method." *Psychological Methods* 6: 18–34.

Nagin, Daniel S., and Richard E. Tremblay. 2005. "Developmental Trajectory Groups: Fact of Fiction?" *Criminology* 43: 873–904.

Odgers, Candice L., Avshalom Caspi, Jonathan M. Broadbent, Nigel Dickson, Robert J. Hancox, HonaLee L. Harrington, Richie Poulton, Malcolm R. Sears, W. Murray Thomson, and Terrie E. Moffitt. 2007. "Prediction of Differential Health Burden by Conduct Problem Subtypes in Males." *Archives of Psychiatry* 64: 476–484.

Odgers, Candice L., Terrie E. Moffitt, Jonathan M. Broadbent, Nigel Dickson, Robert J. Hancox, HonaLee L. Harrington, Richie Poulton, Malcolm R. Sears, W. Murray Thomson, and Avshalom Caspi. 2008. "Female and Male Antisocial Trajectories: From Childhood Origins to Adult Outcomes." *Development and Psychopathology* 20: 673–716.

Osgood, D. Wayne. 2005. "Making Sense of Crime and the Life Course." *Annals of the American Academy of Political and Social Science* 602: 196–211.

Paternoster, Ray, Ronet Bachman, Shawn Bushway, Erin Kerrison, and Daniel O'Connell. 2015. "Human Agency and Explanations of Criminal Desistance: Arguments for a Rational Choice Theory." *Journal of Developmental and Life Course Criminology* 1: 209–235.

Patterson, Gerald R., and Karen Yoerger. 1993. "Developmental Models for Delinquent Behavior." In *Mental Disorder and Crime*, edited by Sheilagh Hodgins, 140–172. Newbury Park, CA: Sage.

Patterson, Gerald R., and Karen Yoerger. 1997. "A Developmental Model for Late-Onset Delinquency." In *Motivation and Delinquency: Nebraska Symposium on Motivation*, Vol. 44, edited by D. Wayne Osgood, 119–177. Lincoln, NE: University of Nebraska Press.

Patterson, Gerald R., and Karen Yoerger. 2002. "A Developmental Model for Early- and Late-Onset Antisocial Behavior." In *Antisocial Behavior in Children and Adolescents: A Developmental Analysis and Model for Intervention*, edited by John B. Reid, Gerald R. Patterson, and James Snyder, 147–172. Washington, DC: American Psychological Association.

Pepler, Debra J., Depeng Jiang, Wendy M. Craig, and Jennifer Connolly. 2010. "Developmental Trajectories of Girls' and Boys' Delinquency and Associated Problems." *Journal of Abnormal Child Psychology* 38: 1033–1044.

Petras, Hanno, and Katherine E. Masyn. 2010. "General Growth Mixture Analysis with Antecedents and Consequences of Change." In *Handbook of Quantitative Criminology*, edited by Alex R. Piquero, and David Weisburd, 69–100. New York: Springer.

Piquero, Alex R. 2008. "Taking Stock of Developmental Trajectories of Criminal Activity over the Life Course." In *The Long View of Crime: A Synthesis of Longitudinal Research*, edited by Akiva M. Liberman, 23–78. New York: Springer.

Piquero, Alex R. 2009. "Self-Control Theory: Research Issues." In *Handbook on Crime and Deviance*, edited by Marvin D. Krohn, Alan J. Lizotte and Gina P. Hall, 153–168. New York: Springer.

Piquero, Alex R. 2015. "Understanding Race/Ethnicity Differences in Offending Across the Life Course: Gaps and Opportunities." *Journal of Developmental and Life Course Criminology* 1: 21–32.

Piquero, Alex R., Alfred Blumstein, Robert Brame, Rudy Haapanen, Edward P. Mulvey, and Daniel S. Nagin. 2001. "Assessing the Impact of Exposure Time and Incapacitation on Longitudinal Trajectories of Criminal Offending." *Journal of Adolescent Research* 16: 54–74.

Piquero, Alex R., Robert Brame, Paul Mazerolle, and Rudy Haapanen. 2002. "Crime in Emerging Adulthood." *Criminology* 40: 137–169.

Piquero, Alex R., David P. Farrington, and Alfred Blumstein. 2003. "The Criminal Career Paradigm." *Crime and Justice: A Review of Research* 30: 359–506.

Piquero, Alex R., David P. Farrington, and Alfred Blumstein. 2007. *Key Issues in Criminal Career Research: New Analyses of the Cambridge Study in Delinquent Development.* Cambridge, UK: Cambridge University Press.

Piquero, Alex R., David P. Farrington, Daniel S. Nagin, and Terrie E. Moffitt. 2010. "Trajectories of Offending and their Relation to Life Failure in Late Middle Age: Findings from the Cambridge Study in Delinquent Development." *Journal of Research in Crime and Delinquency* 47: 151–173.

Piquero, Alex R., Jennifer M. Reingle-Gonzalez, and Wesley G. Jennings. 2015. "Developmental Trajectories and Antisocial Behavior over the Life Course." In *The Development of Criminal and Antisocial Behavior: Theory, Research and Practical Applications*, edited by Julien Morizot and Lila Kazemian, 75–88. New York: Springer.

Raine, Adrian. 2013. *The Anatomy of Violence: The Biological Roots of Crime.* New York: Vintage.

Raudenbush, Stephen W., and Anthony S. Bryk. 2002. *Hierarchical Linear Models.* 2nd ed. Thousand Oaks, CA: Sage.

Robins, Lee N. 1966. *Deviant Children Grown Up: A Sociological and Psychiatric Study of Sociopathic Personality.* New York: Krieger.

Rowe, David C., D. Wayne Osgood, and W. Alan Nicewander. 1990. "A Latent Trait Approach to Unifying Criminal Careers." *Criminology* 28: 237–270.

Sampson, Robert J., and John H. Laub. 2003. "Life-Course Desisters? Trajectories of Crime Among Delinquent Boys Followed to Age 70." *Criminology* 41: 555–592.

Sampson, Robert J., and John H. Laub. 2005. "A Life-Course View of the Development of Crime." *Annals of the American Academy of Political and Social Science* 602: 12–45.

Schaeffer, Cindy M., Hanno Petras, Nicholas Ialongo, Katherine E. Masyn, Scott Hubbard, Jeanne Poduska, and Sheppard Kellam. 2006. "A Comparison of Girls' and Boys' Aggressive-Disruptive Behavior Trajectories Across Elementary School: Prediction to Young Adult Antisocial Outcomes." *Journal of Consulting and Clinical Psychology* 74: 500–510.

Shaw, Daniel S., Éric Lacourse, and Daniel S. Nagin. 2005. "Developmental Trajectories of Conduct Problems and Hyperactivity from Ages 2 to 10." *Journal of Child Psychology and Psychiatry* 46: 931–942.

Sher, Kenneth J., Kristina M. Jackson, and Douglas Steinley. 2011. "Alcohol Use Trajectories and the Ubiquitous Cat's Cradle: Cause for Concern?" *Journal of Abnormal Psychology* 120: 322–335.

Skardhamar, Torbjorn. 2009. "Reconsidering the Theory of Adolescent-Limited and Life-Course Persistent Antisocial Behavior." *British Journal of Criminology* 49: 863–878.

Skardhamar, Torbjorn. 2010. "Distinguishing Facts and Artifacts in Group-Based Modelling." *Criminology* 48: 295–320.

Skinner, Harvey A. 1981. "Toward the Integration of Classification Theory and Methods." *Journal of Abnormal Psychology* 90: 68–87.

Sterba, Sonya K., and Daniel J. Bauer. 2010. "Matching Method with Theory in Person-Oriented Developmental Psychopathology Research." *Development and Psychopathology* 22: 239–254.

Tackett, Jennifer L., Robert F. Krueger, William G. Iacono, and Matt McGue. 2005. "Symptom-Based Subfactors of DSM-Defined Conduct Disorder: Evidence for Etiologic Distinctions." *Journal of Abnormal Psychology* 114: 483–487.

Tofighi, Davood, and Craik K. Enders. 2008. "Identifying the Correct Number of Classes in Growth Mixture Models." In *Advances in Latent Variable Mixture Models*, edited by Gregory R. Hancock and Karen M. Samuelsen, 317–341. Charlotte, NC: Information Age.

Tremblay, Richard E. 2010. "Developmental Origins of Disruptive Behavior Problems: The 'Original Sin' Hypothesis, Epigenetics and their Consequences for Prevention." *Journal of Child Psychology and Psychiatry* 51: 341–367.

Tremblay, Richard E., Christa Japel, Daniel Perusse, Pierre McDuff, Michel Boivin, Mark Zoccolillo, and Jacques Montplaisir. 1999. "The Search for the Age of 'Onset' of Physical Aggression: Rousseau and Bandura Revisited." *Criminal Behaviour and Mental Health* 9: 8–23.

Trim, Ryan S., Matthew J. Worley, Tamara L. Wall, Christian J. Hopfer, Thomas J. Crowley, John K. Hewitt, and Sandra A. Brown. 2015. "Bivariate Trajectories of Substance Use and Antisocial Behavior: Associations with Emerging Adult Outcomes in a High-Risk Sample." *Emerging Adulthood* 3: 265–276.

van de Rakt, Marieke, Joseph Murray, and Paul Nieuwbeerta. 2012. "The Long-Term Effects of Paternal Imprisonment on Criminal Trajectories of Children." *Journal of Research in Crime and Delinquency* 49: 81–108.

van der Geest, Victor, Arjan Blokland, and Catrien Bijleveld. 2009. "Delinquent Development in a Sample of High-Risk Youth: Shape, Content, and Predictors of Delinquent Trajectories from Age 12 to 32." *Journal of Research in Crime and Delinquency* 46: 111–143.

Van Dulmen, Manfred H. M., Elizabeth A. Goncy, Andrea Vest, and Daniel J. Flannery. 2009. "Group-Based Trajectory Modeling of Externalizing Behavior Problems from Childhood through Adulthood: Exploring Discrepancies in the Empirical Findings." In *The Development of Persistent Criminality*, edited by Joan Savage, 288–314. New York: Oxford University Press.

Viding, Essi, R. James Blair, Terrie E. Moffitt, and Robert Plomin. 2005. "Evidence for Substantial Genetic Risk for Psychopathy in 7-Year-Olds." *Journal of Child Psychology and Psychiatry* 46: 592–597.

West, Stephen G., Aaron B. Taylor, and Wei Wu. 2012. "Model Fit and Model Selection in Structural Equation Modeling." In *Handbook of Structural Equation Modeling*, edited by Rick H. Hoyle, 209–231. New York: Guilford.

White, Helen R., Marsha E. Bates, and Steven Buyske. 2001. "Adolescence-Limited Versus Persistent Delinquency: Extending Moffitt's Hypothesis into Adulthood." *Journal of Abnormal Psychology* 110: 600–609.

Wiesner, Margit, and Deborah M. Capaldi. 2003. "Relations of Childhood and Adolescent Factors to Offending Trajectories of Young Men." *Journal of Research in Crime and Delinquency* 40: 231–262.

Wiesner, Margit, Deborah M. Capaldi, and Hyoun K. Kim. 2007. "Arrest Trajectories Across a 17-Year Span for Young Men: Relation to Dual Taxonomies and Self-Reported Offenses Trajectories." *Criminology* 45: 835–863.

Wolfgang, Marvin E., Robert M. Figlio, and Thorsten Sellin. 1972. *Delinquency in a Birth Cohort*. Chicago: University of Chicago Press.

Wood, A. L. 1969. "Ideal and Empirical Typologies for Research in Deviance and Control." *Sociology and Social Research* 53: 227–241.

Zara, Georgia, and David P. Farrington. 2010. "A Longitudinal Analysis of Early Risk Factors for Adult Onset Offending: What Predicts a Delayed Criminal Career?" *Criminal Behaviour and Mental Health* 20: 257–273.

Zara, Georgia, and David P. Farrington. 2013. "Assessment of Risk for Juvenile Compared with Adult Criminal Onset: Implications for Policy, Prevention, and Intervention." *Psychology, Public Policy, and Law* 19: 235–249.

Zucker, Robert A. 1987. "The Four Alcoholisms: A Developmental Account of the Etiologic Process." In *Nebraska Symposium on Motivation: Alcohol and Addictive Behavior*, edited by P. Clayton Rivers, 27–83. Lincoln: Nebraska.

Zucker, Robert A. 2006. "Alcohol Use and the Alcohol Use Disorders: A Developmental-Biopsychosocial Systems Formulation Covering the Life Course." In *Developmental Psychopathology:* Vol. 3. *Risk, Disorder, and Adaptation*, 2nd ed., edited by Dante Cicchetti and Donald J. Cohen, 620–656. New York: Wiley.

CHAPTER 8

··

CO-OFFENDING

··

SARAH B. VAN MASTRIGT
AND PETER J. CARRINGTON*

ONE of the most frequent observations about crime is that it is often a joint venture, particularly among young people. Evidence for co-offending—the act of committing crime together with one or more other offenders—is long-standing (Breckinridge and Abbott 1917; Shaw and McKay 1931) and consistent across countries and jurisdictions (Erickson 1971; Reiss and Farrington 1991; Sarnecki 2001; Carrington 2002; Warr 1996; Carrington and van Mastrigt 2013). It is also robust across self-report and official data (Warr 2002). Since the first formal descriptions of co-offending emerged nearly a century ago, several empirical regularities of the phenomenon have been identified, including its strong and negative relationship with the offender's age, its overrepresentation in crimes such as burglary, robbery, and theft of motor vehicles and relative rarity in cases of sexual assault, and the general tendency for offending groups to be small, homogeneous, and transitory (for recent reviews, see Warr 2002; Weerman 2003; Carrington 2014; Lantz and Ruback 2017).

To date, however, most co-offending research has been cross-sectional in nature. As Carrington (2009, p. 1296) noted, with few exceptions "published research on co-offending . . . has made only limited (or no) reference to the criminal careers of its subjects . . . and the vast body of research on delinquent and criminal careers has made little or no reference to co-offending." This is unfortunate, as the empirical fact that many individuals' criminal careers intersect via joint offending has potentially profound implications for developmental and life-course (DLC) criminology. Although Shaw and McKay (1931) highlighted the apparent role of accomplices in shaping both the nature and frequency of offending in their early account of the development of Sidney Boltzman's criminal career, the first paper devoted to the relationship between co-offending and criminal careers was not published until 55 years later. In that work, Reiss

* Preparation of this chapter was supported by a grant from the Social Sciences and Humanities Research Council of Canada.

(1986, 1988) outlined basic knowledge about co-offending and called for more research on its role in the onset, persistence, and desistance of offending, arguing that "understanding co-offending is central to understanding the etiology of crime and the effects of intervention strategies" (1988, p. 117).

Unfortunately, progress in answering Reiss's call has been slow, not least due to the shortage of longitudinal and linkable datasets needed to explore such issues. Until recently, nearly all of the (limited) research on co-offending from a criminal career perspective relied on data from only two studies—the Cambridge Study in Delinquent Development (Reiss and Farrington 1991) and the Philadelphia Co-offending Study (McCord and Conway 2002, 2005; McGloin et al. 2008). While hugely influential, both studies are based on relatively small and specific samples (411 London males in the former and 400 urban juveniles in the latter), which, as the authors themselves acknowledge, limits their statistical power and generalizability. Although some scholars have begun to cast wider nets in search of additional co-offending data that allow for at least some degree of longitudinal within-individual analysis (Warr 1996; Sarnecki 2001; Carrington 2009; van Mastrigt and Farrington 2009, 2011; McGloin and Stickle 2011; McGloin and Nguyen 2012), follow-up periods in these datasets tend to be short and the ability to link co-offenders into multiplex co-offending networks is also typically limited (for recent advances, see Charette and Papchristos 2017; Grund and Morselli 2017). As a result, "the role of co-offending generally, and within-individual criminal careers in particular, has been one of the most ill-studied of all criminal career dimensions" (Piquero, Farrington, and Blumstein 2007, p. 120).

Recent developments suggest that the tide may be turning, however. Over the past decade, publication of co-offending studies in a number of top-tier journals has been on a steady rise, and although only a handful of these studies have adopted an explicit criminal career perspective, the growing literature on co-offending appears to have reached the critical mass necessary to have gained the attention of mainstream developmental and life-course criminology. In their state-of-the-art review of developments and gaps in criminal career research from 2000–2011, DeLisi and Piquero (2011, p. 293) identified research on the "role and importance of co-offenders" as one of the 16 most pressing areas in which additional "theoretical, empirical, and policy-relevant research" is needed. This is certainly still the case, but with increasing recognition of the value of adopting a developmental framework from which to explore the phenomenon, the knowledge base in this area has the potential for rapid growth.

This chapter reviews existing theory and empirical evidence on changes in co-offending patterns over the life course, links these patterns to other key criminal career parameters, and highlights important areas for future research. In order to set the stage for the remainder of the chapter, Section I reviews the few theoretical insights that relate joint offending to the development of criminal careers. Section II focuses on the age–co-offending curve, outlining what is known about changes in both co-offending prevalence and form across the life course and considering implications for more general DLC discussions of age and offending. Section III examines how co-offending is related to other features of the criminal career including onset, specialization, seriousness, frequency, duration, persistence, and desistance. Finally, Section IV briefly outlines outstanding issues and next steps for advancing DLC theory and research on group crime.

I. THEORETICAL PERSPECTIVES

As Weerman (2014, p. 5173) has argued, "co-offending is not only an interesting subject for empirical study, it also poses many interesting and profound theoretical questions." Unfortunately, formal theorizing about co-offending is relatively scarce, and this is particularly so from an integrated DLC perspective. Nonetheless, a handful of theoretical perspectives of relevance to the current chapter can be identified. There are two types of theories that include both concepts referring to co-offending and concepts associated with developmental and life-course criminology: developmental and life-course theories of crime that treat co-offending as an aspect of the criminal career and theories of co-offending that incorporate concepts from developmental and life-course criminology.

A. Developmental and Life-Course Theories

For most of the core criminal career parameters addressed in this volume (e.g., onset, persistence), DLC theories have provided both explicit hypotheses and explanations for empirical findings. However, despite being identified as one of 13 "key empirical issues that need to be addressed by any DLC theory" (Farrington 2005, p. 9), mention of co-offending is largely absent from even the most well-articulated developmental and life-course theories. Although many DLC theories remark on the importance of "peers" in the development of offending, few distinguish between general peer influences and co-offending specifically. In Farrington (2005), the authors of eight leading DLC theories responded to a common set of empirical and theoretical questions posed by the editor: one question was why co-offending decreases from adolescence to adulthood (see Section II). Only three authors addressed this question, most only briefly. In his own integrated cognitive antisocial potential (ICAP) theory, Farrington views co-offending as one socio-situational context through which individual antisocial potential may be realized. Linking criminal cooperation with changing patterns of social influence across the life course, he suggests that co-offending decreases with age because "boys offend mainly with male peers, and peer influence is more important in adolescence" (p. 86). Catalano and colleagues (p. 116) alternatively argue that according to their social development model, co-offending declines in early adulthood because "the *rewards for antisocial involvement* from social approval in the teenage years are greater than in young adulthood" (emphasis in original).

Piquero and Moffitt (2005, p. 58) also highlighted the importance of accomplices in their reply, but only for certain types of offenders. According to Moffitt's (1993) taxonomic account, co-offending is a key risk factor for adolescence-limited (AL) delinquency but not life-course–persistent (LCP) offending because "unlike adolescence-limited offenders, who appear to need peer support for crime, life-course persistent offenders are willing to offend alone" (p. 668). Aggregate decreases in co-offending across the life course are thus to be expected because "as ALs begin to desist in early adulthood, the majority of offending activity that occurs in mid-life, past the early 20s, is committed by LCPs, who do not need co-offenders to offend" (Piquero and Moffitt 2005, p. 58). We return to this point below.

Another relevant and (implicitly) developmental theory worth mention—although not one of the DLC theories included in Farrington's (2005) analysis—is Mark Warr's peer influence (companions in crime) theory of crime. This theory explains age-varying crime rates in terms of age-varying exposure and susceptibility to peer influence, noting "*the age distribution of crime stems primarily from age-related changes in peer relations*" (Warr 2002, p. 99; emphasis in the original). Unlike many others, Warr distinguishes peer influence from co-offending directly, noting that "'peer influence' and 'group delinquency,' . . . are not necessarily analogous concepts. They may entail different etiological processes . . . and adolescents may be affected by persons outside the immediate circle of co-offenders who accompany them on any given occasion" (Warr 2002, pp. 7–8). However, in distinguishing the two, he assigns little or no etiological significance to co-offending in itself.

B. Theories of Co-offending

Nearly all co-offending theories are non-developmental in nature. However, a few scholars draw directly on concepts from developmental and life-course criminology or, more generally, from life-course theory (Elder, Johnson, and Crosnoe 2003). These theorists primarily attempt to explain the consistent empirical finding of a relationship between co-offending and the offender's age (see Section II). For example, according to Carrington (2002, 2009), the age–co-offending relationship may be explained by age-varying maturity, such that "children and teenagers like to do things with their peers and in groups, and committing crimes is just another of their group activities. With maturity comes greater autonomy, and, therefore, more solo offending" (Carrington 2009, p. 1299). A closely related theory identifies age-varying gregariousness as the explanation of the age–co-offending relationship as "youths tend to be more gregarious than adults and, as a consequence, are more apt than adults to commit crimes in groups than alone" (Stolzenberg and D'Alessio 2008, p. 81).

In addition to the aforementioned theories that make explicit reference to developmental ideas, a number of traditional co-offending theories also have the possibility to be incorporated into a developmental or life-course view of co-offending because their proposed causal factors either have been, or potentially could be, shown to vary over the life course. For example, the "functional" (Reiss 1988), "instrumental" (Weerman 2003), or "rational choice" (Lantz and Ruback 2017) theory explains co-offending as the result of a rational decision-making process in which a potential offender considers the costs and benefits of solo versus co-offending. Variations in the prevalence of co-offending across types of crime are explained by the contingencies related to the offense: for example, crimes such as burglary, robbery, and vehicle theft are more easily committed by a pair or group than by a single offender, whereas the same may not be true of crimes such as sexual assault (Reiss 1988; Tremblay 1993; Warr 2002; West 1978). As research has found that the types of crimes typically committed by offenders vary over the life course, and developmental explanations have been offered for this finding (Le Blanc and Fréchette 1989; Piquero, Blumstein, and Farrington 2003, pp. 451–453), it follows from the functional theory of co-offending that the prevalence of co-offending will also vary over the life course for reasons that are ultimately developmental (Carrington 2009). Even for a given type of crime such as burglary, the perceived value of co-offending may diminish with the offender's age and experience (Lantz and Ruback 2017; van Mastrigt 2017).

The social exchange theory of co-offending (Weerman 2003) can also be framed in this way. In its traditional form, the theory simply proposes that co-offending involves exchange among co-offenders. The "exchange goods" or "criminal capital" (McCarthy and Hagan 1995) that may be exchanged by co-offenders are diverse (Weerman 2003, p. 406), including tangible goods such as loot or payment, tangible services such as assisting with the execution of the crime, and less tangible goods such as information, appreciation, and acceptance. As possession of most forms of criminal capital that are exchanged in Weerman's (2003) theory varies over the life course, it is likely that the nature of co-offending exchange also has, at least partly, developmental antecedents.

Other, situational, theories explain co-offending by the context within which it occurs; for example, D'Alessio and Stolzenberg (2010) show the role of urbanity and Schaefer (2012; Schaefer, Rodriguez, and Decker 2014) highlights the role of neighborhoods in co-offending. Other contextual factors theorized to affect co-offending include embeddedness in networks of delinquent or criminal friends and relatives, which fosters trust (McCarthy and Hagan 1995; Weerman 2003); and "regular meeting places" (Weerman 2003, p. 408), or what Felson (2003) calls "convergence settings," where potential co-offenders can become acquainted, exchange information, and assess one another's potential as accomplices. Many of these contexts are also likely to vary across the life course.

In summary, although very few co-offending theories are explicitly developmental, and even fewer DLC theories specifically address co-offending, there is obvious potential for the integration of these two theoretical fields—likely to the benefit of both.

II. Changes in Co-offending Across the Life-Course: The Age–Co-offending Curve

As noted above, one of the most well-established and empirically robust facts about co-offending is its strong and negative correlation with the offender's age (Weerman

2003; van Mastrigt 2014). Like the aggregate age–crime curve, the aggregate age–co-offending curve typically rises to a peak in mid-adolescence, decreases rapidly through the twenties, and reaches a stable low later in life, a pattern observed fairly consistently across samples and when controlling for both gender and crime type (for the few types of crime that do not conform to this pattern, see Carrington 2002, p. 303; Piquero, Farrington, and Blumstein 2007, p. 105). While this relative pattern is observed across all major studies, some uncertainty has emerged in recent years as to the absolute prevalence of co-offending at different ages and, of particular interest to the DLC agenda, whether the aggregate age–co-offending curve reflects between-individual or within-individual changes in co-offending over time. This section reviews research on changes in both the prevalence and nature of co-offending associated with aging and outlines the implications of these patterns for more general DLC discussions of age and crime.

A. Co-offending Prevalence and Age

Research dating back to the early 20th century has highlighted the fundamentally social nature of much offending early in the criminal career. In their now classic study of juvenile offenders appearing in Cook County Court, Breckinridge and Abbott (1917, p. 35) noted that "there is scarcely a delinquent boy who is not associated with others in his wrongdoing," a finding echoed in later studies by Shaw and McKay (1931), Erickson (1971), McCord and Conway (2002) and others (Reiss and Farrington 1991; Sarnecki 2001; Andresen and Felson 2012; Zimring and Laqueur 2015) who have reported general co-offending rates over 50 percent, and often higher, among juveniles. These findings underlie the common assertion that co-offending is normative in youth and that "solo offending . . . does not become the modal form of offending until the late teens or early twenties" (Reiss 1988, p.151). In the Cambridge Study in Delinquent Development, one of the only prospective longitudinal studies to have tracked co-offending from childhood to adulthood, the correlation between age (up to 40 years) and the percentage of offenses committed alone was extremely strong ($r = 0.916$); whereas 75 percent of offense participations committed by boys aged 10 to 13 years involved co-offenders, solo offending became the norm between ages 21 and 24, and only 28 percent of offense participations at ages 37 to 40 involved multiple offenders (Piquero, Farrington, and Blumstein 2007, p. 104).

Although the bulk of published work supports the conclusion that the majority of youths offend in groups while the opposite is true for adults, a growing body of evidence suggests that lone offending may become typical at earlier ages than previously thought, at least in some samples (Carrington 2002; Stolzenberg and D'Alessio 2008, 2016; van Mastrigt and Farrington 2009). In a recent cross-national study of officially recorded co-offending patterns in the United States, United Kingdom, and Canada, for example, solo offending participations were predominant at even the youngest recorded ages for the United States and England, and from the mid-teens onwards in Canada (Carrington and van Mastrigt 2013, Figure 1). Further, only 16 to 25 percent of incidents in which the offenders were exclusively under 18 years of age were co-offenses, leading the authors to conclude that "the majority of crimes, even youth crimes, are *not* co-offenses in any of these three countries" (p. 135). The reasons for the varied prevalence rates reported by age in the extant literature are somewhat unclear but might have to do with different inclusion requirements applied across studies, ranging from suspicion to conviction, varied crime type profiles, and/or lack of clarity in reporting statistics based on counts of offenders, offense participations, or offenses (van Mastrigt and Farrington 2009; Stolzenberg and D'Alessio 2016). In any case, as Andresen and Felson (2012) have noted, whether or not co-offending is reported to be the norm at any given age, all existing research agrees that on the whole it is more common among younger as compared to older offenders.

As scholars sensitive to the developmental and life-course approach have argued, however, "aggregate indicators of co-offending over time can be analytically insensitive and misleading since they mask unique and varying developmental trajectories" (McGloin et al. 2008, p. 177). From a criminal career perspective, the real question of interest is what drives the aggregate age co-offending curve at the individual level. Does the familiar shape of the age–co-offending curve reflect changes in the population of offenders—that is, selective early desistance of individuals who co-offend—or within-individual shifts from predominately co-offending at younger ages to lone offending later in the criminal career?

Moffitt's (1993) theory would predict the former, as adolescence-limited offenders, who primarily engage in group crime, tend to selectively desist around the same time that the drop in the aggregate age–co-offending curve is observed. Other developmental and functional accounts of co-offending would likely support the latter hypothesis on the basis that changing patterns of social relations with age (i.e., decreased normative influence and time spent with peers) and/or the accumulation of criminal confidence and capital over time may limit the availability and advantages of joining with accomplices, and thereby increase the individual likelihood of lone offending with age (Tremblay 1993; Warr 2002; Weerman 2003). Current evidence suggests that a combination of selective desistance and within-individual change likely underpins the aggregate age–co-offending curve. In the Cambridge Study, Reiss and Farrington (1991) observed a strong negative correlation between co-offending and age for even the most chronic offenders, leading them to conclude that the observed decline in co-offending with age was due to a developmental process that was "not caused by the persistence of solo offenders and/or the dropping out of co-offenders, but instead . . . changes within individual criminal careers" (p. 382; Piquero, Farrington, and Blumstein 2007). However, a recent trajectory analysis of juvenile co-offending careers in Philadelphia (McGloin et al. 2008) revealed that only half of the juveniles who demonstrated a pattern of decreasing co-offending in late adolescence shifted their criminal careers toward solo offending, while the other half desisted (a few atypical offenders also exhibited a pattern of increased co-offending behavior over time). Similarly complex findings were observed in Carrington's (2009) study of the development of 55,000 delinquent careers in Canada and Lantz and Ruback's (2017) study of 270 adult burglars in Pennsylvania, both of which found offending trajectories with divergent combinations of offending frequency, experience, and age (see Section III). These recent findings, in particular, emphasize the value of exploring the age–co-offending relationship at the within-individual level.

B. Variations in Co-offending Groups with Age

In addition to bringing changes in the prevalence of co-offending, aging also appears to shape the character of offending groups. Although age-graded variations in the nature of co-offending have received far less empirical attention than fluctuations in co-offending rates, a number of studies suggest that, on average, co-offending groups become smaller and more heterogeneous as co-offenders age (Lantz and Ruback 2017).

With respect to size, for example, while most investigations indicate that the vast majority of joint offenses at all ages are committed in pairs—75 percent on average in Carrington and van Mastrigt's 2014 cross-national comparison—offending in collectives of three or more is particularly unusual from late adolescence onward (Reiss and Farrington 1991; Sarnecki 2001, p. 53). Despite being (slightly) larger, youths' offending groups also tend to be more age and sex homogeneous than those of adults. Studies done in England (van Mastrigt and Farrington 2009), Sweden (Sarnecki 2001), and the United States (Warr 1996, 2002) all reveal that as age increases, so do the mean age differences between co-offenders—typically from under a year for the youngest offenders to up to a decade for older offenders. This tendency toward increased age heterophily was explored in more detail in recent studies in Canada and England (van Mastrigt and Carrington 2014; Carrington 2015, 2016). In both studies a tendency toward age homogeneity was found at all ages but, compared to adults, children and young people exhibited significantly greater "inbreeding homophily"—the tendency to offend with accomplices of the same age or age range—even when controlling for chance expectations based on the age distribution of the offending population.

Diversification with age has also been observed with respect to the gender composition of offending groups. In Sarnecki's (2001, p. 54) network study of youth co-offending in Stockholm, most of the over 4,000 suspected co-offending dyads up to age 20 were unisexual (and, in particular, all-male), however, the likelihood of committing crimes with accomplices of the opposite sex was significantly increased for the oldest offenders. Similar evidence emerged in an English study in which adults (≥18) were found to have more than twice the odds of offending in mixed-sex groups as compared to youths (van Mastrigt 2008).

It has been hypothesized that the differences observed in co-offender groupings across age likely reflect the changing constellations of individuals' social networks, routine activities, and the "offender convergence settings" that facilitate co-offender selection at different ages (Reiss and Farrington 1991; Warr 2002; Felson 2003; Andresen and Felson 2010; van Mastrigt and Carrington 2014). However, to the authors' knowledge, this has yet to be explored empirically. Future research would benefit from exploring the changing character of co-offending groups formed at different stages within individual criminal careers and relating this to the changing social contexts in which offenders find themselves across the life course.

C. Implications of the Age–Co-offending Curve

The relationship between age and co-offending is not only of interest to specific discussions regarding the role of joint offending within individual criminal careers, but also has important implications for more general DLC discussions of the age–crime curve. Co-offending could impact the age–crime curve in two ways. First, from the perspective of social influence theory, the curvilinear shape of the age–crime curve could be directly and causally related to the age–co-offending curve (see Section I; Warr 2002). Stolzenberg and D'Alessio (2008, p. 71) refer to this as the companion crime hypothesis, which proposes "that the proportion of co-offending to solo offending is higher among juveniles than adults because of the enhanced salience of peer pressure during adolescence, and that this difference accounts for the age-crime curve." Research conducted by Warr (1993) has provided indirect support for the theory. However, Stolzenberg and D'Alessio's test of this hypothesis using National-Incident-Based-Reporting-System data was not supportive, leading the authors to conclude that co-offending plays an incidental rather than causal role in offending and that "the relationship between age and crime cannot be attributed solely or even in large measure to differential co-offending patterns by age" (2008, p. 74, 2016).

The second way in which co-offending may impact the age–crime curve relates to the arithmetic of co-offending. Typically, plots of the age–crime curve are constructed using statistics on offenders (or, more precisely, offender-offense participations). That is, a single crime involving two individuals is counted twice, once for each offender. Because co-offending is more common during youth, however, this double (or more) counting is not uniform across age. This has important implications for the common conclusion drawn from the standard age–crime curve that offending peaks in the teenage years and that youth are responsible for a disproportionate amount of crime. As a number of scholars have stressed, counts of offenders and counts of offenses do not equate where co-offending is concerned (Reiss and Farrington 1991; McCord and Conway 2005; van Mastrigt and Farrington 2009). The standard age–crime curve is thus best understood as an age–offending curve. In order to draw valid conclusions about the number of crimes committed at different ages, the standard age–crime curve must be adjusted to take account of the average number of co-offenders involved in offenses committed at different ages. When such adjustments are made, it appears that whereas "the number of offenders (based on offense participations) peaks in adolescence, the number of offenses clearly peaks later, in adulthood (van Mastrigt and Farrington 2009, p.574). In correcting their age–crime curve for co-offending in the Cambridge Study, Reiss and Farrington's (1991, p. 372) peak age of offending increased from 17 to 20. A replication of this technique in a later U.K. study using a larger and more inclusive dataset similarly resulted in an upward shift from age 17 to 22, a finding that led the authors to conclude that "the high proportion of crimes so often attributed to teenagers in official statistics is, at least in part, an artefact of co-offending" (van Mastrigt and Farrington 2009, p. 574). Such findings highlight the central importance of considering co-offending when computing and comparing criminal statistics across the life course.

To summarize, while co-offending clearly declines rapidly with age in the aggregate, considerable variations are observed in the age–co-offending curves of individual offenders across the life course. The factors that underlie these individual differences in co-offending trajectories are not yet fully understood.

III. Co-offending and the Criminal Career

Although longitudinal studies of co-offending are relatively rare, a small body of research has identified within-individual relationships between co-offending and a number of other parameters of the criminal career, including the onset of offending, specialization and versatility in offending and co-offending, the seriousness of offending, and offender activity (that is, the total number of offenses in the career). These are reviewed below.

A. The Onset of Offending

Most of the scant research on the role of co-offending in the onset of the criminal career falls into one of two categories: specific explorations of "recruitment" into a criminal career by more experienced co-offenders, and more broad assessments of the prevalence and impacts of general co-offending in the first offense.

The notion that criminal careers (may) begin when neophytes are inducted into crime by older, more experienced offenders has a long history, beginning with Shaw (1931; Shaw and McKay 1931, p. 204), and Sutherland (1937, 1947). However, onset was first explicitly linked to co-offending by Reiss, who distinguished between (1) recruitment "into a [criminal] group, either to a loose affiliation with an informal group or, in the limiting case, to a structured position in an organized criminal syndicate" and (2) "recruiting accomplices in crimes" (1988, p. 143), pointing out that accomplices (i.e., co-offenders) do not necessarily come from the same criminal group, or indeed from any criminal group. Empirical literature on the phenomenon of criminal recruiting—and the closely related concepts of mentoring or tutelage—has subsequently developed, but it is mainly directed to the first type of recruitment identified by Reiss—initiation into a criminal group or lifestyle.[1] However, it is primarily the second type of recruitment—in which a criminal neophyte begins a criminal career as a result of being recruited as a co-offender in a specific crime—that is relevant to this review.[2] To date, analyses of this type of recruitment have been almost exclusively based on official records of co-offending, which raise serious problems in identifying the "true" onset of the criminal career and in operationalizing the theoretical concepts associated with recruitment.[3]

Despite these limitations, a number of studies seem to support the existence of at least some recruiters and recruitment. In the Cambridge study sample of 153 convicted offenders in London, England, Reiss and Farrington (1991, pp. 384–385) identified six (3.9 percent of offenders) recruiters, on the basis of their persistent offending, multiplicity of co-offenders, and the relative lack of criminal experience of most of their co-offenders. These six recruiters were tied to a remarkable 68 percent of the 51 co-offenders in the study who were recorded for their first offense (typically a burglary or motor vehicle theft). Beyond playing a potential role in onset, however, they found "no relationship" between co-offending with a more experienced offender at the first (recorded) offense and the frequency of offending in the subsequent criminal career (1991, p. 381). Other research suggests that offending with more experienced co-offenders at onset may, however, impact the character of one's future offending. Conway and McCord (2002) analyzed arrest records from 1976 to 1994 of 235 juvenile offenders in Philadelphia and their co-offenders. They found that juveniles whose first recorded offense was a co-offense with a previously violent offender had a higher probability of future violent offending, even if their first offense itself was not violent, a finding the authors attributed to some form of social learning.

Other evidence for recruitment comes from Sarnecki's Swedish study in which "just under 5 percent" (2001, p. 64) of the suspected co-offending pairs recorded by police in Stockholm in 1995 consisted of one experienced offender with at least four offenses and one with no previous (recorded) delinquency. Using two variants of Reiss and Farrington's (1991) operationalization, van Mastrigt and Farrington (2011, p. 349) also identified a small number of recruiters in their study (less than 1 percent of the offending population), based on approximately 62,000 offenders recorded by a large British police force in 2002–2005. As in the Cambridge Study, motor vehicle theft and burglary featured prominently among these recruiters' offenses (p. 343). In sum, while there appears to be consistent evidence for occasional "recruitment" into offending careers by more experienced co-offenders, it is unlikely that this plays a role in offending onset for most individuals and perhaps only for some offending types (see also Englefield and Ariel 2017).

In addition to analyses targeting recruitment specifically, there have also been a limited number of investigations exploring the general prevalence of co-offending at onset and the impacts of early co-offending for later development of the criminal career. For example, in the Cambridge study, Reiss and Farrington compared rates of co-offending at first and later offenses and found that "first offenses were only slightly more likely to involve co-offenders than the remaining offenses" and that the incidence of co-offending was fairly constant from the first to the eighth offense in the career, then decreased. Furthermore, co-offending did not predict subsequent recidivism (1991, pp. 376–378).

In another study, Carrington (2009) analyzed the police-reported delinquent careers of approximately 55,000 Canadian young offenders born in 1995, using multivariate analyses to disentangle the relationships of co-offending with the offender's age, criminal experience, and total criminal activity. He found that the prevalence of co-offending was highest at the (recorded) onset of the criminal career (55 percent of participations). However, co-offending was slightly higher at the onset of "low-activity" careers (with 7 or fewer recorded offenses) than at the onset of "high-activity" careers (with 8 or more recorded offenses) (Carrington 2009, Figure 8), suggesting that "co-offending *may* be a mechanism through which [low activity offenders] are inducted into delinquency, and by which their delinquent career is nurtured in its early stages" (2009, p. 1321; emphasis added). In contrast, Lantz and Ruback (2017) found that co-offenders tended to be of similar age and experience, suggesting that there was little mentorship in their sample of adult burglars.

As noted above, exclusive reliance on official records may be problematic in attempts to assess offending onset. It is therefore important to also consider findings from self-report studies. Here, too, evidence for co-offending (and possibly also recruitment) at onset is found. Mullins and Wright interviewed a snowball sample of 54 "active residential burglars . . . recruited in the early 1990s on the streets of St. Louis, Missouri" (2003, p. 817). They found that "with few exceptions, [the respondents] committed their first burglary with older friends, family members, or street associates" and that "many of the women said they were coerced by a boyfriend into their first, and sometimes their subsequent, residential burglaries" (2003, pp. 819–820). In another study, Mullins and Cherbonneau interviewed a purposive, snowball sample of 35 active motor vehicle thieves in St. Louis, Missouri, in 2006–2007; 32 of the 35 reported having experienced "a period of learning how to steal a car," and approximately half of the sample reported that their first theft offense consisted of acting as a lookout for an older co-offender who performed the actual theft (2011, p. 286).

In the only study of co-offending and career onset known to the authors that studied both recorded and self-reported onset, Eynon and Reckless (1961) analyzed official offending records and interviews with all 363 white inmates admitted for the first time to a juvenile prison in Ohio in 1958. Seventy-five percent of the sample had "companions" at their first recorded offense; companions were present at between 56 percent (for "run away from home") and 100 percent (for "gang fight") of their first self-reported "delinquent behaviors" (Eynon and Reckless 1961, Tables 2, 4). However, it is not possible to determine from the reported results whether the "companions" were co-offenders, or whether the prevalence of "companions" at onset was higher or lower than at subsequent offenses (if there were any), or whether recruitment or initiation was involved.

In summary, although substantial proportions of offenders report the influence of mentors and/or co-offenders at the onset and in the early stages of their criminal career, it has proved very difficult to quantify the prevalence of co-offending and recruitment at onset, as well as their respective impacts on subsequent criminal careers. Studies relying on interviews with offenders are marred by small, non-representative samples, possible recall error, and the near-impossibility of quantifying the impact of mentors with qualitative data. On the other hand, studies relying on official co-offending data are unable to identify the (real) onset of the criminal career, which is often known to be well before "official" onset, and have had serious difficulty operationalizing the processes of recruitment. Mixed-method studies on the role of co-offending and recruitment in the onset and continuation of criminal careers should be a priority for future work.

B. Specialization and Versatility

Co-offending can be related to offending specialization and versatility in two ways. First, offenders may demonstrate varied levels of specialization in a particular form of offending (joint or lone) across the criminal career. In 1988, Reiss proposed a tripartite typology of co-offending careers: exclusively lone careers in which individuals only offend alone, exclusively co-offending careers in which all offenses are committed with others, and mixed careers. Although a number of subsequent empirical studies have confirmed the existence of these three basic co-offending subgroups (Reiss and Farrington 1991; Warr 1996; Sarnecki 2001), recent work suggests that reliance on this static and aggregated categorization may fail to capture important time-varying patterns of co-offending across the criminal career.

It is clear that when followed over a sufficient period of time, "the typical criminal career is a mix of offenses committed alone and with others" (Reiss 1988, p. 117) and that few offenders specialize exclusively in one form or the other. However, against this backdrop of versatility, most offenders nonetheless exhibit "a style of offending" (i.e., predominantly group or lone) over time (Reiss and Farrington 1991, p. 381; Warr 1996, p. 22; Weerman 2003). In the most comprehensive study to explore co-offending specialization to date, McGloin and colleagues found evidence for both consistency and versatility in a sample of juvenile offending careers in Philadelphia, such that "some classes [of offenders] contain relatively high-rate co-offenders . . . whereas others comprise relatively low-rate co-offenders" (2008, p. 174). Still others exhibited a high degree of versatility in their co-offending behavior, with some increasing and others decreasing their co-offending activity over time (see also Goldweber et al. 2011). Attempts to explore whether similar patterns persist into adulthood would be welcome. A challenge in further developing and testing these typologies, however, is that relatively detailed data and long follow-up periods are needed to detect patterns of increasing and decreasing co-offending over time and to relate these changes to other relevant features of the criminal career including the accumulation of criminal experience and changes in crime types.

The second, related, way that co-offending is connected to offending versatility is with respect to its potential to promote or reduce specialization in particular offense types over the course of the criminal career. Two conflicting theoretical hypotheses regarding the relationship between co-offending and offense type specialization can be advanced. On the one hand, the functional theory's suggestion that co-offending is more advantageous for particular types of crimes would lead to an expectation that offenders with predominantly or exclusively co-offending careers would primarily commit the types of offenses most likely to benefit from joint participation. According to this logic, a chronic burglar would be more likely to demonstrate an exclusively (or primarily) co-offending career as compared to a repeat sexual offender, who might be more likely to demonstrate an exclusively lone offending style.

On the other hand, theories that highlight the role of co-offending for the accumulation and exchange of criminal capital would suggest that criminal cooperation should expand individuals' criminal awareness, skills, and networks, thereby presenting opportunities for greater versatility in offending. While empirical evidence on this topic is scant, some support for the latter hypothesis is found in recent longitudinal research suggesting that American juveniles embedded in larger, non-redundant co-offending networks exhibit more versatile offending careers as compared to solo offenders (McGloin and Piquero 2009) and in aggregated official crime patterns in British Columbia, Canada, showing that the distribution of co-offending is more varied across crime type than solo offending (Andresen and Felson 2012).

What remains to be shown, however, is whether periods marked by relative specialization in a particular offending style (lone or co-offending) align with periods characterized by greater degrees of offense type versatility/specialization within individual criminal careers. This is an empirical question for future research. As Grund and Moreslli (2017) have recently illustrated, widening the scope of such research to also explore the stability and specialization of specific dyadic co-offending ties over time and across crime types, may additionally prove valuable in identifying distinctive trajectories for co-offending relationships.

C. The Seriousness of Offending

The relationship between co-offending and the seriousness of offending is not straightforward. Co-offending is more prevalent than solo offending in some serious offenses like robbery, burglary, arson, and motor vehicle theft but relatively rare in other serious offenses such as aggravated assault and sexual assault. At the same time, it is also relatively prevalent in a range of less serious offenses like minor theft, possession of stolen property, property damage (vandalism), drug-related offenses, and gambling (Reiss 1988; Reiss and Farrington 1991; Carrington 2002; van Mastrigt and Farrington 2009; Carrington et al. 2013; Carrington and van Mastrigt 2013).

In general, however, research suggests that co-offenses tend to be more serious than solo offenses (Erickson 1973; Conway and McCord 2002; Felson 2003; Porter and Alison 2006; Bijleveld et al. 2007; Carrington et al. 2013). Carrington (2002; Carrington et al. 2013) found that co-offenses in Canada were more likely than solo offenses to involve a firearm or other weapon and to result in injury or death to a victim. They were also more likely to be classified by police as a hate crime and have a higher average "seriousness weight," based on judges' sentencing decisions (Carrington et al. 2013, pp. 19–20). McGloin and Piquero (2009, p. 347) similarly demonstrated a relationship between violence and the presence of co-offenders in a youthful American sample, noting that "the likelihood of a co-offense being violent increased with each additional accomplice present, independent of whether these co-offenders had a history of prior violence." Even within specific crime types, studies suggest that group offenses are more serious. In a pair of recent studies examining group and solo robberies in the United States, the use of weapons, levels of violence, and property yields were all increased for group crimes in one or both samples (Alarid, Hochstetler, and Burton 2009; Tillyer and Tillyer 2014). Well-established social psychological tendencies toward social amplification, diffusion of responsibility, and deindividuation in groups might explain these results (see Moffitt et al. 2001; McGloin and Piquero 2009). However, all of the findings reported above are based on aggregated analyses of offenses; it would be valuable to disentangle selection and influence effects by exploring how the seriousness of individual offenders' crimes vary for lone and co-offenses within criminal careers.

D. Frequency, Duration, Persistence, and Desistance in Offending

Theoretical work on the relationship between co-offending and the duration and ac-tivity (number of offenses) in the criminal career has stated, or implied, conflicting hypotheses. According to Moffitt's (1993, p. 688) typology, adolescence-limited (AL) offenders "need support for crime," whereas life-course–persistent (LCP) offenders "are willing to offend alone." Consequently, one would expect an inverse relationship between co-offending and criminal career length: those with short careers should have a high proportion of co-offenses in their careers, and vice versa for those with long careers. On the other hand, as noted above, co-offenders are thought to provide access to the diverse criminal contacts, information, and opportunities that should result in a longer, more active criminal career (Andresen and Felson 2010; McGloin and Nguyen 2012; van Mastrigt 2014). Reiss's review advanced both (contradictory) hypotheses. He proposed that "a substantial proportion of very young delinquents who have short careers offend only with others" (1988, p. 151), that is, a negative relationship between co-offending and career length, but also that "high-rate" offenders tend also to have high rates of co-offending (1988, p. 148), that is, a positive relationship. Furthermore, he suggested that high-rate offenders "are not precluded from also committing some siz-able proportion of offenses alone" (1988, p. 149), that is, a negative relationship between co-offending and career length.

Empirical research on the topic has also produced mixed and conflicting results, probably due in part to the use of widely varied samples and outcome measures. Co-offending was found to be associated with an increase in career length ("persistence") by Conway and McCord (2002) and co-offending in larger groups was associated with "increased criminal careers" in a recent sample of adult burglars (Lantz and Hutchison 2015, p. 682). However, Knight and West (1975) found that co-offending was associated with "temporary" delinquency (i.e., a short criminal career, similar to Moffitt's (1993) AL offender); van Mastrigt (2008) found a negative relationship between career ac-tivity (number of offenses) and a measure of co-offending (the mean number of co-offenders in each offense); and McGloin and Piquero (2009) found that predominantly solo offenders tended to desist later (i.e., have longer careers) than predominantly co-offenders. In addition, Metcalfe and Baker (2014, p. 75) found a relationship between co-offending and intermittency, such that among offenders who committed a mix of lone and solo offenses, "an immediately prior co-offense was related to a significantly lower risk of re-offending (longer time between offenses)." Finally, Reiss and Farrington (1991) and McGloin and Stickle (2011) found no relationship between co-offending and career activity.

The problem, as Reiss (1988) pointed out, is that career activity (the total number of offenses in the career), criminal experience (the number of past offenses at a given point in the career), and the offender's age may all affect the probability of co-offending (or be affected by prior co-offending, in the first two instances), but their effects are interrelated. Carrington's (2009) study of a large population of juvenile offenders (aged 5 to 17) attempted to disentangle these interrelationships. He found four distinct trajectories of offending: "low-activity" (one to seven recorded offenses in the career) and "high-activity" (8 or more recorded offenses) aged 5 to 11 years, and low- and high-activity 12- to 17-year-olds. For low-activity 12- to 17-year-olds (73 percent of the population of offenders) and both types of 5- to 11-year-olds (8 percent of the population), co-offending and career activity are negatively related, but for high-activity 12- to 17-year-olds (20 percent of the population), co-offending and career activity are positively associated, but only weakly (2009, Table 2).

Another problem with assessing relationships between co-offending and career duration and activity is that most of the existing research has relied on data on official, recorded contacts with police (arrests, apprehensions, charges) or courts (convictions). However, the number of official contacts is a reliable estimate (albeit an underestimate) of the number of actual offenses only if all offenses and offenders have an equal probability of resulting in an official contact, which is patently untrue. For research on the relationship between co-offending and career activity and duration, the salient issue is whether a co-offender and a solo offender have the same probability of being recorded in official data, all other things being equal. Erickson (1973, p. 128) proposed and found supporting evidence for the "group hazard" hypothesis—that "violating the law in groups increases the likelihood of official detection and reaction (e.g., apprehension, arrest, court appearances, and so on)." Although van Mastrigt's 2008 review (pp. 244–245) concluded that the weight of the relevant evidence at the time did not support the hypothesis, more recent research (Ouellet et al. 2013) has found support for the group hazard hypothesis, again raising questions regarding use of official contact data to study the relationship between co-offending and career activity and duration. Analyses of alternative data sources may be particularly important in clarifying these relationships, as "research based on official data will classify 'desisters' and successful recidivists in the same category of offenders: those who are not re-arrested" (Ouellet et al. 2013, p. 149).

Another metric of criminal career success that may be related to co-offending, but has only recently been explored in this context, is illegal earnings. Using data from the Pathways to Desistance study, Rowan and colleagues (2018) found that both current and historical co-offending predicts non-zero criminal earnings, but not the amount of criminal earnings. These mixed findings, together with those noted above, point to the need for additional work exploring the complex relationships between co-offending and multiple measures of criminal career activity, duration, and success.

IV. Outstanding Issues

To date, the slow progress in integrating co-offending and developmental and life-course perspectives has largely been due to a lack of longitudinal and linkable co-offending data. As awareness of the importance of co-offending for criminal careers increases and as samples from an increasing number of DLC studies mature, developments in this area are likely to accelerate. At present, however, there are many aspects of co-offending and its implications for DLC criminology that are poorly understood. Throughout this chapter a number of specific avenues for future research have been identified in the areas where co-offending and DLC studies have already begun to converge. However, there are many other co-offending and DLC topics that have yet to be linked.

For example, a number of criminal career parameters including early/late age of onset and acceleration/escalation have yet to be explicitly and empirically associated to co-offending patterns. Knowledge regarding developmental risk/protective factors for co-offending is also lacking. In fact, as van Mastrigt (2014) has noted, relatively little is known about how variations in the tendency to co-offend relate to family risk factors and other individual differences, such as personality (for a recent contribution, see Goldweber et al. 2011). Another outstanding DLC issue that requires further empirical clarification is whether changes in one's co-offending network (including the arrest or victimization of one's accomplices) may act as a turning point promoting desistance and, if so, how this process can be harnessed to encourage individual change (Reiss 1988; Ouellet et al. 2013; Charette and Papachristos 2017).

Underlying all of these issues is the need for more explicit integration of co-offending and developmental and life-course theories. A comprehensive DLC theory of crime must account for the fact that many offenses are committed in groups and should further be able to explain the developmental relationships outlined above. Similarly, a convincing theory of co-offending must embrace the variations observed in criminal cooperation across the life course and within individual criminal careers.

Notes

1. Morselli, Tremblay, and McCarthy (2006) provide a comprehensive bibliography of earlier life-history accounts of criminal mentoring.
2. Research on the related phenomenon of leadership in, or the instigation of, individual crimes (Hochstetler 2001; McGloin and Nguyen 2012; Reiss 1988; Warr 1996) is not reviewed

here, because instigation refers not to the onset of the criminal career but to crimes that may occur at any point in the leader's (i.e., instigator's) or followers' criminal careers.

3. For example, official records do not allow for an assessment of the extent to which more experienced offenders seek out novice accomplices or vice versa.

REFERENCES

Alarid, Leanne. F., Andy L. Hochstetler, and Velmer S. Burton. 2009. "Group and Solo Robberies: Do Accomplices Shape Criminal Form?" *Journal of Criminal Justice* 37: 1–9.

Andresen, Martin A., and Marcus Felson. 2010. "The Impact of Co-offending." *British Journal of Criminology* 50(1): 66–81.

Andresen, Martin A., and Marcus Felson. 2012. "Co-offending and the Diversification of Crime Types." *International Journal of Offender Therapy and Comparative Criminology* 56(5): 811–829.

Bijleveld, Catrien C. J. H., Frank M. Weerman, Daphne Looije, and Jan Hendriks. 2007. "Group Sex Offending by Juveniles." *European Journal of Criminology* 4(1): 5–31.

Breckinridge, Sophonisba P., and Edith Abbott. (1917). *The Delinquent Child and the Home.* New York: Arno Press.

Carrington, Peter J. 2002. "Group Crime in Canada." *Canadian Journal of Criminology* 44(3): 277–315.

Carrington, Peter J. 2009. "Co-offending and the Development of the Delinquent Career." *Criminology* 47(4): 1295–1329.

Carrington, Peter J. 2014. "Co-offending." In *Encyclopedia of Criminology and Criminal Justice*, edited by Gerben Bruinsma and David Weisburd, 548–558. New York: Springer-Verlag.

Carrington, Peter J. 2015. "The Structure of Age Homophily in Co-offending Groups." *Journal of Contemporary Criminal Justice* 31(3): 337–353.

Carrington, Peter J. 2016. "Gender and Age Segregation and Stratification in Criminal Collaborations." *Journal of Quantitative Criminology* 32(4): 613–649.

Carrington, Peter J., Shannon Brennan, Anthony Matarazzo, and Marian Radulescu. 2013. "Co-offending in Canada, 2011." *Juristat.* Ottawa: Canadian Centre for Justice Statistics, Statistics Canada.

Carrington, Peter J., and Sarah B. van Mastrigt. 2013. "Co-offending in Canada, England and the United States: A Cross-National Comparison." *Global Crime* 14(2–3): 123–140.

Charette, Yanick, and Andrew V. Papachristos. 2017. "The Network Dynamics of Co-offending Careers." *Social Networks* 51: 3–13.

Conway, Kevin P., and Joan McCord. 2002. "A Longitudinal Examination of the Relation Between Co-Offending with Violent Accomplices and Violent Crime." *Aggressive Behavior* 28(2): 97–108.

D'Alessio, Stewart J., and Lisa Stolzenberg. 2010. "Do Cities Influence Co-offending?" *Journal of Criminal Justice* 38(4): 711–719.

DeLisi, Matt, and Alex R. Piquero. 2011. "New Frontiers in Criminal Careers Research, 2000–2011: A State-of-the-Art Review." *Journal of Criminal Justice* 39(4): 289–301.

Elder, Glen H., Jr., Monica K. Johnson, and Robert Crosnoe. 2003. "The Emergence and Development of Life Course Theory." In *Handbook of the Life Course*, edited by Jeylan T. Mortimer and Michael J. Shanahan, 3–19. New York: Springer.

Englefield, Ashley, and Barack Ariel. 2017. "Searching for Influential Actors in Co-offending Networks: The Recruiter." *International Journal of Social Science Studies* 5(5): 24–45.

Erickson, Maynard L. 1971. "The Group Context of Delinquency." *Social Problems* 19: 114–129.

Erickson, Maynard L. 1973. "Group Violations and Official Delinquency. The Group Hazard Hypothesis." *Criminology* 11(2): 127–160.

Eynon, Thomas G., and Walter C. Reckless. 1961. "Companionship at Delinquency Onset." *British Journal of Criminology* 2: 162–170.

Farrington, David P. 2005. *Integrated Developmental and Life Course Theories of Offending.* New Brunswick, NJ: Transaction.

Felson, Marcus. 2003. "The Process of Co-offending." In *Theory for Practice in Situational Crime Prevention*, edited by Martha J. Smith and Derek B. Cornish, 149–168. Monsey, NY: Criminal Justice Press.

Goldweber, Asha, Julia Dmitrieva, Elizabeth Cauffman, Alex R. Piquero, and Laurence Steinberg. 2011. "The Development of Criminal Style in Adolescence and Young Adulthood: Separating the Lemmings from the Loners." *Journal of Youth and Adolescence* 40(3): 332–346.

Grund, Thomas, and Carlo Morselli. 2017. "Overlapping Crime: Stability and Specialization of Co-offending Relationships." *Social Networks* 51: 14–22.

Hochstetler, Andrew L. 2001. "Opportunities and Decisions: Interactional Dynamics in Robbery and Burglary Groups." *Criminology* 39(3): 737–763.

Knight, Barry J., and Donald J. West. 1975. "Temporary and Continuing Delinquency." *British Journal of Criminology* 15: 43–50.

Lantz, Brendan, and Robert Hutchison. 2015. "Co-offender Ties and the Criminal Career: The Relationship Between Co-offender Group Structure and the Individual Offender." *Journal of Research in Crime and Delinquency* 52(5): 658–690.

Lantz, Brendan, and R. Barry Ruback. 2017. "The Relationship Between Co-offending, Age, and Experience Using a Sample of Adult Burglary Offenders." *Journal of Developmental and Life Course Criminology* 3(1): 76–97.

Le Blanc, Marc, and Marcel Fréchette. 1989. *Male Criminal Activity from Childhood Through Youth: Multilevel and Developmental Perspectives.* New York: Springer-Verlag.

McCarthy, Bill, and John Hagan. 1995. "Getting into Street Crime—The Structure and Process of Criminal Embeddedness." *Social Science Research* 24(1): 63–95.

McCord, Jean, and Peter K. Conway. 2002. "Patterns of Juvenile Delinquency and Co-offending." In *Crime and Social Organization*, edited by Elin J. Waring and David Weisburd, 15–30. New Brunswick, NJ: Transaction.

McCord, Jean, and Peter K. Conway. 2005. *Co-offending and Patterns of Juvenile Justice.* Research in Brief NCJ 210360. Washington, DC: National Institute of Justice.

McGloin, Jean M., and Holly Nguyen. 2012. "It Was My Idea: Considering the Instigation of Co-offending." *Criminology* 50(2): 463–494.

McGloin, Jean M., and Alex R. Piquero. 2009. "'I Wasn't Alone': Collective Behaviour and Violent Delinquency." *Australian and New Zealand Journal of Criminology* 42(3): 336–353.

McGloin, Jean M., and Wendy P. Stickle. 2011. "Influence or Convenience? Disentangling Peer influence and Co-offending for Chronic Offenders." *Journal of Research in Crime and Delinquency* 48(3): 419–447.

McGloin, Jean M., Christopher J. Sullivan, Alex R. Piquero, and Sarah Bacon. 2008. "Investigating the Stability of Co-offending and Co-offenders Among a Sample of Youthful Offenders." *Criminology* 46: 155–188.

Metcalfe, Christi Falco, and Thomas Baker. (2014). "The Drift from Convention to Crime: Exploring the Relationship Between Co-offending and Intermittency. *Criminal Justice and Behavior* 41(1): 75–90.

Moffitt, Terrie E. 1993. "Adolescence-Limited and Life-Course Persistent Antisocial Behavior: A Developmental Taxonomy." *Psychological Review* 100: 674–701.

Moffitt, Terrie E., Avshalom Caspi, Michael Rutter, and Phil A. Silva. 2001. *Sex Differences in Antisocial Behaviour: Conduct Disorder, Delinquency, and Violence in the Dunedin Longitudinal Study.* Cambridge, UK: Cambridge University Press.

Morselli, Carlo, Pierre Tremblay, and Bill McCarthy. 2006. "Mentors and Criminal Achievement." *Criminology* 44(1): 17–43.

Mullins, Christopher W., and Michael G Cherbonneau. 2011. "Establishing Connections: Gender, Motor Vehicle Theft, and Disposal Networks." *Justice Quarterly* 28(2): 278–302.

Mullins, Christopher W., and Richard Wright. 2003. "Gender, Social Networks, and Residential Burglary." *Criminology* 41(3): 813–840.

Nguyen, Holly, and Jean M. McGloin. 2013. "Does Economic Adversity Breed Criminal Cooperation? Considering the Motivation Behind Group Crime." *Criminology* 51: 833–870.

Ouellet, Frédéric, Rémi Boivin, Chloé Leclerc, and Carlo Morselli. 2013. "Friends With(out) Benefits: Co-offending and Re-arrest." *Global Crime* 14(2–3): 141–154.

Piquero, Alex R., David P. Farrington, and Alfred Blumstein. 2003. "The Criminal Career Paradigm." *Crime and Justice* 30: 359–506.

Piquero, Alex R., David P. Farrington, and Alfred Blumstein. 2007. *Key Issues in Criminal Career Research. New Analyses of the Cambridge Study in Delinquent Development.* Cambridge, UK: Cambridge University Press.

Piquero, Alex R., and Terri E. Moffitt. 2005. "Explaining the Facts of Crime: How the Developmental Taxonomy Replies to Farrington's Invitation." In *Integrated Developmental and Life Course Theories of Offending,* edited by David P. Farrington, 51–72. New Brunswick, NJ: Transaction.

Porter, Louise E., and Laurence J. Alison. 2006. "Behavioural Coherence in Group Robbery: A Circumplex Model of Offender and Victim Interactions." *Aggressive Behavior* 32(4): 330–342.

Reiss, Albert J. 1986. "Co-offender Influences on Criminal Careers." In *Criminal Careers and Career Criminals,* edited by Alfred Blumstein, Jacqueline Cohen, Jeffrey A. Rother, and Christy A. Visher, 121–160. Washington, DC: National Academy Press.

Reiss, Albert J. 1988. "Co-offending and Criminal Careers." *Crime and Justice* 10: 117–170.

Reiss, Albert J., and David P. Farrington. 1991. "Advancing Knowledge About Co-offending—Results from a Prospective Longitudinal Survey of London Males." *Journal of Criminal Law and Criminology* 82(2): 360–395.

Rowan, Zachary, R., Jean Marie McGloin, and Holly Nguyen. 2018. "Capitalizing on Criminal Accomplices: Considering the Relationship Between Co-offending and Illegal Earnings." *Justice Quarterly* 35(2): 280–308.

Sarnecki, Jerzy. 2001. *Delinquent Networks: Youth Co-Offending in Stockholm.* Cambridge, UK: Cambridge University Press.

Schaefer, David R. 2012. "Youth Co-offending Networks: An Investigation of Social and Spatial Effects." *Social Networks* 34(1): 141–149.

Schaefer, David R., Nancy Rodriguez, and Scott H. Decker. 2014. "The Role of Neighborhood Context in Youth Co-offending." *Criminology* 52(1): 117–139.

Shaw, Clifford R. 1931. *The Natural History of a Delinquent Career*. Chicago: University of Chicago Press.

Shaw, Clifford R., and Henry D. McKay. 1931. *Report on the Causes of Crime, Volume II*. Washington, DC: U.S. Government Printing Office.

Stolzenberg, Lisa, and Stewart J. D'Alessio. 2008. "Co-offending and the Age-Crime Curve." *Journal of Research in Crime and Delinquency* 45(1): 65–86.

Stolzenberg, Lisa, and Stewart J. D'Alessio. 2016. "A Commentary on Zimring and Laqueur (2015): Juveniles and Co-offending and Why the Conventional Wisdom Is Wrong" *Journal of Crime and Justice* 39(4): 550–555.

Sutherland, Edwin H. 1937. *The Professional Thief: By a Professional Thief*. Chicago: University of Chicago Press.

Sutherland, Edwin H. 1947. *Principles of Criminology*. 4th ed. Chicago: Lippincott.

Tillyer, Marie Shubak, and Rob Tillyer. 2014. "Maybe I Should Do This Alone: A Comparison of Solo and Co-offending Robbery Outcomes." *Justice Quarterly* 32(6): 1064–1088.

Tremblay, Pierre. 1993. "Searching for Suitable Co-offenders." In *Routine Activity and Rational Choice*, edited by Ronald V. Clarke and Marcus Felson, 17–36. New Brunswick, NJ: Transaction.

van Mastrigt, Sarah B. 2008. *Co-offending: Relationships with Age, Gender and Crime Type*. PhD dissertation, University of Cambridge, Cambridge, UK.

van Mastrigt, Sarah B. 2014. "Co-offending and Offender Attributes." In *Encyclopedia of Criminology and Criminal Justice*, edited by Gerben Bruinsma and David Weisburd, 559–570. New York: Springer-Verlag.

van Mastrigt, Sarah B. 2017. "Co-offending and Offender Decision Making" In *Oxford Handbook of Offender Decision Making*, edited by Wim Bernasco, Henk Elffers, and Jean-Louise van Gelder, 338–360. Oxford: Oxford University Press.

van Mastrigt Sarah B. and Peter J. Carrington. 2014. "Sex and Age Homophily in Co-offending Networks: Opportunity or Preference?" In *Crime and Networks*, edited by Carlo Morselli, 28–51. New York: Routledge.

van Mastrigt, Sarah B., and David P. Farrington. 2009. "Co-offending, Age, Gender and Crime type: Implications for Criminal Justice Policy." *British Journal of Criminology* 49(4): 552–573.

van Mastrigt, Sarah B., and David P. Farrington. 2011. "Prevalence and Characteristics of Co-offending Recruiters." *Justice Quarterly* 28(2): 325–359.

Warr, Mark. 1993. "Age, Peers, and Delinquency." *Criminology* 31(1): 17–40.

Warr, Mark. 1996. "Organization and Instigation in Delinquent Groups." *Criminology* 34(1): 11–37.

Warr, Mark. 2002. *Companions in Crime: The Social Aspects of Criminal Conduct*. Cambridge, UK: Cambridge University Press.

Weerman, Frank. 2003. "Co-offending as Social Exchange: Explaining Characteristics of Co-offending." *British Journal of Criminology* 43: 398–416.

Weerman, Frank. 2014. "Theories of Co-offending." In *Encyclopedia of Criminology and Criminal Justice*, edited by Gerben Bruinsma and David Weisburd, 5173–5184. New York: Springer-Verlag.

West, W. Gordon. 1978. "The Short Term Careers of Serious Thieves." *Canadian Journal of Criminology* 20(2): 169–190.

Zimring, Franklin E., and Hannah Laqueur. 2015. "Kids, Groups, and Crime: In Defense of Conventional Wisdom." *Journal of Research in Crime and Delinquency* 52(3): 403–413.

SECTION III

DEVELOPMENTAL AND LIFE-COURSE THEORIES

CHAPTER 9

....

THE DEVELOPMENTAL
TAXONOMY

....

TARA RENAE MCGEE AND TERRIE E. MOFFITT

THE relationship between age and crime was observed in the early 1800s by Quetelet (1833). Since then many researchers studying the relationship between age and crime have observed that the aggregate pattern is such that criminal activity tends to peak in the late teens and declines throughout adulthood. Therefore, age is inversely related to criminality with younger people being more likely to be involved in crime. The observed relationship between age and crime raises, however, the question of whether the peak in the age–crime curve is a function of active offenders committing more crime during adolescence or a function of more individuals actively offending in the peak years?

Moffitt's theory (Moffitt 1993; Moffitt et al. 1996; Moffitt 2006; Moffitt 2018) is an assimilation of two "robust but incongruous facts about age and antisocial behavior" (Moffitt 1994, p. 3). These are that research shows a strong continuity of antisocial behavior over time and that there is a huge peak in delinquency and offending during adolescence. Moffitt considers that these two observations represent two very different groups of people. In the original conceptualization of the taxonomy (Moffitt 1993), the first is a group of people that exhibit a persistence of antisocial behaviors in one way or another at every stage of life, whereas the other is a group of individuals that only exhibit antisocial behaviors temporarily during adolescence. This led to the development of two theoretical explanations to account for continuity and discontinuity of individuals' antisocial behavior: the life-course persistent (LCP) and adolescence-limited (AL) models. The theory fits with Patterson et al. (1989) idea of early and late starters, but it expands considerably on this idea to include groups of those who are never antisocial (abstainers) and those who start out with antisocial behavior in childhood but desist by adolescence (low-level chronic). Given that the model is based on data representative of the general population, it also includes a group of individuals who do not meet the criteria for the other groups (unclassified).

The organization of this chapter is as follows. Sections I to IV include descriptions of some of the main groupings in Moffitt's typology. The two main and most empirically tested typological groupings, the life-course persistent group and the adolescence-limited group, are discussed in Sections I and II, respectively. Section III includes a review of the evidence on a theoretically interesting grouping—those who abstain from antisocial and offending behavior. The debate regarding whether those who were originally thought to recover from early-onset antisocial behavior have childhood-limited antisocial behavior or exhibit low-level chronic antisocial behavior across the life course is the focus of Section IV. Section V discusses how the theory accounts for adult-onset offending, and Section VI considers whether there are gender differences that need to be accounted for by the theory.

I. Life-Course persistent Antisocial Behavior

Life-course persistent (LCP) behavior is characterized by stability and continuity through varying manifestations of antisocial behavior across time, for example, "biting and hitting at four, shoplifting and truancy at ten, selling drugs and stealing cars at 16, robbery and rape at 22, and fraud and child abuse at 30" (Moffitt 1994, p. 12). Moffitt argues that there is also uniformity in the prevalence rates of various expressions of serious antisocial behavior, with many studies showing prevalence at around 5 to 10 percent. Longitudinal research suggests that the small proportion of people exhibiting antisocial behavior at each stage in the life course are actually the same group of life-course persistent people (Moffitt 1994, p.11). The 1993 taxonomy described life-course persistent offenders as those whose crimes persist well past the normative age of desistence, but how far into the life course such offenders continue antisocial activities is unclear. Some studies emphasize capacity for reform in old age (Laub and Sampson 2003), others emphasize antisocial acts by elderly individuals (Blokland, Nagin, and Nieuwbeerta 2005), but data are sparse because few cohorts have been followed beyond mid-life.

The first step in the life-course persistent trajectory, according to Moffitt's theory, is inherited or acquired neuropsychological deficits. Neuropsychological deficits can be acquired via a range of mechanisms including the absence of breastfeeding (Rogan and Gladen 1993; Golding, Rogers, and Emmett 1997; Quinn et al. 2001), pregnancy/birth problems (Arseneault et al. 2002), and maternal smoking (Raine 2002) and alcohol consumption (Streissguth et al. 1989) during pregnancy.

Moffitt cites research demonstrating that even minor neuropsychological deficits can result in a myriad of developmental problems that may contribute to dysfunctional parent–child relationships in even the most loving families (Moffitt 1994, p.15). Neuropsychological damage also leads to poor language development and self-control behaviors, and Moffitt (1994) observes that the link between verbal impairment and antisocial outcomes is one of the largest and most robust effects in the study of antisocial behavior.

It is proposed that children with such deficits induce a series of failed parent–child interactions and that their difficult temperament contributes to a socialization environment that seems to exacerbate their difficulties (Moffitt 1994, p. 20). Over the life course a series of failed interactions leads to a growing repertoire of antisocial behaviors, and as the individual has learned few prosocial behaviors, the options for change are few (Moffitt 1993, p. 683). These individuals are more likely to be rejected by both adults and peers and as a result may withdraw or strike out preemptively, causing further social isolation.

Persistence of this antisocial behavior is perpetuated by the interaction between individuals' traits and the environmental reactions to them. Any opportunities for change in this cycle are often transformed into opportunities for continuity in antisocial behavior. These individuals, whose behavior consists of pathological antisocial behavior across the life course, are quite distinct from those whose behavior is short term and situational (Moffitt 1994, p. 29). It is this phenomenon, with antisocial behavior that is limited predominantly to the teen years, that Moffitt refers to as adolescence-limited antisocial behavior (1993, p. 676).

II. Adolescence-Limited Antisocial Behavior

To demonstrate this short-term antisocial behavior, Moffitt (1993, p. 676) cites English and American research that demonstrates that the huge peak in the rate of offenses in adolescence is due to an increase in prevalence of offenders rather than an increase in the rate of offending. The behavior of adolescents in this category is characterized by discontinuity, having never been antisocial during their childhood and being unlikely to remain antisocial into their adulthood (Moffitt 1993, p. 685). The decreasing age of biological maturity and increasing age of social maturity is responsible for adolescence-limited antisocial behavior.

A "maturity gap" is the result, with adolescents becoming "chronological hostages of a time warp between biological age and social age" (Moffitt 1994, p. 31). Consequently, adolescents trapped in the maturity gap are denied access to mature status, whereas the life-course persistent antisocial adolescents will be perceived as having attained maturity. The life-course persistent individuals will possibly have their own small business in the underground economy, have fathered or mothered children, and appear to be free of their family of origin (Moffitt 1994, p. 28). The mechanism then, through which previously non-antisocial adolescents become antisocial is through a process of social mimicry. The life-course persistent antisocial individuals are viewed by other teens as having access to a precious resource: mature status and the adolescence-limited individuals mimic their behaviors in an attempt to achieve this status.

According to the theory, once adolescence-limited individuals have reached a stage where they can access legitimate forms of responsibility, for example, through marriage or entering the workforce, their antisocial behavior will cease. For them, the cost of antisocial behavior becomes too high and they will revert back to the prosocial behavior skills learned early in life. (Life-course persistent individuals, on the other hand, will use opportunities such as marriage or employment as new opportunities for antisocial behavior.) There is some evidence to suggest that this adolescence-onset group of individuals also has high levels of internalizing problems and life stress that may prevent this (Aguilar et al. 2000). There is a small number of adolescence-limited individuals who became trapped in a snare such as a drug addiction, imprisonment, teenage pregnancy, and/or interrupted education, which increases the likelihood of maintaining antisocial behavior across the life course (Moffitt 1993, p. 61). Empirical testing of this concept has shown that one-third of individuals identified as having an adolescent onset of antisocial behavior persisted with this antisocial behavior as young adults and that this continuity can in part be attributed to experiencing snares (McGee et al. 2015). Moreover, when the taxonomy was written, studied cohorts showed desistence by their early twenties, and thus the group was named "adolescence-limited," but contemporary cohorts are desisting older, possibly because signs of adulthood such as marriage, children, and independent living are now delayed until the thirties.

III. Abstainers

Moffitt (1996) recognizes that these theories of development would seem to indicate that every adolescent will engage in delinquency, and many self-report studies indicate that most adolescents do participate in some delinquent activities (Moffitt et al. 1996, 2001; Prior et al. 2000; Bor, McGee, and Fagan 2004). In spite of this, there are some individuals who refrain from delinquent behavior entirely. These individuals are categorized in Moffitt's typology as abstainers. She proposes that abstaining from antisocial behavior may be a result of pathological characteristics that exclude an individual from peer networks; skipping the maturity gap, through late puberty or early initiation into adult roles; or a lack of opportunities for social mimicry (Moffitt 1993, p. 695). However, analyses of the National Longitudinal Survey of Youth found that the abstainers were not depressed and had prosocial peers (Piquero, Brezina, and Turner 2005). Moffitt and colleagues' (2002) own analyses of the Dunedin data showed that although they were awkward in their teenage years, they grew into successful adults (age 26)—settling into marriage, well educated, with good jobs. Recent research by Mercer and colleagues (2016) somewhat reconciles these disparate findings using data from the Cambridge Study in Delinquent Development. They identified two different types of abstainers: those who are adaptive and characterized by high honesty and those who are maladaptive characterized by low popularity and low school achievement.

IV. Childhood-Limited Aggression or Low-Level Chronic (Formerly Recovery)

Studies that followed participants only through childhood reported that some children with early-onset antisocial behavior seemed to recover, but now that studies have followed cohorts longer, these childhood recoveries can be observed to reappear in offending data as adults. Thus, another group of adolescents embedded in Moffitt's theory (2006) is the low-level chronic group (formerly identified as "recoveries"; Moffitt et al. 1996). This group (and the abstainer group) are of interest because they may hold the key to prevention (Moffitt et al. 1996, p. 402). Those categorized as low-level chronic are the individuals who seem to start on the life-course persistent trajectory during childhood and then by adolescence "have apparently spontaneously recovered" (Moffitt et al. 1996, p. 402). These individuals are not entirely free of conduct disorder in their teens, but they have not followed the predicted outcome. That is, they fail to make the criterion for serious self-reported delinquency and they have not had involvement in the justice system. The original theory offers little explanation of the causes of this outcome, and it is noted that these high-risk individuals need to be further researched to determine why they have outcomes that are less extreme than expected (Moffitt et al. 1996, p. 419).

In Moffitt's (2006) review of her theory, in light of the limited research conducted on the desistence in adolescence from early-onset antisocial behavior (Raine et al. 2005; Moffitt 2006), she argued that the term "recovery" was a misnomer. Instead she noted that those who were initially identified as having recovered actually show a pattern of persistence when examined in adulthood and argues that a more appropriate name for this group is "low-level chronic" (Moffitt 2006). The identification of a group with persistent but lower-level antisocial behavior is consistent with the findings of other studies (Nagin, Farrington, and Moffitt 1995; D'Unger et al. 1998; Fergusson, Horwood, and Nagin 2000). Some research suggests that most individuals first convicted as adults (adult-onset offenders) have childhood histories of antisocial behavior and risk factors characteristic of recoveries/low-level chronics (Beckley et al. 2016).

While Moffitt's reconsideration of her theory suggests that examining those individuals with an early onset of antisocial behavior in hope of finding recovery is futile, it is important to note that even within her data she found some individuals had truly recovered in adulthood (Moffitt 2006). While it was only a small proportion, she found that 15 percent of those in the recovery (low-level chronic) group were free of adjustment problems at age 26 (Moffitt 2006). As Wilson (1991) has highlighted, desisters can be found among even the most troubled youth, and predictors of this process are best studied from conception onward. Indeed, Veenstra and his colleagues (2009) have shown that recovery from antisocial behavior is possible and is accompanied by an absence of academic failure, peer rejection, and internalizing problems.

V. How Does the Theory Account
for Adult-Onset Offending?

Two different explanations of adult-onset offending are embedded within Moffitt's (2006) theory, but it should be noted that these explanations would only apply to adult-onset offending that *was identified using official records*, with the assumption that there was prior offending that for some reason did not come to the attention of the criminal justice system. The first explanation, noted above, is that adult-onset offending could be the result of low-level chronic offending. The low-level chronic group (previously labeled the "recovery" group; Moffitt et al. 1996) includes individuals who are intermittent offenders from childhood through to adulthood (Moffitt 2006). Using official measures of offending, these individuals would be identified as adult-onset offenders if they were first detected by the criminal justice system as adults.

The other individuals who, within this theory, would account for those identified in analyses of official statistics as adult-onset offenders are those individuals who initially are identified as adolescence-limited self-reported offenders but who get caught in a snare (e.g. drug addiction) that prevents them from returning to the previous pro-social behaviors they learned as children (Moffitt 1993). Their ongoing offending would then lead to detection by the criminal justice system in adulthood. Within this perspective, a key question is why the childhood or adolescent offending was not detected or, alternatively, why official adult-onset offenders (who were offending previously) were not detected until adulthood.

Empirical testing has shown that adult-onset offending is sometimes an artifact of official measurement, but that adult onset offenders commit offenses that are less likely to be detected and commit different type of offenses, that require access to adult roles, compared to those who were first detected by the criminal justice system in adolescence (McGee and Farrington 2010). In examining whether a specific theory for adult offending is required, Beckley and colleagues (2016) found that, during adolescence, adult-onset offenders were more socially inhibited and had fewer delinquent peers. Once they reached adulthood, they had weaker social bonds, anticipated fewer informal sanctions, and self-reported more offenses. They conclude that existing developmental and life-course theories of crime adequately account for adult-onset offenders in existing accounts of onset and persistence.

VI. Are There Important
Gender Differences?

The evidence for the applicability of the theory to girls is mixed. Early research examining the pathways of females found support for a delayed adolescent-onset group of females but not the life-course persistent typology (Silverthorn and Frick 1999). One way to em-pirically identify different types of offenders is using latent class trajectory analysis and a review of studies using these analyses show fewer offending trajectories for female compared to samples (Piquero 2008). In contrast to earlier research, when examining females' trajectories of self-reported offending in the Pittsburgh Girls Study, researchers found a small group of high-rate, versatile offending girls who resemble the male group of life-course persistent offenders, but they did not find evidence for the adolescence-limited offenders (Ahonen et al. 2016). While the evidence shows that many of the risk factors for antisocial behavior and offending are similar for both males and females (Moffitt et al. 2001), it is clear that further research is needed on the gendered nature of developmental pathways of antisocial behavior and offending over the life course.

VII. Summary

Moffitt developed her theoretical perspective based on the robust yet incongruous em-pirical facts of the stability of antisocial behavior across the life course and the huge peak in delinquency and offending during adolescence. To explain this, she developed the life-course persistent and adolescence-limited typologies of antisocial behavior. Life-course persistent behavior is characterized by early neuropsychological damage, a his-tory of failed social interactions, and the development of antisocial behavior at an early age. On the other hand, adolescence-limited antisocial behavior is believed to be the result of the maturity gap between biological maturity and social maturity. Adolescents are believed to overcome this maturity gap through mimicry of the behavior of the life-course persistent individual, who is viewed as already having the coveted access to the resources of social maturity.

Moffitt also states that there are individuals who abstain completely from antisocial behavior due to not experiencing the maturity gap through late onset of puberty and early onset of adult roles, possessing pathological characteristics that exclude them from peer networks, and the lack of opportunities for social mimicry. There are also individuals who begin on the life-course persistent trajectory and appear to recover by the time they reach adolescence but go on to have low-level chronic problems. This is an area that needs further research.

Empirical research tends to generally support the typologies proposed in Moffitt's theory (Kratzer and Hodgins 1999; Fergusson, Horwood, and Nagin 2000; Mazerolle et al. 2000; Moffitt et al. 2001). In addition to this, compared to other elements of the theory, very little research has been conducted into the characteristics of those individuals who abstain from antisocial and delinquent behavior and those who exhibit low-level chronic problem behavior. Overall, recent empirical tests of the background factors of both males and females generally support the proposals put forth in 1993 (for a summary see Moffitt 2006, 2018), but future research should examine the differences in gendered pathways of antisocial behavior and offending.

REFERENCES

Aguilar, Benjamin, L. Alan Sroufe, Byron Egeland, and Elizabeth Carlson. 2000. "Distinguishing the Early-Onset/Persistent and Adolescence-Onset Antisocial Behavior Types: From Birth to 16 Years." *Development and Psychopathology* 12: 109–132.

Ahonen, Lia, Wesley G. Jennings, Rolf Loeber, and David P. Farrington. 2016. "The Relationship Between Developmental Trajectories of Girls' Offending and Police Charges: Results from the Pittsburgh Girls Study." *Journal of Developmental and Life-Course Criminology* 2(3): 262–274.

Arseneault, Louise, Richard E. Tremblay, Bernard Boulerice, and Jean-Francois Saucier. 2002. "Obstetrical Complications and Violent Delinquency: Testing Two Developmental Pathways." *Child Development* 73(2): 496–508.

Beckley, Amber L., Avshalom Caspi, Hona Lee Harrington, Renate M. Houts, Tara Renae McGee, Nick Morgan, Felix Schroeder, Sandhya Ramrakha, Richie Poulton, and Terrie E. Moffitt. 2016. "Adult-Onset Offenders: Is a Tailored Theory Warranted?" *Journal of Criminal Justice* 46: 64–81.

Blokland, A. A. J., Daniel S. Nagin, and Paul Nieuwbeerta. 2005. "Life Span Offending Trajectories of a Dutch Conviction Cohort." *Criminology* 43: 919–954.

Bor, William, Tara Renae McGee, and Abigail A. Fagan. 2004. "Early Risk Factors for Adolescent Antisocial Behaviour: An Australian Longitudinal Study." *Australian and New Zealand Journal of Psychiatry* 38: 365–372.

D'Unger, Amy V., Kenneth C. Land, Patricia L. McCall, and Daniel S. Nagin. 1998. "How Many Latent Classes of Delinquent/Criminal Careers?" *American Journal of Sociology* 103: 1593–1630.

Fergusson, David M., L. John Horwood, and Daniel S. Nagin. 2000. "Offending Trajectories in a New Zealand Birth Cohort." *Criminology* 38(2): 525–551.

Golding, Jean, Imogen S. Rogers, and Pauline M. Emmett. 1997. "Association Between Breast Feeding, Child Development and Behavior." *Early Human Development* 49(Suppl.): S175–S184.

Kratzer, Lynn, and Sheilagh Hodgins. 1999. "A Typology of Offenders: A Test of Moffitt's Theory Among Males and Females from Childhood to Age 30." *Criminal Behaviour and Mental Health* 9: 57–73.

Laub, John H., and Robert J. Sampson. 2003. *Shared Beginnings, Divergent Lives: Delinquent Boys to Age 70.* Cambridge, MA: Harvard University Press.

Mazerolle, Paul, Robert Brame, Ray Paternoster, Alex R. Piquero, and Charles Dean. 2000. "Onset Age, Persistence, and Offending Versatility: Comparisons Across Gender." *Criminology* 38(4): 1143–1172.

McGee, Tara Renae, and David P. Farrington. 2010. "Are There Any True Adult Onset Offenders?" *British Journal of Criminology* 50(3): 530–549.

McGee, Tara Renae, Mohammed R. Hayatbakhsh, William Bor, Rosemary L. Aird, Angela J. Dean, and Jake M. Najman. 2015. "The Impact of Snares on the Continuity of Adolescent-Onset Antisocial Behaviour: A Test of Moffitt's Developmental Taxonomy." *Australian and New Zealand Journal of Criminology* 48(3): 345–366.

Mercer, Natalie, David P. Farrington, Maria M. Ttofi, Loes Keijsers, Susan Branje, and Wim Meeus. 2016. "Childhood Predictors and Adult Life Success of Adolescent Delinquency Abstainers." *Journal of Abnormal Child Psychology* 44(3): 613–624.

Moffitt, Terrie E. 1993. "Adolescence-Limited and Life-Course Persistent Antisocial Behavior: A Developmental Taxonomy." *Psychological Review* 100(4): 674–701.

Moffitt, Terrie E. 1994. "Natural Histories of Delinquency." In *Cross-National Longitudinal Research on Human Development and Criminal Behavior*, edited by E. G. M. Weitekamp and H. J. Kerner, 3–61. Dordrecht, The Netherlands: Kluwer Academic.

Moffitt, Terrie E. 2006. "Life-Course Persistent Versus Adolescence-Limited Antisocial Behavior." In *Developmental Psychopathology*, edited by Dante Cicchetti and Donald J. Cohen, 570–598. New York: Wiley.

Moffitt, T. E. 2018. "Male Antisocial Behaviour in Adolescence and Beyond." *Nature Human Behaviour* 2(3): 177–186.

Moffitt, Terrie E., Avshalom Caspi, Nigel Dickson, Phil Silva, and Warren Stanton. 1996. "Childhood-Onset Versus Adolescent-Onset Antisocial Conduct Problems in Males: Natural History from Ages 3 to 18 Years." *Development and Psychopathology* 8: 399–424.

Moffitt, Terrie E., Avshalom Caspi, Honalee Harrington, and Barry J. Milne. 2002. "Males on the Life-Course Persistent and Adolescence-Limited Antisocial Pathways: Follow-Up at Age 26 Years." *Development and Psychopathology* 14 (1): 179–207.

Moffitt, Terrie E., Avshalom Caspi, Michael Rutter, and Phil A. Silva. 2001. *Sex Differences in Antisocial Behaviour: Conduct Disorder, Delinquency, And Violence in the Dunedin Longitudinal Study*. New York: Cambridge University Press.

Nagin, Daniel S., David P. Farrington, and Terrie E. Moffitt. 1995. "Life-Course Trajectories of Different Types of Offenders." *Criminology* 33: 111–139.

Patterson, Gerald R., Barbara DeBaryshe, and Elizabeth Ramsey. 1989. "A Developmental Perspective on Antisocial Behavior." *American Psychologist* 44: 329–335.

Piquero, Alex. 2008. "Taking Stock of Developmental Trajectories of Criminal Activity Over the Life Course." In *The Long View of Crime: A Synthesis of Longitudinal Research*, edited by Akiva M. Liberman, 23–79. New York: Springer.

Piquero, Alex R., Timothy Brezina, and Michael G. Turner. 2005. "Testing Moffitt's Account of Delinquency Abstention." *Journal of Research in Crime and Delinquency* 42(1): 27–54.

Prior, Margot, Ann Sanson, Diana Smart, and Frank Oberklaid. 2000. *Pathways from Infancy to Adolescence: Australian Temperament Project 1983–2000*. Melbourne: Australian Institute of Family Studies.

Quetelet, Adolphe. 1833. *Research on The Propensity for Crime at Different Ages*. 2nd ed. Brussels: M. Hayez, Printer to the Royal Academy.

Quinn, P. J., Michael O'Callaghan, Gail M. Williams, Jake M. Najman, Margaret J. Andersen, and William Bor. 2001. "The Effect of Breastfeeding on Child Development at 5 Years: A Cohort Study." *Journal of Pediatrics and Child Health* 37: 465–469.

Raine, Adrian. 2002. "The Role of Prefrontal Deficits, Low Autonomic Arousal, and Early Health Factors in the Development of Antisocial and Aggressive Behavior in Children." *Journal of Child Psychology and Psychiatry* 43(4): 417–434.

Raine, Adrian, Terrie E. Moffitt, Avshalom Caspi, Rolf Loeber, Magda Stouthamer-Loeber, and Don Lynam. 2005. "Neurocognitive Impairments in Boys on the Life-Course Persistent Antisocial Path." *Journal of Abnormal Child Psychology* 114(1): 38–49.

Rogan, Walter J., and Beth C. Gladen. 1993. "Breast-Feeding and Cognitive Development." *Early Human Development* 31: 181–193.

Silverthorn, Persephanie, and Paul J. Frick. 1999. "Developmental Pathways to Antisocial Behavior: The Delayed-Onset Pathway in Girls." *Development and Psychopathology* 11: 101–126.

Streissguth, Ann P., Helen M. Barr, Paul D. Sampson, Betty L. Darby, and Donald C. Martin. 1989. "IQ At Age 4 in Relation to Maternal Alcohol Use and Smoking During Pregnancy." *Developmental Psychology* 25(1): 3–11.

Veenstra, René, Siegwart Lindenberg, Frank C. Verhulst, and Johan Ormel. 2009. "Childhood-Limited Versus Persistent Antisocial Behavior: Why Do Some Recover and Others Do Not? The TRAILS Study." *Journal of Early Adolescence* 29(5): 718–742.

Wilson, James Q. 1991. "Thinking About Cohorts." *The Journal of Criminal Law and Criminology* 82(1): 119–124.

CHAPTER 10

....

DEVELOPMENTAL PATHWAYS TO CONDUCT PROBLEMS AND SERIOUS FORMS OF DELINQUENCY

....

ROLF LOEBER*

"You," said my mother to me [when I was five to six years old], "have naturally a violent temper: if you grow up to be a man without learning to govern it, it be impossible for you then to command yourself; and there no knowing what crime you may in a fit of passion commit, and how miserable you may in consequence of it become. You are but a very young child, yet I think you can understand me. Instead of speaking to you as I do at this moment, I might punish you severely; but I think it better to treat you like a reasonable creature. My wish is to teach to command your temper; nobody can do that for you, so well as you can do it for yourself."

Edgeworth 1821, pp. 11–12

THIS recollection was written by Richard Lovell Edgeworth of Edgeworthstown, Co. Longford, Ireland, an enlightened landowner, brilliant educator, father of 22 children (spread over four successive wives), inventor, surveyor, and critic of and collaborator

* This work is supported by grants from the Commonwealth of Pennsylvania (SAP 4100043365) to Dr. Loeber and Dr. Burke, the National Institute of Mental Health (MH 074148) to Dr. Burke and (MH056630 and MH056630) to Dr. Loeber, and the National Institute on Alcohol Abuse and Alcoholism (AA016798) to Dr. White.

with his famous daughter/author Maria. Edgeworth as a child had a bad temper but managed to subsequently restrain his temper and lead a productive life.

The quote illustrates a main point of this chapter: both a developmental sequence from "violent temper" to violence and a pathway to crime. Studies show that youth who commit acts of violence or serious theft rarely do so de novo. Instead, many criminologists, child psychologists, and psychiatrists agree that the majority of youth who commit acts of violence or serious theft practiced less serious forms of conduct problems or delinquency earlier in life (e.g., Elliott 1994; Elliott and Menard 1996; Loeber et al. 1992, 1993). The key question is what type of model(s) best fit the fact that not all juveniles escalate to the most serious behaviors (e.g., Loeber and Le Blanc 1990; White, Jackson, and Loeber 2009). Thus, the onset of violence is usually preceded by a history of escalation in the severity of aggression, which often, but not always, starts in childhood (Loeber et al. 1993; Moffitt 1993), but many youth with the earlier problem behavior do not escalate to violence (Tremblay and Côté 2005).

The following are definitions to capture developmental phenomena of interest here. A developmental sequence is defined as the orderly behavioral development between two problem behaviors different from chance, whereas a developmental pathway is defined as the orderly behavioral development between more than two problem behaviors, again different from chance.

Developmental pathways refer to differences among individuals in their propensity to escalate along successive problem behaviors, which are called pathways. Thus, pathways are a window into dynamic and developmental rather than static differences in individuals' progression to serious forms of delinquency. It should be understood that the conceptualization of a developmental pathway consists of the formulation of a probabilistic, testable model, which does not have to be deterministic (i.e., does not have to stipulate that a given individual will definitely become violent later in life). Finally, the study of developmental pathways among problem behaviors is necessary to improve etiological models of problem behavior and is a key step in identifying targets for early interventions.

Developmental pathways differ from developmental trajectories. As mentioned, pathways primarily concern sequences of multiple behaviors, while trajectories primarily refer to classes of individuals who differ in their behavioral development over time (e.g., Nagin 2005). Typically, studies on developmental trajectories have focused on a single broad category of behavior (e.g., aggression or violence, but not both), whereas studies on developmental pathways have concentrated on sequences among different kinds of problem behaviors (e.g., minor aggression, gang fighting, breaking and entering, violence). Similarly, pathways differ from developmental types (e.g., early-onset vs. late-onset offenders, or life-course–persistent vs. adolescence-limited offenders) in that pathways concern the successive development and escalation of problem behaviors within individuals, whereas developmental types concern categories of individuals with distinct developmental trajectories over time (Moffitt 1993; Piquero et al. 2005).

Researchers have queried whether individuals' successive development between different forms of oppositional behavior, conduct problems, delinquency, and crime (together called externalizing problems) over many years is orderly rather than random, and what type of models best explain the fact that not all juveniles escalate to the most serious behaviors (e.g., Le Blanc and Loeber 1998; Loeber and Le Blanc 1990).

This essay addresses the following questions:

1. What is a parsimonious model of developmental pathways from oppositional behaviors and conduct problems to serious property crime, violence, and homicide? And do the data best fit a single or multiple pathways?
2. What are methods to identify pathways?
3. What are some other key aspects of developmental pathways?
4. What are some of the limitations of developmental pathways?
5. What are some applications of pathways?

Section I reviews defining characteristics of developmental pathways and the methods used to identify them. Section II reviews other key aspects of developmental pathways, including developmental pathways between substance use and delinquency. Section III discusses some limitations of developmental pathways, and Section IV discusses applications of these concepts.

I. Developmental Pathways

Several researchers have proposed that the development toward delinquency can be explained by a single pathway (e.g., Elliott 1994; Gottfredson and Hirschi 1990; Osgood et al. 1988) and have questioned whether there is a need to formulate and test several pathways. A single pathway implies that each or any of individuals' development of offending unfolds with development to incorporate different forms of delinquency, including different forms of property crime and different severity levels of violence. Whether there are single or multiple pathways does not only depend on different outcomes but may also depend on whether oppositional behaviors, conduct problems, and delinquency are best represented along single or multiple dimensions.

The question of whether there are single or multiple pathways to serious outcomes is important. Data on delinquency careers show that, by adulthood, offending outcomes of offenders are far from uniform. For example, a category of violent chronic offenders emerges who also engage in a variety of other types of offenses (Loeber and Farrington 1998), as do more specialized property offenders with little or no history of violent offenses, while a third group may consist of repeat property offenders without a history of violence but an onset in adolescence (Loeber 1985; Moffitt 1993). Thus, some youth mostly engage in property crime, others in violence, and a third group in both. In addition, some youth develop conduct problems but do not become property offenders, violent offenders, or both, but a proportion of those with early conduct problems develop into delinquent offenders. In other words, individuals' life course of conduct problems and delinquency varies on several basic parameters—oppositional behavior, conduct problems, and delinquency—and these individuals differ in terms of the severity of the conduct problems and delinquency they display during development. This is one of the reasons why Loeber and colleagues (Loeber et al. 1993) proposed an escalation model of multiple pathways rather than a single pathway.

Developmental pathways focus those youth who develop a succession of specific problem behaviors versus those who develop fewer behavior problems. Representations of developmental pathways tend to fall under the rubric of escalation models with less serious problem behaviors tending to precede more serious behaviors (Loeber and Le Blanc 1990). Thus, developmental pathways chart how individuals progress from innocuous to very serious problem behaviors. Because violence and serious crime tend to emerge in late adolescence and early adulthood, we are interested in the identification of individuals who are at risk for engaging in these more serious behaviors years before this actually takes place. Rather than waiting for more serious problem behaviors to emerge, the documentation of steps within pathways allows the identification at an early stage of those with a significant probability of escalating to serious problem behaviors.

A. Methods to Identify Developmental Pathways

Prospective longitudinal data, rather than cross-sectional or retrospective longitudinal data, are required for analysis of developmental pathways. It should be understood that the choice of measurements can reveal or conceal the presence of developmental pathways. For example, official records of delinquency notoriously underreport actual offending patterns, and use of official data may fail to indicate when the true onset of specific offense types takes place, thereby obfuscating developmental pathways between different forms of delinquency (Farrington et al. 2007). Similarly, reliance on parent ratings of problem behaviors (compared with self-reports of juveniles) may lead to an underestimation of covert or concealing problem behaviors, and parental data also may be a less valid indicator of onset and developmental sequences. The best studies on developmental pathways rely on multiple sources and informants (e.g., Loeber et al. 1993, 2008).

The identification of developmental pathways can become overwhelming when the possible developmental sequences between dozens of problem behaviors are considered. For example, even with 20 different problem behaviors the number of possible combinations of developmental sequences is 2.43×10^{18}. Only vast studies with tens of thousands of participants studied over decades could possibly address such complexity.

Since there are many possible developmental sequences, it is essential to reduce their number by several types of data-reduction techniques (Loeber et al. 1993; Loeber and Le Blanc 1990). The steps in this data-reduction process are:

1. Examine whether factor analyses and meta-analyses of oppositional behaviors, conduct problems, and delinquency have documented a single externalizing

factor or whether they resulted in more than one factor. Evidence of two or more factors can then mean that there should be a search for several distinct pathways.

2. Establish whether the age-of-onset curves for different behaviors are similar, providing a rationale for grouping such behaviors in a single step in a single pathway.

3. Establish whether groupings of behaviors differ in their age of onset, which then can lead to a hypothesized developmental pathway starting with behavior grouping 1 (called step 1) to behavior grouping n (called step n). One criterion for establishing a stage model is that the transition between stages follow an invariant sequence, but transitions within a stage can occur less systematically.

4. Compute backward probabilities between successive behaviors in developmental pathways. This involves the calculation of the proportion of individuals who had displayed problem behavior B by a certain age who had also displayed problem behavior A at a younger age. If significantly more of those displaying behavior B had also displayed behavior A at a younger age (compared to those displaying behavior B prior to behavior A), then one might propose a developmental sequence from A to B (Loeber et al. 1993, 2008). The establishment of developmental pathways is more convincing if few individuals skip steps in a pathway (e.g., where behavior A is not followed by behavior B but is followed by behavior C).

In the first stage of the pathway analyses, Loeber and Schmaling (1985) undertook a multidimensional scaling of problem behaviors based on 28 factor analytic studies covering over 11,000 children. The main aim was to establish the extent to which two behavior problems loaded on the same factor in factor analytic studies. The results showed a single externalizing dimension with two poles: one of overt, confrontational behaviors and the other consisting of covert, concealing behaviors, with disobedience being situated at an equal distance between overt and covert acts. Frick et al. (1993) repeated this analysis based on a larger sample of factor analytic studies and confirmed the presence of the overt–covert dimension of externalizing behaviors, but they also documented a destructive versus nondestructive dimension. Since that time, the distinction between overt and covert externalizing behaviors has been accepted by many researchers (e.g., Vassallo et al. 2002).

Using the factor analytic evidence, pathways of different problem behaviors (based on the Pittsburgh Youth Study) were specified according to these overt and covert externalizing dimensions (called the overt and covert pathways). On the basis of research findings described below, three pathways in externalizing behaviors were formulated (Figure 10.1). The first pathway is called the Overt Pathway and concerns confrontational acts. This pathway starts with minor aggression (e.g., bullying, annoying others), has physical fighting (physical fighting and gang fighting) as a second step, and serious violence (rape, attack, robbery) as a third step.

The second pathway is called the covert pathway and concerns concealing acts. This pathway starts prior to age 15 with minor covert acts (shoplifting and frequent lying), has property damage (e.g., vandalism and fire-setting) as a second step, moderate

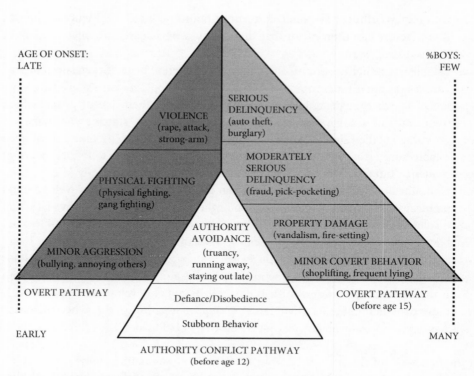

FIGURE 10.1 Three Developmental Pathways in Externalizing Behaviors

Source: Loeber et al. (1993)

delinquency (e.g., fraud, pick-pocketing) as a third step, and has serious delinquency (e.g., auto theft and burglary) as a fourth step.

The third pathway is called the authority conflict pathway. This pathway takes place prior to the age of 12, usually starts with stubborn behavior, has defiance/disobedience as a second step, and authority avoidance (e.g., truancy, running away from home, and staying out late at night) as a third step.

Based on analyses using longitudinal data from the Pittsburgh Youth Study (PYS), Loeber et al. (1993) showed that the development of externalizing problems in boys took place systematically rather than randomly and best fitted three pathways rather than a single pathway. These boys typically followed an orderly progression (escalation) from less to more serious problem behaviors from childhood to adolescence (Loeber, Keenan, and Zhang 1997; Loeber et al. 2005).

The pathways are hierarchical in that those youth who have advanced to the most serious behavior in each of the pathways have usually displayed persistent problem behavior characteristics at the earlier stages in each pathway. By a process of selection, increasingly smaller groups of youth become at risk for the more serious behaviors. The pathways are also related to neighborhoods. For example, a higher percentage of youth in the most disadvantaged neighborhoods escalates from minor aggression to violence than youth living in more advantaged neighborhoods (Loeber and Wikström, 1993). The three-pathway model has been subsequently replicated across two other samples in the Pittsburgh Youth Study (Loeber et al. 1993, 1998). In addition, several other studies have replicated the pathways model (Gorman-Smith and Loeber 2005; Loeber et al. 1999; Tolan, Gorman-Smith, and Loeber 2000).

Boys could be on each of the three pathways at the same time. Thus, the pathways are not mutually exclusive. However, escalation in either the overt or covert pathway was often preceded by escalation in the authority conflict pathway (Loeber et al. 1993). In other words, conflict with authority figures was either a precursor or a concomitant of escalation in overt or covert acts. Also, an early-age-of-onset of problem behavior or delinquency, compared to an onset at a later age, was more closely associated with escalation to more serious behaviors in the overt and covert pathways (Tolan, Gorman-Smith, and Loeber 2000).

The pathways model was evaluated in several ways. First, the backward probabilities were computed to establish the extent to which individuals who had reached a later step in a pathway had also gone through the preceding steps (vs. the forward probabilities). The results showed that most of those who reached a higher step in a pathway also had manifested problem behaviors characteristic of a lower step in the pathway. This applied to each of the three pathways. Second, the pathways model accounted for the majority of the most seriously affected boys, i.e., the self-reported high-rate offenders and court-reported delinquents.

The pathways model has been replicated in four other longitudinal data sets (Loeber et al. 1998, 1999; Tolan et al. 2000) and has been featured in publications of the Office of Juvenile Justice and Delinquency Prevention (e.g., Kelley et al. 1997).

II. Some Other Key Aspects of Developmental Pathways

In this section we will discuss how pathways apply differently to youth who offend rarely compared to those who show persistent externalizing problems, whether pathways apply to homicide, whether there are gender differences in externalizing and delinquent pathways, what the relevance is of early problem behaviors during the preschool years, and developmental sequences between substance use and delinquency.

A. Experimenters and Persisters

Developmental pathways to serious forms of delinquency should be studied in the context of normal development, including the fact that many youth show some externalizing problems at some time in their early life. Several of the early steps in the pathways take into account the frequency and persistence of behaviors in that step. An example is disobedience, which does not refer to rare incidents of disobedience but to a pattern of persistent disobedience. Therefore, in the evaluation of pathways, it is important to make a distinction between experimenters (those who show a less serious problem at a low frequency) and persisters. Loeber et al. (1997) found that more persisters, compared to experimenters, entered a pathway at the first step. Also, fewer persisters, compared to experimenters, entered a pathway at a second or later step. Thus, the identification of pathways was better when experimenters were omitted from the data and was improved by concentrating on persisters.

B. Homicide as an Extension of the Violence Pathway

In the early stages of the development of the pathways model, few of the boys in the PYS had committed homicide (Loeber and Farrington 2011). Although we speculated that violence was a stepping stone toward homicide offending, this hypothesis could only be tested in recent years when the homicide rate among the young males in the PYS increased. Longitudinal analyses (Loeber et al. 2005; Loeber and Farrington 2011) showed that 94 percent of the homicide offenders had been violent (e.g., engaged in aggravated assault, robbery or rape) earlier in their life (as evident from self-reports and official records of violence). Thus, it is proposed that homicide offending among these inner-city young males is an additional, fourth step in the overt pathway, with other forms of violence being a necessary condition for later homicide offending.

C. Developmental Pathways in Girls' Externalizing Behaviors

The research reported thus far concerns males only. Do girls show similar pathways in externalizing behaviors? Using longitudinal data from the first five waves of the National Youth Survey (which is a nationally representative sample), Gorman-Smith and Loeber (2005) found similar developmental patterns of externalizing and delinquent involvement among girls. Approximately 70 percent of involved girls followed most steps in the three pathways that had been identified for boys.

D. Pathways to Early Externalizing Problems

The formulation of developmental pathways in externalizing problems for boys and girls started with data collected after preschool. This limitation of the preceding studies does not do justice to the fact that externalizing problems often emerge during the preschool period (Goodenough 1931; Tremblay and Côté 2005). Keenan and Shaw (2003) proposed a stage escalation model with two externalizing pathways for the preschool period. One pathway, called the pathway to reactive antisocial behavior, starts with irritable behavior during infancy. Children displaying persistent irritability are thought to be at risk of developing emotional difficulties as toddlers (low frustration tolerance, overactivity, and being demanding) and in turn are at risk of developing disruptive, angry behaviors as preschoolers, including reactive aggression, crying, whining, and defiance.

A second pathway, called the pathway to proactive antisocial behavior, starts with children displaying underarousal (i.e., underresponsiveness to stimulation) who are at risk of developing behavior difficulties as toddlers (as demonstrated by persistent unresponsiveness to punishment and a high level of sensation-seeking) and who in turn are at risk of developing oppositional behaviors and conduct problems later. The Keenan and Shaw model may provide a link with the pathways model in that the first two steps in the authority conflict pathway in the pathways model (stubborn behavior and defiance/disobedience) may link to oppositional behaviors in the two Keenan and Shaw pathways. However, the Keenan and Shaw model needs to be tested empirically.

E. Developmental Pathways Between Substance Use and Delinquency

Research shows that the use of different forms of substance use also tends to follow a developmental pathway. Known as the "stage model," most youth begin their substance use with alcohol or tobacco, then proceed to marijuana, and then to harder drugs (e.g., psychedelics, cocaine, and heroin and nonmedical use or prescription medications) (Kandel 2002). Whereas this sequence has been supported in a number of studies, the generalizability of this sequence to all types of drug users, especially those who develop addiction, has been questioned (for a discussion see Labouvie and White 2002).

Because substance use is often directly related to several other forms of serious delinquency (White et al. 2009), it is possible that there is a single developmental sequence that includes substance use and externalizing problems. Therefore, the developmental sequences among substance use, serious offending, and other problem behaviors (i.e., gang membership, gun carrying, and drug dealing) were examined in the youngest and oldest cohorts of the PYS. These different forms of delinquency were selected because they tend to be serious and they were not included in our initial developmental model of pathways when the participants in the Pittsburgh Youth Study were relatively young. For ease of presentation, the earliest age for alcohol and tobacco was counted as the onset of legal drugs and the earliest age for marijuana and hard drug use was counted as the age of onset of illegal drugs (see White, Loeber, and Farrington, 2008, for details of the following results).

For both PYS cohorts, a significantly greater proportion of boys first used legal drugs (alcohol) before they initiated serious violence (i.e., robbery, attaching to hurt or kill, and forced sex), and legal drug use preceded serious violence by 2½ to 3½ years. On the other hand, the mean age of onset of serious violence proceeded the mean age of onset of illegal drug use (marijuana, hard drugs) by only a few months, and boys were equally as likely to first use illegal drugs as they were to first engage in serious violence. Therefore, developmentally, using illegal drugs did not necessarily lead to serious violence.

In both cohorts, the onset of legal drug use preceded the onset of serious theft (i.e., breaking and entering and theft); however, the onset of serious theft preceded the onset of illegal drug use, dealing, and gun carrying. All of these sequences were significantly different from chance in the oldest cohort but in the youngest cohort were only significantly different for theft with legal drugs use and dealing. The sequencing of gang membership and serious theft differed between the cohorts. In the youngest cohort, an equal proportion of boys first joined gangs before as after they committed their first serious theft offense, whereas in the oldest cohort three times as many boys had engaged in theft before joining a gang than had joined a gang before engaging in theft. In summary, there are some developmental sequences between legal and illegal substance use and serious forms of violence and theft. Whether these constitute developmental pathways of multiple problems remains to be established.

III. Some Limitations of Developmental Pathways

There are several limitations to the pathway models, which can be addressed in future research. One is that only a restricted number of behaviors are included in several of the pathway models. For example, in the PYS, the reason is that the initial approach to identifying steps in the pathways depended on charting onset curves for different behaviors based on longitudinal data (Loeber et al. 1993). Those behaviors that showed similar onset curves were placed on the same step in a pathway. The onsets of several externalizing behaviors were less consistent, and for that reason they were excluded from the formulation of the pathways model. Another set of delinquent acts (gang membership, gun carrying, and drug dealing) had a relatively low base rate when the developmental model was first investigated (Loeber et al. 1993) and for that reason were not included at that time.

The analyses of pathways in the PYS were inherently limited by the fact that the youngest boys in the study were age 6 at the beginning of the assessments. Although retrospective information from the parent was collected, this source of information often is incomplete, and therefore prospective information from infancy needs to form the basis for future formulations of developmental pathways in externalizing behavior during the preschool period. Such work needs to take advantage of information about temperament as a precursor to externalizing behaviors (e.g., Frick and Morris 2004; Keenan and Shaw 2003).

Much more needs to be known about de-escalation models of change, showing the order in which individuals shed problem behaviors as they improve or desist (Loeber and Le Blanc 1990; Loeber, Stouthamer-Loeber, and Ahonen. 2016). Pathways in externalizing problems should be seen in the context of incomplete development of so-cial skills and competencies incompatible with externalizing problems. In addition, it is likely that developmental pathways overlap with poor impulse control, poor moral de-velopment, and cognitions favorable to rule and law breaking.

IV. APPLICATIONS OF DEVELOPMENTAL PATHWAYS

We believe that knowledge about developmental pathways is relevant for the assess-ment, prevention, and evaluation of interventions. This is the case no matter what child-serving system is involved. Schools, juvenile justice agencies, and medical and mental health providers all struggle to find the most efficient ways to provide primary, sec-ondary, and tertiary modes of intervention. Assessments of juvenile externalizing be-havior are justified when results are relevant for an appraisal of current behaviors and future risk. Knowledge of developmental pathways can help with the prediction of the future risk of escalation by specifying two important parameters: which behaviors are linked to later progression to serious outcomes and which populations of youth are at risk of progressing to more serious acts. Assessment instruments based on knowledge of developmental pathways can also aid in the identification of those youth whose problem behavior is temporary compared with those whose problem behavior is likely to persist and escalate in severity (Loeber et al. 1997; Loeber, Slot, and Stouthamer-Loeber 2006).

Developmental pathways are also important for specifying targets in preventive interventions. For instance, if the presence of antisocial behavior or conduct problems (as distinguished from more general and less serious externalizing behavior) is a key predictor of the later emergence of delinquency, this would have dramatic implications for the search for reliable early indicators of high risk for later severe externalizing be-havior. If severe antisocial and delinquent behavior in late childhood or adolescence was predicted not by oppositionality or defiance but by more specific early antisocial or conduct problems, or by specific types of temperament or dimensions of dysregulation, it would be much easier to identify those children who are likely to develop antisocial behavior problems and avoid making false-positive predictions. Accordingly, well-targeted and specifically tailored prevention strategies could be delivered.

Developmental pathways can also help to increase the ways by which intervention success is evaluated. Evidence suggests that developmental cascades, or related sets of developmental failures, describe individual pathways to undesirable outcomes. On the other hand, typically the success of a given intervention is evaluated in more of an all-or-nothing and immediate fashion. We argue that, instead, the change in individual propensity to escalate along a developmental pathway is a more refined and, possibly, a more developmentally informed intervention outcome.

REFERENCES

Edgeworth, Richard Lovell. 1821. *Memoirs of Richard Lovell Edgeworth, Esq. begun by himself and concluded by his daughter Maria Edgeworth*. Boston: Wells and Lilly.

Elliott, Delbert S. 1994. "Longitudinal Research in Criminology: Promise and Practice." In *Cross-National Longitudinal Research on Human Development and Criminal Behavior*, edited by Elmar Weitekamp, and Hans-Jürgen Kerner, 189–201. Dordrecht, The Netherlands: Kluwer Academic.

Elliott, Delbert S., and Scott S. Menard. 1996. "Delinquent Friends and Delinquent Behavior: Temporal and Developmental Patterns." In *Delinquency and Crime: Current Theories*, edited by J. David Hawkins, 28–69. Cambridge, UK: Cambridge University Press.

Farrington, David. P., Darrick Jolliffe, Rolf Loeber, and D. Lynn Homish. 2007. "How Many Offenses Are Really Committed per Juvenile Court Offender?" *Victims and Offenders* 2: 227–249.

Frick, Paul J., Benjamin B. Lahey, Rolf Loeber, Lynne Tannenbaum, Yolanda Van Horn, Mary A. G. Christ, Elizabeth A. Hart, and Kelly Hanson. 1993. "Oppositional Defiant Disorder and Conduct Disorder: A Meta-Analytic Review of Factor Analyses and Cross-Validation in a Clinic Sample." *Clinical Psychology Review* 13: 319–340.

Frick, Paul J., and Amanda S. Morris. 2004. "Temperament and Developmental Pathways to Conduct Problems." *Journal of Clinical and Adolescent Psychology* 33: 54–68.

Goodenough, Florence. 1931. *Anger in Young Children*. Minneapolis: University of Minnesota Press.

Gorman-Smith, Deborah, and Rolf Loeber. 2005. "Are Developmental Pathways in Disruptive Behaviors the Same for Girls and Boys?" *Journal of Child and Family Studies* 14: 15–27.

Gottfredson, Michael, and Travis Hirschi. 1990. *A General Theory of Crime*. Stanford, CA: Stanford University Press.

Kandel, Denise B. 2002. "Examining the Gateway Hypothesis: Stages and Pathways of Drug Involvement." In *Stages and Pathways of Drug Involvement: Examining the Gateway Hypothesis*, edited by Denise B. Kandel, 3–11. New York: Cambridge University Press.

Keenan, Kate, and Daniel S. Shaw. 2003. "Development of Conduct Problems During the Preschool Years." In *Causes of Conduct Disorder and Juvenile Delinquency*, edited by Benjamin B. Lahey, Terrie E. Moffitt, and Avshalom Caspi, 76–117. New York: Guilford.

Kelley, Barbara T., Rolf Loeber, Kate Keenan, and Mary DeLamatre. 1997. *Developmental Pathways in Disruptive and Delinquent Behavior*. Washington, DC: U.S. Office of Juvenile Justice and Delinquency Prevention (Juvenile Justice Bulletin).

Labouvie, Erich, and Helene R. White. 2002. "Drug Sequences, Age of Onset, and Use Trajectories as Predictors of Drug Abuse/Dependence in Young Adulthood." In *Stages and Pathways of Drug Involvement: Examining the Gateway Hypothesis*, edited by Denise B. Kandel, 19–41. New York: Cambridge University Press.

Le Blanc, Marc, and Rolf Loeber. 1998. "Developmental Criminology Updated." In *Crime and Justice: A Review of Research*, Vol. 23, edited by Michael Tonry, 115–198. Chicago: University of Chicago Press.

Loeber, Rolf. 1985. "Patterns and Development of Antisocial Child Behavior." In *Annals of Child Development*, Vol. 2, edited by Graver J. Whitehurst. Greenwich, 77–116. CT: JAI Press.

Loeber, Rolf, and David P. Farrington. 2011. *Young Homicide Offenders and Victims: Development and Prediction from Childhood to Adulthood*. New York: Springer.

Loeber, Rolf, Mary DeLamatre, Kate Keenan, and Quanwu Zhang. 1998. "A Prospective Replication of Developmental Pathways in Disruptive and Delinquent Behavior." In *Methods and Models for Studying the Individual*, edited by Robert Cairns, Lars Bergman, and Jerome Kagan, 185–218. Thousand Oaks, CA: Sage.

Loeber, Rolf, and David P. Farrington, eds. 1998. *Serious and Violent Juvenile Offenders: Risk Factors and Successful Interventions*. Thousand Oaks, CA: Sage.

Loeber, Rolf, David P. Farrington, Magda Stouthamer-Loeber, and Helene R. White. 2008. *Violence and Serious Theft: Development and Prediction from Childhood to Adulthood.* New York: Routledge.

Loeber, Rolf, Stephanie M. Green, Benjamin B. Lahey, Mary Anne G. Christ, and Paul J. Frick. 1992. "Developmental Sequences in the Age of Onset of Disruptive Child Behaviors." *Journal of Child and Family Studies* 1: 21–41.

Loeber, Rolf, Kate Keenan, and Quanwu Zhang. 1997. "Boys' Experimentation and Persistence in Developmental Pathways Toward Serious Delinquency." *Journal of Child and Family Studies* 6: 321–357.

Loeber, Rolf, and Marc Le Blanc. 1990. "Toward a Developmental Criminology." In *Crime and Justice: A Review of Research*, Vol. 12, edited by Michael Tonry and Norval Morris, 375–473. Chicago: University of Chicago Press.

Loeber, Rolf, Dustin Pardini, D. Lynn Homish, Evelyn Wei, Anne M. Crawford, David P. Farrington, Magda Stouthamer-Loeber, Judith Creemers, Stephen A. Koehler, and Richard Rosenfeld. 2005. "The Prediction of Violence and Homicide in Young Men." *Journal of Consulting and Clinical Psychology* 73: 1074–1088.

Loeber, Rolf, and Karen B. Schmaling. 1985. "Empirical Evidence for Overt and Covert Patterns of Antisocial Conduct Problems." *Journal of Abnormal Child Psychology* 13: 337–352.

Loeber, Rolf, and Magda Stouthamer-Loeber. 1998. "The Development of Juvenile Aggression and Violence: Some Common Misconceptions and Controversies." *American Psychologist* 53: 242–259.

Loeber, Rolf, Magda Stouthamer-Loeber, and Lia Ahonen. 2016. "Key Behavioural Aspects of Desistance from Conduct Problems and Delinquency." In *Global Perspectives on Desistance: Reviewing What We Know and Looking to the Future,* edited by Joanna Shapland, Stephen Farrall, and Anthony Bottoms, 85–98. London: Routledge.

Loeber, Rolf, Evelyn Wei, Magda Stouthamer-Loeber, David Huizinga, and Terence P. Thornberry. 1999. "Behavioral Antecedents to Serious and Violent Juvenile Offending: Joint Analyses from the Denver Youth Survey, Pittsburgh Youth Study, and the Rochester Youth Development Study." *Studies on Crime and Crime Prevention* 8: 245–263.

Loeber, Rolf, and Per-Olof Wikström. 1993. "Individual Pathways to Crime in Different Types of Neighborhoods." In *Integrating Individual and Ecological Aspects of Crime*, edited by David P. Farrington, Robert J. Sampson, and Per-Olof Wikstrom, 169–204. Stockholm: Swedish National Council for Crime Prevention.

Loeber, Rolf, Phen Wung, Kate Keenan, Bruce Giroux, Magda Stouthamer-Loeber, Welmoet B. Van Kammen, and Barbara Maughan. 1993. "Developmental Pathways in Disruptive Child Behavior." *Development and Psychopathology* 5: 101–132.

Moffitt, Terrie E. 1993. "Adolescence-Limited and Life-Course-Persistent Antisocial Behavior: A Developmental Taxonomy." *Psychological Review* 100: 674–701.

Nagin, Daniel S. 2005. *Group-Based Modeling of Development.* Cambridge, MA: Harvard University Press.

Osgood, D. Wayne, Lloyd D. Johnston, Patrick M. O'Malley, and Jerald G. Bachman. 1988. "The Generality of Deviance in Late Adolescence and Early Adulthood." *American Sociological Review* 53: 81–93.

Piquero, Alex R., Jeffrey A. Fagan, Edward P., Mulvey, Laurence Steinberg, and Candice Odgers. 2005. "Developmental Trajectories of Legal Socialization Among Serious Adolescent Offenders." *Journal of Criminal Law and Criminology* 96: 267–298.

Tolan, Patrick. H., Deborah Gorman-Smith, and Rolf Loeber. 2000. "Developmental Timing of Onsets of Disruptive Behaviors and Later Delinquency of Inner-City Youth." *Journal of Child and Family Studies* 9: 203–230.

Tremblay, Richard E., and Sylvana Côté. 2005. "The Developmental Origins of Aggression: Where Are We Going?" In *Developmental Origins of Aggression,* edited by Richard E. Tremblay, Willard W. Hartup, and John Archer, 447–464. New York: Guilford.

Vassallo, Suzanne, Diana Smart, Ann Sanson, Inez Dussuyer, and Bill McKendry. 2002. *Patterns and Precursors of Adolescent Antisocial Behaviour.* Melbourne, Australia: Crime Prevention Victoria.

White, Helene R., Kristina M. Jackson, and Rolf Loeber. 2009. "Developmental Sequences and Comorbidity of Substance Use and Violence." In *Handbook on Crime and Deviance,* edited by Marvin D. Krohn and Alan J. Lizotte, 433–468. Dordrecht, The Netherlands: Springer.

White, Helene R., Rolf Loeber, and David P. Farrington. 2008. "Substance Use, Drug Dealing, Gang Membership, and Gun Carrying and Their Predictive Associations with Serious Violence and Serious Theft." In *Violence and Serious Theft: Development and Prediction from Childhood to Adulthood,* by Rolf Loeber and David P. Farrington, 137–168. New York: Routledge.

CHAPTER 11

THE INTEGRATED COGNITIVE ANTISOCIAL POTENTIAL (ICAP) THEORY

New Empirical Tests

DAVID P. FARRINGTON AND TARA RENAE MCGEE

DEVELOPMENTAL and life-course criminology (DLC) focuses on the development of offending and antisocial behavior, the importance of risk and protective factors, and the effect of life events on the course of development of offending. The integrated cognitive antisocial potential (ICAP) theory specifies risk factors that influence the development of long-term antisocial potential (varying between individuals) and situational factors that influence short-term antisocial potential (varying within individuals over time). It also specifies the cognitive processes that influence whether antisocial potential becomes actual offending in any situation and the consequences of offending that have feedback influences on antisocial potential. This chapter describes an empirical test of the ICAP theory based on the Cambridge Study in Delinquent Development (CSDD), which is a prospective longitudinal survey of 411 South London males beginning at age 8.

Section I describes the ICAP theory and its contrasting of between-individual differences in long-term antisocial potential and within-individual variations in short-term antisocial potential. Section II describes the CSDD, its research on two generations of males, and its measurement of comparable risk factors in the two generations. Section III presents a new test of the development of long-term antisocial potential in the ICAP theory, using the same antisocial attitude (AA) scale to measure antisocial potential in both generations. It also investigates the relationship between antisocial attitudes and convictions and childhood risk factors for later antisocial attitudes. Section IV concludes that predictions from the ICAP theory have generally been supported. It also makes recommendations about how to improve the ICAP theory, about research needed to advance knowledge about DLC theories, and about interventions to reduce offending.

I. The ICAP Theory

The ICAP theory was primarily designed to explain offending by lower-class males, and it was influenced by results obtained in the CSDD (Farrington 2005; Zara 2010). It integrates ideas from many other theories, including strain, control, learning, labeling, and rational choice approaches. Its key construct is antisocial potential (AP), and it assumes that the translation from antisocial potential to antisocial behavior depends on cognitive (thinking and decision-making) processes that take account of opportunities and victims. Figure 11.1 is deliberately simplified in order to show the key elements of the

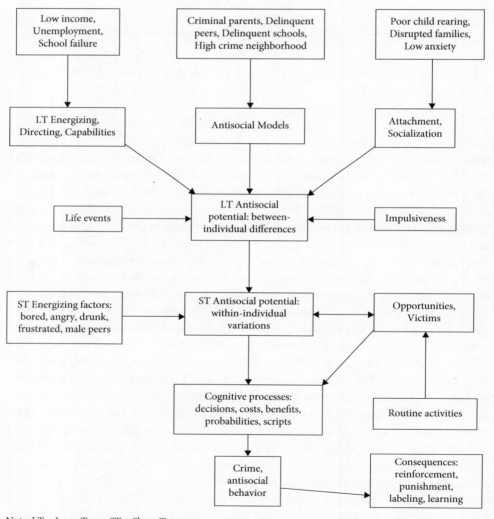

Note: LT = Long-Term; ST = Short-Term

FIGURE 11.1 The Integrated Cognitive Antisocial Potential (ICAP) Theory

ICAP theory on one page; for example, it does not show how the processes operate differently for onset compared with desistance or at different ages.

The key construct underlying offending is antisocial potential (AP), which refers to the potential to commit antisocial acts. Long-term persisting between-individual differences in AP are distinguished from short-term within-individual variations in AP. Long-term AP depends on impulsiveness; on strain, modeling, and socialization processes; and on life events, while short-term variations in AP depend on motivating and situational factors.

Regarding long-term AP, people can be ordered on a continuum from low to high. The distribution of AP in the population at any age is highly skewed; few people have relatively high levels of AP. People with high AP are more likely to commit many different types of antisocial acts, including different types of offenses. Therefore, offending and antisocial behavior are versatile rather than specialized. The relative ordering of people on AP (long-term between-individual variation) tends to be consistent over time, but absolute levels of AP vary with age. AP peaks in the teenage years because of within-individual changes in the factors that influence long-term AP (e.g., from childhood to adolescence, the increasing importance of peers, and the decreasing importance of parents).

A key issue is whether the model should be the same for all types of crimes or whether different models are needed for different types of crimes. With their focus on the development of offenders, DLC researchers have concluded that offenders are versatile rather than specialized, and so it is not necessary to have different models for different types of crimes. For example, it is believed that the risk factors for violence are essentially the same as those for property crime or substance abuse. However, researchers who have focussed on situational influences have argued that different models are needed for different types of crimes. It is suggested that situational influences on burglary may be very different from situational influences on violence.

One possible way to resolve these differing viewpoints would be to assume that long-term potential was very general (e.g., a long-term potential for antisocial behavior), whereas short-term potential was more specific (e.g., a short-term potential for violence). The top half of the model in Figure 11.1 could be the same for all types of crimes, whereas the bottom half could be different (with different situational influences) for different types of crimes.

In the interests of simplification, Figure 11.1 makes the ICAP theory appear static rather than dynamic. For example, it does not explain changes in offending at different ages. Since it might be expected that different factors would be important at different ages or life stages, it seems likely that different models would be needed at different ages. Perhaps parents are more important in influencing children, peers are more important in influencing adolescents, and spouses and partners are more important in influencing adults.

A. Long-Term Risk Factors

A great deal is known about risk factors that predict long-term persisting between-individual differences in antisocial potential. For example, in the CSDD, the most important childhood risk factors for later offending were hyperactivity-impulsivity-attention deficit, low school attainment, family criminality, family poverty, large family size, poor child-rearing, and disrupted families (see, e.g., Farrington 1995). Figure 11.1 shows how risk factors are hypothesized to influence long-term AP. This figure could be expanded to specify protective factors and to include influences on onset, persistence, escalation, de-escalation, and desistance.

Measures of antisocial behavior (e.g., aggressiveness or dishonesty) are not included as risk factors in the ICAP theory because of the concern with explanation, prevention, and treatment. These measures do not cause offending, rather they predict offending because of the underlying continuity over time in AP. Measures of antisocial behavior are useful in identifying risk groups but less useful in identifying causal factors to be targeted by interventions. Similarly, variables that cannot be changed, such as gender or ethnicity, are not included. It is assumed that their relationships with offending are mediated by changeable risk factors (Farrington, Loeber, and Stouthamer-Loeber 2003).

A major problem is to decide which risk factors are causes and which are merely markers or correlated with causes (Murray, Farrington, and Eisner 2009). Ideally, interventions should be targeted at risk factors that are causes. Interventions targeted at risk factors that are merely markers will not necessarily lead to any decrease in offending. Unfortunately, when risk factors are highly intercorrelated (as is usual), it is very difficult to establish which are causes in between-individual research. For example, the particular factors that appear to be independently important as predictors in any analysis may be greatly affected by measurement error and by essentially random variations between samples.

It is also important to establish how risk factors have sequential or interactive effects on offending. Figure 11.1 shows how risk factors are hypothesized to influence long-term AP. Following strain theory, the main energizing factors that potentially lead to high long-term AP are desires for material goods, status among intimates, excitement, and sexual satisfaction. However, these motivations only lead to high AP if antisocial methods of satisfying them are habitually chosen. Antisocial methods tend to be chosen by people who find it difficult to satisfy their needs legitimately, such as people with low income, unemployed people, and those who fail at school. However, the methods chosen also depend on physical capabilities and behavioral skills; for example, a 5-year-old would have difficulty in stealing a car. For simplicity, energizing and directing processes and capabilities are shown in one box in Figure 11.1.

Long-term AP also depends on attachment and socialization processes. AP will be low if parents consistently and contingently reward good behavior, for example, by praising, and punish bad behavior, for example, by withdrawing love. Children with low anxiety will be less well socialized because they care less about parental punishment. AP will be high if children are not attached to (prosocial) parents, for example, if parents are cold and rejecting. Disrupted families (broken homes) may impair both attachment and socialization processes.

Long-term AP will also be high if people are exposed to and influenced by antisocial models, such as criminal parents, delinquent siblings, and delinquent peers, for example, in high-delinquency-rate schools and neighborhoods. Long-term AP will also be high for impulsive people because they tend to act without thinking about the consequences. Also, life events affect AP; it decreases (at least for males) after people get married or move out of high-crime areas, and it increases after separation from a partner. Theobald and Farrington (2009), in the CSDD, found that offending decreased after men got married.

There may also be interaction effects between the influences on long-term AP. For example, people who experience strain or poor socialization may be disproportionally antisocial if they are also exposed to antisocial models. In the interests of simplicity, Figure 11.1 does not attempt to show such interactions.

Figure 11.1 shows some of the processes by which risk factors are hypothesized to have effects on AP. It does not show biological factors, but these could be incorporated in the theory at various points. For example, the children of criminal parents could have high AP partly because of genetic transmission, excitement-seeking could be driven by low cortical arousal, school failure could depend partly on low intelligence, and high impulsiveness and low anxiety could both reflect biological processes.

Many researchers have measured only one risk factor (e.g., impulsiveness) and have shown that it predicts or correlates with offending after controlling for a few other "confounding factors," often including social class. The message of Figure 11.1 is: Don't forget the big picture. The particular causal linkages shown in Figure 11.1 require empirical testing; it is important to measure, analyze, and explain all important risk factors in trying to draw conclusions about the causes of offending or the development of offenders. The main aim of this chapter is to test hypotheses about childhood risk factors that influence AP.

Ideally, protective factors as well as risk factors should be included in the ICAP theory. The risk factor prevention paradigm (Farrington 2000) suggests that risk factors should be reduced while protective factors are enhanced. Often, programs focussing on protective factors (e.g., building on strengths, promoting healthy development) are more attractive to communities and consequently easier to implement than programs focusing on risk factors (which seem to emphasize undesirable features of communities and imply blame). Of course, a key question is whether the risk and protective factors for offending (or for the onset of offending) are the same as or different from the risk and protective factors for reoffending (or for the persistence of offending). Perhaps different models are needed in Figure 11.1 for onset, persistence, escalation, de-escalation, and desistance (Farrington and Hawkins 1991).

B. Explaining the Commission of Crimes

According to the ICAP theory, the commission of offenses and other types of antisocial acts depends on the interaction between the individual (with an immediate level of AP) and the social environment (that provides criminal opportunities and victims). Short-term AP varies within individuals according to short-term energizing factors such as being bored, angry, drunk, or frustrated or being encouraged by peers. Criminal opportunities and the availability of victims is determined by routine activities. Encountering a tempting opportunity or victim may cause a short-term increase in AP, just as a short-term increase in AP may motivate a person to seek out criminal opportunities and victims.

Whether a person with a certain level of AP commits a crime in a given situation depends on cognitive processes, including considering the subjective benefits, costs, and probabilities of the different outcomes, and stored behavioral repertoires or scripts. The subjective benefits and costs include immediate situational factors such as the material goods that can be stolen and the likelihood and consequences of being caught by the police. They also include social factors such as likely disapproval by parents or female partners and encouragement or reinforcement from peers. In general, people tend to make decisions that seem rational to them, but those with low levels of AP will not commit offenses even when (on the basis of subjective expected utilities) it appears rational to do so. Equally, high short-term levels of AP (e.g., caused by anger or drunkenness) may encourage people to commit offenses when it is not rational for them to do so.

The consequences of offending may, as a result of a learning process, lead to changes in long-term AP and in future cognitive decision-making processes. This is especially likely if the consequences are reinforcing (e.g., gaining material goods or peer approval) or punishing (e.g., receiving legal sanctions or parental disapproval). Also, if the consequences involve labeling or stigmatizing the offender, this may make it more difficult for him to achieve his aims legally and therefore may lead to an increase in AP (Farrington 1977). (It is difficult to show these feedback effects in Figure 11.1 without making it very complex.)

A further issue that needs to be addressed is to what extent types of offenders should be distinguished. Perhaps some people commit crimes primarily because of their high long-term AP (e.g., the life-course–persistent offenders of Moffitt 1993), others primarily because of situational influences (e.g., getting drunk frequently) and high short-term AP, while still others offend primarily because of the way they think and make decisions when faced with criminal opportunities. From the viewpoint of both explanation and prevention, research is needed to classify types of people according to their most influential risk factors and most important reasons for committing crimes.

C. Testing the ICAP Theory

The first independent test of the ICAP theory was carried out by Van Der Laan, Blom, and Kleemans (2009) in The Netherlands. Nearly 1,500 youth ages 10 to 17 completed a survey that enquired about long-term and short-term (situational) risk factors for delinquency. Nearly 300 youth answered questions about the circumstances of their last offense. In agreement with the ICAP theory, Van Der Laan and colleagues found that long-term individual, family, and school factors correlated with serious delinquency and the probability of serious delinquency increased with the number of risk factors.

However, after controlling for long-term factors, short-term situational factors such as the absence of tangible guardians and using alcohol or drugs prior to the offense were still important.

II. The Cambridge Study in Delinquent Development

While the results of this test are very encouraging, it is important to test the ICAP theory in a prospective longitudinal survey. This chapter describes an extensive test of the ICAP theory in the CSDD. It builds on three previous papers. Farrington and McGee (2017) tested the ICAP theory on the original sample of CSDD males, who are now termed generation 2, or G2. Farrington and his colleagues (2015) compared risk factors for convictions of the G2 males and also of their sons, termed generation 3, or G3. Farrington, Ttofi, and Crago (2017) investigated the intergenerational transmission of convictions from G2 males to G3 males. The present chapter studies the extent to which predictions from the ICAP theory are verified in G2 males and then replicated in G3 males.

The CSDD is a prospective longitudinal survey of the development of offending and antisocial behavior in 411 London males (G2) from age 8 onwards. The CSDD began in 1961. Results of the study have been described in six books (West 1969; West and Farrington 1973, 1977; West 1982; Piquero, Farrington, and Blumstein 2007; Farrington, Piquero, and Jennings 2013) and in five summary articles (Farrington and West 1981, 1990; Farrington 1995, 2003; Farrington, Coid, and West 2009). These works should be consulted for more information about the CSDD.

A. Generation 2 (G2) Males

At the time they were first contacted in 1961–1962, the G2 boys were all living in a working-class area of South London. The vast majority of the sample was chosen by taking all the boys who were then aged 8 to 9 and on the registers of six state primary schools within a one-mile (1.6-km) radius of a research office which had been established. In addition to 399 boys from these 6 schools, 12 boys from a local school for children with special educational needs were included in the sample in an attempt to make it more representative of the population of boys living in the area. Therefore, the boys were not a probability sample drawn from a population, but rather a complete population of boys of that age in that area at that time.

Most of the G2 boys (357, or 87 percent) were white in appearance and of British origin, in the sense that they were being brought up by parents who had themselves been brought up in England, Scotland, or Wales. Of the remaining 54 boys, 12 were

Afro-Caribbean, having at least one parent of West Indian (usually) or African origin. Of the remaining 42 boys of non-British origin, 14 had at least one parent from the North or South of Ireland, 12 had parents from Cyprus, and the other 16 boys were white and had at least one parent from another Western industrialized country.

On the basis of their occupations of their fathers (generation 1, or G1) when they were aged 8, 94 percent of the G2 boys could be described as working class (categories III, IV, or V on the Registrar General's scale, describing skilled, semi-skilled, or unskilled manual workers) in comparison with the national figure of 78 percent at that time. The majority of the boys were living in conventional two-parent families with both a father and a mother figure; at age 8 to 9, only 6 percent of the boys had no operative father and only 1 percent had no operative mother. This was, therefore, overwhelmingly a traditional white, urban, working-class sample of British origin.

The G2 males have been interviewed nine times, at ages 8, 10, 14, 16, 18, 21, 25, 32, and 48. At all ages except 21 and 25, the aim was to interview all the males who were still alive, and it was always possible to interview a high proportion: 405 (99 percent) at age 14, 399 (97 percent) at age 16, 389 (95 percent) at age 18, 378 (94 percent) at age 32, and 365 (93 percent) at age 48. At ages 8, 10, and 14, the G2 boys were assessed in their schools. The tests in schools measured individual characteristics such as intelligence, attainment, personality, and psychomotor impulsivity.

In addition to interviews and tests with the G2 boys, interviews with their G1 parents were carried out by female psychiatric social workers who visited their homes. These took place about once a year from when the boy was age 8 until when he was age 14 to 15 and was in his last year of compulsory education. The primary informant was the mother, although many fathers were also seen. The parents provided details about such matters as the boy's daring, family income, family size, their child-rearing practices, their closeness of supervision of the boy, and his temporary or permanent separations from them.

The teachers completed questionnaires when the G2 boys were aged about 8, 10, 12, and 14. These furnished data about their troublesome school behavior, their restlessness and poor concentration, their school achievement, and their truancy. Ratings were also obtained from the boys' classmates when they were in the primary schools about such topics as their daring, dishonesty, troublesomeness, and popularity.

The G2 males have been repeatedly searched in criminal records (see, e.g., Farrington, Barnes, and Lambert 1996; Farrington, Lambert, and West 1998). The minimum age of criminal responsibility in England and Wales is 10. Recent searches of criminal records of the males took place in July 2002 and December 2004 in the Police National Computer (PNC), at which time most of the males were aged 51. A Home Office report (Farrington et al. 2006) and many previous analyses were based on the criminal records up to age 50 derived from these searches. A further search of the PNC was completed in March 2011, when most males were aged 57. The criminal records of the G2 males are therefore now known up to age 56 (Farrington et al. 2013).

Up to age 56, 177 out of the 404 G2 males at risk (44 percent) were convicted. Seven males were not at risk of conviction because they emigrated before age 21 and their criminal records were not searched abroad. The present chapter focuses on convictions before age 21, and 34 percent of G2 males (137 out of 404) were convicted up to age 20.

B. Generation 3 (G3) Males

Between 2004 and 2013, efforts were made to interview the biological children of the G2 males. These interviews were carried out over a nine-year period because of intermittent funding. There were 691 G3 children whose name and date of birth were known. Only children aged at least 18 (born up to 1995) were targeted. The ethical requirements of the South-East Region Medical Ethics Committee required that we contact the G2 male and/or his female partner in trying to interview the G3 children. Therefore, 20 G3 children whose G2 fathers refused at age 48, and seven G3 children whose G2 father was dead at age 48 (and where no female partner was available) were not eligible to be interviewed. An additional six G3 children who had died, and three who were disabled, together with two who did not know that the G2 male was their father, were also considered to be not eligible. Of the 653 eligible G3 children, 551 were interviewed (84 percent) at an average age of 25; 291 of the 343 G3 males (85 percent) and 260 of the 310 G3 females (84 percent).

As mentioned, there were 691 children whose name and date of birth were known. Their median year of birth was 1981, and more than half were born between 1977 and 1985. They were first searched in microfiche records in 1994, and they were then searched in the PNC in 2003, 2006, and 2011–2012. The 31 G3 children who had been abroad since birth could not be searched, but 656 of the remaining 660 were searched, comprising 343 G3 males and 313 G3 females. The median age at which they were last searched was 29, and more than half were last searched between ages 25 and 33; 95 of the 343 G3 males (28 percent) were convicted, and 27 of the 313 G3 females (9 percent) were convicted. The present chapter focuses on convictions of G3 males before age 21, since less than 10 percent of G3 males were aged 20 or less when they were last searched; 20 percent of G3 males (70 out of 343) were convicted up to age 20. The lower prevalence of convictions among G3 males compared to G2 males may be partly attributable to the general decrease in convictions in England over time and partly attributable to the fact that the G3 children were relatively less deprived than their G2 fathers.

C. Childhood Risk Factors for G2 Males

For comparability, all risk factors were dichotomized, as far as possible, into the "worst" quarter versus the remainder (see Farrington and Loeber 2000). Where there were assessments at both ages 8 and 10, these were combined. The risk factors that were measured at age 8 to 10 for the G2 males were as follows.

Socioeconomic: Low family income, large family size (five or more children in the family), poor housing (dilapidated slum conditions) and low socioeconomic status (an unskilled manual job of the family breadwinner, usually the father) were rated by the social workers on the basis of their interviews with the boy's parents. Based on the relationships with other variables, Farrington and McGee (2017) classified large family size as a socioeconomic risk factor rather than a family risk factor.

Parental: Convictions of G1 parents were obtained from criminal record searches. The other parental and family risk factors were rated by the social workers on the basis of their interviews with the G1 parents. Young mothers had their first child under age 21, while young fathers had their first child under age 23. Young parents were not explicitly included in the statement of the ICAP theory, but Nagin, Pogarsky, and Farrington (1997) in the CSDD found that they predicted offending by the G2 boys and that this was mediated by family factors such as poor supervision.

Family: Poor supervision was rated when the parents did not know where the boy was when he went out. Harsh and/or erratic discipline identified cold, punitive G1 parents, and parental conflict reflected chronic tension or raging conflicts. Disruptive families (separation from a parent up to the boy's tenth birthday) indicated permanent or temporary (over one month) separations of a boy from a G1 parent that were not caused by death or hospitalization.

Individual: Low junior school attainment was based on scores in standard tests of arithmetic, english, and verbal reasoning at age 10 to 11. High daring was based on parent and peer ratings of taking many risks in traffic, climbing, and so on. High hyperactivity was based on teacher ratings of restlessness or poor concentration in class. High troublesomeness is also included in the analysis, although it is not an explanatory risk factor. It was based on a combination of ratings by peers and teachers.

D. Childhood Risk Factors for G3 Males

The main aim of Farrington and his colleagues (2015) was to measure G3 risk factors that were as comparable as possible to G2 risk factors. Some of the G3 risk factors were based on the interview with the G2 male when he was age 32. Since the vast majority of G3 children (96 percent) were age 10 or less at this time, these variables are prospective and predictive. Other G3 risk factors were retrospectively reported by the G3 children during their interviews at the average age of 25. The G3 risk factors were as follows.

Socioeconomic: Low take-home pay was reported by the G2 male at age 32. Large family size referred to the number of people living in the G2 male's household when he was age 32. Poor housing of the G2 male at age 32 was rated by the interviewer, based on whether the home was dirty, smelly, damp, neglected, overcrowded, inadequately furnished, had vermin, or had structural problems. Low socioeconomic status at age 32 indicated that the G2 male had a semiskilled or unskilled manual job.

Parental: Convictions of the G2 father and G2 mother up to age 32 were obtained from criminal record searches. As for G1 parents, young fathers referred to G2 males who were under age 23 at the time of the birth of their first child, and young mothers referred to G2 mothers who were under age 21 at the birth of their first known child. (We only have records of children that the G2 female had with the G2 male.)

Family: Poor parental supervision referred to the G2 parents not knowing where their children were when they were out, as reported by the G3 male. Physical punishment referred to the G2 parent hitting or smacking their children when they misbehaved, as reported by the G3 male. Parental conflict was based on the G2 father's report at age 32 of frequent rows with his female partner, and the G2 father also reported at age 32 about whether he had a child living elsewhere.

Individual: Early school leaving was based on the report of the G3 male that he had left school before age 16. The G3 male also reported on whether he often or very often took many risks under age 12, and on whether he always had difficulty paying attention at school. He also reported on whether he had ever been suspended or expelled from school.

III. Testing the ICAP Theory

According to the ICAP theory, a number of childhood risk factors contribute to the development of long-term antisocial potential (between-individual differences) because they cause strain, provide antisocial models, or impair attachment or socialization (Figure 11.1). These risk factors include socioeconomic factors (e.g., low family income, poor housing), parental factors (e.g., convicted parents), family factors (e.g., poor parental supervision, disrupted families), and individual factors (e.g., school failure, high impulsiveness).

A. The Antisocial Attitude Scale

Farrington and McGee (2017) measured the crucial theoretical construct of antisocial potential using an Antisocial Attitude (AA) scale, which was completed by the G2 males at ages 18, 32, and 48. They began with two existing scales of aggressive attitudes and anti-establishment attitudes (totaling 24 items) and dropped four items that were not very strongly related to the other 20 items. Table 11.1 shows the 20 items comprising the AA scale. This scale had quite high internal consistency; alpha = .72 at age 18, alpha = .67 at age 32, and alpha = .71 at age 48.

There was relative stability in the AA scores at different ages, since they were significantly intercorrelated; $r = .47$ from age 18 to age 32, $r = .44$ from age 18 to age 48, and $r = .54$ from age 32 to age 48. After correcting for the reliability of the scores, the correlations increased to $r = .68$ (18 to 32), $r = .62$ (18 to 48), and $r = .78$ (32 to 48). Therefore, the most antisocial G2 males at one age tended also to be the most antisocial

Table 11.1 Antisocial Attitude Items

Anti-establishment

1. The police are always roughing people up
2. Boys who get the chance should stay on at school
3. Civil servants are too full of their own importance
4. Rich people are usually very lazy
5. The police should get more support from the public
6. This country would be run better by young people
7. School did me very little good
8. Anyone who works hard is stupid
9. Civil servants are usually quite helpful

Aggression

10. If someone does the dirty on me I always try to get my own back
11. I enjoy watching people getting beaten up on TV
12. I sometimes like to frighten people
13. I enjoy a punch-up
14. Anyone who insults me is asking for a fight
15. Sometimes I am a bit of a bully
16. When I've had a few drinks, I sometimes feel like starting a fight
17. It takes a lot to make me lose my temper
18. I am often cruel to people
19. I've sometimes hit someone without being angry with him
20. If someone hits me first I really let him have it

Four items that reduced internal consistency were removed from the scale: Hard work is the only way to get on in life; I get on well with the man who tells me what to do at work; Even if someone hit me first I would never hit back; I try to keep out of fights. Items 2, 5, 9, and 17 were reverse-coded.

at later ages, in agreement with the ICAP theory postulating relative stability in antisocial potential over time.

There was, however, absolute change in the AA scores at different ages, since they steadily decreased, from mean = 5.70 at age 18 to mean = 4.30 at age 32 and mean = 3.56 at age 48. These scores are meaningful, as they indicate the number of items (out of 20) endorsed in the antisocial direction. Therefore, the G2 males tended to become less antisocial as they got older. The distribution of AA scores was rather flat and not skewed at age 18 (skewness = 0.66, kurtosis = 0.14) and age 32 (skewness = 0.69, kurtosis = 0.60), but it was slightly more peaked and slightly more skewed at age 48 (skewnness = 1.14, kurtosis = 1.49).

In this chapter, two main hypotheses from the ICAP theory are tested:

1. The AA scale is significantly related to convictions (up to age 20) for G2 males and G3 males.
2. Socioeconomic, parental, family, and individual factors significantly predict scores on the AA scale for G2 males and G3 males.

B. Antisocial Attitude Scores Versus Convictions

Table 11.2 shows AA scores versus convictions up to age 20. The left-hand side of the Table shows results for G2 males; 387 males had AA scores and were at risk of conviction in this analysis. It can be seen that the percentage convicted increased irregularly with AA scores, from 20.9 percent convicted of those scoring 0 to 3 to 51.0 percent convicted of those scoring 8 or more. The percent convicted was especially high (75 percent) for G2 males who scored 12 or more. Because the relationship between AA scores and convictions seemed nonlinear, the G2 males with the highest AA scores were investigated in the analyses. Dichotomizing the AA scores into the worst quarter versus the remainder, 51.0 percent of G2 males scoring 8 or more were convicted, compared with 27.7 percent of G2 males scoring 7 or less (odds ratio [OR] = 2.71, $p < .001$; one-tailed statistical tests are used here because of directional predictions). In comparing AA scores with the convicted/nonconvicted dichotomy, the area under the ROC Curve (AUC) was 0.65 ($p < .001$).

The AA scale was completed by 273 G3 males who were at risk of conviction up to age 20, at the average age of 25. Fortunately, AA scores were not correlated with age ($r = .03$) for these males, so it was not necessary to control for age in analyses. It is possible that the previously discovered (in G2 males) tendency for AA scores to decrease with age

Table 11.2 Antisocial Attitude Scores Versus Convictions

Generation 2			Generation 3		
Score	% Conv	N	Score	% Conv	N
0–3	20.9	115	0–2	9.4	85
4–5	33.3	90	3–4	22.9	70
6–7	31.3	80	5–6	22.4	58
8+	51.0	102	7+	31.7	60
Total	33.9	387	Total	20.5	273
8–9	46.8	47	7	29.2	24
10–11	42.9	35	8–9	25.9	27
12+	75.0	20	10+	55.6	9
0–7	27.7	285	0–6	17.4	213
8+	51.0	102	7+	31.7	60
OR = 2.71, CI = 1.83 to 4.00			OR = 2.20, CI = 1.21 to 4.00		
Mean = 5.67, SD = 3.38			Mean = 4.28, SD = 2.76		
AUC = .65, SE = .03			AUC = .63, SE = .04		

OR = odds ratio; CI = confidence interval (based on one-tailed test); SD = standard deviation; AUC = area under the ROC curve; SE = standard error.

was counteracted by the tendency of older G3 males to be more antisocial, possibly be-cause G2 males became their fathers at younger ages. As mentioned, young G1 parents were more likely to have delinquent G2 males in the CSDD (Nagin et al. 1997). The in-ternal consistency of the AA scale for G3 males was alpha = .62, and the mean AA score was 4.28. The distribution of AA scores was rather flat and not skewed (skewness = -0.19, kurtosis = 0.54).

The right-hand side of Table 11.2 shows that the results for G2 males were largely replicated for G3 males, although AA scores and percentages convicted were some-what lower for G3 males. The percentage convicted increased irregularly with AA scores, from 9.4 percent of those scoring 0 to 2 to 31.7 percent of those scoring 7 or more. The percent convicted was especially high (55.6 percent) for G3 males who scored 10 or more. The AUC was 0.63 (p < .001). Dichotomizing the AA scores into the worst quarter versus the remainder, 31.7 percent of G3 males scoring 7 or more were convicted, compared with 17.4 percent of G3 males scoring 6 or less (OR = 2.20, p = .015). In agreement with the ICAP theory, AA scores were significantly related to convictions.

C. Risk Factors Versus AA Scores

Table 11.3 shows the extent to which the risk factors predicted AA scores of G2 males. There were significant relationships within all four categories, and 11 of the 16 risk factors significantly predicted AA scores. The strongest predictors were low junior school attainment (OR = 3.46), low family income (OR = 3.32), large family size (OR = 3.29), high troublesomeness (OR = 3.22), and poor parental supervision (OR = 3.18).

For comparison, the extent to which these risk factors predicted convictions is also shown in Table 11.3 (see also Farrington et al. 2015); 13 risk factors predicted convictions. The biggest differences concerned parental conflict and disrupted families, which predicted convictions but not AA scores. Nevertheless, the ORs for AA scores were significantly correlated (r = .64, p = .007) with the ORs for convictions. (Because the OR is a ratio variable, the logarithms of the ORs were correlated.) The mean ORs (based on logarithms) were 2.06 for AA scores and 2.35 for convictions.

Table 11.4 shows the extent to which the risk factors were related to AA scores of G3 males. There were significant relationships within all four categories, but only 7 of the 16 risk factors were significantly related to AA scores. (In testing the significance of the logarithm of the odds ratio, its standard error was increased by 10 percent be-cause of the clustering of sons in families; see Farrington et al. 2015, p. 57.) Of course, the smaller sample size and the correction for clustering of G3 males mean that some ORs (e.g., 1.88 for poor attention and 1.72 for large family size) were not significant for G3 males but would have been significant for G2 males. The strongest relationships

Table 11.3 Risk Factors Versus AA Scores and Convictions for G2 Males

	AA Scores			Convictions		
	% NR	% R	OR	% NR	% R	OR
Socioeconomic						
Low family income	20.5	46.1	3.32*	29.3	49.5	2.37*
Large family size	20.3	45.7	3.29*	28.8	50.0	2.48*
Poor housing	22.5	32.9	1.68*	27.6	44.7	2.12*
Low SES	25.7	28.9	1.18	32.3	40.5	1.43
Parental						
Convicted G1 father	22.6	41.6	2.44*	26.9	61.7	4.38*
Convicted G1 mother	24.8	46.4	2.63*	31.8	60.0	3.21*
Young G1 father	25.5	30.1	1.26	33.0	35.5	1.12
Young G1 mother	24.2	31.0	1.41	31.4	39.2	1.41
Family						
Poor supervision	21.4	46.4	3.18*	28.6	51.4	2.64*
Harsh discipline	23.8	32.7	1.56*	29.0	42.9	1.83*
Parental conflict	25.8	27.2	1.07	28.1	46.6	2.24*
Disrupted family	24.7	32.2	1.45	29.0	51.1	2.56*
Individual						
Low junior attainment	20.4	47.1	3.46*	28.3	52.2	2.77*
High daring	22.1	36.0	1.98*	26.0	53.3	3.26*
High hyperactivity	22.7	41.6	2.43*	30.4	48.1	2.12*
High troublesomeness	20.9	45.9	3.22	26.4	60.0	4.17*

AA = antisocial attitude; % NR = % of non-risk category; % R = % of risk category; OR = odds ratio; * $p < .05$, one-tailed; SES = socioeconomic status.

were for early school leaving (OR = 4.04), suspended/expelled (OR = 2.74), convicted Gq2 mother (OR = 2.59), poor housing (OR = 2.55), and poor parental supervision (OR = 2.15).

For comparison, the extent to which these risk factors were related to convictions of G3 males is also shown in Table 11.4 (see also Farrington et al. 2015); 11 risk factors were significantly related to convictions. The biggest differences were in low take-home pay and physical punishment, which were related to convictions but not to AA scores. Nevertheless, the ORs for AA scores were significantly correlated (r = .57, p = .021) with the ORs for convictions. The mean ORs were 1.73 for AA scores (lower than for G2 males) and 2.39 for convictions (very similar to G2 males).

Table 11.4 Risk Factors Versus AA Scores and Convictions for G3 Males

	AA Scores			Convictions		
	% NR	% R	OR	% NR	% R	OR
Socioeconomic						
Low take-home pay 32	21.6	18.2	0.81	13.6	33.3	3.17*
Large family size 32	19.6	29.6	1.72	16.9	31.8	2.30*
Poor housing 32	16.0	32.8	2.55*	15.9	37.7	3.19*
Low SES 32	20.8	27.8	1.46	17.3	30.3	2.08*
Parental						
Convicted G2 father	18.5	28.0	1.71*	13.2	30.9	2.94*
Convicted G2 mother	19.7	38.9	2.59*	19.3	43.3	3.20*
Young G2 father	20.5	27.0	1.44	20.3	20.8	1.03
Young G2 mother	20.3	24.5	1.28	19.5	23.7	1.28
Family						
Poor supervision G3	15.7	28.6	2.15*	11.3	30.6	3.47*
Physical punishment G3	22.3	21.3	0.94	15.6	32.2	2.58*
Parental conflict 32	20.7	21.7	1.06	19.2	19.8	1.04
Disrupted family 32	20.4	29.8	1.65	19.4	26.8	1.52
Individual						
Early school leaving G3	18.1	47.2	4.04*	16.4	48.6	4.83*
High risk taking G3	18.2	30.9	2.00*	14.4	35.8	3.33*
Poor attention G3	20.3	32.4	1.88	19.2	29.7	1.78
Suspended/Expelled G3	16.8	35.5	2.74*	13.0	40.8	4.61*

AA = antisocial attitude; % NR = % of non-risk category; % R = % of risk category; OR = odds ratio; * $p < .05$, one-tailed; SES = socioeconomic status; 32 = derived from G2 male at age 32; G3 = derived from G3 male.

IV. CONCLUSIONS

This chapter has presented both the ICAP theory and an empirical test of the ICAP theory using CSDD data on two generations of males. The key construct of long-term antisocial potential (AP) was operationally defined and measured by antisocial attitude (AA) scores. As expected on the ICAP theory, these scores correlated with convictions of the males in both generations.

Deductions from the ICAP theory in regard to which childhood risk factors predict AA scores were also tested. As expected, socioeconomic factors (low family income, large family size, poor housing), parental factors (convicted fathers and mothers), family factors (poor parental supervision, harsh parental discipline), and individual factors (low junior school attainment, high daring, high hyperactivity) all predicted high AA scores for G2 males; and a socioeconomic factor (poor housing), parental factors (convicted fathers and mothers), a family factor (poor parental supervision), and individual factors (early school leaving, high risk taking under age 12) were all related to high AA scores for G3 males.

It should be noted that this analysis has some limitations. In particular, several of the G3 risk factors were measured retrospectively rather than prospectively. Also, while we did our best to measure similar risk factors in the two generations, some are not very comparable. For example, G2 harsh discipline (reflecting harsh and erratic discipline and cold parental attitudes, based on prospective information from G1 parents) was not exactly the same as G3 physical punishment (based on retrospective information from G3 males); and G2 hyperactivity (reflecting poor concentration and restlessness in class, based on prospective information from teachers) was not exactly the same as G3 attention problems (reported retrospectively by G3 males).

The ICAP theory could be improved in several ways. First, different models could be specified at different ages, based on the relative importance of various long-term risk factors (strain, modeling, socialization, impulsiveness, and life events). It might be expected that parental and peer influences would be differentially important at different ages, and the same is true of life events such as leaving school, getting a job, leaving home, and getting married. Second, other risk factors that are not currently in the theory could be incorporated (e.g., biological factors or empathy). Third, the theory could be modified to explain differences in offending by age, gender, race, and nationality or country (Farrington and Loeber 1999). Fourth, different models could be proposed to explain the prevalence and frequency of offending, persistence versus desistance, and the length of criminal careers. Fifth, different models of short-term situational influences could be proposed to explain the commission of different types of crimes. Potential offenders could be asked about their likelihood of committing crimes in different situations to investigate their cognitive processes and motivations (Farrington 1993), and efforts could be made to study the learning processes involved in the development of criminal careers.

In further testing the ICAP theory in the CSDD, the next analysis should study the relationship between AA scores and self-reported delinquency for G2 and G3 males. One problem with convictions is that they reflect not only antisocial potential but also official biases in the arrest, charging, and court processes. These official biases will tend to mask and reduce the relationship between AA scores and convictions. Self-reported delinquency may provide a less biased measure of offending, although it will be affected by the willingness to admit offenses. Farrington and his colleagues (2014) systematically compared convictions and self-reported offenses of the G2 males from age 10 to age 48.

In order to advance knowledge about DLC theories and test them more adequately, new prospective longitudinal studies are needed with repeated self-report and official record measures of offending. Future longitudinal studies should follow people up to later ages and focus on desistance processes. Because past studies have generally focused on onset and on ages up to 30, little is known about life-course–persistent offenders (see Jolliffe et al. 2017a, 2017b). Future studies should compare risk factors for early onset, continuation after onset (compared with early desistance), frequency, seriousness, later onset, and later persistence versus desistance. DLC theories should make explicit empirical predictions about all these topics. Also, future studies should make more effort to investigate protective factors and biological and neighborhood risk factors, since most is known about individual and family risk factors. And future research should compare development, risk factors, and life events for males versus females and for different ethnic and racial groups in different countries.

The ICAP theory and other DLC theories have many policy implications for the reduction of crime. For example, it is clear that children at risk can be identified with reasonable accuracy at an early age. The worst offenders tend to start early and to have long criminal careers. The ICAP theory specifies intervention targets in childhood, including children from low-income families, with poor school attainment, with criminal parents, who are impulsive, and who receive poor child-rearing. It is desirable to intervene early to prevent the later escalation into chronic or life-course–persistent offending and to develop risk-needs assessment instruments to identify children at risk of becoming chronic offenders. These instruments could be administered soon after school entry, at ages 6 to 8 (see, e.g., Augimeri et al. 2011).

The fact that offenders tend to be antisocial in many aspects of their lives means that any measure that succeeds in reducing offending will probably have wide-ranging benefits in reducing, for example, accommodation problems, relationship problems, employment problems, alcohol and drug problems, and aggressive behavior. Consequently, it is very likely that the financial benefits of successful programs will greatly outweigh their financial costs (see, e.g., Farrington and Koegl 2015). The time is ripe to mount a new program of research to compare, contrast, and test predictions from the ICAP and other DLC theories in the interests of developing more valid theories and more effective crime-prevention measures.

References

Augimeri Leena K., Margaret M. Walsh, Angela D. Liddon, and Carla R. Dassinger. 2011. "From Risk Identification to Risk Management: A Comprehensive Strategy for Young Children Engaged in Antisocial Behavior." In *Juvenile Justice and Delinquency*, edited by David W. Springer and Albert R. Roberts, 117–140. Sudbury, MA: Jones and Bartlett.

Farrington, David P. 1977. "The Effects of Public Labelling." *British Journal of Criminology* 17: 112–125.

Farrington, David P. 1993. "Motivations for Conduct Disorder and Delinquency." *Development and Psychopathology* 5: 225–241.

Farrington, David P. 1995. "The Development of Offending and Antisocial Behaviour from Childhood: Key Findings from the Cambridge Study in Delinquent Development." *Journal of Child Psychology and Psychiatry* 36: 929–964.

Farrington, David P. 2000. "Explaining and Preventing Crime: The Globalization of Knowledge—The American Society of Criminology 1999 Presidential Address." *Criminology* 38: 1–24.

Farrington, David P. 2003. "Developmental and Life-Course Criminology: Key Theoretical and Empirical Issues—The 2002 Sutherland Award Address." *Criminology* 42: 211–255.

Farrington, David P. 2005. "The Integrated Cognitive Antisocial Potential (ICAP) Theory." In *Integrated Developmental and Life-Course Theories of Offending*, edited by David P. Farrington, 73–92. New Brunswick, NJ: Transaction.

Farrington, David P., Geoffrey Barnes, and Sandra Lambert. 1996. "The Concentration of Offending in Families." *Legal and Criminological Psychology* 1: 47–63.

Farrington, David P., Jeremy W. Coid, Louise Harnett, Darrick Jolliffe, Nadine Soteriou, Richard Turner, and Donald J. West. 2006. *Criminal Careers up to Age 50 and Life Success up to Age 48: New Findings from the Cambridge Study in Delinquent Development.* London: Home Office (Research Study No. 299).

Farrington, David P., Jeremy W. Coid, and Donald J. West. 2009. "The Development of Offending from Age 8 to Age 50: Recent Results from the Cambridge Study in Delinquent Development." *Monatsschrift fur Kriminologie und Strafrechtsreform (Journal of Criminology and Penal Reform)* 92: 160–173.

Farrington, David P., and J. David Hawkins. 1991. "Predicting Participation, Early Onset, and Later Persistence in Officially Recorded Offending." *Criminal Behaviour and Mental Health* 1: 1–33.

Farrington, David P., and Christopher J. Koegl. 2015. "Monetary Benefits and Costs of the Stop Now And Plan Program for Boys Aged 6–11, Based on the Prevention of Later Offending." *Journal of Quantitative Criminology* 31: 263–287.

Farrington, David P., Sandra Lambert, and Donald J. West. 1998. "Criminal Careers of Two Generations of Family Members in the Cambridge Study in Delinquent Development." *Studies on Crime and Crime Prevention* 7: 85–106.

Farrington, David P., and Rolf Loeber. 1999. "Transatlantic Replicability of Risk Factors in the Development of Delinquency." In *Historical and Geographical Influences on Psychopathology*, edited by Patricia Cohen, Cheryl Slomkowski, and Lee N. Robins, 299–329. Mahwah, NJ: Lawrence Erlbaum.

Farrington, David P., and Rolf Loeber. 2000. "Some Benefits of Dichotomization in Psychiatric and Criminological Research." *Criminal Behaviour and Mental Health* 10: 100–122.

Farrington, David P., Rolf Loeber, and Magda Stouthamer-Loeber. 2003. "How Can the Relationship Between Race and Violence Be Explained?" In *Violent Crime: Assessing Race and Ethnic Differences*, edited by Darnell F. Hawkins, 213–237. Cambridge, UK: Cambridge University Press.

Farrington, David P., and Tara R. McGee. 2017. "The Integrated Cognitive Antisocial Potential (ICAP) Theory: Empirical Testing." In *Routledge International Handbook of Life-Course Criminology*, edited by Arjan A. J. Blokland and Victor Van Der Geest, 11–28. London: Routledge.

Farrington, David P., Alex R. Piquero, and Wesley G. Jennings. 2013. *Offending from Childhood to Late Middle Age: Recent Results from the Cambridge Study in Delinquent Development.* New York: Springer.

Farrington, David P., Maria M. Ttofi, and Rebecca V. Crago. 2017. "Intergenerational Transmission of Convictions for Different Types of Offenses." *Victims and Offenders* 12: 1–20.

Farrington, David P., Maria M. Ttofi, Rebecca V. Crago, and Jeremy W. Coid. 2014. "Prevalence, Frequency, Onset, Desistance and Criminal Career Duration in Self-Reports Compared with Official Records." *Criminal Behaviour and Mental Health* 24: 241–253.

Farrington, David P., Maria M. Ttofi, Rebecca V. Crago, and Jeremy W. Coid. 2015. "Intergenerational Similarities in Risk Factors for Offending." *Journal of Developmental and Life-Course Criminology* 1: 48–62.

Farrington, David P., and Donald J. West. 1981. "The Cambridge Study in Delinquent Development." In *Prospective Longitudinal Research: An Empirical Basis for the Primary Prevention of Psychosocial Disorders,* edited by Sarnoff A. Mednick and Andre E. Baert, 137–145. Oxford: Oxford University Press.

Farrington, David. P., and Donald J. West. 1990. "The Cambridge Study in Delinquent Development: A Long-Term Follow-Up of 411 London Males." In *Kriminalität: Personlichkeit, Lebensgeschichte und Verhalten (Criminality: Personality, Behaviour and Life History),* edited by Hans-Jurgen Kerner and Gunter Kaiser, 115–138. Berlin: Springer-Verlag.

Jolliffe, Darrick, David P. Farrington, Alex R. Piquero, John F. MacLeod, and Steve Van de Weijer. 2017a. "Prevalence of Life-Course-Persistent, Adolescence-Limited, and Late-Onset Offenders: A Systematic Review of Prospective Longitudinal Studies." *Aggression and Violent Behavior* 33: 4–14.

Jolliffe, Darrick, David P. Farrington, Alex R. Piquero, Rolf Loeber, and Karl G. Hill. 2017b. "Systematic Review of Early Risk Factors for Life-Course-Persistent, Adolescence-Limited, and Late-Onset Offenders in Prospective Longitudinal Studies." *Aggression and Violent Behavior* 33: 15–23.

Moffitt, Terrie E. 1993. "Adolescence-Limited and Life-Course-Persistent Antisocial Behavior: A Developmental Taxonomy." *Psychological Review* 100: 674–701.

Murray, Joseph, David P. Farrington, and Manuel P. Eisner. 2009. "Drawing Conclusions About Causes from Systematic Reviews of Risk Factors: The Cambridge Quality Checklists." *Journal of Experimental Criminology* 5: 1–23.

Nagin, Daniel S., Greg Pogarsky, and David P. Farrington. 1997. "Adolescent Mothers and the Criminal Behavior of their Children." *Law and Society Review* 31: 137–162.

Piquero, Alex R., David P. Farrington, and Alfred Blumstein. 2007. *Key Issues in Criminal Career Research: New Analyses of the Cambridge Study in Delinquent Development.* Cambridge, UK: Cambridge University Press.

Theobald, Delphine, and David P. Farrington. 2009. "Effects of Getting Married on Offending: Results from a Prospective Longitudinal Survey of Males." *European Journal of Criminology* 6: 496–516.

Van Der Laan, Andre, Martine Blom, and Edward R. Kleemans. 2009. "Exploring Long-Term and Short-Term Risk Factors for Serious Delinquency." *European Journal of Criminology* 6: 419–438.

West, Donald J. 1969. *Present Conduct and Future Delinquency.* London: Heinemann.

West, Donald J. 1982. *Delinquency: Its Roots, Careers and Prospects.* London: Heinemann.

West, Donald J., and David P. Farrington. 1973. *Who Becomes Delinquent?* London: Heinemann.

West, Donald J., and David P. Farrington. 1977. *The Delinquent Way of Life.* London: Heinemann.

Zara, Georgia. 2010. "David P. Farrington: The Integrated Cognitive Antisocial Potential Theory." In *Encyclopedia of Criminological Theory,* Vol. 1, edited by Francis T. Cullen and Pamela Wilcox, 313–322. Thousand Oaks, CA: Sage.

CHAPTER 12

....

THE INTERCONNECTED DEVELOPMENT OF PERSONAL CONTROLS AND ANTISOCIAL BEHAVIOR

....

MARC LE BLANC

In 1969, my mind was seized by the Travis Hirschi book *Causes of Delinquency*. I thought it was theoretically and empirically greatly innovative. Today, criminologists would agree that it was the most important book in criminology of the 20th century. Then I decided to undertake a longitudinal replication of his empirical test and an axiomatic formalization of his discursive theory. These initial endowers became, during the next 40 years, the Montreal Two Samples Four Generations Longitudinal Studies (MTSFGLS). This chapter is a summary and update of our multidisciplinary, multilayered, and developmental theoretical journey. Section I recalls our conceptual roots and our meta-control theory. Section II presents a definitive statement of our systemic theory of the development of antisocial behavior, particularly the argument that the mechanisms and courses of the development of offending apply to all forms of antisocial behaviors. Section III specifies the content of our integrative personal control theory and the development of self-control and social control. Section IV reviews the mechanism of the developmental interaction between the self and social control systems based on the chaos-order perspective; to do so, examples of the functioning of attractors, bifurcations, self-organization, and interdependence will be exposed. Finally, Section V discusses the importance of our personal control theory for criminology and sequels of our theoretical and empirical journey. Many propositions in this chapter are more thoroughly detailed in Le Blanc (1997a, 2006).

I. Conceptual Roots

In the 1980s we started to design and test three control theories: the explanation of the rate of criminality in a community, the criminal behavior of a person, and a criminal event. They became a multilayered, multidisciplinary, and integrative developmental control meta-theory of the criminal phenomenon (Le Blanc 1997a). It was argued that the three layers of the criminal phenomenon were embedded. Criminal events form the criminal behavior of a person, which becomes the criminality rate of a community. In addition, it was hypothesized that continuity and changes at one layer were a context that influenced growth and decline at higher and lower layers. It was multidisciplinary and integrative because at each layer explanatory notions came from various disciplines and from many perspectives within behavioral sciences. Developmental principles were stated according to existing knowledge in psychology, sociology, and the chaos-order systemic perspective (Le Blanc and Janosz 1998).

We use the term "control" according to its third literal definition in *Webster's* (p. 245), that is, "a mechanism used to regulate and guide the operation of a system." Comte (1842) introduced this notion in sociology (Le Blanc 2004); it is central in psychology (Lytton 1990) and compatible with Gibbs's sociological definition: ". . . control is *overt* behavior by human in belief that (1) the behavior increases the probability of some subsequent condition and (2) the increase or decrease is desirable" (Gibbs 1989, p. 23).

Our meta-control is rooted in Quételet (1831), who wrote "the first scientific treatise ever published on crime" (Sylvester 1984, p. V). During his career he launched developmental criminology. First, he proposed and tested the developmental law of the propensity for crime, the age–crime curve or the crime meta-trajectory. Second, he suggested a developmental mechanism of the criminal career, the aggravation process from minor to major crimes.

> Although it is around the age of 25 that the *maximum* number of different types appears, this *maximum* is found advanced or retarded by some years. However, for certain crimes according to more or less tardy development of some qualities which are in relationship with these crimes. Thus, man pushed by violence and his passions at first yields to rape and indecent assaults. He enters almost at the same time into a career of theft, which he seems to follow as by instinct until his last breath. The development of his strength carries him to all acts of violence, to homicide, rebellion, and thefts on the public ways. Later, reflection turns manslaughter into murder and poisoning. Finally, man, advancing in his career of crime, substitutes more cunning for strength and becomes a forger more than at any other period of his life. (translation by Sylvester 1984, p. 65)

Third, Quételet anticipated an explanation of the propensity for crime, the changes over time in the biological and the psychological characteristics of the criminal; in parenthesis we indicate the terminology now in use in criminology:

> This fatal propensity (*participation*) seems to develop in proportion to the intensity of physical strength (*biological factors*) and passion (*psychological or self-control*)

of man. It attains its maximum around 25 years (*his official data began with age 16*), a period where physical development is pretty nearly ended. Intellectual (*IQ*) and moral development (*beliefs for Hirschi*), which takes place with more slowness, then moderates the propensity for crime which diminishes still more slowly by the weakening of man's physical strength (*biological factors*) and passions (*low self-control*). (translation by Sylvester 1984, p. 65)

In the same direction, Reiss (1951) proposed a distinction between social and personal controls. For his part, Hirschi (1969) limits the notion of social control to Durkheim's definition of the bond to society in his book *Le suicide* (1960; lecture in 1897). Kornhauser (1978) sets the origin of a community control theory with Thrasher (1927), Shaw and McKay (1969), and Sutherland, while Empey (1978) emphasizes Freud's psychodynamic formulation of psychological control. Nevertheless, much of the recent criminological literature forgets the formulations of control preceding Hirschi's statement and test of social control theory. Precursors and followers of Hirschi would probably agree with Empey's statement that the core of control theories is "their emphasis upon the idea that delinquent and conformist behavior is a function of the ability of the child to control his antisocial impulses. They start from the assumption that children require training if they are to behave socially. Delinquent behavior will result either if a child lacks the ability for effective training or because he has been trained badly" (1978, p. 207).

This statement fits particularly well with Durkheim's definition of his personal control theory in *L'éducation morale* (1963; lecture in 1934), which includes bonds and constraints in addition to psychological characteristics. He used the terms temperament, intelligence, and personality in his text. The last version of such theory introduces the notion of low self-control and its relation with social controls (Gottfredson and Hirschi 1990) and opportunities (Gottfredson and Hirchi 2003).

II. A META-CONTROL THEORY OF THE CRIMINAL PHENOMENON

A meta-theory reflects on "what concepts should be included, about how these concepts should be linked, and about how the theory should be studied" (Wagner 1984, p. 26). Our meta-control theory states that "in a favorable context, control mechanisms are operand and they change in harmony with social expectations, as a consequence conformity results and maintains itself over time. Conversely, in an unfavorable context, control mechanisms are insufficient and inappropriate and the criminal phenomenon emerges and persists" (Le Blanc 1997a, p. 224). We propose that there are four general categories of meta-mechanism in the system of control of antisocial behavior: bonding, unfolding, modeling, and constraining. Two conditions modulate their functioning, the environment and the background. Each of these six notions portrays a particular systems composed of concepts that are operationalized by numerous constructs measured by variables. They have an empirically established or a potential impact for the explanation of each level of the phenomenon of antisocial behavior, criminality, criminal activity, and crime.

In our meta-control theory, bonding, in the Durkheim tradition, refers to the various ways by which individuals are held together as a group or a community. Unfolding, in the Binet (1903) and Sorokin (1928) traditions, is the natural growth and development toward a desirable state of greater quality, the growth of a community or the development of the person according to societal expectations. Modeling, in the Tarde (1924) and Sutherland (1960) tradition, is the existence of patterns that can shape conformity, opportunities that are available to individuals in a community, and activities and model persons to be used by them. Constraining, also in the Durkheim tradition, is the regulation of conformity through various direct and indirect restrains; they are formal or informal limits defined by a community or imposed by institution or the social network of the person.

The formulation of the meta-control theory takes the following forms. At the community layer, a low rate of crime persists in a community when the social organization is sound and the cultural organization robust, when direct controls are efficient, and when there are sufficient legitimate opportunities. These states are conditional on the quality of the setting and on the position of the community in the social structure (see Le Blanc 1997a, p. 239). At the individual layer, the fractal notions of the personal control theory are bonds, self-control, models, and constraints, and there are three conditions that modulate these interacting notions: the social status of the family or the individual, the physical and biological environment of the person, and the biological and psychological skills of the individual. At the layer of the act, the central notions are routines activities, immediate control, occasions, and guardianship and the external conditions are the community control and the personal control (Le Blanc 1997a, p. 248).

We hypothesize that the four central mechanisms, at each layer, are simultaneously and longitudinally interacting as a system to produce antisociality. They also have their own ontogeneticity. This meta-control theory is systemic because it defines a structure between components, as well as direct and indirect, reciprocal, and feedback relationships. This structure states the relative position of the mechanisms into three strata. The dynamic dimension, ages, is present because over time there is continuity and change within the mechanisms and, in turn, in antisocial behavior. The distal position of the bonding and unfolding mechanisms depends on the principle of prerequisites in development and on the distinction between continuity and change. Our theory states that there are exogenous or contextual conditions without a direct impact on antisocial behavior, the environment, and the backgrounds. The four central mechanisms of the system of control mediate their impact.

Two mechanisms of control, bonding and unfolding, are prerequisite; their impact is direct and indirect on antisocial behavior. They are the foundations of the control system, the intermediate causes. Without bonds, models cannot be significant and constraints cannot be operand. In consequence, an unbounded individual cannot be sensitive to constraints or influenced by the available prosocial models. In addition, since mechanism refers to a desirable state, what ought to be, it precedes the influence of available models and constraints, whether direct and indirect and formal and informal. In addition, the bonding and unfolding mechanisms modulate the antisocial behavior through the mechanisms of modeling and constraining. These mechanisms are proximal causes of antisocial behavior. Models and constraints are more specific to the space-time dimension. They are not the permanent dimensions of control such as bonding and unfolding. They are in a situation of reciprocal causation at a specific point in time. The modeling and the constraining mechanisms are in the same situation; a causal order cannot be established theoretically at each ages.

In sum, this meta-control theory states that the bonding and unfolding mechanisms are the foundations and the continuity component of control, while the modeling and constraining mechanisms are the actualizing catalysts. These four mechanisms of the central control system are in synergetic relations, while these relations are modulated by external conditions, that is, the backgrounds and the environmental contexts; this modulation operates in a particular space-time and historical context. All these elements interact to produce an overall state of control, in turn to produce a level of forms of antisocial behavior. Before specifying this meta-theory for the explanation of the criminal activity of the individual, let's formulate the unit theory of the development of antisocial behavior system.

III. A UNIT SYSTEM THEORY OF THE COURSE OF ANTISOCIAL BEHAVIOR

In the context of a formal theory, as in this chapter, a unit theory is derived from a meta-theory according to Le Blanc and Caplan's (1993) review of the literature of the methodology of theoretical formulation. It concerns a specific phenomenon, the antisocial behaviors of an individual along his life span. A unit theory formulates definitions of notions and concepts, developmental mechanisms, and propositions of a structure and dynamic relations between components of the antisocial behavior system along the ages.

This section synthesizes our empirical tests (Fréchette and Le Blanc 1987; Le Blanc and Fréchette 1989; Le Blanc and Kaspy 1998; Le Blanc and Bouthillier 2003; Le Blanc 1993, 2009, 2019) and updates our reviews and theoretical formulations of our descriptive theory of the development of antisocial behavior (Loeber and Le Blanc 1990; Le Blanc and Loeber 1998; Le Blanc and Janosz 1998; Le Blanc 2012; Le Blanc 2015a).

A.   From Criminal Behavior to Antisocial Behavior

Since the early 1980s, the MTSFGLS[1] evolved with a developmental perspective. The descriptive parameters of criminal activity were defined, the mechanisms of growth and decline were identified, and trajectories were explored. In 1990, with Rolf Loeber, we proposed the developmental criminology paradigm for the understanding of *"within individual change in criminal behavior."* Our notion of conformity to conventional standards of behavior was the dominant sociological position in criminology (Hirschi 1969). It is delimited by population behavioral norms in a particular society for a specific historical period. Laws and governmental regulations from various levels codify many behavioral norms. These antisocial behaviors are legally subdivided into delinquent and problem behavior. They have been measured, since the 1940s, with self-reported questionnaires or interviews, and many forms of antisocial behaviors were assessed with official records of numerous agencies, such as police, courts, driving, medical, school, welfare, protection, etc.

Over the last 50 years, criminologists accepted the axiom that all types of antisocial behavior are part of a latent construct and that they are equivalent to crime (Gottfredson and Hirschi 1990). That position received support from numerous empirical studies of official crimes and measures of self-reported antisocial behavior (Hindelang, Hirschi, and Weis 1981; Loeber, Keenan, and Zhang 1997). Hierarchical confirmatory factor analysis of sets of data from the MTSFGLS, particularly with measures of onset and frequency, confirmed that antisocial behavior is a hierarchical construct in more than 20 previous studies (Le Blanc and Bouthillier 2003). Our construct of antisocial behavior progressively took the following form—a structure composed of four subconstructs: covert, overt, authority conflict, and reckless behaviors. These subconstructs were formed with 12 types of antisocial behavior (scales composed of at least four acts of the same kind): reckless behavior (motor vehicle use, sexual promiscuity, drugs use, disorderly conducts), authority conflict (at home and at school or work), covert criminal activities (minor and major thefts, motor vehicle theft, fraud), and overt or violent behaviors (vandalism, physical and psychological violence, sexual aggression). Our data show that this theoretical model is empirically valid for measures of official and self-reported antisocial behavior, for females and males, from normative and adjudicated samples of adolescents, and four generations from 1960 (Le Blanc 2019). In addition, for all the antisocial behavior scales cited above, we calculated their internal consistency and criterion validity, and they were excellent far all the samples across generations (Le Blanc 1995c, 2015b).

Antisocial behavior is also recognized as a heteromorphous phenomenon because many of these forms of criminal and problem behavior manifest themselves with different acts during childhood, adolescence, and adulthood according to developmental and life-course criminologists (Le Blanc 2015a). For example, measures should include questions on online acts, such as cyber pornography, gambling, bullying, frauds, and so on. In addition, the inventory and measurement of forms of antisocial behavior typical of adults is far from exhaustive concerning deviant acts at work, with a motor vehicle, during sexual activities, abuse of substances, violence with an intimate partner and family members, personal and commercial frauds, etc.

B. The Course of Antisocial Behavior

The criminological literature reviews on criminal careers (Blumsteim et al. 1986; Piquero, Farrington, and Blumstein 2003, 2007; DeLisi 2015; see also Chapters 2 through 6) and the development of offending (Le Blanc and Fréchette 1989; Loeber and Le Blanc 1990; Le Blanc and Loeber 1998) propose numerous generalizations on descriptive (participation, frequency, variety, seriousness, and crime mix) and boundary (onset, offset, and duration) parameters enumerated in Table 12.1. This table also states that these parameters could be adapted to measure the state and development of self and social controls (right-hand column). In addition, following Quételet observations on the

Table 12.1 The Analytical Tools to Study the Course of Antisocial Behavior and Self– and Social Controls: Descriptive Parameters, Developmental Mechanisms, and Trajectories

Antisocial Behavior	Social and Self Controls
Descriptive Parameters	
Participation: an individual takes part in at least one behavior: current, during last year for example, or cumulative, for a specific time period.	The minimal score of one on a scale
Frequency: number of acts within a given time period: annual (Lambda) or cumulative, for a specific time window.	The score of an individual on a scale
Mix: a combination of acts at a particular point in time.	A combination of scores on social or self-controls scales at an age
Seriousness: a score based on legal classifications, the harmfulness of an act, or by ratings of severity by experts or the population.	An extreme score at an age, for example, a score of two standard deviations or more
Variety: the number of categories of behaviors at a particular point in time.	The number of different non-zero scale at a particular age
Boundary Parameters	
Onset: the age of an individual at his first act	The state of a scale at age one
Offset: the age of an individual when he carried out his last act.	The state of a scale at a subsequent age
Duration: the time interval between the first and the last act.	The quantity of change for a scale between ages
Developmental Mechanisms	
Activation: the process by which the development of a behavior or a characteristic progress or regress with age.	

(continued)

Table 12.1 Continued

Antisocial Behavior	Social and Self Controls
Acceleration: increase in frequency with age.	Increase of a score on a scale with age
Diversification: increase in variety of acts with age.	Increase in variety with age
Developmental sequence: the hierarchical stages of increase of the seriousness on a type of antisocial behavior.	This question is controversial theoretically and empirically.
Escalation: the progression of an individual on a developmental sequence.	
Stabilization: increase in duration with age of onset.	Increase in duration on a scale with age of onset
Deactivation: the process by which the growths of a behavior or a scale regress with age.	
Deceleration: decrease in frequency with age.	Decrease of a score of a scale with age
Specialization: decrease in variety of acts in function of age.	Decrease in variety with age
Ceiling: reaching a plateau of seriousness.	Reaching its maximum score on a scale
Reversal sequence: the hierarchical stages of decrease of the seriousness on a type of antisocial behavior.	Hierarchical stages of decline on a characteristic
De-escalation: the regression of an individual on a developmental sequence.	The regression of an individual on a developmental sequence
Course: the result of the cumulative synergy of the simultaneous action of the developmental mechanisms.	
Meta-trajectory: the individual life span development of all types of antisocial behavior takes the form of a reverse U shape cycle (age-crime curve law).	The individual life span progressive development of any social and self controls characteristics (Glenn aging-stability law)
Meso-trajectories: we called them common, transitory (adolescent-limited, Moffitt 1993), and persistent (life-course-persistent, Moffitt 1993).	Social control meso-trajectories are unknown. Some self-control meso-trajectories are identified: normative, progression, cyclic, etc.
Micro-trajectories: the number varies with the age window, the type of community, the characteristics of the sample, the type of antisocial behavior, etc.	Social control micro-trajectories are unknown. Some self-control micro-trajectories are identified in our data.

Source: Adapted and updated from Le Blanc and Fréchette (1989) and Le Blanc and Loeber (1998).

age–crime curve and today's empirical confirmations (see Chapter 2), our unit theory of antisocial behavior proposes the following generalization: the course of all individual forms of antisocial behaviors takes the shape of a reverse U curve for every individual during their life course. Individuals vary in the timing, length, and height of their reverse U-shape meta-trajectory (Le Blanc 2015a, 2019). However, the tests of this statement are mostly limited to crime—rarely do they consider other forms of antisocial behavior, the exception being alcohol and drug use.

Quételet (1842, 1869) noted the existence of the developmental mechanism of aggravation of individual criminal activity. In Table 12.1 it is claimed that this mechanism operates in between two devices, activation and deactivation, to create the course of all antisocial behaviors or their reverse U curve. Again, we think that it applies to all forms of antisocial behavior, and we are currently investigating this phenomenon (Le Blanc 2019). The task of criminology is still the identification of the mechanisms that result in quantitative and qualitative changes in that meta-trajectory and specific trajectories across the life course. In addition, Table 12.1 proposes ways to measure the action of these mechanisms on antisocial behavior as well as on self- and social controls (for more on self-control, see Morizot and Le Blanc 2003, 2005a, 2005b).

Criminologists have also addressed, for many years, the empirical question of identifying micro-trajectories under the reverse U-shape macro-trajectory of delinquency. Many methodologies were used to conduct such investigations (Le Blanc 2002). They started with transition matrices in the landmark longitudinal study of Wolfgang, Figlio, and Sellin (1972). Then they employed ad hoc dynamic classification such as cross-tabulation of measures of self-reported delinquency at two or more times. Later, researchers experimented with group detection methods with statistical models such as cluster analysis, group-based modeling, growth curve modeling, latent trajectory modeling, etc. There are so many studies of micro-trajectories with general or specific measures of delinquency and problem behavior that it is now difficult to keep track of all of them (see, e.g., Piquero 2008; Piquero, Reingle Gonzalez, and Jennings 2015). Studies have detected between 3 and 10 micro-trajectories from the abstinence to the persistence and the violent persistent trajectories. The number and nature of the trajectories vary with beginning age, gender, stage of the system of justice considered, the type of sample and analytical method used, and the life span window. In the MTSFGLS we identified five micro-trajectories in a representative sample of adolescents and in a sample of adjudicated delinquents.

We proposed that the micro-trajectories could be grouped into three meso-offending trajectories (Fréchette and Le Blanc 1987; Le Blanc and Fréchette 1989; Le Blanc 1995b) that we named the persistent, the transitory, and the common delinquents. The first two meso-trajectories were later named life-course and adolescence-limited delinquents by Moffit (1993). The common trajectory is composed of offenses that are occasional and committed around the middle adolescence in an otherwise law-abiding existence—an epiphenomenon of adolescence manifested by acts of vandalism, shoplifting, minor theft, or public mischief and the exploration of soft drugs. Our hypothesis, under empirical test, is that these three meso-trajectories are observable in the development of all forms of antisocial behavior (Le Blanc 2015a).

Our theory states that the development of antisocial behaviors is systemic in the sense that it is self-regulated in a chaos-order perspective. The interconnections between forms of antisocial behavior over time, for example, crime and drug use, runs according of the developmental mechanism of the chaos-order perspective. This functioning of the system of antisocial behavior was tested empirically for developmental interconnections between crime and drug use along the life course using latent trajectory modeling to identify launch, contemporary, and causal effects (Le Blanc 2009). Section IV explains in more detail unit self and social control theories.

IV. An Explanatory Multidisciplinary and Integrative Unit Control Theory of the Development of Antisocial Behavior in an Individual

Our theory states that the level of individual criminal activity is as follows: "conformity to conventional standards of behavior occurs and persists, on one hand, if an appropriate level of allocentrism exists and the bond to society is firm and, on the other hand, if constraints are appropriate and models of prosocial behavior are available. The personal and social regulation of conformity is conditioned by the biological capacity of the person and his position in the social structure" (Le Blanc 1997a, pp. 228–229). This first formal version of our personal control theory of the development of antisocial behavior proposed four central control explanatory notions shown in Figure 12.1: bonds, self-control, models, and constraints (for changes, compare to Figure 6.3 in Le Blanc, 1997a, p. 230). All notions had their constructs upgraded except for the notion of social status of the family or the individual that is maintained with measures of socioeconomic and occupational status. First, a new aspect, the environment, is introduced, which is composed of two constructs, physical milieu and biological environment. Second, the concept of biological capacities is also subdivided into two constructs, biological capacity and psychological skills. Third, the term community control (top center of Figure 12.1) adds the conditions modulating the action of bonds, self-controls, models, and constraints affected by the nature and degree of the community control system. This last update was introduced in Le Blanc (2006, pp. 226–229) and substantially elaborated in Wikström and Sampson (2006). These eight explanatory notions synthesized constructs that are measured by numerous risks and protective, promotive, and desistance factors that have been empirically identified as having a potential

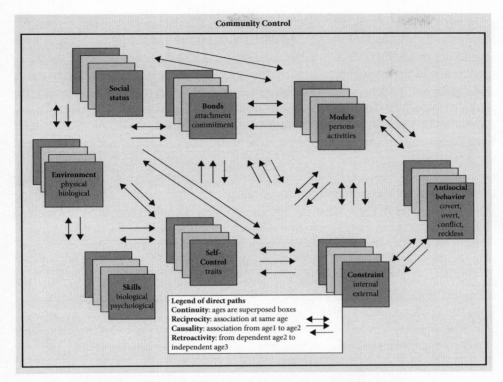

FIGURE 12.1 The Personal Control Explanatory Theory of Antisocial Behavior

Source: Adapted and updated from Le Blanc (1997a, 2006)

or statistical impact on future antisocial behavior. These are reviewed in Morizot and Kazemian (2015; see also Chapters 17 to 22).

Based on our reading of reviews and our own empirical work, our theory states that models and constraints are proximal causes of the development of antisocial behavior; the environment, the skills, and the social status are distal causes; while bonds and self-control become intervening causes. In Figure 12.1, two major systems of control are interacting. The sociological dimension is represented by the social control system composed of the community control system, the social status, the bonds, the models, and the constraints. The psychological dimension is included in the three concepts of individuality: environments, skills, and self-control or personality.

In the social control system, bonding refers to the various ways by which an individual is held together with others (constructs: attachment to persons, such as parents, peers, teachers, adults, etc.; commitment to institutions, e.g., school, religion, work, sport, peers, etc.). Their importance rests in the fact that they reflect the primary need of integration into the group, which grounds the individual in a social and cultural milieu. Second, modeling is the existence of prosocial or antisocial patterns that shape behavior (constructs: routine activities; persons and groups that are exemplars, e.g., scouts, gang members, teacher, coach, etc.). Third, the regulation of behavior through direct and indirect restrains imposed on an individual by social institutions includes socializing tools that one faces in one's family, at school or work, with peers and gangs, in the community, and in society (constructs: rules, discipline, attitudes, reinforcements, informal and formal and direct and indirect sanctions, etc.). Fourth, social status refers to the position of the individual and his or her family in the social structure (construct: racial and ethnic group, sex, immigration, social prestige, socioeconomic status, etc.). Fifth, the state of the community in which the person lives act upon previous constructs according to our community control theory (Le Blanc 1997a, 2006) (construct: setting, background, social and cultural organization, opportunities, direct and indirect controls, and level of community antisocial behavior).

In the self-system, there are three notions in Figure 12.1: the changing physical and biological environments, the biological and psychological skills of the person, and the person's personality or self. The physical setting (deterioration of neighborhood, household quality, etc.) and the biological environment (concepts: what you eat, your sleep, pollution [air, noise, lead, etc.], substance use, media use [television, Internet, etc.]) are composed of many conditions known to be associated with antisocial behavior. The biological and psychological skills are affected by the nature and level of continuity control and changes in the environments. The environment and skills have an impact on the ongoing psychological maturation (concept: the egocentric personality, low level of self-control, impulsivity and other personality traits, etc.).

The first axiom of our theory is that the components of the self- and social control systems are active through the process of learning, successive changes in behavioral potentiality that occur as a result of reinforced practices. The impact of this learning process on antisocial behavior is referred to as differential association in criminology (Sutherland and Cressey 1960) or social learning in psychology (Bandura 1976). The second axiom is that the mechanisms of control are simultaneously and causally interacting and they have their own life—they are state dependent. The third axiom is that these systems are organized in a structure (see boxes in Figure 12.1). The fourth axiom is that the relationships between the constructs are (1) reciprocal, i.e., represented by correlations at each age between the measures of the constructs, (2) directional, i.e., manifested by the correlations between the measures of the constructs from age 1 to age 2 that reflect a statistical causality, and (3) retroactive, i.e., visualized by the correlations between a dependent measure of a construct at age 1 with an independent measure at age 2—for example age 1 antisocial behavior has an impact on age 2 bonds, models, constraints, and self-control. In Figure 12.1, all of these theoretical relationships have to be imagined as part of the pipe that runs between the four central control notions with the three external conditions. Such a completed theoretical model is subsequently corrected with empirical data, as in Le Blanc (2009) for the longitudinal relationships between crime and drugs and other family, school, and peer control models. The fifth axiom is that the systems are dynamic because they are characterized by continuity and change. The relative position of the control mechanisms depends on the principles of prerequisites and the distinction between continuity and change.

In sum, Figure 12.1 illustrates that there are exogenous components of personal control that do not have a direct impact on antisocial behavior, social status, the environment, and skills. Two mechanisms of control, bonding and self-control, are the foundations of the overall control mechanism; they modulate antisocial behavior through models and constraints. The four mechanisms of the central system of control interact and are modulated by external conditions to produce an overall level of personal control of anti-social behavior in the context of a particular community control.

A. The Autonomous Development of the Self-Control System

From its birth, criminology has been looking for a criminal personality. After the Second World War it was replaced by personality traits that were then psychometrically rigorous, and most of the numerous comparisons of delinquents with non-delinquents showed that the later were developmentally delayed (Fréchette and Le Blanc 1987). In 1990, Gottfredson and Hirschi provided a new impetus to criminological theory and research by restating that the psychological dimension is a crucial explanation of crime. That position was ours since the beginning of the MTSFGLS (Fréchette and Le Blanc 1987). Their low-self-control theory became a dominant tested position according to meta-analysis and other reviews (Pratt and Cullen, 2000; Miller and Lyman, 2001; Turner and Piquero, 2002; see Chapter 18). It formulated two laws: low self-control is the most important causal factor in explaining criminal behavior, and it remains stable in criminal individuals' life course. Turner and Piquero (2002) found mixed support for these. This section is a summary of our papers on the development of the self-control system (Fréchette and Le Blanc 1987; Le Blanc 1997a, 1997b; Morizot and Le Blanc, 2003, 2005a, 2005b; see also Morizot 2015; see Chapter 18).

We prefer the comprehensive definition of self in the Robert and Collins dictionaries it refers to personality traits making up the individual as a whole, that is, "the ability to exercised restraint or control over one's feelings, emotions, reactions, etc." This defini-tion was adopted by Drever's *Dictionary of Psychology* (1969). In addition, we argued that Gottfredson and Hirschi's (1990) definition of self-control is clearly behavioral be-cause they refer to impulsive, risk-taking, non-verbal, short-sighted, lack of sensitivity to others, physical, temper, and insensitive acts (Le Blanc 1997b). It is also established that the Gottfredson and Hirschi construct is multidimensional (Pratt and Cullen, 2000; Miller and Lyman, 2001). In addition, many dimensions clearly correspond to traits composing commonly used structural personality models, often called the Big Three or Big Five personality traits (Morizot and Le Blanc 2003). Our personal control theory adopts an epigenetic perspective with the notion of allocentrism. It is the move-ment of the individual away from the natural egocentrism of the infant. It manifests it-self by a genuine consideration of what surrounds a person, a disposition to think about others and behave in relation to them. This egocentrism-allocentrism axis of the devel-opment of humans is present in all theories of human development.

Our operational definition of self-control is the result of a reanalysis of 356 items from the Jesness and Eysenck personality tests (Morizot and Le Blanc 2003, 2005a, 2005b). These data were gathered longitudinally from men 12 to 40 years of age born around 1960 in a population sample and an adjudicated population in Montreal. Using an analytical strategy made up of exploratory factor analysis and hierarchical confirmatory factor analysis, we obtained a four-level hierarchical self-control construct composed of three main traits: disinhibition, negative emotionality, and extraversion. These traits were subdivided into two or three secondary traits: for dishinbition, tough-mindness and antisocial values; for negative emotionality, alienation, maladaptive inhibition, and emotional reactivity; for extraversion. These six traits were subdivided into two or three tertiary traits. In consequence of this hierarchical structure, researcher can choose between primary, secondary, or tertiary traits for their empirical analysis. We calculated the internal consistency and criterion validity for these scales, and they were excellent for all the samples across generations (Le Blanc 2015b).

Since we proposed that the course of antisocial behavior should be analyzed in terms of quantitative and qualitative changes and developmental trajectories (see Table 12.1), we applied some of these analytical tools to the development of self-control (for details, see Le Blanc, 2006). Quantitative changes are defined in terms of growth (acceleration) and decline (deceleration). Studies show that the growth personality traits is governed by the aging-stability law (Glenn 1980), while a different law, the reverse U-shape curve, applies for crime. It has been observed that self-control tends to grow and progressively stabilize to become less likely to change with age. Reviewing the literature and analyzing the development of self-control with MTSTGLS data, we concluded that both stability and change were observable. First, individual differences tend to be more stable as age increases. Second, we observed a non-trivial maturational trend or metatrajectory, a better psychological adjustment in the population generally and for antisocial individuals. Self-control traits are not developmentally static; they are adapted to the particular demands of the phases of the life. Moreover, the measurement invariance of our above operational definition, across groups and time, suggested that a specific self-control structure is a meaningful tool for studying very different types of individuals. However, adjudicated males and men from the general population show clear differences in self-control trajectories.

Qualitative changes refer to something new and more complex according to the ontogenetic principle. These changes in nature are often subdivided into a developmental sequence of hierarchical stages. Even if the results of quantitative change studies support the hypothesis of a normative maturation in the direction of allocentrism, they do not favor stage-based theories. However, the marked slowing of the maturation rate after age 30 may be an indication that men have reached some sort of qualitatively distinct psychological adaptation (a ceiling in Table 12.1). It is plausible that this phenomenon is closely associated with the fact that the majority of men and delinquents have desisted from the typical adolescent lifestyle and gained new social bounds through involvement in adult social roles.

In sum, the quantitative improvements in self-control with age form a maturational meta-trajectory, not a reverse U-shape crime curve. Our review of typological studies of personality concluded that despite differences in age, gender, ethnicity, language, culture, historical period, and geographic region, three replicable personality meso-trajectories are identified: adjusted, overcontrolled, and undercontrolled. In addition, a number of cross-sectional and longitudinal studies examined their antecedents, concurrent correlates, and consequences and concluded that they display differentiated profiles in personality traits in cognitive, behavioral, and social adjustment variables. Some studies also showed that they can be identified at different periods of the life span, but the membership is not always stable across time. However, the scientific community has paid little attention to the task of identifying micro-trajectories of self-control development. With the MTSFGLS data, we were able to identify four self-control developmental micro-trajectories, and the level of antisocial behavior increased from the better to the less mature micro-trajectories. Similar micro-trajectories were identified in the adjudicated sample of men, and each was differentially related to antisocial behavior across time.

In conclusion, there is ample information on quantitative and qualitative changes in self-control, and there is emerging knowledge on the meso- and micro-trajectories of self-control. The impact of the self system is represented by the interactions between the physical and biological environment, biological and psychological skills, and the maturation of the self. As for antisocial behavior, self-control is systemic in the sense that it is self-regulated in a chaos-order perspective. The interconnections between self-control traits over time runs according of the developmental mechanism of the chaos-order perspective (see Section V). We are testing the functioning of the system of self-control

B. The Autonomous Development of the Social Control System

Durkheim (1934) was the first to formulate a general theory of social control. He proposed two mechanisms: attachment to a group and social constraints. He stated that socialization has attachment as its base, identification with his family, corporation, country, and humanity. This type of bond necessitates the attachment to persons, which, in turn, is a source of commitment to the morality of the group. If attachment is the first mechanism of socialization, to be effective it needs the support of social constraints. They are forces that impose restraints and limits on the behavior of individuals. These forces are coercive because they apply to behaviors that are prohibited and could be sanctioned by authorities. They manifest themselves by rules that dictate what are the appropriate behaviors and by sanctions that are applied formally or informally when rules are violated. For Durkheim, the individual adhesion to norms and the probability of being sanctioned create an obligation to behave according to social rules. Criminology has been redefining Durkheim's social control notions for more than a century.

Hirschi (1969) redefined the social bond as attachment, commitment, involvement, and beliefs, and Nye (1958) stated that constraints were formal and informal and direct and indirect. During the MTSFGLS, we replicated Hirschi's results in Montreal (Le Blanc and Caplan 1985), we updated his theory after an axiomatic formalization (Le Blanc and Caplan 1993), and we revised Nye's typology of informal and formal social reactions (Le Blanc 1995a). We also took into account the landmark propositions of Wiatrowski and Anderson (1987) on the measurement of bonds. As a consequence, contrary to Hirschi's definition of social control, which includes internal constraints or beliefs but not external constraints, we proposed that the notion of social control is composed of two notions, bonds and constraints. From a measurement point of view, we now define the social control construct as hierarchical and composed of four categories of measures: attachment to different types of persons, commitment to various institutions, models as persons and involvement in routine activities, and internal constraints and external sanctions from institutions.

In criminology, very few theoretical statements have proposed interdependencies between the community controls and the personal controls, self and social. Kornhauser (1978) synthesizes Shaw and McKay's theory in a graph where social disorganization implies weak personal controls and, on the basis of these weak controls, youths become delinquent with or without the influence of organized crime and delinquent companions. Kornhauser then elaborates her theory by adding that cultural disorganization implies a loss of direct external control by the family and that the resulting defective socialization will produce weaker direct internal control. She also indicates that social disorganization implies that the attachment and commitment of the child, as well as the instrumental bond to institutions, will be attenuated and, as a consequence, direct control will suffer at school and in the family. Twenty years later, Elliott et al. (1996) rightly observed that the theoretical discussion of the neighborhood effects is rudimentary, and they proposed new avenues of thought, as did Wikström and Sampson (2006)

In the MTSFGLS, we conducted empirical studies of the functioning the middle range or meso social control system, most of them with at least two waves of data: family (Le Blanc 1992, 1994; Le Blanc, McDuff, and Kaspy 1998), school (Le Blanc, Vallière, and McDuff 1992, 1993), family and school (Le Blanc 1994), and constraints (Le Blanc 1995a). The structure of social control in Figure 12.1 takes into account these studies. In sum, an adolescent bond to society is manifested toward several institutions: family, school, peers, and religion. It is replaced for adults by marriage, work, children, intimate friends, and religion. A person relates to them through two avenues: attachment to persons and commitment to institutions. First, the level of attachment to parents determines an individual's attachment to other persons, while their cumulative impact protects the person against antisocial influences and discourages antisocial behavior. The second element of the bond, the commitment to institutions, refers to an affective investment in education, work, religion, etc. and to what the person hopes to achieve. Therefore, when a person faces the temptation to commit an antisocial act, he or she evaluates the costs of this act relative to their cognitive investments and commitments to institutions. Finally, following Durkheim's classic distinction between norms, defined as rules of law, and moral values, and discipline, circumscribed as monitoring and punishment, we proposed that there are four major sources of restraint (Figure 12.1): internal (beliefs, perception of risk of arrest, respect to persons in authority, neutralization, etc.) and external (parental supervision and sanction; peer sanction, school discipline from peers and teachers; peers restraints; etc.) and formal (expulsion from school or a peer group, a gang, police arrest, fine, etc.). While bonds and constraints can be defined as components of social control, criminology demonstrated that prosocial and antisocial opportunities have to be taken into account (Gottfredson and Hirschi 2003). There are of two types of modeling: individual as models that exemplar persons (parents, teachers, best friend, coach, significant others) and normative or deviant routine activities. When antisocial models and deviant routine activities are dominant in the life of an individual, antisocial behavior increases, as showed by many studies and reviews (Warr 2002; Vitaro, Brendgen, and Lacourse 2015; see Chapter 20). In addition, for all the social control scales cited above, we calculated internal consistency and criterion validity—they were excellent for all the samples across generations of the MTSFGLS (Le Blanc 1995c, 2015b).

In sum, our notion of social controls involves three constructs modulated by the community control context— social status and the physical and biological environment (Figure 12.1). They are indirect explanations of antisocial behavior; they influence the degree of bonding, which, in turn, affects the evaluation of the appropriateness of constraints and the receptivity to models before impacting antisocial behavior. We have argued, in our review of the literature in the above papers, that the direct impact, not the indirect links, of social status on the social control system is most often tested in criminology. These tests are narrow and static since they use few constructs and they test interactions between them mainly with cross-sectional data. Very few studies address the following question: How does social control develop during the life course?

In 2006, we reviewed quantitative changes in social control along the life course and concluded that the aging-stability law governs their growth as for changes in self-control. The literature on quantitative and qualitative changes on social controls was scant for our 2006 paper, and it has not grown significantly since. The meta-developmental trend is an improvement of attachment to parents and other figures and less conflict with them during late adolescence. In addition, there seems to be a deterioration of the relations with single parents during the same period. The commitment to schooling and work improves. Turning to models, we noted an age trend in routine activities: more involvement in leisure activities and in activities with family members and a decrease in loitering. Concerning antisocial peers, we found a decrease in attachment and an increase in the percentage of youths in less delinquent groups and a declining percentage of individuals in tight groups during late adolescence. However, there was a considerable stability in the type of adolescents they affiliated with from one year to the next, and, when change occurred, it was a gradual transition from one peer group type to a type that was not too dissimilar. In addition, the relevance of peers decreased during adolescence and the importance of intimates increased. Finally, there are very few indications of change in external constraints. Physical punishment decreased, while poor supervision and low-level positive parenting increased. Internal controls, beliefs, also increase during adolescence, and there seems to be a decrease in perceived parental control.

In sum, due to the lack of longitudinal studies there are few generalizations on the continuity and change in the social controls during the life course. Bonds, models, and constraints seem to evolve according to the maturational hypothesis. However, there is little evidence of developmental sequences except for peer relations, external control, and play. In addition, we are not able to identify meso- and micro-trajectories of social control, in general, for bonds, constraints, or models. However, we think that changes could be investigated with the analytical tools indicated in Table 12.1. Criminology has made considerable conceptual efforts in defining social controls and studying their association with all forms of antisocial behavior. However, knowledge is scant on quantitative changes and virtually non-existent concerning qualitative changes and trajectories, and social control models tested are rarely complex.

We conclude with a final note on the role of community control in our personal control theory (grey background in Figure 12.1). We follow the dominant position in developmental psychology that states that the milieu never has a direct effect on individual behavior; it is mediated by individual characteristics that activate or deactivate the characteristics of the milieu. Lerner (2002) reviews a variety of models illustrating the developmental interaction between the milieu and the individual in developmental psychology. In criminology, very few theoretical statements have proposed interdependencies between the neighborhood and personal controls. Some studies concluded that the direct impact of community variables on individual antisocial behavior is marginal. However, there is clear indication that the level of community organization mediates the effect of individual structural characteristics. In addition, there are good indications that social disorganization variables have an indirect impact on the individual social control system. Sampson (1993) shows that community-level differences in social cohesion and indirect controls do have significant effects on individual-level variations in offending, antisocial attitude, and association with delinquent peers through family management techniques.

With this state of knowledge in mind, we adopted a theoretical unification perspective for the understanding of the interactions between community and personal controls (Le Blanc 2006; Figure 12.1). There are six categories of factors that compose each layer of community and individual control: the grounds (setting vs. environments and skills), the milieus (social position of the community vs. social status of the individual), the expectations (cultural organization vs. allocentrism), the social conditions (collective efficacy vs. social bonds), the constraints (direct controls vs. internal and external constraints), and the situation (illegal opportunities vs. routine activities). This fractal principle is illustrated in Le Blanc (1997a, p. 259; Figure 6.7) and updated in Le Blanc (2006, p. 229 Figure 6.6). The following theoretical statement about the interdependencies between community and individual layer constructs can be stated: the constructs of the community layer directly induce the range of variation in the constructs of the personal layer.

More precisely, first, the quality of the community setting (space, quality of air, etc.) affects the biological and psychological skills of individuals. Second, the social structure of the community limits the range of individual and family social and ethnic status. Third, the level of social organization in the community entails the level of individual social bonding. In addition, social disorganization narrows the possibilities of self-maturation. Furthermore, social disorganization implies a wider range of antisocial model, and, as a consequence, more persons will have an increased opportunity to associate with antisocial peers and gangs. It is also possible that the level of social organization will limit the level of internal and external constraints on individuals. Fourth, the community level of the cultural organization restricts expectations for the development of an individual in terms of social bond and self-control. Cultural expectations and opportunities mold internal constraints, while external constraints depend on the quality of the social organization and the nature of direct controls in the community. Fifth, the level of formal control in a community will influence the level of internal and external constraints on individuals. Sixth, the available antisocial and prosocial influences that the individual chooses are dependent on the range of legitimate and illegitimate opportunities in the community and the level of social and cultural organization. In sum, the community-layer phenomenon is a contextual condition of the individual-level phenomenon, which, in turn, modulates antisocial behavior.

Remember that the phenomenon of social control is systemic as antisocial behavior and self-control in the sense that it is self-regulated in a chaos-order perspective. The interconnections between measures of social control over time take place according to the developmental mechanism of that perspective. This functioning of the system of social control is under test. The last section will elaborate on their interconnected development among social control, self-control, and antisocial behavior.

V. Developmental Interactions Between Self-Control, Social Control, and Antisocial Behavior Systems

In 1963, Freud and Durkheim independently proposed an interrelation between self and social controls. For Freud, the interdependence between the ego and the superego regulates antisocial behavior. For Durkheim, three interconnected instances produce morality: the power of inhibition (temperament, intelligence, personality), attachment to the group, and social constraints. Gottfredson and Hirschi (1990, 2003) restated the integrative personal control theory of these pioneers; they paraphrased the link between self-control and social control. Social control, in terms of bonding, is no longer the major cause of offending. Low self-control is the principal cause, and it is moderated by criminal opportunities. Bonding becomes a necessary condition of successful child-rearing, and internal and external constraints intervene between low self-control and offending as well as situational conditions. These opportunities may be normative routine activities, antisocial opportunities, or exposure to antisocial role models and delinquent peers. In sum, Gottfredson and Hirschi are proposing that a tenuous bond to society accompanied by ineffective child-rearing practices favor the maintenance of low self-control, which, in turn, result in offending if constraints are ineffective and if the situation is favorable to offending. Our studies confirmed some of these links with cross-sectional and longitudinal data from representative and delinquent samples (MTSFGLS). However, controlling for all constructs, the models displayed the most important direct effect followed by constraints, self-control, and bonds (Fréchette and Le Blanc 1987; Le Blanc, Ouimet, and Tremblay 1988; Le Blanc 1997b; Lanctôt and Le Blanc 2002). We will describe these interactions in a chaos-order developmental perspective, starting by enumerating basic developmental premises (Le Blanc and Janosz 1998; Le Blanc 1997a, 2006).

We accept the orthogenesis principle that "whenever development occurs it proceeds from a state of relative globalism and lack of differentiation to a state of increasing differentiation, articulation, and hierarchic integration" (Werner 1957, p. 126). This principle is compatible with the contextual perspective in developmental psychology, the chaos-order perspective, and the life-course paradigm in developmental criminology. The contextual perspective states that every phenomenon is historic. Constant changes at all age levels characterize life and embeddedness is a particularity of all human phenomena. Development is probabilistic. The influence of the changing context on the trajectory of development is uncertain, and it must be defined in terms of "organism-context reciprocal or dynamic-interactional relations" (Lerner 1986, p. 69). However, the organization and the internal coherence of the organism limit the developmental probabilities of trajectories. The chaos-order view acknowledges the same type of contextuality (Briggs and Peat 1989). In hard science, chaos refers to a relative state of disorder, uncertainty, non-linearity, and unpredictability. Systems include open, complex, fractal, self-organized, conservation of energy, structured randomness, non-linear dynamics, inner rhythms, and sensitivity to the initial condition. However, one limitation in the chaos-order perspective is that in a chaotic state there is never pure randomness or chance: "statements clarifying the limits and likelihood of future behaviors can still be made for a chaotic process" (Peak and Frame 1994, p. 158). In consequence, chaos refers to a state where there is a low probability of many types of antisocial behavior but there is a high level of uncertainty about which antisocial behavior will occur next. This statement is confirmed by a landmark study of crime switching (Wolfgang, Figlio, and Sellin 1972). All these premises are compatible with Thornberry (1987) interactional theory.

This interactional synergy is the result of at least four types of quantitative relationships between self and social controls and antisocial behavior (Figure 12.1). First, each is state dependent (superimposed boxes); second, there are reciprocal relations between them at a specific point in time; third, the directional relations mean that

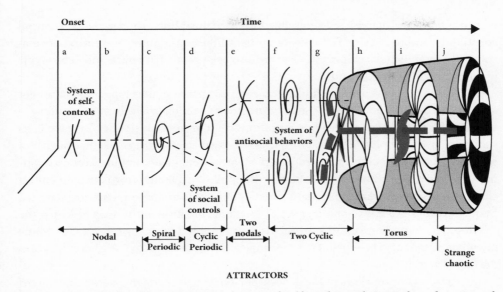

FIGURE 12.2 The Developmental Interrelations of Self- and Social Controls and Antisocial Behavior, a Chaos-Order Perspective

This illustration can be applied to all subsystems of these major systems.

Source: Adapted from Abraham (1995)

variables will become alternatively independent and dependent along the life course; and fourth, as a consequence, there are retroactive effects between them, for example time one antisocial behavior (dependent variable) affects time two models, constraints, bonds, and self-controls (independent variables). We will use an instrument to illustrate the construction of the dynamical interaction of self and social controls in a community context on antisocial behavior, the Briggs and Peat (1989) phase space map. This tool (adapted from Abraham 1995) reinforces the above thinking and serves as a metaphor that may help us understand the interconnected development (superimposed boxes in Figure 12.2). A phase map is composed of attractors, bifurcations, and the logistics of self-organization and interdependence.

A. Attractors and Bifurcations

An attractor is a sort of magnet that structures a phenomenon by the tendency, once initiated, to repeat itself. This is the case in the eight notions of personal control theory shown in Figure 12.1. This state dependency has been amply documented for antisocial behavior and self- and social controls. These attractors are not operating at the same age for each individual or necessarily in the same sequence and fashion. Each attractor is normative. Most individuals have the opportunity to attach to persons, to commit to institutions, to encounter various types of prosocial and antisocial models, to participate in various routine activities, to develop internal constraints, to experience external constraints, and to develop self-control traits. All these components are magnets that concur to their own development. They are also age-graded by society and heterotypic phenomena along the life course.

In Figure 12.2, a self-control nodal attractor, in section *a*, develops into a stronger attractor in section *b*. A social control attractor in section *e* develops in section *f*—similarly for the antisocial behavior in sections *h* and *i*. Not only do they have the constant capacity to duplicate themselves, they are normative in the sense that the list of risk and protective factors that compose them are absent or present in a certain quantity or quality from time to time. Finally, the pull of each attractor is dependent on changes in its own parameters (characteristics of particular control—nature, quantity, frequency, etc.; Table 12.1) and degrees of freedom (the number of ways in which the developmental mechanisms or subsystems have the ability to change; Table 12.1). Some phenomena may also be repellors, for example, the opportunity to use a hard drug and the fear of arrest.

The attractors or repellors in the generic personal control system and its subsystems can produce disequilibrium or chaos in their own and other systems. This disequilibrium is represented by the interactions between the self-control and the social control systems in sections *f* and *g* and subsequent ones. To illustrate this process, we will use delinquent friends as a periodic (section *c*) or a cyclic attractor (section *d*) depending on the number of delinquent peers or the time spent with them (for other examples, see Le Blanc 1997a; Le Blanc 2006). All attractors produce positive and negative feedback. Positive feedback can come from the delinquent peer system itself, for example, delinquent peers introduces the adolescent to a good experience, or from other components of the personal control system, for example, inappropriate parental management techniques or negative emotionality. It is the same for negative feedback. As age increases, opportunities and constraints are modified, and affiliation to a gang is added to the delinquent peer subsystem. Association with delinquent peers and affiliation with a delinquent gang are then two attractors (section *e*). If the association with delinquent peers and the affiliation with a delinquent gang become solid, we have then two cyclic attractors (section *f* and *g*). Later, the system will go through different phases of uncertainty, i.e., the torus attractor situation (sections *h* and *i*). A strong attachment to delinquent friends and affiliation with a delinquent gang become cyclic attractors and they interact. Their interactions form a torus attractor or a high turbulence, which results in increased unpredictability of the impact of the peer subsystem on the antisocial behavior system. Because of this trajectory, a high level of unpredictability can result in antisocial behavior, and we have then a strange attractor, the dark portion in section *j*. This situation of chaos happens when a person has only delinquent friends and is a member of the core group of a structured gang. Then the peer system loses its ability to regulate itself toward a normative situation, the association with prosocial peers. This example can be reformulated with all the components of the personal control theory. It should be noted that some attractors are only minor nodal attractors (e.g., a neighbor) while others are major nodal attractors (e.g., the parents). Other attachments could be chaotic, for example, if the attachment to the mother is very insecure, the child will have difficulties relating to other figures in the attachment subsystem.

As age increases and opportunities change, controls are transformed; systems go through different phases of uncertainty. The torus attractor in *h* and *i* and subsequent sections represents this situation. Self-control, social control, and antisocial behavior have become cyclic attractors, and, in addition, they interact. The interactions form a torus attractor in *h*; high turbulence then exists in the personal control system. The interactions between the self and social control systems and with the antisocial behavior system wrap themselves around the surface of a torus. There is then an increase in un-predictability in the personal system of control of antisocial behavior. In addition, their interactions will cause perturbations in the initial conditions of these systems; the result will then be an amplification of the key parameters. Because of this evolution, a high level of unpredictability can result, and we have then a strange attractor *j*. This situation of chaos happens when a person offends frequently and regularly, when self-control is low, and when social controls are tenuous; it is the persistent delinquent meso-trajectory. In this case, the system loses the ability to regulate itself toward conventional behavior.

Nevertheless, there exist also decline and de-escalation. The level of uncertainty decreases in the systems of control, and the self-control and social control systems move toward an increased conformity, maturation. This is illustrated when we reverse Figure 12.2 by reading it from sections *j* to *a*; this is a phase of de-activation according to Table 12.1. The consequence of these changes is the appearance of critical periods at the intersections of these stages when the systems are in a state of disequilibrium (discussed in Chapters 23 to 30). Then a bifurcation is a forking or a splitting due to a change in one or more parameter that regulates an attractor (Abraham 1995). In sections *e* and *h*, the splitting of a system could be represented by the presence of a new attachment figure, going to day care, or attending elementary school. Attachment to the mother has attained a certain degree, and the attachment to a day-care worker becomes a possibility. We are here referring to changes in internal parameters of the attachment sub-system. In section *h*, the commission of the first antisocial act is a fork that results from the state of the personal control system. The forking is necessarily reinforced by changes in components of the self- and social control system parameters. When there is a bi-furcation in a system, the attractor basin is increased as are the degrees of freedom and parameters. In consequence, the uncertainty level and turbulence are also increased. Abraham (1995) proposes many types of bifurcation for a phase space map (Le Blanc and Janosz 1998; Le Blanc 2006).

B. Self-Organization and Interdependence

Self-organization is a characteristic of systems as well as all living and human beings. It is a basic principle of developmental theories (Lerner 2002). Developmentalists recognize the importance of the self-regulating process when they state that the individual is active in his or her development. The individual gives form to his or her experience by activating or deactivating milieus or personal characteristics. In the social control system, individuals can modify the parameters, for example, by altering the quantity and the nature of the attachment to parents. Individuals are not obliged to attach to all adult figures even if they are attached to their parents, a possible bifurcation in the attachment subsystem. Individuals can learn from their experience, for example, they can stop being attached to a particular antisocial friend. The complexity can take the form of chaos (Figure 12.2).

The self- and social control systems, like all the components of their subsystems, are subject to interactions. In the chaos-order paradigm, interactions are feedback loops (Figure 12.2). These feedback loops are governed by the autopoietic paradox (Briggs and Peat 1989). This paradox says that the degree of autonomy of a system is a function of the number of feedback loops that maintain this system (there is a difference in the number of loops between c and d). However, the number of feedback loops increases opportunities for other systems to enter in the movement. In the model subsystem of social control, we could say that the low frequency of contact with antisocial friends preserves the habit of associating with such friends in the future. In this case, each additional activity with antisocial peers is a supplementary positive-feedback loop. These feedback loops will open avenues for the affiliation with a delinquent gang.

Figure 12.3 integrates the process of the developmental course of self-controls, social controls, and antisocial behavior, their developmental processes (Table 12.1), and

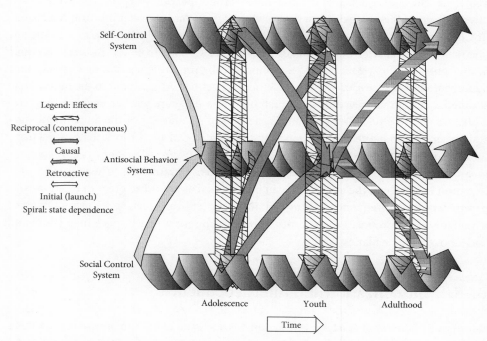

FIGURE 12.3 A Personal Control Theory of the Development of Antisocial Behavior: Interconnection Between Self- and Social Controls and Antisocial Behavior Systems

Source: Adapted from Le Blanc (2006)

their dynamic interactions. It shows the combined action of continuity and change, co-evolution, and the interlocking of systems. First, the horizontal reading in Figure 12.3 represents continuity and change over time. Each spiral is a system: social control, self-control, and antisocial behavior, or their subsystems of constructs because of the fractal nature of the world. They are metaphors for the process we proposed that specify the course and the dynamics of their development (Table 12.1). The time dimension associated with the spirals shows orthogenesis. The beginning of the spirals represents the initial condition, while the rest of the spirals introduce the sensitivity to the initial condition and the state dependence. The independent spirals are there to indicate that each system is a self-organizing phenomenon. Convolution is indicated by the placement of the spirals on three dimensions. Finally, along each spiral there are probabilistic quantitative and qualitative changes and meta-, meso-, and micro-trajectories.

Second, the interactions between self- and social controls and antisocial behavior are illustrated in the vertical reading of Figure 12.3. We are then thinking in terms of interdependencies between the systems, embeddedness, and reciprocal relations. Embeddedness is represented by the fact that each system spiral is part of the personal control theory. As an example, attachment to persons is a subsystem of the bonding subsystem, which in turn is a subsystem of the social control system, which in turn is a subsystem of the personal control system. In Figure 12.3, the white arrows show these interactions at a phase of the life span, in this case childhood, adolescence, and youth. They are in a synergistic interaction. Lighter arrows with lines indicate reciprocal relations; darker arrows show causal relations; grey arrows are retroactive effects. These dark and grey arrows emerge from intersections in the spirals to indicate critical periods in the course of the development of the personal control of antisocial behavior. Notwithstanding these relationships between systems and subsystems, there are also some independent changes relative to the initial condition. The use of spirals implies state dependency. For example, a change in a person's level of self- and social controls will alter the subsequent level of antisocial behavior and, in turn, the subsequent level of self-and social controls, and so on. In fact, these interactions exist all along the time dimension.

VI. Summary and Sequels

The discipline of criminology has been very creative at conceptualizing and measuring antisocial behavior and exploring its life course. In addition, behavioral sciences have been imaginative in advancing the notions of self- and social controls, operationalizing their construct, and testing empirical models. Notwithstanding numerous investigations of the criminal career, criminology has accomplished very little in describing the course of self- and social controls and studying the developmental dynamics between them and antisocial behavior in the context of community control.

The developmental perspective in behavioral sciences offers meaningful tools to describe the course of the personal control system interacting with antisocial behavior. However, they have not helped us to gain a genuine understanding of the processes that support continuity and change in antisocial behavior. With the tools of the chaos-order perspective, we have tried to illustrate the dynamic processes between self- and social controls and antisocial behavior. There is a large gap between our perception of the complexities of these interactions, our discursive statements of these phenomena, the complexity of operational models, and the scarce results of our empirical tests of these complex models.

The discursive theoretical statements and the empirical models in behavioral sciences, as in criminology, are characterized by oversimplification. Until recently, most of the theoretical statements and the quantitative models have been dominated by linear thinking. Linearity is only part of the puzzle. On the one hand, they do not take completely into account the numerous and complex interactions and the random component that is part of development. On the other hand, studies have shown us repeatedly that our theories are reductionist and that our empirical tests are minimally longitudinal since most studies rarely use more than two wave datasets.

In this chapter we explored a different way of overcoming these difficulties by showing that some tools of developmental psychology and the chaos-order perspective could help us to describe the complexity of the conjoint development of personal controls and antisocial behavior. After applying these tools, their heuristic utility is convincing. We believe that the description of the developmental processes of self- and social controls, as well as antisocial behavior, have improved our existing knowledge. In particular, we showed that principles, such as continuity-discontinuity, equilibrium-disequilibrium, probabilistic determinism, and self-organization–interdependence, are compatible with developmental theories in criminology.

Chaos-order tools open a new avenue of investigation for the improvement of our perceptions, theoretical statements, and empirical models. We can more fully consider the complexities of the interactional development of self- and social controls with antisocial behavior. The chaos-order perspective offers a new way of thinking about the probabilistic nature of development and the notion of fractality; it draws our attention to the possibility that structures are reproduced at multiple layers of explanation of the phenomenon of antisocial behavior. Chaos-order tools do not provide a miraculous solution to our difficulties in understanding the complexity of development, only a possible avenue of thinking in criminology. An important heuristic task for criminology would be to simulate mathematically the developmental process that is understood through the phase map. Existing knowledge is sufficient for defining parameters of the course of self- and social controls and antisocial behavior and understanding what new heuristic knowledge would be produced.

NOTE

1. The Montreal Two-Samples Four-Generations Longitudinal Study (MTSFGLS) was supported from 1972 until 2010 by numerous grants, mainly from the Social Sciences and Humanities Research Council of Canada (SSHRC), the Fonds pour la Formation des Chercheurs et l'Aide à la Recherche (Fonds FCAR), and the Conseil Québécois de la Recherche Sociale (CQRS), that were awarded to Marc Le Blanc and collaborators.

REFERENCES

Abraham, Frederick D. 1995. "Introduction to Dynamics: A Basic Language; a Basic Meta-Modeling Strategy." In *Chaos Theory in Psychology*, edited by Frederick D. Abraham and Albert R. Gilgen, 31–50 Westport, CT: Greenwood Press.

Bandura, Albert. 1976. *Social Learning Theory*. Englewood, Cliffs, NJ: Prentice-Hall.

Binet, A. 1903. *L'étude expérimentale de l'intelligence*. Paris: Schleicher.

Briggs, John, and David F. Peat. 1989. *Turbulent Mirror*. New York: Harper & Row.

Comte, A. 1842. *Le Complément de la philosophie sociale, et les conclusions générales*. Paris: Bachelier.

DeLisi, Matt. 2015. "Age-crime Curve and Criminal Career." In *The Development of Criminal and Antisocial Behavior*, edited by Julien Morizot and Lila Kazemian, 51–64. New York: Springer.

Drever, James. 1969. *Dictionary of Psychology*. Baltimore, MD: Penguin Books.

Durkheim, Émile. 1934. *De l'éducation morale*. Paris, France: Alcan. (1963 Édition, Presses Universitaire de France).

Elliott, Delbet S., William J. Wilson, David Huizinga, Robert J. Sampson, Amanda Elliott, and Bruce Rankin. 1996. "The Effects of Neighborhood Disadvantage on Adolescent Development." *Journal of Research in Crime and Delinquency* 33: 389–426.

Empey, Lamat T. 1978. *American Delinquency: Its Meaning and Construction*. Homewood, IL: Dorsey Press.

Fréchette, Marcel, and Marc Le Blanc. 1987. *Délinquances et Délinquants*. Chicoutimi, Quebec: Gaétan Morin.

Gibbs, John P. 1989. *Control Sociology's Central Notion*. Chicago: University of Illinois Press.

Glenn, Norval D. 1980. "Values, Attitudes, and Beliefs." In *Constancy and Change in Human Development*, edited by Orville G. Brim and Jerome Kagan, 596–640. Cambridge, MA: Harvard University Press.

Gottfredson, Michael R., and Travis Hirschi. 1990. *A General Theory of Crime*. Stanford, CA: Stanford University Press.

Gottfredson, Michael R., and Travis Hirschi. 2003. "Self-Control and Opportunity." In *Advances in Theoretical Criminology*, Vol. 12, edited by Chester L. Britt and Micheal R. Gottfredson, 5–20. New Brunswick, NJ: Transaction.

Hindelang, Michael J., Travis Hirschi, and Joseph G. Weis. 1981. *Measuring Delinquency*. Beverly Hills, CA: Sage.

Hirschi, Travis. 1969. *Causes of Delinquency*. Berkeley, CA: University of California Press.

Kornhauser, Ruth R. 1978. *Social Sources of Delinquency: An Appraisal of Analytic Models*. Chicago: University of Chicago Press.

Lanctôt, Nadine, and Marc Le Blanc. 2002. "Explaining Adolescent Females' Involvement in General Deviance: Towards an Integration of Theoretical Perspectives." *Crime and Justice* 26: 113–202.

Le Blanc, Marc. 1992. "Family Dynamics, Adolescent Delinquency, and Adult Criminality." *Psychiatry* 55: 336–353.

Le Blanc, Marc. 1993. "Late Adolescence Deceleration of Criminal Activity and Development of Self and Social Controls, Concomitant Changes for Normative and Delinquent Samples." *Studies on Crime and Crime Prevention* 2: 51–68.

Le Blanc, Marc. 1994. "Family, School, Delinquency, and Criminality, the Predictive Power of an Elaborated Social Control Theory for Males." *Criminal Behavior and Mental Health* 4: 101–117.

Le Blanc, Marc. 1995a. "The Relative Importance of Internal and External Constraints in the Explanation of Late Adolescence Delinquency and Adult Criminality." In *Coercion and*

Punishment in Long-Term Perspectives, edited by Joan McCord, 272–288. New York: Cambridge University Press.

Le Blanc, Marc. 1995b. "Common, Temporary, and Chronic Delinquencies: Prevention Strategies During Compulsory School." In *Integrating Crime Prevention Strategies: Motivation and Opportunity*, edited by Per-Olof H. Wikström, Joan McCord, and Ronald W. Clarke, 160–205. Stockholm: Swedish National Council for Crime Prevention.

Le Blanc, Marc. 1995c. *MASPAQ: Mesures de l'Adaptation Sociale et Personnelle pour les Adolescents Québécois. Manuel et Guide d'Utilisation*. 3rd ed. Montréal, École de Psychoéducation, Université de Montréal.

Le Blanc, Marc. 1997a. "A Generic Control Theory of the Criminal Phenomenon, the Structural and Dynamical Statements of an Integrative Multilayered Control Theory." *Advances in Theoretical Criminology* 7: 215–286.

Le Blanc, Marc. 1997b. "Socialization or Propensity, a Test of an Integrative Control Theory with Adjudicated Boys." *Studies in Crime and Crime Prevention* 6: 200–224.

Le Blanc, Marc. 2002. "The Offending Cycle, Escalation and De-escalation in Delinquent Behavior, a Challenge for Criminology." *International Journal of Comparative and Applied Criminal Justice* 26: 53–84.

Le Blanc, Marc. 2004. "Théories de la Régulation de la Déviance." In *Dictionnaire Critique des Sciences Criminelles*, edited by Gérard Lopez et Stamatios Tiztzis, 245–249. Paris: Dalloz.

Le Blanc, Marc. 2005. "An Integrative Personal Control Theory of Deviant Behavior: Answers to Contemporary Empirical and Theoretical Developmental Criminology Issues." *Advances in Criminological Theory* 14: 125–164.

Le Blanc, Marc. 2006. "Self-Control and Social Control of Deviant Behavior in Context, Development and Interactions Along the Life-Course." In *The Social Contexts of Pathways in Crime, Development, Context, and Mechanisms*, edited by Per-Olof H. Wikstrom and Robert Sampson, 195–242. Cambridge, UK: Cambridge University Press.

Le Blanc, Marc. 2009. "The Development of Deviant Behavior, Its Self-Regulation." *Monatsschrift fur Kriminologie und Strafrechtsreform* 91: 117–136.

Le Blanc, Marc. 2012. "Twenty-Five Years of Developmental Criminology: What We Know, What We Need to Know." In *The Future of Criminology*, edited by Rolf Loeber and Brandon C. Welsh, 124–133. Oxford: Oxford University Press.

Le Blanc, Marc. 2015a. "Developmental Criminology: Thoughts on the Past and Insights for the Future." In *The Development of Criminal and Antisocial Behavior*, edited by Julien Morizot and Lila Kazemian, 507–538. New York: Springer.

Le Blanc, Marc. 2015b. *MASPAQ: Mesures de l'Adaptation Sociale et Personnelle pour les Adolescents Québécois. Manuel et Guide d'Utilisation*, 5th ed. Montréal, École de Psychoéducation, Université de Montréal.

Le Blanc, Marc. 2019. *Antisocial Behavior, A Fifty Years Scientific Journey*. London: Springer Briefs in Criminology.

Le Blanc, Marc, and Christiane Bouthillier. 2003. "A Developmental Test of the General Deviance Syndrome with Adjudicated Girls and Boys Using Hierarchical Confirmatory Factor Analysis." *Criminal Behavior and Mental Health* 1: 81–105.

Le Blanc, Marc, and Aaron Caplan. 1985. "A Cross-Cultural Verification of Hirschi Social Control Theory." *International Journal of Comparative and Applied Criminal Justice* 9: 123–138.

Le Blanc, Marc, and Aaron Caplan. 1993. "Theoretical Formalization, a Necessity: The Example of Hirschi's Social Control Theory." *Advances in Criminological Theory* 4: 329–431.

Le Blanc, Marc, and Marcel Fréchette. 1989. *Male Criminal Activity, from Childhood Through Youth Multilevel and Developmental Perspectives*. New York: Springer-Verlag.

Le Blanc, Marc, and Michel Janosz. 1998. "The Development of Control and General Deviance. The Methodological Contribution of the Chaos-Order Paradigm." Unpublished paper. Montreal, School of Criminology and School of Psychoeducation, Université de Montréal.

Le Blanc, Marc, and Nathalie Kaspy. 1998. "Trajectories of Delinquency and Problem Behavior: Comparison of Synchronous and Non-synchronous Paths on Social and Personal Control Characteristics of Adolescent." *Journal of Quantitative Criminology* 14: 181–214.

Le Blanc, Marc, and Rolf Loeber. 1998. "Developmental Criminology Updated." *Crime and Justice* 23: 115–198.

Le Blanc, Marc, Pierre McDuff, and Nathaly Kaspy. 1998. "Family and Preadolescence Delinquency: A Comprehensive Sequential Family Control Model." *Early Child Development and Care* 42: 63–91.

Le Blanc, Marc, Marc Ouimet, and Richard E. Tremblay. 1988. "An Integrative Control Theory of Delinquent Behavior, a Validation 1976–1985." *Psychiatry* 51: 164–176.

Le Blanc, Marc, Evelyne Vallières, and Pierre McDuff. 1992. "Adolescents' School Experience and Self-Reported Offending, A Longitudinal Test of a Social Control Theory." *International Journal of Adolescence and Youth* 3–4: 197–247.

Le Blanc, Marc, Evelyne Vallières, and Pierre McDuff. 1993. "The Prediction of Males' Adolescent and Adult Offending from School Experience." *Canadian Journal of Criminology* 35: 459–478.

Lerner, Richard M. 1982. *Concepts and Theories of Human Development*. New York: Random House.

Lerner, Richard M. 2002. *Concepts and Theories of Human Development*. 5th ed. New York: Random House.

Loeber, Rolf, Kate Keenan, and Qanwu Zhang. 1997. "Boys' Experimentation and Persistence in Developmental Pathways Toward Serious Delinquency." *Journal of Child and Family Study* 6: 321–357.

Loeber, Rolf, and Marc Le Blanc. 1990. "Toward a Developmental Criminology." *Crime and Justice* 12: 373–473.

Lytton, Hugh. 1990. "Child and Parent Effects in Boys' Conduct Disorder, a Reinterpretation." *Developmental Psychology* 26: 683–697.

Miller, Josuha D., and Donald Lynam. 2001. "Structural Models of Personality and Their Relation to Antisocial Behavior, a Meta-Analytic Review." *Criminology* 39: 765–798.

Moffitt, Terrie E. 1993. "Life-Course-Persistent" and "Adolescent-Limited" Antisocial Behavior, a Developmental Taxonomy." *Psychological Review* 100: 674–701.

Morizot, Julien. 2015. "The Contribution of Temperament and Personalité traits to Criminal and Antisocial Behavior Development and Desistance." In *The Development of Criminal and Antisocial Behavior*, edited by Julien Morizot and Lila Kazemian, 137–166. New York: Springer.

Morizot, Julien, and Lila Kazemian. 2015. *The Development of Criminal and Antisocial Behavior*. New York: Springer.

Morizot, Julien, and Marc Le Blanc. 2003. "Continuity and Change in Personality from Mid-Adolescence to Mid-life, a 25-Years Longitudinal Study Comparing Conventional and Adjudicated Men." *Journal of Personality* 7: 705–755.

Morizot, Julien, and Marc Le Blanc. 2005a. "Searching for a Developmental Typology of Personality in Its Relations to Antisocial Behaviors, a 25-Years Longitudinal Study of an Adjudicated Men Sample." *Criminal Behavior and Mental Health*, 13: 241–277.

Morizot, Julien, and Marc Le Blanc. 2005b. "Searching for Developmental Typology of Personality and Its Relation to Antisocial Behaviors: A 25-Years Longitudinal Study of a Representative Sample of Men." *Journal of Personality* 73: 139–182.

Nye, Ivan F. 1958. *Family Relationships and Delinquent Behavior*. New York: Wiley.

Peak, David, and Micheal Frame. 1994. *Chaos Under Control*. New York: Freeman.

Piquero, Alex R. 2008. "Taking Stock of Developmental Trajectories of Criminal Activity Over the Life-Course." In *The Long View of Crime: A Synthesis of Longitudinal Research*, edited by Akiva M. Liberman, 23–78. New York: Springer.

Piquero, Alex R., David P. Farrington, and Alfred Blumstein. 2003. "The Criminal Career Paradigm." *Crime and Justice* 30: 359–506.

Piquero, Alex R., David P. Farrington, and Alfred Blumstein. 2007. *Key Issues in Criminal Career Research*. Cambridge, UK: Cambridge University Press.

Piquero, Alex R., Jennifer M. Reingle Gonsalez, and Wesley G. Jennings. 2015. "Developmental Trajectories and Antisocial Behavior Over the Life-Course." In *The Development of Criminal and Antisocial Behavior*, edited by Julien Morizot and Lila Kazemian, 75–88. New York: Springer.

Pratt, Travis C., and Francis C. Cullen. 2000. "The Empirical Status of Gottfredson and Hirschi's General Theory of Crime, Meta-analysis." *Criminology* 38: 932–964.

Quételet, A. (1831). *Recherches sur le Penchant au Crime aux Différents Âges*. Brussels: M. Hayez, Imprimeur de l'Académie Royale.

Quételet, A. (1842). *Sur l'Homme et le Développement de ses Facultés, ou Essai de Physique Sociale*. Paris: Bachelier.

Quételet, A. (1869). *Physique Sociale, Essai sur le Développement des Facultés de l'Homme*. Brussels: C. Muquardt.

Reiss, Albert J. 1951. "Delinquency as a Failure of Individual and Social Controls." *American Sociological Review* 16: 196–207.

Sampson, Robert J. 1993. "Family and Community-Level Influences on Crime." In *Integrating Individual and Ecological Aspects of Crime*, edited by David P. Farrington, Robert J. Sampson, and Per-Olof H. Wikström, 31–60. Stockholm: Swedish National Council on Crime Prevention.

Shaw, C. R., and McKay, H. D. 1969. *Juvenile Delinquency and Urban Areas*. 2nd ed. Chicago: University of Chicago Press.

Sorokin, P. 1928. *Contemporary Sociological Theories*. New York: Harper & brothers.

Sutherland, Edwin H., and Donald R. Cressey. 1960. *Principles of Criminology*. 6th ed. Chicago: Lippincott.

Sylvester, Sawyer F. 1984. *Research on the Propensity for Crime at Different Ages*. Cincinnati: Anderson.

Tarde, G. 1924. *La criminalité comparée*. Paris: Alcan.

Thornberry, Terence P. 1987. "Toward an Interactional Theory of Delinquency." *Criminology* 25: 863–892.

Thrasher, F. M. 1927. *The Gang*. Chicago: University of Chicago Press.

Turner, M. G., and Alex Piquero. 2002. "The Stability of Self-Control." *Journal of Criminal Justice* 30: 457–471.

Vitaro, Frank, Mara Brendgen, and Eric Lacourse. 2015. "Peers and Delinquency: A Genitally Informed Developmentally Sensitive Perspective." In *The Development of Criminal and Antisocial Behavior*, edited by Julien Morizot and Lila Kazemian. 221–236. New York: Springer.

Wagner, David G. 1984. *The Growth of Sociological Theories*. Beverly Hills, CA: Sage.

Warr, Mark. 2002. *Companions in Crime: The Social Aspect of Criminal Conduct*. Cambridge, UK: Cambridge University Press.

Werner, H. 1957. "The Concept of Development from a Comparative and Organismic Point of View." In *The Concept of Development*, edited by Dale B. Harris. Minneapolis: University of Minnesota Press.

Wiatrowski, Michael, and Kristine L. Anderson, K.L. 1987. "The Dimensionality of the Social Bond." *Journal of Quantitative Criminology* 3: 63–81.

Wikstrom, Per-Olof H., and Robert Sampson. 2006. *The Social Contexts of Pathways in Crime: Development, Context, and Mechanisms*. Cambridge, UK: Cambridge University Press.

Wolfgang, Marvin E., Robert M. Figlio, and Thorsten Sellin. 1972. *Delinquency in a Birth Cohort*. Chicago: University of Chicago Press.

CHAPTER 13

THE SOCIAL
DEVELOPMENT MODEL

CHRISTOPHER CAMBRON, RICHARD F. CATALANO, AND J. DAVID HAWKINS

THIS chapter presents an overview of the social development model (SDM)—a general theory of human behavior that integrates research on risk and protective factors into a coherent model. Section I specifies the model constructs and their hypothesized relationships to prosocial and antisocial behaviors. Section II provides a synthesis of what we have learned from empirical tests of social development hypotheses for predicting pro- and antisocial behaviors. Section III highlights interventions derived from the SDM and summarizes their impact on pro- and antisocial behaviors. The chapter concludes with a final section presenting future directions for SDM-based research.

I. THEORETICAL BACKGROUND

Much progress has been made over the last 30 years in the discovery of predictors of antisocial behavior. Longitudinal studies have identified these predictors in the individual and in family, school, community, and peer group environments (Farrington 1989; Hawkins, Catalano, and Miller 1992; Farrington and Loeber 1999). However, to utilize these advances in the discovery of longitudinal predictors, the mechanisms by which the development of antisocial behavior is cultivated or inhibited requires a theoretical understanding of the relationships among this array of predictors (Bursik and Grasmick 1996). The goal of any theory of antisocial behavior should be to explain and predict the onset, escalation, maintenance, de-escalation, and cessation or desistance from patterned behaviors that are of concern to society, including illegal drug use, violence, and crime.

The SDM is a general theory of human behavior that attributes the etiology of both prosocial and antisocial behaviors to similar developmental processes (Hawkins and Weis 1985; Catalano and Hawkins 1996b). Rooted in criminological theory, the SDM organizes research on risk and protective factors (Hawkins, Catalano, and Miller 1992) and integrates the strongest empirically supported elements of control theory (Hirschi 1969), social learning theory (Bandura 1977), and differential association theory (Sutherland 1973; Matsueda 1988) into a model of human behavior. The goal of this synthesis is to provide more explanatory power its component theories (Catalano and Hawkins 1996b). Consistent with the tradition of integrated theories in criminology, the SDM attends to underlying theoretical assumptions of human behavior and recognizes the importance of understanding behavior in a developmentally appropriate context (Farrington 2011).

Control theory contributes the etiology of both delinquency and conformity to the SDM. The strength of bonds to prosocial groups such as families or schools and commitment to conventional lines of behavior lead to the adoption of the beliefs of those groups that inhibit antisocial behavior (Hirschi 1969). The SDM incorporates this perspective but departs from control theory by hypothesizing a similar process of antisocial bonds, commitment, and beliefs as a plausible causal mechanism in the development of antisocial behavior. The SDM recognizes that bonds among typically prosocial entities like families may in fact contribute to antisocial behavior if the beliefs and actions of those groups are antisocial. Alternatively, control theory hypothesizes that antisocial behavior emanates from weak, inconsistent, or nonexistent social bonds to families, schools, communities, or peers. In an additional departure from control theory, the SDM hypothesizes that involvement, while playing a role in the theory, is not a part of the social bond itself. Involvement with prosocial others has seen the least empirical support for its ability to inhibit antisocial behavior (Kempf 1993).

Social learning theory (Akers 1977; Bandura 1977; Krohn, Massey, and Skinner 1987) hypothesizes that antisocial behavior is learned in group settings through processes of rewards and punishment. Social learning informs the SDM as a means of identifying which patterns of behavior are adopted, reinforced, and discouraged and the mechanism by which this occurs. Social, emotional, and cognitive skills are also acquired through group interaction. These skills influence the development and application of emotional and behavioral self-regulation necessary for inhibiting antisocial behavior. As applied to the field of criminology by Akers, deviance is conceptualized from a social learning perspective as an interactional process of imitating and modeling observed deviance in society. The SDM hypothesizes syntheses of social learning and control theory that allows stable and interactional antisocial processes to take shape among antisocial groups bonded by shared commitment and beliefs. In the SDM, skills derived from social learning are necessary to access rewards from group interactions.

Sutherland's differential association theory (Sutherland and Cressey 1970; Sutherland 1973; Matsueda 1988) is incorporated into the SDM as an impetus for parallel but separate causal paths for prosocial and antisocial processes. Similar to social learning at its core, humans are hypothesized to learn deviant behavior socially and act out deviance once they have accrued antisocial associations of a sufficient quantity and quality. Antisocial bonds may overcome prosocial bonds in an individual's life and tip the scales toward antisocial behavior. Each operates concurrently within the SDM, with antisocial bonds increasing the likelihood of antisocial behavior and prosocial bonds increasing the likelihood of prosocial behavior. The SDM includes pathways from either antisocial rewards or beliefs to antisocial behavior apart from the influence of deviant others as postulated by differential association.

The SDM hinges on basic assumptions about human nature that coincide with key assumptions made by control theory, social learning, and differential association. First, humans are hypothesized to be satisfaction seekers who primarily act in accordance with their perceived self-interest. Pure self-interest in the Hobbesian sense is unlikely possible given the constraints of ability, opportunity, and prior socializing experiences and the interplay of long- and short-term perceived self-interest. As such, constrained self-interest is thought to influence both prosocial and antisocial behaviors. Second, a normative consensus for prosocial and antisocial behavior exists in society, and prosocial behaviors are typically preferred by individuals. The strength and content of pro- and antisocial motivations makes value conflicts inevitable even if everyone knows the "rules of the game." Even in the presence of a consensus for normative behavior, antisocial behavior has three separate sufficient conditions for development. Antisocial behavior arises when (1) prosocial socialization breaks down, prosocial opportunities are not available, or lack of skills preclude effective involvement with prosocial groups or the environment fails to reinforce prosocial behavior; (2) antisocial behavior develops in the presence of prosocial bonding when perceived benefits of the antisocial behavior outweigh potential costs; or (3) individuals are bonded to antisocial families, schools, communities, or peers and, in turn, act in accordance with the norms and beliefs of these groups (Catalano and Hawkins 1996b).

The SDM hypothesizes two socialization paths through which pro- and antisocial behavior arises. Behavior is ultimately determined by an individual's beliefs and values. Strong beliefs in the moral order or prosocial values lead to prosocial behaviors, while lack of belief in the moral order or beliefs in antisocial values lead to antisocial behaviors. The path to antisocial behavior is afforded two more avenues not contingent on antisocial beliefs. If sufficient rewards exist for antisocial behavior or sufficient pressures to maintain antisocial bonds are felt, an individual with a strong belief in the moral order may still commit antisocial acts. Beliefs and values are derived from strong bonds to social groups and the accompanying commitment that an individual feels to that social group. On each path, four socialization processes establish a social bond between an individual and a socialization unit: (1) perception of opportunities for pro- or antisocial behavior; (2) involvement with pro- or antisocial groups; (3) social, emotional, and cognitive skills that enhance involvements and make recognition or reward more likely; and (4) the perception of rewards for interactions with pro- or antisocial groups. Skills are hypothesized as necessary to access rewards from either pro- or antisocial interaction. An individual will become bonded and committed to prosocial or antisocial socialization units depending on the prosocial or antisocial nature of these opportunities, involvements, and reward. The more strongly an individual is bonded to a socialization unit, the more likely he or she is to adopt its beliefs. Behavior will be prosocial or antisocial depending on the strengths of prosocial and antisocial beliefs of those to whom they are bonded (Catalano and Hawkins 1996b).

The social development process is affected by three exogenous factors: position in the social structure, individual constitutional factors, and external constraints. These factors have demonstrated their ability to predict antisocial behavior (Gottfredson and Hirschi 1990; Dishion et al. 1991; Loeber and Stouthamer-Loeber 1998; Herrenkohl, Hawkins et al. 2001; Wasserman et al. 2003; Moffitt et al. 2011). The SDM hypothesizes that these factors exert influence on perceived opportunities for involvement with a group, skills for interacting with that group, and perceived rewards for interaction. These exogenous factors are hypothesized to be fully mediated by social development processes (Catalano and Hawkins 1996b).

The SDM is explicitly developmental, originally with four submodels for developmental phases defined by major contextual changes that take place in development: birth to school entry, elementary school, middle school, and high school. While the same general social development processes operate, each submodel specifies the socialization units involved and the form of prosocial or antisocial behavior most prevalent during the developmental period. Environmental changes between submodels lead to a new mix of opportunities and rewards and, as a result, new paths toward pro- or antisocial behavior. For example, the shift from middle school to high school typically provides access to a wider array of perceived opportunities to use illegal drugs that were not perceived as available during middle school or earlier developmental periods. Conversely, new prosocial opportunities are also available with the expansion of extracurricular, educational, and civic opportunities as youth mature and are able to negotiate these new opportunities and transportation becomes more independent. These new sources of environmental opportunities, involvement, skills, and recognition can significantly alter social bonds, beliefs, and behaviors. Typically, families are the dominant socializing unit during the preschool period, while peer groups take on a more prominent socializing role as children reach middle school.

Across developmental periods, perceptions of rewards, social bonds, beliefs, and behaviors in earlier developmental periods make their presence felt in later developmental periods through conditioning perceptions of opportunities for pro- and antisocial behavior in the new developmental period. For example, a child who has a strong, prosocial family bond in the preschool period will perceive more prosocial opportunities during the elementary school period. Even as this reciprocal effect across developmental periods is noted, transitions into new and novel environments provide significant potential for new pro- or antisocial bonding as previous opportunity and reward structures may lose their immediacy and new influences move in to occupy that space (Catalano and Hawkins 1996b). The general model is depicted in Figure 13.1. See Catalano and Hawkins (1996b) for a depiction of the developmental submodels.

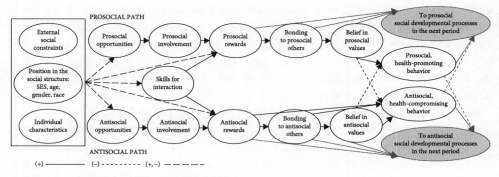

FIGURE 13.1 The Social Development Model

II. EMPIRICAL TESTS OF THE SDM

The SDM has sparked empirical studies investigating pro- and antisocial behaviors among a variety of populations. These studies have operationalized social development indicators (skills, opportunities, involvement, rewards, and bonds) across multiple developmental periods and within family, school, community, and peer domains and tested hypothesized relationships of these constructs and behavioral outcomes. Tests of SDM hypotheses have demonstrated significant utility in understanding the causal mechanisms and correlates of violence (Herrenkohl, Huang, et al. 2001; Huang et al. 2001; Choi et al. 2005; Kim 2009), drug use and abuse (O'Donnell, Hawkins, and Abbott 1995a; Catalano et al. 1996, 2005; Kim 2000; Choi et al. 2005), alcohol use, abuse, and dependence (Guo et al. 2001; Lonczak et al. 2001; Kosterman et al. 2014), delinquency (O'Donnell et al. 1995a; Ayers et al. 1999; Kim 2000; Brown et al. 2005b; Catalano et al. 2005; Deng and Roosa 2007; Jacob 2008), child problem behaviors (Catalano et al. 1999; Kim 2000; Fleming et al. 2002; Laundra, Kiger, and Bahr 2002; Kosterman et al. 2004; Sullivan and Hirschfield 2011), civic engagement (da Silva et al. 2004), prosocial learning (Duerden and Witt 2010), and positive adult social engagement (Kosterman et al. 2014).

Beyond these hypothesis tests, other studies have used the SDM to organize inquiries into a variety of behaviors and incorporated one or more social development constructs into empirical models. These projects do not explicitly test the hypothesized relationships among social development constructs, yet they contribute evidence in support of the utility of the social development perspective for understanding human behavior. Social development constructs and partial model hypotheses have been employed by studies investigating criminal convictions and recidivism (Farrington and Hawkins 1991), violence in adolescence and adulthood (Kosterman, Graham, et al. 2001; Williams et al. 2001), smoking behavior (Hill et al. 2005; Drapela and Mosher 2007), substance use (Fleming et al. 1997; Locke and Newcomb 2004; Drapela and Mosher 2007; Fleming, White, and Catalano 2010), delinquency and problem behavior during childhood (Fleming et al. 2008; Jacob 2008; Roosa et al. 2011), sexually transmitted infections (Hill et al. 2014), family attachment (Oxford et al. 2000), criminal offending trajectories (Chung et al. 2002), and school bonding (O'Donnell, Michalak, and Ames 1997).

No empirical test has attempted to operationalize all social development constructs across more than two developmental periods and among all socializing domains. Twelve published studies to date have conducted full model tests whereby both social development constructs and hypothesized relationships among constructs were tested across one or more domains. Structural equation modeling has been employed in each of these studies to test hypothesized paths from socialization factors to bonding, beliefs, and behaviors. Only studies that operationalized socialization (opportunities, involvement, and rewards), bonding, beliefs, and behaviors are considered full model tests. Five studies using the SDM as an organizing principle have employed social development constructs and hypothesized relationships but have not operationalized one or more aspects of the full model or have modeled additional relationships not hypothesized by the SDM. These tests are considered partial model tests. Further research has been conducted using social development constructs without testing specific social development hypotheses. These are considered construct-only tests. Table 13.1 provides a snapshot of studies drawing constructs and hypotheses directly from the SDM. Considered collectively, a picture emerges of the explanatory power of SDMs as hypothesized by Catalano and Hawkins (1996b).

Full model tests have provided the strictest metric by which to assess the SDM. These 12 tests have shown a general utility for the SDM in predicting pro- and antisocial behaviors in elementary school, high school, and adulthood while also highlighting key developmental considerations. Seven full model tests have been conducted during elementary school and middle school periods. In a comparative test of the SDM and its constituent theories, Brown et al. (2005b) predicted 51 percent of variance in antisocial behavior (e.g., illegal drug use, violence, delinquency) for a primarily white, suburban longitudinal sample in seventh and eighth grade drawn from the Raising Health Children (RHC) project. These analyses considered both prosocial and antisocial socialization paths across all four domains as a mediator of fourth-/fifth-grade antisocial behavior and seventh-/eighth-grade antisocial behavior. All SDM hypotheses were supported, excluding a direct effect from antisocial beliefs to antisocial behavior. Analyses revealed a significant direct path from increased skills to reduced problem behaviors, as hypothesized by social learning theory. SDM hypotheses, however, posit that the relationship of skills and behaviors is fully mediated by social development processes.

Catalano et al. (1999) also found support for SDM hypotheses during the elementary school period among the RHC sample, predicting 25 percent of the variance in externalizing problem behaviors among 9- and 10-year olds. Modeling family domain socialization only, these analyses did not find the hypothesized path from skills to family rewards to be significant. Paths from improved skills to both reduced problem behaviors and increased prosocial beliefs, however, were significant and increased the

Table 13.1 Empirical Tests of Social Development Model Hypotheses and Constructs

Article	Behavioral Outcome	Variance Explained*	Outcome Ages	Developmental Periods	Socialization Domains
Full Model Tests of the SDM					
Catalano et al. (1996)	Alcohol use and abuse, marijuana use, hard drug use	9–11%	17–18	Middle into High School	Family, School, Peers
Catalano et al. (1999)	Child problem behavior	25%	9–10	Elementary School	Family
Lonczak et al. (2001)	Alcohol misuse	45%	16	High School	Family, Community, Peers
Huang et al. (2001)	Violence	18–27%	18	Middle into High School	Family, School, Peers
Herrenkohl, Huang, et al. (2001)	Violence among early initiators of violence	8%	18	Middle into High School	Family, School, Community, Peers
Fleming et al. (2002)	Child problem behavior	32–34%	9–10	Elementary School	Family
Kosterman et al. (2004)	Increases in antisocial behavior	8%	11–12	Elementary School	Family
Brown et al. (2005b)	Antisocial behavior, drug use	51%	13–14	Elementary School	Family, School, Community, Peers
Catalano et al. (2005)	Alcohol, tobacco, marijuana, and hard drug use; violence; nonviolent delinquency; school problems	49%	13–14	Elementary School	Family, School, Community, Peers
Kim (2009)	Violence	42%	15–18	Middle into High School	Family, School, Community, Peers
Sullivan and Hirschfield (2011)	Delinquency, substance use, problem behaviors	22%	10–14	Elementary to Middle School	Family, School
Kosterman et al. (2014)	Alcohol use disorder, civic engagement, constructive engagement, exercise	27%	30	Adult	School, Community, Peers
Partial Model Tests of the SDM					
Kim (2000)	School problems, aggression, delinquency, substance use		10–12	Elementary into Middle School	Family, School

Study	Outcome	Age	School level	Domains
Laundra et al. (2002)	Serious delinquency	15–18	High School	Family, School, Peers
Choi et al (2005)	Alcohol, tobacco, marijuana, and hard drug use; violence	12–14	Elementary School	Family, Peers
Deng and Roosa (2007)	Delinquency, antisocial behavior, aggression	11–17	Middle into High School	Family
Duerden and Witt (2010)	Prosocial learning	12–17	Middle into High School	Peers
Roosa et al. (2011)	Externalizing behavior	12–13	Middle School	Family, Peers
SDM Construct Tests				
Farrington and Hawkins (1991)[a]	Criminal offense: participation, early onset and persistence	10–32	Elementary to Adult	Family, School, Peers
O'Donnell, Hawkins, and Abbott (1995a)	Delinquency, substance use, arrest	13–14	Middle School	Family, School, Peers
Ayers et al. (1999)	Increases or decreases in delinquency	14–15	Middle into High School	Family, School, Community, Peers
Guo et al. (2001)	Alcohol use and abuse	21	Elementary to Young Adult	Family, School, Community, Peers
Locke and Newcomb (2004)	Alcohol involvement, dysphoria	17–37	High School into Adult	Family, School, Community, Peers
da Silva et al. (2004)	Civic engagement and responsiblity	16–17	High School	Family, School, Community, Peers
Jacob (2008)	Delinquency	12–17	Middle into High School	Family, School, Peers
Iranpour et al. (2015)[b]	Alcohol, tobacco, opium use	14–15	High School	Family, School, Peers
Jones et al. (2016)	Substance abuse, mental health, positive functioning	10–33	Middle School into Adult	Family, Peers
Kim et al. (2016)	Violence	13–18	Middle into High School	Family, School, Community

Studies showing a range of variance explained tested more than one iteration of the SDM: [a] United Kingdom sample; [b] Iran sample.

variance explained to 35 percent. Subsample analyses concluded that the relationship of skills to problem behavior was stronger for children with parents modeling problem behaviors (i.e., heavy drinking, illicit drug use, domestic violence). Similar to Brown et al. (2005b), these analyses also found that the direct path from antisocial beliefs to problem behaviors was not significant, but only for the subsample of children whose parents modeled problem behaviors. These results suggest that positive skills may be more important as an inhibitor of antisocial behavior for children in families who exhibit antisocial behaviors. For children not subjected to the antisocial behavior of their parents, prosocial beliefs are more directly related to a reduction in problem behaviors. Fleming et al. (2002), comparing the utility of the prosocial path of the SDM during elementary school by gender and income status for the RHC sample, explained roughly 34 percent of the variance in externalizing problem behaviors among 9- and 10-year-olds. In conjunction with Catalano et al. (1999), the path from skills to family rewards was not significant, while the paths from skills to prosocial beliefs and skills to problem behaviors were both significant.

Catalano et al. (2005), employing the RHC sample, accounted for 49 percent of the variance in the development of antisocial behavior between grades 3–4 and grades 7–8, considering both pro- and antisocial paths across family, school, community, and peer domains. While this test demonstrated support for all socialization hypotheses during the elementary school period, including the paths from pro- and antisocial beliefs to antisocial behavior, some exogenous factors did not operate as hypothesized. Neither gender nor low-income status showed a significant effect on pro- or antisocial opportunities as hypothesized, nor were exogenous factors fully mediated by social development. SDM hypotheses accounted for two-thirds of the effect of gender, one-half of the effect of low-income status, and one-third of the effect of individual constitutional factors of depression, poor concentration, shyness/withdrawal, and early antisocial behavior on antisocial behavior.

Kosterman et al. (2004) tested the SDM on a sample of primarily white, two-parent families of sixth-grade children in a Midwestern state. Analyses of the prosocial path in the family domain indicated unique relationships of mothers and fathers on increases in antisocial behavior (i.e., illegal drug use, delinquency, violence) across six months. While the SDM fits this full sample well, prosocial beliefs were highly predictive of boys' antisocial behavior but demonstrated little impact on girls' antisocial behavior. Nonsignificance of the hypothesized paths from prosocial beliefs to behavior for girls in this sample echoed the results of Brown et al. (2005b) and Catalano et al. (1999). Further analyses reported in Kosterman et al. (2004) suggest that increases in girls' antisocial behavior were influenced by the quality of prosocial socialization with their father but not their mother. Also in the middle school period, Sullivan and Hirschfield (2011) applied a prosocial path SDM across school and family domains to a primarily minority sample (70 percent African American, 24 percent Latino, 4 percent East Asian) from socially and economically disadvantaged neighborhoods in Chicago. The SDM with paths from skills to beliefs and skills to behavior added accounted for 22 percent of self-reported problem behaviors (e.g., illegal drug use, delinquent behavior); significant effects of skills in both increases of prosocial beliefs and reductions in problem behaviors were found.

Five full-model tests of the SDM have been conducted with outcomes of interest measured during the high school period. These studies have all employed data from the Seattle Social Development Project (SSDP). SSDP is a multiethnic, gender-balanced, high-risk longitudinal sample originating in Seattle public schools. While the SDM hypothesizes separate paths from prosocial bonding to prosocial beliefs and antisocial bonding to antisocial beliefs, the measurements used with this sample allow for the operationalization of only one belief construct measuring prosocial beliefs, called "belief in the moral order." Lonczak et al. (2001) measured pro- and antisocial paths in the family, community, and peer domains to predict alcohol misuse at age 16. Analyses explained 45 percent of the variance in alcohol misuse between age 14 and 16 and supported all SDM hypotheses when opportunities, skills, and rewards were modeled as a second-order latent factor to account for their common variance. Catalano et al. (1996) investigated the development of alcohol, marijuana, and other drug use along pro- and antisocial socialization paths at age 17 to 18 among the SSDP sample. Modeling socialization across all four domains as both sequential factors and a single second-order latent factor produced similar support for all SDM hypotheses, excluding a negative path from antisocial bonding to belief in the moral order.

Three studies have employed a full SDM to investigate violent behavior during high school. Huang et al. (2001) predicted violence at age 18 among the SSDP sample, employing pro- and antisocial socialization paths across family, school, and peer domains. Modeling socialization experiences as a single second-order latent factor indicated strong support for all social development hypothesis, excluding a direct path from antisocial bonding and violent behavior. Results suggest that violence at this age may derive more from the socialization processes leading to antisocial bonding than from antisocial bonding itself. Huang et al. (2001) tested mediation of violence by social development processes from age 10 to age 18 and age 13 to age 18 in two separate models. SDM hypotheses fully mediated violence from age 10 to 18 but not from age 13 to 18, indicating the potential importance of socialization during ages 10 to 13 for later violence. Kim (2009), using the RHC sample, demonstrated that pro- and antisocial socialization hypotheses across family, school, community, and peer domains partially mediated the relationship of age 10 to 11 bullying to high school violence measured from age 15 to 18. Modeling socialization as a second-order latent factor and including a direct path from positive skills to reduced violence, these analyses explained 42 percent of the variance of high school violence. Herrenkohl, Huang, et al. (2001) applied the SDM across pro- and antisocial paths in the family, school, community, and peer domains to two models of violence at age 18. Employing separate subsamples of early initiators (age 10 to 11) and adolescent initiators (age 12 to 16) of violence, results indicated support for SDM processes. The SDM model fit equally well for early and adolescent initiators of violence, but the hypothesized paths from antisocial bonding to belief in the moral order as well as antisocial bonding to violence were not significant.

One published study employing the SSDP sample has applied SDM hypotheses to adults. Modeling positive adult functioning as indicated by civic engagement, productive use of time in work or school, and time spent exercising, and problem behavior as indicated by symptoms of alcohol use disorder at age 30 across pro- and antisocial socialization paths, Kosterman et al. (2014) found significant stability between alcohol use disorder at ages 21 and 30. Social development hypotheses considering adult alcohol socialization opportunities and rewards as a single latent factor still accounted for 27 percent of the variance in alcohol use disorder at age 30. While the SDM is yet to be explicitly hypothesized for adults, the shared variance of prosocial opportunities, involvement, and rewards demonstrated significant utility in predicting positive adult behavior at age 30.

The initial full model test of the SDM was conducted with a multiethnic, gender-balanced, high-risk population originating from Seattle, Washington (Catalano et al. 1996). Since that time, multiple studies have specifically investigated the generalizability of the SDM across geographically and demographically diverse samples and subsamples. These tests have found comparable fit for the SDM and its constructs across socioeconomic status and gender (Fleming et al. 2002; Laundra, Kiger, and Bahr 2002; Sullivan and Hirschfield 2011) as well as racial and ethnic groups (Choi et al. 2005; Deng and Roosa 2007; Roosa et al. 2011; Sullivan and Hirschfield 2011). Testing the full model across family, school, community, and peer domains, Fleming et al. (2002) found similar construct and path validity by gender and socioeconomic status in predicting problem behaviors at ages 9 and 10. Laundra, Kiger, and Bahr (2002) also found no gender differences for a partial model test of serious delinquency in the seventh through twelfth grades within the family, school, and peer domains. As mentioned above, Kosterman et al. (2004) identified some gender differences among sixth-graders by modeling two separate family socialization constructs. Unique socialization constructs for mothers and fathers in these analyses showed differential effects on the behaviors of sons and daughters. These analyses did not test a full family socialization construct for differences by gender. Deng and Roosa (2007) predicted nonviolent delinquency for a sample of seventh- to ninth-grade students in Beijing, China, using a partial SDM from the family domain. These analyses found that antisocial family socialization process hypothesized by the SDM explained 45 percent of the variance in adolescent delinquent behavior. Roosa et al. (2011) applied a partial SDM across family, school, and peer domains to predict externalizing behaviors among Mexican American adolescents during the transition to high school. Employing a partial model of SDM constructs and hypotheses from the family domain, Choi et al. (2005) predicted alcohol, tobacco, marijuana, and hard drug use and violence among 12- to 14-year-olds across ethnic groups self-identifying as European American, African American, Asia Pacific Islander, or multiracial. The strongest relationships were found among European American and multiracial groups when controlling for neighborhood and peer influences. Social development constructs and hypotheses have also proven useful in understanding future violence, delinquency, and crime among subsamples of previous offenders (Farrington and Hawkins 1991; O'Donnell et al. 1995a; Herrenkohl, Huang, et al. 2001).

While tests of the SDM have demonstrated that the mechanisms suggested by the model generally operate as hypothesized, three additions to Catalano and Hawkins' 1996 model have emerged from empirical testing. Seven studies have identified the ability of social, emotional, and/or cognitive skills to directly inhibit antisocial behaviors (Ayers et al. 1999; Catalano et al. 1999; Fleming et al. 2002; Brown et al. 2005b; Deng and Roosa 2007; Kim 2009; Sullivan and Hirschfield 2011). While Catalano and Hawkins hypothesized the influence of skills to be fully mediated by socialization processes, analyses suggest only partial mediation and that skills play a direct role in the development of antisocial behavior in addition to their influence on the socialization process. The emergence of social, emotional, and cognitive skills as a mechanism for inhibiting antisocial development provides support for social learning theory hypotheses and highlights the importance of skills for interventions seeking to prevent antisocial behavior (Brown et al. 2005b). Second, three studies have conceptualized the socialization process as a second-order latent factor to capture the common variance among opportunities, involvement, and rewards (Catalano et al. 1996; Lonczak et al. 2001; Huang et al. 2001). These highly correlated factors likely work in conjunction to direct the socialization experience and, as such, may have utility as second-order latent indicators. This indicates that the shared variance among opportunities, involvement, and rewards is important for socialization, suggesting that all three should be built simultaneously to foster prosocial bonds, beliefs, and behavior. Finally, three analyses employing SDM constructs have also demonstrated its utility for predicting adult problem and positive behavior (Farrington and Hawkins 1991; Guo et al. 2001; Kosterman et al. 2014). These results call for the incorporation of additional submodels based on adult development into a new articulation of the SDM.

III. SDM-Inspired Interventions

Interventions provide an important means by which to test theory (Farrington, Ohlin, and Wilson 1986; Farrington, Loeber, and Welsh 2010). These tests require that the theory has guided the design of intervention components to impact specific theoretical constructs. Well-designed experimental or quasi-experimental research trials must demonstrate direct evidence of observed changes to these constructs, direct impact of the intervention on these constructs, and confirmation that changes in theoretical constructs subsequently altered positive or problem behaviors. As such, rigorous testing of interventions developed to alter theoretical constructs can provide strong causal evidence for a theory (Lacourse et al. 2002). The intervention studies summarized below have many of these elements. The SDM has functioned as an explicit theoretical backbone for each intervention.

The hypotheses of the SDM have directed the construction and implementation of interventions aimed at increasing healthy adolescent behaviors and reducing problems including drug use, crime and violence, reduced mental health, and risky sexual activity (Hawkins, Von Cleve, and Catalano 1991; Hawkins, Catalano, and Associates 1992; Catalano and Hawkins 1996a; Catalano et al. 1998; Haggerty et al. 1999). These programs have sought to enhance prosocial opportunities, involvement, and rewards for children among families, schools, and individuals and to enhance skillful performance such that involvement is more likely to be recognized or rewarded. Increasing prosocial opportunities, involvement, skills, and rewards is expected to increase prosocial bonding and beliefs and, ultimately, prosocial behaviors. The constructs and hypothesized relationships on the prosocial path of the SDM are referred to as the social development strategy (Catalano and Hawkins 1996a). In addition, these programs have addressed antisocial opportunities, involvement, skills, and rewards to reduce the likelihood of antisocial bonding, beliefs, and behavior. The social development strategy provides parents, teachers, and community members more broadly with specific tools to maximize prosocial opportunities, involvement, skills, rewards, bonding, and beliefs and reduce antisocial constructs on the antisocial path in classrooms, families, and the community. Classroom strategies for teachers include proactive classroom management, interactive teaching, and cooperative learning (Abbott et al. 1998); parent and family strategies include behavior management skills founded on clear and consistent communication and application of boundaries of behavior, positive reinforcement, academic support skills, and cooperative family engagement to build developmentally appropriate opportunities and reduce opportunities for antisocial behavior (Kosterman, Hawkins, et al. 2001). Strategies taught to children and reinforced by parents and teachers include interpersonal problem-solving skills such as communication, decision making, negotiation, and conflict resolution, and refusal skills encompassing awareness of antisocial social influences, identification of consequences of risky behaviors, and generation of alternatives to antisocial behaviors among peers (Hawkins, Von Cleve, and Catalano 1991; Hawkins et al. 1992). In community efforts, stakeholders apply the social development strategy in their daily interactions with children and youth (Kim et al. 2015).

Empirical research evaluating intervention effects of SDM-inspired interventions provides further evidence of the utility of social development constructs and hypotheses for understanding and improving child and adolescent physical, mental, and social health. Four prevention programs guided by the social development strategy have been evaluated: the Seattle Social Development Project (SSDP), Guiding Good Choices (GGC; formerly titled Preparing for the Drug Free Years), Raising Healthy Children (RHC), and Communities That Care (CTC). SSDP provided a social development intervention to teachers, parents, and children in the first through sixth grades in selected Seattle public schools. Evaluations have been based on a non-randomized controlled trail of 808 individuals classified into four treatment conditions: full intervention (n = 156), consisting of social development strategies for teachers, parents, and children across grades 1–6; late intervention (n = 267), consisting of the same intervention for fifth- and sixth-graders; control group (n = 220), receiving no intervention; and a parent-only training group (n = 141). Comparisons between the full intervention group and the control group have found a broad array of positive significant outcomes from age 7 through age 30 (Hawkins, Kosterman, et al. 2008). Elementary school effects showed reductions in externalizing behaviors and initiation of alcohol use and delinquency for the full intervention group and improved school-based outcomes specifically among low-income students (Hawkins, Von Cleve, and Catalano 1991; Hawkins et al. 1992; O'Donnell et al. 1995b; Abbott et al. 1998; Hawkins et al. 2001). For teachers who were able to successfully incorporate the social development strategy into their teaching practices, classroom-specific analyses found increases in positive student reports of school opportunities, involvement, rewards, and bonding at the end of grade 6 for the full intervention group as compared to the control group. Overall intervention effects on educational achievement at the end of grade 6 were partially mediated by improvements in SDM constructs as hypothesized and can, therefore, be partially attributed to successful implementation of the social development strategy (Abbott et al. 1998). Significant outcomes observed by age 18 included lower lifetime violence and sexual activity, reduced current heavy alcohol use, improved school bonding, and increased academic achievement among the full intervention group; lower rates of teen pregnancy and parenthood among middle-income students; and decreased grade repetition among low-income students (Abbott et al. 1998; Hawkins et al. 1999). From ages 21 to 27, the full intervention group showed reduced mental and emotional health problems, more consistent condom use, and higher levels of constructive engagement as indicated by positive school and employment outcomes (Lonczak et al. 2002; Hawkins et al. 2005; Hawkins, Kosterman, et al. 2008). By age 30, students in the full intervention condition of SSDP had significantly lower incidence of sexually transmitted infections (STI), with larger effects for African Americans. Further analyses investigated mediation of intervention effects by SDM constructs specifically for African Americans. Positive family environment as measured by family bonding, clear rules, parental monitoring, and low family conflict; school bonding; and delayed initiation of sexual behavior mediated the influence of the SSDP intervention on STI hazard (Hill et al. 2014).

Guiding Good Choices is a five-session parenting skills intervention based on the social development strategy designed to mitigate family-based substance use risks (Catalano et al. 1998; Haggerty et al. 1999). A randomized controlled trial of GGC among two economically stressed, rural Midwestern communities recruited 429 families (221 for the intervention, 208 as a control). Sixty-nine percent of families completed follow-ups at one, two, and three and a half years with no differential attrition by intervention condition, sociodemographics, or pretesting scores (Spoth, Redmond, and Shin 1998; Mason et al. 2003). Investigations of treatment effects have indicated significant improvements in targeted SDM behaviors for intervention group parents compared to controls. These include increases in clear communication of standards for behavior, rewards for prosocial behavior, involvement with their children, parental monitoring of children's substance use, as well as significant reductions in spousal conflict (Kosterman, Hawkins, et al. 2001). These early changes in social development constructs were followed by later inhibition of growth in alcohol use, delinquency, and depressive symptoms in the children of families in the GGC condition (Mason et al. 2003, 2007). While alcohol use is expected to increase as children move into high school, the GGC intervention group showed significantly lower rates of growth in alcohol use from age 12 to 15.5, improvements in parental norms against substance use, and improved stability for proactive family management practices compared to controls (Park et al. 2000). By grade 12, children of intervention families demonstrated reduced symptoms of depression and an overall lower rate of growth in depressive symptoms throughout adolescence compared to control families (Mason et al. 2007). Long-term follow-up indicated that young women whose families participated in the intervention at age 12 demonstrated significantly lower rates of alcohol abuse disorder at age 22 (Mason et al. 2009). Reduced alcohol abuse at age 22 was partially mediated by improved prosocial skills.

Raising Healthy Children (RHC) employed the social development strategy across parent, teacher, individual, and peer domains to universally support positive youth development and prevent substance use among students in first through eighth grade of public schools and in parents and teens from grades 9 to 12 in a suburban district near Seattle, Washington (Catalano et al. 2003). For evaluations of RHC, schools were randomly assigned to treatment and control conditions, and a panel of 938 first- and second-grade students was established and followed prospectively. Examinations of outcomes found significant early improvements in parent and teacher reports of academic performance and commitment to school, as well as significant increases in teacher-reported social competency and significant decreases in teacher-reported antisocial behaviors of students in the experimental condition compared to controls at 18-month follow-up (Catalano et al. 2003). These early changes in elementary school social development constructs preceded subsequent inhibited growth of alcohol use and marijuana use from middle into high school for the intervention group compared to the control. Intervention effects were substantial, with reductions of .91 standard deviations for alcohol use and 1.44 standard deviations for marijuana use for the intervention group compared to the control group (Brown et al. 2005a).

Communities That Care (CTC) is a community-focused system for preventing and reducing adolescent delinquency and alcohol, tobacco, and other drug use through training community stakeholders to target elevated risk factors in the community and implement evidence-based preventive interventions and the social development strategy (Hawkins, Catalano, and Associates 1992; Catalano and Hawkins 1996a). The Community Youth Development Study (CYDS) is a randomized controlled trial of CTC implemented in 24 towns across seven states. Towns were matched within state and subsequently assigned to the CTC or control condition, and a longitudinal panel was initiated for fifth graders in all communities (Hawkins, Catalano, et al. 2008). By the eighth grade, youths in the longitudinal panel in CTC communities were found to have significantly higher levels of overall protection using an omnibus test to assess all protective factors specified in the SDM, and significantly higher mean levels of community opportunities for prosocial involvement, school recognition for prosocial involvement, interaction with prosocial peers, and social skills as compared to control communities after adjusting for fifth-grade levels (Kim et al. 2015). In addition to increases in prosocial SDM constructs, CYDS analyses have found significant reductions for CTC as compared with control communities for alcohol and delinquency initiation in the eighth grade, with sustained effects at tenth grade, as well as reduced risk of violence at twelfth grade (Hawkins, Brown, et al. 2008; Hawkins et al. 2009). Significant differences between CTC and control communities in sustained abstinence from alcohol, tobacco, other drugs, and delinquency were found at the end of the twelfth grade (Hawkins et al. 2012). Community-level analyses also determined that CTC communities employed more science-based approaches to prevention and saw increased levels of collaboration across community sectors; specifically improving their collaboration on prevention-related services (Brown et al. 2007; Gloppen et al. 2016). Service system factors are important proximal outcomes of CTC that are related to more effective prevention strategies, increased community protective factors, reduced risk factors, and improved adolescent health and behavior outcomes.

Several of the studies described above have found that intervention effects impacted both SDM constructs and subsequent positive and problem behavior. Explicit mediational hypotheses have been examined by three studies; evidence of partial mediation by SDM constructs was found by two studies investigating SSDP outcomes (Abbott et al. 1998; Hill et al. 2014). Analyses of GGC outcomes indicated that positive intervention effects were partially mediated by enhanced prosocial skills, a construct important in the SDM (Mason et al. 2009).

IV. FUTURE OF THE SDM

The SDM has been tested by multiple studies examining an array of outcomes across developmental periods corresponding to different developmental submodels. Partial as well as full tests have been examined. Family, school, and community interventions have been developed using the model and, in rigorous tests of these interventions, an impact on SDM constructs and positive and problem behavior has been demonstrated. In this section we summarize what we have learned and suggest recommendations for future studies of the SDM.

The broad utility of the SDM has been demonstrated across developmental periods for both problem and positive behaviors and among urban, rural, European American, African American, multiethnic, and international groups. While most SDM hypotheses have been repeatedly confirmed, there are several findings that require more thoughtful theorizing and potential adjustments to the specification or testing of the model. First and most prominently, in multiple studies the skills for interaction construct has demonstrated a direct effect of reducing problem behavior beyond its impact on rewards. Given that the construct has been measured in a variety of ways across studies, it is unlikely that these results are dependent on a particular measure. Skills have also been identified as a mechanism through which the effects of an SDM-inspired intervention improved behavioral outcomes. The scope and content of this construct should be more specifically explicated in the SDM; a direct path from skills to behaviors may need to be added or at least fully investigated in future tests of the SDM.

Second, the opportunities, involvement, and rewards constructs have often re-quired modeling as a second-order latent factor given the high degree of correlation among them. While this socialization construct has still performed as expected in mul-tiple tests, these concepts have been measured at the same time point in order to cap-ture time-specific socialization. Measurement points may need to be separated to more specifically investigate the relationships among these constructs. The SDM, however, specifies that these concepts work together; temporal separation may sacrifice some of this hypothesized socialization synergy.

Third, as hypothesized in the SDM, empirical tests confirm that antisocial rewards, bonding, and beliefs each provide a unique potential pathway to antisocial behav-ior. Given the exclusion of antisocial bonding from control theory, much debate has surrounded its importance. Tests of the SDM have found strong support for a direct effect of antisocial bonding on problem behaviors in elementary school children and al-cohol misuse in high school. Results are mixed for a direct path from antisocial bonding to youth violent behavior. SDM tests finding no direct path from antisocial bonding to antisocial behavior have found significant mediation of antisocial bonding by antisocial beliefs in all but one case (Herrenkohl, Huang, et al. 2001). These results warrant further investigation into the unique effects of antisocial rewards, bonding, and beliefs on spe-cific antisocial behaviors.

While elementary, middle, and high school submodels of the SDM have been investigated, we know of no tests of the SDM during preschool. Investigating this de-velopmental period would be fruitful to further understanding SDM processes. Given that there are fewer environments to which a child is directly exposed, simplification of some environmental complexities can potentially allow for a clearer view of social-ization processes as compared to later stages of development. Furthermore, improved understanding of the mechanisms through which secure attachment is established or frustrated in early childhood is important for healthy future development. We have de-veloped a behavior observation system to track manifestations of SDM constructs in response to play activities between parents and young children that might be helpful to these studies. We are eager to collaborate in longitudinal investigations of the SDM in this developmental period.

Also, while we have investigated the usefulness of the SDM in adulthood, we have not bent our theorizing to this developmental period. While no theoretical statement about the young adult submodel has been explicitly made, a full model test of the SDM in young adulthood by Kosterman and colleagues (2014) suggests the promise of extending a theoretical statement of the SDM to young adulthood. As adults ma-ture through the late twenties, critical environmental transitions begin taking shape as many individuals tackle important developmental tasks and assume adult roles; tasks including the establishment of strong relationships, marriage, family creation, com-pletion of school, career employment, and financial responsibility are all likely to be closely intertwined with hypothesized mechanisms of the SDM. Accomplishment of these developmental tasks is also often associated with decreasing drug use, risky sex, mental health problems, and antisocial behavior. However, for some, failure to achieve these tasks is associated with substance misuse, continuing sexual risk behavior, financial and employment instability, difficulty establishing meaningful relationships, and deteriorating mental health. New adult family, work, and home environments necessarily alter the mix of pro- and antisocial opportunities and rewards for involvement in pro- and antisocial behavior. It will be important for concerted thought to fully develop a theoretical exposition of the SDM for young adulthood.

Importantly, the SDM has been used to develop and test interventions, unlike many theories of antisocial behavior. Through analyzing interventions based on the SDM, strong empirical tests of the theory have been possible. These interventions have had plausible effects on antecedent constructs in the theory as well as on positive and problem behavior. This both provides important intervention effectiveness information and strengthens theory testing through manipulation of the antecedent constructs in the theory. However, specific investigations of SDM constructs as mediators of intervention effects have been conducted in only three cases. We think this is an important direction for future research and recognize that more thorough investigations of these issues are needed.

In sum, the SDM has survived nearly 30 years of conception, development, and testing, and, in the process, researchers have found support for many of its hypotheses. As we have recognized here, there has also been some consistency among specific hypotheses that have not been confirmed. Perhaps most importantly, the SDM has been used to design, implement, and test preventive interventions, which has both provided stronger support for causal hypotheses and improved the health and well-being of numerous individuals, families, schools, and communities.

REFERENCES

Abbott, Robert D., Julie O'Donnell, J. David Hawkins, Karl G. Hill, Rick Kosterman, and Richard F. Catalano. 1998. "Changing Teaching Practices to Promote Achievement and Bonding to School." *American Journal of Orthopsychiatry* 68(4): 542–552.

Akers, Ronald L. 1977. *Deviant Behavior: A Social Learning Approach.* 2nd ed. Belmont, CA: Wadsworth.

Ayers, Charles D., James Herbert Williams, J. David Hawkins, Peggy L. Peterson, Richard F. Catalano, and Robert D. Abbott. 1999. "Assessing Correlates of Onset, Escalation, Deescalation, and Desistance of Delinquent Behavior." *Journal of Quantitative Criminology* 15(3): 277–306.

Bandura, Albert. 1977. *Social Learning Theory.* Englewood Cliffs, NJ: Prentice-Hall.

Brown, Eric C., Richard F. Catalano, Charles B. Fleming, Kevin P. Haggerty, and Robert D. Abbott. 2005a. "Adolescent Substance Use Outcomes in the Raising Healthy Children Project: A Two-Part Latent Growth Curve Analysis." *Journal of Consulting and Clinical Psychology* 73(4): 699–710.

Brown, Eric C., Richard F. Catalano, Charles B. Fleming, Kevin P. Haggerty, Robert D. Abbott, Rebecca C. Cortes, and Jisuk Park. 2005b. "Mediator Effects in the Social Development Model: An Examination of Constituent Theories." *Criminal Behaviour and Mental Health* 15(4): 221–235.

Brown, Eric C., J. David Hawkins, Michael W. Arthur, John S. Briney, and Robert D. Abbott. 2007. "Effects of Communities That Care on Prevention Services Systems: Outcomes from the Community Youth Development Study at 1.5 Years." *Prevention Science* 8(3): 180–191.

Bursik, Robert J., Jr., and Harold G. Grasmick. 1996. "The Use of Contextual Analysis in Models of Criminal Behavior." In *Delinquency and Crime: Current Theories*, edited by J. David Hawkins, 236–267. New York: Cambridge University Press.

Catalano, Richard F., and J. David Hawkins. 1996a. *Communities That Care: Risk-Focused Prevention Using the Social Development Strategy.* Seattle, WA: Developmental Research and Programs.

Catalano, Richard F., and J. David Hawkins. 1996b. "The Social Development Model: A Theory of Antisocial Behavior." In *Delinquency and Crime: Current Theories*, edited by J. David Hawkins, 149–197. New York: Cambridge University Press.

Catalano, Richard F., Rick Kosterman, Kevin P. Haggerty, J. David Hawkins, and Richard Spoth. 1998. "A Universal Intervention for the Prevention of Substance Abuse: Preparing for the Drug-Free Years." In *NIDA Research Monograph No. 177: Drug Abuse Prevention through Family Interventions*, edited by Rebecca S. Ashery, Elizabeth B. Robertson and Karol L. Kumpfer, 130–159. Rockville, MD: National Institute on Drug Abuse.

Catalano, Richard F., Rick Kosterman, J. David Hawkins, Michael D. Newcomb, and Robert D. Abbott. 1996. "Modeling the Etiology of Adolescent Substance Use: A Test of the Social Development Model." *Journal of Drug Issues* 26(2): 429–455.

Catalano, Richard F., James J. Mazza, Tracy W. Harachi, Robert D. Abbott, Kevin P. Haggerty, and Charles B. Fleming. 2003. "Raising Healthy Children Through Enhancing Social Development in Elementary School: Results after 1.5 Years." *Journal of School Psychology* 41(1): 143–164.

Catalano, Richard F., Monica L. Oxford, Tracy W. Harachi, Robert D. Abbott, and Kevin P. Haggerty. 1999. "A Test of the Social Development Model to Predict Problem Behaviour During the Elementary School Period." *Criminal Behaviour and Mental Health* 9(1): 39–56.

Catalano, Richard F., Jisuk Park, Tracy W. Harachi, Kevin P. Haggerty, Robert D. Abbott, and J. David Hawkins. 2005. "Mediating the Effects of Poverty, Gender, Individual Characteristics, and External Constraints on Antisocial Behavior: A Test of the Social Development Model and Implications for Developmental Life-Course Theory." In *Advances in Criminological Theory: Vol. 14. Integrated Developmental and Life-Course Theories of Offending*, edited by David P. Farrington, 93–123. New Brunswick, NJ: Transaction.

Choi, Yoonsun, Tracy W. Harachi, Mary Rogers Gillmore, and Richard F. Catalano. 2005. "Applicability of the Social Development Model to Urban Ethnic Minority Youth: Examining the Relationship Between External Constraints, Family Socialization, and Problem Behaviors." *Journal of Research on Adolescence* 15(4): 505–534.

Chung, Ick-Joong, Karl G. Hill, J. David Hawkins, Lewayne D. Gilchrist, and Daniel S. Nagin. 2002. "Childhood Predictors of Offense Trajectories." *Journal of Research in Crime and Delinquency* 39(1): 60–90.

da Silva, Lisa, Ann Sanson, Diana Smart, and John Toumbourou. 2004. "Civic Responsibility Among Australian Adolescents: Testing Two Competing Models." *Journal of Community Psychology* 32(3): 229–255.

Deng, Shiying, and Mark W. Roosa. 2007. "Family Influences on Adolescent Delinquent Behaviors: Applying the Social Development Model to a Chinese Sample." *American Journal of Community Psychology* 40(3–4): 333–344.

Dishion, Thomas J., Gerald R. Patterson, Mike Stoolmiller, and Martie L. Skinner. 1991. "Family, School, and Behavioral Antecedents to Early Adolescent Involvement with Antisocial Peers." *Developmental Psychology* 27(1): 172–180.

Drapela, Laurie A., and Clayton Mosher. 2007. "The Conditional Effect of Parental Drug Use on Parental Attachment and Adolescent Drug Use: Social Control and Social Development Model Perspectives." *Journal of Child and Adolescent Substance Abuse* 16(3): 63–87.

Duerden, Mat D., and Peter A. Witt. 2010. "The Impact of Socialization on Youth Program Outcomes: A Social Development Model Perspective." *Leisure Sciences* 32(4): 299–317.

Farrington, David P. 1989. "Early Predictors of Adolescent Aggression and Adult Violence." *Violence and Victims* 4(2): 79–100.

Farrington, David P., ed. 2011. *Integrated Developmental and Life-Course Theories of Offending*, Vol. 1. New Brunswick, NJ: Transaction Publishers.

Farrington, David P., and J. David Hawkins. 1991. "Predicting Participation, Early Onset and Later Persistence in Officially Recorded Offending." *Criminal Behaviour and Mental Health* 1(1): 1–33.

Farrington, David P., and Rolf Loeber. 1999. "Transatlantic Replicability of Risk Factors in the Development of Delinquency." In *Historical and Geographical Influences on Psychopathology*, edited by Patricia Cohen, Cheryl Slomkowski, and Lee N. Robbins, 299–329. Mahwah, NJ: Lawrence Erlbaum.

Farrington, David P., Rolf Loeber, and Brandon C. Welsh. 2010. "Longitudinal-Experimental Studies." In *Handbook of Quantitative Criminology*, edited by Alex R. Piquero and David Weisburd, 503–518. New York: Springer.

Farrington, David P., Lloyd E. Ohlin, and James Q. Wilson. 1986. *Understanding and Controlling Crime: Toward a New Research Strategy*. New York: Springer-Verlag.

Fleming, Charles B., Devon D. Brewer, Randy R. Gainey, Kevin P. Haggerty, and Richard F. Catalano. 1997. "Parent Drug Use and Bonding to Parents as Predictors of Substance Use in Children of Substance Abusers." *Journal of Child and Adolescent Substance Abuse* 6(4): 75–86.

Fleming, Charles B., Richard F. Catalano, James J. Mazza, Eric C. Brown, Kevin P. Haggerty, and Tracy W. Harachi. 2008. "After-School Activities, Misbehavior in School, and Delinquency from the End of Elementary School Through the Beginning of High School: A Test of Social Development Model Hypotheses." *The Journal of Early Adolescence* 28(2): 277–303.

Fleming, Charles B., Richard F. Catalano, Monica L. Oxford, and Tracy W. Harachi. 2002. "A Test of Generalizability of the Social Development Model Across Gender and Income Groups with Longitudinal Data from the Elementary School Developmental Period." *Journal of Quantitative Criminology* 18(4): 423–439.

Fleming, Charles B., Helene R. White, and Richard F. Catalano. 2010. "Romantic Relationships and Substance Use in Early Adulthood: An Examination of the Influences of Relationship Type, Partner Substance Use, and Relationship Quality." *Journal of Health and Social Behavior* 51(2): 153–167.

Gloppen, Kari M., Eric C. Brown, Bradley H. Wagenaar, J. David Hawkins, Isaac C. Rhew, and Sabrina Oesterle. 2016. "Sustaining Adoption of Science-Based Prevention Through Communities That Care." *Journal of Community Psychology* 44(1): 78–98.

Gottfredson, Michael R., and Travis Hirschi. 1990. *A General Theory of Crime*. Stanford, CA: Stanford University Press.

Guo, Jie, J. David Hawkins, Karl G. Hill, and Robert D. Abbott. 2001. "Childhood and Adolescent Predictors of Alcohol Abuse and Dependence in Young Adulthood." *Journal of Studies on Alcohol* 62(6): 754–762.

Haggerty, Kevin P., Rick Kosterman, Richard F. Catalano, and J. David Hawkins. 1999. "Preparing for the Drug Free Years." *OJJDP Juvenile Justice Bulletin*, June.

Hawkins, J. David, Eric C. Brown, Sabrina Oesterle, Michael W. Arthur, Robert D. Abbott, and Richard F. Catalano. 2008. "Early Effects of Communities That Care on Targeted Risks and Initiation of Delinquent Behavior and Substance Use." *Journal of Adolescent Health* 43(1): 15–22.

Hawkins, J. David, Richard F Catalano, Michael W. Arthur, Elizabeth Egan, Eric C. Brown, Robert D. Abbott, and David M. Murray. 2008. "Testing Communities That Care: The Rationale, Design and Behavioral Baseline Equivalence of the Community Youth Development Study." *Prevention Science* 9(3): 178–190.

Hawkins, J. David, Richard F. Catalano, Jr., and Associates. 1992. *Communities That Care: Action for Drug Abuse Prevention*. San Francisco: Jossey-Bass.

Hawkins, J. David, Richard F. Catalano, Rick Kosterman, Robert Abbott, and Karl G. Hill. 1999. "Preventing Adolescent Health-Risk Behaviors by Strengthening Protection During Childhood." *Archives of Pediatrics and Adolescent Medicine* 153(3): 226–234.

Hawkins, J. David, Richard F. Catalano, and Janet Y. Miller. 1992. "Risk and Protective Factors for Alcohol and Other Drug Problems in Adolescence and Early Adulthood: Implications for Substance Abuse Prevention." *Psychological Bulletin* 112(1): 64–105.

Hawkins, J. David, Richard F. Catalano, Diane M. Morrison, Julie O'Donnell, Robert D. Abbott, and L. Edward Day. 1992. "The Seattle Social Development Project: Effects of the First Four Years on Protective Factors and Problem Behaviors." In *Preventing Antisocial Behavior: Interventions from Birth through Adolescence*, edited by Joan McCord and Richard Ernest Tremblay, 136–161. New York: Guilford.

Hawkins, J. David, Jie Guo, Karl G. Hill, Sara Battin-Pearson, and Robert D. Abbott. 2001. "Long-Term Effects of the Seattle Social Development Intervention on School Bonding Trajectories." *Applied Developmental Science* 5(4): 225–236.

Hawkins, J. David, Rick Kosterman, Richard F. Catalano, Karl G. Hill, and Robert D. Abbott. 2005. "Promoting Positive Adult Functioning Through Social Development Intervention in Childhood: Long-Term Effects from the Seattle Social Development Project." *Archives of Pediatrics and Adolescent Medicine* 159(1): 25–31.

Hawkins, J. David, Rick Kosterman, Richard F. Catalano, Karl G. Hill, and Robert D. Abbott. 2008. "Effects of Social Development Intervention in Childhood 15 Years Later." *Archives of Pediatrics and Adolescent Medicine* 162(12): 1133–1141.

Hawkins, J. David, Sabrina Oesterle, Eric C. Brown, Michael W. Arthur, Robert D. Abbott, Abigail A. Fagan, and Richard F. Catalano. 2009. "Results of a Type 2 Translational Research Trial to Prevent Adolescent Drug Use and Delinquency: A Test of Communities That Care." *Archives of Pediatrics and Adolescent Medicine* 163(9): 789–798.

Hawkins, J. David, Sabrina Oesterle, Eric C. Brown, Kathryn C. Monahan, Robert D. Abbott, Michael W. Arthur, and Richard F. Catalano. 2012. "Sustained Decreases in Risk Exposure and Youth Problem Behaviors After Installation of the Communities That Care Prevention System in a Randomized Trial." *Archives of Pediatrics and Adolescent Medicine* 166(2): 141–148.

Hawkins, J. David, Elizabeth Von Cleve, and Richard F. Catalano, Jr. 1991. "Reducing Early Childhood Aggression: Results of a Primary Prevention Program." *Journal of the American Academy of Child and Adolescent Psychiatry* 30(2): 208–217.

Hawkins, J. David, and Joseph G. Weis. 1985. "The Social Development Model: An Integrated Approach to Delinquency Prevention." *Journal of Primary Prevention* 6(2): 73–97.

Herrenkohl, Todd I., J. David Hawkins, Ick-Joong Chung, Karl G. Hill, and Sara Battin-Pearson. 2001. "School and Community Risk Factors and Interventions." In *Child Delinquents: Development, Intervention, and Service Needs*, edited by Rolf Loeber and David P. Farrington, 211–246. Thousand Oaks, CA: Sage.

Herrenkohl, Todd I., Bu Huang, Rick Kosterman, J. David Hawkins, Richard F. Catalano, and Brian H. Smith. 2001. "A Comparison of Social Development Processes Leading to Violent Behavior in Late Adolescence for Childhood Initiators and Adolescent Initiators of Violence." *Journal of Research in Crime and Delinquency* 38(1): 45–63.

Hill, Karl G., Jennifer A. Bailey, J. David Hawkins, Richard F. Catalano, Rick Kosterman, Sabrina Oesterle, and Robert D. Abbott. 2014. "The Onset of STI Diagnosis Through Age 30: Results from the Seattle Social Development Project Intervention." *Prevention Science* 15(Suppl. 1): S19–S32.

Hill, Karl G., J. David Hawkins, Richard F. Catalano, Robert D. Abbott, and Jie Guo. 2005. "Family Influences on the Risk of Daily Smoking Initiation." *Journal of Adolescent Health* 37(3): 202–210.

Hirschi, Travis. 1969. *Causes of Delinquency*. Berkeley: University of California Press.

Huang, Bu, Rick Kosterman, Richard F. Catalano, J. David Hawkins, and Robert D. Abbott. 2001. "Modeling Mediation in the Etiology of Violent Behavior in Adolescence: A Test of the Social Development Model." *Criminology* 39(1): 75–107.

Iranpour, Abedin, Ensiyeh Jamshidi, Nouzar Nakhaee, Ali Akbar Haghdoost, Davoud Shojaeizadeh, Mehrdad Eftekhar-Ardabili, and Hassan Eftekhar-Ardabili. 2015. "Development and Psychometric Properties of Risk and Protective Factors of Substance Use Scale in Iran: An Application of Social Development Model." *Addiction and Health* 7(3–4): 117–129.

Jacob, Marilyn. 2008. "The Significance of Gender in Choosing an Etiological Model of Delinquency." *Dissertation Abstracts International Section A: Humanities and Social Sciences* 68: 3591.

Jones, Tiffany M., Karl G. Hill, Marina Epstein, Jungeun Olivia Lee, J. David Hawkins, and Richard F. Catalano. 2016. "Understanding the Interplay of Individual and Social-Developmental Factors in the Progression of Substance Use and Mental Health from Childhood to Adulthood." *Development and Psychopathology* 28(3): 721–741.

Kempf, Kimberly L. 1993. "The Empirical Status of Hirschi's Control Theory." In *New Directions in Criminological Theory: Advances in Criminological Theory*, Vol. 4, edited by Freda Adler and William S. Laufer, 143–185. New Brunswick, NJ: Transaction.

Kim, B. K. Elizabeth, Amanda B. Gilman, Karl G. Hill, and J. David Hawkins. 2016. "Examining Protective Factors Against Violence Among High-Risk Youth: Findings from the Seattle Social Development Project." *Journal of Criminal Justice* 45: 19–25.

Kim, B. K. Elizabeth, Kari M. Gloppen, Isaac C. Rhew, Sabrina Oesterle, and J. David Hawkins. 2015. "Effects of the Communities That Care Prevention System on Youth Reports of Protective Factors." *Prevention Science* 16(5): 652–662.

Kim, Min Jung. 2009. "Youth Violence Prevention: Social Development Model Approaches to Predicting and Preventing the Progression of Childhood Aggression into Youth Violence." *Dissertation Abstracts International Section A: Humanities and Social Sciences* 69: 3320.

Kim, Sunah. 2000. *The Effects of Parent Bonding, School Bonding, Belief on the Structure of Problem Behaviors in Elementary School-Age Children*. Doctoral dissertation, University of Washington, Seattle.

Kosterman, Rick, John W. Graham, J. David Hawkins, Richard F. Catalano, and Todd I. Herrenkohl. 2001. "Childhood Risk Factors for Persistence of Violence in the Transition to Adulthood: A Social Development Perspective." *Violence and Victims* 16(4): 355–369.

Kosterman, Rick, Kevin P. Haggerty, Richard Spoth, and Cleve Redmond. 2004. "Unique Influence of Mothers and Fathers on Their Children's Antisocial Behavior." *Journal of Marriage and Family* 66(3): 762–778.

Kosterman, Rick, J. David Hawkins, Kevin P. Haggerty, Richard Spoth, and Cleve Redmond. 2001. "Preparing for the Drug Free Years: Session-Specific Effects of a Universal Parent-Training Intervention with Rural Families." *Journal of Drug Education* 31(1): 47–68.

Kosterman, Rick, Karl G. Hill, Jungeun Olivia Lee, Meredith C. Meacham, Robert D. Abbott, Richard F. Catalano, and J. David Hawkins. 2014. "Young Adult Social Development as a Mediator of Alcohol Use Disorder Symptoms from Age 21 to 30." *Psychology of Addictive Behaviors* 28(2): 348–358.

Krohn, Marvin D., James L. Massey, and William F. Skinner. 1987. "A Sociological Theory of Crime and Delinquency: Social Learning Theory." In *Behavioral Approaches to Crime and Delinquency: A Handbook of Application, Research, and Concepts*, edited by Edward K. Morris and Curtis J. Braukmann, 455–475. New York: Plenum Press.

Lacourse, Eric, Sylvana Coté, Daniel S Nagin, Frank Vitaro, Mara Brendgen, and Richard E Tremblay. 2002. "A Longitudinal–Experimental Approach to Testing Theories of Antisocial Behavior Development." *Development and Psychopathology* 14(4): 909–924.

Laundra, Kenneth H., Gary Kiger, and Stephen J. Bahr. 2002. "A Social Development Model of Serious Delinquency: Examining Gender Differences." *Journal of Primary Prevention* 22(4): 389–407.

Locke, Thomas F., and Michael D. Newcomb. 2004. "Adolescent Predictors of Young Adult and Adult Alcohol Involvement and Dysphoria in a Prospective Community Sample of Women." *Prevention Science* 5(3): 151–168.

Loeber, Rolf, and Magda Stouthamer-Loeber. 1998. "Development of Juvenile Aggression and Violence: Some Common Misconceptions and Controversies." *American Psychologist* 53(2): 242–259.

Lonczak, Heather S., Robert D. Abbott, J. David Hawkins, Rick Kosterman, and Richard F. Catalano. 2002. "Effects of the Seattle Social Development Project on Sexual Behavior, Pregnancy, Birth, and Sexually Transmitted Disease Outcomes by Age 21 Years." *Archives of Pediatrics and Adolescent Medicine* 156(5): 438–447.

Lonczak, Heather S., Bu Huang, Richard F. Catalano, J. David Hawkins, Karl G. Hill, Robert D. Abbott, Jean A. M. Ryan, and Rick Kosterman. 2001. "The Social Predictors of Adolescent Alcohol Misuse: A Test of the Social Development Model." *Journal of Studies on Alcohol* 62(2): 179–189.

Mason, W. Alex, Rick Kosterman, Kevin P. Haggerty, J. David Hawkins, Cleve Redmond, Richard L. Spoth, and Chungyeol Shin. 2009. "Gender Moderation and Social Developmental Mediation of the Effect of a Family-Focused Substance Use Preventive Intervention on Young Adult Alcohol Abuse." *Addictive Behaviors* 34(6–7): 599–605.

Mason, W. Alex, Rick Kosterman, J. David Hawkins, Kevin P. Haggerty, and Richard L. Spoth. 2003. "Reducing Adolescents' Growth in Substance Use and Delinquency: Randomized Trial Effects of a Preventive Parent-Training Intervention." *Prevention Science* 4(3): 203–312.

Mason, W. Alex, Rick Kosterman, J. David Hawkins, Kevin P. Haggerty, Richard L. Spoth, and Cleve Redmond. 2007. "Influence of a Family-Focused Substance Use Preventive

Intervention on Growth in Adolescent Depressive Symptoms." *Journal of Research on Adolescence* 17(3): 541–564.

Matsueda, Ross L. 1988. "The Current State of Differential Association Theory." *Crime and Delinquency* 34(3): 277–306.

Moffitt, Terrie E., Louise Arseneault, Daniel Belsky, Nigel Dickson, Robert J. Hancox, HonaLee Harrington, Renate Houts, Richie Poulton, Brent W. Roberts, Stephen Ross, Malcolm R. Sears, W. Murray Thomson, and Avshalom Caspi. 2011. "A Gradient of Childhood Self-Control Predicts Health, Wealth, and Public Safety." *PNAS Proceedings of the National Academy of Sciences of the United States of America* 108(7): 2693–2698.

O'Donnell, Julie, J. David Hawkins, and Robert D. Abbott. 1995a. "Predicting Serious Delinquency and Substance Use Among Aggressive Boys." *Journal of Consulting and Clinical Psychology* 63(4): 529–537.

O'Donnell, Julie, J. David Hawkins, Richard F. Catalano, Robert D. Abbott, and L. Edward Day. 1995b. "Preventing School Failure, Drug Use, and Delinquency Among Low-Income Children: Long-Term Intervention in Elementary Schools." *American Journal of Orthopsychiatry* 65(1): 87–100.

O'Donnell, Julie, Elizabeth A. Michalak, and Ellen B. Ames. 1997. "Inner-City Youths Helping Children: After-School Programs to Promote Bonding and Reduce Risk." *Children and Schools* 19(4): 231–241.

Oxford, Monica L., Tracy W. Harachi, Richard F. Catalano, Kevin P. Haggerty, and Robert D. Abbott. 2000. "Early Elementary School-Aged Child Attachment to Parents: A Test of Theory and Implications for Intervention." *Prevention Science* 1(2): 61–69.

Park, Jisuk, Rick Kosterman, J. David Hawkins, Kevin P. Haggerty, Terry E. Duncan, Susan C. Duncan, and Richard Spoth. 2000. "Effects of the "Preparing for the Drug Free Years" Curriculum on Growth in Alcohol Use and Risk for Alcohol Use in Early Adolescence." *Prevention Science* 1(3): 125–138.

Roosa, Mark W., Katherine H. Zeiders, George P. Knight, Nancy A. Gonzales, Jenn-Yun Tein, Delia Saenz, Megan O'Donnell, and Cady Berkel. 2011. "A Test of the Social Development Model During the Transition to Junior High with Mexican American Adolescents." *Developmental Psychology* 47(2): 527–537.

Spoth, Richard, Cleve Redmond, and Chungyeol Shin. 1998. "Direct and Indirect Latent-Variable Parenting Outcomes of Two Universal Family-Focused Preventive Interventions: Extending a Public Health-Oriented Research Base." *Journal of Consulting and Clinical Psychology* 66(2): 385–399.

Sullivan, Christopher J., and Paul Hirschfield. 2011. "Problem Behavior in the Middle School Years: An Assessment of the Social Development Model." *Journal of Research in Crime and Delinquency* 48(4): 566–593.

Sutherland, Edwin Hardin. 1973. "Development of the Theory." In *Edwin Sutherland on Analyzing Crime*, edited by Karl Schuessler, 13–29. Chicago: University of Chicago Press.

Sutherland, Edwin Hardin, and Donald R. Cressey. 1970. *Criminology*. New York: Lippincott.

Wasserman, Gail A., Kate Keenan, Richard E. Tremblay, John D. Coie, Todd I. Herrenkohl, Rolf Loeber, and David Petechuk. 2003. "Risk and Protective Factors of Child Delinquency." *OJJDP Juvenile Justice Bulletin, Child Delinquency Bulletin Series*, April.

Williams, James Herbert, Richard A. Van Dorn, J. David Hawkins, Robert D. Abbott, and Richard F. Catalano. 2001. "Correlates Contributing to Involvement in Violent Behaviors Among Young Adults." *Violence and Victims* 16(4): 371–388.

CHAPTER 14

....

INTERACTIONAL THEORY

....

TERENCE P. THORNBERRY
AND MARVIN D. KROHN

THE first published statement of interactional theory appeared in 1987 (Thornberry 1987). The theory was presented as a theoretical elaboration (Thornberry 1989) of a social control perspective, using the elements of the social bond as the core of the theory and then examining both theoretical and empirical literature to address: what leads to variation in those elements and what additional consequences (other than delinquent behavior itself) the weakening of the social bond might have. These consequences were, in turn, examined to determine if they mediated the relationship between the elements of the social bond and delinquent behavior. The result of this exercise was a theory suggesting that structural position such as social class, living in a disorganized neighborhood, and race affected the initial level of the social bond, which, in turn, was reciprocally related to association with delinquent peers, delinquent values, and delinquent behavior.

In addition to articulating a causal structure in which the above constructs were featured, Thornberry's interactional theory had three important assumptions on which the structure of the theory was built. These assumptions had seldom been emphasized in previous theoretical perspectives. First, Thornberry (1987) asserted that the effect of key theoretical constructs on delinquent behavior varied across developmental stages. Therefore, it was essential that any explanation of delinquent behavior take into account how factors such as the influence of parents or peers may vary depending on the age or developmental stage of the person. Later, in dealing with a broader age range and viewing the process through the lens of a life-course perspective, this notion was extended to recognize the degree to which what occurred at earlier developmental stages could affect what occurs at later stages (Thornberry and Krohn 2005).

The second assumption that underlies the theory is an interactional process whereby adolescents interact with people and institutions resulting in behavioral outcomes. Just as the adolescent is affected by the behaviors of others, his or her own behaviors are likely to affect their behaviors as well. Importantly, participation in delinquent behavior is predicted to influence the quality of interaction between parents, peers, and the adolescent and between the adolescent and conforming institutions such as the school. This called for examining bidirectional or reciprocal causality among the variables specified in the theory.

The third building block of the theory is the proportionality of cause and effect and the related principle of equifinality (Cicchetti and Rogosch 1996). Proportionality of cause and effect states that as the magnitude of the causal force increases, so too does the likelihood of and magnitude of the outcome. There are potentially multiple causes of the same outcome (equifinality), and not all causal factors are needed to produce an outcome. When there are multiple causal influences at play, especially when some are at extreme levels, the likelihood of antisocial behavior is maximized (Thornberry and Krohn 2005).

Interactional theory has had a life course of its own. Prompted by the ongoing research conducted by Thornberry and associates (Thornberry et al. 1991, 2003c) known as the Rochester Youth Development Study (RYDS) and its related intergenerational study (the Rochester Intergenerational Study, or RIGS), the scope of the theory was expanded to include the emerging adult years, the early childhood years, and an explanation of intergenerational concordance and discordance of antisocial behavior. Presentations of the theory to date (Thornberry and Krohn 2001, 2005), have not necessarily reflected the chronology of the hypothesized events and processes. This chapter affords us the opportunity to discuss the full scope of theory over the life course in such a manner.

Section 1.A begins with the processes that occur in early childhood when individual and social structural deficits, parental factors, and the home environment play key roles in child development. Section 1.B then moves to the school-age years when factors outside the home such as the neighborhood environment, school commitment and involvement, and peer interaction play prominent roles. During the later teenage and early adulthood years, these factors continue to be important, but the major focus of our theory turns toward the timing and success of the transition to adult status. In Section 1.C, the question of what might lead to desistance and continuation in adulthood is considered. To address this question, an examination of the interplay across life-course trajectories and the role of cumulative continuity are key points of discussion. Section II concludes our exposition of the theory by examining how the lives of one generation are linked to the next in generating both continuity and discontinuity in deviant behavior between parent and child. As we provide a statement of our theory, we pay particular attention to the research specifically addressing interactional theory but also include studies that examine hypotheses consistent with those of our theory, although not necessarily focusing solely on it.

I. INTERACTIONAL THEORY

Longitudinal research has demonstrated that antisocial and delinquent behavior is evident across the full life course (Piquero, Farrington, and Blumstein 2003), although its manifestation varies at different developmental stages (Patterson 1993). Consistent with this view, interactional theory offers an explanation for antisocial behavior that occurs across the life course, starting with early onset antisocial behavior during childhood.

A. Childhood Delinquency

Tremblay and colleagues (Tremblay et al. 1996; Tremblay and Nagin 2005) found aggression and antisocial behavior to frequently emerge during toddlerhood and early childhood. According to interactional theory (Thornberry and Krohn 2001, 2005), childhood onset of offending is accounted for by three broad factors— social disadvantage, individual characteristics, and ineffective parenting. First, the theory hypothesizes that children who exhibit early involvement in antisocial behavior are more likely to be born to families experiencing severe structural adversity such as chronic poverty, unemployment, and residence in areas of concentrated poverty as compared to non-delinquents and youth with a more age-normative onset of delinquency. Second, they are also likely to suffer from a variety of negative developmental traits and neuropsychological deficits, such as impulsivity, risk-taking, and negative emotionality (Moffitt 1993). Finally, they are more likely to experience less effective parenting styles such as low affective ties with parents, ineffective monitoring and discipline, and, at the extreme, child maltreatment. Although serious deficits in any one of these conceptual domains can lead to antisocial behavior, early-onset antisocial behavior is likely to be brought about by the intense coupling and interaction of these influences. These causal influences themselves are likely to co-occur, and, consistent with the principle of the proportionality of cause and effect, when they accumulate in the child's life course they are likely to lead to early-onset, more persistent involvement in antisocial behavior. In addition, even at these early ages the reciprocal causal influences that are at the heart of interactional theory are evident. Bidirectional influences between the child's temperament and conduct problems, on the one hand, and the parent's child management style, on the other, have been observed as early as toddlerhood and are quite common throughout childhood (Patterson, Reid, and Dishion 1992; Shaw and Bell 1993; Larsson et al. 2008; Hawes et al. 2011).

At somewhat older ages as children enter school and gain a modicum of independence from the family, other social influences come into play and add to the influences of parents on antisocial behavior. In particular, interactional theory focuses on two broad causal pathways—the strength of the persons' bond to conventional society and the person's embeddedness in delinquent networks—to account for offending. Youth who are strongly bonded to conventional society are unlikely to have the behavioral freedom to engage in delinquency, drug use, and other problem behaviors. In particular, youth who are strongly attached to their parents and family, who are committed to conventional institutions like school, and who have strong beliefs in conventional values are constrained from engaging in antisocial behaviors. These elements of the bond to society are likely to prevent any prolonged and serious involvement in antisocial behavior.

In contrast, youth who have weak social bonds have more behavioral freedom and a higher probability of engaging in antisocial behavior.

In interactional theory weak bonds to conventional society are viewed as creating increased behavioral freedom; that is, they allow individuals to deviate from conventional activities, but they do not necessarily lead directly to involvement in delinquent behavior. For that to occur, a learning environment is required that channels the behavioral freedom specifically into delinquent behavior such as violence and theft, as opposed to other maladaptive responses such as mental health problems including depression, anxiety, and social isolation, retreatist behaviors, school disengagement, adopting a "corner-boy" lifestyle with little prosocial engagement as described by Cohen (1955), alienation and withdrawal, and so forth. This learning environment, which channels behavior toward actual delinquency, is represented by two key concepts—association with delinquent peers and delinquent beliefs. Associating with others who engage in delinquent behavior provides role models for imitation and social reinforcements for engaging in delinquent behavior (Akers et al. 1979; Akers 1998). It also increases the likelihood of spending unstructured and unsupervised time with peers, which increases delinquent behavior (Osgood and Anderson 2004). In addition, a set of beliefs that it is acceptable to engage in delinquent behavior in certain circumstances, or at least that it is not morally wrong to engage in those behaviors, also increase the likelihood of delinquent behavior (Payne and Salotti 2007; Cohn et al. 2010; Wikstrom and Svennson 2012).

A core aspect of interactional theory is its reciprocal and dynamic nature. First, these central causes of delinquency are likely to become reciprocally related over time. For example, youth who are poorly attached to their parents are likely to be less engaged and less successful in school, and, in turn, youth who fail in school are likely to grow more distant from their parents. Second, delinquent behavior is not viewed as a mere outcome of earlier factors, such as weak commitment to school or associations with delinquent peers, as it is in many traditional theories. In contrast, delinquency is viewed as embedded in a set of mutually reinforcing causal relationships that develop over time and that create trajectories toward or away from prolonged involvement in delinquency. For example, associating with delinquent peers via learning processes and changes in routine activities increases the chances of delinquent behavior. But the more the individual engages in delinquent behavior, the more likely they are to associate with fellow delinquents, in part because of social selection processes and in part because delinquent youths are often rejected from prosocial peer groups. Similarly, weak social bonds such as attachment to parents increase the likelihood of delinquent behavior as youth are less constrained to follow the wishes and values of parents, but involvement in delinquency is likely to further erode the bond to parents since it is typically antithetical to parental wishes and desires.

Thus, delinquent behavior is not merely the outcome of earlier risk factors and causal processes. It is part and parcel of its own development. Weak bonds to conventional society allow for the emergence of delinquent behavior, values, and associations. But as individuals become enmeshed in these delinquent influences, it is likely that their bonds to the conventional order will become further eroded. As a result, alienation from parents and family is likely to increase, as does school disengagement. The orientation of the theory as a state-dependence model (Nagin and Paternoster 1991) is evident. Past delinquent behavior is correlated with future delinquent behavior because of the consequences—the erosion of bonds to conventional society and embeddedness in deviant networks—that it generates.

This core contention of interactional theory, that delinquency is embedded in a set of mutually reinforcing reciprocal relationships, has received a considerable amount of empirical support. In 1996 Thornberry reviewed 17 studies of delinquency and crime that examined bidirectional relationships. Overwhelmingly, they provided empirical data consistent with the notion of reciprocity: while weak social bonds increase delinquent behavior, involvement in delinquency further attenuates the strength of social bonds. Similarly, association with delinquent peers and delinquent beliefs increased the likelihood of delinquent behavior, but delinquency further cemented those associations and beliefs.

In the context of the Rochester Youth Development Study, Thornberry and colleagues conducted several empirical assessments of interactional theory (see Thornberry et al. 2003b for a summary). For example, Jang and Smith (1997) found that delinquency and parental supervision are involved in mutually reinforcing relationships over time. In contrast, the relationship between attachment to parents and delinquency is unidirectional, but interestingly, delinquent behavior was found to attenuate attachment while attachment was not significantly related to later delinquency. The finding that child effects are significant while parent effects are not is not unique to the Rochester study. Other assessments of bidirectional relationships also demonstrate this. For example, Fite et al. (2006) reported that, during early adolescence, externalizing behavior is related to poor monitoring and inconsistent discipline, but those core parenting skills are not related to the child's externalizing behavior (see also Huh et al. 2006; Burke, Pardini, and Loeber 2008). Other studies of bidirectional relationships between delinquency and various parenting skills do, however, find bidirectional relationships (Hipwell et al. 2008; Pardini, Fite, and Burke, 2008). Interestingly, none of these studies show a unidirectional impact of parenting on child behavior—the most commonly assumed causal impact; they either demonstrate bidirectional influences or a unidirectional impact of child behavior on parenting behavior.

Thornberry et al. (1991) and Thornberry and Henry (2009) demonstrated that disengagement from school and delinquency are also reciprocally interrelated. Hoffmann, Erickson, and Spence (2013) find partial support for interactional theory's hypotheses in this regard. Academic achievement and school attachment both reduce delinquent behavior, but delinquent behavior is only reciprocally related to school attachment, not academic achievement.

Finally, relationships among beliefs, association with deviant peers, and antisocial behavior were investigated in several studies. Thornberry et al. (1994) focused on delinquent behavior, while Krohn et al. (1996) focused on drug use. In both cases support for interactional theory hypotheses was evident. Reciprocal influences between associations and behavior, beliefs and behavior, as well as associations and beliefs were generally evident. More recently, Rebellion et al. (2014) found a reciprocal relationship between attitudes toward delinquency and delinquent behavior, with the relationship between delinquency and attitudes being stronger than that between attitudes and delinquency. Overall, there is little evidence to suggest that the major causal influence is simply from social bonds to delinquency or from peer associations to delinquency. In contrast, there is abundant evidence that these relationships are bidirectional and that delinquent careers develop over time both because of these influences and because of the feedback effects of delinquency on those influences.

B. Middle to Late Adolescence

Adolescence is one of the most dynamic stages of the life course, a time when youth are expected to begin the transition from childhood to adulthood. As such the processes, events, and decisions that occur during this time can be determinative of a successful transition and, ultimately, a conforming and productive adult life.

The major developmental tasks of adolescence include establishing age-appropriate autonomy, an integrated sense of self, and separation from parents in order to set the stage for a successful transition to adulthood (Collins and Steinberg 2006; Scott and Steinberg 2010). However, parents are still charged with the responsibility of guiding and supporting their children. Balancing the adolescent's need for autonomy with parental concern for the safety and welfare of their children may lead to dysfunctional parenting (Silverberg and Steinberg 1990) and an attenuation (albeit often temporary) of the element of the social bond typically created by the relationship between parent and child.

With the increased mobility afforded adolescents and the reduction in parental restrictions (or the youth's adherence to them), adolescents gravitate toward one another. Peer groups replace parents as the most influential social network, and those groups grow in importance as a major source of rewards and approval of behavior (Thornberry 1987; Steinberg and Monahan 2007). They often engage in precocious behaviors typically considered appropriate for adults only such as smoking, drinking, reckless driving, and minor forms of delinquent behavior (Spear, 2010). Given the growing importance of interaction among themselves and the reduced involvement of their parents in their daily lives, peers serve to reinforce these behaviors and establish definitions of them as appropriate, or at least as justified. Engaging in antisocial behavior leads to embeddedness in deviant social networks (Hagan 1992) evincing the reciprocal nature of the relationships among peer associations, definitions, and delinquent behavior predicted by Thornberry (1987).

For adolescents from disadvantaged settings or who manifested early individual deficits, the impact of decreasing parental control coupled with increasing peer influence will be more problematic than for those who were not beset with such disadvantages and deficits. In part this is because disadvantaged families have less ability to provide for alternative activities that could keep their children away from problematic influences (Ambert 1997). In addition, earlier participation in delinquent behavior may lead to additional negative consequences such as school failure and rejection by conventional peers and adults that enhance the deviance-producing effect of striving for independence. Thus, the frequency and seriousness of delinquent behavior among these youth are expected to be greater than among those who did not face structural disadvantages or early deficits.

The reciprocal nature of interactional theory emphasizes the impact that involvement in delinquent behavior during adolescence may have for successful transitions into adult roles. As stated above, adolescents are attempting to increase their autonomy from parental control in anticipation of accepting adult obligations and privileges, and difficulty arises when they make those transitions prematurely. Precocious or disorderly transitions are those that take place either before the normal course of adolescent development would warrant or in a sequence that makes it more difficult for the adolescent to eventually succeed in the adult world (Rindfuss, Swicegood, and Rosenfeld 1987). For example, becoming pregnant (or impregnating someone) or becoming a parent during adolescence places the youth at a disadvantage in completing their education and eventually getting a good job. Participation in delinquent activities and interaction with delinquent peers, especially in locations where adult control is not present, increases the probability that precocious transitions will occur. Krohn, Lizotte, and Perez (1997) found that adolescent involvement in delinquent behavior and drug use increased the risk of early pregnancy, teenage parenthood, high school dropout, and living independently from one's parents during the teenage years. Other longitudinal studies have also found that involvement in antisocial behavior leads to later disruption in the transition to adult roles (Newcomb and Bentler 1988; Huizinga et al. 2003). Relatedly, participation in a gang also increases the probability of those precocious transitions (Thornberry et al. 2003; Krohn et al. 2011; Melde and Esbensen, 2011; Decker, Melde, and Pyrooz 2013; Pyrooz 2014).

Involvement in delinquent behavior also places adolescents at risk for official intervention. Interactional theory recognizes the potential for official intervention becoming a turning point in the lives of adolescents, affecting their chances of success in other life course trajectories. In a series of studies using the RYDS data, police contact early in adolescence was found to decrease the probability of completing high school and acquiring steady employment as young adults (Bernburg and Krohn 2003; Lopes et al. 2012), to decrease the opportunities for successful partnering (Schmidt et al. 2015), and to increase the probability of being in a delinquent social network (Bernburg, Krohn, and Rivera 2006), all of which leads to increased involvement in offending.

C. Late Bloomers

The focus thus far has been on individuals who either had an early start to their offending or who began offending at an age-normative stage in their development. Attention now is turned to a group of offenders whose antisocial behavior onset is during the later adolescent or early adulthood years. We label these offenders as late bloomers in order to distinguish them from the term "late starters," which is often used simply to distinguish those who do not onset at very early ages (Patterson, Capaldi, and Bank 1991; Moffitt 1993).

Bushway, Thornberry, and Krohn (2003), using semi-parametric group based trajectory analysis (Nagin 2005), identified a criminal behavior trajectory path, which initially had a low rate of offending consistent with the non-offender group. But, at about 16.5 to 17 years of age, their offending trajectory began to slope upward rapidly. This was surprising since at these ages most adolescents are beginning to desist from offending. Other studies have found patterns of offending consistent with the late bloomer or adult-onset group (Eggleston and Laub 2002; Krohn, Gibson, and Thornberry 2013; Simpson et al. 2016). For example, Eggleston and Laub (2002) report that averaged across 18 studies, 17.2 percent of non-delinquents begin offending in adulthood. Approximately half of the adult offender population is comprised of these late bloomers. Moreover, the late bloomers continue their offending well into adulthood and tend to be serious offenders (Farrington 1983; Wolfgang, Thornberry, and Figlio 1987; Sampson and Laub 1993; Nagin, Farrington, and Moffitt 1995).

To explain why a group of offenders who have not offended through the early adolescent years, when offending is quite common, suddenly initiate in their later teenage years and then continue serious offending, we focused on the basic tenets of interactional theory. Recall that interactional theory predicts that those who have temperamental deficits will have high rates of delinquent behavior and are more likely to continue offending into the adult years. The theory also suggests that those who have low rates of offending or no offending will have a strong social bond with parents and school and prosocial peer networks. Applying those expectations to late bloomers, we hypothesize that this group of offenders is more likely to have reduced human capital especially in terms of intelligence and cognitive competence. Such deficits make it more difficult for them to establish the social capital necessary for successful adult development than it is for other adolescents. However, during adolescence they are buffered from the effects of these deficits by a supportive family and school environment perhaps because of a more advantageous structural position.

As these adolescents age they are expected, like all youth, to begin the process of establishing autonomy and to become more independent from family and school environments. In that process, however, they are likely to lose the earlier assets that had insulated them from the consequences of their deficits. Deficits in human capital now become a serious disadvantage for acquiring meaningful employment, establishing a quality relationship with a partner, and forming their own family. Additionally, the loss of protection provided by the parental environment and the support from and routine of the school may make them more vulnerable to the influence of delinquent friends. All of these factors increase the likelihood for the onset and maintenance of delinquency, drug use, and related problem behaviors.

Although there has been little research on late bloomers or adult-onset offenders, the findings suggest that the above explanation is plausible. Nagin, Farrington, and Moffitt (1995) found that late bloomers had low IQs at ages 8 to 11 and low academic achievement in early adolescence. Pukkinen, Lyyra, and Kolko (2009) found that adult-onset offenders did as well in school as non-offenders but were more neurotic and more likely to be high risk-takers. In addition, when compared with persistent offenders, adult-onset offenders had more social capital in their family backgrounds. Van der Geest, Blokland, and Bijleveld (2009) compared late bloomers with high-frequency chronics and high-frequency desistors. The late-blooming group was more likely to have a constellation of psychopathological characteristics than the high chronic group. However, parents of late bloomers were less likely to have a delinquent record and more likely to be employed, suggesting that they may have been more capable of buffering their children from criminal behavior in spite of the child's psychopathological deficits. Mata and van Dulmen (2012) compared an adult-onset trajectory group to abstainers and adolescent-limited and chronic offending groups. They found that the adult-onset group was closer to their fathers during adolescence than chronic offenders. Moreover, during emerging adulthood, the adult-onset groups were less likely to be employed, had poorer physical health, and were less likely to be involved in romantic relationships. Preliminary work using the RYDS (Thornberry and Matsueda 2011) found that during adolescence late bloomers were more likely than non-offenders to have delinquent beliefs and experience negative life events than non-offenders were. They also found that they were more likely to have close ties to school and value the importance of education and to be more attached to their parents, who were more likely to be financially secure. Importantly, late bloomers were more likely to be closely supervised by their parent than were high-level offenders. Simpson et al. (2016), using a sample of female prisoners, report that late bloomers (those who initiated offending at 18 to 20 or at 21 plus) had more childhood social bonds then offenders who initiated at earlier ages. Zara and Farrington (2009) compared late starters to non-offenders and to earlier starters on a number of childhood and adolescent characteristics. Among their findings, they report that, compared to non-offenders, late starters had a number of individual deficits such as low concentration, impulsivity, low IQ, and low school attainment. At the same time, compared to those who started offending at earlier ages, late starters were less likely to have a criminal parent, to be exposed to poor child-rearing, and to come from families with low family incomes.

Although there is not an extensive research literature on what we have labeled the late-blooming group of offenders, evidence to date is largely consistent with our hypotheses. Late bloomers are more likely than non-offenders to have early deficits. However, they are more likely than chronic high-level offenders to come from families with the necessary social capital to provide a supportive environment. In addition, some studies find that late bloomers do better in school than do chronic offenders. This research suggests that the early deficits experienced by late bloomers are being buffered by family and school factors delaying the onset of criminal behavior.

D. Continuity and Change

As one moves into the adult years, the focus of attention turns to the twin topics of continuity and change. At that point in the life course, many previous offenders change and desist from active involvement in crime. At the same time other offenders continue and, often escalate, their involvement in criminal behavior.

Continuity in offending is somewhat more likely for those who start early than for those who start later. Unlike taxonomic theories (e.g., Patterson, Capaldi, and Bank 1991; Moffitt 1993), however, interactional theory assumes that continuity is not tightly linked to age of onset. Although there is a positive correlation between onset and persistence, the magnitude of the correlation is, at best, moderate (Krohn et al. 2001). Regardless of when one's delinquent career begins, it is possible for that career to continue. Continuity is accounted for by two general processes. The first, which is more important for those with an early onset of offending, is the stability of factors associated with delinquency. For example, negative temperamental qualities, ineffective parenting styles, and extreme social disadvantage are all relatively stable over time. Therefore, these factors are likely to continue causing involvement in delinquency at later ages, offering a partial explanation for persistence. The second general process, which is important for all offenders regardless of age of onset, stems from the bidirectional relationships within which delinquency is embedded. As we argued earlier, delinquency has feedback effects that further intensify the factors associated with its causality. Delinquency, especially serious delinquency, erodes social bonds with family, school, and prosocial peers and embeds the individual in deviant social networks and belief systems. All of these factors make escape from involvement in crime more difficult and substantially increase the likelihood of persistent involvement in offending during the adult years.

Although some offenders do indeed persist in antisocial behavior throughout long portions of their lives, most offenders stop or desist from involvement in crime. Involvement in delinquent and criminal behavior peaks during adolescence and desistance from crime typically unfolds during the transition from adolescence to adulthood. This transition affords new opportunities for social bonds that can reverse previous patterns of behavior. In particular, successfully establishing one's own family of procreation and stable patterns of work are likely to lead to reductions in involvement in antisocial behavior. First, all of these transitions increase bonds to conventional society—especially the roles of partner, parent, and worker. Second, as individuals become enmeshed in the conventional roles, they are less likely to associate with deviant peers or to engage in risky time with friends; friendships gradually change to prosocial networks organized around family and work. All of these changes are likely to reduce involvement in antisocial behavior, and at this point reciprocal influences begin to work, but in this case in reverse—increasing social bonds enhances prosocial behavior patterns, and those behavior patterns feed back to increase prosocial bonds. Of course, smooth and successful transitions to adulthood are not available to all and are closely related to the person's earlier development. In particular, the more extensive an individual's delinquent career, the harder it is to move from antisocial to prosocial behavior patterns. Nevertheless, most youth come through adolescence with enough human and social capital to give them entrée to successful transitions to adulthood. It may be through a "good marriage" or a set of skills that opens employment opportunities, but once those transitions are initiated, the movement away from antisocial behavior is enhanced. The work of Laub and Sampson (Laub and Sampson 1993, 2003; Sampson and Laub 1993, 2003) has been at the forefront of examining the "turning points" in one's life that can lead to desisting from criminal behavior. Using data originally collected by Sheldon and Eleanor Glueck (1968) and following up part of their original sample, Laub and Sampson examined the factors that facilitated desistance. Their research has identified the importance of a quality marriage, joining the military, being sent to reform school, acquiring a meaningful job, and neighborhood change. They conclude that these turning points all involve new situations that (1) knife off the past from the present, (2) provide both supervision and monitoring as well as new opportunities of social support and growth, (3) change the structure of routine activities, and (4) provide the opportunity for identity transformation (Sampson and Laub 2005, p. 172).

Laub and Sampson's emphasis on time-varying factors in changing trajectories of crime is consistent with the framework provided by interactional theory. Our theory views desistance as a process and not necessarily a dichotomous outcome— crime versus no crime—that gradually unfolds over time in response to changing life circumstances such as life-course transitions and changing social networks (Bushway et al. 2001; Bushway, Thornberry, and Krohn 2003). Warr's research (1998), which shows that the impact of life-course transitions such as marriage on desistence are mediated by changes in peer networks, is also quite consistent with interactional theory's hypotheses concerning the desistance process.

II. Intergenerational Extensions

One of the unique aspects of interactional theory is its formal extension to account for intergenerational continuity and discontinuity in antisocial behavior. There is growing evidence of intergenerational continuity in delinquency, drug use, and other antisocial behaviors. That is to say, children born to parents who have a history of involvement in delinquent behavior are themselves at significantly increased risk of also becoming involved in delinquent behavior (Thornberry 2005, 2009; Farrington 2011; Besemer 2012). At the same time, however, there are also substantial levels of discontinuity, especially intergenerational resilience. That is, there are many children whose parents were involved in delinquency but who are not also involved in delinquency. Interactional theory offers an explanation both for continuity and discontinuity in offending across the generations.

A. Intergenerational Continuity

Linked lives, a basic premise of the life-course perspective, argues that an individual's life course does not unfold independently of that of others. Quite the contrary, the life courses of intimate relations—husbands and wives, best friends, parents and children—become interwoven over time and mutually influence one another. For the topic of intergenerational continuity we are particularly concerned with the manner in which the life courses of parents and children become interwoven. There are a number of possible explanations for intergenerational continuity in delinquency ranging from purely genetic influences to shared environmental influences. Interactional theory's (Thornberry et al. 2003; Thornberry 2005, 2009) explanation for how parental behavior can influence child behavior is firmly rooted in the life-course perspective.

One of the basic premises of interactional theory is that antisocial behavior has important causal influences on subsequent aspects of the person's development. As discussed above, involvement in delinquency during childhood and adolescence, especially if it is prolonged and serious, is not cost free; it has negative consequences for the individual and, eventually, for the individual's children. First, there is considerable evidence that delinquent careers are associated with disorderly transitions from adolescence to adulthood. Delinquency interferes with the successful completion of the major developmental tasks of adolescence, and delinquents are significantly more likely to drop out of high school, to become teen parents, to cohabit, and to have higher rates of unemployment or underemployment. Both a history of delinquency and experiencing these disorderly transitions increase the likelihood of experiencing structural adversity during early adulthood as indicated by such factors as poverty, receipt of welfare, disrupted patterns of family formation, and residence in areas of concentrated disadvantage (Conger, Conger, and Martin 2010). All of these influences increase stressors such as depression, financial stress, aversive life events, and partner conflict. In other words, delinquent careers can initiate a cascade of negative influences that interfere with adolescent development, disrupt an orderly transition to adult roles, and create stress and disadvantage during the period of early or emerging adulthood. These outcomes are not preordained by delinquent careers, but they are significantly more likely to occur for serious delinquents as compared to non-delinquents. Young adults experiencing this constellation of factors are poorly prepared to enter the role of parent and to provide a safe, stable, and nurturing environment for their children. They are more likely to remain involved in antisocial behaviors including substance use and to remain embedded in deviant social networks (Kerr et al. 2011). In addition, they are less likely to develop strong prosocial bonds to conventional institutions, in particular in the arenas of family and work.

These problematic developmental processes have important intergenerational implications. The most potent pathway by which they influence the offspring's development and likelihood of delinquency is via their effect on family processes such as family conflict, hostility, and especially the quality of parenting behaviors (Scaramella et al. 2008). Less effective parenting styles include low affective ties and reduced involvement with the child, inconsistent monitoring and standard-setting, explosive and inconsistent disciplinary styles, and, at the extreme, child maltreatment. A robust literature describes the impact of ineffective parenting on the onset and maintenance of delinquent careers (Patterson, Reid, and Dishion 1992; Smith and Thornberry 1993; Conger, Conger, and Martin 2010). Children exposed to this style of parenting are more apt to be involved in delinquency, drug use, and other antisocial behaviors. They are also, unfortunately, less likely to develop prosocial competencies that may buffer them from these parental risk factors.

And, at this point, we have in a sense come full circle. The children initiate involvement in delinquent behavior in part because they are linked to their parent's history and prior behaviors and to the consequences of those behaviors. But once initiated, their own delinquency is also caused by the contemporary influences, such as peer relationships, social bonding, and so forth, discussed above. Consistent with this view, in a study of adolescent drug use, Krohn et al. (2016) show that the key predictors of adolescent antisocial behavior contained in interactional theory apply equally well to the parent generation studied in RYDS and the child generation studied in RIGS. Also, at this point the reciprocal effects described earlier in our discussion of the original version of interactional theory begin to apply to the next generation of children. Their delinquency is likely to weaken their bonds to society and enhance their embeddedness in deviant networks, thereby increasing the likelihood of an escalating level of involvement in delinquent careers.

Core aspects of this intergenerational theory have been examined in the context of the Rochester Intergenerational Study, which has been following the oldest biological child of the original adolescent participants in the RYDS with annual assessments for the past 19 years. Based on this three-generation study, there is clear evidence of intergenerational continuity for both general antisocial behavior and for drug use. Parental involvement in these behaviors significantly increases the likelihood of child involvement in these behaviors (Thornberry et al. 2003a; Thornberry 2005, 2009; Thornberry, Krohn, and Freeman-Gallant 2006; Thornberry, Freeman-Gallant, and Lovegrove 2009). Interestingly, the level of intergenerational continuity is often moderated by the level of ongoing parental contact with the child in a manner that is quite consistent with interactional theory's emphasis on environmental influences. In particular, the impact of parental criminality on child criminality is statistically significant for mothers, virtually all of whom are primary caretakers of their children, as it is for supervisory fathers, who have ongoing contact with their children. In contrast, for non-supervisory fathers—those who have little or no contact with their children—the relationship is not statistically significant and is quite close to zero (Thornberry et al. 2003a; Thornberry 2005, 2009; Thornberry, Krohn and Freeman-Gallant 2006; Thornberry, Freeman-Gallant, and Lovegrove 2009). A similar pattern also appears to emerge between the drug use patterns of grandparents and grandchildren (Thornberry, Krohn, and Freeman-Gallant 2006). Overall, the pattern of findings in the Rochester study suggests that ongoing contact between the parent and child is essential for the intergenerational transfer of risk for antisocial behavior to occur (see also Jaffee et al. 2003).

The intergenerational analyses from the Rochester study also offer strong support for the mediational model of intergenerational continuity. These studies (Thornberry et al. 2003a; Thornberry 2005, 2009; Thornberry, Freeman-Gallant, and Lovegrove 2009) examined different aspects of parental antisocial behavior; different disorderly transitions; varying types of stressors such as depression, financial stress, exposure to negative life events, and parenting stress; different aspects of parenting styles some-times based on interview data and sometimes based on observational data; and different aspects of the child's antisocial behavior measured by different reporters. Despite these methodological and measurement variations, the results are uniformly supportive of in-teractional theory's predictions. Adolescent antisocial behavior on the part of the parent leads to later life-course disorder that, in turn, leads to ineffective parenting styles that increase the chances of the child's antisocial behavior.

The findings presented by Thornberry, Freeman-Gallant, and Lovegrove (2009) il-lustrate this general pattern. For mothers, they found that parental drug use and de-linquency during adolescence, as well as being a teenage mother, significantly increased their early adult depressive symptoms. In turn, depressive symptoms sig-nificantly reduced their attachment to the child and significantly increased the child's externalizing behavior problems. In addition, maternal depression had a direct impact on the child's behavior. For the supervisory fathers, adolescent involvement in drugs and delinquency increased their early-adult depressive symptoms, depressive symptoms reduced the father's level of attachment to the child, and that, in turn, increased the child's externalizing behavior problems.

A number of other intergenerational studies also report results that confirm interac-tional theory's basic explanation for intergenerational continuity in antisocial behavior (e.g., Conger et al. 2003; Smith and Farrington 2004; Bailey et al. 2009; Martin et al. 2010; Capaldi, Pears, and Kerr 2012). First, these studies find that a history of parental delinquency increases the likelihood of child delinquency. More importantly, they also find that this intergenerational impact is largely indirect, mediated by the types of de-velopment processes hypothesized by interactional theory. Of particular importance are disorderly transitions to adult roles, continued involvement in antisocial behavior, and, especially, parenting behaviors. Ineffective parenting style—low attachment, poor monitoring, harsh discipline, etc.—is the strongest and most proximal mediator of the impact of a parent's history of delinquency on the likelihood of delinquent involvement by their offspring.

B. Intergenerational Resilience

Intergenerational resilience occurs when the child exhibits substantially lower levels of involvement in delinquency (or other problem behaviors) as compared to the parent (Loughran, Larroulet, and Thornberry 2017). Interactional theory (Thornberry and

Krohn, 2005) suggests several developmental domains that are likely to mute or buffer the impact of parental delinquency on their child's subsequent delinquency. In particular, we comment on protective factors in three main clusters that are consistent with the general literature on resilience (Luthar, Cicchetti, and Becher 2000; Jessor and Turbin, 2014; Krohn et al. 2014; Masten 2014) and are capable of explaining intergenerational resilience.

First, there are likely to be changes—turning points—in the parent's own life course that have the potential to reduce the negative impact that their earlier antisocial behavior creates for their children. Among these protective factors are involvement in/commitment to prosocial institutions (college and educational attainment, military service, employment, and marriage), desistance/de-escalation from drug use and related problem behaviors, association with prosocial peers, religiosity and spiritual beliefs, and positive parenting styles (e.g., affective ties, monitoring, consistent discipline, positive parenting, and involvement) (Werner 1986; Edwards, Eiden, and Leonard 2006). Each of these characteristics is likely to provide benefits to children, especially when these characteristics co-occur. In addition, infrequent contact between a parent with a history of serious antisocial behavior and his or her children is likely to be protective for the children (Jaffee et al. 2003; Thornberry 2009); this is particularly important for the relationship between fathers and their children.

Second, characteristics and behaviors of the child's other parent or caregiver can also reduce the likelihood of behavioral continuity between a parent with a history of delinquency and the child. More prosocial other parents/caregivers are likely (1) to have stronger commitment to prosocial institutions such as education, work, and family; (2) to have positive parenting styles; (3) to refrain from or at least have low involvement in drug use and related problem behaviors; (4) to espouse conventional beliefs; and (5) to receive social and material support from parents, partners, and friends. All of these factors improve the chances of prosocial outcomes for children and can help account for discontinuity between a focal parent with a history of antisocial behavior and his or her children.

Finally, characteristics of the child can also be a source of intergenerational resilience. The prosocial assets, strengths, and competencies of the child are likely to both reduce their delinquency and buffer the negative consequences of the parent's earlier drug use. Specific protective factors are positive temperamental characteristics, self-control, cognitive competence, school engagement, attachment to parents, religious involvement, involvement in supervised prosocial activities, social competence; and prosocial peers.

Clearly, there are other arenas that could help account for intergenerational discontinuity such as neighborhood influences and the broader family context (e.g., positive partner relationships). But the broader point is that, in addition to accounting for intergenerational continuity, there are also substantial levels of discontinuity that require explanation. Intergenerational resilience is likely to increase when there are multiple protective factors across these domains, that is, when there are "cumulative advantages" (Thornberry and Krohn 2005). Also there are likely to be indirect effects, where protection in one domain generates additional protection in others (Jessor and Turbin 2014).

For example, Conger, Schofield, and Neppl (2012) demonstrate that a co-parent with a warm/supportive parenting style improves the quality of the focal parent's parenting style, both of which can serve as protective factors for the G3 child.

We have investigated intergenerational resilience in externalizing behaviors in the context of the Rochester Intergenerational Study. Dong and Krohn (2015) focused on delinquent behavior and found that strong affective ties and consistent discipline exhibited by the parent were direct protective factors, mediating the impact of parental delinquency on child externalizing behaviors in both childhood and adolescence; interaction effects were not significant, however. Lovegrove (2010) used trajectory models to identify parents involved in adolescent delinquency and children (age 8 to 11) involved in externalizing problems. He conditioned on parental delinquency by only analyzing children of parents with a history of delinquency and compared children in the trajectory group with the lowest level of externalizing behaviors (32 percent) with all others. Several parental characteristics were associated with discontinuity—lower levels of family poverty, older onset of parenthood, less parenting stress, and better parenting behaviors (supervision, attachment, and consistent discipline). Characteristics of the child's other primary caregiver were also important: less parenting stress, lower levels of violent behavior, less financial stress, less depression, and better parenting skills. Lizotte et al. (2013) examined discontinuity between parental violent offending and child externalizing behavior, as well as an important parent turning point—age at first parenthood—as a source of discontinuity. Parental violence, especially high levels of violence, increased the child's externalizing behavior, while an older age at which the individual first became a parent reduced externalizing behavior. Moreover, in some models an older age at first parenthood served as a buffering protective factor and in others as a direct protective factor. These findings are consistent with interactional theory's model of intergenerational resilience just summarized.

III. CONCLUSION

Interactional theory was first proposed by Thornberry in 1987 and expanded by Thornberry and Krohn in 2001 and 2005. The theory offers a broad explanation for involvement in antisocial behavior across the life course as well as for intergenerational continuity and discontinuity in antisocial behavior. It attempts to account both for the major causal processes associated with the onset of delinquent careers at different stages of the life course as well as for the consequences of involvement in delinquent behavior. This theoretical approach views delinquency as part of a dynamic development process in which factors like individual characteristics, family processes, and peer networks bring about delinquency, but involvement in delinquency also has causal impacts on those factors and, more generally, the person's later development. Those consequences help to account for levels of change and continuity in offending patterns as individuals move through adolescence and into the adult years.

The long-term consequences of earlier antisocial behavior also help explain the manner in which the lives of parents and their children are linked with respect to antisocial behavior. Children of parents with a history of antisocial behavior during adolescence are significantly more likely to engage in adolescent antisocial behavior than children of non-delinquent parents. From an interactional theory perspective this impact is largely indirect, mediated by disruption and stressors in the parent's life course that ultimately interfere with a safe, stable, and nurturing family environment (Mercy and Saul 2009) as well as effective parenting behaviors, thereby increasing the likelihood of the child's involvement in delinquency. At the same time, these cascading consequences of the parent's adolescent antisocial behavior do not necessarily lead to involvement in delinquency and related problem behaviors by their children. There are also substantial levels of intergenerational resilience in which children do not follow in their parents footsteps. Interactional theory also addresses the protective factors associated with this form of discontinuity.

Finally, we note that there is a body of empirical support for the basic tenets of interactional theory and its explanation of offending across the life course and across generations. Longitudinal studies demonstrate that delinquent behavior is, indeed, a function of weak bonds and association with delinquent peers and beliefs. In turn, involvement in delinquency further weakens the individual's social bonds and strengthens their embeddedness in deviant networks. Longitudinal studies also demonstrate the long-term negative consequences of involvement in serious delinquency and embeddedness in delinquent networks such as street gangs (Thornberry et al. 2003b). Intergenerational studies of continuity are, by and large, consistent with the mediated model of intergenerational continuity presented here. Although there have been fewer studies of discontinuity, they are consistent with interactional theory's hypotheses about the protective factors that help account for discontinuity.

Although these core causal processes identified by interactional theory are consistent with empirical findings, there is still much work left to be done to develop the theory more fully and to test its hypotheses. For example, there is little research examining our proposed processes concerning late bloomers or in investigating intergenerational discontinuity with respect to antisocial behavior. These and related topics will be the focus of our continued work using data from the Rochester Youth Development Study and the Rochester Intergenerational Study.

ACKNOWLEDGMENT

Support for the Rochester Youth Development Study has been provided by the National Institute on Drug Abuse [R01DA020195] and the Office of Juvenile Justice and Delinquency Prevention [86-JN-CX-0007]. Work on this project was also aided by grants to the Center for Social and Demographic Analysis at the University at Albany from NICHD [P30HD32041] and NSF [SBR-9512290]. Points of view or opinions in this document are those of the authors and do not necessarily represent the official position or policies of the funding agencies.

References

Akers, Ronald L. 1998. *Social Learning and Social Structure: A General Theory of Crime and Deviance*. Boston: Northeastern University Press.

Akers, Ronald L., Marvin D. Krohn, Lonn Lanza-Kaduce, and Marcia Radosevich. 1979. "Social Learning and Deviant Behavior: A Specific Test of a General Theory." *American Sociological Review* 4: 636–655.

Ambert, Ann-Marie. 1997. *Parents, Children, and Adolescents: Interactive Relationships and Development in Context*. New York: The Haworth Press.

Bailey, Jennifer A., Karl G. Hill, Sabrina Oesterle, and J. David Hawkins. 2009. "Parenting Practices and Problem Behavior Across Three Generations: Monitoring, Harsh Discipline, and Drug Use in the Intergenerational Transmission of Externalizing Behavior." *Developmental Psychology* 45: 1214–1226.

Bernburg, Jón Gunnar, and Marvin D. Krohn. 2003. "Labeling, Life Chances, and Adult Crime: The Direct and Indirect Effects of Official Intervention in Adolescence on Crime in Early Adulthood." *Criminology* 41: 1287–1318.

Bernburg, Jón Gunnar, Marvin D. Krohn, and Craig J. Rivera. 2006. "Official Labeling, Criminal Embeddedness, and Subsequent Delinquency: A Longitudinal Test of Labeling Theory." *Journal of Research in Crime and Delinquency* 43: 67–88.

Besemer, Sytske. 2012. *Intergenerational Transmission of Criminal and Violent Behaviour*. Leiden, The Netherlands: Sidestone Press.

Burke, Jeffrey D., Dustin Pardini and Rolf Loeber. 2008. "Reciprocal Relationships Between Parenting Behavior and Disruptive Psychopathology from Childhood through Adolescence." *Journal of Abnormal Child Psychology* 36:679–692.

Bushway, Shawn D., Alex R. Piquero, Lisa M. Broidy, Elizabeth Cauffman, and Paul Mazerolle. 2001. "An Empirical Framework for Studying Desistance as a Process." *Criminology* 39: 49–515.

Bushway, Shawn D., Terence P. Thornberry, and Marvin D. Krohn. 2003. "Desistance as a Developmental Process: A Comparison of Static and Dynamic Approaches." *Journal of Quantitative Criminology* 19: 129–153.

Capaldi, Deborah M., Katherine C. Pears, and David C. R. Kerr. 2012. "The Oregon Youth Study Three-Generational Study: Theory, Design, and Findings." *The International Society for the Study of Behavioural Development Bulletin* 62: 29–33.

Cicchetti, Dante, and Fred A. Rogosch. 1996. "Equifinality and Multifinality in Developmental Psychopathology." *Development and Psychopathology* 8: 597–600.

Cohen, Albert K. 1955. *Delinquent Boys*. Glencoe, NY: Free Press.

Cohn, Ellen S., D. Bucolo, Cesar J. Rebellion, and Karen Van Gundy. 2010. "An Integrated Model of Legal and Moral Reasoning and Rule-Violating Behavior: The Role of Legal Attitudes." *Law and Human Behavior* 34: 295–309.

Collins, W. Andrew, and Laurence Steinberg. 2006. "Adolescent Development in Interpersonal Context." In *Handbook of Child Psychology: Vol. 3, Social, Emotional, and Personality Development*, edited by Nancy Eisenberg, William. Damon, and Richard. M. Lerner, 1003–1067. Hoboken, NJ: John Wiley.

Conger, Rand D., Katherine J. Conger, and Monica J. Martin. 2010. "Socioeconomic Status, Family Processes, and Individual Development." *Journal of Marriage and Family* 72: 685–704.

Conger, Rand D., Tricia Neppl, Kee Jeong Kim, and Laura V. Scaramella. 2003. "Angry and Aggressive Behavior Across Three Generations: A Prospective, Longitudinal Study of Parents and Children." *Journal of Abnormal Child Psychology* 31(2): 143–160.

Conger, Rand D., Thomas J. Schofield, and Tricia K. Neppl. 2012. "Intergenerational Continuity and Discontinuity in Harsh Parenting." *Parenting: Science and Practice* 12: 222–231.

Decker, Scott H., Chris Melde and David C. Pyrooz. 2013. "What We Know About Gangs and Gang Members and Where Do We Go From Here." *Justice Quarterly* 30: 369–403.

Dong, Beidi, and Marvin D. Krohn. 2015. "Exploring Intergenerational Discontinuity in Problem Behavior: Bad Parents with Good Children." *Youth Violence and Juvenile Justice*. 13: 99–122.

Edwards, Ellen P., Rina Das Eiden, and Kenneth E. Leonard. 2006. "Behavior Problems in 18- to 36-Month-Old Children of Alcoholic Fathers: Secure Mother-infant Attachment as a Protective Factor." *Development and Psychopathology* 18: 395–407.

Eggleston, Elaine P., and John H. Laub. 2002. "The Onset of Adult Offending: A Neglected Dimension of the Criminal Career." *Journal of Criminal Justice* 30(6): 603–622.

Farrington, David P. 1983. "Offending from 10 to 25 Years of Age." In *Prospective Studies of Crime and Delinquency*, edited by Katherine T. van Dusen and Sarnoff. A. Mednick, 17–37. Boston: Kluwer-Nihoff.

Farrington, David P. 2011. "Families and Crime." In *Crime and Public Policy*, edited by James Q. Wilson and Joan Petersilia, 130–157. Oxford: Oxford University Press.

Fite, Paula J., Craig R. Colder, John E. Lochman, and Karen C. Wells, 2006. "The Mutual Influence of Parenting and Boys' Externalizing Behavior Problems." *Applied Developmental Psychology* 27: 151–164.

Glueck, Sheldon, and Eleanor Glueck. 1968. *Delinquents and Non-delinquents in Perspective*. Cambridge, MA: Harvard University Press.

Hagan, John. 1992. "The Poverty of a Classless Criminology—The American Society of Criminology 1991 Presidential Address." *Criminology* 30: 1–19.

Hawes, David J., Mark R. Dadds, Aaron D. J. Frost, and Penelope A. Hasking. 2011. "Do Childhood Callous-Unemotional Traits Drive Change in Parenting Practices?" *Journal of Clinical Child and Adolescent Psychology* 40: 507–518.

Hipwell, Alison E., Kate Keenan, Kristen E. Kasza, Rolf Loeber, Magda Stouthamer-Loeber, and Tammy Bean. 2008. "Reciprocal Influences Between Girls' Conduct Problems and Depression, and Parental Punishment and Warmth: A Six Year Prospective Analysis." *Journal of Abnormal Child Psychology* 36: 663–677.

Hoffmann, John P., Lance D. Erickson, and Karen R. Spence. 2013. "Modeling the Association Between Academic Achievement and Delinquency: An Application of Interactional Theory." *Criminology* 51: 629–660.

Huh, David, Jennifer Tristan, Emily Wade, and Eric Stice. 2006. "Does Problem Behavior Elicit Poor Parenting? A Prospective Study of Adolescent Girls." *Journal of Adolescent Research* 21: 185–204.

Huizinga, David, Anne Weiher, Rachele Espiritu, and Finn Esbensen. 2003. "Delinquency and Crime: Some Highlights from the Denver Youth Survey." In *Taking Stock of Delinquency*, edited by Terence P. Thornberry and Marvin D. Krohn, 47–92. New York: Kluwer-Academic/Plenum.

Jaffee, Sara R., Terrie E. Moffitt, Avshalom Caspi, and Alan Taylor. 2003. "Life with (or Without) Father: The Benefits of Living with Two Biological Parents Depend on the Father's Antisocial Behavior." *Child Development* 74(1):109–126.

Jang, Sung Joon, and Carolyn A. Smith. 1997. "A Test of Reciprocal Causal Relationships Among Parental Supervision, Affective Ties, and Delinquency." *Journal of Research in Crime and Delinquency* 34: 307–336.

Jessor, Richard, and Mark S. Turbin. 2014. "Parsing Protection and Risk for Problem Behavior Versus Pro-social Behavior Among US and Chinese Adolescents." *Journal of Youth and Adolescence* 43: 1037–1051.

Kerr, David C. R., Deborah M. Capaldi, Lee D. Owen, Margit Wiesner, and Katherine C. Pears. 2011. "Changes in At-Risk American Men's Crime and Substance Use Trajectories Following Fatherhood." *Journal of Marriage and Family* 73: 1101–1116.

Krohn, Marvin D., Chris L. Gibson, and Terence P. Thornberry. 2013. "Under the Protective Bud the Bloom Awaits: A Review of Theory and Research on Adult-Onset and Late-Blooming Offenders." In *Handbook of Life-Course Criminology*, edited by Chris L. Gibson and Marvin D. Krohn, 183–200. New York: Springer.

Krohn, Marvin D., Alan J. Lizotte, Shawn D. Bushway, Nicole M. Schmidt, and Matthew D. Phillips. 2014. "Shelter During the Storm: A Search for Factors that Protect At-Risk Adolescents from Violence." *Crime and Delinquency* 60: 379–401.

Krohn, Marvin D., Alan J. Lizotte, and Cynthia M. Perez. 1997. "The Interrelationship Between Substance Use and Precocious Transitions to Adult Statuses." *Journal of Health and Social Behavior* 38: 87–103.

Krohn, Marvin D., Alan J. Lizotte, Terence P. Thornberry, Carolyn Smith, and David McDowall. 1996. "Reciprocal Causal Relationships Among Drug Use, Peers, and Beliefs: A Five-wave Panel Model." *Journal of Drug Issues* 26: 405–428.

Krohn, Marvin D., Thomas A. Loughran, Terence P. Thornberry, Daniel Wonho Jang, Adrienne Freeman-Gallant, and Erin D. Castro. 2016. "Explaining Adolescent Drug Use in Adjacent Generations: Testing the Generality of Theoretical Explanations." *Journal of Drug Issues.* 46: 373–395.

Krohn, Marvin D., Terence P. Thornberry, Craig Rivera, and Marc LeBlanc. 2001. "Later Delinquency Careers." In *Child Delinquents: Development, Intervention, and Service Needs*, edited by Rolf Loeber and David P. Farrington, 67–94. Thousand Oaks, CA: Sage.

Krohn, Marvin D., Jeffrey T. Ward, Terence P. Thornberry, Alan J. Lizotte, and Rebekah Chu. 2011. "The Cascading Effects of Adolescent Gang Involvement Across the Life Course." *Criminology* 49: 991–1028.

Larsson, Henrik, Essi Viding, and Fruhling V. Rijsdijk. 2008. "Relationships Between Parental Negativity and Childhood Antisocial Behavior over Time: A Bidirectional Effects Model in a Longitudinal Genetically Informative Design." *Journal of Abnormal Child Psychology* 36: 633–645.

Laub, John H., and Robert J. Sampson. 1993. "Turning Points in the Life Course: Why Change Matters to the Study of Crime." *Criminology* 31: 301–325.

Laub, John H., and Robert J. Sampson. 2003. *Shared Beginnings, Divergent Lives: Delinquent Boys to Age 70.* Cambridge, MA: Harvard University Press.

Lizotte, Alan J., Mathew Phillips, Marvin D. Krohn, Terence P. Thornberry, Shawn D. Bushway, and Nicole M. Schmidt. 2015. "Like Parent Like Child? The Role of Delayed Childbearing in Breaking the Link Between Parent's Offending and Their Children's Antisocial Behavior." *Justice Quarterly* 32: 410–444.

Lopes, Giza, Marvin D. Krohn, Alan J. Lizotte, Nicole M. Schmidt, Bob Edward Vasquez, and Jon Gunnar Bernburg. 2012. "Labeling and Cumulative Disadvantage: The Impact of Formal

Police Intervention on Life Chances and Crime During Emerging Adulthood." *Crime and Delinquency* 58: 456–488.

Loughran, Thomas A., Pilar Larroulet, and Terence P. Thornberry. 2017. "Definitional Elasticity in the Measurement of Intergenerational Continuity in Substance Use." Child Development. Published online first June 22, 2017. https://doi.org/10.1111/cdev.12849

Lovegrove, Peter J. 2010. *Explaining Discontinuous Cross-Generational Patterns of Delinquency*. Department of Sociology, University of Colorado, Boulder. Dissertation.

Luthar, Suniya S., Dante Cicchetti, and Bronwyn Becker. 2000. "The Construct of Resilience: A Critical Evaluation and Guidelines for Future Work." *Child Development* 71(3): 543–562.

Martin, Monica J., Rand D. Conger, Thomas J. Schofield, Shannon J. Dogan, Keith F. Widaman, M. Brent Donnellan, and Tricia K. Neppl. 2010. "Evaluation of the Interactionist Model of Socioeconomic Status and Problem Behavior: A Developmental Cascade Across Generations." *Development and Psychopathology* 22: 697–715.

Masten, Ann S. 2014. *Ordinary Magic: Resilience in Development*. New York: Guilford.

Mata, Andrea D., and Manfred H. van Dulmen. 2012. "Adult-onset Antisocial Behavior Trajectories: Associations with Adolescent Family Processes and Emerging Adulthood Functioning." *Journal of Interpersonal Violence* 27: 177–193.

Melde, Chris., and Finn A. Esbensen. 2011. "Gang Membership as a Turning Point in the Life Course." *Criminology* 49: 513–552.

Mercy, James A., and Janet Saul. 2009. "Creating a Healthier Future through Early Interventions for Children." *Journal of the American Medical Association* 301: 2262–2264.

Moffitt, Teri E. 1993. "Life Course Persistent" and "Adolescence-Limited" Antisocial Behavior: A Developmental Taxonomy." *Psychological Review* 100: 674–701.

Nagin, Daniel S. 2005. *Group-Based Modeling of Development*. Cambridge, MA: Harvard University Press.

Nagin, Daniel S., David P. Farrington, and Terie E. Moffitt. 1995. "Life-Course Trajectories of Different Types of Offenders." *Criminology* 33: 111–139.

Nagin, Daniel S., and Raymond Paternoster. 1991. "On the Relationship of Past and Future Participation in Delinquency." *Criminology* 29: 163–189.

Newcomb, Michael D., and Peter M. Bentler. 1988. *Consequences of Adolescent Drug Use: Impact on the Lives of Young Adults*. Newbury Park, CA: Sage.

Osgood, D. Wayne, and Amy L. Anderson. 2004. "Unstructured Socializing and Rates of Delinquency." *Criminology* 42(3): 519–547.

Pardini, Dustin, Paula J. Fite, and Jeffrey D. Burke. 2008. "Bidirectional Associations Between Parenting Practices and Conduct Problems in Boys from Childhood to Adolescence: The Moderating Effect of Age and African-American Ethnicity." *Journal of Abnormal Child Psychology* 36: 647–662.

Patterson, Gerald R. 1993. "Orderly Change in a Stable World: The Antisocial Trait as a Chimera." *Journal of Consulting and Clinical Psychology* 61: 911–919.

Patterson, Gerald R., Deborah. Capaldi, and Lew Bank. 1991. "An Early Starter Model for Predicting Delinquency." In *The Development and Treatment of Childhood Aggression*, edited by Debra J. Pepler and Kenneth H. Rubin, 139–168. Hillsdale, NJ: Lawrence Erlbaum.

Patterson, Gerald R., John B. Reid, and Thomas J. Dishion. 1992. *Antisocial Boys*. Eugene, OR: Castalia.

Payne, Allison A., and Steven Salotti. 2007. "A Comparative Analysis of Social Learning and Social Control Theories in the Prediction of College Crime." *Deviant Behavior* 28: 553–573.

Piquero, Alex R., David P. Farrington, and Alfred Blumstein. 2003. "The Criminal Career Paradigm." In *Crime and Justice: A Review of Research,* Vol. 30, edited by Michael Tonry, 359–506. Chicago: University of Chicago Press.

Pukkinen, Lea., Anna-Lisa Lyyra, and Katja. Kolko. 2009. "Life Success of Males on Non-offender, Adolescence-Limited, Persistent, and Adult-Onset Antisocial Pathways: Follow-Up from 8 to 42." *Aggressive Behavior* 35: 117–135.

Pyrooz, David C. 2014. "From Colors and Guns to Caps and Gowns? The Effects of Gang Membership on Educational Attainment," *Journal of Research in Crime and Delinquency* 51: 56–87.

Rebellion, Cesar J., Michelle E. Manasse, Karen T. Van Gundy, and Ellen S. Cohn. 2014. "Rationalizing Delinquency: A Longitudinal Test of the Reciprocal Relationship Between Delinquent Attitudes and Behavior." *Social Psychology Quarterly* 77: 361–386.

Rindfuss, Ronald R., C. Gray Swicegood, and Rachel Rosenfeld. 1987. "Disorder in the Life Course: How Common and Does It Matter?" *American Sociological Review* 52: 785–801.

Sampson, Robert J., and John H. Laub. 1993. *Crime in the Making: Pathways and Turning Points Through Life.* Cambridge, MA: Harvard University Press.

Sampson, Robert J., and John H. Laub. 2003. "Life Course Desisters? Trajectories of Crime Among Delinquent Boys Followed to Age 70. *Criminology* 41: 301–339.

Sampson, Robert J., and John H. Laub. 2005. "A General Age-Graded Theory of Crime." In *Integrated Developmental and Life-Course Theories of Offending,* edited by David P. Farrington, 165–181. New Brunswick, NJ: Transaction.

Scaramella, Laura V., Tricia K. Neppl, Lenna L. Ontai, and Rand D. Conger. 2008. "Consequences of Socioeconomic Disadvantage Across Three Generations: Parenting Behavior and Child Externalizing Problems." *Journal of Family Psychology* 22: 725–733.

Schmidt, Nicole M., Giza Lopes, Marvin D. Krohn, and Alan J. Lizotte. 2015. "Getting Caught and Getting Hitched: An Assessment of the Relationship Between Police Intervention, Life Chances, and Romantic Unions." *Justice Quarterly* 32: 976–1005.

Scott, Elizabeth S., and Laurence Steinberg. 2010. *Rethinking Juvenile Justice.* Cambridge, MA: Harvard University Press.

Shaw, Daniel S., and R. Q. Bell. 1993. "Developmental Theories of Parental Contributors to Antisocial Behavior." *Journal of Abnormal Child Psychology* 21: 35–49.

Silverberg, Susan B., and Lawrence Steinberg. 1990. "Psychological Well-Being of Parents with Early Adolescent Children." *Developmental Psychology* 26: 658–666.

Simpson, Sally S., Mariel Alper, Laura Dugan, Julie Horney, Candace Kruttschnitt, and Rosemary Gartner. 2016. "Age-Graded Pathways into Crime: Evidence from a Multi-Site Retrospective Study of Incarcerated Women." *Journal of Developmental and Life-Course Criminology* 2: 296–320.

Smith, Carolyn A., and David P. Farrington. 2004. "Continuities in Antisocial Behavior and Parenting Across Three Generations." *Journal of Child Psychology & Psychiatry & Allied Disciplines* 45(2): 230–248.

Smith, Carolyn A., and Terence P. Thornberry. 1995. "The Relationship Between Childhood Maltreatment and Adolescent Involvement in Delinquency." *Criminology* 33: 451–481.

Spear, Linda P. 2010. *The Behavioral Neuroscience of Adolescence.* New York: W. W. Norton.

Steinberg, Laurence, and Kathryn C. Monahan. 2007. "Age Differences in Resistance to Peer Influence." *Developmental Psychology* 43: 1531–1543.

Thornberry, Terence P. 1987. "Toward an Interactional Theory of Delinquency." *Criminology* 25: 863–891.

Thornberry, Terence P. 1989. "Reflections on the Advantages and Disadvantages of Theoretical Integration." In *Theoretical Integration in the Study of Deviance and Crime*, edited by Steven F. Messner, Marvin D. Krohn, and Allen E. Liska, 51–60. Albany: State University of New York Press.

Thornberry, Terence P. 1996. "Empirical Support for Interactional Theory: A Review of the Literature." In *Delinquency and Crime: Current Theories*, edited by J. David Hawkins, 198–235. New York: Cambridge University Press.

Thornberry, Terence P. 2005. "Explaining Multiple Patterns of Offending Across the Life Course and Across Generations." *The Annals of the American Academy of Political and Social Science* 602: 156–195.

Thornberry, Terence P. 2009. "The Apple Doesn't Fall Far from the Tree (Or Does It?): Intergenerational Patterns of Antisocial Behavior." *Criminology* 47: 297–325.

Thornberry, Terence P., and Kimberly L. Henry. 2009. "The Interplay of School Disengagement and Drug Use: An Interactional Perspective." *Monatsschrift für Kriminologie und Strafrechtsreform (Criminology and Criminal Law Reform)* 92: 240–252.

Thornberry, Terence P., and Marvin D. Krohn. 2001. "The Development of Delinquency: An Interactional Perspective." In *Handbook of Youth and Justice*, edited by Susan O. White, 289–305. New York: Plenum.

Thornberry, Terence P., and Marvin D. Krohn. 2005. "Applying Interactional Theory to the Explanation of Continuity and Change in Antisocial Behavior." In *Integrated Developmental and Life-Course Theories of Offending.*, edited by David P. Farrington, 183–209. New Brunswick, NJ: Transaction.

Thornberry, Terence P., and Mauri Matsuda. 2011. "Why Do Late Bloomers Wait? An Examination of Factors That Delay the Onset of Offending." Paper presented at the Stockholm Criminology Symposium, Stockholm, Sweden, June 13–15.

Thornberry, Terence P., Adrienne Freeman-Gallant, Alan J. Lizotte, Marvin D. Krohn, and Carolyn A. Smith. 2003a. "Linked Lives: The Intergenerational Transmission of Antisocial Behavior." *Journal of Abnormal Child Psychology* 31: 171–184.

Thornberry, Terence P., Marvin D. Krohn, Alan J. Lizotte, Carolyn A. Smith, and Kimberly Tobin. 2003b. *Gangs and Delinquency in Developmental Perspective*. New York: Cambridge University Press.

Thornberry, Terence P., M. D. Krohn, Carolyn A. Smith, Alan J. Lizotte, and Pamela K. Porter. 2003c. "Causes and Consequences of Delinquency: Findings from the Rochester Youth Development Study." In *Taking Stock of Delinquency: An Overview of Findings from Contemporary Longitudinal Studies*, edited by T. P. Thornberry and M. D. Krohn, 11–46. New York: Kluwer Academic/Plenum.

Thornberry, Terence P., Adrienne Freeman-Gallant, and Peter J. Lovegrove. 2009. "The Impact of Parental Stressors on the Intergenerational Transmission of Antisocial Behavior." *Journal of Youth and Adolescence* 38: 312–322.

Thornberry, Terence P., M. Krohn, and Adrienne Freeman-Gallant. 2006. "Intergenerational Roots of Early Onset Substance Use." *Journal of Drug Issues* 36: 1–28.

Thornberry, Terence P., Alan J. Lizotte, Marvin D. Krohn, Margaret Farnworth, and Sung Joon Jang. 1991. "Testing Interactional Theory: An Examination of Reciprocal Causal Relationships Among Family, School, and Delinquency." *Journal of Criminal Law and Criminology* 82: 3–35.

Thornberry, Terence P., Alan J. Lizotte, Marvin D. Krohn, Margaret Farnworth, and Sung Joon Jang. 1994. "Delinquent Peers, Beliefs, and Delinquent Behavior: A Longitudinal Test of Interactional Theory." *Criminology* 32: 47–83.

Tremblay, Richard E., Louise C. Masse, Linda Pagani, and Frank Vitaro. 1996. "From Childhood Physical Aggression to Adolescent Maladjustment: The Montreal Prevention Experiment." In *Preventing Childhood Disorders, Substance Abuse & Delinquency*, edited by R. De V. Peters and R. J. McMahon, 268–298. Thousand Oaks, CA: Sage.

Tremblay, Richard E., and Daniel S. Nagin. 2005. "The Developmental Origins of Physical Aggression in Humans." In *Developmental Origins of Aggression*, edited by Richard E. Tremblay, Willard W. Hartup, and John Archer, 83–106. New York: The Guilford Press.

Van der Geest, Victor, Arjan Blokland, and Catrien Bijleveld. 2009. "Delinquent Development in a Sample of High Risk Youth: Shape, Content and Predictors of Delinquent Trajectories from Age 12 to 32." *Journal of Research in Crime and Delinquency* 46: 111–142.

Warr, Mark. 1998. "Life-Course Transitions and Desistance from Crime." *Criminology* 36: 183–216.

Werner, Emmy. E. 1986. "Resilient Offspring of Alcoholics: A Longitudinal Study from Birth to Age 18." *Journal of Studies on Alcohol* 47: 34–40.

Wikstrom, Per-Olof H., and Robert Svensson. 2012. "When Does Self-Control Matter: The Interaction Between Morality and Self-Control in Crime Causation." *Journal of Criminology* 7: 395–410.

Wolfgang, Marvin E., Terence P. Thornberry, and Robert M. Figlio. 1987. *From Boy to Man, from Delinquency to Crime*. Chicago: University of Chicago Press.

Zara, Georgia, and David P. Farrington. 2009. "Childhood and Adolescent Predictors of Late Onset Criminal Careers." *Journal of Youth and Adolescence* 38: 287–300.

CHAPTER 15

THE DYNAMICS OF CHANGE

Criminogenic Interactions and Life-Course Patterns in Crime

PER-OLOF H. WIKSTRÖM AND KYLE TREIBER

TRADITIONAL explanations of stability and changes in crime involvement tend to limit our recognition of the more fluid nature of this phenomenon and the fact that people's movement in and out of crime involvement can be understood through a single theoretical framework. Onset, persistence, and desistance, for example, are often studied as separate and distinct processes with different etiologies and therefore implications for policy and practice, but we argue they can be much more effectively analyzed as the result of changes in key causal factors and, crucially, their interaction. We posit that a robust general explanatory model of change in crime involvement—focusing on key personal and environmental explanatory factors and the process that links them to action—will provide a better foundation for studying and ultimately understanding why people's crime involvement changes, for better or for worse. We suggest that situational action theory (SAT) may be particularly useful due to its integration of individual and environmental levels of explanation, its focus on action and action mechanisms, and the fact that it has developed situational and developmental models to explain short- and long-term patterns of crime involvement.

SAT argues that people are the source of their actions—people perceive, choose, and execute actions—but that the causes of those actions are situational—people's perception, choice, and execution of action alternatives is initiated and guided by relevant input from their interaction with the immediate environment (the person–environment interaction). Moreover, SAT insists that without a proper understanding of which situational factors and processes are causally relevant (as causes) it is difficult to identify with any certainty which developmental and life-course factors and processes are causally relevant (as causes of the causes) in the explanation of development, stability, and change in people's crime involvement.

SAT insists that acts of crime are always an outcome of the interaction between people's crime propensities and settings' criminogenic features (a setting being the part of the environment a person can access with his or her senses at a given point in time). People's crime propensities are triggered by specific environmental inducements, and environmental inducements are made relevant by people's particular propensities (although the relative importance of propensities and inducements may vary by circumstance).

SAT suggests that a person's crime propensity (the tendency to see and choose crime as an action alternative in response to particular opportunities and frictions) essentially depends on his or her law-relevant personal morals (rules of conduct and supporting moral emotions such as shame and guilt) and ability to exercise self-control (to withstand external inducements to act against his or her personal morals)[1] and that the criminogenic features of a setting (environmental features which may induce people to see and choose crime as an action alternative in response to particular opportunities and frictions) depend on its law-relevant moral norms (shared rules of conduct) and their strength and level of enforcement.

Against this backdrop, the basic argument of SAT is that stability and change in people's crime involvement is an outcome of stability and changes in their crime propensities and criminogenic exposure (encounters with criminogenic settings). The theory specifically maintains that (1) development, stability, and change in crime propensity depends on psychosocial processes of moral education and cognitive nurturing and (2) stability and change in exposure to criminogenic settings depends on socioecological processes of social and self-selection. These core arguments are captured in SAT's development ecological action (DEA) model of individual stability and change in crime involvement. This chapter develops and refines the key suppositions of this model, which was originally described in Wikström (2005). Section I discusses some limitations of key developmental theories of crime, arguing that there is a neglect of, and therefore a need for, a stronger focus on the crime event and the criminogenic person–environment interactions that cause acts of, and drives pathways in, crime. Section II introduces the basic propositions of situational action theory, arguing that to understand what drives stability and change in people's crime involvement, we need to first explicate the situational factors and processes involved in crime causation. Section III introduces the DEA model, arguing that changes in people's crime involvement, its nature and frequency, are mainly an outcome of changes in people's crime propensities and exposure to criminogenic settings (because these change the nature and frequency of the criminogenic interactions people experience). Section IV explores the DEA model in more depth, explicating the role of psychosocial and socioecological processes in stability and change in people's crime propensities and criminogenic exposure. Finally, Section V sums up the key arguments and their implications for the study of criminal careers.

I. Key Developmental Theories and Their Main Limitations

Developmental theories of crime involvement have historically neglected the influence of the wider social context. This is because most theories have focused on crime propensities, which is perhaps not surprising as most developmental criminologists are psychologists by training. In doing so, they have tended to overlook the role of the wider social environment in how people acquire different propensities (via processes of socialization and habituation) and express those propensities (in response to external inducements and constraints). Many of these theories are essentially theories of criminality (propensity) rather than theories of criminal behavior, the difference being that a theory of criminality addresses the characteristics of the actor while a theory of criminal behavior needs to also address the context in which the behavior takes place and the role of agency. The few theories that have taken the role of social environments into account have tended to focus their attention on the family context and underexplored the role of other contexts in development and action (Brooks-Gunn et al. 1993).

Developmental theories of crime have also generally failed to specify the processes by which individual or any considered environmental factors exert their effects on crime involvement. The dominant risk-factor paradigm has not encouraged interest in processes and mechanisms, and the lack of integration between individual and environmental levels of explanation has meant that simultaneous (interactive) effects remain particularly neglected (Farrington, Sampson, and Wikström 1993).

Gottfredson and Hirschi's (1990) self-control theory, Moffitt's (1993) dual developmental taxonomy, and Sampson and Laub's (2003) age-graded theory of informal social control represent three of the most prominent developmental theories of crime from the past 25 years and often provide the theoretical groundwork for research on change and stability in crime involvement. While each of these theories has made unique and important contributions to the field of criminology, they all suffer from a number of shared limitations (Wikström and Treiber 2009):

1. They ultimately suggest (implicitly or explicitly) that offending is driven by individual-level factors (be it self-control, antisocial personality traits, or weak internalized social bonds).
2. They posit a similar causal mechanism—the consideration of consequences—which relies on questionable assumptions about motivation and decision processes.
3. They say little about the interaction between people and environments at the point of action.
4. They fail to adequately address the role of agency.

Self-control theory ultimately disregards the role of the social environment in the expression of propensity (in this case low self-control; Gottfredson and Hirschi, 2003) but gives almost complete credit to external input for its development (Gottfredson and Hirschi 1990, pp. 96–98); in doing so this theory fails to address the interactive nature of both developmental and situational processes. Once low self-control is established, its expression in acts of crime is relatively stable, although Gottfredson and Hirschi have qualified this with an age effect to keep the implications of the theory in line with the age–crime curve (Gottfredson and Hirschi 1990; see also Hirschi and Gottfredson 1983). As a control theory, self-control theory ignores differential motivation and engages with agency only so far as to use the language of probability and discuss tendencies and likelihoods.

Unlike self-control theory, Moffitt's dual developmental taxonomy emphasizes the interaction between individual and environmental factors in the development of crime propensities (here antisocial personality traits; Moffitt 1993, 1997, 2003). In this theory, certain social environments reinforce emerging crime propensities. In early childhood, neurocognitive and related behavioral deficits are reinforced by negative or inadequate social responses. During subsequent developmental stages, emerging antisocial personality traits are reinforced in evocative, proactive, and reactive person–environment interactions which facilitate expression of crime propensities. The theory is less clear about the interactive nature of situational processes and, like self-control theory, ultimately disregards the role of the social environment in the expression of crime propensity; once antisocial personality traits are established, they determine the outcome of person–environment interactions. As in self-control theory, the role of agency remains unexplored.

On the surface, Sampson and Laub's age-graded theory of informal social control appears quite different from the two previous theories (Laub and Sampson 2003; Sampson and Laub 1993, 2003, 2005). It takes a more life-course rather than typological perspective. However, the main determining factor in crime causation, while more variable over time, is internalized constraints, or social bonds. As in both previous theories, contextual factors (in this case weak social controls) lead to the developmental of an antisocial personality; however, unlike those theories, the expression of this crime propensity depends on more malleable social bonds and routine activities, which determine a person's exposure to informal social controls. While this framework appears to be heading in the right direction in incorporating the role of social environments, this role is not fully developed. Sampson and Laub focus on differences in lifestyle (e.g., marriage) and their impact on social bonds and routines, but they fail to engage with key features of social environments, such as collective efficacy, and how lifestyle factors such as marriage may only serve as general proxies for exposure to these features. As a control theory, the age-graded theory does not explore differential motivation in terms of inducements to offend, but it does pay attention to the concept of agency and its influence on established patterns of behavior (Laub and Sampson 2003); however, it does not fully address how agency exerts its influence at the point of action.

There remains a need for developmental theories of crime to explicitly address the role of social environments in crime causation, and the processes through which social environmental factors, in interaction with personal characteristics, may lead people to commit acts of crime. This includes better specification of their role in differential motivation, perception, and choice, taking agency into account. The DEA model of SAT aims to advance this enterprise.

II. SITUATIONAL ACTION THEORY—THE BASICS

Situational action theory (SAT) is a dynamic, general, and mechanism-based theory of crime causation (e.g., Wikström 2006, 2010b, 2014, 2017) that analyzes crime as acts of rule-breaking (focusing on but not being limited to the rules of law) and underscores the fact that to explain why acts of crime occur requires specification of the person–environment interaction and the action mechanism that links people and their immediate environments to action.

Most mainstream criminological theories, such as control theories (Gottfredson and Hirschi 1990; Hirschi 1969) and opportunity theories (Cohen and Felson 1979; Cornish and Clarke 2008) rely (explicitly or implicitly) on the assumption that people's acts of crime revolve mainly around serving their own self-interests (Agnew 2014). Situational action theory, on the other hand, suggests that humans are essentially rule-guided creatures and that society (social order) is based on shared rules of conduct (Wikström 2010a, 2017). People express their desires and respond to frictions within the context of rule-guided choice. Therefore, rules of conduct (moral rules) and how people respond to them play a central role in guiding people's action in decision-making (whether they agree with those rules or not).

SAT defines moral rules as "value-based rules of conduct specifying what is the right or wrong thing to do, or not do, in response to particular motivations in particular circumstances"[2] (Wikström 2014). Importantly, crimes are moral actions, i.e., actions guided by moral rules. Specifically, crimes are moral actions that break a specific set of moral rules—those of the law. In fact, all acts of crime, in all places, at all times, share the common characteristic of breaking legal rules of conduct specifying what it is right or wrong to do. Although SAT was initially developed to explain acts that break legal rules of conduct, it is also applicable to other types of moral rule-breaking, including why people break informal rules of conduct.

Criminology typically lacks an integrative approach to the study of crime and its causes (Wikström and Sampson 2006). Most leading explanations of crime, and hence changes in crime involvement, focus on either personal or environmental factors, and even the few that acknowledge that both are important largely fail to address how such factors interact in the explanation of crime,[3] whereas SAT argues that crimes are always an outcome of a person–environment (propensity–exposure) interaction and cannot be fully understood by focusing on either in isolation. To explain why crime happens we need to know what makes people crime prone and environments criminogenic and, crucially, how person–environment interactions generate acts of crime (it is, for instance, not enough to make general claims that crimes occur as an outcome of the convergence of "likely offenders" and "suitable targets in the absence of capable guardians"; e.g., Cohen and Felson 1979; Felson and Boba 2010). We can then begin to piece apart what leads to changes in personal propensities, the criminogeneity of settings, and people's exposure to criminogenic settings, and how this leads to changes in crime involvement.

We would argue that, as a result of their preoccupation with either personal or environmental factors, and their reliance on assumptions about action decision-making, which are increasingly undermined by behavioral research (both social and biological, e.g., the debatable ubiquity of self-interest; see Treiber 2017a), criminologists have not been very successful in identifying factors that convincingly predict, let alone explain, people's crime involvement.

At the core of SAT's explanation of acts of crime is the PEA model (P × E → A), suggesting that people's acts of crime (A) are an outcome of a perception–choice process (→) initiated and guided by the interaction of a person's crime propensities (P) and criminogenic exposure (E).

SAT suggests that people and settings are linked to acts of crime via a perception–choice process. This process begins with motivation (goal-directed attention): settings present opportunities and frictions to which people are more or less susceptible (e.g., a hungry person might find a hamburger tempting, but a person who is not hungry, or a vegetarian, might not) and which may act as sources of temptation or provocation. Once a person is motivated, key personal and environmental factors then interact, creating a filter that determines what action alternatives he or she perceives as potential responses (the perception process) and which alternative he or she ultimately chooses to pursue (the choice process). Rule-breaking, including law-breaking, may be one of those alternatives; understanding more about how people's actions are rule-guided can help us better understand when they may consider breaking rules and how they may be encouraged to follow them (given that more traditional approaches, such as deterrence, which are based on assumptions of rational self-interest, have proven insufficient; see, e.g., Hirtenlehner and Wikström 2017; Wikström, Tseloni, and Karlis 2011). The perception–choice process (action mechanism) is described in detail elsewhere (e.g., Wikström 2006, 2010b, 2014, 2017), but it is an important starting point for identifying which personal and environmental factors may be most relevant to crime involvement and its changes over time.

Building upon this perception–choice framework and the assertions that people are fundamentally rule-guided and crime is an act of rule-breaking, SAT forwards that people's crime propensities depend largely on (1) their law-relevant personal morals (internalized rules of conduct and supporting moral emotions, such as shame and guilt) and (2) their ability to exercise self-control (to withstand external inducements to act against their personal morals). The greater the correspondence between a person's personal morals and the rules of conduct stated in law, the less prone he or she will be to considering breaking those rules; the stronger a person's ability to exercise self-control, the less prone he or she will be to breaking a personal moral rule when he or she is externally pressured to do so. Hence, people with strong law-relevant personal morals and a strong ability to exercise self-control (low crime propensity) will be largely resistant to immediate criminogenic environmental influences, whereas those who have weak law-relevant personal morals and a poor ability to exercise self-control (high crime propensity) may be vulnerable.[4]

SAT argues that people acquire their crime propensities in the main through psychosocial processes of moral education and cognitive nurturing ("causes of the causes"[5]), and therefore these processes are the key to understanding why people develop different (and change) crime propensities.

Criminogenic features of a setting (those that promote the perception and choice of crime as an action alternative) depend largely on its perceived[6] law-relevant moral context (the moral norms that apply and their enforcement relevant to the motivations—temptations and provocations—people may experience). Settings are criminogenic to the extent that their perceived moral norms and enforcement encourage (or do not discourage) acts of crime in response to the opportunities they present and/or the frictions they create.

SAT suggests that settings acquire their criminogenic features through historic socioecological processes, which determine the presence of particular populations and activities in particular places at particular times. These processes are consequently key to understanding why settings vary in their moral contexts (spatially and temporally), and thus in their criminogeneity.

Beyond the questions of how people acquire propensities and settings acquire criminogenic features is the question of how certain people come to take part in (be exposed to) certain kinds of settings—in other words, how certain situations, or person–environment interactions, come about. SAT posits that this may be explained by contemporaneous processes of social and self-selection that place certain people, or groups of people, in certain kinds of settings (Wikström 2014, p. 84). The constellation of settings to which a particular person is exposed as a consequence of selection forms his or her activity field. Change in a person's activity field may be one source of change in his or her crime involvement.

All in all, people's crime involvement (and its nature) is seen in SAT to result from their criminogenic interactions (through the effects of those interactions on the perception–choice process), depending on their crime propensities, which in turn depend on past relevant psychosocial processes (primarily moral education and cognitive nurturing) and their criminogenic exposure, which in turn depends on contemporaneous relevant socioecological processes (primarily processes of social and self-selection; Figure 15.1).[7]

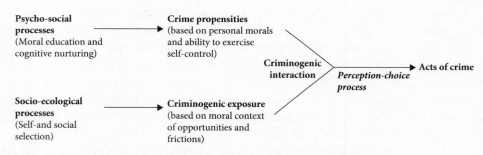

FIGURE 15.1 Key Basic Processes in Crime Causation According to SAT

III. INTRODUCING THE DEA MODEL

Situational action theory's DEA model explicates the dynamics of change in people's crime involvement and criminal careers. Understanding processes of change is crucial for understanding how to prevent or promote relevant changes in crime propensity, criminogeneity, and criminogenic exposure. We have already posited that few criminological theories address the person–environment interaction, so it will not come as a surprise that even fewer do so from a developmental perspective; those that do fall particularly short in explicating the role of social environments (see Wikström and Treiber 2009 for a critical discussion of key theories). We have also argued that few criminological theories posit a compelling situational model of crime involvement. This means they cannot adopt a truly life-course approach, as SAT does, and study sequences of person–environment interactions, each influencing the next, which create specific patterns of stability and change in crime involvement over time. Only once we understand what personal and environmental characteristics are relevant to crime involvement at any given point in time can we begin to assess how they influence relevant characteristics and therefore crime involvement at each subsequent point. SAT attempts to address this dynamic through its DEA model (Wikström 2005; see also Wikström and Treiber 2009; Treiber 2017b).

The drivers of change in the DEA model (Figure 15.2) can be summarized in seven propositions stated below and briefly elaborated in subsequent sections.

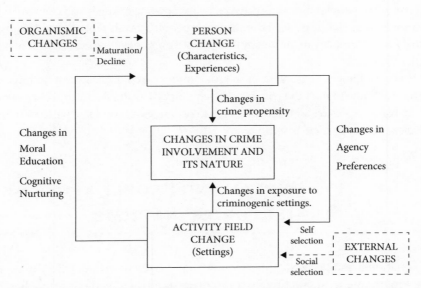

FIGURE 15.2 The Developmental Ecological Action (DEA) Model: Key Basic Processes of Stability and Change in People's Crime Involvement (and Its Nature)

Changes in Crime Involvement and Its Nature

1. Changes in people's crime involvement, its nature and frequency, are mainly driven by changes in people's crime propensities and their exposure to criminogenic settings (because these change the nature and frequency of the criminogenic interactions people experience).

Personal Changes (Influencing Crime Propensities)

2. Organismic changes occur as a result of general processes of biological maturation and decline or instances of illness and injury, which may lead to changes in basic personal capacities (to understand and apply rules and exercise agency and self-control) or the ability for those capacities to be changed.

3. Changes in people's crime propensities are mainly driven by relevant aspects of their moral education and cognitive nurturing (facilitated or impeded by relevant aspects of organismic change) because people's crime propensities are largely based on their law-relevant personal morals and ability to exercise self-control.

4. Changes in people's moral education and cognitive nurturing are mainly driven by changes in their activity field (exposure to particular configurations of settings) because people develop and change their propensities in response to the settings in which they take part.

Activity Field Changes (Influencing Criminogenic Exposure)

5. Changes in people's exposure to criminogenic settings (its nature and frequency) are mainly driven by changes in their activity fields as a result of changes in processes of self-selection (based on agency and activity preferences) and social selection (based on rules and resources).

6. Changes in people's agency are driven by organismic changes and changes in their human, financial, and social capital, while people's development of and changes in activity preferences are driven by their positive and negative experiences of particular activities.

7. External changes (e.g., as a result of political, economical and technological changes) may impact the nature and frequency of available settings (in a jurisdiction) or the rules regulating and access to resources relevant to a particular person taking part in particular settings.

IV. EXPLAINING PEOPLE'S TRAJECTORIES IN CRIME

SAT's situational model, which argues that the causes of crime arise through the person–environment interaction, is the cornerstone of the theory and has been well tested (see Wikström et al. 2012; Wikstrom, Mann, and Hardie 2018). Because situations (person–environment interactions) are central to the explanation of crime, they are also central to the explanation of stability and change in crime involvement: if crime results from people's intersections with different settings (their action contexts), stability or change in crime involvement must result from stability and change in people's intersections with different settings (their action contexts) (Wikström 2005, p. 212). Action contexts may be affected by changes in a person's characteristics and/ or changes in the settings to which he or she is exposed, i.e., his or her activity field. Sources of personal and activity field change are subsequently detailed.

When crime-relevant personal characteristics (personal morality and the ability to exercise self-control) and features of settings (motivators and moral contexts) change, whether people see and choose crime as an action alternative may change. However, it is important to stress the fact that because crime results from the interaction of people and settings, changes in crime-relevant characteristics will not always lead to changes in people's perception and choice of crime as an option. Low crime propensity confers situational resistance; hence people with a low crime propensity may remain unlikely to see crime as an option even if their activity fields change to encompass more criminogenic settings (although exposure to criminogenic settings may over time lead to changes in their propensity). Similarly, people whose activity fields do not encompass any criminogenic settings may not be any more likely to see and choose crime as an alternative even if their crime propensity increases.

Hence it is important to consider not just changes in propensity or changes in exposure, but changes in situations (how propensity and exposure interact) and initial levels. While more complex than person or environment centered frameworks, this framework may help us better understand what kinds of changes, and hence interventions, are most relevant for particular individuals.

A. Personal Changes

SAT posits that moral education and cognitive nurturing are key psychosocial processes that lead to change in crime propensity (Wikström 2005; see further Wikström et al. 2012, pp. 31–32). These processes play a direct role in the acquisition of personal morality and the ability to exercise self-control, respectively. More indirectly, organismic changes (e.g., resulting from biological maturation) may influence the efficacy of moral education and cognitive nurturing, while changes in activity fields (contexts of development) may lead to changes in exposure to moral education and cognitive nurturing.

Moral education and cognitive nurturing can typically be expected to lead to changes in propensity gradually and when people are regularly exposed to relevant influences over an extended period of time. This means propensity generally demonstrates stability, and therefore changes in propensity may have an enduring impact on behaviors such as crime involvement.

When analyzing psychosocial processes it is important to differentiate between content and machinery. Psychosocial content refers to any information, external or internal, which plays a role in cognition; psychosocial machinery refers to the neurocognitive substrates that process (e.g., interpret, evaluate, encode, store, retrieve, and integrate) that information. Psychosocial content is gleaned from the external environment through the senses and from the internal environment through memory and self-monitoring. Faulty machinery may distort psychosocial content by affecting how it is perceived, interpreted, evaluated, and integrated with prior content. Prior content, of course, may likewise influence the activation of psychosocial machinery, e.g., as a result of acquired expectations and associations.

1. *Personal Changes: Organismic Change.* The role of organismic change in crime causation is mainly foundational. Organismic change refers to changes in a person's biological make-up and functioning; typical sources are (1) the general physiological processes associated with growth and maturation and subsequent decline and (2) illnesses and injuries. When these changes affect personal morality and the ability to exercise self-control, they may do so indirectly by moderating a person's receptivity to moral education and cognitive nurturing or directly by moderating a person's ability to apply moral rules and exercise self-control.

Maturation represents a sequence of biological events associated with aging that generally unfold in a predictable pattern so long as any biological and environmental constraints (e.g., gene expression, nutrition) fall within a prescribed range (Goldman 2012; Gottlieb, Wahlsten, and Lickliter 2006; Johnson and de Haan 2011; Westermann et al. 2007). However, variations in the timing of maturation events may lead to significant, and cumulative, differences in people's personal characteristics and capacities across the life span (Elder and Shanahan 2006).

The typical sequence of maturation involves the incremental development of capacities to perceive and interact with one's environment, increasing one's behavioral autonomy and agency (Blakemore and Choudhury 2006; Johnson, Sudhinaraset, and Blum 2010; Wahlstrom et al. 2010). This sequence is characterized by the development of capacities that support the ability to learn and act under the guidance of rules of conduct and to exercise self-control (Blakemore and Robbins 2012; Crone and Dahl 2012; Luna, Padmanabhan, and O'Hearn 2010; Nelson et al. 2005; Tremblay 2006).

Childhood may be an important time window for moral education as it is characterized by organismic changes that promote the rapid acquisition of knowledge and skill, especially in the social domain (Johnson and de Haan 2011; Shonkoff and Phillips 2000). Circumstances that interfere with typical development may impede early moral education, with long-term implications for social behaviors (Anderson et al. 1999, 2000; Eslinger, Flaherty-Craig, and Benton 2004; Eslinger, Gratten, and Damasio 1992). Childhood is also an important time window for the development of the executive capabilities that underlie the ability to exercise self-control (Bunge et al. 2002; Case 1992; Fuster 1997; Hofmann, Schmeichel, and Baddeley 2012; Tranel, Anderson, and Benton 1994). However, more advanced executive capabilities (e.g., integrative and extrapolative functions) may not be fully developed until adolescence (Casey, Giedd, and Thomas 2000; Chelune and Baer 1986; Luciana et al. 2005; Spear 2000).

During adolescence, young people assert their independence in social and behavioral spheres. It is now understood that this transition from dependence to independence is supported by the "rewiring" of cognitive machinery with particular implications for the coordination of motivation and executive control and, therefore, self-control (Blakemore 2012; Blakemore and Choudhury 2006; Casey, Getz, and Galvan 2008; Crone and Dahl 2012; Heatherton and Wagner 2011; Luna, Padmanabhan, and O'Hearn 2010; Steinberg 2008; Sturman and Moghaddam 2011; Wahlstrom et al. 2010).

Adulthood has received little attention in relation to developmental change, and it is often assumed that people enter a developmental "holding pattern," although some evidence suggests that executive processes continue to increasingly dominate action guidance (Christakou et al. 2013; Eppinger et al. 2013a, 2013b; Samanez-Larkin et al. 2012; Worthy et al. 2011; Worthy and Maddox 2012). Late adulthood is characterized by neurodegeneration, the timing and speed of which varies depending on both biological and environmental constraints (Rossini et al. 2007). This may have implications for the ability to exercise self-control but can be offset by internalized moral content (Anderson et al. 1999).

This is how maturational processes unfold under typical circumstances (i.e., normal constraints), but some people are subject to abnormal circumstances and life events that may push their development off the normal track (e.g., developmental disorders or illnesses and injuries). Early deviations from the typical developmental trajectory can have a knock-on, cumulative effect as subsequent development remains out of sync with age-related life experiences (Elder and Shanahan 2006). By contrast, events and circumstances that impact on development later in life may have more "localized" effects and be cushioned by previously acquired knowledge and capacities (Anderson et al. 2000; Eslinger, Flaherty-Craig, and Benton 2004).

In conclusion, organismic change can have an impact on crime propensity by affecting the underlying machinery that processes moral content and supports the exercise of self-control. Organismic changes also influence agency—the power to make things happen intentionally. Key outcomes of biological maturation are increasing autonomy, which requires the ability to act independently, and increasing abilities to perceive and interact with different action contexts, both of which increase agency (Blakemore and Choudhury 2006). On the other hand, illness and injury can reduce agency and people's ability to act upon their environments.

2. *Personal Changes: Moral Education.* People's personal morals are the key determinant of their crime propensity and largely a result of their moral education. Moral education refers to "the learning and evaluation process by which people come to adopt and change value-based rules of conduct about what is the right or wrong thing to do in particular circumstances." This process has three submechanisms: people learn about the rules of conduct that apply in different circumstances through instruction, observation of others' actions and their consequences (personal and social), and trial and error (experimenting with actions and experiencing others' reactions and the consequences).

The more consistent this education (e.g., how homogeneous the instructions, observations, and trial and error incidents a person experiences are), the more effective it will be. Of course people are not simply passive recipients of moral experiences but rather actively evaluate (and re-evaluate) those experiences in the context of their previously acquired personal morals and cognitive capabilities. And as they grow older they do so increasingly, allowing them to refine and actively change their existing personal morality, with the potential to directly influence their crime propensity and potentially their crime involvement.

Effective moral education can have substantial crime preventive effects as it can facilitate the acquisition of a strong value basis for making moral judgments and strong moral habits supporting law abidance. Social institutions with a key stake in moral education are the family and schools, with parents and teachers representing the most potent moral educators of children and adolescents as well as possessing the capacity to control young people's exposure to criminogenic moral contexts, although their influence lessens with age (Wikström 2011).

3. *Personal Changes: Cognitive Nurturing.* People's ability to exercise self-control reflects their ability to act in accordance with their personal morals when challenged to act otherwise and depends on a person's inherent cognitive potential and its nurturing (the extent to which its realization is successfully facilitated). Cognitive nurturing refers to the experiential processes that positively influence neurocognitive abilities (capacities and their expression) (Wikström 2005). It can be argued that two main criteria determine a person's cognitive abilities at any given time: his or her basic neurological constitution and the extent to which his or her specific capabilities have been exercised.

A person's neurological constitution will depend on whether he or she receives adequate nutrition and (neural) stimulation; if he or she does not, the fundamental requirements of specific capacities (e.g., energy, information) may not be met, leading to short- or long-term deficits (Johnson and de Haan 2011; Westermann et al. 2007). If these requirements are met, the main mechanism for changing a specific cognitive capacity is exercise.

Cognitive capacities are strengthened when they are exercised; the underlying neural pathways become established (e.g., through synaptogenesis—neurons which fire together wire together) and potentiated (demonstrating stronger synaptic responses) (Constantine-Paton and Cline 1998; Malenka and Nicoll 1999; Zito and Svoboda 2002). Thus a key aspect of cognitive nurturing is the provision of opportunities to exercise the cognitive capacities that underlie the ability to exercise self-control—i.e., the executive capabilities (Wikström and Treiber 2007).

Executive capabilities are higher-order cognitive functions implicated in attention, inhibition, and the activation, evaluation, organization, and integration of (internally and externally derived) action-relevant information (Fuster 1997; Goldberg 2009; Hofmann, Schmeichel, and Baddeley 2012; Tranel, Anderson, and Benton 1994; Wikström and Treiber 2007). Although these functions are often presented as an aggregate of discrete capabilities that support abstract, goal-oriented, prospective thinking, they have also been associated with the unitary function of internalizing action guidance by organizing and integrating relevant internal and external information to create an internal representation of the action context, which can then be used to guide deliberate action choices (Fuster 1997; Treiber 2011, 2013; Wikström 2007).

The ability to exercise self-control draws heavily on executive capabilities that inhibit impulsive or prepotent actions (e.g., habits) by suppressing motivational and emotive responses (exerting cognitive control) and facilitate the management of conflict between personal morals and motivations by organizing action-relevant information (e.g., relating to personal morals and the moral context as well as personal desires and commitments and external motivators) to evaluate which action alternative is preferred and morally acceptable. Consequently, it can be strengthened through tasks that exercise relevant functions, such as directed or selective attention, inhibition, working memory, the use of rules and switching between rules, and problem-solving. These capabilities are naturally exercised, for the most part unintentionally, through everyday activities like social problem-solving, exercising patience, concentration, and restraint. They can also be deliberately strengthened through activities such as cognitive skills training (e.g., "brain training"). If undertaken on a regular basis, these exercises can increase existing executive capacities, the level of self-control one can exhibit, and one's resistance to "ego-depletion" (reductions in the ability to exercise self-control after repeated use) (Baumeister et al. 2006; Baumeister, Vohs, and Tice 2007; Hagger et al. 2010; Inzlicht and Gutsell 2007; Klingberg 2010; Morrison and Chein 2011; Muraven 2010a, 2010b; Muraven, Baumeister, and Tice 1999; Muraven and Slessareva 2003; Olesen, Westerberg, and Klingberg 2004; Vohs, Baumeister, and Schmeichel 2012). The extent of change that such activities can induce may depend on a person's initial level of executive functioning and the developmental timing.

The extent to which people encounter opportunities to exercise their executive capabilities may differ depending on the kinds of settings in which they act and develop. As with moral education, the family and schools represent key social institutions which may nurture young people's cognitive capacities as well as their basic neurological constitution. Healthcare services may also play an important role in identifying and counteracting emerging cognitive deficiencies. As with moral education, then, mobilizing families and schools to support cognitive nurturing may potentially present a very useful goal for crime-prevention practices.

4. *Personal Changes: Activity Fields.* People grow up and live in different environments. People acquire their personal morals and experience cognitive nurturing through their active engagement with the settings in which they take part (developmental contexts). People's exposure to particular kinds of moral educational and nurturing influences will depend on their activity fields and the extent to which the settings they take part in encourage (or discourage) law-relevant moral rules and emotions and promote (or restrict) the exercise of executive capabilities. This means that people's activity fields play an important developmental role in their crime propensity and may therefore provide another important direction for intervention.

B. Activity Field Changes

SAT proposes that social and self-selection are key socioecological processes that may lead to changes in criminogenic exposure (e.g., Wikström 2014). These processes play a direct role in shaping people's activity fields and consequently the kinds of settings they take part in. People are likely to have widely divergent activity fields; even those who live in the same house (e.g., partners or siblings) may display significant differences in the configuration of settings they are exposed to, and hence the environmental influences they are subjected to, with implications for differences in their development and actions. Particular types of settings (e.g., family, school, work, and leisure settings), which exhibit different environmental features, may have a different impact on people's subsequent development and actions depending on their previous life histories and current personal characteristics. Different environmental influences may also be stronger during different stages of development, often referred to as time windows (Bloom 1964).

Changes in people's activity fields lead to changes in their contexts of action, which may lead to changes in their exposure to criminogenic settings, and their contexts of development, which may lead to changes in their exposure to moral education and cognitive nurturing. The effects of these changes on people's actions and development depend on their baseline characteristics and experiences.

Changes in activity fields typically result from changes in the social and self-selective forces people are subject to or can exert, respectively. Social selection refers to social forces, exerted through a jurisdiction's rules and distribution of resources, which constrain or compel the participation of certain kinds of people in particular time and place-based activities. Changes in social selection typically occur as a result of external changes in wider social conditions (e.g., political, economical, or technological changes). Self-selection refers to people's preference-based choices to participate in particular time and place-based activities within the constraints of social selective forces. Changes in self-selection occur as a result of changes in people's agency and preferences. Unlike changes in crime propensity (which are typically gradual), changes in activity fields can be immediate (e.g., as a result of moving house or leaving school) and therefore lead to immediate changes in behavior. However, because those changes in behavior can just as immediately be reversed, changing people's activity fields often leads to less enduring changes in crime involvement than changing their crime propensities.

The life course may be thought of as a sequence of activity fields (configuration of settings) that a person has taken part in and that have formed and shaped his or her development and actions. A person's particular life-course trajectories may therefore be seen as an outcome of processes of social and self-selection.

1. *Activity Field Changes: Social Selection (External Changes)*. People's lives are embedded in a wider social, political, and economic context that determines the nature and distribution of the settings to which they may be exposed. This wider context encompasses a certain distribution of social and economic resources and enforces certain rules and regulations which, through the process of social selection, influence

people's routines (activity patterns) and consequently their intersections with different kinds of settings (e.g., Wikström, 2017; Wikström and Sampson 2003).

Changes in processes of social selection (e.g., following changes in the law or distribution of resources) create changes in people's activity fields. The wider distribution of resources influences what personal resources (e.g., in terms of human, financial, and social capital) particular people can obtain (at particular stages of their lives) and what resources are required to take part in particular time and place-based activities, which may lead to certain kinds of people being placed in certain kinds of contexts and excluded from others. The rules and regulations stipulated and enforced by a jurisdiction also characterize the settings within that jurisdiction, and in particular the nature and distribution of different moral contexts. These contexts will influence people's action and development.

Thus, together rules and resources influence personal routines and subsequently the extent to which different kinds of people are selected into, and therefore exposed to, different moral contexts. Changes to the wider context (e.g., political, economic, and technological changes) may affect rules, resources, and routines and consequently people's access to different kinds of settings, with implications for the kinds of situations created by social selection.

Social selection is what links human development and action to cultural (rule-based) and structural (resource-based) features of the jurisdiction in which a person operates. It is the main mechanism through which culture and structure (through social rules and the distribution of resources) influence the configuration of settings people take part in, thereby affecting their development and actions. In other words, social selection may be regarded as the main mechanism that connects macro and micro levels in the explanation of human development and action (including the development of crime propensities and exposure to criminogenic settings).

2. *Activity Field Changes: Self-Selection (Changes in Activity Preferences and Agency).* Within the constraints of social selective processes, people are able to exert some control over the settings in which they take part, though some can exert more control than others. This self-selection is facilitated by a person's agency and guided by his or her activity preferences. Agency may be defined as "the power to make things happen intentionally" and depends on factors such as human, financial, and social capital.[8] Greater capital may confer greater access to different settings and ease constraints. Preferences help direct the expression of agency in determining into which time and place-based activities people self-select. Preferences are acquired through experience and may be influenced by moral considerations. People gain increasing agency and form more definitive preferences as they age and their activity fields expand. However, agency tends to be context-dependent, and people will have greater agency in some domains of life than others.

Early in the life course, people (e.g., infants and young children) have very little say in their own activity fields, as these are determined for the most part by the circumstances of their birth (their parents' culture and social class, the historical time period, etc.) and how their caregivers manage the settings to which they are exposed. As people age, however, their activity fields broaden and they acquire preferences along with increasing agency (within existing social constraints). The stronger a person's agency, the more he or she can overcome the pressures of social selection and act upon his or her preferences to shape his or her activity field, lessening the influence of the environment, and increasing the influence of the person–environment interaction. This process is, of course, sequential; preferences, agency, and activity fields at any given time enable or constrain subsequent change.

V. Conclusions

We have argued that changes in crime involvement are more dynamic than is often presented in the criminological literature. That dynamic centers on the interplay between the crime-relevant characteristics of people and settings in both developmental and action contexts. We have forwarded situational action theory (SAT) as a constructive framework for analyzing that dynamic. SAT's development ecological action (DEA) model suggests that changes in crime involvement arise through changes in criminogenic action contexts—interactions between people with certain crime propensities and settings with certain criminogenic features. Changes in action contexts arise from change in people's crime propensities and exposure to criminogenic settings. Changes in people's crime propensities arise through moral education and cognitive nurturing, which depend on people's activity fields and may be moderated by organismic changes; changes in criminogenic action contexts arise from changes in self and social selection, which depend on people's agency and activity preferences, and the wider context, respectively. Analyses of the PADS+ data over the ages 13 to 24 supports the basic propositions of the DEA model (Wikström, Treiber, and Roman 2019).

The DEA model of change has interesting implications for understanding key features of criminal careers. For example, the early-onset behavioral problems often observed in persistent offenders may reflect the criminogenic developmental contexts to which these young people are exposed and generally constrained at a time when they have little agency and are rapidly acquiring information from their environments. The peak in offender prevalence during adolescence may reflect young people's exposure and particular vulnerability to an expanding range of criminogenic action contexts. On the other hand, increasing rates of desistence in early adulthood may reflect significant changes in young adults' activity fields and propensities as they reach full physical and mental maturity, become more self-sufficient, and acquire work and family responsibilities. Each of these effects, of course, will reflect the cumulative nature of each person's life experiences, hence the timing and the outcomes may vary significantly.

Notes

1. SAT's conceptualization of self-control differs in fundamental ways from Gottfredson and Hirschi's (Gottfredson 2011; Gottfredson and Hirschi 1990, 2003; Hirschi 2004; for a discussion see Wikström and Treiber 2007).

2. Moral values are defined as "generalised rules of conduct."
3. See Wikström and Treiber (2007) regarding self-control theory and (2015) regarding opportunity theory (routine activities and rational choice).
4. To study the causes of specific types of crime requires the study of specific propensities and environmental features, as people vary in how acceptable they find breaking different rules of conduct, generally and under different conditions.
5. See Wikström (2011) on the importance of distinguishing between "causes" (proximal or direct) and "causes of the causes" (distal or indirect).
6. While different actors may pay attention to different aspects of a setting (through selective perception) and may wrongly perceive its real characteristics (through distorted or biased perception), environmental features and actors' perceptions of those features typically do not qualitatively differ.
7. Broader historic socioecological processes determine the layout and content of the environments available in the jurisdiction in which a person operates.
8. Human capital refers to personal skills, such as one's level of education; financial capital refers to monetary assets; and social capital refers to resourceful relationships upon which one can draw.

REFERENCES

Agnew, Robert. 2014. "Social Concern and Crime: Moving Beyond the Assumption of Simple Self-Interest." *Criminology* 52(1): 1–32.

Anderson, Steven W., Antoine Bechara, Hanna Damasio, Daniel Tranel, and Antonio R. Damasio. 1999. "Impairment of Social and Moral Behavior Related to Early Damage in Human Prefrontal Cortex." *Nature Neuroscience* 2(11): 1032–1037.

Anderson, Steven, W., Hanna Damasio, Daniel Tranel, and Antonio R., Damasio. 2000. "Long-Term Sequelae of Prefrontal Cortex Damage Acquired in Early Childhood." *Developmental Neuropsychology* 18(3): 281–296.

Baumeister, Roy F., Matthew Gailliot, C. Nathan DeWall, and Megan Oaten. 2006. "Self-Regulation and Personality: How Interventions Increase Regulatory Success, and How Depletion Moderates the Effects of Traits on Behavior." *Journal of Personality* 74(6): 1773–1801.

Baumeister, Roy F., Kathleen D. Vohs, and Dianne M. Tice. 2007. "The Strength Model of Self-Control." *Current Directions in Psychological Science* 16(6): 351–355.

Blakemore, Sarah-Jayne. 2012. "Imaging Brain Development: The Adolescent Brain." *Neuroimage* 61(2): 397–406.

Blakemore, Sarah-Jayne, and Suparna Choudhury. 2006. "Development of the Adolescent Brain: Implications for Executive Function and Social Cognition." *Journal of Child Psychology and Psychiatry* 47(3–4): 296–312.

Blakemore, Sarah-Jayne, and Trevor W. Robbins. 2012. "Decision-Making in the Adolescent Brain." *Nature Neuroscience* 15(9): 1184–1191.

Bloom, Benjamin Samuel. 1964. *Stability and Change in Human Characteristics*. New York: John Wiley.

Brooks-Gunn, Jeanne, Greg J. Duncan, Pamela Kato Klebanov, and Naomi Sealand. 1993. "Do Neighborhoods Influence Child and Adolescent Development?" *American Journal of Sociology* 99(2): 353–395.

Bunge, Silvia A., Nicole M. Dudukovic, Moriah E. Thomason, Chandan J. Vaidya, and John D. E. Gabrieli. 2002. "Immature Frontal Lobe Contributions to Cognitive Control in Children: Evidence from fMRI." *Neuron* 33(2): 301–311.

Case, Robbie. 1992. "The Role of Frontal Lobe Maturation in Cognitive and Social Development." *Brain and Cognition* 20(1): 51–73.

Casey, B. J., Jay N. Giedd, and Kathleen M. Thomas. 2000. "Structural and Functional Brain Development and Its Relation to Cognitive Development." *Biological Psychology* 54: 241–257.

Casey, B. J., Rebecca M. Jones, and Todd A. Hare. 2008. "The Adolescent Brain." *Annals of the New York Academy of Sciences* 1124(1): 111–126.

Chelune, Gordon J., and Ruth A. Baer. 1986. "Developmental Norms for the Wisconsin Card Sorting Test." *Journal of Clinical and Experimental Neuropsychology* 8(3): 219–228.

Christakou, Anastasia, Samuel J. Gershman, Yael Niv, Andrew Simmons, Mick Brammer, and Katya Rubia. 2013. "Neural and Psychological Maturation of Decision-Making in Adolescence and Young Adulthood." *Journal of Cognitive Neuroscience* 25(11): 1807–1823.

Cohen, Lawrence E., and Marcus Felson. 1979. "Social Change and Crime Rate Trends: A Routine Activity Approach." *American Sociological Review* 44(4): 588–608.

Constantine-Paton, Martha, and Hollis T. Cline. 1998. "LTP and Activity-Dependent Synaptogenesis: The More Alike They Are, the More Different They Become." *Current Opinion in Neurobiology* 8(1): 139–148.

Cornish, Derek B., and Ronald V. Clarke. 2008. "The Rational Choice Perspective." In *Environmental Criminology and Crime Analysis*, edited by Richard Wortley and Lorraine Green Mazerolle, 29–61. Abingdon, UK: Routledge.

Crone, Eveline A., and Ronald E. Dahl. 2012. "Understanding Aolescence as a Period of Social-Affective Engagement and Goal Flexibility." *Nature Review Neuroscience* 13(9): 636–650.

Elder, Glen H., and Michael J. Shanahan. 2006. "The Life Course and Human Development." In *Handbook of Child Psychology*, Vol. 1: *Theoretical Models of Human Development*, edited by William Damons and Richard M. Lerner, 665–715. Hoboken, NJ: Wiley.

Eppinger, Ben, Nicolas W. Schuck, Leigh E. Nystrom, and Jonathan D. Cohen. 2013a. "Reduced Striatal Responses to Reward Prediction Errors in Older Compared with Younger Adults." *Journal of Neuroscience* 33(24): 9905–9912.

Eppinger, Ben, Maik Walter, Hauke R. Heekeren, and Shu-Chen Li. 2013b. "Of Goals and Habits: Age-Related and Individual Differences in Goal-Directed Decision-Making." *Frontiers in Neuroscience* 7: 253.

Eslinger, Paul J., Claire V. Flaherty-Craig, and Arthur L. Benton. 2004. "Developmental Outcomes After Early Prefrontal Cortex Damage." *Brain and Cognition* 55(1): 84–103.

Eslinger, Paul J., Lynn M. Grattan, Hanna Damasio, and Antonio R. Damasio. 1992. "Developmental Consequences of Childhood Frontal Lobe Damage." *Archives of Neurology* 49: 764–769.

Farrington, David P., Robert J. Sampson, and Per-Olof H. Wikström. 1993. *Integrating individual and ecological aspects of crime*. National Council for Crime Prevention.

Felson, Marcus, and Rachel L. Boba. 2010. *Crime and Everyday Life*. London: Sage.

Fuster, Joaquin M. 1997. *The Prefrontal Cortex: Anatomy, Physiology and Neuropsychology of the Frontal Lobe*. 3rd ed. Philadelphia: Lippincott-Raven.

Goldberg, Elkhonon. 2009. *The New Executive Brain: Frontal Lobes in a Complex World*. Oxford: Oxford University Press.

Goldman, David. 2012. *Our Genes, Our Choices: How Genotype and Gene Interactions Affect Behavior*. London: Elsevier.

Gottfredson, Michael. 2011. "Sanctions, Situations, and Agency in Control Theories of Crime." *European Journal of Criminology* 8(2): 128–143.

Gottfredson, Michael, and Travis Hirschi. 1990. *A General Theory of Crime*. Stanford, CA: Stanford University Press.

Gottfredson, Michael, and Travis Hirschi. 2003. "Self-Control and Opportunity." In *Control Theories of Crime and Delinquency. Advances in Criminological Theory*, Vol. 12, edited by Chester L. Britt and Michael Gottfredson, 5–19. New Brunswick, NJ: Transaction.

Gottlieb, Gilbert, Douglas Wahlsten, and Robert Lickliter. 2006. "The Significance of Biology for Human Development: A Developmental Psychobiological Systems View." In *Handbook of Child Psychology*, Vol. 1: *Theoretical Models of Human Development*, 6th ed., edited by Richard M. Lerner, 210–257. Hoboken, NJ: John Wiley.

Hagger, Martin S., Chantelle Wood, Chris Stiff, and Nikos L. D. Chatzisarantis. 2010. "Ego Depletion and the Strength Model of Self-Control: A Meta-Analysis." *Psychological Bulletin* 136(4): 495–525.

Heatherton, Todd F., and Dylan D. Wagner. 2011. "Cognitive Neuroscience of Self-Regulation Failure." *Trends in Cognitive Sciences* 15(3): 132–139.

Hirschi, Travis. 1969. *Causes of Delinquency*. Berkeley: University of California Press.

Hirschi, Travis. 2004. "Self-Control and Crime." In *Handbook of Self-Regulation: Research, Theory, and Applications*, edited by Kathleen D. Vohs and Roy F. Baumeister, 537–552. London: Guilford.

Hirschi, Travis, and Michael Gottfredson. 1983. "Age and the Explanation of Crime." *American Journal of Sociology* 89(3): 552–584.

Hirtenlehner, Helmut, and Per-Olof H. Wikström. 2017. "Experience or Deterrence? Revisiting an Old but Neglected Issue." *European Journal of Criminology* 14(4): 485–502. http://journals.sagepub.com/doi/full/10.1177/1477370816671750.

Hofmann, Wilhelm, Brandon J. Schmeichel, and Alan D. Baddeley. 2012. "Executive Functions and Self-Regulation." *Trends in Cognitive Sciences* 16(3): 174–180.

Inzlicht, Michael, and Jennifer N. Gutsell. 2007. "Running on Empty: Neural Signals for Self-Control Failure." *Psychological Science* 18(11): 933–937.

Johnson, Mark H., and Michelle De Haan. 2011. *Developmental Cognitive Neuroscience: An Introduction*. 3rd ed. Chichester, UK: John Wiley.

Johnson, Sara B., May Sudhinaraset, and Robert Wm. Blum. 2010. "Neuromaturation and Adolescent Risk-Taking: Why Development Is Not Determinism." *Journal of Adolescent Research* 25(1): 4–23.

Klingberg, Torkel. 2010. "Training and Plasticity of Working Memory." *Trends in Cognitive Sciences* 1(7): 317–324.

Laub, John H., and Robert J. Sampson. 2003. *Shared Beginnings, Divergent Lives: Delinquent Boys to Age 70*. Cambridge, MA: Harvard University Press.

Luciana, Monica, Heather M. Conklin, Catalina J. Hooper, and Rebecca S. Yarger. 2005. "The Development of Nonverbal Working Memory and Executive Control Processes in Adolescents." *Child Development* 76(3): 697–712.

Luna, Beatriz, Aarthi Padmanabhan, and Kirsten O'Hearn. 2010. "What Has fMRI Told Us About the Development of Cognitive Control Through Adolescence?" *Brain and Cognition* 72(1): 101–113.

Malenka, Robert C., and Roger A. Nicoll. 1999. "Long-Term Potentiation: A Decade of Progress?" *Science* 285(5435): 1870–1874.

Moffitt, Terrie. 1993. "Adolescence-Limited and Life-Course-Persistent Antisocial Behavior: A Developmental Taxonomy." *Psychological Review* 100(4): 674–701.

Moffitt, Terrie. 1997. "Adolescence-Limited and Life-Course-Persistent Offending: A Complementary Pair of Developmental Theories." In *Developmental Theories of Crime and Delinquency: Advances in Criminological Theory*, Vol. 7, edited by Terence P. Thornberry, 11–54. London: Transaction.

Moffitt, Terrie. 2003. "Life-Course Persistent and Adolescence-Limited Antisocial Behavior: A 10-Year Research Review and a Research Agenda." In *Causes of Conduct Disorder and Juvenile Delinquency*, edited by Benjamin B. Lahey, Terrie E. Moffitt, and Avshalom Caspi, 49–75. New York: Guilford.

Morrison, Alexandra B., and Jason. M. Chein. 2011. "Does Working Memory Training Work? The Promise and Challenges of Enhancing Cognition by Training Working Memory." *Psychonoimic Bulletin and Review* 18: 46–60.

Muraven, Mark. 2010a. "Building Self-Control Strength: Practicing Self-Control Leads to Improved Self-Control Performance." *Journal of Experimental Social Psychology* 46(2): 465–468.

Muraven, Mark. 2010b. "Practicing Self-Control Lowers the Risk of Smoking Lapse." *Psychology of Addictive Behaviors* 24(3): 446–452.

Muraven, Mark, Roy F. Baumeister, and Dianne M. Tice. 1999. "Longitudinal Improvement of Self-Regulation Through Practice: Building Self-Control Strength through Repeated Exercise." *Journal of Social Psychology* 139(4): 446–457.

Muraven, Mark, and Elisaveta Slessareva. 2003. "Mechanisms of Self-Control Failure: Motivation and Limited Resources." *Personality and Social Psychology Bulletin* 29(7): 894–906.

Nelson, Eric E., Ellen Leibenluft, Erin B. McClure, and Daniel S. Pine. 2005. "The Social Re-orientation of Adolescence: A Neuroscience Perspective on the Process and its Relation to Psychopathology." *Psychological Medicine* 35(2): 163–174.

Olesen, Pernille J., Helena Westerberg, and Torkel Klingberg. 2004. "Increased Prefrontal and Parietal Activity After Training of Working Memory." *Nature Neuroscience* 7(1): 75–79.

Rossini, Paolo M., Simone Rossi, Claudio Babiloni, and John Polich. 2007. "Clinical Neurophysiology of Aging Brain: From Normal Aging to Neurodegeneration." *Progress in Neurobiology* 88(6): 375–400.

Samanez-Larkin, Gregory R., Sara M. Levens, Lee M. Perry, Robert F. Dougherty, and Brian Knutson. 2012. "Frontostriatal White Matter Integrity Mediates Adult Age Differences in Probabilistic Reward Learning." *Journal of Neuroscience* 32(15): 5333–5337.

Sampson, Robert J., and John H. Laub. 1993. *Crime in the Making: Pathways and Turning Points Through Life*. Cambridge, MA: Harvard University Press.

Sampson, Robert J., and John H. Laub. 2003. "Life-Course Desisters? Trajectories of Crime Among Delinquent Boys Followed to Age 70." *Criminology* 41(3): 555–592.

Sampson, Robert J., and John H. Laub. 2005. "A Life-Course View of the Development of Crime." *Annals of the American Academy of Political and Social Science* 602: 12–45.

Shonkoff, Jack P., and Deborah A. Phillips. 2000. *From Neurons to Neighborhoods: The Science of Early Childhood Development*. Washington, DC: National Academy Press.

Spear, Linda P. 2000. "The Adolescent Brain and Age-Related Behavioral Manifestations." *Neuroscience and Biobehavioral Reviews* 24(4): 417–463.

Steinberg, Laurence. 2008. "A Social Neuroscience Perspective on Adolescent Risk-Taking." *Developmental Review* 28(1): 78–106.

Sturman, David A., and Bita Moghaddam. 2011. "The Neurobiology of Adolescence: Changes in Brain Architecture, Functional Dynamics, and Behavioral Tendencies." *Neuroscience and Biobehavioral Reviews* 35(8): 1704–1712.

Tranel, Daniel, Steven W. Anderson, and Arthur Benton. 1994. "Development of the Concept of 'Executive Function' and its Relationship to the Frontal Lobes." In *Handbook of Neuropsychology*, Vol. 9, *Section 12: The Frontal Lobes*, edited by Francois Boller and Hans Spinnler, 125–148. Oxford: Elsevier.

Treiber, Kyle. 2011. "The Neuroscientific Basis of Situational Action Theory." In *The Ashgate Research Companion to Biosocial Theories of Crime*, edited by Kevin M. Beaver and Anthony Walsh, 213–246. Aldershot, UK: Ashgate Press.

Treiber, Kyle. 2013. "A Neuropsychological Test of Criminal Decision Making: Regional Prefrontal Influences in a Dual Process Model." In *Affect and Cognition in Criminal Decision Making*, edited by Jean-Louis Van Gelder, Henk Elffers, Danielle Reynauld, and Daniel Nagin, 193–220. Abingdon, UK: Routledge.

Treiber, Kyle. 2017a. "Biosocial Criminology and Models of Criminal Decision Making." In *Oxford Handbook of Offender Decision Making*, edited by Wim Bernasco, Henk Elffers, and Jean-Louis van Gelder, 87–120. Oxford: Oxford University Press.

Treiber, Kyle. 2017b. "Situational Action Theory and PADS+: Theoretical and Methodological Advances in the Study of Life-Course Criminology." In *International Handbook of Life Course Criminology*, edited by Arjan Blokland and Victor van der Geest, 50–73. Abingdon, UK: Routledge.

Tremblay, Richard E. 2006. "Tracking the Origins of Criminal Behavior: Back to the Future." *The Criminologist* 31(1): 1.

Vohs, Kathleen. D., Roy F. Baumeister, and Brandon J. Schmeichel. 2012. "Motivation, Personal Beliefs, and Limited Resources All Contribute to Self-Control." *Journal of Experimental Social Psychology* 48(4): 943–947.

Wahlstrom, Dustin, Paul Collins, Tonya White, and Monica Luciana. 2010. "Developmental Changes in Dopamine Neurotransmission in Adolescence: Behavioral Implications and Issues in Assessment." *Brain and Cognition* 72(1): 146–159.

Westermann, Gert, Denis Mareschal, Mark H. Johnson, Sylvain Sirois, Michael W. Spratling, and Michael S. C. Thomas. 2007. "Neuroconstructivism." *Developmental Science* 10(1): 75–83.

Wikström, Per-Olof H. 2005. "The Social Origins of Pathways in Crime: Towards a Developmental Ecological Action Theory of Crime Involvement and Its Changes." In *Integrated Developmental and Life Course Theories of Offending. (Advances in Criminological Theory, Vol. 14)*, edited by David P. Farrington, 211–246. New Brunswick, NJ: Transaction.

Wikström, Per-Olof H. 2006. "Individuals, Settings, and Acts of Crime: Situational Mechanisms and the Explanation of Crime." In *The Explanation of Crime: Context, Mechanisms and Development*, edited by Per-Olof H. Wikström and Robert J. Sampson, 61–107. Cambridge, UK: Cambridge University Press.

Wikström, Per-Olof H. 2007. "The Social Ecology of Crime: The Role of the Environment in Crime Causation." In *Internationales Handbuch der Kriminologie*, edited by Hans J. Schneider. 333–358. Berlin: de Gruyter.

Wikström, Per-Olof H. 2010a. "Explaining Crime as Moral Action." In *Handbook of the Sociology of Morality*, edited by Steven Hitlin and Stephen Vaysey, 211–239. New York: Springer-Verlag.

Wikström, Per-Olof H. 2010b. "Situational Action Theory." In *Encyclopedia of Criminological Theory*, edited by Francis T. Cullen and Pamela Wilcox, 1001–1008. London: Sage.

Wikström, Per-Olof H. 2011. "Social Sources of Crime Propensity: A Study of the Collective Efficacy of Families, Schools and Neighborhoods." In *Antisocial Behavior and Crime: Contributions of Developmental and Evaluation Research to Prevention and Intervention*, edited by Thomas Bliesener, Andreas Beelmann, and Mark Stemmler, 109–122. Cambridge, MA: Hogrefe Publishing.

Wikström, Per-Olof H. 2014. "Why Crime Happens: A Situational Action Theory." In *Analytical Sociology: Actions and Networks*, edited by Gianluca Manzo, 74–94. Chichester, UK: Wiley.

Wikström, Per-Olof H. 2017. "Character, Circumstances, and the Causes of Crime: Towards an Analytical Criminology." In *The Oxford Handbook of Criminology*, 6th ed., edited by Alison Liebling, Shadd Maruna and Lesley McAra, 501–521. Oxford, UK: Oxford University Press.

Wikström, Per-Olof H., Dietrich Oberwittler, Kyle Treiber, and Beth Hardie. 2012. *Breaking Rules: The Social and Situational Dynamics of Young People's Urban Crime*. Oxford, UK: Oxford University Press.

Wikström, Per-Olof H., Richard P. Mann, and Beth Hardie. 2018. "Young People's Differential Vulnerability to Criminogenic Exposure: Briding the Gap Between People- and Place-Oriented Approaches in the Study of Crime Causation." *European Journal of Criminology* 15(1): 10–31.

Wikström, Per-Olof H., and Robert J. Sampson. 2003. "Social Mechanisms of Community: Influences on Crime and Pathways in Criminality." In *Causes of Conduct Disorder and Juvenile Delinquency*, edited by Benjamin B. Lahey, Terrie E. Moffitt, and Avshalom Caspi, 118–148. New York: Guilford.

Wikström, Per-Olof H., and Robert J. Sampson. 2006. "Introduction: Toward a Unified Approach to Crime and Its Explanation." In *The Explanation of Crime: Context, Mechanisms and Development*, edited by Per-Olof Wikström and Robert J. Sampson, 1–7. Cambridge, UK: Cambridge University Press.

Wikström, Per-Olof H., and Kyle Treiber. 2007. "The Role of Self-Control in Crime Causation: Beyond Gottfredson and Hirschi's General Theory of Crime." *European Journal of Criminology* 4(2): 237–264.

Wikström, Per-Olof H., and Kyle Treiber. 2009. "What Drives Persistent Offending? The Neglected and Unexplored Role of the Social Environment." In *The Development of Persistent Criminality*, edited by Joanna Savage, 389–420. Oxford: Oxford University Press.

Wikström, Per-Olof H., and Kyle Treiber. 2015. "Situational Theories: The Importance of Interactions and Action Mechanisms in the Explanation of Crime." In *Handbook of Criminological Theory*, edited by Alex R. Piquero, 415–444. Hoboken, NJ: Wiley-Blackwell.

Wikström, Per-Olof H., Kyle Treiber, and Gabriela Roman. 2019. *Character, Circumstances and Criminal Careers: Towards a Dynamic Developmental and Life Course Criminology*. Oxford: Oxford University Press.

Wikström, Per-Olof., Andromachi Tseloni, and Dimitris Karlis. 2011. "Do People Comply with the Law Because They Fear Getting Caught?" *European Journal of Criminology* 8(5): 401–420.

Worthy, Darrell A., Marissa A. Gorlick, Jennifer L. Pacheco, David M. Schnyer, and W. Todd Maddox. 2011. "With Age Comes Wisdom: Decision Making in Younger and Older Adults." *Psycholological Science* 22(11): 1375–1380.

Worthy, Darrell A., and W. Todd Maddox. 2012. "Age-Based Differences in Strategy Use in Choice Tasks." *Frontiers in Neuroscience* 5: 145.

Zito, Karen, and Karel Svoboda. 2002. "Activity-Dependent Synaptogenesis in the Adult Mammalian Cortex." *Neuron* 35(6): 1015–1017.

CHAPTER 16

....

THE AGE-GRADED THEORY OF INFORMAL SOCIAL CONTROL

....

JOHN H. LAUB, ZACHARY R. ROWAN, AND ROBERT J. SAMPSON

OVER the past 20 years, research on life-course and developmental criminology has grown rapidly. Numerous research journals, policy agendas, symposiums, the American Society of Criminology (ASC) Division, award categories, and handbooks all reflect the rise of a life-course or developmental perspective on crime—what Sampson and Laub (1995a) dubbed "life-course criminology." Evidence of this trend can be seen in Figure 16.1, which depicts the number of life-course publications on crime across major social science journals in the past 14 years.[1] The degrees of separation of scholars conducting work related to this topic have also been reduced and now reach across disciplines and oceans.

Life-course criminology, although situated in the relatively burgeoning field of criminology, has successfully contributed to the description and explanation of major criminological questions and challenges. This work has led to the examination of trajectories of offending across the life course, identification of causes of crime and delinquency, evaluation of macro- and micro-level relationships, exploration of variation in persistent offending and desistance from crime and has broadly accommodated an interdisciplinary perspective on antisocial behavior (see review in Laub 2006). Although life-course and developmental criminology have garnered the attention and contributions of many well-respected scholars, the work by Robert Sampson and John Laub and their age-graded theory of informal social control served as one of the catalysts for the growth in research. Utilizing one of the most comprehensive datasets of the time, Sampson and Laub (1993; Laub and Sampson 2003) reassess data collected by Sheldon and Eleanor

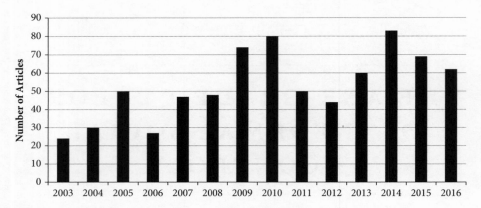

FIGURE 16.1 Frequency of Life-Course Publications, 2003–2016

Glueck in their *Unraveling Juvenile Delinquency* study to develop a theoretical frame-work that explains childhood antisocial behavior, adolescent delinquency, and crime in early adulthood.

The overarching framework for Sampson and Laub's age-graded theory of informal social control is that crime is more likely to occur when an individual's bond to con-ventional society is weakened. Although this framework shares a similar foundation with classical control theory (Hirschi 1969), it emphasizes the salience of later life-course milestones, or "turning points," that require modification of the static nature of classical control theory. Despite early differences in childhood experiences and de-linquency, adult social bonds to work and family are significantly related to changes in adult crime. This position largely contrasts with the age-invariance thesis of Hirschi and Gottfredson (1983), which argues that that crime declines similarly with age for all offenders and is due solely to the underlying propensity to offend known as self-control.

For the purposes of this chapter, we will primarily focus on the theoretical developments and empirical assessments after the publication of Laub and Sampson's *Shared Beginnings, Divergent Lives* (2003) to provide a current review of updates and challenges to the age-graded theory of informal social control.[2] Section I will briefly consider Sampson and Laub's (1993) *Crime in the Making,* followed by the re-sponse to remaining questions with a summary of the revised version of the theory in *Shared Beginnings, Divergent Lives* (Laub and Sampson 2003). Section II will pro-vide an updated theoretical and empirical assessment of the core principles of the theory, namely a review of current research on turning points and human agency. Section III will detail current challenges to the importance of turning points in adult-hood. Section IV will review contemporary barriers to mechanisms of desistance. Lastly, Section V will conclude with our own commentary and final thoughts on the theory.[3]

I. Age-Graded Theory of Informal Social Control and Turning Points in the Life Course

Crime in the Making serves as a first step toward developing a theoretical framework that explains childhood antisocial behavior, adolescent delinquency, and crime in adulthood. As stated, the primary organizing principle is that crime is more likely to occur when an individual's bond to society is attenuated. Following Elder (1975, 1985), Sampson and Laub (1993) differentiate the life course of individuals on the basis of age and argue that salient institutions of both formal and informal social control vary across the life span. In addition, Sampson and Laub (1993) explicitly account for processes of continuity and change in criminal behavior over the life course. Thus, despite the importance of the effects of cumulative continuity and state dependence of prior antisocial behavior, salient life events and socialization experiences in adulthood are capable of modifying trajectories of crime. Still, *Crime in the Making* left several unanswered questions and set the stage for additional directions for future research.

For example, Sampson and Laub (1993) called for further integration of quantitative and qualitative research, a more nuanced understanding of the relationship between age and crime over the full life course, and further unpacking of the mechanisms underlying persistent offending and desistance from crime. Beyond the "natural sanctions" or health costs associated with criminal offending (i.e., early mortality), there are shifts in the salience of formal and informal social controls over time. For instance, scholars have generally found that there needs to be an "accumulation of losses" before informal social controls can catalyze an inhibition toward engaging in anti-social behavior (Graham and Bowling 1995; Shover 1996). Additional emphases on the dimensionality of turning points called for further investigation into the precise nature of turning point processes (Rutter 1996). For instance, not all turning points can be equated with major life experiences, nor can all transitions lead to changes in life trajectories. As such, contextualizing turning points and group processes for explaining continuity and change in criminal behavior became of primary interest.

These motivations led Laub and Sampson (2003) to follow up the Glueck men with a 35-year follow-up and to supplement the existing data with three new sources of data collection—criminal record checks (local and national), death record checks (local and national), and personal interviews with a sample of 52 of the original Glueck men. These cases were selected on the basis of their trajectories of adult offending in order to maximize variation. This new compilation of data encompasses data on crime and life experiences of the Glueck men from age 7 to 70. Although not abandoning the importance of informal social controls, the revised version of the theory recognizes that "social actors are always embedded in space and time [and] respond to specific situations (opportunities as well as constraints) rather than pursuing lines of conduct in purely solipsistic fashion." (Emirbayer 1997, p. 307). It is necessary to contextualize concepts such as crime and how they relate to particular turning points because their meaning and significance varies by context. Thus, *Shared Beginnings* reflects an effort to further unpack the processes of persistence and desistance and illuminate why and how adult social institutions and roles have the capacity to reorder life-course trajectories.

A. Age and Crime over the Life Course

Through a series of within-individual trajectories of age and crime, Laub and Sampson (2003) find support for the variability in the age–crime curve among individuals but confirm that that crime declines for all, even among the active offenders. Thus, the aggregate age–crime curve does not mirror individual age–crime trajectories as the evidence demonstrates important variation in the peak in offending and age at desistance (Laub and Sampson 2003). Nonetheless, across all offenders the underlying process of desistance follows a fairly similar path as all offenses decline systemically. Stated differently, even the serious delinquents of the Glueck sample desist but do so at varying time points across the life course and at different rates. As such, although child prognoses are relatively accurate in terms of predicting criminal behavior between individuals through their twenties, they do not yield distinct groupings that are prospectively valid over the entire life course. This finding holds regardless if offenders are grouped or identified prospectively or ex post (Laub and Sampson 2003). These findings give credence to a middle-ground position with respect to the criminal careers debate in that there is variability among individual age–crime curves and that age has a direct effect on offending such that "life-course desister" is the more accurate label. Further, this suggests that a general desistance processes is at work across the life course and that these processes can only be understood through the full interplay of childhood, adolescent, and adult experiences.

B. Mechanisms of Desistance

Given the heterogeneity in adult criminal trajectories that could not be predicted from childhood, Laub and Sampson (2003) argue that institutions play an important role in understanding crime over the life course. Laub and Sampson (2003) utilize hierarchical linear models and qualitative interviews with a subsample of the Glueck men to assess and describe turning points throughout the course of their lives. Consistent with evidence found in *Crime in the Making*, several turning points emerge as part of the process of desistance from crime to include marriage/spouses, military service, reform school, work, and residential change. Laub and Sampson (2003) exploit the longitudinal nature of the data to examine within-individual change, holding stable characteristics of the person constant and evaluate the impact of changes in social location (e.g., marriage) on criminal trajectories. Laub and Sampson (2003) conclude that, when employed, in military service, or married, the Glueck men are less likely to engage in criminal behavior. These models provide strong statistical evidence of the probabilistic enhancement of desistance associated with turning points such as marriage, military service, and employment.

The qualitative narratives in *Shared Beginnings* further illuminate the mechanisms underlying the desistance process. In particular, these institutional or structural turning points to varying degrees involve (1) new situations that "knife off" the past from the present, (2) new situations that provide both supervision and monitoring as well as new opportunities for social support and growth, (3) new situations that change and structure routine activities, and (4) new situations that provide the opportunity for identity transformation (Laub and Sampson 2003). Thus, although several institutions and turning points emerge frequently throughout the Glueck men narratives, other life experiences characterized by these similar processes are likely to trigger movement toward desistance. Overall, these institutions tend to reorder short-term situational inducements to crime and, over time, redirect long-term commitments to conformity.

C. Agency

In addition, Laub and Sampson (2003) identify the importance of offenders choosing to desist in response to structurally induced turning points that serve as a catalyst or work to sustain shifts in criminal behavior. Consistent with notions of agency, offenders engage in the purposeful execution of choice and individual will that lead to projective actions either toward persistence in crime or toward disengaging from criminal activity Although not all of the Glueck men explicitly describe choosing to desist from crime, many Glueck men indicate examples of sidebets that ultimately result in desistance. That is, before they knew it, the men had invested resources and time in a marriage or a job such that risking this investment became non-negotiable (Becker 1960). Even if below the surface of active consciousness, actions to desist are in a fundamental sense willed by the offender, leading to what Laub and Sampson (2003) refer to as "desistance by default" (Sampson and Laub 2003). The Glueck men were thus seen to be active participants in their own desistance, especially when their actions projected a new sense of one's self-concept.

Human agency was also seen as critical for understanding persistent offending. Several of the Glueck men insisted on a criminal lifestyle due to the rewards of crime (Katz 1988) or because of a willful resistance to perceived domination (Sherman 1993). Several of the life history narratives illuminate the sense of injustice present in the Glueck men's perspective of the criminal justice system driven by their acerbic contacts with the system. Persistence in offending is more than the weakening of social bonds, and desistance is more than the presence of or strengthening of social bonds. Therefore, agency plays a critical role across the full spectrum of offending patterns and infuses a random component into life-course turning points that make "neat prediction" a difficult task.

II. Current Empirical Assessment

Beyond the evidence provided in *Shared Beginnings*, numerous other researchers have taken up the task of evaluating the strength of claims that age-graded roles later in adult life are significantly related to persistence and desistance in offending. The following sections will discuss current evidence that evaluates the role of marriage, employment, and the military as turning points in the desistance process.

A. Marriage

Perhaps the most studied turning point process has been marriage. The marriage effect was originally posited by Sampson and Laub (1993). Furthermore, the relationship between marriage and crime was assessed in Laub, Nagin, and Sampson (1998) using rigorous controls to account for heterogeneity. This finding has been fairly robust across a range of studies and methods including within-individual analyses using self-report and official arrest measures and with both cross-sectional and longitudinal studies (e.g., Farrington and West 1995; Horney, Osgood, and Marshall 1995; Shover 1996; Piquero, MacDonald, and Parker 2002; Blokland and Nieuwbeerta 2005; King, Massoglia, and MacMillan 2007; Beaver et al. 2008; Bersani, Laub, and Nieuwbeerta 2009). Further, more recent evaluations use propensity scores to address concerns over selection and identify consistent effects of marriage on crime reduction (Sampson, Laub, and Wimer 2006; King, Massoglia, and MacMillan 2007; Theobald and Farrington 2009). Although a marriage effect persists, such an effect may not be distributed equally across the population. Evidence suggests that it is strongest for males with the lowest propensity to marry and among men who marry earlier (King, Massoglia, and MacMillan 2007; Theobald and Farrington, 2009, 2011). Additionally, Bersani and DiPetro (2016) demonstrate that the crime-reducing benefits of marriage do not apply consistently across racial and ethnic groups but are more pronounced among black and Hispanic men compared to white men despite the declining prevalence of marriage among minorities (see also Piquero, MacDonald, and Parker 2002; Harris, Lee, and DeLeone 2010).

Evidence in support for the role of marriage is also not tied to findings in the United States. Evaluating the role of marriage in the Netherlands, Bersani, Laub, and Nieuwbeerta (2009) utilize the Criminal Career and Life Course Study (5,000 men and women convicted in the Netherlands) and find support for the effect of marriage to reduce offending across gender and a contemporary socio-historical context. Utilizing data from official population registries in Finland, Savolainen (2009) finds that union formation, which includes being married or cohabiting, is significantly associated with crime leading to approximately a 10 percent reductions in the number of new convictions; however, when separated out it appears that cohabitation drives the reduction in recidivism. Thus, the "good marriage effect" persists among offenders in several geographic and historical contexts (see also Blokland and Nieuwbeerta 2005).

Recent work additionally contributes to establishing causality and to substantiating how marriage matters in the desistance process (e.g., Sampson, Laub, and Wimer, 2006; Bersani and Doherty, 2013). Sampson, Laub, and Wimer (2006) conceptualize the potential causal effect of being in the state of marriage (which hypothetically could be randomly or exogenously induced) with the state of non-marriage for the same person within a counterfactual modeling strategy. Results indicate that being married is associated with a 35 percent average reduction in the probability of crime among the sample of 52 Glueck men assessed from ages 17 to 70. Additional support is found through a prospective twin study that sought to similarly present a counterfactual approach to identify the causal effect of marriage (Burt et al. 2010). Using a longitudinal sample of male twins, analyses by Burt et al. (2010) suggest that although there is some evidence of selection among those twins who marry, a significant effect of marriage toward desistance exists.

Bersani and Doherty (2013) utilize an enduring-versus-treatment model to assess how and why marriage matters. In particular, Bersani and Doherty (2013) focus on the changes in offending when a marriage ends. They argue that although there are several posited mechanisms to explain the marriage effect, each mechanism carries a specific type of change process. These change processes are characterized on a spectrum of being either a stable or enduring change (e.g., social bonds) or a situational or temporary change (e.g., knifing off, supervision). Initial analyses suggest that upon entering a state of divorce, individuals have a higher likelihood of arrest that is stable during the months of being divorced. As Hirschi (1969) described, without the external tie of a spouse, "the divorced man is more likely after divorce to commit a number of deviant acts" (p. 19). In order to account for the fact that marriage likely reflects an investment process that occurs gradually over time, analyses were disaggregated by the length of marriage. Evidence suggests here that for longer marriages there is an immediate increase in offending after divorce, indicating the salience of situational contributors to desistance (e.g., direct supervision, routine activities). This finding contrasts with expectations that lengthier marriages that dissolve would not lead to an immediate increase in offending due to the accumulation of invested social bonds and capital. Ultimately, Bersani and Doherty (2013) contribute to the understanding of Laub and Sampson's (2003) notion that there are underlying mechanisms triggered by turning points such as marriage. In the case of these analyses, the change processes associated with marriage are more strongly supportive of situational shifts associated with marriage (i.e., knifing off, routine activities).

Most recently, Skardhamar, Savolainen, Aase, and Lyngstad (2015) conducted a review of the literature evaluating the marriage–crime relationship. Motivated by skepticism surrounding the causal effect of marriage on criminal behavior, these scholars include 58 publications between 1990 and 2014 in their review. In total, 36 of the 58 publications (62 percent) find marriage to be associated with desistance from crime. An additional 9 studies provide mixed support for the relationship between marriage and desistance, leading to a total of 45 out of 58 studies (78 percent) that demonstrate some support for the negative association. Skardhamar and colleagues (2015) summarize key patterns found in the literature that further specify or contextualize the relationship. These patterns include findings previously discussed related to the role of cohabitation, gender-conditioned impacts of the marriage effect, and the extent to which the marriage effect can be generalized to contexts outside of the United States and United Kingdom. Further, Skardhamar et al. (2015) criticize the validity of existing research that seeks to identify the causal relationship between marriage and desistance. In essence, they argue that a sizable portion of the current literature "is equally consistent with noncausal theories" (p. 426), as there are no studies that provide evidence of counterfactual causal evidence as "defined by prevailing methodological standards" (p. 429) and an accurate consideration of time-ordering between marriage and desistance.

As previously mentioned, both Sampson et al. (2006) and King et al. (2007) attempt to isolate the causal effect of marriage through their respective applications of inverse probability of treatment weighting and propensity score matching. While both of these studies generally conclude that the evidence is consistent with a causal effect of marriage on crime in the expected direction, Skardhamar et al. (2015) suggest that neither of these approaches can derive causal conclusions that would be found in randomized experiments or methodological alternatives such as instrumental variables. But Skardhamar et al. (2015) also concede that both randomized experiments and instrumental variable approaches are likely implausible with respect to studying marriage and recommend scholars "pursue the next-best approach" (p. 430), which includes quasi-experimental methods such as instrumental variable estimation. Skardhamar et al. (2015) clearly are unsatisfied with existing studies that attempt to address concerns surrounding causality, however, they do not offer viable alternatives to build on this existing knowledge.

Our point here is not to diminish efforts that can help triangulate or refine existing causal arguments in support of the marriage effect on crime, but rather to recognize the inherent difficulties in aligning causal identification with the social nature of the research question under inquiry. Consistent with the efforts of Sampson et al. (2006) and King et al. (2007), it would seem to be more important to continue to focus on understanding the assumptions made in methodological decisions, assess the robustness of findings, and provide conceptual transparency in the evident "marriage effect" in lieu of an arguably impossible search for a randomized experiment of marriage. Put differently and more generally, to rule out evidence that only comes from non-randomized experiments is to rule out most of criminology.

B. Employment

Findings from several other studies have mixed support for the capacity of entry into employment to reduce offending, with several noted caveats. The majority of research on this relationship has been cross-sectional and clearly prevents a firm understanding of the causal relationship between employment and crime (see Uggen and Wakefield 2008).[4] Longitudinal analyses that focus on individual-level data are much more limited and tend to find mixed results (Uggen and Wakefield 2008). For example, among a sample of incarcerated drug offenders, O'Connell (2003) finds that employment is negatively associated with drug use and arrest. Tripodi, Kim, and Bender (2010) evaluate the relationship between employment and recidivism among parolees released from Texas prisons and find that although employment is not necessarily associated with a reduction in the likelihood of reincarceration, it does lead to increases in the amount of time spent in the community crime-free before returning to prison.

Additional support has been found for the notion that the subjective quality of employment, as compared to simply being employed, explains the relationship between employment and a reduction in offending. Wadsworth (2006) finds that among a sample from the National Longitudinal Survey of Youth, the quality of employment matters over and beyond the income from and stability of employment in explaining involvement in a variety of criminal behavior. Mesters, van der Geest, and Bijleveld (2016) utilize a dynamic discrete choice modeling strategy to understand the mechanism that explains the employment–crime relationship and find that regular, as opposed to temporary employment drives the negative relationship with crime.

Parallel to the results for marriage, the effects of employment on antisocial behavior are found outside the United States as well. Evaluating the impact of employment on crime in the Netherlands, Verbruggen, Blokland, and van Der Geest (2012) find that after controlling for between-person differences associated with both crime and employment, employment has both an immediate and gradual effect on crime for both high-risk men and women—although effects for women were not as strong, particularly when compared to those men who experienced continuous employment. In Finland, Savolainen (2009) finds that obtaining employment is the strongest predictor of desistance reflected by the 40 percent reduction in the rate of recidivism. Despite some mixed results, the addition of new socio-historical contexts and empirical evaluations employment does seem to explain part of the complex processes of desistance.[5]

C. Military Service

Scholars generally describe military service as a potentially important life event that serves to redirect trajectories of behaviors across a variety of domains (see MacLean and Elder 2007 for review). To some extent, military service serves as the quintessential life-course event, as it encapsulates many of the core principles of the life-course paradigm. The decision to join (or being drafted) into military service is rooted in a particular time and place, which carries developmental consequences upon return from service. As it relates to crime and deviance, scholars have noted that military service may serve as a "knifing-off" experience from social disadvantage, provide new structure to routine activities, reduce criminal opportunities, and provide additional job training or opportunities (Browning, Lopreato, and Poston 1973; Elder 1999; Laub and Sampson

2003). Earlier work that focuses on the experience of military service during World War II generally finds positive effects of military service reflected in reductions in offending (Sampson and Laub 1996). Still, qualitative evidence from interviews with the Glueck men demonstrate that entry into the military may also disrupt existing social roles and expectations and also may provide another environment in which deviant behavior can persist (Sampson and Laub 1993; Laub and Sampson 2003).

More recent endeavors have sought to further our understanding of the role of military service in trajectories of criminal behavior by studying participants of the Vietnam War (Bouffard 2003; Bouffard and Laub 2004; Wright, Carter, and Cullen 2005; Bouffard 2014). To be sure, World War II and the Vietnam War reflect very different experiences in U.S. military history, and therefore it is anticipated that such differences may play out in the outcomes of analyses. Public sentiment and support for World War II was significantly stronger than for the Vietnam War, as there was confusion over U.S. involvement (Moskos 1971; Mueller 1971; Janowitz 1978; Scott 2004). Challenges over the inequality of the draft and the overall treatment of the Vietnamese further exacerbated the negative views over U.S. involvement and perceptions of the military (Moskos 1971; Scott 2004). Lastly, the postwar period of World War II was characterized by economic growth, whereas the years after the Vietnam War were plagued by economic instability. Research confirms this instability; servicemen experience poorer labor market outcomes and acquire less education when compared to nonveterans (Angrist 1990; Cohen, Warner, and Segal 1995). Given the context of the Vietnam War, studying the effect of Vietnam military service as a turning point for criminal behavior provides a chance to evaluate the similarities and differences with prior findings on the role of World War II military service.

Bouffard (2003) considers the differential influence of military service during the Vietnam War through an evaluation of Wolfgang's 1945 Philadelphia birth cohort (see Wolfgang, Figlio, and Sellin 1994) and Lyle Shannon's 1949 Racine birth cohort (see Shannon 1994). After accounting for key differences in the likelihood of entering the military, results indicate that service during the Vietnam War led to reductions in subsequent offending; however, there is no relationship with violent behavior. Subsequent work by Bouffard (2014) extends these analyses to further investigate whether the historical period of military service conditions the relationship with criminal behavior. Bouffard (2014) finds that the effect of military service depends on when the men in both the Philadelphia and Racine cohorts start their service. Specifically, those whose service started post-1968 had significantly lower rates of offending compared to those who did not serve in the military and those who began military service in Vietnam during other time periods. This finding is consistent with Sampson and Laub's (1996) conclusion that military service is dependent on the age of entry into service during World War II.

The experience of military service as it relates to criminal behavior also is demonstrated to vary by subgroups. In an evaluation of the National Longitudinal Survey of Youth, Bouffard (2005) investigates the interaction between military service and individual demographics. Although military service generally predicts an increase in violent behavior, this finding is limited to specific subgroups in the sample (Bouffard 2005). Specifically, results indicate that military service in Vietnam had detrimental impacts for Hispanic, lower-class, and delinquent subjects. Although Bouffard (2005) is not able to empirically test why these groups of individuals differed, it is suggested that the military may only serve as a "bridging environment" to successful opportunities and change for certain groups (Browning, Lopreato, and Poston 1973). Ultimately, military service appears to be a turning point for criminal behavior; however, the direction and intensity of this process varies by socio-historical context and does not seem to have a constant effect across all those in the armed forces.

D. Physical Relocation

As stated, in an effort to explore the underlying mechanisms of structural turning points, *Shared Beginnings* expands the age-graded theory of informal social control. One such life event that illuminates these mechanisms is physical relocation. For example, some of the Glueck men who desisted indicate the importance of shifts in their residential location as being critical for changing their behavior, which may suggest that residential change activates these underlying processes. One Glueck man (Henry) indicates that he could not return to his previous neighborhood because he would end up either dead or in jail (Laub and Sampson 2003).

More recent work additionally supports the notion that residential shifts serve as turning points in the life course, particularly because they implicate these underlying processes. Kirk (2009) uses the consequences of the damage caused by Hurricane Katrina in New Orleans as a natural experiment to evaluate whether residential changes affected recidivism among ex-prisoners and finds a reduction in rate of reincarceration among those ex-offenders who subsequently move out of their prior parish. This effect persisted in a follow-up study indicating that the reduction in the risk of reincarceration due to a change in residential location for these ex-offenders was not temporary and in fact endured over a 3-year observational period (Kirk 2012). Additional work by Sharkey and Sampson (2010) find Chicago adolescents who move to a neighborhood outside of Chicago experience a reduction in the likelihood of violent offending. These findings reinforce the notion that desistance is more likely to occur in contexts that remove individuals from criminal lifestyles, associates, and structures.

E. Summary of Current Empirical Literature

These more recent assessments of criminal behavior across the life course highlight the extent of heterogeneity in longitudinal patterns of offending, undercutting claims of age-invariance for the relationship between age and crime (Hirschi and Gottfredson 1983). Additionally, these findings reflect the goal of life-course criminology to situate the entire life course into an understanding of criminal behavior. Thus, rather than assuming that the relationship between age and crime is "inherent, invariant, and inexplicable" (Tittle and Grasmick 1997, p. 310), these results provide evidence that "behavioral change matters" and cannot be overlooked (Ezell and Cohen 2005, p. 255). In a thorough assessment of behavioral stability and change across the life course, for example, Ezell and Cohen (2005, p. 259) evaluate three independent serious offending samples from the California Youth Authority and conclude that "(1) behavioral change is evident among serious chronic offenders, (2) that the heterogeneity in criminal propensity among the chronic offender population is often underreported, and (3) that there is considerable post-adolescent heterogeneity in the arrest rates of offenders that cannot be explained purely as a consequence of earlier individual differences."

Although not an empirical test of theoretical mechanisms, the conclusions drawn by Ezell and Cohen (2005) succinctly depict several of the core theoretical abstractions and predictions of the age-graded theory of informal social control that are assessed in the preceding paragraphs. In order to further situate and appreciate the sizeable empirical support for this theory, we must contemplate the available criticisms and empirical challenges. The following section provides a current overview of major challenges to this life-course perspective and will be supplemented with our own responses to these challenges.

III. CHALLENGES TO THE CAUSAL IMPORTANCE OF TURNING POINTS

A potential challenge to the importance of turning points in the processes of desistance is that transitions into marriage, employment, or military service may be to due non-random selection into these states. Asked simply, are turning points the chicken or the egg in the desistance process (LeBel, Burnett, Maruna, and Bushway 2008)? Characteristics of the individual including prior experience, individual traits, subjective factors, and other non-random factors may influence entry into marriage or other key turning point processes, thereby confounding the marriage–desistance relationship (see also Gottfredson and Hirschi 1990). Additionally, scholars have argued that "[past studies] do not address the critical issue of time order with sufficient precision" (Skardhamar and Savolainen 2014). Such challenges are paramount to determining the validity of the causality of turning points in explaining age-graded changes in offending behavior. Although Laub and Sampson (2003) attempt to address these concerns, several scholars have levied criticisms of the efforts of Sampson and Laub (1993) and Laub and Sampson (2003) to establish the causality of turning points (see Lyngstad and Skardhamar 2013; Skardhamar and Savolainen 2014).

A. Selection into Marriage and Employment

Lyngstad and Skardhamar (2013) argue that Sampson and Laub compare average offending levels before and after marriage leading to an overstatement of the marriage effect and an understatement of selection. Using data from the Norwegian administrative registrar, these scholars find that changes in offending largely occur prior to marriage followed by a small increase in offending after marriage. Thus, according to Lyngstad and Skardhamar (2013), because changes in offending for those who get married occur largely before marriage and the effect of getting married is negligible, "it is time to stop viewing marriage as a particularly important turning point in the process of desistance when considering contexts from contemporary industrialized societies" (p. 14). Further, given the reported increase in offending after marriage, Lyngstad and Skardhamar (2013) emphasize the importance of understanding the processes leading up to marriage (e.g., courtship, cohabitation, parenthood).[6]

Along similar lines, Barnes et al. (2014) argue that the relationship between crime and turning points are likely reciprocal, such that offenders' criminal behavior may impact their marital propensity. Sampson and Laub (1993) address this specific issue through their discussion of simultaneous modeling of adult social bonds and crime and deviance. Sampson and Laub (1993) find that the role of adult social bonds "is both instantaneous and predictive in nature, independent not only of childhood deviance but of the simultaneous effects of adult crime as well" (pp. 170–171).

Skardhamar and Savolainen (2014) report similar results for the role of employment as a turning point in the life course (see also Mesters et al. 2016). Again, using the Norwegian registrar data, Skardhamar and Savolainen (2014) find that although employment matters in explaining changes in criminal behavior, significant changes in behavior occur largely prior to job entry and for only a small percentage of the sample (2 percent) do changes in offending occur after employment. Laub and Sampson acknowledge that turning points are not singular events and are more realistically part of a gradual process (Laub, Nagin, and Sampson 1998; Laub and Sampson 2003). Further, the mechanisms associated with turning points such as marriage and employment are not a constant once set in motion, and they vary through time. As such, Sampson and Laub have adopted several different methodological approaches to account for selection processes and to identify the impact of the structural turning points responsible for desistance. It would appear that nothing short of a true randomized experiment would address many of the criticisms levied against the importance of marriage and employment. Of note, in an evaluation of the experimental National Supported Work Demonstration Project, Uggen (2000) finds that employment reduces reports of crimes and arrest among those aged 27 or older. But of course, it is difficult if not impossible to randomize marriage, and even if were, experiments have their own limitations with respect to external validity (Sampson 2010). Overall, we conclude that the results to date indicate more support for the marriage effect than employment effect, with the main outlier coming from administrative records in Norway. Whether there is something unique to Norway, the peculiarities of their sample and data, or the analysis in the work of Skardhamar and Savolainen (2014) is beyond the scope of our review but bears further inquiry.

B. Human Agency Across the Life Course

Laub and Sampson (2003) conclude that for a majority of their sample it is normative to desist and that there is a "desistance by default" process. This process is criticized as being an "anti-agentic" process in comparison to the underlying notion of agency as an actionable choice-based process. In fact, Paternoster and Bushway (2009) go so far to criticize Laub and Sampson (2003) for continuing to rely on a structuralist theory that ignores the importance of human agency and rational choice in explanations of change and stability in offending. Additionally, Paternoster and Bushway (2004) claim that believing in agency requires a rational choice perspective. From a rational choice perspective, agency is simply a matter of preferences and how preferences can be used to change or modify inputs or exogenous events like employment and marriage (Paternoster and Bushway 2004).

Our assessment is that the revolution in behavioral economics has rendered the pure rational choice model invalid. The evidence is now overwhelming that humans make decisions "beneath the radar screen" of conscious choice, with mechanisms such as confirmation bias and implicit bias well documented (Sunstein and Thaler 2008; Kahneman 2011). Laub and Sampson (2003) also argue that rational choice ignores the fact that we choose, discover, and construct preferences over the course of time to generate new preferences that are not yet known (March 1978). Choice is not exogenous, in other words. Agency is situated in context and is therefore a dynamic, rather than static, construct which is a relational characteristic rather than a property of the person or the environment. Agency is composed of an ongoing interaction between person and environment that is a crucial ingredient of causation.

Further, in contrast to other theories of desistance that focuses on cognitive transformations or identity shifts as being necessary for the process of desistance to occur, Laub and Sampson (2003) find that may offenders can and do desist without a conscious decision to "make good," as claimed in works such as Maruna (2001), Giordano, Cernkovich, and Rudolph (2002), Farrall (2005), and Paternoster and Bushway (2009). For instance, Paternoster and Bushway's (2009) identity theory argues that individual offenders possess a working self, positive possible self, and feared self. Individuals are tied to their working self, which may be criminal in nature, and will only change through a process of crystallization of discontent. This process involves recognition of the potential feared self and a realization that the costs of crime and a criminal identity are too high. The accumulation and linking of negative experiences associated with a criminal lifestyle leads to further motivation for self-change (Paternoster and Bushway 2009).

Giordano and colleagues (2002) similarly develop a theory of cognitive transformation that involves significant upfront work to ensure desistance. Specifically, individuals must be open to change that either coincides or is followed by "hooks for change" or turning points (Giordano, Cernkovich, and Rudolph 2002). Upon acting on this turning point, the individual is able to envision and adopt a replacement self that triggers a re-evaluation of how an individual perceives deviant behavior. In this depiction of desistance, "the actor creatively and selectively draws upon elements of the environment in order to affect significant life changes'" (Giordano, Cernkovich, and Rudolph 2002, p. 1003).

Laub and Sampson (2003) acknowledge that the original age-graded theory of informal social control was an incomplete response to explaining desistance and consequently have recognized the relevance of recognizing human social action in the lives of the Glueck men. Combinations of both objective and subjective factors are implicated in the process of desistance and persistence. The qualitative narratives facilitate Laub and Sampson's (2003) understanding of the "situated choice(s)" made as a result of the interaction between life-course transitions, macro-level events, situational context, and individual will of the Glueck men. This is illuminated by the fact that the data collected on the Glueck men indicate that desistance is primarily facilitated by turning points in combination with individual actions. Most importantly, desistance is not necessarily a conscious or deliberate decision, but rather a series of "side bets" that are fostered through the experience of socially embedded life events such as marriage, employment, and the military (Becker 1960, p. 38). Generally speaking, this hypothesis is consistent with the research on behavioral economic that moves beyond a pure rational choice model (Sunstein and Thaler 2008; Kahneman 2011).

C. Additional Challenges Regarding Human Agency

Laub and Sampson (2003) state that agency is the "missing link" in desistance research; however, our understanding of the precise definition of agency and how individuals are able to act "agentically" are less clear (Emirybayer and Mische 1998). Several scholars offer very different definitions of agency that produce a lack of consensus among researchers on how to measure this concept. For instance, Bottoms et al. (2004, p. 376) defines agency as "choices . . . taken within specific social contexts," whereas Paternoster and Pogarsky (2009, p. 111) describe agency as an "intentional activity directed toward some goal" (see Healy 2013 for further review). Given these different conceptualizations, we are left with a lack of clarity on whether any of these definitions actually encapsulate the "missing link" in desistance research or can be operationalized without succumbing to post hoc interpretation. Without proper guidance, empirical evaluations that seek to incorporate human agency may also largely be based on previous research efforts or the availability of particular measures in the data. Similar criticisms of this approach have been levied by Farnworth, Thornberry, Krohn, and Lizotte's (1994) discussion of measurement issues of the relationship between social class and delinquency. In particular, they argue that, if scholars seek to test theory, "[i]nadequate measures may lead to research-based rejection of theories, despite the fact that theory falsification is only as valid as the indicators used to represent key concepts" (Farnworth, Krohn, and Lizotte 1994, p. 34).

Given the current state of agency and its use in empirical work, we would like to offer commentary on the future of agency in the field of criminology. First, as referenced above, agency has not been well defined and is filled with ambiguity. Right now agency has become in many ways all things to all people, reminiscent of what happened to the term social capital a decade or so ago. Of course, people have agency to choose, but we are not convinced that all the attempts to examine agency have borne much fruit or yielded clear support for any one theory over another. Second, when the focus is on what starts inside one's head, in our view, the subsequent theory cannot be fully tested. Recall that Hirschi (1969) dismissed the "internalization of norms" in *Causes of Delinquency* and turned to Durkheim to argue for the idea that it was in the relationship that attachment existed (i.e., the external tie). Third, even if we can define and measure agency with validity, as a concept it makes no sense absent a full understanding of the context within which decisions or choices are made.

In sum, based on the accumulation of available evidence, it is our contention that behavioral change is most likely to occur when external changes precede internal changes. In this view, agency is contingent on the situation/context/structure, a view we believe that is consistent with research emerging from the field of behavioral economics.

IV. Contemporary Desistance

Criminological research has struggled to situate data into historical context and consequently has limited our understanding of how lives develop in time and space. Such an approach reflects what Dannefer (1984) terms the "ontogenetic" model, which assumes a maturational unfolding irrespective of socio-historical context. Sampson and Laub's (1993) analysis of the Glueck data explicitly brings in the surrounding context of the Glueck men to recognize that "[s]ocial facts are located" in a bounded historical and spatial context (Abbott 1997, p. 1152). The Glueck data and the historical context in which the data were collected serve as a baseline to identifying consistencies or differences in research findings over time.

The Glueck men grew up during the 1930s and early 1940s in the city of Boston and experienced a specific macro- and micro-level historical context. Drugs, such as crack cocaine, were not as widespread as they are today. Criminal violence, particularly gun violence, was at much lower levels during the Glueck men's lives. The military experiences of some of the Glueck subjects included the last few years of World War II, the stationing of troops in Japan and West Germany, and the Korean War. Such widespread involvement in several wars, growth in the use of the GI Bill of Rights, and use of the draft simply does not exist in today's world. Comparisons of the transition between adolescence and adulthood have also found that there has been a lengthening in the time period with which adolescents developmentally achieve adulthood. Arnett (2000, 2004, 2011) refers to these years as emerging adulthood during which individuals may feel like they are no longer adolescents but have yet to reach adult status. This is driven largely by the fact that traditional markers of adult status (marriage, jobs, children, moving out of the home) occur later in the life course than traditionally experienced in the past.

Although Laub and Sampson (1995b) argue that the "age" of the Glueck data serves as strength to exploit, it is important to consider how current socio-historical contexts shape and alter desistance processes related to notions of age-graded social controls and structurally induced turning points. The following section will discuss two major shifts in today's world that may influence the capacity of men such as those in the Glueck study to desist from crime.

A. Cohabitation and the Decline of Marriage

Recent trends suggest that the nature of marriage is changing in two key ways. First, marriage rates in the United States are at record lows, and this decline in marriage is more pronounced in racial and low-socioeconomic-status communities (Pew Research 2010; Cruz 2013; Wang and Parker 2014). Further, among those who do marry, divorce rates are significantly higher among segments of society with lower income and have remained fairly stable among those with higher levels of income (Bramlett and Mosher 2002). These factors suggest that there is increasing stratification of the experience of marriage, with a noticeable decline in the experience of marriage for communities at higher risk for crime. Still, despite differences in the prevalence of marriage, empirical evidence suggests that minority groups are likely to experience the reductions in offending associated with marriage (e.g., Bersani and DiPetro 2016). These social factors warrant consideration of the role of this transition as it is embedded in the changing socio-macro context of the United States.

Second, there has been growth in the proportion of "first unions" between heterosexual couples that begin as cohabitation. Research suggests that between 2006 and 2010, 48 percent of women cohabitated with men as a first union (Copen, Daniels, and Mosher 2013). This figure has grown significantly since 1995, when only 34 percent of women's first unions was characterized by cohabitation. To be sure, cohabitation is not necessarily replacing marriage but is rather delaying the age at first marriage and contributing to the notion of emerging adulthood and the overall decline in marriage rates (Arnett 2000; Bramlett and Moher 2002).

It is also not yet clear whether or not cohabitation and marriage should be placed on equal ground with respect to desistance. Both forms of relationship carry vastly different legal implications and also possess potentially very different social norms by which behavior and expectations are guided (Bowman 2004; Nock 1995; Waite and Gallagher 2001). These legal and social differences may contribute to the nature and quality of the relationship between individuals. For example, evidence suggests that those individuals cohabitating indicate less-than-desirable relationship satisfaction, stability, and commitment (Nock 1995; Brown and Booth 1996; Forste and Tanfer 1996; Hansen, Moum and Shapiro 2007). Thus, the question posed by Laub and Sampson (2003) of whether the crime-suppression benefits of marriage would translate to those couples who are involved in cohabitation or other arrangements remains an important step for current life-course research to address. Earlier work concludes that cohabitation was a criminogenic experience as it served to increase offending (Horney, Osgood, and Marshall 1995). Yet more recent efforts to assess this "new normal" of first unions between couples offers mixed evidence for the role of cohabitation in explaining change in criminal behavior.

As part of Sampson, Laub, and Wimer's (2006) reanalysis of the Glueck data to determine the causal effect of marriage, additional analyses assess the effect of being in a stable relationship not characterized by the arrangement of marriage. Although cohabitation among the Glueck men was relatively rare, cohabitation exhibits a statistically negative relationship with crime even after controlling for marriage. Savolainen (2009) evaluates the core tenets of the theory among a Finnish sample and includes a specific test of the role of cohabitation, particularly due to the high degree of cohabitation in Finland. Perhaps most surprisingly, once cohabitation and marriage are both controlled for, cohabitation is associated with larger reductions in criminal behavior than getting married. Savolainen (2009) attributes this finding to the fact that it is customary for partners to cohabitate before marriage; therefore, among a sample of offenders, those who choose to quickly get married may reflect a higher degree of tolerance for criminal behavior and lifestyles choices. Thus, a higher proportion of prosocial mates are among those who are interested in cohabitating as compared to those who choose to marry.

Several other studies present mixed findings with respect to cohabitation. For instance, Duncan, Wilkerson, and England (2006) evaluate whether cohabitation influences behavior in the same manner as marriage or whether it could be characterized as an "incomplete institution" that does not contain the same structure, normative guidance, and commitment as marriage (Cherlin 1978). Utilizing the NLSY 1979, Duncan, Wilkereson, and England (2006) find that cohabitation only appears to reduce binge drinking among women, whereas marriage appears to reduce both male substance use (i.e., binge drinking and marijuana use) and female binge drinking. Similarly using the NLSY, Forrest (2014) attempts to further understand the role of marriage and cohabitation by evaluating whether the effect of these experiences varied by the relationship quality. Regardless of relationship quality, cohabitation leads to a reduction in the number of drug offenses,[7] whereas property crime offenses are only reduced among those couples who are characterized as having a medium-quality relationship. Despite these patterns, marriage is consistently found to be related to reductions in all offense categories and additionally related to the cessation of criminal activity (Forrest 2014). The association between marriage and criminal behavior also varies by strength and quality of the marital relationship (Forrest 2014).

Although much of these findings provide support for the importance of marriage as a turning point in the desistance process, the extent of overlap between the underlying processes triggered by marriage and by cohabitation is unclear. The reality of relationship formation in contemporary society is ahead of theoretical explanations and systematic data collection; however, future work should continue to investigate the current state of marriage and how transitions between being single, cohabitation, marriage, and divorce affect the development of socially integrative bonds that facilitate behavioral change. Further, given evidence of the stratification of marriage, future work should evaluate how such processes emerge among different segments of the population.

B. Collateral Consequences and the Growth in Incarceration

> Conviction of a felony imposes a status upon a person which not only makes him vulnerable to future sanctions through new civil disability statutes, but which also seriously affects his reputation and economic opportunities.
>
> —Chief Justice Warren, *Parker v. Ellis,*
> 362 U.S. 574 (1960)

Over the past few decades, the notion that once an individual serves his or her time their debt to society has been repaid has become a forgotten practice. Collateral consequences include a host of barriers—both legal and social—that occur subsequent to criminal convictions. These consequences include denial of government licenses, welfare benefits, parental rights, the right to vote, housing opportunities, and employment and ineligibility for education programs (Mauer and Chesney-Lind 2002). Although we do not have space to discuss the history of collateral consequences in the context of the United States, several factors are worth mentioning to describe the factor that led to shifts in U.S. crime policy.

Largely since the passage of several legislative reforms in the 1970s and 1980s, both the federal government and states implemented policies that led to the proliferation of collateral sanctions and post-release disqualifications among those convicted of felonies and even misdemeanors (Love 2011). Evaluation of the rehabilitation of prisoners during this time period also led to the conclusion that "nothing works" further justified penalization of offenders (Martinson 1974). The establishment of the "war on drugs" has led to the growth in insurmountable deficits among socially disadvantaged minority communities. These challenges have further been supplemented by specific "invisible punishments" which penalize drug offenders (Travis 2002). Lastly, the nation's welfare system has undergone significant changes through the reduction in individual access to welfare and imposition of time limits to benefits (Travis 2002). Each of these shifts coalesces around adding layers of punishment to involvement with the criminal justice system for segments of the most marginalized and defenseless population in our country. Perhaps most troubling is the net widening impacts these consequences have due to the unparalleled growth in state and federal prison and community supervision populations among these disadvantaged groups (National Research Council 2014). Between 1978 and 2009, the number of prisoners held in both state and federal facilitates increased from roughly 200,000 to 1.5 million (Carson and Golinelli 2013; National Research Council 2014).

Thus, given that most of these individuals who are incarcerated will be released and subsequently faced with barriers to access to health, employment, and housing, to what degree are mechanisms of desistance available to contemporary offenders? To be sure, barriers to desistance likely vary by state, as different state statues govern the reintegrative experiences of offenders. We will briefly discuss how the collateral consequences movement has affected access to structural turning points with a particular emphasis on employment and marriage.

The effects of cumulative disadvantage and mortgaging one's future through engaging in criminal behavior are likely felt hardest when discussing employment. In conjunction with the systematic and more permanent identification of individuals involved with the criminal justice system, increased use of background checks among employers has led to difficult employment prospects for individuals with a criminal record (Albright and Denq 1996; Pager 2003). Further, access to and the cost of maintaining criminal records among the public and private sector has been facilitated by advances in information technology (Solove 2004). The effects of imprisonment on securing employment are also conditioned by race and ethnicity, with the majority of stigmatization being attached to blacks or Hispanics (Pager 2003; Pager et al. 2009). In an interesting methodological approach, Pager (2003) uses matched pairs of white and black job applicants to submit resumes to employers, with the only difference being that one of the members in each pair indicates that they have a criminal record. Pager (2003) finds that employers are less likely to call back black applicants compared to white applicants regardless of whether a white applicant has a criminal record, but the effect of a criminal record is significantly more pronounced among black applicants. Black non-offenders are three times more likely to get a call back from the employer than black ex-offenders, whereas white non-offenders are only two times more likely to get a callback compared to white ex-offenders. Even if an individual with a record manages to get their foot into the door, research finds that employers perceive ex-offenders to be the least desirable applicants largely due to potential liability issues (Holzer, Raphael, and Stoll 2003). Thus, among those most affected by mass incarceration, enormous barriers act to disenfranchise them from access to employment.

Although collateral consequences have not explicitly targeted individuals because they are married, the effects of collateral consequences clearly contribute to the nature of relationship formation among those involved with the criminal justice system. For instance, as the previous section discussed, having a criminal record may preclude an individual from obtaining employment, which may in turn place an individual at a disadvantage for marriage prospects (Western 2004). Research findings have generally supported the relative salience of marriage as a prosocial turning point; however, research on the effects of mass incarceration and marriage have also found that both men who are incarcerated and their potential pool of women in the "marriage market" are less likely to marry and in some cases cohabitate (Western and McLanahan 2004; Charles and Luoh 2010). Even among those who are married, incarcerated men are at higher risk of divorce (Western 2004; Siennick, Stewart, and Staff 2014). Lastly, at least some states allow for a partner to dissolve a marriage due to a spouse's incarceration. It appears that the shifts in American penal policy have triggered an assault on the for-mation of the key social bonds for contemporary offenders. Achieving what Giordano, Cernkovich, and Rudolph (2002) refer to as the "respectability package" of marriage and employment is encumbered by various collateral consequences. The implications of this process are still underexplored, but it is probably fair to conclude that the cur-rent landscape of desistance is likely different than the landscape during the lives of the Glueck men.

V. Conclusion

In a recent review of desistance research, Kazemian (2007) describes several dimensions of criminological approaches to investigating desistance processes. Chief among these are the identification of causal factors underlying the process of desistance, pro-viding a comprehensive view of the entire life course, and exploring within-individual changes in behavior. It is our contention that the work by Sampson and Laub on the age-graded theory of informal social control initiated over 20 years ago encapsulates these dimensions. Through an assessment of perhaps one of the longest studies of crim-inal behavior ever collected, these authors have provided clear guidance on how and why some individuals persist and eventually desist from anti-social behavior. Further, recent methodological advances have allowed Laub and Sampson to not only address between-and-within individual change but further explore the causal relationship of turning points through the use of counterfactual-based analyses. Many other scholars have followed suit and largely with similar results. Challenges certainly remain, such as integrating qualitative and quantitative evaluations of behavior, assessing the under-lying mechanisms and dimensions of turning points, accounting for choice processes, and evaluating age-graded trajectories in a contemporary social landscape. Ultimately, however, the age-graded theory of informal social control offers a guidepost for ana-lytic investigation and potential resolution to these challenges in life-course and devel-opmental criminology.

Notes

1. Search terms included "Life-Course," "Life-Course Criminology," "Desistance," "Trajectories," "Transition/s," "Turning Point/s," "Criminal Career/s" in the title for the ProQuest Criminal Justice Database. This review did not include recent book publications, technical reports, or other types of manuscripts. We thank Katie Kozey for her research as-sistance in gathering these publications.
2. For a full review of the findings from *Crime in the Making* by Sampson and Laub (1993), see Laub, Sampson, and Sweeten (2006).
3. Disclaimer: Two of the authors of this chapter are originators of the theory and thus have an obvious interest in the outcome of any evaluation. All three authors recognize this conflict

and strive to consult independent sources and provide a dispassionate account of the evidence. We also recognize that this problem is endemic to most if not all assessments of the literature because scholars have theoretical commitments that they bring to the task, even if implicit. Fortunately, the ultimate arbiter of a theory is the scholarly field and not any individual scholar.

4. One notable exception is Uggen's (2000) experimental evaluation of the National Right to Work Project that will be discussed in a subsequent section of this chapter.

5. Criticisms offered by scholars on the causal importance of turning points will be discussed in a subsequent section (e.g., Lyngstad and Skardhamar 2013; Skardhamar and Savolainen 2014).

6. It is not at all clear what mechanism would lead to an increase in offending as the result of marriage. It is also possible that the decline in offending prior to marriage was the result of cohabitation. It is also not clear why "individual-level visceral factors such as proneness to addictions and temperament" would only be applicable in the post-marriage period (Lyngstad and Skardhamar 2013, p. 613). Finally, the failure to control for age looms large here.

7. Forrest (2014) acknowledges that these associations are not significant at conventional levels.

REFERENCES

Abbott, Andrew. 1997. "Of Time and Space: The Contemporary Relevance of the Chicago School." *Social Forces* 75(4): 1149–1182.

Albright, Shelley, and Furjen Denq. 1996. "Employer Attitudes Toward Hiring Ex-Offenders." *The Prison Journal* 76(2): 118–137.

Angrist, Joshua. 1990. "Lifetime Earnings and the Vietnam Era Draft Lottery: Evidence from Social Security Administrative Records." *American Economic Review* 80(3): 313–336.

Arnett, Jeffrey J. 2000. "Emerging Adulthood: A Theory of Development from the Late Teens Through the Twenties." *American Psychologist* 55(5): 469–480.

Arnett, Jeffrey J. 2004. *Emerging Adulthood: The Winding Road from Late Teens Through the Twenties.* New York: Oxford University Press.

Arnett, Jeffrey. 2011. "Emerging Adulthood(s): The Cultural Psychology of a New Life Stage." In *Bridging Cultural and Developmental Approaches to Psychology, New Syntheses in Theory, Research, and Policy*, edited by Lene Arnett Jensen, 255–275. New York: Oxford University Press.

Barnes, J. C., Kristin Golden, Christina Mancini, Brian B. Boutwell, Kevin M. Beaver, and Brie Diamond. 2014. "Marriage and Involvement in Crime: A Consideration of Reciprocal Effects in a Nationally Representative Sample." *Justice Quarterly* 31(2): 229–256.

Beaver, Kevin M., John Paul Wright, Matt DeLisi, and Michael G. Vaughn. 2008. "Desistance from Delinquency: The Marriage Effect Revisited and Extended." *Social Science Research* 37(3): 736–752.

Becker, Howard. 1960. "Notes on the Concept of Commitment." *American Journal of Sociology* 66(1): 32–40.

Bersani, Bianca E., John H. Laub, and Paul Nieuwbeerta. 2009. "Marriage and Desistance from Crime in the Netherlands: Do Gender and Socio-Historical Context Matter?" *Journal of Quantitative Criminology* 25(1): 3–24.

Bersani, Bianca E., and Elaine Eggleston Doherty. 2013. "When the Ties That Bind Unwind: Examining the Enduring and Situational Processes of Change Behind the Marriage Effect." *Criminology* 51(2): 399–433.

Bersani, Bianca E., and Stephanie M. DiPetro. 2016. "Examining the Salience of Marriage to Offending for Black and Hispanic Men." *Justice Quarterly* 33(3): 510–537.

Blokland, Arjan A. J., and Paul Nieuwbeerta. 2005. "The Effects of Life Circumstances on Longitudinal Trajectories of Offending." *Criminology* 43(4): 1203–1240.

Bottoms, Anthony, Joanna Shapland, Andrew Costello, Deborah Holmes, and Grant Muir. 2004. "Towards Desistance: Theoretical Underpinnings for an Empirical Study." *The Howard Journal* 43(4): 368–389.

Bouffard, Leana Allen. 2003. "Examining the Relationship Between Military Service and Criminal Behavior During the Vietnam Era: A Research Note." *Criminology* 41(2): 491–510.

Bouffard, Leana Allen. 2005. "The Military as a 'Bridging Environment': Differential Outcomes of the Military Experience." *Armed Forces and Society* 31(2): 273–295.

Bouffard, Leana Allen. 2014. "Period Effects in the Impact of Vietnam-Era Military Service on Crime over the Life Course." *Crime and Delinquency* 60(6): 859–883.

Bouffard, Leana Allen, and John H. Laub. 2004. "Jail or the Army: Does Military Service Facilitate Desistance?" In *After Crime and Punishment: Pathways to Offender Reintegration*, edited by Shadd Maruna and Russ Immarigeon, 129–151. Portland, OR: Willian.

Bowman, Cynthia Grant. 2004. "Legal Treatment of Cohabitation in the United States." *Law and Policy* 26(1): 119–151.

Bramlett, Matthew D., and William D. Mosher. 2002. "Cohabitation, Marriage, Divorce, and Remarriage in the United States." *National Center for Health Statistics. Vital Health Stat* 23(22): 1–32.

Brown, Susan L., and Alan Booth. 1996. "Cohabitation Versus Marriage: A Comparison of Relationship Quality." *Journal of Marriage and the Family* 58(3): 668–678.

Browning, Harley L., Sally C. Lopreato, and Dudley L. Poston. 1973. "Income and Veteran Status: Variations Among Mexican Americans, Blacks, and Anglos." *American Sociological Review* 38(1): 219–226.

Burt, S. Alexandra, M. Brent Donnellan, Mikhila N. Humbad, Brian M. Hicks, Matt McGue, and William G. Iacono. 2010. "Does Marriage Inhibit Antisocial Behavior: An Examination of Selection vs Causation via a Longitudinal Twin Design." *Archive of General Psychiatry* 67(12): 1309–1315.

Carson, Ann E., and Daniela Golinelli. 2013. *Prisoners in 2012: Trends in Admissions and Releases, 1991–2012.* Washington, DC: Bureau of Justice Statistics, U.S. Department of Justice.

Charles, Kerwin and Ming Luoh. 2010. "Male Incarceration, the Marriage Market, and Female Outcomes." *The Review of Economics and Statistics* 92(3): 614–627.

Cherlin, Andrew. 1978. "Remarriage as an Incomplete Institution." *American Journal of Sociology* 84(3): 634–650.

Cohen, Jere, Rebecca L. Warner, and David R. Segal. 1995. "Military Service and Educational Attainment in the All-Volunteer Force." *Social Science Quarterly* 76(1): 88–104.

Copen, Casey E., Kimberly Daniels, and William D. Mosher. 2013. "First Premarital Cohabitation in the United States: 2006–2010 National Survey of Family Growth." *National Health Statistics Report.* Washington, DC: National Center for Health Statistics, U.S. Department of Health and Human Services.

Cruz, Julissa. 2013. *Marriage: More Than a Century of Change.* Bowling Green, OH: National Center for Family and Marriage Research.

Dannefer, Dale. 1984. "The Role of the Social in Life-Span Developmental Psychology, Past and Future: Rejoinder to Baltes and Nesselroade." *American Sociological Review* 49(6): 847–850.

Duncan, Greg J., Bessie Wilkerson, and Paula England. 2006. "Cleaning Up Their Act: The Effects of Marriage and Cohabitation on Licit and Illicit Drug Use." *Demography* 43(4): 691–710.

Elder, Glen H., Jr. 1975. "Age Differentiation and the Life Course." *Annual Review of Sociology* 1(1): 65–190.

Elder, Glen H., Jr. 1985. "Perspectives on the Life Course." In *Life Course Dynamics*, edited by G. H. Elder Jr. Ithaca, NY: Cornell University Press.

Elder, Glen H., Jr. 1999. *Children of the Great Depression: Social Changes in Life Experience*. Boulder, CO: Westview.

Emirbayer, Mustafa. 1997. "Manifesto for a Relational Sociology." *American Journal of Sociology* 103(2): 281–317.

Emirbayer, Mustafa, and Ann Mische. 1998. "What Is Agency?" *American Journal of Sociology* 103(4): 962–1023.

Ezell, Michael, and Lawrence E. Cohen. 2005. *Desisting from Crime: Continuity and Change in Long-Term Crime Patterns of Serious Chronic Offenders*. Oxford: Oxford University Press.

Farnworth, Margaret, Terence P. Thornberry, Marvin D. Krohn, and Alan J. Lizotte. 1994. "Measurement in the Study of Class and Delinquency: Integrating Theory and Research." *Journal of Research in Crime and Delinquency* 31(1): 32–61.

Farrall, Stephen. 2005. "On the Existential Aspects of Desistance from Crime." *Symbolic Interaction* 28(3): 367–386.

Farrington, David P., and Donald J. West. 1995. "Effects of Marriage, Separation, and Children on Offending by Adult Males." In *Current Perspectives on Aging and the Life Cycle*. Vol. 4: *Delinquency and Disrepute in the Life Course*, edited by Zena Blau Smith and John Hagan, 249–281. Greenwich, CT: JAI Press.

Forrest, Walter. 2014. "Cohabitation, Relationship Quality, and Desistance from Crime." *Journal of Marriage and Family* 76(3): 539–556.

Forste, Renata, and Koray Tanfer. 1996. "Sexual Exclusivity Among Dating, Cohabitating, and Married Women." *Journal of Marriage and the Family* 58(1): 33–47.

Giordano, Peggy C., Stephen A. Cernkovich, and Jennifer L. Rudolph. 2002. "Gender, Crime, and Desistance: Toward a Theory of Cognitive Transformation." *American Journal of Sociology* 107(4): 990–1064.

Gottfredson, Michael R., and Travis Hirschi. 1990. *A General Theory of Crime*. Stanford, CA: Stanford University Press.

Graham, John, and Benjamin Bowling. 1995. *Young People and Crime*. Research Study 145. London: Home Office.

Hansen, Thomas, Torbørn Moum, and Adam Shapiro. 2007. "Relational and Individual Well-Being Among Cohabitors and Married Individuals in Midlife: Recent Trends from Norway." *Journal of Family Issues* 28(7): 910–933.

Harris, Kathleen M., Hedwig Lee, and Felicia Yang DeLeone. 2010. "Marriage and Health in the Transition to Adulthood: Evidence for African Americans in Add Health." *Journal of Family Issues* 31(8): 1106–1143.

Healy, Dierdre. 2013. "Changing Fate? Agency and the Desistance Process." *Theoretical Criminology* 17(4): 557–574.

Hirschi, Travis. 1969. *Causes of Delinquency*. Berkeley: University of California Press.

Hirschi, Travis, and Michael Gottfredson. 1983. "Age and the Explanation of Crime." *The American Journal of Sociology* 89(3): 552–584.

Holzer, Harry J., Steven Raphael, and Michael A. Stoll. 2003. *Employment Barriers Facing Ex-Offenders*. Washington, DC: The Urban Institute.

Horney, Julie D., Wayne Osgood, and Ineke Haen Marshall. 1995. "Criminal Careers in the Short Term: Intra-individual Variability in Crime and Its Relation to Local Life Circumstances." *American Sociological Review* 60(5): 655–673.

Janowitz, Morris. 1978. *The Last Half-Century: Societal Change and Politics in America.* Chicago: University of Chicago Press.

Kahneman, Daniel. 2011. *Thinking Fast and Slow*. New York: Farrar, Straus and Giroux.

Katz, Jack. 1988. *Seductions of Crime*. New York: Basic Books.

Kazemian, Lila. 2007. "Desistance from Crime: Theoretical, Empirical, Methodological, and Policy Considerations." *Journal of Contemporary Criminal Justice* 23(1): 5–27.

King, Ryan D., Michael Massoglia, and Ross MacMillan. 2007. "The Context of Marriage and Crime: Gender, the Propensity to Marry, and Offending in Early Adulthood." *Criminology* 45(1): 33–65.

Kirk, David S. 2009. "A Natural Experiment on Residential Change and Recidivism: Lessons from Hurricane Katrina." *American Sociological Review* 74(3): 484–505.

Kirk, David S. 2012. "Residential Change as a Turning Point in the Life Course of Crime: Desistance or Temporary Cessation?" *Criminology* 50(2): 329–358.

Laub, John H. 2006. "Edwin H. Sutherland and the Michael-Adler Report: Searching for the Soul of Criminology Seventy Years Later." *Criminology* 44(2): 235–258.

Laub, John H., and Robert J. Sampson. 2003. *Shared Beginnings, Divergent Lives: Delinquent Boys to Age 70*. Cambridge, MA: Harvard University Press.

Laub, John H., and Robert J. Sampson. 1995b. "Crime and Context in the Lives of 1,000 Boston Men, Circa 1925–1955." In *Current Perspectives on Aging and the Life Cycle: Delinquency and Disrepute in the Life Course: 1995*, edited by Zena Smith Blau and John Hagan, 119–139. Greenwich, CT: JAI Press.

Laub, John H., Daniel Nagin, and Robert J. Sampson. 1998. "Trajectories of Change in Criminal Offending: Good Marriages and the Desistance Process." *American Sociological Review* 63(2): 225–238.

Laub, John H., Robert J. Sampson, and Gary A. Sweeten. 2006. "Assessing Sampson and Laub's Life-Course Theory of Crime." In *Taking Stock*, edited by Francis T. Cullen, John Paul Wright, and Kristie R. Belvins, 313–333. New Brunswick, NJ: Transaction.

LeBel, Thomas P., Ros Burnett, Shadd Maruna, and Shawn Bushway. 2008. "The 'Chicken and Egg' of Subjective and Social Factors in Desistance from Crime." *European Journal of Criminology* 5(2): 131–159.

Love, Margaret Colgate. 2011. "Paying their Debt to Society: Forgiveness, Redemption, and the Uniform Collateral Consequences of Conviction Act." *Howard Law Journal* 54(3): 753–793.

Lyngstad, Torkild H., and Torbørn Skardhamar. 2013. "Changes in Criminal Offending Around the Time of Marriage." *Journal of Research in Crime and Delinquency* 50(4): 608–615.

MacLean, Alair, and Glen H. Elder Jr. 2007. "Military Service in the Life Course." *Annual Review of Sociology* 33: 175–196.

March, James G. 1978. "Bounded Rationality, Ambiguity, and the Engineering of Choice." *Bell Journal of Economics* 9(2): 587–608.

Martinson, Robert. 1974. "What Works? Questions and Answers About Prison Reform." *The Public Interest* 35(2): 22–54.

Maruna, Shadd. 2001. *Making Good: How Ex-Offenders Reform and Reclaim Their Lives.* Washington, DC: American Psychological Association Books.

Mauer, Marc, and Meda Chesney-Lind. 2002. *Invisible Punishment: The Collateral Consequences of Mass Imprisonment*. New York: The New Press.

Mesters, Geert, Victor van der Geest, and Catrien Bijleveld. 2016. "Crime, Employment and Social Welfare: An Individual-Level Study on Disadvantaged Males." *Journal of Quantitative Criminology* 32(2): 159–190.

Moskos, Charles C. 1971. "Armed Forces and American Society: Convergence or Divergence?" In *Public Opinion and the Military Establishment. Sage Research Progress Series*: Vol. 1. *On War, Revolution, and Peacekeeping*, edited by Charles C. Moskos, 271–272. Beverly Hills, CA: Sage.

Mueller, John E. 1971. "Trends in Popular Support for the Wars in Korea and Vietnam." *American Political Science Review* 65(2): 358–375.

National Research Council. 2014. *The Growth of Incarceration in the United States: Exploring Causes and Consequences,* Committee on the Causes and Consequences of High Rates of Incarceration, edited by Jeremy Travis and Bruce Western. Washington, DC: National Academy of Sciences.

Nock, Steven L. 1995. "A Comparison of Marriages and Cohabitating Relationships." *Journal of Family Issues* 16(1): 53–76.

O'Connell, Daniel J. 2003. "Investigating Latent Trait and Life Course Theories as Predictors of Recidivism Among an Offender Sample." *Journal of Criminal Justice* 31(5): 455–467.

Pager, Devah. 2003. "The Mark of a Criminal Record." *American Journal of Sociology* 108(5): 937–975.

Pager, Devah, Bruce Western, and Naomi Sugie. 2009. "Sequencing Disadvantage: Barriers to Employment facing Young Black and White Men with Criminal Records." *Annual American Academy of Political Sciences* 623(1): 195–213.

Parker v. Ellis, 362 U.S. 574, 593–594. 1960. Warren, C.J., dissenting.

Paternoster, Ray, and Shawn D. Bushway. 2004. "Rational Choice, Personal Agency, and Us." Paper presented at the annual meeting of the American Society of Criminology, Nashville, TN.

Paternoster, Raymond, and Shawn D. Bushway. 2009. "Desistance and the 'Feared Self': Toward an Identity Theory of Criminal Desistance." *Journal of Criminal Law and Criminology* 99(4): 1103–1155.

Pew Research Center. 2010. *The Decline of Marriage and Rise of New Families*. Washington, DC: Pew Research Center.

Piquero, Alex R., John M. MacDonald, and Karen F. Parker. 2002. "Race, Local Life Circumstances, and Criminal Activity." *Social Sciences Quarterly* 83(3): 654–670.

Rutter, Michael. 1996. "Transitions and Turning Points in Developmental Psychopathology: As Applied to the Age Span between Childhood and Mid-adulthood." *International Journal of Behavioral Development* 19(3): 603–626.

Sampson, Robert J. 2010. "Gold Standard Myths: Observations on the Experimental Turn in Quantitative Criminology." *Journal of Quantitative Criminology* 46(4): 489–500.

Sampson, Robert J., and John H. Laub. 1993. *Crime in the Making: Pathways and Turning Points Through Life*. Cambridge, MA: Harvard University Press.

Sampson, Robert J., and John H. Laub. 1995a. "Understanding Variability in Lives Through Time: Contributions of Life-Course Criminology." *Studies on Crime and Crime Prevention* 4(2): 143–158.

Sampson, Robert J., and John H. Laub. 1996. "Socioeconomic Achievement in the Life Course of Disadvantaged Men: Military Service as a Turning Point, Circa 1940–1965." *American Sociological Review* 61(3): 347–367.

Sampson, Robert J., John H. Laub, and Christopher Wimer. 2006. "Does Marriage Reduce Crime? A Counterfactual Approach to Within-Individual Causal Effects." *Criminology* 44(3): 465–508.

Savolainen, Jukka. 2009. "Work, Family, and Criminal Desistance: Adult Social Bonds in a Nordic Welfare State." *The British Journal of Criminology* 49(3): 285–304.

Scott, Wilbur J. 2004. *Vietnam Veterans Since the War: The Politics of PTSD, Agent Orange, and the National Memorial.* Norman: University of Oklahoma Press.

Shannon, Lyle W. 1994. "Juvenile Delinquency and Adult Crime, 1948–1977 [Racine, Wisconsin]: Three Birth Cohorts." Conducted by University of Iowa, Iowa Urban Community Research Center. 2nd ICPSR Ed. Ann Arbor, MI: Inter-university Consortium for Political and Social Research.

Sharkey, Patrick, and Robert J. Sampson. 2010. "Destination Effects: Residential Mobility and Trajectories of Adolescent Violence in Stratified Metropolis." *Criminology* 48(3): 639–681.

Sherman, Lawrence W. 1993. "Defiance, Deterrence, and Irrelevance: A Theory of the Criminal Sanction." *Crime and Delinquency* 30(4): 445–473.

Shover, Neal. 1996. *Great Pretenders: Pursuits and Careers of Persistent Thieves.* Boulder, CO: Westview Press.

Siennick, Sonja E., Eric A. Stewart, and Jeremy Staff. 2014. "Explaining the Association Between Incarceration and Divorce." *Criminology* 52(3): 371–398.

Skardhamar, Torbørn, and Jukka Savolainen. 2014. "Changes in Criminal Offending Around the Time of Job Entry: A Study of Employment and Desistance." *Criminology* 52(2): 263–291.

Skardhamar, Torbørn, Jukka Savolainen, Kjersti N. Aase, and Torkild H. Lyngstad. 2015. "Does Marriage Reduce Crime?" *Crime and Justice* 44(1): 385–446.

Solove, Daniel J. 2004. *The Digital Person: Technology and Privacy in the Information Age.* New York: NYU Press.

Sunstein, Cass R., and Richard Thaler. 2008. *Nudge: Improving Decisions About Health, Wealth, and Happiness.* New Haven, CT: Yale University Press.

Theobald, Delphine, and David P. Farrington. 2009. "Effects of Getting Married on Offending Results from a Prospective Longitudinal Survey of Males." *European Journal of Criminology* 6(6): 496–516.

Theobald, Delphine, and David P. Farrington. 2011. "Why Do the Crime-Reducing Effects of Marriage on Offending Vary with Age?" *British Journal of Criminology* 51(1): 136–158.

Tittle, Charles R., and Harold G. Grasmick. 1997. "Criminal Behavior and Age: A Test of Three Provocative Hypotheses." *Journal of Criminal Law and Criminology* 88(1): 309–342.

Travis, Jeremy. 2002. "Invisible Punishment: An Instrument of Social Exclusion." In *Invisible Punishment: The Collateral Consequences of Mass Imprisonment*, edited by Marc Mauer and Meda Chesney-Lind. New York: The New Press.

Tripodi, Stephen J., Johnny S. Kim, and Kimberly Bender. 2010. "Is Employment Associated with Reduced Recidivism? The Complex Relationship Between Employment and Crime." *International Journal of Offender Therapy and Comparative Criminology* 54(5): 706–720.

Uggen, Christopher, and Sara Wakefield. 2008. "What Have We Learned from Longitudinal Studies of Work and Crime?" In *The Long View of Crime: A Synthesis of Longitudinal Research*, edited by Akiva M. Liberman, 191–219. New York: Springer.

Uggen, Christopher. 2000. "Work as a Turning Point in the Life Course of Criminals: A Duration Model of Age, Employment, and Recidivism." *American Sociological Review* 65(4): 529–546.

Verbruggen, Janna, Arjan A. J. Blokland, and Victor R. van der Geest. 2012. "Effects of Employment and Unemployment on Serious Offending in a High-Risk Sample of Men and Women from Ages 18 to 32 in the Netherlands." *The British Journal of Criminology* 52(5): 845–869.

Wadsworth, Tim. 2006. "The Meaning of Work: Conceptualizing the Deterrent Effect of Employment on Crime Among Young Adults." *Sociological Perspectives* 49(3): 343–368.

Waite, Linda J., and Maggie Gallagher. 2001. *The Case for Marriage: Why Married People Are Happier, Healthier, and Better off Financially.* New York: Broadway Books.

Wang, Wendy, and Kim Parker. 2014. "Record Share of Americans Have Never Married: As Values, Economics and Gender Patterns Change." Washington, DC: Pew Research Center's Social and Demographic Trends Project.

Western, Bruce, and Sara McLanahan. 2000. "Fathers Behind Bars: The Impact of Incarceration on Family Formation." *Contemporary Perspectives in Family Research* 2: 309–324.

Western, Bruce. 2004. "Incarceration, Marriage, and Family Life." Unpublished manuscript. Princeton University, Department of Sociology.

Wolfgang, Marvin E., Robert M. Figlio, and Thorsten Sellin. 1994. "Delinquency in a Birth Cohort in Philadelphia, Pennsylvania, 1945–1963." Conducted by University of Pennsylvania, Wharton School. 3rd ICPSR ed. Ann Arbor, MI: Inter-university Consortium for Political and Social Research.

Wright, John Paul, David E. Carter, and Francis T. Cullen. 2005. "A Life Course Analysis of Military Service in Vietnam." *Journal of Research in Crime and Delinquency* 42(1): 55–83.

SECTION IV

DEVELOPMENTAL CORRELATES AND RISK/PROTECTIVE FACTORS

CHAPTER 17

....

BIOSOCIAL INFLUENCES
ON OFFENDING ACROSS
THE LIFE COURSE

....

OLIVIA CHOY, JILL PORTNOY, ADRIAN RAINE,
RHEANNA J. REMMEL, ROBERT SCHUG,
CATHERINE TUVBLAD, AND YALING YANG

SINCE the late 20th century, the field of criminology has become increasingly aware of the contributions of biological sciences. Through longitudinal studies and research on different age groups, the role of biological factors in offending has been examined in a developmental context. Findings document that biological factors are associated with offending across the life span, although the strength of the associations may differ across development and between types of offenders. It is proposed that incorporating such factors into future developmental and life-course research and theories can lead to a better understanding of the etiology of offending.

In this chapter, major biological and biosocial findings in relation to the development of offending are presented. Offending is referred to as not only the violation of legal codes but also the broader spectrum of antisocial behavior. Section I reviews empirical findings on the association between two psychophysiological factors, heart rate and skin conductance, and offending. Section II discusses the heritability of antisocial behavior and the contribution of genetics to the understanding of developmental trajectories, stability, and change in offending. Section III describes structural and functional brain abnormalities in antisocial individuals across different age groups. Section IV covers research on hormones and neurotransmitters. It examines the role of cortisol, testosterone, serotonin, and dopamine on offending. Section V highlights the applications of neuropsychology in the understanding of offending across the life span, particularly in the domains of verbal and spatial intelligence and executive functioning. Section VI reviews research on pre- and perinatal factors related to later offending, including prenatal alcohol, nicotine, and lead exposure, minor physical anomalies, and birth complications. Each of the six sections aims to address issues important to the developmental and life-course criminological literature including whether the biological factor is consistently associated with offending throughout the life course and whether persistent offenders differ from other offenders in terms of biological influences. Section VII concludes with potential areas for future research.

I. Psychophysiology

Psychophysiology is the study of cognition, behavior, and emotions as revealed through bodily events (Hugdahl 2001). Heart rate and skin conductance are psychophysiological measures that have been frequently examined in relation to offending.

A. Heart Rate

Heart rate is controlled by both the parasympathetic and sympathetic branches of the autonomic nervous system. A meta-analysis concluded that low resting heart rate is likely the best-replicated correlate of antisocial behavior in children and adolescents (Ortiz and Raine 2004). Although more commonly examined in youths, low resting heart rate is also a risk factor for antisocial behavior in adults (Lorber 2004; Armstrong et al. 2009; Portnoy and Farrington 2015), making low resting heart rate a biological risk factor for offending across the life course.

Importantly, low resting heart rate has been found to predict future levels of antisocial behavior in prospective longitudinal research (Farrington 1997; Raine, Venables, and Mednick 1997; Sijtsema et al. 2010; Jennings, Piquero, and Farrington 2013). One study found that low resting heart rate as young as at age 3 years predicted aggression at age 11 years (Raine et al., 1997). Findings from the Cambridge Study in Delinquent Development showed that low resting heart rate at age 18 years predicted offending up to age 50 years independent of covariates including smoking, sports participation, impulsivity, binge drinking, body mass index, and early childhood individual and environment risk factors (Jennings et al. 2013). This study demonstrated for the first time that the predictive utility of low resting heart rate could extend into late adulthood.

It has also been found that low resting heart rate is only important in explaining initial levels rather than change in antisocial behavior over time. Baker et al. (2009) found that children with low resting heart rate at age 9 years were significantly more antisocial overall, but the reduction in antisocial behavior with age as the children entered early adolescence was not associated with heart rate. This suggests that low heart rate is a fixed, static neurobiological risk factor for antisocial behavior that does not predict desistance from offending throughout early adolescence.

Several theoretical explanations have been proposed to explain the relationship between resting heart rate and antisocial behavior. According to stimulation-seeking theory, low autonomic nervous system arousal is an unpleasant physiological state, leading those with low resting heart rates to seek stimulating behaviors, including antisocial behaviors, in order to increase their level of physiological arousal to a more optimal level (Quay 1965; Raine 2002a). An alternative theory argues that low resting heart rate may reflect a relative lack of fear, which could predispose some individuals to commit antisocial acts that require a degree of fearlessness to complete. Low heart rate could also impede early childhood fear conditioning to socializing punishments (Raine 1993, 2002a). While support for these two theories has been broadly found (Latvala et al. 2015), recent studies documented that stimulation seeking, but not fearlessness, mediated the relationship between low heart rate and antisocial behavior (Sijtsema et al. 2010; Portnoy et al. 2014). Thus, a stimulation-seeking mechanism may be more likely to underlie this relationship.

B. Skin Conductance

Skin conductance is an index of sympathetic nervous system activity that can be measured at rest or during laboratory tasks. Reduced skin conductance reactivity during fear conditioning paradigms has been associated with psychopathy (Birbaumer et al. 2005) and antisocial behavior, particularly persistent proactive aggression (Gao et al. 2015). Conditioning during childhood is thought to be central to socialization and conscience development. It has been suggested that the failure to condition could be a factor that predisposes some individuals to offend later in life (Eysenck 1977). Findings for skin conductance measured at rest tend to be less consistent. A meta-analysis found that low resting skin conductance was significantly associated with higher levels of psychopathy in adults and conduct problems in children, but not aggression or conduct problems in adolescence (Lorber 2004).

Like heart rate, reduced skin conductance has been documented to predict future levels of antisocial behavior. One study found that reduced skin conductance arousal at age 15 years predicted criminal behavior at age 24 years (Raine, Venables, and Williams 1990). Reduced skin conductance fear conditioning as early as age 3 years has been found to predict offending at age 23 years (Gao et al. 2010). These findings suggest that childhood and adolescent skin conductance can help to explain future levels of criminal behavior.

C. Biosocial Interactions Involving Psychophysiology

Some studies have found that low resting heart rate combined with high social risk increases the likelihood of antisocial behavior (Raine et al. 2014). Similarly, skin conductance has been found to interact with social adversity to predict antisocial behavior, though patterns of interaction are not always consistent, with high skin conductance serving as a risk factor for antisocial behavior among children at high social risk in several studies (e.g., Cummings et al. 2007). In general, psychophysiological studies suggest a reduced pattern of autonomic arousal across the life course in antisocial individuals, although results may be partly dependent on the individual's social context.

II. GENETICS

Compelling evidence from behavioral genetic research, which broadly includes twin, adoption, and family studies, shows that heritable influences also contribute to the development of offending. A review on 19 twin and adoption studies between ages 1 and 18 years found that heritability explained 65 percent and 48 percent of the variance in aggressive behavior and delinquent/rule-breaking behavior, respectively (Burt 2009). Additionally, summarizing results from 51 twin and adoption studies in children, adolescents, and adults, Rhee and Waldman (2002) found that genetic factors explained 41 percent of the variance in antisocial behavior. Given findings on the heritability of offending, molecular genetic research has identified candidate genes for offending. Lower monoamine oxidase A (MAOA) gene activity has been associated with violent behaviors and offending over the life course (e.g., Beaver et al. 2013). Other genes suggested to be associated with child and adult antisocial behavior include the catechol-O-methyltransferase (COMT) gene (Volavka, Bilder, and Nolan 2004; Hirata et al. 2013), the vasopressin receptor 1B (Zai et al. 2012) gene, the oxytocin receptor (OXTR) gene (Malik et al. 2012), the human dopamine transporter (DAT1) gene (Guo, Roettger, and Shih 2007), the D2 receptor polymorphism (DRD2) gene, and the D4 receptor polymorphism (DRD4) gene (Beaver et al. 2007; Boutwell et al. 2014).

Reviews have also found that aggressive and delinquent/rule-breaking behavior exhibit different etiological patterns across age (Burt 2009). Genetic influences on aggressive behavior increased across development, while shared environmental factors decreased. In contrast, delinquent/rule-breaking behavior showed a decrease in genetic influences across development, while shared environmental influences remained stable. The results show that aggressive behavior is primarily influenced by genetic factors, while delinquent/rule-breaking behavior is influenced by both genetic and shared environmental factors.

Since 2003, several studies have examined the genetic and environmental influences on psychopathic personality in children, adolescents, and adults (e.g., Viding et al. 2005; Viding, Frick, and Plomin 2007; Brook et al. 2010; Bezdjian et al. 2011; Hicks et al. 2012). According to the average twin correlations across these studies, the heritability of psychopathic personality in males is approximately 64 percent. For females, the heritability of psychopathic personality is approximately 48 percent (Tuvblad 2013). A longitudinal study reported that 58 percent and 62 percent of the stable variance in two features of psychopathic personality, fearless dominance and impulsive antisociality, respectively, from ages 17 to 24 years were explained by genetic factors (Blonigen et al. 2006; Tellegen and Waller 2008).

With regards to different developmental trajectories for offending, twin studies have shown that genetic influences are more important for stable-high/childhood-onset than for increasing/transitory antisocial behavior (e.g., Taylor, Iacono, and McGue 2000; Tuvblad et al. 2011). For example, in one study, genetic influences contributed more strongly to early-onset rather than late-onset delinquent behavior in 11-year-old boys (Taylor et al. 2000).

Longitudinal twin studies have also examined the contribution of genetics to stability in antisocial behavior. One study that measured antisocial behavior from ages 8 to 20 years showed that the stability of antisocial behavior was explained by a common latent antisocial behavior factor, for which genetics accounted for 67 percent of the variance (Tuvblad et al. 2011).

Other twin studies have examined the genetic contribution to change in antisocial behavior. This line of research has generally reported that change or "new" variance in antisocial behavior is primarily due to non-shared environmental factors (e.g., Haberstick et al. 2006). Analysis of three waves of data from the Minnesota Twin and Family Study showed that while genetic influences were to a large extent responsible for the initial level of antisocial personality disorder symptoms, non-shared environmental influences were largely responsible for change (Burt et al. 2007).

A. Biosocial Interactions Involving Genetic Factors

As in molecular genetic studies, such as that by Caspi et al. (2002), which found that childhood maltreatment led to violence in adulthood among individuals with low levels of MAOA expression, behavioral genetic studies have generated a large number of gene–environment interaction (G×E) studies (for a review, see Dick 2011). Specifically, social factors such as family dysfunction, family warmth, high paternal punitive discipline, parental monitoring, religiosity, regional residency, and socioeconomic status have been found to moderate the genetic and environmental influences on antisocial behavior (Koopmans et al. 1999; Rowe, Almeida, and Jacobson 1999; Rose et al. 2001; Button et al. 2005; Tuvblad, Grann, and Lichtenstein 2006; Dick et al. 2007; Button et al. 2008; Middeldorp et al. 2014). Some studies have found higher heritability of antisocial behavior in individuals with low rather than high levels of social risk (Button et al. 2005), while others document that genetic influences contributed more to antisocial behavior when social risk was present (Dick et al. 2007).

III. Brain Imaging

Regarding structural abnormalities associated with offending, studies have largely focused on regions involved in decision-making (e.g., prefrontal cortex), emotion regulation (e.g., amygdala, hippocampus), and reward-processing (e.g., striatum). One of the first structural brain imaging studies of antisocial adults documented an 11 percent reduction in gray matter volume in the prefrontal cortex of men with antisocial personality disorder compared to normal controls and a psychiatric control group (Raine et al. 2000). Yang et al. (2005, 2009, 2010a) found reduced gray matter volume and thickness in the middle frontal and orbitofrontal cortex and reduced volume and surface deformations in the amygdala in psychopaths with prior convictions (i.e., unsuccessful psychopaths) compared to psychopaths without convictions (i.e., successful psychopaths) and non-psychopathic controls. More recently, violent offenders were shown to have abnormal hippocampal structure compared to non-violent controls (Boccardi et al. 2010; Yang et al. 2010b). These frontal and limbic deficits were similarly found in a large sample of nearly 300 incarcerated criminal offenders (Ermer et al. 2012). Using vivo diffusion tensor magnetic resonance imaging tractography, Craig et al. (2009) further showed impaired amygdala-orbitofrontal connections in psychopaths with convictions. However, findings for the striatum are not conclusive, as some studies have documented enlarged putamen, nucleus accumbens, and caudate (Schiffer et al. 2011), while others showed smaller nucleus accumbens in offenders (Boccardi et al. 2013).

In addition to structural imaging research, functional imaging studies have presented evidence for impaired brain functioning in criminal offenders, especially in the prefrontal and temporal cortex. A meta-analysis by Yang and Raine (2009) of 43 studies revealed that increased antisocial behavior was associated with reduced prefrontal structure and function, particularly in the right orbitofrontal, left dorsolateral prefrontal, and right anterior cingulate cortex. Employing a neurocognitive task, the non-verbal Stroop task, Schiffer et al. (2014) found reduced function in the anterior cingulate, dorsolateral prefrontal, superior temporal, putamen, and amygdala in violent offenders with antisocial personality disorder compared to non-offenders. One recent study using resting-state functional magnetic resonance imaging (fMRI) also revealed reduced activity, measured by the amplitude of low-frequency fluctuation, in the right orbitofrontal cortex as well as the left temporal pole, right inferior temporal gyrus, and left cerebellum in these offenders with antisocial personality disorder (Liu et al. 2014). In line with these findings, Ly et al. (2012) found thinner cortices in the right inferior frontal cortex, anterior temporal cortex, and anterior cingulate cortex, which also corresponded to reduced functional connectivity between the left insula and left dorsal anterior cingulate cortex in psychopathic compared to non-psychopathic criminal offenders.

Recently, in a longitudinal study, males with lower amygdala volumes at age 26 years were found to exhibit increased aggression, violence, and psychopathic traits at a 3-year follow-up (Pardini et al. 2014). Similarly, in a study on adult male offenders, lower anterior cingulate activity was associated with a greater likelihood of rearrest (Aharoni et al. 2013). These findings suggest that brain deficits can predict later offending.

Consistent with research on adult offenders, studies of delinquent children and adolescents have revealed abnormal brain structures and function. For example, in a sample of female adolescents with conduct disorders, aggressive symptoms were negatively correlated with right dorsolateral prefrontal cortex volume, while callous-unemotional traits correlated positively with bilateral orbitofrontal cortex volume (Fairchild et al. 2013). Delinquents with high psychopathy scores also showed higher activity in the anterior cingulate cortex, insula, and amygdala during fear conditioning compared to healthy controls (Cohn et al. 2013). Longitudinally, a thicker temporal cortex was linked to higher rates of change in psychopathy during childhood and adolescence (Yang et al. 2015). Taken together, meta-analyses document that youths with disruptive behavior disorder or conduct problems show consistent functional deficits in the dorsal and rostral anterior cingulate and the medial prefrontal cortex (Alegria, Radua, and Rubia 2016), as well as reduced gray matter volume in the insula, left amygdala, and frontal and temporal regions (Rogers and De Brito 2016). One study documented that limbic structural deficits such as in the amygdala were associated with not only early-onset but also adolescent-onset conduct disorder (Fairchild et al. 2011). However, more recently, evidence has been found for quantitative differences in structural brain organization between childhood-onset and adolescence-onset conduct disorder (Fairchild et al. 2016) and for different growth trajectories of cortical thickness for distinct conduct problem pathways (Oostermeijer et al. 2016).

A. Biosocial Interactions Involving Brain Imaging

Although few brain imaging studies to date have addressed the role of psychosocial risk and protective factors on offending, several studies have begun to address two related issues concerning whether home background moderates the relationship between violence and brain functioning and whether brain deficits combine with psychosocial deficits to predispose one to violence. Regarding the first issue, two studies using brain functioning as the outcome variable have demonstrated a moderating effect of home background, but in opposing directions. In one study, murderers from non-deprived home backgrounds showed a 14.2 percent reduction in functioning of the right orbitofrontal cortex relative to murderers from deprived home backgrounds characterized by abuse, neglect, and marital violence (Raine et al. 1998). It was argued that neurobiological deficits are more pronounced among violent individuals who lack the psychosocial deprivation that normally provides a "social push" toward violence. In contrast, a second fMRI study showed that violent offenders who had been severely abused as children were more likely to show poor temporal lobe functioning compared to violent offenders lacking abuse (Raine et al. 2001).

Turning to the second issue, using violence as an outcome variable, an anatomical magnetic resonance imaging study of individuals with antisocial personality disorder and high psychopathy scores showed that the combination of reduced prefrontal gray volume, low autonomic responsivity, and a set of 10 psychosocial deficits correctly classified 88.5 percent of subjects into antisocial personality disorder or control groups (compared to 73 percent for psychosocial predictors only and 76.9 percent for biological predictors only; Raine et al. 2000). A second structural imaging study on the corpus callosum in psychopaths showed that the combination of psychosocial risk factors with callosal measures accounted for 81.5 percent of the variance (Raine et al. 2003). Structural brain measures accounted for a significant increase in the variance in psychopathic/antisocial behavior over and above psychosocial risk factors in both studies.

IV. Hormones and Neurotransmitters

Compared to brain imaging research, fewer studies have examined the relationship between hormones and offending. Two most frequently studied hormones in relation to antisocial behavior are cortisol and testosterone, regulated by the hypothalamus-pituitary-adrenal (HPA) axis and hypothalamus-pituitary-gonadal (HPG) axis, respectively.

A. Cortisol

Studies in children and adolescents have shown that cortisol may be related to antisocial behavior early in life. One meta-analysis found a mean effect size of $d = -.40$ for the relationship between basal cortisol levels and disruptive behavior or aggressive symptoms in children after study sample sizes were taken into account (van Goozen et al. 2007). The mean effect size for cortisol reactivity in response to a stressor across 4 studies after correcting for sample sizes was $d = .42$. A second meta-analysis on 72 study outcomes found that in preschoolers (aged 0 to 5 years), higher basal cortisol was associated with externalizing behavior ($d = .18$). Low basal cortisol was associated with externalizing behavior ($d = -.28$) in elementary school-aged children (aged 5 to 12 years; Alink et al. 2008). However, no significant association was found between basal cortisol and externalizing behavior in adolescents or between cortisol reactivity to stress and externalizing behaviors. Thus, despite smaller relations in the second meta-analysis, there is some evidence of a significant relationship between basal levels of cortisol and antisocial behavior.

Similar findings were obtained for adults as low cortisol levels were found in offenders with psychopathy compared to non-psychopathic offenders (Holi et al. 2006; Cima, Smeets, and Jelicic 2008). In a study on cortisol reactivity using a social stressor, a significant difference in cortisol levels from pre- to post-stressor was observed, but only in males with low rather than high levels of psychopathy (O'Leary, Loney, and Eckel 2007).

Several studies have examined cortisol levels in relation to different categories of offenders. Fairchild et al. (2008) found that basal cortisol level or cortisol reactivity to a stressor did not differ between male adolescents with early-onset and adolescence-onset conduct disorder. It has been proposed that structural abnormalities in the amygdala may underlie the finding that early- and adolescent-onset conduct disorder are associated with lower cortisol responses to stress as the amygdala is involved in initiating HPA responses to stress (Fairchild et al. 2011). However, another study on boys aged 7 to 12 years found that lower cortisol was more strongly related to persistently aggressive boys as well as those with childhood-onset conduct disorder compared to adolescence-onset conduct disorder (McBurnett et al. 2000). This is bolstered by findings that low basal cortisol levels predicted disruptive behavior in boys and girls only if conduct problems were already present at age 10 to 12 years (Sondeijker et al. 2008) and that persistently high-aggressive adolescents exhibited decreased cortisol levels consistently over time compared to low-aggressive adolescents (Platje et al. 2013). Such findings suggest that cortisol levels are related to the persistent trajectory of antisocial behavior rather than the prediction of the onset of behavior problems at later ages.

B. Testosterone

Experimental studies have shown that increased testosterone levels are associated with increased levels of aggression (Pope, Kouri, and Hudson 2000) and decreased levels of empathy (van Honk et al. 2011), which are associated with offending. Associations between higher levels of testosterone and antisocial behavior have been reported in children and adolescents. For example, adolescents with high levels of externalizing behaviors have been documented to have higher levels of testosterone than individuals with low levels of externalizing behaviors (Maras et al. 2003). Furthermore, testosterone levels were found to be higher in a disruptive behavior disorder group than in normal controls for an older subset of participants (aged 9 to 11 years) compared to those of younger ages (aged 5 to 8 years; Chance et al. 2000). However, some other studies have found mixed results on the testosterone–antisocial behavior relationship among children and adolescents (e.g., van Goozen et al. 1998; Dorn et al. 2009).

Additional studies have found a positive relationship between testosterone levels in adulthood and retrospectively reported severity of conduct disorder symptoms in childhood (e.g., Mazur 1995). Longitudinal studies have documented that testosterone levels in a community sample at ages 12 and 14 years predicted antisocial norm-violating behaviors at age 16 years (Tarter et al. 2009), and testosterone levels in conduct disordered boys at age 13 years predicted delinquency and criminal behavior at ages 16 and 21 years (Van Bokhoven et al. 2006). In adults, meta-analytic evidence suggests that testosterone is positively associated with aggression, with higher associations found for the age group of 22 to 35 years and in offender compared to non-offender populations (Archer et al. 2005). Higher testosterone levels also correlated positively with psychopathy scores in convicted criminals (Stålenheim et al. 1998). On the other hand, Glenn et al. (2011) found that instead of baseline testosterone, the ratio of baseline testosterone to cortisol reactivity after stress was significantly related to psychopathy. Generally, research suggests there is a small positive correlation between testosterone and antisocial behavior throughout the life span. Relationships seem to be weakest in young children and get stronger as individuals age (Yildirim and Derksen 2012).

C. Serotonin and Dopamine

Serotonin and dopamine are neurotransmitters that have been implicated in anti-social behavior and specifically in psychopathy. Most commonly, researchers have examined neurotransmitter metabolite levels in cerebrospinal fluid, such as HVA, a metabolite of dopamine, and 5-HIAA, a metabolite of serotonin (Freedman and Verdun-Jones 2010).

Studies have found that examining serotonin and dopamine levels together provides a better prediction of psychopathy scores. In a sample of violent offenders, the ratio of HVA to 5-HIAA was positively associated with psychopathy scores, particularly the Factor 2 Antisocial/Lifestyle score, which has been linked to life-course–persistent offending (Soderstrom et al. 2001; Yildirim and Derksen 2012). In a follow-up study, these results were replicated in a forensic sample. The HVA:5-HIAA ratio was positively related to childhood-onset disruptive disorders (Soderstrom et al. 2003).

Other research has suggested that serotonin levels are generally low in antisocial populations. One meta-analysis on 20 reports revealed reduced 5-HIAA in antisocial populations, particularly for individuals younger than 30 years, supporting the possibility that age-related increases in serotonin correlate with age-related declines in crime (Moore, Scarpa, and Raine 2002). Significantly lower serotonin levels were also found in boys with high levels of callous-unemotional traits (Moul et al. 2013). In children and adolescents with obsessive-compulsive disorder, participants with comorbid disruptive behavior disorders had significantly lower blood serotonin concentrations than participants with no comorbid behavior disorder (Hanna, Yuwiler, and Coates 1995). In the same study, a negative relationship was also found between serotonin concentration and externalizing and aggression scores. Additionally, reduced concentrations of somatostatin, a peptide which stimulates the release of serotonin, have been found in the cerebrospinal fluid of children with disruptive behavior disorders compared to children with obsessive-compulsive disorder (Kruesi et al. 1990). Although reduced serotonin levels have been found in children, findings suggest that the strongest serotonin effects on offending occur in young adulthood (Moore et al. 2002). All in all, despite some mixed findings (Hughes et al. 1996), there is reasonably strong evidence that serotonin and dopamine play a role in the development of offending.

D. Biosocial Interactions Involving Hormones and Neurotransmitters

Limited research has been conducted on biosocial interactions involving hormones and neurotransmitters. In one study, maltreatment was a significant moderator of the cortisol dysregulation–antisocial behavior relationship, such that low cortisol levels were more strongly associated with antisocial behavior in nonmaltreated children compared to maltreated peers (Hawes, Brennan, and Dadds 2009). In a similar vein, Hawes et al.

(2009) suggested that early adversity plays a role in the development of antisocial behavior in children with low levels of callous-unemotional traits and higher basal cortisol levels, while high levels of callous-unemotional traits and low basal cortisol levels characterize a particularly severe subgroup for whom antisocial behavior develops somewhat independently of social adversity. A study on Dutch adolescents documented that among individuals who experienced low levels of an environmental stressor, namely neighborhood density, lower cortisol activity significantly predicted higher levels of delinquency and aggression (Yu et al. 2016). Thus, HPA-axis dysfunction may play a more significant role in the development of chronic antisocial behavior for individuals who have not been exposed to adversity.

V. NEUROPSYCHOLOGICAL FACTORS

Neuropsychology, the indirect, behavior-based assessment of brain dysfunction, has also been used to understand offending across the life span. Neuropsychological investigations of various forms of antisociality have largely targeted deficits in specific domains of cognitive functioning such as verbal and spatial intelligence and executive abilities.

A. Verbal and Spatial Intelligence

To date, the best-replicated cognitive correlate of antisocial, violent, and criminal behavior among non–mentally ill individuals is general intelligence (e.g., IQ or Full Scale IQ) deficits (Wilson and Herrnstein 1985). Reduced verbal relative to spatial/performance IQ—a possible marker for left hemispheric dysfunction—has generally been documented to characterize both males and females from different age groups across studies of antisocial individuals (Raine 1993; Isen 2010). However, some antisocial individuals, such as those with antisocial personality disorder and psychopathy, have not consistently shown intellectual performance or verbal intelligence deficits (Barkataki et al. 2006; Kosson et al. 2007), although relationships have been noted between some specific psychopathic traits (i.e., criminal versatility and violence) and verbal dysfunction (Rasmussen, Almvik, and Levander 2001). Thus, while global and/or verbal intellectual dysfunction may characterize adult antisocial individuals in general, they may not characterize specific constellations of criminogenic and antisocial traits.

Reduced verbal intelligence also appears largely characteristic of antisocial children and adolescents (e.g., Barker et al. 2007). Moffitt, Lynam, and Silva (1994) found that verbal deficits in early adolescence predicted delinquency in later adolescence for persistent, high-level offenders who began offending in pre-adolescence. However, mixed results have been found for juvenile psychopathy. Loney et al. (1998) found no verbal deficits in children with conduct problems and callous-unemotional traits, while Salekin et al. (2004) found that verbal intelligence was positively related to the superficial and deceitful interpersonal style traits and inversely related to the affective processing-disturbance traits of psychopathy in juvenile inmates. In summary, verbal deficits in populations of antisocial youth overall appear relatively consistent, though continued studies of psychopathic youth may assist in clarifying heterogeneous verbal IQ findings among antisocial juveniles as in adults.

Longitudinal studies of community-based samples may call into question the classic view of verbal but not performance IQ deficits in antisocial individuals. In a Pittsburgh youth sample including childhood-limited, adolescent-limited, and life-course–persistent offenders, Raine et al. (2005) found both spatial and verbal impairments. In another sample from Mauritius, Raine et al. (2002c) found early spatial but not verbal deficits at age 3, and later spatial and verbal deficits at age 11 in persistently antisocial individuals. These results suggest that while early spatial deficits contribute to persistent antisocial behavior, verbal deficits may be developmentally acquired. Results support a proposed early starter spatial impairment model of life-course offending, in which early deficits in visuospatial functioning may interfere with mother–infant bonding, possibly reflecting right hemispheric dysfunction that disrupts emotional processing and regulation and, in turn, contributes to persistent offending.

B. Executive Functioning

Executive functioning deficits are thought to represent impairment in frontal lobe functioning and are indicated by performance errors on neuropsychological tests of strategy formation, cognitive flexibility, or impulsivity (i.e., category, maze-tracing, Stroop interference, card sorting, verbal fluency and tower tests, and go/no-go and gambling tasks). In Morgan and Lilienfeld's (2000) classic quantitative review of 39 studies, overall executive functioning deficits were observed in antisocial individuals compared to controls. Strongest effects were found for the Porteus Mazes test and antisociality defined by judicial status. More recently, executive dysfunction has been associated with aggressive, violent, and antisocial personality-disordered populations (e.g., Stanford et al. 2007; Hancock, Tapscott, and Hoaken 2010; Dolan 2012), property criminality (Barker et al. 2007), child molesters with and without pedophilia (Schiffer and Vonlaufen 2011), single as opposed to multiple homicide victims in indigent murder defendants and death row inmates (Hanlon et al. 2010), murderers with schizophrenia compared to non-violent men with schizophrenia (Hanlon et al. 2012), mentally challenged versus non-impaired forensic hospital patients (Bastert et al. 2012), and offenders characterized by reactive as opposed to instrumental violence (Broomhall 2005).

Psychopathy in adults has not been consistently associated with general executive functioning deficits (e.g., Kosson et al. 2007). Some neuropsychological studies have shown that psychopathy may be characterized more by orbitofrontal dysfunction, which is associated with processing rewards and punishments, and emotion

(Rolls 2000; Blair et al. 2006). Additionally, successful, uncaught psychopaths have demonstrated significantly better dorsolateral prefrontal task performance relative to unsuccessful psychopaths and controls (Ishikawa et al. 2001), while white-collar criminals have been found to show increased executive functioning compared to offender controls (Raine et al. 2012). Furthermore, violent antisocial personality disordered offenders with and without psychopathy have demonstrated similar deficits in terms of "cool executive functioning," namely top-down processes subsumed by the dorsolateral and ventrolateral prefrontal cortex, that are distinctly cognitive in nature, such as working memory, response inhibition, planning, sustained attention, and attentional set-shifting, and "hot executive functioning," namely processes with an affective, motivational, or incentive/reward component subsumed by ventromedial connections between the mesolimbic reward pathway and the ventromedial prefrontal cortex, such as appraisal of the motivational significance of a stimulus in emotional decision-making (De Brito et al. 2013).

Findings on children and adolescents have been more mixed, with executive functioning deficits characterizing some antisocial youths (e.g., Cauffman et al. 2005) and not others (Moffitt et al. 1994; Nigg et al. 2004). The development of executive functions along with the ongoing myelination of the frontal cortex into and beyond adolescence (Raine 2002b) may explain differential patterns of executive functioning deficits among children and adults. This is supported by findings of executive functioning impairments in older maximum security hospital patients (Nestor 1992) and more pronounced impairments on an orbitofrontal neuropsychological task in psychopathic adults than psychopathic children (Blair 2006).

C. Biosocial Interactions Involving Neuropsychology

In a study examining biosocial interactions, Gao et al. (2009) found that neurocognitive deficits indicated by more risky decision-making in the Iowa Gambling Task were associated with psychopathic tendencies only in children with higher socioeconomic status. Additionally, progressive cognitive dysfunction affected by adverse psychosocial experience may explain early-onset antisocial behavior (Aguilar et al. 2000) and lifetime, cumulative biosocial risk interactions may be stronger predictors of persistent aggression than risks only occurring in childhood or adolescence (Brennan et al. 2003). More specifically, Brennan et al. (2003), in a study of 370 Australian adolescents, identified that an interaction of biological risk factors including neuropsychological deficits and social risk factors predicted life-course–persistent aggression in boys and girls. Alternatively, the late-developing prefrontal cortex may be overloaded by the social and executive functioning demands of late adolescence, possibly leading to prefrontal dysfunction, behavioral inhibition failure, and significantly increased antisocial behavior (Raine 2002b). In sum, the neuropsychological literature demonstrates how the study of behavioral expressions of brain dysfunction has informed developmental neurobiological perspectives of offending across the life span.

VI. Early Health Risks

Evidence suggests that risk factors experienced early in life, such as during the prenatal and perinatal periods of development, are associated with longitudinal patterns of offending and may lead to the most detrimental effects over the life span (Day, Wanklyn, and Yessine 2014). Prenatal and perinatal factors that have been most closely linked to antisocial behavior include prenatal nicotine, alcohol, and lead exposure, minor physical anomalies, and birth complications.

A. Prenatal Nicotine, Alcohol, and Lead Exposure

Children who are exposed to maternal smoking during pregnancy have been documented to have an elevated risk of offending throughout the life course (Wakschlag et al. 2002). Numerous studies have found associations between prenatal maternal smoking and juvenile offending, delinquency, conduct disorder, and violent offending (e.g., Wakschlag et al. 1997; Brennan, Grekin, and Mednick 1999; Paradis et al. 2015). In particular, a dose-response relationship was observed between the degree of prenatal maternal smoking and the extent of offspring's nonviolent and violent offending assessed at age 34 years (Brennan et al. 1999). However, there is current debate regarding whether the nicotine exposure–offending association involves a genetic confound (Glenn and Raine 2014).

Prenatal exposure to alcohol results in cognitive, behavioral, social, and physical deficits and can lead to a diagnosis of fetal alcohol syndrome (FAS). Fetal alcohol exposure has been documented as a risk factor for antisocial behavior in children, adolescents, and adults (Olson et al. 1997; Fast, Conry, and Loock 1999). However, even without FAS, high rates of delinquency have been found in children and adolescents with heavy fetal alcohol exposure (Mattson and Riley 2000).

Besides nicotine and alcohol exposure, a prospective study found that prenatal maternal blood lead concentrations during the first and second trimesters of pregnancy were associated with higher rates of criminal arrests measured at ages 19 to 24 years (Wright et al. 2008). Another longitudinal study on 195 adolescents found that lead levels from the prenatal period to 6.5 years of age were associated with delinquent and antisocial behavior in middle adolescence (Dietrich et al. 2001). Although few longitudinal studies in this area exist, these studies demonstrate that prenatal lead exposure is associated with the development of offending.

B. Minor Physical Anomalies

Minor physical anomalies (MPAs) such as low-seated ears, single palmar crease, and furrowed tongue are considered indicators of fetal neural maldevelopment near the end of the first trimester or the beginning of the second trimester of pregnancy (Firestone and Peters 1983). Studies have found that MPAs are associated with greater antisocial behavior in children, adolescents, and adults, particularly for violent as opposed to non-violent offending (Glenn and Raine 2014). For example, MPAs measured at age 14 years predicted violent delinquency in 170 males at age 17 years, independent of childhood physical aggression or family adversity (Arseneault et al. 2000). Other studies have found that a larger number of MPAs is associated with recidivistic violent criminal be-havior. One study documented that recidivistic violent offenders at ages 20 to 22 years had more MPAs between ages 11 to 13 years compared to individuals with one or fewer violent offenses (Kandel et al. 1989).

C. Birth Complications

Birth complications, such as pre-eclampsia, preterm birth, and breech fetal positioning, have also been found to predispose to later offending (e.g., Liu et al. 2009). For example, Kandel and Mednick (1991) found that high delivery complications were associated with adult violent offending. Additionally, findings from a longitudinal study, the Fragile Families and Child Well-Being Study, showed that low birthweight was linked to serious aggression and destructive behavior at age 5 years and the relationship was mediated by verbal skills (Vaske, Newsome, and Boisvert 2013). Other perinatal risk factors for later offending include being small for gestational age and a small head circumference (Babchishin et al. 2017).

D. Biosocial Interactions Involving Early Health Risks

Studies have documented that prenatal nicotine exposure, MPAs, and birth complications interact with social factors to predispose to later offending. For example, prenatal nicotine exposure was found to lead to an 11.9-fold and 14.2-fold increase in recidivistic violent offending in adulthood when combined with the individual social risk factor of being raised in a single-parent family and with a group of psychosocial risk factors, respectively (Räsänen et al. 1999). Increased risk has particularly been observed for persistent violent offending (Brennan et al. 1999; Gibson and Tibbetts 2000; Brennan et al. 2002). Moreover, MPAs in boys at age 12 years were related to vio-lent, but not non-violent property offending at age 21 years, but only among individuals reared in unstable homes (Mednick and Kandel 1988). Similarly, Brennan, Mednick, and Raine (1997) and Pine et al. (1997) found higher rates of adult violent crime in males and greater risk for disruptive behavior and conduct disorder at age 17 years among individuals with both MPAs and social risk factors. A recent study documented that individuals born at low birthweight were at an increased risk of adult offending if they were born to adolescent mothers (Vaske et al. 2015). This is consistent with the finding that birth complications combined with early maternal rejection measured at age 1 year increased the likelihood of violent offending at ages 18 and 34 years (Raine, Brennan, and Mednick 1994, 1997). Birth complications have also been found to interact with other psychosocial factors such as poor parenting (Hodgins, Kratzer, and McNeil 2001), family adversity (Arseneault et al. 2002), and being an only child (Kemppainen et al. 2001) to lead to adult violent offending. These studies suggest that increased offending is observed when both early health risks and environmental risk factors are present.

VII. Conclusion

Through a review of extant research, this chapter sheds light on the development of antisocial behavior and risk factors for offending at different ages, issues central to developmental and life-course criminology. Despite some null findings, many biological risk factors such as autonomic underarousal, genetics, structural and functional brain abnormalities (particularly in the prefrontal and temporal cortex), low basal cortisol, high testosterone, low serotonin, neuropsychological deficits, and early health risks are associated with antisocial behavior in children, adolescents, and adults. The strength of the risk factor–antisocial behavior associations may differ across development. For example, genetic influences increased across development for aggressive behavior and decreased across development for delinquent/rule-breaking behavior. Brain deficits predisposed individuals to more severe antisocial behavior if damage occurred earlier rather than later in life. In terms of hormones and neurotransmitters, cortisol levels were found to decrease across development for aggressive individuals. The relationship between high testosterone and antisocial behavior was weakest in young children and strongest in adults, while the effect of low serotonin on antisocial behavior was strongest in young adulthood. Furthermore, antisocial adults seem to suffer a greater degree of executive functioning deficits than younger antisocial populations. Studies examining biosocial interactions have also found that antisocial individuals exposed to fewer social stressors are more likely to exhibit biological risk factors compared to those with high social risk and that individuals are most likely to offend over the life course when both social and biological risk factors are present. Such interaction effects have been found in relation to child, adolescent, and adult offending.

The studies also revealed some differences in the associations between biological factors and offending for different types of offenders. For example, genetic influences were more important for childhood-onset compared to late-onset offending, brain deficits were associated with both early- and adolescent-onset offending, and a higher ratio of HVA to 5-HIAA was associated with life-course–persistent and child-onset offending. Additionally, it has been suggested that low heart rate, early spatial deficits, and perinatal complications may contribute particularly to life-course–persistent offending.

A. Future Directions

Despite these findings, greater research is needed to advance understanding of the role of biology in developmental and life-course criminology. One area of future research involves protective factors for offending. Although psychological and social factors such as attachment (Farrington 2005a) and life events (Wikström 2005) have been proposed in developmental and life-course theories as variables that inhibit offending, such theories do not consider the role of biological factors as possible protective factors. Studies such as that by Raine, Venables, and Williams (1995, 1996) have documented that high resting heart rate and skin conductance can serve as protective factors. For example, antisocial adolescents who desisted from adult crime had significantly better skin conductance conditioning at age 15 years than persisters who were criminal at age 29 years (Raine, Venables, and Williams 1996). Nonetheless, research on biological protective factors is very much more limited compared to that on risk factors. Additional research can provide much-needed insight on the topic of desistance.

Developmental and life-course criminology is also concerned with the effects of life events on the development of offending (Farrington 2005b). Recent findings have provided support for a social neurocriminology perspective, in which biological factors are influenced by social environmental processes to affect antisocial behavior, by documenting that low heart rate partly mediated the social adversity–antisocial behavior relationship (Choy et al. 2015; Fagan, Zhang, and Gao 2017). Given that marriage is associated with lower levels of testosterone in males (Gray et al. 2002) and the finding that adolescents who experience adversity in the form of maltreatment early in life exhibited lower gray matter volumes in corticostriatal-limbic regions such as the dorsolateral prefrontal cortex and amygdala (Edmiston et al. 2011), future efforts could be directed at understanding how social environmental factors can affect offending through changes in biology.

In addition, although several developmental models such as that of Moffitt (1993) and Lahey and Waldman (2005) recognize some biological influences, they do not necessarily emphasize the interactive effects between biological and psychosocial variables. Many theories still fail to incorporate biological factors such as genetics or hormones in understanding the etiology of offending (Barnes et al. 2014). More biological testing should be conducted particularly in prospective longitudinal studies to examine within-individual differences in offending and to investigate biosocial interaction effects. In light of the proposed notion that criminological variables are affected by genetic influences, longitudinal research can be beneficial in accounting for some genetic influences as respondents serve as their own control over many observation points (Barnes et al. 2014). Such efforts can greatly contribute to a better understanding of the role of biology in models of offending and pave the way for the development of early intervention and prevention strategies for crime reduction.

References

Aguilar, Benjamin, L. Alan Sroufe, Byron Egeland, and Elizabeth Carlson. 2000. "Distinguishing the Early-Onset/Persistent and Adolescence-Onset Antisocial Behavior Types: From Birth to 16 Years." *Development and Psychopathology* 12: 109–132.

Aharoni, Eyal, Gina M. Vincent, Carla L. Harenski, Vince D. Calhoun, Walter Sinnott-Armstrong, Michael S. Gazzaniga, and Kent A. Kiehl. 2013. "Neuroprediction of Future Rearrest." *Proceedings of the National Academy of Sciences* 110: 6223–6228.

Alegria, Analucia A., Joaquim Radua, and Katya Rubia. 2016. "Meta-Analysis of fMRI Studies of Disruptive Behavior Disorders." *The American Journal of Psychiatry* 173: 1119–1130.

Alink, Lenneke R. A., Marinus H. van IJzendoorn, Marian J. Bakermans-Kranenburg, Judi Mesman, Femmie Juffer, and Hans M. Koot. 2008. "Cortisol and Externalizing Behavior in Children and Adolescents: Mixed Meta-Analytic Evidence for the Inverse Relation of Basal Cortisol and Cortisol Reactivity with Externalizing Behavior." *Developmental Psychobiology* 50: 427–450.

Archer, John, Nicola Graham-Kevan, and Michelle Davies. 2005. "Testosterone and Aggression: A Reanalysis of Book, Starzyk, and Quinsey's (2001) Study." *Aggression and Violent Behavior* 10: 241–261.

Armstrong, Todd A., Shawn Keller, Travis W. Franklin, and Scott N. MacMillan. 2009. "Low Resting Heart Rate and Antisocial Behavior: A Brief Review of Evidence and Preliminary Results from a New Test." *Criminal Justice and Behavior* 36: 1125–1140.

Arseneault, Louise, Richard E. Tremblay, Bernard Boulerice, and Jean-François Saucier. 2002. "Obstetrical Complications and Violent Delinquency: Testing Two Developmental Pathways." *Child Development* 73: 496–508.

Arseneault, Louise, Richard E. Tremblay, Bernard Boulerice, Jean R. Séguin, and Jean-François Saucier. 2000. "Minor Physical Anomalies and Family Adversity as Risk Factors for Violent Delinquency in Adolescence." *American Journal of Psychiatry* 157: 917–923.

Babchishin, Kelly M., Michael C. Seto, Amir Sariaslan, Paul Lichtenstein, Seena Fazel, and Niklas Långström. 2017. "Parental and Perinatal Risk Factors for Sexual Offending in Men: A Nationwide Case-Control Study." *Psychological Medicine* 46: 305–315.

Barkataki, Ian, Veena Kumari, Mrigendra Das, Pamela Taylor, and Tonmoy Sharma. 2006. "Volumetric Structural Brain Abnormalities in Men with Schizophrenia or Antisocial Personality Disorder." *Behavioural Brain Research* 169: 239–247.

Baker, Laura A., Catherine Tuvblad, Chandra Reynolds, Mo Zheng, Dora Isabel Lozano, and Adrian Raine. 2009. "Resting Heart Rate and the Development of Antisocial Behavior from Age 9 to 14: Genetic and Environmental Influences." *Development and Psychopathology* 21: 939–960.

Barker, Edward D., Jean R. Séguin, Helene Raskin White, Marsha E. Bates, Eric Lacourse, Rene Carbonneau, and Richard E. Tremblay. 2007. "Developmental Trajectories of Male Physical Violence and Theft: Relations to Neurocognitive Performance." *Archives of General Psychiatry* 64: 592–599.

Barnes, J. C., Brian B. Boutwell, Kevin M. Beaver, Chris L. Gibson, and John P. Wright. 2014. "On the Consequences of Ignoring Genetic Influences in Criminological Research." *Journal of Criminal Justice* 42: 471–482.

Bastert, Eva, Detlef Schläfke, Annika Pein, Franziska Kupke, and Jörg M. Fegert. 2012. "Mentally Challenged Patients in a Forensic Hospital: A Feasibility Study Concerning the Executive Functions of Forensic Patients with Organic Brain Disorder, Learning Disability, or Mental Retardation." *International Journal of Law and Psychiatry* 35: 207–212.

Beaver, Kevin M., J. C. Barnes, and Brian B. Boutwell. 2013. "The 2-Repeat Allele of the MAOA Gene Confers an Increased Risk for Shooting and Stabbing Behaviors." *Psychiatric Quarterly*, 85: 257–265.

Beaver, Kevin M., John Paul Wright, Brian B. Boutwell, J. C. Barnes, Matt DeLisi, and Michael G. Vaughn. 2013. "Exploring the Association between the 2-Repeat Allele of the MAOA Gene Promoter Polymorphism and Psychopathic Personality Traits, Arrests, Incarceration, and Lifetime Antisocial Behavior." *Personality and Individual Differences* 54: 164–168.

Beaver, Kevin M., John Paul Wright, Matt DeLisi, Anthony Walsh, Michael G. Vaughn, Danielle Boisvert, and Jamie Vaske. 2007. "A Gene x Gene Interaction Between Drd2 and Drd4 Is Associated with Conduct Disorder and Antisocial Behavior in Males." *Behavioral and Brain Functions* 3: 1186–1193.

Bezdjian, Serena, Catherine Tuvblad, Adrian Raine, and Laura A. Baker. 2011. "The Genetic and Environmental Covariation Among Psychopathic Personality Traits, and Reactive and Proactive Aggression in Childhood." *Child Development* 82: 1267–1281.

Birbaumer, Niels, Ralf Veit, Martin Lotze, Michael Erb, Christiane Hermann, Wolfgang Grodd, and Herta Flor. 2005. "Deficient Fear Conditioning in Psychopathy: A Functional Magnetic Resonance Imaging Study." *Archives of General Psychiatry* 62: 799–805.

Blair, R. J. R. 2006. "The Emergence of Psychopathy: Implications for the Neuropsychological Approach to Developmental Disorders." *Cognition* 101: 414–442.

Blair, K. S., Chris Newman, Derek GV Mitchell, R. A. Richell, Alan Leonard, John Morton, and R. J. R. Blair. 2006. "Differentiating Among Prefrontal Substrates in Psychopathy: Neuropsychological Test Findings." *Neuropsychology* 20: 153–165.

Blonigen, Daniel M., Brian M. Hicks, Robert F. Krueger, Christopher J. Patrick, and William G. Iacono. 2006. "Continuity and Change in Psychopathic Traits as Measured via Normal-Range Personality: A Longitudinal-Biometric Study." *Journal of Abnormal Psychology* 115: 85–95.

Boccardi, Marina, Martina Bocchetta, Hannu J. Aronen, Eila Repo-Tiihonen, Olli Vaurio, Paul M. Thompson, Jari Tiihonen, and Giovanni B. Frisoni. 2013. "Atypical Nucleus Accumbens Morphology in Psychopathy: Another Limbic Piece in the Puzzle." *International Journal of Law and Psychiatry* 36: 157–167.

Boccardi, Marina, Rossana Ganzola, Roberta Rossi, Francesca Sabattoli, Mikko P. Laakso, Eila Repo-Tiihonen, Olli Vaurio, et al. 2010. "Abnormal Hippocampal Shape in Offenders with Psychopathy." *Human Brain Mapping* 31: 438–447.

Boutwell, Brian B., Scott Menard, J. C. Barnes, Kevin M. Beaver, Todd A. Armstrong, and Danielle Boisvert. 2014. "The Role of Gene-Gene Interaction in the Prediction of Criminal Behavior." *Comprehensive Psychiatry* 55: 483–488.

Brennan, Patricia A., Emily R. Grekin, and Sarnoff A. Mednick. 1999. "Maternal Smoking During Pregnancy and Adult Male Criminal Outcomes." *Archives of General Psychiatry* 56: 215–219.

Brennan, Patricia A., Emily R. Grekin, Erik Lykke Mortensen, and Sarnoff A. Mednick. 2002. "Relationship of Maternal Smoking During Pregnancy with Criminal Arrest and Hospitalization for Substance Abuse in Male and Female Adult Offspring." *American Journal of Psychiatry* 159: 48–54.

Brennan, Patricia A., Jason Hall, William Bor, Jake M. Najman, and Gail Williams. 2003. "Integrating Biological and Social Processes in Relation to Early-Onset Persistent Aggression in Boys and Girls." *Developmental Psychology* 39: 309–323.

Brennan, Patricia A., Sarnoff A. Mednick, and Adrian Raine. 1997. "Biosocial Interactions and Violence: A Focus on Perinatal Factors." In *Biosocial Bases of Violence,* edited by

Adrian Raine, Patricia A. Brennan, David P. Farrington, and Sarnoff A. Mednick, 163–174. New York: Plenum.

Brook, Michael, Matthew S. Panizzon, David S. Kosson, Elizabeth A. Sullivan, Michael J. Lyons, Carol E. Franz, Seth A. Eisen, and William S. Kremen. 2010. "Psychopathic Personality Traits in Middle-Aged Male Twins: A Behavior Genetic Investigation." *Journal of Personality Disorders* 24: 473–486.

Broomhall, Luke. 2005. "Acquired Sociopathy: A Neuropsychological Study of Executive Dysfunction in Violent Offenders." *Psychiatry, Psychology and Law* 12: 367–387.

Burt, S. Alexandra. 2009. "Are There Meaningful Etiological Differences within Antisocial Behavior? Results of a Meta-Analysis." *Clinical Psychology Review* 29: 163–178.

Burt, S. Alexandra, Matt McGue, Latanya A. Carter, and William G. Iacono. 2007. "The Different Origins of Stability and Change in Antisocial Personality Disorder Symptoms." *Psychological Medicine* 37: 27–38.

Button, Tanya M. M., Jennifer Y. F. Lau, Barbara Maughan, and T. C. Eley. 2008. "Parental Punitive Discipline, Negative Life Events and Gene–Environment Interplay in the Development of Externalizing Behavior." *Psychological Medicine* 38: 29–39.

Button, Tanya Maria May, Jane Scourfield, Neilson Martin, Shaun Purcell, and Peter McGuffin. 2005. "Family Dysfunction Interacts with Genes in the Causation of Antisocial Symptoms." *Behavior Genetics* 35: 115–120.

Caspi, Avshalom, Joseph McClay, Terrie E. Moffitt, Jonathan Mill, Judy Martin, Ian W. Craig, Alan Taylor, and Richie Poulton. 2002. "Role of Genotype in the Cycle of Violence in Maltreated Children." *Science* 297:851–854.

Cauffman, Elizabeth, Laurence Steinberg, and Alex R. Piquero. 2005. "Psychological, Neuropsychological and Physiological Correlates of Serious Antisocial Behavior in Adolescence: The Role of Self-Control." *Criminology* 43: 133–176.

Chance, Susan E., Ronald T. Brown, James M. Dabbs Jr., and Robert Casey. 2000. "Testosterone, Intelligence and Behavior Disorders in Young Boys." *Personality and Individual Differences* 28: 437–445.

Choy, Olivia, Adrian Raine, Jill Portnoy, Anna Rudo-Hutt, Yu Gao, and Liana Soyfer. 2015. "The Mediating Role of Heart Rate on the Social Adversity-Antisocial Behavior Relationship." *Journal of Research in Crime and Delinquency* 52: 303–341.

Cima, Maaike, Tom Smeets, and Marko Jelicic. 2008. "Self-Reported Trauma, Cortisol Levels, and Aggression in Psychopathic and Non-Psychopathic Prison Inmates." *Biological Psychology* 78: 75–86.

Cohn, M. D., A. Popma, W. van den Brink, L. E. Pape, M. Kindt, L. van Domburgh, T. A. H. Doreleijers, and D. J. Veltman. 2013. "Fear Conditioning, Persistence of Disruptive Behavior and Psychopathic Traits: An fMRI Study." *Translational Psychiatry* 3: e319.

Craig, M. C., M. Catani, Q. Deeley, R. Latham, E. Daly, R. Kanaan, M. Picchioni, P. K. McGuire, T. Fahy, and D. G. M. Murphy. 2009. "Altered Connections on the Road to Psychopathy." *Molecular Psychiatry* 14: 946–953.

Cummings, E. Mark, Mona El-Sheikh, Chrystyna D. Kouros, and Peggy S. Keller. 2007. "Children's Skin Conductance Reactivity as a Mechanism of Risk in the Context of Parental Depressive Symptoms." *Journal of Child Psychology and Psychiatry* 48: 436–445.

Day, David M., Sonya G. Wanklyn, and Annie K. Yessine. 2014. "A Review of Terminological, Conceptual, and Methdological Issues in the Developmental Risk Factor Literature for Antisocial and Delinquent Behavior." *Child and Youth Care Forum* 43: 97–112.

De Brito, Stephane A., Essi Viding, Veena Kumari, Nigel Blackwood, and Sheilagh Hodgins. 2013. "Cool and Hot Executive Function Impairments in Violent Offenders with Antisocial Personality Disorder With and Without Psychopathy." *PloS One* 8: e65566.

Dick, Danielle M. 2011. "Gene-Environment Interaction in Psychological Traits and Disorders." *Annual Review of Clinical Psychology* 7: 383–409.

Dick, Danielle M., Richard Viken, Shaun Purcell, Jaakko Kaprio, Lea Pulkkinen, and Richard J. Rose. 2007. "Parental Monitoring Moderates the Importance of Genetic and Environmental Influences on Adolescent Smoking." *Journal of Abnormal Psychology* 116: 213–218.

Dietrich, Kim N., Ris M. Douglas, Paul A. Succop, Omer G. Berger, and Robert L. Bornschein. 2001. "Early Exposure to Lead and Juvenile Delinquency." *Neurotoxicology and Teratology* 23: 511–518.

Dolan, Margaret. 2012. "The Neuropsychology of Prefrontal Function in Antisocial Personality Disordered Offenders with Varying Degrees of Psychopathy." *Psychological Medicine* 42: 1715–1725.

Dorn, Lorah D., David J. Kolko, Elizabeth J. Susman, Bin Huang, Howard Stein, Edvin Music, and Oscar G. Bukstein. 2009. "Salivary Gonadal and Adrenal Hormone Differences in Boys and Girls With and Without Disruptive Behavior Disorders: Contextual Variants." *Biological Psychology* 81: 31–39.

Edmiston, Erin E., Fei Wang, Carolyn M. Mazure, Joanne Guiney, Rajita Sinha, Linda C. Mayes, and Hilary P. Blumberg. 2011. "Corticostriatal-Limbic Gray Matter Morphology in Adolescents with Self-Reported Exposure to Childhood Maltreatment." *Archives of Pediatrics & Adolescent Medicine* 165: 1069–1077.

Ermer, Elsa, Lora M. Cope, Prashanth K. Nyalakanti, Vince D. Calhoun, and Kent A. Kiehl. 2012. "Aberrant Paralimbic Gray Matter in Criminal Psychopathy." *Journal of Abnormal Psychology* 121: 649–658.

Eysenck, Hans. J. 1977. *Crime and Personality*. London: Routledge & Kegan Paul.

Fagan, Shawn E., Wei Zhang, and Yu Gao. 2017. "Social Adveristy and Antisocial Behavior: Mediating Effects of Autonomic Nervous System Activity." *Journal of Abnormal Child Psychology* 45: 1–12.

Fairchild, Graeme, Cindy C. Hagan, Nicholas D. Walsh, Luca Passamonti, Andrew J. Calder, and Ian M. Goodyer. 2013. "Brain Structure Abnormalities in Adolescent Girls with Conduct Disorder." *Journal of Child Psychology and Psychiatry* 54: 86–95.

Fairchild, Graeme, Luca Passamonti, Georgina Hurford, Cindy C. Hagan, Elisabeth AH von dem Hagen, Stephanie H. M. van Goozen, Ian M. Goodyer, and Andrew J. Calder. 2011. "Brain Structure Abnormalities in Early-Onset and Adolescent-Onset Conduct Disorder." *American Journal of Psychiatry* 168: 624–633.

Fairchild, Graeme, Nicola Toschi, Kate Sully, Edmund J. S. Sonuga-Barke, Cindy C. Hagan, Stefano Diciotti, Ian M. Goodyer, Andrew J. Calder, and Luca Passamonti. 2016. "Mapping the Structural Organization of the Brain in Conduct Disorder: Replication of Findings in Two Independent Samples." *Journal of Child Psychology and Psychiatry* 57: 1018–1026.

Fairchild, Graeme, Stephanie H. M. van Goozen, Sarah J. Stollery, Jamie Brown, Julian Gardiner, Joe Herbert, and Ian M. Goodyer. 2008. "Cortisol Diurnal Rhythm and Stress Reactivity in Male Adolescents with Early-Onset or Adolescence-Onset Conduct Disorder." *Biological Psychiatry* 64: 599–606.

Farrington, David P. 1997. "The Relationship Between Low Resting Heart Rate and Violence." *Biosocial Bases of Violence*, edited by Adrian Raine, Patricia A. Brennan, David P. Farrington, and Sarnoff A. Mednick, 89–105. New York: Plenum.

Farrington, David P. 2005a. "The Integrated Cognitive Antisocial Potential (ICAP) Theory." In *Integrated Developmental & Life-Course Theories of Offending: Advances in Criminological Theory*, Vol. 14, edited by David P. Farrington, 73–92. New Brunswick, NJ: Transaction.

Farrington, David P. 2005b. "Introduction to the Integrated Developmental and Life-Course Theories of Offending." In *Integrated Developmental & Life-Course Theories of Offending: Advances in Criminological Theory*, Vol. 14, edited by David P. Farrington, 1–14. New Brunswick, NJ: Transaction.

Fast, Diane K., Julianne Conry, and Christine A. Loock. 1999. "Identifying Fetal Alcohol Syndrome Among Youth in the Criminal Justice System." *Journal of Developmental & Behavioral Pediatrics* 20: 370–372.

Firestone, Philip, and Susan Peters. 1983. "Minor Physical Anomalies and Behavior in Children: A Review." *Journal of Autism and Developmental Disorders* 13: 411–425.

Freedman, Lauren F., and Simon N. Verdun-Jones. 2010. "Blaming the Parts Instead of the Person: Understanding and Applying Neurobiological Factors Associated with Psychopathy." *Canadian Journal of Criminology and Criminal Justice* 52: 29–53.

Gao, Yu, Laura A. Baker, Adrian Raine, Henry Wu, and Serena Bezdjian. 2009. "Brief Report: Interaction Between Social Class and Risky Decision-Making in Children with Psychopathic Tendencies." *Journal of Adolescence* 32: 409–414.

Gao, Yu, Adrian Raine, Peter H. Venables, Michael E. Dawson, and Sarnoff A. Mednick. 2010. "Association of Poor Childhood Fear Conditioning and Adult Crime." *The American Journal of Psychiatry* 167: 56–60.

Gao, Yu, Catherine Tuvblad, Anne Schell, Laura Baker, and Adrian Raine. 2015. "Skin Conductance Fear Conditioning Impairments and Aggression: A Longitudinal Study." *Psychophysiology* 52: 288–295.

Gibson, Chris L., and Stephen G. Tibbetts. 2000. "A Biosocial Interaction in Predicting Early Onset of Offending." *Psychological Reports* 86: 509–518.

Glenn, Andrea L., and Adrian Raine. 2014. "Neurocriminology: Implications for the Punishment, Prediction and Prevention of Criminal Behaviour." *Nature Reviews Neuroscience* 15: 54–63.

Glenn, Andrea L., Adrian Raine, Robert A. Schug, Yu Gao, and Douglas A. Granger. 2011. "Increased Testosterone-to-Cortisol Ratio in Psychopathy." *Journal of Abnormal Psychology* 120: 389–999.

Gray, Peter B., Sonya M. Kahlenberg, Emily S. Barrett, Susan F. Lipson, and Peter T. Ellison. 2002. "Marriage and Fatherhood Are Associated with Lower Testosterone in Males." *Evolution and Human Behavior* 23: 193–201.

Guo, Guang, Michael E. Roettger, and Jean C. Shih. 2007. "Contributions of the DAT1 and DRD2 Genes to Serious and Violent Delinquency Among Adolescents and Young Adults." *Human Genetics* 121: 125–136.

Haberstick, Brett C., Stephanie Schmitz, Susan E. Young, and John K. Hewitt. 2006. "Genes and Developmental Stabiltiy of Aggressive Behavior Problems at Home and School in a Community Sample of Twins Aged 7–12." *Behavior Genetics* 36: 809–819.

Hancock, Megan, Jennifer L. Tapscott, and Peter NS Hoaken. 2010. "Role of Executive Dysfunction in Predicting Frequency and Severity of Violence." *Aggressive Behavior* 36: 338–349.

Hanlon, Robert E., Joseph J. Coda, Derin Cobia, and Leah H. Rubin. 2012. "Psychotic Domestic Murder: Neuropsychological Differences Between Homicidal and Nonhomicidal Schizophrenic Men." *Journal of Family Violence* 27: 105–113.

Hanlon, Robert E., Leah H. Rubin, Marie Jensen, and Sarah Daoust. 2010. "Neuropsychological Features of Indigent Murder Defendants and Death Row Inmates in Relation to Homicidal Aspects of Their Crimes." *Archives of Clinical Neuropsychology* 25: 1–13.

Hanna, Gregory L., Arthur Yuwiler, and Janice K. Coates. 1995. "Whole Blood Serotonin and Disruptive Behaviors in Juvenile Obsessive-Compulsive Disorder." *Journal of the American Academy of Child & Adolescent Psychiatry* 34: 28–35.

Hawes, David J., John Brennan, and Mark R. Dadds. 2009. "Cortisol, Callous-Unemotional Traits, and Pathways to Antisocial Behavior." *Current Opinion in Psychiatry* 22: 357–362.

Hicks, Brian M., Marie D. Carlson, Daniel M. Blonigen, Christopher J. Patrick, William G. Iacono, and Matt MGue. 2012. "Psychopathic Personality Traits and Environmental Contexts: Differential Correlates, Gender Differences, and Genetic Mediation." *Personality Disorders: Theory, Research, and Treatment* 3: 209–227.

Hirata, Yuko, Clement C. Zai, Behdin Nowrouzi, Joseph H. Beitchman, and James L. Kennedy. 2013. "Study of the Catechol-O-Methyltransferase (COMT) Gene with High Aggression in Children." *Aggressive Behavior* 39: 45–51.

Hodgins, Sheilagh, Lynn Kratzer, and Thomas F. McNeil. 2001. "Obstetric Complications, Parenting, and Risk of Criminal Behavior." *Archives of General Psychiatry* 58(8): 746–752.

Holi, Matti, Laura Auvinen-Lintunen, Nina Lindberg, Pekka Tani, and Matti Virkkunen. 2006. "Inverse Correlation Between Severity of Psychopathic Traits and Serum Cortisol Levels in Young Adult Violent Male Offenders." *Psychopathology* 39: 102–104.

Hugdahl, Kenneth. 2001. *Psychophysiology*. Cambridge, MA: Harvard University Press.

Hughes, Carroll W., Frederick Petty, Sabri Sheikha, and Gerald L. Kramer. 1996. "Whole-Blood Serotonin in Children and Adolescents with Mood and Behavior Disorders." *Psychiatry Research* 65: 79–95.

Isen, Joshua. 2010. "A Meta-Analytic Assessment of Wechsler's P>V Sign in Antisocial Populations." *Clinical Psychology Review* 30: 423–435.

Ishikawa, Sharon S., Adrian Raine, Todd Lencz, Susan Bihrle, and Lori Lacasse. 2001. "Autonomic Stress Reactivity and Executive Functions in Successful and Unsuccessful Criminal Psychopaths from the Community." *Journal of Abnormal Psychology* 110: 423–432.

Jennings, Wesley G., Alex R. Piquero, and David P. Farrington. 2013. "Does Resting Heart Rate at Age 18 Distinguish General and Violent Offending up to Age 50? Findings from the Cambridge Study in Delinquent Development." *Journal of Criminal Justice* 41: 213–219.

Kandel, Elizabeth, Patricia A. Brennan, Sarnoff A. Mednick, and N. M. Michelson. 1989. "Minor Physical Anomalies and Recidivistic Adult Violent Criminal Behavior." *Acta Psychiatrica Scandinavica* 79(1): 103–107.

Kandel, Elizabeth, and Sarnoff A. Mednick. 1991. "Perinatal Complications Predict Violent Offending." *Criminology* 29: 519–529.

Kemppainen, Liisa, Jari Jokelainen, Marjo-Riitta Järvelin, Matti Isohanni, and Pirkko Räsänen. 2001. "The One-Child Family and Violent Criminality: A 31-Year Follow-Up Study of the Northern Finland 1966 Birth Cohort." *American Journal of Psychiatry* 158: 960–962.

Koopmans, Judith R., Wendy S. Slutske, G. Caroline M. Van Baal, and Dorret I. Boomsma. 1999. "The Influence of Religion on Alcohol Use Initiation: Evidence for Genotype X Environment Interaction." *Behavior Genetics* 29: 445–453.

Kosson, David S., Sarah K. Miller, Katherine A. Byrnes, and Catherine L. Leveroni. 2007. "Testing Neuropsychological Hypotheses for Cognitive Deficits in Psychopathic Criminals: A Study of Global–Local Processing." *Journal of the International Neuropsychological Society* 13: 267–276.

Kruesi, Markus J. P., Susan Swedo, Henrietta Leonard, David R. Rubinow, and Judith L. Rapoport. 1990. "CSF Somatostatin in Childhood Psychiatric Disorders: A Preliminary Investigation." *Psychiatry Research* 33: 277–284.

Lahey, Benjamin B., and Irwin D. Waldman. 2005. "A Developmental Model of the Propensity to Offend During Childhood and Adolescence." In *Integrated Developmental & Life-Course Theories of Offending: Advances in Criminological Theory*, Vol. 14, edited by David P. Farrington, 15–50. New Brunswick, NJ: Transaction.

Latvala, Antti, Ralf Kuja-Halkola, Catarina Almqvist, Henrik Larsson, and Paul Lichtenstein. 2015. "Heart Rate and Violent Criminality in More Than 700,000 Men." *JAMA Psychiatry* 72: 971–978.

Liu, Huasheng, Jian Liao, Weixiong Jiang, and Wei Wang. 2014. "Changes in Low-Frequency Fluctuations in Patients with Antisocial Personality Disorder Revealed by Resting-State Functional MRI." *PloS One* 9: e89790.

Liu, Jianghong, Adrian Raine, Anne Wuerker, Peter H. Venables, and Sarnoff Mednick. 2009. "The Association of Birth Complications and Externalizing Behavior in Early Adolescents: Direct and Mediating Effects." *Journal of Research on Adolescence* 19 :93–111.

Loney, Bryan R., Paul J. Frick, Mesha Ellis, and Monique G. McCoy. 1998. "Intelligence, Callous-Unemotional Traits, and Antisocial Behavior." *Journal of Psychopathology and Behavioral Assessment* 20: 231–247.

Lorber, Michael F. 2004. "Psychophysiology of Aggression, Psychopathy, and Conduct Problems: A Meta-Analysis." *Psychological Bulletin* 130: 531–552.

Ly, Martina, Julian C. Motzkin, Carissa L. Philippi, Gregory R. Kirk, Joseph P. Newman, Kent A. Kiehl, and Michael Koenigs. 2012. "Cortical Thinning in Psychopathy." *American Journal of Psychiatry* 169: 743–749.

Malik, Ayesha I., Clement C. Zai, Zihad Abu, Behdin Nowrouzi, and Joseph H. Beitchman. 2012. "The Role of Oxytocin and Oxytocin Receptor Gene Variants in Childhood-Onset Aggression." *Genes, Brain and Behavior* 11: 545–551.

Maras, Athanasios, Manfred Laucht, Dirk Gerdes, Cindy Wilhelm, Sabina Lewicka, Doris Haack, Lucie Malisova, and Martin H. Schmidt. 2003. "Association of Testosterone and Dihydrotestosterone with Externalizing Behavior in Adolescent Boys and Girls." *Psychoneuroendocrinology* 28: 932–940.

Mattson, Sarah N., and Edward P. Riley. 2000. "Parent Ratings of Behavior in Children with Heavy Prenatal Alcohol Exposure and IQ-Matched Controls." *Alcoholism: Clinical and Experimental Research* 24: 226–231.

Mazur, Allan. 1995. "Biosocial Models of Deviant Behavior Among Male Army Veterans." *Biological Psychology* 41: 271–293.

McBurnett, Keith, Benjamin B. Lahey, Paul J. Rathouz, and Rolf Loeber. 2000. "Low Salivary Cortisol and Persistent Aggression in Boys Referred for Disruptive Behavior." *Archives of General Psychiatry* 57: 38–43.

Mednick, Sarnoff A., and Elizabeth S. Kandel. 1988. "Congenital Determinants of Violence." *Journal of the American Academy of Psychiatry and the Law Online* 16: 101–109.

Middeldorp, Christel M., Diane J. Lamb, Jacqueline M. Vink, Meike Bartels, Catharina E. M. van Beijsterveldt, and Dorret I. Boomsma. 2014. "Child Care, Socio-Economic Status and Problem Behavior: A Study of Gene–Environment Interaction in Young Dutch Twins." *Behavior Genetics* 44: 314–325.

Moffitt, Terrie E. 1993. "Adolescence-Limited and Life-Course-Persistent Antisocial Behavior: A Developmental Taxonomy." *Psychological Review* 100: 674–701.

Moffitt, Terrie E., Donald R. Lynam, and Phil A. Silva. 1994. "Neuropsychological Tests Predicting Persistent Male Delinquency." *Criminology* 32: 277–300.

Moore, Todd M., Angela Scarpa, and Adrian Raine. 2002. "A Meta-Analysis of Serotonin Metabolite 5-HIAA and Antisocial Behavior." *Aggressive Behavior* 28: 299–316.

Morgan, Alex B., and Scott O. Lilienfeld. 2000. "A Meta-Analytic Review of the Relation Between Antisocial Behavior and Neuropsychological Measures of Executive Function." *Clinical Psychology Review* 20: 113–136.

Moul, Caroline, Carol Dobson-Stone, John Brennan, David Hawes, and Mark Dadds. 2013. "An Exploration of the Serotonin System in Antisocial Boys with High Levels of Callous-Unemotional Traits." *PloS One* 8: e56619.

Nestor, Paul G. 1992. "Neuropsychological and Clinical Correlates of Murder and Other Forms of Extreme Violence in a Forensic Psychiatric Population." *The Journal of Nervous and Mental Disease* 180: 418–423.

Nigg, Joel T., Jennifer M. Glass, Maria M. Wong, Edwin Poon, Jennifer M. Jester, Hiram E. Fitzgerald, Leon I. Puttler, Kenneth M. Adams, and Robert A. Zucker. 2004. "Neuropsychological Executive Functioning in Children at Elevated Risk for Alcoholism: Findings in Early Adolescence." *Journal of Abnormal Psychology* 113: 302–314.

O'Leary, Megan M., Bryan R. Loney, and Lisa A. Eckel. 2007. "Gender Differences in the Association Between Psychopathic Personality Traits and Cortisol Response to Induced Stress." *Psychoneuroendocrinology* 32: 183–191.

Olson, Heather Carmichael, Ann P. Streissguth, Paul D. Sampson, Helen M. Barr, Fred L. Bookstein, and Keith Thiede. 1997. "Association of Prenatal Alcohol Exposure with Behavioral and Learning Problems in Early Adolescence." *Journal of the American Academy of Child & Adolescent Psychiatry* 36: 1187–1194.

Oostermeijer, Sanne, Sarah Whittle, Chao Suo, Nicholas B. Allen, Julian G. Simmons, Nandita Vijayakumar, Peter M. van de Ven, Lucres M. C. Jansen, Murat Yücel, and Arne Popma. 2016. "Trajectories of Adolescent Conduct Problems in Relation to Cortical Thickness Development: A Longitudinal MRI Study." *Translational Psychiatry* 6: e841.

Ortiz, Jame, and Adrian Raine. 2004. "Heart Rate Level and Antisocial Behavior in Children and Adolescents: A Meta-Analysis." *Journal of the American Academy of Child & Adolescent Psychiatry* 43: 154–162.

Paradis, Angela D., Garrett M. Fitzmaurice, Karestan C. Koenen, and Stephen L. Buca. 2015. "A Prospective Investigation of Neurodevelopmental Risk Factors for Adult Antisocial Behavior Combining Official Arrest Records and Self-Reports." *Journal of Psychiatric Research* 68: 363–370.

Pardini, Dustin A., Adrian Raine, Kirk Erickson, and Rolf Loeber. 2014. "Lower Amygdala Volume in Men Is Associated with Childhood Aggression, Early Psychopathic Traits, and Future Violence." *Biological Psychiatry* 75: 73–80.

Pine, Daniel S., David Shaffer, Irvin Sam Schonfeld, and Mark Davies. 1997. "Minor Physical Anomalies: Modifiers of Environmental Risks for Psychiatric Impairment?" *Journal of the American Academy of Child & Adolescent Psychiatry* 36: 395–403.

Platje, Evelien, Lucres Jansen, Adrian Raine, Susan J. T. Branje, Theo A. H. Doreleijers, Marjan de Vries-Bouw, Arne Popma, et al. 2013. "Longitudinal Associations in Adolescence Between Cortisol and Persistent Aggressive or Rule-Breaking Behavior." *Biological Psychology* 93: 132–137.

Pope, Harrison G., Elena M. Kouri, and James I. Hudson. 2000. "Effects of Supraphysiologic Doses of Testosterone on Mood and Aggression in Normal Men: A Randomized Controlled Trial." *Archives of General Psychiatry* 57: 133–140.

Portnoy, Jill, Adrian Raine, Frances R. Chen, Dustin Pardini, Rolf Loeber, and J. Richard Jennings. 2014. "Heart Rate and Antisocial Behavior: The Mediating Role of Impulsive Sensation Seeking." *Criminology* 52: 292–311.

Portnoy, Jill and David P. Farrington. 2015. "Resting Heart Rate and Antisocial Behavior: An Updated Systematic Review and Meta-analysis." *Aggression and Violent Behavior* 22: 33–45.

Quay, Herbert C. 1965. "Psychopathic Personality as Pathological Stimulation-Seeking." *American Journal of Psychiatry* 122: 180–183.

Raine, Adrian. 1993. *The Psychopathology of Crime: Criminal Behavior as a Clinical Disorder.* San Diego, CA: Academic Press.

Raine, Adrian. 2002a. "Annotation: The Role of Prefrontal Deficits, Low Autonomic Arousal, and Early Health Factors in the Development of Antisocial and Aggressive Behavior in Children." *Journal of Child Psychology and Psychiatry* 43: 417–434.

Raine, Adrian. 2002b. "Biosocial Studies of Antisocial and Violent Behavior in Children and Adults: A Review." *Journal of Abnormal Child Psychology* 30: 311–326.

Raine, Adrian, Annis Lai Chu Fung, Jill Portnoy, Olivia Choy, and Victoria L. Spring. 2014. "Low Heart Rate as a Risk Factor for Child and Adolescent Proactive Aggressive and Impulsive Psychopathic Behavior." *Aggressive Behavior* 40: 290–299.

Raine, Adrian, Patricia Brennan, and Sarnoff A. Mednick. 1994. "Birth Complications Combined with Early Maternal Rejection at Age 1 Year Predispose to Violent Crime at Age 18 Years." *Archives of General Psychiatry* 51: 984–988.

Raine, Adrian, Patricia Brennan, and Sarnoff A. Mednick. 1997. "Interaction Between Birth Complications and Early Maternal Rejection in Predisposing Individuals to Adult Violence: Specificity to Serious, Early-Onset Violence." *American Journal of Psychiatry* 154: 1265–1271.

Raine, Adrian, William S. Laufer, Yaling Yang, Katherine L. Narr, Paul Thompson, and Arthur W. Toga. 2012. "Increased Executive Functioning, Attention, and Cortical Thickness in White-Collar Criminals." *Human Brain Mapping* 33: 2932–2940.

Raine, Adrian, Todd Lencz, Susan Bihrle, Lori LaCasse, and Patrick Colletti. 2000. "Reduced Prefrontal Gray Matter Volume and Reduced Autonomic Activity in Antisocial Personality Disorder." *Archives of General Psychiatry* 57: 119–127.

Raine, Adrian, Todd Lencz, Kristen Taylor, Joseph B. Hellige, Susan Bihrle, Lori Lacasse, Mimi Lee, Sharon Ishikawa, and Patrick Colletti. 2003. "Corpus Callosum Abnormalities in Psychopathic Antisocial Individuals." *Archives of General Psychiatry* 60: 1134–1142.

Raine, Adrian, Terrie E. Moffitt, Avshalom Caspi, Rolf Loeber, Magda Stouthamer-Loeber, and Don Lynam. 2005. "Neurocognitive Impairments in Boys on the Life-Course Persistent Antisocial Path." *Journal of Abnormal Psychology* 114: 38–49.

Raine, Adrian, Sohee Park, Todd Lencz, Susan Bihrle, Lori LaCasse, Cathy Spatz Widom, Louai Al-Dayeh, and Manbir Singh. 2001. "Reduced Right Hemisphere Activation in Severely Abused Violent Offenders During a Working Memory Task: An fMRI Study." *Aggressive Behavior* 27: 111–129.

Raine, Adrian, Jacqueline Stoddard, Susan Bihrle, and Monte Buchsbaum. 1998. "Prefrontal Glucose Deficits in Murderers Lacking Psychosocial Deprivation." *Cognitive and Behavioral Neurology* 11: 1–7.

Raine, Adrian, Peter H. Venables, and Sarnoff A. Mednick. 1997. "Low Resting Heart Rate at Age 3 Years Predisposes to Aggression at Age 11 Years: Evidence from the Mauritius Child Health Project." *Journal of the American Academy of Child & Adolescent Psychiatry* 36: 1457–1464.

Raine, Adrian, Peter H. Venables, and Mark Williams. 1990. "Relationships Between Central and Autonomic Measures of Arousal at Age 15 Years and Criminality at Age 24 Years." *Archives of General Psychiatry* 47: 1003–1007.

Raine, Adrian, Peter H. Venables, and Mark Williams. 1995. "High Autonomic Arousal and Electrodermal Orienting at Age 15 Years as Protective Factors Against Criminal Behavior at Age 29 Years." *American Journal of Psychiatry* 152: 1595–1600.

Raine, Adrian, Peter H. Venables, and Mark Williams. 1996. "Better Autonomic Conditioning and Faster Electrodermal Half-Recovery Time at Age 15 Years as Possible Protective Factors Against Crime at Age 29 Years." *Developmental Psychology* 32: 624–630.

Raine, Adrian, Pauline S. Yaralian, Chandra Reynolds, Peter H. Venables, and Sarnoff A. Mednick. 2002c. "Spatial but Not Verbal Cognitive Deficits at Age 3 Years in Persistently Antisocial Individuals." *Development and Psychopathology* 14: 25–44.

Räsänen, Pirkko, Helinä Hakko, Matti Isohanni, Sheilagh Hodgins, Marjo-Riitta Järvelin, and Jari Tiihonen. 1999. "Maternal Smoking During Pregnancy and Risk of Criminal Behavior Among Adult Male Offspring in the Northern Finland 1966 Birth Cohort." *American Journal of Psychiatry* 156: 857–862.

Rasmussen, Kirsten, Roger Almvik, and Sten Levander. 2001. "Performance and Strategy Indices of Neuropsychological Tests: Relations with Personality, Criminality and Violence." *Journal of Forensic Neuropsychology* 2: 29–43.

Rhee, Soo Hyun, and Irwin D. Waldman. 2002. "Genetic and Environmental Influences on Antisocial Behavior: A Meta-Analysis of Twin and Adoption Studies." *Psychological Bulletin* 128: 490–529.

Rogers, Jack C., and Stéphane A. De Brito. 2016. "Cortical and Subcortical Gray Matte Volume in Youths with Conduct Problems: A Meta-Analysis." *JAMA Psychiatry* 73: 64–72.

Rolls, Edmund T. 2000. "The Orbitofrontal Cortex and Reward." *Cerebral Cortex* 10: 284–294.

Rose, Richard J., Danielle M. Dick, Richard J. Viken, and Jaakko Kaprio. 2001. "Gene-Environment Interaction in Patterns of Adolescent Drinking: Regional Residency Moderates Longitudinal Influences on Alcohol Use." *Alcoholism: Clinical and Experimental Research* 25: 637–643.

Rowe, David C., David M. Almeida, and Kristen C. Jacobson. 1999. "School Context and Genetic Influences on Aggression in Adolescence." *Psychological Science* 10: 277–280.

Salekin, Randall T., Craig S. Neumann, Anne-Marie R. Leistico, and Alecia A. Zalot. 2004. "Psychopathy in Youth and Intelligence: An Investigation of Cleckley's Hypothesis." *Journal of Clinical Child and Adolescent Psychology* 33: 731–742.

Schiffer, Boris, Bernhard W. Müller, Norbert Scherbaum, Sheilagh Hodgins, Michael Forsting, Jens Wiltfang, Elke R. Gizewski, and Norbert Leygraf. 2011. "Disentangling Structural Brain Alterations Associated with Violent Behavior from Those Associated with Substance Use Disorders." *Archives of General Psychiatry* 68: 1039–1049.

Schiffer, Boris, Christina Pawliczek, Michael Forsting, Elke Gizewski, Norbert Leygraf, Sheilagh Hodgins, et al. 2014. "Neural Mechanisms Underlying Cognitive Control of Men with Lifelong Antisocial Behavior." *Psychiatry Research: Neuroimaging* 222: 43–51.

Schiffer, Boris, and Corinne Vonlaufen. 2011. "Executive Dysfunctions in Pedophilic and Nonpedophilic Child Molesters." *The Journal of Sexual Medicine* 8: 1975–1984.

Sijtsema, Jelle J., René Veenstra, Siegwart Lindenberg, Arie M. van Roon, Frank C. Verhulst, Johan Ormel, and Harriëtte Riese. 2010. "Mediation of Sensation Seeking and Behavioral

Inhibition on the Relationship Between Heart Rate and Antisocial Behavior: The TRAILS Study." *Journal of the American Academy of Child & Adolescent Psychiatry* 49: 493–502.

Soderstrom, Hendrik, Kaj Blennow, Anna Manhem, and A. Forsman. 2001. "CSF Studies in Violent Offenders." *Journal of Neural Transmission* 108: 869–878.

Soderstrom, Hendrik, Kaj Blennow, A. K. Sjodin, and A. Forsman. 2003. "New Evidence for an Association Between the CSF HVA: 5-HIAA Ratio and Psychopathic Traits." *Journal of Neurology, Neurosurgery & Psychiatry* 74: 918–921.

Sondeijker, Frouke E. P. L., Robert F. Ferdinand, Albertine J. Oldehinkel, Henning Tiemeier, Johan Ormel, and Frank C. Verhulst. 2008. "HPA-Axis Activity as a Predictor of Future Disruptive Behaviors in Young Adolescents." *Psychophysiology* 45: 398–404.

Stålenheim, E. Gunilla, Elias Eriksson, Lars von Knorring, and Leif Wide. 1998. "Testosterone as a Biological Marker in Psychopathy and Alcoholism." *Psychiatry Research* 77: 79–88.

Stanford, Matthew S., Sarah M. Conklin, Laura E. Helfritz, and Tim R. Kockler. 2007. "P3 Amplitude Reduction and Executive Function Deficits in Men Convicted of Spousal/Partner Abuse." *Personality and Individual Differences* 43: 365–375.

Tarter, Ralph E., Levent Kirisci, Judith S. Gavaler, Maureen Reynolds, Galina Kirillova, Duncan B. Clark, Jionglin Wu, Howard B. Moss, and Michael Vanyukov. 2009. "Prospective Study of the Association Between Abandoned Dwellings and Testosterone Level on the Development of Behaviors Leading to Cannabis Use Disorder in Boys." *Biological Psychiatry* 65: 116–121.

Taylor, Jeanette, William G. Iacono, and Matt McGue. 2000. "Evidence for a Genetic Etiology of Early-Onset Delinquency." *Journal of Abnormal Psychology* 109: 634–643.

Tellegen, Auke, and Niels G. Waller. 2008. "Exploring Personality Through Test Construction: Development of the Multidimensional Personality Questionnaire." In *The SAGE Handbook of Personality Theory and Assessment*, Vol. 2, edited by Gregory J. Boyle, Gerald Matthews, and Donald H. Saklofske, 261–292. London: Sage.

Tuvblad, Catherine. 2013. "Genetic Influences on Antisocial Behavior over the Life Course." In *Routledge Handbook of Biosocial Criminology*, edited by Matt DeLisi and Michael G. Vaughn, 77–100. New York: Routledge.

Tuvblad, Catherine, Martin Grann, and Paul Lichtenstein. 2006. "Heritability for Adolescent Antisocial Behavior Differs with Socioeconomic Status: Gene–Environment Interaction." *Journal of Child Psychology and Psychiatry* 47: 734–743.

Tuvblad, Catherine, Jurgita Narusyte, Martin Grann, Jerzy Sarnecki, and Paul Lichtenstein. 2011. "The Genetic and Environmental Etiology of Antisocial Behavior from Childhood to Emerging Adulthood." *Behavior Genetics* 41: 629–640.

van Goozen, Stephanie H. M., Graeme Fairchild, Heddeke Snoek, and Gordon T. Harold. 2007. "The Evidence for a Neurobiological Model of Childhood Antisocial Behavior." *Psychological Bulletin* 133: 149–182.

Van Goozen, Stephanie H. M., Walter Matthys, Peggy T. Cohen-Kettenis, Jos H. H. Thijssen, and Herman van Engeland. 1998. "Adrenal Androgens and Aggression in Conduct Disorder Prepubertal Boys and Normal Controls." *Biological Psychiatry* 43: 156–158.

Van Bokhoven, Irene, Stephanie H. M. Van Goozen, Herman Van Engeland, Benoist Schaal, Louise Arseneault, Jean R. Séguin, Jean-Marc Assaad, Daniel S. Nagin, Frank Vitaro, and Richard E. Tremblay. 2006. "Salivary Testosterone and Aggression, Delinquency, and Social Dominance in a Population-Based Longitudinal Study of Adolescent Males." *Hormones and Behavior* 50: 118–125.

Van Honk, Jack, Dennis J. Schutter, Peter A. Bos, Anne-Wil Kruijt, Eef G. Lentjes, and Simon Baron-Cohen. 2011. "Testosterone Administration Impairs Cognitive Empathy in Women Depending on Second-to-Fourth Digit Ratio." *Proceedings of the National Academy of Sciences* 108: 3448–3452.

Vaske, Jamie, Jamie Newsome, and Danielle Boisvert. 2013. "The Mediating Effects of Verbal Skills in the Relationship Between Low Birth Weight and Childhood Aggressive Behaviour." *Infant and Child Development* 22: 235–249.

Vaske, Jamie, Jamie Newsome, Danielle L. Boisvert, Alex R. Piquero, Angela D. Paradis, and Stephen L. Buka. 2015. "The Impact of Low Birth Weight and Maternal Age on Adulthood Offending." *Journal of Criminal Justice* 43: 49–56.

Viding, Essi, R. James R. Blair, Terrie E. Moffitt, and Robert Plomin. 2005. "Evidence for Substantial Genetic Risk for Psychopathy in 7-Year-Olds." *Journal of Child Psychology and Psychiatry* 46: 592–597.

Viding, Essi, Paul J. Frick, and Robert Plomin. 2007. "Aetiology of the Relationship Between Callous–Unemotional Traits and Conduct Problems in Childhood." *The British Journal of Psychiatry* 190: s33–38.

Volavka, J. A. N., Robert Bilder, and Karen Nolan. 2004. "Catecholamines and Aggression: The Role of COMT and MAO Polymorphisms." *Annals of the New York Academy of Sciences* 1036: 393–398.

Wakschlag, Lauren S., Benjamin B. Lahey, Rolf Loeber, Stephanie M. Green, Rachel A. Gordon, and Bennett L. Leventhal. 1997. "Maternal Smoking During Pregnancy and the Risk of Conduct Disorder in Boys." *Archives of General Psychiatry* 54: 670–676.

Wakschlag, Lauren S., Kate E. Pickett, Edwin Cook Jr, Neal L. Benowitz, and Bennett L. Leventhal. 2002. "Maternal Smoking During Pregnancy and Severe Antisocial Behavior in Offspring: A Review." *American Journal of Public Health* 92: 966–974.

Wikström, Per-Olof H. (2005). "The Social Origins of Pathways in Crime: Towards a Developmental Ecological Action Theory of Crime Involvement and Its Changes. In *Integrated Developmental & Life-Course Theories of Offending: Advances in Criminological Theory,* Vol. 14, edited by David P. Farrington, 211–245. New Brunswick, NJ: Transaction.

Wilson, James Q. and Richard Herrnstein. 1985. *Crime and Human Nature.* New York: Simon & Schuster.

Wright, John Paul, Kim N. Dietrich, M. Douglas Ris, Richard W. Hornung, Stephanie D. Wessel, Bruce P. Lanphear, Mona Ho, and Mary N. Rae. 2008. "Association of Prenatal and Childhood Blood Lead Concentrations with Criminal Arrests in Early Adulthood." *PLoS Medicine* 5: e101.

Yang, Yaling, and Adrian Raine. 2009. "Prefrontal Structural and Functional Brain Imaging Findings in Antisocial, Violent, and Psychopathic Individuals: A Meta-Analysis." *Psychiatry Research: Neuroimaging* 174: 81–88.

Yang, Yaling, Adrian Raine, Patrick Colletti, Arthur W. Toga, and Katherine L. Narr. 2010a. "Morphological Alterations in the Prefrontal Cortex and the Amygdala in Unsuccessful Psychopaths." *Journal of Abnormal Psychology* 119: 546–554.

Yang, Yaling, Adrian Raine, Chen-Bo Han, Robert A. Schug, Arthur W. Toga, and Katherine L. Narr. 2010b. "Reduced Hippocampal and Parahippocampal Volumes in Murderers with Schizophrenia." *Psychiatry Research: Neuroimaging* 182: 9–13.

Yang, Yaling, Adrian Raine, Todd Lencz, Susan Bihrle, Lori LaCasse, and Patrick Colletti. 2005. "Volume Reduction in Prefrontal Gray Matter in Unsuccessful Criminal Psychopaths." *Biological Psychiatry* 57: 1103–1108.

Yang, Yaling, Adrian Raine, Katherine L. Narr, Patrick Colletti, and Arthur W. Toga. 2009. "Localization of Deformations Within the Amygdala in Individuals with Psychopathy." *Archives of General Psychiatry* 66: 986–994.

Yang, Yaling, Pan Wang, Laura A. Baker, Katherine L. Narr, Shantanu, H. Joshi, George Hafzalla, Adrian Raine, Paul M. Thompson. 2015. "Thicker Temporal Cortex Associates with a Developmental Trajectory for Psychopathic Traits in Adolescents." *PloS One* 10: e0127025.

Yildirim, Baris O. and Jan J. L. Derksen. 2012. "A Review on the Relationship Between Testosterone and Life-Course Persistent Antisocial Behavior." *Psychiatry Research* 200: 984–1010.

Yu, Rongqin, Jaap Nieuwenhuis, Wim Meeus, Pieter Hooimeijer, Hans M. Koot, and Susan Branje. 2016. "Biological Sensitivity to Context: Cortisol Awakening Response Moderates the Effects of Neighbourhood Density on the Development of Adolescent Externalizing Problem Behaviours." *Biological Psychology* 120: 96–107.

Zai, Clement C., Katherine E. Muir, Behdin Nowrouzi, Sajid A. Shaikh, Esther Choi, Laura Berall, Marc-Olivier Trépanier, Joseph H. Beitchman, and James L. Kennedy. 2012. "Possible Genetic Association Between Vasopressin Receptor 1B and Child Aggression." *Psychiatry Research* 200: 784–788.

CHAPTER 18

PERSONALITY AND OTHER INDIVIDUAL INFLUENCES ON OFFENDING

DARRICK JOLLIFFE AND DAVID P. FARRINGTON

It is a basic assumption of psychology that behavior arises out of an interaction between an individual and the environment. Interestingly, the importance that criminologists have placed on the individual side of this equation in explaining criminal behavior has varied throughout the history of the discipline (for a review, see Hollin 2007). Theoretical viewpoints have evolved from placing the causes of crime wholly within the individual (as in early biological positivism) to viewing the individual as a passive vessel through which larger social or environmental factors exert their influence (such as conflict theories). However, as the methodological sophistication of research examining the causes and correlates of offending has increased, these two extreme views have been moderated. As evidenced by the reviews of the main developmental and life-course theories earlier in this volume, the most influential theories of criminal behavior acknowledge that both the individual and the environment have a role to play in understanding the development of offending. It is now widely acknowledged that offending is the result of a complex interaction between types of individuals and types of environments with reciprocal effects (Lynam et al. 2000; Zimmerman 2012).

Two key research findings that have been replicated in numerous studies make the individual aspect of this individual/ environment equation essential to fully understand the development of offending. First, research has clearly demonstrated that individuals differ in their potential to commit criminal and antisocial acts given a particular opportunity, situation, or victim (Farrington 2009). As crime is a socially and legally defined concept, any potential to commit crime is probably part of a broader potential to commit antisocial acts, but this chapter focuses on crime. Second, a great deal of criminal career research has demonstrated that the relative ordering of individuals on this potential is remarkably stable over time even though the absolute level of offending and the types of offending vary with age. That is, individuals who tend to be "worst" at one age also tend to be "worst" at later ages (Farrington 1998; Farrington and McGee 2017).

It is essential to distinguish between descriptions of criminal potential, the results of criminal potential, and the likely causes of criminal potential. Terms such as anti-social, aggressive, or hostile seem essentially to refer to people with high criminal potential, while behavioral variables such as truanting, physical fighting and oppositional behavior, as well as delinquency and offending seem to be the outcomes or behavioral manifestations of underlying criminal potential. However, constructs such as low guilt, weak conscience, low self-control, high impulsivity, emotional coldness, callousness, low empathy, fearlessness, egocentricity (self-centeredness), poor conditionability, and a poor ability to manipulate abstract concepts seem more likely to be causes of high criminal potential. Obviously, it is important to establish the key underlying constructs that are linked to individual differences in offending behavior.

Long-term between-individual differences in criminal potential (intended to ex-plain why some people are more likely to commit offenses than other people in a par-ticular situation) can be distinguished from short-term within-individual variations in criminal potential (intended to explain why people are more likely to commit crimes at some times and in some situations than at other times and in other situations). Long-term criminal potential is likely to be influenced by biological, individual, family, peer, school, community, and societal factors. Short-term criminal potential is likely to be influenced by situational events such as being insulted or frustrated, getting drunk, or seeing a tempting criminal opportunity. While both topics are important, the focus in this chapter is on explaining long-term between-individual differences in criminal potential.

Specifically, this chapter summarizes knowledge about the key individual difference factors that have been proposed to underlie criminal potential. Section I discusses tem-perament and personality; Section II explores the relation between impulsivity and offending, and Section III investigates low intelligence and offending. Sections IV and V examine the evidence for low empathy and cognitive (decision-making) factors, re-spectively. In isolation, these (or any other) individual differences cannot fully explain the development of offending, but the strength of the evidence suggests that any com-plete theory would need to take account of at least some of these factors, as all are po-tential "risk factors" for later offending. Risk factors are defined as factors that predict a high likelihood of later offending (e.g., Kazdin et al. 1997). By definition, risk factors require longitudinal data in order to be identified. While there are different ways of conceptualizing a risk factor (see Farrington and Welsh 2008), generally it refers to an extreme category of an explanatory variable. For example, the risk factor of low intelli-gence is an extreme category of the explanatory variable of intelligence.

It is important to try to establish which risk factors are causally related to offending. To the extent that a risk factor causes offending, interventions could be designed to re-duce its impact and in turn reduce offending. However, it is extremely difficult to estab-lish causal influences in non-experimental research. It is widely accepted that the main criteria for establishing that X causes Y are (1) X is correlated with Y, (2) X can change or be changed within individuals, (3) X precedes Y, and (4) X predicts Y after controlling for confounding variables (Kraemer, Lowe, and Kupfer 2005; Murray, Farrington, and Eisner 2009). Therefore, in trying to draw conclusions about whether any factors might have a causal influence on offending, this chapter will focus on especially on knowledge gained in major prospective longitudinal studies of offending, in which community samples of at least several hundred people are followed up from childhood into adolescence and adulthood, with repeated personal interviews as well as the collection of record data.

I. Personality and Temperament

Personality is defined as an individual's typical pattern of thinking, feeling, and behaving across situations and time (Kenrick and Funder 1988) and is proposed to be composed of a set of traits such as impulsiveness, sensation seeking, assertiveness, modesty, and dutifulness. There is, however, no definitive list of personality traits, and in some cases different terms are probably used to describe the same underlying construct. Furthermore, many constructs that are assumed to underlie behavior are not included under the heading of personality. This is true, for example, of intelligence and moral reasoning and of cognitive processes such as thinking, reasoning, and decision-making. However, the boundaries between personality and all of these constructs are not well defined. For example, it has been suggested that neuropsychological deficits in the executive functions of the brain (i.e., reasoning, planning, sustaining attention, and concentration) can cause both low intelligence and high impulsiveness (Moffitt 1990). Higher-order personality dimensions, such as extraversion, are clusters of personality traits that are typically found to be associated with one another (e.g., impulsiveness and sensation seeking). In their meta-analysis of 152 longitudinal studies, Roberts and Del Vecchio (2000) reported that average test-retest correlations for personality traits increased from .31 in childhood to .54 in the college years to .74 in adulthood (for an average time interval of seven years).

Temperament is basically the early childhood equivalent of personality, although there is more emphasis in the temperament literature on constitutional predisposition and on genetic and biological factors that influence temperament. The modern study of child temperament began with the New York Longitudinal Study of Chess and Thomas (1984). Children in their first five years of life were rated on temperamental dimensions by their parents, and these dimensions were combined into three broad categories of easy, difficult, and "slow-to-warm-up" temperament. Having a difficult temperament at ages 3 to 4 (frequent irritability, low amenability and adaptability, irregular habits) predicted poor adult psychiatric adjustment at ages 17 to 24.

Remarkably, Bates (1989) found that mothers' ratings of difficult temperament as early as age 6 months (defined primarily as frequent, intense expressions of negative emotions) predicted mothers' ratings of child conduct problems between the ages of

3 and 6 years. Similar results were obtained in the Australian Temperament Project, which found that children who were rated as irritable, not amenable, or showing behavior problems at ages 4 to 8 months tended to be rated as aggressive at ages 7 to 8 years (Sanson et al. 1993). When information at each age comes from the same source, it is possible that the continuity lies in the rater, rather than the child. However, in a sample of 103 children followed up from age 2 to 17, Guerin et al. (2003) found that difficult temperament in infancy, rated by mothers, predicted a greater frequency of attention problems, aggressive problems, and thinking problems in the elementary school years, as reported by teachers.

Other researchers have investigated more specific dimensions of temperament than the rather vague "difficult temperament." For example, Kagan, Reznick, and Snidman (1988) in Boston classified children as inhibited (shy or fearful) or uninhibited at age 21 months on the basis of their observed reactions to a strange situation and concluded that about 10 to 20 percent of children were inhibited, while about 30 to 40 percent were uninhibited. They found that children were significantly stable on this classification up to age 7 years. Furthermore, the uninhibited children at age 21 months significantly tended to be identified as aggressive at age 13 years, according to self and parent reports (Schwartz, Snidman, and Kagan 1996).

There are several systems for classifying childhood temperament. Evans and Rothbart (2007) identified three important dimensions: (1) effortful control (including planning ahead and the suppression of inappropriate responses), which was related to the Big Five dimension of conscientiousness in adulthood (see later); (b) negative affect (including frustration, fear, and sadness), which was related to the Big Five dimension of neuroticism; and (c) extraversion (including impulsiveness and low shyness), which was related to the Big Five dimension of extraversion. Lahey et al. (2006) also identified three important dimensions (low prosociality, negative emotionality, and high daring) and showed that all three, measured at age 7, predicted delinquency up to age 17 in the Pittsburgh Youth Study, which is a prospective longitudinal survey of over 1,500 Pittsburgh boys.

The most important results on the link between childhood temperament and later offending have been obtained in the Dunedin longitudinal study in New Zealand, which followed up over 1,000 children from age 3 years into their thirties. Temperament at age 3 was rated by observing the child's behavior during a testing session involving cognitive and motor tasks. The most important dimension of temperament was being undercontrolled (restless, impulsive, with poor attention), which predicted aggression, self-reported delinquency, and convictions at ages 18 to 21 and problem gambling at age 32 (Caspi 2000; Slutske et al. 2012).

Before 1990, the most influential theory of personality and crime was that of Eysenck (1996). He viewed offending as natural and even rational, on the assumption that human beings were hedonistic, sought pleasure, and avoided pain. He assumed that delinquent acts, such as theft, violence, and vandalism, were essentially pleasurable or beneficial to the offender. In order to explain why everyone was not a criminal, Eysenck suggested that the hedonistic tendency to commit crimes was opposed by the conscience, which was viewed as a conditioned fear response.

Eysenck proposed that the conscience was built up in childhood. Each time a child committed a disapproved act and was punished by a parent, the pain and fear aroused in the child tended to become associated with the act by a process of classical (automatic) conditioning. After children had been punished several times for the same act, they felt fear when they next contemplated it, and this fear tended to stop them from committing it. According to the theory, this conditioned fear response was the conscience, and it would be experienced subjectively as guilt if the child committed a disapproved act.

On the Eysenck theory, the people who commit offenses are those who have not built up strong consciences, either because their conditioning was poor (i.e., they had not been taught right from wrong) or because they have inherently poor conditionability. Poor conditionability is linked to Eysenck's three dimensions of personality: extraversion (E; sensation-seeking, sociability), neuroticism (N; anxiety, depression), and psychoticism (P; toughmindedness, low empathy).

According to Eysenck, people who are high on E build up conditioned responses less well because they have low levels of cortical arousal. People who are high on N also condition less well, because their high resting level of anxiety interferes with their conditioning. Also, since N acts as a drive, reinforcing existing behavioral tendencies, neurotic extraverts should be particularly criminal. Eysenck also predicted that people who are high on P would tend to be offenders, because the traits included in his definition of psychoticism (emotional coldness, low empathy, high aggression) were typical of criminals. However, the meaning of the P scale is unclear, and it might perhaps be more accurately labeled as psychopathy.

A review of studies relating Eysenck's personality dimensions to official and self-reported offending concluded that high N (but not E) was related to official offending, while high E (but not N) was related to self-reported offending (Farrington, Biron, and LeBlanc 1982). High P was related to both, but this could have been a tautological result, since many of the items on the P scale are connected with antisocial behavior or were selected in light of their ability to discriminate between prisoners and nonprisoners. In a prospective longitudinal study of over 400 London boys, those high on both E and N tended to be juvenile self-reported offenders, adult official offenders, and adult self-reported offenders but not juvenile official offenders. These relationships held independently of other criminogenic risk factors, such as low family income, low intelligence, and poor parental child-rearing behavior.

When individual items of the personality questionnaire were studied, however, it was clear that the significant relationships were caused by the items measuring impulsiveness (e.g., doing things quickly without stopping to think). Therefore, it seems likely that research inspired by the Eysenck theory essentially confirms the link between impulsiveness and offending (see later). More recent empirical studies (e.g., Carrasco et al. 2006) and meta-analyses (e.g., Cale 2006) that have compared Eysenck's dimensions with crime and antisocial behavior have given further support to this conclusion.

In recent years the Five Factor Model (FFM) of personality has replaced Eysenck's three-factor theory as the primary model of personality traits (McCrae and Costa 1997). The FFM includes the dimensions of E and N (defined similarly to those of Eysenck), as well as agreeableness (A; altruism, modesty), openness (O; imagination, aesthetic sensitivity), and conscientiousness (C; self-discipline, competence). Research has suggested that Eysenck's P is inversely related to both A and C (Costa, McRae, and Dye 1991). McCrae and Costa (1997) also found that the same five factors emerged in several different countries.

A number of studies have related the Big Five personality dimensions to offending. In the Pittsburgh Youth Study, John et al. (1994) found that the most delinquent boys scored significantly lower on agreeableness, conscientiousness, and openness and significantly higher on extraversion. In Australia, Heaven (1996) reported that agreeableness and conscientiousness were most strongly (negatively) correlated with delinquency, while Van Dam, Janssens, and De Bruyn (2005) in the Netherlands reported that students scored significantly higher on agreeableness and openness than juvenile delinquents. In England, Jolliffe (2013) similarly found that low conscientiousness and low agreeableness were independently related to self-reported offending of adolescent males (controlling for low socioeconomic status and coming from a single-parent family). Interestingly, while low agreeableness also characterized adolescent female self-reported offending, so did extraversion and openness, but only when combined with coming from a single-parent family. Generally research has suggested that environmental factors might be more important for explaining female as opposed to male offending (Hedderman and Jolliffe 2015).

In their meta-analysis relating a number of personality scales to antisocial behavior, Miller and Lynam (2001) concluded that low agreeableness and low consciousness were significantly related to antisocial behavior, while neuroticism was only weakly related and extraversion was not related. In the most recent meta-analysis, Jones, Miller, and Lynam (2011) concluded that agreeableness and conscientiousness were negatively related to antisocial behavior and aggression, while neuroticism was positively correlated. The most important facets that were related to antisocial behavior were hostility and impulsiveness (N), straightforwardness and compliance (A; negatively), and dutifulness and deliberation (C; negatively).

II. Impulsiveness

Impulsiveness is one of many terms in the literature that refers to a general reduction in people's ability to control their behavior. Other similar terms include low self-control, hyperactivity, inattention, a poor ability to delay gratification, risk-taking, sensation seeking, and not considering the consequences before acting. There are differences in the specific definitions of many of these terms, but it is safe to say that a relationship has been identified between these variables and poor life outcomes such as smoking (Burke et al. 2007), gambling (Clarke 2006), drinking (Klinteberg et al. 1993), and offending (White et al. 1994).

High impulsiveness might contribute to an increased likelihood of offending directly, indirectly, or though some intermediate combination. By the direct pathway, impulsiveness would have a fundamental impact on the way in which an individual acts in any given situation. With shorter time horizons, less foresight, and less cognitive energy available for the contemplation of potential responses, an impulsive individual would, on balance, select the option that provides the most immediate perceived benefit. Numerous researchers and theorists have detailed how criminal offending tends to satisfy immediate urges at the risk of later, uncertain, and occasionally hypothetical negative consequences (e.g., Gottfredson and Hirschi 1990; Farrington and Welsh 2008)

Wilson and Herrnstein (1985) developed a criminological theory that was based on the premise that individuals differ in their underlying criminal tendencies and that whether a person chooses to commit a crime in a situation depends on whether the perceived benefits of offending are considered to outweigh the perceived costs. They focused on how the importance of later consequences varied with the time horizons of different individuals. They further argued that those with a significant degree of impulsiveness were more likely to commit offenses because their calculation of the costs and benefits of offending were biased by their desire for immediate reinforcement. That is, an impulsive individual gives the most weight to the benefits of offending that offer instant rewards (e.g., material gain, peer approval, etc.), and is less influenced by the later potential costs of offending (e.g., the risk of being apprehended, loss of reputation or employment, etc.).

The General Theory of Crime proposed by Gottfredson and Hirschi (1990) is similar to the theory of Wilson and Herrnstein in the importance that it places on impulsiveness as a key explanatory factor. The key construct of their theory was termed "low self-control," which referred to the extent to which individuals were vulnerable to the temptations of the moment. People with low self-control were impulsive, took risks, had low cognitive and academic skills, were self-centered, had low empathy, and had short time horizons. Hence, they found it hard to defer gratification, and their decisions to offend were insufficiently influenced by the future possible painful consequences of offending.

Other researchers have suggested that high impulsiveness may also contribute to an increased likelihood of offending indirectly through a person–environment interaction (e.g., Moffitt 1993). For example, an impulsive child may prove to be a challenge to even the most conscientious parent, over time eliciting poor parenting, which is in itself an established risk factor for later offending (Farrington and Welsh 2008). Similarly, impulsivity may lead to offending by reducing the likelihood of school success. Using the repeated assessments of the Pittsburgh Youth Study, Defoe, Farrington, and Loeber (2013) used a cross-lagged panel analysis to investigate the interrelations between delinquency, hyperactivity, low academic achievement, depression, and socioeconomic status. The results suggested that hyperactivity and low socioeconomic status caused low achievement, which in turn caused delinquency. In contrast, delinquency was found to be the cause of depression.

Pratt and Cullen (2000) undertook a review and meta-analysis to empirically test the relationship between low self-control and crime. In their review, low self-control was operationalized using the definition provided by Gottfredson and Hirschi (1990) in their General Theory of Crime; that is, someone who is "impulsive, insensitive, physical as opposed to mental, risk-taking, short sighted, and non-verbal" (Gottfredson and Hirschi, 1990, p. 90). Pratt and Cullen (2000) analyzed the results of 21 empirical studies, which measured low self-control, and found that this was strongly associated with crime, with mean effect sizes (d) ranging from .47 to .58. Many of the studies included in the review of Pratt and Cullen (2000) assessed low self-control using the Grasmick self-control scale (Grasmick et al., 1993). While corresponding well with the original conceptualization of low self-control, this measure does not allow for the separation of hyperactivity, impulsiveness, and inattention, and it is not possible to separate these features of impulsiveness from a number of other concepts included in this very specific definition (e.g., lack of sympathy).

Another review was undertaken by Pratt et al. (2002), who examined the relationship between attention deficit hyperactivity disorder (ADHD) and crime and delinquency. Usefully, Pratt et al. (2002) disaggregated the ADHD construct into four subcategories (attention deficit (AD) excluding hyperactivity, AD plus hyperactivity, hyperactivity, and an additional category for ADHD concepts such as attention problems or emotional or behavioral problems, which are often cited as proxies of AD or ADHD) and examined their relationships to crime and delinquency. The AD excluding hyperactivity category had the strongest relationship with crime and delinquency, and the ADHD concepts category had the weakest relationship. Pratt et al. (2002) concluded that ADHD in its various forms appeared to have a general relationship with crime and delinquency.

A major limitation of these reviews is that, because they included studies where the key construct (self-control or ADHD) was assessed retrospectively, it was not possible to determine causal ordering. That is, self-control or ADHD might contribute to an increased likelihood of offending, but it is also possible that delinquent activity may cause a reduction in people's self-control or make them more impulsive and hyperactive (Moffitt 1990). The precise form of causal ordering can only be established in prospective longitudinal studies where impulsiveness is measured before offending.

A number of prospective longitudinal surveys show that early measures of impulsiveness are related to later offending. In a study of over 4,000 males in Copenhagen, hyperactivity (restlessness and poor concentration) measured at ages 11 to 13 significantly predicted arrests for violence up to age 22, especially among boys whose mothers had experienced delivery complications. More than half of those with both hyperactivity and delivery complications were arrested for violence, compared to less than 10 percent of the remainder (Brennan, Mednick, and Mednick 1993). In another prospective longitudinal study of over 7,000 children followed from pregnancy in Australia, problems of attention and restlessness at age 5 more than doubled the risk of delinquency at age 14 (Bor, McGee, and Fagan 2004).

In the Cambridge Study in Delinquent Development of 411 males followed up from age 8 to age 48, boys who were identified by teachers as lacking in concentration or restless, those identified by parents, peers, or teachers as the most daring or risk-taking, and those who were the most impulsive on psychomotor tests at age 8 to 10 all tended to become offenders later in life. Later self-report measures of impulsiveness were also related to offending. Daring, poor concentration, and restlessness all predicted both official convictions and self-reported delinquency, and daring was consistently one of the best independent predictors (Farrington 1992).

A multi-method, multi-source assessment of impulsivity was conducted using data from over 400 males in a prospective longitudinal study of the development of antisocial behavior in Pittsburgh (White et al. 1994). The measures that were most strongly related to self-reported delinquency at ages 10 and 13 were teacher-rated impulsiveness (e.g., "acts without thinking"), self-reported impulsiveness (e.g., scores on the Eysenck impulsivity scale), self-reported undercontrol (e.g., "unable to delay gratification"), motor restlessness (from videotaped observations), and psychomotor impulsiveness (from the Trail Making Test). Generally, the verbal behavior rating tests produced stronger relationships with offending than the psychomotor performance tasks, suggesting that cognitive impulsiveness (based on thinking processes) was more relevant to delinquency than was behavioral impulsiveness (based on psychomotor test performance). Future time perception and delay of gratification tasks were only weakly related to self-reported offending.

Jolliffe and Farrington (2009) undertook a systematic review and meta-analysis of the relationship between early measures of impulsiveness and later violence using only data from prospective longitudinal studies. The results suggested that early measures of impulsiveness (measured as early as age 5) were quite strongly related to later violence (measured as late as age 40). While all measures of impulsiveness were associated with later violence, measures of daring and risk-taking had a particularly strong relationship with later violence. The authors suggested that daring and risk-taking might influence offending via a direct pathway linking impulsiveness and later offending (e.g., Wilson and Herrnstein, 1985; Gottfredson and Hirschi, 1990), whereas the other forms of impulsiveness (e.g., poor concentration) might have a more muted effect through mediating variables (e.g., school failure).

III. Intelligence

Intelligence is usually measured according to the ability to manipulate abstract concepts, and these measures often include assessments of both verbal intelligence (e.g., producing synonyms of given words) and performance intelligence (e.g., replicating a picture pattern using blocks). Intelligence measures are designed to predict later success at school, and they appear to do this well (Barchard 2005). There is strong evidence to suggest that offenders score low on measures of intelligence (e.g., Hirschi and Hindelang 1977; Wilson and Herrnstein 1985; Lynam et al. 1993), and this is especially true of verbal measures of intelligence (West and Farrington 1973). However, the mechanism that connects low intelligence and offending is still hotly debated. Some researchers have asserted that the relationship between low intelligence and offending is actually spurious, while others suggest that indirect mechanisms provide the best account of the research findings. There are also some who believe that the relationship between low intelligence and offending is direct and causal.

The argument that the relationship between low intelligence and offending is spurious is largely based on the assumption that intelligence tests are biased against persons from lower social classes or ethnic minorities. Intelligence tests are designed to measure school success, which is proposed to be a value of the middle and upper classes (e.g., Cohen 1955). Because of wider socio-political forces, less affluent and more marginalized social groups are more likely to be offenders and will also be less successful in intelligence tests, perhaps lacking motivation to complete them properly. This could create an illusory link between poor results on intelligence tests and offending. These suggestions, however, are not supported by the research. There is little evidence showing bias against social or ethnic groups on measures of intelligence (Cole 1981; Reynolds 1995), and while motivation does appear to have some influence on the results of intelligence tests, the relationship between low intelligence and offending holds up after controlling for the observed level of motivation (Lynam et al. 1993).

Some have suggested that it is not offenders generally who are less intelligent, but only those offenders who come to the attention of the criminal justice system (and are therefore included in most studies of "offenders"). In other words, it is suggested that low intelligence leads to an increased likelihood of detection among offenders. Again however, there is little evidence for this so-called differential detection hypothesis. For example, Farrington (1992) found that low intelligence was almost as strongly related to self-reported offending as it was to officially recorded convictions. Also, Moffitt and Silva (1988) discovered that the average intelligence score of self-reported offenders who had, or had not, been detected by the police was similar, and that both of these groups had significantly lower scores than those of a comparison group who did not self-report offenses. There may be a relationship between intelligence and the depth of penetration into the criminal justice system, such that those with lower levels of intelligence are more likely to be convicted and imprisoned than those with higher levels of intelligence, but this might also reflect a relationship between low intelligence and an increase in the frequency or seriousness of offending.

Another less widely explored hypothesis is that the relationship between low intelligence and offending is actually reversed, and rather than low intelligence increasing the likelihood of offending, offending might actually decrease measured intelligence (e.g., Lynam et al. 1993). Many aspects of a criminal lifestyle, such as drug/alcohol use and physical injury (especially head trauma incurred in fights), could result in impaired cognitive functioning (Moffitt 1990). While it is plausible that offending could decrease measured intelligence, this does not provide a full explanation of the observed relationship. This is because of the overwhelming evidence from prospective longitudinal studies (see below) where intelligence was measured well before offending and antisocial behavior had started (e.g., Denno 1990; Schweinhart et al. 1993; Stattin and Klackenberg-Larson 1993).

It has also been suggested that the low intelligence–offending relationship is actually produced by an alternative variable that results in both low intelligence and offending. Social class has most commonly been suggested as this alternative variable (e.g., Lynam et al. 1993), although other variables such as social bonding (Hirschi 1969) and impulsivity (Felson and Staff 2006) have also been proposed. According to this argument, it is not that low intelligence causes offending, but rather that an individual's low social class (or poor bonding/high impulsivity) causes both lower scores on measures of intelligence and an increased likelihood of offending. To a great extent, however, this argument has also not been supported by the research findings. This is because studies have continued to identify a link between low intelligence and offending while controlling for these (and other) plausible alternative variables (e.g., Hirschi and Hindelang 1977; Lynam et al. 1993; Farrington and Welsh 2008).

Clearly there is little, if any, evidence to support the suggestion that intelligence and offending are not functionally linked. In fact the results of a number of prospective longitudinal studies (where intelligence was measured early in life) clearly show that intelligence is an important predictor of later offending. For example, Stattin and Klackenberg-Larson (1993) in Sweden reported that low intelligence measured at age 3 significantly predicted officially recorded offending up to age 30. Frequent offenders (with four or more offenses) were found to have particularly low intelligence, and, importantly, all of these results held up after controlling for social class. Likewise, Schweinhart, Barnes, and Weikart (1993) found that low intelligence measured at age 4 significantly predicted the number of arrests up to age 27, and Lipsitt, Buka, and Lipsitt (1990) also showed that low intelligence at age 4 predicted later juvenile delinquency.

Similar results have been obtained with other samples. In Philadelphia, Denno (1990) used multiple measures of intelligence to demonstrate the link with offending. In her study, low verbal and performance intelligence, measured at ages 4 and 7, as well as low scores on the California Achievement tests at ages 13 to 14 (vocabulary, comprehension, math, language, spelling), all predicted arrests for violence up to age 22. In Chicago, McCord and Ensminger (1997) discovered that low intelligence at age 6 predicted arrests for violent crimes up to age 32. In Copenhagen, Hogh and Wolf (1983) found that low intelligence at age 12 significantly predicted police-recorded violence between ages 15 and 22. The link between low intelligence and violence was strongest among lower class boys.

In the Cambridge Study in Delinquent Development, low intelligence and low school attainment both predicted juvenile and adult convictions (Farrington 1992). Low intelligence at ages 8 to 10 was also an important independent predictor of spouse assault at age 32 (Farrington 1994). In addition, low intelligence and attainment predicted aggression and bullying at age 14 (Farrington 1989, 1993). Low non-verbal intelligence was especially characteristic of juvenile recidivists and those first convicted at the earliest ages (10 to 13). This factor was about as strong a predictor of juvenile convictions as other important early risk factors (low family income, large family size, poor parental child-rearing behavior, poor parental supervision, and poor concentration or restlessness), but it was a weaker predictor than having a convicted parent and daring or risk-taking. Measures of intelligence and school attainment predicted measures of offending independently of other risk factors such as low family income and large family size (Farrington 1990).

Because of the commonly found association between low intelligence, school failure, and offending, some researchers have suggested that low intelligence may have an influence on offending indirectly by increasing the probability of school failure (e.g., Hirschi and Hindelang 1977). It is argued that low intelligence leads to failure at school, and it is this failure, and the potential secondary effects on associating with similarly situated others (e.g., peer delinquency) and later employment opportunities, that actually result in offending. Support for this hypothesis comes from the fact that measures of intelligence and school failure are strongly correlated with one another and both predict later offending (West and Farrington 1973; Farrington 1992). Lynam et al. (1993) undertook an important test of this relationship using data from the Pittsburgh Youth Study. The results suggested that different mechanisms might operate between low intelligence and offending based on ethnicity. For African American boys, the evidence was supportive of a relationship between low intelligence and self-reported offending that was mediated by school failure. For Caucasian boys, school failure only marginally reduced the observed relationship between low intelligence and self-reported offending, suggesting that a direct relationship was the best explanation of the data.

A number of other variables have been suggested as potentially mediating the relationship between low intelligence and later offending. For example, low intelligence could lead to being allocated to different curriculum tracks in school. Being placed on a remedial curriculum track could have detrimental impact on self-esteem, which could increase the likelihood of offending (McGloin and Pratt 2003). Also, low intelligence could have its influence indirectly by leading to greater impulsivity. Koolhof et al. (2007) investigated the role of impulsivity in the offending of 428 boys from the Pittsburgh Youth Study. The sample was divided into four groups: low-IQ serious delinquents, higher-IQ serious delinquents, low-IQ non- to moderate delinquents, and higher-IQ non- to moderate delinquents. The research showed that both intelligence and impulsivity were related to later offending and that those with higher intelligence demonstrated lower impulsivity. Other research supports the close link between impulsivity, intelligence, and offending (Lynam et al. 1993; White et al. 1994; Felson and Staff 2006).

The conceptualization of the intelligence-offending relationship as indirectly mediated by another variable tends to be viewed more favorably among those who are concerned about the deterministic implications of a direct link between low intelligence and offending. An indirect pathway offers an additional point to intervene, so, regardless of the mutability or heritability of intelligence, given appropriate intervention with this indirect variable, the effect of low intelligence on offending could theoretically be reduced.

The relationship between low intelligence and offending has been viewed as direct and causal by some theorists (e.g., Wilson and Herrnstein 1985). On this view, those of lower intelligence have a limited capacity to devise non-criminal solutions to problems, which limits their ability to understand and appreciate the impact of their behavior on others. This is linked to the suggestion that offenders possess neurological deficits, specifically in executive functioning (see below), with intelligence as a proxy measure of this (Moffitt et al. 2001).

IV. EMPATHY

There is strong support for the belief that low empathy is related to an increased likelihood of offending (e.g., Marcus and Gray 1998; Burke 2001). For example, empathy is included in Gottfredson and Hirschi's general theory (1990, pp. 89–90), and a "lack of empathy" is included as a key, and possibly, defining characteristic of the concept of psychopathy (e.g., Hare 1999; Blair 2007). There is also conceptual overlap between empathy and a host of factors that have been associated with explaining crime, such as poor social cognition (Bennett, Farrington, and Huesmann 2004) and lack of guilt (Loeber et al. 2008), among others. In addition, empathy enhancement (through role-play and various perspective-taking exercises) is viewed as standard practice in many offender rehabilitation programs (e.g., Mulloy, Smiley, and Mawson 1991).

Currently there are many definitions of the term empathy in the literature, and these tend to either emphasize the proposed emotional component of empathy (i.e., being able to experience the emotions of another person) or the cognitive component (i.e., being able to understand the emotions of another person). However, a broad consensus seems to be forming that empathy contains both affective and cognitive components (e.g., Davis 1983; Cohen and Strayer 1996; Jolliffe and Farrington 2006a).

The theoretical relationship between low empathy and offending is seductively simplistic. Individuals who have lower levels of empathy are more likely to offend because they are free from experiencing or understanding the emotional consequences of their actions on others. Whereas people with relatively high empathy may comprehend or experience another's fear, distress, or sadness when committing antisocial acts, these are not factored in as a cost or consequence of the antisocial act for those with low empathy. Thus, people with relatively low levels of empathy do not have the same behavioral inhibitions imposed by these internal experiences and cognitive representations. A number of more detailed models of the relationship between empathy and antisocial behavior exist (e.g., Hoffman 2000; Hanson 2003), but in essence these models all have the same overall formula: low empathy increases the likelihood of committing criminal offenses. Clearly, the relationship between low empathy and offending should be somewhat stronger for more serious and interpersonal offences such as violence and sex offenses than for offenses where the victim is less obvious (e.g., shoplifting or drug possession).

Support for the inverse relationship between empathy and offending also comes from the study of psychopathy. Psychopathy is a constellation of psychological and behavioral traits linked to an increased likelihood of criminal and antisocial behavior (Harpur, Hakstian, and Hare 1988). Those classified as psychopaths tend to be glib, superficial, and manipulative, but it is the lack of appropriate emotionality and empathy that is said to characterize this condition. It is well established that psychopaths are more violent and more likely to recidivate than non-psychopaths, and it is the conspicuous lack of empathy of psychopaths that is often used to explain these behavioral outcomes (e.g., Hare 1999).

While there is clearly a strong theoretical relationship between low empathy and offending, the empirical evidence for this relationship is less impressive. For example, studies comparing the scores on measures of empathy of offenders and non-offenders have proven inconclusive. This is true among studies comparing general offenders to non-offenders (e.g., Goldstein and Higgins-D'Alessandro 2001) as well as sex offenders to non-offenders (e.g., Hayashino et al. 1995). These findings were contrary to expectation, especially as sex offenders have long been assumed to possess significant deficits in empathy, which directly contribute to their chosen method of offending (Marshall et al. 2009).

The inability to consistently identify deficits in empathy among sex offenders has led some to question the usefulness of global or trait-based measures of empathy in sex offenders. Instead, some researchers have suggested that the empathy deficits of sex offenders might be specific to certain victims (e.g., women or children; Finkelhor and Lewis 1988) or even that these deficits might be micro-specific to the victims of their own offenses (Marshall and Marshall 2011). When conceptualized in this way, however, it is very difficult to determine if victim empathy is separable from post-offense cognitive distortions (e.g., justifications and neutralizations) that have long been identified among offenders (Sykes and Matza 1957). The fact that victim empathy was not related to the recidivism of sex offenders in two large-scale meta-analyses suggests that victim empathy may not be a useful construct (Hanson and Bussiere 1998; Hanson and Morton-Bourgon 2005), although some would dispute this (Marshall and Marshall 2011).

Fortunately, more promising results have been obtained when focusing on trait empathy and general offenders. Jolliffe and Farrington (2004) undertook a systematic review and meta-analysis, which included 35 studies comparing questionnaire measures of empathy with official records of offending. The results showed that low cognitive empathy was strongly related to offending, but low affective empathy was only weakly related. Jolliffe and Farrington (2004) suggested that the magnitude of the relationship between cognitive empathy and offending might have been elevated by the widespread use of a weak measure of cognitive empathy. The results of their systematic review also suggested that younger offenders and violent offenders tended to have low empathy. Most important, however, the relationship between low empathy and offending was greatly reduced after controlling for intelligence or socioeconomic status, suggesting that they might be more important risk factors or that low empathy might mediate the relationship between these risk factors and offending.

A recent meta-analysis replicated the key findings of this earlier study by showing that the difference between offenders and non-offenders was greatest for cognitive empathy as opposed to affective empathy, for younger as opposed to older offenders, and that the more closely matched the offender/nonoffender groups were, the less likely there were to be empathic differences (van Langen et al. 2014). The authors also suggested that the questionnaire measures of empathy used in the primary studies might be not be measuring empathy very well because of the method of development of the scales or because they might be including similar but separable constructs (e.g., sympathy).

Jolliffe and Farrington (2006a) created the Basic Empathy Scale to measure both the cognitive and affective components of empathy. An example of a cognitive item would be "It is hard for me to understand when my friends are sad," and an example of an affective item would be "After being with a friend who is sad about something, I usually feel sad." This scale was administered to 720 adolescents about age 15 and compared to self-reported offending (Jolliffe and Farrington 2007). The results showed that males who had reported any offense in the last year had lower empathy, and this was especially the case for affective empathy. Females who reported committing any offense did not have low empathy, but both males and females who reported committing violence did have low empathy. Also, males and females who were high-rate offenders also had significantly lower empathy (especially affective), compared to low-rate male and female offenders.

A similar pattern of results was evident when empathy was compared to self-reported bullying (Jolliffe and Farrington 2006b). Both males and females who took part in frequent bullying tended to have low affective empathy. In addition, males who took part in violent bullying and females who took part in indirect bullying also had low empathy. Subsequent analyses suggested that affective empathy was related to frequent bullying by males and bullying by females independently of impulsivity, intelligence, socioeconomic status, parental supervision, alexithymia (difficulty in understanding and expressing emotions), and coming from a broken home (Jolliffe and Farrington 2011).

These results provide support for a relationship between low empathy (especially affective empathy) and offending. However, in the absence of prospective longitudinal studies, it is impossible to determine whether low empathy precedes offending or whether offending, and experiencing what one believes to be the minimal consequences of offending, precedes low empathy. There is also limited evidence to suggest that low empathy is related to offending independently of other important social and individual background characteristics (e.g., intelligence, impulsivity, or low socioeconomic status). Hence, additional prospective longitudinal research is required to conclusively establish that low empathy is a risk factor for offending.

Despite the serious limitations in the research linking low empathy and offending, empathy training is a key component of many interventions for general offenders (e.g., Mulloy, Smiley, and Mawson 1999), and sex offenders (Marshall and Marshall, 2011). In the United Kingdom, empathy enhancement remains a treatment target for accredited programs for offenders delivered both in prison and the community (e.g., Enhanced Thinking Skills, Sex Offender Treatment Programs). However, there has been increasing acknowledgment by the Ministry of Justice, a U.K. government body responsible for criminal justice, that the evidence linking empathy and later reoffending is not strong (Ministry of Justice, 2013).

V. Socio-Cognitive Factors

Cognition refers to an individual's knowledge and perception of the world, while cognitive processes refer to the complex set of mechanisms that make such knowledge possible (Bennett, Farrington, and Huesmann 2005). Therefore social cognition refers to interpersonal knowledge, perceptions, and attitudes toward the wider social world, and social information processing refers to mechanisms such as coding, rehearsing, storage, and retrieval that are employed in interpreting social cues and guiding behavior (Bennett, Farrington and Huesmann 2005). It has been argued by many researchers that both social cognition and social information processing are different among those who commit offenses, particularly violent and aggressive offenses (e.g., Huesmann and Eron 1984; Dodge and Crick 1990; Gannon 2009).

Perhaps the best developed theory to explain the development of social cognitive skills in relation to aggressive behavior is the social information processing model of Dodge (1991). According to this, children respond to an environmental stimulus by encoding relevant cues, interpreting those cues, retrieving possible behavioral responses from long-term memory, considering the possible consequences of alternative responses, and selecting and performing a behavior. According to Dodge, aggressive children are more likely to interpret cues as hostile, to retrieve aggressive alternative responses, and to evaluate the consequences of aggression as beneficial. Huesmann and Eron (1989) put forward a somewhat similar cognitive scripts model, in which aggressive behavior depended on stored behavioral repertoires (cognitive scripts) that were learned during early development.

Addressing the proposed deficits in socio-cognitive functioning forms the basis of the most successful offender rehabilitation programs (Ross, Antonowicz, and Dhaliwal 1995; Lipsey 2009). These programs use cognitive-behavioral approaches employing role-play, Socratic questioning, and other cognitive approaches such as relapse prevention, all of which are designed to teach offenders how to think before they act, to consider the consequences of their behavior on others, and to recognize that other people might think or perceive differently than they do (Jolliffe and Farrington 2009).

Some researchers have suggested that the limited socio-cognitive functioning of offenders might be the result of underlying neuropsychological deficits. For example, neurological impairments can affect an individual's cognitive information processing capabilities, contribute to a difficult temperament, increase impulsivity, and result in other learning problems that place individuals at an increased risk of antisocial behavfior (Moffitt 1990; Moffitt et al. 2001). Moffitt et al. (2001) suggested that a child's risk of developing antisocial behavior emerged from a combination of acquired neuropsychological problems, manifested as subtle cognitive deficits, difficult temperament, or hyperactivity, along with deprived environmental conditions, such as poor parenting and low socioeconomic status. These researchers also used data from the Dunedin, New Zealand, longitudinal study to show that, while boys and girls had similar levels of family risk factors (e.g., poor parenting), males were more likely to show neurocognitive deficits, hyperactivity, poor impulse control, and undercontrolled temperaments. It was these deficits that were proposed to account for the fact that males are much more likely than females to engage in criminal and antisocial behavior.

It is noteworthy that many of the personality, individual difference, and socio-cognitive factors discussed above appear to be linked to one another by a diminished ability to understand concepts, such as the likely consequences of actions and the emotions of other people. These abilities, along with sustaining attention, concentrating, and self-monitoring, are often linked with the executive functions of the brain that are located in the pre-frontal cortex. This suggests that this area of the brain may have an important role to play in fully understanding these features, their interrelations, and their respective contributions to criminal behavior (e.g., Lynam et al. 1993; Moffitt et al. 2001; Farrington and Welsh 2008)

Offenders often do better on non-verbal performance tests such as object assembly and block design than on verbal tests (Farrington 1989). This suggests that they find it easier to deal with concrete objects than abstract concepts, which some have suggested may be the key explanatory factor underlying the link between intelligence and delinquency (Farrington and Welsh 2008). People who are poor at abstract reasoning tend to do badly in intelligence tests and at school, and they also tend to commit offenses, possibly because of their poor ability to foresee the consequences of their offending (e.g., high impulsiveness) and to appreciate the feelings of victims (e.g., low empathy). Clearly, some family backgrounds are less conducive than others to the development of abstract reasoning. For example, lower-class, economically deprived parents tend to talk in terms of the concrete rather than the abstract and tend to live for the present rather than the future (Cohen, 1955).

VI. Conclusion

Any comprehensive theory that attempts to explain crime should incorporate the temperamental, individual, and socio-cognitive features that have been found to differentiate those who go on to commit offenses from those who do not. The evidence from prospective longitudinal studies is particularly strong in showing that high impulsivity and low intelligence measured early in life are associated with later offending. Because empathy was not included in classic prospective longitudinal studies, it is difficult to determine how, or indeed if, low empathy is related to later offending. Many of the key personality and individual differences factors have been incorporated into socio-cognitive approaches to understand the decision-making of offenders and have been used to develop successful approaches to reducing the reoffending of offenders.

Future research should continue to move from studying the risk factors for offending to identifying the actual causal mechanisms by investigating changes within individuals in longitudinal studies. It is likely that some of the personality, individual, and socio-cognitive factors that have been identified by researchers are causal, and therefore viable targets for interventions, while others are not.

REFERENCES

Barchard, Kimberly A. 2005. "Does Emotional Intelligence Assist in the Prediction of Academic Success?" *Educational and Psychological Measurement* 63: 840–858.

Bates, John E. 1989. "Applications of Temperament Concepts." In *Temperament in Childhood*, edited by G. Adolph Kohnstamm, John. E Bates, and Mary K. Rothbart, 321–355. Chichester, UK: Wiley.

Bennett, Sarah, David P. Farrington, and L. Rowell Huesmann. 2004. "Explaining Gender Differences in Crime and Violence: The Importance of Social Cognitive Skills." *Aggression and Violent Behavior* 10: 263–288.

Bennett, Sarah, David P. Farrington, and L. Rowell Huesmann. 2005. "Explaining gender differences in crime and violence: The importance of social cognitive skills." *Aggression and Violent Behavior* 10: 263–288.

Blair, James R. 2007. "Empathy Dysfunction in Psychopathic Individuals." In *Empathy in Mental Illness*, edited by Tom Farrow. New York: Cambridge University Press.

Bor, William, Tara R. McGee, and Abigail A. Fagan. 2004. "Early Risk Factors for Adolescent Antisocial Behaviour: An Australian Longitudinal Study." *Australian and New Zealand Journal of Psychiatry* 38: 365–372.

Brennan, Patricia A., Birgitte R. Mednick, and Sarnoff A. Mednick. 1993. "Parental Psychopathology, Congenital Factors, and Violence." In *Mental Disorder and Crime*, edited by Sheilagh Hodgins, 244–261. Newbury Park, CA: Sage.

Burke, David M. 2001. "Empathy in Sexually Offending and Nonoffending in Adolescent Males." *Journal of Interpersonal Violence* 16: 222–233.

Burke, Jeffrey D., Rolf Loeber, Helene R. White, Magda Stouthamer-Loeber, and Dustin Pardini. 2007. "Inattention as a Key Predictor of Tobacco Use in Adolescence." *Journal of Abnormal Psychology* 116: 249–259.

Cale, Ellison M. 2006. "A Quantitative Review of the Relations Between the "Big 3" Higher Order Personality Dimensions and Antisocial Behavior." *Journal of Research in Personality* 40: 250–284.

Carrasco Miguel, Edward, D. Barker, Richard, E. Tremblay, and Frank Vitaro. 2006. "Eysenck's Personality Dimensions as Predictors of Male Adolescent Trajectories of Physical Aggression, Theft and Vandalism." *Personality and Individual Differences* 41: 1309–1320.

Caspi, Avshalom. 2000. "The Child Is Father of the Man: Personality Continuities from Childhood to Adulthood." *Journal of Personality and Social Psychology* 78: 158–172.

Chess, Stella, and Alexander Thomas.1984. *Origins and Evolution of Behavior Disorders: From Infancy to Early Adult Life*. New York: Brunner-Mazel.

Clarke, Dave. 2006. "Impulsivity as a Mediator in the Relationship Between Depression and Problem Gambling." *Personality and Individual Differences* 40: 5–15.

Cohen, Albert K. 1955. *Delinquent Boys: The Culture of the Gang*. Glencoe, IL: Free Press.

Cohen, Douglas, and Janet Strayer. 1996. "Empathy in Conduct-Disordered and Comparison Youth." *Developmental Psychology* 32: 988–998.

Cole, Nancy S. 1981. "Bias in Testing." *American Psychologist* 36: 1067–1077.

Costa Paul T., Robert R. McRae, and David A. Dye. 1991. "Facet Scales for Agreeableness and Conscientiousness: A Revision of the NEO Personality Inventory." *Personality and Individual Differences* 12: 887–898.

Davis, Mark. H. 1983. "Measuring Individual Differences in Empathy: Evidence for a Multidimensional Approach." *Journal of Personality and Social Psychology* 44: 113–126.

Defoe, Ivy, N., David P. Farrington, and Rolf Loeber. 2013. "Disentangling the Relationship Between Delinquency and Hyperactivity, Low Achievement, Depression, and Low Socioeconomic Status: Analysis of Repeated Longitudinal Data." *Journal of Criminal Justice* 41: 100–107.

Denno, Deborah W. 1990. *Biology and Violence: From Birth to Adulthood.* Cambridge, UK: Cambridge University Press.

Dodge, Kenneth A. 1991. "The Structure and Function of Reactive and Proactive Aggression." In *Development and Treatment of Childhood Aggression,* edited by Debra J. Pepler and Kenneth H. Rubin. Hillsdale, NJ: Lawrence Erlbaum.

Dodge, Kenneth A., and Nicki R. Crick. 1990. "Social Information-Processing Bases of Aggressive Behavior in Children." *Personality and Social Psychology Bulletin* 16: 8–22.

Evans, David, and Mary K. Rothbart. 2007. "Developing a Model for Adult Temperament." *Journal of Research in Personality* 41: 868–888.

Eysenck, Hans J. 1996. "Personality and Crime: Where Do We Stand?" *Psychology, Crime and Law* 2: 143–152.

Finkelhor, David, and I. A. Lewis. 1988. "An Epidemiologic Approach to the Study of Child Molestation." *Annals of the New York Academy of Sciences* 528: 64–78.

Farrington, David P. 1989. "Early Predictors of Adolescent Aggression and Adult Violence." *Violence and Victims* 4: 79–100.

Farrington, David P. 1990. "Implications of Criminal Career Research for the Prevention of Offending." *Journal of Adolescence* 13: 93–113.

Farrington, David P. 1992. "Explaining the Beginning, Progress and Ending of Antisocial Behavior from Birth to Adulthood." In *Facts, Framework and Forecasts* (*Advances in Criminological Theory,* Vol. 3), edited by Joan McCord, 253–286. New Brunswick, NJ: Transaction.

Farrington, David P. 1993. "Childhood Origins of Teenage Antisocial Behaviour and Adult Social Dysfunction." *Journal of the Royal Society of Medicine* 86: 13–17.

Farrington, David P. 1994. "Childhood, Adolescent and Adult Features of Violent Males." In *Aggressive Behavior: Current Perspectives,* edited by L. Rowell Huesmann, 215–240. New York: Plenum.

Farrington, David P. 1998. "Predictors, Causes and Correlates of Male Youth Violence." In *Youth Violence,* (*Crime and Justice: A Review of Research,* Vol. 24), edited by Michael Tonry and Mark H. Moore, 421–475. Chicago: University of Chicago Press.

Farrington, David P. 2009. "Conduct, Disorder, Aggression and Delinquency." In *Handbook of Adolescent Psychology,* 3rd ed., edited by Richard M. Lerner and Laurence Steinberg, 683–722. Hoboken, NJ: Wiley.

Farrington David P., Louise Biron, and Marc LeBlanc. 1982. "Personality and Delinquency in London and Montreal." In *Abnormal Offenders, Delinquency, and the Criminal Justice System,* edited by John Gunn and David P. Farrington, 153–201. Chichester, UK: Wiley.

Farrington, D. P., and McGee, Tara R. (2017). "The Integrated Cognitive Antisocial Potential (ICAP) Theory: Empirical Testing." In *Routledge International Handbook of Life-Course Criminology,* edited by Arjan A. J. Blokland and Victor R. Van Der Geest, 11–28. London: Routledge.

Farrington, David P., and Brandon C. Welsh. 2008. *Saving Children From a Life of Crime: Early Risk Factors and Effective Interventions*. Oxford: Oxford University Press.

Felson, Richard, B., and Jeremy Staff. 2006. "Explaining the Academic Performance-Delinquency Relationship." *Criminology* 44: 299–319.

Gannon, Theresa A. 2009. "Social Cognition in Violent and Sexual Offending: An Overview." *Psychology, Crime and Law* 15: 97–118

Goldstein, Harold, and Ann Higgins-D'Allessandro. 2001. "Empathy and Attachment in Relation to Violent vs. Nonviolent Offense History Among Jail Inmates." *Journal of Offender Rehabilitation* 32: 31–53.

Gottfredson, Michael R., and Travis Hirschi. 1990. *A General Theory of Crime*. Stanford, CA: Stanford University Press.

Grasmick, Harold G., Charles R. Tittle, Robert J. Bursik, and Bruce Arneklev. 1993. "Testing the Core Empirical Implications of Gottfredson and Hirschi's General Theory of Crime." *Journal of Research in Crime and Delinquency* 30: 5–29.

Guerin, Diana W., Allen W. Gottfried, Pamella H. Oliver, and Craig W. Thomas. 2003. *Temperament: Infancy Through Adolescence*. New York: Kluwer Academic/Plenum.

Hanson, Karl. R. 2003. "Empathy Deficits of Sexual Offenders: A Conceptual Model." *Journal of Sexual Aggression* 9: 13–23.

Hanson, Karl, R. and Monique Bussiere. 1998. "Predicting Relapse: A Meta-Analysis of Sexual Offender Recidivism Studies." *Journal of Consulting and Clinical Psychology* 66: 348–362.

Hanson, Karl, R., and Kelly E. Morton-Bourgon. 2005. "The Characteristics of Persistent Sexual Offenders: A Meta-Analysis of Recidivism Studies." *Journal of Consulting and Clinical Psychology* 73: 1154–1163.

Hare, Robert D. 1999. "Psychopathy as a Risk Factor for Violence." *Psychiatric Quarterly* 70: 181–197.

Harpur, Timothy J., Ralph A. Hakstian, and Robert D. Hare. 1988. "Factor Structure of the Psychopathy Checklist." *Journal of Consulting and Clinical Psychology* 56: 741–747.

Hayashino, Diane., Sandy K. Wurtele, and Kelli J. Klebe. 1995. "Child Molesters: An Examination of Cognitive Factors." *Journal of Interpersonal Violence* 10:106–116.

Hoffman, Martin L. 2000. *Empathy and Moral Development: Implications for Caring and Justice*. New York: Cambridge University Press.

Heaven, Patrick C. L. 1996. "Personality and Self-reported Delinquency: Analysis of the 'Big Five' Personality Dimensions." *Personality and Individual Differences* 20: 47–54

Hedderman, Carol, and Darrick Jolliffe. 2015. "The Impact of Prison on Women: Paying the Price for Wrong Decisions." *Victims and Offenders* 10: 152–178.

Hirschi, Travis. 1969. *Causes of Delinquency*. Berkeley: University of California Press.

Hirschi, Travis, and Michael J. Hindelang. 1977. "Intelligence and Delinquency: A Revisionist Review." *American Sociological Review* 42: 571–587.

Hogh, Erik, and Preben Wolf. 1983. "Violent Crime in a Birth Cohort: Copenhagen 1953–1977." In *Prospective Studies of Crime and Delinquency*, edited by Katherine T. van Dusen and Sarnoff A. Mednick. Boston: Kluwer.

Hollin, Clive R. 2007. "Criminological Psychology." In *The Oxford Handbook of Criminology*, edited by Michael Maguire, Rod Morgan, and Robert Reiner, 43–77. Oxford: Oxford University Press.

Huesmann, L. Rowell, and Leonard D. Eron. 1989. "Individual Differences and the Trait of Aggression." *European Journal of Personality* 3: 95–106.

Huesmann, L. Rowell, and Leonard D. Eron. 1984. "Cognitive Processes and the Persistence of Aggressive Behavior." *Aggressive Behavior* 10: 243–251.

John, Oliver P., Avshalom Caspi, Richard W. Robins, Terrie E. Moffitt, and Magda Stouthamer-Loeber. 1994. "The 'Little Five': Exploring the Nomological Network of the Five-Factor Model of Personality in Adolescent Boys." *Child Development* 65: 160–178.

Jolliffe, Darrick. 2013. "Exploring the Relationship Between the Five-Factor Model of Personality and Self-Reported Offending." *Personality and Individual Differences* 55: 47–52.

Jolliffe, Darrick, and David P. Farrington. 2004. "Empathy and Offending: A Systematic Review and Meta-Analysis." *Aggression and Violent Behavior* 9: 441–476.

Jolliffe, Darrick, and David P. Farrington. 2006a. "The Development and Validation of the Basic Empathy Scale." *Journal of Adolesc*ence 29: 589–611.

Jolliffe, Darrick, and David P. Farrington 2006b. "Examining the Relationship Between Low Empathy and Bullying." *Aggressive Behavior* 32: 540–550.

Jolliffe, Darrick, and David P. Farrington 2007. "The Relationship Between Low Empathy and Self-Reported Offending." *Legal and Criminological Psychology* 12: 265–286.

Jolliffe, Darrick, and David P. Farrington. 2009. "A Systematic Review of the Relationship Between Childhood Impulsiveness and Later Violence." In *Personality, Personality Disorder and Violence*, edited by Mary McMurran and Richard C. Howard, 40–61. London: Wiley.

Jolliffe, Darrick, and David P. Farrington. 2011. "Is Low Empathy Related to Bullying Controlling for Other Factors?" *Journal of Adolescence* 34: 59–71.

Jones, Shayne, E., Joshua D. Miller, and Donald R. Lynam. 2011. "Personality, Antisocial Behavior, and Aggression: A Meta-Analytic Review." *Journal of Criminal Justice* 39: 329–337.

Kagan, Jerome, J., Steven Reznick, and Nancy Snidman. 1988. "Biological Bases of Childhood Shyness." *Science* 240: 167–171.

Kazdin, Alan E., Helena C. Kraemer, Ronald C. Kessler, David J. Kupfer, and David R. Offord. 1997. "Contributions of Risk-Factor Research to the Development of Psychopathology." *Clinical Psychology Review* 17: 375–406.

Kenrick, Douglas T., and David C. Funder. 1988. "Profiting from Controversy: Lessons from the Person–Situation Debate." *American Psychologist* 43: 23–34.

Klinteberg, Britt, A., Tommy Andersson, David Magnusson, and Hakin Stattin. 1993. "Hyperactive Behavior in Childhood as Related to Subsequent Alcohol Problems and Violent Offending: A Longitudinal Study of Male Subjects." *Personality and Individual Differences* 15: 381–388.

Koolhof, Roos, Rolf Loeber, Evelyn H. Wei, Dustin Pardini, and Annematt C. D'escury. 2007. "Inhibition Deficits of Serious Delinquent Boys of Low Intelligence." *Criminal Behaviour and Mental Health* 17: 274–292.

Kraemer, Helena C., Karen K. Lowe, and David J. Kupfer. 2005. *To Your Health? How to Understand What Research Tells Us About Risk*. Oxford: Oxford University Press.

Lahey, Benjamin B., Rolf Loeber, Irwin D. Waldman, and David P. Farrington. 2006. "Child Socioemotional Dispositions at School Entry that Predict Adolescent Delinquency and Violence." *Impuls: Tidsskrift for Psykologi* 3: 40–51.

Lipsey, Mark W. 2009. "The Primary Factors That Characterize Effective Interventions with Juvenile Offenders: A Meta-Analytic Overview." *Victims and Offenders* 4: 124–147.

Lipsitt, Paul D., Stephen L. Buka, and Lewis P. Lipsitt. 1990. "Early Intelligence Scores and Subsequent Delinquency: A Prospective Study." *American Journal of Family Therapy* 18: 197–208.

Loeber, Rolf, David P. Farrington, Magda Stouthamer-Loeber, and Helene Raskin White. 2008. *Violence and Serious Theft: Development and Prediction from Childhood to Adulthood*. New York: Routledge.

Lynam, Donald R., Avshalom Caspi, Terrie E. Moffitt, Per-Olof Wikström, Rolf Loeber, and Scott Novak. 2000. "The Interaction Between Impulsivity and Neighborhood Context on Offending: The Effects of Impulsivity Are Stronger in Poorer Neighborhoods." *Journal of Abnormal Psychology* 109: 563–574.

Lynam, Donald R., Terrie E. Moffitt, and Magda Stouthamer-Loeber. 1993. "Explaining the Relation Between IQ and Delinquency: Class, Race, Test Motivation, School Failure, or Self-Control?" *Journal of Abnormal Psychology* 102: 187–196.

Marcus, Robert F., and Lewis Gray 1998. "Close Relationships of Violent and Nonviolent African American Delinquents." *Violence and Victims* 13: 31–46.

Marshall, Liam E., and William L. Marshall. 2011. "Empathy and Antisocial Behavior." *Journal of Forensic Psychiatry and Psychology* 22: 742–759.

Marshall, William L, Liam E. Marshall, Geris A. Serran, and Dana O'Brien. 2009. "Self-esteem, Shame, Cognitive Distortions and Empathy in Sexual Offenders." *Psychology Crime & Law* 15: 217–234.

McCord, Joan, and Margaret E. Ensminger. 1997. "Multiple Risks and Comorbidity in an African American Population." *Criminal Behaviour and Mental Health* 7: 339–352.

McCrae, Robert R., and Paul T. Costa. 1997. "Personality Trait Structure as a Human Universal," *American Psychologist* 52: 509–516.

McGloin, Jean M., and Travis C. Pratt. 2003. "Cognitive Ability and Delinquent Behavior Among Inner City Youth: A Life-Course Analysis of Main, Mediating, and Interaction Effects." *International Journal of Offender Therapy and Comparative Criminology* 47: 253–271.

Miller, Joshua D., and Donald R. Lynam. 2001. "Structural Models of Personality and Their Relation to Antisocial Behavior: A Meta-analytic Review." *Criminology* 39: 765–798.

Ministry of Justice. (2013). *Transforming Rehabilitation: A Summary of Evidence on Reducing Reoffending.* London: Ministry of Justice. https://www.gov.uk/government/uploads/system/uploads/attachment_data/file/243718/evidence-reduce-reoffending.pdf.

Moffitt, Terrie E. 1993. "Adolescence-Limited and Life-Course-Persistent Antisocial Behavior: A Developmental Taxonomy." *Psychological Review* 100: 674–701.

Moffitt, Terrie E. 1990. "The Neuropsychology of Juvenile Delinquency: A Critical Review." In *Crime and Justice: A Review of Research,* Vol. 12, edited by Michael Tonry and Norval Morris, 99–169. Chicago: University of Chicago Press.

Moffitt, Terrie E., Avshalom Caspi, Michael Rutter, and Phil A. Silva. 2001. *Sex Differences in Antisocial Behaviour.* Cambridge, UK: Cambridge University Press.

Moffitt, Terrie E., and Phil A. Silva. 1988. "IQ and Delinquency: A Direct Test of the Differential Detection Hypothesis." *Journal of Abnormal Psychology* 97: 330–333.

Mulloy, Rachel, Carson W. Smiley, and Diana L. Mawson. 1999. "The Impact of Empathy Training on Offender Treatment." *Focus on Corrections Research* 11: 15–18.

Murray, Joseph, David P. Farrington, and Manuel P. Eisner 2009. "Drawing Conclusions About Causes from Systematic Reviews of Risk Factors: The Cambridge Quality Checklists." *Journal of Experimental Criminology* 5: 1–23.

Pratt, Travis C., and Francis T. Cullen. 2000. "The Empirical Status of Gottfredson and Hirschi's General Theory of Crime: A Meta-Analysis." *Criminology* 38: 931–960.

Pratt, Travis C., Francis T. Cullen, Kristie R. Blevins, Leah Daigle, and James D. Unnever. 2002. "The Relationship of Attention Deficit Hyperactivity Disorder to Crime and Delinquency: A Meta-Analysis." *International Journal of Police Science and Management* 4: 344–360.

Reynolds, Cecil R. 1995. "Test Bias and the Assessment of Intelligence and Personality." In *International Handbook of Personality and Intelligence*, edited by Donald H. Saklofske and Moshe Zeidner, 545–576. New York: Plenum.

Roberts, Brent W., and Wendy F. Del Vecchio. 2000. "The Rank-Order Consistency of Personality Traits from Childhood to Old Age: A Quantitative Review of Longitudinal Studies." *Psychological Bulletin* 126: 3–25.

Ross, Robert R., Daniel H. Antonowicz, and Gurmeet K. Dahliwal, eds. 1995. *Going Straight: The Reasoning and Rehabilitation Program for Delinquency Prevention and Offender Rehabilitation*. Ottawa, Canada: Air Training and Publications.

Sanson, Ann, Diana Smart, Margot Prior, and Frank Oberklaid. 1993. "Precursors of Hyperactivity and Aggression." *Journal of the American Academy of Child and Adolescent Psychiatry* 32: 1207–1226.

Schwartz, Carl E., Nancy Snidman, and Jerome Kagan. 1996. "Early Childhood Temperament as a Determinant of Externalizing Behavior in Adolescence." *Development and Psychopathology* 8: 527–537.

Schweinhart, Lawrence J., Helen V. Barnes, and David P. Weikart. 1993. *Significant Benefits: The High/Scope Perry Preschool Study Through Age 27*. Ypsilanti, MI: High/Scope Press.

Slutske, Wendy S., Terrie E. Moffitt, Richie Poulton, and Avshalom Caspi. 2012. "Undercontrolled Temperament at Age 3 Predicts Disordered Gambling at Age 32: A Longitudinal Study of a Complete Birth Cohort." *Psychological Science* 23: 510–516.

Stattin, Hakan, and Ingrid Klackenberg-Larsson. 1993. "Early Language and Intelligence Development and Their Relationship to Future Criminal Behavior." *Journal of Abnormal Psychology* 102: 369–378.

Sykes, Gresham M., and David Matza. 1957. "Techniques of Neutralization: A Theory of Delinquency." *American Sociological Review* 22: 664–670.

Van Dam, Coleta, Jan M. A. M. Janssens, and Eric E. J. De Bruyn. 2005. "PEN, Big Five, Juvenile Delinquency and Criminal Recidivism." *Personality and Individual Differences* 39: 7–19.

Van Lagen, M. A. M., I. B. Wissink, E.S. van Vugt, T. Van der Stouwe, and G J. J. M. Stams. 2014. "The Relation Between Empathy and Offending: A Meta-Analysis." *Aggression and Violent Behavior* 19: 179–189.

White, Jennifer. L., Terri E. Moffitt, Avshalom Caspi, Dawn J. Bartusch, Douglas J. Needles, and Magda Stouthamer-Loeber. 1994. "Measuring Impulsivity and Examining Its Relationship to Delinquency." *Journal of Abnormal Psychology* 103: 192–205.

Wilson, James Q., and Richard J. Herrnstein. 1985. *Crime and Human Nature*. New York: Simon & Schuster.

West, Donald J., and David P. Farrington. 1973. *Who Becomes Delinquent?* London: Heinemann.

Zimmerman, Gregory M. 2012. "Impulsivity, Offending, and the Neighborhood: Investigating the Person-Context Nexus." *Journal of Quantitative Criminology* 301–332.

CHAPTER 19

··

FAMILY INFLUENCES
ON YOUTH OFFENDING

··

ABIGAIL A. FAGAN AND KRISTEN M. BENEDINI

MANY of the life-course theories reviewed in this book identify the family as playing a significant role in shaping children's potential for delinquency. Several of these theories posit that family factors are particularly influential early in children's development. For example, Terrie Moffitt (1993) identifies adverse family conditions in the prenatal and early childhood periods as contributing to the emergence of a life-course–persistent offending trajectory. Factors such as maternal drug abuse during pregnancy and child maltreatment in the first few years of life contribute directly or indirectly (e.g., via neuropsychological deficits) to an early onset of behavioral problems and an increased likelihood of persistent offending into adulthood. Robert Sampson and John Laub (1990, 1993) highlight the role of strong parent–child relationships in childhood and early adolescence, characterized by emotional closeness and parental monitoring and supervision of youth, in inhibiting crime. They also contend that family influences become less important over time as children's circumstances change and bonds to other social groups and institutions (e.g., peer groups, school, marriage, employment, etc.) emerge and are prioritized. Borrowing from social learning, social bond, and social control theories, interactional theory (Thornberry 1987) and the Social Development Model (Catalano and Hawkins 1996) each consider parents' modeling of positive behaviors, stated disapproval of deviant behavior, supervision and discipline of children, and establishment of close, affective bonds with youth as important in reducing delinquency early in the life course. They also state that such factors may become less important as children age.

This chapter will review the degree to which empirical evidence demonstrates that families influence youth delinquency. Because they are most likely to be emphasized in life-course theories, this chapter focuses on parenting practices such as parental warmth and involvement, supervision and discipline of children, and child maltreatment. We also summarize literature examining the role of children's exposure to parental violence, family criminality, and young (teenage) parents in affecting delinquency. The chapter will not review findings related to family socioeconomic status or parent divorce given space limitations and because these structural factors are often shown to affect delinquency indirectly, often via the parenting processes covered here.

Because life-course theories are ideally tested using longitudinal data (Farrington 2013), which allow examination of, in this case, the impact of parenting practices on children's subsequent behaviors, this chapter focuses on evidence generated from prospective studies conducted in the United States and other countries. We also discuss findings from experimental studies designed to reduce youth substance use and delinquency by improving the family environment. Experiments are better equipped than observational studies to investigate causal relationships given that they can control for the time ordering of key variables (Farrington and Welsh 2005). Ensuring temporal ordering is particularly important because children's behavior has been shown to affect parenting practices (Thornberry 1987; Smith and Stern 1997; Kerr and Stattin 2003). Our review of observational and experimental studies will focus on findings generated from the most rigorous analyses available, such as multivariate models, which control for other risk and protective factors related to delinquency (e.g., low self-control and peer influences), and mediation analyses, which test the degree to which changes in parenting practices lead to changes in delinquency.

This chapter is organized as follows. Section I reviews evidence from longitudinal and experimental studies to identify the degree to which six family characteristics affect delinquency: parental warmth and involvement, supervision and discipline of children, child maltreatment, children's exposure to parental violence, family criminality, and young (teenage) parents. Section II describes the results of four meta-analyses that have calculated average effect sizes of these family characteristics on youth offending based on findings from multiple research studies. Section III draws conclusions about family influences on offending based on all of the research reviewed and provides recommendations for future research projects to better specify how the family context affects children's delinquency.

I. Review of Findings from Longitudinal and Experimental Research

This section reviews evidence obtained from longitudinal and experimental research designed to examine family influences on juvenile delinquency. Although studies may have estimated the impact of multiple family factors on delinquency, each of the six family factors is considered separately in the following subsections.

A. Parental Warmth and Involvement

Life-course theories examining the affective relationship between parents and children largely draw upon Travis Hirschi's (1969) social bond theory. According to Hirschi

(1969), youth who have warm and close relationships with their parents will refrain from delinquency because they do not want to risk losing their approval and affection. These attachments or bonds will help ensure that children regulate their own behaviors to be in compliance with their parents' rules and wishes (Catalano and Hawkins 1996).

The affective bond between parent and youth has been measured in different ways across studies. While some research, following Hirschi (1969), includes items relating to parental supervision of youth, such indicators are reviewed in the next subsection. Here we describe findings from studies investigating the effects of parental warmth and affection, time spent in joint parent/child activities, and parent supportiveness. Research examining a lack of closeness between parents and children, including parental rejection of youth, hostility or "coldness," and conflict between youth and parents (excluding child abuse) is also reviewed.

National longitudinal studies in the United States have provided evidence that greater parent–child attachment reduces substance use and delinquency. According to data from the National Youth Survey (NYS), adolescent reports of time spent with parents and closeness to their family were each negatively associated with delinquency (Jang 1999) and substance use (Jang 2002) throughout adolescence, even controlling for other risk factors like exposure to deviant peers. Positive relationships with both parents (including spending time with parents and having supportive parents) as well as children's relationships with their fathers (Bronte-Tinkew, Moore, and Carrano 2006) reduced delinquency in later adolescence according to youth in the National Longitudinal Survey of Youth (NLSY; Hair et al. 2008).

Data collected from smaller, local samples in the United States also indicate the impact of affective parent–child relationships on youth offending. In a study following boys from low-income families in Pittsburgh, Pennsylvania, those receiving greater observed maternal rejection at age 2 were more likely to have stable compared to decreasing levels of conduct problems from ages 2 to 8 (Shaw et al. 2003). In an Oregon sample, males who were classified as having stable levels of delinquency from ages 9 to 18 were more likely to have experienced declines in parent warmth from ages 9 to 16 compared to non-delinquent boys (Dishion, Nelson, and Bullock 2004). Also relying on data from youth in the Pacific Northwest, Mark Van Ryzin and colleagues (2012) found that parent–child relationship quality predicted substance use in adolescence (ages 12 to 17), but the impact was not significant by early adulthood (age 23).

Other studies have failed to show even a short-term effect of parent warmth and affection. For example, Montreal boys' reports of attachment to parents at ages 11 to 12 did not predict delinquency at ages 13 to 14 (Vitaro, Brendgen, and Tremblay 2000), and youth attachment to parents predicted delinquency when youth participating in the Rochester Youth Development Study (RYDS) were aged 13 to 15, but not when they were aged 14 to 16 (Thornberry et al. 1991). In a study of youth from Christchurch, New Zealand, parental attachment rated by children at age 15 did not predict self-reported offending at ages 15 to 21 (Fergusson, Swain-Campbell, and Horwood 2004).

The few experimental evaluations investigating the degree to which changes in parent–child bonds mediate intervention effects on youth offending have reported mixed evidence. (See Table 19.1 for a summary of all experimental studies referred to

Table 19.1 Prevention Programs Shown in High-Quality Evaluations to Reduce Children's Externalizing Behaviors, Delinquency, or Substance Use via Improvements in Parenting Practices

Program	Program Description	Characteristics of Study Participants at Baseline	Parenting Practice(s) Shown to Mediate Intervention Outcomes
Child–Parent Center (CPC) Program	Provides two years of intensive preschool for youth and support services for the family.	Low income, mostly African American 3-year-olds from high-poverty neighborhoods in Chicago, Illinois	Child maltreatment (Reynolds and Ou 2011)
Incredible Years–Basic Parent Program	Fourteen-week program with weekly, two-hour sessions delivered to small groups of parents to improve parenting practices.	British children aged 2 to 9 with conduct problems, primarily from low-income, female-headed households	Positive parenting (e.g., use of praise and proactive discipline) (Gardner, Burton, and Klimes 2006; Gardner et al. 2010)
New Beginnings Program	Ten-week program with weekly, two-hour sessions delivered to small groups of recently divorced women to improve parenting practices. Concurrent small group sessions for children can also be offered. Mothers also receive two home visits or phone calls to allow personalized services.	Mostly Caucasian mothers of 10-year-old children from Arizona	Mother/child relationship quality (Tein et al. 2004; Zhou et al. 2008) and discipline (McClain et al. 2010; Tein et al. 2004)
Positive Family Support–Family Check Up	Tiered program including a school-based Family Resource Center, a six-week universal classroom curricula for students, and three individualized motivational interviews for parents of youth with behavior problems.	Racially/ethnically diverse middle school students and their parents from the northwestern United States	Parental monitoring (Dishion, Nelson, and Kavanagh 2003) and family conflict (Van Ryzin and Dishion 2012)
Familias Unidas	Program delivered to small groups of parents in eight or nine two-hour weekly sessions to improve parenting practices. Four to 10 home visits are also provided to improve family bonding and communication.	Low-income, Hispanic parents of middle school children in Miami, Florida	Positive parenting (e.g., positive reinforcement, child monitoring, and open communication with children) (Prado et al. 2007; Pantin et al. 2009)
Effekt	Six 20-minute presentations to parents held during parent/teacher meetings at school to emphasize the adverse effects of youth alcohol use and permissive parent attitudes about youth drinking. A four-session, classroom-based program for students was also offered in the Dutch trial.	Parents of junior high school students in Sweden (Ozdemir and Koutakis 2016) and the Netherlands (Koning et al. 2010)	Parent attitudes about youth drinking and rules limiting youth drinking
Multisystemic Therapy	One-on-one intensive therapeutic services for families with youth involved with the juvenile justice system. Treatment lasts three to five months and is delivered by therapists with small caseloads.	Study 1: male White and African American sex offenders aged 11 to 18 from Missouri (Henggeler et al. 2009) Study 2: youth referred for delinquency in the Netherlands, 73 percent male, half Dutch and half from ethnic minority groups (Dekovic et al. 2012)	Parent discipline strategies (Henggeler et al. 2009; Dekovic et al. 2012)

in this essay.) When implemented with recently divorced mothers and middle school children in Arizona, the New Beginnings program improved the quality of the mother/ child relationship (i.e., mothers' acceptance of children, warmth, and open communication). Relationship quality mediated program effects on children's externalizing behaviors in the short term (Tein et al. 2004) and up to age 16 (Zhou et al. 2008), but it did not mediate outcomes on youth substance use (Zhou et al. 2008; McClain et al. 2010). A randomized trial of the Positive Family Support–Family Check Up intervention conducted in the Pacific Northwest with families of middle school students indicated that family conflict mediated program effects on adolescent externalizing at age 19 (Van Ryzin and Dishion 2012). More specifically, those receiving the intervention reported less growth in family conflict (i.e., youth reports of arguing with and being angry at parents) from ages 12 to 15 compared to those in the control group, and this improvement was related to less delinquency. An evaluation of multisystemic therapy (MST), an intensive therapeutic intervention for adolescent offenders and their families, indicated that relationship quality did not mediate program effects on delinquency when implemented with Dutch families (Dekovic et al. 2012).

B. Parental Supervision and Discipline

Many studies have assessed the impact of parental controls on youth delinquency. Such investigations typically operationalize this construct by measuring parental rule-setting, monitoring of children's behaviors, and positive and negative reinforcement of rules and standards. The importance of parental knowledge of children's activities and friends has also been investigated (Kerr and Stattin 2000; Racz and McMahon 2011).

One of the first longitudinal studies in the United States to examine parental controls involved a sample of Caucasian boys from Boston (Glueck and Glueck 1950). A long-term follow-up of these youth indicated that parental supervision and harsh/inconsistent discipline during childhood each predicted subsequent delinquency, controlling for child characteristics and family structural variables (Sampson and Laub 1993). Longitudinal analysis of African Americans in the Rochester study (Jang and Krohn 1995) and males in the Pittsburgh Youth Study (Farrington et al. 2002; Loeber et al. 2007) have also shown a relationship between supervision and delinquency, whereby increased parental control predicts less youth crime. In the Seattle Social Development Project (Herrenkohl et al. 2006), youth who reported consistently strong family management from ages 11 to 14 were less likely to engage in violence and to be chronic violent offenders from ages 13 to 18 compared to those who experienced consistently poor management. Ronald Simons and colleagues (2001) reported that low parental monitoring and supervision at age 13 predicted increases in delinquency from ages 13 to 16 among Caucasian youth from two-parent families in rural Iowa.

Parental attitudes and rules also affect children's substance use. Based on data from the Seattle study collected when youth were ages 10 to 18, lax parental rules regarding children's alcohol use predicted children's initiation of drinking (Kosterman et al. 2000). Similar results were reported in a prospective study of primarily African American and Hispanic adolescents in Chicago (Komro et al. 2007); those who reported permissive parent attitudes about alcohol use were more likely to report drinking.

Studies conducted in Europe and New Zealand have also supported the link between parental controls and delinquency. The Edinburgh Study of Youth Transitions (Neumann et al. 2010) and the Dutch Conflict and Management of Relationships study (Keijsers et al. 2009) both reported a negative relationship between parent knowledge of adolescents' activities and delinquency using prospective data collected from ages 13 to 16. Life-course–persistent offenders from Dunedin, New Zealand were more likely than adolescent-limited offenders to have experienced inconsistent discipline and harsh, physical punishment at ages 7 to 9 (Moffitt and Caspi 2001). Farrington (2002) reported that London males participating the Cambridge Study in Delinquent Development who experienced harsh or inconsistent discipline and poor supervision at ages 8 and 10 had an increased likelihood of a criminal conviction by age 32.

What do we know about the effects of parent controls on delinquency from experimental studies? Such research suggests that this relationship is important at multiple developmental periods and for diverse populations. When implemented in separate trials with British and Welsh parents of children displaying problem behaviors at age 7, the three-month-long Incredible Years parenting program showed positive intervention effects on children's externalizing behaviors in the short term via improvements in "positive parenting," such as the use of praise and proactive discipline techniques (Gardner, Burton, and Klimes 2006; Gardner et al. 2010). Evaluations of the New Beginnings program indicated that improvements in parental discipline when children were aged 11 to 12 mediated intervention effects on youth externalizing behaviors and substance use up to age 16 (Tein et al. 2004; McClain et al. 2010). An evaluation of the Familias Unidas intervention for Hispanic parents of 13-year-olds found that participation increased parents' use of positive reinforcement, child monitoring, and communication with children, and these outcomes mediated intervention effects on substance use at age 16 (Prado et al. 2007; Pantin et al. 2009). A parent-training program shown to reduce alcohol use among middle school students in Sweden (Ozdemir and Koutakis 2016) and the Netherlands (Koning et al. 2010) found that effects were mediated by changes in parents' attitudes and rule-setting about children's drinking. Finally, evaluations of the MST program indicated that reductions in externalizing and delinquency demonstrated among Dutch adolescents were mediated by parents' increased use of positive discipline strategies (Dekovic et al. 2012), and desired effects on delinquency among sex offenders in the United States were mediated by improvements in parent discipline (Henggeler et al. 2009).

C. Child Maltreatment

Although some studies operationalize parental controls by assessing harsh discipline practices like physical punishment (e.g., spanking), in this section we review the impact of severe and often frequent physical abuse of children, as well as other forms of child maltreatment including child emotional abuse, physical neglect, and sexual abuse. These constructs may be measured using official records of alleged or substantiated maltreatment, parent reports of such practices, child reports, or a combination of these measures.

Cathy Widom was one of the first researchers to document a relationship between child maltreatment and subsequent involvement in crime using a well-conducted, longitudinal study design. Her research has shown that youth with official records of maltreatment have a greater likelihood of arrests during adolescence and adulthood, as well as increased substance use and drug dependency, when compared to a matched comparison group (Widom 1989a, 1989b; Maxfield and Widom 1996; Widom, Marmorstein, and White 2006; Widom, Schuck, and White 2006). Other longitudinal studies conducted with national (e.g., the National Youth Survey data; see Fagan 2005) and regional (Smith and Thornberry 1995; Herrenkohl, Egolf, and Herrenkohl 1997; Lansford et al. 2007; Mersky, Topitzes, and Reynolds 2012) samples in the United States have also demonstrated that youth who experience abuse or neglect are more likely to engage in illegal behaviors compared to those who are not maltreated.

However, not all research has established significant and/or substantial relationships between child physical abuse and subsequent violence (Zingraff et al. 1993; Derzon 2010), suggesting that some children are resilient to the negative effects of abuse (DuMont, Widom, and Czaja 2007). In the Dunedin study (Fergusson and Lynskey 1997), retrospective reports of experiencing harsh physical punishment and abuse during childhood were associated with increased violent offending and alcohol dependence at ages 16 to 18, but not with property offending or marijuana dependence. Additional analyses of these data indicated that child maltreatment was most likely to predict criminal convictions at age 26 for those known to carry a genetic risk allele (Caspi et al. 2002), providing additional evidence that the impact of child abuse and neglect may vary across individuals.

Relevant to life-course theory, research has suggested that the impact of maltreatment is sensitive to the developmental stage in which it is experienced. In the Rochester Youth Development Study, Terence Thornberry and colleagues (Thornberry, Ireland, and Smith 2001; Ireland, Smith, and Thornberry 2002; Thornberry et al. 2010) found that abuse and neglect during adolescence had a greater impact on criminal involvement compared to maltreatment experienced only during childhood, although persistent maltreatment (experienced during childhood and adolescence) also increased crime. Findings from the Chicago Longitudinal Study of low-income, African American youth present a somewhat more complicated story (Mersky, Topitzes, and Reynolds 2012). In this study, adolescent-only maltreatment had a stronger impact on adolescent offending compared to childhood-only maltreatment. However, childhood-only maltreatment was more strongly related to offending during adulthood (from ages 18 to 26).

To date, there has been little examination of whether or not reductions in child mal-treatment may mediate family-focused intervention effects on offending. A quasi-experimental evaluation of the Child-Parent Center program (Reynolds and Ou 2011), which provided high-quality preschool services to low-income African American families in Chicago, indicated that reductions in substantiated maltreatment cases at ages 4 to 17 mediated intervention effects on felony arrests at ages 18 to 24. Home visita-tion programs implemented during the prenatal period and in the first few years of life have also been shown to reduce child abuse and neglect (Bilukha et al. 2005; Avellar and Supplee 2013), and evaluations of the Nurse-Family Partnership (NFP) home visitation program have demonstrated intervention effects on maltreatment as well as offending (Olds, Henderson, and Cole 1998; Eckenrode et al. 2010; Kitzman et al. 2010). However, whether or not changes in child maltreatment mediated reductions in crime and sub-stance use among children of NFP participants has not been tested.

D. Exposure to Intimate Partner Violence

Youth who are abused or neglected have an increased risk of also being exposed to intimate partner violence (IPV) between caregivers (Margolin and Gordis 2000; Herrenkohl et al. 2008; Hamby et al. 2010), making it important but also difficult to differentiate the impacts of these types of violence on delinquency. Studies control-ling for child abuse have indicated mixed evidence that IPV has a unique influence on offending. In the Rochester Youth Development Study, children whose parents reported engaging in IPV had greater levels of delinquency during early adulthood, controlling for child abuse (Ireland and Smith 2009). In contrast, findings from the Christchurch study indicated statistically significant bivariate relationships between youth exposure to parent IPV, crime, and drug dependency when participants were aged 18 years old, but these relationships failed to retain statistical significance when child abuse and other control variables were added to the model (Fergusson and Horwood 1998). Similarly, a study of racially diverse youth from Chicago found that parental IPV experienced in early adolescence did not predict youth violence five years later, and effects on drug use were inconsistent (Wright, Fagan, and Crittenden 2011). Finally, prospective data col-lected from youth in Lehigh, Pennsylvania, indicated that those whose parents engaged in IPV but not child physical abuse were more likely than non-victims to report minor assault but not felony assault or general delinquency at age 18 (Sousa et al. 2011). Youth exposed to child physical abuse but not IPV were more likely than non-victims to report status offenses, but not more serious delinquent acts (i.e., minor assault, felony assault, and general delinquency).

Experimental evidence of the influence of IPV on children's illegal behavior is scarce. An evaluation of the New Beginnings program found that parental conflict witnessed by children did not mediate intervention effects on externalizing behaviors (Tein et al. 2004). A randomized trial of the Nurse-Family Partnership program in Denver showed that NFP participants were less likely than those in the control group to report IPV (Olds et al. 2004), but there was no examination of whether or not reductions in IPV mediated the intervention effects on children's delinquency. Other interventions designed to reduce IPV (e.g., Sherman and Berk 1984) have not typically assessed effects on children's offending.

E. Family Criminality and Substance Use

More general forms of family criminality have also been identified as contributing to children's delinquency. The impact of these influences is usually explained by social learning theory (Akers et al. 1979; Akers 1985), whereby children with deviant role models are thought to be at risk for modeling such behaviors and for being positively reinforced for doing so. The Social Development Model (SDM) (Catalano and Hawkins 1996) life-course theory emphasizes that youth who have strong bonds to family members who engage in crime or drug use will be more at risk for offending. The SDM, as well as Moffitt's (1993) dual taxonomy theory, also identifies maternal drug use during pregnancy as increasing the likelihood of children's crime and drug use.

Information from birth cohort studies has shown a relationship between maternal prenatal substance use and children's delinquency. In the Dunedin study, maternal prenatal smoking predicted child conduct disorder at age 12 (Fergusson, Horwood, and Lynskey 1993). However, neither prenatal smoking nor drinking was significantly related to youth externalizing behaviors at age 14 in a cohort study in Brisbane, Australia (Bor, McGee, and Fagan 2004). Long-term, positive relationships between prenatal smoking and children's crime were found in birth cohort studies conducted with males in Copenhagen, Denmark, based on official records collected when participants were age 34 (Brennan, Grekin, and Mednick 1999) and with African American males and females from Philadelphia, Pennsylvania (Piquero et al. 2002), based on official records collected when participants were age 36. Furthermore, these two studies each showed that prenatal smoking predicted life-course–persistent offending. In the 1970 British Cohort Study, maternal smoking during pregnancy predicted conduct disorder at age 10 for both boys and girls and criminal convictions at age 34 for females only (Murray et al. 2010).

In later years of the life course (e.g., after birth), substance use by parents, as well as parent involvement in other types of crime, has been shown to increase children's substance use and criminality (Donovan 2004). For example, data from Caucasian, rural families in Iowa indicated an impact of parental alcohol use on children's alcohol use across four waves of data (Conger and Reuter 1996). In terms of the influence of parent offending on children's crime, data from the Cambridge Study in Delinquent Development have shown that males whose parents had official criminal convictions were more likely to themselves be convicted based on records collected at ages 32 (Farrington 2002) and 50 (Farrington, Coid, and Murray 2009). The Copenhagen cohort study (Brennan, Grekin, and Mednick 1999) reported that parent criminality was associated with increased males' criminal convictions at age 34.

Data from the Pittsburgh Youth Study suggest that parental incarceration is most problematic in leading to crime. In this study, neither parental arrest nor conviction predicted youth offending, while parental incarceration was linked to increased theft (Murray, Loeber, and Pardini 2012). A meta-analysis of 40 studies, conducted mostly in the United States but also in Europe, Australia, and New Zealand, found that parental incarceration was significantly related to children's antisocial behavior (with an odds ratio of 1.9 across prospective studies) but not substance use (Murray, Farrington, and Sekol 2012).

Research has also indicated that sibling substance use and delinquency affect adolescent offending (Lauritsen 1993; Rowe, Linver, and Rodgers 1996; Feinberg, Solmeyer, and McHale 2012), sometimes even more strongly than parental substance use or crime (Fagan and Najman 2003, 2005), although much of this research is based on cross-sectional data. In one of the first longitudinal studies to assess this relationship, Reiss and Farrington (1991) reported that for males in the Cambridge study, having a delinquent sibling at age 8 predicted juvenile arrests and adult offending through age 32. More recent prospective research has shown a relationship between siblings' delinquency among Caucasian youth in Iowa (Slomkowski et al. 2001) and males in Pittsburgh (Farrington et al. 2001). The Iowa study (Conger and Reuter 1996) as well as longitudinal research conducted in the Pacific Northwest (Low, Shortt, and Snyder 2012) has also indicated that one sibling's substance use increases the likelihood of the other's substance use.

Sibling influences on crime are also suggested by research indicating that youth from larger families are more likely to be involved in crime compared to those from smaller families (Loeber and Dishion 1983). For example, in the study of Boston males, those from larger families had greater odds of self-reported and officially recorded crime as adults compared to those from smaller families (Sampson and Laub 1994). The Cambridge study (Nagin, Pogarsky, and Farrington 1997; Farrington 2002) and the 1970 British Cohort Study (Murray et al. 2010) have each shown a positive relationship between the number of siblings in the household and adult criminal convictions. Although other explanations for this relationship are possible, one interpretation is that families with more children may have more deviant sibling role models (Brownfield and Sorenson 1994). Aligned with this view, analysis of 10 years of data from the Hutchinson Smoking Prevention Project conducted in Washington State indicated that the greater the number of siblings who smoked, the higher the probability that the study child would smoke (Bricker et al. 2006).

There is not much experimental research to draw upon when assessing the relationship between parental or sibling crime and youth offending. Most parent-focused programs focus on changing parenting practices and increasing parent–child bonds, rather than reducing parent or sibling criminality, and so do not collect data on the delinquency of family members. An exception is the Nurse-Family Partnership program, which has been shown to reduce prenatal smoking (Olds et al. 1986) and criminal in-volvement (Koning et al. 2010) among mothers who receive services. However, the de-gree to which these positive effects mediate changes in children's delinquency has not been assessed. Evaluations of the MST and Functional Family Therapy (FFT) (Klein, Alexander, and Parsons 1977) programs have shown benefits for siblings of those re-ceiving therapeutic treatment, compared to siblings of those assigned to the con-trol group. For example, siblings of participants in an MST trial conducted in South Carolina reported a greater reduction in substance use compared to the control group siblings (Rowland, Chapman, and Henggeler 2008), and siblings of participants re-ceiving MST services in Missouri had greater reductions in arrests 25 years following treatment (Wagner et al. 2014). While such findings support observational research indicating concordance in sibling crime, they cannot establish that the targeted child played a direct role in affecting his or her sibling's outcomes; instead, it could be that the intervention altered the shared environment of both siblings or improved parents' behaviors (Wagner et al. 2014).

F. Young (Teenage) Parents

The last factor to be considered in this chapter is the impact of being born to a young parent. Longitudinal research has shown that teen parenthood predicts ele-vated externalizing behaviors among children early in the life course as well as de-linquency and crime in later years (Farrington 1996). For example, children of teen parents, compared to those of older parents, had more conduct problems at age 10 in the British Cohort Study (but only among daughters; Murray et al. 2010), more delinquency at age 14 in the Brisbane cohort study (Bor, McGee, and Fagan 2004), and higher levels of aggression from ages 6 to 15 in the Montreal study (Nagin and Tremblay 2001). In addition, studies conducted in Rochester (Pogarsky, Lizotte, and Thornberry 2003), Christchurch (Fergusson and Woodward 1999), and Dunedin (Jaffee et al. 2001) all indicated positive relationships between teen parenthood and children's self-reported offending or official convictions collected through early adulthood. These studies also showed that young mothers had less effective par-enting practices than older mothers, but even controlling for these behaviors, the effect of teen parenthood remained significant. In contrast, analysis of data from the Cambridge study did not show a significant relationship between young par-enthood and adult offending (based on official convictions at age 32) in multivar-iate models that controlled for other family characteristics (Nagin, Pogarsky, and Farrington 1997).

The causal relationship between teen parenthood and children's offending cannot be evaluated based on experimental manipulation. Observational studies that control for factors thought to mediate or be responsible for the impact of early parenthood on children's crime, such as those described above, are thus the best current source of data on this relationship.

II. Summary of Findings
from Meta-analyses

The empirical evidence reviewed to this point has indicated that family characteristics and parenting practices affect children's delinquency. However, it is difficult to determine the strength of this relationship given the disparities in research methods across studies. Furthermore, it is challenging to determine the relative impact of different family characteristics. To help provide answers to these questions, this section summarizes findings from meta-analyses that have reviewed multiple studies investigating the relationship between family characteristics and offending. Meta-analyses allow for more precise estimates of relationship(s) of interest, as this approach produces an average effect size based on findings from multiple studies (Pratt et al. 2010). Moreover, meta-analyses typically involve a systematic and critical review of all studies pertaining to the area of interest and are less subject to researcher bias in selecting particular studies to review.

Table 19.2 provides the effect sizes from four meta-analyses that have examined some or all of the family/parenting characteristics discussed in this chapter. The review by Machteld Hoeve and colleagues (2009) considered outcomes from 161 studies that investigated the relationship between parenting practices and juvenile delinquency, most of which utilized cross-sectional data (69 percent of all studies) and youth self-reports of offending (75 percent of studies). James Derzon's (2010) meta-analysis was based on 119 longitudinal studies that investigated the impact of family characteristics on adolescent delinquency (in about 60 percent of the studies) and crime in young adulthood (40 percent of studies). Mark Lipsey and James Derzon's (1998) review drew upon data from 34 longitudinal studies that included analysis of the impact of family characteristics on serious offending and violence when participants were 15 to 25 years old. Alan Leschield and colleagues (2008) reviewed 19 longitudinal studies with information on children's contact with the criminal justice system when participants were an average age of 25 years.

Taken as a whole, the four meta-analyses indicate that, on average, family factors are moderately associated with delinquency and violence. Leschied et al. (2008) reported an overall effect size on crime of 0.24 based on all the family/parent characteristics they considered (which also included parental mental health and family structure), which is a small to medium-sized impact. Although the other three studies did not calculate overall effect sizes, they all concluded that family influences on children's illegal behaviors were relatively modest. Nonetheless, they also all indicated that reported effect sizes were statistically significant for each parenting/family construct assessed (except the impact of teenaged parenthood in the review by Derzon 2010) and in the expected direction, and thus provided evidence that poor family experiences increase the likelihood of children's offending.

In terms of the relative impact of family characteristics, parental warmth/support, parental supervision/discipline, and parent/family criminality were among the largest

Table 19.2 Effect Sizes Reported in Four Meta-Analyses Based on Multiple Empirical Investigations of the Relationship Between Family Characteristics and Youth Delinquency

Family Characteristic	Hoeve et al. (2009)	Derzon (2010)[a]	Lipsey and Derzon (1998)[b]	Leschield (2008)[b]
Parental Warmth and Involvement	Support: .19 Affection: .21 Open communication: .07	Warmth .17 (PB) .18 (crime) .21 (violence)		
Parental Controls (i.e., Supervision and Discipline)	Discipline: .19 Permissiveness: .09 Monitoring: .23 Knowledge: .26 Psychological control: .23 General control: .21 Physical punishment: .10	Supervision .20 (PB) .06 (crime) Discipline .22 (PB) .17 (crime) .13 (violence) Child-rearing .22 (BP) .26 (crime)	Supervision, discipline and warmth .15 (age 6–11) .19 (age 12–14)	Supervision and discipline .41 (mid-childhood) .12 (adolescence)
Child Maltreatment		Maltreatment .19 (BP) .21 (crime) .10 (violence)	Maltreatment .07 (age 6–11) .09 (age 12–14)	Adverse family environment .16 (early childhood) .17 (mid-childhood) .38 (adolescence)
Exposure to Intimate Partner Violence (IPV)		Family discord .22 (PB) .26 (crime) .10 (violence)		Adverse family environment .16 (early childhood) .17 (mid-childhood) .38 (adolescence)

Family Criminality and Substance Use	Family deviance	Criminal parent
	.22 (PB)	.23 (age 6–11)
	.19 (crime)	.16 (age 12–14)
	Criminal parent	
	.30 (PB)	
	.15 (crime)	
	.17 (violence)	
	Large family size	
	.08 (PB)	
	.11 (crime)	
Teen Parent		
	.11 (PB)	

[a]Calculated separate effect sizes for the relationship between family characteristics and aggression (e.g., based on self, parent, or teacher reports), problem behavior (PB; e.g., alcohol and tobacco use, externalizing, and conduct disorder), criminal behavior (e.g., based on self-reports and official recorded delinquency and crime), and violent behavior. Effect sizes for the last three categories are provided when they were based on five or more studies.

[b]Calculated separate effect sizes according to the developmental/age period in which the family factor was measured.

predictors of offending, with similarly sized effect sizes around 0.20. Of the different parenting practices reviewed by Hoeve et al. (2009), parents' knowledge of children's activities and whereabouts has the strongest relationship with delinquency (with an effect size of 0.26 based on 47 studies), whereas Lipsey and Derzon (1998) reported that parent criminality was the strongest risk factor. The impact of child maltreatment varied across the four studies, perhaps because it was measured in slightly different ways—for example, Leschied et al. (2008) combined exposure to child abuse and parental violence in their measure of the "adverse family environment." Finally, Derzon (2010) was the only study to report effect sizes for family size and teenage parenthood, and each had small effects. He also reported a weak impact of parental substance use, but this conclusion was based on only a few studies (Derzon 2010).

III. CONCLUSION

In this section we draw conclusions regarding the strength and quality of the empirical evidence examining the impact of family influences on youth delinquency and provide recommendations for future research on this topic.

A. Summary of the Evidence

This chapter examined evidence from longitudinal and experimental studies and from meta-analyses to assess the degree to which six parent/family characteristics have been shown to affect youth offending. This information indicates that the family environment matters and that exposure to family risk factors increases the likelihood of delinquency and crime in the short and the long term. Experimental studies not only provide some causal evidence of this relationship but also indicate that it is possible to enhance the family environment in order to prevent children from engaging in substance use, delinquency, and violence.

How does the role of the family compare to other risk factors considered important in the development of crime? According to the meta-analyses shown in Table 19.2, family factors have a small to moderate direct effect on offending, and the size of these associations is similar to, though slightly smaller than, other risk factors (Smith and Stern 1997). For example, meta-analyses conducted by Travis Pratt and colleagues report effect sizes of 0.26 to 0.28 for self-control (Pratt and Cullen 2000), 0.27 for peer delinquency (Pratt et al. 2010), and 0.30 for collective efficacy (Pratt et al. 2006). Lipsey and Derzon (1998) report an effect size of 0.37 for peer delinquency, and they state that peer and individual factors are more strongly associated with offending than are most family characteristics.

Although these comparisons suggest that family influences may be weaker than other risk factors, it is important to realize that studies assessing direct effects do not take into account how family factors may affect or be mediated by other risk factors. For example, Lawrence Steinberg (2001, p. 11) asserts that parents are very likely to influence children's exposure to prosocial and antisocial peers, and "what may appear to the direct effect of peers [e.g., in influencing delinquency] is often the indirect influence of parents." Likewise, many life-course theories point out that negative experiences in the family, especially early on, can lead to increased exposure to delinquent peers or other adverse events (e.g., school failure), which will cumulatively impact risk for offending later in life (Patterson 1982; Moffitt 1993; Sampson and Laub 1993). Research has also indicated that positive family experiences can reduce the impact of other risk factors on offending (Derzon 2010); for example, ameliorating the criminogenic influence of exposure to delinquent peers (Vitaro, Brendgen, and Tremblay 2000; Dishion, Nelson, and Bullock 2004; Barnes et al. 2006). Many studies focus on the direct effects of parenting practices and family characteristics and thus do not capture all of the ways in which families may contribute to delinquency.

B. Suggestions for Future Research

Our review of the evidence indicates that additional research is needed to draw stronger conclusions regarding family influences on youth delinquency. Most relevant to life-course research, more developmentally informed analyses of family influences are warranted. Although longitudinal studies are well equipped for this task, much of the research we reviewed failed to fully capitalize on their prospective data. Such studies often analyzed short-term effects, long-term effects with no analysis of mediating mechanisms, or the impact of static rather than dynamic family factors. As such, this research is unable to fully test hypotheses from life-course theories, such as the assertion that family influences become less important as children age (Thornberry 1987; Sampson and Laub 1993; Catalano and Hawkins 1996) or that different family characteristics may have different relevance depending on the age of the child. Similarly, future research should examine the degree to which parenting practices change over time and how these changes are linked to changes in children's delinquency (Farrington et al. 2002). Such research should also take into account possible reciprocal effects in order to assess how children's behaviors, including delinquency, affect parenting practices (Thornberry 1987; Dishion and McMahon 1998; Dishion, Nelson, and Bullock 2004).

Some life-course theories recognize individual differences in responses to particular life events (Moffitt 1993; Elder 1995), yet attempts to identify individual factors that may moderate the impact of family influences on offending have been relatively uncommon (Fagan et al. 2013). There are some exceptions; for example, gender differences in the impact of parenting practices has received some empirical attention (Kroneman et al. 2009; Fagan et al. 2011). Other factors, such as race/ethnicity and genetic predispositions, have been much less examined. Likewise, although some studies have investigated whether or not family factors are moderated by peer influences (Dishion, Nelson, and Bullock

2004; Barnes et al. 2006), there has been less attention to how neighborhood and school characteristics may affect the family/offending relationship.

Finally, we recommend that criminologists utilize more sophisticated measurement models to model the impact of family processes. Most family-focused studies note the high degree of correlation between the characteristics reviewed in this chapter, yet many studies analyze the impact of only one or two family factors or assess their independent rather than combined effect on offending. Such models are likely to be misspecified and may underestimate the role of the family in predicting delinquency. In contrast, psychological studies are more apt to model parenting as a multi-faceted construct, most often one that captures parent warmth/support, monitoring and disciplining, and parent attempts to foster children's independence (i.e., "authoritative parenting"; see, e.g., Steinberg et al. 1991). Some criminological research has relied on comprehensive measures of the family environment (e.g., Gorman-Smith, Tolan, and Henry 2000; Simons et al. 2001; Hoeve et al. 2008; Fagan et al. 2011; Herrenkohl et al. 2012; Krohn et al. 2014), but this approach is relatively rare. We hope that future research expands upon this line of research and takes advantage of innovative methods and statistical approaches (e.g., latent variables, latent class analyses, etc.) when assessing family influences on crime.

Attention to these issues can advance knowledge of the role of the family in affecting youth offending and help to refine life-course and other theories of crime. In addition, information gleaned from more nuanced empirical investigations of the family can inform the development of new interventions targeting the reduction of family risk factors and promotion of family protective factors. It can also be useful in dissemination of such interventions, to be certain that family-focused programs target for services the populations for whom they will be most beneficial.

REFERENCES

Akers, Ronald L. 1985. *Deviant Behavior: A Social Learning Approach*. 3rd ed. Belmont, CA: Wadsworth.

Akers, Ronald L., Marvin D. Krohn, Lonn Lanza-Kaduce, and Marcia Radosevich. 1979. "Social Learning and Deviant Behavior: A Specific Test of a General Theory." *American Sociological Review* 44: 636–655.

Avellar, Sarah A., and Lauren H. Supplee. 2013. "Effectiveness of Home Visiting in Improving Child Health and Reducing Child Maltreatment." *Pediatrics* 132: S90–99.

Barnes, Grace M., John P. Hoffman, J.W. Welte, Michael P. Farrell, and Barbara A. Dintcheff. 2006. "Effects of Parental Monitoring and Peer Deviance on Substance Use and Delinquency." *Journal of Marriage and the Family* 68(4): 1084–1104.

Bilukha, Oleg, Robert A. Hahn, Alex Crosby, Mindy T. Fullilove, Akiva Liberman, Eve K. Moscicki, Susan Snyder, Farris Tuma, Phaedra Corso, Amanda Schofield, Peter A. Briss, and Task Force on Community Prevention Services. 2005. "The Effectiveness of Early Childhood Home Visitation in Preventing Violence: A Systematic Review." *American Journal of Preventive Medicine* 28(2S1): 11–39.

Bor, William, Tara Renae McGee, and Abigail A. Fagan. 2004. "Early Risk Factors for Adolescent Antisocial Behaviour: An Australian Longitudinal Study." *Australian and New Zealand Journal of Psychiatry* 38: 365–372.

Brennan, Patricia A., Emily R. Grekin, and Sarnoff A. Mednick. 1999. "Maternal Smoking During Pregnancy and Adult Male Criminal Outcomes." *Archives of General Psychiatry* 56(3): 215–219.

Bricker, Jonathan B., Arthur V. Peterson Jr., Brian G. Leroux, M. Robyn Andersen, K. Bharat Rajan, and Irwin C. Sarason. 2006. "Prospective Prediction of Children's Smoking Transitions: Role of Parents' and Older Siblings' Smoking." *Addiction* 101(1): 128–136.

Bronte-Tinkew, Jacinta, Kristin A. Moore, and Jennifer Carrano. 2006. "The Father-Child Relationship, Parenting Styles, and Adolescent Risk Behaviors in Intact Families." *Journal of Family Issues* 27(6): 850–881.

Brownfield, David, and Ann Marie Sorenson. 1994. "Sibship Size and Sibling Delinquency." *Deviant Behavior* 15: 45–61.

Caspi, Avshalom, Joseph McClay, Terrie E. Moffitt, Jonathan Mill, Judy Martin, Ian W. Craig, Alan Taylor, and Richie Poulton. 2002. "Role of Genotype in the Cycle of Violence in Maltreated Children." *Science* 297: 851–859.

Catalano, Richard F., and J. David Hawkins. 1996. "The Social Development Model: A Theory of Antisocial Behavior." In *Delinquency and Crime: Current Theories*, edited by J. David Hawkins, 149–197. New York: Cambridge University Press.

Conger, Rand D., and Martha A. Reuter. 1996. "Siblings, Parents, and Peers: A Longitudinal Study of Social Influences in Adolescent Risk for Alcohol Use and Abuse." In *Sibling Relationships: Their Causes and Consequences*, edited by Gene H. Brody. Norwood, NJ: Ablex.

Dekovic, Maja, Willeke A. Manders, Jessica J. Asscher, Pier J. M. Prins, and Peter van der Laan. 2012. "Within-Intervention Change: Mediators of Intervention Effects During Multisystemic Therapy." *Journal of Consulting and Clinical Psychology* 80(4): 574–587.

Derzon, James H. 2010. "The Correspondence of Family Features with Problem, Aggressive, Criminal, and Violent Behavior: A Meta-Analysis." *Journal of Experimental Criminology* 6: 263–292.

Dishion, Thomas J., and Robert J. McMahon. 1998. "Parental Monitoring and the Prevention of Child and Adolescent Problem Behavior: A Conceptual and Empirical Formulation." *Clinical Child and Family Psychology Review* 1(1): 61–75.

Dishion, Thomas J., Sarah E. Nelson, and Bernadette Marie Bullock. 2004. "Premature Adolescent Autonomy: Parent Disengagement and Deviant Peer Process in the Amplification of Problem Behaviour." *Journal of Adolescence* 27: 515–530.

Donovan, John E. 2004. "Adolescent Alcohol Initiation: A Review of Psychosocial Risk Factors." *Journal of Adolescent Health* 35(6): e7–e18.

DuMont, Kimberly A., Cathy Spatz Widom, and Sally J. Czaja. 2007. "Predictors of Resilience in Abused and Neglected Children Grown-Up: The Role of Individual and Neighborhood Characteristics." *Child Abuse and Neglect* 31: 255–274.

Eckenrode, John, Mary Campa, Dennis W. Luckey, Charles R. Henderson Jr., Robert Cole, Harriet Kitzman, Elizabeth Anson, Kimberly Sidora-Arcoleo, Jane Powers, and David L. Olds. 2010. "Long-Term Effects of Prenatal and Infancy Nurse Home Visitation on the Life Course of Youths: 19-Year Follow-Up of a Randomized Trial." *Archives of Pediatric and Adolescent Medicine* 164(1): 9–15. https://doi.org/10.1007/s11121-009-0126-0.

Elder, Glen H., Jr. 1995. "The Life Course Paradigm: Social Change and Individual Development." In *Examining Lives in Context: Perspectives on the Ecology of Human Development*, edited by Phyllis Moen, Glen H. ElderJr., and Kurt Luscher, 101–139. Washington, DC: APA Press.

Fagan, Abigail A., and Jake M. Najman. 2003. "Sibling Influences on Adolescent Delinquent Behavior: An Australian Longitudinal Study." *Journal of Adolescence* 26(5): 546–558.

Fagan, Abigail A., and Jake M. Najman. 2005. "The Relative Contributions of Parental and Sibling Substance Use to Adolescent Tobacco and Alcohol Use." *Journal of Drug Issues* 35(4): 869–884.

Fagan, Abigail A. 2005. "The Relationship Between Adolescent Physical Abuse and Criminal Offending: Support for an Enduring and Generalized Cycle of Violence." *Journal of Family Violence* 20(5): 279–290.

Fagan, Abigail A., M. Lee Van Horn, Susan Antamarian, and J. David Hawkins. 2011. "How Do Families Matter? Age and Gender Differences in Family Influences on Delinquency and Drug Use." *Youth Violence and Juvenile Justice* 9(2): 150–170.

Fagan, Abigail A., M. Lee Van Horn, Thomas Jaki, and J. David Hawkins. 2013. "Differential Effects of Parental Controls on Adolescent Substance Use: For Whom Is the Family Most Important?" *Journal of Quantitative Criminology* 29(3): 347–368.

Farrington, David P. 1996. "The Explanation and Prevention of Youthful Offending." In *Delinquency and Crime: Current Theories*, edited by J. David Hawkins, 68–148. Cambridge, UK: Cambridge University Press.

Farrington, David P. 2002. "Key Results from the First Forty Years of the Cambridge Study in Delinquent Development." In *Taking Stock of Delinquency: An Overview of Findings from Contemporary Longitudinal Studies*, edited by Terence P. Thornberry and Marvin D. Krohn, 137–184. New York: Kluwer/Plenum.

Farrington, David P. 2013. "Longitudinal and Experimental Research in Criminology." In *Crime and Justice in America*, edited by Michael Tonry, 453–527. Chicago: University of Chicago Press.

Farrington, David P., Jeremy W. Coid, and Joseph Murray. 2009. "Family Factors in the Intergenerational Transmission of Offending." *Criminal Justice and Behavior* 19: 109–124.

Farrington, David P., Darrick Jolliffe, Rolf Loeber, Magda Stouthamer-Loeber, and Larry M. Kalb. 2001. "The Concentration of Offenders in Families, and Family Criminality in the Prediction of Boys' Delinquency." *Journal of Adolescence* 24: 579–596.

Farrington, David P., Rolf Loeber, Yanming Yin, and Stewart J. Anderson. 2002. "Are Within-Individual Causes of Delinquency the Same as Between-Individual Causes?" *Criminal Behaviour and Mental Health* 12: 53–68.

Farrington, David P., and Brandon C. Welsh. 2005. "Randomized Experiments in Criminology: What Have We Learned in the Last Two Decades?" *Journal of Experimental Criminology* 1: 9–38. https://doi.org/10.1007/s11292-004-6460-0.

Feinberg, Mark E., Anna R. Solmeyer, and Susan M. McHale. 2012. "The Third Rail of Family Systems: Sibling Relationships, Mental and Behavioral Health, and Preventive Intervention in Childhood and Adolescence." *Clinical Child and Family Psychology Review* 15: 43–57.

Fergusson, David M., John L. Horwood, and Michael T. Lynskey. 1993. "Maternal Smoking Before and After Pregnancy: Effects on Behavioral Outcomes in Middle Childhood." *Pediatrics* 92: 815–822.

Fergusson, David M., and L. John Horwood. 1998. "Exposure to Interparental Violence in Childhood and Psychosocial Adjustment in Young Adulthood." *Child Abuse and Neglect* 22(5): 339–557.

Fergusson, David M., and Michael T. Lynskey. 1997. "Physical Punishment/Maltreatment During Childhood and Adjustment in Young Adulthood." *Child Abuse and Neglect* 21(7): 617–630.

Fergusson, David M., Nicola Swain-Campbell, and John L. Horwood. 2004. "How Does Childhood Economic Disadvantage Lead to Crime?" *Journal of Child Psychology and Psychiatry* 45(5): 956–966.

Fergusson, David M., and Lianne J. Woodward. 1999. "Maternal Age and Educational and Psychosocial Outcomes in Early Adulthood." *Journal of Child Psychology and Psychiatry* 43(3): 479–489.

Gardner, Frances, Jennifer Burton, and Ivana Klimes. 2006. "Randomised Controlled Trial of a Parenting Intervention in the Voluntary Sector for Reducing Child Conduct Problems: Outcomes and Mechanisms of Change." *Journal of Child Psychology and Psychiatry* 47(11): 1123–1132. https://doi.org/10.1111/j.1469-7610.2006.01668.x.

Gardner, Frances, Judy Hutchings, Tracey Bywater, and Chris Whitaker. 2010. "Who Benefits and How Does It Work? Moderators and Mediators of Outcome in an Effectiveness Trial of a Parenting Intervention." *Journal of Clinical Child and Adolescent Psychology* 39(4): 568–580.

Glueck, Sheldon, and Eleanor Glueck. 1950. *Unraveling Juvenile Delinquency*. Cambridge, MA: Harvard University Press.

Gorman-Smith, Deborah, Patrick H. Tolan, and David B. Henry. 2000. "A Developmental-Ecological Model of the Relation of Family Functioning to Patterns of Delinquency." *Journal of Quantitative Criminology* 16(2): 169–198.

Hair, Elizabeth C., K. A. Moore, Sarah B. Garrett, Thomson Ling, and Kevin Cleveland. 2008. "The Continued Importance of Quality Parent-Adolescent Relationships During Late Adolescence." *Journal of Research on Adolescence* 18(1): 187–200.

Hamby, Sherry, David Finkelhor, Heather A. Turner, and Richard K. Ormrod. 2010. "The Overlap of Witnessing Partner Violence with Child Maltreatment and Other Victimizations in a Nationally Representative Survey of Youth." *Child Abuse and Neglect* 34: 734–741.

Henggeler, Scott W., Elizabeth J. Letourneau, Jason E. Chapman, Paul A. Schewe, Charles M. Borduin, and Michael R. McCart. 2009. "Mediators of Change for Multisystemic Therapy with Juvenile Sexual Offenders." *Journal of Consulting and Clinical Psychology* 77(3): 451–462.

Herrenkohl, Roy C., Brenda P. Egolf, and Ellen C. Herrenkohl. 1997. "Preschool Antecedents of Adolescent Assaultive Behavior: A Longitudinal Study." *American Journal of Orthopsychiatry* 67(3): 422–432.

Herrenkohl, Todd I., Karl G. Hill, J. D. Hawkins, Ick-Joong Chung, and Daniel S. Nagin. 2006. "Developmental Trajectories of Family Management and Risk for Violent Behavior in Adolescence." *Journal of Adolescent Health* 39(2): 206–213.

Herrenkohl, Todd I., Jungeun Olivia Lee, Rick Kosterman, and J. David Hawkins. 2012. "Family Influences Related to Adult Substance Use and Mental Health Problems: A Developmental Analysis of Child and Adolescent Predictors." *Journal of Adolescent Health* 51: 129–135.

Herrenkohl, Todd I., Cindy Sousa, Emiko A. Tajima, Roy C. Herrenkohl, and Carrie A. Moylan. 2008. "Intersection of Child Abuse and Children's Exposure to Domestic Violence." *Trauma, Violence and Abuse* 9(2): 84–99.

Hirschi, Travis. 1969. *Causes of Delinquency*. Berkeley: University of California Press.

Hoeve, Machteld, Arjan Blokland, Judith Semon Dubas, Rolf Loeber, Jan R. M. Gerris, and Peter H. van der Laan. 2008. "Trajectories of Delinquency and Parenting Styles." *Journal of Abnormal Child Psychology* 36: 223–235.

Hoeve, Machteld, Judith Semon Dubas, Veroni I. Eichelsheim, Peter H. Van der Laan, Wilma Smeenk, and Jan R. M. Gerris. 2009. "The Relationship between Parenting and Delinquency: A Meta-Analysis." *Journal of Abnormal Child Psychology* 37: 749–775. https://doi.org/10.1007/s10802-009-9310-8.

Ireland, Timothy O., and Carolyn Smith. 2009. "Living in Partner-Violent Families: Developmental Links to Antisocial Behavior and Relationship Violence." *Journal of Youth and Adolescence* 38: 323–339.

Ireland, Timothy O., Carolyn A. Smith, and Terence P. Thornberry. 2002. "Developmental Issues in the Impact of Child Maltreatment on Later Delinquency and Drug Use." *Criminology* 40(2): 359–400.

Jaffee, Sara R., Avshalom Caspi, Terrie E. Moffitt, Jay Belsky, and Phil Silva. 2001. "Why Are Children Born to Teen Mothers at Risk for Adverse Outcomes in Young Adulthood? Results from a 20-Year Longitudinal Study." *Development and Psychopathology* 13: 377–397.

Jang, Sung Joon. 1999. "Age-Varying Effects of Family, School, and Peers on Delinquency: A Multilevel Modeling Test of Interactional Theory." *Criminology* 37(3): 643–686.

Jang, Sung Joon. 2002. "The Effects of Family, School, Peers, and Attitudes on Adolescent's Drug Use: Do They Vary with Age?" *Justice Quarterly* 19(1): 97–126.

Jang, Sung Joon, and Marvin D. Krohn. 1995. "Developmental Patterns of Sex Differences in Delinquency Among African American Adolescents: A Test of the Sex-Invariance Hypothesis." *Journal of Quantitative Criminology* 11(2): 195–222.

Keijsers, Loes, Tom Frijns, Susan J. T. Branje, and Wim Meeus. 2009. "Developmental Links of Adolescent Disclosure, Parental Solicitation, and Control with Delinquency: Moderation by Parental Support." *Developmental Psychology* 45(5): 1314–1327.

Kerr, Margaret, and Hakan Stattin. 2000. "What Parents Know, How They Know It, and Several Forms of Adolescent Adjustment: Further Support for a Reinterpretation of Monitoring." *Developmental Psychology* 36(3): 366–380.

Kerr, Margaret, and Hakan Stattin. 2003. "Parenting of Adolescents: Action or Reaction?" In *Children's Influence on Family Dynamics: The Neglected Side of Family Relationships*, edited by Ann C. Crouter and Alan Booth, 121–152. Mahwah, NJ: Lawrence Erlbaum.

Kitzman, Harriet J., David L. Olds, Robert E. Cole, Carole A. Hanks, Elizabeth A. Anson, Kimberly J. Arcoleo, Dennis W. Luckey, Michael D. Knudtson, Charles R. Henderson Jr., and John R. Holmberg. 2010. "Enduring Effects of Prenatal and Infancy Home Visiting by Nurses on Children: Follow-Up of a Randomized Trial among Children at Age 12 Years." *Archives of Pediatric and Adolescent Medicine* 164(5): 412–418.

Klein, Nanci C., James F. Alexander, and Bruce V. Parsons. 1977. "Impact of Family Systems Intervention on Recidivism and Sibling Delinquency: A Model of Primary Prevention and Program Evaluation." *Journal of Consulting and Clinical Psychology* 45(3): 469–474.

Komro, Kelli A., Mildred M. Maldonado-Molina, Amy L. Tobler, Jennifer R. Bonds, and Keith E. Muller. 2007. "Effects of Home Access and Availability of Alcohol on Young Adolescents' Alcohol Use." *Addiction* 102: 1597–1608.

Koning, Ina M., Regina J. J. M. Van den Eijnden, Rutger C. M. E. Engels, Jacqueline E. E. Verdurmen, and Wilma A. M. Vollebergh. 2010. "Why Target Early Adolescents and Parents in Alcohol Prevention? The Mediating Effects of Self-Control, Rules and Attitudes About Alcohol Use." *Addiction* 106: 538–546.

Kosterman, Rick, J. David Hawkins, Jie Guo, Richard F Catalano, and Robert D. Abbott. 2000. "The Dynamics of Alcohol and Marijuana Initiation: Patterns and Predictors of First Use in Adolescence." *American Journal of Public Health* 90(3): 360–366.

Krohn, Marvin D., Alan J. Lizotte, Shawn D. Bushway, Nicole M. Schmidt, and Matthew D. Phillips. 2014. "Shelter During the Storm: A Search for Factors That Protect At-Risk Adolescents from Violence." *Crime and Delinquency* 60(3): 379–401.

Kroneman, Leoniek, Rolf Loeber, Alison E. Hipwell, and Hans M. Koot. 2009. "Girls' Disruptive Behavior and Its Relationship to Family Functioning: A Review." *Journal of Child and Family Studies* 18: 259–273.

Lansford, Jennifer E., Shari Miller-Johnson, Lisa J. Berlin, Kenneth A. Dodge, John E. Bates, and Gregory S. Pettit. 2007. "Early Physical Abuse and Later Violent Delinquency: A Prospective Longitudinal Study." *Child Maltreatment* 12(3): 233–245.

Lauritsen, Janet L. 1993. "Sibling Resemblance in Juvenile Delinquency: Findings from the National Youth Survey." *Criminology* 31(3): 387–409.

Leschied, Alan, Debbie Chiodo, Elizabeth Nowicki, and Susan Rodger. 2008. "Childhood Predictors of Adult Criminality: A Meta-Analysis Drawn from the Prospective Literature." *Canadian Journal of Criminology and Criminal Justice* 50: 435–467.

Lipsey, Mark W., and James H. Derzon. 1998. "Predictors of Violent or Serious Delinquency in Adolescence and Early Adulthood: A Synthesis of Longitudinal Research." In *Serious and Violent Juvenile Offenders: Risk Factors and Successful Interventions*, edited by Rolf Loeber and David P. Farrington, 86–105. Thousand Oaks, CA: Sage.

Loeber, Rolf, and Thomas J. Dishion. 1983. "Early Predictors of Male Delinquency: A Review." *Psychological Bulletin* 94(1): 68–99.

Loeber, Rolf, Dustin A. Pardini, Magda Stouthamer-Loeber, and Adrian Raine. 2007. "Do Cognitive, Physiological, and Psychosocial Risk and Promotive Factors Predict Desistance from Delinquency in Males?" *Development and Psychopathology* 19: 867–887.

Low, Sabina, Joann Wu Shortt, and James Snyder. 2012. "Sibling Influences on Adolescent Substance Use: The Role of Modeling, Collusion, and Conflict." *Development and Psychopathology* 24(1): 287–300.

Margolin, Gayla, and Elana B. Gordis. 2000. "The Effects of Family and Community Violence on Children." *Annual Review of Psychology* 51: 445–479.

Maxfield, Michael G., and Cathy Spatz Widom. 1996. "The Cycle of Violence: Revisited Six Years Later." *Archives of Pediatrics and Adolescent Medicine* 150: 390–395.

McClain, Darya Bonds, Sharlene A. Wolchik, Emily Winslow, Jenn-Yun Tein, Irwin Sandler, and Roger E. Millsap. 2010. "Developmental Cascade Effects of the New Beginnings Program on Adolescent Adaptation Outcomes." *Development and Psychopathology* 22: 771–784.

Mersky, Joshua P., James Topitzes, and Arthur J. Reynolds. 2012. "Unsafe at Any Age: Linking Childhood and Adolescent Maltreatment to Delinquency and Crime." *Journal of Research in Crime and Delinquency* 49: 295–318.

Moffitt, Terrie E. 1993. "Adolescence-Limited and Life-Course Persistent Anti-Social Behavior: A Developmental Taxonomy." *Psychological Review* 100(4): 674–701.

Moffitt, Terrie E., and Avshalom Caspi. 2001. "Childhood Predictors Differentiate Life-Course Persistent and Adolescence-Limited Antisocial Pathways Among Males and Females." *Development and Psychopathology* 13: 355–375.

Murray, Joseph, David P. Farrington, and Ivana Sekol. 2012. "Children's Antisocial Behavior, Mental Health, Drug Use, and Educational Performance After Parental Incarceration: A Systematic Review and Meta-Analysis." *Psychological Bulletin* 138(2): 175–201.

Murray, Joseph, Barrie Irving, David P. Farrington, Ian Colman, and Claire A. J. Bloxsom. 2010. "Very Early Predictors of Conduct Problems and Crime: Results from a National Cohort Study." *The Journal of Child Psychology and Psychiatry* 51(11): 1198–1207.

Murray, Joseph, Rolf Loeber, and Dustin A. Pardini. 2012. "Parental Involvement in the Criminal Justice System and the Development of Youth Theft, Marijuana Use, Depression, and Poor Academic Performance." *Criminology* 50(1): 255–302.

Nagin, Daniel S., Greg Pogarsky, and David P. Farrington. 1997. "Adolescent Mothers and the Criminal Behavior of Their Children." *Law and Society Review* 31(1): 137–162.

Nagin, Daniel S., and Richard E. Tremblay. 2001. "Parental and Early Childhood Predictors of Persistent Physical Aggression in Boys from Kindergarten to High School." *Archives of General Psychiatry* 58: 389–394.

Neumann, Anna, Edward D. Barker, Hans M. Koot, and Barbara Maughan. 2010. "The Role of Contextual Risk, Impulsivity, and Parental Knowledge in the Development of Adolescent Antisocial Behavior." *Journal of Abnormal Psychology* 119(3): 534–545.

Olds, David L., Charles R. Henderson Jr., and Robert Cole. 1998. "Long-Term Effects of Nurse Home Visitation on Children's Criminal and Antisocial Behavior: 15-Year Follow-Up of a Randomized Controlled Trial." *Journal of the American Medical Association* 280(14): 1238–1244.

Olds, David L., Charles R. Henderson Jr., Robert Tatelbaum, and Robert Chamberlin. 1986. "Improving the Delivery of Prenatal Care and Outcomes of Pregnancy: A Randomized Trial of Nurse Home Visitation." *Pediatrics* 77(1): 16–28.

Olds, David L., JoAnn Robinson, Lisa M. Pettitt, Dennis W. Luckey, John Holmberg, Rosanna K. Ng, Kathy Isacks, Karen Sheff, and Charles R. Henderson Jr. 2004. "Effects of Home Visits by Paraprofessionals and by Nurses: Age 4 Follow-up Results of a Randomized Trial." *Pediatrics* 114: 1560–1568.

Ozdemir, Metin, and Nikolaus Koutakis. 2016. "Does Promoting Parents' Negative Attitudes to Underage Drinking Reduce Adolescents' Drinking? The Mediating Process and Moderators of the Effects of the Örebro Prevention Programme." *Addiction* 111: 263–271.

Pantin, Hilda, Guillermo Prado, Barbara Lopez, Shi Huang, Maria I. Tapia, Seth J. Schwartz, Eduardo Sabillon, C. Hendricks Brown, and Jennifer Branchini. 2009. "A Randomized Controlled Trial of Familias Unidas for Hispanic Adolescents with Behavior Problems." *Psychosomatic Medicine* 71(9): 987–995.

Patterson, Gerald R. 1982. *A Social Learning Approach.* Vol. 3: *Coercive Family Practices.* Eugene, OR: Castalia Publishing.

Piquero, Alex R., Chris L. Gibson, Stephen G. Tibbetts, Michael G. Turner, and Solomon H. Katz. 2002. "Maternal Cigarette Smoking During Pregnancy and Life-Course-Persistent Offending." *International Journal of Offender Therapy and Comparative Criminology* 46(2): 231–248.

Pogarsky, Greg, Alan J. Lizotte, and Terence P. Thornberry. 2003. "The Delinquency of Children Born to Young Mothers: Results from the Rochester Youth Development Study." *Criminology* 41(4): 1249–1286.

Prado, Guillermo, Hilda Pantin, Ervin Briones, Seth J. Schwartz, Daniel Feaster, Shi Huang, Summer Sullivan, Maria I. Tapia, Eduardo Sabillon, Barbara Lopez, and Jose Szapocznik. 2007. "A Randomized Controlled Trial of a Parent-Centered Intervention in Preventing Substance Use and HIV Risk Behaviors in Hispanic Adolescents." *Journal of Consulting and Clinical Psychology* 75(6): 914–926.

Pratt, Travis C., and Francis T. Cullen. 2000. "The Empirical Status of Gottfredson and Hirschi's General Theory of Crime: A Meta-Analysis." *Criminology* 38(3): 931–964.

Pratt, Travis C., Francis T. Cullen, Kristie R. Blevins, Leah E. Daigle, and Tamara D. Madensen. 2006. "The Empirical Status of Deterrence Theory: A Meta-Analysis." In *Taking Stock: The*

Status of Criminological Theory, edited by Francis T. Cullen, John Paul Wright, and Kristie R. Blevins, 367–395. New Brunswick, NJ: Transaction.

Pratt, Travis C., Francis T. Cullen, Christine S. Sellers, L. Thomas Winfree, Tamara D. Madensen, Leah E. Daigle, Noelle E. Fearn, and Jacinta M. Gau. 2010. "The Empirical Status of Social Learning Theory: A Meta Analysis." *Justice Quarterly* 27(6): 765–802. https://doi.org/10.1080/07418820903379610.

Racz, Sarah Jensen, and Robert J. McMahon. 2011. "The Relationship between Parental Knowledge and Monitoring and Child and Adolescent Conduct Problems: A 10-Year Update." *Clinical Child and Family Psychology Review* 14:377–398.

Reiss, Albert J., and David P. Farrington. 1991. "Advancing Knowledge About Co-Offending: Results from a Prospective Longitudinal Survey of London Males." *The Journal of Criminal Law and Criminology* 82(2): 360–395.

Reynolds, Arthur J., and Suh-Ruu Ou. 2011. "Paths of Effects from Preschool to Adult Well-Being: A Confirmatory Analysis of the Child-Parent Center Program." *Child Development* 82(2): 555–582.

Rowe, David C., Miriam R. Linver, and Joseph Lee Rodgers. 1996. "Delinquency and IQ: Using Siblings to Find Sources of Variation." In *Sibling Relationships: Their Causes and Consequences*, edited by Gene H. Brody, 147–172. Norwood, NJ: Ablex.

Rowland, Melisa D., Jason E. Chapman, and Scott W. Henggeler. 2008. "Sibling Outcomes from a Randomized Trial of Evidence-Based Treatments with Substance Abusing Juvenile Offenders." *Journal of Child and Adolescent Substance Abuse* 17(3): 11–26.

Sampson, Robert J., and John H. Laub. 1990. "Crime and Deviance over the Life Course: The Salience of Adult Social Bonds." *American Sociological Review* 55: 609–627.

Sampson, Robert J., and John H. Laub. 1993. *Crime in the Making: Pathways and Turning Points Through Life*. Cambridge, MA: Harvard University Press.

Sampson, Robert J., and John H. Laub. 1994. "Urban Poverty and the Family Context of Delinquency: A New Look at Structure and Process in a Classic Study." *Child Development* 65(2): 523–540.

Shaw, Daniel S., Miles Gilliom, Erin M. Ingoldsby, and Daniel S. Nagin. 2003. "Trajectories Leading to School-Age Conduct Problems." *Developmental Psychology* 39(2): 189–200.

Sherman, Lawrence W., and Richard A. Berk. 1984. "The Specific Deterrent Effects of Arrest for Domestic Assault." *American Sociological Review* 49(2): 261–272.

Simons, Ronald L., Wei Chao, Rand D. Conger, and Glen H. Elder. 2001. "Quality of Parenting as Mediator of the Effect of Childhood Defiance on Adolescent Friendship Choices and Delinquency: A Growth Curve Analysis." *Journal of Marriage and the Family* 63: 63–79.

Slomkowski, Cheryl, Richard Rende, Katherine Jewsbury Conger, Ronald L. Simons, and Rand Conger. 2001. "Sisters, Brothers, and Delinquency: Evaluating Social Influence During Early and Middle Adolescence." *Child Development* 72(1): 271–283.

Smith, Carolyn A., and Susan B. Stern. 1997. "Delinquency and Antisocial Behavior: A Review of Family Processes and Intervention Research." *Social Service Review* 71(3): 382–420.

Smith, Carolyn, and Terence P. Thornberry. 1995. "The Relationship between Childhood Maltreatment and Adolescent Involvement in Delinquency." *Criminology* 33: 451–477.

Sousa, Cindy, Todd I. Herrenkohl, Carrie A. Moylan, Emiko A. Tajima, Bart Klika, Roy C. Herrenkohl, and M. Jean Russo. 2011. "Longitudinal Study on the Effects on Child Abuse and Children's Exposure to Domestic Violence, Parent-Child Attachments, and Antisocial Behavior in Adolescence." *Journal of Interpersonal Violence* 26(1): 111–136.

Steinberg, Laurence. 2001. "We Know Some Things: Parent-Adolescent Relationships in Retrospect and Prospect." *Journal of Research on Adolescence* 11(1): 1–19.

Steinberg, Laurence, Nina S. Mounts, Susie D. Lamborn, and Sanford M. Dornbusch. 1991. "Authoritative Parenting and Adolescent Adjustment Across Varied Ecological Niches." *Journal of Research on Adolescence* 1(1): 19–36.

Tein, Jenn-Yun, Irwin N. Sandler, David P. MacKinnon, and Sharlene A. Wolchik. 2004. "How Did It Work? Who Did It Work For? Mediation in the Context of a Moderated Prevention Effect for Children of Divorce." *Journal of Consulting and Clinical Psychology* 72(4): 617–624.

Thornberry, Terence P. 1987. "Toward an Interactional Theory of Delinquency." *Criminology* 25: 863–891.

Thornberry, Terence P., Kimberly L. Henry, Timothy O. Ireland, and Carolyn A. Smith. 2010. "The Causal Impact of Childhood-Limited Maltreatment and Adolescent Maltreatment on Early Adult Adjustment." *Journal of Adolescent Health* 46(4): 359–365.

Thornberry, Terence P., Timothy O. Ireland, and Carolyn A. Smith. 2001. "The Importance of Timing: The Varying Impact of Childhood and Adolescent Maltreatment on Multiple Problem Outcomes." *Development and Psychopathology* 13: 957–979.

Thornberry, Terence P., Alan J. Lizotte, Marvin D. Krohn, Margaret Farnworth, and Sung Joon Jang. 1991. "Testing Interactional Theory: An Examination of Reciprocal Causal Relationships among Family, School, and Delinquency." *The Journal of Criminal Law and Criminology* 82(1): 3–35.

Van Ryzin, Mark J., and Thomas J. Dishion. 2012. "The Impact of a Family-Centered Intervention on the Ecology of Adolescent Antisocial Behavior: Modeling Developmental Sequelae and Trajectories During Adolescence." *Development and Psychopathology* 24(3): 1139–1155. https://doi.org/10.1017/S0954579412000582.

Van Ryzin, Mark J., Gregory M. Fosco, and Thomas J. Dishion. 2012. "Family and Peer Predictors of Substance Use from Early Adolescence to Early Adulthood: An 11-Year Prospective Analysis." *Addictive Behaviors* 37: 1314–1324.

Vitaro, Frank, Mara Brendgen, and Richard E. Tremblay. 2000. "Influence of Deviant Friends on Delinquency: Searching for Moderator Variables." *Journal of Abnormal Child Psychology* 28(4): 313–325.

Wagner, David V., Charles M. Borduin, Aaron M. Sawyer, and Alex R. Dopp. 2014. "Long-Term Prevention of Criminality in Siblings of Serious and Violent Juvenile Offenders: A 25-Year Follow-Up to a Randomized Clinical Trial of Multisystemic Therapy." *Journal of Consulting and Clinical Psychology* 82(3): 492–499.

Widom, Cathy Spatz. 1989a. "Child Abuse, Neglect, and Violent Criminal Behavior." *Criminology* 27(2): 251–271.

Widom, Cathy Spatz. 1989b. "The Cycle of Violence." *Science* 244: 160–166.

Widom, Cathy Spatz, Naomi R. Marmorstein, and Helene Raskin White. 2006. "Childhood Victimization and Illicit Drug Use in Middle Adulthood." *Psychology of Addictive Behaviors* 20(4): 394–403.

Widom, Cathy Spatz, Amie M. Schuck, and Helene Raskin White. 2006. "An Examination of Pathways from Childhood Victimization to Violence: The Role of Early Aggression and Problematic Alcohol Use." *Violence and Victims* 21(6): 675–690.

Wright, Emily M., Abigail A. Fagan, and Courtney A. Crittenden. 2011. *Exposure to Intimate Partner Violence: Gendered and Contextual Effects on Adolescent Interpersonal Violence, Drug Use, and Mental Health Outcomes.* Washington, DC: National Institute of Justice.

Zhou, Qing, Irwin N. Sandler, Roger E. Millsap, Sharlene A. Wolchik, and Spring R. Dawson-McClure. 2008. "Mother-Child Relationship Quality and Effective Discipline as Mediators of the 6-Year Effects of the New Beginnings Program for Children from Divorced Families." *Journal of Consulting and Clinical Psychology* 76(4): 579–594.

Zingraff, Matthew T., Jeffrey Leiter, Kristen A. Myers, and Mathew C. Johnsen. 1993. "Child Maltreatment and Youthful Problem Behavior." *Criminology* 31(2): 173–202.

CHAPTER 20

PEER INFLUENCES ON OFFENDING

CHRISTOPHER J. SULLIVAN, KRISTINA K. CHILDS, AND SHAUN GANN

THE relationship between peers, crime, and human development converges around two recurrent findings in the criminological literature. First, the age and crime relationship is well founded going back to the work of Quetelet (1984) in the 1800s and suggests that offending behavior ebbs and flows over time with an increase in engagement population-wide during the adolescent years (Farrington 1986). Second, "co-offending," especially in adolescence, has been established as a core "fact of crime" (Warr 2002, 2011), with immersion in street gangs and serious offender networks proving especially criminogenic (Huff 1998; Gordon et al. 2004). Although there has been considerable growth in knowledge on the subject, owing in part to the emergence of developmental and life-course perspectives, there are reasons to look more closely at the prior literature in criminology and related fields to synthesize what is known about the ways in which peers might influence behavior, particularly deviance in adolescence. This sets the stage for an examination of questions that must be investigated further in order to fully specify the mechanisms that link peers, development, and criminal behavior.

This chapter consists of four main sections. Section I briefly details some important literature related to peers, delinquency, and development, offering a sense of how those parallel findings should be viewed in relation to one another when considering offending behavior. In Section II we consider the theoretical perspectives that have incorporated peer influences in their core tenets—focusing especially on how those theories may have made their way into integrated developmental, life-course explanations for offending. Given the empirical relationship between peers and delinquency, a number of theorists have incorporated accounts of those processes into their core propositions about the etiology of delinquent behavior. In Section III we assess the ways in which peers and gangs fit into the practical literature on crime prevention, which has become increasingly linked to key perspectives and findings from developmental and life-course criminology. We also look at how justice response might account for peer influences on offending behavior. Using the prior discussion as a catalyst, Section IV describes some areas that offer opportunities for growth in knowledge with respect to the role of peers in offending over the life course. Within this final section we explore opportunities to expand the empirical evidence base and also discuss the prospects of this specific area of this literature for contributing more generally to the understanding of crime and societal response. We then summarize some key points in a brief conclusion.

I. Delinquency, Development, and Peers

While criminologists generally point to the peer social environment as a facilitator of delinquency, the developmental literature has also considered the role of peer influence on various behaviors at different stages of the life course. For example, Bronfenbrenner's (1979) often-cited ecological model of development situates peers in the "micro-system," which means that, along with family, they are among those influences most proximal to multiple dimensions of individual development. In particular, peer influences are apt to have a great deal of salience during adolescence (Steinberg and Morris 2001; Smetana, Campione-Barr, and Metzger 2006). Research shows that by early adolescence (ages 11 to 12), a large portion of children's social activity involves other same-age children, and by the time they reach high school, adolescents report spending significantly more time with their peers than with their parents (Csikzentmihalyi and Larson 1974; Collins and Laursen 2004). Thus, during this period of life, time spent with peers increases dramatically while time spent with parents decreases. It is not surprising then that research also suggests that conformity to parental attitudes and beliefs declines from early to mid-adolescence as the leverage of peer attitudes and beliefs increases (Berndt 1979; Krosnick and Judd 1982).

Still, despite the commonly held view that parent and peer influences are in competition, more recent research has suggested that these influences are much more complementary than previously thought (Laible, Carlo, and Raffaelli 2000; Goldstein, Davis-Kean, and Eccles 2005). More importantly, parent–child relationships may even set the stage for the selection of friends as well as the nature and quality of peer associations (Steinberg and Morris 2001; Collins and Laursen 2004; Goldstein et al. 2005). A number of studies have shown that an affective and supportive parent–child relationship, as well as parental monitoring, is associated with youths' inclination towards more prosocial relationships (Mounts and Steinberg 1995; Carson and Parke 1996; Ary et al. 1999; Kiesner, Poulin, and Dishion 2010). On the other hand, adolescents who actively seek out antisocial friends are more likely to come from families with severe and persistent problems (Ingoldsby et al. 2006; Kirillova et al. 2008). Adolescents' beliefs about autonomy have also been shown to predict peer selection. If adolescents perceive that they are not receiving freedom that they desire, they are more likely to seek out friendships, often with an antiauthoritarian orientation, that will enable them to achieve autonomy (Fuligni and Eccles 1993; Goldstein et al. 2005). This can in turn lead to involvement in antisocial behavior. Thus, although the direct impact of the parent–child relationship on behavior may decline during adolescence, it remains a key factor in the selection of peers and the quality of friendships—both of which are strong predictors of adolescent behavior. This implies that peer influences on behavior cannot be fully understood without considering earlier developmental influences that may affect friendship selection and interaction, serving as a reminder of the linkage between experiences within and across life stages.

While peers are often viewed as a less-than-constructive influence on adolescent behavior, it is clear that adolescent culture can affect youth development and behavior in a host of ways (Coleman 1961). Many developmental psychologists argue that healthy peer interaction is an essential element in the successful transition from childhood to adulthood (Warr 2002; Collins and Laursen 2004), and peer groups provide the setting in which adolescents establish their first identity outside of the family of origin. As a result, peers provide an independent source of self-esteem, autonomy from family, and emotional support during a time when rapid biological, cognitive, and social changes are taking place. In addition, during early to mid-adolescence, peer groups provide the context for the transition from same-sex friendships to opposite-sex friendships and, eventually, romantic relationships (Connolly, Furman, and Konarski 2000; Steinberg and Morris 2001). Thus, it is believed that peer groups are important for the development of social competence, empathy, and intimacy (Hartup and Laursen 1993; Connolly et al. 2000). Positive peer relationships have been linked to a number of factors associated with healthy adolescent adjustment, including positive self-worth (Armsden and Greenberg 1987), emotional stability (Garneski and Diekstra 1996; Hay and Ashman 2003), moral development (Piaget 1965; Walker, Henning, and Krettenauer 2000), and academic achievement (Mounts and Steinberg 1995; Caprara et al. 2000; Ryan 2001). Quality friendships have also been found to improve social skills as well as individual competence and efficacy (Collins and Steinberg 2006).

Still, there are good reasons for the commonly held perception that peers can help foster deviant behavior. For decades, juvenile delinquency has been considered a group-level phenomenon (McCord and Conway 2002; Stolzenberg and D'Alessio 2008) because risky and boundary-pushing behavior has a strong social component at that stage of the life course (Erickson and Jensen 1977). Compared to adulthood, antisocial acts are substantially more likely to be committed while in a group (Warr 2002, 2011). Association with risk-taking friends in adolescence is consistently found to be related to a number of problem behaviors including substance use (Wills and Cleary 1999; Windle 2000), dangerous driving (Allen and Brown 2008), risky sexual activity (Metzler et al. 1994; Henry et al. 2007), and delinquency (see Warr 2002).

Not surprisingly, the degree of contact with delinquent peers is one of the most robust predictors of individual delinquency during adolescence. This is commonly referred to as the crime companion hypothesis, and it asserts that the increased time spent with peers during adolescence amplifies group participation in delinquent behavior due to elevated exposure to delinquent peers (Haynie 2002; Warr 2002; Stolzenberg and D'Alessio 2008). As a result, the strong link between antisocial peers and engaging in antisocial behavior is often explained by the presence of peer influence. However, in moving from questions of "whether" peers have an impact to "how" and "why," a number of explanations regarding the ways in which peers influence behavior, particularly delinquent behavior, have been proposed. These explanations are often framed around the controversial question, which has a lengthy history in the criminological literature (see, e.g., Sutherland 1947; Glueck and Glueck 1950), of whether "birds of a feather flock together" (peer selection), or does having antisocial peers "cause" adolescents to engage in delinquent behavior in some way (peer socialization)? A third perspective, which is predicated on the impact of routine activities and the convergence of unsupervised adolescents in time and space, has emerged in recent years as well (Osgood et al. 1996; Haynie and Osgood 2005).

A. Peer Selection

A number of studies have suggested that peer affiliation is not a random process (Kandel 1978). That is, adolescents typically select friends that are similar to themselves in behaviors, attitudes, and beliefs, and personality—a process referred to as homophily. For example, Burk et al. (2011) found that adolescents in three different age groups (4th grade, 7th grade, and 10th grade) selected peers with similar drinking behaviors. When friends are similar on characteristics that are collectively valued (e.g., engagement in delinquent behavior), peer influence occurs through reinforcement of both attitudes and behaviors. High correspondence in attitudes or behaviors that are considered important to the peer group will result in either high pressure to stay the same or no pressure to change, while low correspondence results in pressure to change (Ryan 2000; McGloin 2009).

Criminological theories that support the principle of homophily include social control (Hirschi 1969) and subcultural (Staff and Kreager 2008) theories of delinquency. For example, Gottfredson and Hirschi's General Theory of Crime (1990) posits that both peer selection and delinquent behavior are caused by low self-control. Adolescents with low self-control are more likely to self-select peers who also have low self-control. Research consistently finds that low self-control is a concurrent (e.g., Gibson, Wright, and Tibbetts 2000) and longitudinal predictor of having delinquent peers (e.g., McGloin and Shermer 2009), which suggests that it may play a role in friendship selection. Subcultural theories point to shared experiences and similarities that bring youth together to form subcultures that are often based on delinquent or violent behavior as a way of opposing "mainstream" culture. These shared experiences and similarities may include prior involvement in delinquent behavior that has resulted in labeling (Becker 1963; Lemert 1974) or strain (Cohen 1955; Cloward and Ohlin 1960). The selection hypothesis for the peer–delinquency relationship has parallels in the population heterogeneity explanation for continuity in delinquent behavior (see Nagin and Paternoster 2000).

B. Peer Socialization

The peer socialization explanation argues that, regardless of their prior similarity, individuals who associate with one another will influence each other's behavior (Kandel 1978). Many scholars believe that adolescents are particularly vulnerable to negative peer influence because they are experiencing (often stressful) changes such as puberty, increasing social demands, and a desire to demonstrate some self-sufficiency (Maxwell 2002). Of particular interest to criminologists is Moffitt's (1993) identification of a "maturity gap" as an external pressure that serves as a structural push toward adolescent delinquency (see also Greenberg 1977). Through interaction with peers, adolescents experience pressures to conform to certain behaviors, receive reinforcement for behaviors (sometimes risky) that are accepted by their peers, and employ social comparisons as a way to measure whether their behavior is appropriate. Thus, this perspective suggests that antisocial peers can guide or "cause" adolescents to develop antisocial beliefs and values that promote their engagement in associated behaviors.

There are a number of ways that peers exert influence on behavior (see Ryan 2000; Brown 2004). Peer pressure involves direct and overt efforts to foster certain attitudes and behaviors while discouraging others. This involves the exchange of information that may provide an adolescent with new ideas or perspectives regarding behavior (Berndt, Laychak, and Park 1990). Any changes in an individual's cognition, behavior, or affect that result from the observation of others would be attributed to a "modeling effect" from others (Ryan 2000). Observing friends engage in certain behaviors can inform an adolescent of new behaviors and viewpoints and alert them to the consequences of that behavior or viewpoint (or lack thereof). Depending on the rewards or consequences, the likelihood of repeating that behavior may increase or decrease according to what was observed (Bandura, 1986). Normative regulation involves reinforcement of the expectations of the peer group through informal mechanisms such as shaming, taunting, or gossiping (Dishion et al. 1996; Steinberg and Monahan 2007). Attitudes and behaviors that are not supported by the peer group are less likely to be maintained, while beliefs and behaviors that are positively reinforced are significantly more likely to recur in the presence of the peer group (Brown, Clasen, and Eicher 1986). Normative regulation can also occur as a result of the adolescent's perception of negative or positive reinforcement. Perception of reinforcement can play a vital role in determining how information (reinforcement or perceived reinforcement) is processed and the selection of appropriate responses (subsequent delinquent behavior).

Social learning theory, which is arguably the most prominent criminological theory on the link between peers and antisocial behavior, posits that deviant peers cause delinquent behavior through modeling, normative regulation, and peer pressure. More specifically, according to social learning theory, association with delinquent peers causes adolescents to learn pro-delinquent attitudes and behaviors, imitate others' delinquent behavior, and receive positive reinforcement for their own delinquent acts (Akers 1985). A large body of research has provided support for these propositions (Pratt et al. 2010).

C. Peers and Delinquent Opportunities

A third, emerging perspective on the "peer effect" suggests that the social context structures opportunities to engage in certain behaviors through the amount of time spent socializing, the settings where peer interaction takes place, and the degree of supervision over their activities (Gardner and Steinberg 2005). This argument incorporates components of the Routine Activities Theory (Cohen and Felson 1979) and Risky Lifestyle Theories (Hindelang et al. 1978) to explain how time spent with delinquent peers increases opportunities to engage in delinquent behavior. For example, Osgood and colleagues (1996, 2004) argue that situations conducive to delinquent behavior are most prevalent during unsupervised socializing with peers. According to these authors, the presence of peers, in the absence of authority figures, provides opportunities to engage in delinquent behavior that are easier and more rewarding. Using data from the Monitoring the Future study, Osgood et al. (1996) showed that within-individual changes in unstructured socializing predicted delinquency and substance use. More recently, Haynie and Osgood (2005) found that adolescents who spent more time socializing with peers in unsupervised settings reported greater involvement in delinquent behavior. According to this perspective, it is not the type of friends that one chooses (peer selection) or the pressure that is exerted to behave in a certain way (socialization) that is important, but rather the mere time spent in the presence of peers (opportunities). As described above, these opportunities tend to increase as youths gradually limit the time spent with their family of origin in favor of adolescent peer groups. Subsequently, there may be a movement back to more conventional activities in late adolescence and early adulthood where individuals begin to migrate into relationships and families of choice—which then restrict opportunity for delinquent behavior (Warr 1998; Laub and Sampson 2003).

D. Mixed DLC Perspective on Peers and Offending

A mixed perspective on the peer–delinquency relationship suggests that adolescents might initially choose others who share similar behavior and attitudes (selection), and in turn they may become more similar to each other over time (socialization) (Kandel 1978; Thornberry et al. 1993; Brechwald and Prinstein 2011). Adolescents who exhibit antisocial behaviors may seek out others who embody these behaviors, which causes antisocial behavior to proliferate (Thornberry et al. 1993; Gatti et al. 2005). They might also knowingly or unwittingly seek parity with those peers, which affects stability or change in their behavioral patterns over time (McGloin 2009). As an example, gangs, which embody the idea of the antisocial peer network, can reinforce criminogenic tendencies among adolescents (Lynam and Gudonis 2005; Dupéré et al. 2007). Battin and colleagues (1998) assessed the delinquent acts of gang members, non-gang youths with delinquent friends, and non-gang youths with no delinquent friends. They found that, across all violent, non-violent, and general delinquency outcomes, youths with no delinquent friends scored lowest on all outcome measures, while youths with delinquent friends scored significantly higher, and gang members scored the highest. This suggests that gang membership provides a criminogenic influence where joining a gang contributes to delinquency and drug use independent of prior propensity toward delinquency (see also Esbensen and Huizinga 1993).

Youth who exhibit antisocial personality traits, such as impulsivity and lack of empathy, may self-select these social networks or are restricted to them by virtue of evocative relationships with their social environment (Caspi, Bem, and Elder 1989). Involvement with these groups can then heighten the development of delinquent behavior and entrench the individual in a longer-term pattern of antisocial attitudes and behavior. This can occur through both selection and socialization processes, but it also may be a manifestation of the type of cumulative continuity present in particular developmental, life-course theories of offending (e.g., Moffitt 1993; Sampson and Laub 1993). Involvement with a gang also reflects a particular lifestyle wherein exposure to criminogenic situations, such as drug market encounters and weapon carrying, is considerably greater (e.g., Huff 1998), offering another means by which peer affiliations might affect individual behavior.

From a broader developmental and life-course perspective, Caspi, Bem, and Elder (1989) discuss similar person–environment interaction processes that impact behavioral patterns across the life course. Similar to peer selection, the notion of cumulative continuity proposes that there is a "selection" into environments that reinforce and sustain initial or existing patterns of behavior through the "progressive accumulation of its own consequences" (p. 377). Similar to peer socialization, the interactional process involves reciprocity between the person and the environment: "The youth acts, the environment reacts, and the person reacts back" (p. 378). For example, following engagement in an antisocial act, youth will consider the reaction of their peers to the behavior. If it is positively reinforced, the behavior is validated and will be maintained by the youth. Additionally, the entrenchment in a particular lifestyle that is a byproduct of cumulative continuity would also affect youths' routine activities.

Given the empirical evidence to support all three perspectives (selection, socialization, and opportunity), it is clear that the ways in which peers influence behavior are complex and multifaceted. Longitudinal studies tend to support reciprocal effects where engagement in delinquent behavior leads to association with delinquent peers (selection) and these associations lead to continued or increased delinquent behavior through increased opportunities and socialization (Matsueda and Anderson 1998; Simons-Morton 2007; Monahan et al. 2009). Thus, peer influence during adolescence is best viewed as a dynamic process in which selection, socialization, and opportunity work together to produce change and continuity in behavior (Urberg et al. 2003). This means that the peer micro-system within Bronfenbrenner's (1979) model comprises a complex set of possible influences on individual development.

Regardless of the complexity of peer influence on behavior, there is little doubt that effects are stronger in adolescence than in adulthood (Gardner and Steinberg 2005; Steinberg and Monahan 2007). Developmental research has consistently shown that susceptibility to negative peer pressure begins in early adolescence and continues to increase throughout mid- and late adolescence (Brown 2004). Around late adolescence or early adulthood, susceptibility to peer pressure substantially declines (Monahan et al. 2009). For example, Steinberg and Monahan (2007) found that resistance to peer influence increased linearly from ages 14 through 18 but did not find evidence for significant peer influence from ages 10 through 14 or 18 through 30. This curvilinear trend is most prominent when the behaviors in question are antisocial acts such as substance use or delinquency (Erickson, Crosnoe, and Dornbusch 2000). Not surprisingly, a similar curvilinear pattern is also found in studies examining the relationship between having delinquent friends and engagement in delinquent behavior (Brown 2004; Monahan et al. 2009).

The longstanding evidence of an "age–crime curve" in which delinquency increases during early to mid-adolescence and then declines thereafter also suggests a linkage between the prevalence of antisocial behavior and developmental stage—in particular, delinquency is far more prominent in adolescence (Farrington 1986; Moffitt 1993). This trend in delinquent behavior coincides with the levels of susceptibility to peer pressure discussed above and the strength of the association among delinquent peers and behavior during adolescence (Elliott and Menard 1996). It also corresponds with findings on trajectories of co-offending across adolescence (McGloin et al. 2008). Given the broad, and complementary, trends in delinquency and peer influence in adolescence, as well as the role that peers play in individual development, it is clear that delinquency, development, and peers are intertwined in ways that are important to understanding each on its own as well as their intersection. These broader perspectives and findings mean that peers have a firm place in the developmental and life-course criminology literature and, in fact, most core theories in criminology have something to say about the relationship between peers and individual offending. The next section considers that literature in terms of its key propositions on peer influences on offending.

II. Developmental Life-Course Criminology and Peers: Theory and Empirical Research

Section II of this *Handbook* presents a number of key developmental and life-course theories of crime. Whether explicit or implicit, nearly all contain some propositions about the role of peers in offending. This section presents a small sampling of these important theories, describes the role of peers in each theory's core propositions, reviews related empirical evidence where available, and considers the broader developmental, life-course concepts inherent in their place in that theory. In some cases, these theories do not focus primarily on the role of peers in defining the processes that underlie patterns of offending, but their core tenets with respect to age-graded peer effects can be examined nevertheless.

A. Developmental Taxonomy of Antisocial Behavior

Although there are a number of relevant accounts of the development of offending over time, Moffitt's (1993, 1997) developmental taxonomy is one of the most prominent theories in criminology. The developmental taxonomy envisions at least two potential roles for peer influences, which can be seen as complementary (Moffitt 1997). For life-course–persistent (LCP) offenders, early relationships with peers are marked by rejection due to their enduring antisocial disposition, and this likely limits their chances for developing alternative interactional styles and forming prosocial adolescent friendships (see also Caspi, Bem, and Elder 1989). Laird and colleagues (2001) identified a group of youth with early externalizing behavior problems that appeared to follow such a trend. Cillessen and Mayeux (2004) also conducted a longitudinal study of aggression and social status in early adolescence and saw results that reflect the over-time peer rejection and popularity dynamics suggested by Moffitt (1993).

A second mechanism within the taxonomy sees those life-course persisters, who were rejected by prosocial peers at one time, as potential behavioral reference points for the broader population of adolescents a few years later. This is the notion of "social mimicry," where LCP offenders appear—at least to other teens—to be managing the widely experienced "maturity gap" fairly effectively. This proposition is distinct from a pure socialization perspective as it does not necessitate direct transfer of attitudes and behaviors from LCP offenders (Barnes, Beaver, and Piquero 2011). Other adolescents may observe them from afar and see those behaviors as a way to deal with some of the angst that they experience during that time period. Young (2014) found some support for this proposition in observed upticks in LCP-type individuals' social status in early to mid-adolescence. While there are a few studies on this aspect of the taxonomy of antisocial behavior, the role of peer dynamics within Moffitt's taxonomic groups has been less a point of emphasis than most of the theory's other propositions. Nevertheless, the role of peers in potentially closing off prosocial opportunities for LCP offenders and subsequently facilitating antisocial behavior on the part of onlooking adolescence-limited offenders is central to the processes affecting the patterns associated with each group.

B. Age-Graded Social Control Theory

Sampson and Laub's age-graded social control theory (1993; Laub and Sampson 2003) includes a role for peers and other social influences in affecting individual offending under the bigger umbrella of "social connectedness" (Sampson and Laub 2005, p. 15). While Sampson and Laub (1993) found that attachment to delinquent peers exerted a consistent, significant effect on individual delinquency, they were cognizant of some methodological limitations in disentangling the two (see also Warr 2002; Haynie and Osgood 2005). At the same time, they strongly assert the importance of social influences that emerge in adolescence and adulthood in affecting offending patterns (Sampson and Laub 2005) and, like Moffitt (1993), indicate that early peer rejection and bonding with delinquent friends can be part of a "cumulative" process that fosters continued antisocial behavior over time among some individuals (Sampson and Laub 1997). Additionally, they consider the implications of shifts in social capital investment and routine activities that occur after adolescence as a facilitator of desistance (Laub, Sampson, and Sweeten 2006). In part, this occurs due to a relative disinvestment in peers and a reduction in time spent with them as a consequence of greater engagement in adult relationships (see also Warr 1998). Laub and Sampson's (2003) re-analysis of the Gluecks' data and intensive interviews with a subsample of those cases helped provide empirical grounding for this revised version of their theory, one that contains strands of individual agency (selection), social control (socialization), and change in routine activities (opportunity).

C. The Social Development Model

The social development model (SDM) is a general theory of behavior that incorporates both anti- and prosocial outcomes (Catalano and Hawkins 1996). Using the literature on developmental risk and protective factors as a foundation, the theoretical underpinnings and practical implications of the model have been refined and studied over multiple decades. Given that association with deviant peers is among the most prominent risk factors for delinquency, SDM incorporates that as a possible mechanism affecting antisocial development and associated behavior. Catalano and Hawkins (1996) assert that socialization is the main vehicle by which youth become involved with antisocial (or prosocial) behavioral patterns. SDM draws on control, social learning, and differential association theories, which have each made assertions about the role of peer relationships in delinquent behavior.

There are a few dimensions of the socialization process outlined in SDM, including opportunities and interactions with particular individuals or groups, degree of involvement and interaction with others, development of skills for interaction, and reinforcements that come from these interactions. This process results in a bond that may perpetuate a given prosocial or antisocial behavioral pattern (Catalano and Hawkins

1996). While SDM encompasses multiple domains of social influence (e.g., family, neighborhoods), the theory's propositions assert the importance of peers in the socialization process as early as elementary school (though parents and other adults retain primacy then). Catalano and his colleagues (2005) examined the different mechanisms by which peers might influence antisocial behavior, such as via perceived opportunities for antisocial behavior through peers, involvement with deviant friends, or bonding to antisocial peers. In each case, their model estimates showed that the peer-related measure had the expected effect in terms of the chain of relationships outlined in SDM.

D. Interactional Theory

Like the social development model, Thornberry's interactional theory (Thornberry 1987; 1996; Thornberry and Krohn 2005) draws on and integrates existing criminological theories—in particular social control and social learning—but utilizes their propositions in a "dynamic," developmental framework (Thornberry 1996, p. 199). As its label suggests, the theory posits a series of interactive relationships between individuals and their environment that plays out over time (Thornberry 1987). Delinquent behavior inherently rests on weakened controls where bonds are not static over time and can be made weaker or stronger by an interactional process. Attenuated social controls within the family or school lead to delinquency (indirectly) as there must also be an interactive setting where it is learned, carried out, and reinforced over time. Often this setting involves the peer group. In that sense, the theory suggests interplay among attachment and commitment to conventional others (e.g., parents, schools) and belief in conventional values, association with delinquent peers, and adoption of delinquent values. This process in turn leads to delinquent behavior, which then further weakens conventional beliefs, attachments, and commitments while shoring up associations with delinquent others and reinforcing delinquent attitudes.

Thornberry (1996) identifies a number of studies that provide support for the propositions of interactional theory. This includes several studies that evaluated reciprocal relationships between involvement and bonding with deviant peers and delinquent behavior. He finds evidence for propositions within the interactional theory in a review of existing criminological literature, asserting in particular that the learning component of the theory (i.e., delinquent association and delinquent beliefs variables) receives consistent support. Direct tests by Thornberry and colleagues also found some support for the peer-centered aspects of the theory. In particular, Thornberry (1987) established support for interactional and reciprocal relationships in social influences in criminal behavior as he found evidence of an over-time, reciprocal relationship between heightened contact with delinquent peers, marijuana use, and loosened religious commitment. Later, Thornberry and Krohn (2005) found that conventional bonds were weakened by delinquent behavior at the same time that ties to delinquent peers were strengthened. This, in turn, helped generate continuity in antisocial behavior associated with the early onset of delinquency.

E. Situational Action Theory

Wikström's (2005, 2006) situational action theory (SAT) has gained more prominence in recent years. Like the other theories discussed here, it draws on existing principles and research in criminology and related disciplines. It is, however, somewhat distinct from others in the scope and nature of its underlying propositions (Farrington 2006). Wikström's (2005) general theory views both individual and ecological factors as important in driving "moral rule-breaking." In particular, the theory sees change/stability in moral transgressions as owing to the individual's change/stability in terms of interaction with the settings to which he or she is exposed. In that sense, an individual's propensity for rule-breaking (e.g., morality, self-control) is influential, but it is applied such that different individuals will respond to the same setting in distinct ways. In short, the theory explicitly distinguishes propensity for criminal behavior from the actual commission of criminal acts.

Within the theory, an "activity field" represents a setting where the individual develops and acts, and it can be viewed as the social space where an individual chooses to engage in delinquent and criminal behavior (Wikström 2006). An individual's decision-making process is then linked to environmental signals via their perceptions. This generates a sense of the available alternatives for action. In particular, unstructured time spent in the presence of peers may offer opportunities and temptations for offending. In work with data from the Peterborough Youth Study, Wikström and Butterworth (2006) found that individual variation in lifestyle factors—in particular time spent with peers—was a strong predictor of offending levels.

It is important that developmental and life-course theories in criminology account for both why individuals become offenders and the reasons that they commit criminal acts (Farrington 2005b). SAT may prove to be important in providing a link between developmental and life-course principles with those that focus on lifestyles, routine activities, and criminogenic situations in terms of understanding the ways that peers might affect antisocial behavior. Thus, the theory makes a very important contribution to the DLC literature in terms of expanding its scope in a way that parallels the broader literature on peers and delinquency discussed earlier.

III. Peers, Prevention, and Juvenile Justice

The evolution of developmental and life-course theories in criminology from the risk and protective factor and criminal career paradigms was in part an effort to create more vigorous explanations for patterns of offending over time (Farrington 2003). This move from a focus on describing aspects of offending and identifying associated risk markers to generating theoretical propositions about how different patterns emerge was essential in propelling the area of study forward (Catalano and Hawkins 1996). While seemingly "less practical" in an immediate sense, a move from an emphasis on description and identification of risk markers to prioritization of explanation and risk mechanisms is in line with theoretical development that is often necessary for creating solid interventions that are responsive to important social problems (Weiss 1995; Wikström 2007). To that end, a better understanding of how peers influence delinquency and criminal behavior from a developmental perspective can identify when and how it might be best to intervene to prevent offending. This section considers the topic of practical intervention in the context of the insights about peers, development, and antisocial behavior discussed to this point of the chapter.

A. Prevention and Peer Risk

Multiple types of prevention programs aim to reduce the negative peer influences that contribute to delinquent behavior. Two examples that tie into the peer influence mechanisms described earlier are activity-based intervention programs (e.g., Boys and Girls Clubs, sports leagues) and classroom-based programs designed to teach students universal social skills to reduce rejection and foster positive engagement with peers (van Lier, Vitaro, and Eisner 2007; Sullivan and Jolliffe 2012).

Many unstructured prevention programs attempt to keep at-risk youth off the street and away from the "wrong crowd" by providing them with structured conventional activities via community centers, sports leagues, and after-school programs (Warr 2011). While well intentioned, studies suggest that these types of programs are typically not successful in reducing—and may actually increase—delinquency (Dodge, Dishion, and Lansford 2006; van Lier et al. 2007). One reason that these programs tend to have negligible or iatrogenic effects is that they may become forums for antisocial youth to come together and actually stimulate the peer–delinquency relationship rather than extinguish it. Indeed, Mahoney, Stattin, and Lord (2004) concluded that antisocial youths and those with poor bonds with their parents or school were more likely to frequent these types of programs than normative youths and that, all other things equal, the frequency of participation in these programs was positively related to antisocial and delinquent behavior.

Given that peers are consistently identified as a risk factor for delinquent behavior, a number of prevention programs have focused on social skills and "peer refusal" as a part of their intervention strategy. A recent review by Sullivan and Jolliffe (2012) identified 13 of these programs. These tend to be school-based primary or secondary prevention efforts with a stated objective of targeting decisions made regarding peer association and behavior in groups. They are often implemented in school settings where there are high numbers of at-risk youth and involve a skill-building, curriculum-based instructional approach. Some programs utilize situational role-playing and coaching with feedback, however. The studies tended to show positive effects on reductions in exposure to deviant peers in the short-term, but there was less evidence about whether that in turn affected delinquent behavior. An experimental study of the Aban Aya program (Chicago) by Flay and colleagues (2004) did, however, find treatment effects on later violent behavior. This was a classroom-based instructional program with role-playing that emphasized social development, problem-solving, and refusal skills. A companion study found that the program affected the level of exposure to delinquent peers, which had a mediating effect on long-term violent behavior (Ngwe et al. 2004).

The social nature of delinquency is also addressed in mentoring programs. Frequently, these programs expose at-risk or delinquent youths to an older, more experienced role model who provides assistance and encouragement aimed at reducing delinquency and increasing positive developmental outcomes (Sullivan and Jolliffe 2012). Mentoring programs are believed to have an effect on delinquency via the social bond formed between mentor and mentee, a reduction in the amount of available idle time for at-risk youths, and the peer-refusal skills taught to the mentee, which in turn help youths resist the negative peer pressure of antisocial peers. Mentoring programs are widely used, but research is still emerging. Some early reviews report small to moderate effects on offending (Jolliffe and Farrington 2008).

Often, programs that are not explicitly focused on peer risk still attempt to disrupt some of the problematic developmental pathways that may lead to later involvement with antisocial peers. Because youths depend on their parents for guidance and support, poor or inept parenting and weakened family bonds can lead to association with delinquent peers and a subsequent increase in the probability of delinquency (Simons et al. 1994; Alleyne and Wood 2014). As described above, studies have consistently found that quality parenting has a long-lasting negative relationship with delinquent peer association (Calkins and Keane 2009; Sitnick, Shaw, and Hyde 2014). These results suggest that interventions focused on reducing early antisocial behaviors and increasing familial bonds and parental efficacy can cultivate "social acceptance by the normative peer group and/or associations with non-deviant friends" (van Lier et al. 2007, p. 281), thus altering the developmental chain leading to association with deviant peers.

B. Gang Prevention and Intervention

Gang members are consistently found to commit more delinquent acts—especially serious and violent acts—than their non-gang member counterparts (Esbensen and Huizinga 1993; Thornberry et al. 1993; Huff 1998). Gang membership can also intensify delinquent behavior. Given these findings, identifying the small group of serious juvenile offenders and treating them with intense, long-term intervention programs has the potential to drastically reduce serious and violent crime. Jeffery (1998, p. 25) argues that although common family, peer, school, and community interventions may be adequate to deter and prevent the majority of youthful offending, this small group of serious offenders "will not be helped by such interventions since they have major neurological defects which make working with the families or with the school system futile."

The fact that violent youth gangs (as well as other forms of social disorganization) are more common in certain communities and non-existent in others can also have an effect on the types and efficacy of treatment programs aimed at reducing the negative consequences of delinquent peer associations. For example, in communities where gangs are pervasive, affiliation with delinquent peers may manifest as severe delinquency and/or violence, whereas in communities with no gangs, any delinquency resulting from delinquent peer associations may be relatively less severe (Simons et al. 1994). Put simply, if there are no delinquent peer groups or gangs present in a certain community, youths residing there will be less able to associate with deviant peers and more likely to associate with normative peers. As such, prevention programs should also address neighborhood gangs and community-level social disorganization so as to possibly reduce the severity of delinquency among those youths who seek strong peer group affiliations during adolescence. Hawkins and colleagues' (2009) work on Communities That Care provides one case in point where individual, group, and community-level risk factors might be identified and considered in possible interventions.

Because a large number of the most violent gang members have a history of justice contact and are well known to law enforcement, intervention efforts likely require a collaborative effort among police and other community agencies to prevent gang violence at the community level and redirect individual trajectories. One promising program is the American Probation and Parole Association's collaboration, analysis, re-entry, and evaluation (CARE) model (Matz et al. 2011). Cities that incorporate the CARE model start by forming collaborative partnerships among multiple adult and juvenile justice agencies and community organizations. This necessitates analysis of community-level crime data to develop an understanding of the distribution of gang-related activities (i.e., crime mapping) and develop strategies and programs to address the problem. Because a large number of gang members are arrested and imprisoned, CARE also addresses the rehabilitative and re-entry needs of incarcerated gang members to reduce the likelihood they return to their gang-related activities post-incarceration.

Another strategy used to combat gang-related violence is the "pulling levers," or focused deterrence, approach. First introduced in Boston's Operation Ceasefire in the 1990s, these programs attempt to combat gang violence through the collaborative efforts of police, social service providers, neighborhood street advocates, and other community agencies (Braga and Weisburd 2011). Its primary objectives are to increase the costs of involvement in gang violence (i.e., increased severity of punishment for new crimes), increase the certainty of punishment for that violence, and communicate consequences directly to gang members in offender notification meetings. Importantly, in addition to the formal intervention, focused deterrence programs attempt to use a degree of informal social leverage based on the nature of gangs in an attempt to affect the norms and values of gang members and reduce their criminal acts (Kennedy 2009). Since their introduction, evaluation studies have provided some promising evidence regarding the deterrent effect of "pulling levers" programs. In their meta-analysis of 11 focused deterrence programs, Braga and Weisburd (2011) found an overall effect size of .60, indicating that these programs had a moderately strong effect on community-level crime rates.

Clearly, understanding how to respond to peer risk and the important role that it can play within adolescence has important implications for addressing criminal behavior—especially in light of the patterns observable in the age–crime curve, co-offending prevalence levels, and the elevation of offending behavior among members of delinquent peer networks. This also implies that furthering the understanding of important theoretical and empirical questions pertinent to peers, development, and delinquency will pay dividends in addressing broader delinquency and crime problems. The final section of this chapter considers some areas that might be important in this regard as well as some challenges that could arise in pursuing a greater understanding of peers, development, and delinquency.

IV. Developmental and Life-Course Criminology and Peers: Future Directions

Despite the tremendous growth in understanding the relationship between peers and delinquency—and concurrent integration of developmental and life-course perspectives—there are still a number of areas where growth in basic knowledge and related practical responses is needed. Some of these future directions pertain to theoretical or explanatory questions, and others relate to the possibilities of the empirical study of peers from these perspectives. Regardless of the present limitations and future challenges, consideration of peer influences in the context of developmental and life-course criminology has a great deal to offer in enhancing the field's understanding of the processes that contribute to delinquent and criminal behavior.

A. Peers, Situations, and Development

Although they are often seen as separate developmental mechanisms, the progression of the literature on peer influences on offending suggests that it is important to blend an understanding of the multiple possible mechanisms (e.g., socialization, selection, situational) by which peers influence individual development and situational behavior. This must also be considered in data collection, measurement, and analysis. An important place for growth is in what Warr (2002, p. 128) has termed the "micro-life course." Horney (2001) highlights the importance of incorporating shorter-term situational events into the longer longitudinal window often used in understanding crime across the life course. This provides a framework where each of the purported peer influence mechanisms might be considered alongside different developmental and life-course explanations for change and stability in behavior. To this end, some have begun to introduce space-time budgets into developmental studies in order to understand situational influences on behavior, including peer effects (Wikström and Butterworth 2006).

Implicit in these types of investigations is the question of how the propensity of the adolescent toward delinquent behavior interacts with particular peer influences in the short or long term. This is particularly important with respect to how within-individual change and stability may affect such interactions (Childs, Sullivan, and Gulledge 2010) as a lot of what is known about the risks for delinquent behavior is based on measures and analysis of between-individual differences (Farrington 2005a). While some studies have considered this question (e.g., Wright et al. 2001; Ousey and Wilcox 2007), this is an area that could use further investigation as it has implications for propositions within multiple DLC theories and also might provide a more extensive understanding of vulnerability and resilience to inform intervention.

B. The Multifaceted Nature of the "Peer Group" in Time and Space

Peers take on a number of roles in terms of their possible influence on individual behavior. In addition to the individual factors mentioned above, their influence can be conditioned on the closeness of relationships (e.g., best friend, weak or strong network, broader school-level social influences), the composition of the group (e.g., same vs. mixed-sex, romantic partnerships, siblings, age-structure), the nature of the immediate situation (e.g., school vs. unsupervised party), or developmental timing (e.g., when an individual encounters particular peers). For example, previous developmental studies have identified differences in the degree of correspondence in antisocial behavior across same-sex versus opposite-sex friendships (Arndorfer and Stormshak 2008; Deutsch, Steinley, and Slutske 2014) and have highlighted the influential role that romantic partners play in shaping behavior (Simons et al. 2002; Haynie et al. 2005). The peer group may also be comprised of dyadic relationships, cliques, or crowds that can have enduring or fleeting effects (Brown, Mory, and Kinney 1994; Warr 2002). Individuals, particularly adolescents, generally do not make decisions and establish behavioral patterns in well-defined social space; rather they are likely to simultaneously belong to multiple groups and draw on several referents and motivations in making decisions about delinquent behavior (McGloin, Sullivan, and Thomas 2014). It is important that all of these factors, which reflect the multidimensional nature of peers as a developmental influence, are considered in studying the processes that affect situational decisions and emergent behavioral patterns in social environments with multiple distinct cues.

C. Secular Shifts in Development, Peers, and Delinquency

The discussion of peer influence on antisocial behavior tends to assume traditional views of the life course with respect to role expectations about childhood, adolescence, and adulthood. For instance, some purported mechanisms for desistance from offending assume a migration from the adolescent social environment to one commensurate with adult status (i.e., more conventional social bonds and more conventional routines) (see, e.g., Warr 1998; Laub and Sampson 2003). Recent accounts of developmental patterns and timing of key life events suggest that some traditionally observed pathways may be changing (Arnett 2000). These wide-ranging changes in when and how individuals experience key milestones can have important implications for how criminologists understand the role that peers play in individual behavior. For instance, if emerging adulthood is found to be important in understanding criminal behavior, it is possible that persistent peer effects beyond the teenage years will be a part of the explanation. Future study of peer effects on behavior should account for the role that they may play in contemporary society.

D. Peers and DLC Theories

Although there has been tremendous growth in DLC theories, there is an enduring need to consider the underlying mechanisms that affect delinquent and criminal behavior at different stages of the life course. Farrington (2005a) mentions the questions of learning processes and age-graded changes in co-offending patterns as examples of potential areas of emphasis. In particular, it would be beneficial to tie some of the traditional ways of conceptualizing offending over time (e.g., state dependence, population heterogeneity) with the selection, socialization, and situational frameworks that have been prominent in the discussion of peers and delinquency to try to better specify and test the mechanisms by which peers influence individual behaviors in the short and long term. Just as the question of whether state dependence and population heterogeneity has led to the conclusion that both matter, so too does the discussion of selection or socialization. It has become increasingly clear that both matter and that there also are a number of other possible processes by which peers affect individual behavior (Warr 2002). Further attention to these possible mechanisms as they play out across the life course will be beneficial to the field's understanding of offending at multiple developmental stages.

These studies do pose some challenges, of course. A growing portion of the research on peer influences on delinquent and criminal behavior does utilize longitudinal data with analytic procedures appropriate to the situation (see, e.g., Haynie and Osgood 2005). It is still challenging to clearly identify causal relationships between peer influence (and its numerous possible dimensions; see earlier discussion and Warr 2002) and individual behavior in a conventional sense. In addition, instability of friendship networks poses some problems for conceptualizing, measuring, and analyzing the relationship between peers and individual development. Specifically, even longitudinal studies examining the effect of peers may not be tapping into the same friendships over time so that the estimate of peer influence on an adolescent might be diminished by more proximal relationships (Brown 2004). All of this suggests that future research will need to consider measurement and analysis strategies that capture the complexity of the relationship between a fluid social environment and individual behavior. While there are a number of promising avenues in this regard, longitudinal, adaptive network analysis (Gross and Sayama 2009) and state-space methods within a dynamic systems framework may aid in integrating multiple interdependent influences on individual actions using emerging data sources (Granic and Hollenstein, 2003; Granic and Patterson, 2006).

E. Implications for Policy and Practice

While the literature on peers, development, and delinquency has evolved such that there are important lessons to be learned about how it may be prevented or remedied after its onset, there is definitely room for growth in understanding how best to identify and respond to this link between peers and delinquency (Sullivan and Jolliffe 2012). In particular, the developmental and life-course literature may be useful in considering the optimal timing for intervention to limit the potential effects of negative peer associations. Another aspect of policy and practice that warrants further attention relates to whether and how the peer–delinquency relationship manifests itself in juvenile justice processing—especially in light of the recent influence of modern developmental science (see National Academy of Sciences 2013). The fact that most delinquency is committed in groups should probably affect how cases are processed and disposed of in the juvenile justice system (Warr 2011). For example, judges may attempt to reduce peer influences among co-offending youth by issuing no-contact orders or removing one or more of the youths from the community (e.g., institutional placement). However, there is little to no research on whether or how co-offending affects juvenile court decisions.

V. Conclusion

Recurring findings related to age and crime and peers and crime are mere headlines to a rich story about antisocial behavior and the life course. This chapter has described a number of perspectives and pertinent findings from developmental and life-course criminology and related literatures to provide a sense of the current state of knowledge on these topics. In doing so, it has highlighted several core concepts and empirical results that can shape an enhanced understanding of the relationship between peers and individual behavior, situating it in developmental and life-course frameworks. It then also laid out some possible pathways for future study in the area while acknowledging some of the challenges that the field is likely to face as it moves forward. While there has been considerable development in the general understanding of both of these "facts of crime," it is clear that further consideration of the two—and their interdependence— will be quite valuable in making progress in the general understanding of criminal behavior and the response to it.

REFERENCES

Akers, Ronald L. 1985. *Deviant Behavior: A Social Learning Approach.* 3rd ed. Belmont, CA: Wadsworth.

Allen, Joseph P., and B. Bradford Brown. 2008. "Adolescents, Peers, and Motor Vehicles: The Perfect Storm?" *American Journal of Preventive Medicine* 35: 289–293.

Alleyne, Emma, and Jane L. Wood. 2014. "Gang Involvement: Social and Environmental Factors." *Crime and Delinquency* 60: 547–568.

Arndorfer, Cara Lee, and Elizabeth A. Stormshak. 2008. "Same-Sex Versus Other-Sex Best Friendship in Early Adolescence: Longitudinal Predictors of Antisocial Behavior Throughout Adolescence." *Journal of Youth and Adolescence* 37: 1059–1070.

Arnett, Jeffrey Jensen. 2000. "Emerging Adulthood: A Theory of Development from the Late Teens Through the Twenties." *American Psychologist* 55: 469–480.

Armsden, Gay C., and Mark T. Greenberg. 1987. "The Inventory of Parent and Peer Attachment: Individual Differences and their Relationship to Psychological Well-Being in Adolescence." *Journal of Youth and Adolescence* 16: 427–454.

Ary, Dennis V., Terry E. Duncan, Susan C. Duncan, and Hyman Hops. 1999. "Adolescent Problem Behavior: The Influence of Parents and Peers." *Behavior Research and Therapy* 37: 217–230.

Bandura, Albert. 1986. *Social Foundations of Thought and Action: A Social Cognitive Theory.* Englewood Cliffs, NJ: Prentice-Hall.

Barnes, J. C., Kevin M. Beaver, and Alex R. Piquero. 2011. "A Test of Moffitt's Hypotheses of Delinquency Abstention." *Criminal Justice and Behavior* 38: 690–709.

Battin, Sara R., Karl G. Hill, Robert D. Abbott, Richard F. Catalano, and J. David Hawkins. 1998. "The Contribution of Gang Membership to Delinquency Beyond Delinquent Friends." *Criminology* 36: 93–115.

Becker, Howard S. (1963). *Outsiders: Studies in the Sociology of Deviance.* New York: Macmillan.

Berndt, Thomas J. 1979. "Developmental Changes in Conformity to Peers and Parents." *Developmental Psychology* 15: 608–616.

Berndt, Thomas J., Ann E. Laychak, and Keunho Park K. 1990. "Friends' Influence on Adolescents' Academic Achievement Motivation: An Experimental Study." *Journal of Educational Psychology* 82: 664–670.

Braga, Anthony A., and David L. Weisburd, D. 2011. "The Effects of Focused Deterrence Strategies on Crime: A Systematic Review and Meta-Analysis of the Empirical Evidence." *Journal of Research in Crime and Delinquency* 49: 323–358.

Brechwald, Whitney A., and Mitchell J. Prinstein. "Beyond Homophily: A Decade of Advances in Understanding Peer Influence Processes. 2011." *Journal of Research on Adolescence* 21: 166–179.

Bronfenbrenner, Urie. 1979. *The Ecology of Human Development: Experiments by Nature and Design*. Cambridge, MA: Harvard University Press.

Brown, B. Bradford, Margaret S. Mory, and David Kinney. 1994. "Casting Adolescent Crowds in a Relational Perspective." In *Advances in Adolescent Development, Personal Relationships During Adolescence*, Vol. 6, edited by Raymond Montemary, Gerald R. Adams, and Thomas P. Gullotta, 123–167. Newbury Park, CA: Sage.

Brown, B. Bradford. 2004. "Adolescents' Relationships with Peers." In *The Handbook of Adolescent Psychology*, 2nd ed., edited by Richard M. Lerner and Laurence Steinberg. New York: Wiley.

Brown, B. Bradford, Donna R. Clasen, and Sue A. Eicher. 1986. "Perceptions of Peer Pressure, Peer Conformity Dispositions, and Self-Reported Behavior Among Adolescents. *Developmental Psychology* 22: 521–530.

Burk, William J., Haske van der Vorst, Margaret Kerr, and Hakan Stattin. 2011. "Alcohol Use and Friendship Dynamics: Selection and Socialization in Early-, Middle-, and Late-Adolescent Peer Networks." *Journal of Studies on Alcohol and Drugs* 73: 89–98.

Calkins, Susan D., and Susan P. Keane. 2009. "Developmental Origins of Early Antisocial Behavior." *Development and Psychopathology* 21: 1095–1109.

Caprara, Gian Vittorio, Claudio Barbaranelli, Concetta Pastorelli, Albert Bandura, and Phillip G. Zimbardo. 2000. "Prosocial Foundations of Children's Academic Achievement." *Psychological Science* 11: 302–306.

Carson, James L., and Ross D. Parke. 1996. "Reciprocal Negative Affect in Parent-Child Interactions and Children's Peer Competency." *Child Development* 67: 2217–2226.

Caspi, Avshalom, Daryl J. Bem, and Glen H. Elder. 1989. "Continuities and Consequences of Interactional Styles Across the Life Course." *Journal of Personality* 57: 375–406.

Catalano, Richard F., and J. David Hawkins. 1996. "The Social Development Model: A Theory of Antisocial Behavior." In *Delinquency and Crime: Current Theories*, edited by J. David Hawkins. Cambridge, UK: Cambridge University Press.

Catalano, Richard F., Jisuk Park, Tracy Harachi, Kevin P. Haggerty, Robert D. Abbott, and J. David Hawkins. 2005. "Mediating the Effects of Poverty, Gender, Individual Characteristics, and External Constraints on Antisocial Behavior: A test of the Social Development Model and Implications for Developmental Life-Course Theory." In *Integrated Developmental and Life-Course Theories of Offending, Advances in Criminological Theory*, Vol. 14, edited by David P. Farrington. New Brunswick, NJ: Transaction.

Childs, Kristina K., Christopher J. Sullivan, and Laura M. Gulledge. 2010. "Delinquent Behavior Across Adolescence: Investigating the Shifting Salience of Key Criminological Predictors." *Deviant Behavior* 32: 64–100.

Cillessen, Antonius H. N., and Lara Mayeux. 2004. "From Censure to Reinforcement: Developmental Changes in the Association Between Aggression and Social Status." *Child Development* 75: 147–163.

Cloward, Richard A., and Lloyd E. Ohlin. 1960. *Delinquency and Opportunity*. Glencoe, IL: Free Press.

Cohen, Albert K. (1955). *Delinquent Boys: The Culture of the Gang*. Glencoe, IL: Free Press.

Cohen, Lawrence E., and Marcus Felson. 1979. "Social Change and Crime Rate Trends: A Routine Activity Approach." *American Sociological Review* 44: 588–608.

Coleman, James C. 1961. *The Adolescent Society*. New York: The Free Press.

Collins, W. Andrew, and Brett Laursen. 2004. "Changing Relationships, Changing Youth: Interpersonal Contexts of Adolescent Development." *Journal of Early Adolescence* 24: 55–62.

Collins, W. Andrew, and Laurence Steinberg. 2006. "Adolescent Development in Interpersonal Context." In *The Handbook of Child Psychology*, edited by W. Damon and R. M. Lernor. Hoboken, NJ: Wiley.

Connolly, Jennifer, Wyndol Furman, and Roman Konarski. 2000. "The Role of Peers in the Emergence of Heterosexual Romantic Relationships in Adolescence." *Child Development* 71: 1395–1408.

Csikzentmihalyi, Mihaly, and R. Larson. 1974. *Being Adolescent: Conflict and Growth in the Teenage Years*. New York: Basic Books.

Deutsch, Arielle R., Douglas Steinley, and Wendy S. Slutske. 2014. "The Role of Gender and Friends' Gender on Peer Socialization of Adolescent Drinking: A Prospective Multilevel Social Network Analysis." *Journal of Youth and Adolescence* 43: 1421–1435.

Dishion, Thomas J., Kathleen M. Spracklen, David W. Andrews, and Gerald R. Patterson. 1996. "Deviancy Training in Male Adolescents' Friendships." *Behavioral Therapy* 27: 373–390.

Dodge, Kenneth A., Thomas J. Dishion, and Jennifer E. Lansford. 2006. "Deviant Peer Influences in Intervention and Public Policy for Youth." *Social Policy Report* 20: 3–19.

Dupéré, Véronique, Éric Lacourse, J. Douglas Willms, Frank Vitaro, and Richard E. Tremblay. 2007. "Affiliation to Youth Gangs During Adolescence: The Interaction Between Childhood Psychopathic Tendencies and Neighborhood Disadvantage." *Journal of Abnormal Child Psychology* 35: 1035–1045.

Elliott, Delbert, and Scott Menard. 1996. "Delinquent Friends and Delinquent Behavior." In *Delinquency and Crime: Current Theories*, edited by J. David Hawkins. New York: Cambridge University Press.

Erickson, Kristan Glasgow, Robert Crosnoe, and Sanford M. Dornbusch. 2000. "A Social Process Model of Adolescent Deviance: Combining Social Control and Differential Association Perspectives." *Journal of Youth and Adolescence* 29: 395–425.

Erickson, Maynard L., and Gary F. Jensen. 1977. "Delinquency Is Still Group Behavior: Toward Revitalizing the Group Premise in the Sociology of Deviance." *Journal of Criminal Law and Criminology* 68: 262–273.

Esbensen, Finn-Aage, and David Huizinga. 1993. "Gangs, Drugs, and Delinquency in a Survey of Urban Youth." *Criminology* 31: 565–589.

Farrington, David P. 1986. "Age and Crime." In *Crime and Justice: A Review of Research*, edited by Michael Tonry. Chicago: University of Chicago Press.

Farrington, David P. 2003. "Developmental and Life-Course Criminology: Key Theoretical and Empirical Issues—The 2002 Sutherland Award Address." *Criminology* 41: 221–225.

Farrington, David P. 2005a. "Introduction to Integrated Developmental and Life-Course Theories of Offending." In *Integrated Developmental and Life-Course Theories of Offending: Advances in Criminological Theory*, Vol. 14, edited by David P. Farrington. New Brunswick, NJ: Transaction.

Farrington, David P. 2005b. "Conclusions About Developmental and Life-Course Theories." In *Integrated Developmental and Life-Course Theories of Offending, Advances in Criminological Theory*, Vol. 14, edited by David P. Farrington. New Brunswick, NJ: Transaction.

Farrington, David P. 2006. "Building Developmental and Life-Course Theories of Offending." In *Taking Stock: The Status of Criminological Theory, Advances in Criminological Theory*, Vol. 15, edited by Francis T. Cullen, John Paul Wright, and Kristie R. Blevins. New Brunswick, NJ: Transaction.

Flay, Brian R., Sally Graumlich, Eisuke Segawa, James L. Burns, Michelle Y. Holiday, and Aban Aya. 2004. "Effects of Two Prevention Programs on High-Risk Behaviors Among African-American Youth." *Archives of Pediatric and Adolescent Medicine* 158: 377–84.

Fuligni, Andrew J., and Jaquelynne S. Eccles. 1993. "Perceived Parent-Child Relationships and Early Adolescents' Orientation Toward Peers." *Developmental Psychology* 29: 622–632.

Gardner, Margo, and Laurence Steinberg. 2005. "Peer Influence on Risk Taking, Risk Performance, and Risky Decision-Making in Adolescence and Adulthood: An Experimental Study." *Developmental Psychology* 41: 625–635.

Garneski, Nadia, and Rene F.W. Diekstra. 1996. "Perceived Social Support from Family, School, and Peers: Relationship with Emotional and Behavioral Problems Among Adolescents." *Journal of the American Academy of Child and Adolescent Psychiatry* 35: 1657–1664.

Gatti, Uberto, Richard E. Tremblay, Frank Vitaro, and Pierre McDuff. 2005. "Youth Gangs, Delinquency and Drug Use: A Test of the Selection, Facilitation, and Enhancement Hypotheses." *Journal of Child Psychology and Psychiatry* 46: 1178–1190.

Gibson, Chris L., John Paul Wright, and Stephen G. Tibbetts. 2000. "An Empirical Assessment of the Generality of the General Theory of Crime: The Effects of Low Self-Control on Social Development." *Journal of Crime and Justice* 23:109–134.

Glueck, Sheldon, and Eleanor Glueck. 1950. *Unraveling Juvenile Delinquency*. Cambridge, MA: Harvard University.

Goldstein, Sara E., Pamela E. Davis-Kean, and Jacquelynne S. Eccles. 2005. "Parents, Peers, and Problem Behavior: A Longitudinal Investigation of the Impact of Relationship Perceptions and Characteristics on the Development of Adolescent Problem Behavior." *Developmental Psychology* 41: 401–413.

Gordon, Rachel A., Benjamin B. Lahey, Eriko Kawai, Rolf Loeber, Magda Stouthamer-Loeber, and David P. Farrington. 2004. "Antisocial Behavior and Youth Gang Membership: Selection and Socialization." *Criminology* 42: 55–88.

Gottfredson, Michael R., and Travis Hirschi. 1990. *A General Theory of Crime*. Stanford, CA: Stanford University Press.

Granic, Isabela, and Tom Hollenstein. 2003. "Dynamic Systems Methods for Models of Developmental Psychopathology." *Development and Psychopathology* 15: 641–669.

Granic, Isabela, and Gerald R. Patterson. 2006. "Toward a Comprehensive Model of Antisocial Development: A Dynamic Systems Approach." *Psychological Review* 113: 101–131.

Greenberg, David F. 1977. "Delinquency and the Age Structure of Society." *Contemporary Crises* 1: 189–223.

Gross, Thilo, and Hiroki Sayama. 2009. "Introduction to Adaptive Networks." In *Adaptive Networks: Theory, Models and Applications*, edited by Thilo Gross and Hiroki Sayama. New York: Springer.

Hartup, Willard W., and Brett Laursen. 1993. "Conflict and Context in Peer Relations." In *Children on Playgrounds: Research Perspectives and Applications,* edited by Craig H. Hart. Albany: State University of New York Press.

Hawkins, J. David, Sabrina Oesterle, Eric C. Brown, Michael W. Arthur, Robert D. Abbott, Abigail A. Fagan, and Richard F. Catalano. 2009. "Results of a Type 2 Translational Research Trial to Prevent Adolescent Drug Use and Delinquency: A Test of Communities That Care." *Archives of Pediatrics and Adolescent Medicine* 163: 789–798.

Hay, Ian, and Adrian F. Ashman. 2003. "The Development of Adolescents' Emotional Stability and General Self-Concept: The Interplay of Parents, Peers, and Gender." *International Journal of Disability, Development and Education* 50: 77–91.

Haynie, Dana L. 2002. "Friendship Networks and Delinquency: The Relative Nature of Peer Delinquency." *Journal of Quantitative Criminology* 18: 99–134.

Haynie, Dana L., and D. Wayne Osgood. 2005. "Reconsidering Peers and Delinquency: How Do Peers Matter?" *Social Forces* 84: 1109–1130.

Haynie, Dana L., Peggy C. Giordano, Wendy D. Manning, and Monica A. Longmore. 2005. "Adolescent Romantic Relationships and Delinquency Involvement." *Criminology* 43: 177–210.

Henry, David B., Michael E. Schoeny, Daneen P. Deptula, and John T. Slavick. 2007. "Peer Selection and Socialization Effects on Adolescent Intercourse without a Condom and Attitudes About the Costs of Sex." *Child Development* 78: 825–838.

Hindelang Michael J., Michael R. Gottfredson, and James Garofalo. 1978. *Victims of Personal Crime: An Empirical Foundation for a Theory of Personal Victimization.* Cambridge, MA: Ballinger.

Hirschi, Travis. 1969. *Causes of Delinquency.* Berkeley, CA: University of California Press.

Horney, Julie. 2001. "Criminal Events and Criminal Careers: An Integrative Approach to the Study of Violence." In *The Process and Structure of Crime, Advances in Criminological Theory*, Vol. 9, edited by Robert F. Meier, Leslie W. Kennedy, and Vincent F. Sacco. New Brunswick, NJ: Transaction.

Huff, C. Ronald. 1998. *Comparing the Criminal Behavior of Youth Gangs and At-Risk Youths: Research in Brief.* Washington, DC: National Institute of Justice.

Ingoldsby, Erin M., Daniel S. Shaw, Emily Winslow, Michael Schonberg, Miles Gilliom, and Michael M. Criss. 2006. "Neighborhood Disadvantage, Parent–Child Conflict, Neighborhood Peer Relationships, and Early Antisocial Behavior Problem Trajectories." *Journal of Abnormal Child Psychology* 34: 293–309.

Jeffery, C. Ray. 1998. "Prevention of Juvenile Violence: A Critical Review of Current Scientific Strategies." *Journal of Offender Rehabilitation* 28: 1–28.

Jolliffe, Darrick, and David P. Farrington. 2008. *The Influence of Mentoring on Reoffending.* Stockholm: Swedish National Council on Crime Prevention.

Kandel, Denise B. 1978. "Homophily, Selection, and Socialization in Adolescent Friendships." *American Journal of Sociology* 84: 427–436.

Kennedy, David M. 2009. *Deterrence and Crime Prevention: Reconsidering the Prospect of Sanction.* New York: Routledge.

Kiesner, Jeff, Francois Poulin, and Thomas J. Dishion. 2010. "Adolescent Substance Use with Friends: Moderating and Mediating Effects of Parental Monitoring and Peer Activity Contexts." *Merrill-Palmer Quarterly* 56: 529–556.

Kirillova, Galina P., Michael M. Vanyukov, Levent Kirisci, and Maureen Reynolds. 2008. "Physical Maturity, Peer Environment, and the Ontogenesis of Substance Use Disorders." *Psychiatry Research* 158: 43–53.

Krosnick, Jon A., and Charles M. Judd. 1982. "Transitions in Social Influence at Adolescence: Who Induces Cigarette Smoking?" *Developmental Psychology* 18: 359–368.

Laible, Deborah J., Gustavo Carlo, and Marcela Raffaelli. 2000. "The Differential Relations of Parent and Peer Attachment to Adolescent Adjustment." *Journal of Youth and Adolescence* 29: 45–59.

Laird, Robert D., Kristi Y. Jordan, Kenneth A. Dodge, Gregory S. Pettit, and John E. Bates. 2001. "Peer Rejection in Childhood, Involvement with Antisocial Peers in Early Adolescence, and the Development of Externalizing Behavior Problems." *Development and Psychopathology* 13: 337–354.

Laub, John H., and Robert J. Sampson. 2003. *Shared Beginnings, Divergent Lives: Delinquent Boys to Age 70.* Cambridge, MA: Harvard University Press.

Laub, John H., Robert J. Sampson, and Gary A. Sweeten. 2006. "Assessing Sampson and Laub's Life-Course Theory of Crime." In *Taking Stock: The Status of Criminological Theory, Advances in Criminological Theory,* Vol. 15, edited by Francis T. Cullen, John Paul Wright, and Kristie R. Blevins. New Brunswick, NJ: Transaction.

Lemert, Edwin M. (1974). "Beyond Mead: The Societal Reaction to Deviance." *Social Problems* 21: 457–468.

Lynam, Donald R., and Lauren Gudonis. 2005. "The Development of Psychopathy." *Annual Review of Clinical Psychology* 1: 381–407.

Mahoney, Joseph L., Hakan Stattin, and Heather Lord. 2004. "Unstructured Youth Recreation Centre Participation and Antisocial Behaviour Development: Selection Influences and the Moderating Role of Antisocial Peers." *International Journal of Behavioral Development* 28: 553–560.

Matsueda, Ross L., and Kathleen Anderson. 1998. "The Dynamics of Delinquent Peers and Delinquent Behavior." *Criminology* 36: 269–308.

Matz, Adam K., Nathan C. Lowe, Matthew T. DeMichele, and Carl Wicklund. 2011. "Gangs and Guns a Threat to Public Safety: Introducing the APPA C.A.R.E. Model." *Journal of Community Corrections* 20: 9–15.

Maxwell, Kimberly A. 2002. "Friends: The Role of Peer Influence Across Adolescent Risk Behaviors." *Journal of Youth and Adolescence* 31: 267–277.

McCord, Joan, and Kevin P. Conway. 2002. "Patterns of Juvenile Delinquency and Co-Offending." In *Crime and Social Organization, Advances in Criminological Theory,* Vol. 10, edited by Elin Waring and David Weisburd. New Brunswick, NJ: Transaction.

McGloin, Jean. 2009. "Delinquency Balance: Revisiting Peer Influence." *Criminology* 47: 439–477.

McGloin, Jean Marie, and Lauren O'Neill Shermer. 2009. "Self-Control and Deviant Peer Network Structure." *Journal of Research in Crime and Delinquency* 46: 35–72.

Mcgloin, Jean, Christopher J. Sullivan, Alex R. Piquero, and Sarah Bacon. 2008. "Investigating the Stability of Co-offending and Co-offenders Among a Sample of Youthful Offenders." *Criminology* 46: 155–188.

McGloin, Jean Marie, Christopher J. Sullivan, and Kyle J. Thomas. 2014. "Peer Influence and Context: The Interdependence of Friendship Groups, Schoolmates and Network Density in Predicting Substance Use." *Journal of Youth and Adolescence* 43: 1436–1452.

Metzler, Carol W., John Noell, Anthony Biglan, Dennis Ary, and Keith Smolkowski. 1994. "The Social Context for Risky Sexual Behavior Among Adolescents." *Journal of Behavioral Medicine* 17: 419–438.

Moffitt, Terrie E. 1993. "Adolescent-Limited and Life-Course-Persistent Antisocial Behavior: A Developmental Taxonomy." *Psychological Review* 100: 674–701.

Moffitt, Terrie E. 1997. "Adolescence-Limited and Life-Course Persistent Offending: A Complementary Pair of Developmental Theories." In *Developmental Theories of Crime and Delinquency, Advances in Criminological Theory,* Vol. 7, edited by Terrence P. Thornberry. New Brunswick, NJ: Transaction.

Monahan, Kathryn C., Laurence Steinberg, and Elizabeth Cauffman. 2009. "Affiliation with Antisocial Peers, Susceptibility to Peer Influence, and Antisocial Behavior during the Transition to Adulthood." *Developmental Psychology* 45: 1520–1530.

Mounts, Nina S., and Laurence Steinberg. 1995. "An Ecological Analysis of Peer Influence on Adolescent Grade Point Average and Drug Use. *Developmental Psychology* 31: 915–922.

Nagin, Daniel, and Raymond Paternoster. 2000. "Population Heterogeneity and State Dependence: State of the Evidence and Directions for Future Research." *Journal of Quantitative Criminology* 16: 117–144.

National Research Council [NRC]. 2013. *Reforming Juvenile Justice: A Developmental Approach.* Committee on Assessing Juvenile Justice Reform, Bonnie, R. J., Johnson, R. L., Chemers, B. M., & Schuck, J. A. (Eds.). Committee on Law and Justice, Division of Behavioral and Social Sciences and Education. Washington, DC: The National Academies Press.

Ngwe, Job E., Li C. Liu, Brian R. Flay, Eisuke Segawa, and Aban Aya. 2004. "Violence Prevention Among African American Adolescent Males." *American Journal of Health Behaviors* 28(Suppl.): S24–37.

Osgood, D. Wayne, and Amy L. Anderson. 2004. "Unstructured Socializing and Rates of Delinquency. *Criminology* 42: 519–550.

Osgood, D. Wayne, Janet K. Wilson, Patrick M. O'Malley, Jerald G. Bachman, and Lloyd D. Johnston. 1996. "Routine Activities and Individual Deviant Behavior." *American Sociological Review* 61: 635–655.

Ousey, Graham C., and Pamela Wilcox. 2007. "The Interaction of Antisocial Propensity and Life-Course Varying Predictors of Delinquent Behavior: Differences by Method of Estimation and Implications for Theory." *Criminology* 45: 313–353.

Piaget, Jean. 1965. *The Moral Judgment of the Child.* London: Routledge and Kegan Paul.

Pratt, Travis C., Francis T. Cullen, Christine S. Sellers, Thomas Winfree Jr., Tamara D. Madensen, Leah E. Daigle, Noelle E. Fearn, and Jacinta M. Gau. 2010. "The Empirical Status of Social Learning Theory: A Meta-Analysis." *Justice Quarterly* 27: 765–802.

Quetelet, Adolphe. 1984 [1833]. *Research on the Propensity for Crime at Different Ages.* Cincinnati: Anderson Publishing Company.

Ryan, Allison M. 2000. "Peer Groups as a Context for Socialization of Adolescents' Motivation, Engagement, and Achievement in School." *Educational Psychologist* 35: 101–111.

Ryan, Allison M. 2001. "The Peer Group as a Context for the Development of Young Adolescent Motivation and Achievement." *Child Development* 72: 1135–1150.

Sampson, Robert J., and John H. Laub. 1993. *Crime in the Making: Pathways and Turning Points Through Life.* Cambridge, MA: Harvard University Press.

Sampson, Robert J., and John H. Laub. 2005. "A Life-Course View of the Development of Crime." *Annals of the American Academy of Political and Social Science* 602: 12–45.

Sampson, Robert J., and John H. Laub. 1997. "A Life-Course Theory of Cumulative Disadvantage and the Stability of Delinquency." In *Developmental Theories of Crime and Delinquency, Advances in Criminological Theory,* Vol. 7, edited by Terrence P. Thornberry. New Brunswick, NJ: Transaction.

Simons, Ronald L., Chyi-In Wu, Rand D. Conger, and Frederick O. Lorenz. 1994. Two Routes to Delinquency: Differences Between Early and Late Starters in the Impact of Parenting and Deviant Peers." *Criminology* 32: 247–276.

Simons, Ronald L., Eric Stewart, Leslie C. Gordon, Rand D. Conger, and Glen H. Elder. 2002. "A Test Of Life-Course Explanations for Stability and Change in Antisocial Behavior from Adolescence to Young Adulthood." *Criminology* 40: 401–434.

Simons-Morton, Bruce. 2007. "Social Influences on Adolescent Substance Use." *American Journal of Health Behavior* 31: 672–684.

Sitnick, Stephanie L., Daniel S. Shaw, and Luke W. Hyde. 2014. "Precursors of Adolescent Substance Use from Early Childhood and Early Adolescence: Testing a Developmental Cascade Model." *Development and Psychopathology* 26: 125–140.

Smetana, Judith G., Nicole Campione-Barr, and Aaron Metzger. 2006. "Adolescent Development in Interpersonal and Societal Contexts." *Annual Review of Psychology* 57: 255–284.

Staff, Jeremy, and Derek A. Kreager. 2008. "Too Cool for School? Violence, Peer Status and High School Dropout." *Social Forces* 87: 445–471.

Steinberg, Laurence, and Kathryn C. Monahan. 2007. "Age Differences in Resistance to Peer Influence." *Developmental Psychology* 43: 1531–1543.

Steinberg, Laurence, and Amy Sheffield Morris. 2001. "Adolescent Development." *Annual Review of Psychology* 52: 83–100.

Stolzenberg, Lisa, and Stewart J. D'Alessio. 2008. "Co-offending and the Age-Crime Curve." *Journal of Research in Crime and Delinquency* 45: 65–86.

Sullivan, Christopher J., and Darrick Jolliffe. 2012. "Peer Influence, Mentoring, and the Prevention of Crime." In *The Oxford Handbook of Crime Prevention*, edited by David P. Farrington and Brandon C. Welsh. New York: Oxford University Press.

Sutherland, Edwin H. 1947. *Principles of Criminology*. Philadelphia: J.B. Lippincott.

Thornberry, Terrence P. 1987. "Toward an Interactional Theory of Delinquency." *Criminology* 25: 863–891.

Thornberry, Terrence P. 1996. Empirical Support for Interactional Theory: A Review of the Literature. In *Delinquency and Crime: Current Theories*, edited by J. David Hawkins. Cambridge, UK: Cambridge University.

Thornberry, Terrence P., and Marvin Krohn. 2005. "Applying Interactional Theory to the Explanation of Continuity and Change in Antisocial Behavior." In *Integrated Developmental and Life-Course Theories of Offending, Advances in Criminological Theory*, Vol. 14, edited by David P. Farrington. New Brunswick, NJ: Transaction.

Thornberry, Terence P., Marvin D. Krohn, Alan J. Lizotte, and Deborah Chard-Wierschem. 1993. "The Role of Juvenile Gangs in Facilitating Delinquent Behavior." *Journal of Research in Crime and Delinquency* 30: 55–87.

Urberg, Kathryn A., Qing Luo, Colleen Pilgrim, and Serdar M. Degirmencioglu. 2003. "A Two-Stage Model of Peer Influence in Adolescent Substance Use: Individual and Relationship-Specific Differences in Susceptibility to Influence." *Addictive Behaviors* 28: 1243–1256.

van Lier, Pol, Frank Vitaro, and Manuel Eisner. 2007. "Preventing Aggressive and Violent Behavior: Using Prevention Programs to Study the Role of Peer Dynamics in Maladjustment Problems." *European Journal on Criminal Policy and Research* 13: 277–296.

Walker, Lawrence J., Karl H. Hennig, and Tobias Krettenauer. 2000. "Parent and Peer Contexts for Children's Moral Reasoning Development." *Child Development* 71: 1033–1048.

Warr, Mark. 1998. "Life Course Transitions and Desistance from Crime." *Criminology* 36: 183–215.

Warr, Mark. 2002. *Companions in Crime: The Social Aspects of Criminal Conduct*. New York: Cambridge University Press.

Warr, Mark. 2011. "The Social Side of Delinquent Behavior." In *The Oxford Handbook of Juvenile Crime and Juvenile Justice*, edited by Barry C. Feld and Donna M. Bishop. New York: Oxford University Press.

Weiss, Carol H. 1995. "Nothing as Practical as Good Theory: Exploring Theory Based Evaluation for Comprehensive Community-Based Initiatives for Children and

Families." In *New Approaches to Evaluating Community Initiatives,* Vol. 1, edited by James P. Connell, Anne C. Kubisch, Lisbeth B. Schorr, and Carol H. Weiss. Washington, DC: Aspen Institute.

Wikström, Per-Olof H. 2005. "The Social Origins of Pathways to Crime: Towards a Developmental Ecological Action Theory of Crime Involvement and Its Changes." In *Integrated Developmental and Life-Course Theories of Offending: Advances in Criminological Theory,* Vol. 14, edited by David P. Farrington. New Brunswick, NJ: Transaction.

Wikström, Per-Olof H. 2006. "Individuals, Settings, and Acts of Crime: Situational Mechanisms and the Explanation of Crime." In *The Explanation of Crime: Context, Mechanisms and Development,* edited by Per-Olof Wikström and Robert J. Sampson. Cambridge, UK: Cambridge University Press.

Wikström, Per-Olof H. 2007. "In Search of Causes and Explanations of Crime." In *Doing Research on Crime and Justice,* edited by Roy King and Emma Wincup. Oxford: Oxford University Press.

Wikström, Per-Olof H., and David A. Butterworth. 2006. *Adolescent Crime: Individual Differences and Lifestyle.* Portland, OR: Willan.

Windle, Michael. 2000. "Parental, Sibling, and Peer Influences on Adolescent Substance Use and Alcohol Problems." *Applied Developmental Science* 4: 98–110.

Wills, Thomas Ashby, and Sean D. Cleary. 1999. "Peer and Adolescent Substance Use Among 6th–9th Graders: Latent Growth Analyses of Influence versus Selection Mechanisms. *Health Psychology* 18: 453–463.

Wright, Bradley, R. E., Avshalom Caspi, Terrie E. Moffitt, and Phil A. Silva. 2001. "The Effects of Social Ties on Crime Vary by Criminal Propensity: A Life-Course Model of Interdependence." *Criminology* 39: 321–352.

Young, Jacob T.N. 2014. "'Role Magnets'? An Empirical Investigation of Popularity Trajectories for Life-Course Persistent Individuals During Adolescence." *Journal of Youth and Adolescence* 43: 104–115.

CHAPTER 21

··

SCHOOLS AND THE PATHWAY TO CRIME

A Focus on Relationships

··

DEBRA J. PEPLER

SCHOOLS comprise a primary socializing context for children and youth. In many jurisdictions, schools operate *in loco parentis*—in the place of parents—while students are at school. Baumrind (1991) identified two important dimensions of parenting: providing love and being responsive, as well as guiding and setting expectations and limits for children's behaviors. Therefore, if schools are expected to operate *in loco parentis*, they have some of the same responsibilities as parents for nurturing and supporting students, teaching and guiding them, and keeping them safe. Schools have long served as society's institution for socialization, not only for academic skills, but ideally also for the social-emotional skills and moral development that are essential for healthy development and adaptation across the life span. The critical question at this point is not whether youths' lives in school are linked to delinquency, but why it is that experiences in school can draw youth into the "schools to prison pipeline" (Christle, Jolivette, and Nelson 2005) or fail to support their development onto a healthier pathway.

This chapter focuses on the role of schools in the pathway to crime. Section I begins by highlighting research that points to the importance of relationships in development, followed by a review of theoretical perspectives of relationships and the development of delinquency and a consideration of school violence. Section II focuses on the importance of school connections and relationships, with a consideration of engagement and bonding with school, failing academic performance, and dropout rates. School and classroom organization and relationships with teachers and with peers are identified as potential risk factors that further alienate troubled youth. Conversely, if these systemic and relationship processes are positive, they can mitigate the risk of moving along the pathway to crime. The concluding Section III revisits the theory and research, with a call to identify and intervene with the most vulnerable youth that leads to a discussion of implications for programming and policy.

I. The Importance of Relationships in Development

Over the past 30 years of collaborative research on troubled children, we have highlighted the nature of aggressive children's interactions at school (Pepler, Craig, and Roberts 1998), the peer dynamics in bullying (O'Connell, Pepler, and Craig 1999), the diverse trajectories in the development of delinquency (Pepler et al. 2010), as well as the links between the quality of school relationships and health (Pepler, Craig, and Haner 2012; Craig and Pepler 2014). Through our extended program of research we have come to recognize that relationships at school play a central role in promoting social-emotional development or, conversely, function to marginalize and alienate children and youth within this critical socialization context. Children who lag in the development of both social-emotional and academic skills are at risk of following a troubled pathway, not only because of their deficits in a wide range of academic and social capacities, but also because of the ways that others interact with them, further constraining them on a troubled pathway. This chapter highlights the relational experiences of children and youth at school as a window into the dynamic mechanisms that shape students' pathways to crime. The focus on schools is critical for both programming and policy because experiences in school comprise a central part of the problem and a potential solution to the school-to-crime pathway (Sander et al. 2012).

A. Theoretical Perspectives of Relationships and the Development of Delinquency

From a developmental perspective, relationships are important because they comprise the primary environments in which children grow up (National Scientific Council on the Developing Child 2004). Numerous theories reviewed in earlier chapters of this book point to the importance of children's experiences in relationships within the family, peer group, school, and neighborhood on the development of criminal behavior. For example, Farrington's Integrated Cognitive Antisocial Potential theory (see Chapter 11, this volume) highlights the importance of these relationships in establishing the long-term potential for criminal behavior. Thornberry and Krohn (see Chapter 14) take an interactional perspective on the development of criminal behavior and note that antisocial behavior develops in the early years through interactional experiences within the family. As children move into schools, broader social contexts begin to shape their development. Thornberry and Krohn contend that children shift toward a pathway of delinquency because of structural adversity or a disadvantaged position within the peer group, school, and/or neighborhood.

Drawing from these perspectives, this chapter on the influence of the school on the development of delinquent behavior and the pathway to crime focuses on the reciprocal relationship processes that unfold within school, constrain positive development, and foster antisocial development. Hirschi's (1969) social control theory was among the first to focus on youths' relationships. Hirschi contended that when youths have a weak bond or attachment to the critical social systems in their lives, such as the family, school, and community, they are less inclined to think and behave in ways that are consistent with the expectations of these systems. Another way to think about this perspective is that youths with weak attachments may not be concerned about disappointing the adults in their lives; hence, they may not resist the temptation to engage in antisocial opportunities when they arise (Gottfredson and Hirschi 1990). The social development model extends social control theory by highlighting that social bonds develop when children and youth are raised with opportunities for positive interactions, experiences for positive involvement and associations, adequate skills for social interactions, and reinforcements for positive behaviors (Catalano and Hawkins 1996). When these positive relationship processes are inadequate, children are at risk for developing along a troubled pathway to crime. These theoretical models highlight that it is experiences with and in relationships that enable and motivate youth to develop along a positive pathway or fail to support positive youth development, leaving the youth to drift onto a deviant pathway.

These theoretical perspectives are consistent with the emerging view that "relationships are the 'active ingredients' of the environment's influence on healthy human development" (National Scientific Council on the Developing Child 2004, p. 1). The Search Institute has recently extended its focus beyond individual assets of children and youth to include the relationships that promote their healthy development. They have identified developmental relationships as those that support children and youth to achieve the psychosocial capacities that underlie success in school and in life (Search Institute 2014). They note that developmental relationships can be provided by parents and other family members, school staff, peers, and caring adults in communities. In our own research and knowledge mobilization, we have been focusing on the importance of healthy relationships, which we define as those that provide children with a sense of security and stability, a sense of being valued and belonging, and support and guidance to develop essential skills and understanding. In addition, healthy relationships do not create stress for children and youth but help to buffer the stresses they inevitably encounter (Pepler, Craig, and Haner 2012; Craig and Pepler 2014). Both theory and research on the development of delinquency highlight the importance of youths' relationships and point to the importance of relationships in school—a primary developmental context for children and youth.

In qualitative research with male and female offenders and non-offenders, Skrzypiec (2013) studied youths' perceptions of why adolescents commit crimes. She found that both prosocial and delinquent youths provided explanations about the motivation to commit crime which were aligned with the "big three" criminological theories suggested by Cullen and Agnew (2003): control, differential association, and strain theories. Skrzypiec (2013) noted that youths, themselves, have insightful perceptions of the causes of crime and might also have insights into effective strategies for programming and policy to prevent or intervene to support children and adolescents on a pathway to crime.

B. School Violence

Attention to youth violence and violence in schools has increased markedly over the past two decades. In 1994, the American Psychological Association published a seminal volume entitled *Reason to Hope: A Psychosocial Perspective on Violence and Youth.* The book provided both developmental and sociocultural perspectives on the causes of youth violence, with a consideration of vulnerable youth and the influence of broader societal factors such as the media, availability of guns, and gangs on youth violence. The perspective of hope arises from reports on the promising, evidence-based prevention and intervention strategies that shift youth from a pathway to crime. The mid-1990s represented a high point for youth violence, and it has been decreasing since (Centers for Disease Control, 2015).

Concern for school violence skyrocketed after the Columbine High School shootings in 1999, which have been followed by other school shootings in the United States and elsewhere. In 2002, the *Journal of School Violence* was launched, encouraging research, commentaries, position statements, and knowledge translation on this critical social issue. According to the Centers for Disease Control, rates of violent crimes have dropped substantially from 1995 to 2011 for both male and female youth. Nevertheless, violence perpetrated at school raises concerns not only for the learning environment but also for the well-being and safety of both students and staff. The FBI has studied youths who perpetrated school shootings within the United States (Federal Bureau of Investigation, 2015). It found that 75 percent of these youths felt bullied, persecuted, and/or threatened by others, pointing to a breakdown in relationships within the school system.

These extreme acts of violence are, however, very rare, and the majority of violent episodes at school do not result in death or serious injury, even though they can be physically, psychologically, and socially harmful. The probability of a violent act depends not only on student characteristics but also on the contexts within and outside of school, including the media and Internet, which have the potential to influence youths' attitudes and behaviors. A study by Brezina and colleagues revealed variability among schools in the overall levels of anger and aggression among the students (Brezina, Piquero, and Mazerolle 2001). Consistent with Agnew's macro-level strain theory, they noted that when the student population is relatively high in anger, there are more opportunities for conflict and aggression between individual students. The interaction of diverse individual characteristics and a range of systemic processes experienced by students underlies the propensity for school violence.

C. How Many Youth Become Delinquent and Why?

Concerns for the quality of youths' relationships and the development of delinquency were confirmed by our analyses of the trajectories in delinquency through adolescence (Pepler et al. 2010). We explored the diverse developmental pathways of delinquency with eight waves of data over seven years and examined a range of individual and relationship factors that differentiated youths on the diverse trajectories. When we analyzed girls and boys together, we found that the youths' trajectories were best represented by a five-class model: 60 percent of the youths rarely reported delinquency from age 10 to 17; 27.7 percent reported low initial levels with moderate levels of delinquency developing over time; 6 percent of youths fell in the late-onset group and reported initially low and rising levels of delinquency; and 5 percent were in the early-onset group and reported moderate initial levels, which increased and then began to decrease after age 14. A small group of only boys (1.3 percent), whom we identified as chronic, reported high initial levels of delinquency that increased from age 10 to 17.

When we compared trajectory groups we found that both boys and girls involved in even moderate levels of delinquency generally differed from the low-delinquency group on individual and relationship factors. The youth engaged in delinquency used more substances and had higher levels of internalizing problems compared to those consistently low in delinquency. They also had strained relationships with their parents, with lower monitoring (a proxy for poor communication; Stattin and Kerr 2000) and higher conflict with parents than the low-delinquency youth. The delinquent boys and girls were more likely to have friends who also reported delinquency and were more susceptible to negative peer pressure than low-delinquency youth. Few differences emerged between girls and boys in the nature of delinquent behaviors and in the associated problems with parents and peers. The trajectories were consistent with the age–crime curves that show a general decline in delinquency from early adolescence to early adulthood (Le and Stockdale 2011). Although there are general trends in the development of delinquency, our data highlight the heterogeneity in developmental pathways. This research suggests that the development of delinquency is a dynamic process that occurs in adolescence when some youth have strained relationships that fail to provide important developmental opportunities and may cause them to drift to the margins of social systems, associate with similar peers, and engage in antisocial behavior.

II. The Importance of School Connections and Relationships

A. Engagement with Schools

There is mounting evidence that students' attachment to teachers and their engagement or connection with schools are related not only to their academic achievement but also to their social, moral, and behavioral development (Kuperminc, Leadbeater, and Blatt 2001). It is important to recognize, however, that the development of bonds with school and the links between school bonds and delinquency are dynamic and transactional. In other words, delinquency may be both the cause and consequence of the weakening of attachment or bonds to school (Hoffman, Erickson, and Spence 2013). When students are disengaged at school, their detached orientation may foster strained relationships with school staff and peers alike. Conversely, if school staff and peers are not supportive, accepting, and including of youth who are struggling, the experiences of being rejected may underlie youths' migration to the margins of the school social context and promote their disengagement. According to Hirschfeld and Gasper (2011), the process of disengagement from school, which is linked to the development of delinquency, may start at the moment of school entry and comprise the primary developmental process that underlies school failure and dropout.

At school entry, there is a group of children who are unprepared for the academic, behavioral, and social demands in the school setting and consequently vulnerable to experiencing problems and not engaging with school. Based on inadequate socialization within the family and/or daycare context, these children enter the school system with an inability to regulate their behaviors and emotions, poorly developed executive functions, a lack of social skills, weak moral understanding and attitudes, and mental health problems (e.g., anxiety, oppositional behavior). As Dodge and colleagues (2009) note, the combination of difficult child factors and adverse social contexts sets up a developmental cascade of failure in family, peer, and school contexts and risk of movement into antisocial and illegal behaviors, where alternate reinforcement processes attract the youth into crime. For children with these initial vulnerabilities, society depends on schools to be the socializing institution and to pick up where parents left off or were unable to establish a foundation for adaptive regulation and learning.

Experiences in the early school years are important because this is the time when school commitment and connectedness is generally highest. Jang (1999) found a developmental trend in school commitment, measured by reports of studying/homework, attachment to school/teachers, and grades. Prior to high school (ages 12 and 13), students reported more commitment to school than during high school. With Canadian data, we measured the quality of school connectedness and relationships using the response to three statements: the rules in this school are fair; our school is a nice place to be; and I feel I belong at this school (Pepler et al. 2012). We found that youths' reports of the quality of school relationships were related to all outcomes in the emotional health and academic domains. We also found a consistent developmental decline in the quality of relationships with schools for both boys and girls from grade 6 to grade 10. Jang (1999) noted that schools become more important as youth move into adolescence, when parental influences decline and peer influences increase. Schools can only perform this role and support academic success and school completion if students are engaged and have positive relationships with school staff and peers.

In a recent longitudinal study, Hirschfeld and Gasper (2011) measured three forms of school engagement: behavioral (participation in academic and extracurricular activities), emotional (positive thoughts and emotions about school activities and those in school), and cognitive (willingness to engage with the cognitive challenges of the academic curriculum). They were interested in testing whether the relationship between school engagement and misconduct is bidirectional. In other words, they were interested in seeing whether delinquency places students at risk to become disengaged from school or whether being disengaged from school places youth at risk for delinquency. They found that the students who were emotionally and behaviorally engaged at school were less delinquent. Conversely, the students who were delinquent became less cognitively engaged with school.

The "school to prison pipeline" was identified by Christle, Jolivette, and Nelson (2005) as the process through which students become disengaged from school and drift into delinquency and crime. At the school level, Christle and colleagues found that school-level characteristics such as supportive leadership, dedicated and collegial staff, and school-wide behavior management were important protective factors. In an analysis of national data from the United States, Gottfredson and colleagues (2005) found lower rates of student delinquency and student victimization in the schools where students reported greater fairness and clarity of rules. Of note, the psychosocial climate, as measured by teacher reports of organizational focus, morale, planning, and administrative leadership was unrelated to students' reports of delinquency and victimization. The school-level factors that were linked to delinquency in this study fall into the two dimensions of Baumrind's (1991) model of parenting: love and responsivity, as well as guiding and setting expectations and limits for students' behaviors within the school.

When weak school engagement is combined with a school system that does not meet vulnerable students' developmental needs, the process of failure is set into motion. In many countries, there is a strong emphasis within education to focus almost exclusively on literacy, numeracy, and science knowledge to bolster rankings on the Organization for Economic Cooperation and Development's Program for International Student Assessment (PISA). Teachers, schools, school systems, and countries are measured and judged on students' performance in these academic areas. This concentrated academic focus contrasts with the principle of educating the whole child and has led to a strong call for a renewed focus on children and youths' social-emotional development in school (Collaborative for Academic, Social, and Emotional Learning [CASEL], 2015).

The challenge for students, especially those lacking a strong foundation at home, is that developing social-emotional capacity is much more difficult than developing numeracy and literacy. In learning to work with numbers or read letters, there are consistent 1:1 patterns that can be recognized, acquired, and repeated: 2 + 2 always equals 4 and b-o-o-k always represents book. In learning how to get along with others, diverse skills and strategies are required for relationships with familiar and unfamiliar adults and peers; furthermore, an approach that is generally successful with a specific individual may not be successful on a given day because of the circumstances (e.g., the teacher is highly stressed). Many children acquire complex social-emotional skills through naturally occurring learning opportunities in the early years; others require specific supports for social-emotional development to enable them to succeed at school and beyond.

B. Schools, Academic Performance, and Dropout

Students who perform well in academic subjects move through the school years rela-tively smoothly. In contrast, students who struggle because they lack the regulation capacity to concentrate, have had limited opportunities to learn, or have a learning dis-ability and/or mental health challenges; as a result they increasingly fall behind. A crit-ical question is why does failure in school lead to marginalization and a move into delinquency? In a foundational study, Ward and Tittle (1994) tested two competing hypotheses about why IQ and delinquency are linked. The first, "school performance" hypothesis was that students' IQ was related to their inability to perform to the standards expected of middle-class mainstream students, which fosters negative attitudes about school and, in turn, leads to delinquency. The second, "school reaction" hypothesis was that students' IQ was related to their experiences of being streamed into less challenging classrooms, resulting in lowered self-esteem, which leads to delinquency. The analyses showed that when assessed separately, both these mechanisms linking IQ and delin-quency were upheld by the data; however, when they were tested in an integrated model, the school performance hypothesis was upheld because school reaction was linked to IQ through school performance. The authors acknowledge that the associations among IQ, school performance, school bonding, and delinquency are complex, but this research points to the importance of supporting and engaging every student to achieve optimal performance and satisfaction within the school setting.

There has been a continued focus on poor school achievement and links to delin-quency. In a recent paper, Hoffman, Erickson, and Spence (2013) assessed the link be-tween academic performance and delinquent behavior by building on Thornberry and Krohn's interactional theory (see Chapter 14). With longitudinal analyses, they examined reciprocal associations among delinquent behavior, school attachment, and academic achievement. They found that academic achievement was associated with less delinquent behavior over time, as well as with higher school attachment. When examined from the reciprocal direction, delinquency was only linked to lower school attachment and did not relate directly to change in academic achievement. They sug-gest that a common cause, self-regulation, may account for the well-established link between delinquency and subsequent problems in school performance. The lack of self-regulation may also underlie youths' susceptibility to negative influences in their relationships with peers and in the broader community context.

Values may also play a role in the link between academic performance and delin-quency. Felson and colleagues (1994) found that students who value academic perfor-mance are also those who tend to have negative values against interpersonal violence, theft, vandalism, and school delinquency. They suggest that the groups who value var-ious forms of delinquency are likely to be the same groups that reject other positive values of society, such as doing well in school.

The process of disengaging from school cognitively, emotionally, and behaviorally is prolonged. In a study examining engagement, delinquency, and school dropout, Wang and Fredricks (2014) found that dropping out of school is predicted by lower behavioral and emotional engagement and higher problem behaviors. The result of this process is that the most at-risk and vulnerable youth in society become truant and eventually drop out of the school system. As indicated above, the process of disengagement that leads to truancy and dropout is dynamic, bi-directional, and embedded in the relationships that youth experience in school. In a qualitative study of early school leavers, Ferguson and colleagues (2005) found that relationships figured prominently in students' perceptions of why they had dropped out of school. Many youths who had dropped out reported that they received both direct and indirect messages from principals, vice-principals, teachers, and guidance counselors indicating that they were not wanted in the school system. Relationships with other students were also strained and were perceived as contributing to the process of disengagement from school. According to Ferguson and colleagues, "young people described troubled school cultures due to severe and on-going bullying and violence. When these issues were not clearly and swiftly addressed, students began the process of skipping school, detentions, suspensions and early leaving" (2005, p. 27). In this research, relationships were also identified as part of the protective processes that kept youth engaged with school, including caring and supportive teachers and caring, flexible, and proactive school climates.

In a study of the trajectories of school engagement and school dropout, Janosz and colleagues (2008) found that that students who experienced a rapid decrease in school engagement over the high school years, as well as those who reported low levels of school engagement at the beginning of adolescence, were more likely to drop out. There was heterogeneity among the students on the unstable engagement trajectories; however, the majority of students on these trajectories had more psychosocial and academic difficulties than those following a steady engagement path. Although boys dropped out of school at a higher rate than girls, Janosz and colleagues found that when girls follow an unstable school engagement trajectory, they are at as much risk of dropping out of schools as boys. In a subsequent study, Archambault et al. (2009) confirmed the importance of student disengagement as a factor that predicts dropout above and beyond the effects of individual and family risk factors. They found that the behavioral component of disengagement, compliance and attendance, predicted dropout better than students' cognitive or affective engagement with school. Archambault and colleagues noted that behaviors such as impoliteness, truancy, and absenteeism are related to alienation from school. Furthermore, when students are punished for these behaviors, they are further alienated, with the end result being a high probability of school dropout.

C. School and Classroom Organization

Students' experiences at school are shaped by both the quality of the interactions and the general organization of the school and classroom environments. At the classroom level, Christle and colleagues (2005) found that effective academic instruction was related to a lower level of delinquency. Similarly, Gottfredson (2001) highlighted many classroom- and school-based factors related to delinquency including a general climate of emotional support and classroom management. At the school level, she identified a strong academic mission and administrative leadership as important in preventing the move to delinquency and maintaining school engagement. Gottfredson also noted that schools can provide opportunities for students to drift into delinquency if drugs and alcohol are available and weapons are present.

Classroom climate was highlighted in a longitudinal study by Sprott (2004). She found that young people who behaved violently during early adolescence had often been in elementary school classrooms with limited emotional support from teachers and classmates. In a subsequent study, Sprott, Jenkins, and Doob (2005) found that students' strong attachment to school was associated with less violent offending in early adolescence. They concluded that school relationships may be protective if they are able to engage students for whom relationships within the family are strained.

School organization can serve a preventive function by mitigating the influences of deviant peer relationships. Zimmerman and Rees (2014) found that schools with strict policies regarding delinquency had lower levels of problem behaviors within the school. Students in schools with strict policies were less exposed to delinquent peers and thereby less susceptible to negative peer influences for smoking, drinking, and fighting. Zimmerman and colleagues suggested that school policies can serve to prevent crime by reducing the effects of associating with delinquent peers. Maimon, Antonaccio, and French (2012) found similar results regarding structured school environments with high and consistent levels of sanctions. In their research, however, the strict sanctions reduced delinquency primarily among those students who were weak in thoughtfully reflective decision-making. In other words, youths who have limited cognitive capacities fare better in schools where the expectations and rules are clear and sanctions are consistently applied. Maimon and colleagues postulated that students with weak cognitive skills may fare better in highly structured school environments with consistent sanctioning because the increased social control and sanctions serve as disincentives and limit their perspectives of available delinquent responses.

Research by Danbrook, Hymel, and Waterhouse (2012) highlighted the supportive function of positive relationships within the school context. They tested three aspects of school climate: school involvement, perceived peer support, and perceived adult support. They found that perceived peer and adult support, but not school involvement, moderated the relationship between victimization and school violence. Specifically, highly victimized students were more likely to engage in physical violence as their perceived levels of peer and adult support at school diminished. The quality of relationships was particularly important with regard to weapon carrying: highly victimized students were more likely to report bringing weapons to school when they had reported low support from other students. Conversely, students who reported low levels of victimization and high levels of adult support were less likely to bring weapons to school. Danbrook and colleagues (2012) concluded that support from both adults and peers in the school context appeared to mitigate the link between victimization and school violence. They noted that for marginalized and victimized students, high-quality school relationships can reduce the likelihood of high-risk behaviors for vulnerable students, including the use of physical aggression and carrying weapons to protect themselves from the ongoing abuse of their peers.

D. Relationships with Teachers

In their landmark longitudinal study, Werner and Smith (1982) examined the factors that enabled children to thrive in spite of many challenges in their lives. They found that those children who thrived had positive relationships with their teachers. Their teachers were not only supportive academically but also provided caring, compassionate support and served as positive role models for the vulnerable children. Werner and Smith's research reveals that the teachers were operating *in loco parentis* by providing both dimensions of Baumrind's model: care and guidance. The challenge in providing these two dimensions of support may be overwhelming for teachers when dealing with undersocialized students.

Our observational research of aggressive elementary school students revealed this challenge in that these students are most likely to be involved in disruptive and bullying behaviors in the classroom (Atlas and Pepler 1998). Without a high level of awareness about the needs of specific children and mindfulness about one's own responses to troubled children, teachers may experience difficulties engaging and supporting the students who are most disruptive and defiant. As Boyce and colleagues (2012) have shown, teachers' child-centered teaching practices mitigate the psychosocial difficulties of children who are vulnerable because of their social position within a classroom. When teachers were able to create supportive classroom climates for the most vulnerable children, the deleterious effects of being marginalized within the peer social structure were mitigated, leading Boyce and colleagues to call for "more supportive, egalitarian, and generous social environments" (2012, p. 17171).

Farmer, Lines, and Hamm (2011) reintroduced Robert Cairns's concept of the teacher having an "invisible hand" as a way to describe teachers' subtle influences on their students' academic learning, emotional and behavioral development, and peer relationships. They note that teachers have two essential roles in the classroom. First, teachers are responsible for promoting learning, reinforcing appropriate behaviors, and correcting inappropriate behaviors. Their second role relates to students' social interactions and positive peer dynamics, which they can shape by managing classroom activities and organizing students' groupings to include marginalized students and ensure that groupings mitigate deviant peer processes. We have described this responsibility as social architecture—organizing children's peer groupings to promote optimal peer dynamics (Pepler 2006).

The World Health Organization's Health Behaviors of School-Aged Children survey assesses the quality of students' relationships with their teachers with five statements: I feel that my teachers care about me as a person; I feel that my teachers accept me as I am; I feel a lot of trust in my teachers; My teachers are interested in me as a student; and My teachers listen to how I would like to do things. The proportion of students who report high-quality relationships with their teachers decreases from the middle school to high school years (Pepler et al. 2012); therefore, it is important that high-quality teacher–student relationships are established in the early school years. When students have a positive relationship with their teachers, they can thrive throughout their school careers. For aggressive children, however, a strained relationship with teachers starts at school entry and increases over the course of the school year (Doumen et al. 2008). Teachers' low preference for students relates not only to declining grades but also to increased loneliness (Mercer and DeRosier 2008). Therefore, a conflictual teacher–student relationship may exacerbate vulnerable children's behavioral and emotional adjustment problems and initiate the process of alienation and marginalization from both staff and peers within the school context.

The quality of the teacher–student relationship arises, as with other relationships, through bi-directional processes. Liljeberg and colleagues (2011) studied the links between teacher–student relationships and delinquency through a longitudinal study. Students' attachment was measured by their interpersonal relations with school staff, including the feeling of being supported and understood by them. They also measured students' defiance of teachers in terms of hostile attitudes toward teachers. They found reciprocal effects between delinquency and general school connectedness for both boys and girls. In terms of the teacher–student relationships, students who had poor attachments to their teachers at Time 1 were more likely to be delinquent at Time 2. Conversely, students who were high on delinquency at Time 1 were more likely to have poor teacher attachment at Time 2. Poor teacher attachment was more strongly associated with delinquency for boys than for girls.

The researchers analyzed further to determine whether defiance toward teachers underlies the link between delinquent behavior at Time 1 and poor teacher attachment at Time 2. They found that when defiance toward teachers was entered into the model testing the links between teacher attachment and delinquency, delinquency no longer predicted worse teacher attachment over time, whereas teacher defiance did. Liljeberg and colleagues (2011) discussed gender differences in the links between attachment and delinquency. For boys, it appears that the likelihood of increasing in delinquency is related to all aspects of school bonding—the connectedness to school, academic engagement, and the quality of relationships with teachers. For girls, it was the quality of relationships with teachers that most strongly predicted the likelihood to engage in delinquency.

The quality of the teacher–student relationship was one focus of Brendgen and colleagues' (2011) research on gene by environment interactions. They assessed the effects of this important relationship for children with a genetic vulnerability to be aggressive. They found the expected genetic effects accounting for a significant proportion of the variance in children's aggressive behaviors. The genetic effects, however, were exacerbated when the children had a high-conflict and distant relationship with their teachers. Conversely, the genetic effects on children's aggressive behaviors were reduced for children who had a close and low-conflict relationship with their teachers.

Consistent with Boyce and colleagues' (2012) research, this study indicates that high-quality teacher–student relationships may be especially important for the most vulnerable students.

Research points to the important impact that teachers can have on children's developmental pathway into problem behavior and delinquency. The evidence points to the importance of Baumrind's two parenting dimensions—warmth and responsivity—as well as guidance and setting expectations and limits. When teachers are able to foster warm relationships with their students (particularly those at risk for aggressive behavior problems) and are able to create and manage a classroom context that promotes positive behaviors and engagement, then students are able to flourish. The paradox is that these two dimensions of the teacher–student relationship are most important for those students who are most vulnerable for moving onto a pathway to crime and these are the students who are often least likable and most troublesome in the classroom. Without warm, reflective, and effective teachers, vulnerable students are at risk of becoming increasingly alienated and marginalized within the classroom and broader school context.

E. Relationships with Peers

Peer relationships also play an important role in exacerbating or mitigating children's risk of moving into delinquency and crime. In their seminal review of peer influences in two interventions and a summer program, Dishion, McCord, and Poulin (1999) concluded that high-risk youth were susceptible to "deviancy training" within their peer groups and that friendships among deviant peers predicted increases in delinquency, substance use, violence, and maladjustment in adulthood. They highlighted two mechanisms within deviancy training that may propel youth along a troubled pathway: first, when youth are reinforced for their deviant behavior by peers who laugh or pay attention, it is likely to increase the problem behavior; second, high-risk youths value the deviancy training and become increasingly motivated to engage in problem behavior.

The peer processes at school that potentially contribute to a pathway to crime occur through both commission and omission. Our observations of bullying at school provide evidence for the behaviors committed within peer dynamics that promote deviant peer processes. We found that peers were present in 85 percent of bullying episodes and they spent 75 percent of the time paying attention to the child who is bullying (Craig and Pepler 1997). They played an active role in exacerbating the aggression: when a peer joined in bullying, the child who had initiated the bullying became increasingly aggressive and aroused (O'Connell, Pepler, and Craig 1999). Furthermore, the deviant peer influences were bi-directional: bystanders were much more likely to join the bullying when incited to do so by the child who had initiated the episode (O'Connell et al. 1999).

Another problem is that peers may respond negatively toward aggressive children. Our observations of aggressive children on the school playground indicated that they have higher rates of verbal and physical aggression than nonaggressive children (Pepler, Craig, and Roberts 1998). Since 22 percent of aggressive behaviors elicit an aggressive response from peers, it follows that aggressive children are on the receiving end of aggressive behaviors more often than their nonaggressive peers. In their research on young elementary school children, Brendgen and colleagues (2011) found that the likelihood of being victimized by peers was in part related to the genetic vulnerability for aggressive behavior. In other words, those children who have a genetic predisposition to be aggressive are more vulnerable to being bullied by their peers.

Within peer groups at school, there may also be natural processes of omission that contribute to aggressive children's drifting to the margins and becoming alienated. Given aggressive children's dysregulated interactional style, other children may not actively choose to play with them. Through our observations in elementary schools, we discovered that aggressive children have less predictable interaction styles than their non-aggressive peers (Pepler et al. 1998). They exhibit more mixed behaviors in which they initiate an aggressive (or prosocial) behavior, fail to wait for the peer to respond, and immediately follow with a prosocial (or aggressive) behavior directed at a peer. Therefore, classmates may be similar to teachers in finding aggressive children difficult to interact with and challenging to have in the classroom. When aggressive children are marginalized in the classroom or peer group, they may find that the available peers are those who are similar to themselves, with a tendency for aggression and problem behaviors. This association with similarly deviant peers was true of students who maintained high levels of bullying over the course of elementary and high school: they were significantly more likely than non-bullying students to have friends who were also involved in bullying (Pepler et al. 2008).

The nature of peer relations and the link to the pathway to crime is dynamic and multi-determined. First, students' individual characteristics play a role: those students who have low engagement with school become less connected to peers, which in turn leads to processes of peer rejection (Hirschfeld and Gasper 2011). Second, teachers' preferences, or more accurately their lack of preference for aggressive students, is linked to increases in peer disliking and rejection (Mercer and DeRosier 2008). Conversely, peer rejection also predicted lower teacher preference. Third, classroom norms shape the levels of individual students' aggression and experiences of victimization (Mercer, McMillan, and DeRosier 2010). Fourth, in special education classrooms where aggressive students are aggregated, deviancy training tends to flourish and students' problem behaviors are exacerbated (Dodge, Dishion, and Lansford 2006). Finally, there are school-level effects on students' likelihood of being influenced by peers to engage in delinquent activities. Zimmerman and Rees (2014) found that in schools with strict and consistently applied policies regarding smoking, drinking, and fighting, the peer effects on delinquency were attenuated. They noted that the mechanisms are complex and interactive but suggest that strict school-level policies may not only signal to students the potential discipline consequences but also the school staff's concern for students' well-being, thereby shaping individual students' decisions to participate or not in criminal behavior.

III. CONCLUSION

A. Theory and Research

In considering the role of schools in the pathway to crime, the theoretical perspectives focus our attention on social bonds (Hirschi 1969), the importance of relationships in establishing the long-term potential for criminal behavior (see Chapter 11), and on interactions within the family and beyond that shape the development of criminal behavior. In her book *Schools and Delinquency*, Gottfredson (2001) highlights functional and structural aspects of schools that relate to delinquency. The current research focuses attention on students' experience in relationships with their principals, teachers, other school staff, and peers within the school context. At this point, there is a need to advance both the theory and research to understand the moment-to-moment interactions in these relationships that shape students' knowledge, attitudes, and behaviors throughout the formative school years and either engage them in the socialization process or fail to connect with them. Theory and research need to take heterogeneity into account: some students within the system are more vulnerable than others. If children enter school with a genetic vulnerability and inadequate socialization experiences from home and/or daycare, they place a burden on an already stressed school system. Nevertheless, there is tremendous potential to identify these vulnerable children early in their school careers and provide the ongoing instrumental and social-emotional support that they require to be diverted from a troubled pathway.

The research on the development of delinquency raises a critical question: Whose responsibility is it to help children when their families have not been able to socialize them and pass on society's moral values (Skrzypiec, 2013)? If schools are to operate *in loco parentis*, then we need to consider schools' roles in ensuring that children experience being valued, cared for, guided, directed, and corrected. Schools have a critical role in collaborating with families in meeting children's basic needs—to be educated not only for academic capacities, but also for social-emotional capacities. The research reviewed in this chapter on the role of schools in the development of criminality points to both practice and policy implications to ensure that all children, especially the most vulnerable, are nurtured and supported within the school system.

B. Practice

Loeber, Farrington, and Petechuk (2003) have written about the seven years of warning signs before a youth enters delinquency. They note that most youths who become serious, violent, and chronic juvenile offenders by age 15 have a history of problem behaviors that started about seven years earlier in childhood. Loeber and colleagues note that it is not possible to identify which children will proceed from initial problem behavior to serious offending. They argue, therefore, that it is better to tackle problem behaviors during the preschool and elementary school years, before these children develop serious and consolidated antisocial behavior patterns.

There are now many prevention and early intervention programs that have been documented as effective. One such program, Stop Now and Plan®—SNAP, has recently been evaluated with a randomized controlled treatment effectiveness trial (Burke and Loeber 2015). The SNAP® program for 6- to 12-year-old boys was compared to treatment as usual. The boys in the SNAP® program had significantly decreased aggression, conduct, externalizing behavior, oppositional defiant disorder, and attention deficit hyperactivity disorder symptoms, compared to boys in treatment as usual. The SNAP® program boys were also lower on internalizing symptoms (depression and anxiety) than comparison boys. The greatest improvement among the SNAP® boys was found for those who were at highest risk. The effect sizes associated with the SNAP® program were .29 and .31 for externalizing and internalizing problems, respectively. Farrington and Koegl (2015) assessed the monetary benefits and costs of the SNAP® program as related to boys' future criminal involvement. The cost savings with the recorded and undetected offenses included were between $17.33 and $31.77 for every $1 spent on the program. Farrington and Koegl argue for early identification and intervention for youth at risk of following the pathway to crime.

The highest-risk children in schools present with multiple individual, family, school, and peer problems. In many cases, these children and families may need intensive services to meet their needs. Data from the SNAP® program reveal that high-risk boys who received an enhanced relationship intervention improved the most (Augimeri et al. 2006). These boys had received a "befriending" intervention through which they developed a relationship with a caring mentor who met with them weekly and engaged them in community activities. Interventions for high-risk youth need to scaffold for their diverse and interrelated social-emotional, academic, and relational needs (Pepler 2006).

The peer context within the school plays an important role in shaping antisocial behaviors (Dodge et al. 2006). Children with behavior problems are often aggregated in special classrooms—a practice that creates a context for deviance training as described by Dishion and colleagues (1999). For school staff and other organizations, such as juvenile detention centers, aggregating difficult students may be easier than having them integrated into regular classrooms; however, for these students and for society, this strategy presents a grave concern if it accelerates the move to deviance and crime (Dodge et al., 2006). New research on teachers' "invisible hand" in managing the classroom highlights the importance of attunement to individual students and the peer dynamics (Farmer et al., 2011). We have described teachers' responsibility for social architecture, which we identify as strategically organizing peer groupings to minimize deviant peer processes and maximize inclusion, acceptance, and positive interactions among peers (Pepler 2006). A reorientation to the social world of students within schools rather than a singular focus on academic performance will require a reorientation of post-secondary education of prospective teachers and a redirection of educational policy.

C. Policy

The critical question for policy in education is: What is the goal for all students? If the goal is to educate "the whole child" and provide a socialization experience to prepare all children and youth for a productive and happy adulthood, then there is a moral dilemma to be considered. At present the relationship dynamics within the school system often appear to marginalize and alienate those children and youth who most need the support from caring adults. The discipline system may also comprise a process that contributes to students' disengagement and alienation from the one system that may be safe and able to support them.

Over the past two decades, there has been a growing concern about school violence, bullying, harassment, and safe schools. The policies that have been developed to ensure safety at school identify the problem behaviors exhibited by students and assign discipline consequences for these behaviors. The consequences often intensify with repeated offenses, leading to exclusionary practices of suspension and expulsion. Morrison and Vaandering (2012) have analyzed the differences in punitive and restorative practices, both of which are focused on accountability when there has been a problem. They illustrate how the predominant policy paradigm in school systems focuses on a framework of rules and regulations, with clearly stated punitive consequences for a range of transgressions. The desired outcome of the punitive approach is for the offender to be punished; decisions about the offense and consequences are made by a third party (e.g., principal), who works to bring students' behaviors into line with the rules through punishment. In contrast, the desired outcome for restorative processes is to repair the harm and restore damaged relationships. Restorative processes include the perpetrator(s), the individual(s) harmed, other community members, and relevant school staff. Decisions are facilitated with the individuals involved to achieve an appropriate resolution of the problem, with strong emotional engagement to build understanding and move toward reconciliation. The restorative process is primarily educational and instructive for the students who have offended, and the goal is repair, restitution, and restoring relationships.

The challenge for policy is to find the balance between the critical concern to ensure that students and staff in schools are safe and the critical need to educate and rehabilitate children and youth who have started along the pathway to crime. Given the mounting evidence regarding the importance of school relationships for children and youths' healthy development, the time has come to re-examine educational policies and legislation in light of children's social-emotional development. It is essential to consider what children need to support their holistic development and what is required for schools to operate effectively *in loco parentis*. The challenge is to find the balance in setting expectations, limits, and consequences. Troubled students need to understand expectations and experience consequences when they do not meet or transgress these expectations; however, as Baumrind (1991) points out, consequences need to be meted out in a way that is balanced with warmth, care, and concern.

The cost of not intervening to support children who have started into the seven- year warning period is too great (Loeber et al. 2003). Those children and youth who are not engaged and connected with school are most likely to drop out. Dropping out of school is associated with a myriad of poor health and quality of life outcomes (Freudenberg and Ruglis 2007). Recent research helps to reveal that the school-to-prison pipeline is essentially a process of being marginalized and alienated within the school system; it is the sense of disconnection from important school relationships that leads youth to follow a pathway to crime. A recent analysis of the prison population in Canada demonstrated the costs of school alienation and dropout: whereas about one-third of the population in British Columbia has dropped out of high school, three-fourths of those in prison are high school dropouts. The costs of failing to ensure that children have adequate socialization and education experiences are too high at individual, family, community, and societal levels. The solutions lie in enhancing the moment-to-moment interactions with children and youth in the school context to ensure that they have healthy relationships to promote their healthy development.

The research reviewed in this chapter indicates that vulnerable children and youths' propensity to follow a pathway to crime is shaped or diverted to a large extent by the quality of relationships that they experience within multiple systems in the home, at school, and in the community over the course of their school career. As Loeber and Farrington (2001) highlighted in their edited volume, *Child Delinquents*, the risk and protective processes that operate to draw children into delinquency begin in the early years and compound through strained relationships and risky contexts over time. In the school setting, the process of disengagement and the associated pathway to delinquency may begin at the moment of school entry (Hirschfeld and Gasper 2011). A focus on relationships highlights the potential moment-to-moment experiences in students' lives at school, which either engage them in the school community and learning process or accumulate to alienate them and enable them to drift to the margins.

The field of developmental criminology has made great strides over the past few decades and the rates of youth violence have decreased. Nevertheless, there are children and youth in society who are vulnerable and often very challenging. These are the children who need to be identified early and supported in schools with a true *in loco parentis* approach, with an appropriate balance of care and guidance, to accelerate their social-emotional development and their capacity to engage in healthy relationships for their healthy development through the life span.

REFERENCES

Archambault, Isabelle, Michel Janosz, Jean-Sébastien Fallu, and Linda S. Pagani. 2009. "Student Engagement and Its Relationship with Early High School Dropout." *Journal of Adolescence* 32: 651–670.

Atlas, Rona, and Pepler, Debra J. 1998. "Observations of Bullying in the Classroom." *Journal of Educational Research* 92: 86–99.

Augimeri, Leena K., Depeng Jiang, Christopher J. Koegl, and John Carey. 2006. "Differential Effects of the Under 12 Outreach Project (ORP) Associated with Client Risk and Treatment Intensity." Report prepared for the Child Development Institute, Toronto, Canada.

Baumrind, Diana. 1991. "The Influence of Parenting Style on Adolescent Competence and Substance Use." *Journal of Early Adolescence* 11: 56–95.

Boyce, W. Thomas, Jelena Obradović, Nicole R. Bush, Juliet Stamperdahl, Young Shin Kim, and Nancy Adler. 2012. "Social Stratification, Classroom Climate, and the Behavioral Adaptation of Kindergarten Children." *Proceedings of the National Academy of Sciences* 109: 17168–17173.

Brendgen, Mara, Michel Boivin, Ginette Dionne, Edward D. Barker, Frank Vitaro, Alain Girard, Richard Tremblay, and Daniel Pérusse. 2011. "Gene–Environment Processes Linking Aggression, Peer Victimization, and the Teacher–Child Relationship." *Child Development* 82: 2021–2036.

Brezina, Timothy, Alex R. Piquero, and Paul Mazerolle. 2001. "Student Anger and Aggressive Behavior in School: An Initial Test of Agnew's Macro-Level Strain Theory." *Journal of Research in Crime and Delinquency* 38: 362–386.

Burke, Jeffrey D., and Rolf Loeber. 2015. "Mechanisms of Behavioral and Affective Treatment Outcomes in a Cognitive Behavioral Intervention for Boys." *Journal of Abnormal Child Psychology* 44: 1–11.

Collaborative for Academic, Social, and Emotional Learning (CASEL). 2015. "Policy Recommendations to Sustain SEL." http://www.casel.org/policy/recommendations.

Catalano, Richard F., and J. David Hawkins. 1996. "The Social Development Model: A Theory of Antisocial Behavior." In *Delinquency and Crime: Current Theories*, edited by David J. Hawkins, xxx–xxx. Cambridge, UK: Cambridge University Press.

Centers for Disease Control. 2015. "Youth Violence: National Statistics." http://www.cdc.gov/violenceprevention/youthviolence/stats_at-a_glance/vca_temp-trends.html.

Christle, Christine A., Kristine Jolivette, and C. Michael Nelson. 2005. "Breaking The School-to-Prison Pipeline: Identifying School Risk and Protective Factors for Youth Delinquency." *Exceptionality* 13: 69–88.

Craig, Wendy M., and Debra J. Pepler. 1997. "Observations of Bullying and Victimization in the School Yard." *Canadian Journal of School Psychology* 13: 41–59.

Craig, W., and D. Pepler. 2014. *Trends in Healthy Development and Healthy Relationships*. Report submitted to the Public Health Agency Canada. www.prevnet.ca.

Cullen, Francis T., and Robert Agnew. 2003. *Criminological Theory. Past to Present. Essential Readings*. 2nd ed. Los Angeles: Roxbury.

Danbrook, M. C., Shelley Hymel, and Terry Waterhouse. 2012. "Peer Victimization and School Violence: Does School Climate Matter?" Paper presented at the biennial meeting of the International Society for the Study of Behavioural Development. Edmonton, AB.

Dishion, Thomas J., Joan McCord, and Francois Poulin.1999. "When Interventions Harm: Peer Groups and Problem Behavior." *American Psychologist* 54: 755.

Dodge, K. A., T. J. Dishion, and J. E. Lansford. 2006. "Deviant Peer Influences in Intervention and Public Policy for Youth." *Social Policy Report* 20: 1–19.

Dodge, K. A., Patrick S. Malone, Jennifer E. Lansford, Sherry Miller, Gregory S. Pettit, and Jack E. Bates. 2009. "A Dynamic Cascade Model of the Development of Substance-Use Onset." *Monographs of the Society for Research in Child Development* 74: 1–134.

Doumen, Sarah, Karine Verschueren, Evelien Buyse, Veerle Germeijs, Koen Luyckx, and Bart Soenens. 2008. "Reciprocal Relations Between Teacher–Child Conflict and Aggressive

Behavior in Kindergarten: A Three-Wave Longitudinal Study." *Journal of Clinical Child and Adolescent Psychology* 37: 588–599.

Farmer, Thomas W., Meghan McAuliffe Lines, and Jill V. Hamm. 2011. "Revealing the Invisible Hand: The Role of Teachers in Children's Peer Experiences." *Journal of Applied Developmental Psychology* 32: 247–256.

Farrington, David P., and Christopher J. Koegl. 2015. "Monetary Benefits and Costs of the Stop Now and Plan Program for Boys Aged 6–11, Based on the Prevention of Later Offending," *Journal of Quantitative Criminology* 31: 263–287.

Farrington, David P., and Tara R. McGee. 2017. "The Integrated Cognitive Antisocial Potential (ICAP) Theory: New Empirical Tests." In *The Oxford Handbook on Developmental and Life-Course Criminology*, edited by David P. Farrington, Lila Kazemian, and Alex R. Piquero. New York: Oxford University Press.

Federal Bureau of Investigation. 2015. "The School Shooter: A Quick Reference Guide." http://info.publicintelligence.net/FBI_The_School_Shooter_A_Quick_Reference_Guide.pdf.

Felson, Richard B., Allen E. Liska, Scott J. South, and Thomas L. McNulty. 1994. "The Subculture of Violence and Delinquency: Individual vs. School Context Effects." *Social Forces* 73: 155–173.

Ferguson, Bruce, Kate Tilleczek, Katherine Boydell, Joanna Anneke Rummens, Dara Roth Edney, and Jacques Michaud. 2005. *Early School Leavers: Understanding the Lived Reality of Student Disengagement from Secondary School*. Report submitted to the Ontario Ministry of Education and Training, Special Education Branch.

Freudenberg, Nicholas, and Jessica Ruglis. 2007. "Reframing School Dropout as a Public Health Issue." *Preventing Chronic Disease* 4: 4.

Gottfredson, Denise C. 2001. *Schools and Delinquency*. Cambridge, UK: Cambridge University Press.

Gottfredson, Gary D., Denise C. Gottfredson, Allison Ann Payne, and Nisha C. Gottfredson. 2005. "School Climate Predictors of School Disorder: Results from a National Study of Delinquency Prevention in Schools." *Journal of Research in Crime and Delinquency* 42: 412–444.

Gottfredson, Michael R., and Travis Hirschi. 1990. *A General Theory of Crime*. Stanford, CA: Stanford University Press.

Hirschfield, Paul J., and Joseph Gasper. 2011. "The Relationship Between School Engagement and Delinquency in Late Childhood and Early Adolescence." *Journal of Youth and Adolescence* 40: 3–22.

Hirschi, Travis. 1969. "A Control Theory of Delinquency." In *Criminology Theory: Selected Classic Readings*, edited by Frank P. Williams and Marilyn D. McShane. New York: Routledge.

Hoffmann, John P., Lance D. Erickson, and Karen R. Spence. 2013. "Modeling the Association Between Academic Achievement and Delinquency: An Application of Interactional Theory." *Criminology* 51: 629–660.

Jang, Sung Joon. 1999. "Age-Varying Effects of Family, School, and Peers on Delinquency: A Multilevel Modeling Test of Interactional Theory." *Criminology* 37: 643–686.

Janosz, Michel, Isabelle Archambault, Julien Morizot, and Linda S. Pagani. 2008. "School Engagement Trajectories and Their Differential Predictive Relations to Dropout." *Journal of Social Issues* 64: 21–40.

Kuperminc, Gabriel P., Bonnie J. Leadbeater, and Sidney J. Blatt. 2001. "School Social Climate and Individual Differences in Vulnerability to Psychopathology Among Middle School Students." *Journal of School Psychology* 39: 141–159.

Le, Thao N., and Gary Stockdale. 2011. "The Influence of School Demographic Factors and Perceived Student Discrimination on Delinquency Trajectory in Adolescence." *Journal of Adolescent Health* 49: 407–413.

Liljeberg, Jenny Freidenfelt, Jenny M. Eklund, Marie Väfors Fritz, and Britt af Klinteberg. 2011. "Poor School Bonding and Delinquency Over Time: Bidirectional Effects and Sex Differences." *Journal of Adolescence* 34: 1–9.

Loeber, Rolf, and David P. Farrington, eds. 2001. *Child Delinquents: Development, Intervention, and Service Needs.* Thousand Oaks, CA: Sage.

Loeber, Rolf, David P. Farrington, and David Petechuk. 2003. *Child Delinquency: Early Intervention and Prevention.* Washington, DC: US Department of Justice, Office of Justice Programs, Office of Juvenile Justice and Delinquency Prevention.

Maimon, David, Olena Antonaccio, and Michael T. French. 2012. "Severe Sanctions, Easy Choice? Investigating the Role of School Sanctions in Preventing Adolescent Violent Offending." *Criminology* 50: 495–524.

Mercer, Sterett H., and Melissa E. DeRosier. 2008. "Teacher Preference, Peer Rejection, and Student Aggression: A Prospective Study of Transactional Influence and Independent Contributions to Emotional Adjustment and Grades." *Journal of School Psychology* 46: 661–685.

Mercer, Sterett H., Janey Sturtz McMillen, and Melissa E. DeRosier. 2009. "Predicting Change in Children's Aggression and Victimization Using Classroom-Level Descriptive Norms of Aggression and Pro-Social Behavior." *Journal of School Psychology* 47: 267–289.

Morrison, Brenda E., and Dorothy Vaandering. 2012. "Restorative Justice: Pedagogy, Praxis, and Discipline." *Journal of School Violence* 11: 138–155.

National Scientific Council on the Developing Child. (2004). *Young People Develop in an Environment of Relationships: Working Paper No. 1.* http://www.developingchild.net.

O'Connell, Paul, Debra Pepler, and Wendy Craig. (1999). "Peer Involvement in Bullying: Insights and Challenges for Intervention." *Journal of Adolescence* 22: 437–452.

Pepler, Debra J. 2006. "Bullying Interventions: A Binocular Perspective." *Journal of the Canadian Academy of Child and Adolescent Psychiatry* 15: 16–20.

Pepler, D., W. Craig, and D. Haner. (2012). *Healthy Development Depends on Healthy Relationships.* Report submitted to the Public Health Agency Canada. www.prevnet.ca/sites/prevnet.ca/files/HealthyRelationshipsPaper.pdf.

Pepler, Debra J., Wendy M. Craig, and William L. Roberts. 1998. "Observations of Aggressive and Nonaggressive Children on the School Playground." *Merrill-Palmer Quarterly* 55–76.

Pepler, Debra, Depeng Jiang, Wendy Craig, and Jennifer Connolly. 2008. "Developmental Trajectories of Bullying and Associated Factors." *Child Development* 79: 325–338.

Pepler, Debra J., Depeng Jiang, Wendy M. Craig, and Jennifer Connolly. 2010. "Developmental Trajectories of Girls' and Boys' Delinquency and Associated Problems." *Journal of Abnormal Child Psychology* 38: 1033–1044.

Sander, Janay B., Erika A. Patall, Laura A. Amoscato, Alexandra L. Fisher, and Catherine Funk. 2012. "A Meta-Analysis of the Effect of Juvenile Delinquency Interventions on Academic Outcomes." *Children and Youth Services Review* 34: 1695–1708.

Search Institute. 2014. "Development Relationships." http://www.search-institute.org/what-we-study/developmental-relationships.

Skrzypiec, Grace. 2013. "Adolescents' Beliefs About Why Young People Commit Crime." *Australian Journal of Guidance and Counselling* 23: 185–200.

Sprott, Jane B. 2004. "The Development of Early Delinquency: Can Classroom and School Climates Make a Difference?" *Canadian Journal of Criminology and Criminal Justice* 46: 553–572.

Sprott, Jane B., Jennifer M. Jenkins, and Anthony N. Doob. 2005. "The Importance of School Protecting At-Risk Youth from Early Offending." *Youth Violence and Juvenile Justice* 3: 59–77.

Stattin, Häkan, and Margaret Kerr. 2000. "Parental Monitoring: A Reinterpretation." *Child Development* 71: 1072–1085.

Thornberry, Terence P., and Marvin D. Krohn (2017). "Interactional Theory." In *The Oxford Handbook on Developmental and Life-Course Criminology*, edited by David P. Farrington, Lila Kazemian, and Alex R. Piquero. New York: Oxford University Press.

Wang, Ming-Te, and Jennifer A. Fredricks. 2014. "The Reciprocal Links Between School Engagement, Youth Problem Behaviors, and School Dropout During Adolescence." *Child Development* 85: 722–737.

Ward, David A., and Charles R. Tittle. 1994. "IQ and Delinquency: A Test of Two Competing Explanations." *Journal of Quantitative Criminology* 10: 189–212.

Werner, Emmy E., and Ruth S. Smith. 1982. *Vulnerable but Invincible: A Study of Resilient Children and Youth*. New York: McGraw-Hill.

Zimmerman, Gregory M., and Carter Rees. 2014. "Do School Disciplinary Policies Have Positive Social Impacts? Examining the Attenuating Effects of School Policies on the Relationship Between Personal and Peer Delinquency." *Journal of Criminal Justice* 42: 54–65.

CHAPTER 22

....

DEVELOPMENTAL INFLUENCES OF SUBSTANCE USE ON CRIMINAL OFFENDING

....

HELENE RASKIN WHITE[*]

DEVELOPMENTAL criminology focuses primarily on temporal within-individual changes in criminal offending and other deviant behaviors throughout the life course (Le Blanc and Loeber 1998). This chapter focuses on the developmental influence of substance use on criminal behavior. Although both substance use and criminal offending are considered forms of deviant behavior (Le Blanc 2009), Le Blanc and Loeber (1998) suggested that it is possible to think of all types of deviance as part of a general deviance (or problem behavior) syndrome but at the same time to acknowledge that this general pattern can be subdivided into different types of deviance. By studying these behaviors as two distinct forms of deviance, one can examine how substance use acts as a precursor to offending and, thereby, be in a better position to inform preventive interventions.

Specifically, this chapter will investigate how substance use might increase the risk of offending with an emphasis on developmental trajectories of substance use and their influence on offending. Developmental trajectories are an important parameter of interest to developmental criminologists (Loeber and Le Blanc 1990). A developmental trajectory is the "description of systemic developmental changes in offending" (Loeber

[*] Portions of this essay were excerpted from Helene R. White, 2016. "Substance Use and Crime." In *The Oxford Handbook of Substance Use and Substance Use Disorders*, Vol. 2, edited by Kenneth J. Sher. Oxford: Oxford University Press; and Helene R. White, 2015. "A Developmental Approach to Understanding the Substance Use-Crime Connection." In *The Development of Criminal and Antisocial Behavior: Theory, Research and Practical Applications*, edited by Julien Morizot and Lila Kazemian. New York: Springer.

and Le Blanc 1990, p. 382). Loeber and Le Blanc (1990) argued that there are multiple trajectories that reflect individual differences in the development of deviance. An advantage of studying trajectories is that they allow for the study of individual differences within a developmental perspective. An ultimate goal of studying trajectories is to identify etiological factors for and precursors of various developmental stages so that they can be targeted in preventive interventions (Le Blanc and Loeber 1998).

There are three primary ways (although not mutually exclusive) by which substance use can directly impact criminal offending: (1) acute and chronic psychopharmacological effects of drugs on behavior; (2) the need for drugs creating an economic motivation for criminal offending; and (3) socioenvironmental/contextual influences, specifically involvement in drug-using and drug-selling networks (Goldstein 1985; White and Gorman 2000). This essay focuses on the developmental influences of substance use on criminal offending with the acknowledgment that criminal behavior can influence substance use and that the association between these two behaviors can be reciprocal or spurious. For example, criminal behavior can induce drug use because of having extra money to spend, reinforcement from deviant peers groups, and other lifestyle factors (Bennett and Holloway 2006; Brunelle et al. 2014; Collins and Messerschmidt 1993; Welte et al. 2005). Furthermore, some offenders use drugs to justify or excuse their criminal behavior, to give themselves the courage to commit a crime, or simply to have fun while committing a crime (Brunelle, Brochu, and Cousineau 2010; Brunelle et al. 2014; Zhang, Welte, and Wieczorek 2002).

For some individuals (especially adolescents), the relationship between substance use and criminal offending may be spurious or coincidental because both forms of deviance share similar underlying predictors (e.g., impulsivity, low self-control, childhood victimization, poor parenting) (Brunelle et al. 2014; Hawkins, Catalano, and Miller 1992; Kirschbaum et al. 2013; White 2016). This essay does not focus on this "common cause" model (but see White 2016 for details); instead, it focuses on the influence of substance use on offending.

There are two main sections of this chapter. Section I describes three models that explain how substance use directly influences criminal offending: the psychopharmacological model, the economic motivation model, and the socioenvironmental/contextual model. Section II provides an overview of empirical studies examining developmental influences of substance use on criminal behavior. First, studies examining contemporaneous and lagged associations are briefly summarized. Then, studies that have examined how trajectories of alcohol and marijuana use predict later criminal offending are reviewed. The section ends with a brief discussion of the effects of substance use on desistance and persistence of criminal offending. The concluding section (Section III) summarizes the previous two sections and recommends areas for future research. For this chapter, substance use includes alcohol, illicit drugs (e.g., marijuana, cocaine, heroin), and non-medical use of prescription drugs (e.g., pain killers, tranquilizers, amphetamines, sedatives, etc.). Criminal offending includes adolescent delinquent behavior (e.g., fighting, theft, vandalism, assault) and adult criminal behavior (e.g., armed robbery, rape, assault, theft). Drug dealing and its influence on non–drug-related offending is also addressed.

I. Explanatory Models

A. The Psychopharmacological Model

The psychopharmacological model proposes that the effects of intoxication (including disinhibition, cognitive-perceptual distortions, attention deficits, bad judgment, and neurochemical changes) increase the risk for criminal (especially violent and impulsive) behavior (White 2016). In other words, intoxication causes cognitive disruption and impairs cognitive processes that would normally inhibit aggressive responding (Giancola 2002). Whereas experimental studies provide strong support for a relationship between alcohol intoxication and aggression, findings also indicate that the effects of alcohol use on aggression are moderated by subject characteristics (e.g., propensity toward aggression), experimental design conditions (e.g., alternatives to aggression), and beverage characteristics (e.g., dose, type) (Chermack and Giancola 1997; Gustafson 1993; Ito, Miller, and Pollock 1996).

Although the psychopharmacological model has been mostly attributed to alcohol and violent crime, other drugs with similar psychoactive properties to alcohol (e.g., barbiturates and tranquilizers) may have similar effects on violence (Lundholm et al. 2013). In addition, some studies suggest that stimulants (e.g., crack cocaine and amphetamines) and various steroids increase violence (Pihl and Sutton 2009), although the results have been mixed (Lundholm et al. 2013). Intoxication from marijuana and heroin generally has not been found to increase aggression, although the effects of specific drugs on violence often depend on dosage (Haggård-Grann et al. 2006; Lundholm et al. 2013; Miczek et al. 1994). Furthermore, few laboratory studies of drug effects on aggression have been conducted with the sophisticated controls that alcohol studies have included (MacCoun, Kilmer, and Reuter 2003). Cognitive disruptions caused by alcohol and other drugs may also influence decisions to commit property crimes, especially impulsive decisions (Fergusson and Horwood 2000; Kirschbaum et al. 2013).

Chronic alcohol and drug use may also contribute to aggression and crime due to factors such as withdrawal, sleep deprivation, nutritional deficits, impairment of neuropsychological functioning, or enhancement of psychopathologic personality disorders (Virkkunen and Linnoila 1993). Furthermore, chronic administration of alcohol or drugs (or withdrawal among those addicted) can lead to physiological or neuropsychological changes that result in mood changes, such as increased negative affect (Miczek et al. 1994). These mood changes can increase the risks for aggressive behavior (for greater detail, see White 2016).

Besides the pharmacological effects of alcohol, another broad explanation for the impact of alcohol on aggression focuses on the beliefs and expectations of the drinker regarding alcohol (Leonard 2008). Those individuals who believe that alcohol causes aggression will be more likely than those without such beliefs to become aggressive after drinking. Whereas cross-cultural studies provide some evidence for expectancy effects on aggression (e.g., McAndrew and Edgerton 1969), laboratory studies do not provide strong support for a pure expectancy model of alcohol and physical aggression (Leonard 2008).

B. The Economic Motivation Model

The economic motivation model assumes that drug users need to generate illicit income to support their drug habit. Therefore, they engage in crimes such as robbery, burglary, prostitution, and shoplifting to get drugs or the money to buy drugs. Support for the economic motivation model originated from literature on heroin addicts, which indicated that raising or lowering the frequency of substance use among addicts raised or lowered their frequency of crime, especially property crime (e.g., Anglin and Perrochet 1998). In addition, criminal activity was significantly greater following addiction to drugs than before addiction (Nurco et al. 1988). McGolothin (1985) found that addicts commit more property crime but not more violent crime compared to those who use less drugs (see also Gottfredson, Kearley, and Bushway 2008; Jofre-Bonet and Sindelar 2001; Thompson and Uggen 2012). The fact that treatment reduces income-generating crimes rather than all crimes lends support for the economic motivation model (Anglin and Perrochet 1998).

Anglin and Perrochet (1998) argued that in countries where drug maintenance and treatment are provided by the government (e.g., the Netherlands and the United Kingdom), many fewer property crimes are attributed to narcotics use. On the other hand, studies in the United Kingdom and Australia have found that economic motivation accounts for a substantial amount of criminal activity (Bennett and Holloway 2006). For example, in a U.K. study, Bennett and Holloway (2006) found that a large majority (approximately 60 to 80 percent) of drug-using offenders reported that there was a connection between their offending and their drug use. Those criminals using heroin and cocaine generally claimed an economic connection, whereas alcohol, barbiturates, stimulant, and PCP use were most often associated with crime due to the pharmacological properties of these substances (see also Manzoni, Fischer, and Rehm 2007). In contrast, in the United States only about 17 percent of 2004 state prisoners reported having committed a crime in order to get money for drugs (Mumola and Karberg 2006).

In sum, the economic motivation model is more applicable to property rather than violent crimes. Overall, this model has been attributed primarily to drugs that are addictive and expensive (e.g., heroin and crack). Nevertheless, Brunelle and colleagues (2014) claimed that, due to limited funds during adolescence, young drug users often commit crimes to cover their drug expenses, even for relatively inexpensive drugs. Conversely, other studies of adolescents have not found much support for an economic motivation model (Menard and Mihalic 2001). Inconsistencies in findings regarding the relative strength of the economic model probably reflect differences in the age composition of the samples, the stage of substance use (e.g., recreational vs. dependent), and type of substance used. Furthermore, historical, geographical, and social policy factors affect the need for income-generating crime.

C. Socioenvironmental/Contextual Model

The socioenvironmental/contextual model proposed here primarily encompasses the influence of drug-using peers and drug-selling environments on criminal behavior. Substance users and offenders often share similar social networks in which subcultural norms reinforce both criminal behavior and substance use (Fagan 1990). In fact, Brunelle et al. (2010) found that, among adolescents, substance use and offending are tightly linked within a wider deviant lifestyle.

Substance use and crime also share common environmental and situational influences. For example, drug exposure and use are more common among residents of neighborhoods with high rates of crime (White and Gorman 2000). Certain places and situations where substances are consumed also generate greater rates of crime. For instance, crime rates are high when and where people (especially young males) are drinking (e.g., at bars and sports stadiums) (Fagan 1993). In addition, characteristics of certain bars (e.g., loud noise, inconvenient access routes, poor ventilation, overcrowding, permissive social environments, and aggressive staff) make them more conducive for fighting and aggression than other bars (Graham, Schmidt, and Gillis 1996; Home Office 2004; Roberts 2007). In the United Kingdom violence occurs most often around pubs and clubs on weekend nights and rates of violence are especially high around pub closing times as crowds of intoxicated strangers (mostly young males) converge on the street at the same time (Home Office 2004; see also Brower and Carroll 2007).

There is also "systemic violence" connected with drug markets (Goldstein 1985). That is, the system of drug distribution is inherently connected with crime and violence, including fights over organizational and territorial issues, enforcement of rules, punishments of and efforts to protect buyers and sellers, and transaction-related crimes (Miczek et al. 1994). Further, drug markets can create community disorganization, which in turn may be associated with increases in crime that are not directly related to drug selling (see Blumstein 1995; Gorman, Zhu, and Horel 2005).

Although drug dealing is strongly related to criminal offending, studies indicate that individuals drawn to dealing were already violent and delinquent prior to dealing, and once involved in drug use or dealing, their level of violent behavior increased (Fagan and Chin 1990; Van Kammen and Loeber 1994). Research conducted in the 1990s consistently showed that crack users were heavily involved in dealing, but they were also involved in nondrug criminality (Inciardi and Pottieger 1994). In a study of in-custody, inner-city male adolescents, researchers found that large percentages of dealers did not use cocaine or crack but that few crack or cocaine users did not also deal (Lipton and Johnson 1998).

In an at-risk sample of young men from the Pittsburgh Youth Study (PYS), White, Loeber, and Farrington (2008) found that, among those who engaged in both behaviors, serious violent offending preceded drug dealing by about one year. Serious theft preceded dealing by one to three years depending on cohort. They also found that, controlling for earlier violent offending, drug dealing was significantly related to later violent offending during adolescence and emerging adulthood. In general, dealing, compared to drug use, is more strongly related to violence (De Li, Priu, and MacKenzie 2000; Menard and Mihalic 2001). Nevertheless, not all drug dealers are violent, and levels of violence differ depending on types of drug markets, types of drugs, and geographical areas (Curtis and Wendel 2007; Desroches 2007; Sales and Murphy 2007) as well as national policies regarding drug control (White and Gorman 2000).

II. Developmental Associations

Developmental researchers are interested in the comorbidity or contemporaneous occurrence of two or more behaviors as well as their sequential covariation. Loeber and Le Blanc (1990, p. 432) defined sequential covariation as "when increases and decreases in the frequency of an independent variable are associated with increases and decreases in offending." This section briefly summarizes results from studies that have examined contemporaneous and cross-lagged associations between substance use and criminal offending. Then it describes how various substance use trajectories are related to later criminal offending, including persistence and desistance of offending.

A. Contemporaneous and Cross-Lagged Associations

Several within-individual analyses have examined sequential covariation and found that individuals commit more offenses at the same time in their lives when they are most involved with substances (Gottfredson et al. 2008; Horney, Osgood, and Marshall 1995; Welte et al. 2005). For example, among a high-risk sample of adolescents and young adults, Mulvey and colleagues (2006) found that violent days were more likely to be substance-using days, and substance-using days were more likely to be violent days (see also Chermack and Blow 2002; Felson, Teasdale, and Burchfield 2008). The findings for marijuana use were weaker than for alcohol and other illicit drugs. Among a sample of male offenders, Horney and colleagues (1995) found that periods of illegal drug use but not alcohol use were related to increases in drug dealing, property crime, and assault. Margolin and colleagues (2013) found that, although most occasions of aggression perpetration for male college students occurred on days without alcohol or drug use, on days when men used substances, they had a significantly greater chance of being aggressive than on days when they did not. For women, there was no significant association between aggressive behavior and days of substance use, suggesting that the association between substance use and aggression may differ by gender (see also Swan and Goodman-Delahunty 2013; but see Brunelle et al. 2014 and Ogders et al. 2008 for conflicting findings).

Using the PYS data, White and colleagues (2013) found that within-individual annual increases in alcohol use quantity from one's own typical levels of drinking between ages 13 and 18 were concurrently associated with within-individual increases in aggressive behavior and vice versa. This association did not differ by race; however, increases in alcohol use and aggression were more strongly associated among boys with attitudes favoring violence and those who lived in high-crime neighborhoods. On the other hand, within-individual increases in marijuana use were associated with decreases in aggressive behavior. Overall, their results indicated that individual and contextual factors affect the strength of the sequential covariation of alcohol use and aggressive behavior during adolescence.

Longitudinal studies indicate that heavy drinking in adolescence is predictive of both violent and property offending in later adolescence and adulthood (e.g., Fergusson and Horwood 2000; Menard and Mihalic 2001). Conversely, individuals, especially males, who were aggressive in childhood or adolescence were more likely to be heavier drinkers in adolescence and adulthood (e.g., Farrington 1995; Popovici et al. 2012). Overall, studies examining cross-lagged associations indicate that there are reciprocal relationships of alcohol use with delinquency and aggression over time during adolescence (e.g., Huang et al. 2001; Wei, Loeber, and White 2004; White et al. 1999). Nevertheless, these associations differ depending on individual characteristics, such as age, race/ethnicity, gender, and socioeconomic status (Loeber et al. 2010; Mason et al. 2010). In general, the literature has demonstrated that early delinquency is a stronger predictor of later alcohol use than early alcohol use is of later delinquency and criminal offending (Mason et al. 2010).

Several studies have found that marijuana and/or other illicit drug use in adolescence predicts criminal offending later on (e.g., Menard, Mihalic, and Huizinga 2001; Mulvey, Schubert, and Chassin 2010). Similarly, studies have found that adolescent delinquency predicts later drug use (e.g., Doherty, Green, and Ensminger 2008; Hayatbaksh et al. 2008). Overall, as with alcohol, it appears that the relationship between drug use and delinquency/violence is reciprocal during adolescence (e.g., D'Amico et al. 2008; Estévez and Emler 2011; Mason and Windle 2002; Wei et al. 2004; White et al. 1999). D'Amico and colleagues (2008) argued that neither substance use nor delinquency is the driving force behind the other; they suggested, instead, that each behavior influences the other.

B. Trajectory Analyses

Whereas there have been numerous studies examining developmental trajectories of delinquency and aggression/violence and trajectories of alcohol and marijuana use during adolescence or from adolescence into adulthood (for a review, see White 2015), only studies examining the influence of developmental trajectories of substance use on criminal offending are reviewed here. Although not the focus of this chapter, it should be noted that trajectories of offending have also been found to predict later substance use and abuse (e.g., Brook et al. 2013; Odgers et al. 2008; Wiesner, Kim, and Capaldi 2005).

Several studies have examined criminal outcomes in young adulthood of adolescent alcohol use trajectories. For example, Tucker et al. (2005) found that early adolescent high-binge drinkers were significantly more likely to sell drugs and commit violent crimes at age 23 than adolescent non-binge drinkers. In contrast, Hill and colleagues (2000) reported that once they controlled for adolescent drug use, there was no effect of adolescent binge drinking trajectories on self-reported criminal behavior at age 21. Similarly, Lynne-Landsman, Bradshaw, and Ialongo (2010) found no adolescent alcohol or marijuana trajectory group differences in violent or nonviolent criminal records at age 21.

In a joint trajectory analysis with the PYS data, White, Jackson, and Loeber (2009) identified moderate associations between trajectories of drinking (based on frequency) and violence (a binary indicator) during adolescence (ages 13 to 18), but no significant associations during emerging adulthood (ages 18 to 25). In addition, adolescent trajectories of drinking did not predict emerging adult violent offending and adolescent trajectories of violence did not predict emerging adult drinking. They argued that heavy drinking is normative in emerging adulthood and, thus, cannot differentiate violent offenders from non-offenders. Although not a trajectory analysis, Fergusson, Harwood, and Swain-Campbell (2002) also found a stronger association between marijuana use and offending in adolescence than in emerging adulthood.

Several studies have examined how trajectories of marijuana use beginning in adolescence affect later criminal behavior in young adulthood. For example, Brook, Zhang, and Brook (2011) examined developmental trajectories of marijuana use from ages 14 to 32 and found that early-onset chronic marijuana users and increasers reported significantly more symptoms of antisocial personality disorder (ASPD) at age 37 than never and occasional users, even with controls for early personality and behavioral factors associated with antisocial behavior. There were no differences between the quitters/decreasers and the non- and occasional users. Tucker et al. (2005) found that individuals in all marijuana-using trajectories, compared to abstainers, were more likely to sell drugs in emerging adulthood. Steady marijuana increasers, compared to abstainers, were also more likely to steal in emerging adulthood. In a minority sample, Brook, Lee and colleagues (2011) identified four marijuana trajectory groups from ages 14 to 29 and examined self-reported criminal behavior at age 29. The chronic high, late-onset, and maturing out groups were all significantly higher than the non-/low users. Furthermore, the chronic high group was significantly higher than the maturing out group. Brown and colleagues (2004) examined trajectories of marijuana use from the sixth to the tenth grade separately for blacks and whites. For blacks, they identified an early-onset group, a later-onset group, and a very-late-onset group. The later-onset group reported more arrests at age 20 than the very-late-onset group. For whites, they identified a non-user group, a later-onset chronic group, and an early-onset chronic group, across which arrest rates significantly increased in a linear fashion. For both races, the early-onset and later-onset groups reported more aggression at age 20 than the non-user or very-late-onset groups.

Pardini, Bechtold, Loeber, and White (2015) identified four marijuana use trajectory groups from adolescence through the mid-twenties in the PYS older cohort: non-users or very light users, adolescence-limited users, late increasing users, and early-onset chronic users. They used both official records and self-reports of offending in young adulthood (through the mid-thirties) and controlled for race, socioeconomic status, other substance use, and several confounding variables related to propensity for offending. Early-onset chronic and late increasing marijuana users were more likely to engage in drug-related offending (self and official report) during their mid-thirties, compared to non-users. Compared to non-users, adolescence-limited users were more likely to be arrested for drug-related crimes. There were no trajectory group differences for violence or theft. Although blacks scored higher than whites on several criminal outcomes, none of the race by trajectory group interactions were significant.

Overall, the trajectory studies generally indicate that early-onset, chronic substance users exhibit more antisocial personality features, aggression, and criminal behavior in adulthood than non-/low users. This finding is more consistent for marijuana than alcohol users, although when substance-related offenses are excluded and confounding factors are included, results are more ambiguous.

C. Desistance

Le Blanc and Loeber (1998; Loeber and Le Blanc 1990) highlighted the importance of developmental criminologists studying desistance as part of an offending trajectory. Desistance has been defined in many ways (see Kazemian 2007). Loeber and Le Blanc (1990, p. 407) defined it as the processes that lead to cessation, either in part or entirely. Here, research on the role of alcohol and drugs in desistance from offending is briefly summarized.

Due to age normative changes in substance use and offending, these two types of deviance peak at different stages in the life cycle and desistance for most individuals occurs earlier for offending than for substance use. Desistance from criminal offending often begins in late adolescence (Elliott 1994), a time when substance use is generally escalating (Bachman et al. 1997). For the most part, youth do not mature out of heavy drinking and illicit drug use until they take on adult roles, such as marriage and career (Labouvie 1996).

Nevertheless, studies have shown that reductions in substance use in young adulthood may play a key role in de-escalation of offending (Kazemian, Farrington, and Le Blanc 2009; Stoolmiller and Blechman 2005). Some research also suggests that chronic use of substances impedes the natural desistance from offending (e.g., Farrington and Hawkins 1991; Hussong et al. 2004; Morizot and Le Blanc 2007; Welte et al. 2005). Hussong et al. (2004, p. 1043) suggested that substance abuse may impede desistance by entrenching individuals into antisocial patterns of behavior, increasing the occurrence of snares (e.g., incarceration), and reducing the accumulation of protective factors (e.g., good marriages). They also suggested that abuse of different types of substances may impede maturation out of offending in different ways. For example, dependence on illicit drugs may push individuals into drug markets where antisocial behavior is expected, whereas heavy drinking may cause acute cognitive impairments, which increase the likelihood of antisocial behavior. In contrast, White and colleagues (2012) found that, during emerging adulthood, heavy drinking for both black and white young men was not related to persistence of serious violent offending. They attributed this finding to the fact that heavy drinking is normative during this developmental period. Furthermore, in a follow-up study, White, Buckman, Pardini, and Loeber (2015) found no differences in alcohol, marijuana, or hard drug use at age 36 between persisters and desisters of violent offending. Maruna (2001) argued, however, that desistance from crime goes hand in hand with desistance from substance use.

III. Conclusion

The nature of the associations between substance use and offending is developmental and evolves through adolescence and adulthood (Brunelle et al. 2014). As discussed earlier, there are clear age differences generally suggesting a stronger relationship in adolescence than adulthood (Fergusson et al. 2002; White et al. 2009, 2012), although heavy use or addiction can interfere with the natural desistance out of offending in young adulthood (Hussong et al. 2004). Besides stage in the life cycle, the nature of the relationship between substance use and offending depends on the stage of drug use. Faupel and Klockars (1987) suggested that during the initial user stage, the association is spurious; during the more intense user stage, drug use is facilitated by criminal behavior; and finally during the street addict career stage, drug use directly influences crime (see also Brunelle et al. 2014).

The literature reviewed above indicates that substance use and crime are strongly related. Nevertheless, the substance-using/crime-committing population is heterogeneous, and there are multiple paths that lead from substance use to crime as well as connect the two forms of behavior. For some individuals, instances of acute intoxication increase the risks for violent and impulsive crime; for some, the need for expensive and addictive drugs increases the risks for income-generating crime; for some, exposure to drug cultures and drug markets increases all types of crime, especially violent crime; for some, the criminal lifestyle increases substance use; and, finally, for some, common underlying characteristics (e.g., family, personality, genetics, neighborhoods) increase the risks for both substance use and crime. Not only do substance use and crime associations vary across individuals, they also vary across occasions, types of substance use, and types of crimes. Nonetheless, heavy drinking and illicit drug use do not lead to offending for many users. Protective factors may include higher financial status, greater social control, and prosocial families and peers. In addition, individual temperament factors, such as lower impulsivity or greater harm avoidance, may protect some substance users from offending. More research is needed to understand the individual and situational factors that increase the risk that substance use will result in criminal offending.

There are several gaps in knowledge regarding substance use and crime. For example, although some studies have found that there are ethnic/racial and gender differences in the nature and extent of the drug–crime relationship, more research is needed to explain these differences. In particular, longitudinal studies with larger populations of ethnic/racial minorities and women are needed to understand developmental changes in substance use and crime and to identify proximal and distal risk and protective factors. More research is also needed on environmental contexts (e.g., societal norms toward specific drugs, availability, and laws prohibiting use of certain drugs) and how they influence the drug–crime association (MacCoun et al. 2003). Further, much of the research on substance use and criminal offending has focused on lower-class addicts and street crime with little research on the role of substance use in white-collar crime (McBride, VanderWaal, and Terry-McElrath 2003). In addition, it is well documented that drug-using criminal offenders often have comorbid mental health problems (Sacks et al. 2009). Therefore, more research is needed on the relationships among alcohol and drug use, mental illnesses, and crime and on appropriate interventions within the community and within the criminal justice system to deal with these co-existing problems. Most importantly, better-designed prevention and intervention research is needed to determine which components of which interventions work for which individuals under which conditions.

In summary, the studies reviewed above make it clear that the associations between substance use and criminal offending depend on drug type; crime type; contextual, cultural, and historical factors; and individual differences in gender, age, race/ethnicity, expectancies, reactions to drugs, and temperament. There is, therefore, a need for researchers to collect data across multiple domains and use multidimensional models to examine mediators and moderators (Chermack and Giancola 1997).

Acknowledgment

The writing of this chapter was supported in part by a grant from the National Institute on Drug Abuse (R01 DA034608). The content is solely the responsibility of the author and does not necessarily represent the official views of the National Institute on Drug Abuse or the National Institutes of Health. I thank Judit Ward and William Bejarano for their help with the literature search and Kathy Unmanzor for her help with the references. I am also indebted to Dennis Gorman, Stephen Hansell, Kristina Jackson, Rolf Loeber, Eun-Young Mun, Robert Pandina, Dustin Pardini, and Magda Stouthamer-Loeber for their intellectual contributions to my research and writing on drug use and crime.

References

Anglin, Douglas M., and Brian Perrochet. 1998. "Drug Use and Crime: A Historical Review of Research Conducted by the UCLA Drug Abuse Research Center." *Substance Use and Misuse* 33(9): 1871–1914.

Bachman, Jerald G., Katherine N. Wadsworth, Patrick M. O'Malley, Lloyd D. Johnston, and John E. Schulenberg. 1997. *Smoking, Drinking and Drug Use in Young Adulthood: The Impacts of New Freedoms and New Responsibilities.* Mahwah, NJ: Erlbaum.

Bennett, Trevor, and Katy Holloway. 2006. "Variations in Drug Users' Accounts of the Connection Between Drug Misuse and Crime." *Journal of Psychoactive Drugs* 38(3): 243–254.

Blumstein, Alfred. 1995. "Youth Violence, Guns and the Illicit-Drug Industry." *The Journal of Law and Criminology* 86(1): 10–36.

Brook, Judith S., Jung Yeon Lee, Elaine N. Brown, Stephen J. Finch, and David W. Brook. 2011. "Developmental Trajectories of Marijuana Use from Adolescence to Adulthood: Personality and Social Role Outcomes." *Psychological Reports* 108(2): 339–357.

Brook, Judith S., Jung Yeon Lee, Elaine N. Brown, Stephen J. Finch, and David W. Brook. 2013. "Long-Term Consequences of Membership in Trajectory Groups of Delinquent Behavior in an Urban Sample: Violence, Drug Use, Interpersonal, and Neighborhood Attributes." *Aggressive Behavior* 39(6): 440–452.

Brook, Judith S., Chenshu Zhang, and David W. Brook. 2011. "Antisocial Behavior at Age 37: Developmental Trajectories of Marijuana Use Extending from Adolescence to Adulthood." *The American Journal on Addiction* 20(6): 509–515.

Brower, Aaron M., and Lisa Carroll. 2007. "Spatial and Temporal Aspects of Alcohol-Related Crime in a College Town." *Journal of American College Health* 55(5): 267–275.

Brown, Tamara L., Kate Flory, Donald R. Lynam, Carl Leukefeld, and Richard R. Clayton. 2004. "Comparing the Developmental Trajectories of Marijuana Use of African American and Caucasian Adolescents: Patterns, Antecedents, and Consequences." *Experimental and Clinical Psychopharmacology* 12(1): 47–56.

Brunelle, Natacha, Serge Brochu, and Marie-Marthe Cousineau. 2010. "Drug-Crime Relations Among Drug-Consuming Juvenile Delinquents: A Tripartite Model and More." *Contemporary Drug Problems* 57: 835–866.

Brunelle, Natacha, Joël Tremblay, Nadine Blanchette-Martin, Annie Gendron, and Mélanie Tessier. 2014. "Relationships Between Drugs and Delinquency in Adolescence: Influence of Gender and Victimization Experiences." *Journal of Child and Adolescent Substance Abuse* 23: 19–28.

Chermack, Stephen T., and Frederic C. Blow. 2002. "Violence Among Individuals in Substance Abuse Treatment: The Role of Alcohol and Cocaine Consumption." *Drug and Alcohol Dependence.* 66(1): 29–37.

Chermack, Stephen T., and Peter R. Giancola. 1997. "The Relation Between Alcohol and Aggression: An Integrated Biopsychosocial Conceptualization." *Clinical Psychology Review* 17(6): 621–649.

Collins, James J., and Pamela M. Messerschmidt. 1993. "Epidemiology of Alcohol-Related Violence." *Alcohol Health and Research World* 17(2): 93–100.

Curtis, Ric, and Travis Wendel. 2007. "'You're Always Training the Dog': Strategic Interventions to Reconfigure Drug Markets." *The Journal of Drug Issues* 37: 867–891.

D'Amico, Elizabeth J., Maria Orlando Edelen, Jeremy N. V. Miles, and Andrew R. Morral. 2008. "The Longitudinal Association Between Substance Use and Delinquency Among High-Risk Youth." *Drug and Alcohol Dependence* 93(1): 85–92.

De Li, Spencer De, Heidi D. Priu, and Doris L. MacKenzie. 2000. "Drug Involvement, Lifestyles and Criminal Activities among Probationers." *Journal of Drug Issues* 30(3): 593–619.

Desroches, Frederick. 2007. "Research on Upper Level Drug Trafficking: A Review." *Journal of Drug Issues* 37(4): 827–844.

Doherty, Elaine E., Kerry M. Green, and Margaret E. Ensminger. 2008. "Investigating the Long-Term Influence of Adolescent Delinquency on Drug Use Initiation." *Drug and Alcohol Dependence* 93(1–2): 72–84.

Elliott, Delbert S. 1994. "Serious Violent Offenders: Onset, Developmental Course, and Termination—The American Society of Criminology 1993 Presidential Address." *Criminology* 32(1): 1–21.

Estévez, Estefania, and Nicholas P. Emler. 2011. "Assessing the Links Among Adolescent and Youth Offending, Antisocial Behaviour, Victimization, Drug Use, and Gender." *International Journal of Clinical and Health Psychology* 11(2): 269–289.

Fagan, Jeffrey. 1990. "Intoxication and Aggression." In *Drugs and Crime,* edited by Michael Tonry and James Q. Wilson. Chicago: University of Chicago Press.

Fagan, Jeffrey. 1993. "Influence of Alcohol and Illicit Drugs on the Social Context of Violent Events." In *Alcohol and Interpersonal Violence: Fostering Multidisciplinary Perspectives,* edited by Susan E. Martin. Rockville, MD: National Institute of Health.

Fagan, Jeffrey, and Kolin Chin. 1990. "Violence as Regulation and Social Control in the Distribution of Crack." In *Drugs and Violence: Causes, Correlates and Consequences,* edited by Mario De La Rosa, Elizabeth Y. Lambert, and Bernard Gropper. Rockville, MD: National Institute on Drug Abuse.

Farrington, David P. 1995. "The Development of Offending and Antisocial Behaviour from Childhood: Key Findings from the Cambridge Study in Delinquent Development." *Journal of Child Psychology and Psychiatry* 36(6): 929–964.

Farrington, David P., and J. David Hawkins. 1991. "Predicting Participation, Early Onset, and Later Persistence in Officially Recorded Offending." *Criminal Behaviour and Mental Health* 1(1): 1–33.

Faupel, Charles E., and Carl B. Klockars. 1987. "Drugs-Crime Connections: Elaborations from Life Histories of Hard-Core Heroin Addicts." *Social Problems* 34(1): 54–68.

Felson, Richard B., Brent Teasdale, and Keri B. Burchfield. 2008. "The Influence of Being Under the Influence: Alcohol Effects on Adolescent Violence." *Journal of Research in Crime and Delinquency* 45(2): 119–139.

Fergusson, David M., and L. John Horwood. 2000. "Alcohol Abuse and Crime: A Fixed-Effects Regression Analysis." *Addiction* 95(10): 1525–1536.

Fergusson, David M., L. John Horwood, and Nicola Swain-Campbell. 2002. "Cannabis Use and Psychosocial Adjustment in Adolescence and Young Adulthood." *Addiction* 97: 1123–1135.

Giancola, Peter R. 2002. "Alcohol-Related Aggression During the College Years: Theories, Risk Factors, and Policy Implications." *Journal of Studies on Alcohol, Supplement* 14:129–139.

Goldstein, Paul J. 1985. "The Drugs/Violence Nexus: A Tripartite Conceptual Framework." *Journal of Drug Issues* 15(4): 493–506.

Gorman, Dennis M., Li Zhu, and Scott Horel. 2005. "Drug 'Hot-Spots,' Alcohol Availability and Violence." *Drug and Alcohol Review* 24(6): 507–513.

Gottfredson, Denise C., Brook W. Kearley, and Shawn D. Bushway. 2008. "Substance Use, Drug Treatment, and Crime: An Examination of Intra-Individual Variation in a Drug Court Population." *Journal of Drug Issues* 38(2): 601–630.

Graham, Kathryn, Gail Schmidt, and Kelly Gillis. 1996. "Circumstances When Drinking Leads to Aggression: An Overview of Research and Findings." *Contemporary Drug Problems* 23: 493–557.

Gustafson, Roland. 1993. "What Do Experimental Paradigms Tell Us About Alcohol-Related Aggressive Responding?" *Journal of Studies on Alcohol* 11(Suppl.): 20–29.

Haggård-Grann, Ulrika, Johan Hallqvist, Niklas Långström, and Jette Möller. 2006. "The Role of Alcohol and Drugs in Triggering Criminal Violence: A Case-Crossover Study." *Addiction* 101(1): 100–108.

Hawkins, J. David, Richard F. Catalano, and Janet Y. Miller. 1992. "Risk and Protective Factors for Alcohol and Other Drug Problems in Adolescence and Early Adulthood. Implications for Substance Abuse Prevention." *Psychological Bulletin* 112: 64–105.

Hayatbakhsh, Mohammad R., Tara R. McGee, Konrad Jamrozik, William Bor, Abdullah A. Mamun, and Jake M. Najman. 2008. "Child and Adolescent Externalizing Behavior and Cannabis Use Disorders in Early Adulthood: An Australian Prospective Birth Cohort Study." *Addictive Behaviors* 33: 422–438.

Hill, Karl G., Helene R. White, Ick-Joong Chung, J. David Hawkins, and Richard F. Catalano. 2000. "Early Adult Outcomes of Adolescent Alcohol Use: Person and Variable Centered Analyses of Binge Drinking Trajectories." *Alcoholism: Clinical and Experimental Research* 24: 892–901.

Home Office. 2004. *Violence in the Night-Time Economy.* Key Findings from the Research, no. 214. London: Home Office.

Horney, Julie, D. Wayne Osgood, and Ineke Haen Marshall. 1995. "Criminal Careers in the Short-Term: Intra-Individual Variability in Crime and Its Relation to Local Life Circumstances." *American Sociological Review* 60: 655–673.

Huang, Bu, Helene R. White, Rick Kosterman, Richard F. Catalano, and J. David Hawkins. 2001. "Developmental Associations Between Alcohol and Interpersonal Aggression During Adolescence." *Journal of Research in Crime and Delinquency* 38:64–83.

Hussong, Andrea M., Patrick J. Curran, Terrie E. Moffitt, Avshalom Caspi, and Madeline M. Carrig. 2004. "Substance Abuse Hinders Desistance in Young Adults' Antisocial Behavior." *Development and Psychopathology* 16: 1029–1046.

Inciardi, James A., and Ann E. Pottieger. 1994. "Crack-Cocaine Use and Street Crime." *Journal of Drug Issues* 24: 273–292.

Ito, Tiffany A., Norman Miller, and Vicki E. Pollock. 1996. "Alcohol and Aggression. A Meta-Analysis on the Moderating Effects of Inhibitory Cues, Triggering Events, and Self-Focused Attention." *Psychological Bulletin* 120: 60–82.

JofreBonet, Mireia, and Jody L. Sindelar. 2001. "Drug Treatment as a Crime Fighting Tool." *Journal of Mental Health Policy and Economics* 4(4): 175–188.

Kazemian, Lila. 2007. "Desistance from Crime: Theoretical, Empirical, Methodological, and Policy Considerations." *Journal of Contemporary Criminal Justice* 23: 5–27.

Kazemian, Lila, David P. Farrington, and Marc Le Blanc. 2009. "Can We Make Accurate Long-Term Predictions About Patterns of De-Escalation in Offending Behavior?" *Journal of Youth and Adolescence* 38: 384–400.

Kirschbaum, Katrin M., Lisa Grigoleit, Cornelius Hess, Burkhard Madea, and Frank Musshoff. 2013. "Illegal Drugs and Delinquency." *Forensic Science International* 226(1–3): 230–234.

Labouvie, Erich.1996. "Maturing Out of Substance Use: Selection and Self-Correction." *Journal of Drug Issues* 26: 457–476.

Le Blanc, Marc. 2009. "The Development of Deviant Behavior, Its Self-Regulation." *MschrKrim*, ABH_09_0007: 1–20.

Le Blanc, Marc, and Rolf Loeber. 1998. "Developmental Criminology Updated." In *Crime and Justice: A Review of Research*, Vol. 23, edited by Michael Tonry. Chicago: University of Chicago Press.

Leonard, Kenneth E. 2008. "The Role of Drinking Patterns and Acute Intoxication in Violent Interpersonal Behaviors." In *Alcohol and Violence: Exploring Patterns and Responses*, edited by International Center for Alcohol Policies. Washington, DC: International Center for Alcohol Policies.

Lipton, Douglass S., and Bruce D. Johnson. 1998. "Smack, Crack, and Score: Two Decades of NIDA-Funded Drugs and Crime Research at NDRI 1974–1994." *Substance Use and Misuse* 33(9): 1779–1815.

Loeber, Rolf, and Marc Le Blanc. 1990. "Toward a Developmental Criminology." In *Crime and Justice: A Review of Research*, Vol. 12, edited by Michael Tonry and Norvil Morris. Chicago: University of Chicago Press.

Loeber, Rolf, Stephanie D. Stepp, Tammy Chung, Alison E. Hipwell, and Helene R. White. 2010. "Time-Varying Associations Between Conduct Problems and Alcohol Use in Adolescent Girls: The Moderating Role of Race." *Journal of Studies on Alcohol and Drugs* 71(4): 544–553.

Lundholm, Lena, Ulrika Haggård, Jette Möller, Johan Hallqvist, and Ingemar Thiblin. 2013. "The Triggering Effect of Alcohol and Illicit Drugs on Violent Crime in a Remand Prison Population: A Case Crossover Study." *Drug and Alcohol Dependence* 129(1): 110–115

Lynne-Landsman, Sarah D., Catherine P. Bradshaw, and Nicholas S. Ialongo. 2010. "Testing a Developmental Cascade Model of Adolescent Substance Use Trajectories and Young Adult Adjustment." *Development and Psychopathology* 22: 933–948.

MacAndrew, Craig, and Edgerton, Robert B. (1969). *Drunken Comportment: A Social Explanation*. Chicago: Aldine.

MacCoun, Robert, Beau Kilmer, and Peter Reuter. 2003. "Research on Drugs-Crime Linkages: The Next Generation." In *Towards a Drugs and Crime Research Agenda for the 21st Century*. National Institute of Justice Special Report. Washington, DC: Department of Justice, Office of Justice Programs.

Manzoni, Patrik, Benedikt Fischer, and Jürgen Rehm. 2007. "Local Drug–Crime Dynamics in a Canadian Multi-site Sample of Untreated Opioid Users." *Canadian Journal of Criminology and Criminal Justice* 49(3): 341–373.

Margolin, Gayla, Michelle C. Ramos, Brian R. Baucom, Diana C. Bennett, and Elyse L. Guran. 2013. "Substance Use, Aggression Perpetration, and Victimization: Temporal Co-occurrence in College Males and Females." *Journal of Interpersonal Violence* 28(14): 2849–2872.

Maruna, Shadd. 2001. *Making Good: How Ex-Offenders Reform and Reclaim Their Lives*. Washington, DC: American Psychological Association Books.

Mason, W. Alex, Julia E. Hitch, Rick Kosterman, Carolyn A. McCarty, Todd I. Herrenkohl, and J. David Hawkins. 2010. "Growth in Adolescent Delinquency and Alcohol Use in Relation to Young Adult Crime, Alcohol Use Disorders, and Risky Sex: A Comparison of Youth from Low- Versus Middle-Income Backgrounds." *Journal of Child Psychology and Psychiatry* 51: 1377–1385.

Mason, W. Alex, and Michael Windle. 2002. "Reciprocal Relations Between Adolescent Substance Use and Delinquency: A Longitudinal Latent Variable Analysis." *Journal of Abnormal Psychology* 111: 63–76.

McBride, Duane C., Curtis J. VanderWaal, and Yvonne M. Terry-McElrath. 2003. "The Drug-Crime Wars: Past, Present, and Future Directions in Theory, Policy, and Program Interventions." In *National Institute of Justice: Towards a Drugs and Crime Research Agenda for the 21st Century*. National Institute of Justice Special Report. Washington, DC: Department of Justice, Office of Justice Programs.

McGolothin, William H. 1985. "Distinguishing Effects from Concomitants of Drug Use: The Case of Crime." In *Studying Drug Abuse: Series in Psychosocial Epidemiology*, Vol. 6, edited by Lee N. Robins. New Brunswick, NJ: Rutgers University Press.

Menard, Scott, and Sharon Mihalic. 2001. "The Tripartite Conceptual Framework in Adolescence and Adulthood: Evidence from a National Sample." *Journal of Drug Issues* 31: 905–940.

Menard, Scott, Scott Mihalic, and David Huizinga. 2001. "Drugs and Crime Revisited." *Justice Quarterly* 18: 269–299.

Miczek, Klaus A., Joseph F. DeBold, Margaret Haney, Jennifer Tidey, Jeffrey Vivian, and Elise M. Weerts. 1994. "Alcohol, Drugs of Abuse, Aggression, and Violence." In *Understanding and Preventing Violence*, Vol. 3, edited by Albert J. Reiss and Jeffrey A. Roth. Washington, DC: National Academy Press.

Morizot, Julien, and Le Blanc, Marc. 2007. "Behavioral, Self, and Social Control Predictors of Desistance from Crime: A Test of Launch and Contemporaneous Effect Models." *Journal of Contemporary Criminal Justice* 23: 50–71.

Mulvey, Edward P., Candice Odgers, Jennifer Skeem, William Gardner, Carol Schubert, and Charles Lidz. 2006. "Substance Use and Community Violence: A Test of the Relation at the Daily Level." *Journal of Consulting and Clinical Psychology* 74(4): 743–754.

Mulvey, Edward P., Carol A. Schubert, and Laurie Chassin. 2010. *Substance Use and Delinquent Behavior Among Serious Adolescent Offenders*. Juvenile Justice Bulletin. Washington, DC: U.S. Department of Justice, Office of Justice Programs, Office of Juvenile Justice and Delinquency Prevention.

Mumola, Christopher J., and Jennifer C. Karberg. 2006. *Drug Use and Dependence, State, and Federal Prisoners, 2004*. Bureau of Statistics Special Report. Washington, DC: U.S. Department of Justice Office of Justice Programs.

Nurco, David N., Hanlon, Thomas. E., Timothy W. Kinlock, and Karen R. Duszynski. 1988. "Differential Criminal Patterns of Narcotic Addicts over an Addiction Career." *Criminology* 26(3): 407–423.

Odgers, Candace L., Terrie E. Moffitt, Jonathan M. Broadbent, Nigel Dickson, Robert J. Hancox, Honalee Harrington, Malcolm R. Poulton, W. Murray Thomson Sears, and Avshalom Caspi. 2008. "Female and Male Antisocial Trajectories: From Childhood Origins to Adult Outcomes." *Development and Psychopathology* 20: 673–716.

Pardini, Dustin, Jordan Bechtold, Rolf Loeber, and Helene White. 2015. "Developmental Trajectories of Marijuana Use Among Males: Examining Linkages with Criminal Behavior and Psychopathic Features into the Mid-30s." *Journal of Research in Crime and Delinquency* 52(6): 797–828.

Pihl, Robert O., and Rachel Sutton. 2009. "Drugs and Aggression Readily Mix; So What Now?" *Substance Use and Misuse* 44: 1188–1203.

Popovici, Ioana, Jenny F. Homer, Hai Fang, and Michael T. French. 2012. "Alcohol Use and Crime: Findings from a Longitudinal Sample of U.S. Adolescents and Young Adults." *Alcoholism: Clinical and Experimental Research* 36(3): 532–543.

Roberts, James C. 2007. "Barroom Aggression in Hoboken, New Jersey: Don't Blame the Bouncers!" *Journal of Drug Education* 37(4): 429–445.

Sacks, S., Charles M. Cleland, Gerald Melnick, Patrick M. Flynn, Kevin Knight, Peter D. Friedmann, Michael L. Prendergast, and Carrie Coen. 2009. "Violent Offenses Associated with Co-Occurring Substance Use and Mental Health Problems: Evidence from CJDATS," *Behavioral Sciences and the Law* 27: 51–69.

Sales, Paloma, and Sheigla Murphy. 2007. "San Francisco's Freelancing Ecstasy Dealers: Towards a Sociological Understanding of Drug Markets." *Journal of Drug Issues* 37: 919–949.

Stoolmiller, Mike, and Elaine A. Blechman. 2005. "Substance Abuse Is a Robust Predictor of Adolescent Recidivism." *Criminal Justice and Behavior* 32: 302–328.

Swan, Angeline C., and Jane Goodman-Delahunty. 2013. "The Relationship Between Drug Use and Crime Among Police Detainees: Does Gender Matter?" *The International Journal of Forensic Mental Health* 12(2): 107–115.

Thompson, Melissa, and Christopher Uggen. 2012. "Dealers, Thieves, and the Common Determinants of Drug and Nondrug Illegal Earnings." *Criminology* 50(4): 1057–1087.

Tucker, Joan S., Phyllis L. Ellickson, Maria Orlando, Steven C. Martino, and David J. Klein. 2005. "Substance Use Trajectories from Early Adolescence to Emerging Adulthood: A Comparison of Smoking, Binge Drinking, and Marijuana Use." *Journal of Drug Issues* 35(2): 307–331.

Van Kammen, Welmoet, and Rolf Loeber. 1994. "Are Fluctuations in Delinquent Activities Related to the Onset and Offset in Juvenile Illegal Drug Use and Drug Dealing?" *Journal of Drug Issues* 24:9 –24.

Virkkunen, Matti, and Markku Linnoila. 1993. "Brain Serotonin, Type II Alcoholism and Impulsive Violence." *Journal of Studies on Alcohol* 11(Suppl.): 163–169.

Wei, Evelyn H., Rolf Loeber, and Helene R. White. 2004. "Teasing Apart the Developmental Associations Between Alcohol and Marijuana Use and Violence." *Journal of Contemporary Criminal Justice* 20: 166–183.

Welte, John, Grace Barnes, Joseph Hoffman, William Wieczorek, and Lening Zhang. 2005. "Substance Involvement and the Trajectory of Criminal Offending in Young Males." *American Journal of Drug and Alcohol Abuse* 31(2): 267–284.

White, Helene R. 2015. "A Developmental Approach to Understanding the Substance Use-Crime Connection." In *The Development of Criminal and Antisocial Behavior: Theory, Research and Practical Applications*, edited by Julien Morizot and Lila Kazemian. New York: Springer.

White, Helene R. 2016. "Substance Use and Crime." In *The Oxford Handbook of Substance Use and Substance Use Disorders*, Vol. 2, edited by Kenneth J. Sher. Oxford: Oxford University Press.

White, Helene R., Jennifer Buckman, Dustin Pardini, and Rolf Loeber. 2015. "The Association of Alcohol and Drug Use with Persistence of Violent Offending in Young Adulthood." *Journal of Developmental and Life Course Criminology* 1: 289–303.

White, Helene R., Paula Fite, Dustin Pardini, Eun-Young Mun, and Rolf Loeber. 2013. "Moderators of the Dynamic Link Between Alcohol and Aggressive Behavior Among Adolescent Males." *Journal of Abnormal Child Psychology* 41: 211–222.

White, Helene R., and Dennis M. Gorman. 2000. "Dynamics of the Drug-Crime Relationship." In *Criminal Justice 2000. The Nature of Crime: Continuity and Change,* Vol. 1, edited by Gary LaFree. Washington, DC: U.S. Department of Justice.

White, Helene R., Kristina Jackson, and Rolf Loeber. 2009. "Developmental Sequences and Comorbidity of Substance use and Violence." In *Handbook of Deviance and Crime*, edited by Marvin Krohn, Alan Lizotte, and Gina Penly Hall. New York: Springer.

White, Helene R., Chioun Lee, Eun-Young Mun, and Rolf Loeber. 2012. "Developmental Patterns of Alcohol Use in Relation to Persistence and Desistance of Serious Violent Offending Among African American and Caucasian Young Men." *Criminology* 50: 391–426.

White, Helene R., Rolf Loeber, and David P. Farrington. 2008. "Substance Use, Drug Dealing, Gang Membership, and Gun Carrying and Their Predictive Associations with Serious Violence and Serious Theft." In *Violence and Serious Theft: Development and Prediction from Childhood to Adulthood,* edited by Rolf Loeber, David P. Farrington, Magda Stouthamer-Loeber, and Helene Raskin White. New York: Routledge.

White, Helene R., Rolf Loeber, Magda Stouthamer-Loeber, and David P. Farrington. 1999. "Developmental Associations Between Substance Use and Violence." *Development and Psychopathology* 11: 785–803.

Wiesner, Margit, Hyoun K. Kim, and Deborah M. Capaldi. 2005. "Developmental Trajectories of Offending: Validation and Prediction to Young Adult Alcohol Use, Drug Use, and Depressive Symptoms." *Development and Psychopathology* 17: 251–270.

Zhang, Lening, John W. Welte, and William W. Wieczorek. 2002. "The Role of Aggression-Related Alcohol Expectancies in Explaining the Link Between Alcohol and Violent Behavior." *Substance Use and Misuse* 37(4): 457–471.

SECTION V

LIFE TRANSITIONS AND TURNING POINTS

CHAPTER 23

....

THE IMPACT OF CHANGES IN FAMILY SITUATIONS ON PERSISTENCE AND DESISTANCE FROM CRIME

....

DELPHINE THEOBALD, DAVID P. FARRINGTON, AND ALEX R. PIQUERO

THE family environment is one of the most important factors associated with the onset, persistence, and desistance from offending, and many individual-level criminological theories have acknowledged the importance of families in socializing children and in deterring antisocial behavior (Patterson et al. 1989; Gottfredson and Hirschi 1990; Agnew 1992; Moffitt 1993; Hirschi 1995). Consequently, family effects have been empirically examined in the criminological literature for several decades (Loeber and Stouthamer-Loeber 1986), with the most recent attention devoted to the effects of marriage on patterns of desistance. In their resurrection and re-analysis of the classic Glueck study of delinquents, Sampson and Laub (1993) suggested that attachments to social institutions such as marriage could act as key "turning points" in the process of desistance.

This chapter is organized as follows: Section I reviews literature on the effects of getting married but also considers the relatively limited evidence on the effects of cohabitation. Section II considers the evidence on the effects of parenthood, and Section III reviews the effect of separation/divorce on offending. Much of the empirical work in this area has studied effects on men, but the relatively limited literature on the effects on women is also reviewed.

I. The Effects of Getting Married

As mentioned, Sampson and Laub (1993) suggested that marriage can act as a turning point in the criminal career, especially when characterized by high levels of attachment (see also Laub and Sampson 2003). These authors argued that the quality of the marriage is a significant factor and may serve as the probable mechanism underlying the association. There is now a relatively consistent body of research from both Europe and the United States that supports this marriage effect (Piquero et al. 2002; Sampson, Laub, and Wimer 2006; King, Massoglia, and MacMillan 2007; Beaver et al. 2008; Bersani et al. 2009; Theobald and Farrington 2009; Burt et al. 2010; McGloin et al. 2011; Barnes and Beaver 2012; Zoutwelle-Terovan et al. 2012; Craig and Foster 2013; Doherty and Ensminger 2013; Craig 201; Forrest 2014; Siennick et al. 2014; but see Lyngstad and Skardhamar 2013; Skardhamar, Monsbakken, and Lyngstad 2014). There are, however, differences across studies in the measures of crime, population type, age range, and methodology. These findings show that the marriage effect holds when considering both cross-cultural studies and the socio-historical context, but the exact mechanisms are still not clearly understood.

This body of evidence can be explained to some extent by the theory that offending is affected by the strength of bonding to conventional institutions. Turning points reflect transitions that can substantially change an individual's trajectory and are accompanied by behavioral and cognitive transformations. It is important to consider these transitions in a life-course framework, and research studies with a longitudinal design are needed to properly address questions relating to continuity and change in criminal behavior (Farrington 1992, 2003; Paternoster et al. 1997). Prospective longitudinal studies allow for between-individual analyses, but more importantly they allow for analyses of within-individual change over time. The Cambridge Study in Delinquent Development (CSDD), which has spanned over 40 years, is one such study, and it has shed light on continuity and change in criminal behavior. A number of factors were measured from when boys were age 8 to when they had reached mid-life at age 50 (Farrington et al. 2009, 2013). These factors give some insight into why individuals become criminals; what individual, family, and environmental risk factors predict offending; and which life transitions (pertinent to this essay) impact persistence or desistance.

A. Marriage and Selection

When investigating the effects of getting married on offending, the most important issue centers on selection effects. Those individuals who marry can be different from those who do not in many variables that may influence their future offending behavior, and it is also important to determine whether getting married is a cause or a consequence of a reduction in offending (see Hirschi and Gottfredson 1995). Some recent studies have analyzed data using statistical methods in an attempt to overcome the problem of selection effects and temporal sequences (Sampson, Laub, and Wimer 2006; King, Massoglia, and MacMillan 2007; Theobald and Farrington 2009). In order to convincingly demonstrate a causal effect of getting married, individuals would need to be randomly allocated to the intervention (in this case getting married), as this would equate married and unmarried individuals on all possible (measured and unmeasured) variables before the marriage.[1] This is clearly not possible. However, propensity score matching is one method that can be used to control for extraneous variables and aims to overcome the problem of selection effects by matching married and unmarried individuals on their prior probability of getting married. Thus, propensity score matching aims to mimic random allocation in a non-experimental study. This is a quasi-experimental method, with analysis of the change in offending after marriage compared with before (see e.g., Murray, Farrington, and Eisner 2009).

A few important studies on the marriage effect have used similar statistical methods. Sampson et al. (2006) utilized a counterfactual life-course approach using the same Glueck and Glueck (1950, 1968) data comprising 500 delinquent boys followed prospectively to age 32. They also conducted a follow-up study of these men through state and national record searches for both crime and death (to rule out false desistance) and included in-depth interviews with a stratified subsample of 52 men at about age 70 (Laub and Sampson 2003). They were therefore able to track variations in offending within individuals over time, controlling for the effects of stable background characteristics. Using within-individual analyses to determine the effect of getting married compared with being unmarried, they demonstrated that marriage had a deterrent effect. This applied to offending behavior for each man from age 17 to 32 in the full delinquent group and from age 17 to 70 in the small interviewed group. In contrast to the selection argument put forward by Hirschi and Gottfredson (1995), Laub and Sampson (2003) argued that the findings from this more recent study gave support to their theory that marriage itself is greatly responsible for reductions in offending, with an average reduction of 35 percent in the odds of crime. They did not, however, dismiss selection effects completely, and acknowledged that these effects will be acting at some level, although most individuals "couple" from chance meetings rather than from opportunistic arrangements. In this sample specifically, wives acted as "social controllers," aiding the men to live more conventional lives.

On further examination of the quality of marital attachment at age 25 and the deviant character of the spouse also at age 25 (within the subgroup of 225 men who were married by that age), Laub and Sampson (2003) still found that within-individual differences in criminality were associated with being married compared with being unmarried. Although their previous results suggested that the quality of the attachment was very important, these findings support the idea that even those who are at high risk for criminality do marry, and often marry very successfully. Also, if they marry antisocial individuals and attachment is low, there is still a deterrent effect of marriage, but not as strong. This may depend on the individual's propensity to marry; those who find it difficult to maintain relationships in adolescence may be those who are less able to form the attachments needed for an enduring relationship (Moffitt et al. 2002).

More recently King, Massoglia, and MacMillan (2007) addressed the issue of desistance using propensity score matching and extended their analysis to include the effects of marriage on women. In their analyses, they included variables from the U.S. National Youth Survey that predicted an individual's likelihood of getting married in order to calculate a propensity (to marry) score. Individuals were then matched on these propensity scores to examine the effect of marriage on offending. They found that there was a small but significant effect of marriage on offending for men but a less significant effect for women. When they introduced a propensity-to-marry score, based on background characteristics, they found a big effect for those men who had a low propensity to marry; their mean self-reported offending score went down significantly from 23.36 to 7.65 (67 percent). For women, there was more of a reducing effect for those with a moderate propensity to marry; their mean score went down significantly from 6.19 to 2.22 (64 percent).

The findings of King, Massoglia, and MacMillan (2007) suggest that desistance may not depend so much on getting married as on an investment process, on the concept of a respectability package, on the propensity to change, and on the personal characteristics of the spouse and the quality of the relationship (Farrington and West 1995; Giordano et al. 2002; Laub and Sampson 2003; Theobald and Farrington 2009; van Schellen, Apel, and Niewbeerta 2012; Bersani and Doherty 2013). With the exception of the work by Sampson and Laub (1990, 1993) and Laub, Nagin, and Sampson (1998, 2003), the most notable prior research on the effects of marriage is that of Farrington and West (1995). These authors found, using both within-individual and between-individual analyses of the males in the CSDD, that getting married had a reducing effect on offending compared to remaining single. From a selection perspective, offenders were no less likely to marry than were non-offenders.

Theobald and Farrington (2009), in a follow-up study to Farrington and West (1995), used more recent data from the CSDD to investigate the effects of getting married on offending. A propensity (to marry) score, based on key childhood and adolescent risk factors and the number of convictions before marriage, was used to match married and unmarried men. Boys who at age 8 to 10 came from a low-income family, had few friends, were unpopular, and came from a broken home were less likely to marry. In order to take account of the stability of the marriage, Theobald and Farrington (2009) only examined those men who remained married for five years or more. They found that, for those marriages which took place between ages 18 and 24, there was a 70 percent reduction in the conviction rate (from an average of 1.48 in the five years before to 0.44 in the five years after). In contrast, early marriages that did not last five years were followed by a small 9 percent increase in the conviction rate (from an average of 1.18 in the five years before to 1.29 in the five years thereafter; Theobald and Farrington 2010). Farrington and West (1995, p. 277) had earlier concluded that "short-lived marriages were less effective in inhibiting offending than longer-lasting ones."

Theobald and Farrington (2009) found no strong effect of marriage, however, for those who married later, that is from age 25 onward, even for enduring marriages. There may be many reasons why this result was obtained. Those men who married later had fewer convictions before marriage on average than those who married earlier, so it was more difficult to detect any effect. It may be the case that their marriages coincided with a natural aging out of crime. Further analyses to test for regression to the mean suggested that, even when the number of convictions before marriage was controlled, there was still no appreciable effect of marriage on offending for those men who married at age 25 or later. It is likely that these men were very different from those who married earlier. They were almost twice as likely to come from a broken home as those who married earlier, and this may well have impacted the way that they were able to form attachments (Moffitt et al. 2002) and thus participate in the investment process of marriage. Behaviors that are less conducive to a good marital relationship tended to predominate in these men; they were less likely to have experienced intimate relationships with women by age 18, and they were much more likely to continue to go out with their male friends, to participate in binge drinking, and to take marijuana at ages 18 and 32. Compared to those who married earlier, these men were more likely to persist in aggressive attitudes over time. Interestingly, none of these men were married to women with criminal convictions, so their continued offending could not be explained by the undesirable effects of a criminal spouse. It seems likely that the later-marrying men were more set in their ways and less changeable by their wife.

The effects of marriage on offending have been studied in a variety of populations using different methodologies, but overall the findings suggest that there is a robust effect of getting married in reducing offending behavior. However, there is a need for more research in longitudinal studies to investigate the possible mechanisms.

B. Differential Effects of Marriage on Women

There has been much debate about the effects of marriage on female offenders, since most evidence for the beneficial effects of marriage is based on large samples of men. The institution of marriage is generally beneficial for men (Waite and Gallagher 2000), but it is also beneficial for women (Lillard and Waite 1995). With regard to offending behavior in women, however, there is little evidence of the beneficial effects of marriage. In Craig, Diamond, and Piquero's (2014) review of the marriage effect, 87 percent of the findings demonstrated significant reductions in offending for men, whereas only 55 percent of findings showed similar reductions for women. These results may reflect the smaller number of criminal women and the consequent greater difficulty of finding a significant effect.

Sampson, Laub, and Wimer's (2006) explanation that men tend to marry "up" and women marry "down" seems plausible, while others argue that the orientation of the spouse is more important. Farrington and West (1995), among others, suggest that men's offending is, to a greater or lesser extent, influenced by persons they are involved with at any time in their lives, and that in a marriage the influence originates in the spouse. These authors also suggest that there is most probably an association between the personal characteristics of a spouse and the quality of the relationship. Some female partners may have a prosocial influence, but if the spouse has antisocial tendencies, this may encourage continuity in offending (Farrington and West 1995; Simons et al. 2002). Therefore, it is difficult to suggest that marriage acts as a deterrent if the personal characteristics of the partner and the quality of the relationship are not taken into account. The chosen partner can contribute considerably to continuity or discontinuity in offending (Elder 1998; Sampson and Laub 1993; Engfer et al. 1994; King, Massoglia, and MacMillan 2007).

In the CSDD, an enduring first marriage was followed by a decrease in the offending of convicted women. Of 32 convicted women who got married to a man in the study, 29 married a convicted man. For the 25 marriages that lasted at least five years, the offending rate of the women decreased by 54 percent (from an average of 0.52 offenses in the five years before to an average of 0.24 offenses in the five years after). In contrast, for the seven marriages that did not last five years, the offending rate of the women increased by half (from 1.14 offenses in the five years before to 1.71 offenses in the five years after). These analyses are severely limited, of course, by the small number of convicted married women and their offenses (Theobald and Farrington 2010).

Because only three convicted women in the CSDD married an unconvicted man, it was not possible to compare the effects on women of marrying a convicted versus an unconvicted man. However, it was possible to compare the effects on men of marrying a convicted versus an unconvicted woman, and overall there was little difference. Of 77 men who married between ages 18 and 24, 55 married an unconvicted woman, and the offending rate of these men decreased by 71 percent (from an average of 1.40 convictions in the five years before to 0.40 convictions in the five years after). Similarly, the offending rate of the 22 men who married a convicted woman decreased by 67 percent (from 1.68 convictions in the five years before to 0.55 convictions in the five years after).

Larger comparisons of the effects of marriage on men and women were completed by King, Massoglia, and MacMillan (2007) and Bersani, Apel, and Nieuwbeerta (2009). Both studies found that marriage was associated with a decrease in offending for women as well as men but that the effect for men was larger. For example, in the Dutch study of Bersani, Apel, and Nieuwbeerta (2009), marriage was associated with a 36 percent decrease in the odds of a conviction for men and with a 21 percent decrease in the odds of a conviction for women. In a more recent study, the impact of the spouse's criminal history was investigated, and women were less likely to be convicted regardless of the criminal conviction history of their spouse (vanSchellen, Apel, and Nieuwbeerta 2012). In contrast, the future convictions of the men were reduced by 30 percent if they married a woman with no criminal history compared with marrying a criminal woman. Evidence for the differential effects of marriage for women are mixed and are hindered to some extent by the size of the samples investigated, and other methodological limitations, compared to studies of men. As for men, more research is needed to establish the mechanisms that might explain such differences between the genders and the effect of marriage on offending by women.

C. Cohabitation

Much of the evidence on the effects of marriage arises primarily from studies where the participants were reaching early adulthood when marriage was almost the sole family structure. Since those times, family structures have changed in many ways, and one important change is the increased popularity of cohabitation. Existing evidence of the effect of cohabitation on offending is generally inconsistent. Some researchers have found that it is associated with a decrease in crime but less so than for marriage (Sampson, Laub, and Wimer 2006), that it can increase crime for some offenses (Horney, Osgood, and Marshall 1995), or that it increases all types of crime for non-whites but has an insignificant effect for white individuals (Piquero, MacDonald, and Parker 2002).

In an Australian study, Forrest (2014) found that cohabitation had no effect on criminal activity in within-individual analyses, regardless of the quality of the relationship. Savolainen (2009), however, reported that cohabitation had a bigger effect than marriage in predicting the five-year recidivism of felony offenders in Finland. He explained this result by suggesting that the women who rushed into marriage might have been more antisocial and less antagonistic to the men's criminal behavior than were the women who cohabited. Again, it is suggested that the quality of the relationship might be a key factor in whether intimate relationships have an effect on the reduction of offending or not. The evidence suggests, however, that cohabiting relationships are less stable than marriages (but see Skardhamar and Lyngstad 2009). It has been reported that even those who cohabit before marriage tend to have lower marital satisfaction (Brown and Booth 1996), poorer interpersonal communication (Cohan and Kleinbaum 2002), higher marital conflict (Thomson and Colella 1992), and a greater perceived risk of marital dissolution (Amato and Booth 1997; Cohan and Kleinbaum 2002; Kiernan 2002), compared with those who get married without cohabiting beforehand.

Those who cohabit without subsequently getting married seem to have the most unstable relationships, possibly because they have lower commitment to the relationship than those who marry or go on to marry after a period of cohabitation (Kiernan 2000; Forrest 2014; Siennick et al. 2014). Siennick et al. (2014) found that the transition with the most effect on offending behavior, after that of marriage, was getting engaged. These authors found that those individuals who cohabit with the intention of getting married are more likely to show a decline in offending than single individuals, but not to the same extent as for marriage. Siennick et al. (2014, p. 749) raise the question about the continuing impact of the meanings and changes in the effects of marriage or marriage-like unions on offending behavior. Undoubtedly, as they suggest, increases in responsibility, changes in routine activities, and changes in identities (Osgood et al. 1996) clearly play a part. It may be the case that, where cohabitation is stable, it may have similar beneficial effects on offending to those of marriage. However, to date, the body of evidence on the effects of cohabitation is limited.

II. PARENTHOOD

One aspect of the family that has received somewhat less empirical attention has been the effect of having a child on continued or reduced offending. Several important questions arise: for example, does having a child somehow alter a parent's orientation to their lives and their social network patterns, as might be suggested by age-graded social control theory (Sampson and Laub 1993), in much the same way as marriage is suggested to do? As stated previously, there have been few studies to date that have considered the effect of the birth of a child on a parent's offending. With a few exceptions (see Zoutewelle-Terovan, van der Geest, Liefbroer, and Bijleveld 2012; Monsbakken, Lyngstad, and Skardhamar 2013; Zoutewelle-Terovan and Skardhamar, 2016), most report little or no effect on offending (Sampson and Laub 1993; Stouthamer-Loeber and Wei, 1998; Uggen and Kruttschnitt 1998; Warr 1998; Wakefield and Uggen 2004; Blokland and Nieuwbeerta 2005; Skardhamar and Lyngstad 2009; Kreager, Matsueda, and Erosheva 2010). These studies include analyses of men, women, and mixed samples, and generally the results are inconsistent.

There may, of course, be differential effects for men and women, as for marriage with regard to reduced offending. Just as many factors may influence the effect of marriage, it might also be expected that the effect of having a child would also depend on many factors, such as whether the child was planned or unplanned, the time period of the parental life course, the quality of parental relationships, coping skills, marital status, financial resources, and social support (Cox et al. 1999; Nomaguchi and Milkie 2003; Huston and Holmes 2004; Ganem and Agnew 2007; Giordano et al. 2011).

In one study, Stouthamer-Loeber and Wei (1998) found that, compared to matched controls (on age, race, and neighborhood), those who fathered children before the age of 19 were significantly more likely to engage in a variety of serious acts of delinquency in the year of fatherhood and the year after. This might suggest, for example, that young age and all the problems surrounding early fatherhood might influence the effect of having a child, or that these young men were on an increasing offending trajectory. Another study, carried out by Blokland and Nieuwbeerta (2005) in the Netherlands, suggested that becoming a parent seemed to increase convictions for some offenders, notably those who were sporadic offenders, but the authors suggested that these results may have been affected by the few offenses committed by these offenders. Drawing on a Norwegian sample, Skardhamar and Lyngstad (2009) found that men who were in cohabiting and married relationships decreased their offending in the five years prior to the birth but that this decrease in offending was not permanent, and increases in offending occurred in the five years after the birth. On the other hand, in Finland, Savolainen (2009) reported that offending did decrease after a child's birth but only for cohabiting or married couples and that "union forma-tion and parenthood . . . typically go hand in hand" (p. 299). Although this study did not examine the interaction effects between parenthood and the type of relationship, an additive effect of the "full family package" (having a stable relationship and chil-dren) was observed.

It is difficult to determine whether the effects of having a child, or partnership for-mation such as getting married or cohabiting, have direct effects on offending. For ex-ample, in Sampson and Laub's (1993) qualitative narratives of the Glueck offenders, the importance of social capital in adult relationships "especially between husbands and wives" seemed paramount in encouraging change. However, having a child or children was also relevant, especially if the man had strong social bonds to them (p. 220). In a na-tional survey from the United States, Ganem and Agnew (2007) showed that, regardless of age and gender, parents were significantly less likely to be involved in crime if they had high-quality relationships with their children.

The timing of parenthood further complicates the assessment of "child-on-crime" effects. Farrington and West (1995) found that the men who had their first child after at least nine months of marriage were less likely to be convicted than those who had their first child before marriage or before nine months of marriage, but this result could reflect selection effects. Recent work using data from the CSDD suggests that there are reductions in offending from several years before the first child's birth to several years after the first child's birth, but the effects are not large. Theobald, Farrington, and Piquero (2015) found that there was little effect of having a child on offending for births occurring at later ages (age 25 or later). When men were matched on propensity scores for the likelihood of having a child using childhood and adolescent risk factors, the greatest effect size (d = 0.27) was observed for earlier births. It may be that the father's relationship with his child(ren) is dependent on his relationship with their mother, so that the parental relationship is the most important. Data constraints prevented these authors from investigating any qualitative aspects of these relationships at or around the time of the birth. Future research should examine issues related to relationship quality, marriage, childbirth, and offending, comparing those who remain with the same partner and those who change partners.

In further analyses examining "shotgun" marriages (defined as conception outside of wedlock), the reductions in offending after the first birth were larger than for non-shotgun marriages (Theobald et al. 2015). In the early 1970s, when most of the CSDD males were forming intimate relationships, the social expectation was that a couple would marry if the girl became pregnant, and men may have considered it their duty within the traditional interpretations of the male role at that time. It is important to note that in the CSDD the majority of shotgun marriages occurred at a young age (see Besemer et al. 2016). This may be a reflection of the time period, since in 1971 when the majority of males were age 18, 68 percent of CSDD males agreed that "you should be pre-pared to marry a girl if you get her pregnant" (West and Farrington 1977, p. 189). It might be the case that commitment to a partner was less if the man felt obliged to marry and changes in attitudes to offending consequently might not occur.

Research on the family suggests that it is the relationship with the partner that is most important but it may be the case that it is the whole package, of having a wife and children, that is most important (see also Giordano et al. 2002; Zoutwelle-Terovan et al. 2012). It may be the case that males who marry early due to shotgun marriages may have experienced family breakdown as a child/adolescent, which may result in their precocious role exits. The stress often experienced in family breakdown can lead adolescents to spend more time outside the family environment, to mix with delinquent friends, to become sexually active earlier, and to form relationships that lead to early marriages (Hill, Yeung, and Duncan 1996; Armour and Haynie 2007). Interestingly, Theobald et al. (2015) also found that the men who did not experience a shotgun marriage had similar percentage reductions before and after the birth to the matched controls, suggesting that the birth of the child had little effect on offending in these marriages. These authors also found that if a man remained with the child for at least five years, the reduction in his convictions was greater than if he did not.

The evidence for the differential effects of parenthood are therefore mixed, with some studies suggesting an effect for certain populations and other studies finding no effect. Clearly, the effect of parenthood will be determined by a complex interaction of many factors, which include socioeconomic status, gender, age, the stability of the relationship, cognitive processes, and maturation.

A. Differential Effects of Parenthood on Women

Studies of women often show that it is the birth of the child, rather than getting married, that acts as a turning point in their lives (Ganem and Agnew 2007; Kreager, Matsueda, and Erosheva 2010; but see Giordano, Cernkovich, and Rudolf 2002; Giordano 2010). For women, motherhood can provide a cognitive transformation that may lead to enduring changes in behavior, especially if social networks and systems of social support are in place. However, the evidence is inconsistent. Qualitative studies using high-risk samples suggest that motherhood can cause changes in identity, stakes in conformity, and attachment to social institutions (Edin and Kefalas 2005; Kreager et al. 2010).

Kreager et al.'s (2010) longitudinal study provides strong evidence that the transition to motherhood is followed by decreases in crime. These authors suggest that this may be due to decreases in substance misuse and changes in social networks. However, in a more recent study Giordano et al. (2011) found that the level of criminal behavior after becoming a parent was moderated by the level of disadvantage in terms of socioeconomic status. Both socioeconomic status and cognitive factors influenced changes in offending for the most disadvantaged males and females in this study. Life history narratives demonstrated that the promise of parenthood, while inducing hope, was affected by the personal and structural limitations associated with levels of disadvantage. These authors did find, however, that, regardless of socioeconomic status, pregnancies that were wanted reduced female involvement in crime. For those with higher socioeconomic status, there was some prosocial benefit of motherhood even when the child was not wanted.

Monsbakken et al. (2013), as mentioned previously, found that offending decreased prior to the birth, when examining five years before to five years after, but that the offending resumed at a lower level after the birth. Other authors have found that having a child was not systematically related to reductions in offending in long-term follow-ups of delinquent girls (Giordano et al. 2002; Thompson and Petrovic 2009; Zoutewelle-Terovan et al. 2012). The postbirth situation may of course impact on any prebirth prosocial transformations, possibly due to the breakdown of intimate relationships, loss of employment, or inadequate housing. Of course, as Kreager et al. (2010) suggest, the inconsistency in results may be attributed to differences in study populations, with the effects being more pronounced in some samples than others. It should also not be forgotten that women are usually the primary caregivers for children, and this brings added stressors to what can sometimes be a fraught situation and may well impact on whether offending recurs. Support with regard to housing, addiction, and mental health needs may well provide an environment where hope and positive cognitive transformations with regard to reoffending may be nurtured.

The current evidence on the effect of parenthood on offending is inconsistent, and this may be attributable to the fact that it is difficult to disentangle the birth of a child from the timing of the union. However, it might be expected that marriages at earlier ages, especially shotgun marriages, may have different effects than those marriages that follow a more traditional format, in a sequential way where the first child is conceived sometime after the marriage. Marriages and childbirth at early ages, particularly in the teenage years, are often rife with problems that are not necessarily conducive to successful outcomes in the social, family, health, and financial spheres (Dahl 2010). However, regardless of the timing, many other factors may be confounded with the birth of a child.

It could be argued that having a child or getting married could be as much an outcome as a cause of any change in criminal behavior. Importantly, methods that allow researchers to study the change in offending after having a child within individuals, compared to the period before having a child, may help to address the problem of causal order and better establish whether the change in offending occurred after the birth of the child. Recent work on employment, another social institution, suggests that longitudinal research may well show the temporality between offending and an event such as parenthood, but it does not necessarily take into account maturational processes (Skardhamar and Savolainen 2014). It is often difficult to say whether changes in offending occur as a cause or a consequence of a particular life transition. If change is a function of maturational processes, then parenthood may well follow the onset of desistance, which might suggest that parenthood is a consequence rather than a cause of a reduction in offending behavior. Recall that desistance should be considered as a process rather than an event (Bushway et al. 2001). Future research should consider the cognitive transformations that may well occur prior to any life transition. It is important that future studies are able to disaggregate the effects of having a child from the formation of a stable union, and the whole package may be the most effective in the reduction of offending.

III. Separation and Divorce

Few studies have investigated the effects of separation or divorce on offending, and most studies that have addressed this issue have done so in the context of studying the effects of marriage. As discussed in Section I, the marriage effect has reasonably robust support in the literature thus far, but it is clear from a societal point of view that marriages have become increasingly unstable over the last 50 years. Family structures have changed dramatically in Western societies. The ending of a marriage is a stressful experience for the majority of people, whether they are the prime instigator or not. The breakdown of a relationship is not a discrete event, and problems are often obvious years before the actual separation or divorce (Amato 2000). The breakdown is a process that often begins with one or both partners disengaging emotionally from the relationship (Rodgers and Pryor 1998).

The effects of separation can be devastating on the individuals involved (e.g., negative emotional, behavioral, and health outcomes) but are really dependent on a number of individual characteristics, such as coping mechanisms and post-separation adjustment (Hetherington 1999). If individuals have good emotional stability and psychological functioning prior to the divorce, then they are more likely to adjust well in the aftermath (Wang and Amato 2000). The effects can be mediated by the loss of contact with children (most often by the man), continuing conflict with the ex-partner, loss of emotional support, and a decline in economic resources, especially if two homes are being supported (Rutter 1987). Booth and Amato (1991) have shown that the success of the adjustment to the stress caused by divorce is positively associated with the level of education and with the formation of new supportive intimate relationships (see also Hetherington et al. 1997).

With regard to the effects on the two adults in the marriage, there is little information about their offending behavior after the marital breakdown. In earlier analyses of the CSDD, Farrington and West (1995) found that offending increased if there was a breakdown in the relationship and the men were no longer living with their spouse. In contrast, staying married was associated with a decrease in offending. In between-individual analyses, 43 percent fewer men who had enduring marriages were convicted up to age 32 compared with those whose marriage broke down. Separation by the age of 26 significantly predicted conviction between ages 27 and 32; 24 percent of the separated men were convicted after the separation, compared with only 9 percent of married men who did not separate. These results were replicated in self-reported offending, independent of all other variables.

In regression analyses, Farrington and West (1995) found that three life events predicted later convictions: an unmarried conception, an unstable marriage, and separation from a spouse. In within-individual analyses, where each individual acts as his own control, they found that offending rates increased by 44 percent during the periods when the men were separated compared with periods when they were married.

These authors concluded that separation leads to an increase in offending compared with marriage. In their retrospective analysis of short-term month-to-month changes in criminality of incarcerated offenders, Horney et al. (1995) reported that, regardless of the men's overall offending, when men lived separately from their wives it resulted in higher rates of their offending. However, this was based on a high-risk sample, and measurements were in the short term, which suggests that the results are not necessarily generalizable.

In more recent analyses of the CSDD, Theobald and Farrington (2013) found that 74 (56 percent) of the convicted men had marriages that resulted in separation, whereas 59 (44 percent) did not. Of those 74 men, 58 (78 percent) had marriages that lasted three years or more. After matching on the number of convictions before separation, those men who separated showed an increase of 19 percent in their offending rate (an average of 0.42 convictions in the five years before separation compared with an average of 0.50 convictions in the five years after). In contrast, men who did not separate showed a reduction of 80 percent in their offending rate (from an average of 0.46 convictions in the five years before separation to an average of 0.09 in the five years after). When a propensity score was introduced, based on risk factors at ages 8 to 10 and 18 predicting separation, the results were even more convincing; those who separated showed a 91 percent increase in their offending rate (from an average of 0.33 convictions in the five years before separation to an average of 0.63 convictions in the five years after). Conversely, those who did not separate showed a decrease of 64 percent (from an average of 0.33 convictions in the five years before separation to an average of 0.12 convictions in the five years after).

Theobald and Farrington (2013) were not able to assess the circumstances surrounding the separation, and these may have had an effect on the man's offending. It may be the case that a man who maintains a strong bond with his children and a reasonable, low-conflict relationship with his spouse and/or finds a new supportive partner after a separation and/or divorce is less likely to offend than a man who loses all contact with his children or has high conflict with his spouse. Another recent study by Bersani and Doherty (2013) examined the association between separation, divorce, and offending behavior and found that divorce was detrimental for both men (55 percent) and women (48 percent), with both experiencing a significantly increased likelihood of arrest. These authors also found that legal separation and divorce functioned differently for men and women, with legal separation having no significant association with arrest for men but associated with an increased likelihood of arrest for women. Bersani and Doherty (2013) also investigated whether the increased risk of offending was temporary, resulting from difficulties associated with marital breakdown, or whether the divorce was associated with a stable return to offending. Their findings suggest that there was a stable and sustained return to offending. Further analyses investigated the length of the marriage before the divorce, and those who had experienced longer marriages (longer than two years) were more influenced by the breakdown in terms of their offending. Those in shorter marriages offended at higher rates when married compared with when single, and the authors suggest that this might indicate unstable marriages of poor quality. Bersani and Doherty (2013) could only speculate as to why these results were obtained but suggested that short-term marriages may reflect "general delinquent tendencies of the individual" (p. 424).

Clearly, relationship breakdown is very complex, and factors such as the length of the marriage and post-separation outcomes such as the formation of new relationships and continued conflict are important. As with the effect of marriage, further research is required with different populations to fully understand the mechanisms involved.

IV. CONCLUSION

There is strong evidence to suggest that getting married is associated with a reduction in offending. Without a systematic review of the evidence and randomized trials, we cannot categorically state that getting married causes a decrease in offending, but the evidence is quite convincing by the standards of other topics in criminological research. It seems clear, therefore, that encouraging stable marriages is important in order that both parents and children can benefit. It may be the case that in some countries stable cohabitations have similar beneficial effects to those of stable marriages, but there is not yet a body of convincing evidence on this topic. Further work on the effect of having a child on persistence or desistance from crime is warranted. This should consider a wide range of samples varying in gender and race/ethnicity and the effect of the timing of having a child, especially given the demographic changes of the past decades with respect to both marriage and childbirth.

The key causal mechanisms that mediate the effect of getting married, having a child, and becoming separated or divorced on offending are not clear. Longitudinal studies do not always contain the necessary information to assess the important mediators of these associations. Up to the present time, the effects of marriage and other life transitions have to a greater or lesser extent been interpreted via social control theory and to some extent attachment theory. Although the quality of the marriage relationship may be one pathway to desistance, other possible mechanisms might be explained by other theories such as rational choice theory (Cusson and Pinsonneault 1986) and social learning theory (Warr 1998). More recent studies have suggested that the effects of life-course transitions depend primarily on changes in attitudes and values that affect the self-identity of the offender (Giordano et al. 2002). It is possible that the most complete explanation of the effects of changes in family situations would involve an integration of all of the above theories (Laub and Sampson 2003), but any integration of theories would be difficult to evaluate empirically.

NOTE

1. Within the limits of statistical fluctuation, providing that a reasonably large number of individuals were allocated.

REFERENCES

Agnew, Robert. 1992. "Foundation for a General Strain Theory of Crime and Delinquency." *Criminology* 30: 47–87.

Amato, Paul R. 2000. "The Consequences of Divorce for Adults and Children." *Journal of Marriage and the Family* 62: 1269–1287.

Amato, Paul R., and Alan Booth. 1997. *A Generation at Risk: Growing Up in an Era of Family Upheaval.* Cambridge, MA: Harvard University Press.

Armour, Stacy, and Dana L. Haynie. 2007. "Adolescent Sexual Debut and Later Delinquency." *Journal of Youth and Adolescence* 36: 141–152.

Barnes, J. C., and Kevin M. Beaver. 2012. "Marriage and Desistance from Crime: A Consideration of the Gene-Environment Correlation." *Journal of Marriage and the Family* 74: 19–33.

Beaver, Kevin M., John P. Wright, Matt DeLisi, and Michael G. Vaughn. 2008. "Desistance from Delinquency: The Marriage Effect Revisited and Extended." *Social Science Research* 37: 736–752.

Bersani Bianca E., and Elaine E. Doherty. 2013. "When the Ties That Bind Unwind: Examining the Enduring and Situational Processes of Change Behind the Marriage Effect." *Criminology* 51: 399–433.

Bersani, Bianca E., John H. Laub, and Paul Nieuwbeerta. 2009. "Marriage and Desistance from Crime in the Netherlands: Do Gender and Socio-Historical Context Matter?" *Journal of Quantitative Criminology* 25: 3–24.

Besemer, Sytske, David P. Farrington, and Delphine Theobald. 2016. "Relationship Between a Parental Conviction and a Son's Family Formation." *Advances in Life Course Research* 28: 52–64.

Blokland, Arjan A. J., and Paul Nieuwbeerta. 2005. "The Effects of Life Circumstances on Longitudinal Trajectories of Offending." *Criminology* 43: 1203–1240.

Booth, Alan, and Paul R. Amato.1991. "Divorce and Psychological Stress." *Journal of Health and Social Behavior* 32: 396–407.

Brown, Susan L., and Alan Booth. 1996. "Cohabitation Versus Marriage: A Comparison of Relationship Quality." *Journal of Marriage and the Family* 58: 668–678.

Burt, S. Alexandra, M. Brent Donnellan, Mikhila N. Humbad, Brian M. Hicks, Matt McGue, and William G. Iacono. 2010. "Does Marriage Inhibit Antisocial Behavior? An Examination of Selection vs Causation via a Longitudinal Twin Design." *Archives of General Psychiatry* 67: 1309–1315.

Bushway, Shawn D., Alex R. Piquero, Lisa M. Broidy, Elizabeth Cauffman, and Paul Mazerolle. 2001. "An Empirical Framework for Studying Desistance as a Process." *Criminology* 39: 491–515.

Cohan, Catherine L., and Stacey Kleinbaum. 2002. "Toward a Greater Understanding of the Cohabitation Effect: Premarital Cohabitation and Marital Communication." *Journal of Marriage and the Family* 64: 180–192.

Cox, Martha J., Blair Paley, Margaret Burchinal, and C. Chris Payne. 1999. "Marital Perceptions and Interactions Across the Transition to Parenthood." *Journal of Marriage and the Family* 61: 611–616.

Craig, Jessica M. 2015. "The Effects of Marriage and Parenthood on Offending Levels over Time Among Juvenile Offenders Across Race and Ethnicity." *Journal of Crime and Justice* 38:163–182.

Craig, Jessica M., Brie Diamond, and Alex. R. Piquero. 2014. "Marriage as an Intervention in the Lives of Criminal Offenders." In *Effective Interventions in the Lives of Criminal Offenders*, edited by John A. Humphrey and Peter Cordella, 19–37. New York: Springer.

Craig, Jessica, and Holly Foster. 2013. "Desistance in the Transition to Adulthood: The Roles of Marriage, Military, and Gender." *Deviant Behavior* 34: 208–223.

Cusson, Maurice, and Pierrre Pinsonneault. 1986. "The Decision to Give Up Crime." In *The Reasoning Criminal: Rational Choice Perspectives on Offending*, edited by Derek B. Cornish and Ronald V. Clarke, 72–82. New York: Springer-Verlag.

Dahl, Gordon B. 2010. "Early Teen Marriage and Future Poverty." *Demography* 47: 689–718.

Doherty, Elaine E., and Margaret E. Ensminger. 2013. "Marriage and Offending Among a Cohort of Disadvantaged African Americans." *Journal of Research in Crime and Delinquency* 50: 104–131.

Edin, Kathryn, and Maria Kefalas. 2005. *Promises I Can Keep: Why Poor Women Put Motherhood Before Marriage*. Berkeley: University of California Press.

Elder, Glen H. 1998. "The Life Course as Developmental Theory." *Child Development* 6: 1–12.

Engfer, Annette., Sabine Walper, and Michael Rutter. 1994. "Individual Characteristics as a Force in Development." In *Development Through Life: A Handbook for Clinicians*, edited by Michael Rutter and David Hay, 79–111. Oxford: Blackwell.

Farrington, David P. 1992. "Criminal Career Research in the United Kingdom." *British Journal of Criminology* 32: 521–536.

Farrington, David P. 2003. "Key Results from the First Forty Years of the Cambridge Study in Delinquent Development." In *Taking Stock of Delinquency: An Overview of Findings from Contemporary Longitudinal Studies*, edited by Terence P. Thornberry and Marvin D. Krohn. New York: Kluwer/Plenum.

Farrington, David P., Jeremy W. Coid, and Donald J. West. 2009. "The Development of Offending From Age 8 to age 50: Recent Results From the Cambridge Study in Delinquent Development." *Monatsschrift fur Kriminologie und Strafrechtsreform* 92: 160–173.

Farrington, David P., Alex R. Piquero, and Wesley G. Jennings. 2013. *Offending from Childhood to Late Middle Age: Recent Results from the Cambridge Study in Delinquent Development*. New York: Springer.

Farrington, David. P., and Donald West. 1995. "Effects of Marriage, Separation and Children on Offending by Adult Males." In *Current Perspectives on Aging and the Life Cycle*, Vol. 4, *Delinquency and Disrepute in the Life Course*, edited by John L. Hagan. Greenwich CT: JAI Press.

Forrest, Walter. 2014. "Cohabitation, Relationship Quality, and Desistance from Crime." *Journal of Marriage and the Family* 76: 539–556.

Ganem, Natasha M., and Robert Agnew. 2007. "Parenthood and Adult Criminal Offending: The Importance of Relationship Quality." *Journal of Criminal Justice* 35: 630–643.

Giordano, Peggy C. 2010. *Legacies of Crime: A Follow-up of the Children of Highly Delinquent Girls and Boys*. Cambridge, MA: Cambridge University Press.

Giordano, Peggy C., Patrick M. Seffrin, Wendy D. Manning, and Monica A. Longmore. 2011. "Parenthood and Crime: The Role of Wantedness, Relationships with Partners, and SES." *Journal of Criminal Justice* 39: 405–416.

Giordano, Peggy C., Stephen A. Cernkovich, and Jennifer L. Rudolph. 2002. "Gender, Crime, and Desistance: Toward a Theory of Cognitive Transformation." *American Journal of Sociology* 107: 990–1064.

Glueck, Sheldon, and Eleanor T. Glueck. 1950. *Unraveling Juvenile Delinquency*. New York: Commonwealth Fund.

Glueck, Sheldon, and Eleanor T. Glueck. 1968. *Delinquents and Nondelinquents in Perspective*. Cambridge, MA: Harvard University Press.

Gottfredson, Michael R., and Travis Hirschi. 1990. *A General Theory of Crime*. Stanford, CA: Stanford University Press.

Henry, Bill, Avshalom Caspi, Terrie E. Moffitt, and Phil A. Silva. 1996. "Temperamental and Familial Predictors of Violent and Nonviolent Criminal Convictions: Age 3 to Age 18." *Developmental Psychology* 32: 614–623.

Hetherington, E. Mavis. 1999. *Coping with Divorce, Single Parenting, and Remarriage: A Risk and Resiliency Perspective*. Hillsdale, NJ: Lawrence Erlbaum.

Hetherington, E. Mavis, T. C. Law, and Thomas G. O'Connor. 1997. "Divorce: Challenges, Changes and New Chances." In *Family in Transition*, edited by Arlene S. Skolnick and Jerome H. Skolnick. New York: Longman.

Hill, Martha S., Wei Jun J. Yeung, and Greg J. Duncan. 1996. "Timing of Childhood Events and Early-Adult Household Formation." *New Directions for Child and Adolescent Development* 71: 87–109.

Hirschi, Travis. 1969. *Causes of Delinquency*. Berkeley: University of California Press.

Hirschi, Travis. 1995. "The Family." In *Crime*, edited by James Q. Wilson and Joan Petersilia. San Francisco: ICS.

Hirschi, Travis, and Michael R. Gottfredson. 1995. "Control Theory and the Life-Course Perspective." *Studies on Crime and Crime Prevention* 4: 131–142.

Horney, Julie, D. Wayne Osgood, and Ineke H. Marshall. 1995. "Criminal Careers in the Short-Term: Intra-individual Variability in Crime and Its Relation to Local Life Circumstances." *American Sociological Review* 60: 655–673.

Huston, Ted. L., and Erin K. Holmes. 2004. "Becoming Parents." In *Handbook of Family Communication*, edited by Anita L. Vangelisti. Mahwah, NJ: Erlbaum.

Kiernan, Kathleen, E. 2000. "European Perspectives on Union Formation." In *Ties That Bind: Perspectives on Marriage and Cohabitation*, edited by Linda Waite, Christine Bachrach, Michelle Hindin, Elizabeth Thomson, and Arland Thornton. Hawthorne, NY: Aldine de Gruyter.

Kiernan, Kathleen E. 2002. "Cohabitation in Western Europe: Trends, Issues and Implications." In *Just Living Together: Implications of Cohabitation for Children, Families, and Social Policy*, edited by Alan Booth and Anne. C. Crouter. Mahwah, NJ: Lawrence Erlbaum.

King, Ryan D., Michael Massoglia, and Ross Macmillan. 2007. "The Context of Marriage and Crime: Gender, the Propensity to Marry, and Offending in Early Adulthood." *Criminology* 45: 33–65.

Kreager, Derek A., Ross L. Matsueda, and Elena A. Erosheva. 2010. "Motherhood and Criminal Desistance in Disadvantaged Neighbourhoods." *Criminology* 48: 221–258.

Laub, John H., Daniel S. Nagin, and Robert J. Sampson. 1998. "Trajectories of Change in Criminal Offending: Good Marriages and the Desistance Process." *American Sociological Review* 63: 225–238.

Laub, John H., and Robert J. Sampson. 2003. *Shared Beginnings, Divergent Lives: Delinquent Boys to Age 70.* Cambridge, MA: Harvard University Press.

Lillard, Lee A., and Linda J. Waite. 1995. "Till Death Do Us Part: Marital Disruption and Mortality." *American Journal of Sociology* 100: 1131–1156.

Loeber, Rolf, and Magda Stouthamer-Loeber. 1986. "Family Factors as Correlates and Predictors of Juvenile Conduct Problems and Delinquency." In *Crime and Justice: An Annual Review of Research*, edited by Michael Tonry and Norval Morris. Chicago: University of Chicago Press.

Lyngstad, Torkild H., and Tobjorn Skardhamar. 2013. "Changes in Criminal Offending Around the Time of Marriage." *Journal of Research in Crime and Delinquency* 50: 608–614.

McGloin, Jean M., Christopher J. Sullivan, Alex R. Piquero, Arjan A. J. Blokland, and Paul Nieuwbeerta. 2011. "Marriage and Offending Specialization: Expanding the Impact of Turning Points and the Process of Desistance." *European Journal of Criminology* 8: 361–376.

Moffitt, Terrie E. 1993. "Adolescence-Limited and Life-Course Persistent Antisocial Behavior: A Developmental Taxonomy." *Psychological Review* 100: 674–701.

Moffitt, Terrie E., Avshalom Caspi, Honalee Harrington, and Barry J. Milne. 2002. "Males on the Life-Course-Persistent and Adolescent-Limited Pathways: Follow-Up at Age 26 Years." *Development and Psychopathology* 14: 179–207.

Monsbakken, Christian W., Torkild H. Lyngstad, and Torbjørn Skardhamar. 2013. "Crime and the Transition to Parenthood: The Role of Sex and Relationship Context." *British Journal of Criminology* 3: 129–148.

Murray, Joseph, David P. Farrington, and Manuel P. Eisner. 2009. "Drawing Conclusions About Causes from Systematic Reviews of Risk Factors: The Cambridge Quality Checklists." *Journal of Experimental Criminology* 5: 1–23.

Nomaguchi, Kei M., and Melissa A. Milkie. 2003. "Costs and Rewards of Children: The Effects of Becoming a Parent on Adults'Lives." *Journal of Marriage and Family* 65: 356–374.

Osgood, D. Wayne, Janet K. Wilson, Patrick M. O'malley, Jerald G. Bachman, and Lloyd D. Johnston. 1996. "Routine Activities and Individual Deviant Behavior." *American Sociological Review* 61: 635–655.

Patterson, Gerald R., Barbara DeBaryshe, and Elizabeth Ramsey. 1989. "A Developmental Perspective on Antisocial Behavior." *American Psychologist* 44: 329–335.

Paternoster, Raymond, Charles W. Dean, Alex R. Piquero, Paul Mazerolle, and Robert Brame. 1997. "Generality, Continuity and Change in Offending." *Journal of Quantitative Criminology* 13: 231–266.

Piquero, Alex R., Robert Brame, Paul Mazerolle, and Rudy Haapanen. 2002. "Crime in Emerging Adulthood." *Criminology* 40: 137–169.

Piquero, Alex R., John M. MacDonald, and Karen F. Parker. "Race, Local Life Circumstances, and Criminal Activity." *Social Science Quarterly* 83: 654–670.

Rodgers, Brian, and Jan Pryor. 1998. *Divorce and Separation: The Outcomes for Children.* York, UK: Joseph Rowntree Foundation.

Rutter, Michael. 1987. "Psychosocial Resilience and Protective Mechanisms." *American Journal of Orthopsychiatry* 57: 316–331.

Sampson, Robert J., and John H. Laub. 1990. "Crime and Deviance Over the Life Course: The Salience of Adult Social Bonds." *American Sociological Review* 55: 608–627.

Sampson, Robert J., and John H. Laub. 1993. *Crime in the Making: Pathways and Turning Points Through Life.* Cambridge, MA: Harvard University Press.

Sampson, Robert J., John H. Laub, and Christopher Wimer. 2006. "Does Marriage Reduce Crime? A Counterfactual Approach to Within-Individual Causal Effects." *Criminology* 44: 465–508.

Savolainen, Jukka. 2009. "Work, Family and Criminal Desistance: Adult Social Bonds in a Nordic Welfare State." *British Journal of Criminology* 49: 285–304.

Siennick, Sonja E., Jeremy Staff, D. Wayne Osgood, John E. Shulenberg, Jerald G. Bachman, and Matthew Van Eseltine. 2014. "Partnership Transitions and Antisocial Behavior in Young Adulthood: A Within-Person, Multi-Cohort Analysis." *Journal of Research in Crime and Delinquency* 51: 735–758.

Simons, Ronald L., Eric Stewart, Lesley C. Gordon, Rand D. Conger, and Glen H. Elder. 2002. "A Test of Life-Course Explanations for Stability and Change in Antisocial Behaviour from Adolescence to Young Adulthood." *Criminology* 40: 401–434.

Skardhamar, Torbjorn, and Torkild H. Lyngstad. 2009. "Family Formation, Fatherhood and Crime: An Invitation to a Broader Perspective on Crime and Family Transitions." Discussion Papers 579. Statistics Norway, Research Department.

Skardhamar, Torbjorn, Christian W. Monsbakken, and Torkild H. Lyngstad. 2014. "Crime and the Transition to Marriage: The Role of the Spouse's Criminal Involvement." *British Journal of Criminology* 54: 411–427.

Skardhamar, Torbjorn, and Jukka Savolainen. 2014. "Changes in Criminal Offending Around the Time of Job Entry: A Study of Employment and Desistance." *Criminology* 52: 263–291.

Stouthamer-Loeber, Magda and Wei, E. H. 1998. "The Precursors of Young Fatherhood and Its Effect on Delinquency of Teenage Males. *Journal of Adolescent Health* 22: 56.

Theobald, Delphine, and David P. Farrington. 2009. "Effects of Getting Married on Offending: Results from a Prospective Longitudinal Survey of Males." *European Journal of Criminology* 6: 496–516.

Theobald, Delphine, and David P. Farrington. 2010. "Should Policy Implications Be Drawn from Research on the Effects of Getting Married on Offending?" *European Journal of Criminology* 7: 239–247.

Theobald, Delphine, and David P. Farrington. 2013. "The Effects of Marital Breakdown on Offending: Results from a Prospective Longitudinal Survey of Males." *Psychology Crime and Law* 19: 391–408.

Theobald, Delphine, David P. Farrington, and Alex R. Piquero. 2015. "Does the Birth of a First Child Reduce the Father's Offending?" *Australian and New Zealand Journal of Criminology* 48: 3–23.

Thompson, Melissa, and Milena Petrovic. 2009. "Gendered Transitions: Within-Person Changes in Employment, Family, and Illicit Drug Use." *Journal of Research in Crime and Delinquency* 46: 377–408.

Thomson, Elizabeth, and Ugo Colella. 1992. "Cohabitation and Marital Stability: Quality or Commitment?" *Journal of Marriage and the Family* 54: 259–267.

Uggen, Christopher, and Candace Kruttschnitt. 1998. "Crime in the Breaking: Gender Differences in Desistance." *Law and Society Review* 32: 339–366.

van Schellen, Marieke, Robert Apel, and Paul Nieuwbeerta. 2012. "Because You're Mine, I Walk the Line? Marriage, Spousal Criminality, and Criminal Offending Over the Life Course." *Journal of Quantitative Criminology* 28: 701–723.

Waite, Linda J., and Maggie Gallagher. 2000. *The Case for Marriage: Why Married People Are Happier, Healthier and Better Off Financially.* New York: Random House.

Wang, Hongyu, and Paul R. Amato. 2000. "Predictors of Divorce Adjustment: Stressors, Resources and Definitions." *Journal of Marriage and the Family* 62: 655–668.

Wakefield, Sara, and Christopher Uggen. 2004. "Having a Kid Changes Everything? The Effects of Parenthood on Subsequent Crime." Paper presented at the Annual Meeting of the American Sociological Association, San Francisco, August.

Warr, Mark. 1998. "Life-Course Transitions and Desistance from Crime." *Criminology* 36: 183–216.

West, Donald J., and David P. Farrington. 1977. *The Delinquent Way of Life.* London: Heinemann.

Zoutewelle-Terovan, Mioara, Victor van der Geest, Aart Liefbroer, and Catrien Bijleveld. 2012. "Criminality and Family Formation: Effects of Marriage and Parenthood on Criminal Behavior for Men and Women." *Crime and Delinquency* 60: 1209–1234.

Zoutewelle-Terovan, Mioara, and Torbjorn Skardhamar. 2016. "Timing of Change in Criminal Offending Around Entrance into Parenthood: Gender and Cross-Country Comparisons for At-Risk Individuals." *Journal of Quantitative Criminology* 32: 695–722.

CHAPTER 24

··

EMPLOYMENT, CRIME, AND THE LIFE COURSE

··

JUKKA SAVOLAINEN, MIKKO AALTONEN,
AND TORBJØRN SKARDHAMAR

THE association between employment and crime has been examined widely in the social scientific literature (Uggen and Wakefield 2008; Bushway 2011; Crutchfield 2014). The appeal of this topic is easy to understand given that several perspectives expect employment to limit criminal offending. The proverb "idle hands are the devil's workshop" is particularly consistent with Routine Activities Theory as it suggests that involvement in legitimate work protects from criminal temptations (Felson 1998). From the perspective of social bonding theory (Hirschi 1969), employment has the potential to restrain individuals from offending because going to work increases involvement in conventional activities, attachment to conventional peers, and commitment to conventional life goals, such as a steady paycheck. Some theories, such as anomie theory and rational choice theory, view crime and work as alternative methods of making ends meet. Merton's (1938) anomie theory argues that by failing to provide legitimate opportunities to pursue normative success goals, some social systems create pressures for the disadvantaged classes to use illegal means of securing those goals. Research by economists and ethnographers alike suggests that lack of attractive job opportunities among disenfranchised youth contributes to their widespread participation in the illegal economy (Sullivan 1989; Freeman 1996).

Crutchfield (1995, 2014) has argued that having a low-quality job is not any less criminogenic than having no job at all, especially among those living in disadvantaged communities. The idea that the effect of employment depends on job characteristics is consistent with several theories of crime. Social control theory argues that the restraining effect of employment is contingent on its capacity to generate prosocial capital (Laub and Sampson 2003). A dead-end job is unlikely to produce such effects. Jobs that do not pay well and are inherently undignified or taxing are more likely to rather increase than reduce economic and psychological strain (Grogger 1998; Agnew 2006).

Rational choice theory suggests that people may choose to commit crime even at the risk of punishment if the benefits of work are exceedingly low compared to the rewards of crime (Fagan and Freeman 1999). An adequate study of employment effects should examine those characteristics of the job that are expected to produce the hypothesized effects. As a sophisticated example of such research, Wadsworth (2006) examined the impact of several theoretically grounded job characteristics on criminal offending using data from the National Longitudinal Study of Youth. His results highlight the importance of two characteristics above others: rewarding job attributes (subjective quality) and benefits (paid leave, health insurance, etc.). By contrast, job stability and earnings were unrelated to either property crime or violent crime in the fully specified model.

Although most perspectives expect crime to be negatively related to employment, some question the causal nature of the association. The general theory of crime (Gottfredson and Hirschi 1990) argues that low self-control, a stable dispositional characteristic emerging in early childhood, is the fundamental cause of individual differences in criminal offending. Under this theory, we should expect crime-prone individuals to fare poorly in the labor market as a predictable consequence of low self-control: "The instability of offenders' careers in the legitimate labor market is consistent with the absence of persistence in most ordinary obligations whether they be interpersonal or school- or job-related" (Gottfredson and Hirschi 1990, p. 165). In support of this argument, developmental research on socioeconomic attainment has shown that childhood deficits in behavioral regulation are strongly related to the risk of unemployment in adulthood (Caspi et al. 1998; Kokko, Pulkkinen, and Puustinen 2000). A key challenge to life-course research of employment effects is to address the selection of antisocial individuals into unemployment and unstable working careers. We should expect a great deal of spuriousness in the longitudinal association between criminal offending and employment outcomes.

The idea that criminal behavior may affect employment, rather than vice versa, is also suggested by labeling theory, which draws attention to how social reactions to formal punishment shape individual life outcomes (Fagan and Freeman 1999; Bernburg and Krohn 2003). Using data from an experimental employment audit, Pager (2003) studied the impact of criminal record on labor market success. Employment audit involves sending matched pairs of individuals to apply for real jobs in order to see if employers respond differently to applicants based on the characteristics manipulated in the experiment (Pager 2003, p. 945). In this case, the pairs were identical with the exception of one characteristic—the appearance of a (fabricated) criminal record, which was randomly assigned so that by the end of the experiment, each member of the pair had served in the criminal condition an equal number of times. The results from this experiment are compelling. Among the job applicants of white ethnicity, having a criminal record reduced the probability of callbacks by 50 percent. The effect was even larger among African Americans because employers were three times more likely to contact those without a criminal record.

It is, of course, possible for both sets of influences to contribute to the negative association between employment and crime: employment may reduce crime and crime may reduce employment. Evidence for reciprocal effects of this kind has been documented in prior research on unemployment and crime (Thornberry and Christenson 1984). This bidirectional perspective is also consistent with the interactionist theory of desistance articulated recently by Massoglia and Uggen (2010).

So far we have focused on theories that expect employment to reduce crime, crime to reduce employment, as well as theories that assume no causal association between the two. Are there any perspectives that would expect employment to increase crime? Drawing on differential association theory (Warr 2002), one can identify examples where participation in legitimate work might stimulate offending. A historical study of "occasional" offenders in an English railroad town found that rather than suppressing crime, getting a job in the railway industry facilitated participation in a lifestyle of heavy drinking with male peers, which, as a rule, increased rather than decreased criminal offending (Godfrey, Cox, and Farrall 2007, p. 108). Studies of frontier violence offer several examples of situations where employment opportunities attract large concentrations of single men to distant or isolated locations (Savolainen, Lehti, and Kivivuori 2008; Courtwright 2009). These men spend much of their time drinking, gambling, and competing over women, who tend to be in short supply. Settings like these are particularly conducive to interpersonal violence. Cowboys of the Wild West are perhaps the most famous example of this phenomenon. Initial reports focusing on the recent energy boom in North Dakota finds that the sudden influx of mostly male migrant labor may be linked to increased levels of both violent and property crime in shale-rich counties (James and Smith 2014; Ruddell et al. 2014).

Research on the effects of adolescent part-time work on delinquency is another example of a literature that considers employment as potentially criminogenic. Theoretical reasons for expecting a positive association between employment and crime at this stage of the life course include increased exposure to delinquent peers, increased availability of alcohol and drugs due to increased earnings and associations with older peers, and increased strain due to the dual demands of working and going to school. Early research by Steinberg et al. (1982) found that working long hours (at least 15 to 20 hours per week) in a job while going to school was associated with a variety of risky outcomes, including increased use of cigarettes and marijuana. Although the association between work intensity and delinquency has been replicated in a number of subsequent studies (e.g., Steinberg, Fegley, and Dornbusch 1993; Ploeger 1997; Staff and Uggen 2003), recent evidence from more rigorous designs suggests that the association is likely to be spurious rather than causal (Apel et al. 2008; Staff et al. 2010).

The focus of this review is on life-course studies of employment and crime. The relevant research engages longitudinal data at the individual level of analysis. In basic terms, we are interested in studies that examine criminal behavior from the point of view of employment transitions: job entries and job exists. Thus, cross-sectional and aggregate-level studies of (un)employment and crime are outside the scope of this chapter. The review draws predominantly on quantitative results, but we discuss evidence from qualitative life-course studies as well. The purpose is to provide an informed assessment of the state-of-the-art scholarship. Although we wish to be comprehensive, the goal is not to mention every longitudinal study that has examined employment and criminal outcomes. Instead, the focus is on key studies with an emphasis on evidence on causality. Thus, we prioritize studies that are methodologically sophisticated with respect to causal inference and theoretical mechanisms.

The chapter is organized into two main sections. Section I reviews studies that examine the capacity of employment (job entries) to curb criminal involvement. There are strong theoretical reasons to expect transitions to stable employment to contribute to the desistance process. Section II reviews life-course studies of unemployment effects on criminal behavior (job exits). Section III concludes the chapter by summarizing the evidence and discussing implications for the next generation of studies on employment and crime.

I. Job Entries: Does Employment Reduce Crime?

A. Experimental Evidence

From the perspective of causal analysis, employment is an advantageous variable because it lends itself to random assignment. To study the effect of, say, marriage on criminal offending, it would not be feasible to randomly "assign" spouses for unmarried offenders. By contrast, not only are experimental designs possible in studies of job effects, there is an extensive literature evaluating the effectiveness of labor market programs on criminal offending, and some of those studies use data from randomized controlled trials (Wilson, Gallagher, and MacKenzie 2000; Bushway and Reuter 2001; Visher, Winterfield, and Coggeshall 2005).

Overall, the results from job experiments have been disappointing. According to Bushway and Apel (2012, p. 28), "the most defensible conclusion from experimental evaluations of work programs is that the programs have a dismal record of jointly improving employment outcomes and of lowering recidivism." A meta-analysis of the effects of employment programs on recidivism echoes this pessimistic conclusion: following the protocol endorsed by the Campbell Collaboration, Visher, Winterfield, and Coggeshall (2005) identified eight methodologically rigorous randomized controlled trials. The average effect size calculated from this set of studies was not statistically different from zero, which implies that employment programs tend to have no impact on offending. Only one of the eight studies reported a statistically significant negative effect on recidivism (Uggen 2000), but this effect was limited to the older members of the sample and based on data collected in the 1970s.

Because age is likely related to increased motivation to "go straight," the result could mean that employment programs are effective among sufficiently motivated clients (Uggen and Wakefield 2008). To temper this conclusion, many of the relevant programs require evidence of motivation or readiness to change as a prerequisite for participation. For example, in order to be eligible for Job Corps, one of the programs included in the meta-analysis, applicants must "be free of serious behavioral problems" and "have the capability and aspirations to participate in Job Corps." Despite these and nine additional screening criteria, Job Corps has not proven to be effective in curbing crime among participants with prior criminal history (Visher, Winterfield, and Coggeshall 2005).

Using the data from the same 1970s experiment as Uggen (2000), a recent study by Uggen and Shannon (2014) focused on participants who were heavy drug users. In this hard-to-employ population, participation in supported work was found to reduce predatory property crime (robberies and burglaries) substantially but had no impact on drug use. The finding is interesting because it suggests that the effect of employment may be crime-dependent. It makes sense that having access to steady income would reduce motivation for economic crime. An optimistic interpretation is that work helps transform drug use from a crime problem into a health problem. On the other hand, if employment sustains the drug habit, there is a strong possibility these individuals will eventually lose their jobs and presumably recidivate as predatory offenders. Also, Uggen and Shannon (2014) did not examine other forms of property crime, such as theft. Perhaps participation in employment provides opportunities to steal valuable items, making it less necessary for motivated offenders to commit robberies or burglaries—crimes that are arguably more risky than, say, embezzlement or larceny.

Although randomized experiments are methodologically compelling, a major limitation with the evidence from job programs is that the jobs they provide tend to be of low quality (Uggen and Wakefield 2008; Apel and Horney 2017). They are almost invariably what Crutchfield (1995) has described as "secondary-sector" jobs, i.e., menial jobs that offer low pay, no health care benefits or retirement plan, and limited opportunities for career advancement. As discussed earlier, most criminological perspectives expect jobs to reduce offending only in so far as they increase bonds to conformity and/or increase the economic benefits of legitimate work relative to the gains from crime. To appreciate the importance of job quality in the desistance process, consider the life history of Wes Moore (Moore 2010), a persistent offender from the Baltimore area who enrolled in Job Corps, a program that has been described as "the most prominent" residential program providing vocational and life skills training, general education, and job placement after graduation (Bushway and Reuter 2001, p. 210).

Wes Moore learned about Job Corps through a friend who was about to enter the program. At this time of his life, Wes, too, was ready to turn his life around: "I'm done, man. I want to get out. Do something different with my life. But I'm not sure what. I'm not going back to high school. I'm too old for that. But I'm tired of running these streets" (Moore 2010, p. 138). This quote conveys heightened awareness of being in the wrong path and increased openness to change. In the vernacular of desistance research, Wes was going through cognitive transformation (Giordano, Cernkovich, and Rudolph 2002)—a perfect moment for entering a high-end program targeting disadvantaged dropouts like him. When he arrived at the campus of the Job Corps Center in Maryland, he could not have been more impressed with the physical setting, a sharp contrast to the streets of the ghetto. He excelled as a student, earning his GED near the top of his class. He selected carpentry as his vocational specialty and enjoyed "the quiet thrill of a job well done" (Moore 2010, p. 142). After seven months in the residential program, Wes graduated from Job Corps and was excited to face the real world. However, despite doing everything right in the program, finding consistent work proved difficult.

Wes moved from landscaping to home construction to working in a food court of a shopping mall. None of these jobs paid living wages: "He worked ten hours a day and came home with barely enough energy to play with his kids and barely enough money to feed and clothe them" (Moore 2010, p. 144). After trying to stay straight for more than a year, the temptation of making money from cooking and selling crack proved too hard to resist, and eventually Wes resumed his criminal activities. Soon after, he was arrested and convicted for his (alleged) involvement in an armed robbery of a jewelry store during which the security guard was killed. Wes Moore was sentenced to life in prison without the possibility of parole.

Aside from being tragic, the story of Wes Moore is instructive in many different ways, but here our focus is on the observation that his promising path toward desistance was interrupted by the failure of the labor market to provide him with an opportunity to support his family through hard work. The effectiveness of Job Corps in reducing criminal offending has been evaluated in a nationally representative randomized trial (Schochet, Burghardt, and Glazerman 2001). This research found a small beneficial treatment effect in the general client population but no statistically significant differences between the control and the treatment groups among those with prior convictions. Consistent with the experience of Wes Moore, this otherwise model program was found to have one major shortcoming: "placement services provided after participants left the centers were found to be limited in scope and substance" (Schochet, Burghardt, and McConnell 2008, p. 1866). Recent evidence from a randomized re-entry experiment suggests that employment programs are more effective when bolstered with a comprehensive system of services that not only prepare ex-offenders for the labor market but continue to support them with equal vigor during the transition process (Cook et al. 2015). The research by Cook et al. (2015) evaluated the effectiveness of the Milwaukee Safe Street Prisoner Release Initiative (PRI) and found improvements in both employment and recidivism outcomes in the treatment group. The unique aspect of the PRI was the provision of frequent and multi-systemic assistance to the clients during the critical post-release period.

B. Work as a Turning Point: The Effect of Good Jobs

Sampson and Laub's (1993) age-graded theory of informal social control is arguably the most influential contemporary life-course theory of desistance from crime. As the term "age-graded" suggests, this perspective is focused on explaining changes in the criminal trajectory at different stages of the life course. Although Sampson and Laub do not deny the role of stable individual differences (e.g., low self-control) in criminal behavior, their goal is to elucidate the social-environmental processes that sustain or modify the effect of such propensities. As far as desistance, the age-graded theory has emphasized the role of marriage and employment as two adult social bonds with the potential to redirect behavior away from crime. A key aspect of the argument is that the level of bonding must be sufficiently strong and of high quality in order to contribute to the process of desistance.

With regard to employment, the initial research by Sampson and Laub (1993) underscored job stability as an influential factor in promoting desistance: having a stable job in early adulthood was found to restrain criminal offending at later stages. The relevant regression models were estimated controlling for individual differences in cognitive ability, antisocial traits, and other potential sources of spuriousness. However, critical examinations of Sampson and Laub's (1993) index of job stability have revealed that labor market bonding was not the only thing it measured (Uggen 2000; Wright and Cullen 2004). One of the items included in this construct is "work habits." It indicates the level of reliability and effort in the job performance and the degree to which the employer considered the subject as "an asset to the organization" (Sampson and Laub 1993, p. 144). As observed by Uggen (2000, p. 531): "If employment effects are conditional on good work habits, the putative 'job effects' are tainted by 'person effects' or pre-existing worker characteristics." In other words, instead of measuring job stability, this index appears to capture individual differences in such characteristics as maturity, sobriety, and motivation.

Attempts to replicate the employment effects reported by Sampson and Laub (1993) have produced mixed results. Using contemporary data on juvenile offenders in the United States, Giordano, Cernkovich, and Rudolph (2002) found no association between job stability and offending rates. On the other hand, studies using nationally representative data from the United States (Wright and Cullen 2004) and Finland (Savolainen 2009) report longitudinal evidence of reduced offending as a function of labor market attachment. Although the Finnish study did not attend to employment quality, the argument was made that in a generous welfare state, such as Finland, where even the chronically unemployed are guaranteed a decent standard of living, choosing to work in the absence of economic necessity can be interpreted as a signal of job quality. Another European study from the Netherlands found that "regular" jobs were more effective than jobs acquired through a temporary work agency (van der Geest, Bijleveld, and Blokland 2011). As the jobs of the former variety are associated with better prospects of long-term employment, this result is consistent with the age-graded theory of informal social control. On the other hand, this same study did not find any association between employment duration and offending rate. It may be that the "regular" jobs are not only more stable but also more rewarding in terms of pay as well as non-economic attributes (Wadsworth 2006).

Evidence from ethnographic research suggests that regular paycheck may not be the only mechanisms that helps offenders remain in the straight and narrow (Laub and Sampson 2003). One of the "persistent thieves" interviewed in Shover's (1996) monograph underscores the importance of interpersonal bonding with a conventional other as the key factor in his employment experience: "The guy liked me from the jump. And that's when I hooked up with him. And I went straight a long time without the intentions of going straight" (Shover 1996, p. 127). Similar to quantitative studies of observational data, ethnographic research offers conflicting accounts concerning the role of employment in desistance. Giordano, Cernkovich, and Rudolph (2002, p. 1033) report that both male and female respondents "were very unlikely to build a story of change around the development of a rewarding career, and only a few focus heavily on stable employment." Maruna (2001, p. 25) has argued that it would be unrealistic to expect employment to trigger self-transformation among most addicts and offenders.

C. Selection Bias in Observational Studies

If the results from labor market experiments have been mostly dismal, the evidence from observational studies is mixed. Some studies find evidence that work matters while others do not. The main challenge for non-experimental research is addressing selection bias. The decision to seek employment, the employer's decision to hire a person, and the worker's ability to hold on to a job are not random outcomes but exhibit a great deal of selectivity. It is safe to say that an offender who gets a job and manages to stay employed is different from an offender that fails to do so. For example, we might expect the employed offender to be more motivated to change, less likely to struggle with addiction problems, and more likely to have children.

Traditional methods of multivariate analysis reduce selection bias by adjusting for differences in observable characteristics presumed to influence the association between employment and crime. For example, in their research showing a link between stable employment and desistance, Sampson and Laub (1993) estimated models controlling for differences in childhood antisocial tendencies, family socioeconomic status, educational attainment, prior offending, and many other potential sources of bias. In addition to using control variables, the study by Savolainen (2009) reduced selection bias by focusing on a homogeneous sample of offenders, all of whom were weakly tied to conventional institutions (including the labor market) and had similar criminal histories at the start of tracking. Propensity score matching is a more sophisticated way to harmonize the employment and comparison groups. Under this technique, the comparisons of the employment effect are limited to cases that are individually matched using information from observable covariates, and those without an acceptable match are excluded from the analysis (Apel and Sweeten 2010).

Although these approaches are useful, it is ultimately unrealistic to expect any data set to be able to capture all the relevant differences that might bias the comparisons. As a matter of logic, critics may always point to variables that were not held constant or included in the matching procedure. Unobserved heterogeneity is the technical term for this problem. Cognizant of the limits of between-individual comparisons, a number of scholars have gravitated to designs in which the employed individual him- or herself serves as the comparison case. This is possible with sufficiently frequent longitudinal observations of within-individual change over time. For example, using data generated by retrospective life-history calendars over a three-year period, Horney, Osgood, and Marshall (1995) linked monthly changes in life circumstances, such as employment, to self-reported rates of criminal offending in a sample of men released from prison. In this path-breaking study, within-individual changes in employment status were unrelated to all measures of criminal activity except one. Contrary to expectations, the odds of property crime were higher during periods of employment. As discussed above, in the context of Uggen and Shannon (2014), it is possible that, for crime-prone individuals, work settings present superior opportunities for theft and other non-predatory property offenses. (Because studies that examine within-individual changes in employment status can be understood as studies of job exits as well as job entries, we discuss this literature in more detail in the next section, which is dedicated to unemployment effects.)

Focusing on within-individual change is an effective way to eliminate selection bias in such time-stable characteristics as cognitive ability, personality, educational failure, and exposure to childhood maltreatment. However, as most scholars recognize, this approach is limited in its ability to address unobserved heterogeneity in time-variant individual differences, such as motivation or recovery from addiction. To illustrate this point, consider a recent within-person analysis of life history calendar data from the Second Nebraska Inmate Study (Apel and Horney 2017). In an effort to shed light to the mechanisms responsible for the inverse association between employment and crime, the study examined which job characteristics mediated the association. The results showed that objective job characteristics (income and hours worked) did not matter, but that the person's subjective commitment to the job did. Although it is possible, as the authors seem to assume, that increased commitment was caused by the employment experience (such as bonding with coworkers), the results cannot rule out the possibility that these individuals express more commitment to their jobs because they are more committed to changing their lives, and they realize employment supports this goal. Thus, it is possible that commitment to change precedes the decision to become and remain employed. As we demonstrate below, because results from intra-individual models compare average rates of offending between states of employment and unemployment, they are unable to demonstrate the correct time order between the employment event and the onset of desistance.

To appreciate the point about time order, consider, once more, the case of Wes Moore. Recall that he enrolled in Job Corps after a period of initial desistance and then cleaned up his act by the time of program graduation. However, after a series of failed attempts to secure stable employment with living wage, he returned to selling drugs and eventually became involved in a robbery-homicide. The criminal trajectory related to this sequence of events is depicted in Figure 24.1, along with a trajectory representing the turning point hypothesis derived from the age-graded theory. The two pathways are very different. The curve representing the turning point hypothesis depicts active but fluctuating levels of criminality during the pre-employment period, followed by gradual but steady decline in the offending rate during the employment period. This pattern is consistent with the hypothesis that employment has a causal effect on desistance. The

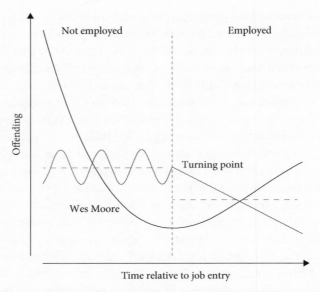

FIGURE 24.1 Two Ideal-Typical Offending Trajectories Around the Point of Job Entry: Wes Moore and The Turning Point Process. (The Dotted Line Shows the Average Offending Rate During the Pre- and Post-Employment Periods.)

curve describing Wes Moore's offending trajectory is clearly inconsistent with the causal effect because his offending increases after the employment transition. However, if we compare the rates of criminal offending between the two trajectories, we find that, in each situation, the average rates (represented by the dotted horizontal lines) are lower in post-employment period than on the pre-employment period. In this example, the amount of reduction (i.e., the effect size) is identical across the two hypothetical trajectories.

The point of this example is to show why standard methods of estimation used in observational research are inadequate for addressing a key element of causal inference— the timing of change in the criminal trajectory. In order for a job to qualify as a turning point it is obvious that the employment transition must take place before desistance rather than vice versa. This critical issue was addressed in an article by Skardhamar and Savolainen (2014). Using monthly data on recidivist male offenders from Norway, the authors examined changes in criminal trajectories around the point of entry to stable employment (defined as a job lasting for a minimum of 6 months). The results showed that most offenders had desisted long before the employment transition and that becoming employed was not associated with additional reductions in criminal behavior. The study further examined if these patterns varied depending on the age of the offender and the stage of the criminal career. They did not observe meaningful evidence of age interaction but were able to identify a subset of offenders who became employed during an active phase of the criminal career, and who experienced substantial reductions in criminal offending thereafter. To the extent this can be interpreted as evidence in support of the turning point hypothesis, it is marginal to say the least: this trajectory described less than 2 percent of the sample. The main conclusion from this research is that that transition to employment is best viewed as a consequence rather than a cause of desistance.

In a more recent contribution to this literature, Loughran, Nagin, and Nguyen (2016) attempted to salvage the turning point hypothesis by emphasizing the gradual and interdependent nature of the association between legal employment and criminal offending. Modeling desistance as a discrete-time Markovian process, they found that the probability of "transitioning to a crime-free state" increased with the number and length of prior employment periods. In other words, the results show that the longer or more frequently the individuals were working in legal employment, the more likely they were to end up desisting from crime. However, as the authors acknowledge, these results have no direct bearing on the causal effect on employment crime since the reported pattern does not rule out the selection hypothesis.

Instead, the main implication seems to be that if employment does have an effect on crime, this effect is likely to unfold gradually via a mutually reinforcing process. This kind process is not, however, consistent with the turning point hypothesis, which does indeed assume a gradual process of desistance, but only in response to an exogenous "triggering event," such as a transition to marriage or employment (e.g., Laub, Nagin, and Sampson 1998).

The process described by Loughran, Nagin, and Nguyen (2016) is rather more consistent with the interactionist theory of desistance advanced by Massoglia and Uggen (2010), which, similar to Loughran, Nagin, and Nguyen's (2016) research, is focused on adolescent transitions to adulthood. By contrast, the focus of the turning point hypothesis is on adult offenders' disengagement from career criminality. Thus, contrary to what the authors claim, none of the evidence presented in their research "calls into question the conclusions of Skardhamar and Savolainen" (Loughran, Nagin, and Nguyen 2016, p. 49) because, consistent with the turning point hypothesis, that research was concerned with investigating the timing of change in criminal offending vis-à-vis a transition to stable employment—a hypothetical turning point –within a population of recidivistic adult offenders.

II. Job Exits: Research on Unemployment and Crime

Although criminological research on unemployment is extensive, there are surprisingly few studies with an explicit focus on job loss as a life-course event. This may have to do with the fact that most longitudinal studies of crime are based on high-risk (offender) samples where unemployment is the "normal" starting point. Whatever the reason, life-course criminologists have been far more interested in estimating the effect of employment on desistance than the effect of unemployment on offending. As a notable exception from the early days of modern life course criminology, Farrington et al. (1986) analyzed the crime rates of late adolescent males in the Cambridge Study, finding that levels of property crime were higher during unemployment, while rates of violent crime did not vary by employment status. Using birth cohort data from New Zealand, Fergusson, Horwood, and Woodward (2001) examined the longitudinal within-individual association between unemployment and a number of problem outcomes during late adolescence and emerging adulthood. Similar to the Farrington study, they found rates of property crime to be higher during periods of unemployment. As noted in the previous section, studies of within-individual change can be understood as estimating either the effects of employment or unemployment. More often than not, the relevant studies are not framed as studies of "job entries" or "job exits," as they simply examine the time-varying association between (un)employment and offending using one of the two possible states as the focal category.

Research on short-term changes in "local life circumstances" have utilized the life history calendar method to create longitudinal data sets. Using monthly data from Second Nebraska Inmate Study (Horney 2001), Felson et al. (2012) found unemployment to be positively related to drug dealing but unrelated to violent and property crimes during the three-year observational period. In the same study, a measure of financial stress (which could be related to employment quality) was associated with increases in both drug dealing and property crime. Slocum et al. (2005) examined monthly changes in employment and crime in a sample drawn from a women's detention center and found rates of property crime and drug use to be higher during times of unemployment. Meanwhile, Griffin and Armstrong (2003) found that only drug dealing increased during periods of unemployment in their female jail inmate sample. Piquero, MacDonald, and Parker (2002) examined within-individual changes in employment status and violent and non-violent offending during a seven-year follow-up, finding a positive association between unemployment and violent offending only for whites; none of the other associations were statistically significant. In their updated re-analysis of the Glueck study, Laub and Sampson (2003) found levels of both alcohol/drug crime and predatory crime to be higher during unemployment in a 16-year follow-up of 419 delinquent men. However, as they point out, because the reference category includes not just employment but also incarceration, the results could be inflated (Laub and Sampson 2003, p. 270).

Drawing on individual-level data from administrative records, Aaltonen et al. (2013) examined a large sample of Finnish men (n = 15,658) with at least one recorded criminal offense over a six-year observational period. Results from fixed-effects regression models of within-individual change showed that unemployment was associated with higher levels of property crime but unrelated to violent crime or drunk driving. This study also found evidence suggesting that the duration of unemployment was positively related to property crime. Similar patterns were observed in a Dutch study (Mesters, van der Geest, and Bijleveld 2014), where regular employment (but not temporary employment) was negatively associated with property crime but unrelated to violent crime. Attending to the duration of both employment and unemployment, and using both random and fixed effects models, Verbruggen, Blokland, and van der Geest (2012) found employment to be associated with lower levels of offending among males and females, but employment duration was significant only for males. On the other hand, the duration of unemployment was associated with increased offending among females but decreased offending among males. According to the authors, this surprising finding may be caused by the higher likelihood of institutionalization (incapacitation) among the chronically unemployed men.

Unlike with job entries, there are no randomized experiments manipulating job exits. The reasons are obvious: it would be highly unethical to ask employers to fire their workers in order to study the effects of unemployment. However, some scholars have used data generated from natural experiments to approximate a randomized design (Mustard 2010). Most of these studies have been conducted at the aggregate level and thus fall outside the scope of this essay. For example, Raphael and Winter-Ebmer (2001) used state-level measures for defense contracts and exposure to oil price shocks as instruments for state-level unemployment rate and found that levels of property crime increased when unemployment rates went up as a consequence of these exogenous shocks. We are aware of two individual-level studies of unemployment and crime that exploit data from natural experiments. Both are based on administrative microdata tracking officially recorded criminal offending before and after large-scale layoffs.

Using data from Norway, Rege et al. (2014) showed that men who became unemployed as a consequence of plant downsizing had higher offending rates after job displacement compared to men working in similar plants who did not experience layoffs (see also Rege et al. 2009). Although the relative increases in crime rates were large, the base rates were low in this normal population study. For example, the 60 percent increase in property offending was produced by a change from approximately 0.1 to 0.16 crimes per 100. Using similar data from Denmark, Bennett and Ouazad (2016) examined changes in crime among individuals who had lost their jobs as a result of mass layoffs (defined as a termination of more than 30 percent of the employees). This study identified causal effects similar in magnitude to the Norwegian study. A comparison of persons who were laid off and those who kept their jobs showed no differences in pre-displacement levels of recorded offending, indicating that the layoff experience was not systematically related to individual differences in criminal propensity. Among those who lost their jobs, the offending rate increased by 0.5 percentage point and remained at a higher level during the entire four year tracking period. Most of this effect was related to increased involvement in property crime by individuals with low educational attainment. This pattern points to material hardship as the mechanisms accounting for the increased offending levels. Together, these two Scandinavian studies offer the most compelling evidence to date regarding the causal effect of unemployment on criminal behavior at the individual level of analysis.

Scholars in the Nordic countries have also examined the link between unemployment benefits and crime. A Danish evaluation study of active labor market programs (ALMPs) found that individuals randomly assigned to the treatment group receiving more intensive activation measures (including a 2-week job search program and more meetings with caseworkers) committed fewer crimes than those in the control group of standard ALMP (Andersen 2012). Similar results were obtained in a Finnish (non-experimental) study that showed that the same individuals committed more property crimes during "passive" unemployment periods when compared to activation periods (Aaltonen et al. 2013). These Nordic results are consistent with the previously noted evaluation study from Milwaukee showing the potential for employment to reduce recidivism when coupled with enduring and comprehensive assistance toward successful labor market attachment (Cook et al. 2015).

III. Conclusion

The assumption that employment reduces crime is both logical and attractive. As noted above, employment is an outcome that can be targeted through realistic policy interventions. It would be comforting if it turned out that problems of crime and violence can be addressed effectively by offering training and jobs for individuals with antisocial tendencies. From the perspective of public good, turning criminals into taxpayers amounts to a win-win proposition. Unfortunately, evidence from life-course criminology finds little support for the hypothesis that work reduces crime.

The evidence from observational (i.e., non-experimental) studies is mixed. The most consistent finding emerging from the literature suggests that employment is associated with reductions in economic crime, although notable exceptions to this generalization exist. This finding is intuitive: given that work provides a source of income, there is less need to resort to crime as a means to earn a living or to finance a drug habit, for example. On the other hand, it is not surprising if changes in employment status are weakly related to interpersonal violence given that most jobs do not prevent aggressive people from having disputes or developing grievances with other people (Felson 2014). However, the main shortcoming of observational studies is their inability to demonstrate causality. Studies of within-individual change are superior to between-individual comparisons because they rule out the confounding influence of unobserved heterogeneity in time-stable individual differences, but this is not sufficient because such time-varying characteristics as motivation or maturation are likely to bias the longitudinal association between employment and criminal offending.

As long as the research design allows for systematic (i.e., non-random) selection into employment, the problem of unobserved heterogeneity is going to be a factor. However, it is a problem that can be managed more effectively with additional investment in data collection. Most criminological studies of within-individual change rely on two kinds of sources: life-history calendars and official statistics. The former are typical in the Anglo-American context dominated by survey data, while scholars in northern European countries (e.g., Finland, Norway, and the Netherlands) are able to create individual-level data sets drawing on interlinked population registries (Lyngstad and Skardhamar 2011). If the purpose of research is to establish associations between objective life circumstances, such as employment, and criminal offending, both of these methods of data collection are good options. However, it is clear that data available from population registries are limited in their capacity to measure changes in motivation, maturity, and other time-varying psychological characteristics assumed to influence the association between employment transitions and desistance. These types of measures can be included in life history surveys, but we suspect that retrospective self-reports of psychological change are unreliable because one's life circumstances at a given time are likely to bias subjective assessments of pre-transition psychological states. For example, all else equal, a person who is currently working in a stable job is likely to see him- or herself as having been more motivated prior to the employment transition than a person who remained unemployed or lost their job (Massoglia and Uggen 2010).

Thus, as an improvement to the status quo, we propose prospective data collection of short-term change in both objective life circumstances and psychological states implicated in theories of desistance. Although this approach would not eliminate the problem of unobserved heterogeneity, it could reduce it significantly. For example, a prospective study that controls for weekly changes in motivation to "go straight" is less vulnerable to the claim that the association between employment and desistance is spurious than a study that fails to attend to this confounder. Moreover, in addition to addressing spuriousness, this analytic strategy could be used to examine the mechanisms expected to produce the employment effect: changes in peer context, income, time use, etc. Methodological examples of this kind of research can be found in the literature on college drinking and its consequences (Patrick and Maggs 2008; Patrick, Maggs, and Lefkowitz 2014).

Although observational data are not ideal for demonstrating causality, they can be used productively to evaluate causal claims. This point is illustrated well by Skardhamar and Savolainen's (2014) study focusing on the timing of employment entries in the criminal trajectory. In order for employment to serve as a turning point, or to assist in the desistance process, we should observe reductions in criminal offending after the transition to employment. This basic point was largely ignored in prior research focusing on changes in the average offending rate (see Figure 24.1). The evidence from Skardhamar and Savolainen (2014) showed that an overwhelming majority of offenders had desisted from crime before they were able to make transitions to stable employment. Moreover, their analysis found virtually no evidence of reduced offending following the point of job entry. Because a single study is never a sufficient foundation for drawing firm conclusions, we encourage replications of this style of analysis using data from different national contexts. We also call for an end to studies that ignore the timing component in the longitudinal association between employment and crime.

In terms of methodological rigor, randomized controlled trials are the best option to study the causal effect of employment on crime. As discussed above, the weight of experimental evidence favors the null hypothesis by an overwhelming margin, especially among studies focusing on individuals with prior criminal history. There is some evidence that employment may protect at-risk individuals from criminal temptations, but even these effects are relatively small. Although it would be a mistake for life-course criminologists to ignore this literature, results from experimental research are devastating only if you assume that merely providing jobs to crime-prone individuals will have a significant impact, regardless of the quality of the job and the readiness of the person. We find this assumption naïve and inconsistent with most theories of criminal desistance.

There is occasional evidence suggesting that, under the right conditions, participation in high-quality training and employment programs may help individuals reduce their involvement in crime (Uggen and Wakefield 2008; Bushway 2011; Andersen 2012; Cook et al. 2015). The challenge for future research is to specify these conditions. As an innovative step, Bushway and Apel (2012) have proposed using evidence of clients' performance in an employment program as an objective signal that could be used to sort "good bets" from those who may not be ready to take on steady job. In addition, as illustrated in the case of Wes Moore, once the "good bet" has been identified, it is important to connect the person to a job with qualities that help sustain the process of desistance. Given that employment quality has been widely recognized as an important factor, it is striking how little attention has been devoted to this issue in either experimental or observational research. Following Sampson and Laub's (1993) original formulation, most studies have focused on job stability as the only aspect of employment quality. It would seem that such additional characteristics as wages, autonomy, benefits, and how well the job matches the worker's skills and aspirations merit more systematic scrutiny in future research (Wadsworth 2006).

While the evidence for the crime restraining effect of becoming employed is weak, the best available evidence—from two quasi-experimental studies—supports the assumption that involuntary unemployment increases the rate of criminal offending (Rege et al. 2014; Bennett and Ouazad 2016). This observation suggests that the effect of employment on crime may be asymmetrical (Lieberson 1985). In other words, the causal effect of employment may be limited to a situation where regularly employed people become criminally active when coping with reduced income and increased leisure. Employment is far less likely to have a crime-reducing effect on the behavior on antisocial individuals whose personal history indicates weak attachment to the labor market.

In conclusion, life-course research on employment and crime remains a vibrant field of inquiry. The literature has made a great deal of progress in the past 30 years or so. The current state of knowledge offers limited evidence of causality in the longitudinal association between employment transitions and rates of criminal offending. However, there are several ways in which the evidence base can be improved by the next generation of studies. We find this agenda worth pursuing because it has the potential to inform policies that are politically feasible, cost-effective, and morally superior to the more punitive alternatives.

References

Aaltonen, Mikko, John MacDonald, Pekka Martikainen, and Janne Kivivuori. 2013. "Examining the Generality of the Unemployment-Crime Association." *Criminology* 51(3): 561–594.

Agnew, Robert. 2006. *Pressured into Crime: An Overview of General Strain Theory*. New York: Oxford University Press.

Andersen, Signe Hald. 2012. *Unemployment and Crime: Experimental Evidence of the Causal Effects of Intensified ALMPs on Crime Rates Among Unemployed Individuals*. Rockwool Foundation Study Paper No. 38. Odense: University Press of Southern Denmark.

Apel, Robert, Shawn D. Bushway, Raymond Paternoster, Robert Brame, and Gary Sweeten. 2008. "Using State Child Labor Laws to Identify the Causal Effect of Youth Employment on Deviant Behavior and Academic Achievement." *Journal of Quantitative Criminology* 24(4): 337–362.

Apel, Robert, and Julie Horney. 2017. "How and Why Does Work Matter? Employment Conditions, Routine Activities, and Crime Among Adult Male Offenders." *Criminology* 55(2): 307–343.

Apel, Robert, and Gary Sweeten. 2010. "Propensity Score Matching in Criminology and Criminal Justice." In *Handbook of Quantitative Criminology*, edited by Alex R. Piquero and David Weisburd, 543–562. New York: Springer.

Bennett, Patrick, and Amine Ouazad. 2016. *Job Displacement and Crime: Evidence from Danish Microdata*. INSEAD Working Paper No. 2016/55/EPS. Available at SSRN: https://ssrn.com/abstract=2815312 or http://dx.doi.org/10.2139/ssrn.2815312/.

Bernburg, Jön Gunnar, and Marvin D. Krohn. 2003. "Labeling, Life Chances, and Adult Crime: The Direct and Indirect Effects of Official Intervention in Adolescence on Crime in Early Adulthood." *Criminology* 41(4): 1287–1318.

Bushway, Shawn D. 2011. "Labor Markets and Crime." In *Crime and Public Policy*, edited by James Q. Wilson and Joan Petersilia, 183–209. New York: Oxford University Press.

Bushway, Shawn D., and Peter Reuter. 2001. "Labor Markets and Crime." In *Crime: Public Policies for Crime Control*, edited by James Q. Wilson and Joan Petersilia, 191–224. San Francisco: ICS Press.

Bushway, Shawn D., and Robert Apel. 2012. "A Signaling Perspective on Employment-Based Reentry Programming." *Criminology and Public Policy* 11: 21–50.

Caspi, Avshalom, Bradley R. Wright, Terrie E. Moffitt, and Phil A. Silva. 1998. "Early Failure in the Labor Market: Childhood and Adolescent Predictors of Unemployment in the Transition to Adulthood." *American Sociological Review* 63: 424–451.

Cook, Philip J., Songman Kang, Anthony A. Braga, Jens Ludwig, and Mallory E. O'Brien. 2015. "An Experimental Evaluation of a Comprehensive Employment-Oriented Prisoner Re-Entry Program." *Journal of Quantitative Criminology* 31(3): 355–382.

Courtwright, David T. 2009. *Violent Land: Single Men and Social Disorder from the Frontier to the Inner City*. Cambridge, MA: Harvard University Press.

Crutchfield, Robert D. 2014. *Get a Job: Labor Markets, Economic Opportunity, and Crime*. New York: NYU Press.

Crutchfield, Robert D. 1995. "Ethnicity, Labor Markets and Crime." In *Ethnicity, Race and Crime: Perspectives Across Time and Place*, edited by Darnell F. Hawkins, 194–211. New York: State University of New York Press.

Fagan, Jeffrey, and Richard B. Freeman. 1999. "Crime and Work." *Crime and Justice* 25: 225–290.

Farrington, David, Bernard Gallagher, Lynda Morley, Raymond St. Ledger, and Donald West. 1986. "Unemployment, School Leaving, and Crime." *British Journal of Criminology* 26(4): 335–356.

Felson, Marcus. 1998. *Crime and Everyday Life*. 2nd ed. Thousand Oaks, CA: Pine Forge Press.

Felson, Richard B. 2014. "What Are Violent Offenders Thinking?" In *Cognition and Crime: Offender Decision-Making and Script Analyses*, edited by Benoit Leclerc and Richard Wortley, 12–25. Abingdon, UK: Routledge.

Felson, Richard, Wayne D. Osgood, Julie Horney, and Craig Wiernik. 2012. "Having a Bad Month: General Versus Specific Effects of Stress on Crime." *Journal of Quantitative Criminology* 28(2): 347–363.

Fergusson, David, John Horwood, and Lianne Woodward. 2001. "Unemployment and Psychosocial Adjustment in Young Adults: Causation or Selection?" *Social Science and Medicine* 53(3): 305–320.

Freeman, Richard B. 1996. "Why Do So Many Young American Men Commit Crimes and What Might We Do About It?" *Journal of Economic Perspectives* 10(1): 25–42.

Giordano, Peggy C., Stephen A. Cernkovich, and Jennifer L. Rudolph. 2002. "Gender, Crime, and Desistance: Towards a Theory of Cognitive Transformation." *American Journal of Sociology* 107: 990–1064.

Godfrey, Barry S., David J. Cox, and Stephen Farrall. 2007. *Criminal Lives: Family Life, Employment, and Offending.* Oxford: Oxford University Press.

Gottfredson, Michael R., and Travis Hirschi. 1990. *A General Theory of Crime.* Stanford, CA: Stanford University Press.

Griffin, Marie, and Gaylene Armstrong. 2003. "The Effect of Local Life Circumstances on Female Probationers' Offending." *Justice Quarterly* 20(2): 213–239.

Grogger, Jeffrey 1998. "Market Wages and Youth Crime." *Journal of Labor Economics* 16(4): 756–791.

Hirschi, Travis. 1969. *Causes of Delinquency.* Berkeley: University of California Press.

Horney, Julie. 2001. "Criminal Events and Criminal Careers: An integrative approach to the study of violence." In *The Process and Structure of Crime: Criminal Events and Crime Analysis,* edited by Robert F. Meier, Leslie W. Kennedy, and Vincent F. Sacco, 141–168. New Brunswick, NJ: Transaction.

Horney, Julie, D. Wayne Osgood, and Ineke Haen Marshall. 1995. "Criminal Careers in the Short-Term: Intra-Individual Variability in Crime and Its Relation to Local Life Circumstances." *American Sociological Review* 60: 655–673.

James, Alexander, and Brock Smith. 2014. *There Will Be Blood: Crime Rates in Shale-Rich US Counties.* No. 140. Oxford Centre for the Analysis of Resource Rich Economies, University of Oxford, UK.

Kokko, Katja, Lea Pulkkinen, and Minna Puustinen. 2000. "Selection into Long-Term Unemployment and Its Psychological Consequences." *International Journal of Behavioral Development* 24(3): 310–320.

Laub, John H., Daniel S. Nagin, and Robert J. Sampson. 1998. "Trajectories of Change in Criminal Offending: Good Marriages and the Desistance Process." *American Sociological Review* 63(2): 225–238.

Laub, John H., and Robert J. Sampson. 2003. *Shared Beginnings, Divergent Lives: Delinquent Boys to Age 70.* Cambridge, MA: Harvard University Press.

Lieberson, Stanley. 1985. *Making It Count: The Improvement of Social Research and Theory.* Berkeley: University of California Press.

Loughran, Thomas A., Daniel S. Nagin, and Holly Nguyen. 2016. "Crime and Legal Work: A Markovian Model of the Desistance Process." *Social Problems* 64: 30–52.

Lyngstad, Torkild Hovde, and Torbjorn Skardhamar. 2011. "Nordic Register Data and Their Untapped Potential for Criminological Knowledge." In *Crime and Justice: A Review of Research,* Vol. 40, edited by Michael H. Tonry and Tapio Lappi-Seppälä, 613–645. Chicago: University of Chicago Press.

Maruna, Shadd. 2001. *Making Good. How Ex-Convicts Reform and Rebuild Their Lives.* Washington, DC: American Psychological Association Books.

Massoglia, Michael, and Christopher Uggen. 2010. "Settling Down and Aging Out: Toward an Interactionist Theory of Desistance and the Transition to Adulthood." *American Journal of Sociology* 116: 543–582.

Merton, Robert K. 1938. "Social Structure and Anomie." *American Sociological Review* 3: 672–682.

Mesters, Geert, Victor van der Geest, and Catrien Bijleveld. 2014. "Crime, Employment and Social Welfare: An Individual-Level Study on Disadvantaged Males." Unpublished working paper. http://geertmesters.nl/wp-content/uploads/2014/07/EmpBenOff_v2.pdf.

Moore, Wes. 2010. *The Other Wes Moore: One Name, Two Fates.* New York: Random House.

Mustard, David. 2010. *How Do Labor Markets Affect Crime? New Evidence on an Old Puzzle.* IZA Discussion Paper No. 4856. Bonn: Institute for the Study of Labor.

Pager, Devah. 2003. "The Mark of a Criminal Record." *American Journal of Sociology* 108:937–975.

Patrick, Megan E., and Jennifer L. Maggs. 2008. "Short-Term Changes in Plans to Drink and Importance of Positive and Negative Alcohol Consequences." *Journal of Adolescence* 31(3): 307–321.

Patrick, Megan E., Jennifer L. Maggs, and Eva S. Lefkowitz. 2014. "Daily Associations Between Drinking and Sex Among College Students: A Longitudinal Measurement Burst Design." *Journal of Research on Adolescence* 25(2): 377–386.

Piquero, Alex, John MacDonald, and Karen Parker. 2002. "Race, Local Life Circumstances, and Criminal Activity." *Social Science Quarterly* 83(3): 654–670.

Ploeger, Matthew. 1997. "Youth Development and Delinquency: Reconsidering a Problematic Relationship." *Criminology* 35(4): 659–675

Raphael, Steven, and Rudolf Winter-Ebmer. 2001. "Identifying the Effect of Unemployment on Crime." *Journal of Law and Economics* 44(1): 259–283.

Rege, Mari, Torbjørn Skardhamar, Kjetil Telle, and Mark Votruba. 2009. "The Effect of Plant Closure on Crime." Statistics Norway Discussion Papers no 593. http://www.ssb.no/a/publikasjoner/pdf/DP/dp593.pdf.

Rege, Mari, Torbjørn Skardhamar, Kjetil Telle, and Mark Votruba. 2014. "Job Displacement and Crime. Results from Norwegian Register Data." Unpublished manuscript.

Ruddell, Rick, Dheeshana S. Jayasundara, Roni Mayzer, and Thomasine Heitkamp. 2014. "Drilling Down: An Examination of the Boom-Crime Relationship in Resource-Based Boom Counties." *Western Criminology Review* 15(1): 3–17.

Sampson, Robert J., and John H. Laub. 1993. *Crime in the Making: Pathways and Turning Points Through Life.* London: Harvard University Press.

Savolainen, Jukka. 2009. "Work, Family, and Criminal Desistance: Adult Social Bonds in a Nordic Welfare State." *British Journal of Criminology* 49: 285–304.

Savolainen, Jukka, Martti Lehti, and Janne Kivivuori. 2008. "Historical Origins of a Cross-National Puzzle Homicide in Finland, 1750 to 2000." *Homicide Studies* 12(1): 67–89.

Schochet, Peter Z., John Burghardt, and Steven Glazerman. (2001) "National Job Corps Study: The Impacts of Job Corps on Participants' Employment and Related Outcomes." Princeton, NJ: Mathematica Policy Research.

Schochet, Peter Z., John Burghardt, and Sheena McConnell. 2008. "Does Job Corps Work? Impact Findings from the National Job Corps Study." *The American Economic Review* 98(5): 1864–1886.

Shover, Neal. 1996. *Great Pretenders: Pursuits and Careers of Persistent Thieves.* Boulder, CO: Westview Press.

Skardhamar, Torbjørn, and Jukka Savolainen. 2014. "Changes in Criminal Offending Around the Time of Job Entry: A Study of Employment and Desistance." *Criminology* 52(2): 263–291.

Slocum, Lee Ann, Sally Simpson, and Douglas Smith. 2005. "Strained Lives and Crime: Examining Intra-Individual Variation in Strain and Offending in a Sample of Incarcerated Women." *Criminology* 43(4): 1067–1110.

Staff, Jeremy, and Christopher Uggen. 2003. "The Fruits of Good Work: Early Work Experiences and Adolescent Deviance." *Journal of Research in Crime and Delinquency* 40(3): 263–290.

Staff, Jeremy., D. Wayne Osgood, John E. Schulenberg, Jerald G. Bachman, and Emily E. Messersmith. 2010. "Explaining the Relationship Between Employment and Juvenile Delinquency." *Criminology* 48(4): 1101–1131.

Steinberg, Laurence D., Ellen Greenberger, Mary Ruggiero, Laurie Garduque, and Alan Vaux. 1982. "Effects of Working on Adolescent Development." *Developmental Psychology* 18(3): 385–395.

Steinberg, Laurence, Suzanne Fegley, and Sanford M. Dornbusch. 1993. "Negative Impact of Part-Time Work on Adolescent Adjustment: Evidence from a Longitudinal Study." *Developmental Psychology* 29(2): 171–180.

Sullivan, Mercer L. 1989. *"Getting Paid." Youth, Crime and Work in the Inner City*. Ithaca, NY: Cornell University Press.

Thornberry, Terence P., and Robert L. Christenson. 1984. "Unemployment and Criminal Involvement: An Investigation of Reciprocal Causal Structures." *American Sociological Review* 49(3): 398–411.

Uggen, Christopher. 2000. "Work as a Turning Point in the Life Course of Criminals: A Duration Model of Age, Employment, and Recidivism." *American Sociological Review* 67: 529–546.

Uggen, Christopher, and Sara Wakefield. 2008. "What Have We Learned from Longitudinal Studies of Work and Crime?" In *The Long View of Crime: A Synthesis of Longitudinal Research*, edited by Akiva M. Liberman, 191–219. New York: Springer.

Uggen, Christopher, and Sarah K. S. Shannon. 2014. "Productive Addicts and Harm Reduction: How Work Reduces Crime–But Not Drug Use." *Social Problems* 61(1): 105–130.

van der Geest, Victor R., Catrien C. J. H. Bijleveld, and Arjan A. J. Blokland. 2011. "The Effects of Employment on Longitudinal Trajectories of Offending: A Follow-Up of High-Risk Youth from 18 to 32 Years of Age." *Criminology* 49(4): 1195–1234.

Verbruggen, Janna, Arjan Blokland, and Victor van der Geest. 2012. "Effects of Employment and Unemployment on Serious Offending in a High-Risk Sample of Men and Women from Ages 18 to 32 in the Netherlands." *British Journal of Criminology* 52(5): 845–869.

Visher, Christy A., Laura Winterfield, and Mark B. Coggeshall. 2005. "Ex-Offender Employment Programs and Recidivism: A Meta-Analysis." *Journal of Experimental Criminology* 1(3): 295–316.

Wadsworth, Tim. 2006. "The Meaning of Work: Conceptualizing the Deterrent Effect of Employment on Crime among Young Adults." *Sociological Perspectives* 49(3): 343–368.

Warr, Mark. 2002. *Companions in Crime: The Social Aspects of Criminal Conduct*. Cambridge, UK: Cambridge University Press.

Wilson, David B., Catherine A. Gallagher, and Doris L. MacKenzie. 2000. "A Meta-Analysis of Corrections-Based Education, Vocation, and Work Programs for Adult Offenders." *Journal of Research in Crime and Delinquency* 37(4): 347–368.

Wright, John P., and Francis T. Cullen. 2004. "Employment, Peers, and Life-Course Transitions." *Justice Quarterly* 21: 183–205.

CHAPTER 25

THE EFFECTS OF NEIGHBORHOOD CONTEXT AND RESIDENTIAL MOBILITY ON CRIMINAL PERSISTENCE AND DESISTANCE

DAVID S. KIRK

ONE in every 100 adults in the United States is in prison or jail at this very moment, with approximately 1.6 million individuals serving time in state and federal prisons and another 745,000 in local jails (Pew Center on the States 2008; Carson and Golinelli 2013; Minton 2013). Most of these individuals are not "lifers" and will eventually be released from incarceration. Although the War on Drugs and the "tough-on-crime" sentencing policies of the 1980s and 1990s facilitated the mass removal of criminals from many U.S. metropolitan neighborhoods, the most recent decade has been characterized by a growing number of individuals returning to these very same neighborhoods following their exit from prison. As shown in Figure 25.1, in 1977, roughly 150,000 individuals were released from U.S. prisons. By 1987, releases had increased to more than 300,000. By 2007, they surpassed 720,000, representing a nearly 400 percent increase in three decades (Bureau of Justice Statistics 2000; West and Sabol 2008). In total there are roughly 5 million formerly incarcerated individuals residing in U.S. neighborhoods, and 15 million former felons (Bonczar 2003; Shannon et al. 2017).

Research suggests that up to one-half of individuals released from prison have been in prison on at least one other occasion, and that more than two-thirds of returning prisoners are rearrested within three years of prison release and almost one-half are reincarcerated (Langan and Levin 2002; Durose, Cooper, and Snyder 2014). In fact, recidivism rates have remained essentially unchanged over the past decade, despite an increasing societal recognition of the failures of mass incarceration and the collateral consequences of criminal stigmas.

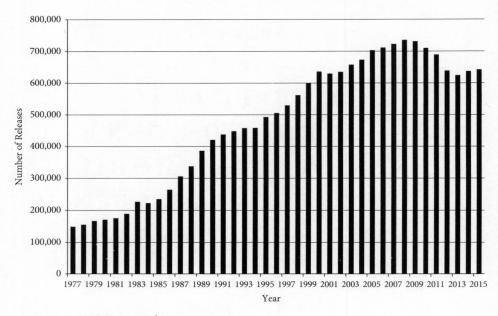

FIGURE 25.1 U.S. Prison Releases, 1977–2015

Source: Bureau of Justice Statistics, National Prisoner Statistics

It is important to note that stable recidivism rates are not necessarily the result of the futility of rehabilitation, as Robert Martinson (1974) prematurely concluded decades ago. Critics of Martinson's report subsequently concluded that the implementations of many of the programs reviewed by Martinson were so poor that it was unrealistic to expect a significant reduction in recidivism (Cullen and Gendreau 2000; MacKenzie 2002). Moreover, many of the reviewed studies suffered from weak research designs, thus prohibiting sound conclusions. Whereas rehabilitation efforts have far more promise than Martinson concluded, many programs and services for ex-prisoners are limited to addressing individual determinants of recidivism (e.g., education levels, drug addiction, cognitive thinking) and generally neglect the importance of social context for promoting desistance from crime. Nonetheless, a convincing and growing body of knowledge in criminology reveals just how important social context is to criminal desistance. Hence, there is an unfortunate disconnect between criminological theory on social correlates of desistance and programs to reduce recidivism.

With the preceding discussion in mind, this chapter seeks to describe the relevance of neighborhood context in the explanation of persistence in and desistance from criminal offending, with a particular focus on the behavior of former prisoners. Section I of the chapter presents facts about the geographic distribution of returning prisoners. Section II draws upon extant research to examine in what ways the conditions of residential neighborhoods influence persistence and desistance among formerly incarcerated individuals. Similarly, Section III draws upon theoretical perspectives and corresponding empirical evidence to examine how residential mobility might exert an impact on persistence and desistance. The distinction between these two sections is that the former focuses on neighborhood effects whereas the latter focuses on individual-level mobility effects. Section IV concludes with a focus on criminal justice policy and practice, including a discussion of the implications of the lessons learned from research on neighborhood effects and residential mobility for the re-entry and re-integration of formerly incarcerated individuals. This chapter focuses on research largely from the United States, in part because many of the recent studies of the relationship between neighborhood conditions and persistence and desistance draw upon data from the United States. However, I would suggest that many of the conclusions of the chapter generalize to countries and their neighborhood environments outside of the United States.

I. THE GEOGRAPHY OF PRISONER RE-ENTRY

Understanding the neighborhood context of persistence and desistance requires appreciation of the facts surrounding the geography of prisoner re-entry. Despite the sheer magnitude of returning prisoners in the United States, most neighborhoods are untouched by prisoner re-entry. The geographic distribution of prisoner re-entry is highly concentrated in a relatively small number of neighborhoods within metropolitan areas. For instance, research reveals that more than one-half of prisoners released from Illinois prisons in 2001 returned to the city of Chicago; among these, one-third were concentrated in just 6 of 77 community areas (La Vigne et al. 2003). These six communities are among the most economically and socially disadvantaged in the city.

Interestingly, while metropolitan areas, particularly inner cities, continue to be the modal destination for returning prisoners, evidence reveals considerable geographic shifts in the urbanization and suburbanization of returning prisoners over the past two decades. For instance, in an analysis of the geography of prisoner re-entry in Illinois, Kirk (2016) found that the percentage of Illinois prison releases returning to the City of Chicago declined incrementally between 1996 and 2005 (from 52 percent to 50 percent) and then declined dramatically between 2005 and 2009 before leveling off at roughly 39 percent in 2013. Increasingly over time, former prisoners in Illinois are residing in suburban and exurban areas.[1] That being said, despite recent shifts in the geography of prisoner re-entry, evidence suggests that returning prisoners are still highly concentrated into relatively few neighborhoods. That is, for individuals returning from prison to the City of Chicago, they are clustered into a select few neighborhoods on the west and south side of the city. Similarly, those former prisoners residing in suburban areas are located in relatively few suburban neighborhoods. The fact that returning prisoners tend to be geographically clustered into resource-deprived neighborhoods has important implications for the persistence of criminal behavior.

II. The Role of Neighborhood Context in Explanations of Persistence and Desistance

Several different theoretical perspectives can be used to explain the effect of neighborhood conditions on criminal persistence and desistance. The discussion to follow focuses on the following mechanisms: criminal opportunity, social disorganization and informal social control, social and cultural isolation, and legal cynicism.[2]

A. Criminal Opportunities

One perspective explaining the effect of neighborhood conditions on persistence and desistance comes from routine activity theory (Cohen and Felson 1979). As Cohen and Felson (1979) argue, crime is the result of the convergence of motivated offenders and suitable targets in the absence of capable guardians. The implication is that to truly understand criminal behavior, we must model routine activities of offenders, victims, and guardians. Regarding offenders, Osgood and colleagues (1996) argue that motivation for crime is situational rather than fixed in the individual. Many criminal offenders are not wholly committed to crime, and therefore persistence is a function of the situational contingencies that provide opportunities for crime and weaken social controls (Farrall et al. 2014). For instance, in their qualitative longitudinal study of a random sample of 199 probationers in the United Kingdom, Farrall and colleagues (2014) find that sample members who persisted in crime spent more time in situations conducive to crime and had far fewer structured routines in their lives (i.e., with respect to family time and work).

To understand the availability of criminal opportunities, it is pertinent to examine how the structure of neighborhoods influence the amount of activity that takes place in a space and what influences the convergence of offenders and victims in space (Sampson, Morenoff, and Gannon-Rowley 2002). From this perspective, neighborhood characteristics such as land use, the location of schools and public transportation stops, population density, and the prevalence of nighttime visitors are consequential to the convergence of offenders and targets in the absence of guardians. For instance, residence in proximity to bars and taverns, which have been shown to be magnets for crime (Roncek and Maier 1991), could contribute to the persistence of crime.

One factor influencing the availability of criminal opportunities is the presence of criminal peers. I noted in the discussion of the geography of prisoner re-entry that former prisoners and individuals with previous contact with the criminal justice system tend to cluster in geographic space. Accordingly, residence in a neighborhood housing many former prisoners may facilitate an individual's persistence in criminal activity through expansion of criminal opportunities. As Osgood and colleagues (1996, p. 639) suggest, "Being with peers can increase the situational potential for deviance by making deviance easier and rewarding. . . . Friends are a common source of illicit drugs; being accompanied by friends reduces the danger in challenging a rival to a fight; and having a partner to serve as look-out can enhance the chances of success at theft." Hence, the greater the prevalence of potential partners in crime in a neighborhood, the greater the exposure to criminal opportunities.

B. Social Disorganization

Social disorganization theory provides another perspective on the neighborhood context of persistence and desistance. Shaw and McKay (1942) propose that variations in crime and delinquency across neighborhoods are a function of the extent of social disorganization across these areas. Social disorganization refers to the breakdown in the social institutions of a neighborhood community (e.g., family, schools, churches, political groups), rendering them ineffective at maintaining social order and control. The implication is that to prevent or reduce crime (and relatedly, recidivism), we need to alter conditions of neighborhoods and not simply focus on the rehabilitation of individuals within those neighborhoods (Shaw and McKay 1942).

The most widely tested aspect of Shaw and McKay's thesis stems from their argument that low socioeconomic status (SES), ethnic heterogeneity, and residential mobility all lead to disruption of local community social organization, which ultimately accounts for neighborhood variation in rates of crime and delinquency. High recidivism rates are a predictable outcome given that ex-prisoners and other former offenders often reside in disorganized neighborhoods characterized by these types of factors.

Central to Shaw and McKay's (1942) theoretical claims about the relation between disorganization and crime is their emphasis on "differential systems of values." Shaw and McKay do note that in both high- and low-SES areas the dominant value system is conventional, but in low-SES areas there is a competing system of values with which residents must contend. This is not to say that the more affluent and less-crime-ridden areas do not have unconventional values and behavior; rather, there is greater uniformity and consensus on values in those areas, which insulates individuals from the criminal element. In contrast, in high-crime areas, individuals are routinely brought into contact with unconventional attitudes and behaviors that conflict with the dominant (conventional) value systems. These unconventional attitudes still emphasize the achievement of status and economic gain, but different means to achieve these ends are formulated and transmitted. In other words, these unconventional values support criminal and delinquent behavior. By residing in disorganized neighborhoods marked by unconventional values, past offenders may be discouraged or dissuaded from following the necessary path to successful re-integration into society and therefore persist with their criminal activities.

More recent formulations of the social disorganization thesis have come to define social disorganization as the inability of a community structure to realize the common values of its residents and maintain effective social controls (Kornhauser 1978; Bursik 1988; Sampson and Groves 1989). With an emphasis on the importance of relational networks to facilitate social control, current formulations of the social disorganization thesis have utilized the systemic model, which identifies the social organization of communities by focusing on the local community networks (Kasarda and Janowitz 1974). Related to social control, the systemic model posits that the structure and characteristics of these networks determines the capacity with which a neighborhood can engage in control.

Whereas social network ties facilitate the creation and maintenance of social capital and informal social control, Sampson (2001) argues that social networks and the strength of social ties alone cannot explain social control given that strong ties are not always conducive to action. Evidence of the limits of social ties can be seen in the findings of Whyte (1993 [1943]) and more recently in research by Warner and Rountree (1997). Accordingly, Morenoff and colleagues (2001; see also Sampson, Morenoff, and Earls 1999) argue that researchers must move beyond a reliance on social capital and density of ties when examining the determinants of crime. They describe social capital as a "resource potential," but one that must be activated and utilized. To move beyond social capital and strong ties and associations, these authors use the "task-specific" construct of collective efficacy to explain neighborhood variations in violent crime (Sampson, Raudenbush, and Earls 1997; Morenoff, Sampson, and Raudenbush 2001). Collective efficacy is defined as the process of activating or converting social ties among neighborhood residents in order to achieve collective goals, such as public order or the control of crime (Sampson, Raudenbush, and Earls 1997).

Clear and colleagues' (Rose and Clear 1998; Clear et al. 2003; Clear 2007) coercive mobility thesis is a variant of the social disorganization model that similarly emphasizes the role of social networks in the control of crime. In the first articulation of the coercive mobility thesis, Rose and Clear (1998) examine the implications of incarceration on neighborhood social networks and put forth the argument that high neighborhood incarceration rates disrupt familial and neighborhood social networks, thus undermining efforts to informally control neighborhood crime. In other words, extensive use of formal social controls through the incarceration of neighborhood residents may ultimately undermine a neighborhood's capacity for informal social control by fragmenting the social networks upon which informal control depends. Neighborhoods that disproportionately send individuals to prison are also typically the neighborhoods that receive released prisoners, thereby creating a process known as "churning" that is disruptive to the stability of neighborhoods (Clear 2007). Thus, released prisoners often return to neighborhoods lacking in informal social controls, making crime and recidivism more likely.

C. Social and Cultural Isolation

A third perspective on the neighborhood context of persistence and desistance can be garnered from the seminal work of William Julius Wilson. In *The Truly Disadvantaged*,

Wilson (1987) argues that the socioeconomically disadvantaged in the United States circa the 1980s were qualitatively different than the urban poor of prior periods, or, more specifically, their social contexts were different. Prior to the 1960s, he notes, "lower-class, working-class, and middle-class black families all lived more or less in the same communities (albeit in different neighborhoods), sent their children to the same schools, availed themselves of the same recreational facilities, and shopped at the same stores" (Wilson 1987, p. 7). In contrast, Wilson suggests that the contemporary poor are drastically more likely to live in social isolation from mainstream society. This social isolation, he argues, creates a fundamentally different urban milieu than in eras when the poor lived among other socioeconomic classes. To Wilson, the "truly disadvantaged" refers to more than just poverty; it refers to the geographic isolation of the underclass— that is, the unskilled, the undereducated, the unemployed, the poor, and the criminal— from working- and middle-class segments of society.

Why is the social isolation Wilson described so consequential? He (Wilson 1987, p. 56) argues:

> the exodus of middle- and working-class families from many ghetto neighborhoods removes an important 'social buffer' that could deflect the full impact of the kind of prolonged and increasing joblessness that plagued inner-city neighborhoods in the 1970s and early 1980s . . . this argument is based on the assumption that even if the truly disadvantaged segments of an inner-city area experience a significant increase in long-term spells of joblessness, the basic institutions in that area (churches, schools, stores, recreational facilities, etc.) would remain viable if much of the base of their support comes from the more economically stable and secure families.

Yet when the middle-class base of support vacated the inner city, mainstream institutions of informal social control weakened. Wilson (1987) argues that the exodus of the middle class and the resulting social isolation of the disadvantaged resulted in a cultural isolation: neighborhood residents are isolated from mainstream cultural norms, particularly those associated with steady work.

As Harding (2010) points out, Wilson's theory of cultural isolation diverges from Shaw and McKay's theory of a "differential system of values" even though each one is a variant of a control model. For Shaw and McKay, unconventional values gain traction in a neighborhood because the weakened institutions of social control (e.g., churches, schools, and families) cannot fend them off; yet Shaw and McKay contend that the conventional value system is still dominant.[3] Thus, disorganized neighborhoods are said to be characterized by a differential system of values, or cultural heterogeneity, rather than cultural isolation of just unconventional norms and values. As Harding (2010) explicates, because of neighborhood cultural heterogeneity, an individual's commitment to any particular cultural model is weak—e.g., he or she is less likely to follow his or her stated goals or to act in accordance with one particular cultural frame. In sum, the cultural mechanism of the disorganization and isolation models diverge—i.e., cultural isolation away from mainstream values versus cultural heterogeneity of mainstream and unconventional values in the same neighborhood; yet they are united by the notion that structural conditions breed cultural adaptations that undermine the control of crime. This leads to a focus on one particular cultural adaptation linking neighborhood context and persistence in crime: legal cynicism.

D. Legal Cynicism

Legal cynicism is a cultural orientation in which the law and the police are viewed as illegitimate, unresponsive, and ill-equipped to ensure public safety (Kirk and Papachristos 2011). In contrast to an attribute solely of individuals, Kirk and Papachristos (2011, p. 1201) suggest that legal cynicism can become part of the social fabric of neighborhoods: "Cynicism becomes cultural through social interaction. In this sense, individuals' own experiential-based perception of the law becomes solidified through a collective process whereby residents develop a shared meaning of the behavior of the law." Prior research on legal cynicism has demonstrated that cynical views of the law in a neighborhood are generally the product of the structural conditions of the neighborhood, particularly socioeconomic disadvantage, and variation in criminal justice practices, especially the legitimacy of the police (Sampson and Bartusch 1998; Kirk and Papachristos 2011; Kirk et al. 2012). Building on the work of Kapsis (1978), Sampson and Bartusch (1998) argue that the economic and political marginalization of neighborhoods, combined with racial segregation, breeds cynicism of the law in those neighborhoods.

Cynicism of the law helps answer the question of why the concentration of offenders and former offenders in geographic space may lead to the persistence of criminal behavior. The funneling of massive numbers of formerly incarcerated individuals back to select neighborhoods likely reproduces a cultural ethos in those areas characterized by a severe cynicism of the law (Kirk and Papachristos 2011, 2015; Kirk 2016).

One basis for this assertion can be found in recent work by Weaver and Lerman (2010). Their findings reveal that direct experiences with incarceration or police harassment fundamentally influence an individual's distrust of the law. They find that involvement with the criminal justice system significantly depresses a person's trust in government, with trust becoming increasingly damaged as criminal sanctions become more severe (see also Muller and Schrage 2014). Given that ex-prisoners are relatively more distrustful of the criminal justice system, concentrated prisoner re-entry may have a devastating effect on perceptions of the law and authority among a community of residents. Concentrating ex-prisoners in the same neighborhood saturates residents' social networks with criminals and potentially leads to the contagious spread of legal cynicism and distrust of the police.

Evidence of this contagion process can be seen in recent work by Papachristos, Meares, and Fagan (2012). These authors point out that among individuals with a history of criminal behavior there is great variation in the frequency of criminal offending and that most criminals actually spend the majority of their time complying with the law. The authors thus wonder why criminals do, in fact, obey the law most of the time, and they look to the import of criminal social networks for an answer. Papachristos and colleagues (2012) find that members of street gangs—particularly, those whose social networks are inundated with criminal associates—are more likely to view the law and the police as illegitimate and therefore are more likely to engage in criminal behavior. Conversely, criminals who do not generally associate with other criminals are far more likely to have positive views of the criminal justice system than those who associate primarily with other criminals. As a consequence, criminals embedded in networks with noncriminals engage less often in criminal activity than those embedded in social networks with many other criminals. In relation to concentrated prisoner re-entry, if association with non-criminals is vital for desisting from crime, then residing in a neighborhood with limited access to prosocial peers would appear to thwart turning points in the life course of crime even if an individual is motivated to change. Accordingly, it is plausible to assume that ex-prisoners who reside in a neighborhood with many other former prisoners are more likely to recidivate than ex-prisoners who are not routinely exposed to other criminals. Recent research by Kirk (2015) provides support for this hypothesis. He finds that ex-prisoners are more likely to be re-incarcerated if they reside in proximity to many other former prisoners (see also Mennis and Harris 2011; Stahler et al. 2013; Chamberlain and Wallace 2016).

E. Person–Context Interactions

Largely absent from the discussion thus far is consideration of how individual characteristics bear upon persistence and desistance. While it is out of the scope of this chapter to review all of the various individual-level risk and protective factors predictive of persistence and desistance, it is relevant to discuss the interaction between person and contextual characteristics. As Wikström and Loeber (2000, p. 1110) suggest, "Individuals' perceptions of alternatives and process of decision making will be seen as a result of the interaction of the individual's set of characteristics (dispositions and social situation) and the characteristics of the community context (structural characteristics and their related social processes) in which he or she lives and acts." Accordingly, in his explication of situational action theory, Wikström (2006, p. 61) argues, "people are moved to action (including acts of crime) by how they *see their action alternatives and make their choices when confronted with the particularities of a setting*" (emphasis in original).

Strands of this argument can be found in the preceding discussions of criminal opportunity and legal cynicism. Many criminal offenders are weakly motivated to commit crime. When they do engage in criminal conduct, it is often because a good opportunity to do so came along. For instance, in their qualitative study of persisting and desisting offenders, Farrall and colleagues (2014) recount the story of a former probationer named Danny. Danny was working in legitimate employment and was relatively content with his lifestyle. However, Danny willingly noted that should an illegal opportunity for "big money" come along, he'd take it. He was not firmly committed to criminal behavior, nor was he staunchly opposed to it. Danny's persistence in crime very much depended upon the presentation of criminal opportunities. An individual with a different cognitive orientation and firm commitment to desistance could perhaps more readily withstand the temptation of a "big money" opportunity.

In their conception of legal cynicism, Kirk and Papachristos (2011) similarly conceive of behavior as the product of individual choices influenced by the characteristics of the social environment. In discussing the consequences of legal cynicism, they suggest, "the consequence is constraint—that is, cynicism constrains choices for resolving grievances and protecting oneself because individuals are more likely to presume that the law is unavailable or unresponsive to their needs. In the face of such constraints, individuals may choose to engage in their own brand of social control because they cannot rely upon the law to assist them" (Kirk and Papachristos 2011, pp. 1202–1203). When faced with a threatening situation, individuals may choose to avoid the situation or otherwise run from the situation, seek protection from older neighborhood peers, call the police for protection, or resort to violence to resolve a conflict. Individuals with negative perceptions of the criminal justice system may view reliance on the police as an ineffective strategy for handling the threatening situation, thus making it more likely that they choose a different strategy. Ultimately an individual's behavior will depend upon the interaction of situational opportunities and individual characteristics.

F. Empirical Tests of the Link Between Neighborhood Context and Persistence/Desistance

Whereas there are several theoretical perspectives offering testable hypotheses related to the effect of neighborhood context on persistence and desistance, there is a relative dearth of research undertaking such tests, particularly related to the behavior of returning prisoners. Perhaps one reason is that methodological advances in GIS and spatial modeling have just recently opened the research avenues for exploring the question of the spatial distribution of prisoner re-entry. Even with such methodological advances, however, empirical studies are still dependent upon the availability of spatial and geographic data of crime, prisoner re-entry, and neighborhood characteristics. Thus, researchers have often been constrained by a lack of data. With that said, a few noteworthy studies have applied the arguments of the aforementioned neighborhood perspectives to understand the correlates of recidivism.

As one fruitful example, through a series of both theoretical and empirical publications, Rose, Clear, and a number of colleagues have examined the effects of high rates of incarceration in a given neighborhood on social disorganization and social control (see, e.g., Rose and Clear 1998; Clear, Rose, and Ryder 2001; Clear et al. 2003). As noted, Rose and Clear (1998) argue that high neighborhood incarceration rates disrupt familial and neighborhood social networks, thus undermining efforts to informally control neighborhood crime. In one empirical test, Clear and colleagues (2003) assess the repercussions of high rates of prisoner re-entry to Tallahassee neighborhoods on subsequent crime rates. They find a positive effect of neighborhood rates of prisoner re-entry on neighborhood crime rates in the following year, even after controlling for neighborhood characteristics like poverty, residential mobility, racial heterogeneity, and prior crime rate. Similarly, a study of census tracts in Seattle finds that the rates of prisoner re-entry in neighborhoods are positively associated with subsequent violent crime rates and that the relative percentage of former prisoners in a neighborhood negatively influences collective efficacy by increasing housing and employment instability in the neighborhood (Drakulich et al. 2012).

While the aforementioned research examines the effect of neighborhood context (measured through the concentration of returning prisoners) on an aggregate indicator of crime, Kubrin and Stewart (2006) examine the effect of neighborhood context on an individual's likelihood of recidivism. In a study of recidivism in Multnomah County, Oregon, the authors find that offenders under community supervision who resided in disadvantaged neighborhoods following criminal sanctioning were significantly more likely to recidivate than those offenders who resided in more affluent neighborhoods. Offenders living in the least disadvantaged neighborhoods still had a 0.42 probability of recidivating, but those living in the most disadvantaged neighborhoods had a 0.60 probability (where recidivism is defined as a rearrest within twelve months following admission to community supervision). These results hold even after controlling for individual-level factors such as gender, age, race, ethnicity, and criminal history as well as sanctioning information.

In more recent research, Mears and colleagues (2008) find a positive association between county-level resource deprivation and reconviction from violent offending among male offenders released from Florida prisons. Hipp, Petersilia, and Turner (2010) find that multiple dimensions of neighborhood context predict reincarceration among a sample of California parolees, including concentrated disadvantage and the number of social service providers within two miles of parolees.

III. Residential Mobility, Persistence, and Desistance

As noted in the introductory section, estimates suggest that two-thirds of returning prisoners will be rearrested within three years, and roughly one-half will be back in prison (Durose, Cooper, and Snyder 2014). A likely contributor to high levels of recidivism is the fact that many released prisoners return home to the same environment with the same criminal opportunities and criminal peers that proved so detrimental to their behavior prior to incarceration. Recent estimates from Michigan suggest that the first post-prison place of residence for roughly one-third of newly released prisoners is within one-half mile of their pre-prison place of residence, and that a full 60 percent reside within five miles of their pre-prison place of residence (Harding, Morenoff, and

Herbert 2013). Hence, a sizable percentage of newly released prisoners reside in relatively close proximity to their pre-prison place of residence.

John Laub and Robert Sampson's (2003; see also Sampson and Laub 1993) life-course theory of desistance from crime provides a theoretical basis for understanding why separating from old neighborhoods through residential mobility could promote desistance and, conversely, why returning to home neighborhoods is predictive of the persistence in criminal offending. Among the notable findings from their multi-decade project are that offenders desist from crime in response to structurally induced turning points, such as work and marriage. Turning points serve as catalysts for sustained behavioral change by providing opportunities for individuals to separate from the settings, situations, and criminal peers that facilitated their prior criminal behavior.

Sampson and Laub's (2005) life-course theory of criminal desistance highlights several commonalities among turning points that foster desistance from crime. They (2005, pp. 17–18) note:

> What appears to be important about institutional or structural turning points is that they all involve, to varying degrees, (1) new situations that "knife off" the past from the present, (2) new situations that provide both supervision and monitoring as well as new opportunities of social support and growth, (3) new situations that change and structure routine activities, and (4) new situations that provide the opportunity for identity transformation.

At a theoretical level, residential relocation would seem to fit these four commonalities. In particular, residential moves may be turning points in the life course of crime, but the moves must include enough physical and social separation from previous neighborhood environments to allow an individual to "knife off" from his or her criminal past and prior criminal associates (Sampson 2008; Kirk 2009; Sharkey and Sampson 2010; Kirk 2012, 2020). In other words, the mere act of moving may be insufficient for desistance; rather, the degree of move is consequential. The more separation an individual has from his or her criminal past—both geographically and socially—the better. Thus, moving next door may have little effect on behavioral change, but moving to an entirely different city may allow an individual to truly separate from the past and therefore lead to long-term behavioral change.

Recent quantitative research supports this assertion. Kirk (2009, 2012, 2020) used the neighborhood destruction in New Orleans following Hurricane Katrina as a natural experiment to investigate the effects of residential change on recidivism. He found substantial reductions in rates of re-incarceration among ex-offenders who moved away from their former parishes. His most conservative estimates (Kirk 2012) reveal that ex-prisoners who moved were 14 percentage points less likely to be reincarcerated within three years of prison release. In another study, Sharkey and Sampson (2010) found that among Chicago adolescents who moved to a different neighborhood within the city, their likelihood of violent offending increased. However, moving outside of Chicago reduced violent behavior.[4]

With respect to qualitative research, in their study of the life course of crime through age 70, Laub and Sampson (2003) find through qualitative interviews that residential change is often a fundamental turning point that leads to desistance from crime. Similarly, Farrall and colleagues (2014) find, particularly among drug users, that desistance was often achieved by moving far away from the people and situations conducive to drug use. These quantitative and qualitative studies suggest that residential change may lead to shifts in prior behavioral patterns, especially if the new residence is a considerable distance from the old neighborhood.

The Moving to Opportunity (MTO) housing mobility demonstration offers important insights about the consequences of residential relocation and the importance of residential moves that provide a true separation between origin and destination locations. MTO is a program sponsored by the U.S. Department of Housing and Urban Development, which was initiated in 1994 in Baltimore, Boston, Chicago, Los Angeles, and New York (Katz, Kling, and Liebman 2001; Kling, Liebman, and Katz 2007). It has been described as the "most ambitious randomized social experiment ever conducted by HUD," with over 4,600 low-income families with children participating (Sanbonmatsu et al. 2011, foreword). The question driving the MTO studies is whether an individual would behave differently, in terms of crime and other individual outcomes, if he or she lived in a non-poor neighborhood instead of a poor neighborhood. MTO families were randomly assigned to one of three groups: (1) an experimental group, which received a housing voucher and relocation assistance to move to homes only in areas with less than 10 percent poverty; (2) a Section 8 comparison group, which received a housing voucher that could be used in any neighborhood; and (3) a control group, which received no housing assistance (but were free to move if they wished). Researchers compared the three groups on a variety of outcomes, including crime, earnings, and health.

For many tested outcomes in the MTO demonstration, the residential moves were inconsequential, or in some cases detrimental. Mid- and long-term impact evaluations from MTO revealed that male youth in the experimental group showed a greater likelihood of engaging in problem behavior than control group youth (Kling, Ludwig, and Katz, 2005; Kling, Liebman, and Katz 2007). Thus, the results would suggest that there are limits to the potential benefits of relocation, particularly for male youth. Yet, as findings from Kirk's (2009, 2012, 2020) work on New Orleans and Sharkey and Sampson's (2010) research on Chicago allude, it may be the case that the residential moves in the MTO program were not, on average, substantial enough to produce a turning point in behavioral trajectories.

As noted, turning points can serve as catalysts for behavioral change by providing individuals a fresh start or a new situation to change their behavior. Importantly, Sampson (2008) points out through his analysis of families from the Chicago MTO site that a vast majority of MTO experimental families in Chicago moved a relatively short distance from their origin neighborhoods, with most of the families moving from one South Side neighborhood to a nearby neighborhood. Thus, it is questionable whether moving really severed the peer social networks of those youth. If a family moved just a short distance, then a youth could easily maintain ties with his or her criminogenic social network despite the move. On this point, Briggs, Popkin, and Goering (2010, p. 18) note in their thorough evaluation of MTO: "Changing the social relations of participants was not a primary aim of the MTO experiment. . . . But many of the hoped-for positive outcomes anticipated changes in exposure to particular kinds of peers, adult role models, and more successful neighbors." In other words, MTO was not specifically designed to provide participants a fresh start in life by altering their social networks, but many of the hypothesized changes in behavior seemingly required just that. Because the MTO program did not require that families move a minimum distance, the program may have had little chance of separating youths from anti-social peers or with reducing criminal behavior. By implication, residential relocation may still foster desistance from crime, but there must be enough distance between the origin and destination locations to provide a true catalyst for change.

Summarizing the implications of the MTO results, it is critical to note that the intervention of the MTO program was the opportunity to move out of poverty. Moving to "opportunity" may in fact be advantageous to desisting from crime, but this opportunity may be enhanced if the move truly allows for a fresh start. In this sense, the greatest reductions in the likelihood of recidivism may be found when an ex-prisoner moves a considerable distance away from his or her old neighborhood and the new neighborhood is characterized by an abundance of social and economic resources.

There is, of course, a counterargument to any claims that residential mobility is uniformly beneficial if it means separation from familial resources. Research reveals that reuniting ex-offenders with families often provides critical support to ex-offenders as they work to desist from crime (Visher, La Vigne, and Travis 2004). Families often provide housing, financial support, assistance with job searches, and emotional support for formerly incarcerated persons. That being said, reuniting with family members is not universally beneficial. Families can be supportive, but that is not always the case. One of the well-known facts of criminology is that crime runs in the family for a variety of reasons. Many ex-prisoners have family members who are actively involved in criminal activity and drug use, and the vast majority of ex-prisoners have at least one family member who has been convicted of a crime (Visher, La Vigne, and Travis 2004). Still, to the extent that residential mobility leads to the desistance from crime, it is arguably more effective when criminogenic ties are severed and prosocial ties are maintained.

Whereas residential mobility may serve some benefit in terms of separating former offenders from the people and places associated with their past criminal activity, too many residential moves can be destabilizing, which can potentially lead to persistence of crime and recidivism (Meredith et al. 2003; Roman and Travis 2006; Geller and Curtis 2011; Harding, Morenoff, and Herbert 2013). One factor explaining the link between housing instability and recidivism is employment—the lack of stable housing makes it challenging to secure and maintain employment. Research on prisoner re-entry in Michigan suggests that parolees move frequently—an estimated 2.6 times per year for the median parolee (Harding, Morenoff, and Herbert 2013). Hence, it is important to recognize the conditions by which residential mobility may promote desistance from crime. Infrequent moves that sever criminogenic ties while maintaining supportive ties are more likely to promote desistance from crime than the alternatives.

IV. RESIDENTIAL IMPLICATIONS FOR OFFENDER RE-ENTRY AND RE-INTEGRATION EFFORTS

Most rehabilitation programs and services for ex-prisoners are dedicated to addressing individual determinants of criminal recidivism (e.g., education levels, drug addiction, cognitive thinking). As this chapter has revealed, there are a variety of mechanisms by which social context, and mobility away from those contexts, contribute to the persistence of, and desistance from, criminal offending. Hence, it would be fruitful to direct prisoner re-entry and re-integration efforts toward both individual and contextual determinants of behavior.

Upon exiting prison, ex-offenders most often return to the same general areas where they resided before incarceration. Many ex-prisoners still end up moving back to their former counties and neighborhoods despite an expressed interest to avoid such places (Visher and Farrell 2005). These patterns are anything but random. In fact, many states legally require parolees to return to their county of conviction or last residence when they exit prison (National Research Council 2007). There are many additional reasons why ex-prisoners are likely to return to disadvantaged neighborhoods in proximity to their former places of residence, including family and social ties as well as familiarity and attachment to particular places. Of course residence with family members may be the result of more than preference; it may also result because of limited options for other housing. The lack of housing for ex-offenders is certainly a function of the limited income, wealth, and job prospects of the typical offender, and it is also the product of the unwillingness of owners and landlords in the private housing market to rent to felons and the combination of long waiting lists for public housing assistance and the unwillingness of public housing authorities to provide units or vouchers to formerly incarcerated individuals. Also of importance is the fact that the availability of affordable housing in the United States has shrunk over the past decade at the same time that the number of households with extremely low incomes has drastically increased. For all these reasons, individuals exiting prison tend to cluster into the same few resource-deprived neighborhoods, often times returning in close proximity to the very same neighborhoods where they resided when they got into trouble with the law.

To lower recidivism, there are a number of remedies government agencies can pursue that are targeted at connecting formerly incarcerated individuals to those neighborhood contexts conducive to desistance from crime. Per the discussion above, the expansion of housing opportunities for formerly incarcerated individuals into more affluent and resourced areas with an abundance of collective efficacy should reduce the likelihood of recidivism. However, because of politics and NIMBYism, the feasibility of such a strategy is doubtful, at least on a large scale.

To the extent that a criminal record limits access to certain housing opportunities and neighborhood environments, another possibility for reform is to limit the sale and release of mug shots and criminal record information by the government. The government could adopt an automatic expunction of criminal records for low-level offenders successfully completing deferred adjudications. The government might also prohibit public access to all non-conviction criminal records. Again, to the extent that a criminal record reduces an individual's chances of residing in a neighborhood environment characterized by socioeconomic opportunity and institutions of informal social control, one possibility for bringing about a change in behavior is to enable access to a residential environment conducive to behavioral change. There are numerous possibilities for opening up such access, but the political will for reform must exist.

Notes

1. Trends in the suburbanization and exurbanization of prisoner re-entry are not limited to the Chicago metropolitan area. While few research studies to date have examined this geographic shift in re-entry, there is also evidence of the suburbanization of prisoner re-entry in Austin, Texas (Austin/Travis County Reentry Roundtable 2014).
2. For discussion of additional causal mechanisms linking neighborhood conditions and behavior, see Jencks and Mayer (1990), Leventhal and Brooks-Gunn (2000), and Sampson, Morenoff, and Gannon-Rowley (2002).
3. Shaw and McKay (1942) suggest that affluent areas will have unconventional values and behavior to some extent, yet there is greater uniformity and consensus on values in those areas that insulates individuals from the criminal element.
4. This distinction between the effects of suburban versus intracity moves is consistent with research from the Gautreaux housing mobility program, a court-ordered residential desegregation program that resulted from a 1976 U.S. Supreme Court ruling. Male youths from the Gautreaux families who moved to the Chicago suburbs were less likely to be arrested for drug, theft, and violent offenses than male youths who moved internally within Chicago (Keels 2008).

References

Austin/Travis County Reentry Roundtable. 2014. *Austin/Travis County Reentry Report Card, 2014.* Austin, TX: Austin/Travis County Reentry Roundtable. http://www.reentryroundtable.net/wp-content/uploads/2014/08/ATCRRT-report-card-revised-Sept14-Final.pdf.

Bonczar, Thomas P. 2003. *Prevalence of Imprisonment in the U.S. Population, 1974–2001.* Washington, DC: U.S. Department of Justice.

Briggs, Xavier de Souza, Susan J. Popkin, and John Goering. 2010. *Moving to Opportunity: The Story of an American Experiment to Fight Ghetto Poverty.* New York: Oxford University Press.

Bureau of Justice Statistics. 2000. *Total Sentenced Prisoners Released from State or Federal Jurisdiction*. Washington, DC: Bureau of Justice Statistics, U.S. Department of Justice. http://www.bjs.gov/content/dtdata.cfm.

Bursik, Robert J., Jr. 1988. "Social Disorganization and Theories of Crime and Delinquency: Problems and Prospects." *Criminology* 26: 519–551.

Carson, E. Ann, and Daniela Golinelli. 2013. *Prisoners in 2012: Trends in Admissions and Releases, 1991–2012*. Bureau of Justice Statistics Bulletin. Washington, DC: U.S. Department of Justice.

Chamberlain, Alyssa W., and Danielle Wallace. 2016. "Mass Reentry, Neighborhood Context and Recidivism: Examining How the Distribution of Parolees Within and Across Neighborhoods Impacts Recidivism." *Justice Quarterly* 33: 912–941.

Clear, Todd R. 2007. *Imprisoning Communities: How Mass Incarceration Makes Disadvantaged Neighborhoods Worse*. New York: Oxford University Press.

Clear, Todd R., Dina R. Rose, and Judith Ryder. 2001. "Incarceration and the Community: The Problem of Removing and Returning Offenders." *Crime and Delinquency* 47: 335–351.

Clear, Todd R., Dina R. Rose, Elin Waring, and Kristen Scully. 2003. "Coercive Mobility and Crime: A Preliminary Examination of Concentrated Incarceration and Social Disorganization." *Justice Quarterly* 20: 33–64.

Cohen, Lawrence E., and Marcus Felson. 1979. "Social Change and Crime Rate Trends: A Routine Activity Approach." *American Sociological Review* 44: 588–607.

Cullen, Francis T., and Paul Gendreau. 2000. "Assessing Correctional Rehabilitation." In *Policies, Processes, and Decisions of the Criminal Justice System*, Vol. 3, edited by Julie Horney, 109–175. Washington, DC: U.S. Department of Justice.

Drakulich, Kevin M., Robert D. Crutchfield, Ross L. Matsueda, and Kristin Rose. 2012. "Instability, Informal Control, and Criminogenic Situations: Community Effects of Returning Prisoners." *Crime, Law and Social Change* 57: 493–519.

Durose, Matthew R., Alexia D. Cooper, and Howard Snyder. 2014. *Recidivism of Prisoners Released in 30 States in 2005: Patterns from 2005 to 2010*. Washington, DC: Bureau of Justice Statistics.

Farrall, Stephen, Ben Hunter, Gilly Sharpe, and Adam Calverley. 2014. *Criminal Careers in Transition: The Social Context of Desistance from Crime*. New York: Oxford University Press.

Geller, Amanda, and Marah A. Curtis. 2011. "A Sort of Homecoming: Incarceration and the Housing Security of Urban Men." *Social Science Research* 40: 1196–1213.

Harding, David J. 2010. *Living the Drama: Community, Conflict, and Culture Among Inner-City Boys*. Chicago: University of Chicago Press.

Harding, David J., Jeffrey D. Morenoff, and Claire W. Herbert. 2013. "Home Is Hard to Find: Neighborhoods, Institutions, and the Residential Trajectories of Returning Prisoners." *Annals of the American Academy of Political and Social Science* 647: 214–236.

Hipp, John R., Joan Petersilia, and Susan Turner. 2010. "Parole Recidivism in California: The Effect of Neighborhood Context and Social Service Agency Characteristics." *Criminology* 48: 947–979.

Jencks, Christopher, and Susan E. Mayer. 1990. "The Social Consequences of Growing Up in a Poor Neighborhood." In *Inner-City Poverty in the United States*, edited by L. E. Lynn Jr. and M. G. H. McGeary, 111–185. Washington, DC: National Academy Press.

Kapsis, Robert E. 1978. "Black Ghetto Diversity and Anomie: A Sociopolitical View." *American Journal of Sociology* 83: 1132–1153.

Kasarda, John D., and Morris Janowitz. 1974. "Community Attachment in Mass Society." *American Sociological Review* 39: 328–339.

Katz, Lawrence F., Jeffrey R. Kling, and Jeffrey B. Liebman. 2001. "Moving to Opportunity in Boston: Early Results of a Randomized Mobility Experiment." *Quarterly Journal of Economics* 116 :607–654.

Keels, Micere. 2008. "Second-Generation Effects of Chicago's Gautreaux Residential Mobility Program on Children's Participation in Crime." *Journal of Research on Adolescence* 18: 305–352.

Kirk, David S. 2009. "A Natural Experiment on Residential Change and Recidivism: Lessons from Hurricane Katrina." *American Sociological Review* 74: 484–505.

Kirk, David S. 2012. "Residential Change as a Turning Point in the Life Course of Crime: Desistance or Temporary Cessation?" *Criminology* 50: 329–358.

Kirk, David S. 2015. "A Natural Experiment of the Consequences of Concentrating Former Prisoners in the Same Neighborhoods." *Proceedings of the National Academy of Sciences* 112: 6943–6948.

Kirk, David S. 2016. "Prisoner Reentry and the Reproduction of Legal Cynicism." *Social Problems* 63: 222–243.

Kirk, David S. 2020. *Home Free: Residential Change and Redemption After Hurricane Katrina.* New York: Oxford University Press.

Kirk, David S., and Andrew V. Papachristos. 2011. "Cultural Mechanisms and the Persistence of Neighborhood Violence." *American Journal of Sociology* 116: 1190–1233.

Kirk, David S., and Andrew V. Papachristos. 2015. "Concentrated Disadvantage, the Persistence of Legal Cynicism, and Crime: Revisiting the Conception of 'Culture' in Criminology." In *Challenging Criminological Theory: The Legacy of Ruth Kornhauser,* edited by Francis T. Cullen, Pamela Wilcox, Robert J. Sampson, and Brendan Dooley, 259–274. New Brunswick, NJ: Transaction.

Kirk, David S., Andrew V. Papachristos, Jeffrey Fagan, and Tom R. Tyler. 2012. "The Paradox of Law Enforcement in Immigrant Communities: Does Tough Immigration Enforcement Undermine Public Safety?" *The Annals of the American Academy of Political and Social Science* 641: 79–98.

Kling, Jeffrey R., Jeffrey B. Liebman, and Lawrence F. Katz. 2007. "Experimental Analysis of Neighborhood Effects." *Econometrica* 75: 83–119.

Kling, Jeffrey R., Jens Ludwig, and Lawrence F. Katz. 2005. "Neighborhood Effects on Crime for Female and Male Youth: Evidence from a Randomized Housing Voucher Experiment." *Quarterly Journal of Economics* 120: 87–130.

Kornhauser, Ruth. 1978. *Social Sources of Delinquency.* Chicago: University of Chicago Press.

Kubrin, Charis E., and Eric A. Stewart. 2006. "Predicting Who Reoffends: The Neglected Role of Neighborhood Context in Recidivism Studies." *Criminology* 44: 165–197.

La Vigne, Nancy G., Cynthia A. Mamalian, Jeremy Travis, and Christy Visher. 2003. *A Portrait of Prisoner Reentry in Illinois.* Washington, DC: Urban Institute.

Langan, Patrick A., and David J. Levin. 2002. *Recidivism of Prisoners Released in 1994.* Washington, DC: Bureau of Justice Statistics.

Laub, John H., and Robert J. Sampson. 2003. *Shared Beginnings, Divergent Lives: Delinquent Boys to Age 70.* Cambridge, MA: Harvard University Press.

Leventhal, Tama, and Jeanne Brooks-Gunn. 2000. "The Neighborhoods They Live In: The Effects of Neighborhood Residence on Child and Adolescent Outcomes." *Psychological Bulletin* 126: 309–337.

MacKenzie, Doris L. 2002. "Reducing the Criminal Activities of Known Offenders and Delinquents: Crime Prevention in the Courts and Corrections." In *Evidence-Based Crime*

Prevention, edited by Lawrence W. Sherman, David P. Farrington, Brandon C. Welsh, and Doris L. MacKenzie, 330–404. London: Routledge.

Martinson, Robert. 1974. "What Works? Questions and Answers About Prison Reform." *The Public Interest* 10: 22–54.

Mears, Daniel P., Xia Wang, Carter Hay, and William D. Bales. 2008. "Social Ecology and Recidivism: Implications for Prisoner Reentry." *Criminology* 46: 301–340.

Mennis, Jeremy, and Philip Harris. 2011. "Contagion and Repeat Offending Among Urban Juvenile Delinquents." *Journal of Adolescence* 34: 951–963.

Meredith, Tammy, John Speir, Sharon Johnson, and Heather Hull. 2003. *Enhancing Parole Decision-Making Through the Automation of Risk Assessment*. Atlanta: Applied Research Services, Inc.

Minton, Todd D. 2013. *Jail Inmates at Midyear 2012—Statistical Tables*. Washington, DC: U.S. Department of Justice.

Morenoff, Jeffrey D., Robert J. Sampson, and Stephen W. Raudenbush. 2001. "Neighborhood Inequality, Collective Efficacy, and the Spatial Dynamics of Homicide." *Criminology* 39: 517–560.

Muller, Christopher, and Daniel Schrage. 2014. "Mass Imprisonment and Trust in the Law." *The Annals of the American Academy of Political and Social Science* 651: 139–158.

National Research Council, 2007. *Parole, Desistance from Crime, and Community Integration*. Committee on Community Supervision and Desistance from Crime. Committee on Law and Justice, Division of Behavioral and Social Sciences and Education. Washington, DC: The National Academies Press.

Osgood, D. Wayne, Janet K. Wilson, Jerald G. Bachman, Patrick M. O'Malley, and Lloyd D. Johnston. 1996. "Routine Activities and Individual Deviant Behavior." *American Sociological Review* 61: 635–655.

Papachristos, Andrew V., Tracey L. Meares, and Jeffrey Fagan. 2012. "Why Do Criminals Obey the Law? The Influence of Legitimacy and Social Networks on Active Gun Offenders." *Journal of Criminal Law and Criminology* 102: 397–440.

Pew Center on the States. 2008. *One in 100: Behind Bars in America 2008*. Washington DC: The Pew Charitable Trusts.

Roman, Caterina G., and Jeremy Travis. 2006. "Where Will I Sleep Tomorrow? Housing, Homelessness, and the Returning Prisoner." *Housing Policy Debate* 17: 389–418.

Roncek, Dennis W., and Pamela A. Maier. 1991. "Bars, Blocks, and Crime Revisited: Linking the Theory of Routine Activities to the Empiricism of 'Hot Spots.'" *Criminology* 29: 725–753.

Rose, Dina R., and Todd R. Clear. 1998. "Incarceration, Social Capital and Crime: Examining the Unintended Consequences of Incarceration." *Criminology* 36: 441–480.

Sampson, Robert J. 2001. "How Do Communities Undergird or Undermine Human Development? Relevant Contexts and Social Mechanisms." In *Does It Take A Village? Community Effects on Children, Adolescents, and Families*, edited by Alan Booth and Ann C. Crouter. Mahwah, NJ: Lawrence Erlbaum.

Sampson, Robert J. 2008. "Moving to Inequality: Neighborhood Effects and Experiments meet Social Structure." *American Journal of Sociology* 114: 189–231.

Sampson, Robert J., and Dawn Jeglum Bartusch. 1998. "Legal Cynicism and (Subcultural?) Tolerance of Deviance: The Neighborhood Context of Racial Differences." *Law and Society Review* 32: 777–804.

Sampson, Robert J., and W. Byron Groves. 1989. "Community Structure and Crime: Testing Social Disorganization Theory." *American Journal of Sociology* 94: 744–802.

Sampson, Robert J., and John H. Laub. 1993. *Crime in the Making: Pathways and Turning Points Through Life*. Cambridge, MA: Harvard University Press.

Sampson, Robert J., and John H. Laub. 2005. "A Life Course View of the Development of Crime." *Annals of the American Academy of Political and Social Science* 602: 12–45.

Sampson, Robert J, Jeffrey D Morenoff, and Felton Earls. 1999. "Beyond Social Capital: Spatial Dynamics of Collective Efficacy for Children." *American Sociological Review* 64: 633–660.

Sampson, Robert J., Jeffrey D. Morenoff, and Thomas P. Gannon-Rowley. 2002. "Assessing 'Neighborhood Effects': Social Processes and New Directions in Research." *Annual Review of Sociology* 28: 443–478.

Sampson, Robert J., Stephen W. Raudenbush, and Felton Earls. 1997. "Neighborhoods and Violent Crime: A Multilevel Study of Collective Efficacy." *Science* 227: 918–924.

Sanbonmatsu, Lisa, Jens Ludwig, Lawrence F. Katz, Lisa A. Gennetian, Greg J. Duncan, Ronald C. Kessler, Emma Adam, Thomas W. McDade, and Stacy Tessler Lindau. 2011. *Moving to Opportunity for Fair Housing Demonstration Program: Final Impacts Evaluation*. Washington, DC: U.S. Department of Housing and Urban Development, Office of Policy Development and Research.

Shannon, Sarah K.S., Christopher Uggen, Jason Schnittker, Michael Massoglia, Melissa Thompson, and Sara Wakefield. 2017. "The Growth, Scope, and Spatial Distribution of People with Felony Records in the United States, 1948–2010." *Demography* 54: 1795–1818.

Sharkey, Patrick, and Robert J. Sampson. 2010. "Destination Effects: Residential Mobility and Trajectories of Adolescent Violence in a Stratified Metropolis." *Criminology* 48: 639–682.

Shaw, Clifford, and Henry McKay. 1942. *Juvenile Delinquency and Urban Areas*. Chicago: University of Chicago Press.

Stahler, Gerald J., Jeremy Mennis, Steven Belenko, Wayne N. Welsh, Matthew L. Hiller, and Gary Zajac. 2013. "Predicting Recidivism for Released State Prison Offenders: Examining the Influence of Individual and Neighborhood Characteristics and Spatial Contagion on the Likelihood of Reincarceration." *Criminal Justice and Behavior* 40: 690–711.

Visher, Christy, and Jill Farrell. 2005. *Chicago Communities and Prisoner Reentry*. Washington, DC: Urban Institute.

Visher, Christy, Nancy La Vigne, and Jeremy Travis. 2004. *Returning Home: Understanding the Challenges of Prisoner Reentry: Maryland Pilot Study: Findings from Baltimore*. Washington, DC: Urban Institute.

Warner, Barbara D., and Pamela W. Rountree. 1997. "Local Social Ties in a Community and Crime Model: Questioning the Systemic Nature of Informal Social Control." *Social Problems* 44: 520–546.

Weaver, Vesla M., and Amy E. Lerman. 2010. "Political Consequences of the Carceral State." *American Political Science Review* 104: 817–833.

West, Heather C., and William J. Sabol. 2008. *Prisoners in 2007*. Washington, DC: Bureau of Justice Statistics, U.S. Department of Justice.

Whyte, William F. 1993 [1943]. *Street Corner Society*. 4th ed. Chicago: University of Chicago Press.

Wikström, Per-Olof. 2006. "Individuals, Settings, and Acts of Crime: Situational Mechanisms and the Explanation of Crime." In *The Explanation of Crime: Context, Mechanisms, and Development*, edited by Per-Olof H. Wikström and Robert J. Sampson, 61–107. Cambridge, UK: Cambridge University Press.

Wikström, Per-Olof, and Rolf Loeber. 2000. "Do Disadvantaged Neighborhoods Cause Well-Adjusted Children to Become Adolescent Delinquents? A Study of Male Juvenile Serious Offending, Individual Risk and Protective Factors, and Neighborhood Context." *Criminology* 38: 1109–1142.

Wilson, William J. 1987. *The Truly Disadvantaged: The Inner City, the Underclass, and Public Policy.* Chicago: University of Chicago Press.

CHAPTER 26

RELIGION AND THE MILITARY

LEANA A. BOUFFARD AND HAE RIM JIN

THEORIES of desistance point to a number of potential factors that may lead offenders away from criminal trajectories. While some suggest a simple aging out or maturational reform process, others point to the influence of turning points that encourage a "knifing-off" from past experiences and behaviors (Sampson and Laub 1993; Laub and Sampson 2003), that offer a choice-structuring environment that discourages criminal behavior (Laub and Sampson 2003), or that foster cognitive transformation or a change in identity (Giordano et al. 2008; Paternoster and Bushway 2009). Religion and the military as social institutions seem likely to foster desistance through all of these mechanisms, but relatively little research has examined their influence on offending and desistance as compared to other life events, like marriage and employment.

The purpose of this essay is to provide an overview of the literature examining the role of religion and military service in the desistance process and to identify outstanding issues and directions for future research. Section I presents an overview of research examining the role of religion in desistance and highlights measurement issues, potential intervening mechanisms, and a consideration of faith-based programs as criminal justice policy. Section II covers the relationship between military service and offending patterns, including period effects that explain variation in the relationship, selection effects, and the incorporation of military factors in criminal justice policy and programming. The chapter concludes in Section III by highlighting general conclusions from these two bodies of research and questions to be considered in future research.

I. RELIGION, RELIGIOSITY, AND DESISTANCE

Religion may deter antisocial behavior by promoting belief systems that focus on interpersonal morality and long-term goals (Pirutinsky 2014). Consistent with a learning perspective, Giordano et al. (2008) also note the importance of rewards and consequences for deviance. At an individual level, adherence to religious belief systems coupled with expectations for prosocial behavior may inspire individual identity change and the development of a new prosocial identify for former offenders (Giordano et al. 2008). Strong bonds to religion and religious institutions may also contribute to desistance, and close adherence to a religious belief system may inspire shame when deviance occurs, reducing deviant involvement (see Evans et al. 1995).

Some of the earliest research on religion in a criminological context cited the assumption that "religious training and commitment produce moral character," leading to reform and desistance (Hirschi and Stark 1969, p. 202). Hirschi and Stark (1969), as well as other scholars more recently, cite the ability of religion to socialize youth to conventional norms and the incorporation of a supernatural system of rewards and punishments to reinforce a commitment to conformity (see also McCullough and Willoughby 2009). Contrary to this hypothesis, however, Hirschi and Stark (1969) found no relationship between church attendance and delinquency among a sample of high school students. Early ecological studies generally found lower rates of deviance in areas with higher rates of church attendance (see Evans et al. 1995). In a cross-national comparison, Ellis and Peterson (1996) examined the relationship between religiosity and crime at the aggregate level across 13 industrial nations and found that countries with more religious citizens (as indicated by church membership and attendance) had lower rates of property crimes than less religious countries. No aggregate level relationship was found, however, for violent crime.

In a meta-analysis of 60 studies assessing the relationship between religion and crime at both the aggregate and individual levels, Baier and Wright (2001) identified a significant moderate effect of religion in reducing offending. More recent studies, however, suggest that this relationship may be more nuanced. For example, Evans et al. (1995) found that a significant relationship between general religiosity and self-reported offending became non-significant with the addition of controls for other factors, like parental and peer attachment. The authors comment that "religiosity factors . . . are apparently overwhelmed or duplicated in their influence on crime by other secular sources of morality" (Evans et al. 1995, p. 210), echoing earlier suggestions that the social and community benefits of religion may be redundant with other social controls (Tittle and Welch 1983). Similarly, a longitudinal study by Stansfield et al. (2017), using four waves from the Serious and Violent Offender Reentry Initiative, found that religion had direct effects on increased levels of employment and lower levels of substance use, however, it failed to decrease recidivism. The exception in the Evans et al. (1995) study appeared to be religious activity, which maintained a significant relationship. A recent study of religion and violence among a nationally representative sample of American adolescents also found a strong and significant effect of frequency of religious service attendance on violence but weaker associations for religious beliefs. Interestingly, the effect of religious service attendance was stronger for females than for males (Salas-Wright, Vaughn, and Maynard 2014b). Evans et al. (1995) theorized that a greater degree of religious activity implies more personal contact with a social community, which enhances monitoring and sanctioning of deviant behavior.

In a longitudinal study of juvenile offenders in Ohio, Giordano et al. (2008) also found no relationship between religiosity/spirituality and desistance or persistence in their quantitative analyses when controlling for social networks, marriage, employment, and other factors. Their qualitative analyses, on the other hand, did identify some patterns in which religiosity exerted some influence in former offenders' lives. In particular, individuals identified their religion or religious beliefs as a source of guidance for behavior, as a social support, and as an important coping mechanism for dealing with stress and strain (Giordano et al. 2008). Salas-Wright and colleagues (2013) also highlight religious coping in their study of the relationship between religion and spirituality and adolescent delinquency in a sample of 290 high-risk adolescents and young adults involved in a gang in El Salvador. In general, the authors found that spirituality (i.e., perceived relationship with God) was associated with a decreased likelihood of weapon carrying, property destruction, and public disturbances, but this relationship was entirely mediated by social developmental factors, like bonding. In contrast, no direct or mediated relationships were found when looking at religious coping.

Following from the social disorganization framework, recent ecological studies have examined the covariation between crime rates and the presence and type of churches. Triplett, White, and Gainey (2013) examined the roles of denomination (evangelical and non-evangelical churches), stability, and heterogeneity on both street and domestic violent crimes. Contrary to expectations, the presence of churches, both evangelical and non-evangelical, significantly increased the number of both street and domestic assaults. Consistent with findings from Desmond, Kikuchi, and Morgan (2010), Triplett et al. (2013) explained that since many of the churches were located in non-residential commercial areas, this could have contributed to the increase in residential heterogeneity and future criminal opportunities. In addition, as churches were vacant much of the week, they may be attractive targets of crime (Triplett et al. 2013).

While strong bonds to religion may contribute to desistance, religious beliefs can also be used to promote and justify use of violence. For example, religious extremists embrace theologies that sanction violence and are willing to sacrifice their own lives in the service of God (Sprinzak 2000; Iannaccone and Berman 2006). Violent religious extremism tends to thrive in countries where governments and economies are deteriorating. Thus, when religious extremists become better protectors and providers than the governments, they gain more supporters who are willing to use violence to preserve their religious beliefs (Iannnaccone and Berman 2006). Of course, as "extremist groups constitute just one segment of the religious marketplace" (Iannaccone and Berman 2006, p. 110), the effects of religion and extremism should be interpreted with caution.

In general, the body of research in this area does tend to find weak to moderate effects of religion/religiosity on reduced offending. More specifically, the relationship appears to vary depending on a variety of factors, including sample size (Baier and Wright 2001), gender (Salas-Wright, Vaughn, and Maynard 2014b), and measure of religiosity (Evans et al. 1995; Giordano et al. 2008; Salas-Wright, Olate, and Vaughn 2013; Salas-Wright, Vaughn, and Maynard 2014b). As Giordano et al. (2008, p. 125) comment, the evidence points to a conclusion of "positive effects of religion and spirituality for some individuals and under some conditions."

A. Organized Religion Versus Spirituality

Given the differences in measuring religion and religiosity noted above, it is important to recognize a potential distinction between organized religion or religious affiliation and a more general spirituality. McCullough and Willoughby (2009, p. 3) define religion as "cognition, affect, and behavior that arise from awareness of, or perceived interaction with, supernatural entities that are presumed to play an important role in human affairs." The practical aspect of measuring religion, however, varies widely. Religion implies a group affiliation and may be measured as membership and/or involvement in religious activities (frequency of prayer, attendance at religious services, etc.), while religiosity tends to reflect more individual identification with a particular religious belief system or beliefs about the existence of god(s) and their role in human lives (McCullough and Willoughby 2009). Likewise, Giordano et al. (2008) distinguish between religious participation (i.e., attendance) and spirituality, as indicated by perceived closeness to God. Pirutinsky (2014), however, argues that these different elements of the definition of religion are highly intercorrelated.

The distinction may be important, though, to questions of how religion or religious beliefs facilitate the desistance process. While both religion and spirituality may include a set of moral values and beliefs that guide an individual toward conventional behavior, organized religion emphasizes traditional expectations such as church membership, attendance, and practices (Wink et al. 2007; Pepper, Jackson, and Uzzell 2010). Spirituality, on the other hand, may be more individualized, emphasizing the individual's search for meaning outside of a traditional church context (Wink et al. 2007; Pepper et al. 2010), which may be more in line with an identity change model of desistance. On the other hand, religion as an institution, incorporating time constraints on individual behavior (through attendance at church activities) and a more organized social support or control system through church membership, may structure routine activities and choices, providing direct as well as indirect social controls to discourage offending. For example, Kewley et al.'s (2016) in-depth interview with four sex offenders post-release indicated that through their religious affiliations, participants were exposed to new and different prosocial networks, had opportunities to ask for forgiveness, and had an increased sense of belonging to the community and to their faith. Giordano et al. (2008) note that individual spirituality plays a part in the narratives of offenders trying to desist, but those efforts may be less successful unless paired with a more organized religious membership and attendance, which offers accountability and a support network.

The consideration of spirituality versus organized religion echoes similar factors that may be at work when examining desistance related to other type of social institutions.

For example, the distinction between marriage and cohabitation further emphasizes that organized institutions have greater impact on promoting desistance. Recognizing increasing rates of cohabitation, Forrest (2014) examined the relationship between co-habitation and criminal behavior using the National Longitudinal Survey of Youth 1997. While cohabitation was linked with reduction in property and drug offending, it did not lead to a termination of these offenses. On the other hand, marriage was associated with both reduction and termination of violent, property, and drug offenses, illustrating that the institution of marriage has a stronger influence than cohabitation in regards to desistance from crime (Forrest 2014).

In order to better understand any distinction between spirituality and religion in their relationship with criminal behaviors, some researchers have incorporated separate measures, allowing "for an overlap of the constructs for those respondents who have both an institutional religious faith as well as an individual invested spiritual approach to faith" (Jang and Franzen 2013, p. 599). This type of survey can distinguish between individuals who are either spiritual or religious, those who identify as both, and those who identify as neither (Giordano et al. 2008; Jang and Franzen 2013). Jang and Franzen (2013) examined the differences in crime among young adults in the third wave of the National Longitudinal Study of Adolescent Health, according to four groups: "religious and spiritual," "spiritual but not religious," "religious but not spiritual," and "neither." The authors found that the individuals self-identifying as "spiritual only" had more risk factors for delinquency compared to individuals in the other groups. Additionally, those "spiritual only" individuals tended to have lower levels of religious involvement and self-control. Jang and Franzen (2013) suggest that the "religious" and "religious and spiritual" groups imply a commitment to more normative conventional values, while "spiritual only" without religious involvement may be adopted by young adults in opposition to conventional values.

B. How Religion and Spirituality Lead to Desistance

While studies have found evidence of a link between religion/religiosity and prosocial behavior, the question remains as to what elements of religious affiliation or spiritual/moral beliefs contribute to desistance. To further explore these mechanisms, researchers have examined the interplay of religiosity with various sociodemographic factors as well as possible mediating factors, like self-control. Empirical studies tested the relationship between religion and violence among adolescents across sociodemographic factors such as race/ethnicity, gender (Salas-Wright, Vaughn, and Maynard 2014a), and family processes (Simons, Simons, and Conger 2004; Pickering and Vazsonyi 2009). Salas-Wright and colleagues (2014a) examined the use of violence among youth across demographic differences and found that adolescent religious service attendance was associated with the decreased likelihood of violence across a variety of sociodemographic subgroups. Additionally, the relationship between religiosity and criminal behavior was consistent across gender and developmental periods (Salas-Wright, Vaughn, and

Maynard 2014a). Pickering and Vazsonyi (2009) examined variation in the religiosity effect among a sample of high school students and found that family processes, including monitoring and attachment, did not mediate the relationship between religiosity and deviance. They concluded that religiosity is an important independent predictor of deviance (Pickering and Vazsonyi 2009). Simons, Simons, and Conger (2004), on the other hand, found that religiosity increased the likelihood that youth would view delinquency as morally wrong, reducing the likelihood that they would participate in delinquent behaviors. Additionally, religiosity structured social networks such that youth who identified as more religious had more conventional peer groups and less exposure to delinquent peers (Simons, Simons, and Conger 2004).

Other studies have examined the role of self-control as a potential mediator of the link between religiosity and crime, suggesting that religiosity reduces offending by promoting self-control through commitment to a set of supernatural rewards and punishments and social group monitoring and accountability (Johnson et al. 2000; Baier and Wright 2001; McCullough and Willoughby 2009; Laird, Marks, and Marrero 2011; Reisig, Wolfe, and Pratt 2012; Pirutinsky 2014). Despite methodological differences across studies, various authors have found that the protective effects of religion on criminal and delinquent behavior are partially mediated by higher self-control (Welch, Tittle, and Grasmick 2006; Walker et al. 2007; Laird, Marks, and Marrero 2011; Desmond, Ulmer, and Bader 2013). To address the limitations of cross-sectional mediation studies such as confounding variables and reverse causality, Pirutinsky (2014) used longitudinal data from 1,354 adolescent offenders in the Pathways to Desistance Study. Consistent with previous research, results suggested that individual religiosity was negatively correlated with impulsivity and offending. Additionally, short-term reductions in impulsivity were correlated with reduced offending at later time periods, suggesting that self-control does mediate the relationship between religiosity and offending to some extent (Pirutinsky 2014).

C. Faith-Based Programs to Promote Desistance

Reflecting assumptions that religion increases morality and self-control, the criminal justice system has increasingly incorporated faith-based programming. According to Johnson (2004), "beyond work, education, or vocational training, religious activities attract more participants than any other personal enhancement program offered inside a prison" (p. 330). Studies have consistently found that faith-based programs in prisons reduce recidivism (Young et al. 1995; Johnson, Larson, and Pitts 1997; Johnson 2004). Many religious programs assist individuals that meet their program goals and expect the participants to be responsible and abide by the moral expectations, and research on prison re-entry illustrates that religious institutions and other faith-based organizations play an important role with successful transition out of prison (Johnson 2004).

In general, prior studies on religion, religiosity, and desistance have indicated mixed findings with weak to moderate effects on reduced offending. In addition, compared to the idea of spirituality, affiliation with organized religion affiliations was found to have a stronger effect in reducing offenses with emphasis on accountability to self and the community for both youth and adults. Furthermore, religion as an institution may strengthen self-control in adolescents during crucial developmental periods. Additionally, faith-based programs are promising avenues to promote desistance by providing education and vocational trainings as well as religious activities that divert individuals from future criminal offenses.

II. Military Service and Desistance

Military service was originally identified by Sampson and Laub (1993) in their age-graded theory as one of the primary forces of social control that contribute to desistance. The military has traditionally been seen by society as an experience that promotes maturity and that makes "men" out of boys (Arkin and Dobrofsky 1978). Anecdotally, it has been an accepted practice for parents to send troublesome and delinquent male children to a military academy or boarding school in order to emulate a military way of life, and judges and other criminal justice officials have ordered some offenders to join the military as an alternative to trial or prison (Bryant 1979). Following the advent of the all-volunteer force and declining numbers of people exposed to military service, the view of the military as an arena for behavioral change faded. More recently, with large numbers of service members returning from combat experiences, the question of whether and how military service impacts behavior has become more relevant.

Military service is a life event that "knifes-off" individuals from previous environments, substituting a structured environment that provides prosocial behavioral models as well as systematic consequences for deviance. Additionally, the military as an institution provides individuals with education, training, and other opportunities they may have had less access to in the civilian world (Bookwala, Frieze, and Grote 1994; Sampson and Laub 1996; MacLean and Elder 2007). This combination of factors may contribute to improved self and social controls that foster desistance from offending. As with the consideration of religious extremism fostering violence, there is also a counterargument as to the relationship between military service and offending. As an institution built on the use of violence and that trains its member to be aggressive and to use weapons, service may also contribute to increased offending, especially violence and substance abuse (Archer and Gartner 1976; Bryant 1979; White et al. 2012). Laub and Sampson (2003) also point out that the military may serve as an arena for service members to merely continue preexisting behavior patterns.

Until the start of the Vietnam War, results on the long-term offending patterns of men who served during the early draft era, such as World War II and the Korean War, indicated a beneficial impact of service, including increased educational attainment, socioeconomic status, and reduced offending (Xie 1992; Sampson and Laub 1993; Sampson and Laub 1996). In contrast, research on the impact of military service on criminal activity using samples from the Vietnam War era or the AVF (all-volunteer force) has been more mixed. Sampson and Laub (1996) linked factors such as overseas duty, in-service schooling, and GI Bill training to increased socioeconomic achievements later in life. While the conclusion of World War II led to one of the largest and most sustained economic expansions in U.S. history, the Vietnam era (1965–1975) led to a significant decrease in employment opportunities and deterioration of the civilian labor market (Berger and Hirsch 1983; Angrist 1990). Individual differences prior to military service, economic strain, and unfavorable social contexts of the era led more Vietnam veterans to experience more psychological problems, alcohol and substance use, and a greater propensity to commit crime (Wright, Carter, and Cullen 2005).

Bouffard (2005) utilized longitudinal data from 1979 to 1994 to examine the relation-ship between individual characteristics and military service prior to the AVF. Findings emphasized the importance of individual characteristics when analyzing the protective effects of military service. While some groups of individuals did experience the military as a beneficial turning point (e.g., African Americans), others did not (Bouffard, 2005). Similarly, Bouffard and Laub (2004) found that military service may foster desistance especially for serious delinquents. Rohlfs (2010) examined the relationship between the Vietnam draft and combat exposure on later violent and criminal behavior using data from the National Vietnam Veterans Readjustment Study, finding a reduction in arrests among men who served in the military. Rohlfs (2010), however, suggests that this ef-fect may be a result of incapacitation in that service during this period of time typically removed men from the purview of the U.S. criminal justice system. Wright, Carter, and Cullen (2005) similarly point to a "latency effect" whereby men who served in Vietnam were subject to less criminal involvement. Bouffard (2014) highlights additional com-plexity in the relationship between Vietnam-era military service and offending, finding that a beneficial effect of service was limited to those who served towards the end of the war, providing additional evidence that the influence of military service varies by histor-ical period.

Using more recent data from Current Population Survey (CPS) and the Surveys of Inmates in State and Federal Correctional Facilities, Culp and colleagues (2013) compared the probability of imprisonment of veterans from the draft era to those in the AVF era. The findings suggest that "military service in general does not elevate the prob-ability of imprisonment at all, but if the service occurred during the AVF era rather than the draft era, the odds of imprisonment increased" (Culp et al. 2013, p. 675). However, the authors caution that this finding may reflect a greater degree of combat exposure among veterans of the draft era as compared to those who served in the AVF. Using the Longitudinal Study of Adolescent Health (Add Health) and a sample experiencing more recent military service during the AVF, Craig and Foster (2013) examined the effects of military enlistment and marriage over the life course by gender. While marriage was sig-nificantly associated with delinquency in their sample, Craig and Foster (2013) found no relationship between military service and delinquency, but they did identify a protec-tive effect of service for females. Studies also suggest desistance due to military service may vary depending on the race of the individual. Greenberg, Rosenbeck, and Desai

(2007), for example, found that nonwhite veterans were less likely than white veterans to be incarcerated. Craig and Connell (2013) also found that racial minorities had a greater likelihood of desistance.

A. Mental Health, Military Service, and Offending

Research in this area suggests that military service may not act as a beneficial turning point for some individuals. For example, it is possible that stressful working environments, such as the military, and combat exposure could impact the psychological well-being of service members, which in turn could explain changes in personality and behavior over time. More specifically, stressful experiences during military service and/or combat may increase the likelihood of developing posttraumatic stress disorder (PTSD) (Kline et al. 2010). This may lead to adjustment problems upon return, and research has found that male veterans with PTSD symptomatology were at greater risk for perpetrating intimate partner violence (Jordan et al. 1992; Byrne and Riggs 1996; Bell and Orcutt 2009). Other research has found that service members with PTSD were more likely to have anger issues, violent outbursts, and aggressive behaviors (Lasko et al. 1994; Beckham et al. 1997; McFall et al. 1999). Using a sample of arrestees in Arizona, White et al. (2012) also found that veteran arrestees were more likely to have been arrested for a violent offense and many of the veterans reported having suffered an injury during their service, having a PTSD diagnosis, or having other mental health problems. Thus, individuals who are exposed to combat and related physical (e.g., traumatic brain injury) and mental (e.g., PTSD) health issues may experience more negative outcomes as a result of their service. In contrast, using data from the 1997 National Longitudinal Survey of Youth, Teachman and Tedrow (2016) found that while military service significantly decreased the risk of arrest and being convicted for violent and non-violent crimes, combat exposure did not influence participants' contact with the criminal justice system.

B. Selection Effects in the Impact of Military Service

Even during the draft era, service in the military was not randomly assigned. With the advent of the AVF, it is even more likely that individual differences determine who is likely to enter military service. In particular, individuals from lower socioeconomic backgrounds and males are more likely to join the military rather than attending college compared to those from higher socioeconomic backgrounds (Elder et al. 2010). African Americans are also more likely to enter military service as they face more challenges in securing civilian employment (Elder et al. 2010). In addition, prior research has highlighted the personality differences between those who enlist and their civilian counterparts in that those who join the military tend to be less agreeable, less neurotic, and less open to experience prior to their service (Jackson et al. 2012). After their military training, the same respondents were found to be even less agreeable, with further change continuing even after leaving the military (Jackson et al. 2012). Thus, pre-existing personality differences may also affect the individual's likelihood to either persist or desist in delinquency. While the issue of selection is especially pertinent to understanding the relationship between military service and offending and researchers have recognized this (see Bouffard 2003, 2014; Wright, Carter, and Cullen 2005), few studies have explicitly attempted to control for selection effects. Bouffard (2014) presented a supplemental analysis using propensity score matching and demonstrated that the military effects were robust after accounting for some elements of selection. These analyses, however, were limited by the available data, and much work remains to be done regarding selection to determine whether the relationship between military service and offending/desistance is spurious.

C. Desistance and Military Training as Correctional Policy

While the research evidence on the relationship between military service and offending remains somewhat mixed, correctional philosophy has frequently incorporated military-style training and discipline to punish and reform offenders (Morash and Rucker 1990). The military basic training model was also the basis for the development of shock incarceration, or "boot camp" prison, which was developed as a "get tough" approach to crime during the 1980s and early 1990s (MacKenzie et al. 1995; MacKenzie, Wilson, and Kider 2001). Boot camp prison programs add to the traditional prison experience by incorporating components of military basic training, including military drill and ceremony, physical training, physical labor, and strict discipline (MacKenzie et al. 1995; MacKenzie and Souryal 1995). Guards at correctional boot camps are called drill instructors and are often trained by military personnel in how to effectively manage inmates in a military atmosphere, and those incarcerated in boot camp prisons also follow a military lifestyle. Inmates spend at least part of their day in physical training and military style drill exercises (MacKenzie et al. 1995). The military components of boot camp prisons are expected to deter offenders and to teach them how to live a structured, disciplined lifestyle, which should translate to life after boot camp (Morash and Rucker 1990; MacKenzie and Souryal 1995). Generally, evaluations of boot camp prison programs have found that they are not effective in reducing recidivism or facilitating desistance (MacKenzie, Wilson, and Kider 2001).

More recently, criminal justice jurisdictions have begun implementing specialty courts to address veterans in the system and unique issues these offenders may face. The first Veterans Treatment Court was established in Buffalo, New York, in 2008, and the use of veterans courts has expanded dramatically since (Clark, McGuire, and Blue-Howells 2014). Adapted from a drug court model, veterans courts are designed specifically to address the needs of offenders who are veterans, typically including mental health and substance abuse treatment, staff with an understanding of military culture and experiences (and connections to the U.S. Department of Veterans Affairs), and peer mentoring (Clark, McGuire, and Blue-Howells 2014). As a very recent development, little information is available as to the effectiveness of the veterans court model in reducing recidivism and facilitating desistance.

In addition, transitioning from prison and the military back into the community may be difficult despite the opportunities and trainings that were offered by the institutions. The adjustment after reintegration depends on both individual and social factors, such as personal and situational characteristics, peers, family, and community (Visher and Travis 2003). Travis (2007) stated that in order for individuals to successfully reenter the community, the tone of the public toward criminals and prisoners must change. All of the beneficial opportunities that were once provided by the military and corrections department will be meaningless if returning individuals cannot successfully adjust to civilian life. Finally, maladjustment may increase the likelihood of recidivism, delaying or preventing desistance.

Overall, military service functions as a "turning point" for many individuals by providing them with an experience to promote maturity as well as vocational and educational training. There is also, however, great psychological risk that comes with serving in the military that may be conducive to future offending behaviors. Prior studies have found that prior military service and exposure to stressful and traumatic events increase the likelihood of developing PTSD, which in turn may lead to developing violent behaviors such as violent outbursts and uncontrollable anger. With the advent of the AVF and individual differences determining selection into the armed forces, more recent research on military service and desistance calls into questions whether military service continues to be a positive turning point. Currently, there is a need to examine the relationship between military service and offending/desistance in regards to selection. Similarly, future studies should examine the relationship between desistance and military service as correctional policy accounting for recent developments such as veterans courts.

III. Conclusions and Future Directions

Religion and military service are two institutions with the potential to facilitate desistance from offending, but these institutions have received less attention in the criminological literature as compared to other potential turning points, like work and marriage. Both religion and military service may provide the opportunity for identity change by offering a set of moral values and behavioral expectations. In addition, religious attendance and military service occur within organized environments that structure time and choices and that incorporate consequences for deviance. While religion does have some influence on criminal offending, studies continue to demonstrate mixed findings, which may be due to the substantial differences in methodology. However, the positive and protective influences of religion as an institution on adolescent behavior cannot be overlooked. The relationship between military service and offending, however, remains somewhat inconclusive, with results varying by historical period especially. In both cases, lingering questions remain, and further research is needed to address these concerns.

Individual experiences of religion and military service vary, and it remains unclear what particular aspects of these two institutions may be responsible for facilitating desistance. For religion, individuals adhere to different specific religions, practice different rituals, and hold different beliefs. Addressing the question of religion versus spirituality, research has yet to fully answer whether the moral value system, the social control and support of group membership, or the reinforcement of supernatural rewards and punishments is responsible for any desistance effect, or whether all or some of these elements interact. Likewise, it is unclear which aspect of military service (e.g., educational and job opportunities, structured environment, combat-related mental health issues, etc.) may be specifically correlated with either increased or decreased offending. Of course, both sources of social control may facilitate desistance or may serve as risk factors for continued offending. Religion emphasizes moral values and provides opportunities to develop mentorship and support groups. However, religion can also have a detrimental effect when those moral values are used to support extremist beliefs and behaviors. Similarly, military service may provide structure as well as financial and educational opportunities, but there is also a risk of developing psychological disorders. Furthermore, future studies should examine whether religion and military service are more effective in promoting desistance when they occur in conjunction with other sources of social control and whether effects vary by individual characteristics.

Another lingering issue is the question of selection, which is true not just for considerations of religion and the military but for the impact of other social institutions as well. The military currently relies on an all-volunteer force, and evidence suggests that certain types of individuals are more likely to self-select into the military. To the extent that the factors influencing military entry are also correlated with offending behavior, it is possible that any relationship between military service and offending is spurious. Few studies have explicitly accounted for selection, and future research must carefully consider selection effects. Selection may be even more difficult to assess in the relationship between religion and offending, but the same concerns are present. It may be that individuals with a lower propensity for offending and greater commitment to conventional values are more likely to be involved in religious organizations. This involvement likely begins at an early age with parents encouraging their children's attendance and involvement, making it difficult to address issues of selection. Similar factors may be at play, however, in the relationship between involvement in faith-based treatment programs and recidivism or desistance. Truly understanding the causal relationship between both military service and religious involvement will require addressing these issues in future research.

Despite a growing body of research in this area, a number of questions remain regarding the relationship between religion, military service, and offending. Studies of religion and desistance must be especially concerned with the definition and measurement of religiosity to understand any true causal impact. Additionally, the components of religiosity and military service that contribute to a possible desistance effect (or a crime-promoting effect, for that matter) remain unclear. It is possible that the military is a social institution that provides access to educational opportunities and stable employment that are less readily available for disadvantaged individuals in civilian society. The organization of religion and military life may structure individual choices in such a way as to discourage offending or may provide conventional role models and values for members to adhere to. Alternatively, in the case of the military, service may expose individuals to stressful and traumatic experiences, including combat, that foster mental health issues, including posttraumatic stress disorder, substance abuse, and offending. It is also possible that the military is viewed as an arena in which to legitimately engage in violence, becoming a career of choice for those predisposed to aggression. The contradictory findings suggest that while military service demonstrates a protective effect to a certain extent, individual differences and historical period influence how the military contributes to desistance. Similarly, contradictory findings within the body of literature on the effect of religion highlight the individual and socio-religious context in determining the specific relationship between religion and desistance. As institutions that impact the lives of large segments of the population, it is important to better understand how military service and religion affect trajectories of offending behavior.

REFERENCES

Angrist, Joshua D. 1990. "Lifetime Earnings and the Vietnam Era Draft Lottery: Evidence from Social Security Administrative Records." *The American Economic Review* 80: 313–336.

Archer, Dane, and Rosemary Gartner. 1976. "Violent Acts and Violent Times: A Comparative Approach to Postwar Homicide Rates." *American Sociological Review* 41: 937–963.

Arkin, William, and Lynne R. Dobrofsky 1978. "Military Socialization and Masculinity." *Journal of Social Issues* 34: 151–155.

Baier, Colin J., and Bradley R. E. Wright. 2001. "'If You Love Me, Keep My Commandments': A Meta-Analysis of the Effect of Religion on Crime." *Journal of Research in Crime and Delinquency* 38(1): 3–21.

Beckham, Jean C., Michelle E. Feldman, Angela C. Kirby, Michael A. Hertzberg, and Scott D. Moore. 1997. "Interpersonal Violence and Its Correlates in Vietnam Veterans with Chronic Posttraumatic Stress Disorder." *Journal of Clinical Psychology* 53: 859–869.

Bell, Kathryn M., and Holly K. Orcutt. 2009. "Posttraumatic Stress Disorder and Male-Perpetrated Intimate Partner Violence." *Journal of the American Medical Association* 302: 562–564.

Berger, Mark C., and Barry T. Hirsch. 1983. "The Civilian Earnings Experience of Vietnam-Era Veterans." *Journal of Human Resources* 18: 455–479.

Bookwala, Jamila, Irene Frieze, and Nancy Grote. 1994. "The Long-Term Effects of Military Service on Quality of Life: The Vietnam Experience." *Journal of Applied Social Psychology* 24: 529–545.

Bouffard, Leana A. 2003. "Examining the Relationship between Military Service and Criminal Behavior During the Vietnam Era: A Research Note." *Criminology* 41(2): 491–510.

Bouffard, Leana A. 2005. "The Military as a Bridging Environment in Criminal Careers: Differential Outcomes of the Military Experience." *Armed Forces & Society* 31: 273–295.

Bouffard, Leana A. 2014. "Period Effects in the Impact of Vietnam-Era Military Service on Crime over the Life Course." *Crime and Delinquency* 60: 859–883.

Bouffard, Leana A., and John H. Laub. 2004. "Jail or the Army: Does Military Service Facilitate Desistance from Crime?" In *After Crime and Punishment: Pathways to Offender Reintegration*, edited by Shadd Maruna and Russell Immarigeon, 129–151. Portland, OR: Willan.

Bryant, Clifton D. 1979. *Khaki-Collar Crime: Deviant Behavior in the Military Context*. New York: Free Press.

Byrne, Christina A., and David S. Riggs. 1996. "The Cycle of Trauma: Relationship Aggression in Male Vietnam Veterans with Symptoms of Posttraumatic Stress Disorder." *Violence and Victims* 11(3): 213–225.

Clark, Sean, James McGuire, and Jessica Blue-Howells. 2014. "What Can Family Courts Learn from Veterans Treatment Courts?" *Family Court Review* 52: 417–424.

Craig, Jessica M., and Nadine M. Connell. 2013. "The All-Volunteer Force and Crime: The Effects of Military Participation on Offending Behavior." *Armed Forces & Society* 41: 1–23.

Craig, Jessica, and Holly Foster. 2013. "Desistance in the Transition to Adulthood: The Roles of Marriage, Military, and Gender." *Deviant Behavior* 34(3): 208–223.

Culp, Richard, Tasha J. Youstin, Kristin Englander, and James Lynch. 2013. "From War to Prison: Examining the Relationship Between Military Service and Criminal Activity." *Justice Quarterly* 30(4): 651–680.

Desmond, Scott A., Jeffery T. Ulmer, and Christopher D. Bader. 2013. "Religion, Self Control, and Substance Use." *Deviant Behavior* 34(5): 384–406.

Desmond, Scott, G. Kikuchi, and K. Morgan. 2010. "Congregation and Crime: Is the Spatial Distribution of Congregations Associated with Neighborhood Crime Rates?" *Journal for the Scientific Study of Religion* 49: 37–55.

Elder, Glen H., Lin Wang, Naomi J. Spence, Daniel E. Adkins, and Tyson H. Brown. 2010. "Pathways to the All-Volunteer Military." *Social Science Quarterly* 91(2): 455–475.

Ellis, Lee, and James Peterson. 1996. "Crime and Religion: An International Comparison Among Thirteen Industrial Nations." *Personality and Individual Differences* 20(6): 761–768.

Evans, T. David, Francis T. Cullen, R. Gregory Dunaway, and Velmer S. Burton Jr. 1995. "Religion and Crime Reexamined: The Impact of Religion, Secular Controls, and Social Ecology on Adult Criminality." *Criminology* 33: 195–224.

Forest, Walter. 2014. "Cohabitation, Relationship Quality, and Desistance from Crime." *Journal of Marriage and Family* 76: 539–556.

Giordano, Peggy C., Monica A. Longmore, Ryan D. Schroeder, and Patrick M. Seffrin. 2008. "A Life-Course Perspective on Spirituality and Desistance from Crime." *Criminology* 46(1): 99–132.

Greenberg, Greg A., Robert A. Rosenheck, and Rani A. Desai. 2007. "Risk of Incarceration among Male Veterans and Nonveterans Are Veterans of the All Volunteer Force at Greater Risk?" *Armed Forces & Society* 33(3): 337–350.

Hirschi, Travis, and Rodney Stark. 1969. "Hellfire and Delinquency." *Social Problems* 17: 202–213.

Iannaccone, Laurence R., and Eli Berman. 2006. "Religious Extremism: The Good, The Bad, and The Deadly." *Public Choice* 128: 109–129.

Jackson, Joshua J., Felix Thoemmes, Kathrin Jonkmann, Oliver Lüdtke, and Ulrich Trautwein. 2012. "Military Training and Personality Trait Development Does the Military Make the Man, or Does the Man Make the Military?" *Psychological Science* 23(3): 270–277.

Jang, Sung Joon, and Aaron B. Franzen. 2013. "Is Being 'Spiritual' Enough Without Being Religious? A Study of Violent and Property Crimes among Emerging Adults." *Criminology* 51(3): 595–627.

Johnson, Byron R. 2004. "Religious Programs and Recidivism Among Former Inmates in Prison Fellowship Programs: A Long-Term Follow-Up Study." *Justice Quarterly* 21(2): 329–354.

Johnson, Byron R., Spencer De Li, David B. Larson, and Michael McCullough. 2000. "A Systematic Review of the Religiosity and Delinquency Literature: A Research Note." *Journal of Contemporary Criminal Justice* 16(1): 32–52.

Johnson, Byron R., David B. Larson, and Timothy C. Pitts. 1997. "Religious Programs, Institutional Adjustment, and Recidivism among Former Inmates in Prison Fellowship Programs." *Justice Quarterly* 14(1): 145–166.

Jordan, B. Kathleen, Charles R. Marmar, John A. Fairbank, William E. Schlenger, Richard A. Kulka, Richard L. Hough, and Daniel S. Weiss. 1992. "Problems in Families of Male Vietnam Veterans with Posttraumatic Stress Disorder." *Journal of Consulting and Clinical Psychology* 60(6): 916–926.

Kewley, Stephanie, Michael Larkin, Leigh Harkins, and Anthony R. Beech. (2016). "Restoring Identity: The Use of Religion as a Mechanism to Transition Between an Identity of Sexual Offending to a Non-Offending Identity." *Criminology and Criminal Justice* 17(1): 79–96.

Kline, Anna, Maria Falca-Dodson, Bradley Sussner, Donald S. Ciccone, Helena Chandler, Lanora Callahan, and Miklos Losonczy. 2010. "Effects of Repeated Deployment to Iraq and Afghanistan on the Health of New Jersey Army National Guard Troops: Implications for Military Readiness." *American Journal of Public Health* 100(2): 276–283.

Laird, Robert D., Loren D. Marks, and Matthew D. Marrero. 2011. "Religiosity, Self-Control, and Antisocial Behavior: Religiosity as a Promotive and Protective Factor." *Journal of Applied Developmental Psychology* 32(2): 78–85.

Lasko, Natasha B., Tamara V. Gurvits, Arthur A. Kuhne, Scott P. Orr, and Roger K. Pitman. 1994. "Aggression and Its Correlates in Vietnam Veterans With and Without Chronic Posttraumatic Stress Disorder." *Comprehensive Psychiatry* 35(5): 373–381.

Laub, John H., and Robert J. Sampson. 2003. *Shared Beginnings, Divergent Lives: Delinquent Boys to Age 70*. Cambridge, MA: Harvard University Press.

MacKenzie, Doris Layton, Robert Brame, David McDowall, and Claire Souryal. 1995. "Boot Camp Prisons and Recidivism in Eight States." *Criminology* 33: 327–357.

MacKenzie, Doris Layton, and Clair Souryal. 1995. "Inmates' Attitude Change During Incarceration: A Comparison of Boot Camp with Traditional Prison." *Justice Quarterly* 12: 325–354.

MacKenzie, Doris Layton, David B. Wilson, and Suzanne B. Kider. 2001. "Effects of Correctional Boot Camps on Offending." *Annals of the American Academy of Political and Social Science* 578:126–143.

MacLean, Alair, and Glen H. Elder Jr. 2007. "Military Service in the Life Course." *Sociology* 33(1): 175–196.

McCullough, Michael E., and Brian L. B. Willoughby. 2009. "Religion, Self-Regulation, and Self-Control: Associations, Explanations, and Implications." *Psychological Bulletin* 135(1): 69–93.

McFall, Miles, Alan Fontana, Murray Raskind, and Robert Rosenheck. 1999. "Analysis of Violent Behavior in Vietnam Combat Veteran Psychiatric Inpatients with Posttraumatic Stress Disorder." *Journal of Traumatic Stress* 12(3): 501–517.

Morash, Merry, and Lila Rucker. 1990. "A Critical Look at the Ideal of Boot Camp as Correctional Reform." *Crime and Delinquency* 36: 204–222.

Paternoster, Raymond, and Shawn Bushway. 2009. "Desistance and the 'Feared Self': Toward an Identity Theory of Criminal Desistance." *The Journal of Criminal Law and Criminology* 99: 1103–1156.

Pepper, Miriam, Tim Jackson, and David Uzzell. 2010. "A Study of Multidimensional Religion Constructs and Values in the United Kingdom." *Journal for the Scientific Study of Religion* 49(1): 127–146.

Pickering, Lloyd E., and Alexander T. Vazsonyi. 2010. "Does Family Process Mediate the Effect of Religiosity on Adolescent Deviance? Revisiting the Notion of Spuriousness." *Criminal Justice and Behavior* 37(1): 97–118.

Pirutinsky, Steven. 2014. "Does Religiousness Increase Self-Control and Reduce Criminal Behavior? A Longitudinal Analysis of Adolescent Offenders." *Criminal Justice and Behavior* 41: 1290–1307.

Reisig, Michael D., Scott E. Wolfe, and Travis C. Pratt. 2012. "Low Self-Control and the Religiosity-Crime Relationship." *Criminal Justice and Behavior* 39(9): 1172–1191.

Rohlfs, Chris. 2010. "Does Combat Exposure Make You a More Violent or Criminal Person? Evidence from the Vietnam Draft." *Journal of Human Resources* 45(2): 271–300.

Salas-Wright, Christopher P., René Olate, and Michael G. Vaughn. 2013. "The Protective Effects of Religious Coping and Spirituality on Delinquency Results Among High-Risk and Gang-Involved Salvadoran Youth." *Criminal Justice and Behavior* 40(9): 988–1008.

Salas-Wright, Christopher P., Michael G. Vaughn, and Brandy R. Maynard. 2014a. "Buffering Effects of Religiosity on Crime Testing the Invariance Hypothesis Across Gender and Developmental Period." *Criminal Justice and Behavior* 41(6): 673–691.

Salas-Wright, Christopher P., Michael G. Vaughn, and Brandy R. Maynard. 2014b. "Religiosity and Violence Among Adolescents in the United States: Findings from the National Survey on Drug Use and Health 2006–2010." *Journal of Interpersonal Violence* 29(7): 1178–1200.

Sampson, Robert J., and John H. Laub. 1993. *Crime in the Making; Pathways and Turning Points Through Life*. Cambridge, MA: Harvard University Press.

Sampson, Robert J., and John H. Laub. 1996. "Socioeconomic Achievement in the Life Course of Disadvantaged Men: Military Service as a Turning Point, Circa 1940–1965." *American Sociological Review* 61(3): 347–367.

Simons, Leslie Gordon, Ronald L. Simons, and Rand D. Conger. 2004. "Identifying the Mechanisms Whereby Family Religiosity Influences the Probability of Adolescent Antisocial Behavior." *Journal of Comparative Family Studies* 35: 547–563.

Sprinzak, Ehud. 2000. "Rational Fanatics." *Foreign Policy* 120(5): 66–73.

Stansfield, Richard, Thomas J. Mowen, Thomas O'Connor, and John H. Boman. 2017. "The Role of Religious Support in Reentry Evidence from the SVORI Data." *Journal of Research in Crime and Delinquency* 54(1): 111–145.

Teachman, Jay, and Lucky Tedrow. (2016). "Altering the Life Course: Military Service and Contact with the Criminal Justice System." *Social Science Research* 60: 74–87.

Tittle, Charles R., and Michael R. Welch. 1983. "Religiosity and Deviance: Toward a Contingency Theory of Constraining Effects." *Social Forces* 61: 653–682.

Travis, Jeremy. 2007. "Reflections on the Reentry Movement." *Federal Sentencing Reporter* 20(2): 84–87.

Triplett, Ruth A., Garland White, and Rand Gainey. 2013. "Churches as Neighborhood Organizations and Their Relationship to Street and Domestic Violent Crime: The Role of Denomination, Stability, and Heterogeneity." *Deviant Behavior* 34(10): 803–823.

Visher, Christy A., and Jeremy Travis. 2003. Transitions from Prison to Community: Understanding Individual Pathways." *Annual Review of Sociology* 29: 89–113.

Walker, Carmella, Michael G. Ainette, Thomas A. Wills, and Don Mendoza. 2007. "Religiosity and Substance Use: Test of an Indirect-Effect Model in Early and Middle Adolescence." *Psychology of Addictive Behaviors* 21(1): 84–96.

Welch, Michael R., Charles R. Tittle, and Harold G. Grasmick. 2006. "Christian Religiosity, Self-Control and Social Conformity." *Social Forces* 84(3): 1605–1623.

White, Michael D., Philip Mulvey, Andrew M. Fox, and David Choate. 2012. "A Hero's Welcome: Exploring the Prevalence and Problems of Military Veterans in the Arrestee Population." *Justice Quarterly* 29: 258–286.

Wink, Paul, Lucia Ciciolla, Michele Dillon, and Allison Tracy. 2007. "Religiousness, Spiritual Seeking, and Personality: Findings from a Longitudinal Study." *Journal of Personality* 75(5): 1051–1070.

Wright, John Paul, David E. Carter, and Francis T. Cullen. 2005. "A Life-Course Analysis of Military Service in Vietnam." *Journal of Research in Crime and Delinquency* 42(1): 55–83.

Xie, Yu. 1992. "The Socioeconomic Status of Young Male Veterans, 1964–1984." *Social Science Quarterly* 73(2): 379–396.

Young, Mark C., John Gartner, Thomas O'Connor, David Larson, and Kevin N. Wright. 1995. "Long-Term Recidivism Among Federal Inmates Trained as Volunteer Prison Ministers." *Journal of Offender Rehabilitation* 22: 97–118.

CHAPTER 27

....

THE EFFECTS OF JUVENILE SYSTEM PROCESSING ON SUBSEQUENT DELINQUENCY OUTCOMES

....

ANTHONY PETROSINO, CAROLYN PETROSINO, SARAH GUCKENBURG, JENNA TERRELL, TREVOR A. FRONIUS, AND KYUNGSEOK CHOO

JUVENILE offenses can be thought of as being on a wide continuum. At either extreme end of the continuum, discretion exercised by agents of the justice system is less varied. Very minor offenses will probably be overlooked by the police; very serious offenses are almost always handled using the full weight of arrest and prosecution powers. But where justice practitioners have tremendous discretion is on how to handle offenses and offenders that move further from the edges of the continuum. Less serious juvenile offenders are defined here as those that commit offenses of moderate or low severity. In addition, such offenders usually have had little or no prior contact with legal authorities, as prior record is a strong factor in how severe the system response will be.

The juvenile justice system can be thought of as a conveyor belt (see Figure 27.1). Once a youth is officially contacted by the police through arrest or referral, he or she then enters a system where there is either progression to the next stage or diversion out of the system. The United States Office of Juvenile Justice and Delinquency Prevention (OJJDP) provided an illustration of this conveyor belt, with progression or diversion at many points along the process (OJJDP, no date).

Once youth are contacted, police officers, district attorneys, juvenile court intake officers, juvenile and family court judges, and other officials have broad discretion regarding how to handle such juveniles. Ultimately, these gatekeepers determine which juvenile offenders should be "officially processed" through the juvenile justice system,

Processing/Progression

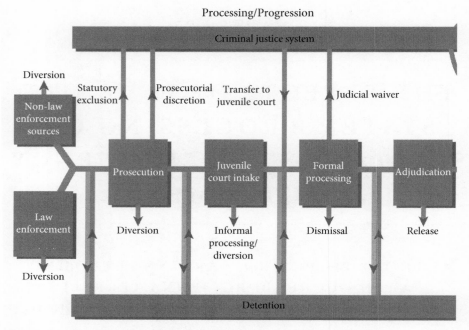

FIGURE 27.1 How Cases Flow Through the Juvenile Justice System

with the eventual end being an appearance before a juvenile judge to receive a disposition (sentence). The youth could also be diverted from the formal juvenile justice system at any point from police contact to final disposition through some type of diversion program.[1]

Such divergent courses of action beg an important policy question: Which strategy leads to reduced recidivism and engagement with the justice system? Because very similar low- to moderate-severity juveniles are being given quite different interventions (formally processed, diverted to a program, or released altogether), there is obviously some confusion among juvenile justice practitioners about which strategy is best. Such situations of policy confusion are fertile ground for constructing rigorous studies to shed light on the question, and nearly 30 (through 2008) randomized controlled trials have been conducted that collectively provide evidence on the effectiveness of these alternative methods for handling juveniles. This chapter summarizes these experiments using meta-analytic techniques and reports findings. Section I discusses the theoretical and empirical literature on the impact of juvenile criminal justice processing on subsequent juvenile criminal behavior. We also discuss the policy question of interest. In Section II we discuss our methodology to systematically gather and analyze randomized trials that test the efficacy of justice-processing methods on subsequent juvenile outcomes. We report the results of our meta-analysis using 29 randomized controlled trials in Section III and the implications for researchers, policymakers, and practitioners in Section IV.

I. Study Background

We began our review with a summary of the literature on the impact of alternative methods for juvenile criminal justice processing on future juvenile criminal behavior. We also reviewed the evidence available to answer the policy question of interest—specifically, which processing method is more effective at reducing recidivism.

A. The Impact of Criminal Justice Processing on Subsequent Criminal Behavior: Alternative Views

There are arguments for each of the different approaches to handling juveniles who commit less serious offenses. Some experts believe that formal juvenile justice system processing can help deter future criminal behavior by juveniles. For example, some officials believe that less serious offenses are a "gateway" to more serious offending (e.g., Musacari 2010) and should be dealt with intensively at their first occurrence to prevent the juvenile from becoming a more serious offender. Others advocate that the formal system will deter or "scare" low-level offenders from future misconduct (Cullen and Wright 2002). Some officials also believe that the primary role of the juvenile or family court is to rehabilitate the child, and thus it is necessary that juveniles be processed into the formal juvenile justice system to be able to administer to them needed treatment or services (Crime Solutions 2015).

Opponents, however, argue that formal processing could lead juveniles to commit more crimes in the future, perhaps due to a "labeling" effect (e.g., Schur 1973; Farrington and Murray 2014), and that low-level offenders should be handled in as non-intrusive a manner as possible. For example, a juvenile court petition results in an official label of the child as a delinquent, and institutions and people involved in the youth's life will now begin to treat him or her differently. For example, such a juvenile may receive increased police scrutiny and end up being rearrested more often than juveniles who are not under the same surveillance, even though both sets of youths are misbehaving in similar manner. The same actions that resulted in police turning a blind eye to misconduct by one juvenile may also result in an official arrest of another youth. Labeling is theorized to have other potential impacts, including economic or educational losses, and marginalization by significant others such as family and friends.

There are other theories, apart from labeling, that could explain why further processing in the juvenile system may increase crime. For example, formal processing could further criminogenic exposure to more deviant peers who are also being moved along the system, resulting in a harmful effect (e.g., Dishion et al. 1999).

Another important issue raised by opponents is that certain youths, usually from minority racial and ethnic subgroups, are more likely to be officially processed for the same offenses than white youth (Cullen and Wright 2002). The end result is that a disproportionate number of minority youth end up with more "official" police and court contacts, which impacts perceptions about "prior record," and this, in turn, impacts dispositions (which tend to be harsher for youth with more significant prior records). It is this early penalty that is paid by minority youths, at the official processing stage, that may be a contributing factor to the disproportionate minority representation among juveniles in confinement.

B. Evidence to Answer the Policy Question

The key policy question is whether it is better to formally process the child through the juvenile justice system or to divert the child out altogether. To answer which policy alternative is more effective in reducing recidivism (or not), we have to examine the scientific evidence regarding the question. For questions like this, the evidence comes from prior assessments, or evaluations, of the subsequent outcomes of these decisions. Due to the problems that plague many outcome evaluations, particularly threats to internal validity such as selection bias, many criminologists have long advocated for randomized controlled trials (Farrington 1983). This is because such trials, when implemented with good integrity, provide statistically unbiased estimates of the effect of a policy alternative, such as traditional processing or diversion (Boruch 1997).

Fortunately for those concerned with using good evidence to answer the policy question, a number of relevant rigorous trials have been conducted since the 1960s that can be systematically gathered to rigorously examine the impact of the processing decision on subsequent offending by juveniles. Most of these trials have examined the efficacy of diversion programs and compared it to outcomes for youths officially processed. Despite the fact that a number of such experiments have been conducted, there has not been any prior attempt to systematically gather the data from these experiments and analyze it to determine what the crime deterrent impact is for traditional system processing on low-level juvenile offenders. There was one prior meta-analysis reported on the effects of juvenile diversion programs; this review is now over 20 years old, included quasi-experiments of varying levels of rigor (including pre-post designs without a comparison group), and reported an average reduction in delinquency for diversion programs of about 13 percent (Gensheimer et al. 1986).

II. Methodology

To provide sound evidence to respond to the policy question, we systematically identified, collected, and analyzed experiments relevant to the effectiveness of formal juvenile system processing on subsequent delinquency (Petrosino et al. 2010, 2014).

A. Criteria for Study Eligibility

For this project, we included only those studies that had the following characteristics: (1) used random or quasi-random (e.g., alternation) assignment; (2) randomly assigned juvenile delinquents (ages 17 and younger) who have not yet been "officially adjudicated" for their current offense to juvenile system processing (e.g. "juvenile system processing," "traditional handling by the juvenile court," "traditional processing," or "regular petition and processing by the juvenile court")—or to an alternative non-system condition; (3) included at least one quantifiable outcome measure of crime (e.g., arrest, conviction); and (4) report published or available through July 2008, without regard to language.

B. Search Strategy for Identification of Relevant Studies

To identify randomized trials, we relied on three main strategies:

1. Our existing collections of experiments.
2. Electronic searches of bibliographic databases. We searched 44 electronic databases and two Internet search engines (Google and Google Scholar). After a series of pilot searches, we were most successful in searching the databases by combining three sets of keywords: (1) those associated with rigorous evaluation (e.g., words like "controlled," "randomly," and "experiment"); (2) words like "juvenile" or "delinquent" and their derivatives; and (3) more focused keywords to identify components of the juvenile justice system (e.g., words such as "diversion," "adjudication," "processing," "system," and "court").
3. Existing reviews. We also searched through the bibliographies of over 50 prior reviews of research (e.g., Weisburd, Sherman, and Petrosino 1990) for references to potential experiments meeting our criteria.

As noted in the eligibility criteria, we did not exclusively seek English reports. We asked colleagues from Spain, Germany, Denmark, Israel, the Netherlands, and other nations for help in identifying any non-English studies. None were identified. Our efforts resulted in a final sample of 29 randomized experiments that included a comparison of juvenile system processing to either a release or a diversion program condition.

C. Extracting Information from Each Study

Informed by our prior research (Petrosino 1997; Petrosino, Turpin-Petrosino, Hollis-Peel, and Lavenberg 2013), we designed a preliminary instrument to guide us in extracting data from each study. In some sense, extracting data is like interviewing, or as Wilson (2009) wryly stated, "interrogating the studies." The instrument included items in the following areas: (1) researcher and study characteristics (e.g., type of publication); (2) study methods and methodological quality (e.g., if randomization integrity was substantially violated or there was large attrition from the study sample); (3) treatment and control conditions data (e.g., type of condition, and number of participants assigned to the condition); (4) participants in the trial data (e.g., race, gender, and prior record); and (5) outcome data (prevalence, incidence, severity, latency, and self-report).

D. How Decisions About Studies Were Made

It is important in a systematic review to be very explicit about the procedures we followed and how we made decisions so that readers can interpret and judge the work accordingly. For example, when we encountered studies that reported more than one comparison or control condition, our standard principle was to select the least intrusive or least harsh condition as the control group, i.e., diversion over diversion with services. Our unit of analysis was the individual experiment and not the individual research article, and we extracted information from all relevant documents (i.e., multiple articles) to complete the coding instrument for one experiment. Most studies in our sample, however, issued only one report. Moreover, each study is represented in the analyses by a single effect size to prevent the analysis from being compromised by non-independence (multiple effect sizes from one study).

We conducted analyses of four outcomes of all offending behavior (recidivism): prevalence, incidence, severity, and self-report (there was only one study that reported on latency data). Because the follow-up intervals were so disparate, with some studies reporting just one follow-up and a few studies reporting multiple follow-ups over many years, we decided to conduct three separate analyses for each of the four crime outcomes:[2]

- *First follow-up effect*: the earliest post-intervention follow-up outcome reported in the study
- *Longest follow-up effect*: the post-intervention follow-up outcome that had the longest time interval
- *Strongest follow-up effect*: the post-intervention follow-up that reported the strongest effect for juvenile system processing

Because of the relatively small differences between the outcomes of these three analyses, we only report on the strongest effects for processing in this chapter. This provides the strongest benefit of the doubt to the processing condition. It should be noted that some studies reported only one follow-up interval (meaning that first effect = longest effect = strongest effect).

When multiple types of data on the same outcome (e.g., prevalence or incidence) might be reported at the same follow-up period (e.g., police data, petitions), we selected the outcome that represented the earliest point of contact in the juvenile justice system (i.e., usually police contact).

E. Statistical Procedures and Conventions

We report standardized mean differences (Cohen's *d*). Cohen's *d* provides the flexibility in that many types of outcome data can be used to estimate the standardized mean difference (e.g., the test statistic or probability level and sample size). We used the transformation formulae provided in *Comprehensive Meta-Analysis* (see Borenstein et al. 2006) or as reported by Lipsey and Wilson (2001) to make these conversions.

We reported effect sizes assuming both fixed and random effects models for meta-analyses across the 29 studies. We conducted one sensitivity analysis, examining the impact of two studies with substantial methodological problems on the overall results by dropping them from the analyses. We also conducted several exploratory moderator analyses to determine if variables such as the type of control condition or extent of prior record in the sample have any impact on the meta-analytic results. Of course, moderator analyses must be viewed with caution for two reasons. First, as moderator analysis is done, the number of studies remaining in each of the cells can drop precipitously. The analyses are therefore based on very small numbers of studies in many instances. Second, as the number of analyses increases, the likelihood of a chance finding that a variable is moderating the result increases (i.e., more likely to be statistically significant).

III. Results

We summarized the descriptive statistics about the 29 studies included in our review. Then, we reported our meta-analysis results by outcome and the results from our sensitivity and moderator analyses as described above.

A. Descriptive Analyses

The studies included in the review were published over a 35-year period between 1973 and 2008 and included 7,304 juveniles across 29 experiments. Also, note that the time intervals for follow-up of outcomes ranged from just 2 months to a full 108 months. Studies reported between one and seven different types of crime outcomes.

Table 27.1 provides a summary of some of the descriptive data on the included studies. Most trials were reported before 1990 (76 percent). The importance of not overlooking grey literature was underscored by the fact that only 38 percent of the primary documents used to code the studies were published in peer review journals or books. Only two studies were conducted outside of the United States (Australia). In fact, nearly

Table 27.1 Characteristics of Included Studies

Selected Items	Responses	N	Percent
Where were the studies conducted?	Midwest (USA)	11	37.9%
	West (USA)	7	24.1%
	South (USA)	4	13.8%
	East (USA)	3	10.3%
	Unknown (USA)	2	6.9%
	Outside USA	2	6.9%
Who did the studies?	Michigan State University	12	41.4%
	Others	17	58.6%
When were the studies conducted?	Before January, 1990	22	76.0%
	After January, 1990	7	24.0%
Where were studies reported?	Journals/Books	11	37.9%
	Unpublished	18	62.1%
How many study groups were included?	Two groups	10	34.5%
	Three groups	13	44.8%
	Four or more groups	6	20.7%
What was the processing condition?	Traditional processing	19	65.5%
	Other	10	34.5%
What was the control condition?	Diversion with services	15	51.7%
	Diversion	14	48.3%
Was the assignment random or quasi-random?	Random	17	85.0%
	Quasi-random	3	15.0%
	Missing	9	
At what stage in the process did randomization occur?	Following police contact	9	37.5%
	After referral to program	8	33.3%
	Other	7	29.2%
	Missing	5	
What was the combined sample size of treatment and control groups?	1–100	6	21.4%
	101–200	9	32.1%
	201–300	6	21.4%
	301–400	3	10.7%
	401–500	1	3.6%
	501+	3	10.7%
	Missing	1	
What was the mean age of juveniles?	14.73 (7 cases missing)		
What was the average percentage of whites?	61.0% (10 cases missing)		
What was the average percentage of males?	74.2% (7 cases missing)		
What was the level of prior offending?	High	8	34.8%
	Moderate	3	13.0%
	Low	9	39.1%
	None	3	13.0%
	Missing	6	
Did the study include specific or general offending types?	Specific	5	17.8%
	General	23	82.2%
	Missing	1	

40 percent were conducted in the Midwest, largely because Michigan State University conducted many of them.

Most of the studies had two or three study groups (79 percent). The intervention or treatment in this review was described as "processing" in nearly two-thirds (65.5 percent) of the experiments; other descriptions of the included treatments were "petition," "adjudication," or "appear before magistrate." The type of control condition was nearly evenly split across the review sample. Fifteen studies (51.7 percent) assigned juveniles to diversion with services, including such conditions as family counseling, restorative justice conferencing, or an education program. The remaining 14 studies (48.3 percent) assigned juveniles to diversion alone, such as counsel and release or outright release. This provided the data for an interesting moderator analyses described later.

The randomization procedures were often not described explicitly enough to determine how they were done. In the 20 experiments in which enough detail was provided, only 15 percent used quasi-random allocation procedures such as alternation. Randomization most often occurred following police contact or arrest (37.5 percent) or after referral to a diversion program (33 percent).[3] Most studies included 300 or fewer juvenile participants in the treatment and control condition (74.9 percent).[4]

The average age of participants across these 29 experiments was about 14 years old. Studies in the review sample were comprised of large percentages of white (61 percent on average) and male (74 percent on average) participants. Surprisingly, although most studies included juveniles with prior offending records rates as "low" (nine studies, 39.1 percent), there were eight studies (34.8 percent) that included juveniles with prior offending records rated as "high." Only five studies (17.8 percent) targeted specific offending types (for the current or instant offense) such as shoplifters; the majority included juvenile offenders of all types.

B. Meta-Analysis Results

1. Prevalence of Offending

Prevalence data capture how many or the percentage of each treatment group that fails or succeeds according to the outcome of interest. Twenty-seven of the 29 included studies reported prevalence data on subsequent delinquency that could be analyzed using meta-analysis. As Table 27.2 shows, 15 of the 27 studies reporting the "strongest effects" for system processing were negative in direction. The overall effect size was $-.10$ for the random effects model ($-.15$ for the fixed effects model). In short, processing was associated with an increase in the number of youth who recidivated.

2. Incidence of Offending

Another question that is of interest to policymakers is whether juvenile system processing reduces the total number of offenses committed by the group, that is, the mean number of offenses per person in the group. This is especially important for

Table 27.2 Strongest Effect Reported on Prevalence Outcomes for Formal System Processing

Model	Study name	Outcome	Statistics for each study							Std diff in means and 95% CI
			Std diff in means	Z-Value	Standard error	Variance	Lower limit	Upper limit	p-Value	
	Patrick & Marsh (2005)	Strongest Effect–P	0.278	0.947	0.294	0.086	-0.298	0.854	0.344	
	Severy & Whitaker (1982)	Strongest Effect–P	0.095	1.038	0.091	0.008	-0.084	0.274	0.299	
	Klein (1986)	Strongest Effect–P	-0.479	-2.618	0.183	0.033	-0.837	-0.120	0.009	
	Smith, et al. (1979)	Strongest Effect–P	0.000	0.000	0.312	0.097	-0.612	0.612	1.000	
	Baron & Feeney (1976) 602	Strongest Effect–P	-0.428	-2.546	0.168	0.028	-0.757	-0.098	0.011	
	Baron & Feeney (1976) 601	Strongest Effect–P	-0.253	-3.853	0.066	0.004	-0.382	-0.124	0.000	
	Dunford, et al. (1982) KC	Strongest Effect–P	0.100	0.642	0.156	0.024	-0.206	0.407	0.521	
	Dunford, et al. (1982) NY	Strongest Effect–P	-0.296	-2.224	0.133	0.018	-0.557	-0.035	0.026	
	Dunford, et al. (1982) FL	Strongest Effect–P	0.097	0.591	0.163	0.027	-0.224	0.417	0.555	
	Koch (1985)	Strongest Effect–P	-0.275	-0.991	0.277	0.077	-0.818	0.268	0.322	
	Blakely (1981)	Strongest Effect–P	0.065	0.116	0.559	0.312	-1.031	1.160	0.908	
	Davidson II, et al. (1987)	Strongest Effect–P	-0.226	-0.896	0.252	0.063	-0.720	0.268	0.370	
	Davidson II, et al. (1990)	Strongest Effect–P	-0.936	-3.630	0.258	0.067	-1.442	-0.431	0.000	
	Quay & Love (1977)	Strongest Effect–P	-0.113	-1.022	0.110	0.012	-0.329	0.104	0.307	
	Bauer et al. (1980)	Strongest Effect–P	-0.512	-1.505	0.340	0.116	-1.179	0.155	0.132	
	Quincy (1981)	Strongest Effect–P	-0.282	-1.304	0.217	0.047	-0.707	0.142	0.192	
	Hintzen, et al. (1979)	Strongest Effect–P	0.999	2.196	0.455	0.207	0.107	1.890	0.028	
	Smith, et al. (2004)	Strongest Effect–P	-0.050	-0.341	0.146	0.021	-0.336	0.236	0.733	
	Povitsky Stickle, et al. (2008)	Strongest Effect–P	0.161	0.670	0.241	0.058	-0.310	0.632	0.503	
	University Associates (1986) OTSEGO	Strongest Effect–P	-0.192	-0.345	0.557	0.310	-1.283	0.899	0.730	
	University Associates (1986) BAY	Strongest Effect–P	-0.027	-0.133	0.200	0.040	-0.418	0.365	0.894	
	University Associates (1986) KALAMAZOO	Strongest Effect–P	0.029	0.205	0.141	0.020	-0.248	0.306	0.837	
	University Associates (1986) DETROIT	Strongest Effect–P	-0.050	-0.342	0.146	0.021	-0.336	0.236	0.732	
	Curran, et al. (1977)	Strongest Effect–P	-0.635	-6.730	0.094	0.009	-0.820	-0.450	0.000	
	Sherman, et al. (2000) JPP	Strongest Effect–P	0.649	2.939	0.221	0.049	0.216	1.081	0.003	
	McCold & Wachtel (1998)	Strongest Effect–P	0.368	1.922	0.191	0.037	-0.007	0.743	0.055	
	True (1973)	Strongest Effect–P	0.684	1.092	0.626	0.392	-0.543	1.911	0.275	
Fixed			-0.153	-5.042	0.030	0.001	-0.212	-0.093	0.000	
Random			-0.095	-1.443	0.066	0.004	-0.224	0.034	0.149	

Criminogenic Effect   Deterrent Effect

understanding whether intervention impacted high-rate offenders, that is, juveniles who go on to commit more than one offense after being exposed to processing.

Unfortunately, only seven experiments reported data that we could use to compute effect sizes for incidence measures. Because five of these seven studies only report incidence measures at one time interval, the outcomes for the first effect, longest effect, and strongest effect are very similar. Table 27.3 presents the results for the strongest positive effect for juvenile system processing.

As indicated, processing has an even larger negative effect on incidence of subsequent delinquency than demonstrated on the prevalence measures above, at least according to these seven experiments. As Table 27.3 indicates, six of the seven incidence measures are negative in direction. The overall effect size is −.23 when assuming a random effects model and −.21 when assuming a fixed effects model. Processing is associated with an increase in the average number of subsequent delinquent offenses per youth.

3. Severity of Offending

Policymakers may also be interested in whether or not an intervention like juvenile system processing reduces the seriousness of offending. An intervention may not impact the number of offenders who commit new offenses (prevalence) or the number of offenses committed by each person (incidence) but could be considered effective if it reduced the severity or harm caused by those new offenses (e.g., fewer violent offenses).

Unfortunately, only nine experiments reported severity data. As with incidence data, very few experiments reported more than one follow-up of a severity outcome measure, so that the effect sizes for the first effect, longest effect, and strongest effect were very similar. Table 27.4 presents the strongest effect for juvenile system processing for the nine experiments that reported such data that could be used in a meta-analysis. Again, these data were generated from official crime measures such as police contact or arrest. The average length of follow-up across these nine studies was 24 months. This is because one study reported its only severity measure at 108 months follow-up.

As Table 27.4 indicates, of the nine experiments, five are negative and four are positive in direction. However, the overall effect size is again negative in direction, with −.13 assuming a random effects model and −.20 when a fixed effects model is assumed. Processing is associated with an increase in the number of youth who commit more serious types of delinquency.

4. Self-Reported Offending

Because only one study reported a latency or "time to failure" outcome, our final analyses of crime data draw upon self-report data. Self-report data are valuable because relying on official arrest or other data could be the result of labeling and greater police scrutiny rather than any real increase in delinquent recidivism. One way to examine this is to look at self-reported crime by the juveniles in the studies. Only five experiments, however, captured self-report data that could be used in the meta-analysis. The average length of follow-up for these five studies is 11 months. As Table 27.5 indicates, in four of these five studies, the effect for juvenile system processing is negative in direction. The

Table 27.3 Strongest Effect Reported on Incidence Outcomes for Formal System Processing

Model	Study name	Outcome	Statistics for each study							Std diff in means and 95% CI
			Std diff in means	Z-Value	Standard error	Variance	Lower limit	Upper limit	p-Value	
	Klein (1986)	Strongest Effect-I	-0.742	-3.569	0.208	0.043	-1.149	-0.334	0.000	
	Baron & Feeney (1976) 601	Strongest Effect-I	-0.190	-2.672	0.071	0.005	-0.330	-0.051	0.008	
	Dunford, et al. (1982) KC	Strongest Effect-I	0.041	0.201	0.205	0.042	-0.361	0.443	0.841	
	Dunford, et al. (1982) NY	Strongest Effect-I	-0.210	-1.155	0.182	0.033	-0.567	0.147	0.248	
	Emshoff & Blakely (1983)	Strongest Effect-I	-0.500	-2.017	0.248	0.061	-0.986	-0.014	0.044	
	Sherman, et al. (2000) JPP	Strongest Effect-I	-0.070	-0.541	0.130	0.017	-0.324	0.184	0.589	
	Sherman, et al. (2000) JPS	Strongest Effect-I	-0.190	-1.098	0.173	0.030	-0.529	0.149	0.272	
Fixed			-0.205	-4.019	0.051	0.003	-0.305	-0.105	0.000	
Random			-0.228	-2.878	0.079	0.006	-0.383	-0.073	0.004	

Std diff in means and 95% CI

-1.00 -0.50 0.00 0.50 1.00

Criminogenic Effect   Deterrent Effect

Table 27.4 Strongest Effect Reported on Severity Outcomes for Formal System Processing

Model	Study name	Outcome	Statistics for each study							Std diff in means and 95% CI
			Std diff in means	Z-Value	Standard error	Variance	Lower limit	Upper limit	p-Value	
	Severy & Whitaker (1982)	Strongest Effect-S	1.090	2.561	0.425	0.181	0.256	1.924	0.010	
	Klein (1986)	Strongest Effect-S	-0.198	-1.260	0.157	0.025	-0.506	0.110	0.208	
	Baron & Feeney (1976) 602	Strongest Effect-S	-0.557	-3.115	0.179	0.032	-0.907	-0.207	0.002	
	Baron & Feeney (1976) 601	Strongest Effect-S	-0.290	-3.519	0.082	0.007	-0.452	-0.129	0.000	
	Dunford, et al. (1982) KC	Strongest Effect-S	0.020	0.105	0.188	0.035	-0.349	0.389	0.917	
	Dunford, et al. (1982) NY	Strongest Effect-S	-0.204	-1.319	0.155	0.024	-0.508	0.099	0.187	
	Dunford, et al. (1982) FL	Strongest Effect-S	0.184	0.701	0.262	0.069	-0.330	0.697	0.483	
	Quay & Love (1977)	Strongest Effect-S	-0.194	-0.989	0.196	0.038	-0.578	0.190	0.323	
	Hintzen, et al. (1979)	Strongest Effect-S	0.032	0.129	0.250	0.062	-0.458	0.522	0.898	
Fixed			-0.205	-3.838	0.053	0.003	-0.310	-0.100	0.000	
Random			-0.134	-1.445	0.093	0.009	-0.315	0.048	0.148	

Criminogenic Effect   Deterrent Effect

-1.00   -0.50   0.00   0.50   1.00

Table 27.5 Strongest Effect Reported on Self-Report Outcomes for Formal System Processing

Model	Study name	Outcome	Statistics for each study							Std diff in means and 95% CI
			Std diff in means	Z-Value	Variance	Standard error	Lower limit	Upper limit	p-Value	
	Klein (1986)	SELF-REPORT	−0.321	−2.034	0.025	0.158	−0.630	−0.012	0.042	
	Quincy (1981)	SELF-REPORT	−0.260	−1.168	0.050	0.223	−0.696	0.176	0.243	
	Povitsky Stickle, et al. (2008)	SELF-REPORT	0.515	2.178	0.056	0.236	0.051	0.978	0.029	
	Sherman, et al. (2000) JPP	SELF-REPORT	−0.230	−1.771	0.017	0.130	−0.485	0.025	0.077	
	Sherman, et al. (2000) JPS	SELF-REPORT	−0.507	−2.890	0.031	0.175	−0.851	−0.163	0.004	
Fixed			−0.230	−2.994	0.006	0.077	−0.380	−0.079	0.003	
Random			−0.190	−1.335	0.020	0.142	−0.469	0.089	0.182	

−1.00   −0.50   0.00   0.50   1.00

Criminogenic Effect   Deterrent Effect

overall effect size is −.19 assuming a random effects model and −.23 assuming a fixed effects model. Again, processing is associated with an increase in self-reported delinquency, supporting the notion that the results here are not just the function of law enforcement scrutiny and labeling but that there is likely a real criminogenic effect to the intervention.

C. Sensitivity Analysis

Although our review sample is comprised of experiments that randomly (or, in three studies, quasi-randomly) assigned participants, some factors may impede the interpretation of findings in evaluation research, including experiments. The two most common methodological factors that can compromise the findings in the types of experiments reported here are randomization failure and attrition. Although a small number of experiments reported randomization or attrition problems, only two studies were determined to have significant methodological problems because of breakdowns that would potentially undermine the reported findings.

In the Povitsky et al. (2008) study, youths were randomly assigned to traditional processing or to a diversion program featuring a "teen court." Randomization was done before juvenile participants (and their parents) agreed to participate. Therefore, a large number of juveniles were dropped from the initial randomization sample. In the Bethlehem, Pennsylvania, restorative justice experiment, youths were randomly assigned to traditional processing or a diversionary program featuring victim conferencing (McCold and Wachtel 1998). However, over half of the youths assigned to the diversionary program refused to participate and were officially processed.

Sensitivity analyses are one method that can be used by reviewers to determine the impact of studies that report methodological compromises on the overall meta-analysis findings by dropping studies to determine what impact they made on the findings. Using prevalence data at the first, longest, and strongest effects (for the 27 studies that reported such data), we dropped the McCold and Wachtel (1998) and Povitsky et al. (2008) studies to determine how that impacted effect size. After dropping the two studies, the effect sizes remain negative and increase only trivially in magnitude (about .01 change in Cohen's d), regardless of which effect model is assumed. The inclusion, therefore, of these particular two studies does not substantively impact the conclusions of the review.

D. Moderator Analyses

Juvenile system processing, at least given the experimental evidence presented here, appears to have consistently negative effects on the crime measures of prevalence, incidence, and severity, as well as crime measured by self-report. However, the results are not universal across every study, and some experiments do report positive impact of system processing. In addition, the size of the effect varies across the studies. In such

Table 27.6 Results of Moderating Analyses

Moderator	Characteristic	Effect Size—Random (Fixed)
Type of control group	Diversion Alone (n = 14)	−.04 (−.05)
	Diversion with Services (n = 13)	−.16 (−.28)
Did Michigan State University researchers conduct the study?	Yes (n = 12)	−.20 (−.16)
	No (n = 15)	−.03 (-.17)
Was the experiment reported before or after 1990?	Before 1990 (n = 21)	−.17 (−.20)
	1990 and Beyond (n = 6)	.09 (.09)
Was the report published or unpublished?	Published (n = 11)	−.18 (−.11)
	Unpublished (n = 16)	−.06 (−.19)
What was the extent of the study sample's prior record?	High (n = 8)	−.29 (−.27)
	Moderate (n = 2)	−.30 (−.30)
	Low (n = 9)	−.06 (−.13)
	None (n = 3)	.31 (.22)

cases, moderator analyses (examining how the effect varies across dimensions of the studies) can be helpful in illuminating these differences. Because prevalence data were reported in such a way that they could be used in meta-analysis by 27 of the 29 included studies, we rely on prevalence data reported at the first follow-up time interval for these moderating analyses. We have also limited our initial set of moderating analyses to five. We should also again note that the average follow-up time interval for the first prevalence outcome measurement is between 10 and 11 months.

Table 27.6 provides the results for five moderating analyses. Because analyses conducted assuming random effects models are considered more conservative, we report those and place those effect sizes computed while assuming fixed effects models in parentheses.

An important moderator is the type of control group that juvenile system processing is being compared to. There are two basic alternative groups in these experiments: (1) groups in which juveniles are diverted from the system to receive "services" ("diversion with services"); and (2) groups in which juveniles are diverted from the system and are simply released with no services (e.g., "counsel and release"). As Table 27.6 indicates, there are 14 experiments that reported prevalence data that compared juvenile system processing with diversion and 13 experiments that have a diversion with services alternative group. The overall effect for juvenile system processing is slightly negative when compared to "doing nothing," with effect sizes of −.04 (random) and −.05 (fixed). When system processing is compared to "doing something," the effect sizes are larger and remain negative, with −.16 (random) and −.28 (fixed).

Researchers and Ph.D. students from Michigan State University, generally under the supervision of Professor William Davidson, conducted 12 of the experiments in the review sample. Davidson was part of a team that developed a particular approach to juvenile diversion that included behavioral contracting and child advocacy (the Adolescent Diversion Program). Given the long program of research that he and others established at MSU, they generated a number of the randomized trials in this review sample (over 40 percent). To explore the influence of MSU studies on the sample, we compared effect size for the 12 MSU experiments with the 15 non-MSU studies that comprised the remaining 27 reports in this prevalence, first-effect analysis. Table 27.6 indicates that, like the control group moderator analysis, all of the effects are negative in direction. However, the effect size for juvenile system processing in non-MSU studies varies widely depending on whether a fixed (−.17) or random effects (−.03) model is assumed. System processing in the 12 studies reported by William Davidson and his colleagues at MSU had a larger negative effect regardless of which effects model is assumed (−.20 assuming a random effects model and −.16 assuming a fixed effects model).

Because this systematic review did not have eligibility criteria to limit it to more recent studies, experiments that were conducted and reported from 1973 through 2008 were included. This exploratory moderating analysis examines the effect for juvenile system processing in studies reported before January 1, 1990, and those reported after January 1, 1990. We should note that only six experiments were reported in 1990 or later; 21 of the studies of the 27 reporting prevalence data that could be used in meta-analysis were conducted before 1990. As Table 27.6 also indicates, the effect size varies according to the year of publication. For those studies reported before 1990, the effect size is −.17 assuming a random effects model and −.20 assuming a fixed effects model. However, for the six studies reported in 1990 or beyond, the effect size for juvenile system processing is positive in direction at .09 assuming either a random or fixed effects model. It should be noted, however, that the two studies that experienced the greatest threats to the experimental design were more recent studies (McCold and Wachtel 1998; Povitsky et al. 2008), and both reported large and positive effects for juvenile system processing. When these two studies are removed from the analysis, leaving just four post-1990 studies, the positive results dissipate (0 assuming a random effects model and −.01 assuming a fixed effects model).

This systematic review included searches for reports published in peer-reviewed journals and books as well as reports located in the grey or fugitive literature (e.g., dissertations, conference papers, government reports, technical reports, etc.). This provides an opportunity to explore the difference in effect size between published and unpublished reports. It should be noted that 11 studies in this analysis were published in peer-reviewed journals or books and 16 were reported in the fugitive literature. As Table 27.6 indicates, the overall effect sizes for juvenile system processing as reported in both published and unpublished studies are negative in direction. However, the magnitude of that negative effect is larger for published findings than for unpublished reports. For published findings, the effect size is −.18 assuming a random effects model and −.11

assuming a fixed effects model. For unpublished studies, the effect is −.06 assuming a random effects model and −.19 when assuming a fixed effects model.

Although the reports did not have an extensive amount of information on prior record, some studies did permit us to rate the extent of the sample's prior record of offending into four categories: none, low, moderate, or high. The distinctions between the categories are that if one-third or less of the study sample has a prior offense (in addition to the current offense), we rated that as "low." If the report indicated that between one-third and two-thirds of the study sample had a prior record, we rated that as "moderate." If the report indicated that over two-thirds of the study sample had a prior record, we rated that as "high." These are subjective criteria, but they provide one method to ascertain the influence of how extensive the prior record of study participants was and how that might influence the magnitude of the effect size for juvenile system processing. For example, it might be that juvenile system processing is more effective with more serious juveniles (those who have a prior record) than those who have not been in trouble before. Or perhaps the inverse is the case. Table 27.6 also presents the effect sizes for the categories of the extensiveness of the individual study sample's prior record. It should be noted that 22 studies reported enough data to allow us to rate the extensiveness of prior record in the studies, with eight rated as "high," two as "moderate," nine as "low," and three as "none." As Table 27.6 indicates, the effect sizes for juvenile system processing are larger and negative in direction when the extensiveness of prior offending in the study sample is rated as "high" or "moderate." For example, when the sample is rated as having a "high" amount of prior offending, the effect size is −.29 assuming a random effects model and −.27 for fixed effects. For the two "moderate" rated studies, the effect size is exactly −.30 regardless of which effects size model is assumed. Although the effect sizes for the nine "low"-rated studies are still negative in direction, it reduces in size to −.06 when assuming the random effects model and −.13 when assuming the fixed effects model. We should note that the two studies dropped in the sensitivity analysis involved samples rated as having "low" degree of prior offending. When they are dropped here, the effect sizes are −.15 (random) and −.18 (fixed). Finally, in the three studies that included first-time offenders only (no prior offending record), juvenile system processing has positive and much larger effects (.31 assuming a random effects model and .22 assuming a fixed effects model).

IV. IMPLICATIONS

These findings have implications for researchers, policymakers, and practitioners. For researchers, we outlined future directions for evaluation and research studies. We then described implications for policymakers and practitioners who influence juvenile system processing decisions in their jurisdictions.

A. Implications for Research

One common question in response to a review that reports an overall negative impact for a policy or practice intervention is "why?" What is the mechanism responsible for negative or crime enhancing effects for juvenile system processing? It is possible, of course, that labeling is still the key ingredient, but the meta-analysis of five experiments that included self-report data indicated that system processing also had an overall negative impact on crime when measured by self-report data. Although moderating variable analyses can shed light on this, insufficient data were reported in the studies to allow researchers to unpack the key ingredients that would help explain why system processing had consistently negative impacts on juveniles.

Research that unpacks the potential criminogenic effect of formal system processing would be important to a developmental or life-course perspective. What is it about the experience of being formally processed through the juvenile justice system that leads it be become a negative and significant event in the youth's developmental path?

Because the investigators conducting the experiments collected for this review were more interested in the effects of the diversion program (diversion was the "treatment" group), scant information is reported on the juvenile system processing condition. In fact, many of the trials simply labeled the condition as "official processing" or "traditional processing" with no further details. Better descriptions of the control conditions in randomized trials are needed in such experiments to permit a better assessment of exactly what the treatment is being compared to. In our review, in which we were ultimately concerned with the juvenile system processing condition (it became our "treatment" group), data on the eventual outcomes in the process would have been helpful. For example, how many of the juvenile cases that were officially processed ended up being dismissed? It is possible that system processing is not a deterrent because most cases end up being dismissed or assigned to a weak or informal probation condition. The diversion program may actually end up being a stronger deterrent because juveniles may view the condition as being more onerous or intrusive. There is also a "black box" problem with the meta-analysis. Although the treatment group was traditional system processing, there was often little description of what this meant in each jurisdiction where a rigorous study was implemented. For example, did the processing result in any formal dispositions and sentences to facilities? A processing condition in which most cases are eventually dismissed might be a contributing factor as to why processing does not demonstrate positive impact.

B. Implications for Policy

Given the overall negative results for juvenile system processing across these studies and outcome measures, jurisdictions should review their own policies regarding the handling of juvenile coming to the attention of legal authorities. First, although the results are not uniform across the 29 experiments, the main effect shows that system processing results in more subsequent delinquency. Rather than providing a public safety benefit, processing a juvenile through the system appears to have a negative effect. This was especially true in those studies that compared system processing with a diversion program or services. Even if the diversion program were more expensive than system processing, which is not likely the case, the crime reduction benefit associated with the diversion program would likely persuade any cost-benefit analysis to favor the implementation of diversion programs.

But, as the moderating analysis indicated, even those studies that compared juvenile system processing with "doing nothing" averaged a slightly negative impact. Even if the impact were zero, given that the evidence indicates that there is no public safety benefit to system processing and its greater costs when compared to release, the most conservative cost-benefit analyses would favor release over system processing. One could argue that interventions achieve other important goals, but other than crime reduction, we are not sure what other potential benefits of system processing should be measured. The studies included here all too infrequently examined the impacts of system processing on education and other measures.

None of the findings here provide guidance on what the juvenile system should do with an individual juvenile offender. This review captured aggregate data from 29 experimental studies. It is most appropriate for guiding larger local, state, and national policies regarding juveniles. This systematic review does not specifically identify the particular type of offender that could benefit from further processing in the juvenile justice system.

It should be noted that these experiments compared system processing with a diversion program or simple release. Thus, the data from these studies do not support a policy of establishing diversion programs for juveniles that normally would not have been officially processed (i.e., "net-widening").

V. Conclusion

This chapter, examining the results of 29 randomized controlled trials, finds that juvenile system processing has an overall negative impact on crime. This was consistent across measures of prevalence, incidence, severity, and self-report and consistent even when giving juvenile system processing the benefit of the doubt and looking only at the strongest positive effect for processing. The effects are even more negative for juvenile system processing when the two trials experiencing significant randomization or attrition issues are removed from the analysis.

Moderating analyses indicated that effect sizes were more negative for processing in studies that compared it to a diversion program or provision of services than in those trials that compared processing to simple release ("doing nothing"). Effect sizes were also larger and more negative in direction for older studies (before 1990), those conducted by Michigan State University researchers, and those reported in unpublished documents such as dissertations and technical reports. An interesting moderating variable was the extent of prior record of offending in the study sample. When the study sample was rated as having a low, moderate, or high amount of prior offending, system processing had consistently negative effects. However, for the three studies that were rated as having no prior record because they were comprised of first-time offenders, system processing has a positive crime-reduction effect.

Given the lack of positive effects for system processing, and the consistently negative impacts on subsequent delinquency outcomes, jurisdictions should review their policies regarding the handling of juveniles. Not only does the evidence identified in the review indicate harmful effects, there are also additional financial costs associated with system processing. Except for the most intensive diversion programs, system processing is likely to be the more expensive option. Thus, jurisdictions that officially process a high percentage of low- to moderate-severity juveniles may cause harm to both youthful offenders and taxpayers.

ACKNOWLEDGMENT

The Norwegian Knowledge Centre for the Health Sciences and an unnamed U.S. organization provided funding, in part, for the systematic review reported on in this chapter. Note that this chapter draws on prior published works, including a Campbell Collaboration review (Petrosino, Turpin-Petrosino, and Guckenburg 2010) and a chapter in a 2014 volume of the Advances in Criminological Theory series (Petrosino, Turpin-Petrosino, and Guckenburg 2014).

NOTES

1. These programs range in their components, intensity, and requirements and usually include counseling but sometimes include other services. The youth may be released from the system altogether to be taken home by his or her parents (sometimes with a stern warning by police, often called "counsel and release").
2. We also conducted analyses with a "standardized one year follow-up," i.e., the outcome closest to 12 months. However, we found the difference in effect sizes between the one-year and longest follow-up for the prevalence data to be negligible. For incidence, severity, and self-report data, so few follow-up periods were included that first effect, longest effect, and strongest effect meta-analyses yielded very similar estimates.
3. In these trials assignment was then made to processing or to stay in the diversion program.
4. This represents the total number of the juveniles in the processing condition and the control condition used in the meta-analysis. This would not reflect the total study sample if multiple comparison groups were involved that were not collapsed into a single comparison group.

References

Borenstein, Michael, Larry Hedges, Julian Higgins, and Hannah Rothstein. 2006. Comprehensive Meta-Analysis (Version 2.2.027) [computer software]. Englewood, NJ: Biostat.

Boruch, Robert. 1997. *Randomized Experiments for Planning and Evaluation: A Practical Guide.* Thousand Oaks, CA: Sage.

Crime Solutions. 2015. *Practice Review: Formal System Processing for Juveniles.* https://www.crimesolutions.gov/PracticeDetails.aspx?ID=9.

Cullen, Francis, and John Paul Wright. 2002. Criminal Justice in the Lives of American Adolescents: Choosing the Future. In *The Future of the Adolescent Experience: Societal Trends and the Transition to Adulthood in the 21st Century,* edited by J. Mortimer and R. Larson, 88–128. New York: Cambridge University Press.

Dishion, Thomas, Joan McCord, and Francois Poulin. 1999. "When Interventions Harm: Peer Groups and Problem Behavior." *American Psychologist* 54: 755–764.

Farrington, David P. 1983. "Randomized Experiments on Crime and Justice." In *Crime and Justice: An Annual Review of Research,* Vol. 4, edited by Michael Tonry and Norval Morris. Chicago: University of Chicago Press.

Farrington, David, and Joseph Murray. 2014. *Advances in Criminological Theory,* Vol. 18, *Labeling Theory: Empirical Tests.* New Brunswick, NJ: Transaction.

Gensheimer, Leah K., Jeffrey P. Mayer, and Rand Gottschalk. 1986. "Diverting Youth from the Juvenile Justice System: A Meta-Analysis of Intervention Efficacy." In *Youth Violence: Problems and Prospects,* edited by Stephen Apter and Arnold Goldstein. Elmsford, NY: Pergamon.

Lipsey, Mark W., and David B. Wilson. 2001. *Practical Meta-Analysis.* Applied Social Research Methods Series, Vol. 49. Thousand Oaks, CA: SAGE.

McCold, Paul, and Benjamin Wachtel. 1998. *Restorative Policing Experiment: The Bethlehem Pennsylvania Police Family Group Conferencing Project.* Bethlehem, PA: Community Service Foundation.

Muscari, Mary E. 2010. What Should I Know About Status Offenses? *Medscape Experts: Ask the Nurses.* http://www.medscape.com/viewarticle/723866.

Petrosino, Anthony. 1997. *What Works? Revisited Again: A Meta-Analysis of Randomized Experiments in Rehabilitation, Deterrence and Prevention.* Ph.D. dissertation, Rutgers University. Ann Arbor, MI: University Microfilms.

Petrosino, Anthony, Carolyn Turpin-Petrosino, M. Hollis-Peel, and J. G. Lavenberg. 2013. "Scared Straight and Other Juvenile Awareness Programs for Preventing Juvenile Delinquency: A Systematic Review." *Campbell Systematic Reviews* 5. doi: 10.4073/csr.2013.5.

Petrosino, Anthony, Carolyn Turpin-Petrosino, and Sarah Guckenburg. 2010. "Formal System Processing of Juveniles: Effects on Delinquency." *Campbell Systematic Reviews* 1. doi: 10.4073/csr.2010.1.

Petrosino, Anthony, Carolyn Turpin-Petrosino, and Sarah Guckenburg. 2014. "The Impact of Juvenile System Processing on Delinquency." In *Labeling Theory: Empirical Tests* (Advances in Criminological Theory, Vol. 18), edited by David Farrington and Joseph Murray. New Brunswick, NJ: Transaction.

Povitsky-Stickle, Wendy, Nadine Connell, Denise Wilson, and Denise Gottfredson. 2008. "An Experimental Evaluation of Teen Courts." *Journal of Experimental Criminology* 4(2):137–163.

Schur, Edwin. 1973. *Radical Nonintervention: Rethinking the Delinquency Problem.* Englewood Cliffs, NJ: Prentice-Hall.

U.S. Office of Juvenile Justice & Delinquency Prevention. no date. Juvenile Justice System and Process. Case Flow Diagram. *Statistical Briefing Book.* https://www.ojjdp.gov/ojstatbb/structure_process/case.html.

Weisburd, David, Lawrence Sherman, and Anthony Petrosino. 1990. *Registry of Randomized Criminal Justice Experiments in Sanctions.* Unpublished report. Rutgers University, University of Maryland and Crime Control Institute.

Wilson, David B. 2009. "Systematic Coding." In *The Handbook of Research Synthesis and Meta-Analysis*, 2nd ed., edited by Harris Cooper, Larry Hedges, and Jeff Valentine, 159–176. New York: Russell Sage Foundation.

CHAPTER 28

....

EFFECTS OF INCARCERATION

....

LILA KAZEMIAN AND ALLYSON WALKER

INCARCERATION rates have generally been on the rise in most developed countries over the course of the past decades (International Centre for Prison Studies), and this increase has been particularly pronounced in the United States (National Research Council 2014). There are approximately 2.2 million people incarcerated in U.S. state and federal prisons and jails; these figures reflect a nearly 500 percent increase in the incarceration rate over the past three decades (National Research Council 2014). This dramatic increase in the recourse to imprisonment has highlighted the importance of better understanding the impact of the incarceration experience on crime rates, criminal careers, and desistance from crime.

The potential harmful effects of imprisonment have been discussed by many researchers. According to Sykes (1958, pp. 286–292), the "pains of imprisonment" include the deprivations of liberty, goods and services, heterosexual relationships, autonomy, and security. Liebling (2011, p. 536) describes a "new and distinctive kind of 'prison pain' . . . consisting of a kind of existential and identity crisis brought on by both the length and uncertainty of contemporary sentences, but also by the restricted facilities available." Clemmer (1958) introduced the concept of prisonization, which refers to the process by which prisoners adopt the customs, values, and norms of prison, some of which may be incompatible with life on the outside.

In this chapter, we offer an overview of research findings relating to the impact of incarceration on subsequent offending and other risk factors. Section I examines the empirical evidence on the impact of incarceration on aggregate crime rates, followed by a discussion of the effect of imprisonment on subsequent reoffending (Section II). Section III explores the link between incarceration and risk factors extending beyond behavioral outcomes, including psychological well-being and mental health issues as well as housing and employment outcomes. In Section IV, the collateral consequences of imprisonment on the families of prisoners are discussed. These include the impact of incarceration on family ties, family housing, and income and the potentially adverse effects on the children of prisoners. The chapter concludes with a discussion of the imprisonment–desistance link and the methodological intricacies pertinent to the study of this relationship.

I. The Impact of Incarceration on Aggregate Crime Rates

In order to test the premise that imprisonment leads to reductions in crime through incapacitation and deterrence, several studies have investigated the incarceration–crime link. Incapacitation relates to crimes prevented through the physical removal of an individual from the community. Specific deterrence designates the process by which any given sanction prevents the punished individual from committing further offenses, whereas general deterrence refers to crimes averted as a result of the threat of punishment.

From the viewpoint of policymakers who are concerned with rapid reductions in crime rates, the idea that increased incarceration produces immediate declines in crime is certainly appealing. Much of the research that has assessed the incapacitation effects of incarceration has relied on elasticity estimates, which measure the change in crime rate for every 1 percent increase in imprisonment rate. Some studies have suggested that increased incarceration rates result in short-term decreases in aggregate crime rates (Marvell and Moody 1994; Levitt 2004; Spelman 2006). Levitt (1996, p. 348) found that the incapacitation of each additional offender prevents about 15 crimes per year, and concluded that "the marginal costs of incarceration are at or below the accompanying social benefits of crime reduction." Spelman (2006) estimated that a quarter of the crime decline of the 1990s occurred as a result of higher incarceration rates. Fabelo (1995) found that a 30 percent increase in incarceration is associated with a 5 percent decrease in crime, highlighting the drastic increases in imprisonment rates required to produce changes in crime rates. Drawing on data from a longitudinal Dutch study, Blokland and Nieuwbeerta (2007) created "two hypothetical societies": an experimental society subject to a selective incapacitation policy and a control society with no exposure to any specific policy. Blokland and Nieuwbeerta (2007) found that targeting high-rate offenders for incapacitation resulted in considerable reductions in crime, although this effect was somewhat attenuated over time (as a result of prison releases). Their analyses also showed a "25 percent decrease in crime under the strictest regime" (p. 348), but this decline required a substantial increase in the prison population (up to 45 times higher than the control group).

Notwithstanding these results, most studies have found that incarceration does not significantly reduce crime. In a comprehensive review of research that has investigated the link between crime and incarceration, the National Research Council (2014) found that there was a great deal of variation in elasticity estimates across studies and as a result, the magnitude of the impact of incarceration on crime rates cannot be determined on the basis of existing research. While incarceration rates rose rather steadily between the 1970s and the 2000s in the United States (especially between the mid-1980s and early 1990s), this increase did not always coincide with a decline in crime rates (King, Mauer, and Young 2005). Incarceration rates were on the rise in the 1980s, but this was also true for violent crimes rates (i.e., robbery and murder). These trends suggest that factors other than incarceration may have contributed to these fluctuations in crimes rates.

King et al. (2005) suggested that after a certain threshold, incarceration produces diminished returns and even adverse consequences (see also Johnson and Raphael 2012; The Pew Center on the States 2012; National Research Council 2014). This is the case when incarcerated individuals are replaced by others who engage in offending, when the deterrent effect of incarceration is attenuated because an increasing number of individuals become exposed to the prison experience, directly or indirectly (see also Nagin 1998), and when incarceration contributes to the development of other risk factors for crime (social disorder, impact on families, mental health impediments, etc.). These findings have prompted scholars to conclude that "the deterrent return to increasing already long sentences is modest at best" (National Research Council 2014, p. 139). In short, the evidence emerging from prior research on the effects of incarceration on aggregate crime rates has suggested that incarceration has limited crime-reduction benefits.

II. The Impact of Incarceration on Reoffending

Most empirical studies and meta-analyses that have investigated the impact of incarceration on recidivism have found that imprisonment has either no impact or undesirable effects on subsequent offending (Gendreau, Goggin, and Cullen 1999; Villettaz, Killias, and Zoder 2006; Nagin, Cullen, and Jonson 2009; Nieuwbeerta, Nagin and Blokland 2009; Weatherburn 2010; Bales and Piquero 2012; Petrosino, Turpin-Petrosino, and Guckenburg 2013). However, without comparison samples that provide an estimate of the magnitude of reoffending rates in the absence of imprisonment, it is difficult to truly assess the impact of incarceration on subsequent changes in individual offending rates. Very few studies have employed experimental designs or minimally a comparison group, in large part due to the ethical concerns associated with this approach. These studies tend to be dated, rely on juvenile samples (Schneider 1986; Barton and Butts 1990) or focus on short-term incarceration (Killias, Aebi, and Ribeaud 2000; Killias et al. 2010), but they have consistently found that incarceration either has a null or aggravating effect on subsequent offending behavior.

In their updated systematic review of the state of knowledge on the link between reoffending and custodial versus non-custodial sanctions, Villettaz, Gillieron, and Killias's (2015) findings confirmed the central result of their first review (see Villettaz et al. 2006): recidivism rates are generally lower after a non-custodial sanction versus a custodial sanction. Interestingly, this finding was more frequently observed in studies employing weaker research designs when compared with experimental evaluations and natural experiments. In fact, the meta-analysis did not show significant differences in reoffending rates between custodial and non-custodial sanctions in the experimental evaluations and natural experiments (though this analysis was based on a small number of studies: n = 5). Villettaz et al. (2015, p. 7) concluded that "results in favour of non-custodial sanctions in the majority of quasi-experimental studies may reflect insufficient control of pre-intervention differences between prisoners and those serving 'alternative' sanctions." More research drawing on experimental designs and extended follow-up periods is needed in order to conduct more through and accurate comparisons of reoffending rates between incarceration and community sanctions.

Some studies have relied on natural experiments, which involved cases that were randomly assigned to judges with varying sentencing practices (Green and Winik 2010; Loeffler 2013; Nagin and Snodgrass 2013); these studies have found that sentencing disparities were not associated with subsequent reoffending rates. For instance, in a study of randomly assigned criminal cases in Chicago state courts, Loeffler (2013) did not find a significant relationship between the punitiveness of the judge (i.e., the type of sentence imposed) and 5-year reoffending rates. These findings suggest that sentence type does not significantly predict recidivism and that more severe sentences have limited crime-reduction benefits.

These empirical findings are consistent with systematic reviews of research. Gendreau et al. (1999) conducted a meta-analysis of studies that have investigated the link between prison and recidivism. Their analysis was based on 50 studies (336,052 offenders) that have assessed the effect of incarceration (compared with community sanctions) and length of time in prison on recidivism. Controlling for relevant risk factors, the authors found that both these conditions led to increases in recidivism. Similarly, drawing on Dutch data, Wermink et al. (2017, p. 1) found that the "length of imprisonment exerts an overall null effect on future rates of recidivism." The National Research Council (2014, pp. 155–156) concluded that "the evidence base demonstrates that lengthy prison sentences are ineffective as a crime control measure," and that "statutes mandating lengthy prison sentences cannot be justified on the basis of their effectiveness in preventing crime" (see also Mauer, King, and Young 2004; Nellis and King 2009; Wermink et al. 2017). Nagin, Cullen, and Jonson's (2009) review reached a similar conclusion and suggested that prison either has no impact on crime, or exerts criminogenic effects. Gendreau et al. (1999, p. 7) concluded that prison may promote offending behavior by damaging the "psychological and emotional well-being of inmates." Imprisonment may lead to reoffending through the various psychological, social, or financial consequences of incarceration. These effects will be explored in the following sections.

One major caveat of the research findings discussed in this chapter relates to the common assumption that correctional settings are homogeneous across different prisons, which is not the case. Just like recidivism can vary in intensity and seriousness (e.g., violent versus non-violent recidivism, new offense versus technical violation, etc.), conditions of confinement can vary significantly across facilities, and "not all prisons are created equal" (National Research Council, 2014, p. 158). Few studies have investigated the impact of quality of life in prisons on crime and recidivism rates. Katz, Levitt, and Shustorovich (2003) tested the deterrent effect of the low quality of prison life on aggregate crime rates. Using prisoner death rates as a proxy for prison conditions, the authors found that poorer prison conditions were associated with lower crime rates, though the aggregate impact was quite small ("a doubling of the prison death rate would reduce the crime rate by only a few percentage points") (Katz et al. 2003, p. 340). Katz et al. (2003) acknowledged that their findings may simply reveal selective incapacitation effects. In addition, the measure of prison conditions employed in Katz et al.'s (2003) study is very broad and does not capture the intricacies of the quality of life inside facilities.

Drawing on a sample of approximately 20,000 released Italian prisoners, Drago, Galbiati, and Vertova (2011) investigated whether the harshness of prison conditions influenced subsequent offending. The authors used a more comprehensive measure of prison conditions (i.e., prison deaths, overcrowding, and isolation from the rest of society). Unlike Katz et al.'s aggregate analyses, Drago et al.'s (2011) study included individual-level data. Using data from the Italian Department of Prison Administration on 25,814 released prisoners from prisons across Italy, Drago et al. (2011) found that all indicators of harsh prison conditions and isolation were associated with increased recidivism in the year following release. In the United States, because there is no comprehensive and systematic assessment of the conditions of confinement (National Research Council 2014), the underlying (and erroneous) assumption of most research on the effects of incarceration is that imprisonment is a standardized experience across different individuals and facilities.

III. The Impact of Incarceration on Other Risk Factors

Policymakers and researchers tend to focus on recidivism as an outcome variable in assessments of the effectiveness of intervention programs or sanctions. One caveat of a recidivism-favored approach is that it disregards changes and progress exhibited in other social and cognitive domains. Imprisonment does not exclusively exert an effect on offending. It also impacts the psychological well-being of incarcerated individuals, as well as social, economic, and health outcomes that may be associated with offending behavior (for a more detailed discussion of these indicators, see Liebling and Maruna 2005). Because long-term follow-ups of prisoners are infrequent, there remain important gaps in our knowledge regarding the long-term impact of incarceration on prisoners.

A. The Impact of Incarceration on Psychological Well-Being and Mental Health

Some studies have highlighted the link between serious mental illness and offending behavior (Fisher, Silver, and Wolff 2006; Frank and McGuire 2011). In addition, the significant prevalence of serious traumatic experiences and mental health disorders among the prisoner population has been highlighted by various scholars (e.g., Fazel and Danesh 2002; Haney 2006; James and Glaze 2006; Wolff Blitz and Shi 2007; Wolff, Shi, and Siegel 2009; Dudeck et al. 2011; National Research Council 2014). The National Research Council (2014) identified several harmful conditions of incarceration, all of which can produce adverse psychological outcomes; these include extreme overcrowding, boredom, and isolation. The constant feeling of loneliness can cause significant distress to prisoners (Johnson and McGunigall-Smith 2008). Dudeck et al. (2011) examined the prevalence of trauma and mental health problems among prisoners serving long sentences (minimum sentences of 5 years) in 11 European countries. The authors found that participants were exposed to an average of three traumatic experiences during their sentences; 14 percent of the sample consequently developed symptoms characteristic of posttraumatic stress disorder (PTSD). The researchers argued that more than half of the sample was in need of treatment. Liem and Kunst (2013) also reported that PTSD and other forms of mental illness were common among former prisoners who had served long sentences. Turney, Wildeman, and Schnittker (2012) drew on data from the Fragile Families and Child Wellbeing Study to explore major depression among current and former prisoners. Controlling for financial situation, substance use, and relationship quality, the authors found immediate and persistent effects of incarceration on major depression among study participants.

Official statistics suggest higher suicide rates among prisoners when compared to the general population (Mumola 2005; Mumola and Noonan 2009). Approximately 30 percent of Dudeck et al.'s (2011) sample reported that they had attempted suicide at some point during their incarceration. Research has also suggested that former prisoners are at a high risk of suicide immediately after their release from prison. A meta-analysis conducted by Jones and Maynard (2013) revealed that the risk of suicide was 6.76 times greater among released prisoners when compared with the general population, highlighting the persistence of mental health issues upon release.

It remains unclear whether incarceration causes the development of mental illness or whether it simply exacerbates a pre-existing condition (Schnittker, Massoglia, and Uggen 2012). A noteworthy study by Massoglia (2008) examined the effects of incarceration on various health outcomes. Controlling for health issues prior to incarceration, the study matched incarcerated participants with individuals in the general population. Massoglia (2008) found that incarcerated individuals were more likely to suffer from infectious diseases and stress-related illnesses, including anxiety, depression, and insomnia. Schnittker et al. (2012) examined the effects of incarceration on psychiatric disorders while controlling for various confounding health outcomes, childhood background characteristics, and other early risk factors prior to incarceration. The authors found that the prevalence of mental health disorders was higher among individuals with histories of incarceration; however, these individuals also had a higher rate of exposure to early risk factors such as substance abuse, child abuse and neglect, and childhood poverty. Although incarceration was found to be linked to mood disorders, some of the psychiatric disorders that were prevalent among former prisoners emerged earlier in the life course and prior to incarceration. In addition, further analyses suggested that the association between incarceration and psychiatric disorders dissipated over time. These findings highlight the complexity of the incarceration–mental health link and underline the need to better understand the long-term effects of incarceration.

Not all research has suggested deterioration in the well-being and adjustment of prisoners over extended periods of incarceration (e.g., MacKenzie and Goodstein 1985). Some research has suggested that prisoners may learn to adapt to the circumstances of long-term incarceration (Zamble and Porporino 1988; Zamble 1992; Leigey 2010), though this body of research tends to be dated. In a more recent study, Dettbarn (2012) compared forensic-psychiatric examinations conducted with a sample of 87 long-term German prisoners at the beginning and at the end of their sentences (with an average sentence length of 14.6 years). The author found a decline in the prevalence of psychiatric disorders over time. Emotional stability improved between the first and last assessments, and depression and aggressiveness decreased. The author concluded that "there was no evidence that longer duration of sentence per se led to physical illness or a diminution of cognitive capacity" (Dettbarn 2012, p. 238). This study is, however, limited by mainly descriptive analyses, the absence of a control group, and only two data collection points. In addition, it is unclear to what extent findings drawn from the German prison setting are generalizable to correctional facilities in other parts of the world, especially the United States. Liebling (1999, p. 287) argued that research that has found minimal effects of incarceration on prisoner well-being is partly biased by issues of operationalization of harm and "the failure of research on the effects of prison life to ask the right questions or to ask in an appropriate kind of way how imprisonment is experienced."

In short, while most research has suggested that incarceration adversely affects the well-being of prisoners, several questions remain unanswered. Our understanding of how psychological well-being and other health outcomes vary during periods of incarceration (particularly long sentences) remains limited due to the lack of longitudinal follow-ups of contemporary samples of prisoners (Kazemian and Travis 2015). In addition, given that few studies have employed strong methodological frameworks that control for risk factors prior to incarceration, more research is needed in order to assess whether mental health impediments are a result of the incarceration experience or whether they precede prison and merely reflect selection effects.

B. The Impact of Incarceration on Housing and Employment Outcomes

Employment is key to a successful reintegration into the community after release from prison. Individuals who cannot secure employment after release from custody are at an increased risk of recidivism (Petersilia 2003; Wang, Mears, and Bales 2010; D'Alessio, Stolzenberg, and Eitle 2014). Former prisoners face significant barriers to employment. They often experience economic disadvantage prior to incarceration: they are likely to have lower levels of education and more limited employment history when compared to the general population (Pew Charitable Trusts 2010). The experience of incarceration results in a decreased likelihood of securing a job, especially one with reasonable pay (Western 2002), and this is particularly true for racial minorities (Pager 2003). A study commissioned by the Pew Charitable Trusts (2010) found that employment disadvantage resulting from incarceration reduced wages by an average of $179,000 by age 48, excluding wages lost during incarceration.

Beyond laws explicitly barring individuals with criminal records from certain employment opportunities, former prisoners are faced with a number of other barriers. Research has shown that employers are less likely to hire individuals with a criminal record when compared with those from other stigmatized groups with low levels of skill, such as those receiving welfare benefits or workers with large gaps in their employment histories (Pager 2007; Schmitt and Warner 2011). Some surveys have suggested that approximately 40 percent of employers would not hire an individual with a criminal record (Holzer et al. 2007; Pager 2007).

Pager (2007) described three distinct processes by which former prisoners are barred from employment: selection, labeling, and transformation. Selection occurs when formerly incarcerated individuals possess individual characteristics that simultaneously impact the risk of incarceration and the access to financial/employment opportunities. Labeling refers to the reduced likelihood of employment resulting from the stigma associated with a criminal record. Transformation is the process by which incarceration changes individuals over time and adversely impacts their skillset or ability to adapt to the workforce. For instance, trauma experienced in prison may impair a former prisoner's ability to work. Haney (2006) argued that individuals who become acclimated to the prison environment may experience difficulties in adjusting to the unstructured and unpredictable character of life on the outside, and that some former prisoners may find it challenging to make decisions and initiate plans autonomously.

Studies drawing on administrative data show mixed results with regard to the effects of incarceration on subsequent employment and earnings outcomes. Several studies using data on unemployment insurance records reported decreases in long-term employment after incarceration (Waldfogel 1994; Grogger 1995; Sabol 2007; Pettit and Lyons 2009). Other studies (Lalonde and Cho 2008) failed to detect significant short-term effects of incarceration on employment and earnings. Pettit and Lyons (2009) and Sabol (2007) reported an increase in employment shortly after release (when compared with employment levels prior to incarceration), though these effects were not lasting. The National Research Council report (2014) speculated that the emerging finding of short-term positive effects of incarceration on employment may be a result of parole conditions.

The ability to secure housing after release has also been associated with lower rates of recidivism (Petersilia 2003; Makarios, Steiner, and Travis 2010). As a result of local, state, and federal policies, returning offenders face multiple barriers in seeking housing (Geller and Curtis 2011). Ethnographic research conducted in San Francisco and St. Louis showed that incarceration resulted in the dissolution of social networks, which in turn led to periods of homelessness after release (Gowan 2002). Geller and Curtis (2011) used data from the Fragile Families and Child Wellbeing Study to explore the effects of confinement on post-incarceration housing stability. Controlling for a variety of demographic and socioeconomic variables (including marriage, cohabitation, education, income, and substance abuse history), the researchers found that individuals with a history of incarceration were twice as likely to face housing insecurity; this association was more pronounced for individuals who had been recently incarcerated.

IV. The Collateral Consequences of Incarceration

The effects of incarceration extend beyond the prison walls. Scholars have highlighted the collateral consequences of incarceration (e.g., see Travis and Waul 2003; National Research Council 2014). Empirical evidence has suggested that incarceration adversely impacts the well-being of families and communities. Drawing on Clemmer's (1958) work, Comfort (2008) introduced the concept of "secondary prisonization," which refers to the extended effects of confinement on the families of prisoners.

A. The Adverse Impact of Incarceration on Family Ties

The negative impact of incarceration on social bonds (e.g., work, school, community, etc.) has been highlighted by many researchers (Orsagh and Chen 1988; Sampson and Laub 1997; Travis and Petersilia 2001; Burnett 2004; Richards and Jones 2004; Sabol and Lynch 2004; King et al. 2005; Travis 2005; National Research Council 2014). Gust (2012) summarized the ways in which imprisonment impacts the family. It exerts an adverse effect on family structure and living arrangements, strains family relationships, creates a financial burden, causes significant emotional stress resulting from the experience of incarceration, and leads to stigma, which impacts the prisoner as well as his or her family members. Mothers with incarcerated partners are more likely to experience economic and housing insecurity (Geller et al. 2009; Schwartz-Soicher et al. 2011; Geller and Franklin 2014). They are also more likely to be exposed to increased levels of stress and to develop mental health issues (namely, major depression and life dissatisfaction; see Wildeman et al. 2012). Dyer, Pleck, and McBride's (2012) review underlined the fact that incarceration leads to reduced self-identification as a parent as well as a decreased ability to play a central role in family life, thus disconnecting incarcerated men from their children and partners.

Incarceration removes family members from their homes, often to a facility that is not easily accessible. On average, women are incarcerated in prisons that are located 160 miles away from their children; for men, the average distance is 100 miles (Western and Wildeman 2009). Researchers have documented numerous barriers to maintaining contact with family members in prison (Grinstead et al. 2001; Braman 2004; Comfort 2008). Christian (2005) described some of these barriers: high costs of transportation and food for visitors and prisoners, lengthy travel time to and from the facilities, and rigid rules (such as dress codes and ID requirements) that may result in some visitors being turned away upon arrival at the facility.

Turney and Wildeman (2013) investigated the effects of incarceration on family relationships while controlling for a host of covariates, including relationship quality, trust, and emotional and socioeconomic variables. The authors found that partners of incarcerated individuals were seven times more likely to separate from their partners compared with couples who were not affected by incarceration. Braman (2004) further argued that incarceration can impact the extent to which partners are perceived as being trustworthy and selfish. Western (2006) also found that men who are married when entering prison are more likely to separate from their partners compared with their counterparts in the general population, and those who are unmarried are less likely to get married later in life (Western 2006). In contrast, research conducted by Lopo and Western (2005) found that incarceration was not significantly associated with the men's likelihood of marrying later in life, although a positive relationship was observed between incarceration and divorce (see also Apel et al. 2010, for similar results in a Dutch sample).

La Vigne et al. (2005) suggested that the maintenance of contacts with an incarcerated parent during the period of incarceration may be effective in reducing the negative consequences of imprisonment on children, but others have found that these visits may exert negative effects (e.g., stress, anxiety, humiliation) on family members and particularly children (Hairston, 1998; Comfort, 2008). In addition, Edin et al. (2004) argued that incarceration was not necessarily detrimental to relationships that were harmed by the incarcerated partner's lifestyle choices prior to prison (see also Dyer et al. 2012). Despite the growing literature on this topic, much remains unknown about the mechanisms underlying the effects of incarceration on families (Dyer et al. 2012), especially over prolonged periods of incarceration (Kazemian and Travis 2015).

B. The Impact of Incarceration on Family Housing and Income

Given that most incarcerated parents are often the primary breadwinners in the family (Travis, McBride, and Solomon 2005; Glaze and Maruschak 2008) and that prison salaries, when accessible, are low, it is not surprising that incarceration exerts a significant impact on the economic situation of the family. Walker (2011) found that mothers with incarcerated partners were more likely to receive Temporary Assistance for Needy Families (TANF), as well as food stamps, when compared with mothers without incarcerated partners. Similarly, mothers with recently incarcerated partners have been found to be more likely to be enrolled in Medicaid/State Children's Health Insurance Program (SCHIP) and to receive food stamps (Sugie 2012).

Stable housing is widely recognized as an integral component of personal and family well-being (Bratt 2001; Postmus et al. 2009; Lee, Tyler, and Wright 2010). In addition to the impact on the physical and emotional health of families, housing security is a key factor in both securing and maintaining employment (Bradley et al. 2001). The incarceration experience has been linked to the housing stability of the prisoners' families. Controlling for various early-life and contemporaneous covariates, Geller and Franklin (2014) found that the likelihood of housing insecurity was 50 percent greater among partners of incarcerated fathers compared with those who did not have an incarcerated partner. The loss of the father's financial contributions to the household explained a large proportion, but not all, of the effect of incarceration on housing insecurity.

Additional research by Wildeman (2014) suggested that the incarceration of fathers (but not mothers) had a significant effect on the likelihood of their partners and children experiencing homelessness and that this issue disproportionally affected black families. Schwartz-Soicher, Geller, and Garfinkel (2011) also showed significant, negative effects of paternal incarceration on the mother's housing security, measured on the basis of eviction or missed rent or mortgage payments. The authors examined the effects of custodial sanctions on the partner's material hardship more generally and found that incarceration resulted in negative outcomes with regard to the ability to pay utility and telephone bills, to afford medical care, and to purchase food without assistance. In short, the empirical evidence suggests that the incarceration experience can adversely impact the housing and financial stability of the families of prisoners.

C. The Negative Effects of Incarceration on the Children of Prisoners

Between 1991 and 2007, the number of incarcerated parents with children under the age of 18 increased by 79 percent in the United States (Glaze and Maruschak 2008). In 2007, 1.7 million American children (representing 2.3 percent of the population of children in the United States) had at least one parent incarcerated in a state or federal facility (Glaze and Maruschak 2008). Unsurprisingly, paternal incarceration has been found to be a stressful experience for children (National Research Council 2014).

Children of incarcerated parents have been found to be at higher risk of exhibiting problems in school, inadequate self-esteem, issues relating to cognitive functioning, behavioral problems and delinquency, as well as later incarceration (Hanlon et al. 2005; Murray and Farrington 2005; Poehlmann 2005; Huebner and Gustafson 2007; Kinner et al. 2007; Murray and Farrington 2008; Wildeman 2009, 2010; Walker 2011; Roettger and Swisher 2011; Wakefield and Wildeman 2011; Johnson and Easterling 2012; Murray, Loeber, and Pardini 2012; National Research Council 2014; Muftić, Bouffard, and Armstrong 2015). Some research has suggested that the strains of the incarceration experience are often transferred to children (Hairston 1998; Comfort 2008), and parental incarceration has been regarded as a traumatic experience for children (Travis and Waul 2003; Arditti 2012). The incarceration of a father may also result in turnovers in the mother's romantic partners, which can be associated with poor parenting practices (Arditti, Burton, and Neeves-Botelho 2010). In addition, the likelihood of attaining upward economic mobility is said to be reduced among children of incarcerated parents (The Pew Charitable Trusts 2010).

Several studies have found a positive association between parental incarceration and subsequent offending behaviors of children (e.g., Hanlon et al. 2005; Kjellstrand and Eddy 2012). Roettger and Swisher (2011) investigated this association. Using data from the National Longitudinal Study of Adolescent Health (Add Health) study and controlling for a variety of demographic, family, and attachment variables, the authors found that adolescents with incarcerated parents were more likely to engage in delinquency and to be arrested in early adulthood. Drawing on a sample of 1,009 boys in the Pittsburgh Youth Study, Murray, Loeber, and Pardini (2012) used propensity score matching to examine the relationship between parental arrest, conviction, and incarceration and children's education, mental health, marijuana use, and involvement in theft. Results showed that parental arrest and conviction did not have a significant effect on any of the four outcomes of child behavior. However, parental incarceration increased the likelihood of engagement in theft, and this effect was more pronounced for white youths when compared with black youths.

The negative experiences of the family members of prisoners are partly shaped by the nature of preexisting relationships and risk factors prior to incarceration (Travis and Waul 2003; Murray and Farrington 2008; Turanovic et al. 2012), though these risk factors may be amplified with the experience of imprisonment (Hagan and Dinovitzer 1999). One of the major challenges in studying the effects of parental incarceration on children relates to the lack of control for background risk factors, thus making it difficult to disentangle the effects of incarceration from the influence of preexisting risk factors (La Vigne, Davies, and Brazzell 2008). Much of the research that has examined the effects of parental incarceration on children is characterized by significant methodological shortcomings (Murray, 2005; Johnson and Easterling 2012). Johnson and Easterling (2012) underlined the fact that most research tends to regard incarceration as a uniform experience and fails to control for sentence length or other variables that would indicate potentially distinctive prison experiences.

Murray et al. (2012) conducted a systematic review to assess the empirical association between parental imprisonment and children's later antisocial behaviors, mental health issues, drug use, and performance in school. Drawing on 40 studies and controlling for relevant covariates, the authors found that parental incarceration increased the risk of child antisocial behavior but was not significantly associated with other outcomes. Murray et al.'s (2012) results also suggested that the association between parental incarceration and antisocial behavior extended beyond the effects of separation between the parent and child; the risk for antisocial behavior was found to be higher among children of incarcerated parents when compared with children separated from their parents for other reasons (see also Murray and Farrington 2008). Parental incarceration is believed to be more challenging for children than parental death, since the latter is "naturally occurring and final, while separation due to incarceration is ambiguous" (Miller 2006, p. 478). Miller added that "[c]hildren are confused about their feelings and unsure how to grieve the loss of a parent who is alive, yet emotionally and physically absent" (p. 478).

Wakefield and Wildeman (2011) concluded that paternal imprisonment generally causes more harm than good, and that it is associated with greater behavioral and mental health problems among children of incarcerated individuals. Offering a more nuanced view, Johnson and Easterling's (2012, p. 347) review did not "support the conclusion that parental incarceration has uniformly unique, negative effects on child well-being." In a similar vein, Turanovic et al. (2012) examined both positive and negative effects of incarceration on caregivers who are responsible for the care of children of incarcerated parents. Through in-depth interviews with a sample of 100 caregivers, Turanovic et al. (2012) reported that most changes experienced by caregivers were detrimental to the family. The range of problematic outcomes included financial hardship, greater emotional stress, strained interpersonal relationships, and increased challenges in monitoring and supervising children. However, the authors also found that "a nontrivial portion of . . . caregivers experienced either positive changes or no change at all as a result of parental incarceration." This finding is consistent with Giordano's (2010) and Turney and Wildeman's (2015) results suggesting that incarceration does not always exert a negative impact if the incarcerated parent is abusive or neglectful or exhibits otherwise poor parenting. The impact of parental incarceration on children's well-being may vary with the quality of the relationship prior to prison, exposure to the parent's arrest, and the ability to visit the parent frequently (Arditti 2012). The research presented above has suggested that imprisonment may yield heterogeneous effects on partners and children, partly resulting from variations in family systems, parenting styles, and individual propensities. More research is needed to better understand the circumstances that may act as a protective factor against the potentially harmful effects of incarceration.

D. The Impact of Incarceration on Communities

Clear (2008) has argued that incarceration can also have dramatic effects on community structure, bonds between neighbors, and community safety. This undermining of neighborhood functioning had a disproportionate effect on certain communities (Lynch and Sabol 2004) due to the geographic spread of crime and incarceration (see National Review Council 2014 for a review).

Social controls and networks in the community are impacted by the removal of large numbers of neighborhood residents, often for lengthy periods of time (Bursik and Grasmick 1993; Lynch and Sabol 2004). Economic effects are also noted due to the removal of individuals who would otherwise contribute to the local economy. In addition, there are fewer legal employment opportunities in neighborhoods where large numbers of residents are removed, due to severed networks (Roberts 2004). This has been shown to disproportionately impact individuals and communities of color (Lynch and Sabol 2004).

Clear (2008) also noted that because the removal of large numbers of men from communities decreases the pool of potential partners, mothers may be less reluctant to end abusive or neglectful relationships, and men show less motivation to stay committed to their roles as partners and parents. Relatedly, Thomas and Torrone (2006) showed that neighborhoods with high incarceration rates also exhibited higher rates of sexually transmitted infections and of teenage pregnancies. Despite these findings, the National Research Council (2014) advised against making conclusions regarding the effects of incarceration on specific neighborhoods, given the methodological challenges in demonstrating causal relationships and the lack of reliable data (for a more detailed overview of the link between incarceration and the neighborhood context, see Chapter 25, this volume).

V. THE INCARCERATION–DESISTANCE LINK

The desistance literature has largely ignored changes that may occur during periods of incarceration (Kazemian and Travis 2015). The effectiveness of prison is usually assessed on the basis of post-release behavior, principally the absence of recidivism. Very few studies have documented the progression (or disintegration) of criminal careers, of the desistance process, and of other social and cognitive changes that occur during periods of incarceration. Liebling (2012) rightfully argued that theories of desistance may not take into account the full context of the prison experience.

Irwin (2009) described the desistance process of 17 incarcerated men serving long sentences (i.e., 20 or more years). He found that most lifers changed drastically over the course of their prison sentence. Irwin described a process of awakening, the point at which individuals understand that their actions have led to their current situation. This is a crucial step in the desistance process and occurs at different points in time depending on a host of factors, such as maturity level, commitment to crime-promoting beliefs and values, and adherence to the prison lifestyle. Many authors have highlighted the importance of identity transformation in the process of desistance (Maruna 2001; Giordano, Cernkovich, and Rudolph 2002; Bottoms et al. 2004; Burnett 2004). In its current form, the prison environment may not be conducive to the development of a reformed, positive self-image and identity. In order to eliminate harmful behaviors and attitudes, individuals must be exposed to alternative (and socially acceptable) models. Very little is known about the identity shifts that occur during periods of incarceration and how these shifts impact their attitudes, behaviors, and relationships over time (Kazemian and Travis 2015).

We know that individuals who serve long sentences tend to be older at release when compared with those who serve shorter sentences and that recidivism rates are lower among older individuals when compared to their younger counterparts. Toch (2010, p. 8) argued that "age is a proxy for whatever transformations have occurred among dedicated middle-aged prisoners that we do not fully understand."

Policymakers and researchers alike favor a results-oriented approach and fixate on recidivism as an outcome variable. A recidivism-focused approach disregards changes and progress exhibited in other social and cognitive outcomes. Criminal careers are characterized by intermittent patterns of offending (Horney, Osgood, and Marshall 1995; Burnett 2004), and several researchers have acknowledged the relevance of perceiving desistance as a gradual process (for a review, see Kazemian 2007). The complete abandonment of offending activities is unlikely to occur suddenly, especially among individuals who have been highly active in crime from a young age. Therefore, focusing solely on the final state of termination provides little guidance for intervention initiatives and neglects to offer support and reinforcement during periods when they are most needed (i.e., periods of reassessment and ambivalence toward desistance/persistence; see Burnett 2004). The scope for change is particularly significant among individuals serving long sentences (Kazemian and Travis 2015).

VI. Conclusion

This chapter offered an overview of the empirical evidence on the impact of imprisonment on crime rates and reoffending, as well as the collateral consequences on the families of incarcerated individuals. While some studies have found that the high rates of incarceration in the United States may have resulted in short-term reductions in crime rates, a comprehensive review of this research has suggested that the magnitude of this effect is unclear and that it is likely to be marginal (National Research Council 2014). The deterrent effect (both general and specific) of prison appears to be limited. In addition, most contemporary research and correctional statistics have suggested that incarceration tends to exert a null or aggravating effect on subsequent offending behavior. Imprisonment also adversely impacts other psychological and social indicators known to be linked to desistance/persistence in crime, namely the access to employment opportunities, the strength of family ties, and mental health outcomes. Finally, the effects of incarceration extend far beyond the prisoner and affect the well-being of the families, children, and communities of incarcerated individuals.

Prisons, at least in their current form, tend to be largely discordant with the outside world. The problem-solving solutions adopted in prison may be incompatible with strategies promoted in the outside world (Haney 2006; Jamieson and Grounds 2005). Haney (2006, p. 179) highlighted that "a tough veneer that precludes seeking help for personal problems, the generalized mistrust that comes from the fear of exploitation, and the tendency to strike out in response to minimal provocations are highly functional in many prison contexts and problematic virtually everywhere else."

If used adequately, prison need not be detrimental to the progress and development of individuals. The National Research Council (2014) highlighted the need to develop and invest in prison programs that may minimize the harmful effects of incarceration. The report concluded that "certain kinds of proactive programs of prison rehabilitation can be effective in neutralizing or even reversing the otherwise criminogenic effects of incarceration" (p. 196), such as interventions based on the risk-need-responsivity (RNR) model (Andrews, Bonta, and Hoge 1990), substance use treatment with post-release follow-up services, and cognitive-behavioral programs. French and Gendreau's (2006) meta-analysis also suggested that intervention programs of a behavioral nature are the most effective in reducing prison misconduct as well as post-release recidivism rates.

Some studies have suggested that the effects of imprisonment grow more pronounced with longer periods of incarceration (Flanagan 1979; Wolff and Draine 2004). However, we know very little about the effects of incarceration over long periods of confinement. We need contemporary, prison-based longitudinal studies in order to assess the effects of prison over prolonged sentences and to better inform policy and practice about how prison time can be used in a productive manner to promote desistance efforts.

REFERENCES

Andrews, Don A., James Bonta, and Robert D. Hoge. 1990. "Classification for Effective Rehabilitation: Rediscovering Psychology." *Criminal Justice and Behavior* 17: 19–52.

Apel, Robert, Arjan A. J. Blokland, Paul Nieuwbeerta, and Marieke van Schellen. 2010. "The Impact of Imprisonment on Marriage and Divorce: A Risk Set Matching Approach." *Journal of Quantitative Criminology* 26(2): 269–300.

Arditti, Joyce A. 2012. "Child Trauma Within the Context of Parental Incarceration: A Family Process Perspective." *Journal of Family Theory & Review* 4(3): 181–219.

Arditti, Joyce, Linda Burton, and Sara Neeves-Botelho. 2010. "Maternal Distress and Parenting in the Context of Cumulative Disadvantage." *Family Process* 49(2): 142–164.

Bales, William D., and Alex R. Piquero. 2012. "Assessing the Impact of Imprisonment on Recidivism." *Journal of Experimental Criminology* 8: 71–101.

Barton, William H., and Jeffrey A. Butts. 1990. "Viable Options: Intensive Supervision Programs for Juvenile Delinquents." *Crime & Delinquency* 36(2): 238–256.

Blokland, Arjan A. J., and Paul Nieuwbeerta. 2007. "Selectively Incapacitating Frequent Offenders: Costs and Benefits of Various Penal Scenarios." *Journal of Quantitative Criminology* 23(4): 327–353.

Bottoms, Anthony, Joanna Shapland, Andrew Costello, Deborah Holmes, and Grant Muir. 2004. "Towards Desistance: Theoretical Underpinnings for an Empirical Study." *The Howard Journal of Criminal Justice* 43(4): 368–389.

Bradley, Katharine H., R. B. Michael Oliver, Noel C. Richardson, and Elspeth M. Slayter. 2001. *No Place Like Home: Housing and The Ex-Prisoner*. Boston: Community Resources for Justice.

Braman, Donald S. 2004. *Doing Time on the Outside: Incarceration and Family Life in Urban America*. Ann Arbor: University of Michigan Press.

Bratt, Rachel G. 2001. "Housing and Family Well-Being." *Housing Studies* 17(1): 13–26.

Burnett, Ros. 2004. "To Reoffend or Not to Reoffend? The Ambivalence of Convicted Property Offenders." In *After Crime and Punishment: Pathways to Offender Reintegration*, edited by Shadd Maruna and Russ Immarigeon, 152–180. Cullompton, Devon, UK: Willan.

Bursik, Robert J., Jr., and Harold G. Grasmick. 1993. "Economic Deprivation and Neighborhood Crime Rates, 1960–1980." *Law & Society Review* 27: 263.

Christian, Johnna. 2005. "Riding the Bus Barriers to Prison Visitation and Family Management Strategies." *Journal of Contemporary Criminal Justice* 21(1): 31–48.

Clear, Todd R. 2008. "The Effects of High Imprisonment Rates on Communities." *Crime and Justice* 37(1): 97–132.

Clemmer, Donald. 1958. *The Prison Community*. New York: Holt, Rinehart & Winston.

Comfort, Megan L. 2008. "In The Tube at San Quentin The 'Secondary Prisonization' of Women Visiting Inmates." *Journal of Contemporary Ethnography* 32(1): 77–107.

D'Alessio, Stewart J., Lisa Stolzenberg, and David Eitle. 2014. "'Last Hired, First Fired': The Effect of the Unemployment Rate on the Probability of Repeat Offending." *American Journal of Criminal Justice* 39(1): 77–93.

Dettbarn, Elisabeth. 2012. "Effects of Long-Term Incarceration: A Statistical Comparison of Two Expert Assessments of Two Experts at the Beginning and the End of Incarceration." *International Journal of Law and Psychiatry* 35(3): 236–239.

Drago, Francesco, Roberto Galbiati, and Pietro Vertova. 2011. "Prison Conditions and Recidivism." *American Law and Economics Review* 13(1): 103–130.

Dudeck, Manuela, Kirstin Drenkhahn, Carsten Spitzer, Sven Barnow, Daniel Kopp, Philipp Kuwert, Harald J. Freyberger, and Frieder Dünkel. 2011. "Traumatization and Mental Distress in Long-Term Prisoners in Europe." *Punishment & Society* 13(4): 403–423.

Dyer, W. Justin, Joseph Pleck, and Brent McBride. 2012. "Using Mixture Regression to Identify Varying Effects: A Demonstration with Paternal Incarceration." *Journal of Marriage and Family* 74(5): 1129–1148.

Edin, Kathryn, Maria J. Kefalas, and Joanna M. Reed. 2004. "A Peek Inside the Black Box: What Marriage Means for Poor Unmarried Parents." *Journal of Marriage and Family* 66(4): 1007–1014.

Fabelo, Tony. 1995. *Testing the Case for More Incarceration in Texas: The Record So Far*. Austin, TX: Criminal Justice Policy Council.

Fazel, Seena, and John Danesh. 2002. "Serious Mental Disorder in 23,000 Prisoners: A Systematic Review of 62 Surveys." *The Lancet* 359: 545–550.

Fisher, William H., Eric Silver, and Nancy Wolff. 2006. "Beyond Criminalization: Toward a Criminologically Informed Framework for Mental Health Policy and Services Research." *Administration and Policy in Mental Health* 33(5): 544–557.

Flanagan, Timothy J. 1979. *Long-Term Prisoners: A Study of the Characteristics Institutional Experience and Perspectives of Long-Term Inmates in State Correctional Facilities.* PhD dissertation, State University of New York, Albany.

Frank, Richard G., and Thomas G. McGuire. 2011. "Mental Health Treatment and Criminal Justice Outcomes." In *Controlling Crime: Strategies and Tradeoffs*, edited by Phillip J. Cook, Jens Ludwig, and Justin McCray, 167–215. Chicago: University of Chicago Press.

French, Shiela A., and Gendreau, Paul. 2006. "Reducing Prison Misconducts: What Works!" *Criminal Justice and Behavior* 33(2): 185–218.

Geller, Amanda, Irwin Garfinkel, Carey E. Cooper, and Ronald B. Mincy. 2009. "Parental Incarceration and Child Well-Being: Implications for Urban Families." *Social Science Quarterly* 90(5): 1186–1202.

Geller, Amanda, and Marah A. Curtis. 2011. "A Sort of Homecoming: Incarceration and the Housing Security of Urban Men." *Social Science Research* 40(4): 1196–1213.

Geller, Amanda, and Allyson W. Franklin. 2014. "Paternal Incarceration and the Housing Security of Urban Mothers." *Journal of Marriage and Family* 76(2): 411–427.

Gendreau, Paul, Claire Goggin, and Francis T. Cullen. 1999. *The Effects of Prison Sentences on Recidivism (User Report No. 24).* Ontario: Department of the Solicitor General Canada.

Giordano, Peggy C. 2010. *Legacies of Crime: A Follow-Up of the Children of Highly Delinquent Girls and Boys.* Cambridge, UK: Cambridge University Press.

Giordano, Peggy C., Stephen A. Cernkovich, and Jennifer L. Rudolph. 2002. "Gender, Crime, and Desistance: Toward a Theory of Cognitive Transformation." *American Journal of Sociology* 107(4): 990–1064.

Glaze, Lauren E., and Laura M. Maruschak. 2008. *Parents in Prison and Their Minor Children.* Bureau of Justice Statistics Special Report. Washington, DC: National Institute of Justice.

Gowan, Teresa. 2002. "The Nexus Homelessness and Incarceration in Two American Cities." *Ethnography* 3(4): 500–534.

Grinstead, Olga, Bonnie Faigeles, Carrie Bancroft, and Barry Zack. 2001. "The Financial Cost of Maintaining Relationships with Incarcerated African American Men: A Survey of Women Prison Visitors." *Journal of African American Men* 6(1): 59–69.

Green, Donald P., and Daniel Winik. 2010. "Using Random Judge Assignments to Estimate the Effects of Incarceration and Probation on Recidivism Among Drug Offenders." *Criminology* 48: 357–387.

Grogger, Jeffrey. 1995. "The Effect of Arrests on the Employment and Earnings of Young Men." *The Quarterly Journal of Economics* 110(1): 51–71.

Gust, Liepa V. 2012. "Can Policy Reduce the Collateral Damage Caused by the Criminal Justice System? Strengthening Social Capital in Families and Communities." *American Journal of Orthopsychiatry* 82(2): 174–180.

Hagan, John, and Ronit Dinovitzer. 1999. "Collateral Consequences of Imprisonment for Children, Communities, and Prisoners." In *Crime and Justice, Vol. 26: Prisons*, edited by Michael Tonry and Joan Petersilia. Chicago: University of Chicago Press.

Hairston, Creasie F. 1998. "The Forgotten Parent: Understanding the Forces That Influence Incarcerated Fathers' Relationships with Their Children." *Child Welfare* 77(5): 617–639.

Haney, Craig. 2006. *Reforming Punishment: Psychological Limits to the Pains of Imprisonment.* Washington, DC: American Psychological Association.

Hanlon, Thomas E., Robert J. Blatchley, Terry Bennett-Sears, Kevin E. O'Grady, Marc Rose, and Jason M. Callaman. 2005. "Vulnerability of Children of Incarcerated Addict Mothers: Implications for Preventive Intervention." *Children and Youth Services Review* 27(1): 67–84.

Holzer, Harry J., Stephen Raphael, and Michael A. Stoll 2007. "The Effect of an Applicant's Criminal History on Employer Hiring Decisions and Screening Practices: Evidence from Los Angeles." In *Barriers to Reentry? The Labor Market for Released Prisoners in Post-Industrial America*, edited by Shawn Bushway, Michael A. Stoll, and David F. Weiman. New York: Russell Sage Foundation.

Horney, Julie, D. Wayne Osgood, and Ineke Haen Marshall. 1995. "Criminal Careers in the Short-Term: Intra-Individual Variability in Crime and its Relation to Local Life Circumstances." *American Sociological Review* 60(5): 655–673.

Huebner, Beth M., and Regan Gustafson. 2007. "The Effect of Maternal Incarceration on Adult Offspring Involvement in the Criminal Justice System." *Journal of Criminal Justice* 35(3): 283–296.

International Centre for Prison Studies. World Prison Brief Online. http://www.prisonstudies.org/info/worldbrief/.

Irwin, John. 2009. *Lifers: Seeking Redemption in Prison*. London: Routledge

James, Doris J., and Lauren E. Glaze. 2006. *Mental Health Problems of Prison and Jail Inmates*. Washington, DC: Bureau of Justice Statistics.

Jamieson, Ruth, and Grounds Adrian. 2005. "Release and Adjustment: Perspectives from Studies of Wrongly Convicted and Politically Motivated Prisoners." In *The Effects of Imprisonment*, edited by Alison Liebling and Shadd Maruna, 33–65. Cullompton: Willan.

Johnson, Robert, and McGunigall-Smith Sandra. 2008. "Life Without Parole, America's Other Death Penalty: Notes on Life Under Sentence of Death by Incarceration." *Prison Journal* 88(2): 328–346.

Johnson, Rucker, and Steven Raphael. 2012. "How Much Crime Reduction Does the Marginal Prisoner Buy?" *Journal of Law and Economics* 55(2): 275–310.

Johnson, Elizabeth I., and Beth Easterling. 2012. "Understanding Unique Effects of Parental Incarceration on Children: Challenges, Progress, and Recommendations." *Journal of Marriage and Family* 74(2): 342–356.

Jones, Daniel, and Alan Maynard. 2013. "Suicide in Recently Released Prisoners: A Systematic Review." *Mental Health Practice* 17(3): 20–27.

Justin Dyer, W., Joseph H. Pleck, and Brent A. McBride. 2012. "Imprisoned Fathers and Their Family Relationships: A 40-Year Review From a Multi-Theory View." *Journal of Family Theory & Review* 4(1): 20–47.

Katz, Lawrence, Steven D. Levitt, S. D. and Ellen Shustorovich. 2003. "Prison Conditions, Capital Punishment, and Deterrence." *American Law and Economics Review* 5(2): 318–343.

Kazemian, Lila. 2007. "Desistance from Crime: Theoretical, Empirical, Methodological, and Policy Considerations." *Journal of Contemporary Criminal Justice* 23(1): 5–27.

Kazemian, Lila, and Jeremy Travis. 2015. "Forgotten Prisoners: Imperative for Inclusion of Long Termers and Lifers in Research and Policy." *Criminology & Public Policy* 14(2): 355–395.

Killias, Martin, Marcelo Aebi, and Denis Ribeaud. 2000. "Does Community Service Rehabilitate Better Than Short-Term Imprisonment?: Results of a Controlled Experiment." *The Howard Journal of Criminal Justice* 39(1): 40–57.

Killias, Martin, Gwladys Gilliéron, Françoise Villard, and Clara Poglia. 2010. "How Damaging Is Imprisonment in the Long-Term? A Controlled Experiment Comparing Long-Term Effects of Community Service and Short Custodial Sentences on Re-Offending and Social Integration." *Journal of Experimental Criminology* 6(2): 115–130.

King, Ryan S., Marc Mauer, and Malcolm C. Young. 2005. *Incarceration and Crime: A Complex Relationship*. Washington, DC: The Sentencing Project.

Kinner, Stuart A., Rosa Alati, Jake M. Najman, and Gail M. Williams. 2007. "Do Paternal Arrest and Imprisonment Lead to Child Behaviour Problems and Substance Use? A Longitudinal Analysis." *Journal of Child Psychology and Psychiatry* 48(11): 1148–1156.

Kjellstrand, Jean M., and J. Mark Eddy. 2012. "Parental Incarceration During Childhood, Family Context, and Youth Problem Behavior Across Adolescence." *Journal of Offender Rehabilitation* 50(1): 18–36.

Lalonde, Robert J., and Rosa M. Cho. 2008. "The Impact of Incarceration in State Prison on the Employment Prospects of Women." *Journal of Quantitative Criminology* 24(3): 243–265.

La Vigne, Nancy G., Elizabeth Davies, and Diana Brazzell. 2008. *Broken Bonds: Understanding and Addressing the Need of Children with Incarcerated Parents.* Washington, DC: The Urban Institute Justice Policy Centre.

La Vigne, Nancy G., Rebecca L. Naser, Lisa E. Brooks, and Jennifer L. Castro. 2005. "Examining the Effect of Incarceration and In-Prison Family Contact on Prisoners' Family Relationships." *Journal of Contemporary Criminal Justice* 21(4): 314–335.

Lee, Barrett A., Kimberly A. Tyler, and James D. Wright. 2010. "The New Homelessness Revisited." *Annual Review of Sociology* 36(1): 501–521.

Leigey, Margaret E. 2010. For the longest time: The Adjustment of Inmates to a Sentence of Life without Parole. *The Prison Journal* 90: 247–268.

Levitt, Steven D. 1996. The Effect of Prison Population Size on Crime Rates: Evidence from Prison Overcrowding Litigation. *The Quarterly Journal of Economics* 111(2): 319–351.

Levitt, Steven D. 2004. "Understanding Why Crime Fell in the 1990s: Four Factors That Explain the Decline and Six That Do Not." *Journal of Economic Perspectives* 18(1): 163–190.

Liebling, Alison. 2012. "Can Human Beings Flourish in Prison?" Paper presented at The Prison Phoenix Trust, London.

Liebling, Alison. 2011. Moral Performance, Inhuman and Degrading Treatment and Prison Pain. *Punishment and Society* 13(5): 530–550.

Liebling, Alison. 1999. "Prison Suicide and Prisoner Coping." In *Crime and Justice, Vol. 26: Prisons,* edited by Michael Tonry and Joan Petersilia. Chicago: University of Chicago Press.

Liebling, Alison, and Shadd Maruna eds. 2005. *The Effects of Imprisonment.* Cullompton, Devon, UK: Willan.

Liem, Marieke, and Maarten Kunst. 2013. "Is There a Recognizable Post-Incarceration Syndrome Among Released 'Lifers'?" *International Journal of Law and Psychiatry,* Special Issue on Prisons and Mental Health 36(3–4): 333–337.

Loeffler, Charles E. 2013. "Does Imprisonment Alter the Life Course? Evidence on Crime and Employment from a Natural Experiment." *Criminology* 51: 137–166.

Lopoo, Leonard M., and Bruce Western. 2005. "Incarceration and the Formation and Stability of Marital Unions." *Journal of Marriage and Family* 67(3): 721–734.

Lynch, James P., and William J. Sabol. 2004. "Assessing the Effects of Mass Incarceration on Informal Social Control in Communities." *Criminology & Public Policy* 3(2): 267–294.

MacKenzie, Doris L., and Lynn Goodstein. 1985. "Long-Term Incarceration Impacts and Characteristics of Long-Term Offenders: An Empirical Analysis." *Criminal Justice and Behavior* 12(4): 395–414.

Makarios, Matthew, Benjamin Steiner, and Lawrence F. Travis. 2010. "Examining the Predictors of Recidivism Among Men and Women Released from Prison in Ohio." *Criminal Justice and Behavior* 37(12): 1377–1391.

Maruna, Shadd. 2001. *Making Good: How Ex-Convicts Reform and Rebuild Their Lives.* Washington, DC: American Psychological Association.

Marvell, Thomas B., and Carlisle E. Moody Jr. 1994. "Prison Population Growth and Crime Reduction." *Journal of Quantitative Criminology* 10(2): 109–140.

Massoglia, Michael. 2008. "Incarceration as Exposure: The Prison, Infectious Disease, and Other Stress-Related Illnesses." *Journal of Health and Social Behavior* 49(1): 56–71.

Mauer, Marc, and Ryan S. King. 2007. *Uneven Justice: State Rates of Incarceration by Race and Ethnicity.* Washington, DC: Sentencing Project.

Mauer, Marc, Ryan S. King, and Malcolm C. Young. 2004. *The Meaning of "Life": Long Prison Sentences in Context.* Washington, DC: The Sentencing Project.

Miller, Keva M. 2006. "The Impact of Parental Incarceration on Children: An Emerging Need for Effective Interventions." *Child and Adolescent Social Work Journal* 23(4): 472–486.

Muftić, Lisa R., Leana A. Bouffard, and Gaylene S. Armstrong. 2016. "The Impact of Maternal Incarceration on the Criminal Justice Involvement of Adult Offspring: A Research Note." *Journal of Research in Crime & Delinquency* 53(1): 93-111.

Mumola, Christopher J. 2005. *Suicide and Homicide in State Prisons and Local Jails.* Washington, DC: U.S. Department of Justice, Bureau of Justice Statistics.

Mumola, Christopher J., and Margaret E. Noonan. 2009. *Deaths in Custody Statistical Tables.* Washington, DC: U.S. Department of Justice, Bureau of Justice Statistics.

Murray, Joseph. 2005. "The Effects of Imprisonment on Families and Children of Prisoners." In *The Effects of Imprisonment,* edited by Alison Liebling and Shadd Maruna. Cullompton, Devon, UK: Willan.

Murray, Joseph, and David P. Farrington. 2005. "Parental Imprisonment: Effects on Boys' Antisocial Behaviour and Delinquency Through the Life-Course." *Journal of Child Psychology and Psychiatry* 46(12): 1269–1278.

Murray, Joseph, and David P. Farrington. 2008. "The Effects of Parental Imprisonment on Children." *Crime and Justice* 37(1): 133–206.

Murray, Joseph, David P. Farrington, and Ivana Sekol. 2012. "Children's Antisocial Behavior, Mental Health, Drug Use, and Educational Performance after Parental Incarceration: A Systematic Review and Meta-Analysis." *Psychological Bulletin* 138(2): 175–210.

Murray, Joseph, Rolf Loeber, and Dustin Pardini. 2012. "Parental Involvement in the Criminal Justice System and the Development of Youth Theft, Marijuana Use, Depression, and Poor Academic Performance." *Criminology* 50(1): 255–302.

Nagin, Daniel S. 1998. "Criminal Deterrence Research at the Outset of the Twenty-First Century." *Crime and Justice* 23: 1–42.

Nagin, Daniel S., Francis T. Cullen, and Cheryl Lero Jonson. 2009. "Imprisonment and Reoffending." *Crime and Justice* 38(1): 115–200.

Nagin, Daniel S., and G. Matthew Snodgrass. 2013. "The Effect of Incarceration on Re-offending: Evidence from a Natural Experiment in Pennsylvania." *Journal of Quantitative Criminology* 29(4): 601–642.

National Research Council. 2014. *The Growth of Incarceration in the United States: Exploring Causes and Consequences.* Washington, DC: The National Academies Press.

Nellis, Ashley, and Ryan King. 2009. *No Exit: The Expanding Use of Life Sentences in America.* Washington, DC: The Sentencing Project.

Nieuwbeerta, Paul, Daniel S. Nagin, and Arjan A. J. Blokland. 2009. "Assessing the Impact of First-Time Imprisonment on Offenders' Subsequent Criminal Career Development: A Matched Samples Comparison." *Journal of Quantitative Criminology* 25(3): 227–257.

Orsagh, Thomas, and Jong-Rong Chen. 1988. "The Effect of Time Served on Recidivism: An Interdisciplinary Theory." *Journal of Quantitative Criminology* 4(2): 155–171.

Pager, Devah. 2003. "The Mark of a Criminal Record." *American Journal of Sociology* 108(5): 937–975.

Pager, Devah. 2007. *Marked: Race, Crime, and Finding Work in an Era of Mass Incarceration*. Chicago: University of Chicago Press.

Petersilia, Joan. 2003. *When Prisoners Come Home: Parole and Prisoner Reentry*. New York: Oxford University Press.

Petrosino, Anthony, Carolyn Turpin-Petrosino, and Sarah Guckenburg. 2013. *Formal System Processing of Juveniles: Effects on Delinquency*. No. 9 of Crime Prevention Research Review. Washington, DC: U.S. Department of Justice, Office of Community Oriented Policing Services.

Pettit, Becky, and Lyons, Christopher. 2009. "Status and the Stigma of Incarceration: The Labor Market Effects of Incarceration by Race, Class, and Criminal Involvement." In *Barriers to Reentry? The Labor Market for Released Prisoners in Post-Industrial America*, edited by Shawn Bushway, Michael A. Stoll, and David F. Weiman. New York: Russell Sage Foundation.

The Pew Center on the States. 2012. *Time Served: The High Cost, Low Return of Longer Prison Terms*. Washington, DC: The Pew Center on the States.

The Pew Charitable Trusts. 2010. *Collateral Costs: Incarceration's Effect on Economic Mobility*. Washington, DC: The Pew Charitable Trusts.

Poehlmann, J. 2005. "Children's Family Environments and Intellectual Outcomes During Maternal Incarceration." *Journal of Marriage & Family* 67: 1275–1285.

Postmus, Judy L., Margaret Severson, Marianne Berry, and Jeong Ah Yoo. 2009. "Women's Experiences of Violence and Seeking Help." *Violence Against Women* 15(7): 852–868.

Richards, Stephen C., and Richard S. Jones. 2004. "Beating the Perpetual Incarceration Machine: Overcoming Structural Impediments to Re-entry." In *After Crime and Punishment: Pathways to Offender Reintegration*, edited by Shadd Maruna and Russ Immarigeon. Cullompton, Devon, UK: Willan.

Roberts, Dorothy E. 2004. "The Social and Moral Cost of Mass Incarceration in African American Communities." *Stanford Law Review* 56(5): 1271–1305.

Roettger, Michael E., and Raymond R. Swisher. 2011. "Associations of Fathers' History of Incarceration with Sons' Delinquency and Arrest Among Black, White, and Hispanic Males in the United States." *Criminology* 49(4): 1109–1147.

Sabol, William J. 2007. "Local Labor-Market Conditions and Post-Prison Employment Experiences of Offenders Released from Ohio State Prisons." In *Barriers to Reentry? The Labor Market for Released Prisoners in Post-Industrial America*, edited by Shawn Bushway, Michael A. Stoll, and David F. Weiman. New York: Russell Sage Foundation.

Sabol, William J., and James P. Lynch. 2003. "Assessing the Longer-Run Consequences of Incarceration: Effects on Families and Employment." *Contributions in Criminology and Penology* 55: 3–26.

Sampson, Robert J., and John H. Laub. 1997. "A Life-Course Theory of Cumulative Disadvantage and the Stability of Delinquency." In *Developmental Theories of Crime and Delinquency*, edited by Terence P. Thornberry (Vol. 7 of Advances in Criminological Theory). New Brunswick, NJ: Transaction.

Schmitt, John, and Kris Warner. 2011. "Ex-offenders and the Labor Market." *Working USA: The Journal of Labor and Society* 14:87–109.

Schneider, A. L. (1986). "Restitution and Recidivism Rates of Juvenile Offenders: Results from Four Experimental Studies." *Criminology* 24: 533–552.

Schnittker, Jason, Michael Massoglia, and Christopher Uggen. 2012. "Out and Down Incarceration and Psychiatric Disorders." *Journal of Health and Social Behavior* 53(4): 448–464.

Schwartz-Soicher, Ofira, Amanda Geller, and Irwin Garfinkel. 2011. "The Effect of Paternal Incarceration on Material Hardship." *Social Service Review* 85(3): 447–473.

Spelman, William. 2006. "The Limited Importance of Prison Expansion." In *The Crime Drop in America*, edited by Alfred Blumstein and Joel Wallman. New York: Cambridge University Press.

Sugie, Naomi F. 2012. "Punishment and Welfare: Paternal Incarceration and Families' Receipt of Public Assistance." *Social Forces* 90(4):1403–1427.

Sykes, Gresham M. 1958. *The Society of Captives: A Study of a Maximum-Security Prison*. Princeton, NJ: Princeton University Press.

Thomas, James C., and Elizabeth Torrone. 2006. "Incarceration as Forced Migration: Effects on Selected Community Health Outcomes." *American Journal of Public Health* 96(10): 1762–1765.

Toch, H. 2010. "'I Am Not Now Who I Used to Be Then:' Risk Assessment and the Maturation of Long-Term Prison Inmates." *The Prison Journal* 90(1): 4–11.

Travis, Jeremy. 2005. *But They All Come Back: Facing the Challenges of Prisoner Reentry*. Washington, DC: The Urban Institute.

Travis, Jeremy, Elizabeth Cincotta McBride, and Amy L. Solomon. 2005. *Families Left Behind: The Hidden Costs of Incarceration and Reentry*. Washington, DC: Urban Institute Policy Brief.

Travis, Jeremy, and Joan Petersilia. 2001. "Reentry Reconsidered: A New Look at an Old Question." *Crime & Delinquency* 47(3): 291–313.

Travis, Jeremy, and Michelle Waul, eds. 2003. *Prisoners Once Removed: The Impact of Incarceration and Reentry on Children, Families, and Communities*. Washington, DC: The Urban Institute.

Turanovic, Jillian J., Nancy Rodriguez, and Travis C. Pratt. 2012. "The Collateral Consequences of Incarceration Revisited: A Qualitative Analysis of the Effects on Caregivers of Children of Incarcerated Parents." *Criminology* 50(4): 913–959.

Turney, Kristin, and Christopher Wildeman. 2013. "Redefining Relationships Explaining the Countervailing Consequences of Paternal Incarceration for Parenting." *American Sociological Review* 78(6): 949–979.

Turney, Kristin, and Christopher Wildeman. 2015. Detrimental for Some? Heterogeneous Effects of Maternal Incarceration on Child Wellbeing. *Criminology & Public Policy* 14: 125–156.

Turney, Kristin, Christopher Wildeman, and Jason Schnittker. 2012. "As Fathers and Felons: Explaining the Effects of Current and Recent Incarceration on Major Depression." *Journal of Health and Social Behavior* 53(4): 465–481.

Villettaz, Patrice, Martin Killias, and Isabel Zoder. 2006. *The Effects of Custodial vs. Non-Custodial Sentences on Re-Offending: A Systematic Review of the State of Knowledge*. Oslo, Norway: The Campbell Corporation.

Villettaz, Patrice, Gwladys Gillieron, and Martin Killias. 2015. *The Effects on Re-offending of Custodial vs. Non-custodial Sanctions: An Updated Systematic Review of the State of Knowledge*. Philadelphia: Campbell Collaboration Crime and Justice Group.

Wakefield, Sarah, and Christopher Wildeman. 2011. "Mass Imprisonment and Racial Disparities in Childhood Behavioral Problems." *Criminology & Public Policy* 10(3): 793–817.

Walker, Sheri Pruitt. 2011. *The Effects of the Incarceration of Fathers on the Health and Wellbeing of Mothers and Children*. PhD dissertation, University of Maryland, College Park.

Waldfogel, Joel. 1994. "The Effect of Criminal Conviction on Income and the Trust 'Reposed in the Workmen.'" *Journal of Human Resources* 29(1): 62–81.

Wang, Xia, Daniel P. Mears, and William D. Bales. 2010. "Race-Specific Employment Contexts and Recidivism." *Criminology* 48(4): 1171–1211.

Weatherburn, Don. 2010. *The Effect of Prison on Adult Re-Offending*. Sydney: NSW Bureau of Crime Statistics and Research.

Wermink, Hilde, Paul Nieuwbeerta, Anke A. T. Ramakers, Jan W. de Keijser, and Anja J. E. Dirkzwager. 2017. "Short-Term Effects of Imprisonment Length on Recidivism in the Netherlands." *Crime & Delinquency* 64(8): 1057–1093.

Western, Bruce. 2002. "The Impact of Incarceration on Wage Mobility and Inequality." *American Sociological Review* 67(4): 526–546.

Western, Bruce. 2006. *Punishment and Inequality in America*. New York: Russell Sage Foundation.

Western, Bruce, and Christopher Wildeman. 2009. "The Black Family and Mass Incarceration." *Annals of the American Academy of Political and Social Science* 621(1): 221–242.

Wildeman, Christopher. 2009. "Parental Imprisonment, the Prison Boom, and the Concentration of Childhood Disadvantage." *Demography* 46(2): 265–280.

Wildeman, Christopher. 2010. "Paternal Incarceration and Children's Physically Aggressive Behaviors: Evidence from the Fragile Families and Child Wellbeing Study." *Social Forces* 89(1): 285–309.

Wildeman, Christopher. 2014. "Parental Incarceration, Child Homelessness, and the Invisible Consequences of Mass Imprisonment." *Annals of the American Academy of Political and Social Science* 651(1): 74–96.

Wildeman, Christopher, Jason Schnittker, and Kristin Turney. 2012. "Despair by Association? The Mental Health of Mothers with Children by Recently Incarcerated Fathers." *American Sociological Review* 77(2): 216–243.

Wolff, Nancy, Cynthia L. Blitz, and Jing Shi. 2007. "Rates of Sexual Victimization in Prison for Inmates With and Without Mental Disorders." *Psychiatric Services* 58(8): 1087–1094.

Wolff, Nancy, and Jeffrey Draine. 2004. "Dynamics of Social Capital of Prisoners and Community Reentry: Ties that Bind?" *Journal of Correctional Health Care* 10(3): 457–490.

Wolff, Nancy, Jing Shi, and Jane A. Siegel. 2009. "Patterns of Victimization Among Male and Female Inmates: Evidence of an Enduring Legacy." *Violence and Victims* 24(4): 469–484.

Zamble, Edward. 1992. "Behavior and Adaptation in Long-Term Prison Inmates: Descriptive Longitudinal Results." *Criminal Justice and Behavior* 19: 409–425.

Zamble, Edward, and Frank J. Porporino. 1988. *Coping, Behavior, and Adaptation in Prison Inmates*. Berlin: Springer-Verlag.

CHAPTER 29

··

DESISTANCE AND COGNITIVE
TRANSFORMATIONS

··

SARAH ANDERSON AND FERGUS MCNEILL

In this chapter we review the state of current knowledge on "cognitive transformations" in the desistance process, a phrase coined by Peggy Giordano and colleagues in the title of their influential paper (Giordano, Cernkovich, and Rudolph 2002). In doing so, we use the term "cognitive" in its broadest sense to include phenomenological and identity transformations, as well as attitudes, beliefs, and intentions. We also consider changes in abilities to act on intentions formed.

Desistance from crime is increasingly understood as more than a one-off event (the cessation of offending) or an absence of events (offenses). Like others (Bushway et al. 2001; Laub and Sampson 2001; Maruna 2001), we understand desistance as a process. For present purposes, we define desistance broadly as a process of human development (inevitably occurring in and affected by particular social contexts) that involves moving away from crime and toward social integration and participation.

The relative importance in this process of the objective socio-structural contexts and correlates of desistance and of the subjectively experienced, internal worlds of desisters is a subject of much debate. Structural turning point explanations of desistance (best exemplified in the seminal work of Sampson and Laub, 1993, 1997; Laub and Sampson 2003) (see Chapter 16) have tended to stress the importance of social bonds (especially those associated with marriage or work), downplaying the role of changes in the internal world of the person desisting from offending. Yet most of us assume that—or at least live as if we believe that—we are active agents in our own lives: we think and reflect and, in turn, make choices, both good and bad. Farrall and Bowling (1999) highlight that the turning point mechanisms through which social control theorists propose that life events promote desistance, appear to treat people as "super-dupes," passively responding to the influence of external forces without recourse to personal agency. This is perhaps an exaggeration, but clearly there is a need to capture the role of personal agency in the desistance process, without falling into the alternative trap of treating people as "super-agents," able to choose their way out of crime, irrespective of the challenging social and structural contexts in which their choices are made.

Accordingly, since the start of the 2000s, a number of studies have sought to refocus desistance studies on the lived experiences and subjectivities of the people involved. In the United States, Giordano, Cernkovich, and Rudolph's (2002) theory of cognitive transformation offered a symbolic interactionist perspective on the desistance process to supplement social control theories. Based on findings from a long-term study of young men and women involved in offending, they argued that four cognitive shifts are integral to the desistance process: (1) a general openness to change; (2) actively seeking out, selecting into or latching onto "hooks for change" within the external environment (e.g., marriage or employment); (3) envisioning and assuming alternative (prosocial) identities; and (4) a change in the meaning and appeal of criminal behavior (Giordano, Cernovich, and Rudolph 2002, pp. 1000–1002). In the United Kingdom, a study based on interviews with people persisting in and desisting from offending in Liverpool identified a number of distinctive features in the transformation narratives, or "redemption scripts," of the desisters (Maruna 2001). These included a sense of acquiring control over one's destiny, an assertion or reassertion of the "real me" as fundamentally good, the reconstruction of both past and future behavior to be narratively coherent with this real me, and an increasingly generative focus on others in an active process of "making good."

Despite challenges to the necessity of either cognitive or identity changes in the desistance process (notably from Laub and Sampson 2003), the work of Giordano and colleagues and of Maruna has stimulated a proliferation of theory and (largely qualitative) research that has explored the role of cognitions, human agency, and narrative identity in the desistance process. It is this literature that we aim to review in this chapter, focusing on cognitive shifts that occur across the life course which might help to support and sustain desistance from crime. In Section I, we consider transformations in the person's narrative identity, which provides an overarching organizing framework for cognitions and a blueprint for non-offending behavior. In Section II, we consider transformations in the content of cognitions: changing pro-criminal attitudes; changing meanings of and emotions surrounding criminal behavior; and the importance of motivation and hope (not just the will to change, but also the ways to change; Burnett and Maruna 2004). In Section III we consider transformations in cognitive skills that enable the person trying to desist to act upon the intentions they have formed. These include changes in self-control, the use of cognitive strategies to support desistance, and changes in executive functioning in adolescence and young adulthood.

In Section IV we argue that an integrated theory of the desistance process must include an understanding of all these cognitive transformations. However, we emphasize throughout that it is not possible to understand either the origins or role of cognitive transformations in the desistance process without considering the complex, dynamic, and often reciprocal interaction of these factors with social events, social relations, and structural factors. In developing this argument, we challenge narrowly psychological-criminological theories, and more particularly their recent applications in offender treatment, which too often treat cognitions in a decontextualized way and target them in isolation from their social circumstances. Finally, in Section V, we conclude by suggesting that further and more methodologically robust empirical exploration of the chronological sequencing of a range of life events and cognitive changes will be critical to developing our understanding of desistance from crime.

I. Transformations in Narrative Identity

Building on a growing body of work in identity psychology, criminology has increasingly focused on the role of identity and shifts in identity in persistence in and desistance from offending. In these theories, identities play an important role, providing an overarching organizing framework for cognitions—attitudes, beliefs, meaning, and emotions—and acting as a blueprint for future behavior (how to act and how not to act in future situations) (Giordano, Cernkovich, and Rudolph 2002).

In an important early example of this work, Lemert (1951) posited a critical role for identity shifts in persistent involvement in offending. His influential labeling theory suggested that negative societal labels become "incorporated as part of the 'me' of the individual" (Lemert 1951, p. 76), leading to the adoption of a personal identity consistent with deviant behavior, which thereby facilitates ongoing participation in such behavior. Identity shifts in desistance may involve shedding this offending identity and/or acquiring a non-offending one. Indeed, one of the four cognitive shifts proposed in Giordano, Cernkovich, and Rudolph's (2002) account of the process of desistance involves the fashioning of a "replacement self" to supplant "the marginalized or deviant one that must be left behind" (p. 1001): e.g., the "thief," the "addict," the "offender." Giordano, Cernkovich, and Rudolph (2002) suggest that adoption of the 'replacement self' makes it "inappropriate for 'someone like me' to do 'something like that,'" (p. 1002), in doing so it provides an organizing framework which "can act as a cognitive filter for decision-making" (p. 1001).

Building on the work of psychologists like Dan McAdams (1985, 1993), Maruna (2001) adopts a narrative understanding of identity, in which the ongoing construction of one's personal narrative is the iterative process through which we find and create meaning and purpose in our lives. Similarly to Lemert, Maruna's analysis suggests that the personal narrative of persisters may include the acceptance and internalization of negative labels applied by society, albeit in a more passive, begrudging way than suggested by Lemert's theory: '"I guess I'm just a thief—no more, no less"' (male, age 28; Maruna 2001, p. 75). Maruna terms this the "condemnation script." In contrast, the desister's narrative is a "redemption script"; one in which the real me is fundamentally good. What is more, that good real me was always there beneath the surface, however hidden. Consequently,

Maruna argues that the desistance process is one of self-reconstruction in which the person must find a way to coherently incorporate this past conduct into their own narrative "as a necessary prelude to a productive and worthy life" (Maruna 2001, p. 87). Our past is (re)made to be coherent with our future, and this future becomes predictable in the light of our remade past (see Maruna 2001; Crewe and Maruna 2006).

In addition, Maruna illustrates and emphasizes the generative components within redemption scripts, which suggest an active process of making good frequently through helping, or even, saving others (see also Gove 1985). These generative activities and concerns enable desisters to infuse meaning or reason into long stretches of their lives for which otherwise they would have nothing to show. Tom LeBel's (2007) research on ex-prisoners suggests that having what was termed a "helper" or "wounded healer" orientation was negatively associated with having a criminal attitude or with their subjective forecast of their likelihood of re-arrest. Such an orientation—which involves sharing one's experiences for the benefit of others, acting as a role model, mentoring others, or having an interest in pursuing a career helping others—was also positively related to higher self-esteem and satisfaction with life.

A dynamic and ongoing process of striving for a meaningful identity is also central to Farrall's (2005) existentialist account of the desistance process. In his case study (Sandra), he suggests that Sandra persists in offending precisely because she cannot envision a future self, and so has no need to care for her current self (p. 380). As with Giordano, Cernkovich, and Rudolph's (2002) respondents, it is only when new social opportunities open up to Sandra and she progressively begins to envision a future identity that she is able to actively move toward it, engaging in what Farrall terms "the ongoing project of 'self'" (2005, p. 369).

In a somewhat similar vein, Paternoster and Bushway's (2009) theory includes the desister envisioning a future self. However, unlike Giordano and colleagues, Paternoster and Bushway (2009) place primary emphasis on the envisioning of a negative future self which acts as a catalyst to desistance by motivating contemplation of and ultimately intentional self-change toward a more positive possible self. According to their theory, this projection of a negative future self is formed through the gradual accumulation of negative experiences (such as relationship breakdown, health problems, involvement in prostitution) linked to their current criminal identity; experiences which are then projected into the future to create an image of what the person does not want to become. Their theory emphasizes the desister as a rational actor who has made choices to offend and following this "crystallization of discontent" makes a conscious choice to desist.

Paternoster and Bushway's theory also has clear differences in emphasis from Maruna's thesis. His research suggests that the person who is desisting manages to hold onto a positive current self, which guides future prosocial behavior. What emerges is the idea that to hold a coherent and consistent "self-story," the past self—and its past motivations and intentions—must also be positively reconstructed so as to make sense of past behavior. Whereas Paternoster and Bushway emphasize fear of the "future me" as a driver for developing a prosocial orientation, Maruna posits that the maintenance of this prosocial orientation involves reflection on, re-scripting of and ultimately integration of the "past me." Of course, this is at least logically compatible with either or both positive or negative future selves being catalysts for initial change.

For our part, while we agree that fear of a future self might provoke cognitive dissonance about one's current lifestyle and thereby attempts to change it, we also tend to agree with Maruna that sustaining change efforts is likely to rely more on positive than negative reinforcement (see also Bottoms and Shapland 2011). Consider, for example, attempts to change one's diet or exercise habits in order to address risks to our long-term health and well-being; the fear may invoke action, but sustaining progress may require both a sense of success in or returns from the effort invested and a progressive shift in identity (from "couch potato" to "fitness freak").

Analysis of in-depth interviews with 14 men as part of a small exploratory study by Healy (2014) sheds further light on these issues. Healy distinguishes between three categories of desister: "imagined," "liminal," and "authentic." These categories are differentiated on two bases: first, whether imagined possible future selves are deemed "credible" (i.e., can a pathway to achieving this be envisioned?), and second, whether these possible selves remain imagined or have been realized. For "imagined desisters," the imagined future self is not deemed credible and therefore provides no blueprint or pathway for change. "Liminal desisters" have imagined a credible future self. Though it is yet to be fully achieved, it offers a pathway for change that can drive action. The final group, "authentic desisters," have followed that pathway and have realized this new self through the enactment of conventional roles. However, Healy (2014) agrees with King (2013), who emphasizes the role of social and structural constraints in limiting the future selves that are actually possible and therefore appear credible to the would-be desister.

Importantly, Healy (2014) envisages these desisters as people at different stages in the desistance process and not as fundamentally different types of person/desister (see also Maruna 2001), thereby allowing for the integration of apparently different theories of narrative identity in desistance. She allows space for both positive and negative future selves as motivators and guides for progression: "The narrative imagination plays a critical role in this process because it allows people to simultaneously inhabit multiple realities, both real and fictional, thereby freeing the self to imagine different ways of being" (Healy 2014, p. 2).

Others have highlighted how aspects of a current identity that are maintained through the offending life cycle can, at different times, promote different (criminal or prosocial) behavior as the meaning attached to these identities undergoes transformation. In particular, research by both Carlsson (2013) and Weaver (2016) demonstrates that, within continuing hegemonic masculine identities, the performance of such masculinities can change through the life course, for example, from violence and anti-authoritarianism in adolescence to being a provider or a role model in adulthood.

An important area of contention is whether or not such shifts are necessary for desistance from offending. Maruna and Farrall (2004) distinguish between a lull or crime-free gap in a criminal career (primary desistance) and crime-free behavior sustained by a change in the way that an ex-offender sees him- or herself (secondary desistance).[1]

In so doing they make identity shift a conceptual or definitional necessity for secondary desistance. Laub and Sampson (2003) found that "some, but by no means all, men [in their study] who desisted changed their identity" (p. 147, emphasis added) linking this to the age-appropriateness of certain social roles—"party boy," "family man"—and the accompanying accumulation of responsibility and (investment in) social bonds. However, they suggest that in many cases the men they interviewed did not undergo identity change, nor did they have the ability to engage in self-reflection. In a similar vein, Bottoms et al. (2004) allow that some desisters may make a conscious decision to move toward a conforming identity, but that for others "behaviour drifts towards conformity" (p. 382). They suggest that Maruna and Farrall's (2004) "approach seems to suggest that if someone has experienced no strong role or identity change, but just stops offending for a significant period, he or she is not a 'true' desister" (Bottoms et al. 2004, p. 371).

More recently, in a study of released lifers, Liem and Richardson (2014) consistently identified a transformation narrative that included a good core self and generative motivations among their interviewees, including those who had persisted in offending behavior. However, they suggested that the focus should be on individual agency rather than identity—with agency conceived of as capability to act independently and to make choices within the social structure. In their analysis agency emerged as the factor that distinguished those who had been re-imprisoned from those who had not (see more on the role of agency below).

Of course, significant empirical questions remain on the causal role of identity transformation within the desistance process. One way of accounting for some of the differences in opinion noted above might be to consider when accounts of desistance were elicited. For example, we might conjecture that Laub and Sampson's (2003) respondents, recalling a process decades past, might telescope their accounts of desistance in such a way as to leave identity change out. Perhaps time lends a sense of inevitability to some of our life transitions, and perhaps the redevelopment of our selves seems less significant when it is long distant. Conversely, for those whose change process is recent and still fragile, an account that invokes identity change may be more necessary. In addition, the need for identity change may depend on the extent to which the individual perceives him or herself as having (or having had) a "spoiled identity," which has incorporated stigmatized and criminal labels. Identity change may be unnecessary for someone who has committed a minor, one-off offense and/or has never been processed through the justice system. But at least where a person has been persistently criminalized, we might question whether it is really possible to imagine a meaningful desistance process that doesn't involve some identity change.

In our assessment, identity transformation—or secondary desistance—may well prompt change for many people and may well help to sustain it for most people, perhaps especially in the first few years of the transition. Emerging prosocial identities (like those of Healy's "liminal desisters") are fragile and their social contexts (opportunities, access to resources, societal reaction to change efforts) are frequently hostile. Many people develop transformation stories, and, yes, agency plays a key part in realizing these. But agency operates in a bounded way—adverse reaction to change efforts can easily diminish agency and stunt change (we discuss this in more detail below in discussing interactive models of desistance).

II. Transformations in Cognitive Content

Those who emphasize the role of identity transformations in the desistance process understand these as critical in helping organize and generate cognitive content—attitudes, beliefs, meaning, and emotions—that can drive change. It is theorized that transformation in cognitive content promotes desistance through the formation of conscious intentions to change behavior or through unconscious dispositions, which guide responses in social situations, although it could be argued that the exact mechanisms involved have received inadequate attention in the desistance literature. While disagreement persists regarding the role of identity within this, the desistance and offender rehabilitation treatment literatures contain extensive discussion of transformations in attitudes, beliefs, meaning, and emotions and their associations with and roles in desistance from offending.

A. Attitudinal Change

Criminal justice practice has been particularly concerned with challenging and changing pro-criminal or antisocial attitudes, loosely theorizing that these play a facilitating role in the persistence of offending, and consequently that changing them should promote desistance.

Although the terms pro-criminal or antisocial attitudes are very widely used, there is no consensus on their definitions. A review of published peer-reviewed empirical articles on intervention programs aimed at such attitudes demonstrates the multiple different general and offense-specific pro-criminal attitudes identified and operationalized in the empirical literature. Nevertheless, Banse et al.'s (2013) review found support for an association between a range of such attitudes and reoffending with weak to moderate effect sizes. This conclusion was said to corroborate findings from previous meta-analyses (Andrews and Bonta 2010; Helmus et al. 2013).

The work of Andrews and Bonta (2010) has been particularly influential. They identify three general categories of pro-criminal attitudes: (1) techniques of neutralization, (2) identification with criminal others, including admiration for, imitation of and valuing of relationships with criminal others, and (3) rejection of convention, particularly rejection of the authority of criminal justice bodies (Banse et al. 2013).

The largest body of theoretical literature relates to techniques of neutralization. Sykes and Matza (1957) famously proposed that juvenile delinquents employed five such techniques, which facilitate both the onset and the maintenance of criminal activity: denial of responsibility, denial of injury, denial of the victim, condemnation of condemners, and the appeal to higher loyalties. Neutralization theory suggests that the employment of these techniques enables the young person to resolve the cognitive dissonance that arises from their (largely) prosocial values and their intended and actual deviant behavior. In their study of young people, Barriga et al. (2000) distinguished between self-debasing cognitive distortions which attack the self, overplaying negative consequences and personal responsibility, and self-serving cognitive distortions which protect the self, but only by minimalizing harm, projecting blame or hostility onto others or by prioritizing one's own needs over others. Both were found to be associated with problem behaviors. In particular the former was associated with internalizing behaviors (e.g., self-harm) and the latter with externalizing behaviors (e.g., aggression), although these cognitions were not mutually exclusive and many of the participants exhibited both.

The literature on sexual offending contains extensive discussion and examination of cognitive distortions that support the initiation or maintenance of such offending (see Gannon and Polaschek 2006, for an extensive review). One of the earliest proponents of cognitive distortion theories in sexual offending, Gene Abel, proposed that a range of offense-supportive beliefs are employed to enable "the offender to justify his ongoing sexual abuse of children without the anxiety, guilt and loss of self-esteem that would usually result from an individual committing behaviors contrary to the norms of society" (Abel et al. 1989, p. 137). Subsequently, Ward and Keenan (1999) have proposed sets of beliefs (or theories), held implicitly or explicitly, which help facilitate engagement in sexual offending against children, with clear similarities to Barriga et al.'s (2000) self-serving cognitive distortions.

Although extensively referenced, the literature differs as to whether cognitive distortions are unconscious or conscious, general or situationally specific beliefs and at what point these beliefs occur in the chronology of offending. Critically, there are differences over whether such distortions precede sexual offending behavior and have a facilitative or etiological role in this behavior, helping overcome internal inhibitions and justifying one's intended actions (Finkelhor 1984; Hartley 1998; Ward and Keenan 1999) or whether they arise after an event, reducing shame and guilt for past behavior (Maruna and Copes 2004). If they are formed after an event, are these simply ad hoc justifications and excuses or are these enduring attitudes that have an ongoing maintenance role, allowing this behavior to continue (Abel et al. 1989; Murphy 1990)?

In relation to offending in general, Shapland and Bottoms (2011) have suggested that attitudinal change cannot sufficiently explain the shape of the age–crime curve. They challenge the view implicitly held by many correctional psychologists that attitudes radically transform across the life course from prosocial in childhood to pro-criminal in late adolescence/young adulthood, returning again to prosocial in adulthood. Their research with young adults involved in crime found that desistance was associated with more conventional attitudes to the law and rating of all offenses as more serious. Their findings corroborate Matza's (1964) thesis that young people involved in crime hold largely prosocial values. However, in contrast to Matza and Sykes's theory, Shapland and Bottoms did not find support among their sample for the idea that techniques of neutralization are employed by those who continue to offend with regards to "the overall moral judgments of acts of criminality" (p. 270), although there were exceptions. They found that young adults involved in very persistent offending did not employ these techniques to justify the commission of criminal offenses in general, although they did not examine whether or not these techniques were used to justify specific instances of their own offending behavior.

As Maruna and Mann (2006) have cogently argued, we all use post hoc justifications and excuses to explain our behavior toward others—and ourselves—when we have transgressed social norms or personal values. Phrases such as "I shouldn't have done it, but . . . ," "I only did it because . . . ," and "I am sorry, I just . . ." are familiar to all of us. Arguably these function to demonstrate that the transgressor is nonetheless aware of and accepts the social and moral order. Maruna and Mann (2006) highlight that the unpalatable alternative to neutralization for the person who has offended is to declare that they committed the offense because they wanted to or because of who they are, in so doing publicly rejecting the social order and their place within it. By enabling the desister to maintain a positive, coherent, and credible sense of self, neutralizations and justifications may support desistance. If criminal behavior is not indicative of "who I really am" ("not what I am like, "was not my fault,") then the repetition of such behavior in the future would also be inconsistent with this "real" me. Challenging such neutralizations or justifications may enforce self-conceptions of an irredeemable deviant, stifling any hope or motivation for change.

The lack of theoretical clarity regarding the definition of pro-criminal attitudes and the role that they play in the persistence of offending is clearly reflected in the empirical literature (see Banse et al. 2013). Yet, in spite of this uncertainty, it seems that correctional and clinical practice has "run ahead of scientific knowledge" (Gannon and Polaschek 2006, p. 1000), with the enthusiastic adoption of an array of cognitive behavioral treatment programs designed to eradicate pro-criminal attitudes, neutralizations, justifications, and excuses for many types of offending behavior.

B. Meaning of and Emotions Surrounding Criminal Behavior

Transformations in the content of cognitions are about more than attitudinal changes. Some researchers have concentrated on phenomenological aspects of offending and desistance—in particular, how the meanings attached to and emotions surrounding criminal behavior change over time.

Strain theorists suggest that emotions such as resentment, dissatisfaction, disappointment, and, particularly, anger play an important role in offending and arise from a mismatch between expectations and achievement (Agnew 1992). Others propose a link between offending and adverse experiences (particularly those occurring in childhood in the family environment), mediated by emotions of anger and fear (Hamilton 2016), rage, humiliation, guilt, and shame (Winlow 2014).

Conversely, Katz (1988) draws our attention to the "the emergence of distinctive sensual dynamics" (p. 6) in offending including the excitement of criminal activity. Bottoms and Shapland (2011) report that the excitement of offending was one of the obstacles to desistance most prominently cited by the young adults they interviewed. As Farrall and Calverley (2006) point out, given that most people ultimately stop offending, these dangers and thrills must lose their appeal, or at least their relative potency, over time (p. 100). Indeed, additional analysis by Giordano and colleagues, which drew on a further wave of interviews and initial data from their study of delinquent youth, supports this. The analysis found empirical support for developmental shifts which see a diminution of both positive and negative emotions associated with crime. These developmental shifts have clear implications for desistance (Giordano, Schroeder, and Cernkovich 2007).

Many studies highlight an increasing dissatisfaction or disillusionment with criminal lifestyles (Paternoster and Bushway 2009; Weaver 2016). Some stress the role of the criminal justice system and experience of (repeated) punishment in this process (Shover and Thompson 1992). Farrall and Calverley (2006) highlighted emotions of relief among those embarking on desistance journeys, as a direct result of avoiding negative emotions associated with offending such as fear of arrest, trepidation of court appearances and "having to look over your shoulder" (p. 105).

While the cumulative impacts of criminal justice intervention are likely to have some impact in generating negative feelings that may stimulate change, Farrall and Caverley's (2006) research identifies positive emotions such as pride, self-worth, and happiness, which emerge later in desistance resulting both from the (re)building of relationships of trust and from recognition of progress by others. In the follow-up study to this work, Farrall and colleagues (2014) suggest that these positive feelings may also, in turn, subside: as distance from offending increases, the achievements of desistance (e.g., periods of non-offending) begin to be seen as mundane. This is part of what they term the "emotional trajectory of desistance."

As the meaning attached to criminal behavior changes, this can lead to former criminal activity being viewed with shame and regret (Farrall and Calverley 2006). Research suggests that shame and regret may play a supportive role in the desistance process (LeBel et al. 2008). However, the role of shame is not uncomplicated: it can be present in the narratives of people still involved in persistent offending (Maruna 2001; Healy 2013) and may facilitate offending if it is linked to hopelessness (see next section). Braithwaite (1989) distinguishes between reintegrative shame and stigmatizing shame, a distinction that sheds light on the different mechanisms with which shame comes into play in persistence and desistance. In the former, the act is distinguished from the actor: the act is denounced while the actor is offered reintegrative pathways back into the moral community. In the latter, the actor perceives not only the act but also him- or herself as condemned. Braithwaite suggests that the subjective perception of such stigmatizing shame may lead to reaction and the perpetuation and entrenchment of deviant behaviors. LeBel et al. (2008) found that perceptions of stigma were associated with reconviction (and marginally statistically significantly associated with reimprisonment). Deeply held shame that permeates and destabilizes the person's sense of self has been particularly associated with violent behavior (Scheff and Retzinger 1991; Gilligan 1996; Beck 1999; Butler 2008). Labeling theories, discussed above, provide a means of understanding how shame can act as a mediator between societal reaction, negative identities, and ongoing deviant behavior (see LeBel 2008, 2012, for more on the role of stigma and labeling). Such an understanding is critical in developing responses to offending that engender potentially desistance-promoting regret but not desistance-inhibiting shame.

Regret, guilt, and shame are not the only negative emotions evoked in desistance. Farrall and colleagues' (2014) work on emotional trajectories tracks a path away from (at least acute) pain of guilt regarding past offending and toward positive emotions, such as a sense of belonging and happiness. However, an important article by Briege Nugent and Marguerite Schinkel (2016) highlights the "pains of desistance" when offending stops but a positive life transformation is not successfully secured. The article draws on two qualitative studies with two distinct groups: one with long-term prisoners (drawing on interviews with those on release licenses) and one with young people with a history of offending in the transition to adulthood. In both groups, Nugent and Schinkel identified three interrelated pains of desistance: the pain of isolation, the pain of goal failure, and the pain of hopelessness. In many cases the respondents had sacrificed former peer groups in pursuit of staying out of trouble, yet failed to secure conventional achievements (e.g., family and employment) or recognition of change by others. The result was a diminished life. Of one group they write: "not feeling able to fully take part in life or to move towards their goals meant that many of the men were slowly giving up hope for anything other than a life of merely existing" (p. 574). As a result, their desistance remained "limited or fragile" (p. 579). This brings us on to the importance of hope.

C. The Will and the Ways: Motivation, Hope, and Self-Efficacy

As the meaning of emotions contributing to changes in criminal behavior evolves, a wish or decision to desist from offending may crystallize. Most desistance theories discuss the importance of motivational factors in the desistance process. As we have seen, however, such a wish may not promote desistance unless accompanied by a belief that change is possible and that some alternative future can be envisioned (Giordano, Cernkovich, and Rudolph 2002). Thus, desistance research has explored the role of hope and optimism in desistance from offending and, conversely, the role of hopelessness and pessimism in persistence. Such ideas are closely linked to the person's subjective perception of their own self-efficacy in achieving goals and their ability to exercise agency, although the relationships between hope, optimism, self-efficacy, and the complex and often poorly defined concept of agency are murky.

Empirical research supports the widely held view that motivation matters in desistance. In a study tracking the progress of 199 men and women on probation and their probation officers, Farrall (2002) identified motivation to stop offending as one key factor associated with desistance. Similarly, Shapland and Bottoms (2011) found that expressing a definite intention to desist significantly predicted lower self-reported offending in subsequent interviews. Further analysis of their data found scores on a self-efficacy scale (measuring beliefs about what one can achieve) were related to expressions of definite intentions to desist, while self-perceived obstacles to desistance were a strong predictor for reoffending (Bottoms and Shapland 2011).

Some studies emphasize that the would-be desister must see realistic avenues for achieving success: they must have both the will and the ways, i.e., realistic hope. In a longitudinal study of 130 prisoners interviewed pre- and post-release, Burnett and Maruna (2004) found that pre-release optimism regarding abilities to avoid reoffending was inversely correlated with self-reported reoffending, even when controlling for static factors and some social problems. Moreover, hope was inversely correlated with re-conviction and re-imprisonment in a 10-year follow-up study. Continuing the earlier tracking study of probationers (Farrall 2002), Farrall and Calverley's (2006) analysis of the emotional trajectory of desistance suggests hope is important but ebbs and flows through the desistance process.

Maruna (2001) identifies the importance of optimism about the future and the narrator's capacity to make it in the non-criminal world. In a later paper, he even suggests that it is the redemption script, with its exaggerated sense of control, which expresses cognitive distortions, albeit highly adaptive ones (Maruna and Mann 2006). In contrast, the persisters' condemnation script suggested powerlessness, fatalism, and even perceptions of victimization, resigned to a fate predetermined by childhood experiences, a lack of resources, and societal prejudice. Farrall et al.'s (2014) latest findings from the qualitative longitudinal tracking study reinforce the importance of hope.

Similarly, in their drawing together of a criminal-coping hypothesis and relapse theory, Zamble and Quinsey (2001) suggest that people who reoffend frequently not only have poor coping abilities for overcoming life's problems but make cognitive appraisals of their own (in)ability to cope with these problems. Self-perceptions that they are unlikely to cope lead to a return to maladaptive strategies and criminal behavior. This was supported by results from their study with Canadian prisoners reincarcerated following release.

Nonetheless, in stark contrast to the picture of persisters as lacking agentic power, some theories depict them as rational agents, choosing to engage in crime on the basis of criminal self-efficacy, i.e., the expectation of successfully meeting goals through criminal means (Brezina and Topalli 2012). In Shover and Thompson's (1992) research, desistance from offending was associated with a decline in these expectations of success through criminal means, as opposed to increased expectations of success through legitimate pursuits. At the very least, one can assume that pessimism about the future and the perceived absence of agentic power may only play a role in sustaining offending behavior for some people and some types of offending. As Healy (2013), points out: "the most serious financial crimes tend to be committed by agentic—and highly successful—individuals" (p. 565).

Following a recent study of prisoners in Norway, which found high levels of optimism regarding post-release desistance efforts despite past failures and severe welfare issues among the sample, Friestad and Hansen (2010) have drawn a distinction between optimism and unrealistic optimism. They suggest that while the former can encourage effort directed at goals (even in the face of obstacles), the latter can lead to inadequate preparation and adoption of prevention measures. Though this appears contrary to Maruna's thesis that such views can act as a form of adaptive cognitive distortion, perhaps the key question concerns the relationship between an optimistic appraisal of future prospects and the availability of practical resources and social supports that might assist the individual in vindicating that optimism and reinforcing a sense of agency. Equally, the ways in which optimism can come unstuck (for example, as a result of legal and social barriers to reintegration) also require further exploration (see Schinkel 2014).

III. Transformations in Cognitive Skills and Strategies

Transformations in identity and in cognitive content—attitudes, motivation, hope, and a sense of agency—are important to the development and maintenance of the broader project of desistance. Once a desire for change exists, identifying clear and realistic pathways to achieving this change (the "ways") is critical in formulating specific intentions on how to act, and we have suggested that envisaging a possible self is important in providing this. However, as well as available social pathways, the person wishing to desist must also have the necessary executive capabilities—cognitive skills or "tools" (Wikström 2006, p. 101)—to effectively deliberate and implement intended positive actions, in particular under pressure and without the time for considered responses. Research suggests that desistance may include transformations in these cognitive skills, for example, in decision-making or emotion regulation—or, alternatively, development of strategies to avoid risky situations altogether.

The ability of those people who are trying to desist to resist temptations and impulses, i.e., cognitive processes related to the exercise of self-control, will clearly play a part in determining whether or not desistance is sustained. In their theory of criminality, Gottfredson and Hirschi (1990) famously attributed offending behavior to low self-control among those committing crime. Importantly, self-control is conceived as a static rather than a dynamic factor in this theory, in that they suggest that individual levels of self-control develop in childhood and remain relatively stable across the life course. With self-control stable, they explained desistance through "inexorable ageing of the organism" (p. 141) and changes in surrounding opportunity structures.

In contrast, Shapland and Bottoms (2011) suggest a role for self-control construed as a dynamic rather than a static concept. They draw attention to cognitive strategies employed by desisters to overcome "weakness of will" or "the condition of acting voluntarily in a way that the actor considers is not in his/her long-term interests, and so something (s)he will regret later" (Shapland and Bottoms 2011, p. 274). In particular, they highlight common practices of what is termed diachronic self-control among their sample, whereby the desister takes steps to avoid potential situations and places where they might be tempted to engage in criminal activity, in some cases even going as far as a self-imposed form of house arrest.

Wikström (2006) similarly proposes that self-control should be understood as a situational concept as opposed to an individual trait, but he challenges the extent to which self-control is relevant to persistent offending, since self-control can only come into play when an individual considering criminal action perceives this as conflicting with his or her personal moral code. Nevertheless, Shapland and Bottoms (2011) found that the young adults in their study involved in very persistent offending did hold largely conventional moral views regarding offending. Desistance, then, can be viewed as a process whereby episodes of temptation have to be resisted, at least in part, through the implementation of cognitive strategies, with varying degrees of success.

Michael Rocque (2015) has tried to rehabilitate the Glueck and Glueck's (1940) "maturational reform" theory which hinted at social, psychological, and biological processes involved in a natural aging out of criminal activity (see Chapter 2). Although it did not offer a comprehensive or satisfactory theory of the maturation process, he argues that the Gluecks' work contains important insights into this process with relevance to desistance, such as the observation that "self-control, foresight, planfulness" increase through the maturation process (Glueck and Glueck 1943, p. 39). Rocque suggests that their work anticipated a number of important recent advances in the developmental sciences, which to date have not been adequately incorporated into desistance theory (see also Collins 2004; Byrne and Lurigio 2008). In a similar vein, a report summarizing the neurodevelopmental literature and its relevance for criminal justice highlights a mismatch in late adolescence/early adulthood between two systems (Williams 2012). Williams reports that the problem-solving system develops by around age 16, enabling the young person to determine what action should and shouldn't be taken in any given circumstance. However, the system that enables the young person to apply this in the light of immediate social and emotional concerns does not develop until later. This neurodevelopmental insight supports Giordano, Schroeder, and Cernkovich's (2007) findings in their follow-up study of delinquent youths. Their interviewees reported improved skills in controlling emotions and developing strategies for coping—emotion regulation and management—that had supported their desistance as they matured into adulthood.

Both Williams (2012) and Rocque (2015) also highlight evidence that brain injury, which occurs with higher prevalence among the prison population, impedes these developmental processes. This may explain persistence of behavior in later life, at least in some cases. Interestingly, Shapland and Bottoms' concept of diachronic self-control implies that desisters utilize problem-solving abilities to avoid situations where immediate social and emotional concerns might override intentions to desist. As such, it might be one means by which they are able to circumvent the limitations of not (yet) fully developed neurocognitive abilities.

IV. Toward an Integrated Interactional Model of Desistance

This chapter has identified a series of linked cognitive transformations that research suggests may occur in the desistance process: transformations in narrative identity, transformations in cognitive content and transformations in cognitive skills and strategies. So far, this chapter has largely treated these cognitive transformations in relative isolation from external social factors. This is, of course, an artificial dichotomy since internal states, social relations and structural factors all influence one another. Although varying significantly from Laub and Sampson's theory, Giordano, Cernkovich, and Rudolph (2002), in their emphasis on the agentic changes within desistance, suggest that their theory can be largely integrated with social control theories of desistance, which provide "an important but incomplete account of the change process" (p. 992). They go on to explain that "while we continue to focus primarily on micro-level processes, we have increasingly recognized that the form and content of these narratives intimately connect to the social addresses of our respondents" (p. 993). That said, commentators have highlighted that the exact nature of this connection and the interaction of these subjective and structural aspects of the desistance process remains both undertheorized and underresearched, although a number of important attempts have been made to begin bridging this gap (Farrall 2005; LeBel et al. 2008; Bottoms and Shapland 2011; Healy 2013; King 2013; Rocque 2015).

A key issue in seeking to disentangle causes and correlates of desistance is the chronological sequencing of subjective and social changes in the desistance process. What comes first? Social control theorists give primacy to social events and the subsequent accumulation of social bonds in the desistance process, leading to changes in thought processes around offending; the desister comes to believe that between his or her job, partner, and family he or she simply has too much to lose (Laub and Sampson 2003). As we have noted, in this account these structural changes (and associated thought processes) may be accompanied by a change in identity, but this is not considered necessary to the desistance process. A second position, held by some cognitive and identity theorists, treats cognitive changes as the prime mover in the desistance process. According to such theories, subjective dispositions toward offending change first and these drive subsequent changes in behavior. As well as reductions or even cessation of offending, this may also include actively seeking out prosocial roles, notably intimate partner and employee, although such social changes may be incidental to the desistance process. However, a third position is that the very concept of a single primary cause

may not be helpful, since it fails to take account of the dynamic, interdependent and potentially reciprocal interaction between internal and external factors (see Weaver and
McNeill 2015; Weaver 2016).

Unraveling the differential impacts of internal and external factors has certainly been
a "thorny methodological point" (Laub and Sampson 2001, p. 41). A study by LeBel et al.
(2008) attempted to use a combination of qualitative and quantitative methods to begin
to distinguish between these positions, termed the strong social model, the strong subjective model, or the interactional model. LeBel et al. were able to consider two forms of
interactional subjective-social model: one in which both subjective and social factors
both play an independent role in the desistance process and a second in which social
events play a role in desistance, but the impact of these events depend on the subjective
state, or mindset of the person. However, data limitations did not enable the authors
to explore how anticipated social problems have an impact on the mindset of the individual (a different form of social-subjective model).

LeBel et al.'s analysis supports the idea of an interaction of subjective and social
factors in at least two ways. Looking specifically at prison release, they suggest that social
problems (e.g., problems with housing, employment, finances, relationships, or alcohol
and drugs) and some subjective states can act independently on the desistance process;
they found regret for past actions promotes, but internalized stigma stifles, desistance.
In addition, they suggest that pre-release belief in one's ability to go straight (hope or
self-efficacy) and perceptions of available alternate identities (or roles) can impact on
desistance by causing social problems post-release not to occur (or reducing their impact). They suggest that having hope may help people to grasp opportunities and to
overcome disappointments, "*so long as the problems are not excessive*" (LeBel et al. 2008,
p. 154, emphasis added). Importantly, the authors found "the complete absence of any
support for the strong subjective model" (p. 150) or the view that one's mindset alone is
all that matters in achieving desistance.

Bottoms and Shapland's (2011) heuristic and interactive model of the early stages
of desistance builds on Giordano, Cernkovich, and Rudolph's (2002) model whereby
the environment provides hooks for change which act as critical scaffolding around
which both life and identity changes can be built. Their model involves a seven-stage
relapsing but forward-oriented process. In this model, current offending is influenced
by a triggering event, which leads to the wish to try to change, which leads the person
to think differently about him- or herself or the surroundings, which leads them to take
action toward desistance. However, these fledgling attempts to desist may be threatened
by obstacles, barriers, and temptations, so the desister must find reinforcing factors
(from within him- or herself or more likely within his or her changing social relations)
to maintain the change which, if successful, may ultimately enable the establishment of
a crime-free identity. Crucially, progression along this journey is affected, for better or
worse, by both the pre-programmed potential of the individual and his social capital
resources.

According to interactive theories, life events are important. This is not just about new
constraints on a person's (unchanged) propensity to offend. It is also because of a change

in meaning accompanying these events. Giordano, Schroeder, and Cernkovich (2007) stress that, beyond mere social control, marital relationships offer positive emotions, which replace the original emotions (both negative and positive) that promoted criminal behavior. Such relationships contribute to a positive sense of self, as well as imbuing life with meaning. In a small-scale narrative inquiry with eight desisting men, Paula Hamilton (2016) found that triggering events in the men's narratives were those in which the meaning of events—dynamic, and specific to that time and context—was such as to generate strong emotional responses (positive or negative). The men in her study, who had previously worked to suppress their emotions, were then "compelled to engage in 'emotional labour'" (p. 35). Following Vaughan (2007), she found that "prompted by these corrective emotional experiences, these men entered into a period of intensive reflexive dialogue" (Hamilton 2016, p. 35) and reappraisal of their lives, in which narrative identities were rewritten.

Drawing on the results of Beth Weaver's (2016) research exploring the interlinked histories of a friendship group of men who had offended together in adolescence and young adulthood, Weaver and McNeill (2015) have demonstrated how the meaning of criminal behavior can gradually change in a group context. For Weaver's respondents, offending was initially an understandable, even necessary, behavior pursued as a means of securing highly valued relational goods (reciprocity, trust, equality, uncritical support, loyalty, and solidarity) within the context of the group and its wider social and cultural environment. Supporting friends caught up in a violent incident could secure or reinforce trust and loyalty, meriting the risk of punishment. Over time, as existing group relationships were played out in a new social context (pursuing employment opportunities in a distant city), and as intimate and working relationships were forged outside of the group, the relational rules of the group were transformed. Within this revised context, offending no longer offered a means to achieve the same relational goods; indeed, increasingly offending became incompatible with the relational goods (including mutual support and encouragement to desist) now generated through new activities.

Similar dynamics are apparent in Farrall's (2005) application of existentialist sociology to the desistance process: "the importance of situated places in the ongoing production of a meaningful self. . . . Who one is, therefore, is not just about one's own feelings, actions or identity, but also partly implied by the places which surround oneself and the sorts of activities which are commonly held to occur in those social spaces" (p. 370). Farrall's case study, Sandra, does not experience a dramatic overnight cognitive transformation—an epiphany—but various social events and changes (such as employment and promotion) act as staging posts from which her initially fragile emerging self could be reinforced. Similarly, Maruna et al. (2009) argue that the personal transformations that take place in the desistance process contain a "looking-glass element" in that internal states are at least partly a reflection of societal and relational factors. Just as labeling theorists propose that the internalization of negative societal labels may promote deviance, Maruna et al. (2009) suggest that internalization of positive societal labels may promote desistance. Rehabilitation is a partner dance: when close relations and the wider community project a genuine belief that the person can and is changing their life for the better, this reinforces self-belief in the person who is trying to desist. People can and do rise to meet expectations—as in the so-called Pygmalion effect in psychology (Rosenthal and Jacobson 1992). In Maruna et al.'s (2009) case study of a drug rehabilitation unit, they demonstrate how trust, responsibility, and recognition of progress are as much a cause of the desister's prosocial mindset and identity as they are a result of it. Concrete external recognition of reform may be necessary for fragile emerging desisting identities to be internalized and desistance maintained—and for desisters to discover and enact a heightened sense of agency in the process.

Carlsson (2016) has also recently emphasized how agency is time and context dependent, suggesting that more must be done to unpack "what causes an individual to intend one thing rather than another" (p. 36) at any given time and why this changes. He argues that the term agency needs significant conceptual development, warning that a failure to do so may be linked to the critique that agency is a residual term for behavior that our theories are unable to explain.

To date, one of the most thoughtful discussions of agency in relation to desistance has been offered by Deirdre Healy. Healy (2013) employed Côté's (1997) "identity capital" model in the natural developmental process to provide a theoretical model for the interaction between agency and structure in desistance processes. Côté suggests that we start life on a default individualization position, whereby our lives are guided by external circumstances and impulses and we do not possess a sense of control over our own destinies. However, as we transition to adulthood, most of us move onto a developmental individualization pathway characterized by high self-esteem, emotional stability, strong coping skills, reflection on choices and consequent sense of responsibility for actions, a sense of purpose, and actively seeking out opportunities for growth and self-improvement (Healy 2013, p. 563). The move onto such a pathway is a result of natural maturation processes that increase many of these agentic capacities, but this maturation takes place only in interaction with the social capital and structural opportunities which often accompany the transition to adulthood and which are necessary for agency to be enacted. However, Healy highlights how structural constraints in late modernity, particularly in the lives of marginalized social groups, may delay the transition to adulthood by denying the possibility for a progressive interaction between developing agency and developing social capital in the complete absence of the latter. Her thesis is that desisters have been able to make a natural—or delayed—move onto a developmental individualization pathway. Emphasizing that "[e]xpressions of agency must always be accompanied by at least the possibility of success if they are to lure people away from a life of crime" (p. 565), she proposes that in many cases such a move may necessitate a lowering of aspirations so that the desister is able to strive toward goals and to engage in the dynamic ongoing process of identity construction (see also Shapland and Bottoms 2011 on this point).

What all these interactive models acknowledge is the debilitating impact of severe social problems on attempts at desistance. To suggest that desistance can be achieved by mind over matter fundamentally misunderstands and ignores the impact of multiple structural disadvantage in creating significant and even insurmountable barriers to attempts to go straight (see Farrall, Bottoms, and Shapland 2010; Nugent and Schinkel, 2016). This is also recognized by Giordano, Cernkovich, and Rudolph (2002) in their theory of cognitive transformations: "Given a relatively 'advantaged' set of circumstances, the cognitive transformations and agentic moves we describe are hardly necessary; under conditions of sufficiently extreme disadvantage, they are unlikely to be nearly enough" (Giordano, Cernkovich, and Rudolph 2002, p. 1026).

V. Conclusion

In this chapter, we have identified a number of cognitive transformations that are associated with the desistance process. We have explored how identity transformation can provide an organizing framework for cognitions and act as a blueprint for evaluating what behavior fits with the (re)emergent prosocial real me. Linked transformations in cognitive content—attitudes, beliefs, meaning, and emotions—may support the formation of unconscious changes in behavior as well as conscious intentions to change. Finally, to carry through with these intentions, people trying to desist may need to improve the skills and develop the strategies to ensure that intentions are not displaced by emotions and temptations in the heat of the moment.

Understanding the internal worlds of people in desistance processes is critical to any full explanation of those processes. These are their journeys—often long and winding. But to continue the analogy, to emphasize their roles as drivers of change is not to deny that the vehicle, the weather conditions, the state of the road, and the responses of other road users don't also influence their prospects of arriving safely.

We argue that cognitive transformations matter in the desistance process. So, the nurturing of motivation and prosocial attitudes is likely to play at least some part in promoting desistance. However, desistance researchers have cautioned about the history of correctional practice, one that too often describes the development and application of interventions that isolate motivational and attitudinal factors from their social and structural contexts and treat people as if, simply by thinking differently or developing other skills, they can move away from a life of crime. The relational context in which offending occurs and the disadvantaged structural contexts within which attempts at desistance are too often thwarted also need to be tackled. Social relations, social events, and structural factors can act to frustrate the desire for change, the belief that change is possible, the perception of realistic pathways for sustaining non-criminal lives (the development of hope), the formation of alternative identities—and ongoing efforts to sustain changes of all these sorts. Penal systems, cultures, and practices can also act in ways that suffocate change processes and/or in ways that breathe life into them (see McNeill 2012, 2014). The practical challenge—both for desistance researchers and for correctional practitioners—is to develop a clearer understanding of how and in what contexts (social and penal) cognitive transformations can be best supported.

NOTE

1. This echoes Lemert's (1951) distinction between the initiation of deviant behavior (primary deviance) and that associated with the assumption of a deviant identity (secondary deviance).

REFERENCES

Abel, Gene G., David K. Gore, C. L. Holland, Nancy Camp, Judith V. Becker, and Jerry Rathner. 1989. "The Measurement of the Cognitive Distortions of Child Molesters." *Annals of Sex Research* 2(2): 135–152.

Agnew, Robert. 1992. "Foundation for a General Strain Theory of Crime and Delinquency." *Criminology* 30(1): 47–88.

Andrews, Donald A., and James Bonta. 2010. *The Psychology of Criminal Conduct.* 5th ed. New Providence, NJ: Matthew Bender.

Banse, Rainer, Judith Koppehele-Gossel, Lisa M. Kistemaker, Verena A. Werner, and Alexander F. Schmidt. 2013. "Pro-criminal Attitudes, Intervention, and Recidivism." *Aggression and Violent Behavior* 18(6): 673–685.

Barriga, Alvaro Q., Jennifer R. Landau, Bobby L. Stinson, II, Albert K. Liau, and John C. Gibbs. 2000. "Cognitive Distortion and Problem Behaviors in Adolescents." *Criminal Justice and Behavior* 27(1): 36–56.

Beck, Aaron T. 1999. *Prisoners of Hate: The Cognitive Basis of Anger, Hostility and Violence.* New York: HarperCollins.

Bottoms, Anthony, Joanna Shapland, Andrew Costello, Deborah Holmes, and Grant Muir. 2004. "Towards Desistance: Theoretical Underpinnings for an Empirical Study." *Howard Journal of Criminal Justice* 43(4): 368–389.

Bottoms, Anthony, and Joanna Shapland. 2011. "Steps Towards Desistance Among Young Adult Recidivists." In *Escape Routes: Contemporary Perspectives on Life After Punishment,* edited by Stephen Farrall, Mike Hough, Shadd Maruna, and Richard Sparks, 43–80. London: Routledge.

Braithwaite, John. 1989. *Crime, Shame and Reintegration.* Cambridge, UK: Cambridge University Press.

Brezina, Timothy, and Volkan Topalli. 2012. "Criminal Self-Efficacy: Exploring the Correlates and Consequences of a "Successful Criminal" Identity." *Criminal Justice and Behavior* 39(8): 1042–1062.

Burnett, Ros, and Shadd Maruna. 2004. "So 'Prison Works,' Does It? The Criminal Careers of 130 Men Released from Prison under Home Secretary, Michael Howard." *Howard Journal of Criminal Justice* 33(4): 390–404.

Bushway, Shawn D., Alex R. Piquero, Lisa M. Broidy, Elizabeth Cauffman, and Paul Mazerolle. 2001. "An Empirical Framework for Studying Desistance as a Process." *Criminology* 39(2): 491–515.

Butler, Michelle. 2008. "What Are You Looking At? Prisoner Confrontations and the Search for Respect." *British Journal of Criminology* 48(6): 856–873.

Byrne, James M., and Arthur Lurigio. 2008. "Victimization and Criminal Behavior in Adolescence and Adulthood." *Victims and Offenders* 3(4): 319–330.

Carlsson, Christoffer. 2013. "Masculinities, Persistence, and Desistance." *Criminology* 51(3): 661–693.

Carlsson, Christoffer. 2016. "Human Agency, Criminal Careers and Desistance." In *Global Perspectives on Desistance*, edited by Joanna Shapland, Stephen Farrall, and Anthony Bottoms, 28–49. Abingdon, UK: Routledge.

Collins, Raymond E. 2004. "Onset and Desistance in Criminal Careers: Neurobiology and the Age–Crime Relationship. *Journal of Offender Rehabilitation* 39(3): 1–19.

Côté, James E. 1997. "An Empirical Test of the Identity Capital Model." *Journal of Adolescence* 20(5): 577–597.

Crewe, Ben, and Shadd Maruna. 2006. "Self-Narratives and Ethnographic Fieldwork." In *The Sage Handbook of Fieldwork*, edited by Dick Hobbs and Richard Wright, 109–123. London: Sage.

Farrall, Stephen. 2002. *Rethinking What Works with Offenders: Probation, Social Context and Desistance From Crime*. Cullompton, UK: Willan.

Farrall, Stephen. 2005. "On the Existential Aspects of Desistance from Crime." *Symbolic Interaction* 28(3): 367–386.

Farrall, Stephen, and Adam Calverley. 2006. *Understanding Desistance from Crime: Emerging Theoretical Directions in Resettlement and Rehabilitation*. Maidenhead, UK: Open University Press.

Farrall, Stephen, Anthony Bottoms, and Joanna Shapland. 2010. "Social Structures and Desistance from Crime." *European Journal of Criminology* 7(6): 546–570.

Farrall, Stephen, and Benjamin Bowling. 1999. "Structuration, Human Development and Desistance from Crime." *British Journal of Criminology* 39(2): 253–268.

Farrall, Stephen, Ben Hunter, Gilly Sharpe, and Adam Calverley. 2014. *Criminal Careers in Transition: The Social Context of Desistance from Crime*. Oxford: Oxford University Press.

Finkelhor, David. 1984. *Child Sexual Abuse: New Theory and Research*. New York: Free Press.

Friestad, Christine, and Inger L. S. Hansen. 2010. "Gender Differences in Inmates' Anticipated Desistance." *European Journal of Criminology* 7(4): 285–298.

Gannon, Theresa A., and Devon L. L. Polaschek. 2006. "Cognitive Distortions in Child Molesters: A Re-examination of Key Theories and Research." *Clinical Psychology Review* 26(8): 1000–1019.

Gilligan, James. 1996. *Violence: Our Deadly Epidemic and Its Causes*. New York: GP Putnam's.

Giordano, Peggy C., Stephen A. Cernkovich, and Jennifer. L. Rudolph. 2002. "Gender, Crime, and Desistance: Toward a Theory of Cognitive Transformation." *American Journal of Sociology* 107(4): 990–1064.

Giordano, Peggy C., Ryan D. Schroeder, and Stephen A. Cernkovich. 2007. "Emotions and Crime over the Life Course: A Neo-Meadian Perspective on Criminal Continuity and Change." *American Journal of Sociology* 112(6): 1603–1661.

Glueck, Sheldon, and Eleanor T. Glueck. 1940. *Juvenile Delinquents Grown Up*. New York: Commonwealth Fund.

Glueck, Sheldon, and Eleanor T. Glueck. 1943. *Criminal Careers in Retrospect*. New York: Commonwealth Fund.

Gottfredson, Michael R., and Travis Hirschi. 1990. *A General Theory of Crime*. Stanford, CA: Stanford University Press.

Gove, Walter. 1985. "The Effect of Age and Gender on Deviant Behavior: A Biopsychosocial Perspective." In *Gender and the Life Course*, edited by Alice S. Rossi, 114–115. New York: Aldine.

Hamilton, Paula. 2016. "Emotions and Identity Transformation." In *Moving on from Crime and Substance Use: Transforming Identities*, edited by Anne Robinson and Paula Hamilton, 19–41. Bristol, UK: Policy Press.

Hartley, Carolyn. C. 1998. "How Incest Offenders Overcome Internal Inhibitions Through the Use of Cognitions and Cognitive Distortions." *Journal of Interpersonal Violence* 13: 25–39.

Healy, Deirdre. 2013. "Changing Fate? Agency and the Desistance Process." *Theoretical Criminology* 17(4): 557–574

Healy, Deirdre. 2014. "Becoming a Desister: Exploring the Role of Agency, Coping and Imagination in the Construction of a New Self." *British Journal of Criminology* 54(5): 873–891.

Helmus, Leslie R., Karl Hanson, Kelly M. Babchishin, and Ruth E. Mann. 2013. "Attitudes Supportive of Sexual Offending Predict Recidivism: A Meta-Analysis." *Trauma, Violence, and Abuse* 14(1): 34–53.

Katz, Jack. 1988. *Seductions of Crime: Moral and Sensual Attractions in Doing Evil*. New York: Basic Books.

King, Sam. 2013. "Transformative Agency and Desistance from Crime." *Criminology and Criminal Justice* 13(3): 317–335.

Laub, John H., and Robert J. Sampson. 2001. "Understanding Desistance from Crime." In *Crime and Justice*, edited by Michael Tonry. Chicago: University of Chicago Press.

Laub, John H., and Robert J. Sampson. 2003. *Shared Beginnings, Divergent Lives: Delinquents Boys to Age 70*. Cambridge, MA: Harvard University Press.

LeBel, Thomas P. 2007. "An Examination of the Impact of Formerly Incarcerated Persons Helping Others." *Journal of Offender Rehabilitation* 46(1/2): 1–24.

LeBel, Thomas P. 2008. "Perceptions of and Responses to Stigma." *Sociology Compass* 2(2): 409–432.

LeBel, Thomas P. 2012. "Invisible Stripes? Formerly Incarcerated Persons' Perceptions of Stigma." *Deviant Behavior* 33(2): 89–107.

LeBel, Thomas P., Ros Burnett, Shadd Maruna, and Shawn Bushway. 2008. "The 'Chicken and Egg' of Subjective and Social Factors in Desistance from Crime." *European Journal of Criminology* 5(2): 130–158.

Lemert, Edwin M. 1951. *Social Pathology: Systematic Approaches to the Study of Sociopathic Behavior*. New York: McGraw-Hill.

Liem, Marieke, and Nicholas J. Richardson. 2014. "The Role of Transformation Narratives in Desistance Among Released Lifers." *Criminal Justice and Behavior* 41(6): 692–712.

Maruna, Shadd. 2001. *Making Good: How Ex-convicts Reform and Rebuild Their Lives*. Washington, DC: American Psychological Association.

Maruna, Shadd, and Heith Copes. 2004. "Excuses, Excuses: What Have We Learned from Five Decades of Neutralization Research." In *Crime and Justice: An Annual Review of Research*, Vol. 32, edited by Michael Tonry, 171–194. Chicago: University of Chicago Press.

Maruna, Shadd, and Ruth Mann. 2006. "A Fundamental Attribution Error? Rethinking Cognitive Distortions." *Legal and Criminological Psychology* 11 (2): 155–177.

Maruna, Shadd, and Stephen Farrall. 2004. "Desistance from Crime: A Theoretical Reformulation." *Kölner Zeitschrift fur Soziologie und Sozialpsychologie* 43.

Maruna, Shadd, Thomas P. LeBel, Michelle Naples, and Nick Mitchell. 2009. "Looking-Glass Identity Transformation: Pygmalion and Golem in the Rehabilitation Process." In *How Offenders Transform their Lives*, edited by Bonita Veysey, Johanna Christian, and Damian J. Martinez, 30–55. Cullompton, UK: Willan.

Matza, David. 1964. *Delinquency and Drift*. New York: John Wiley.

McAdams, Dan P. 1985. *Power, Intimacy and the Life Story: Personological Inquiries into Identity*. Chicago: Dorsey.

McAdams, Dan P. 1993. *The Stories We Live By: Personal Myths and the Making of the Self*. New York: Willam Morrow.

McNeill, Fergus. 2012. "Four Forms of 'Offender' Rehabilitation: Towards an Interdisciplinary Perspective." *Legal and Criminological Psychology* 17(1): 18–36.

McNeill, Fergus. 2014. "Punishment as Rehabilitation." In *Encyclopedia of Criminology and Criminal Justice*, edited by Gerben Bruinsma and David Weisburd, 4195–4206. New York: Springer.

Murphy, William D. 1990. "Assessment and Modification of Cognitive Distortions in Sex Offenders." In *Handbook of Sexual Assault*, edited by William L. Marshall, D. R. Laws, and Howard E. Barbaree, 331–342. New York: Plenum.

Nugent, Briege, and Marguerite Schinkel. 2016. "The Pains of Desistance." *Criminology and Criminal Justice* 16(5): 568–584.

Paternoster, Ray, and Shawn Bushway. 2009. "Desistance and the Feared Self: Toward an Identity Theory of Criminal Desistance." *Journal of Criminal Law and Criminology* 99(4): 1103–1156.

Rocque, Michael. 2015. "The Lost Concept: The (Re)Emerging Link Between Maturation and Desistance from Crime." *Criminology and Criminal Justice* 15(3): 340–360.

Rosenthal, Robert, and Lenore Jacobson. 1992. *Pygmalion in the Classroom*. New York: Irvington.

Sampson, Robert J., and John H. Laub. 1993. *Crime in the Making: Pathways and Turning Points Through Life*. Cambridge, MA: Harvard University Press.

Sampson, Robert J., and John H. Laub. 1997. "A Life-Course Theory of Cumulative Disadvantage and the Stability of Delinquency." In *Developmental Theories of Crime and Delinquency: Advances in Criminological Theory*, Vol. 7, edited by Terence P. Thornberry, 133–161. New Brunswick, NJ: Transaction.

Scheff, Thomas J., and Suzanne M. Retzinger. 1991. *Emotions and Violence: Shame and Rage in Destructive Conflicts*. Lexington, MA: Lexington Books.

Schinkel, Marguerite. 2014. *Being Imprisoned: Punishment, Adaptation and Desistance*. Basingstoke, UK: Palgrave MacMillan.

Shapland, Joanna, and Anthony Bottoms. 2011. "Reflections on Social Values, Offending and Desistance Among Young Adult Recidivists." *Punishment and Society* 13(3): 256–282.

Shover, Neal, and Carol Y. Thompson. 1992. "Age, Differential Expectations, and Crime Desistance. *Criminology* 30(1): 89–104.

Sykes, Gresham M., and David Matza. 1957. "Techniques of Neutralization: A Theory of Delinquency." *American Sociological Review* 22(6): 664–670.

Vaughan, Barry. 2007. "The Internal Narrative of Desistance." *British Journal of Criminology* 47(3): 390–404.

Ward, Tony, and Thomas Keenan. 1999. "Child Molesters' Implicit Theories." *Journal of Interpersonal Violence* 14(8): 821–838.

Weaver, Beth. 2016. *Offending and Desistance: the Importance of Social Relations*. Abingdon, UK: Routledge.

Weaver, Beth, and Fergus McNeill. 2015. "Lifelines: Desistance, Social Relations, and Reciprocity." *Criminal Justice and Behavior* 42(1): 95–107.

Wikström, Per-Olof H. 2006. "Individuals, Settings, and Acts of Crime." In *The Explanation of Crime: Context, Mechanisms and Development*, edited by Per-Olof H. Wikström and Robert J. Sampson, 61–107. Cambridge, UK: Cambridge University Press.

Williams, Huw. 2012. *Repairing Shattered Lives: Brain injury and Its Implications for Criminal Justice*. London: Transition to Adulthood Alliance.

Winlow, Simon. 2014. "Trauma, Guilt and the Unconscious: Some Theoretical Notes on Violent Subjectivity." *Sociological Review* 62: 32–49.

Zamble, Edward, and Vernon L. Quinsey. 2001. *The Criminal Recidivism Process*. Cambridge, UK: Cambridge University Press.

CHAPTER 30

DEVELOPMENTAL AND LIFE-COURSE FINDINGS ON WOMEN AND GIRLS

LISA M. BROIDY AND CARLEEN M. THOMPSON

GENDER and age are two of the most stable correlates of offending. We know that females offend far less frequently than males, particularly when it comes to serious and violent offending (Block et al. 2010; DeLisi and Piquero 2011). We also know that, in the aggregate, males and females both exhibit the typical age–crime curve, with a peak in antisocial behavior in adolescence that begins to taper in early adulthood (Fergusson and Horwood 2002; Macmillan and McCarthy 2014). Considering gender and age together, it is clear that beneath broadly similar aggregate age–crime patterns lay both subtle and obvious differences in the frequency, seriousness, life-course patterning, and mechanisms that characterize the developmental course of offending behavior across males and females. Gender disparities in antisocial behavior emerge in the first few years of life and continue throughout the life course (Russell, Robins, and Odgers 2014).

Despite evidence that gender is a central organizing feature of life-course patterns of offending, we know surprisingly little about how gender conditions life-course developmental processes. Criminologists have become increasingly sensitive to the importance of gender as theoretically and empirically central to the criminological project, but developmental life-course criminology has been slow to keep pace with this shift. This reflects, in part, data limitations that have precluded a focus on questions of gender. Most early longitudinal data collection efforts relied on male samples to maximize the likelihood that the sample would include significant numbers of serious offenders (e.g., Glueck and Glueck 1968; Wolfgang, Figlio, and Sellin 1972; West and Farrington 1973). Even where females were part of the data collection effort, questions of gender were not generally central to related theoretical and empirical projects (e.g., Thornberry, Bjerregaard, and Miles 1993). As a result, much of the theoretical work in developmental life-course criminology either focuses on patterns of offending emergent in male samples or overlooks gender as an organizing principle in samples that do include females.

Moffitt (1993) stands as an exception to this early developmental life-course work. Not only does her sample include females, but she includes gender in her theoretical explanation of the patterns emergent from her data. Specifically, she invokes gendered biopsychosocial mechanisms to explain why the life-course persistent pattern of offending appears as a uniquely male phenomena in her data. As we document below, other studies challenge the empirical finding on which her theoretical arguments are based (that the life-course persistent trajectory is fundamentally a male trajectory). Nonetheless, her work spurred a set of theoretical and empirical questions about gender differences in life-course patterns of offending that, coupled with the broader androcentric critique lodged against criminology as a discipline, made it difficult to defend new male-only data collection efforts.

Recent longitudinal data collection efforts generally do include females, and researchers have begun to exploit these data to examine gender differences in life-course offending patterns and their key correlates. To date, however, the work in this area is difficult to summarize because it is not guided by a set of theoretically driven empirical questions about how gender frames life-course patterns of offending. Instead, the two research questions that have oriented this work to date are descriptive: What are the prominent similarities and differences with respect to how males and females sort into developmental pathways? and Do the correlates of distinct developmental pathways vary across males and females and, if so, how? These are important questions for understanding emergent life-course patterns. However, missing from this body of work is a core theoretical project that can guide these efforts and outline a set of theoretically driven empirical questions about when, why, and how gender should matter for the unfolding of developmental pathways of offending. As a result, the findings are difficult to compare and collate, and it is not clear how, as a group, they contribute to the theory building around the mechanisms through which gender frames and influences life-course offending patterns.

There is, however, a separate body of work that is largely theoretical, focusing on women's pathways in and out of offending and, in some cases, how they compare to men's (Uggen and Kruttschnitt 1998; Gaarder and Belknap 2002; Giordano, Cernkovich, and Rudolph 2002; Hagan and Foster 2003; Carbone-Lopez and Miller 2012; DeHart et al. 2014; Jones et al. 2014). Generally referred to as the gendered pathways literature, this work tends to ignore within and across gender differences in the nature and pattern of life-course offending trajectories and, as such, is rarely invoked to frame studies that detail variation in offending trajectories. As a result, these complementary literatures have evolved independently. However, the gendered pathways literature introduces a number of theoretical principles that are relevant to our interpretation of the growing body of work describing female offending trajectories and comparing them to those evidenced in male samples. Our aim in this chapter is to build on theoretical insights from the gendered pathways literature to interpret the evidence regarding the influence of gender on life-course offending patterns. In doing so, we hope to spur new empirical and theoretical innovation in this area.

Section I summarizes the key theoretical models explaining female offending and highlights what we believe to be the central theoretical principles that should guide research on gender and life-course offending patterns. Section II describes the most prominent life-course offending patterns, how females sort into these patterns, what we know about the relevant correlates, and how these vary across gender. In each instance we also apply core theoretical principles (detailed in Section I) to help make sense of evident patterns. Section III concludes with a call for more research on the theoretical mechanisms that might account for life-course patterns of female offending and the ways in which these patterns diverge from those evidenced by males.

I. Models Explaining Female Offending Over the Life Course

Theoretical explanations of the life-course trajectories that characterize female offending are limited. Moffitt's (1993, 2006) developmental taxonomy (see Chapter 9) reflects patterns of offending among the males and females in her New Zealand birth cohort data. The taxonomy distinguishes a small group of life-course persistent offenders, characterized by a range of individual, social, and contextual risks and disadvantages that present early in life and cumulate throughout life, leading to stable antisocial behavior trajectories that include frequent and serious offending. Moffitt argues that females are much less likely to experience the constellation of risks that characterize this group and, as such, are relatively unlikely to populate this trajectory. In comparison, the adolescent-limited trajectory group is much larger and reflects normative adolescent processes (both biological and social) that accrue to both males and females, leading to more gender parity in this group.

Challenging Moffitt's explanation of female offending trajectories, Silverthorn and Frick (1999) argue that what looks like adolescent-limited offending among females is actually more akin to life-course persistence, but its onset is delayed until adolescence as a function of biopsychosocial constraints on female antisocial behavior in childhood that are relaxed in the transition to adolescence. Both of these models paint a picture of reasonably limited heterogeneity among female offenders. In Moffitt's case, female offending is relatively trivial and constrained to adolescence, and in Silverthorn and Frick's case it is relatively serious but starts in adolescence. As we detail below, the data suggest that female offending patterns are more diverse and complex than either of these models would suggest (Russell, Robins, and Odgers 2014). Still, the processes they outline to explain female offending may be relevant to some of the patterns of offending emergent in female samples. In addition, they overlap with some of the theoretical mechanisms outlined in the gendered pathways literature.

The gendered pathways literature is more squarely situated within feminist criminology than developmental life-course criminology, which helps explain why the two literatures have largely evolved independently despite their obvious overlap. Building on the work of feminist scholars (Daly 1992; Bloom 1996; Chesney-Lind 1997; Owen 1998), the pathways literature highlights both gender-specific and gender-neutral traits, experiences, and contexts that frame girls' and women's risks for victimization and offending over the life course. Clearly this pathways literature is relevant to developmental life-course studies of female offending, and some scholars do integrate the two bodies of scholarship. Sampson and Laub's (1993) age-graded social control theory (see Chapter 16) is central to much of this work. Though developed to account for patterns of male offending over the life course, the theory has broad resonance, and the idea that changes in social control and social capital over the life course, and related transitions and turning points, are linked to changes in offending pathways guides much of the work linking developmental criminology with gendered pathways. This body of work focuses on women's pathways into and out of offending and can be traced to Giordano, Cernkovich, and Rudolph's (2002) gendered critique of Sampson and Laub's work. Giordano and colleagues argue that social control and social capital are important, and their data confirm that both male and female offenders lack ties to the key social institutions that generate social control and social capital. Though access to these institutions can trigger desistance and may be more salient for women (Uggen and Kruttschnitt 1998), such access is not always the key mechanism explaining pathways out of offending. Like their male counterparts, female offenders often cannot successfully link to these institutions, yet Giordano, Cernkovich, and Rudolph (2002) find that many still desist. More central than social capital to women's desistance, they argue, are cognitive shifts triggered by "hooks for change" in the offender's environment that allow her to envision a conforming self and an associated non-criminal identity. This highlights the role of identity and agency in women's offending pathways, echoing Maruna's (2004) explanations of male desistance mechanisms. The influence of identity and agency have been largely overlooked in the developmental life-course literature on offending trajectories, but both are likely relevant for explaining variation in female offending patterns.

The gendered pathways literature also highlights the central role of child maltreatment, particularly physical and sexual abuse, for girls' and women's pathways into offending and drug use (Gaarder and Belknap 2002; Cernkovich, Lanctot, and Giordano 2008; Salisbury and VanVoohris 2009; Wilson and Widom 2009; Topitzes et al. 2011; DeHart et al. 2014) and invokes social control and strain theories to help frame this link. Specifically, the fractured family dynamics as well as the strains and related emotional consequences that victimization introduces trigger antisocial outcomes in adolescence that continue into adulthood (Cernkovich, Lanctot, and Giordano 2008). Certainly child maltreatment is relevant to male offending as well, but research suggests it is more salient for females (Belknap and Holsinger 2006). This introduces the question of why females appear to manage other early risks better than males but are particularly impacted by child maltreatment. It may be that, despite introducing criminogenic risk in the lives of both males and females, strains within the family are particularly challenging for females, while females are either more protected from or comparatively better equipped to deal with strains in other domains. In this vein, Kruttschnitt (2013) proposes that the differential salience of key risk factors may reflect gendered mediation processes and highlights the potential role of emotions in accounting for gender differences in outcomes in response to similar risks and stressors. Building from strain theory explanations of gender differences in offending (Broidy and Agnew 1997), she suggests that not only might gender differences in negative emotional responses to negative life events mute the effects of anger on women's behavioral responses (Broidy 2001; Hay 2003; DeCoster and Zito 2010), but so too might girls' and women's greater tendencies toward empathy (Broidy, Cauffman et al. 2003). In other words, gender differences in emotional responses to risk exposure and negative life events likely frame behavioral responses and shape gender differences in life-course offending trajectories.

In addition to detailing exposure to (or protection from) the core biopsychosocial risk factors that characterize the lives of males and females on various offending trajectories, the developmental life-course literature needs to theorize about the mechanisms that account for gender differences in exposure to key risk factors and in the links between these risks and offending outcomes. Core to this project, we argue, is attention to four theoretical mechanisms: identity, agency, victimization, and emotions. Building from the gendered pathways literature, these four mechanisms may help explain how males and females, exposed to similar risks and negative life events, might process this exposure in ways that lead to distinct offending outcomes in the short and long term, introducing variation in the nature and longitudinal course of their offending patterns. In what follows we outline how gender conditions life-course patterns of offending and speculate how these four theoretical mechanisms might help account for these patterns.

II. Variability in Offending Patterns

A growing body of research documents marked heterogeneity in female offending patterns (Fontaine et al. 2009; Russell, Robins, and Odgers 2014; Cauffman et al. 2015). Like male offenders, female offenders differ considerably across key dimensions of offending, including age of onset, frequency, persistence, versatility, and seriousness (Fontaine et al. 2009; Block et al. 2010; Russell, Robins, and Odgers 2014; Ahonen et al. 2016). This heterogeneity is often summarized in trajectories or typologies of offending. Interestingly, research reveals considerable similarities in the number and shape of trajectories that summarize offending patterns across gender (Fontaine et al. 2009; Ferrante 2013; Russell, Robins, and Odgers 2014; Cauffman et al. 2015). While some researchers report more trajectory groups for males, many identify the same number of trajectories across gender (Russell, Robins, and Odgers 2014). Typically, this ranges between two and four trajectory groups (e.g., D'Unger, Land, and McCall 2002; Broidy, Nagin et al. 2003; Odgers et al. 2008; Blokland and van Os 2010; Andersson et al. 2012

Ferrante 2013; Ahonen et al. 2016; Loeber et al. 2017), although some studies have identified as many as five trajectory groups (e.g., Lahey et al. 2006; Cauffman et al. 2015). The number of groups tends to vary by methodological design, with more trajectories identified in studies with larger samples, longer follow-up periods, and self-reported antisocial behavior (Piquero 2008). The shapes of offending trajectories are usually similar across gender, although male trajectories are typically higher, reflecting higher frequencies of offending among males (Ferrante 2013). Similar to male offenders, the causes and correlates of offending also vary across female offending trajectories (e.g., Fontaine et al. 2009; Russell, Robins, and Odgers 2014; Cauffman et al. 2015).

We broadly group female offending patterns into the following trajectories: low-rate, persistent, adolescent-onset and adult-onset. We use these groups as a mechanism for summarizing the key findings on female offending patterns. We acknowledge that the number, gendered distribution, and the form and content of trajectories vary across studies, but these four groups provide a rough way of summarizing information on the character of male and female criminal careers and the related correlates. For each trajectory pattern we describe the general findings that characterize what we know about females whose offending best fits with aggregate group patterns and discuss how gender conditions membership and patterns within the group. Our summary of the literature identifies both uniform and discrepant findings across studies. Given the general paucity of research on female offending over the life course, we are not well positioned to resolve discrepancies, but rather point them out in the interest of spurring future research on female offending trajectories. To facilitate this, we reference the four theoretical mechanisms described above to help interpret current findings and to frame questions for future research.

A. Low-Rate Offending Trajectory

Most offenders, whether male or female, evidence offending behavior that is consistent with a trajectory characterized by short-lived, sporadic, and not very serious offending behavior (D'Unger, Land, and McCall 2002; Odgers et al. 2008; Blokland and van Os 2010; Jennings et al. 2010; Andersson et al. 2012; Ferrante 2013; Russell, Robins, and Odgers 2014). Regardless of gender, this trajectory accounts for a large portion of offenders but a relatively small proportion of offenses. For example, female low-rate desisters in the Swedish Project Metropolitan Study constituted 64 percent of female offenders but just 33 percent of female offenses (Andersson et al. 2012). While this pathway is common among both male and female offenders, a larger proportion of female offenders populate this pathway compared to males (e.g., 84.5 percent of female offenders versus 69.2 percent of male offenders; Block et al. 2010; see also D'Unger, Land, and McCall 2002; Fergusson and Horwood, 2002; Pepler et al. 2010; Ferrante 2013; Broidy et al. 2015; although see Odgers et al. 2008; Andersson et al. 2012). The overrepresentation of females following a low-rate trajectory is not surprising in light of robust findings that females perpetrate fewer crimes than males (Block et al. 2010).

Low-rate offenders, both male and female, are generally less versatile than other offenders (Blokland and van Os 2010; Andersson et al. 2012). Additionally, their offending is usually not very serious, dominated by property and traffic offenses, as opposed to violent person offenses (Blokland and van Os 2010; Andersson et al. 2012). Research suggests that, for females in this group, fraud is also a characteristic offense (Andersson et al. 2012), though this is typically not the case for low rate male offenders.

1. *Correlates and Theoretical Processes Linked to Low-Rate Offending*

In terms of the key biopsychosocial risk factors, low-rate female offenders are characterized by few risk factors and relatively normative scores on correlates of offending (Fergusson and Horwood 2002; Lahey et al. 2006; Odgers et al. 2008). Like low-rate male offenders, these female offenders usually evidence less risky individual level characteristics and environmental backgrounds than other groups of offenders (e.g., Fergusson and Horwood 2002; Lahey et al. 2006; Odgers et al. 2008; Pepler et al. 2010). When this is not the case, it is because other offender groups are exhibiting relatively low or normative levels of particular correlates and hence cannot be differentiated from low rate females (e.g., Moffitt and Caspi 2001; Lahey et al. 2006). Low-rate offenders have the most promising outcomes of all offender groups, exhibiting quite normative levels of adjustment and functioning in adulthood (e.g., Odgers et al. 2008). In many ways, low-rate offenders are indistinguishable from non-offenders, and some researchers with population data group these individuals together (e.g., Blokland and van Os 2010; Miller et al. 2010).

Overall, then, this trajectory is the least troublesome and the most common regardless of gender. It represents a population of individuals with few biopsychosocial risk factors to navigate. Notably though, a higher proportion of female offenders populate this trajectory than male offenders, suggesting that gender dynamics do play a role here. To begin, the life-course developmental literature provides evidence that females, as a group, are less exposed to the core biopsychosocial risks that drive serious offending (e.g., Moffitt et al. 2001; Jennings et al. 2010). Protection from these risks (detailed in Section IV of this volume) is an obvious and concrete explanation for female's preponderance in the low-rate offending group. But it still begs the question of why females, in similar structural and social contexts as males, experience less risk.

Building from the theoretical principles we outline above, we suggest that these principles can help us further understand what differentiates low-rate offenders from other more serious offender groups and why women especially predominate this group. First, we can surmise from the empirical literature that for this group, offending is situationally driven, opportunistic, and experimental rather than a reaction to cumulative or significant negative life experiences and stressors related to the core biopsychosocial risk factors that trigger more serious offending. We know that childhood victimization does not feature prominently in the lives of males or females populating this group. This group also likely benefits from a range of personal resources that protect against criminal involvement, including ones that generally help explain why females are less inclined toward offending than males. This would include things like self-control, strong family ties, prosocial peers, and attachment to school, all of which distinguish non-offenders from offenders in the criminological literature and also help to explain why females are less inclined toward offending. Specifically relevant to distinguishing this trajectory from others is that these individuals likely have conforming identities inconsistent with serious involvement in offending. Moreover, individuals in this group likely believe that they have control over the course of their lives and their behavior and this degree of agency helps to constrain their criminal involvement. Finally, we would propose that, relative to other more serious offender groups, individuals in this group may be both less inclined toward negative emotions (experiencing fewer of the risks and stressors that trigger these emotions) and have an extensive arsenal of legitimate coping resources to manage negative emotions. For females in particular, inclinations toward empathy may constrain their criminal involvement (Broidy, Cauffman et al. 2003). Again, we propose that these dynamics should help account for group membership in general and to explain gender differences in the distribution of males and females into this trajectory relative to other more serious ones.

B. Persistent Offending Trajectory

The persistent offending trajectory starkly contrasts with the low-rate offending trajectory, irrespective of gender. This pattern of offending is characterized by high rates of offending and continuity of antisocial behavior over time (Fontaine et al. 2009; Russell, Robins, and Odgers 2014). Persistent offenders are likely to onset at a young age (Mofitt and Caspi 2001; Lahey et al. 2006; Odgers et al. 2008; Blokland and van Os 2010; Miller et al. 2010), although this is not always the case for female offenders (Silverthorn, Frick, and Reynolds 2001; DeLisi 2002; Andersson et al. 2012). These offenders are usually more versatile than other groups of offenders (e.g., Kratzer and Hodgins 1999; Mazerolle et al. 2000; Blokland and van Os 2010; Ahonen et al. 2016) and are more likely to perpetrate serious and violent offenses (e.g., Kratzer and Hodgins 1999; Simpson, Yahner, and Dugan 2008; Block at al. 2010; Andersson et al. 2012) and persist for longer durations (e.g., Block at al. 2010). Persistent offenders also display more heterotypic and homotypic continuity over the life course than other offenders (e.g., Odgers et al. 2008; Bergman and Andershed 2009; Estrada and Nilsson 2012) and, compared with other offenders, have the least favorable outcomes in adulthood (e.g., Odgers et al. 2008; Bergman and Andershed 2009; Blokland and van Os 2010; Xie, Drabick, and Chen 2011; Estrada and Nilsson 2012).

In general, females whose offending reflects a high-rate, persistent pattern of offending are rare (Fontaine et al. 2009; Russell, Robins, and Odgers 2014; Joliffe et al. 2017). In fact, there is some debate about whether such a pathway even exists for females (see Goldweber, Broidy, and Cauffman 2009; D'Unger, Land, and McCall 2002; Pepler et al. 2010). After reviewing the extant literature, Fontaine et al. (2009) concluded that approximately 1 to 2 percent of females exhibit a persistent (or early-onset chronic) pattern of antisocial behavior in community samples (i.e., population-based or birth cohorts). More recently, Russell, Robins, and Odgers's (2014) review of 47 trajectory studies identified persistent (or early-onset chronic) patterns of antisocial behavior in at least 1 percent of females in nearly 80 percent of studies. However, given the rarity of persistent female offenders, some studies do not find any females whose offending conforms to this pattern (e.g., Pepler et al. 2010; Ferrante 2013). In fact, the prevalence of persistent offending differs widely according to the sample source (high risk versus population samples), definitions of antisocial behavior (official records versus self-reports, as well as offending versus delinquency or conduct problems), and the method for identifying persistent trajectories (gender-specific versus full-sample trajectory analyses, or cut-points using age, seriousness, or continuity of antisocial behavior) (for review, see Goldweber, Broidy, and Cauffman 2009; Russell, Robins, and Odgers 2014). Nevertheless, there is growing consensus that a small group of persistent female offenders exist that, like their male counterparts, account for a disproportionate amount of crime (e.g., Moffitt and Caspi 2001; Fergusson and Horwood 2002; Lahey et al. 2006; Odgers et al. 2008; Block et al. 2010; Broidy et al. 2015; Joliffe et al. 2017). In the Second Philadelphia Birth Cohort, 0.5 percent of females classified as chronic offenders perpetrated 23 percent of all female offenses (Cohen, Piquero, and Jennings 2010). Similarly, persisters in the Stockholm Birth Cohort Study constituted just 1.3 percent of all females but accounted for 45 percent of all registered female youth crimes and 54 percent of all registered female adult crimes (Estrada and Nilsson 2012).

Clearly there are key similarities in the nature of persistent offending across gender: frequent offending, continuity across the life course, more versatility, greater seriousness and low prevalence (Mazerolle et al. 2000; Russell, Robins, and Odgers 2014). However, there are also important gender differences (Goldweber, Broidy, and Cauffman 2009). Most notably, the prevalence of persistent trajectories differs markedly across gender. Females are far less likely to follow a persistent trajectory than males (e.g., Kratzer and Hodgins 1999; Moffitt and Caspi 2001; Fergusson and Horwood 2002; Soothill, Ackerley, and Francis 2003; Lahey et al. 2006; Bergman and Andershed 2009; Block et al. 2010; Miller et al. 2010; Andersson et al. 2012). This finding is reasonably robust across samples, methodologies, and countries, and DeLisi and Piquero (2011) report the gender ratios across several studies as between 9:1 and 12:1 (male:female) for "career offenders." Cauffman et al. (2017) find this to be the case even when they focus their analysis exclusively on violent male and female offenders. Among violent offenders they find 25 percent of females persist compared to 46 percent of males.

Another important gender difference relates to age of onset. The link between an early onset of offending and persistence is both strong and consistent for males (Kruttschnitt 2013; Russell, Robins, and Odgers 2014). By contrast, the evidence is mixed as to whether persistent female offenders onset early as well as whether an early onset predicts persistence among female offenders (Kruttschnitt 2013; Russell, Robins, and Odgers 2014). While a number of studies identify persistent females who onset early (Mofitt and Caspi 2001; White and Piquero 2004; Lahey et al. 2006; Odgers et al. 2008; Blokland and van Os 2010; Miller et al. 2010), other research documents persistent females who do not onset until adolescence and in some cases late adolescence or even adulthood (Silverthorn and Frick 1999; Silverthorn, Frick, and Reynolds 2001; DeLisi 2002; Andersson et al. 2012). As Silverthorn and Frick (1999) point out, this may be related to early constraints on female behavior that endure through early adolescence, limiting opportunities for early onset, even among females with similar risk profiles as early-onset males. Alternatively, females may experience unique risks for persistence in adolescence and early adulthood, including exposure to physical and sexual victimization, that might trigger a delayed-onset persistent pathway. Salisbury and VanVoorhis (2009) find that depression/anxiety, low-self efficacy, and substance abuse all figure prominently in women's recidivism. These outcomes are linked to early victimization, but also to dysfunctional adult relationships, low educational attainment, employment and financial challenges, and weak family supports later in life.

There are also differences in the rate and nature of offending across male and female persistent offenders. Male persistent offenders offend at much higher rates than female persistent offenders (e.g., Fergusson and Horwood, 2002; Bergman and Andershed 2009; Cohen, Piquero, and Jennings 2010; Jennings et al. 2010; Andersson et al. 2012). While both male and female persistent offenders are versatile, violence may be less characteristic of female persistent offenders (DeLisi 2002; Goldweber, Broidy, and Cauffman 2009; Block et al. 2010). This is not surprising, given that females generally perpetrate far less violence than males (Mazerolle et al. 2000; DeLisi 2002; Broidy, Nagin et al. 2003; Odgers et al. 2007; Fitzgerald et al. 2012). However, Odgers et al. (2008) reported that, although few life-course–persistent females had official convictions for violence in adulthood, 75 percent self-reported perpetrating violence. At a minimum, we know that persistent female offenders perpetrate higher rates of violence than other female offenders. Persistent male and female offenders may also differ on several specific offense types. For instance, DeLisi (2002) reported that, although chronic male and female offenders were similarly versatile, males were more likely to perpetrate rape, robbery, aggravated assault, burglary, weapons offenses, car theft, disorderly conduct, and vagrancy. In contrast, females were more likely than males to perpetrate forgery, theft, and prostitution. Given these gender differences in the nature of persistent offending, it seems likely that the correlates might also evidence some differences across gender.

1. Correlates and Theoretical Processes Linked to Persistent Offending

Like their male counterparts, persistent female offenders have the most problematic risk profiles of all female offenders, exhibiting risks across multiple domains that accumulate over the life course (Lahey et al. 2006; Gunnison and McCartan 2007; Russell, Robins, and Odgers 2014). Both male and female offenders on this trajectory have high levels of individual vulnerability, including lower intellectual ability and academic competence, hyperactivity, and neuropsychological deficits or neurological injuries (Kratzer and Hodgins 1999; Fergusson and Horwood 2002; Leve and Chamberlain 2004; White and Piquero 2004; Lahey et al. 2006; Gunnison and McCartan 2007; Odgers et al. 2008; Bergman and Andershed 2009; Xie, Drabick, and Chen 2011; Russell, Robins, and Odgers 2014). Across gender, persistent offenders have problematic childhoods, characterized by social disadvantage (low social class, low socioeconomic status), parents who abused substances or have mental health issues, criminal parents, histories of child maltreatment or intervention by child services, family conflict, broken or unstable families, young mothers, poor parental monitoring and inconsistent or coercive discipline, difficulties in school, and exposure to violence (Silverthorn, Frick, and Reynolds 2001; Fergusson and Horwood 2002; Leve and Chamberlain 2004; White and Piquero 2004; Lahey et al. 2006; Gunnison and McCartan 2007; Odgers et al. 2008; van de Rakt, Nieuwbeerta, and de Graaf 2008; Bergman and Andershed 2009; Estrada and Nilsson 2012; Jennings et al. 2010; Xie, Drabick, and Chen 2011; Andersson, Levander, and Torstensson Levander 2013). Males and females on this trajectory are also likely to have delinquent peers, abuse substances, and have more favorable attitudes toward antisocial behavior (Gunnison and McCartan 2007; Odgers et al. 2008; Bergman and Andershed 2009; Jennings et al. 2010). Despite remarkable similarities across gender, some risk factors may be unique to females, such as precocious romantic relationships and early pubertal onset (Caspi et al. 1993; Moffitt et al. 2001; Leve and Chamberlain 2004; Carbone-Lopez and Miller 2012). Others, like internalizing problems, may be evident across males and females but be more salient for females (Belknap and Holsinger 2006; Pepler et al. 2010). However, too few longitudinal studies have examined these factors across gender and trajectory groups to draw conclusions.

The research suggests that there are more similarities than differences in the formative experiences of male and female persistent offenders. This begs the question of why there is such a disparity in the proportion of persistent offending across gender and why a handful of females are particularly vulnerable to early risk factors. Both Moffitt (1993) and Silverthorn and Frick (1999) suggest that females may be differentially influenced by early risk exposure than males. For Moffitt, this means they are less likely to become chronic offenders, and for Silverthorn and Frick it means their chronic offending is delayed. However, we know from the literature that some females do evidence both early onset and persistence. We propose that the theoretical processes outlined in the gendered pathways literature are relevant to understanding early onset and persistence among females when it does occur and for explaining its relatively low prevalence compared to males.

There is much evidence to suggest that early and persistent victimization is central to the onset of persistent offending among females in particular (Gaarder and Belknap 2002; McCabe et al. 2004; Belknap and Holsinger 2006; Odgers et al. 2007; Simpson, Yahner, and Dugan 2008; van der Put et al. 2014; Cauffman et al. 2015; Simpson et al. 2016). These victimization experiences, often lead to identities characterized by low self-esteem and limited social competence (Kim and Cicchetti 2004; 2006) and a reduced sense of agency, often manifest in low self-efficacy and learned helplessness, characteristics that seem to endure into adulthood (Gross and Keller, 1992). Salisbury and VanVoorhis (2009) show that early victimization is linked to recidivism through its effects on self-efficacy. For females, it may be this combination of low self-efficacy and learned helplessness that partly explains why they are more vulnerable than other similarly situated females to the biopsychosocial risk factors that characterize persistent offending. Moreover, one of the consequences of childhood maltreatment is antisocial behavior (Belknap and Holsinger 2006; Cernkovich, Lanctot, and Giordano 2008; van der Put et al. 2014), which can lead to an entrenched antisocial identity that is difficult to shed, regardless of intentions. This is because identity transformation, in part, involves a social negotiation. Amidst a backdrop of chronic antisocial behavior, primary and secondary social networks may be leary of change talk, constraining social support for such change. Maltreatment also has emotional consequences. It increases anger and related externalizing behaviors among males and females and as a result complicates transitions to adolescence by interfering with social development and peer attachment (Trickett et al. 2011). Moreover, depression is characteristic of females exposed to early maltreatment and abuse (Belknap and Holsinger 2006; Kim and Cichetti 2006; Fitzgerald et al. 2012), which might also exaggerate the effect of risk exposure by further reducing females' resilience to the risks that characterize offenders on this trajectory. Indeed, Cauffman et al. (2015) find that females who exhibit persistent offending have notably more mental health problems than other female offenders and have more adversarial interpersonal relationships as well. In short, we suggest that, particularly for females, child maltreatment enhances vulnerability to core biopsychosocial risk factors by reducing self-esteem, limiting perceived agency, and enhancing emotions that facilitate antisocial behavior.

Despite evidence of long-term persistence for males and females on this trajectory, we actually have limited data detailing adult outcomes for females, and what we do have suggests that despite the criminogenic processes outlined above, females on this trajectory may be more likely to desist from offending than males (e.g., Giordano 2010). This is despite the fact that, like their male counterparts, this group of females has a hard time accessing the adult social institutions (e.g., quality marriages and stable jobs) that facilitate desistance (Giordano, Cernkovich, and Rudolph 2002; Broidy and Cauffman 2017). Though, Kreager, Matsueda, and Erosheva (2011) do show that motherhood may be an important path out of offending for this group. While some might find motherhood or other "hooks for change" that facilitate desistance via cognitive shifts and reformulated identities, others may desist from offending but not antisocial behavior more broadly. Hagan and Foster (2003), for instance, suggest that early disadvantage, family stress, and adolescent delinquency have significant emotional consequences for females that lead to adult depression. A focus on offending outcomes overlooks other antisocial outcomes that may endure for this group—particularly depression and other mental health outcomes, substance abuse, and exposure to intimate partner violence and other forms of victimization as well as perpetration of child maltreatment (Belknap and Holsinger 2006; Gunnison and McCartan 2007; Odgers et al. 2008), all of which would also be linked to the biopsychosocial risk factors that characterize their childhood and adolescent environments as well as the theoretical processes that we argue link these risk factors to persistent offending outcomes for females. As we amass more data following female offenders into adulthood, it will be important to assess gender differences in the adult lives of persistent offenders. For females in particular, we need to understand the collateral consequences of early-onset serious offending, especially for diverse adult outcomes such as mental health problems, abuse and victimization, and child maltreatment perpetration.

C. Adolescent-Onset Offending Trajectory

Researchers repeatedly identify a group of female offenders who onset in adolescence (Russell, Robins, and Odgers 2014). When these offenders are followed into adulthood, their offending is generally concentrated in adolescence and subsides in late adolescence or early adulthood (Kratzer and Hodgins 1999; Moffitt et al. 2001; D'Unger, Land, and McCall 2002; Fergusson and Horwood 2002; White and Piquero 2004; Odgers et al. 2008; Blokland and van Os 2010; Estrada and Nilsson 2012; Ferrrante 2013). Like adolescent-onset males, adolescent-onset females' offending profiles fall somewhat in between those of low-rate and persistent offenders. These offenders perpetrate fewer, less serious, and less violent offenses than chronic offenders and exhibit less versatility (Kratzer and Hodgins 1999; Mazerolle et al. 2000; Blokland and van Os 2010; Francis, Liu, and Soothill 2012). At the same time, they have higher rates of offending than low-rate offenders (D'Unger, Land, and McCall 2002; Fergusson and Horwood 2002; Lahey et al. 2006; Odgers et al. 2008; Blokland and van Os 2010; Miller et al. 2010; Xie, Drabick, and Chen 2011; Zheng and Cleveland 2013). These offenders primarily perpetrate minor property offenses (predominantly theft and shoplifting) (Blokland and van Os 2010; Francis, Liu, and Soothill 2012). Drug and status offenses are also common (Moffitt et al. 2001; Blokland and van Os 2010; Thompson et al. 2014).

Across gender, adult outcomes are much more favorable for adolescent-onset offenders than persistent offenders (Moffitt and Caspi 2001; Odgers et al. 2008; Bergman and Andershed 2009; Blokland and van Os 2010; Xie, Drabick, and Chen 2011; Estrada and Nilsson 2012). However, these offenders may still experience adjustment problems in adulthood (Moffitt and Caspi 2001; Bergman and Andershed 2009; Miller et al. 2010; Xie, Drabick, and Chen 2011; Estrada and Nilsson 2012). Females may be particularly susceptible to problems with substance abuse and economic stability and in some cases relationship problems/instability (Moffitt et al. 2001; Odgers et al. 2008; Bergman and Andershed 2009; Blokland and van Os 2010; Estrada and Nilsson 2012). Some of these adjustment problems may be associated with "snares" encountered as a result of antisocial behavior in adolescence such as early pregnancy (Odgers et al. 2008; Xie, Drabick, and Chen 2011) or substance abuse problems (Estrada and Nilsson 2012).

The adolescent-onset trajectory is much more prevalent than the persistent trajectory for both males and females, but usually far less frequent than the low-rate trajectory (e.g., Odgers et al. 2008 reported 17.4 percent adolescent-onset females compared with 55.1 percent low and 7.4 percent persistent females; also see Fergusson and Horwood 2002; Lahey et al. 2006; Blokland and van Os 2010). The gender disparity is significantly smaller among adolescent-onset offenders (e.g., 1.5:1 in Moffitt et al. 2001; 1.1:1 in Lahey et al. 2006; see also Bergman and Andershed 2009; Miller et al. 2010) compared to other offending groups. However, males are often still overrepresented in this trajectory, particularly in studies utilizing official records (e.g., 4:1 in Estrada and Nilsson 2012; see also Broidy et al. 2015). The overall shape/pattern of adolescent-onset trajectories is usually fairly similar across gender (e.g., White and Piquero 2004; Lahey et al. 2006; Odgers et al. 2008; Bergman and Andershed 2009). However, in some studies male adolescent-onset offenders exhibit higher rates of offending than their female counterparts (e.g., Kratzer and Hodgins 1999; D'Unger, Land, and McCall 2002; Ferrante 2013).

1. *Correlates and Theoretical Processes Linked to Adolescent-Onset Offending*

Researchers identify few consistent gender differences in the correlates of adolescent-onset offending (Kratzer and Hodgins 1999; Moffitt and Caspi 2001; Fergusson and Horwood 2002; White and Piquero 2004; Lahey et al. 2006; Moffitt 2006; Odgers et al. 2008; Xie, Drabick, and Chen 2011; Ferrante 2013; Zheng and Cleveland 2013; Russell, Robins, and Odgers 2014). As is the case with males, findings are mixed as to whether adolescent-onset females have similarly low-risk childhoods and individual vulnerabilities as low-rate or non-offenders (Moffitt and Caspi 2001; Lahey et al. 2006; Xie, Drabick, and Chen 2011), whether they exhibit an intermediate level of risk in these domains (Kratzer and Hodgins 1999; Bergman and Andershed 2009; Estrada and Nilsson 2010; Zheng and Cleveland 2013) or whether this varies depending on the correlate in question (Fergusson and Horwood 2002; Odgers et al. 2008; Bergman and Andershed 2009). For example, adolescent-onset females from the Dunedin study were comparable to low-rate offenders on 9 of 12 childhood risk factors (e.g., socioeconomic status, familial conflict and discipline, parental convictions) but had significantly higher rates of maltreatment and were more likely to have mothers with lower IQs and poorer mental health (Odgers et al. 2008). It is possible that divergent results reflect different etiologies of different types of adolescent-onset offenders (Fergusson and Horwood 2002; Fontaine et al. 2009; Xie, Drabick, and Chen 2011; Zheng and Cleveland 2013). Indeed, several studies identify different types or levels of adolescent onset across gender (e.g., Fergusson and Horwood 2002; Zheng and Cleveland 2013; Broidy et al. 2015). Of course, divergent results may otherwise reflect different methodologies and correlates across studies. Regardless, across gender and across studies, adolescent-onset offenders experience less risk exposure in childhood and exhibit fewer individual-level vulnerabilities than persistent offenders (Moffitt et al. 2001; Fergusson and Horwood 2002; McCabe et al. 2004; Lahey et al. 2006; Odgers et al. 2008; Bergman and Andershed 2009; Estrada and Nilsson 2012).

Most studies suggest that the risks characterizing this group of offenders are, instead, localized in adolescence, for example, delinquent peers, low parental monitoring or family support, and substance use/abuse (Moffitt and Caspi 2001; Odgers et al. 2008; Bergman and Andershed 2009; Pepler et al. 2010; Estrada and Nilsson 2012; Zheng and Cleveland 2013). Some adolescent factors may be unique to females too, such as early menarche (Caspi et al. 1993; Moffitt et al. 2001) and, relatedly, teen dating (Caspi et al. 1993; Haynie et al. 2005), or more salient for females such as internalizing problems (Pepler et al. 2010). The clustering of risk factors in the adolescent period is consistent with Moffitt's (1994) theory. Agnew (2003) also talks about the specific dynamics of adolescence and how they drive adolescent offending. Both highlight the transitional nature of adolescence and the complexity of navigating the growing need for independence with the enduring need for nurturance and support from parents and other adults. Many of the related risks are associated with the adolescent peer context. Exposure to larger, more diverse peer networks that include peers who model and reinforce antisocial behavior is particularly relevant. These risks are more pervasive for males and are activated for females when they navigate mixed sex social environments (Caspi et al. 1993) and via adolescent dating, which often introduces them to delinquency through their romantic partners (Haynie et al. 2005; Rebellon and Manasse 2006).

These uniquely adolescent risks are easy to interpret within the theoretical lens we apply here. To begin, as Moffitt, Agnew, and others point out, adolescence is a period of identity transformation. For both males and females, delinquency is often part of the boundary testing that accompanies the development of an independent identity in adolescence (Moffitt 1994; Agnew, 2003). Moreover, as they exert this new independent self, adolescents are expected to take responsibility for their behavior and this level of agency can introduce strain, since adolescents often lack the personal and social resources to effectively navigate these new expectations (Agnew 2003). Additionally, navigating new social spaces and new expectations associated with adolescence can trigger a range of negative emotions that adolescents are not well equipped to handle (Agnew 2003). These negative emotions reflect the broadly labile nature of adolescent emotions but are also a reaction to peer victimization, like bullying and harassment that often occurs in adolescent networks (Lahey et al. 2006). Indeed, part of adolescent development is learning to navigate these new situations and emotions. Given the central role of peer networks, peer strains, and emotional processing to adolescent-onset offending, and the primacy females place on social relations as well as the salience of social networks to females' identities, it makes sense that females might cope with the challenges of adolescence in antisocial ways. As adolescents mature, not only do the strains that trigger their offending start to wane, but they gain more prosocial coping skills and they are more cognizant of and responsive to the negative consequences of antisocial behavior, which should help account for desistance among this group (Moffitt 1993; Agnew 2003). So too should their ability to access the key social institutions that are not readily open to persistent offenders.

Unfortunately, few researchers have documented adolescent-onset females' pathways out of offending. While Moffitt hypothesizes that cognitive and emotional maturity reduce the attraction of risky behavior in the transition to adulthood (Moffitt 1993), there are no studies specifically examining these shifts as central to desistance among females who act out in adolescence. In fact, few studies follow representative samples of female offenders into adulthood. There is evidence that desistance among adolescent-onset females coincides with the attainment of adult roles such as marriage and motherhood (Blokland and van Os 2010; Kreager, Matsueda, and Erosheva 2011). These new identities are inconsistent with antisocial behavior, further reinforcing adult desistance. Since adolescent-onset offenders have better prospects in adulthood than persistent offenders (e.g., Odgers et al. 2008; Blokland and van Os 2010; Estrada and Nilsson 2012), and generally less risky backgrounds (e.g., Fergusson and Horwood 2002; Odgers et al. 2008; Bergman and Andershed 2009), these women may be better equipped to navigate the transition into adulthood. For example, these females may have fewer barriers to marrying non-offenders than persistent female offenders and may have more resources to support their transition into parenthood. Consequently, the traditional mechanisms for desistance may be operant for these offenders. These differences in the role and impact of adult transitions on adolescent-onset and persistent offenders may explain inconsistent findings about the role of marriage and motherhood on females' desistance.

D. Adult-Onset Offending Trajectory

In recent years, adult-onset offending has been a subject of criminological debate. Many researchers argue that adult-onset offending is extremely rare or even non-existent and is primarily an artifact of methodological design (e.g., underreporting of earlier offenses in official records or defining adulthood too broadly; Moffitt 2006). However, a growing body of research documents non-trivial numbers of offenders who onset in adulthood. This offending pattern emerges in studies using official data as well as studies using self-report data (Simpson, Yahner, and Dugan 2008; Block et al. 2010; Thompson et al. 2014; Simpson et al. 2016). Despite increasing interest in adult-onset offending, we still know very little about the nature of adult-onset offending, including how this pattern of offending differs across gender.

A major challenge to the examination of adult-onset offending among females is that few longitudinal studies follow female offenders beyond adolescence or young adulthood (Fontaine et al. 2009). However, this is changing, particularly as cohorts age (Russell, Robins, and Odgers 2014). While adult-onset trajectories are identified among both males and females, evidence is accumulating that female offenders are more likely to have an adult onset than male offenders (e.g., DeLisi 2002; Soothill, Ackerley, and Francis 2003; Bergman and Andershed 2009; Block et al. 2010; Andersson et al. 2012; Estrada and Nilsson 2012; Beckley et al. 2016). Indeed, an adult-onset trajectory is only evident for females in the Swedish Project Metropolitan study (Andersson et al. 2012). Nonetheless, an opposing body of research reports comparable or even higher rates of adult-onset offending in males (e.g., Gomez-Smith and Piquero 2005; Thompson et al. 2014).

Importantly, many female adult-onset offenders do not initiate offending before their thirties (DeLisi 2002; Simpson, Yahner, and Dugan 2008; Block et al. 2010; Simpson et al. 2016). Using official records, the Criminal Career and Life-Course Study finds that close to 80 percent of male offenders onset by 30 years of age, yet only around 55 percent of women had onset by this age (Block et al. 2010). In the same sample, Blokland and van Os (2010) reported that females who followed an adult-onset trajectory displayed comparatively high rates of convictions until 60 years of age. In a different sample, 54 percent of incarcerated females self-reported that they onset in adulthood, most of them onsetting after 30 years of age (Simpson, Yahner, and Dugan 2008). Therefore, studies that are truncated at or before 30 years of age, as is the case with most longitudinal samples that include females, potentially miss a substantial number of female offenders and a non-trivial proportion of female offenses.

It is difficult to describe the typical pattern of female adult-onset offending given the paucity of research in this area and because the characteristics of this trajectory vary across samples and length of follow-up. Using official convictions for offenders between 12 and 72 years of age from the Netherlands, female adult-onset offenders averaged fewer convictions than chronic offenders (Blokland and van Os 2010). However, adult-onset females averaged more convictions than offenders who fit the sporadic (low-rate) group, and similar, yet somewhat more, convictions than emerging adulthood desisters (adolescent-limited offenders). Similar patterns have been identified in studies that followed women to 30 and 35 years of age, even though these adult-onset offenders had truncated windows to offend (Kratzer and Hodgins 1999; Bergman and Andershed 2009; Andersson et al. 2012). It is possible that longer follow-up periods may have identified more adult-onset offenders as well as more persistent patterns of adult-onset offending. In fact, adult-onset offenders are common among both males and females in DeLisi's (2002) sample of chronic offenders (30+ offenses). In addition, some of the high-level chronic offenders in Andersson et al.'s (2012) sample did not onset until adulthood. Importantly, there may be variability in the chronicity of offending that onsets in adulthood, as is the case with early-onset offenders (Soothill, Ackerley, and Francis 2003; Thompson et al. 2014). This may be particularly true of females, some of whom may evidence sporadic, situational offending in adulthood while others may onset in adulthood but develop an entrenched pattern of offending that becomes chronic.

The findings regarding diversity and crime types among adult-onset female offenders is limited and inconsistent. However, property crimes dominate female adult-onset offending across studies (DeLisi 2002; Bergman and Andershed 2009; Blokland and Van Os 2010; Andersson et al. 2012; Francis, Liu, and Soothill 2012), as is the case for most types of female offenders, with fraud being particularly common (Andersson et al. 2012). Also like other female offenders, violence is uncommon among adult-onset offenders (Blokland and van Os 2010; Andersson et al. 2012), though at times may be more frequent than it is among adolescent-onset offenders (Kratzer and Hodgins 1999). Clearly, there is a need for more research to examine the nature and patterns of female adult-onset offending, including how this differs to male adult-onset offending.

1. *Correlates and Theoretical Processes Linked to Adult-Onset Offending*

We know very little about the correlates of adult-onset offending for either gender, let alone if or how these factors differ across males and females. This is in large part because researchers have only recently begun to identify and study adult-onset offending. Indeed, an onset of offending in adulthood challenges core assumptions of most developmental and life-course frameworks for describing criminal onset trajectories (e.g., Moffitt 2006). Adding further complexity to this issue is that the correlates of adult-onset offending differ across studies. In addition, the few studies that do examine this phenomenon often do not disaggregate across gender or have used male-only samples. However, evidence of gender differences in risk for adult-onset offending suggests that gendered causal factors are likely relevant. In this section we summarize the limited research that has examined the correlates of female adult-onset offending but recognize that much more research is necessary to really understand this trajectory. We also suggest that, based on the evidence to date, the same theoretical mechanisms implicated in the other three trajectories are likely at play for women who evidence an adult-onset offending pattern.

The limited research that has examined correlates of female adult-onset offending has produced three contrasting stories on the importance of risk factors in childhood and adolescence. Adult-onset offenders in the Swedish Project Metropolitan data have notably risky backgrounds akin to those of persistent offenders (e.g., parental criminality, broken families, child welfare intervention, low socioeconomic status, lower academic performance, psychiatric problems, and drug use; Andersson et al. 2013). In stark contrast, the adult-onset females in Bergman and Andershed's (2009) study are analogous to non-offenders across most adolescent risk factors, including socioeconomic status, low rates of harsh parenting and family conflict, and low rates of adolescent substance use. However, as is the case in Andersson, Levander, and Torstensson Levander (2013), adult-onset females are much more likely to come from broken families and are comparable to early-onset offenders in this regard. A third story emerges from the Stockholm Birth Cohort (Kratzer and Hodgins 1999; Estrada and Nilsson 2010) and Simpson, Yahner, and Dugan's (2008) prison sample. In these cohorts, adult-onset females have intermediate levels of risk that resemble adolescent-onset offenders. More recent work by Simpson et al. (2016) suggests that these inconsistencies may reflect diversity among the adult-onset group, with those who onset in early adulthood exhibiting more extensive risk histories than those who onset later in adulthood.

The question that arises from studies that report high or intermediate levels of childhood risk is why these adult-onset offenders did not onset earlier. While we cannot answer this question with the available data, it is possible that protective factors in childhood and adolescence insulated these individuals from offending (e.g., Silverthorn and Frick 1999; Thornberry and Krohn 2005; Zara and Farrington 2009). Of particular import is attachment to family, especially for girls. Parents tend to restrict their daughters' autonomy more strictly than their sons', especially in adolescence (Svensson 2003). This protects girls from deviant peer influences and reduces their antisocial involvement throughout adolescence (Svensson 2003). However, come adulthood, females may be less equipped to handle new expectations of independence. Central to the transition to adulthood is establishing independence from one's parents and taking responsibility for one's own actions (Arnett, 2001), making identity and agency central to successful transitions to adulthood (Schwartz, Côté, and Arnett 2005). This new independent identity and expectations of personal agency as well as the related role transitions associated with adult institutions like marriage, parenthood, and employment might be difficult for some to acquire or manage, particularly if they come into adulthood with low self-esteem and no clear, goal-driven sense of purpose (Schwartz, Côté, and Arnett 2005). Schwartz and colleagues (2005) link this to aimlessness and anomie, which likely generates criminogenic emotions. Without the parental supervision and support that is particularly influential for females, these new demands and emotions might trigger antisocial responses that manifest as adult-onset offending. This may be particularly the case among those who struggle to enact adult roles and thereby have no clear avenues for securing independence, limiting their sense of personal agency and complicating the acquisition of key markers of adult status.

This is consistent with the limited literature to date. Despite varied findings for childhood and adolescent factors, all studies on female adult-onset offending identify problems/risks in adulthood. Andersson and colleagues (2013) and Bergman and Andershed (2009) both report the salience of mental health problems among adult-onset offenders in young adulthood. Specifically, Andersson and colleagues (2013) reported that 42.7 percent of adult-onset offenders were admitted for psychiatric treatment between 16 and 30 years of age (Andersson et al. 2013), and Bergman and Andershed (2009) reported that 21.2 percent were registered for psychiatric treatment between 20 and 24 years of age. Substance abuse problems have also been identified among adult-onset offenders during young adulthood (Bergman and Andershed 2009; Estrada and Nilsson 2010; Andersson et al. 2013). These mental health and substance use problems are consistent with the profiles of women who struggle to cope with the range of emotional challenges the transition to adulthood introduces. In addition, Simpson, Yahner, and Dugan (2008) identified high rates of violent victimization in adulthood among adult-onset females that far exceeded the victimization experienced by early-onset and adolescent-onset females. Interestingly, these adult-onset offenders experienced significantly less childhood physical and sexual abuse than early-onset females. Therefore, the timing of violent victimization may be important for understanding when female offenders onset. There is also evidence of less successful attainment of traditional adult roles among adult-onset females than non-offenders or low-rate offenders, for example, less stable relationships (e.g., lower rates of marriage and higher rates of divorce at age 30 or 48 years of age; Andersson et al. 2013; Bergman and Andershed 2009; Estrada and Nilsson 2010), higher rates of unemployment or lower-paying jobs (e.g., at age 30 or 48 years of age; Andersson et al. 2013; Bergman and Andershed 2009; Estrada and Nilsson 2010), and lower educational attainment (at 48 years of age; Bergman and Andershed 2009). Marriage may also introduce risks for adult-onset offenders (Simpson, Yahner, and Dugan 2008; Blokland and van Os 2010). For example, marriage and motherhood coincided with desistance for adolescent-onset females but initiation for adult-onset females in the Criminal Career and Life-Course Study (Blokland and van Os 2010).

Together, the limited research on female adult-onset offenders suggests that these offenders may encounter difficulties in the transition to adulthood as well as later in adulthood. There is reason to believe that some of these difficulties may be particularly acute for females. Whether these are causes or consequences of adult-onset offending, however, is still unclear. We suspect a recursive model would best represent the process, where difficulties during the transition to adulthood trigger initial antisocial coping responses. For some, this behavior subsides as they come to understand and adapt to the demands of adulthood. For others, initial adult offending may lead to further difficulties navigating adulthood and a more entrenched adult offending pattern. There is an obvious need for more research on both childhood and adulthood factors associated with adult-onset offending and the mechanisms that explain these linkages.

III. CONCLUSION

Clearly we know more about the basic contours of female offending over the life course and how these overlap with and diverge from those evident in male samples than we do about the mechanisms that drive these patterns. In broad brush, we can summarize life-course patterns of male and female offending with reference to similar trajectory groups, though the distribution of males and females into these groups and the levels and types of behaviors that characterize their offending patterns show some variation across gender. Many of the same biopsychosocial risks and protections correlated with male offending patterns are also correlated with female offending patterns, though there is some evidence that the salience of various correlates vary by gender. And we suspect that there are some gender-specific processes that underpin these differences. Building from the gendered pathways literature, we suggest that protection from or exposure to victimization as well as its timing, nature, and extent play a particularly salient role in women's offending. These experiences often introduce developmental challenges by complicating the age-graded autonomy and identity processes associated with crucial life-course transitions. We argue that when females encounter developmental challenges, their antisocial responses are tightly linked to their emotional resources. In addition to anger, which is central to male offending (Broidy and Agnew 1997; Broidy 2001), a range of other emotions such as depression, anxiety, fear, and guilt frame their responses, prompting not just offending but other antisocial outcomes as well (Broidy 2001; Jang 2007; DeCoster and Zito 2010). These include mental health problems often associated with such outcomes as suicidal ideation, substance abuse, self-harm, and disordered eating, along with relational problems often manifesting in child maltreatment as well as emotional and physical aggression from and toward partners.

Future research should continue to assess life-course patterns of offending in female samples, especially as they mature into adulthood. We hope, however, that this work also begins to more carefully examine similarities and differences in these patterns across males and females. Even more important, we encourage developmental and life-course criminologists to theorize about the mechanisms that account for both gender-invariant and gender-specific processes evident in samples of males and females followed over time. We offer some suggestions for the theoretical processes that might help explain women's life-course offending patterns and how they differ from men's. However, these need testing, and other mechanisms are likely operant as well. Our aim here was not to offer a definitive theoretical account, but to spur interest in the theoretical project and encourage researchers to collect data that can assess not only patterns and correlates of life-course offending but also the theoretical mechanisms that account for them across both males and females.

References

Agnew, Robert. 2003. "An Integrated Theory of the Adolescent Peak in Offending." *Youth & Society* 34: 263–299.

Ahonen, Lia, Wesley G. Jennings, Rolf Loeber, and David P. Farrington. 2016. "The Relationship Between Developmental Trajectories of Girls' Offending and Police Charges: Results from the Pittsburgh Girls Study." *Journal of Developmental and Life-Course Criminology* 2: 262–274.

Andersson, Frida, Sten Levander, Robert Svensson, and Marie Torstensson Levander. 2012. "Sex Differences in Offending Trajectories in a Swedish Cohort." *Criminal Behaviour and Mental Health* 22: 108–121.

Andersson, Frida., Sten Levander, and Marie Torstensson Levander. 2013. "A Life-Course Perspective on Girls' Criminality." In *Girls at Risk Swedish Longitudinal Research on Adjustment*, edited by Anna-Karin Andershed, 119–137. New York: Springer.

Arnett, Jeffrey Jensen. 2001. "Conceptions of the Transition to Adulthood: Perspectives from Adolescence Through Midlife." *Journal of Adult Development* 8: 133–143.

Beckley, Amber, L., Avshalom Caspi, Honalee Harrington, Renate M. Houts, Tara R. McGee, Nick Morgan, Felix Schroeder, et al. 2016. "Adult-Onset Offenders: Is a Tailored Theory Warranted?" *Journal of Criminal Justice* 46: 64–81.

Belknap, Joanne, and Kristi Holsinger. 2006. "The Gendered Nature of Risk Factors for Delinquency." *Feminist Criminology* 1: 48–71.

Bergman, Lars R, and Anna-Karin Andershed. 2009. "Predictors and Outcomes of Persistent or Age-Limited Registered Criminal Behavior: A 30-Year Longitudinal Study of a Swedish Urban Population." *Aggressive Behavior* 35: 164–178.

Block, Carolyn. R., Arjan A. J. Blokland, Cornelia van der Werff, Rianne van Os, and Paul Nieuwbeerta. 2010. "Long-Term Patterns of Offending in Women." *Feminist Criminology* 5: 73–107.

Blokland, Arjan A. J., and Rianne van Os. 2010. "Life Span Offending Trajectories of Convicted Dutch Women." *International Criminal Justice Review* 20: 169–187.

Bloom, Barbara. 1996. *Triple Jeopardy: Race, Class and Gender as Factors in Women's Imprisonment*. Riverside: University of California.

Broidy, Lisa M. 2001. "A Test of General Strain Theory." *Criminology* 39: 9–36.

Broidy, Lisa M., and Robert Agnew. 1997." Gender and Crime: A General Strain Theory Perspective." *Journal of Research in Crime and Delinquency* 34: 275–306.

Broidy, Lisa, and Elizabeth Cauffman. 2017. "The Glueck Women: Using the Past to Assess and Extend Contemporary Understandings of Women's Desistance from Crime." *Journal of Developmental and Life-Course Criminology* 3: 102–125.

Broidy, Lisa M., Daniel S. Nagin, Richard E. Tremblay, John E. Bates, Bobby Brame, Kenneth A. Dodge, David Fergusson et al. 2003. "Developmental Trajectories of Childhood Disruptive Behaviors and Adolescent Delinquency: A Six-Site, Cross-National Study." *Developmental Psychology* 39: 222–245.

Broidy, Lisa, Elizabeth Cauffman, Dorothy L. Espelage, Paul Mazerolle, and Alex Piquero. 2003. "Sex Differences in Empathy and Its Relation to Juvenile Offending." *Violence and Victims* 18: 503–516.

Broidy, Lisa M., Anna L. Stewart, Carleen M. Thompson, Troy Allard, April Chrzanowski, and Susan M. Dennison. 2015. "Assessing Race/Ethnicity and Gender Disaggregated Differences in Life-Course Offending Trajectories." *Journal of Developmental and Life-Course Criminology* 2: 296–320.

Carbone-Lopez, Kristin, and Jody Miller. 2012. "Precocious Role Entry as a Mediating Factor in Women's Methamphetamine Use: Implications for Life-Course and Pathways Research." *Criminology* 50: 187–220.

Caspi, Avshalom, Donald Lynam, Terrie E. Moffitt, and Phil A. Silva. 1993. "Unraveling Girls' Delinquency: Biological, Dispositional, and Contextual Contributions to Adolescent Misbehavior." *Developmental Psychology* 29: 19–30.

Cauffman, Elizabeth, Kathryn C. Monahan, and April Gile Thomas. 2015. "Pathways to Persistence: Female Offending from 14 to 25." *Journal of Developmental and Life-Course Criminology* 1: 236–268.

Cauffman, Elizabeth, Adam Fine, April G. Thomas, and Kathryn C. Monahan. 2017. "Trajectories of Violent Behavior Among Females and Males." *Child Development* 88: 41–54.

Cernkovich, Stephen A., Nadine Lanctôt, and Peggy C. Giordano. 2008. "Predicting Adolescent and Adult Antisocial Behavior among Adjudicated Delinquent Females." *Crime & Delinquency* 54: 3–33.

Chesney-Lind, Meda. 1997. *The Female Offender: Girls, Women, And Crime*. Thousand Oaks, CA: Sage.

Cohen, Mark A., Alex R. Piquero, and Wesley G. Jennings. 2010. "Monetary Costs of Gender and Ethnicity Disaggregated Group-Based Offending." *American Journal of Criminal Justice* 35: 159–172.

Daly, Kathy. 1992. Women's Pathways to Felony Court: Feminist Theories of Lawbreaking and Problems of Representation. *Southern California Review of Law and Women's Studies* 2: 11–52.

DeCoster, Stacy, and Rena Cornell Zito. 2010. "Gender and General Strain Theory: The Gendering of Emotional Experiences and Expressions." *Journal of Contemporary Criminal Justice* 26: 224–245.

DeHart, Dana, Shannon Lynch, Joanne Belknap, Priscilla Dass-Brailsford, and Bonnie Green. 2014. "Life History Models of Female Offending the Roles of Serious Mental Illness and Trauma in Women's Pathways to Jail." *Psychology of Women Quarterly* 38: 138–151.

DeLisi, Matt. 2002. "Not Just a Boy's Club." *Women & Criminal Justice* 13(4): 27–45.

DeLisi, Matt, and Alex R. Piquero. 2011. "New Frontiers in Criminal Careers Research, 2000–2011: A State-of-the-Art Review." *Journal of Criminal Justice* 39: 289–301.

D'Unger, Amy V., Kenneth C. Land, and Patricia L. McCall. 2002. "Sex Differences in Age Patterns of Delinquent/Criminal Careers: Results from Poisson Latent Class Analyses of the Philadelphia Cohort Study." *Journal of Quantitative Criminology* 18: 349–375.

Estrada, Felipe, and Anders Nilsson. 2012. "Does It Cost More to Be a Female Offender? A Life-Course Study of Childhood Circumstances, Crime, Drug Abuse, and Living Conditions." *Feminist Criminology* 7: 196–219.

Fergusson, David M., and L. John Horwood. 2002. "Male and Female Offending Trajectories." *Development and Psychopathology* 14: 159–177.

Ferrante, Anna M. 2013. Assessing Gender and Ethnic Differences in Developmental Trajectories of Offending. *Australian & New Zealand Journal of Criminology* 46: 379–402.

Fitzgerald, Robin., Paul Mazerolle, Alex R. Piquero, and Donna L. Ansara. 2012. "Exploring Sex Differences among Sentenced Juvenile Offenders in Australia." *Justice Quarterly*, 29: 420–447.

Fontaine, Nathalie, Rene Carbonneau, Frank Vitaro, Edward D. Barker, and Richard E. Tremblay. 2009. "Research Review: A Critical Review of Studies on the Developmental Trajectories of Antisocial Behavior in Females." *Journal of Child Psychology and Psychiatry* 50: 363–385.

Francis, Brian, Jiayi Liu, and Keith Soothill. 2012. "Criminal Lifestyle Specialization: Female Offending in England and Wales." *International Criminal Justice Review* 20: 188–204.

Gaarder, Emily, and Joanne Belknap. 2002. "Tenuous Borders: Girls Transferred to Adult Court." *Criminology* 40: 481–517.

Giordano, Peggy C. 2010. *Legacies of Crime: A Follow-Up of Highly Delinquent Girls and Boys.* New York: Cambridge University Press.

Giordano, Peggy C., Steven A. Cernkovich, and Jennifer L. Rudolph. 2002. "Gender, Crime, and Desistance: Toward a Theory of Cognitive Transformation." *American Journal of Sociology* 107: 990–1064.

Glueck, Sheldon, and Eleanor Glueck. 1968. *Delinquents and Nondelinquents in Perspective.* Cambridge, MA: Harvard University Press.

Goldweber, Asha, Lisa M. Broidy, and Elizabeth Cauffman. 2009. "Interdisciplinary Perspectives on Persistent Female Offending: A Review of Theory and Research." In *The Development of Persistent Criminality,* edited by Akiva M. Liberman, 205–230. New York: Springer.

Gomez-Smith, Zenta, and Alex R. Piquero. 2005. "An Examination of Adult Onset Offending." *Journal of Criminal Justice* 33: 515–525.

Gross, Amy B., and Harold R. Keller. 1992. "Long-Term Consequences of Childhood Physical and Psychological Maltreatment." *Aggressive Behavior* 18: 171–185.

Gunnison, Elaine, and Lisa M. McCartan. 2007. "The Role of Different Developmental Experiences." *Women & Criminal Justice* 16: 43–65.

Hagan, John, and Holly Foster. 2003. "S/he's a Rebel: Toward a Sequential Stress Theory of Delinquency and Gendered Pathways to Disadvantage in Emerging Adulthood." *Social Forces* 82: 53–86.

Hay, Carter. 2003. "Family, Strain, Gender and Delinquency. *Sociological Perspectives* 46: 107–135.

Haynie, Dana L., Peggy C. Giordano, Wendy D. Manning, and Monica A. Longmore. 2005. "Adolescent Romantic Relationships and Delinquency Involvement." *Criminology* 43: 177–210.

Jang, Sung Joon. 2007. "Gender Differences in Strain, Negative Emotions, and Coping Behaviors: A General Strain Theory Approach." *Justice Quarterly* 24: 523–553.

Jennings, Wesley G., Mildred M. Maldonado-Molina, Alex R. Piquero, Candice L. Odgers, Hector Bird, and Glorisa Canino. 2010. "Sex Differences in Trajectories of Offending among Puerto Rican Youth." *Crime & Delinquency* 56: 327–357.

Joliffe, Darrick, David P. Farrington, Alex R. Piquero, John F. MacLeod, and Steve van de Weijer. 2017. "Prevalence of Life-Course–Persistent, Adolescence-Limited, and Late-Onset Offenders: A Systematic Review of Prospective Longitudinal Studies." *Aggression and Violent Behavior* 33: 4–14.

Jones, Natalie J., Shelley L. Brown, Kayla A. Wanamaker, and Leigh E. Greiner. 2014. "A Quantitative Exploration of Gendered Pathways to Crime in a Sample of Male and Female Juvenile Offenders." *Feminist Criminology* 9: 113–136.

Kim, Jungmeen, and Dante Cicchetti. 2004. "A Longitudinal Study of Child Maltreatment, Mother–Child Relationship Quality and Maladjustment: The Role of Self-Esteem and Social Competence." *Journal of Abnormal Child Psychology* 32: 341–354.

Kim, Jungmeen, and Dante Cicchetti. 2006. "Longitudinal Trajectories of Self-System Processes and Depressive Symptoms Among Maltreated and Nonmaltreated Children." *Child Development* 77: 624–639.

Kratzer, Lynn, and Sheilagh Hodgins.1999. "A Typology of Offenders: A Test of Moffitt's Theory Among Males and Females from Childhood to Age 30. *Criminal Behaviour and Mental Health* 9: 57–73.

Kreager, Derek A., Ross L. Matsueda, and Elena A. Erosheva. 2011. "Motherhood and Criminal Desistance in Disadvantaged Neighborhoods." *Criminology* 48: 221–258.

Kruttschnitt, Candace. 2013. "Gender and Crime." *Annual Review of Sociology* 39: 291–308.

Lahey, Benjamin B., Carol A. Van Hulle, Irwin D. Waldman, Joseph Lee Rodgers, Brian M. D'Onofrio, Steven Pedlow, Paul Rathouz, and Kate Keenan. 2006. "Testing Descriptive Hypotheses Regarding Sex Differences in the Development of Conduct Problems and Delinquency." *Journal of Abnormal Child Psychology* 34: 737–755.

Leve, Leslie D., and Patricia Chamberlain. 2004. "Female Juvenile Offenders: Defining an Early-Onset Pathway for Delinquency." *Journal of Child and Family Studies* 13: 439–452.

Loeber, Rolf, Wesley G. Jennings, Lia Ahonen, Alex R. Piquero, and David P. Farrington. 2017. *Female Delinquency from Childhood to Young Adulthood*, 29–35. Cham, Switzerland: Springer Nature.

Macmillan, Ross., and McCarthy, B. 2014. "Gender and Offending in a Life Course Context." In *The Oxford Handbook of Gender, Sex, And Crime,* edited by Rosemary Gartner and Bill McCarthy, 343–361. New York: Oxford University Press.

Maruna, Shadd. 2004. "Desistance from Crime and Explanatory Style: A New Direction in the Psychology of Reform." *Journal of Contemporary Criminal Justice* 20: 184–200.

Mazerolle, Paul, Robert Brame, Ray Paternoster, Alex Piquero, and Charles Dean. 2000. "Onset Age, Persistence, and Offending Versatility: Comparisons Across Gender." *Criminology* 38: 1143–1172.

McCabe, Kristen M., Carie Rodgers, May Yeh, and Richard Hough. 2004. "Gender Differences in Childhood Onset Conduct Disorder." *Development and Psychopathology* 16: 179–192.

Miller, Shari, Patrick Malone, Kenneth Dodge, and Conduct Problems Prevention Research Group. 2010. "Developmental Trajectories of Boys' and Girls' Delinquency: Sex Differences and Links to Later Adolescent Outcomes." *Journal of Abnormal Child Psychology* 38: 1021–1032.

Moffitt, Terrie E. 1993. "Adolescence-Limited and Life-Course-Persistent Antisocial Behavior: A Developmental Taxonomy." *Psychological Review* 100: 674–701.

Moffitt, Terrie E. 1994. "Natural Histories of Delinquency." In *Cross-National Longitudinal Research on Human Development and Criminal Behavior*, edited by Elmar Weitekamp and Hans-Jürgen Kerner, 3–64. Dordrecht, The Netherlands: Kluwer.

Moffitt, Terrie E. 2006. "Life-Course Persistent Versus Adolescence-Limited Antisocial Behavior." In *Developmental Psychopathology*: Vol. 3, *Risk, Disorder, and Adaptation*, edited by Dante Cicchetti and Donald J. Cohen, 570–598. Hoboken, NJ: Wiley.

Moffitt, Terrie E., and Avshalom Caspi. 2001. "Childhood Predictors Differentiate Life-Course Persistent and Adolescence-Limited Antisocial Pathways Among Males and Females." *Development and Psychopathology* 13: 355–375.

Moffitt, Terrie E., Avshalom Caspi, Michael Rutter, and Phil A. Silva. 2001. *Sex Differences in Antisocial Behavior: Conduct Disorder, Delinquency, and Violence in the Dunedin Longitudinal Study.* Cambridge, UK: Cambridge University Press.

Odgers, Candice L., Marlene M. Moretti, Mandi L. Burnette, Preeti Chauhan, Dennis Waite, and N. Dickon Reppucci. 2007. "A Latent Variable Modeling Approach to Identifying Subtypes of Serious and Violent Female Juvenile Offenders." *Aggressive Behavior* 33: 339–352.

Odgers, Candice L., Terrie E. Moffitt, Jonathan M. Broadbent, Nigel Dickson, Robert J. Hancox, Honalee Harrington, Richie Poulton, Malcolm R. Sears, W. Murray Thomson, and Avshalom Caspi. 2008. "Female and Male Antisocial Trajectories: From Childhood Origins to Adult Outcomes." *Development and Psychopathology* 20: 673–716.

Owen, Barbara. 1998. *In The Mix: Struggle and Survival in a Woman's Prison.* Albany: State University of New York Press.

Pepler, Debra, Depeng P. Jiang, Wendy Craig, and Jennifer Connolly. 2010. "Developmental Trajectories of Girls' and Boys' Delinquency and Associated Problems." *Journal of Abnormal Child Psychology* 38: 1033–1044.

Piquero, Alex R. 2008. "Taking Stock of Developmental Trajectories of Criminal Activity over the Life Course." In *The Long View of Crime: A Synthesis of Longitudinal Research*, edited by Akiva M. Liberman, 23–78. New York: Springer.

Rebellon, Cesar J., and Michelle Manasse. 2006. "Do 'Bad Boys' Really Get the Girls? Delinquency as a Cause and Consequence of Dating Behavior Among Adolescents." *Justice Quarterly* 21: 355–389.

Russell, Michael A., Summer J. Robins, and Candice L. Odgers. 2014. "Developmental Perspectives: Sex Differences in Antisocial Behavior from Childhood to Adulthood." In *The Oxford Handbook of Gender, Sex, And Crime*, edited by Rosemary Gartner and Bill McCarthy, 286–315. New York: Oxford University Press.

Salisbury, Emily J., and Patricia Van Voorhis. 2009. "Gendered Pathways: A Quantitative Investigation of Women Probationers' Paths to Incarceration." *Criminal Justice and Behavior* 36: 541–566.

Sampson, Robert J., and John H. Laub. 1993. *Crime in the Making: Pathways and Turning Points Through Life.* Cambridge, MA: Harvard University Press.

Schwartz, Seth J., James E. Côté, and Jeffrey Jensen Arnett. 2005. "Identity and Agency in Emerging Adulthood: Two Developmental Routes in the Individualization Process." *Youth & Society* 37: 201–229.

Silverthorn, Persephanie, and Paul J. Frick. 1999. "Developmental Pathways to Antisocial Behavior: The Delayed-Onset Pathway in Girls." *Development and Psychopathology* 11: 101–126.

Silverthorn, Persephanie, Paul J. Frick, and Richard Reynolds. 2001. "Timing of Onset and Correlates of Severe Conduct Problems." *Journal of Psychopathology and Behavioral Assessment* 23: 171–181.

Simpson, Sally S., Jennifer L. Yahner, and Laura Dugan. 2008. "Understanding Women's Pathways to Jail: Analysing the Lives of Incarcerated Women." *The Australian and New Zealand Journal of Criminology* 41: 84–108.

Simpson, Sally S., Mariel Alper, Laura Dugan, Julie Horney, Candace Kruttschnitt, and Rosemary Gartner. 2016. "Age-Graded Pathways into Crime: Evidence from a Multi-Site Retrospective Study of Incarcerated Women." *Journal of Developmental and Life-Course Criminology* 2: 296–320.

Soothill, Keith, Elizabeth Ackerley, and Brian Francis. 2003. "The Persistent Offenders Debate: A Focus on Temporal Changes." *Criminal Justice* 3: 389–412.

Svensson, Robert. 2003. "Gender Differences in Adolescent Drug Use: The Impact of Parental Monitoring and Peer Deviance." *Youth & Society* 34: 300–329.

Thompson, Carleen, Anna Stewart, Troy Allard, April Chrzanowski, Chelsea Luker, and Jerneja Sveticic. 2014. "Examining Adult-Onset Offending: A Case for Adult Cautioning." *Trends & Issues in Crime and Criminal Justice* 488: 1–8.

Thornberry, Terence P., Beth Bjerregaard, and William Miles. 1993. "The Consequences of Respondent Attrition in Panel Studies: A Simulation Based on the Rochester Youth Development Study." *Journal of Quantitative Criminology* 9: 127–158.

Thornberry, Terence P., and Marvin D. Krohn. 2005. "Applying Interactional Theory to the Explanation of Continuity and Change in Antisocial Behavior." In *Integrated Developmental and Life-Course Theories of Offending*, edited by David P. Farrington, 183–209. New Brunswick, NJ: Transaction.

Topitzes, James, Joshua P. Mersky, and Arthur J. Reynolds. 2011. "Child Maltreatment and Offending Behavior: Gender-Specific Effects and Pathways." *Criminal Justice and Behavior* 38: 492–510.

Trickett, Penelope K., Sonya Negriff, Juye Ji, and Melissa Peckins. 2011. "Child Maltreatment and Adolescent Development." *Journal of Research on Adolescence* 21: 3–20.

Uggen, Christopher, and Candace Kruttschnitt. 1998. "Crime in the Breaking: Gender Differences in Desistance." *Law & Society Review* 32: 339–366.

van de Rakt, Marieke., Paul Nieuwbeerta, and Nan Dirk de Graaf. 2008. "Like Father, Like Son: The Relationships Between Conviction Trajectories of Fathers and Their Sons and Daughters." *British Journal of Criminology* 48: 538–556.

van der Put, Claudia E., Maja Dekovic, Machteld Hoeve, Geert Jan J. M. Stams, Peter H. van der Laan, and Femke E. M. Langewouters. 2014. "Risk Assessment of Girls: Are There Any Sex Differences in Risk Factors for Re-offending and in Risk Profiles?" *Crime & Delinquency* 60: 1033–1056.

West, Donald James, and David P. Farrington. 1973. *Who Becomes Delinquent?* London: Heinemann.

White, Norman A., and Alex R. Piquero. 2004. "A Preliminary Empirical Test of Silverthorn and Frick's Delayed-Onset Pathway in Girls Using an Urban, African-American, US-Based Sample." *Criminal Behaviour and Mental Health* 14: 291–309.

Wilson, Helen W., and Cathy Spatz Widom. 2009. "A Prospective Examination of the Path from Child Abuse and Neglect to Illicit Drug Use in Middle Adulthood: The Potential Mediating Role of Four Risk Factors." *Journal of Youth and Adolescence* 38: 340–354.

Wolfgang, Marvin E., Robert M. Figlio, and Thorsten Sellin. 1972. *Delinquency in a Birth Cohort.* Chicago: University of Chicago Press.

Xie, Hongling, Deborah A. G. Drabick, and Diane Chen. 2011. "Developmental Trajectories of Aggression from Late Childhood through Adolescence: Similarities and Differences Across Gender." *Aggressive Behavior* 37: 387–404.

Zara, Georgia, and David P. Farrington. 2009. "Childhood and Adolescent Predictors of Late-Onset Criminal Careers." *Journal of Youth and Adolescence* 38:2 87–300.

Zheng, Yao, and H. Harrington Cleveland. 2013. "Identifying Gender-Specific Developmental Trajectories of Nonviolent and Violent Delinquency from Adolescence to Young Adulthood." *Journal of Adolescence* 36: 371–381.

DEVELOPMENTAL INTERVENTIONS

CHAPTER 31

FAMILY-BASED PROGRAMS FOR PREVENTING DELINQUENCY AND LATER OFFENDING

BRANDON C. WELSH AND STEVEN N. ZANE

FAMILIES matter, and by focusing on families we can go a long way toward improving the effectiveness of programs and policies to prevent delinquency and later criminal offending. We are by no means the first to say this (see e.g., McCord 1991; Tolan 2002; Fagan 2013). Importantly, the voluminous research on the subject bears this out (e.g., Farrington and Welsh 2007). This chapter aims to contribute to this body of research by reviewing the leading family-based programs for preventing delinquency and later offending.

In this chapter we focus on the highest quality research studies (i.e., randomized experiments and quasi-experiments that establish equivalence between groups) as well as the most rigorous reviews of research (i.e., systematic reviews and meta-analyses) that include only high-quality studies. We were also interested in studies with a total sample size of no fewer than 50 individuals and an outcome measure of delinquency or criminal offending; a program would not be considered if it only had outcome measures of risk factors. This helps to ensure that our conclusions are based on the best available evidence. The chapter builds upon some past works by the first author and colleagues (Farrington and Welsh 2003, 2006, 2007; Welsh 2012a, 2012b; Welsh et al. 2012; Welsh and Piquero 2012; Piquero et al. 2016).

The organization of this chapter is as follows. Section I provides some background on family risk factors and family-based prevention programs. Sections II, III, and IV examine, respectively, the research evidence on the leading family-based programs for preventing delinquency and later offending—parent education, parent management training, and family programs for system-involved youth. Section V discusses some implications for research and policy.

I. Risk for Prevention

Family-based prevention programs and policies target risk factors for delinquency and offending associated with the family. After decades of rigorous study—using prospective longitudinal studies—a great deal is known about family risk factors. Farrington (2011) organized these factors into six main categories: (1) criminal and antisocial parents and siblings; (2) large family size; (3) child-rearing methods (poor supervision, inconsistent discipline, parental coldness and rejection, low parental involvement with the child); (4) abuse (physical or sexual) or neglect; (5) parental conflict and disrupted families; and (6) other parental features (especially young parents, parental substance abuse, stress, or depression). The strongest family factor that predicts offending is usually criminal or antisocial parents. Other quite strong and replicable family factors that predict offending are large family size, poor parental supervision, parental conflict, and disrupted families (Farrington and Welsh 2007; Derzon 2010).

Broadly speaking, family-based prevention programs have developed in two major fields of study: psychology and public health. When delivered by psychologists, these programs are often classified into parent management training, functional family therapy, or family preservation (Wasserman and Miller 1998). Typically, they attempt to change the social contingencies in the family environment so that children are rewarded for appropriate or prosocial behaviors and punished for inappropriate or antisocial behaviors. Family-based programs delivered by health professionals such as nurses are typically less behavioral, mainly providing advice and guidance to parents or general parent education. Home visiting with new parents is one of the more popular forms of this type of family intervention.

Within these fields of study, there is an emerging evidence base on the effectiveness of early family-based programs designed to address some of the most important familial risk factors for delinquency. Systematic reviews and meta-analyses incorporating the highest quality studies have shown that a number of program models are effective in preventing delinquency and later offending (see Farrington et al. 2017).

Two recent reviews capture the broad-scale effectiveness of family-based prevention programs targeted on young children. Manning, Homel, and Smith (2010) carried out a meta-analysis of the effects of early developmental prevention programs for children up to age 5 years on delinquency and other outcomes in adolescence. Eleven high-quality studies were included that covered a variety of program modalities: structured preschool, center-based developmental daycare, home visitation, family support services, and parental education (improvement of core parenting skills). Results show significant effects across a number of important domain outcomes, including educational achievement (mean effect size $d = .53$), delinquency/deviance ($d = .48$), cognitive development ($d = .34$), involvement in the justice system ($d = .24$), and family well-being ($d = .18$). Interestingly, program duration and intensity were associated with larger effect sizes but not multi-component programs.

Piquero and his colleagues (2016) reported on an updated systematic review and meta-analysis of the effects of early family/parent training programs for children up to age 5 years on antisocial behavior and delinquency. The review, which included 78 randomized controlled experiments, investigated the full range of these programs, including home visits, parent education plus daycare, and parent management training. Results indicate that early family/parent training is an effective intervention for reducing antisocial behavior and delinquency, with a mean effect size $d = .37$. These programs also produce a wide range of other important benefits for families, including improved school readiness and school performance on the part of children and greater employment and educational opportunities for parents.

II. PARENT EDUCATION

Home visiting with new parents, especially mothers, is a common method of delivering the family-based intervention known as general parent education. Home visits focus on educating parents to improve the life chances of children from a very young age, often at birth and sometimes in the final trimester of pregnancy. Some of the main goals include the prevention of preterm or low-weight births, the promotion of healthy child development and school readiness, and the prevention of child abuse and neglect (Gomby, Culross, and Behrman 1999, p. 4). Home visits also serve to improve parental well-being, linking parents to community resources to help with employment, education, or addiction recovery. Home visitors are usually nurses or other health professionals with a diverse array of skills in working with families.

Farrington and Welsh (2007; see also Farrington and Welsh 2003) carried out a meta-analysis that included four home visitation programs (all randomized controlled experiments). It was found that this form of early intervention was effective in preventing antisocial behavior and delinquency, corresponding to a significant yet small mean effect size ($d = .24$).

Bilukha et al. (2005) carried out a systematic review on the effects of home visitation on violence. Four studies were included that reported the effects of home visitation programs on violence by the visited children. Mixed results were found for effects on criminal violence (in adolescence) and child externalizing behavior across the four programs: two reported desirable but non-significant effects, one reported a significant desirable effect, and one reported mixed results. The review also assessed, using these four and many other studies, the effectiveness of early childhood home visitation on parental violence, intimate partner violence, and child maltreatment. For the first two outcomes, there was insufficient evidence to make a determination of effectiveness. Strong evidence of effectiveness was found for home visiting programs in preventing child abuse and neglect.

The best known home visiting program, and the only one with a direct measure of delinquency, is the Nurse-Family Partnership (NFP) developed by David Olds

(Olds, Sadler, and Kitzman 2007). At its core is the provision of nurse home visits for new parents. NFP was first tested in Elmira, New York, in the early 1980s. Four hundred first-time mothers were randomly assigned to receive home visits from nurses during pregnancy, or to receive visits both during pregnancy and during the first two years of life, or to a control group who received no visits. Each visit lasted just over one hour, and the mothers were visited on average every two weeks. The home visitors gave advice about prenatal and postnatal care of the child, infant development, and the importance of proper nutrition and avoiding smoking and drinking during pregnancy.

The results of the experiment showed that the postnatal home visits caused a significant decrease in recorded child physical abuse and neglect during the first two years of life, especially by poor, unmarried, teenage mothers; 4 percent of visited mothers versus 19 percent of nonvisited mothers of this type were guilty of child abuse or neglect (Olds et al. 1986). In a 15-year follow-up, which included 330 mothers and 315 children, significantly fewer experimental compared to control group mothers were identified as perpetrators of child abuse and neglect (29 percent vs. 54 percent; Olds et al. 1997). At the age of 15, children of the treatment mothers had incurred significantly fewer arrests than their control counterparts (20 as opposed to 45 per 100 children; Olds et al. 1998). In the latest follow-up at age 19, compared to their control counterparts, girls of the full sample of mothers had incurred significantly fewer arrests and convictions and girls of the higher-risk mothers had significantly fewer children of their own and less Medicaid use; few program effects were observed for the boys (Eckenrode et al. 2010). Benefit-cost analyses have repeatedly shown that the program is a worthwhile expenditure of public resources (Welsh, Farrington, and Raffan-Gowar 2015). Large-scale replications in Memphis and Denver are also showing a range of positive effects for children and mothers (Olds, Sadler, and Kitzman 2007).

Today, NFP operates in almost 600 counties in 43 states, serving more than 33,000 families each year. It is also being implemented in many other countries, including Australia, Germany, Norway, and the United Kingdom. Crucial to each of these sites and the program's continued expansion is a commitment by local providers to ensure fidelity to the model. As programs are implemented in new settings or scaled-up for wider public use, there is the very real threat that the program will become diluted and its effectiveness greatly reduced (Dodge 2001; Welsh, Sullivan, and Olds 2010). As a sign of the importance of this concern, a national office was established to work with local providers to make sure that NFP programs are implemented and operated as planned and to help address local needs. This marks a crucial advancement in the local delivery of evidence-based prevention programs.

A small number of parent education programs that include daycare services for children of the participating parents have also measured delinquency. Daycare programs are distinguished from preschool programs in that the former are not focused on the child's intellectual enrichment or necessarily on readying the child for kindergarten and elementary school but serve largely as an organized form of child care to allow parents to return to work. Daycare also provides children with a number of important benefits, including social interaction with other children and stimulation of their cognitive, sensory, and motor control skills.

One of the most successful early family-based prevention programs to combine parent education and daycare services is the Syracuse University Family Development Research Project (Lally, Mangione, and Honig 1988). The project, which took place in Syracuse, New York, aimed to bolster family and child functioning through a comprehensive intervention strategy that focused on parent education, with child care as supplementary. The researchers began with a sample of pregnant women (mostly poor African American single mothers) and gave them weekly help with child-rearing, health, nutrition, and other problems. In addition, their children received free full-time daycare, designed to develop their intellectual abilities, up to age 5. This was not a randomized experiment, but a matched control group was chosen when the children were aged 3. The experimental group consisted of 82 children and the control group of 74.

Ten years later, 119 children were followed up to about age 15. The strongest program effects were on delinquency. Significantly fewer of the experimental group children (2 percent as opposed to 17 percent) had been referred to the juvenile court for delinquency offenses, and the severity of offenses and degree of chronicity was much higher among control group children. Treated girls, compared to their control counterparts, showed better school attendance and school performance; no differences were found among the boys.

III. Parent Management Training

Gerald Patterson (1982) developed behavioral parent management training (PMT). His careful observations of parent–child interaction showed that parents of antisocial children were deficient in their methods of child rearing. These parents failed to tell their children how they were expected to behave, failed to monitor their behavior to ensure that it was desirable, and failed to enforce rules promptly and unambiguously with appropriate rewards and penalties. The parents of antisocial children used more punishment (such as scolding, shouting, or threatening) but failed to make it contingent on the child's behavior.

Patterson attempted to train these parents in effective child-rearing methods, namely, noticing what a child is doing, monitoring behavior over long periods, clearly stating house rules, making rewards and punishments contingent on behavior, and negotiating disagreements so that conflicts and crises did not escalate. His treatment was shown to be effective in reducing child stealing and antisocial behavior over short periods in small-scale studies (Patterson, Chamberlain, and Reid 1982; Patterson, Reid, and Dishion 1992).

Farrington and Welsh (2007; see also Farrington and Welsh 2003) carried out a meta-analysis that included 10 high-quality evaluations of PMT programs and found that this type of early intervention produced a significant and moderate mean effect size ($d = .40$). Each of the 10 programs included in this meta-analysis aimed to teach parents to use rewards and punishments consistently and contingently in child-rearing. The programs were usually delivered in guided group meetings of parents, including role-playing and modeling exercises, and three of the programs were delivered by videotape. Just one of the 10 programs combined PMT with another intervention (child skills training).

Serketich and Dumas (1996) carried out a meta-analysis of 26 controlled studies of behavioral parent training (also called PMT) with young children up to age 10. Most were based on small numbers (average $N = 29$), and most were randomized experiments. They concluded that PMT was effective in reducing child antisocial behavior, since the mean effect size was .86. However, d correlated $-.52$ with sample size, indicating that larger evaluations found smaller effect sizes, and .69 with age, indicating that PMT was more effective for (relatively) older children.

In their narrative review of PMT, Duncan and Magnuson (2004) concluded that it is a "promising intervention strategy" for improving the behavior of children, especially for children with "severe behavior problems" (p. 123). Kazdin's (1997) narrative review of this intervention strategy was more optimistic. He concluded that PMT has led to "marked improvements in child behavior on parent and teacher reports of deviant behavior, direct observation of behavior at home and at school, and institutional records (e.g., school truancy, police contacts, arrest rates, institutionalization)" (p. 1351). He also noted that these programs had produced a number of spin-off benefits, including improvements in behaviors of siblings at home and maternal depression.

Long and her colleagues (1994) carried out the longest follow-up of a PMT program, tracking their experimental children for 14 years after the completion of the program. Seventy-three young children (between 2 and 7 years old) who were referred to the researcher's clinic for noncompliance (to parent requests) and their mothers were randomly allocated to an experimental group that received PMT or to a control group that received no services. Over the course of 8 to 10 sessions, mothers were taught to attend to and reward appropriate behavior and to use clear commands and time-out for non-compliance.

At the completion of treatment, it was found that, compared to the controls, children in the experimental group were less likely to exhibit "deviant" behavior and were more compliant (Long et al. 1994, p. 101). At the latest follow-up, when the experimental group participants were between 16 and 21 years old, Long and her colleagues found that, as adults, they were similar on delinquency, emotional adjustment, and academic progress, compared to controls retrospectively matched on age, gender, ethnicity, and family socioeconomic status. In Farrington and Welsh's (2007) meta-analysis of PMT programs noted earlier, they calculated the effect size $d = .31$ for the program's effect on delinquency. This corresponds roughly to a small-to-moderate but non-significant 15 percent reduction.

One PMT approach that has been widely used is Triple P—the Positive Parenting Program. Developed in Australia by Matthew Sanders, it offers five different levels of intervention, ranging from universal—intended to be useful to any parent—to an intensive clinical intervention, designed for families of children and young people whose multiple behavior problems are especially serious and persistent (Sanders et al. 2000). Triple P emphasizes the importance of developing parents' resilience and capacity for self-regulation as part of a program that helps them acquire skills to become self-sufficient and self-confident in their parenting. Implementation methods have ranged from training through television and other media at the universal level, to the use of home visiting, clinical observations, group work, and self-directed learning. The program has been evaluated at all five levels in both clinical and community settings. A randomized controlled experiment compared three different versions of Triple P—standard, self-directed, and enhanced—with a waiting list control group of disruptive 3-year-olds at high risk of developing conduct problems (Sanders et al. 2000). At one-year follow-up the children in all three Triple P groups had achieved clinically reliable improvements in their behavior compared with the control group. A meta-analysis of Triple P involving 11 studies found that it was effective in reducing children's antisocial behavior (Thomas and Zimmer-Gembeck 2007). A benefit-cost analysis found that for every dollar spent on the program, more than $6 was saved by the government and taxpayers and crime victims (Lee et al. 2012).

Universal PMT also has been found to be effective in preventing delinquency when provided to parents of young people entering adolescence. Mason and his colleagues (2003) evaluated the effectiveness of a universal PMT program for parents of children aged 10 through 14 called Guiding Good Choices. The program involves five weekly parenting sessions, each lasting two hours. Children attend the third session with their parents to learn "refusal skills" together. The program teaches parents about the risk and protective factors that predict substance abuse and delinquent behavior; helps them to develop skills for establishing and communicating clear behavioral expectations, monitoring their children's behavior, and consistently enforcing family rules; provides training in skills to manage and reduce family conflict; and encourages parents to find developmentally appropriate ways for their adolescent children to contribute to family life, thereby maintaining strong family bonds even as adolescents explore new roles. In a randomized experiment involving parents of 429 11-year-old children, adolescents whose parents were assigned to the program had significantly lower rates of delinquent behavior and substance abuse than controls 3.5 years post-intervention (Mason et al. 2003). A benefit-cost analysis found that this program produced benefits for society in reduced costs of crime—almost $3 for every dollar spent on the program (Lee et al. 2012).

IV. Family Programs
for System-Involved Youth

Family-based approaches to delinquency prevention also extend beyond the early years of the life course. While it often focuses on early family prevention, a developmental perspective can also inform intervention programs for older, adjudicated adolescents. As a "last resort," several family therapy programs have been developed to prevent future offending for system-involved youth. Three therapy models have emerged as effective evidenced-based programs: Multisystemic Therapy, Functional Family Therapy, and Multidimensional Treatment Foster Care (Greenwood 2006; Welsh and Greenwood 2015). All three programs follow multisystem-oriented approaches, involving active family participation to combat dysfunctional patterns that may contribute to existing delinquency and antisocial behavior (Baldwin et al. 2012). While other promising family approaches certainly exist—such as Brief Strategic Family Training (Szapocznik et al. 2012)—the programs included in this section are the most widely used and most relevant because they specifically target delinquency and criminal offending outcomes.

A. Multisystemic Therapy

Developed specifically to deal with serious juvenile delinquents, Multisystemic Therapy (MST) embodies an ecological approach toward all aspects of a youth's development that may contribute to delinquency or other antisocial behavior (Henggeler and Schaeffer 2010). At the core of the model is the insight that behavior problems must be assessed according to the particular needs of the youth in question. On a case-by-case basis, treatment may include individual, peer, and community intervention in addition to primary family intervention (Greenwood 2006). The most consistent feature of MST is to discover positive parts of the youth's life and build upon those positive sources to prevent future antisocial behavior. This begins with an identification of reinforcers of such behavior within the youth's home environment. MST therapist teams then provide parents with effective tools for dealing with these environmental triggers. An especially intensive intervention, MST is characterized by low therapist caseloads and on-call emergency services (Hage et al. 2009). Although initially designed for delinquent youth, the model has expanded to other at-risk populations and today serves more than 17,000 families in the United States every year (Henggeler and Sheidow 2012).

MST represents the most evaluated family-based program for system-involved youth and is the main focus of several systematic reviews and meta-analyses (Woolfenden, Williams, and Peat 2002; Farrington and Welsh 2003; Curtis, Ronan, and Borduin 2004; Littell, Popa, and Forsythe 2005; Baldwin et al. 2012; van der Stouwe et al. 2014). The most recent meta-analyses have found that MST is effective in reducing delinquency and future offending. Baldwin et al. (2012) included 12 randomized experiments and reported a significant yet small mean effect size ($d = .22$) for 10 studies comparing MST to treatment-as-usual and a non-significant and moderate mean effect size ($d = .57$) for two studies comparing MST to alternate forms of therapy. The Washington State Institute for Public Policy (2016a) carried out a meta-analysis that included 11 MST studies and found a significant moderate mean effect size ($d = .43$). Most recently, van der Stouwe and colleagues (2014) found that across 22 evaluation studies (containing 32 effect sizes), MST programs produced, on average, a significant yet small effect on delinquency ($d = .20$).

Earlier meta-analyses also demonstrated significant moderate summary effects, although they did not include as many independent evaluations. Curtis, Ronan, and Borduin (2004) found a significant and moderate mean effect size ($d = .55$) based on seven randomized controlled trials performed by MST developers. Farrington and Welsh (2003) summarized six randomized experiments in their meta-analysis—including one independent evaluation—and calculated a significant and moderate mean effect size ($d = .41$). Only one meta-analysis reported non-significant mean effect sizes when eight studies were grouped by specific outcome measures, although each effect size favored the MST condition (Littell, Popa, and Forsythe 2005; see also Littell 2005). A benefit-cost analysis found that for every dollar spent on MST, $1.74 was saved by participants and taxpayers (Washington State Institute for Public Policy 2016a). Dopp et al. (2014) recently conducted a benefit-cost analysis as part of a 25-year follow-up and found that $5.04 was saved by taxpayers and potential crime victims for every dollar spent on MST.

The Missouri Delinquency Project has the longest follow-up of all MST experiments, offering unique insight regarding effects over the life course (Sawyer and Borduin 2011). One hundred and seventy-six serious juvenile offenders were randomly assigned to MST or individual treatment. Results collected after approximately four years showed that 71 percent of the control youth were rearrested, while only 26 percent of the MST youth were rearrested—less than one-third (Borduin et al. 1995). After approximately 14 years, 50 percent of MST youth were rearrested compared to 81 percent of the controls (Schaeffer and Borduin 2005).

Sawyer and Borduin (2011) carried out the most recent follow-up—an average 21.9 years post-treatment when participants were on average 37.3 years old— and found that 35 percent of MST youth had been reconvicted compared to 55 percent of the controls (rearrest rates were not reported in the final follow-up). In other words, non-MST youth were 2.3 times as likely as MST participants to be reconvicted over the life course. Researchers also found that the closest-age siblings of the MST youth had a far lower likelihood of criminal activity. In a 25-year follow-up, Wagner et al. (2014) found that arrest rates were significantly lower for MST siblings compared to siblings of youth in the control condition (43 percent vs. 72 percent). This peripheral effect—what economists would call a positive externality—further demonstrates the benefit of an ecological, family-based approach.

Although program developers have performed most MST evaluations to date, several independent experiments were conducted in the past decade, including studies in the United States (Weiss et al. 2013; Timmons-Mitchell et al. 2006), United Kingdom (Butler et al. 2011), Sweden (Sundell et al. 2008), Norway (Ogden and Halliday-Boykins 2004), and New Zealand (Curtis et al. 2009). The most recent independent evaluation that involved delinquency outcomes was performed in the United Kingdom, with 108 court-referred youth randomized to the MST condition or youth treatment teams (Butler et al. 2011). Delinquency rates decreased dramatically for both groups after 18 months, but the MST group achieved greater reductions. Although MST youth offended less frequently than the control group during every six-month period, the between-group differences in offending did not demonstrate statistical significance until the final six months of the study, a period in which 8 percent of MST youth and 36 percent of the controls reoffended.

B. Functional Family Therapy

Based on the developmental insight that poor family functioning exacerbates adolescent at-risk behaviors and a perceived clinical need to serve a difficult-to-treat population of at-risk adolescents, Functional Family Therapy (FFT) was developed at the University of Utah in the late 1960s (Sexton and Alexander 2003). As its name suggests, FFT is designed to prevent juvenile delinquency by improving the functioning of the family unit. This is accomplished by addressing communication, social problem solving, and exchange of privileges among family members. The therapeutic model moves through three phases. In the first phase, the therapist helps the family move from feelings of frustration to more hopeful attitudes that positive change can occur. In the second phase, the therapist provides concrete resources for guiding this positive change, and in the final phase, the therapist attempts to generalize positive change beyond the immediate family context (Alexander and Sexton 2004). This relatively short-term intervention is delivered over approximately three months, usually within the family home. Compared to MST, it is a far less intensive intervention—making it less expensive (Greenwood 2006).

Although FFT has been implemented nationwide as a leading evidence-based program, it has not been evaluated to the same extent as MST (Henggeler and Sheidow 2012). Baldwin et al. (2012) carried out a meta-analysis of FFT that included four randomized experiments. They found a non-significant and small mean effect size ($d = .29$) for three studies with alternative treatment controls, and a significant and large mean effect size ($d = .82$) for one study with a non-therapy control. The Washington State Institute for Public Policy (2016b; see also Aos et al. 2001) also carried out a meta-analysis of FFT. Based on eight studies, it reported a significant and moderate mean effect size ($d = .59$), but not all of the included studies were randomized experiments. A benefit-cost analysis indicated that for youth on probation, $6.51 was saved by participants and taxpayers for every dollar spent on FFT (Washington State Institute for Public Policy 2016b), while $9.38 was saved for every dollar spent on FFT for institutionalized youth (Washington State Institute for Public Policy 2016c).

Sexton and Turner (2010) conducted the most recent evaluation of FFT, with an 18-month follow-up of a large-scale program in Washington State. Adolescents who had been adjudicated delinquent and sentenced to probation ($N = 917$) were randomly assigned to FFT or usual probation services. Trained therapists provided home visits for three to six months, averaging 12 visits for each participating family. The senior author, an early developer of the FFT model, monitored treatment delivery to assess therapist adherence. Results revealed a null effect, with rearrest rates of 22 percent for both groups after one year. When FFT youth with high therapist adherence were compared to the control group, however, the effect was statistically significant, indicating that high-adherence FFT youth were less likely to reoffend than probation youth (15 percent vs. 22 percent). A post hoc comparison revealed that high-adherence FFT youth had less than half the odds of reoffending compared to low-adherence FFT youth. The starkest conclusion was that the low-adherence FFT group was actually more likely to recidivate than the control group (odds ratio = 1.65), perhaps suggesting that family-based programs can be harmful if not administered correctly.

C. Multidimensional Treatment Foster Care

Programs like MST and FFT are predicated on treating system-involved youth in the context of their natural family environment. In some cases, however, this is not possible. Developed at the Oregon Social Learning Center in the early 1980s, Multidimensional Treatment Foster Care (MTFC) represents a family-focused alternative to group residential treatment for delinquent youth placed out-of-home (Chamberlain, Fisher, and Moore 2002). Because traditional community-based care can facilitate negative bonding between at-risk youth, MTFC foster parents are charged with providing close supervision, monitoring peer associations, setting clear limits, and reinforcing prosocial behaviors through a "point system" (Fisher and Chamberlain 2000). Although foster parents represent the primary agents of treatment, MTFC staff—including youth therapists, family therapists, and case managers—provide support through weekly group meetings as well as daily telephone calls and family therapy (Greenwood 2006). When possible, the youth's natural family is encouraged to participate in these therapy sessions. As treatment progresses, interaction with the natural family can extend to home and even overnight visits, with the ultimate goal of reunification (Fisher and Chamberlain 2000).

Of the three model programs examined in this section, MTFC is the least evaluated to date. Turner and Macdonald (2011) carried out a meta-analysis of five foster care treatment studies, including two MTFC experiments. Compared to group residential treatment, MTFC showed significant and moderate-to-large mean effect sizes for "days in locked settings" ($d = .92$) and "criminal referrals" ($d = .56$) in a two-year follow-up. The only other meta-analysis of MTFC, carried out by the Washington State Institute for Public Policy (2016d), reported a marginally significant ($p = .09$) and moderate effect size ($d = .54$) based on three studies. While further evaluation research on MTFC is needed, research to date demonstrating large treatment effects is promising. This theme tends to be corroborated by several studies too recent to be included in any meta-analysis or systematic review (e.g., Biehal, Ellison, and Sinclair 2011; Rhoades et al. 2013; Green et al. 2014). Also, a benefit-cost analysis indicates that per dollar spent, it saves $1.70 to participants and taxpayers (Washington State Institute for Public Policy 2016d).

Most randomized experiments of MTFC have been small, including samples of fewer than 50 participants in the treatment condition. In Chamberlain, Leve, and

DeGarmo (2007), an all-female sample (N = 81) of serious juvenile offenders in Oregon was randomly assigned to MTFC or community-based group care. After the first year, delinquency rates had reduced by approximately 50 percent for both groups (Leve, Chamberlain, and Reid 2005). After two years, MTFC was associated with lower offending rates based on a "delinquency construct," which was calculated from number of criminal referrals, days in locked settings, and self-reported delinquency (Chamberlain, Leve, and DeGarmo 2007). At baseline the mean delinquency construct score was .47 and .48 for the MTFC and group care conditions, respectively. One year later this had reduced to .22 and .30, and after two years it had reduced to .12 and .25. This translated into a significant and moderate-to-large effect of MTFC, with stronger effects emerging over time. To date, no study has assessed MTFC outcomes beyond a two-year follow-up.

The largest independent evaluation of MTFC with a randomized component occurred as part of the Care Placement Evaluation (CaPE) in the United Kingdom (Green et al. 2014). Between June 2005 and December 2008, 219 youth met inclusion criteria and consented to the trial. Unlike prior studies, adjudicated adolescents made up only approximately one-quarter of the sample of at-risk youth. The youth were separated into an observational arm (N = 185) and a randomized experiment for a small subset (N = 34). For the observational study, 92 youth were placed in MTFC and 93 were placed in usual care; in the randomized trial, 20 youth were assigned to MTFC and 14 to usual care. Propensity scores were used in the observational study to achieve better balance and approximate randomization. After the first year, there was no significant effect for either MTFC group. Researchers observed that this might be due to the lower proportion of delinquents in the sample, suggesting that MTFC may be more effective for adjudicated adolescents who would otherwise be in a custodial setting.

MTFC has been associated with several other positive outcomes. Two recent Swedish experiments found favorable effects of MTFC for antisocial behavior (Westermark, Hansson, and Olsson 2011; Hansson and Olsson 2012). In a nine-year follow-up of a randomized experiment, Kerr et al. (2014) found decreased depressive symptoms and suicidal thinking in females who received MTFC treatment. In a randomized controlled trial of teenage pregnancy, Leve, Kerr, and Harold (2013) found that pregnancy rates were reduced for high-risk youth who had been treated with MTFC. These findings remind us that family-based intervention can have desirable effects on treated youth that go well beyond reductions in delinquency.

V. Discussion and Conclusions

Today, the evidence is stronger than it ever has been in demonstrating that family-based prevention of delinquency is effective and that it is never too early or too late to intervene. Early parent education, especially nurse home visits beginning during pregnancy, has produced a wide range of promising outcomes including reductions in adolescent offending. Parent management training has also proved effective at reducing delinquency in the context of at-risk youth whose parents need to improve their methods of child-rearing. And family-based intervention can still be successful as a "last resort" for system-involved youth, with family therapies such as MST, FFT, and MTFC showing lower recidivism rates for adjudicated adolescents.

Of course, silver bullet solutions are not readily available for crime-prevention efforts, and family-based prevention is no exception (Mears 2007). Our review reveals small-to-moderate mean effect sizes for the leading family-based prevention modalities. Given that even the most effective developmental interventions do not typically reduce the risk of reoffending by more than 40 percent, this should be considered a success (Loeber, Slot, and Stouthamer-Loeber 2006). Nonetheless, there are several important lessons and caveats that may be helpful for future research and public policy.

As a general matter, more program evaluation research of the highest quality is needed to establish widespread effectiveness of family-based prevention programs. The consistency of high-quality evidence to date is promising, yet the number of program evaluation studies leaves something to be desired. This much-needed evaluation research should expand upon existing research by using longer follow-up periods and larger samples. While a few family programs profiled in this chapter have long follow-up periods and large samples, they represent the exception rather than the rule. Similarly, for even the most tested family-based programs, the majority of studies are efficacy trials: small, randomized controlled experiments performed by program developers under ideal conditions. While the results of these efficacy trials represent an important scientific foundation for family-based prevention, they cannot be the end of the story.

For family prevention programs to have a meaningful impact on reducing crime and improving lives, wide-scale dissemination is necessary. This is complicated by the tendency for program effects to attenuate as a program is "scaled up" from efficacy trials to community settings (Dodge 2001; Welsh, Sullivan, and Olds 2010; see also Sullivan, Welsh, and Ilchi 2017). More heterogeneous populations and a loss of treatment fidelity are among the leading explanations for the attenuation of program effects. As noted by Mears (2007, p. 673), treatment fidelity is a "central, if not the primary, contributor" to scaling-up problems. Moreover, as Elliott and Mihalic (2004, p. 51) have noted, there is no guarantee that an efficacious program will prove effective upon dissemination, and "any bargaining away of fidelity will most likely decrease program effectiveness." It is even possible that a program that works in small efficacy trials will have harmful effects if implemented poorly on a larger scale. In Sexton and Turner (2010), for example, the overall effect of the FFT experiment was null—but not because FFT was ineffective. The culprit was implementation fidelity: FFT was effective, but only when therapists properly adhered to the FFT model.

Although several family programs, including NFP, Triple P, and MST, have established methods for promoting fidelity in wide-scale dissemination projects (see, e.g., Sanders et al. 2000; Henggeler 2011; Welsh and Greenwood 2015), implementation studies still make up a small fraction of the research evaluation literature (Irwin and Supplee 2012). This has led some to call for a "science around program implementation"

(Petersilia 2008, p. 350; see also Fixsen et al. 2013). This science would seek to understand and address the difficulty of transporting prevention models to community settings and represents the next horizon in program evaluation research for family-based crime prevention.

A national council to support and monitor local delivery of family-based prevention programs would go a long way toward improving the scaling-up process. While the financial costs of wide-scale dissemination can be prohibitive, the good news is that benefit-cost analyses make clear that family-based prevention is a worthwhile alternative to the status quo. Funding the wide-scale dissemination of effective family programs as well as follow-up research is a long-term investment in preventing crime and improving the life-course development of at-risk families and children.

REFERENCES

Alexander, James F., and Thomas L. Sexton. 2004. "Functional Family Therapy: A Model for Treating High-Risk, Acting-Out Youth." In *Comprehensive Handbook of Psychotherapy: Integrative/Eclectic*, Vol. 4, edited by Florence W. Kaslow and Jay L. Lebow, 111–132. New York: Wiley.

Aos, Steve, Polly Phipps, Robert Barnoski, and Roxanne Lieb. 2001. *The Comparative Costs and Benefits of Programs to Reduce Crime*. Olympia: Washington State Institute for Public Policy.

Baldwin, Scott A., Sarah Christian, Arjan Berkeljon, William Shadish, and Roy Bean. 2012. "The Effects of Family Therapies for Adolescent Delinquency and Substance Abuse: A Meta-Analysis." *Journal of Marital and Family Therapy* 38: 281–304.

Biehal, Nina, Sarah Ellison, and Ian Sinclair. 2011. "Intensive Fostering: An Independent Evaluation of MTFC in an English Setting." *Children and Youth Services Review* 33: 2043–2049.

Bilukha, Oleg, Robert A. Hahn, Alex Crosby, Mindy T. Fullilove, Akiva Liberman, Eve Moscicki, Susan Snyder, Farris Tuma, Phaedra Corso, Amanda Schofield, and Peter A. Briss. 2005. "The Effectiveness of Early Childhood Home Visitation in Preventing Violence: A Systematic Review." *American Journal of Preventive Medicine* 28(2S1): 11–39.

Borduin, Charles M., Barton J. Mann, Lynn. T. Cone, Scott W. Henggeler, Bethany R. Fucci, David M. Blaske, and Robert A. Williams. 1995. "Multisystemic Treatment of Serious Juvenile Offenders: Long-Term Prevention of Criminality and Violence." *Journal of Consulting and Clinical Psychology* 63: 569–578.

Butler, Stephen, Geoffrey Baruch, Nicole Hickey, and Peter Fonagy. 2011. "A Randomized Controlled Trial of Multisystemic Therapy and a Statutory Therapeutic Intervention for Young Offenders." *Journal of the American Academy of Child and Adolescent Psychiatry* 50: 1220–1235.

Chamberlain, Patricia, Philip. A. Fisher, and Kevin Moore. 2002. "Multidimensional Treatment Foster Care: Applications of the OSLC Intervention Model to High-Risk Youth and Their Families." In *Antisocial Behavior in Children and Adolescents: A Developmental Analysis and Model for Intervention*, edited by John B. Reid, Gerald R. Patterson, and James Synder, 203–218. Washington, DC: American Psychological Association.

Chamberlain, Patricia, Leslie D. Leve, and David S. DeGarmo. 2007. "Multidimensional Treatment Foster Care for Girls in the Juvenile Justice System: 2-Year Follow-Up of a Randomized Clinical Trial." *Journal of Consulting and Clinical Psychology* 75: 187–193.

Curtis, Nicola M., Kevin R. Ronan, Naamith Heiblum, and Kylie Crellin. 2009. "Dissemination and Effectiveness of Multisystemic Treatment in New Zealand: A Benchmarking Study." *Journal of Family Psychology* 23: 119–129.

Curtis, Nicola M., Kevin R. Ronan, and Charles M. Borduin. 2004. "Multisystemic Treatment: A Meta-Analysis of Outcome Studies." *Journal of Marital and Family Therapy* 18: 411–419.

Derzon, James H. 2010. "The Correspondence of Family Features with Problem, Aggressive, Criminal, and Violent Behavior: A Meta-Analysis." *Journal of Experimental Criminology* 6: 263–292.

Dodge, Kenneth A. 2001. "The Science of Youth Violence Prevention: Progressing from Developmental Epidemiology to Efficacy to Effectiveness to Public Policy." *American Journal of Preventive Medicine* 20(1S): 63–70.

Dopp, Alex R., Charles M. Borduin, David V. Wagner, and Aaron M. Sawyer. 2014. "The Economic Impact of Multisystemic Therapy Through Midlife: A Cost-Benefit Analysis with Serious Juvenile Offenders and Their Siblings." *Journal of Consulting and Clinical Psychology* 82: 694–705.

Duncan, Greg J., and Katherine Magnuson. 2004. "Individual and Parent-Based Intervention Strategies for Promoting Human Capital and Positive Behavior." In *Human Development Across Lives and Generations: The Potential for Change*, edited by P. Lindsay Chase-Lansdale, Kathleen Kiernan, and Ruth J. Friedman, 93–125. New York: Cambridge University Press.

Eckenrode, John, Mary Campa, Dennis W. Luckey, Charles R. Henderson, Robert Cole, Harriet J. Kitzman, Elizabeth Anson, Kimberly Sidora-Arcoleo, Jane Powers, and David L. Olds. 2010. "Long-Term Effects of Prenatal and Infancy Nurse Home Visitation on the Life Course of Youths: 19-Year Follow-Up of a Randomized Trial." *Archives of Pediatrics and Adolescent Medicine* 164: 9–15.

Elliott, Delbert S., and Sharon Mihalic. 2004. "Issues in Disseminating and Replicating Effective Prevention Programs." *Prevention Science* 5: 47–52.

Fagan, Abigail A. 2013. "Family-Focused Interventions to Prevent Juvenile Delinquency: A Case Where Science and Policy Can Find Common Ground." *Criminology & Public Policy* 12: 617–650.

Farrington, David P. 2011. "Families and Crime." In *Crime and Public Policy*, edited by James Q. Wilson and Joan Petersilia, 130–157. New York: Oxford University Press.

Farrington, David P., Hannah Gaffney, Friedrich Lösel, and Maria M. Ttofi. 2017. "Systematic Reviews of the Effectiveness of Developmental Prevention Programs in Reducing Delinquency, Aggression, and Bullying." *Aggression and Violent Behavior* 33: 91–106.

Farrington, David P., and Brandon C. Welsh. 2003. "Family-Based Prevention of Offending: A Meta-Analysis." *Australian and New Zealand Journal of Criminology* 36: 127–151.

Farrington, David P., and Brandon C. Welsh. 2006. "Family-Based Crime Prevention." In *Evidence-Based Crime Prevention*, rev. ed., edited by Lawrence W. Sherman, David P. Farrington, Brandon C. Welsh, and Doris Layton MacKenzie, 22–55. New York: Routledge.

Farrington, David P., and Brandon C. Welsh. 2007. *Saving Children from a Life of Crime: Early Risk Factors and Effective Interventions*. New York: Oxford University Press.

Fisher, Philip A., and Patricia Chamberlain. 2000. "Multidimensional Treatment Foster Care: A Program for Intensive Parenting, Family Support, and Skill Building." *Journal of Emotional and Behavioral Disorders* 8: 155–164.

Fixsen, Dean L., Karen A. Blase, Allison Metz, and Melissa van Dyke. 2013. "Statewide Implementation of Evidence-Based Programs." *Exceptional Children* 79: 213–230.

Gomby, Deanna S., Patti L. Culross, and Richard E. Behrman. 1999. "Home Visiting: Recent Program Evaluations—Analysis and Recommendations." *The Future of Children* 9(1): 4–26.

Green, J. M., N. Biehal, C. Roberts, J. Dixon, C. Kay, E. Parry, J. Rothwell, A. Roby, D. Kapadia, S. Scot, and I. Sinclair. 2014. "Multidimensional Treatment Foster Care for Adolescents in English Care: Randomized Trial and Observational Cohort Evaluation." *British Journal of Psychiatry* 204: 214–221.

Greenwood, Peter W. 2006. *Changing Lives: Delinquency Prevention as Crime-Control Policy.* Chicago: University of Chicago Press.

Hage, S., B. van Meijel, F. Fluttert, and G. F. M. G. Berden. 2009. "Aggressive Behavior in Adolescent Psychiatric Settings: What Are Risk Factors, Possible Interventions and Implications for Nursing Practice? A Literature Review." *Journal of Psychiatric and Mental Health Nursing* 16: 661–669.

Hansson, Kjell, and Martin Olsson. 2012. "Effects of Multidimensional Treatment Foster Care (MTFC): Results from a RCT Study in Sweden." *Children and Youth Services Review* 34: 1929–1936.

Henggeler, Scott W. 2011. "Efficacy Studies to Large-Scale Transport: The Development and Validation of Multisystemic Therapy Programs." *Annual Review of Clinical Psychology* 7: 351–381.

Henggeler, Scott W., and Cindy Schaeffer. 2010. "Treating Serious Antisocial Behavior Using Multisystemic Therapy." In *Evidence-Based Psychotherapies for Children and Adolescents*, edited by John R. Weisz and Alan E. Kazdin, 259–276. New York: Guilford.

Henggeler, Scott W., and Ashli J. Sheidow. 2012. "Empirically Supported Family-Based Treatments for Conduct Disorder and Delinquency in Adolescents." *Journal of Marital and Family Therapy* 38: 30–58.

Irwin, Molly, and Lauren H. Supplee. 2012. "Directions in Implementation Research Methods for Behavioral and Social Science." *Journal of Behavioral Health Services and Research* 39: 339–342.

Kazdin, Alan E. 1997. "Parent Management Training: Evidence, Outcomes, and Issues." *Journal of the American Academy of Child and Adolescent Psychiatry* 36: 1349–1356.

Kerr, David C. R., David S. DeGarmo, Leslie D. Leve, and Patricia Chamberlain. 2014. "Juvenile Justice Girls' Depressive Symptoms and Suicidal Ideation 9 Years After Multidimensional Foster Care." *Journal of Consulting and Clinical Psychology* 82: 684–693.

Lally, J. Ronald, Peter L. Mangione, and Alice S. Honig. 1988. "The Syracuse University Family Development Research Program: Long-Range Impact of an Early Intervention with Low-Income Children and Their Families." In *Parent Education as Early Childhood Intervention: Emerging Directions in Theory, Research and Practice*, edited by D. R. Powell, 79–104. Norwood, NJ: Ablex.

Lee, Stephanie, Steve Aos, Elizabeth K. Drake, Anne Pennucci, Marna G. Miller, and Laurie Anderson. 2012. *Return on Investment: Evidence-Based Options to Improve Statewide Outcomes.* Olympia: Washington State Institute for Public Policy.

Leve, Leslie D., Patricia Chamberlain, and John B. Reid. 2005. "Intervention Outcomes for Girls Referred from Juvenile Justice: Effects on Delinquency." *Journal of Consulting and Clinical Psychology* 73: 1181–1185.

Leve, Leslie D., David C. R. Kerr, and Gordon T. Harold. 2013. "Young Adult Outcomes Associated with Teen Pregnancy among High-Risk Girls in a Randomized Controlled Trial of Multidimensional Treatment Foster Care." *Journal of Child and Adolescent Substance Abuse* 22: 431–434.

Littell, Julia H. 2005. "Lessons from a Systematic Review of Effect of Multisystemic Therapy." *Children and Youth Services Review* 27: 445–463.

Littell, Julia H., Melanie Popa, and Burnee Forsythe. 2005. "Multisystemic Therapy for Social, Emotional, and Behavioral Problems in Youth Aged 10–17." *Campbell Collaboration*. https://doi.org/10.4073//csr.2005.1.

Loeber, Rolf, N. Wim Slot, and Magda Stouthamer-Loeber. 2006. "A Three-Dimensional, Cumulative Developmental Model of Serious Delinquency." In *The Explanation of Crime: Context, Mechanisms, and Development*, edited by Per-Olof H. Wikström and Robert J. Sampson, 153–194. New York: Cambridge University Press.

Long, Patricia, Rex Forehand, Michelle Wierson, and Allison Morgan. 1994. "Does Parent Training with Young Noncompliant Children Have Long-Term Effects?" *Behavior Research and Therapy* 32: 101–107.

Manning, Matthew, Ross Homel, and Christine Smith. 2010. "A Meta-Analysis of the Effects of Early Developmental Prevention Programs in At-Risk Populations on Non-Health Outcomes in Adolescence." *Children and Youth Services Review* 32: 506–519.

Mason, W. Alex, Rick Kosterman, J. David Hawkins, Kevin P. Haggerty, and Richard L. Spoth. 2003. "Reducing Adolescents' Growth in Substance Use and Delinquency: Randomized Trial Effects of a Parent-Training Prevention Intervention." *Prevention Science* 4: 203–212.

McCord, Joan. 1991. "Family Relationships, Juvenile Delinquency, and Adult Criminality." *Criminology* 29: 397–417.

Mears, Daniel P. 2007. "Towards Rational and Evidence-Based Policy." *Journal of Criminal Justice* 35: 667–682.

Ogden, Terje, and Colleen A. Halliday-Boykins. 2004. "Multisystemic Treatment of Antisocial Adolescents in Norway: Replication of Clinical Outcomes Outside of the US." *Child and Adolescent Mental Health* 9: 77–83.

Olds, David L., Charles R. Henderson, Robert Chamberlin, and Robert Tatelbaum. 1986. "Preventing Child Abuse and Neglect: A Randomized Trial of Nurse Home Visitation." *Pediatrics* 78: 65–78.

Olds, David L., John Eckenrode, Charles R. Henderson, Harriet Kitzman, Jane Powers, Robert Cole, Kimberly Sidora, Pamela Morris, Lisa M. Pettitt, and Dennis W. Luckey. 1997. "Long-Term Effects of Home Visitation on Maternal Life Course and Child Abuse and Neglect: Fifteen-Year Follow-Up of a Randomized Trial." *Journal of the American Medical Association* 278: 637–643.

Olds, David L., Charles R. Henderson, Robert Cole, John Eckenrode, Harriet Kitzman, Dennis W. Luckey, Lisa M. Pettitt, Kimberly Sidora, Pamela Morris, and Jane Powers. 1998. "Long-Term Effects of Nurse Home Visitation on Children's Criminal and Antisocial Behavior: 15-Year Follow-Up of a Randomized Controlled Trial." *Journal of the American Medical Association* 280: 1238–1244.

Olds, David L., Lois Sadler, and Harriet J. Kitzman. 2007. "Programs for Parents of Infants and Toddlers: Recent Evidence from Randomized Trials." *Journal of Child Psychology and Psychiatry* 48: 355–391.

Patterson, Gerald. 1982. *Coercive Family Process*. Eugene, OR: Castalia.

Patterson, Gerald, John B. Reid, and Thomas J. Dishion. 1992. *Antisocial Boys*. Eugene, OR: Castalia.

Patterson, Gerald, Patricia Chamberlain, and John B. Reid. 1982. "A Comparative Evaluation of a Parent Training Program." *Behavior Therapy* 13: 638–650.

Petersilia, Joan. 2008. "Influencing Public Policy: An Embedded Criminologist Reflects on California Prison Reform." *Journal of Experimental Criminology* 4: 335–356.

Piquero, Alex R., Wesley G. Jennings, Brie Diamond, David P. Farrington, Richard E. Tremblay, Brandon C. Welsh, and Jennifer M. Reingle Gonzalez. 2016. "A Meta-Analysis Update on the Effects of Early Family/Parent Training Programs on Antisocial Behavior and Delinquency." *Journal of Experimental Criminology* 12: 229–248.

Rhoades, Kimberly A., Patricia Chamberlain, Rosemarie Roberts, and Leslie D. Leve. 2013. "MTFC for High-Risk Adolescent Girls: A Comparison of Outcomes in England and the United States." *Journal of Child and Adolescent Substance Abuse* 22: 435–449.

Sanders, Matthew R., Carol Markie-Dadds, Lucy A. Tully, and William Bor. 2000. "The Triple P-Positive Parenting Program: A Comparison of Enhanced, Standard, and Self-Directed Behavioral Family Intervention for Parents of Children with Early Onset Conduct Problems." *Journal of Consulting and Clinical Psychology* 68: 624–640.

Sawyer, Aaron M., and Charles M. Borduin. 2011. "Effects of Multisystemic Therapy through Midlife: A Follow-Up to a Randomized Clinical Trial with Serious Juvenile Offenders." *Journal of Consulting and Clinical Psychology* 79: 643–652.

Schaeffer, Cindy M., and Charles M. Borduin. 2005. "Long-Term Follow-Up to a Randomized Clinical Trial of Multisystemic Therapy with Serious and Violent Juvenile Offenders." *Journal of Consulting and Clinical Psychology* 73: 445–453.

Serketich, Wendy J., and Jean E. Dumas. 1996. "The Effectiveness of Behavioral Parent Training to Modify Antisocial Behavior in Children: A Meta-Analysis." *Behavior Therapy* 27: 171–186.

Sexton, Thomas L., and James F. Alexander. 2003. "Functional Family Therapy: A Mature Clinical Model for Working with At-Risk Adolescents and Their Families." In *Handbook of Family Therapy: The Science and Practice of Working with Families and Couples*, edited by Thomas L. Sexton, Gerald R. Weeks, and Michael S. Robbins, 323–348. New York: Brunner-Routledge.

Sexton, Thomas, and Charles W. Turner. 2010. "The Effectiveness of Functional Family Therapy for Youth with Behavioral Problems in a Community Practice Setting." *Journal of Family Psychology* 24: 339–348.

Sullivan, Christopher J., Brandon C. Welsh, and Omeed S. Ilchi. 2017. "Modeling the Scaling Up of Early Crime Prevention: Implementation Challenges and Opportunities for Translational Criminology." *Criminology & Public Policy* 16: 457–485.

Sundell, Knut, Kjell Hansson, Cecilia Andrée Löfholm, Tina Olsson, Lars-Henry Gustle, and Christina Kadesjö. 2008. "The Transportability of Multisystemic Therapy to Sweden: Short-Term Results from a Randomized Trial of Conduct-Disordered Youth." *Journal of Family Psychology* 22: 550–560.

Szapocznik, José, Seth J. Schwartz, Joan A. Muir, and C. Hendricks Brown. 2012. "Brief Strategic Family Therapy: An Intervention to Reduce Adolescent Risk Behavior." *Couple and Family Psychology: Research and Practice* 1: 134–145.

Thomas, Rae, and Melanie J. Zimmer-Gembeck. 2007. "Behavioral Outcomes of Parent-Child Interaction Therapy and Triple P—Positive Parenting Program: A Review and Meta-Analysis." *Journal of Abnormal Child Psychology* 35: 475–495.

Timmons-Mitchell, Jane, Monica B. Bender, Maureen A. Kishna, and Clare C. Mitchell. 2006. "An Independent Effectiveness Trial of Multisystemic Therapy with Juvenile Justice Youth." *Journal of Clinical Child and Adolescent Psychology* 35: 227–236.

Tolan, Patrick. 2002. "Crime Prevention: Focus on Youth." In *Crime: Public Policies for Crime Control*, 2nd ed., edited by James Q. Wilson and Joan Petersilia, 109–127. Oakland, CA: Institute for Contemporary Studies Press.

Turner, William, and Geraldine MacDonald. 2011. "Treatment Foster Care for Improving Outcomes in Children and Young People: A Systematic Review." *Research on Social Work Practice* 21: 501–527.

van der Stouwe, Trudy, Jessica J. Assher, Geert Jan J. M. Stams, Maja, Deković, Peter H. van der Laan. 2014. "The Effectiveness of Multisystemic Therapy (MST): A Meta-Analysis." *Clinical Psychology Review* 34: 468–481.

Wagner, David V., Charles M. Borduin, Aaron M. Sawyer, and Alex R. Dopp. 2014. "Long-Term Prevention of Criminality in Siblings of Serious and Violent Juvenile Offenders: A 25-Year Follow-Up to a Randomized Clinical Trial of Multisystemic Therapy." *Journal of Consulting and Clinical Psychology* 82: 492–499.

Washington State Institute for Public Policy. 2016a. "Multisystemic Therapy." http://www.wsipp.wa.gov/BenefitCost/Program/36.

Washington State Institute for Public Policy. 2016b. "Functional Family Therapy (Youth on Probation)." http://www.wsipp.wa.gov/BenefitCost/Program/32.

Washington State Institute for Public Policy. 2016c. "Functional Family Therapy (Youth in State Institutions." http://www.wsipp.wa.gov/BenefitCost/Program/40.

Washington State Institute for Public Policy. 2016d. "Multidimensional Treatment Foster Care." http://www.wsipp.wa.gov/BenefitCost/ Program/20.

Wasserman, Gail A., and Laurie S. Miller. 1998. "The Prevention of Serious and Violent Juvenile Offending." In *Serious and Violent Juvenile Offenders: Risk Factors and Successful Interventions*, edited by Rolf Loeber and David P. Farrington, 197–247. Thousand Oaks, CA: Sage.

Weiss, Bahr, Susan Han, Vicki Harris, Victoria K. Ngo, Annalise Caron, Robert Gallop, and Carol Guth. 2013. "An Independent Randomized Clinical Trial of Multisystemic Therapy with Non-Court Referred Adolescents with Serious Conduct Problems." *Journal of Consulting and Clinical Psychology* 81: 1027–1039.

Welsh, Brandon C. 2012a. "Delinquency Prevention." In *The Oxford Handbook of Juvenile Crime and Juvenile Justice*, edited by Barry C. Feld and Donna M. Bishop, 395–415. New York: Oxford University Press.

Welsh, Brandon C. 2012b. "Preventing Delinquency by Putting Families First." In *The Future of Criminology*, edited by Rolf Loeber and Brandon C. Welsh, 153–158. New York: Oxford University Press.

Welsh, Brandon C., David P. Farrington, and B. Raffan-Gowar. 2015. "Benefit-Cost Analysis of Crime Prevention Programs." In *Crime and Justice: A Review of Research*, Vol. 44, edited by Michael Tonry, 447–516. Chicago: University of Chicago Press.

Welsh, Brandon C., and Peter Greenwood. 2015. "Making It Happen: State Progress in Implementing Evidence-Based Programs for Delinquent Youth." *Youth Violence and Juvenile Justice* 13: 243–257.

Welsh, Brandon C., Mark W. Lipsey, Frederick P. Rivara, J. David Hawkins, Steve Aos, and Meghan E. Hollis-Peel. 2012. "Promoting Change, Changing Lives: Effective Prevention and Intervention to Reduce Serious Offending." In *From Juvenile Delinquency to Adult Crime: Criminal Careers, Justice Policy, and Prevention*, edited by Rolf Loeber and David P. Farrington, 245–277. New York: Oxford University Press.

Welsh, Brandon C., and Alex R. Piquero. 2012. "Investing Where It Counts: Preventing Delinquency and Crime with Early Family-Based Programs." In *Contemporary Issues in Criminological Theory and Research: The Role of Social Institutions*, edited by Richard Rosenfeld, Kenna Quinet, and Crystal Garcia, 13–28. Belmont, CA: Cengage.

Welsh, Brandon C., Christopher J. Sullivan, and David L. Olds. 2010. "When Early Crime Prevention Goes to Scale: A New Look at the Evidence." *Prevention Science* 11: 115–125.

Westermark, Pia Kyhle, Kjell Hansson, and Martin Olsson. 2011. "Multidimensional Treatment Foster Care (MTFC): Results from an Independent Replication." *Journal of Family Therapy* 33: 20–41.

Woolfenden, Susan, Katrina J. Williams, and Jennifer Peat. 2002. "Family and Parenting Interventions for Conduct Disorder and Delinquency: A Meta-Analysis of Randomized Controlled Trials." *Archives of Disease in Childhood* 86: 251–256.

CHAPTER 32

DEVELOPMENTAL PRESCHOOL AND SCHOOL PROGRAMS AGAINST VIOLENCE AND OFFENDING

IZABELA ZYCH AND DAVID P. FARRINGTON

SCHOOL programs against violence and offending are aimed at children and youth and implemented in educational settings. These programs usually include different components based on knowledge of risk and protective factors and might involve all the members of the school community such as teachers, students, and parents. Programs might be delivered by external agents such as researchers or, on the other hand, by teachers. Some of them are limited to specific workshops or a series of lessons, whereas others are school-wide interventions that are integrated in the curriculum and school policies. The instruments used for evaluation also differ among the interventions. This great variability in design, implementation, and evaluation strategies is also reflected in the outcomes, with some programs being more effective than others.

This chapter reviews knowledge on these programs, providing clues on features and components found to be the most effective, focusing particularly on meta-analytic findings. Interventions to prevent violence have been conducted for more than 50 years. The effectiveness of programs designed in the 1960s was limited, and therefore new programs appeared focusing on specific predictors of problem behaviors. Later interventions started to consider several predictors at the same time and also aimed to promote positive behaviors (Catalano et al. 2012). This approach is very useful since many social problems share similar risk and protective factors.

Among different crime-prevention methods, developmental crime prevention focuses on early-onset risk and protective factors (Welsh and Farrington 2010; Farrington 2015). The scientific research designs necessary to establish these factors are very complex, and it is worth mentioning that only longitudinal designs provide information on the ordering of these factors with respect to the outcomes. Most of the studies of risk and protective factors are correlational in nature, and therefore drawing conclusions from them about cause and effect relationships is rarely possible. Only studies that analyze changes in risk/protective factors over time in relation to changes in outcomes, controlling for confounding variables and investigating within-individual changes, are appropriate for establishing causal risk factors (Murray, Farrington, and Eisner 2009). Even though these factors are difficult to study, a large amount of knowledge has already been gained and can be successfully utilized in designing the intervention programs.

Building on knowledge about these factors, it is possible to design programs to reinforce protective factors and reduce risks (Farrington 2015). Some of these interventions can be successfully implemented in schools. This approach is particularly interesting for many different reasons. On the one hand, there are specific risk and protective factors related to school (see Chapter 21). At the same time, one of the main objectives of formal education itself is not only to enhance academic skills but also to provide education for life, promoting positive interpersonal relationships, civic behavior, solidarity, and responsibility for one's own and others' well-being (Ortega 2005). Another good reason for conducting interventions in schools is that, at least in Organization for Economic Co-operation and Development (OECD) countries, students receive almost 8,000 hours of instruction during their primary and lower secondary education, an average of about 800 hours per year (OCED 2014). Taking into account that this time is spent with personnel who are specifically trained in teaching and learning processes, methodologies and strategies, curriculum planning, and knowledge about child development and needs, the school is a perfect setting for the implementation of prevention programs against violence and offending.

Interventions are conducted in schools all over the world, but there are big differences among these programs regarding the methodologies employed for their design, implementation, and evaluation. A systematic review of anti-bullying programs published by Evans, Fraser, and Cotter (2014) reported that about one in five programs used only one item to evaluate the outcomes. Similar results were found by Ryan and Smith (2009) in another systematic review on evaluation practices used in anti-bullying programs. That review reported that about one-third of the studies were uncontrolled, two-thirds did not report follow-ups, about half included only one informant, and programs rarely met all the criteria of efficacy, effectiveness, or dissemination. For these reasons, choosing an effective program is a big challenge for educators and policy makers. Thus, this chapter describes the most important meta-analytic findings and gives examples of programs that have proved to be effective in reducing violence or delinquency. Section I reviews programs found to be effective in reducing violence and offending in general, while Section II reviews anti-bullying programs, and Section III reviews other related interventions. Examples of interventions found to be successful in reducing bullying, violence, or delinquency are described.

I. School-Based Violence-Prevention Programs

School-based violence-prevention programs are interventions that usually address numerous violent and aggressive behaviors (Farrington 2015). Some of these programs might focus on delinquent or criminal behavior, but in most cases they focus on self-reported or other-reported aggression in school or outside school.

This section describes school-based violence-prevention programs, starting from the most general scientific findings and finishing with descriptions of specific interventions. Thus, findings from a recent systematic review of systematic reviews and meta-analyses on the topic will be described first (Farrington, Lösel, and Ttofi 2016), followed by the findings of other reviews and meta-analyses and, finally, programs proved to be effective in reducing violence or delinquency are described.

A. Systematic Reviews and Meta-Analyses of Violence-Prevention Programs

Recently, reviews of systematic reviews and meta-analyses of developmental prevention programs were published by Farrington and colleagues (Farrington et al. 2016, 2017). These studies are particularly interesting because they brought together findings from research syntheses on the topic that usually include dozens or hundreds of empirical studies each, and therefore they provided a global vision and filled gaps in knowledge by analyzing findings from the whole field. The studies focused on developmental and social prevention programs, including general, individual, family, and school interventions, but since Chapter 31 of this book describes family programs and Chapter 33 focuses on individual programs, only findings from school programs are included in this chapter.

Twenty-five systematic reviews of school programs were included in Farrington et al. (2017), and effect sizes with confidence intervals could be calculated for 11 reports. It was found that 9 out of 11 meta-analyses of school-based prevention programs reported that, overall, the interventions were effective in reducing problem behaviors. The largest effect sizes were found for cognitive-behavioral programs (Farrington et al. 2016). The median odds ratio in these 11 meta-analyses of school-based interventions was 1.22. This overall effect size is not very large (Lipsey and Wilson 2001), but it is very important, since it corresponds to about a 20 percent reduction in aggression.

A systematic review of universal school-based programs to prevent violent and aggressive behavior, conducted by Hahn et al. (2007), reported the effectiveness of different interventions according to the percentage decreases in problem behaviors. The results refer to intervention types and educational levels but do not focus on specific programs.

Overall, the median relative decrease in the intervention group compared with the control group was 15 percent. The biggest decrease were found in pre-kindergarten and kindergarten (32.4 percent), followed by high schools (29.2 percent), elementary schools (18 percent), and middle schools (7.3 percent).

In relation to intervention types, Hahn et al. (2007) found that peer mediation programs worked best (a 61.2 percent decrease), followed by social skills training (19.1 percent), environmental classroom change (15 percent), cognitive/affective programs (14 percent), environmental school change (11.7 percent), and information conveyed programs (8.6 percent). Programs yielded different results also depending on their focus, with the highest percentage of change for dating violence (29.2 percent), followed by disruptive or antisocial behavior (19.1 percent), general violence (10.3 percent), bullying (6.7 percent), and gang activity (5.3 percent). The most effective programs were conducted by peers or students (41.6 percent), administrators/counselors (34.4 percent), and teachers (17.5 percent), with less change in the case of researchers (7.3 percent) and non-school personnel (5.3 percent). The best results were found in high-crime/low-socioeconomic status community environments (29.2 percent). These results should be interpreted with caution, since different numbers of studies were included in each category, ranging from 1 study only (dating violence) to 49 (interventions conducted by teachers). The main conclusion of this review is that school-based programs can be effective in reducing violence.

Although not based on systematic searches or meta-analysis, a thorough review of interventions against youth violence, conducted by the leading spokesperson on matters of public health in the United States, the Surgeon General (U.S. Department of Health and Human Services 2001) provides very useful information on programs and, therefore, is briefly described in this section. This review summarized information on youth violence in the United States, listing interventions as model or promising programs. Interventions were classified as effective or ineffective, and among the former, "model" programs were those that met the highest standards of effectiveness (experimental and quasi-experimental designs with an effect size of 0.30 or larger, with both replication and sustainability of effects), whereas "promising" programs were those that met minimum standards (experimental and quasi-experimental designs with an effect size of 0.10 or greater, with either replication or sustainability of effects). Programs were also classified as those that showed effectiveness on delinquency/violence or risk factors. Only school-based programs are described in this chapter. Programs that were found to be effective in reducing risk factors such as drug and alcohol use are not described, since this chapter focuses specifically on delinquency or violence.

The only school-based program that showed effectiveness in reducing delinquency or violence and was classified by the Surgeon General (U.S. Department of Health and Human Services 2001) as "model" was the Seattle Social Development Project (Hawkins, Von Cleve, and Catalano 1991). The Surgeon General included the following as "promising" programs: the Perry Preschool Program (Weikart et al. 1970), the School Transitional Environmental Program (STEP) (Felner and Adan 1988), the Olweus anti-bullying program (Olweus 1995), Promoting Alternative Thinking Skills (PATHS;

Greenberg and Kusché 2002), Families and Schools Together (FAST track; Conduct Problems Prevention Research Group 1992), the Good Behavior Game (Kellam et al. 1994), and I Can Problem Solve (Spivack and Shure, 1974). All these programs are described in this section, except the Olweus anti-bullying program, which is described together with other anti-bullying interventions.

B. Proven School-Based Violence-Prevention Programs

1. *The Seattle Social Development Project*

This intervention was conducted in public elementary schools in Seattle by Hawkins and colleagues (1991), was aimed at teachers, parents, and students, and was based on the social development model. Teacher training was provided during five days each year in three main domains: proactive classroom management, interactive teaching, and cooperative learning. Proactive classroom management consisted of training teachers in giving clear instructions and rewarding students for desired behaviors and proactively managing classroom discipline with clear routines, rules, and procedures. The interactive teacher training component trained teachers in designing a motivating curriculum and monitoring the learning process. The cooperative learning component consisted of helping teachers to enhance learning in groups focusing on cooperation among the students.

Interventions with students were aimed at fostering their cognitive, social, emotional, and behavioral skills based on an interpersonal cognitive problem-solving curriculum. In grade 6, students received a four-hour training session in refusing to engage in problem behaviors, finding positive alternatives, and suggesting that other students join these positive alternatives. Parent training included behavioral management skills, academic support skills, and helping children to avoid drugs. Behavioral management consisted of learning how to detect positive and negative behaviors, provide expectancies, reinforce positive behaviors, and administer adequate consequences for undesirable behaviors. Academic support skills included learning how to talk with teachers about children's learning, helping children in learning mathematics and language, and creating learning-friendly home environments. Helping children to avoid drugs included increasing family bonds, conflict resolution, family management and child's engagement in the family, and helping children to deal with peer influence.

This program was effective in reducing delinquency in boys and drug use in girls by grade 6 (O'Donnell et al. 1995), and it also reduced violence at age 18 (Hawkins et al. 1999). Nevertheless, at ages 27 (Hawkins et al. 2008) and 30 (Hill et al. 2014), the impact on violence or delinquency was no longer significant, although participants in the experimental group still showed less sexually risky behavior.

2. *The Perry Preschool Program*

This program provided high-quality preschool education for children at high risk of school failure from low-income families at ages 3 and 4. It was started in the 1960s by

Weikart and his colleagues (1970). It implemented the HighScope curriculum, based on general curriculum guidelines, but through an active and participatory learning approach. This curriculum addressed traditional academic subjects together with additional content such as promoting independence, curiosity, decision-making, persistence, cooperation, creativity, and problem solving. The teaching was approached in a way that differs from most of the preschool programs, because children's participation in the learning process was active and based on direct experience, making plans and decisions supported by the teachers. At the same time, teachers provided contexts in which children felt free to explore, but also set limits that were necessary for children's safety. A broad variety of materials relating to student interests and culture were provided, and children were encouraged to use them to promote independence and initiative. There was a relatively flexible daily routine with different individual and group activities, including work, playing, exercising, or cleaning up, among others, based on a so-called "plan–do–review" sequence.

Among other benefits, this program was effective in preventing offending, according to a long-term 40-year follow-up (Schweinhart et al. 2005). Children who participated in the program, compared to the control group, had fewer lifetime arrests in adolescence (7 percent vs. 29 percent had five or more arrests) and at age 40 (36 percent vs. 55 percent had five or more arrests). The percentage of people ever sentenced to jail by age 40 was also lower in the experimental group (28 percent vs. 52 percent). In general, the percentages of all types of crimes were lower in the experimental group.

3. *The School Transitional Environmental Program*

This program (Felner and Adan 1988) was designed to help students during the transition between different levels of education (middle grade schools and junior and senior high schools). There were three main components of the intervention: decreasing the flux and complexity of the new school setting, increasing emotional and academic support during the transition, and fostering connectedness and a sense of belonging to the school. Teachers received specific training on developmental, emotional, and organizational topics. Classes were restructured to create communities within larger schools, homeroom teachers provided help and support to individual students, and they also maintained relationships with the families and other teachers. This program was effective in improving classroom behaviors according to a five-year follow-up (Felner et al. 1993), but no detailed or further evaluation was conducted.

4. *Promoting Alternative Thinking Skills*

The PATHS curriculum (Greenberg and Kusché 2002) is a social and emotional learning program for preschoolers and students in grades 1 to 6. It contains detailed manuals and materials for teachers (pictures, puppets, posters, stickers, cards, novels, dialogs, etc.), packed in attractive suitcases for each grade. These materials are ready to use with a certain degree of flexibility during the classroom hours. It also contains information for parents and some materials that can be used in homes. Lessons are taught for 20 to 30 minutes, two to three times per week. PATHS focuses on five social and emotional domains—self-control, emotional understanding, self-esteem, relationship skills, and interpersonal problem-solving skills—with all of them included in most of the units. The modules include objectives, scripts that can be used in the classroom, and materials to communicate with families. According to the authors, the program is easy to use by teachers, enhances parent involvement, and is appropriate for students with or without special needs. Dozens of articles have been published reporting findings from this program, and a detailed description of the evaluations goes beyond the scope of this chapter. It is worth mentioning that the PATHS curriculum was found to significantly decrease teacher-rated aggressive behaviors and attention deficit hyperactivity disorder in a large-scale randomized controlled trial in elementary schools in Zurich, Switzerland (Malti, Ribeaud, and Eisner 2012).

5. *Fast Track*

This program is a multicomponent intervention aimed at children with a high risk of conduct problems identified in kindergartens, and it was conducted when they were attending grades 1 to 10 (Conduct Problems Prevention Research Group 1992). It was designed with a holistic approach, taking into account risk factors related to school, classroom, and family. In elementary schools (grades 1 to 5), it included the PATHS curriculum described above. It also included parent training, which promoted family–school relationships and behavior management skills, together with home visits. For children, specific social-skills training groups were held, tutoring in reading was provided, and there was a specific component in which friendships among children were promoted. Another phase that was designed for adolescents (grades 6 to 10) included an individualized intervention depending on the needs of each child, parent and adolescent meetings to give support during the transition to middle school, and visits and support for families.

Fast Track provided multiple benefits that have been reported in dozens of research articles whose description goes beyond the scope of the current chapter. In relation to delinquency and the effect on youth arrests (Conduct Problems Prevention Research Group 2010), it should be noted that the percentage of juvenile arrests based on court records in the intervention group was smaller than in the control group (odds ratio = 0.71). There was no significant overall effect on adult arrests based on court records, but for children with the highest risk at pre-test, the program reduced the number of people who were arrested four or more times by 47 percent. There was no significant effect on self-reported offenses, but the onset of juvenile arrests was delayed.

6. *The Good Behavior Game*

Randomized trials of the Good Behavior Game were conducted in the 1980s with first- and second-grade students. This program was designed to help teachers in classroom management and in establishing clear behavioral rules. First, the rules were displayed on posters for some months. Then, students were divided into three teams, and, for 10 minutes three times a week, they were rewarded if all the members followed the rules. Later, the time was increased, individual work was also incorporated into the game, and rewards were progressively changed to be less tangible or immediate. A manual for teachers was provided.

Among other benefits, this program was found to be effective in decreasing disruptive and aggressive behaviors in school (Kellam et al. 1994). The results obtained from self-reports, juvenile courts, and incarceration records among highly aggressive males showed that violent and criminal behavior was 16 percent lower in the experimental group compared to the control condition (Kellam et al. 2011).

7. I Can Problem-Solve

This intervention was designed to prevent problem behaviors through the development of skills in interpersonal problem solving by children between 4 and 12 years of age (Spivack and Shure 1974). For the youngest children, it consisted of a game that enhanced language and thinking skills, including training in a specific vocabulary relating to problem solving (e.g., same vs. different, before vs. after). In the next step, a vocabulary relating to feelings and emotions was taught, and then, in the third step, finding solutions to problems and understanding consequences of behaviors was taught. These skills were then applied to classroom situations in which children were encouraged, through dialogue with teachers, to find solutions to their own daily conflicts. For older children, it was emphasized that a problem can be solved in many different ways and that they should think about different possibilities in order to finally find the best one. It was suggested that the teachers should include at least one 20-minute lesson every day for four months. This program was effective in decreasing impulsive and problem behaviors and in increasing prosocial behavior (Shure 2001), but to our knowledge no specific evaluations of its effects on violence or offending have been conducted.

II. Anti-Bullying Programs

Anti-bullying programs are usually conducted in schools and are designed with the objective of decreasing bullying perpetration and victimization. These programs usually include different components and are targeted to different members of the school community (Zych et al. 2017). This section will start with a description of the findings from reviews of systematic reviews and meta-analyses on the topic, followed by a detailed description of meta-analytic findings and, finally, specific programs.

A. Systematic Reviews and Meta-Analyses of Anti-Bullying Programs

Meta-analyses and systematic reviews of anti-bullying programs were reviewed by Ttofi, Eisner, and Bradshaw (2014), who analyzed six reports taking into account quality criteria regarding literature searches, inclusion criteria, calculation of the effect sizes, definitions of bullying, etc. There were big differences in methodologies and criteria used in these research syntheses. These variations concerned search strategies and intensities, timelines, inclusion criteria and their application, and theoretical approach, and they led to the inclusion of different numbers of studies in each review ranging from 13 to 44. Thus, it is not surprising that the results also differed among the studies, with some of them finding only a very small overall effectiveness of anti-bullying programs (e.g., Ferguson, Miguel, Kilburn, and Sanchez 2007) and others showing that these interventions were generally effective in decreasing bullying (e.g., Farrington and Ttofi 2009). An optimistic finding of this review is that the meta-analysis that included the highest number of empirical studies and was based on the most rigorous criteria and exhaustive analysis found that, overall, these programs were effective in reducing bullying (Farrington and Ttofi 2009).

A systematic review of systematic reviews and meta-analyses on bullying and cyberbullying was conducted by Zych, Ortega-Ruiz, and Del Rey (2015b), including also findings from research syntheses of anti-bullying programs. Once again, it was found that designs, implementations, and, therefore, results varied among the studies, but nevertheless most of the research syntheses showed that the programs were generally effective in reducing bullying. Even though the overall effect sizes were not always large, the practical implications of the impact on participants was high. Ferguson et al. (2007) found an overall effect size on involvement in bullying of $r = .12$, whereas Merrell et al. (2008) found that peer reports showed an overall effect size of $d = .32$ on participation in bullying; $r = .12$ corresponds roughly to an absolute 12 percent decrease, whereas $d = .32$ corresponds roughly to an absolute 16 percent decrease.

These overall effect sizes are usually calculated only from studies with high methodological quality but without taking into account the theoretical standpoint, focus, type of intervention, number of elements, involvement of different members of the school community, and other important variables. Thus, the overall effect sizes only suggest that, in general, these programs might be effective. On the other hand, a detailed analysis of different components and features, as in the meta-analysis conducted by Farrington and Ttofi (2009; Ttofi and Farrington 2011), is necessary for establishing what works and what does not. This meta-analysis was published by the Campbell Collaboration, and therefore it followed strict methodological criteria. Among the meta-analyses of anti-bullying programs, it was based on the most thorough searches and rigorous quality criteria, and therefore it is considered that it produced the most exact results. This meta-analysis synthesized the results from 89 reports of 53 anti-bullying programs conducted all over the world. It was based on broad searches in 18 databases, 35 journals, and contacts with leading research teams. There were strict inclusion and exclusion criteria and coding procedures. Detailed descriptions of each included intervention were provided and overall effect sizes were calculated for bullying perpetration and victimization. Moreover, the effectiveness of different components and design features was also evaluated.

The meta-analysis conducted by Farrington and Ttofi (2009) included 41 programs that provided data allowing the calculation of effect sizes for effectiveness in reducing the perpetration of bullying. Overall, the effect size calculated from all these interventions showed a significant reduction in perpetration (odds ratio = 1.36), which indicates 20 percent to 23 percent fewer bullies in the experimental conditions. Another important finding is that, although some of the interventions were not significantly effective, none of the programs increased perpetration.

Key elements and design features of the programs were coded and dichotomized with the objective of comparing groups of studies (Farrington and Ttofi 2009; Ttofi and Farrington 2011). Sixteen elements were associated with significantly larger effect sizes when they were present. Establishing a formal whole-school policy against bullying showed a significantly larger effect size. Cooperative group work among professionals such as teachers and other experts was also found to be beneficial. Programs that included disciplinary methods referring to the use of somewhat punitive methods to stop bullying situations were significantly more effective in reducing perpetration in comparison to the interventions that did not include these methods. Improved playground supervision during activities and contexts that were found to have a high risk of bullying was also found to be effective. Classroom rules against bullying, frequently designed through cooperation between teachers and students, and displayed in a visible place, together with the emphasis on classroom management of bullying situations, were also elements that were associated with larger effect sizes in decreasing perpetration. Another effective element was a school conference in which programs were announced and students were frequently informed and sensitized about bullying in their schools.

Interventions that included teacher training worked better than those without this element. Also, training for parents that was intended to provide information about the intervention through meetings with teachers or educational presentations, together with information for parents referring to materials such as manuals or newsletters informing them about the program, were features whose presence had larger effect sizes. Programs with longer durations for children (270 days or more) and teachers (4 days or more) and programs with a greater intensity for children (20 hours or more) and teachers (10 hours or more) were found to work better than interventions with shorter durations and lesser intensities. Moreover, a higher total number of elements (11 or more) was found to be beneficial, suggesting a dose-response relationship. Finally, effect sizes were found to be larger in programs inspired by Dan Olweus, whose program will be described in detail in the next section. Table 32.1 shows the percentages of programs that included each of the 16 elements found to be more effective than others according to the meta-analysis (Farrington and Ttofi 2009; Ttofi and Farrington 2011).

The study of design features showed that effect sizes for the programs were larger for older children (aged 11 years or more), for evaluations published in 2003 or earlier, and for evaluations with outcome measures based on bullying two or more times per month. Comparisons of geographic zones showed that programs conducted in Norway were more effective when compared to other areas (possibly because of the Olweus program) and also that programs in Europe yielded larger effect sizes when compared to other

Table 32.1 Percentages of Programs Including Elements That Showed
Larger Effect Sizes for Decreasing Perpetration

Element	Programs Including the Element
Classroom rules	73.2%
Classroom management	68.3%
Information for parents	68.3%
Training for teachers	68.3%
Whole-school policy	58.5%
Intensity for teachers of 10 hours or more	55.6%
Cooperative group work	53.7%
Duration for children of 270 days or more	50%
Duration for teachers of 4 days or more	50%
School conferences	48.8%
Total elements of 11 or more	43.9%
Parent training	41.5%
Intensity for children of 20 hours or more	40.6%
Inspired by Olweus	39%
Disciplinary methods	31.7%
Improved playground supervision	26.8%

Percentages were calculated based on the meta-analysis conducted by Farrington and Ttofi (2009).

zones. Finally, programs with 900 or more participants also worked better than those with smaller samples.

B. Proven Anti-Bullying Programs

Because the current chapter focuses on violent outcomes, only examples of interventions that were effective in decreasing bullying perpetration are described. Nevertheless, it is worth mentioning that some programs that had large effect sizes for reducing victimization (e.g., Alsaker and Valkanover 2001; Ortega, Del Rey, and Mora-Merchán 2004) were not significantly effective in reducing perpetration.

As described in the previous section, programs inspired by Dan Olweus generally showed larger effect sizes than those not inspired by this author. Nevertheless, once again, these results should be interpreted with caution, since analysis of the programs one by one show that many programs that were not inspired by Olweus yielded significant effect sizes. Among the 41 interventions that were included in the meta-analysis conducted by

Farrington and Ttofi (2009), 14 showed significant effect sizes in decreasing perpetration (Whitney et al. 1994; Melton et al. 1998; Olweus 2004; Pepler et al. 2004; Salmivalli et al. 2004; Andreou, Didaskalou, and Vlachou 2007; Ertesveg and Vaaland 2007; Evers et al. 2007; Raskauskas 2007; Menard et al. 2008; Fonagy et al. 2009). Out of these 14 programs, 8 were inspired by the work of Dan Olweus (Whitney et al. 1994; Melton et al. 1998; Pepler et al. 2004; Salmivalli et al. 2004). Even though there are some differences among these programs, taking into account space limitations of this chapter, the Olweus program will be described only once. Detailed descriptions of the programs that were not inspired by Olweus but had significant effect sizes are also included.

1. *The Olweus Bullying Prevention Program*

The Olweus bullying prevention program (Olweus 1995) was originally developed in Norway. The effect sizes of this program were particularly large, and it inspired many other programs that proved to be effective in reducing bullying. It is worth mentioning that this program includes all the 16 elements that were proved to work better than others as described in the previous section (see Table 32.1). This program was aimed at children in primary and junior high schools (ages 11 to 14).

According to Olweus (1995), the program was designed taking into account a series of basic principles applied through different interventions at school, classroom, and individual levels. These principles focus on the necessity of creating contexts with high affect, warmth, and support but, at the same time, clear behavioral limits and non-hostile or non-physical but consistent consequences that are applied in the case of transgressions. The Olweus program was developed in collaboration with the existing school personnel, involving teachers, school psychologists or counselors, parents, and other members of the school community.

At the school level, a survey was conducted and there was a conference day. Supervision during high-risk situations was improved, and coordinating groups were formed. There were also meetings between school personnel and parents. At the classroom level, there were regular class meetings with students, and classroom anti-bullying rules were established. The program also included interventions at the individual level, such as serious talks with bullies and victims, meetings with their parents, and finding specific solutions to each problem. There was a significant relationship between the intensity of dosage and the reduction in bully/victim problems, with greater implementation resulting in bigger changes (Olweus 2004). This program was implemented in different countries and tested in several research projects. Among them, the New National Initiative Against Bullying was probably the project with the greatest number of participants, including 100 schools and 21,000 students. Based on the age-cohort design, the results showed that perpetration decreased by 37 percent, 48 percent, and 49 percent for the three evaluated cohorts (Olweus 2005).

2. *The SPC and CAPSLE Program*

This program (Fonagy et al. 2009) was conducted in the United States and included 10 out of the 16 elements described in Table 32.1. The intervention included two programs. The first, School Psychiatric Consultation (SPC), consisted of implementing a protocol against different problems, such as disruptive behavior, internalizing problems, or poor academic performance. This component was delivered by child psychiatry residents under supervision. At the same time, CAPSLE (Creating a Peaceful School Learning Environment) was developed from the psychodynamic social system theoretical standpoint, focusing on the relationships between bullies, victims, and bystanders, including all members of the school community (a whole-school approach), and promoting the awareness of one's own and other people's mental states. This program was implemented by school staff and was aimed at children from kindergarten to fifth grade. Based on a randomized controlled trial, the analysis of interactions with time between experimental and control groups showed that the program was effective in decreasing perpetration in the post-tests and follow-ups and that CAPSLE yielded better results than SPC (Fonagy et al. 2009).

3. *Greek Anti-Bullying Program*

This intervention (Andreou et al. 2007) was implemented in Greece with fourth- to sixth-grade students (mean age = 10.23). Five out of the 16 elements described in Table 32.1 were included. The program was conducted by trained school teachers and consisted of eight curriculum-based activities. It was inspired by the work of Salmivalli (1999) and focused on raising awareness about bullying and group dynamics, self-reflection on the roles adopted by each student, and commitment to new, positive ways of approaching conflicts. This intervention was based on an ecological approach. The comparison of before and after scores for the experimental group, utilizing *t*-tests, showed no significant decrease in perpetration (Andreou et al. 2007), but before–after, experimental–control odds ratios showed that the program had a significant effect in reducing perpetration (Farrington and Ttofi 2009).

4. *Transtheoretical-Based Tailored Anti-Bullying Program*

This intervention (Evers et al. 2007) also showed significant effects in decreasing bullying perpetration, and it was very different from the rest. This program only included one of the 16 elements (information for parents), and it was conducted in the United States, through information and communication technologies with children in middle (ages 11 to 14) and high schools (ages 14 to 17). The main approach of this intervention was based on a theory of behavior change focusing on decision-making and reinforcement. There were only three sessions for students and optional material for parents and teachers. About 40 percent of children who were identified as perpetrators in the pre-test progressed to be uninvolved after the intervention (vs. 21 percent in the control group) (Evers et al. 2007).

5. *Bully-Proofing Your School*

This program (Menard et al. 2008) included 9 out of the 16 components, and it was conducted in elementary and middle schools in the United States. It was a school-wide program, included in the classroom curriculum, that contained three main elements. It was intended to raise awareness and zero tolerance of bullying, provide skills for dealing with bullying and assisting the victims, create a positive school climate, and change bystanders' behaviors. It also emphasized commitment against bullying, involving all the members of the school community. This intervention was effective in reducing per-petration, although results varied throughout the analyzed years and levels of analysis (e.g., item-level, scale-level per year, scale before-after) (Menard et al. 2008).

6. *Kia Kaha*

This program (Raskauskas 2007) was implemented in New Zealand and included 5 out of the 16 elements. It was aimed at children aged between 8 and 13 years enrolled in ele-mentary schools. It was based on a whole-school approach, educating teachers, parents, students, and administrators about bullying, including curriculum design and resources. One particular feature of this program is that it also involved police officers who were trained as educators. The self-reported perpetration after the program in the experimental group was found to be lower than in the control group, although school-level comparisons showed no significant differences in the percentages of bullies (Raskauskas 2007).

7. *The Respect Program*

This program (Ertesvag and Vaaland 2007) was conducted in Norway in grades 5 to 10 and included 12 out of the 16 elements reported to be the most effective in tackling bullying perpetration. It was designed to target different types of problem behaviors including bullying, disobedience (disturbing or breaking the rules), off-task behavior (disengaging from learning and engaging in other behavior), and aggression in gen-eral. There were several basic principles of the program. According to these principles, adults were considered to be a source of authority, while the intervention was broad and targeted different problem behaviors, including all members of the school community at all levels (individual, classroom, and school). The program was always implemented in the same way by different actors, across times and situations. Additionally, there was also a commitment to continuity among actions, with an established order, rationale, and continuity over time. These principles were implemented within four main strategies: a whole-school approach, classroom leadership, timing adapted to academic activity, and commitment of all the adults. This program was effective in decreasing all of the targeted problem behaviors. Bullying perpetration was reduced in elementary school students and in grade 8 of secondary schools, according to self-reports, and in most of the grades according to teacher ratings. However, these results should be interpreted with caution, since levels of self-reported (but not other reported) reactive aggression (other than bullying) were higher in the intervention group (Ertesvag and Vaaland 2007).

III. OTHER INTERVENTIONS

This chapter focuses on school-based developmental interventions to reduce vio-lence and delinquency. Nevertheless, there are other related interventions, such as after-school programs, mentoring, and interventions against cyberbullying, which are worthwhile mentioning. This section contains some information about these other interventions, although no profound analysis is provided because it would extend the scope of the current chapter.

A. After-School Programs

Formal activities that are not part of the school curriculum are mostly designed with the objective of promoting positive competencies and reducing risks through organized activities and helping children to overcome developmental tasks and challenges. Among these organized activities, after-school programs are supervised by adults, and one of their advantages is reducing self-care during the parents' working hours (Mahoney et al. 2005). Frequently, they are aimed at children in unsafe neighborhoods who, otherwise, would be at risk of associating with delinquent peers. Federal investment in after-school programs in the United States has increased in the last decades, and these programs have been found to be effective in reducing different types of risky behaviors (Afterschool Alliance 2013).

A recent systematic review and meta-analysis of after-school programs for delinquency prevention, conducted by Taheri and Welsh (2016), showed that the overall mean effect size for these programs was not significant. Nevertheless, as in the case of any mean score, the results should be interpreted with caution. In this case, more thorough analysis is needed, because the individual results showed great variation among the studies. Three programs showed significant or large effect sizes in reducing delinquency, two programs increased criminality, and the other programs were not significant. The program characteristics were not related to the overall effect size.

B. Mentoring

The main idea of these programs consists of establishing interpersonal relationships in which mentors provide support for mentees, with the objective of benefiting the latter (DuBois and Karcher 2005). Mentors have more knowledge or skills that can be transmitted to mentees, but both may be equal in roles (e.g., both are students, colleagues, or peers). Mentoring interventions can be conducted in different settings, and some of them are held in schools. A meta-analysis of mentoring programs in relation to juvenile delinquency evaluated the effectiveness of these interventions (Tolan et al. 2013). It was found that mentoring is often effective in decreasing violence (weighted effect size g = 0.21), aggression (weighted effect size g = 0.29), and related risk factors. Altogether, 46 interventions were included in this meta-analysis.

C. Programs Against Cyberbullying

Cyberbullying is a form of bullying that is perpetrated through electronic devices, and research on the topic is relatively recent (Baldry, Farrington, and Sorrentino 2015;

Zych, Ortega-Ruiz, and Del Rey 2015a). Thus, meta-analyses of programs to reduce cy-berbullying are still in progress, as can be seen in the example of the systematic review registered as a title by the Campbell Collaboration that is planned to be published by Fong and Espelage (2015)[1]. A narrative review of programs against cyberbullying can be found in Zych, Baldry, and Farrington (2017). Thus, meta-analytic findings will not be described in this section, and only one example of a program is included.

The ConRed Program (Ortega-Ruiz, Del Rey, and Casas 2012) was designed spe-cifically to reduce cyberbullying. It focused on empathy, face-to-face bullying, and Internet dependency and was based on knowledge about traditional anti-bullying programs and specific characteristics of this new kind of aggression. ConRed is a whole-school intervention involving students, teachers, and parents, targeting the whole school climate and based on a theory of normative social beliefs, which states that behaviors are influenced by social conventions. It included eight sessions during three months, grouped in three units: one focusing on safety and information control, the second related to prosocial Internet use and moral principles, and the third aimed to deal with problems such as technology abuse and cyberbullying. There was direct work with all members of the school community and a campaign to raise awareness, including leaflets, bookmarks, and posters. This program showed promising results, decreasing cyberbullying aggression in boys who were identified as perpetrators both in the treatment group as a whole and in the treatment group of bully victims (Del Rey, Casas, and Ortega 2016).

IV. CONCLUSIONS

This chapter reviewed evaluations of school-based developmental programs to pre-vent violence and offending. Meta-analytic findings were described, providing a global, synthesized vision of the effectiveness of interventions and of their different components and features. Also, specific programs that have been proved to be effective in reducing violence or delinquency were described. The information included in this chapter shows that interventions can be effective but should be chosen with caution, since some components and some specific programs work better than others. Only programs and components that have been proven to be effective for specific outcomes and populations should be implemented. These programs have enormous social benefits, and cost-benefit analysis shows that they can also save a lot of money, given the high monetary costs of crime (Farrington 2015).

NOTE

1. After this chapter was written, a new meta-analysis of cyberbullying programs was completed (Gaffney et al. 2018).

REFERENCES

Afterschool Alliance. 2013. *Evaluations Backgrounder: A Summary of Formal Evaluations of Afterschool Programs' Impact on Academics, Behavior, Safety and Family Life*. Washington, DC: Afterschool Alliance.

Alsaker, Françoise D., and Stefan Valkanover. 2001. "Early Diagnosis and Prevention of Victimization in Kindergarten." In *Peer Harassment in School*, edited by Jaana Juvonen and Sandra Graham, 175–195. New York: Guilford.

Andreou, Elenia, Eleni Didaskalou, and Anastasia Vlachou. 2007. "Evaluating the Effectiveness of a Curriculum-Based Anti-Bullying Intervention Program in Greek Primary Schools." *Educational Psychology* 27: 693–711.

Baldry, Anna C., David P. Farrington, and Anna Sorrentino. 2015. "'Am I at Risk of Cyberbullying?' A Narrative Review and Conceptual Framework for Research on Risk of Cyberbullying and Cybervictimization: The Risk and Needs Assessment Approach." *Aggression and Violent Behavior* 23: 36–51.

Catalano, Richard F., Abigail A. Fagan, Loretta E. Gavin, Mark T. Greenberg, Charles E. Irwin Jr., David A. Ross, and Daniel T. L. Shek. 2012. "Worldwide Application of Prevention Science in Adolescent Health." *The Lancet* 379: 1653–1664.

Conduct Problems Prevention Research Group. 1992. "A Developmental and Clinical Model for the Prevention of Conduct Disorder: The FAST Track Program." *Development and Psychopathology* 4: 509–527.

Conduct Problems Prevention Research Group. 2010. "Fast Track Intervention Effects on Youth Arrests and Delinquency." *Journal of Experimental Criminology* 6: 131–157.

Del Rey, Rosario, José A. Casas, and Rosario Ortega. 2016. "The Impacts of the ConRed Program on Different Cyberbulling Roles." *Aggressive Behavior* 42: 123–135.

DuBois, David L, and Michael J. Karcher. 2005. "Youth Mentoring: Theory, Research, and Practice." In *Handbook of Youth Mentoring*, edited by David L. DuBois and Michael J. Karcher, 2–11. Thousand Oaks, CA: Sage.

Ertesvåg, Sigrun K., and Grete Sørensen Vaaland. 2007. "Prevention and Reduction of Behavioural Problems in School: An Evaluation of the Respect Program." *Educational Psychology* 27: 713–736.

Evans, Caroline B. R., Mark W. Fraser, and Katie L. Cotter. 2014. "The Effectiveness of School-Based Bullying Prevention Programs: A Systematic Review." *Aggression and Violent Behavior* 19: 532–544.

Evers, Kerry E., James O. Prochaska, Deborah F. Van Marter, Janet L. Johnson, and Janice M. Prochaska. 2007. "Transtheoretical-Based Bullying Prevention Effectiveness Trials in Middle Schools and High Schools." *Educational Research* 49: 397–414.

Farrington, David P. 2015. "The Developmental Evidence Base: Psychosocial Research" *In Forensic Psychology*, 2nd ed., edited by David A. Crighton and Graham J. Towl, 161–181. Oxford: Blackwell.

Farrington, David P., Hannah Gaffney, Friedrich A. Lösel, and Maria M. Ttofi. 2017. "Systematic Reviews of the Effectiveness of Developmental Prevention Programs in Reducing Delinquency, Aggression, and Bullying." *Aggression and Violent Behavior*, in press.

Farrington, David P., Friedrich A. Lösel, and Maria M. Ttofi. 2016. "Developmental and Social Prevention." In *What Works in Crime Prevention and Rehabilitation: Lessons from Systematic*

Reviews, edited by David Weisburd, David P. Farrington, and Charlotte Gill, 15–75. New York: Springer.

Farrington, David P., and Maria M. Ttofi. 2009. "School-Based Programs to Reduce Bullying and Victimization." *Campbell Systematic Reviews* 6: 1–148.

Felner, Robert D., and Angela M. Adan. 1988. "The School Transitional Environment Project: An Ecological Intervention and Evaluation." In *14 Ounces of Prevention: A Casebook for Practitioners,* edited by Richard H. Price and Raymond P. Lorion, 111–122. Washington, DC: American Psychology Association.

Felner, Robert D., Stephen Brand, Angela M. Adan, Peter F. Mulhall, Nancy Flowers, Barbara Sartain, and David L. DuBois. 1993. "Restructuring the Ecology of the School as an Approach to Prevention During School Transitions: Longitudinal Follow-Ups and Extensions of the School Transitional Environment Project." *Prevention in Human Services* 10: 103–136.

Ferguson, Christopher J., Claudia San Miguel, John C. Kilburn JR, and Patricia Sanchez. 2007. "The Effectiveness of School-Based Anti-Bullying Programs: A Meta-Analytic Review." *Criminal Justice Review* 32: 401–414.

Fonagy, Peter, Stuart W. Twemlow, Eric M. Vernberg, Jennifer Mize Nelson, Edward J. Dill, Todd D. Little, and John A. Sargent. 2009. "A Cluster Randomized Controlled Trial of Child-Focused Psychiatric Consultation and a School Systems-Focused Intervention to Reduce Aggression." *Child Psychology and Psychiatry* 5: 607–616.

Fong, Carlton J., and Dorothy L. Espelage. 2015. "Title Registration for a Systematic Review: Anti-Cyberbullying Interventions for Reducing Cybervictimization in Youth: A Systematic Review." *Campbell Systematic Reviews.*

Gaffney, Hannah, David P. Farrington, Dorothy L. Espelage, and Maria M. Ttofi 2018. "Are Cyberbullying Intervention and Prevention Programs Effective? A Systematic and Meta-analytical Review." *Aggression and Violent Behavior.* Online First.

Greenberg, Mark T., and Carol A. Kusché. 2002. *Promoting Alternative Thinking Strategies: Blueprint for Violence Prevention,* Vol. 10, 2nd ed. Boulder, CO: University of Colorado.

Hahn, Robert, Dawna Fuqua-Whitley, Holly Wethington, Jessica Lowy, Alex Crosby, Mindy Fullilove, Robert Johnson, Akiva Liberman, Eve Moscicki, LeShawndra Price, Susan Snyder, Farris Tuma, Stella Cory, Glenda Stone, Kaushik Mukhopadhaya, Sajal Chattopadhyay, Linda Dahlberg, and Task Force on Community Preventive Services. 2007. "Effectiveness of Universal School-Based Programs to Prevent Violent and Aggressive Behavior Systematic Review." *American Journal of Preventive Medicine* 33: 114–129.

Hawkins, J. David, Richard F. Catalano, Rick Kosterman, Robert Abbott, Karl G. Hill. 1999. "Preventing Adolescent Health Risk Behaviors by Strengthening Protection During Childhood." *Archives of Pediatrics and Adolescent Medicine* 153: 226–234.

Hawkins, J. David, Rick Kosterman, Richard R. Catalano, Karl G. Hill, and Robert D. Abbott. 2008. "Effects of Social Development Intervention in Childhood 15 Years Later." *Archives of Pediatrics and Adolescent Medicine* 162: 1133–1141.

Hawkins, J. David, Elizabeth Von Cleve, and Richard F. Catalano. 1991. "Reducing Early Childhood Aggression: Results of a Primary Prevention Program." *Journal of the American Academy of Child and Adolescent Psychiatry* 30: 208–217.

Hill, Karl G., Jennifer A. Bailey, J. David Hawkins, Richard F. Catalano, Rick Kosterman, Sabrina Oesterle, Robert D. Abbott. 2014. "The Onset of STI Diagnosis Through Age 30: Results from the Seattle Social Development Project intervention." *Prevention Science* 15: 19–32.

Kellam, Sheppard G., Amelia C. L. Mackenzie, C. Hendricks Brown, Jeanne M. Poduska, Wei Wang, Hanno Petras, Holly C. Wilcox. 2011. "The Good Behavior Game and the Future of Prevention and Treatment." *Addiction Science and Clinical Practice* 6: 73–84.

Kellam, Sheppard G., George W. Rebok, Nicholas Ialongo, and Lawrence S. Mayer. 1994. "The Course and Malleability of Aggressive Behavior from Early First Grade into Middle School: Results of a Developmental Epidemiologically-Based Preventive Trial." *Journal of Child Psychology and Psychiatry* 35: 259–282.

Lipsey, Mark W., and David Wilson. 2001. *Practical Meta-Analysis*. Thousand Oaks, CA: Sage.

Mahoney, Joseph L., Reed W. Larson, Jacquelynne S. Eccles, and Heather Lord. 2005. "Organized Activities as Developmental Contexts for Children and Adolescents." In *Organized Activities as Developmental Contexts: Extracurricular Activities, After-School and Community Programs*, edited by Joseph L. Mahoney, Reed W. Larson, and Jacquelynne S. Eccles, 3–22. Mahwah, NJ: Lawrence Erlbaum.

Malti, Tina, Denis Ribeaud, and Manuel Eisner. 2012. Effectiveness of a Universal School-Based Social Competence Program: The Role of Child Characteristics and Economic Factors. *International Journal of Conflict and Violence* 6: 249–259.

Menard, Scott, Jennifer Grotpeter, Daniella Gianola, and Maura O'Neal. 2008. *Evaluation of Bullyproofing Your School*. Washington, DC: U.S. Department of Justice.

Melton, Gary B., Susan P. Limber, Vicki Flerx, Maury Nation, Wayne Osgood, Jeff Chambers, Scott Henggeler, Phillippe Cunningham, and Dan Olweus. 1998. "Violence Among Rural Youth. Final Report to the Office of Juvenile Justice and Delinquency Prevention." https://www.ncjrs.gov/pdffiles1/Digitization/180334NCJRS.pdf.

Merrell, Kenneth W., Barbara A. Gueldner, Scott W. Ross, and Duane M. Isava. 2008. "How Effective Are School Bullying Intervention Programs? A Meta-Analysis of Intervention Research." *School Psychology Quarterly* 23: 26–42.

Murray, Joseph, David P. Farrington, and Manuel P. Eisner. 2009. "Drawing Conclusions About Causes from Systematic Reviews of Risk Factors: The Cambridge Quality Checklists." *Journal of Experimental Criminology* 5: 1–23.

OCED. 2014. "Education Indicators in Focus." http://www.oecd.org/edu/skills-beyond-school/educationindicatorsinfocus.htm.

O'Donnell, Julie, J. David Hawkins, Richard F. Catalano, Robert D. Abbott, and L. Edward Day. 1995. "Preventing School Failure, Drug Use, and Delinquency Among Low-Income Children: Long-Term Intervention in Elementary Schools." *American Journal of Orthopsychiatry* 65: 87–100.

Olweus, Dan. 1995. "Bullying or Peer Abuse at School: Facts and Intervention." *Current Directions in Psychological Science* 4: 196–200.

Olweus, Dan. 2004. "The Olweus Bullying Prevention Programme: design and implementation issues and a new national initiative in Norway." In *Bullying in Schools: How Successful Can Interventions Be?*, edited by Peter K. Smith, Debra Pepler and Ken Rigby, 13–36. Cambridge, UK: Cambridge University Press.

Olweus, Dan. 2005. "A Useful Evaluation Design, and Effects of the Olweus Bullying Prevention Program." *Psychology, Crime and Law* 11: 389–402.

Ortega, Rosario. 2005. *Psicología de la Enseñanza y Desarrollo de Personas y Comunidades*. Mexico City: Fondo de cultura económica.

Ortega-Ruiz, Rosario, Rosario Del Rey, and José A. Casas. 2012. "Knowing, Building and Living Together on Internet and Social Networks: The ConRed Cyberbullying Prevention Program." *International Journal of Conflict and Violence* 6: 303–313.

Ortega, Rosario, Rosario Del Rey, and Joaquín Mora-Merchan. 2004. "SAVE Model: An Anti-bullying Intervention in Spain." In *Bullying in Schools: How Successful Can Interventions Be?*, edited by Peter K. Smith, Debra Pepler, and Ken Rigby, 167–186. Cambridge, UK: Cambridge University Press.

Pepler, Debra J., Wendy M. Craig, Paul O'Connell, Rona Atlas, and Alice Charach. 2004. "Making a Difference in Bullying: Evaluation of a Systemic School-Based Program in Canada." In *Bullying in Schools: How Successful Can Interventions Be?*, edited by Peter K. Smith, Debra Pepler, and Ken Rigby, 125–140. Cambridge, UK: Cambridge University Press.

Raskauskas, Juliana. 2007. *Evaluation of the Kia Kaha Anti-Bullying Programme for Students in Years 5–8*. Wellington: New Zealand Police.

Ryan, Wendy, and J. David Smith. 2009. "Antibullying Programs in Schools: How Effective are Evaluation Practices?" *Prevention Science* 10: 248–259.

Salmivalli, Christina, Ari Kaukiainen, Marinus Voeten, and Mirva Sinisammal. 2004. Targeting the Group as a Whole: The Finnish Anti-Bullying Intervention. In *Bullying in Schools: How Successful Can Interventions Be?*, edited by Peter K. Smith, Debra Pepler, and Ken Rigby, 251–274. Cambridge, UK: Cambridge University Press.

Salmivalli, Christina. 1999. "Participant Role Approach to School Bullying: Implications for Interventions." *Journal of Adolescence* 22: 453–459.

Schweinhart, Lawrence J., Jeanne Montie, Zongping Xiang, W. Steven Barnett, Clive R. Belfield, and Milagros Nores. 2005. *Lifetime Effects: The HighScope Perry Preschool Study Through Age 40*. Ypsilanti, MI: HighScope Press.

Shure, Myrna B. 2001. "I Can Problem Solve (ICPS): An Interpersonal Cognitive Problem Solving Program for Children." *Residential Treatment for Children & Youth* 18: 3–14.

Spivack, George, and Myrna B. Shure. 1974. *Social Adjustment of Young Children*. San Francisco: Jossey-Bass.

Taheri, Sema A., and Brandon C. Welsh. 2016. "After-School Programs for Delinquency Prevention: A Systematic Review and Meta-Analysis." *Youth Violence and Juvenile Justice* 14: 272–290.

Tolan, Patrick, David Henry, Michael Schoeny, Arin Bass, Peter Lovegrove, Emily Nichols. 2013. "Mentoring Interventions to Affect Juvenile Delinquency and Associated Problems: A Systematic Review." *Campbell Systematic Reviews* 10: 1–148.

Ttofi, Maria M., Manuel Eisner, and Catherine P. Bradshaw. 2014. "Bullying Prevention: Assessing Existing Meta-Evaluations." In *Encyclopedia of Criminology and Criminal Justice*, edited by Gerben Bruinsma, and David Weisburd, 231–242. New York: Springer.

Ttofi, Maria M., and David P. Farrington. 2011. "Effectiveness of School-Based Programs to Reduce Bullying: A Systematic and Meta-Analytic Review." *Journal of Experimental Criminology* 7: 27–56.

U.S. Department of Health and Human Services. 2001. *Youth Violence: A Report of the Surgeon General*. Washington, DC: U.S. Department of Health and Human Services.

Weikart, David P., Dennis J. Deloria, Sara A. Lawser, and Ronald Wiegerink. 1970. *Longitudinal Results of the Ypsilanti Perry Preschool Project*. Ypsilanti, MI: HighScope Press.

Welsh, Brandon C., and David P. Farrington. 2010. "The Future of Crime Prevention: Developmental and Situational Strategies." Washington, DC: U.S. National Institute of Justice. http://www.crim.cam.ac.uk/people/academic_research/david_farrington/nijprev.pdf.

Whitney, Irene, Rivers, Ian, Peter K. Smith, and Sonia Sharp. 1994. "The Sheffield Project: Methodology and Findings." In *School Bullying: Insights and Perspectives*, edited by Peter K. Smith and Sonia Sharp, 20–56. London: Routledge.

Zych, Izabela, Anna C. Baldry, and David P. Farrington. 2017. "School Bullying and Cyberbullying: Prevalence, Characteristics, Outcomes, and Prevention." In *Handbook of Behavioral Criminology: Contemporary Strategies and Issues*, edited by Vincent B. Van Hasselt and Michael L. Bourke, 113–138. New York: Springer.

Zych, Izabela, David P. Farrington, Vicente J. Llorent, and Maria M. Ttofi. 2017. *Protecting Children Against Bullying and Its Consequences*. New York: Springer.

Zych, Izabela, Rosario Ortega-Ruiz, and Rosario Del Rey. 2015a. "Scientific Research on Bullying and Cyberbullying: Where Have We Been and Where Are We Going." *Aggression and Violent Behavior* 24: 188–198.

Zych, Izabela, Rosario Ortega-Ruiz, and Rosario Del Rey. 2015b. "Systematic Review of Theoretical Studies on Bullying and Cyberbullying: Facts, Knowledge, Prevention and Intervention." *Aggression and Violent Behavior* 23: 1–21.

CHAPTER 33

....

COGNITIVE-BEHAVIORAL TREATMENT TO PREVENT OFFENDING AND TO REHABILITATE OFFENDERS

....

GEORGIA ZARA

THIS chapter reviews evidence-based treatments that include cognitive-behavioral interventions to target offending. Identifying what works in reducing recidivism and in preventing crime has proved challenging, not because of the absence of scientific research and valid programs, but because the heterogeneity of offenders makes it difficult to guarantee that what works with some offenders will work in all conditions, and at all times. Differences among offenders (elderly vs. adults vs. juveniles; males vs. females; violent vs. sexual vs. general; one-timers vs. persisters vs. chronics), in different settings (correction vs. probation vs. community), with different needs (intellectually disabled vs. non–intellectually disabled individuals; mentally disordered offenders; ethnic minority offenders), at different times in their criminal careers (early onsetters vs. late onsetters) require the scrupulous assessment of risk, needs, and responsivity and an individualized plan for intervention and treatment.

The work on crime prevention by Welsh and Farrington (2012) emphasizes the prime requirement of an evidence-based approach to treatment and intervention: one that requires a commitment to the use of the most scientific, validated, and evaluated assessment methods and programs. Such a commitment can flourish if no room is left "for moralizing about crime or politicizing what works or does not work" and if "the facts—arrived at by a scrupulous evaluation—are made the centerpiece of the policymaking processes" (Welsh and Farrington, 2012, p. 511).

Two issues are worth some consideration: the methodology and the results. Randomized controlled trials (RCTs) meet the requirement of scientific accuracy. They solve the problem of confounding factors by randomly assigning treatment. The threat to quality research evaluation is posed by confounding factors that bias findings and the estimation of them. As Weisburd and Hinkle (2012) described, "randomized experiments offer a way to get unbiased estimates of treatment impact without requiring knowledge of every possible confounding factor" (p. 450). Reality is very complex, and this is even more true when we attempt to understand or explain criminal behavior and the likelihood of its occurrence. Not even the most scientific method is infallible, and no researcher can know, measure, and control for all the variables that directly or indirectly influence the behavioral outcome under observation. Program evaluation is one of the most challenging and relevant and significant endeavors that scientists embark on. To learn which interventions are the most effective and worthy to pursue is important for at least three reasons: (1) because of its useful, well-being, and health promotion impacts, (2) because of the well-spent public money that will convey renewed confidence in policy and research, and (3) because of its ethical implications (Weisburd 2003). Ethics emerges from preciseness and integrity; ethics promotes transparency between methodology, hypotheses, and results; ethics allows scientific thinking to guide social demands and expectations, and to minimize the risk of accepting false or biased results. Cognitive-behavioral treatment (CBT) interventions that are evaluated within a randomized controlled trial can offer a major guarantee about their effectiveness and the quality of their application. The use of RCTs can ensure that researchers are responsible when they provide policymakers and practitioners with findings, suggestions, and conclusions; nothing can be certain, but everything can be evidence-based.

Effective programs are not only those that influence offending and violent and sexually motivated problem behavior, they are those that target the criminogenic needs that lie at the root of antisocial persistence. Effectiveness is also measured by its impact on preventing offending from its start, by its well-controlled and independent evaluations, accurate risk assessment, quality management, evident behavioral outcomes, and long follow-up periods. All this could be attainable if integrated scientific approaches are combined with long-term policies of developmental crime prevention.

The aims of this chapter are to review cognitive-behavioral skill-enhancing programs in criminological psychology and their efficacy in preventing offending and reducing the risk of reoffending and to explain why they seem to be the most effective programs, both in corrections and in the community. However, a complete description of which programs are most effective does not fall within the scope of this chapter for two reasons: because of space limitations and because previous studies have offered enlightening information about which cognitive-behavioral programs are most effective and which interventions are capable of producing significant reductions in the recidivism of even high-risk offenders. These are studies, to mention just a few, on crime prevention (Welsh and Farrington 2012), what works and what is promising, and what does not work (Sherman, et al. 1998), correctional strategies, policies, and programs (MacKenzie, 2006), benefit-cost analyses (Welsh, Farrington, and Raffan Gowar 2015), the effective applicability of cognitive-behavioral methods (Hollin 2004; Lösel and Schmucker 2005; Zara and Farrington 2014), for both adults (males and females) (Andrews and Dowden 1999; Polaschek et al. 2005; Wilson, Bouffard, and MacKenzie 2005; Lipsey and Landerberg 2006) and juveniles (Lösel 1996; Redondo, Garrido, and

Sanchez-Meca 1999; Latessa 2006; Zara and Gulotta 2014), and numerous reviews and meta-analyses (Andrews et al. 1990; Beelmann and Lösel 2006; Lipsey, Landenberger, and Wilson 2007; Petrosino and Lavenberg 2007) and synthesis of meta-analyses (Gendrau and Andrews 1990; Hollin 1990; Lipsey and Wilson 1998; Lösel 1995, 2001; Lösel and Beelmann 2003).

This chapter is organized in five sections. Section I briefly describes the theoretical principles of CBT and then presents an overview of some of the most effective programs in criminological settings. In Section II, the recognition of criminal behavior as multidetermined by a multiplicity of factors and criminogenic needs requires multimodal types of treatment to respond to the complexity of aspects involved in its onset and its persistence. A critical analysis of research findings is presented by looking first at some of the variations in CBT interventions in Section III, and then by exploring the X factor of their effectiveness in Section IV. Section V discusses the risk-need-responsivity (RNR) model, which integrates scientific accurateness with integrity.

I. An Overview of the Theoretical and Clinical Bases of Cognitive-Behavioral Programs

"Our ability to reason is vital. The better we reason the better our lives" (Johnson-Laird 2008, p. 414). This ability describes the human capacity to recognize, understand, interpret, and respond to interpersonal and social cues that is central to behavior and social adaptation. This key aspect of human functioning lies in how individuals judge specific situations or problems, because people are distressed not by things or situations per se, but by the views they take of them.[1] It is not uncommon that individuals misinterpret situations or events or misread other people's intentions and behavior in ways that are likely to weaken their capacity for coping and their confidence to respond functionally to their social world. Biases in information processing and deficits in problem-solving contribute to consolidate a behavioral pattern that can often be maladjusted and socially unacceptable.

Criminal thinking is likely to blossom in these cognitive and emotional situations. Offenders, especially when persistent and violent, may misjudge benevolent social situations as menacing, perceive their life conditions as mainly a result of unjust events, require unconditional understanding, put great emphasis on the sorrowful destiny that they perceive, and look at victims as willful participants in criminal acts. If these features do not certainly describe all offenders and all of their reactions, criminal thinking, in a quite significant proportion of cases, is tied to these types of distortions and biases that profoundly affect and direct criminal and violent persistent behavior (Zara and Farrington 2016). Thus, in exploring the most significant criminogenic needs that sustain criminal recidivism, it is feasible to specify the cascade of risks put in motion for recidivists and persistent offenders: pro-criminal attitude, distorted thinking, negative emotionality, personality disorders, social support for crime, substance abuse, inadequate parenting, lack of self-control, school/work failure, and unsafe and antisocial recreational activities.

Criminogenic needs, seen as psychological dynamic factors, provide insights into the core of antisociality. Dowden and Andrews (1999b) completed a meta-analysis of human service, risk, need, and responsivity to explore whether programs that addressed these principles were more effective than other programs that dealt with clinical issues and non-criminogenic needs (e.g., personal distress, low self-esteem, hallucinations, anxiety and depression, feelings of alienation and exclusion, victimization, a disorganized community, lack of ambition) (see also Andrews and Bonta 2010). The findings were interesting: programs that addressed criminogenic needs were followed by a significant reduction in recidivism, showing an effect size of .55 in comparison with other programs (−.18). Similar conclusions were drawn in meta-analysis of female offenders (Dowden and Andrews 1999a) and for sex and violent offenders (Hanson et al. 2009). In a meta-analysis carried out by Jolliffe and Farrington (2007) on effectiveness of intervention with violence offenders, there was some evidence to suggest that interventions that addressed cognitive skills, anger control, relapse prevention, and used role play, and had offenders complete homework, were more effective than those interventions that did not. Interventions, which targeted two or three of these areas, had statistically significantly higher effects in reducing general re-offending. Moreover, their meta-analysis suggested that intervention that provided a greater overall duration were more effective, and that the greater duration per session was associated with greater effects for both general and violent re-offending. However, while the relationship among treatment intensity, routine monitoring of the individual's response to treatment, and reduction in re-offending is recognized in clinical psychological treatment (Hansen, Lambert, and Forman 2002; Harnett, O'Donovan, and Lambert 2010) and correctional settings (Chitty 2005), what seems still uncertain is the precise point at which additional treatment duration no longer significantly enhances reduction in re-offending (Jolliffe and Farrington 2007).

Hanson and colleagues (2009) found evidence for the effectiveness of the RNR principles in the treatment of sex offenders. Twenty-three studies were reviewed, reporting that, compared to untreated sex offenders, treated sex offenders had lower general recidivism rates (31.8 percent vs. 48.3 percent), and sexual recidivism rates (10.9 percent vs. 19.2 percent). Studies that did not adhere to any of the RNR principles had the weakest effects, while the effectiveness of the treatments increased with the degree of adherence to RNR, as recidivism decreased significantly when all three principles were tackled. However, only three studies fully implemented all three principles. Violent offenders are likely to have distorted thinking, violent fantasies, criminogenic development and living conditions, and psychopathic and personality disorder traits. In a meta-analysis of 89 studies (Whitaker et al., 2008), it was found that sex offenders were more likely to minimize their responsibility for offending (with an r of about .27) and manifest a more tolerant attitude toward the idea of adult–child sex (with an r of about .25). They also used cognitive distortions to explain their behavior (Egan, Kavanagh, and Blair 2005). For instance, in a study by Prentky and colleagues (1989), 86 percent of 25 serial sexual murderers reported that sadistic fantasies preceded their crime.

The unified proposition of CBT, as pioneered by Beck (1970) and Ellis (1962), is that psychological and behavioral problems arise as a consequence of faulty patterns of thinking, misperceptions and misattribution of intents that affect and direct behavior. Criminal behavior begins and develops in a process in which the individual fails to stop and think before responding to events and situations. When offenders learn to evaluate their thinking in a more truthful and adaptive way, they improve in the way they behave, interact with others, and think about themselves and their lives. Improvement in their emotional and cognitive state seems to stabilize their behavior.

CBT is inspired by seven significant principles that work best in bringing about change and in addressing offending behavior:

1. Cognitive style assessment
2. Skills training
3. Social competence
4. Cognitive restructuring
5. Emotional regulation
6. Problem solving
7. Self-regulation and self-acceptance

CBT is based on an accurate assessment of the cognitive style of the person. It uses a variety of techniques to change thinking, mood, and behavior, and most of all techniques are concrete; their effects can be seen in a short- and medium-term period, so as to create an encouraging anchor of possibilities and new opportunities for many offenders. The treatment varies considerably according to individual offenders, their intellectual abilities and cognitive style, gender, and cultural background, as well as the nature of their difficulties and their stage in life. It also differs depending on offenders' goals, their ability to respond and bond, their motivation and readiness to change, and their previous rehabilitation experiences. CBT involves cognitive skills training and social skills and social competence promotion. At the basis of the former is the aim of challenging the set of cognitive distortions and impulsive, rigid, and egocentric thinking that exert a general and often increasingly pervasive influence over the person's daily functioning. Cullen and Gendreau (2000) recognize that effective cognitive programs attempt to assist offenders in redefining and controlling problems that led them to break the law, identify new goals in their life, reflect on alternative prosocial solutions, and apply these solutions to concrete situations. These programs works at three main levels: cognitive, behavioral, and relational (Lösel and Bender 2012). Cognitive enhancement teaches offenders to learn how to evaluate the consequences of their own behavior, to modulate emotional manifestations according to the situations, to make a more realistic assessment of events in which they are involved, and to start to acknowledge their own responsibility. Social skills improvement focuses on enhancing behavioral manifestations. Developing social competence requires acquiring interpersonal and communication abilities that lead to more adequate interactions with others.

Research evidence indicates that interpersonal inadequacy, relationship failures, and emotional disengagement contribute to low empathy, in other words to a maladjusted way of relating, thinking, and feeling about other people (Zara and Mosso 2014). Empathy failures can trigger offending (Ward and Durrant 2013). According to ethicist Justin D'Arms (2000, cited in Oxley 2011, p. 15) empathy involves "both an act *and* a capacity," which are revealed in an intellectual and emotional understanding of a person or an event. Individuals engage in acts of empathy when they acquire a knowledge of how someone else is likely to be feeling in certain situations, or alternatively, when they anticipate how they would feel in similar circumstances. Offenders do not show empathy either because they lack such a knowledge of others or of events, or because their understanding is biased or altered by distorted thoughts and implicit theories that support offensive and violent behavior, or even because they suffer emotional dysregulation (Zara and Farrington 2016).

In a meta-analysis carried out by Jolliffe and Farrington (2004), a common measure of effect size (the standardized mean difference) was calculated in 35 studies, 21 of cognitive empathy and 14 of affective empathy. It was found that cognitive empathy had a stronger negative relationship with offending than did affective empathy. The relationship between low empathy and offending was relatively strong for violent offenders but relatively weak for sex offenders. An important finding of their meta-analysis was that the empathy differences between offenders and non-offenders disappeared when intelligence and socioeconomic status were controlled for in the offending and non-offending populations. Whether these dysfunctions are causal or consequential is not clear. Nevertheless, treatment research suggests that reducing cognitive and emotional distortions is the primary positive outcome in preventive treatment (Ware and Mann 2012) and in therapeutic interventions (Barnett and Mann 2013), and it may provide an indicator of the risk of recidivism (Hanson and Morton-Bourgon 2005).

CBT is concrete and initially emphasizes the present. CBT is scheduled and time focused. Sessions are structured so that having a specific arrangement in each session maximizes efficiency and effectiveness. Following this format makes the process of intervention more understandable to offenders, promotes their collaborative participation, and increases the likelihood that they will be able to apply what has been learned after termination.

CBT emphasizes collaboration and active participation, and it is built on two forms of reinforcement. The first involves discouraging cognitive processes that are maladaptive and strengthening the thoughts that lead to agreeable and gratifying behavioral choices. The second endorses the process of reinforcing behaviors that involve positive consequences. These aspects contribute to the nature of CBT that is goal oriented and problem focused; it is educative to the extent that it aims to teach offenders to identify, evaluate, and respond to their dysfunctional thoughts and beliefs, encourage them to control these thoughts, and behave accordingly to the situation.

The prototypical models of CBT programs are:

- Aggression Replacement Training® (ART®) (Goldstein and Glick 1987)
- Moral Reconation Therapy® (MRT®) (Little and Robinson 1986)
- Reasoning and Rehabilitation (R&R) (Ross and Fabiano 1985)
- Relapse Prevention Therapy (RPT) (Marlatt and Gordon 1985)
- Thinking for a Change (T4C) (Bush, Glick, and Taymans 1997)

This chapter will briefly describe the prototypical accredited CBT programs[2] and will then present some programs that have been proven to be effective with juvenile and adult offenders. It will conclude with the RNR model, a successful model that integrates risk assessment, treatment, and prevention.

A. ART

Aggression Replacement Training® (ART®)[3] is a multimodal approach to work with aggressive offenders. It was developed in 1980 by Goldstein and Glick, who completed their first publication on ART in 1987. The key element from which ART begins is aggression. Research shows that aggression is difficult to tackle (Goldstein, Glick, and Gibbs 1998). It is learned by repetition, observation, imitation, experiences of victimization, and rehearsal. Different contexts (home, school, neighborhoods, media, and videogames) are the places where children and adolescents learn to be aggressive. What seems to reinforce its use is that aggression is frequently rewarded and has few punishments. When manifested behaviorally, it seems to give energy through the emotional arousal of anger that generates distorted thoughts of control and strength. The shortcoming, however, is that this energy is short lived and requires continual substitution to defuse the sense of inadequacy and frustration that often generates an aggressive reaction. ART is based on the principle that aggressive behavior can be unlearned and replaced by a more constructive, socially competent and efficient attitude and consequent behavior. Three main components make up ART: skillstreaming, anger control training, and moral reasoning training (Goldstein, Glick, and Gibbs 1998). Skillstreaming involves a step-by-step approach that teaches people how to replace destructive and out-of-control behavior with constructive and prosocial behavior. The tenet of this task is modeling, so that social skills are introduced by group leaders and then practiced by offenders. Anger control training is implemented by the antecedent-behavior-consequences (A-B-C) progression, and the aim is to enhance self-awareness. Moral reasoning training focuses on changing moral reasoning and egocentric biases: the person is encouraged to recognize anger cues and to understand what elicits them.

B. MRT

Moral Reconation Therapy® (MRT®)[4] is a cognitive-behavioral treatment based on the moral development theory of Kohlberg (1963) and includes some aspects of the ego and identity theory of Erikson (1959). It was developed and implemented in a prison drug offender therapeutic community in 1985 in Memphis, Tennessee, by Gregory Little and Kenneth Robinson and has since been employed with other high-risk populations, including juvenile offenders. The term conation refers to the association of knowledge and affect with behavior, given that knowledge and affect are critical components for engaging in self-direction and self-regulation. By learning how offenders make decisions, it is possible to work on changing how they make criminal choices. The central tenets of MRT are that attitudes, beliefs, and thoughts are the main determinants of behavior, and that by modifying the way people build up their theories of themselves and their lives it is possible to access the way people behave and to alter it. MRT is designed to facilitate change in the offender's process of conscious decision-making and enhance and reinforce appropriate and responsible behavior through high moral reasoning (Little 2000, 2005). It is a systematic treatment designed to develop and reinforce moral, social, and positive behavior through either a 12- or 16-step-by-step program depending on the different populations involved.

C. R&R and R&R2

Reasoning and Rehabilitation (R&R) (Ross and Fabiano 1985) is a cognitive-behavioral training program for offenders. This program, devised by Ross and Fabiano (1991), aims to train people to stop and think before acting and to consider the consequences of their actions, to conceptualize alternative ways of solving interpersonal problems, to consider the effects of their behavior upon other people. In other words, the aim of R&R is to change the criminogenic thinking of offenders (Ross, Fabiano, and Dimmer-Ewles 1995; McGuire 2001; Tong and Farrington 2008).

The R&R program has been implemented in many different countries. In Ottawa, a randomized experiment testing a R&R intervention led to a significant reoffending reduction in a small sample of followed-up adult offenders after nine months (Farrington 2003a).

R&R is composed of 35 sequential modules that are delivered to small groups of offenders. They include social competence, social skills training, lateral and critical thinking, social perspective taking, the management of emotions, creative problem solving, negotiation skills, value enhancement, critical thinking and cognitive exercises, role-playing and modeling. A shorter version of R&R was specifically developed for adults (Ross and Hilborn 2005), called R&R2. It is a specialized 15-session version that targets behavior that leads to involvement with criminal justice agencies, and it aims to increase prosocial competence among participants by developing new pathways that will encourage prosocial feelings, thoughts, and behavior. This version of the program is based on four key principles: motivational interviewing, prosocial modeling, relapse prevention, and desistance from a criminal career. Long-term interventions are not always suitable for certain types of offenders, because they might tax their responsivity, deplete their motivation, and trigger conflicting reactions that lead offenders to drop out from the program. R&R2 programs are designed to assess offenders and their risk levels in order to focus on promoting prosocial neurological development while fostering prosocial competence. R&R2 programs are part of Ross and Hilborn's (2008) neurocriminology model, which encourages time to think again and promotes new interventions to encourage crime prevention.

D. RPT

In its original design, Relapse Prevention Therapy (RPT) (Marlatt and Gordon 1985) was a maintenance program for the treatment of addictive behaviors. RPT is a behavioral self-control program that teaches individuals how to maintain and enhance changes in their behavior. RPT combines cognitive and behavioral interventions in an overall approach that emphasizes self-management and encourages a detachment from what the individual did, so as to enhance the development of a changed sense of self. Hence, RPT rejects labeling an individual as alcoholic or drug addict or criminal (Marlatt and Donovan 2005) because this fosters stabilizing distorted self-beliefs. RPT interventions include three strategic categories: coping skills training, cognitive therapy, and lifestyle modification. Coping skills training strategies involve cognitive and behavioral techniques. Cognitive therapy procedures provide the individuals with ways to sustain the change process. The principle is simple: the longer the period of successful abstinence or controlled use, the greater will be the individual's perception of self-efficacy. Achieving change is introduced as a learning experience, with errors, failures, and impediments that can nurture the development of a sense of self-mastery. Offenders are taught to understand that relapse is a process and not an event. RPT begins by identifying those high-risk situations that could endanger the individual's recovery and then assesses the individual's capability of coping with those situations and enhances the belief that they can do it. Lifestyle modification strategies are designed to strengthen the individual's overall coping capacity in order to create a more balanced self to maintain the cognitive and behavioral changes.

E. T4C

Offenders can change. Criminal behavior is amenable to prosocial transformation when offenders learn to access the tools from both cognitive restructuring and cognitive skills programs (Bush, Glick, and Taymans 1997). As a result of this learning from restructuring cognitive interventions, Thinking for a Change (T4C) is a National Institute of

Corrections (NIC) program that addresses the cognitive, social, and emotional needs of the offending population. It is designed for both adults and juveniles and has been delivered in prisons, jails, community corrections, probation, and parole supervision settings. The program is composed of 22 lessons and includes self-assessment. The scope is to increase self-awareness and consideration of others and to deepen attentiveness to a person's own beliefs, attitudes, and thinking patterns that are relevant to their present and future needs.

II. The Multi-Modal Nature of Treatment

Research conclusions are unanimous in stating that criminal behavior is multi-determined, so that the way for crime prevention to be effective is to impact simultaneously on the different conditions that influence crime. Timing is also crucial: early interventions seem to have more positive and long-lasting results. The cumulative emotional, human, and economic costs of early criminal careers justify considerable attention to early and multi-modal interventions. Schindler and Black (2015) indicate that the estimated cost that a high-risk youth poses to society, pursuing a life-course–persistent offending trajectory, is approximately $1 to $5 million. Early integrated prevention represents a way to reduce this cost (Munoz et al. 2004; Cohen and Piquero 2009).

Interventions that work at one level (e.g., individual) should be supported by preventive practices applied to other settings as well (e.g., family, school, community, labor market, police agencies, courts, corrections, etc.) and may be more effective if appropriately integrated. "Just as exercise can only work properly on a fit body," crime prevention of all kinds may only be effective when the institutional, familial, and social contexts are structured and prepared to support and encourage it (Sherman et al. 2002, p. 5).

After reviewing 13 meta-analytic studies, Lösel (1995) concluded that the strongest effects in reducing re-offending are mostly achieved by multi-modal programs that include CBT and skills training. Multi-modal programs are most effective with aggressive and generalized antisocial behavior, and they also contain structured guidelines that might facilitate adherence to the program's delivery for populations involved. Purely cognitive or behavioral child skills programs have shown no significant effect sizes (Lösel and Beelmann 2006). In their meta-analysis, Pearson and colleagues (2002) included 69 research studies that covered both behavioral and cognitive-behavioral programs. They found that the cognitive-behavioral programs were more effective in reducing recidivism than the behavioral ones, with an overall recidivism reduction for the treated groups of about 30 percent.

Time seems crucial: the earlier the intervention, the lower the risk that the individual will become entrapped in a long criminal career. Farrington (2015a, 2015b) suggests that three significant protective dimensions are associated with children's resilience: positive and nurturing parenting, social skills and emotional stability, and teacher training. Interventions that involve strengthening the parent–child relationship, reducing harsh parenting, promoting child competence, and enhancing proactive teaching strategies and fair discipline can play an extremely crucial role in the development of children's emotional and social competencies and cognitive and scholastic abilities. These contribute to curtailing behavioral problems and antisociality.

Child-rearing and parenting that take place in an affectionate, positive, and emotionally stable family environment and that reinforce prosocial behavior are associated with self-regulation, conflict control skills, and social competence. Programs that aim to enhance effective parenting also promote collaborative home–school relationships (Webster-Stratton and Taylor 2001). Programs that also focus on building up socio-emotional regulatory skills can provide children with coping skills to help them to counteract various life stressors. Interventions that target the emotional and familial climate of children and parents are likely to reinforce promotive factors that buffer life stressors. Piquero and Jennings (2012) demonstrated that "child behavioral problems can be partially prevented or lessened with the implementation of the appropriate parent training programs" (p. 97). What is crucial is that these programs can provide children, families, and social communities with many other benefits beyond crime reduction that include higher education, employment stability, health enhancement, family harmony, individual life achievements, and social integration (Farrington and Welsh 2007).

The remainder of this chapter describes some of these early intervention programs.[5]

A. The Incredible Years

The Incredible Years Parents, Teachers, and Children's Training Series encompasses a number of programs named The Incredible Years (IY), and they are delivered in a group template that includes child behavior management training, cognitive-behavioral and emotional practices that focus on enhancing problem-solving strategies, self-management principles, and positive self-talk (Brotman et al. 2008; Webster-Stratton, Reid, and Stoolmiller 2008). Strengthening parenting competencies (monitoring positive discipline and increasing parental confidence) and fostering parents' involvement in children's school experiences in order to promote children's academic, social, and emotional competencies and reduce conduct problems are the most targeted aims. The parent programs are grouped according to children's ages: Babies and Toddlers (0 to 3 years), BASIC Early Childhood (3 to 6 years), BASIC School-Age (6 to 12 years) and ADVANCED (6 to 12 years). The IY Child Training curriculum (Dinosaur School) was originally developed to treat clinic-referred children (3 to 7 years) diagnosed with oppositional defiant disorder (ODD) or early-onset conduct disorder (CD). Webster-Stratton and colleagues (2004) suggested that, following completion of the parent program, mothers were more likely to be consistent, more nurturing, and more affective. Their children showed reduced aggressive attitude and more prosocial behavior in comparison with controls. These results were maintained over a one-year follow-up period (Webster-Stratton, Reid, and Hammond 2001). Mothers at risk of mental problems, such as depression and anger, who experienced sexual abuse as children, and who engaged in the program, benefited from it and manifested parental competence at levels comparable with mothers without these risk factors (Baydar, Reid, and Webster-Stratton 2003).

The IY Teachers Series, a videotape-based, group discussion program, was designed to help preschool, child-care, and early school-age teachers to deal with child aggression and behavioral problems, and to promote social and emotional skills in children.

The IY Child Training Program was evaluated with children (4 to 8 years old), diagnosed with ODD or CD, in their classrooms. Webster-Stratton and colleagues (2004) found that children whose teachers received the training were significantly less aggressive and engaged more positively in social interactions than those children whose teachers were not trained. A two-year follow-up revealed that the teacher training was an added value to the program so far as it was mirrored in the child's social and school functioning.

In an RCT of the effectiveness of classroom management within the IY Teacher Training Programs, 61 Head Start teachers of children aged 3 to 5 were involved. The aim was to explore its implications in reducing risk factors leading to delinquency. Fourteen Head Start centers (34 classrooms) were randomly assigned either to an experimental condition, in which parents, teachers, and family service professionals participated in the IY prevention program, or to a control regular Head Start program group. Experimental teachers were better able to initiate parental involvement in classroom events, to encourage a more welcoming classroom atmosphere, and to implement less harsh and severe discipline than teachers in the control group (Webster-Stratton et al. 2001). Children involved in this intervention displayed more compliance and manifested less aggressive behavior and were more socially oriented and developed higher school readiness skills than did control students. The improvements seemed to last over a 12-month period and were visible in the management of the classroom atmosphere and achievements by trained teachers and also in the attitude of parents who attended more than six groups. These findings suggest the importance of trained and supportive teachers as a cost-effective method of improving the social outcomes of young children and of liaising with parents to create a collaborative atmosphere for the cognitive, emotional, and social development of children (Webster-Stratton et al. 2001).

B. SNAP®

The SNAP® Under 12 Outreach Project (SNAP® ORP) served both boys and girls between 1985 and 1996 who displayed aggressive and antisocial behaviors. It was developed in 1985 by the former Earlscourt Child and Family Centre, now called the Child Development Institute, and in conjunction with the Toronto Police Service. ORP is a fully manualized mental health program for children aged 6 to 11 with antisocial problems and their families. In 1996, research findings showed that more specific gender factors were related to these behavioral problems, and since then girls have been served by the SNAP® Girls Connection, launched in October 1996.

The program is theoretically grounded in social learning, cognitive-behavioral, developmental, ecological, and attachment perspectives. The pragmatic keystone of ORP is a cognitive-behavioral and problem solving technique called SNAP® (Stop Now and Plan) (Augimeri et al. 2007) that helps children and their caregivers to stop their disruptive and negative behavioral patterns and replace them with thoughtful and constructive alternatives. The curriculum of the program is organized in conducted discussions and role-playing sections and providing practical modules in which participants acquire new problem-solving skills to distance themselves from provoking and disruptive situations such as aggression and delinquency for children and harsh and unreliable educational practices for parents. The program consists of a 12-week treatment for children and parents, and it is delivered in community-based settings. The primary components are the SNAP® children's group and a 90-minute SNAP® parent group, attended separately. In addition, and depending on the needs of children and families, there are also available a "one-on-one family counseling based on Stop Now and Plan Parenting (SNAPP) (Levene, 1998), individual befriending sections for children in need of additional social support, and academic tutoring for children who are underperforming academically" (Koegl et al. 2008, p. 422).

Different evaluation studies (Augimeri et al. 2007; Koegl et al. 2008) suggest the effectiveness of ORP in reducing the likelihood of police involvement and antisocial behavior in children at risk. Koegl and colleagues (2008) tested the effectiveness of SNAP® with 59 boys and 21 girls aged 6 to 11, who were clinically referred. These children were divided into three groups: 14 controls, who did not receive the ORP; 50 matched, who received the ORP; and 16 experimentals, who received an enhanced version of the ORP. The Child Behavior Checklist (CBCL) was administered as a measure of delinquency and aggression. Results indicated that there were significant pre–post CBCL changes for the experimental and matched children. The magnitude of these changes was higher for the former group who received comparatively more family counseling sections, individual befriending encounters, and academic tutorials over the three months. No improvements were found in the controls. Moreover, there was a positive relationship between the number of individual CBT sessions that were attended by children and the additional clinical benefits (e.g., a decrease in delinquent and minor aggressive behaviors). Children who received eight sessions or less reported almost double the level of delinquent involvement than children who attended nine or more sessions.

Farrington and Koegl (2015) have assessed the monetary benefits and costs of SNAP-ORP in preventing later offending by boys. Their results show that the benefit-to-cost ratio was greatest for the low-risk boys and smallest for the high-risk boys. However, it must be mentioned that all the SNAP-ORP boys were very high risk compared to the rest of the population. Despite the fact that the lower effect of the program on the high-risk boys diverged from prior studies, further analyses indicated that the program was particularly effective for high-risk boys who received intensive treatment, including befriending or mentoring. This finding suggests that there was a dose-response relationship between the intensity of CBT and reduction in antisocial behavior.

III. Heterogeneity in CBT Findings

Since it was found that psychodynamic forms of treatment and counseling did not work well in correctional and criminological settings, cognitive-behavioral and cognitive skills programs have become the common types of interventions most employed in prison settings and probation services since 1990. Various meta-analyses carried out between the 1980s and 1990s revealed that CBT with offenders can lead to a significant effect in reducing recidivism (McGuire 1995; McGuire and Priestley 1995). The mean effect size (d value) was .10 but there were considerable differences between forms of treatment (Lösel 1995); the empirical evidence is not yet consistent (Zara and Farrington 2014), for both juveniles and adults, and this leaves space for further investigations to analyze why. Roughly speaking, d is twice the percentage reduction in recidivism, and r is the same as the percentage reduction in recidivism. Therefore $d = .10$ might correspond to 45 percent recidivism versus 50 percent in a control group.

Lösel and Beelman (2006) carried out a meta-analysis of child skills training as a measure for preventing antisocial behavior in children and youth, based on a large data set of 55 research reports (randomized experiments) and 89 treatment control groups (comparisons) with 9,109 juveniles, 50 percent of whom were assigned to a program. Forty-six of the studies included follow-up data, of which 46 percent reported desirable effects, 39 percent close to zero effects, and 15 percent undesirable effects. The weighted mean effect size was $d = .29$ for post-treatment outcomes and $d = .21$ for follow-ups. Cognitive-behavioral programs were the most successful, having significant effects in all areas of antisocial behavior: for aggressive behavior ($d = .39$), for oppositional-disorder behavior ($d = .73$), for delinquency ($d = .37$), and for unspecified antisocial behavior ($d = .54$). Counseling, care and therapy programs also revealed a significant overall effect, with specific significant effect on aggressive behavior ($d = .53$) and unspecified behavior ($d = .50$). While mono-modal cognitive or behavioral programs had no significant effects either in post-treatment or in follow-up, cognitive-behavioral programs were the only types to report significant follow-up effects ($d = .50$). These findings showed an overall and positive effect of social competence training on antisocial behavior of juveniles. Cognitive-behavioral programs worked best at reducing recidivism and worked better with older children, aged 13 or older. Regarding child skills training as an approach to crime prevention, the follow-up analysis revealed a significant effect size of $d = .19$ on delinquency, which is quite encouraging. As Lösel and Beelman (2006) suggest, "[a] d coefficient of approximately .20 is equivalent to a correlation of $r = .10$, which indicates approximately a ten percentage point more positive outcome in treated groups than in control groups" (p. 45). If the recidivism in the control group is 50 percent, and in the treated group is 40 percent, this is a one-fifth reduction in recidivism.

Falshaw and colleagues (2003) carried out an evaluation and found no difference between the two-year reconviction rates for a sample of 649 adult male prisoners who had participated in a CBT program, between 1996 and 1998, and a matched control group of 1,947 adult males. Ten percent of the treatment sample did not complete the treatment program. This result contrasts with the previous evaluation of cognitive skills programs for prisoners carried out in 1992–1996. Explanations for this finding are diverse and may reflect a lower level of motivation of the delivering staff and participants in the program in comparison with those involved earlier in a CBT program (Friendship et al. 2002). The finding may also reflect a decreased standard in the quality of program delivery and a widening of the criteria for treatment. While prisoners were specially selected for treatment in 1992–1996, there was a push to treat all prisoners afterwards. The involvement of lower-risk offenders in treatment may also help to explain this result. While low-risk offenders may be easier to engage with professionals and correctional staff, and may even be more collaborative to participate and amenable to treatment programs, they may not be necessarily responsive, and it may be difficult to detect any effects on them (Zara and Farrington 2016).

Another investigation, with 1,534 young and 2,195 adult male offenders, obtained similar results (Cann et al. 2003). Enhanced Thinking Skills (ETS) and R&R programs were assessed, between 1998 and 2000, for these separate samples of offenders. One- and two-year reconviction rates were compared with matched control groups. The findings did not show any significant differences between who received the cognitive-behavioral program and those who did not. However, when program dropouts (9 percent of the sample) were excluded from the analysis, the one-year reconviction rates for both young and adult completers were significantly lower than in the matched groups. In numerical terms, this difference can be translated to a 2.5 percentage point difference in reconviction for adult offenders and a 4.1 percentage point reduction for young offenders who completed the treatment. These differences were not maintained two years after release from prison. Adult high-risk program completers also had a statistically significant lower rate of reconviction (a 6.9 percentage point difference). The differences between the low- and medium/high-risk completers for both adult and juvenile offenders and their matched groups were not significant.

Another analyzed aspect was the different impact of ETS and R&R on reconviction. The study showed that ETS had an impact in reducing reconviction but R&R did not. It may be significant to say that ETS was specifically designed for the offender population in England and Wales and that it is a shorter program (22 two-hour sessions vs. 38 for R&R), which may help to keep up the motivation and attention of offenders during the program. It is important to note that this study was limited by the fact that the comparison groups were matched to the participant groups on demographic variables and criminal history. As Cann and colleagues (2003) suggested, it may be possible that the groups differed in other and more relevant aspects related to dynamics risk factors, psychological needs, cognitive deficits, or motivation to change, but these dimensions were not explored. An RCT would be more convincing than these retrospectively matched designs.

The effectiveness of the ETS and R&R programs was also explored to assess their impact upon female prisoners (Cann 2006). The program participants were 180 female offenders, of whom 14 (8 percent) did not complete the program. The comparison group was composed of 540 female offenders who did not take part in the program during their custodial sentence and were matched to program participants on the basis of their predicted reconviction score. All offenders where discharged from prisons in England and Wales during 1996–2000 and spent at least one year in the community. No statistically significant differences were found either overall or within risk groups in the effects of ETS intervention, but statistically significant differences were found between the R&R participants and the controls. The R&R participants fared worse than the controls, with a reconviction rate of 19.7 percent compared with the rate of 10.1 percent of the latter (p = 0.038). There is no clear evidence that the cognitive deficits of the female offenders were causally linked to their offending (Cann 2006), so no one can be sure that involving female offenders in a cognitive-behavioral program is likely to affect their criminal careers more than other offenders. Although ETS and R&R are aimed at, and work better, with high-risk offenders, only one-third of the women involved in this study were medium-high or high-risk. These results can be encouraging if their face value is not misinterpreted. They shed some light on the importance of individualizing intervention and on measuring and addressing the criminogenic needs of different offenders. Female offenders may have different criminogenic needs from male offenders, or some criminogenic needs may impact differently upon female offenders in comparison to other offending populations.

IV. THE X FACTOR OF EFFECTIVENESS

The appropriateness of allocating offenders to the most suitable intervention programs, based on their level of risk and needs, is crucial in achieving effectiveness and accurately investing resources. Research findings suggest that service delivery is likely to improve if offenders are more appropriately allocated to the programs that (1) adhere to their level of risk and needs, (2) work at sustaining their readiness to change, and (3) aim to engage and retain offenders in programs.

Within the Probation Service in England and Wales, the Offender Group Reconviction Scale-2 (OGRS2)[6] is used to indicate the probability of an offender's risk of reconviction within two years (Taylor 1999). In an examination of offender placement, Palmer and colleagues (2009) found that the appropriateness of allocation affected reconviction rates independently of program completion per se. There were interesting findings relating to the extreme (low- and high-risk) groups: no program completion effect was found among the low-risk offenders. It is difficult to achieve a significant reduction in reoffending among offenders who are already low-risk. Despite the very high-risk offenders being the most unlikely to start a program, when they completed the program, there was a larger effect in comparison with the reconviction level of the "appropriate" group, according to the OGRS2 evaluation (i.e., medium- to high-risk offenders).

Travers and colleagues (2013) suggested that the unpublished National Offender Management System (NOMS) figures (ODEAT 2010) indicated that only one third of inmates assessed through the Offender Assessment System (OASys) in 2009/2010 met the risk and need criteria for accredited cognitive skills programs. It follows that the majority of the cohort did not have the elevated risk and criminogenic needs addressed by ETS and this is relevant for two reasons. First, it explains why those individuals were less likely to reoffend; second, it indicates that results for the majority of the inmates could not be compared with those of the ETS participants in 2009–2010.

The relevance of matching suitability requirements to treatment samples emerged in an examination by Sadlier (2010). Sadlier (2010) examined the impact of ETS programs, between 2006 and 2008, on one-year reconviction outcomes of 257 prison-based (male and female) participants, sentenced to between one month and four years; 2,514 inmates did not participate in ETS and were used to select a matched comparison group. ETS has since been replaced by the Thinking Skills Programme (TSP). The results of this evaluation show that ETS was successful in significantly reducing both the reconviction rate and the frequency of general reoffending of participants. The proportion of ETS participants who were reconvicted within one year (27.2 percent) was 5 percentage points lower (statistically significant) than the comparison group (33.5 percent). However, another finding was that the program reported low adherence to the suitability targeting criteria (i.e., meeting simultaneously the need, risk, and responsivity requirements). Only 58 percent of ETS participants were suitable for ETS. While this was a serious drawback, it also suggests that, if the targeting criteria had been respected, the effectiveness of the program in reducing reoffending might have been greater.

Travers and colleagues (2013) carried out a real-world evaluation, with the aim of comparing the reconviction outcomes of the 17,047 ETS participants who were in custody from 2000 to 2005 with a national cohort of 19,792 inmates released over the same period. Individuals involved in ETS were found to reoffend at a rate of 6.4 percentage points less than the national cohort (increasing to 7.5 percentage points for program completers) and 9.5 percentage points less than the predicted rate. According to previous studies, in all but the very highest risk group, the reoffending outcome for ETS participants was significantly better than for the inmates in the cohort. These are encouraging results, not least because there is evidence that real world outcomes typically provide smaller effect sizes than research projects (Andrews and Bonta, 2010) and because various meta-analyses report that delivery in residential settings generally yields a lower effect on reoffending than community based interventions (Lipsey and Cullen, 2007).

Travers, Mann, and Hollin (2014) explored whether the ETS program, delivered over several years to 21,000 male prisoners in England and Wales, reduced reoffending, and whether this reduction was greater for some categories of offenders than others. As before, predicted and actual reconviction rates were compared. The reconviction rate for the whole sample was 47.2 percent, 8.4 percentage points lower than predicted (Travers, Mann, and Hollin 2015). Participating in the program led to reduced reoffending for sexual offenders (13 percent point reduction), violent offenders (17 percent point reduction), and other non-acquisitive offenders (10 to 12 percent point reduction). It is interesting to note that reoffending reduction was not found for offenders convicted of burglary or robbery. After controlling for risk level, age, previous offenses committed, sentence length, and program completion, the current offense type emerged as an independent and significant predictor of reoffending.

According to a previous study, carried out in Canada (Robinson 1995), offense type appears to have an important influence on program impact. Research (Wilson, Attrill, and Nugent 2003) shows that property offenses are likely to be based on rational choices. Acquisitive offenders (such as burglars and robbers), when assessing costs and benefits, consider the likelihood of being rewarded with monetary gains or some other valuable goods compared with that of being convicted, which is a risk ingrained in the equation for engaging in criminal behavior. Such offenders may well be less motivated to apply learned prosocial skills than violent offenders, for whom the cost of their offending might be more detrimental than the benefit. For acquisitive offenders, other criminogenic needs might, in fact, be more crucial than those targeted in thinking skills programs. More relevant factors might be, for example, financial motivation, substance misuse, pro-criminal attitudes, the recognition of peers and group influence, and social status. These results are insightful insofar as they strengthen the importance of investigating the characteristics of offenders and their criminal careers. Offense type is not simply a behavioral cue but acts as a proxy for offenders' characteristics that are relevant to their responsivity to programs.

A. Beyond Mixed Findings

The CDATE project coded studies in 1968–1996 of treatment/intervention programs in prison, jail, probation, or parole settings, and these studies were meta-analyzed by Pearson and colleagues (2002). The findings showed a (weighted mean) r of .11, corresponding to 55.7 percent successes in the experimental groups and 44.3 percent successes in the comparison groups, or an approximately 11 percent reduction in reoffending. The researchers indicated that this effect was mainly due to cognitive-behavioral interventions rather than to standard behavior modification approaches; the specific types of programs that were shown to be effective included cognitive-behavioral social skills development programs and R&R programs.

In a meta-analysis of 32 aggregated European interventions addressing recidivism, Redondo, Sanchez-Meca, and Garrido (1999) found that 9.4 percent of interventions were explicitly cognitive-behavioral in nature. Despite limitations relating to the significant heterogeneity of the programs (e.g., the analysis included only three randomized studies), it was found that cognitive-behavioral interventions were the most successful programs overall. The effect size of the CBT programs ($r = .226$) was nearly double the impact across all types ($r = .120$). In a subsequent multivariate regression analysis, treatment type accounted for 48 percent of the explained variance in the model. Redondo and colleagues (1999, p. 271) explicitly indicated that "the partialised unstandardized regression coefficients for the CBT programs ($\beta = .785$) remained the most effective with regard to overall recidivism."

Tong and Farrington (2008) carried out a review of the effectiveness of the R&R programs in reducing recidivism. A previous systematic review of R&R, using meta-analytic techniques, had been published by Tong and Farrington (2006). Nineteen evaluations (involving 32 separate comparisons) were identified; experimental and control groups were compared. There was a significant 14 percent decrease in recidivism for program participants compared to controls. This result, however, was smaller than in the earlier meta-analysis by Pearson and colleagues (2002) in which the effect size (weighted mean $r = .147$) was converted to a relative 26 percent decrease in recidivism for R&R participants in comparison with controls. Certainly new studies, based on larger samples, may obtain larger effect sizes. Overall, R&R programs seem to be effective. Tong and Farrington (2008) showed that R&R programs were effective in Canada and the United Kingdom, but not in the United States; they were effective in both institutional and community settings, whether given on a voluntary basis or not. R&R programs benefited both low- and high-risk offenders, though the effect size was greater with low-risk offenders. Tong and Farrington (2008) suggested that this is possibly because of the greater likelihood of high-risk offenders dropping out of the program and faring worse than those who had never participated in the program.

Martín and colleagues (2010) conducted a study in Spain to assess the extent to which social and employment integration (SEI) may enhance the efficacy of social-cognitive training carried out in prison through a Spanish adaptation of the R&R program, entitled the Prosocial Thinking Program (PTP) (Ross et al. 1996). A quasi-experimental design was employed to compare a group of inmates who received only the social-cognitive training with a group of inmates who also received social and employment integration and with a comparison group who received neither of these interventions. The findings showed that social-cognitive skills training with the PTP had a desirable effect upon recidivism. This effect was strengthened when the PTP program was combined with the SEI intervention. The likelihood of recidivism was reduced by 18 percent in the PTP group and by 27 percent in the PTP + SEI group, even though these differences were not statistically significant. Nevertheless, these results, obtained through a survival analysis after a 6-year follow-up, are quite encouraging in suggesting that both treatment groups were significantly different from the control group in their recidivism rates. Additional research is needed to examine the efficacy of CBT for RCT studies. RCT studies are the most reliable method to link causes and effects (Farrington 2003b; Farrington and Welsh 2005; Weisburd and Piquero 2008; Weisburd 2010; Ariel and Farrington 2010) and to establish the effects of interventions.

V. ADHERENCE TO THE RISK-NEED-RESPONSIVITY MODEL

Risk assessment is crucial in ascertaining which intervention is best for which offenders, when, at which intensity, and for how long. Risk assessment is more than a practice for screening offenders (Zara and Farrington 2013); it is a practice to inform treatment planning, and foster treatment. Evidence supports the relationship between risk-targeted interventions and large effect sizes (Andrews, Bonta, and Hogue 1990; Zara and Farrington 2016); interventions are successful when, regardless of the context (prison- or community-based), they primarily target offenders' specific risks and needs. Maintaining respect for and attention to individual differences is another aspect to prioritize. It is not sufficient to offer any cognitive-behavioral program to any group of offenders who manifest cognitive deficits or social inadequacy or incompetence. The successful track record of cognitive-behavioral programs is a function of their adherence to the psychosocial reality of offending populations (Zara and Farrington 2014), to the consideration of the RNR model (Andrews 2006), and to the scope of combining the psychology of crime with the requirement of clinical relevance (Brown, 2005).

The risk principle states that offender recidivism can be reduced if the level of treatment provided to the offender is proportional to the offender's level of risk. It specifies "who to treat, and when."

The need principle calls for the focus of treatment to be on criminogenic needs. It targets "what to treat."

The responsivity principle requires that treatment should be delivered responsively, i.e., by matching the type of treatment to the ability, cognitive and emotional resources, and learning style of the offenders. It specifies "how to treat." This means that both the design and delivery of the treatment play a crucial role in its effectiveness, along with the general structure of the program, which should be explicit, and should be delivered in adherence to its rationale and in respect of its design. As introduced before, criminogenic needs or dynamic (psychological) risk factors are factors that, when present, enhance the likelihood of reoffending, while, when they are directly targeted and addressed by treatment, reoffending, is significantly reduced. Criminogenic needs (e.g., antisocial personality patterns, pro-criminal attitudes, social supports for crime, substance abuse, family/marital relationships, school/work, prosocial recreational activities) are dynamic and changeable, unlike static risk factors (e.g., age of onset, the past criminal career). Higher-risk offenders are likely to have a broader range of criminogenic needs and problems than lower-risk offenders, and generally higher-risk offenders will respond better to treatment if the treatment matches the level of risk. One advantage of the psychological assessment of offender risk is that, using Hanson's and Bourgon's (2017) words, "it reminds evaluators to look beyond [. . .] risk factors, and scores and consider the underlying psychological reasons why individuals engage in criminal behavior" (p. 246). Treatments focusing on non-criminogenic needs appear to slightly increase offending rates (Andrews and Dowden 2006), even though they might increase the sense of self-efficacy or self-esteem or reduce the anxiety level of the offenders. More studies are certainly necessary to disentangle these mechanisms that, though positive, do not reduce reoffending (Zara and Farrington 2016).

Studies have found that programs that do not meet or consider less than two of the RNR aspects may slightly increase reoffending rates (Andrews et al. 1990). According to Andrews and Bonta (2010), Bonta (2002), and Bonta and Andrews (2017), programs that adhere to all three principles can achieve a 26 percent reduction in the recidivism rate. The recidivism reduction reached an average of 17 percent if delivered in residential and custodial settings and 35 percent if delivered in community settings. Programs that followed two principles achieved an 18 percent reduction, and those that followed only one principle achieved only a 2 percent reduction.

VI. Conclusion

Cognitive-behavioral interventions are overall the most effective types of programs in preventing reoffending and reducing recidivism in a variety of offending populations. They come in different forms and shapes, with some programs initially being mostly based on addressing distorted thoughts and biased cognitions, while others rely mainly on behavioral intervention. However, all these programs are effective as long as they are implemented properly. Targeting appropriate criminogenic needs, enhancing protective factors and investing in the resources of the offenders, employing evidence-based methodology and scientific risk-assessment instruments, operating within settings of high-quality professional relationships, and adhering to the principle of responsivity are only some of the crucial aspects that are likely to achieve effective results in reducing the risk of criminal recidivism and enhancing the likelihood of desistance. To prevent crime and to rehabilitate offenders requires one step backward and two steps forward: the first implies seeing the person behind the behavior, and beyond the criminal offence, while the second requires scientific knowledge and rigorous methodology. Humanity and ethics are essential for making scientific and clinical interventions effective.

Acknowledgment

This work was supported by PRIN (Ministry of Research and University, Italy) Prot. 2010RP5RNM_004.

NOTES

1. "Men are disturbed not by things but by the views which they take of them . . . when, there-fore, we are hindered, or disturbed, or grieved, let us never blame anyone but ourselves: that is, our own judgments" (Epictetus, Greek philosopher).
2. England and Wales are an example of a system that is interested in the very complex task of joining together criminal justice and scientific knowledge and research evidence to prevent criminal behavior, reduce recidivism, rehabilitate offenders. Accredited Offending Behavior Programs have been run by prison and probation services since the early 1990s. These continue under the new arrangements for delivery of probation services. The Correctional Services Accreditation and Advisory Panel (CSAAP) gives the reassurance that programs are evidence-based. Accredited programs are routinely reviewed. CSAAP can grant accreditation for a period of up to five years, at which point a program must be resubmitted. This process includes reviewing the latest theory and evidence that underpins a program and can require minor changes in a program, or an entirely new program being developed. If there has been a substantial decrease in the need for a program, re-accreditation may not be pursued (see Accredited Offending Behavior Programmes Bulletin 2014/2015 England and Wales 2015). "Accreditation is a system for ensuring that treatment programmes offered to offenders, which aim to reduce reoffending, have a proper theoretical basis, and are designed in accordance with the "What Works" literature" (see Accredited Offending Behavior Programmes Bulletin 2014/2015 England and Wales 2015, p. 3). "In principle, the accreditation of social interventions is analogous to the establishment of norms and quality standards in engineering and technology" (McGuire, Grubin, Lösel et al. 2010). Interventions are, in fact, treated as techniques based on empirical evidence, which are liable to be replicated, evaluated, modified, and certified according to their quality of meeting the required scientific standards. The accredited programs can be grouped into five categories: Domestic Violence, General Offending, Sex Offending, Substance Misuse, and Violence. The following list includes programs designed and developed by the *National Offender Management Service* (NOMS), and also by external providers such as the *Rehabilitation for Addicted Prisoners Trust* (RAPt 12 Step programmes) and *Delight Services* (COVAID):

ART (Aggression Replacement Training) for violent offenders.
ARV (Alcohol Related Violence Programme) for alcohol abusers (NOT severely dependant drinkers) involved in violent offending.
ASRO (Addressing Substance Related Offending) for offenders who misuse drug and alcohol.
Belief in Change for medium to high-risk general offenders.
BBR (Building Better Relationships) for male perpetrators of violence and abuse within heterosexual intimate relationships.
BSR (Building Skills for Recovery) for general offenders with problematic substance misuse and can be delivered in a group setting or on a one-to-one basis.
CALM (Controlling Anger and Learning to Manage it) for offenders with intense emotional anger problems.
CARE (Choices, Actions, Relationships and Emotions) for female prisoners with emotion regulation difficulties.
CDVP (Community Domestic Violence Programme) for male domestic violence perpetrators.

Chromis for high-risk and psychopathic violent offenders.

COVAID Programmes (Control of violence and anger in impulsive drinkers) for violent and impulsive drinkers. The different versions of the COVAID programme can be delivered as group work or on a one to one basis, in either secure or community settings.

CSB (Cognitive Skills Booster) for general offenders.

DID (Drink Impaired Drivers Programme) for drinking problematic offenders.

DTC (Democratic Therapeutic Community) for emotional and psychological needs and personality disorders offenders.

FOCUS Substance misuse programme for drug and alcohol abuser offenders in detention.

FOR (Focus on Resettlement) for offenders in custody. This programme is designed for those serving sentences under 4 years and is only available in custody.

GBP (Generic Booster Programme) for violent offenders.

HRP (Healthy Relationship Programme) for moderate to high-risk and high-need male offenders who committed violent behavior in a domestic setting.

IDAP (Integrated Domestic Abuse Programme) for male offenders who have committed violent behavior in an intimate relationship.

JETS (Juvenile Estate Thinking Skills Programme) for antisocial juveniles aged 14 to 17 years.

Kainos CTC (Kainos "challenge to change") for medium to high-risk offenders. The Kainos Community is a registered charity and currently runs programmes in three prisons: HMP Stocken, HMP Guys Marsh and HMP Haverig.

LIAP (Low Intensity Alcohol Programme) for offenders with alcohol problems to assist relapse prevention.

OSAP (Substance Abuse Programme) for offenders who misuse drugs or alcohol to prevent relapse and reduce offending.

PASRO (Prison Addressing Substance Related Offending) for offenders with substance use problems.

POTO (Priestley One to One Programme) for offenders in the community.

PPTCP (Prison Partnership Therapeutic Community Programme) for offenders with substance misuse problems.

PPTSP (Prison Partnership Twelve Step Programme) for offenders with serious drug and alcohol problems.

RAPt (Rehabilitation of Addicted Prisoners Trust) for offenders involved in an Alcohol Dependency Treatment Programme (ADTP).

RESOLVE for medium risk violent adult male offenders.

RESPOND for offenders eligible for TSP but not suitable for the group format.

SCP (Self Change Programme) for violent high-risk persistent violent offenders.

SDP (Short Duration Programme) for offenders with substance and anger problems.

TSP (Thinking Skills Programme) for general offenders.

The Women's Programme for female offenders who have committed acquisitive offences and are at risk of reconviction for non-violent crimes.

A>Z a "non-accredited yet" program for general offenders.

The following are programs specific for sex offenders, and are delivered according to the level of risk and needs of the offenders:

SOTP (Sex Offender Treatment Programmes)

CSOGP (Community Sex Offenders Group Programme)

NSOGP (Northumbria Sex Offenders Group Programme)

TVSOGP (Thames Valley Sex Offenders Group Programme)

ABLB (Sex Offenders Treatment Programme Adapted Better Lives Booster) for sexual offenders who have completed the Adapted SOTP. It shares the same aims as the Core version but the treatment delivery methods are different to accommodate different learning styles and abilities.

ASOTPCV (Adapted Sex Offender Treatment Programme Community Version) for sexual offenders who have social or learning difficulties. Adapted Community sex offender programme similar to SOTP.

BLB (Better Lives Booster) for sexual offenders who are learning from other SOTPs. It is delivered in the low intensity and high intensity forms, and it is also available for intellectually disabled and non intellectually disabled sex offenders.

BNM (Sex Offenders Treatment Programme Becoming New Me) for medium- and high-risk sexual offenders who have social or learning difficulties. Covers similar areas to Core SOTP.

Core SOTP (Sex Offenders Treatment Programme) for sexual offenders.

Extended SOTP (Extended Sex Offenders Treatment Programme) for high and very high-risk male sexual offenders who have successfully met the treatment targets of the Core programme.

HSF (Healthy Sex Programme)/ HSF (Healthy Sexual Functioning Programme) for high-risk sexual offenders.

i-SOTP (Internet Sex Offender Treatment Programme) for sexual offenders who acted out via the internet.

LNM (Living as New Me) for sex offenders of medium and above risk. It is a maintenance program.

NMC (New Me Coping) for lower risk intellectually disabled sex offenders. It involves a less intense treatment approach.

Rolling Programme (Rolling Programme) for sexual offenders who can join and leave as the program rolls along so members are at different stages of treatment, depending on when they joined the group.

The High and Low Intensity Pilot Sex Offender Treatment Programmes for sex offenders who will be treated in the community. These are new treatment approaches, which are being piloted in the community.

For a complete description visit https://www.justice.gov.uk/offenders/before-after-release/obp and https://www.gov.uk/government/statistics/accredited-programmes-bulletin-2014-to-2015.

3. Aggression Replacement Training® (ART®) was awarded trademarks in 2004 by the U.S. Patent and Trademark Office protected printed matter and training seminars, training programs, and their variants.

4. Moral Reconation Therapy® (MRT®) was awarded its first federal trademark in 1995.

5. For a more complete overview of early interventions to prevent child behavior problems and antisociality, see Zara and Farrington (2014).

6. The OGRS2 score is calculated from nine items that assess the offender's demographic and criminal history, using a scale range between of 0 and 100 (Palmer, McGuire, Hatcher et al. 2009, p. 910). The low and high OGRS2 score cut-off values used by the Probation Service to assess the suitability of programs are usually set at 31 percent and 74 percent, respectively, although there is room for professional discretion to override this.

References

Andrews, Don A. 2006. "Enhancing Adherence to Risk-Need-Responsivity: Making Quality a Matter of Policy." *Criminology and Public Policy* 5: 595–602.

Andrews, Don A., and James Bonta. 2010. *The Psychology of Criminal Conduct*. 5th ed. Cincinnati: Anderson.

Andrews, Don A., James Bonta, and Robert D. Hogue. 1990. "Classification for Effective Rehabilitation: Rediscovering Psychology." *Criminal Justice and Behavior* 17: 19–52.

Andrews, Don A., and Craig Dowden. 1999. "A Meta-Analytic Investigation into Effective Correctional Intervention for Female Offenders." *Forum on Corrections Research* 11: 18–21.

Andrews, Don A., and Craig Dowden. 2006. "Risk Principle of Case Classification in Correctional Treatment: A Meta-Analytic Investigation." *International Journal of Offender Therapy and Comparative Criminology* 50: 88–100.

Andrewson Don A., Ivan Zinger, Robert H. Hoge, James Bonta, Paul Gendreau, and Francis T. Cullen 1990. "Does Correctional Treatment Work? A Clinically Relevant and Psychologically Informed Meta-Analysis." *Criminology* 28: 369–404.

Augimeri, Lina A., David P. Farrington, Christopher J. Koegl, and David M. Day. 2007. "The SNAP® Under 12 Outreach Project: Effects on a Community Based Program for Children with Conduct Problems." *Journal of Family and Child Studies* 16: 799–807.

Barak Ariel, and David P. Farrington. 2010. "Randomized Block Designs." In *Handbook of Quantitative Criminology*, edited by Alex R. Piquero and David Weisburd, 437–454. New York: Springer.

Barnett, Georgia, and Ruth E. Mann. 2013. "Empathy Deficits and Sexual Offending: A Model of Obstacles to Empathy." *Aggression and Violent Behavior* 18: 228–239.

Baydar, Nazli, M. Jamila Reid, and Carolyn Webster-Stratton. 2003. "The Role of Mental Health Factors and Program Engagement in the Effectiveness of a Preventive Parenting Program for Head Start Mothers." *Child Development* 74: 1433–1453.

Beck, Aaron T. 1970. "Cognitive Therapy: Nature and Relation to Behavior Therapy." *Behavior Therapy* 1: 184–200.

Beelmann, Andreas, and Friedrich Lösel. 2006. "Child Social Skills Training in Developmental Crime Prevention: Effects of Antisocial Behavior and Social Competence." *Psicothema* 18: 603–610.

Bonta, James. 2002. "Offender Risk Assessment: Guidelines for Selection and Use." *Criminal Justice and Behavior* 29: 355–379.

Bonta, James, and Don A. Andrews. 2017. *The Psychology of Criminal Conduct*. 6th ed. New York: Routledge.

Brotman, Laura M., Kathleen K. Gouley, Keng-Yeng Huang, Amanda Rosenfelt, Colleen O'Neal, Rachael Klein, and Patrick Shrout. 2008. "Preventive Intervention for Preschoolers at High Risk for Antisocial Behavior: Long-Term Effects on Child Physical Aggression and Parenting Practices." *Journal of Child and Adolescent Psychology* 37: 386–396.

Brown, Sarah. 2005. *Treating Sex Offenders. An Introduction to Sex Offender Treatment Programs*. Cullompton, UK: Willan.

Bush, Jack, Barry Glick, and Juliana Taymans. 1997. *Thinking for a Change: Integrated Cognitive Behavior Change Program*. National Institute of Corrections. Washington, DC: U.S. Department of Justice.

Cann, Jenny. 2006. *Cognitive Skills Programmes: Impact on Reducing Reconviction Among a Sample of Female Prisoners*. London: Home Office. Research, Development and Statistics Directorate Research Findings No. 276.

Cann, Jenny, Louise Falshaw, Francis Nugent, and Caroline Friendship. 2003. *Understanding What Works: Accredited Cognitive Skills Programmes for Adult Men and Young Offenders.* London: Home Office. Research, Development and Statistics Directorate Research Findings No. 226.

Chitty, Chloë. 2005. "The Impact of Corrections on Re-offending: Conclusions and the Way Forward." *The Impact of Corrections on Re-offending: A Review of 'What Works,* edited by Gemma Harper and Chitty Chloë, 75–82, London: Home Office. (Research Study 291).

Cohen, M. A., and Alex R. Piquero. 2009. "New Evidence on the Monetary Value of Saving a High Risk Youth." *Journal of Quantitative Criminology* 25: 25–49.

Cullen, Francis T., and Paul Gendreau. 2000. "Assessing Correctional Rehabilitation: Policy, Practice, and Prospects." In *Criminal Justice 2000,* Vol. 3, edited by Julie Horney, 109–175. Washington, DC: U.S. Department of Justice, Office of Justice Programs, National Institute of Justice, NCJ 182410.

D'Arms, Justin. 2000. "Empathy and Evaluative Inquiry." *Chicago-Kent Law Review* 74: 1467–1500.

Dowden, Craig, and Don A. Andrews. 1999a. "What Works for Female Offenders: A Meta-Analytic Review." *Crime and Delinquency* 45: 438–452.

Dowden, Craig, and Don A. Andrews. 1999b. "What Works in Young Offender Treatment: A Meta-Analysis." *Forum on Corrections Research* 11: 1–24.

Egan, Vincent, Beth Kavanagh, and Mary Blair. 2005. "Sexual Offenders Against Children: The Influence of Personality and Obsessionality on Cognitive Distortions." *Sexual Abuse: A Journal of Research and Treatment* 17: 223–240.

Ellis, Albert. 1962. *Reason and Emotion in Psychotherapy.* New York: Lyle Stuart.

Erikson, Erik H. 1959. *Identity and the Life Cycle.* New York: W.W. Norton.

Falshaw, Louise, Caroline Friendship, Rosie Travers, and Francis Nugent. 2003. *Searching for "What Works": An Evaluation of Cognitive Skills Programmes.* London: Home Office. Research, Development and Statistics Directorate Research Findings No. 206.

Farrington, David P. 2003a. "Advancing Knowledge About the Early Prevention of Adult Antisocial Behaviour." In *Early Prevention of Adult Antisocial Behaviour,* edited by David P. Farrington, and Jeremy W. Coid, 1–31. Cambridge, UK: Cambridge University Press.

Farrington, David P. 2003b. "Methodological Quality Standards for Evaluation Research." *Annals of American Academy of Political and Social Science* 587: 49–68.

Farrington, David P. 2015a. "The Developmental Evidence Base: Psychosocial Research." In *Forensic Psychology,* 2nd ed., edited by G. J. Towl and D. A. Crighton, 161–171. Oxford: Blackwell.

Farrington, David P. 2015b. "Prospective Longitudinal Research on the Development of Offending." *Australian and New Zealand Journal of Criminology* 48: 314–335.

Farrington, David P., and Brandon C. Welsh. 2005. "Randomized Experiments in Criminology: What Have We Learned in the Past 2 Decades?" *Journal of Experimental Criminology* 1: 9–28.

Farrington, David P., and Brandon C. Welsh. 2007. *Saving Children from a Life of Crime.* Oxford: Oxford University Press.

Farrington, David P., and Koegl, Christopher J. 2015. "Monetary Benefits and Costs of the Stop Now and Plan Program for Boys Aged 6–11, Based on the Prevention of Later Offending." *Journal of Quantitative Criminology* 31: 263–287.

Friendship, Caroline, Linda Blud, Matthew Erikson, and Rosie Travers. 2002. *An Evaluation of Cognitive Behavioral Treatment for Prisoners.* London: Home Office. Research, Development and Statistics Directorate Research Findings No. 161.

Gendreau, Paul, and Don A. Andrews. 1990. "Tertiary Prevention: What the Meta-Analyses of the Offender Treatment Literature Tell Us About 'What Works.'" *Canadian Journal of Criminology* 32: 173–184.

Goldstein, Arnold P., and John C. Gibbs. 1987. *Aggression Replacement Training: A Comprehensive Intervention for Aggressive Youth*. Champaign, IL: Research Press.

Goldstein, Arnold P., Barry Glick, and John C. Gibbs. 1998. *Aggression Replacement Training*. Rev. ed. Champaign, IL: Research Press.

Hansen, Nathan B., Michael J. Lambert, and Evan M. Forman. 2002. "The Psychotherapy Dose-Response Effect and Its Implications for Treatment Delivery Services." *Clinical Psychology: Science and Practice* 9: 329–343.

Hanson, R. Karl, and Guy Bourgon. 2017. "Advancing sexual offender risk assessment. Standardized risk levels based on psychologically meaningful offender characteristics." In *Handbook on Risk and Need Assessment. Theory and Practice*, edited by Faye S. Taxman, 244–268. New York: Routledge.

Hanson, R. Karl, Guy Bourgon, Leslie Helmus, and Shannon Hodgson. 2009. "The Principles of Effective Correctional Treatment also Apply to Sexual Offenders: A Meta-Analysis." *Criminal Justice and Behavior* 36: 865–889.

Hanson, R. Karl, and Kelly E. Morton-Bourgon. 2005. "The Characteristics of Persistent Sexual Offenders: A Meta-Analysis of Recidivism Studies." *Journal of Consulting and Clinical Psychology* 73: 1154–1163.

Harnett, Paul, Analise O'Donovan, and Michael J. Lambert. 2010. "The Dose Response Relationship in Psychotherapy: Implications for Social Policy." *Clinical Psychologist* 14: 39–44.

Hollin, Clive R. 1990. *Cognitive–Behavioral Interventions with Young Offenders*. Elmsford, NY: Pergamon Press.

Hollin, Clive R. 2004. "Aggression Replacement Training: The Cognitive-Behavioral Context." In *New Perspectives on Aggression Replacement Training: Practice, Research, and Application*, edited by Arnold P. Goldstein, Rune Nensén, Bengt Daleflod, and Mikael Kalt, 3–19. Chichester, UK: John Wiley.

Johnson-Laird, Philip. 2008. *How We Reason*. Oxford: Oxford University Press.

Jolliffe, Darrick, and David P. Farrington. 2004. "Empathy and Offending: A Systematic Review and Meta-Analysis." *Aggression and Violent Behavior* 9: 441–476.

Jolliffe, Darrick, and David P. Farrington. 2007. *A Systematic Review of the National and International Evidence on the Effectiveness of Interventions with Violent Offenders*. London. Ministry of Justice (Research Series 16/07).

Koegl, Christopher J., Farrington, David P., Augimeri, Lina A., and David M. Day. 2008. "Evaluation of a Targeted Cognitive-Behavioral Program for Children with Conduct Problems—The SNAP® Under 12 Outreach Project: Service Intensity, Age and Gender Effects on Short- and Long-Term Outcomes." *Clinical Child Psychology and Psychiatry* 13: 419–434.

Kohlberg, Lawrence. 1963. "The Development of Children's Orientations toward a Moral Order: I. Sequence in the Development of Moral Thought." *Human Development* 6: 11–33.

Latessa, Edward J. 2006. "Effectiveness of Cognitive Behavioral Interventions for Youthful Offenders. Review of the Research." In *Cognitive Behavioral Interventions for At-Risk Youth*, edited by Barry Glick, 14-1-14-20. Kingston, NJ: Civic Research Institute.

Levene, Kathryne S. 1998. *SNAPP Stop-Now-And-Plan Parenting: Parenting Children with Behavior Problems*. Toronto: Earlscourt Child and Family Centre.

Lipsey, Mark W., and Francis T. Cullen. 2007. "The Effectiveness of Correctional Rehabilitation: A Review of Systematic Reviews." *Annual Review of Law and Social Science* 3: 297–320.

Lipsey, Mark W., and Nana A. Landenberger. 2006. "Cognitive-Behavioral Interventions." In *Preventing Crime. What Works for Children, Offenders, Victims, and Places*, edited by Brandon C. Welsh and David P. Farrington, 57–71. Dordrecht, The Netherlands: Springer.

Lipsey, Mark W., Nana A. Landenberger, and Sandra J. Wilson. 2007. "Effects of cognitive-Behavioral Programs for Criminal Offenders." *Campbell Systematic Reviews* 2007: 6.

Lipsey, Mark W., and David B. Wilson. 1998. "Effective intervention for serious juvenile offenders." In *Serious & Violent Juvenile Offenders: Risk Factors and Successful Interventions*, edited by Rolf Loeber and David P. Farrington, 313–345. Thousand Oaks, CA: Sage.

Little, Gregory. 2000. "Cognitive-Behavioral Treatment of Offenders: A Comprehensive Ten-Year Review of MRT® Research." *Addictive Behaviors Treatment Review* 2: 12–21.

Little, Gregory. 2005. "Meta-Analysis of Moral Reconation Therapy® Recidivism results from Probation and Parole Implementations." *Cognitive Behavioral Treatment Review* 14: 14–16.

Little, Gregory, and Kenneth D. Robinson. 1986. *How to Escape Your Prison*. Memphis, TN: Eagle Wing Books.

Lösel, Friedrich. 1995. "The Efficacy of Correctional Treatment: A Review and Synthesis of Meta-Evaluations." In *What Works: Reducing Reoffending. Guidelines for Research and Practice*, edited by James McGuire, 70–111. Chichester, UK: John Wiley.

Lösel, Friedrich. 1996. "Working with Young Offenders: The Impact of Meta-Analyses." In *Clinical Approaches to Working with Young Offenders*, edited by Clive R. Hollin and K. Howells, 57–82. Chichester, UK: John Wiley.

Lösel, Friedrich. 2001. "Evaluating the Effectiveness of Correctional Programs: Bridging the Gap Between Research and Practice." In *Offender Rehabilitation in Practice*, edited by Gary A. Bernfeld, David P. Farrington, and Alan W. Leschied, 67–92. New York: John Wiley.

Lösel, Friedrich, and Andreas Beelmann. 2003. "Effects of Child Skills Training in Preventing Antisocial Behavior: A Systematic Review of Randomized Evaluations." *Annals of the American Academy of Political and Social Science* 587: 84–109.

Lösel, Friedrich, and Andreas Beelmann. 2006. "Child skills training." In *Preventing Crime: What Works for Children, Offenders, Victims and Places*, edited by Brandon C. Welsh and David P. Farrington, 33–54. Dortrecht, NL: Wadsworth Publishing.

Lösel, Friedrich, and Doris Bender. 2012. "Child Skills Training in the Prevention of Antisocial Development and Crime." In *The Oxford Handbook of Crime Prevention*, edited by Brandon C. Welsh and David P. Farrington, 102–129. New York: Oxford University Press.

Lösel, Friedrich, and Martin Schmucker. 2005. "The Effectiveness of Treatment for Sex Offenders: A Comprehensive Meta-Analysis." *Journal of Experimental Criminology* 1: 117–146.

MacKenzie, Doris L. 2006. *What Works in Corrections: Reducing the Criminal Activities of Offenders and Delinquents*. New York: Cambridge University Press.

Marlatt, Alan G., and Dennis M. Donovan, eds. 2005. *Relapse Prevention: Maintenance Strategies in the Treatment of Addictive Behaviors*. 2nd ed. New York: Guilford.

Marlatt, Alan G., and Judith R. Gordon. 1985. *Relapse Prevention: Maintenance Strategies in the Treatment of Addictive Behaviors*. New York: Guilford Press.

Martín, Ana M., Bernardo Hernández, Estefanía Hernández-Fernaud, José L. Arregui, and Juan A. Hernández. 2010. "The Enhancement Effect of Social and Employment Integration on the Delay of Recidivism of Released Offenders Trained with the R&R Programme." *Psychology, Crime, and Law* 16: 401–413.

McGuire, James. 1995. *What Works: Reducing Reoffending*. Chichester, UK: John Wiley.

McGuire, James. 2001. "What Works in Conventional Intervention? Evidence and Practical Implications." In *Offender Rehabilitation in Practice*, edited by G. A. Bernfeld, David P. Farrington, and A. W. Leschied, 25–43. Chichester, UK: John Wiley.

McGuire, James, and Philip Priestley. 1995. "Reviewing "What Works": Past, Present and Future." In *What Works: Reducing Re-Offending*, edited by James McGuire, 3–34. Chichester, UK: John Wiley.

McGuire, Mike, Don Grubin, Friedrich Lösel, and Peter Raynor. 2010. "'What Works' and the Correctional Services Accreditation Panel: Taking Stock from an Inside Perspective." *Criminology and Criminal Justice* 10: 37–58.

Ministry of Justice 2015. *Accredited Offending Behavior Programmes Bulletin 2014/2015 England and Wales*. London: Ministry of Justice Statistics Bulletin.

Munoz, Rachel, Judy Hutchings, Rhiannon-Tudor Edwards, Barry Hounsome, and Alan O'Ceilleachair. 2004. "Economic Evaluation of Treatments for Children with Severe Behavior Problems." *Journal of Mental Health Policy Economics* 7: 177–189.

ODEAT—National Offender Manager Service. 2010. *Suitability for Accredited Programmes—Custody*. Unpublished report.

Oxley, Julinna C. 2011. *The Moral Dimensions of Empathy: Limits and Applications in Ethical Theory and Practice*. London: Palgrave Macmillan.

Palmer, Emma J., James McGuire, Ruth M. Hatcher, Juliette C. Hounsome, Charlotte A. L. Bilby, and Clive R. Hollin. 2009. "Allocating to Offending Behavior Programs in the English and Welsh Probation Service." *Criminal Justice and Behavior* 36: 909–922.

Pearson, Frank S., Douglas S. Lipton, Charles M. Cleland, and Dorline S. Yee. 2002. "The Effects of Behavioral/Cognitive-Behavioral Programs on Recidivism." *Crime and Delinquency* 48: 476–496.

Petrosino, Anthony, and Julia Lavenberg. 2007. "Systematic Reviews and Metal-Analytic Best Evidence on 'What Works' for Criminal Justice Decision Makers." *Western Criminology Review* 8: 1–15.

Piquero, Alex R., and Wesley J. Jennings. 2012. "Parent Training and the Prevention of Crime." In *The Oxford Handbook of Crime Prevention*, edited by Brandon C. Welsh and David P. Farrington, 89–101. New York: Oxford University Press.

Polaschek, Devon L. L., Nick J. Wilson, Marilyn R. Townsend, and Lorna R., Daly. 2005. "Cognitive-Behavioral Rehabilitation for High-Risk Violent Offenders: An Outcome Evaluation of the Violence Prevention Unit." *Journal of Interpersonal Violence* 20: 1611–1627.

Prentky, Robert A., Ann W. Burgess, Frances Rokous, Austin L. Lee, Carol Hartman, Robert Ressler, and John Douglas. 1989. "The Presumptive Role of Fantasy in Serial Sexual Homicide." *American Journal of Psychiatry* 146: 887–891.

Redondo, Santiago, Julio Sanchez-Meca, and Vicente Garrido. 1999. "The Influence of Treatment Programmes on the Recidivism of Juvenile and Adult Offenders: An European Meta-Analytic Review." *Psychology, Crime and Law* 5: 251–278.

Robinson, D. 1995. *The Impact of Cognitive Skills Training on Post-Release Recidivism among Canadian Federal Offenders* (Report No. R-41). Ottawa, ON: Public Safety Canada.

Ross, Robert R., and Elisabeth A. Fabiano. 1985. *Time to Think: A Cognitive Model of Delinquency Prevention and Offender Rehabilitation*. Johnson City, TN: Institute of Social Sciences and Arts.

Ross, Robert R., and Elisabeth A. Fabiano. 1991. *Reason and Rehabilitation: A Handbook for Teaching Cognitive Skills*. Ottawa, ON: T3 Associates.

Ross, Robert R., Elisabeth A. Fabiano, and Crystal Dimmer-Ewles. 1995. "The Pickering Project for High-Risk Offenders." In *Thinking Straight: The Reasoning and Rehabilitation Program for Delinquency Prevention and Offender Rehabilitation*, edited by Robert R. Ross and Roslynn D. Ross, 145–153. Ottawa, ON: AIR Training and Publications.

Ross, Robert R., Elisabeth A. Fabiano, Vicente Garrido, V., and Ana M. Gómez. 1996. *Programa "El Pensamiento Prosocial": Una Guía de Trabajo Detallada para la Prevención y el Tratamiento de la Delinquencia y la Drogopedencia* ["*The Prosocial Thinking Program*": A Detailed Work Guide for the Prevention and Treatment of Offending Behavior and Drug Abuse]. Valencia, Spain: Cristóbal Serrano Villalba.

Ross, Robert R., and Jim Hilborn 2005. *Reasoning & Rehabilitation Short Version For Adults: Program Overview*. Ottawa: Cognitive Centre of Canada.

Ross, Robert R., and Jim Hilborn. 2008. *Rehabilitating Rehabilitation: Neurocriminology for Treatment of Antisocial Behavior*. Ottawa, ON: Cognitive Centre of Canada.

Sadlier, Greg. 2010. *Evaluation of the Impact of the HM Prison Service Enhanced Thinking Skills Programme on Reoffending. Outcomes of the Surveying Prisoner Crime Reduction (SPCR) Sample*. London: Ministry of Justice (Research Series 19/10).

Schindler, Holly S., and Caroline F. D. Black. 2015. "Early Prevention of Criminal and Antisocial Behavior: A Review of Interventions in Infancy and Childhood." In *The Development of Criminal and Antisocial Behaviour*, edited by Julien Morizot, and Lila Kazemian. New York: Springer.

Sherman, Lawrence W., David P. Farrington, Brandon C. Welsh, and Layton MacKenzie, D. 2002. "Preventing Crime." In *Evidence-Based Crime Prevention*, edited by Lawrence W. Sherman, David P. Farrington, Brandon C. Welsh, and Doris Layton MacKenzie. London: Routledge.

Sherman, Lawrence W., Denise C. Gottfredson, Doris L. MacKenzie, D., John Eck, Peter Reuter, and Shawn D. Bushway. 1998. *Preventing Crime: What Works, What Doesn't, What's Promising*. Washington, DC: U.S. National Institute of Justice.

Taylor, Ricky. 1999. *Predicting Reconvictions for Sexual and Violent Offences using the Revised Offender Group Reconviction Scale*. London: Home Office (Research Findings No. 104).

Tong, L. S. Joy, and David P. Farrington. 2006. "How Effective Is the "Reasoning and Rehabilitation" Program in Reducing Reoffending? A Meta-Analysis of Evaluations in Four Countries." *Psychology, Crime, and Law* 12: 3–24.

Tong, L. S. Joy, and David P. Farrington. 2008. "Effectiveness of 'Reasoning and Rehabilitation' in Reducing Reoffending." *Psicothema* 20: 20–28.

Travers, Rosie, Ruth E. Mann, and Clive R. Hollin. 2014. "Who Benefits from Cognitive Skills Programmes? Differential Impact by Risk and Offence Type." *Criminal Justice and Behavior* 41: 1103–1129.

Travers, Rosie, Ruth E. Mann, and Clive R. Hollin. 2015. *Who Benefits from Cognitive Skills Programmes?* London: National Offender Management Service 1–4.

Travers, Rosie, Helen C. Wakeling, Ruth E. Mann, and Clive R. Hollin. 2013. "Reconviction Following a Cognitive Skills Intervention: An Alternative Quasi-Experimental Methodology." *Legal and Criminological Psychology* 18: 48–65.

Ward, Tony, and Russil Durrant. 2013. "Altruism, Empathy, and Sex Offender Treatment." *International Journal of Behavioral Consultation and Therapy* 8: 66–71.

Ware, Jayson, and Ruth E. Mann. 2012. "How Should 'Acceptance of Responsibility' Be Addressed in Sexual Offending Treatment Programs?" *Aggression and Violent Behavior* 17: 279–288.

Webster-Stratton, Carolyn, and Ted Taylor. 2001. "Nipping Early Risk Factors in the Bud: Preventing Substance Abuse, Delinquency, and Violence in Adolescence Through Interventions Targeted at Young Children (Ages 0–8 Years)." *Prevention Science* 2: 165–192.

Webster-Stratton, Carolyn, M. Jamila Reid, and Mary A. Hammond. 2001. "Preventing Conduct Problems, Promoting Social Competence: A Parent and Teacher Training Partnership in Head Start." *Journal of Clinical Child Psychology* 30: 283–302.

Webster-Stratton, Carolyn, M. Jamila Reid, and Mary A. Hammond. 2004. "Treating Children with Early-Onset Conduct Problems: Intervention Outcomes for Parent, Child, and Teacher Training." *Journal of Clinical Child and Adolescent Psychology* 33: 105–124.

Webster-Stratton, Carolyn, M. Jamila Reid, and Mike Stoolmiller. 2008. "Preventing Conduct Problems and Improving School Readiness: Evaluation of the Incredible Years Teacher and Child Training Programs in High-Risk Schools." *Journal of Child Psychology and Psychiatry* 49: 471–488.

Weisburd, David. 2003. "Ethical Practice and Evaluation of Interventions in Crime and Justice: The Moral Imperative for Randomized Trials." *Evaluation Review* 27: 336–354.

Weisburd, David. 2010. Justifying the Use of Non-Experimental Methods and Disqualifying the Use of Randomized Controlled Trials: Challenging Folklore in Evaluation Research in Crime and Justice. *Journal of Experimental Criminology,* 6: 209–227.

Weisburd, David, and Joshua C. Hinkle. 2012. "The Importance of Randomized Experiments in Evaluating Crime Prevention." In *The Oxford Handbook of Crime Prevention*, edited by Brandon C. Welsh and David P. Farrington, 446–465. New York: Oxford University Press.

Weisburd, David, and Alex P. Piquero. 2008. "How Well Do Criminologists Explain Crime? Statistical Modeling in Published Studies." In *Crime and Justice*, Vol. 37, edited by Michael Tonry, 453–502. Chicago: University of Chicago Press.

Welsh Brandon C., and David P. Farrington. 2012. "The Science and Politics of Crime Prevention: Toward a New Crime Policy." In *The Oxford Handbook of Crime Prevention*, edited by Brandon C. Welsh and D. P. Farrington, 509–520. New York: Oxford University Press.

Welsh Brandon C., David P. Farrington, and B. Raffan Gowar. 2015. "Benefit-Cost Analysis of Crime Prevention Programs." In *Crime and Justice*, Vol. 44, edited by Michael Tonry, 447–516. Chicago: University of Chicago Press.

Whitaker, Daniel J., Brenda Le, R. Karl Hanson, Charlene K. Baker, Pam M. McMahon, Gail Ryan, Alisa Klein, and Deborah Donovan Rice. 2008. "Risk Factors for the Perpetration of Child Sexual Abuse: A Review and Meta-Analysis." *Child Abuse and Neglect* 32: 529–548.

Wilson, Davis B., Leana Allen Bouffard, and Doris L. MacKenzie. 2005. "A Quantitative Review of Structured, Group-Oriented, Cognitive-Behavioral Programs for Offenders." *Criminal Justice and Behavior* 32: 172–204.

Wilson, S., Attrill, G., and Nugent, F. 2003. "Effective Interventions for Acquisitive Offenders: An Investigation of Cognitive Skills Programmes." *Legal and Criminological Psychology* 8: 83–101.

Wilson, David B., and Lipsey, Mark W. 2001. "The Role of Method in Treatment Effectiveness Research: Evidence from Meta-Analysis." *Psychological Methods* 6: 413–429.

Zara, Georgia, and David P. Farrington. 2013. "Assessment of Risk for Juvenile Compared with Adult Criminal Onset: Implications for Policy, Prevention and Intervention." *Psychology, Public Policy and Law* 19: 235–249.

Zara, Georgia, and David P. Farrington. 2014. "Cognitive-Behavioral Skills Training in Preventing Offending and Reducing Recidivism." In *Criminology and Forensic Psychology*, edited by Eva Maria Jiménez González and Jose Luis Alba Robles, 56–103. Charleston, SC: Criminology and Justice.

Zara, Georgia, and David P. Farrington. 2016. *Criminal Recidivism: Explanation, Prediction and Prevention*. Abingdon, UK: Routledge.

Zara, Georgia, and Guglielmo Gulotta. 2014. "Evidence Based Research in Juvenile Delinquency." In *Criminology and Forensic Psychology*, edited by Eva Maria Jiménez González and Jose Luis Alba Robles, 103–155. Charleston, SC: Criminology and Justice.

Zara, Georgia, and Cristina Mosso. 2014. "Empathy." In *Encyclopedia of Criminal Justice Ethics*, edited by Bruce A. Arrigo. Thousand Oaks, CA: Sage.

CHAPTER 34

··

COST-BENEFIT ANALYSIS OF DEVELOPMENTAL PREVENTION

··

JOBINA LI AND CAMERON MCINTOSH*

IN light of burgeoning criminal justice costs, governments the world over are exploring ways to prioritize and allocate resources amid concerns about the viability and sustainability of existing practices. From a life-course perspective, developmental crime prevention offers an intriguing solution to address these concerns, given the growing body of research that suggests that this type of intervention is both results-oriented and fiscally responsible. To this end, Section I of this chapter lays out the case for the economics of developmental crime prevention. Section II provides an overview of the methodological basis, and related considerations, of a cost-benefit analysis, which assigns monetary values to program outcomes relative to program costs so as to provide an estimate of the financial return on investment. Section III reviews the leading cost-benefit analysis studies in developmental crime prevention today, and Section IV offers a glimpse at the future of such research.

I. COST-BENEFIT ANALYSIS OF DEVELOPMENTAL PREVENTION: EXPLORING THE "WHY"

··

Governments across the world are increasingly faced with fiscal challenges and budgetary constraints and, consequently, the dilemma of how to allocate limited resources

* The views expressed are those of the authors and do not necessarily reflect those of the Government of Canada

among multiple competing public sector needs is a constant preoccupation. In the area of criminal justice, the costs to society of crime, offending, victimization, and justice system responses are significant and ever-growing and, to a large extent, unsustainable. Internationally, the costs of crime and traditional criminal justice system responses are staggeringly high. In the United States, for example, the total gross annual cost of crime was estimated at $3.2 trillion in 2010 (with the net cost being almost $1.7 trillion), after the inclusion of such categories as crime-induced production, opportunity costs, risks to life and health, and transfers (Anderson 2011). Another study reported that in 2007, crime resulted in approximately $15 billion in economic losses to the victims and $179 billion in government expenditures on police protection, judicial and legal activities, and corrections (McCollister, French, and Fang 2010). In Canada, the Department of Justice estimated the cost of crime to be $100 billion CAD in 2008, consisting of $31.4 billion in tangible social and economic costs of Criminal Code offenses, and another $68 billion in intangible costs of crime, such as pain and suffering (Zhang 2011). Relatedly, the Parliamentary Budget Officer reported that Canadian criminal justice system expenditures were approximately $20.3 billion in 2011–2012 (Story and Yalkin 2013). In the United Kingdom, the total cost of crimes against individuals and households in 2003–2004 was approximated at £36.2 billion (Dubourg and Hamed 2005), whereas in Australia, the estimated costs of crime for 2005 were $35.8 billion AUD (Rollings 2008).

In addition, the costs of high-risk offenders and their typically lengthy criminal trajectories are particularly high. For instance, the present value of saving a 14-year-old high-risk juvenile from a life of crime and negative social outcomes (e.g., substance use) in the United States is estimated to range from $3.2 to $5.8 million (Cohen and Piquero 2009). Similarly, one Canadian study that predicted future criminal and health outcomes has estimated that a high-risk youth in Ontario will cost society $1.4 million CAD between the ages of 12 and 21, increasing to $2.2 million by age 28. Moreover, early-onset offenders, persistent offenders, prolific offenders, and persistent/prolific offenders cost anywhere between three to five times as much as other offender groups (Koegl 2011). More recently, a Canadian study utilizing a sample of 386 high-risk males sentenced as juvenile offenders in Toronto found that over a 15-year follow-up period, the aggregate cost of offending was $671 million CAD or approximately $1.7 million per person, based on official convictions. Incorporating the costs of undetected crime brought the per-person total to $3.8 million (Day et al. 2015). Lastly, an Australian study of 41,377 offenders born in 1983 and 1984 found that by age 26, chronic offenders (those accumulating 30 or more offenses) cost, on average, between $186,366 and $262,799 AUD, more than 20 times the average cost of low rate offenders (those with only about 2 offenses) (Allard et al. 2014).

A. Developmental Prevention as a Key Theoretical and Economic Approach

So how can decision-makers manage these rising costs without compromising public safety? International research indicates that prevention can be both effective and cost-efficient, and specifically, investing in families, children, and youth significantly reduces crime, provides value for money, and is both economically and socially beneficial in the long term (e.g., Farrington and Welsh 2014; Lee et al. 2012). For example, in a meta-analysis of family-based crime-prevention programs, Farrington and Welsh (2003) found a mean program effect size of 0.3, which translated to an approximately 15 percent reduction in delinquency among participants.

Within this particular context of prevention strategies, developmental prevention, which is primarily predicated on the notion that engagement in criminal behaviors is determined by behavioral and attitudinal patterns learned during development, involves targeting empirically-identified risk factors of delinquency, such as antisocial attitudes and impulsiveness, and/or intervening early in the life course (e.g., Loeber 1990; Murray and Farrington 2010; Day and Wanklyn 2012). As Homel (2005) rightly points out, developmental prevention may indeed encompass a more expansive range of life-course phases and transitions, however, we take the approach of a risk-focused, early intervention framework for this chapter, emphasizing prevention programs that occur during the childhood and adolescent years.

Targeting and intervening early with respect to risk and protective factors for offending makes theoretical sense, given that signs of chronic antisocial behavior tend to emerge early in life and persist, to the point of eventually culminating in serious offending in the adolescent and adult years (e.g., Farrington 1991; Piquero, Farrington, and Bluemstein 2003; Welsh and Farrington 2012). Additionally, the risk factors for criminality affect multiple other domains. For example, substance abuse has been shown to enhance the risk of crime across the life span (Day and Wanklyn 2012) and also has serious health consequences that place additional economic strain on health care systems (Office of National Drug Control Policy 2004; Rehm et al. 2007). Therefore, by modifying offending-related behavioral and attitudinal precursors that emerge during development, criminal behaviors and other adverse outcomes (and their costs) in adolescence and adulthood can be reduced or averted (e.g., Deković et al. 2011).

Developmental prevention also makes sense economically (Lynch 2004). Indeed, research using longitudinal cohorts has quantified the substantial monetary gains that could potentially be realized through early intervention with career criminals. According to Cohen and Piquero (2009), the costs that a high-risk offender imposes on society peaks between the ages of 18 and 24 years, indicating that huge future costs can be avoided with the early detection of high-risk youth. For example, if a high-risk offender can be identified at age 8, when they have only imposed $2,482 in costs, and effective intervention programs are implemented, the value of future costs saved is $4.3 million in current dollars. By age 18, a total of $1.5 million in costs will already have been imposed at this point, yet the value of future costs not yet imposed is still high at $3.7 million in current dollars. Therefore, even if an effective intervention is not implemented until age 18, considerable savings can still be realized. Additional follow-up analyses on the same cohort (the Second Philadelphia Birth Cohort Study) showed that some high-risk offenders incur lifetime costs that greatly exceed the average—the most costly individual in the sample incurred $35,406,000 by age 26 (Cohen, Piquero, and Jennings 2010a). This result highlights the fact that even if early interventions are only successful with a handful of high-risk individuals, preventing or averting these individuals from a criminal career can yield enormous savings. Other studies in Australia (Allard et al. 2014) and Canada (Day et al. 2015) lend support to this finding as well.

Moreover, as Nagin (2001) points out, beyond delinquency and offending, early investments in the cognitive and social development of children confers multiple benefits across the various life-course domains, such as health and mental health, welfare, education, and employment. Thus, not only do developmental prevention programs avert the costs associated with offending, they potentially offer a range of gains that would have positive economic implications that can be monetized. This holds true for children in a variety of countries and across time (Nores and Barnett 2010). Thus, developmental prevention is an area that holds a lot of promise for risk-focused, early intervention strategies (e.g., Karoly, Kilburn, and Cannon 2005). As Jenkins (2014, p. 147) aptly states, "The long-term individual and societal benefits of investing resources during early childhood make it an unrivaled opportunity for policy."

However, the reality is that developmental prevention programs may be incredibly complex and costly to design, implement, and monitor, so any undertaking involving a developmental intervention needs to be informed by evidence on "what works" and also "what's worthwhile" (Welsh, Farrington, and Sherman 2001). In other words, concerns about program effectiveness must be balanced with considerations about fiscal prudence and viability, as not all developmental interventions can be expected to yield worthwhile returns on investment (Dalziel, Halliday, and Segal 2015). Given that both the impacts and the economic benefits of developmental prevention programs are important, these aspects should be considered in tandem for a holistic perspective (Burssens 2016), with one of the most promising tools for providing an economic assessment of developmental prevention programs being benefit-cost (or cost-benefit) analysis.[1]

II. THE METHODOLOGICAL BASICS OF A COST-BENEFIT ANALYSIS

This section presents a brief overview of the main concepts, issues, and challenges of cost-benefit analysis in criminology, only insofar as to acquaint the reader with this area. For more detailed, technical accounts, interested readers are invited to refer to the following works: Barnett (1994); Dhiri and Brand (1999); Welsh, Farrington, and Sherman (2001); Dossetor (2011); McIntosh and Li (2012); and Jacobsen (2013). Another excellent resource is the Cost-Benefit Analysis Toolkit (Henrichson and Rinaldi 2014), developed by the Cost-Benefit Knowledge Bank for Criminal Justice, an initiative of the Vera Institute of Justice.

A cost-benefit analysis (CBA) is a financial assessment of how much society saves from the impact of a program, determined by computing the monetary benefits of a program (or, for that matter, a policy) and comparing them to its costs (Welsh and Farrington, 2000; Welsh, Farrington, and Gowar 2015). An alternative for comparing costs and benefits is the "net value" or "net benefit" method, where the monetary benefits are subtracted from the costs. However, this does not control for differences in currencies or time periods, and unlike the "net benefit" method, a CBA addresses the question of the value of prevention programs in reducing crime or "Has the money been well-spent?" (Dossetor 2011, p. iii). Comparing the quantitative fiscal value of the costs and benefits of a program results in a unit-independent benefit-cost ratio (BCR):

$$\text{Benefit-Cost Ratio} = \frac{\text{Averted Costs/Potential Benefits} \times \text{Net Effects of Program}}{\text{Total Program Costs}}$$

where Averted Costs/Potential Benefits refers to the reduction in costs (e.g., prevention of a robbery) or gain in benefits (e.g., employment) to society of the outcome in question. Net Effects of Program is the difference in the occurrence of the adverse (or beneficial) outcome under the program versus an alternative scenario (e.g., no program at all or a different program). and Total Program Costs is the tabulation of the costs of implementation (e.g., administration, capital, and indirect costs).

In theory, a BCR that exceeds 1.0 translates into a scenario where the monetized benefits from a program's impact outweigh the costs of its implementation, and thus, the program has produced a positive "return on investment," with higher BCRs generally signaling a greater rate of return. For example, a BCR of 1.52 means that the program has produced $1.52 of benefits for every dollar of initial investment. Conversely, BCRs of less than 1.0 signify that program costs eclipse any gain in benefits, and thus, the program is not economically advantageous or worthwhile.

The main steps to conducting a CBA (adapted from Chisholm 2000; Welsh and Farrington 2000) include:

1. Obtaining estimates of program effects
2. Defining the nature, parameters, and limits of the economic analysis
3. Identifying and monetizing relevant program inputs (i.e., the program costs)
4. Identifying and monetizing relevant averted costs or (societal) benefits derived from the program
5. Comparing the value of benefits for program effects with the costs of program inputs
6. Conducting sensitivity analyses

At this juncture, two main variants of CBAs should be noted: cost-savings analysis and social return on investment (SROI). The former refers to situations where the scope of the costs and benefits included in a CBA are limited to those realized by a particular stakeholder, such as a program's funding source (Australian Institute of Criminology 2003). In the latter case, SROIs predominantly focus on benefits that are not easily quantifiable, such as social, environmental and cultural impacts.

A. Links to Evaluation Methodology

As is apparent from the above procedural scheme, one of the fundamental prerequisites of a CBA is the realistic, objective, and rigorous evaluation of the impacts of different policies and interventions (e.g., Welsh, Farrington, and Sherman 2001; Dossetor 2011). Typically, effectiveness outcomes for developmental programs include criminal justice measures as well as other related gains such as changes in attitudes, values, and behaviors on the part of the program participants (Cohen 2000). As Welsh and Farrington (2000) point out, a CBA is essentially "an extension of an outcome evaluation, and is only as defensible as the outline on which it is based" (p. 310). In other words, a CBA will only be as valid and robust as the impact evaluation that forms its premise; the impact evaluation, in turn, is only as sound as the degree of fidelity to which the policy or program is implemented. Thus, the CBA will inherit any shortcomings associated with policy/ program implementation or impact evaluation methodology, which may render it unreliable and possibly fallacious. In situations where study quality standards are poor, monetary benefits cannot be ascribed, and doing so may even be counterproductive or detrimental to the decision-making process (Cohen 2000). Therefore, with regard to evaluation methodology, the following should be considered.

- **What are the impacts that should be measured?** Effectiveness outcomes in crime prevention often relate to data based on official records, for example, police arrest or court convictions. However, self-reported delinquency may be a complementary outcome measure, especially in the case of youth (e.g., Thornberry and Krohn 2000; Farrington et al. 2003; Krohn et al. 2010). Considerations could also include other outcomes that are linked to, or precede, any official or self-reported delinquency and offending behavior, such as antisocial attitudes and behaviors, oppositional defiant and conduct disorders, aggression, anger management, callous-unemotional traits, hyperactivity and impulsivity (e.g., Nagin and Tremblay 1999; Murray and Farrington 2010). In addition, developmental prevention programs have other effects, such as educational success, physical health outcomes, teenage pregnancy, social participation, cognitive/social-emotional development, and family well-being (e.g., Anderson et al. 2003; Cohen, Piquero, and Jennings 2010b; Manninga, Homel, and Smith 2010).
- **How should impacts be measured?** Randomized controlled trials are typically considered the "gold standard" of evaluations (Weisburd and Hinkle 2012). However, in real-world settings, there are numerous challenges[2] to implementing such an evaluation model, such as ethical issues (e.g., participants who could benefit from the intervention will be denied), participant recruitment and retention,

lack of random selection from the target population, lack of random assignment to treatment and control groups, sample size and characteristics, maturation effects, and length of follow-up period. Therefore, these issues, which have received excellent analysis by the Coalition for Evidence-Based Policy, beg the question of "What is the minimally acceptable standard?" At minimum, a pre–post test design with appropriate (i.e., matched) intervention and control groups would appear to be acceptable (e.g., Sherman et al. 1997; Farrington 2003), but others have argued for an experimental or strong quasi-experimental design (e.g., Weimer and Friedman 1979). An additional consideration, although by no means the last, is that emerging research suggests that prevention and intervention efforts have the greatest impact on the highest-risk individuals (e.g., Welsh and Farrington 2007), and so any measurement of impacts should take this differential into account and stratify the results of the CBA by risk level if possible.

B. Calculating Averted Costs and/or Potential Benefits

In addition to impact evaluation considerations, it is also critical to think about issues related to the data being used to assign costs/benefits to outcomes in a CBA, bearing in mind that there exists an endless array of potentially relevant cost elements and ways to measure them. Areas of consideration include the following.

- **What are the averted costs/benefits that should be measured, and from whose perspective?** Crime costs result from impacts at both the micro and macro levels, not only affecting offenders and the criminal justice system, but also victims, families, friends, and communities (Cohen 2000, 2005; Cohen and Bowles 2010). Hence, there may be differences in estimating the economic benefits of a program's impact on crime-related issues, depending on whose perspective is considered (e.g., McIntosh and Li 2012; Dominguez and Raphael 2015; Gabor 2015; Hunt, Anderson, and Saunders 2017). In addition, some costs are easier to monetize than others, and decisions on whether to include tangible or intangible costs will differentially impact the CBA (Welsh and Farrington 2000). Furthermore, as discussed previously, in addition to the savings associated with crime prevention and reduction due to the implementation of developmentally focused policies and programs, there are economic benefits in a myriad of areas, including reductions in social assistance, improvements in health, decreases in need for special education, and increases in income tax revenue due to education, productivity and employment gains (e.g., Reynolds et al. 2001; Homel et al. 2006), and these should be monetized as well.
- **How should averted costs/potential benefits be measured?** In addition to robust evaluation results, accurate crime cost estimates are required for CBAs. However, monetizing benefits is a difficult and imprecise endeavor, especially

given the relative scarcity of reliable costing data. This is particularly true for costs and benefits that are intangible, such as the pain and suffering of victims (McCollister, French, and Fang 2010). Often the choice of monetization is dictated by the parameters of the analysis (e.g., from whose perspective gains in benefits should be considered), as well as data constraints (availability, validity, reliability, etc.). Thus, the "bottom-up" approach, the "top-down" approach, or the "break-down" approach may be used. The bottom-up approach is fairly straightforward and adds up all the direct and indirect losses from crime through an accounting-based process (e.g., DeLisi et al. 2010; McCollister et al. 2010). The top-down approach (also known as willingness-to-pay or contingent valuation) surveys a sample of the general public to discover the extent to which they would be willing to pay for crime-reduction/prevention alternatives (e.g., Cohen et al. 2004). Jury compensation/court awards and quality-adjusted life-years (QALYs) are also some other top-down approaches to specifically get at the hard-to-measure intangible costs. Finally, the break-down method starts with an overall budget (e.g., police, correctional services), eliminates costs for all non-crime-related activities, and then uses administrative data to extract crime-related costs (Moolenaar 2009).

Within this context, the CBA should account for whether average, marginal (incremental) or aggregate costs should be used, if local or national cost estimates are most appropriate, the magnitude of the inflation and/or discount rates to be applied, and whether the benefits are crime specific (e.g., Cohen 2000; Cohen et al. 2004; McCollister, French, and Fang 2010). Finally, given the lack of a standardized approach to CBA and its somewhat arbitrary nature, there is a high degree of variability in BCRs. Instituting a sensitivity analysis protocol will vary the assumptions underlying a CBA to test for the robustness and validity of the results (Leung 2004). In addition, Farrell, Bowers, and Johnson (2004) recommend presenting the analysis in the form of confidence intervals rather than discrete figures.

III. Current CBAs in Developmental Prevention

In line with the theme of this book, this section presents a narrative review of existing CBA studies in developmental prevention, building on earlier seminal work by Welsh and Farrington (2000). Since then, advances have been made in cost-benefit work in the field of developmental prevention. For example, since Welsh and Farrington's early mention of the U.S. Washington State Institute for Public Policy (WSIPP), researchers there have greatly refined their approach to how they systematically assess the evidence on "what works" to improve outcomes and calculate the costs, benefits, and risks for various public policy options (e.g., Lee et al. 2012). Their three-pronged approach is based on the following strategy:

1. A comprehensive and methodical assessment of high-quality studies to identify potentially viable policy alternatives that would produce improved outcomes
2. A determination of the cost, to Washington State taxpayers, to achieve similar results in this state, and the associated benefits of each policy alternative
3. A risk assessment to determine the probability that a specific policy alternative will at least break even

In essence, by pooling effect sizes from many studies, and using a Monte Carlo approach to make hypothetical projections of the costs and benefits that would arise if various programs were implemented in Washington State, the WSIPP has calculated BCRs in a number of program areas, with the last update in December 2017. Specifically, the programs that have more of a developmental focus, whether classified as juvenile justice (e.g., Multisystemic Therapy), child welfare (e.g., Triple P Positive Parenting Program), children's mental health (e.g., Incredible Years), or general prevention (e.g., Seattle Social Development Program), have, for the most part, demonstrated a positive rate of return. The WSIPP's work on systematically assessing the costs and benefits of programs has become the benchmark for many other jurisdictions, including states like Pennsylvania (Jones et al. 2008) and Wisconsin (Small et al. 2005) and cities like Washington, D.C. (Taxy et al. 2012), which have either incorporated the WSIPP's CBA results or followed a similar approach to bolster an evidence-based approach to public policy decision-making.

It is hoped that the selection of emerging economic results discussed below will contribute to furthering the practice of CBAs in developmental prevention programs. To the extent possible, the programs that are included focus on developmental prevention, with a clear description of program components; target children and youth under the age of 18 years; use, at minimum, a pre-test/post-test design with an appropriate control group or acceptable alternative; have an outcome related to antisocial or delinquent behavior (e.g., a reduction in risk factors); clearly state the assumptions, parameters, and limitations of the cost-benefit analysis; provide a cost-benefit ratio; and clearly describe the elements included in the cost-benefit analysis, with reference to the source. However, like Welsh and Farrington (2000), this review is limited by the non-comparability of many CBAs, given the impact and economic evaluation issues discussed in the previous section (e.g., variations in the quality of research designs, lack of standardization in measuring program outcomes, costs and benefits, and scarcity of data). As there is no comprehensive consensus on validity, quality, or comparability for the economic methodology, the results should only be viewed as "indicative" and not as "conclusive."

A. Better Beginnings, Better Futures (Canada)

In 1991, the Ontario Ministry of Community and Social Services adopted the Better Beginnings, Better Futures (BBBF) model in several communities across the province of Ontario. The program intervenes with young children in low-income, high-risk neighborhoods, with the goal of reducing emotional and behavioral problems in children, while promoting healthy and prosocial development. Compared to matched control sites (no BBBF program), both short- and long-term impact evaluations found significant positive results for BBBF participants, including academic achievement, lower levels of hyperactivity/inattention, improved family functioning, and reductions in delinquency. Based on the number of contacts with a variety of publicly-funded agencies (e.g., health care, the criminal justice system, and welfare/disability), a limited CBA was conducted, where only the economic costs and benefits to Canadian government/taxpayers were considered. By the time the participants were in Grade 9, there was a return of $1.31 CAD to the government for every dollar invested in the program. By grade 12, the return had grown to $2.50 per dollar of investment (Peters et al. 2016).

B. The Carolina Abecedarian Project (United States)

The Abecedarian Project involved a sample of 112 children born in the 1970s to low-income families, who were believed to be at risk of delayed intellectual and social development. These children were randomly assigned to an intervention group or a control group; those in the former received year-round, full-day, high-quality, personalized educational programming in a child-care environment, and their activities were designed to promote social, emotional, language, and cognitive development. Follow-up evaluations of the project's impact revealed that there were substantial early, and continued, gains in IQ and scholastic achievement, as well as reduced grade retention, placements in special education classes, and high school dropout. However, there were no statistically significant differences in the incidence of youth crime among the intervention and control groups up to age 21 years. As such, when a CBA of the Abecedarian Project was conducted, benefits for crime and delinquency could not be monetized, and the focus was instead on other benefits such as earnings, use of special education services, postsecondary school costs, smoking, and welfare use. With a program cost of $63,476 and the benefits estimated at $158,278, the Abecedarian Project resulted in a net savings of $94,802 per child, or a return of $2.50 for every dollar invested (Barnett and Masse 2007).

C. Chicago Child-Parent Center Program (United States)

The Chicago Child-Parent Center (CPC) Program is a school-based intervention program that provides comprehensive education, family, and health services for urban children from low-income families. The three enrollment options include preschool participation (1 to 2 years), school-age participation (1 to 3 years), and extended program participation (4 to 6 years). Using a nonrandomized, matched-group design, Reynolds and colleagues (2001) followed a cohort of 1,539 children born in 1980 and enrolled in either a CPC Program or an alternative early childhood program (e.g., full-day kindergarten) in Chicago, Illinois. By the age of 21, children who participated in a CPC Program experienced several positive educational and social effects, including improved school outcomes (e.g., a higher rate of high school completion, less use of remedial education services) and offending (e.g., lower rates of juvenile arrests). In a CBA of the three CPC Programs, economic benefits were measured up to age 21 or projected into the future for five areas: school remedial services, criminal justice system expenditures, child welfare system expenditures, victimization, and earnings. In 1998 dollars, the preschool program provided a return to society of $7.14 per dollar invested, the school-age program yielded a return of $1.66, and the extended intervention program had a societal return of $6.11 per program dollar (Reynolds et al. 2002). A more recent CBA used data collected up to age 26 and found that in 2007 dollars, the preschool program returned $10.83 per dollar invested, the school-age program provided a return of $3.97, and the extended intervention program yielded return of $8.24 (Reynolds et al. 2011).

D. Elmira Prenatal/Early Infancy Project—Nurse–Family Partnership (United States)

The Elmira project (Nurse-Family Partnership, NFP), developed by Olds and colleagues (1997), trained registered nurses providing pre- and post-natal home visitation services (e.g., parent education, referrals to social services) to expectant mothers. Compared to a control group (no services provided), families who participated in the program reported improved health outcomes for both mother and infant, as well as a significant reduction in the number of child abuse reports. Follow-up studies at the age of 15 revealed that the children of the NFP Elmira project displayed better behavioral and developmental outcomes, such as reductions in the use of welfare, child maltreatment rates, and criminal behavior. Studies utilizing randomized controlled trials in Denver and Memphis added supporting evidence to the effectiveness of NFP, as did complementary evaluations in Orange County, California, and Louisiana. A recent cost-benefit analysis by Miller (2013) found that cost savings due to better health outcomes (e.g., reductions in youth violence and substance abuse), reductions in the use of social services (e.g., food stamps), and gains in social benefits (e.g., quality of life) yielded positive results. In general, every dollar invested in NFP yielded a return of $6.20 per family, with the program breaking even within its first year of service. Miller (2015) then conducted a CBA of NFP based on a meta-analysis of six randomized trials and, based on program enrollments between 1996 and 2013, projected $3.0 billion in savings by 2031 compared to about $1.6 billion in program costs, thus producing a benefit-cost ratio of $1.87 for every dollar invested.

E. The High/Scope Perry Preschool Program (United States)

The High/Scope Perry Preschool Program was implemented in the Ypsilanti (Michigan) school district from 1962 to 1965, targeting young African American children 3 to 4 years of age, who came from disadvantaged socioeconomic backgrounds, and who scored low on IQ tests. The goal of the program was to promote cognitive and social development in these at-risk children by using a more autonomous learning approach and promoting greater parent–teacher involvement (Hohmann and Weikart 2002). An early BCA of the High/Scope Perry Preschool Program demonstrated that at age 27, there was a return of $7.16 for every dollar in taxes invested, in terms of economic benefits such as increased earnings, and reductions in criminal activity and welfare reliance (Barnett 1996; also reviewed in Welsh and Farrington 2000). At age 40 the return had increased to $12.90 per tax dollar invested (Belfield et al. 2006). The dollar amounts are expressed in 2000 dollars with a discount rate of 3 percent. In order to be comparable to the figures reported at the age-27 follow-up, the calculation of age-40 benefits only takes into account the general public perspective and not the participants' (Schweinhart et al. 2005a). However, the total return on investment (for both the public and the participants) at age 40 is $16.14 per dollar invested (the initially reported $17.07 figure was erroneous; Schweinhart et al. 2005b).

F. Stop Now and Plan (Canada)

Stop Now and Plan (SNAP®) is a prevention program for children between the ages of 6 and 12 years, who have come into contact, or are at risk of coming into contact, with the criminal justice system, and who have shown early signs of serious antisocial, aggressive, or delinquent behavior. The program uses a cognitive-behavioral, multi-component approach to teach children emotional regulation, self-control, and problem-solving skills. Parents also learn SNAP® skills, as well as cognitive-behavioral parenting techniques for effective child management. Farrington and Koegl (2015) analyzed data for boys (n = 376) treated in the Stop Now And Plan Under 12 Outreach Project (SNAP®-ORP) between the years of 1985 and 1999 in Toronto. Using crime-specific cost estimates, the savings due to averted convictions and averted undetected offenses for low-, moderate-, and high-risk boys were compared to the cost of the program. The results indicated that based on official conviction data, between $2.05 and $3.75 CAD was saved for every dollar spent on SNAP®-ORP. However, when scaling up to undetected offenses, a savings of $17.33 to $31.77 was achieved for every dollar invested, with the greatest BCA observed for the low-risk boys.

G. Communities That Care (United States)

The Communities That Care (CTC) system is a community mobilization strategy aimed at reducing youth substance use, delinquency, violence, and other problem behaviors through a number of avenues: (1) improving collaboration and coordination among community stakeholders; (2) reducing tolerance of delinquency by strengthening community norms; and (3) fostering the adoption of various evidence-based prevention approaches, in particular developmental prevention. In 2003, a cluster-randomized trial of the CTC system was undertaken in 24 communities across seven states, with a total of 4,407 youth in grades 5 to 9. Follow-up analyses focused on a subset of youth who indicated at the baseline assessment that they had not yet initiated substance use (alcohol or tobacco) and delinquent behavior (e.g., vandalism, shoplifting, assault, etc.). By grade 12, youth in the CTC communities showed significantly higher rates of abstinence from all of these behaviors compared to non-CTC communities. The program benefits were measured up to grade 12 or projected into the future in four domains: criminal justice system, victimization, health care, and earnings. With program costs and benefits of, respectively, $556 and $4,477 per youth, the benefit-cost ratio was $8.22 per dollar invested (Kuklinski et al. 2015).

H. YouthBuild Offender Project (United States)

YouthBuild is an international, alternative education program (in the United States and worldwide) for at-risk youth aged 16 to 24 years, who divide their time between the classroom and helping to build or renovate affordable housing, schools, and community centers, allowing those who left high school without receiving a diploma to obtain educational credentials and job skills simultaneously. Participating youth also receive personal counseling and training and often go on to become program leaders. In 2003, the U.S. Department of Labor provided three years of funding for a YouthBuild Offender Project (YBOP), in which 388 recent juvenile or young adult offenders were integrated into the broader YouthBuild program. A comparison of the educational and criminal justice outcomes of the project participants with those of similar groups of offenders (from the Philadelphia Cohort) and high school dropouts (from the National Longitudinal Survey of Youth) revealed that the YBOP was associated with substantial increases in high school graduation rates (or attainment of a General Educational Development degree), as well as large decreases in 2-year rates of police recontact. With a per participant program cost of $24,000 and projected benefits (e.g., earnings, productivity, and improvements in health associated with high school graduation, plus averted costs to taxpayers of specific crimes) ranging from $174,000 to $281,000, the YBOP yielded a benefit-cost ratio ranging from $7.20 to $11.70 per dollar invested (Cohen and Piquero 2015).

I. New Beginnings Program (United States)

The New Beginnings Program (NBP) is a group-based intervention designed to help both parents and children adjust to the aftermath of divorce. The program objectives are to improve parent–child relationship quality, teach effective methods of discipline, and reduce the exposure of children to interparental conflict. In 1992–1993, 240 divorced women from the Phoenix metropolitan area who had a least one cohabitating child aged 9 to 12 years participated in a randomized trial of NBP, in which two versions of the program (mother-only and mother-plus-child) were pitted against a self-study control condition. At a 15-year follow-up assessment, parental use of mental health services (i.e., outpatient and counseling visits, medications) was significantly lower in the preceding year for NBP participants, as was the frequency of the children's (now young adults) criminal justice system encounters (police, courts, corrections). Both versions of the NBP were shown to be equally effective, but had different per-family incremental costs compared to the self-study condition: $633 and $1,381 for the mother-only and mother-plus-child versions, respectively. With benefits estimated at $1,630 per family, the respective benefit-cost ratios for the mother-only and mother-plus-child versions of the program were $2.58 and $1.18, so the mother-only approach can be considered as more economically preferable (Herman et al. 2015).

J. Multisystemic Therapy (United States)

Multisystemic Therapy (MST) is an intensive treatment program for juvenile offenders (12 to 17 years), which targets all systems that affect those youth: their homes and families, schools and teachers, neighborhoods, and friends. Each youth is assigned an on-call, 24/7 clinician who works closely with caregivers to bring about positive change in risk factors, improve quality of life, and reduce recidivism. Clinicians draw largely on a combination of evidence-based, cognitive-behavioral, and family therapies to achieve these treatment goals. One of the earliest implementations of MST was the 1983 Missouri Delinquency Project, in which 176 young offenders and 129 of their closest-in-age siblings were randomly assigned to MST or conventional individual therapy (IT). A recent 25-year follow-up study of criminal records revealed significant reductions in arrests for the MST group relative to the IT group. Outcomes and associated monetary benefits in terms of savings to taxpayers and crime victims were calculated separately for three groups: juvenile offenders (i.e., the MST-referred youth), their siblings, and referred youth–sibling pairs. The per-participant, incremental cost of the program (over and above IT) was $9,405, with no extra cost for siblings, and the benefits were $35,582 per juvenile offender and $7,798 per sibling. Therefore, in the 25-year post-treatment period, MST yielded savings of $5.04 per dollar invested (no benefit-cost ratio could be computed for siblings given that the denominator was zero) (Dopp et al. 2014). Further, specialized variations on MST for subgroups of young offenders have also been shown to be highly economically viable. For example, Borduin and Dopp (2015) found that MST-PSB (i.e., MST for problem sexual behaviors) yielded $48.81 in savings to taxpayers and crime victims over an almost 9-year follow-up period.

IV. Conclusion

This chapter shows that a wide variety of international developmental crime-prevention projects have yielded substantial economic benefits, lending credence to the notion that developmental programs provide value for money in terms not only of preventing crime, but also for other social and health outcomes. By its nature, the focus on risk factors means that there is an opportunity to intervene early in the life course, thereby disrupting entry into, and continuation of, a delinquent pathway. As has been noted previously (e.g., Cohen and Piquero 2009; Day et al. 2015), the potential for benefits to accrue are the greatest when early interventions are effectively implemented for children and youth, prior to the snowball effect of accumulating social, health, and criminal justice costs. Moreover, under certain conditions, even saving one high-risk youth from a life of crime may be worth the initial investment of preventive programs.

The relatively small number of high-quality studies demonstrates that there is considerable room for improvement in both impact and economic evaluation methodologies among developmental prevention programs. There is no doubt that progress has been made in the last decade or so, and there has been more of a movement to bring in economic analysis techniques to bolster the argument for crime prevention in general. Yet, cost-benefit studies in this area remain rare. And even in the case of studies that were judged as sufficiently rigorous to summarize in the present review, cross-study differences in various design and analysis factors, such as the children/youth populations, outcome definitions, costing methodologies and assumptions, and follow-up periods, make it difficult, if not impossible, to compare economic results across studies and develop a ranking of different interventions. However, groundbreaking work being undertaken by organizations like the WSIPP prove that the challenges are not insurmountable, and elevated interest in these types of economic techniques, as evidenced by recent research discussions at the 19th annual conference of the Society for Prevention Research (Crowley et al. 2014), also provide insight into future directions and efforts to improve cost-benefit analysis standards and uptake.

Furthermore, looking forward, the potential for developmental programs and cost-benefit methods to be integrated with other innovative practices in social justice policy like social impact investing (Temple and Reynolds 2015) or decision-tree modeling (Welsh, Rocque, and Greenwood 2014) is tantalizing, as governments will be enabled to expand proven or promising preventive interventions in an empirically and fiscally responsible manner. As such, we would encourage the continued uptake and use of this form of analysis, as well as the undertaking of work to establish a community of practice that aims to create a common methodological framework and standards for the economic evaluation of prevention programs to facilitate decision-making.

NOTES

1. Another popular economic tool is a cost-effectiveness analysis (CEA), which serves to compare the costs of a program or policy to its effects. This results in a cost-effectiveness ratio in the form of a cost per unit of program outcome. For example, in their assessment of the Iowa Strengthening Families Program (ISFP), Spoth et al. (2002) calculated a cost-effectiveness

ratio of $12,459 per case of youth alcohol use prevented. However, given that CEAs do not consider or monetize the range of possible benefits derived from a program/policy, it cannot possibly provide an indication of whether the effect of the program or policy was worth the cost of implementing it (Levin and McEwan 2001; Dossetor 2011). Therefore, the discussion in this chapter shall be limited to cost-benefit analysis.

2. It is beyond the scope of this chapter to delve into the details of evaluation challenges. Interested readers may wish to examine some of the following works: Shadish, Cook, and Campbell (2002), Farrington (2003), and Weisburd (2010).

References

Allard, Troy, Anna Stewart, Christine Smith, Susan Dennison, April Chrzanowski, and Carleen Thompson. 2014. "The Monetary Cost of Offender Trajectories: Findings from Queensland (Australia)." *Australian and New Zealand Journal of Criminology* 47(1): 81–101.

Anderson, David A. 2011. "The Costs of Crime." *Foundations and Trends in Microeconomics* 7(3): 209–265.

Anderson, Laurie M., Carolynne Shinn, Mindy T. Fullilove, Susan C. Scrimshaw, Jonathan E. Fielding, Jacques Normand, and Vilma G. Carande-Kulis. 2003. "The Effectiveness of Early Childhood Development Programs: A Systematic Review." *American Journal of Preventive Medicine* 24(3): 32–46.

Australian Institute of Criminology. 2003. *Measuring Crime Prevention Costs and Benefits* (AIC Crime Reduction Matters, No. 15). Canberra: Australian Institute of Criminology.

Barnett, W. Steven. 1994. "Cost effectiveness and cost-benefit analysis." In *Cost Analysis for Education Decisions: Methods and Examples*, edited by W. Steven Barnettt, 257–276. Greenwich, CT: JAI Press.

Barnett, W. Steven. 1996. *Lives in the Balance: Age-27 Benefit-Cost Analysis of the High/Scope Perry Preschool Program*. Ypsilanti, MI: High/Scope Press.

Barnett, W. Steven, and Leonard N. Masse. 2007. "Comparative Benefit–Cost Analysis of the Abecedarian Program and its Policy Implications." *Economics of Education Review* 26(1): 113–125.

Belfield, Clive R., Milagros Nores, Steve Barnett, and Lawrence Schweinhart. 2006. "The High/Scope Perry Preschool Program: Cost–Benefit Analysis Using Data from the Age-40 Follow-Up." *Journal of Human Resources* XLI(1): 162–190.

Borduin, Charles M., and Dopp, Alex R. 2015. "Economic Impact of Multisystemic Therapy with Juvenile Sexual Offenders." *Journal of Family Psychology* 29(5): 687–696.

Burssens, Dieter. 2016. "Evaluation of Crime Prevention: Escaping the Tunnel Vision on Effectiveness." *The Howard Journal* 55(1–2): 238–254.

Chisholm, John. 2000. "Benefit-Cost Analysis and Crime Prevention." *Trends & Issues in Crime and Criminal Justice, no. 147*. Canberra: Australian Institute of Criminology.

Cohen, Mark A. 2000. "Measuring the Costs and Benefits of Crime and Justice." In *Criminal Justice 2000*, Vol. 4: *Measurement and Analysis of Crime and Justice*, edited by Julie E. Samuels, Eric Jefferis, Janice Munsterman, Robert Kaminski, and Nancy La Vigne, 263–316. Washington, DC: National Institute of Justice, U.S. Department of Justice.

Cohen, Mark A. 2005. *The Costs of Crime and Justice*. New York: Routledge.

Cohen, Mark A., and Roger Bowles. 2010. "Estimating Costs of Crime." In *Handbook of Quantitative Criminology* (Part II), edited by Alex R. Piquero and David Weisburd, 143–162. New York: Springer-Verlag.

Cohen, Mark A., and Alex R. Piquero. 2009. "New Evidence on the Monetary Value of Saving a High Risk Youth." *Journal of Quantitative Criminology* 25: 25–49.

Cohen, Mark A., and Alex R. Piquero. 2015. "Benefits and Costs of a Targeted Intervention Program for Youthful Offenders: The YouthBuild USA Offender Project." *Journal of Benefit Cost Analysis* 6(3): 603–627.

Cohen, Mark A., Alex R. Piquero, and Wesley G. Jennings. 2010a. "Monetary Costs of Gender and Ethnicity: Disaggregated Group-Based Offending." *American Journal of Criminal Justice* 35: 159–172.

Cohen, Mark A., Alex R. Piquero, and Wesley G. Jennings. 2010b. "Estimating the Costs of Bad Outcomes for At-Risk Youth and the Benefits of Early Childhood Interventions to Reduce Them." *Criminal Justice Policy Review* 21(4): 391–434.

Cohen, Mark A., Roland T. Rust, Sara Steen, and Simon T. Tidd. 2004. "Willingness-to-Pay for Crime Control Programs." *Criminology* 42: 89–109.

Crowley, D. Max., Laura G. Hill, Margaret R. Kuklinski, and Damon E. Jones. 2014. "Research Priorities for Economic Analyses of Prevention: Current Issues and Future Directions." *Prevention Science* 15: 789–798.

Dalziel, Kim M., Dale Halliday, and Leonie Segal. 2015. "Assessment of the Cost-Benefit Literature on Early Childhood Education for Vulnerable Children: What the Findings Mean for Policy." *SAGE open* January–March: 1–14.

Day, David M., Christopher J. Koegl, Lianne Rossman, and Sandra Oziel. 2015. *The Monetary Cost of Criminal Trajectories for an Ontario Sample of Offenders. Research Report 2015-R011.* Ottawa, ON: Public Safety Canada.

Day, David M., and Sonya G. Wanklyn. 2012. *Identification and Operationalization of the Major Risk Factors for Antisocial and Delinquent Behaviour Among Children and Youth.* Ottawa, ON: National Crime Prevention Centre, Public Safety Canada.

Dekovića, Maja, Meike I. Slagta, Jessica J. Asscherb, Leonieke Boendermakerc, Veroni I. Eichelsheima, and Peter Prinziea. 2011. "Effects of Early Prevention Programs on Adult Criminal Offending: A Meta-Analysis." *Clinical Psychology Review* 31(4): 532–544.

DeLisi, Matt, Anna Kosloski, Molly Sween, Emily Hachmeister, Matt Moore, and Alan Drury. 2010. "Murder by Numbers: Monetary Costs Imposed by a Sample of Homicide Offenders." *The Journal of Forensic Psychiatry and Psychology* 21(4): 501–513.

Dhiri, Sanjay, and Sam Brand. 1999. *Analysis of Costs and Benefits: Guidance for Evaluators. Crime Reduction Programme Guidance Note 1.* London: Home Office.

Dominguez, Patricio, and Steven Raphael. 2015. "The Role of the Cost-of-Crime Literature in Bridging the Gap Between Social Science Research and Policy Making: Potentials and Limitations." *Criminology and Public Policy* 14(4): 589–632.

Dopp, Alex R., Charles M. Borduin, David V. Wagner, and Aaron M. Sawyer. 2014. "The Economic Impact of Multisystemic Therapy Through Midlife: A Cost-Benefit Analysis with Serious Juvenile Offenders and Their Siblings." *Journal of Consulting and Clinical Psychology* 82(4): 694–705.

Dossetor, Kym. 2011. *Cost-Benefit Analysis and Its Application to Crime Prevention and Criminal Justice Research.* AIC Reports: Technical and Background Paper, 42. Canberra: Australian Institute of Criminology.

Dubourg, Richard, and Joe Hamed. 2005. *Estimates of the Economic and Social Costs of Crime in England and Wales: Costs of Crime Against Individuals and Households, 2003/04.* London: Home Office.

Farrell, Graham, Kate Bowers, and Shane D. Johnson. 2004. "Cost-Benefit Analysis for Crime Science: Making Cost-Benefit Analysis Useful Through a Portfolio of Outcomes." In *Crime*

Science: New Approaches to Preventing and Detecting Crime, edited by Melissa J. Smith and Nick Tilley, 56–84. London: Willan Press.

Farrington, David P. 1991. "Childhood Aggression and Adult Violence: Early Precursors and Later Life Outcomes." In *The Development And Treatment Of Childhood Aggression*, edited by Debra J. Pepler and Kenneth H. Rubin, 5–29. Hillsdale, NJ: Lawrence Erlbaum.

Farrington, David P. 2003. "Methodological Quality Standards for Evaluation Research." *The Annals of the American Academy of Political and Social Science* 587(1): 49–68.

Farrington, David P., Darrick Jolliffe, J. David Hawkins, Richard F. Catalano, Karl G. Hill, and Rick Kosterman. 2003. "Comparing Delinquency Careers in Court Records and Self-Reports." *Criminology* 41(3): 933–958.

Farrington, David P., and Christopher J. Koegl. 2015. "Monetary Benefits and Costs of the Stop Now And Plan Program for Boys Aged 6–11, Based on the Prevention of Later Offending." *Journal of Quantitative Criminology* 31: 263–287.

Farrington, David P., and Brandon C. Welsh. 2003. "Family-Based Prevention of Offending: A Meta-Analysis." *Australian and New Zealand Journal of Criminology* 36:127–151.

Farrington, David P., and Brandon C. Welsh. 2014. "Saving Children from a Life of Crime: the Benefits Greatly Outweigh the Costs!" *International Annals of Criminology* 52(1–2): 67–92.

Gabor, Thomas. 2015. *Costs of Crime and Criminal Justice Responses. Research Report 2015-R022.* Ottawa, ON: Public Safety Canada.

Henrichson, Christian, and Joshua Rinaldi. 2014. *Cost-Benefit Analysis and Justice Policy Toolkit.* New York: Vera Institute of Justice. http://archive.vera.org/sites/default/files/resources/downloads/cba-justice-policy-toolkit.pdf.

Herman, Patricia M., Nicole E. Mahrer, Sharlene A. Wolchik, Michele M. Porter, Sarah Jones, and Irwin N. Sandler. 2015). "Cost-Benefit Analysis of a Preventive Intervention for Divorced Families: Reduction in Mental Health and Justice System Service Use Costs 15 Years Later." *Prevention Science* 16: 586–596.

Hohmann, Mary, and David P. Weikart. 2002. *Educating Young Children: Active Learning Practices for Preschool and Child Care Programs and A Study Guide to Educating Young Children: Exercises for Adult Learners.* 2nd ed. Ypsilanti, MI: High/Scope Press.

Homel, Ross. 2005. "Developmental Crime Prevention." In *Handbook of Crime Prevention and Community Safety*, edited by Nick Tilley. Portland, OR: Willan.

Homel, Ross, Kate J. Freiberg, Cherie Z. Lamb, Marie Leech, Angela E. Carr, Anne Hampshire, Ian Hay, Gordon C. Elias, Matthew Manning, Rosie J. P. Teague, and Sam J. Batchelor. 2006. *The Pathways to Prevention Project: The First Five Years, 1999-2004.* Sydney, Australia: Mission Australia and the Key Centre for Ethics, Law, Justice and Governance, Griffith University.

Hunt, Priscillia, James Anderson, and Jessica Saunders. 2017. "The Price of Justice: New National and State-Level Estimates of the Judicial and Legal Costs of Crime to Taxpayers." *American Journal of Criminal Justice* 42(2): 231–254.

Jacobsen, Rasmus H. 2013. *Hands-On Guide to Cost-Benefit Analysis of Crime Prevention Efforts.* Copenhagen: Centre for Economic and Business Research, Copenhagen Business School.

Jenkins, Jade M. 2014. "Early Childhood Development as Economic Development: Considerations for State-Level Policy Innovation and Experimentation." *Economic Development Quarterly* 28(2): 147–165.

Jones, Damon, Brian K. Bumbarger, Mark T. Greenberg, Peter Greenwood, and Sandee Kyler. 2008. *The Economic Return on PCCD's Investment in Research-Based Programs: A Cost-Benefit Assessment of Delinquency Prevention in Pennsylvania.* University Park: The

Prevention Research Center for the Promotion of Human Development, The Pennsylvania State University.

Karoly, Lynn A., M. Rebecca Kilburn, and Jill S. Cannon. 2005. *Early Childhood Interventions: Proven Results, Future Promise*, Vol. 341. Santa Monica, CA: Rand Corporation.

Koegl, Christopher J. 2011. *High-Risk Antisocial Children: Predicting Future Criminal and Health Outcomes.* Ph.D. dissertation, University of Cambridge.

Krohn, Marvin D., Terence P. Thornberry, Chris L. Gibson, and Julie M. Baldwin. 2010. "The Development and Impact of Self-Report Measures of Crime and Delinquency." *Journal of Quantitative Criminology* 26: 509–525.

Kuklinski, Margaret R., Abigail A. Fagan, J. David Hawkins, John S. Briney, and Richard F. Catalano. 2015. "Benefit–Cost Analysis of a Randomized Evaluation of Communities That Care: Monetizing Intervention Effects on the Initiation of Delinquency and Substance Use Through Grade 12." *Journal of Experimental Criminology* 11: 165–192.

Lee, Stephanie, Steve Aos, Elizabeth Drake, Annie Pennucci, Marna Miller, and Laurie Anderson. 2012. *Return on Investment: Evidence-Based Options to Improve Statewide Outcomes, April 2012 Update.* Olympia: Washington State Institute of Public Policy.

Leung, A. (2004). *The Cost of Pain and Suffering from Crime in Canada.* Ottawa, ON: Research and Statistics Division, Department of Justice Canada.

Levin, Henry M., and Patrick J. McEwan. 2001. *Cost-Effectiveness Analysis: Methods and Applications.* 2nd ed. Thousand Oaks, CA: Sage.

Loeber, Rolf. 1990. "Development and Risk Factors of Juvenile Antisocial Behavior and Delinquency." *Clinical Psychology Review* 10(1): 1–41.

Lynch, Robert G. 2004. *Economic, Fiscal, and Social Benefits of Investment in Early Childhood Development.* Washington, DC: Economic Policy Institute.

Manninga, Matthew, Ross Homel, and Christine Smith. 2010. "A Meta-Analysis of the Effects of Early Developmental Prevention Programs in At-Risk Populations on Non-Health Outcomes in Adolescence." *Children and Youth Services Review* 32(4): 506–519.

McCollister, Kathryn E., Michael T. French, and Hai Fang. 2010. "The Cost of Crime to Society: New Crime-Specific Estimates for Policy and Program Evaluation." *Drug and Alcohol Dependence* 108: 98–109.

McIntosh, Cameron, and Jobina Li. 2012. *An Introduction to Economic Analysis in Crime Prevention: The Why, How and So What? Research Report 2012–5.* Ottawa, ON: National Crime Prevention Centre, Public Safety Canada.

Miller, Ted R. 2013. *Nurse-Family Partnership Home Visitation: Costs, Outcomes, and Return on Investment.* Beltsville, MD: H.B.S.A., Inc.

Miller, Ted R. 2015. "Projected Outcomes of Nurse-Family Partnership Home Visitation During 1996–2013." *Prevention Science* 16: 765–777.

Moolenaar, Debora E. G. 2009. "Modelling Criminal Justice System Costs by Offence: Lessons from The Netherlands." *European Journal on Criminal Policy and Research* 15: 309–326.

Murray, Joseph, and David P. Farrington. 2010. "Risk Factors for Conduct Disorder and Delinquency: Key Findings from Longitudinal Studies." *Canadian Journal of Psychiatry* 55(10): 633–642.

Nagin, Daniel S. 2001. "Measuring the Economic Benefits of Developmental Prevention Programs." *Crime and Justice* 28: 347–384.

Nagin, Daniel, and Richard E. Tremblay. 1999. "Trajectories of Boys' Physical Aggression, Opposition, and Hyperactivity on the Path to Physically Violent and Nonviolent Juvenile Delinquency." *Child Development* 70(5): 1181–1196.

Nores, Milagros, and W. Steven Barnett. 2010. "Benefits of Early Childhood Interventions Across the World: (Under) Investing in the Very Young." *Economics of Education Review* 29: 271–282.

Olds, David L., John Eckenrode, Charles R. Henderson, Harriet Kitzman, Jane Powers, Robert Cole, Kimberly Sidora, Pamela Morris, Lisa M. Pettitt, and Dennis Luckey. 1997. "Long-Term Effects of Home Visitation on Maternal Life Course and Child Abuse and Neglect." *Journal of the American Medical Association* 278(8): 637–643.

Peters, Ray D., Kelly Petrunka, Shahriar Khan, Angela Howell-Moneta, Geoffrey Nelson, S. Mark Pancer, and Colleen Loomis. 2016. "Cost-Savings Analysis of the Better Beginnings, Better Futures Community-Based Project for Young Children and Their Families: A 10-Year Follow-Up." *Prevention Science* 17: 237–247.

Piquero, Alex R., David P., Farrington, and Alfred Blumstein. 2003. "The Criminal Career Paradigm." In *Crime and Justice: A Review of Research* 30: 359–506.

Reynolds, Arthur J., Judy A. Temple, Dylan L. Robertson, and Emily A. Mann. 2001. "Long-Term Effects of an Early Childhood Intervention on Educational Achievement and Juvenile Arrest: A 15-Year Follow-Up of Low-Income Children in Public Schools." *Journal of the American Medical Association* 284(18): 2339–2346.

Rehm, Jürgen, William Gnam, Svetlana Popova, Dolly Baliunas, Serge Brochu, Benedikt Fischer, Jayadeep Patra, Sarnocinska-Hart, and Benjamin Taylor. 2007. "The Costs of Alcohol, Illegal Drugs, and Tobacco in Canada, 2002." *Journal of Studies on Alcohol and Drugs* 68(6): 886–895.

Reynolds, Arthur J., Judy A. Temple, Dylan L. Robertson, and Emily A. Mann. 2002. "Age 21 Cost-Benefit Analysis of the Title I Chicago Child-Parent Centers." *Educational Evaluation and Policy Analysis* 24(4): 267–303.

Reynolds, Arthur J., Judy A. Temple, Barry A. White, Suh-Ruu Ou, and Dylan L. Robertson. 2011. "Age-26 Cost-Benefit Analysis of the Child-Parent Center Early Education Program." *Child Development* 82(1): 379–404.

Rollings, Kiah. 2008. *Counting the Costs of Crime in Australia: A 2005 Update.* Canberra: Australian Institute of Criminology.

Schweinhart, Lawrence J., Jeanne Montie, Zongping Xiang, William S. Barnett, Clive R. Belfield, and Milagros Nores. 2005a. *Lifetime effects: The High/Scope Perry Preschool study through age 40.* (Monographs of the High/Scope Educational Research Foundation, No. 14). Ypsilanti, MI: High/Scope Press.

Schweinhart, Lawrence J., Jeanne Montie, Zongping Xiang, William S. Barnett, Clive R. Belfield, and Milagros Nores. 2005b. *The High/Scope Perry Preschool Study Through Age 40: Summary, Conclusions, and Frequently Asked Questions.* Ypsilanti, MI: High/Scope Press.

Shadish, William R., Thomas D. Cook, and Donald T. Campbell. 2002. *Experimental and Quasi-Experimental Designs for Generalized Causal Inference.* Boston: Houghton-Mifflin.

Sherman, L.W., Denise Gottfredson, Doris MacKenzie, John Eck, Peter Reuter, and Shawn Bushway. 1997. *Preventing Crime: What Works, What Doesn't, What's Promising. A Report to the United States Congress.* College Park: University of Maryland, Department of Criminology and Criminal Justice.

Small, Stephen A., Arthur J. Reynolds, Cailin O'Connor, and Siobhan M. Cooney. 2005. *What Works, Wisconsin. What Science Tells Us About Cost-Effective Programs for Juvenile Delinquency Prevention.* A report to the Wisconsin Governor's Juvenile Justice Commission and the Wisconsin Office of Justice Assistance. Washington, DC: Office of Juvenile Justice and Delinquency Prevention, Office of Justice Programs.

Spoth, Richard L., Max Guyll, and Susan X. Day. 2002. "Universal Family-Focused Interventions in Alcohol-Use Disorder Prevention: Cost-Effectiveness and Cost-Benefit Analyses of Two Interventions." *Journal of Studies on Alcohol and Drugs* 63(2): 219–228.

Story, Rod, and Tolga R. Yalkin. 2013. *Expenditure Analysis of Criminal Justice in Canada.* Ottawa, ON: Office of the Parliamentary Budget Officer.

Taxy, Samuel, Akiva M. Liberman, John K. Roman, and P. Mitchell Downey. 2012. *The Costs and Benefits of Functional Family Therapy for Washington, DC.* Washington, DC: The Urban Institute.

Temple, Judy A., and Arthur J. Reynolds. 2015. "Using Benefit-Cost Analysis to Scale Up Early Childhood Programs Through Pay-for-Success Financing." *Journal of Benefit Cost Analysis* 6(3):628–653.

Thornberry, Terence P., and Krohn, M. D. 2000. "The Self-Report Method for Measuring Delinquency and Crime." In *Criminal Justice 2000,* Vol. 4: *Measurement and Analysis of Crime and Justice,* edited by Julie E. Samuels, Eric Jefferis, Janice Munsterman, Robert Kaminski, and Nancy La Vigne, 33–84. Washington, DC: National Institute of Justice, U.S. Department of Justice.

Vera Institute of Justice. n.d. Cost-Benefit Knowledge Bank for Criminal Justice—Cost-Benefit Analysis Toolkit. http://cbkb.org/toolkit/.

Weimer, David L., and Lee S. Friedman. 1979. "Efficiency Considerations in Criminal Rehabilitation Research: Costs and Consequences." In *The Rehabilitation of Criminal Offenders: Problems and* Prospects, edited by Lee Sechrest, Susan O. White, and Elizabeth D. Brown, 251–272. Washington, DC: National Academy of Sciences.

Weisburd, David. 2010. "Justifying the Use of Non-Experimental Methods and Disqualifying the Use of Randomized Controlled Trials: Challenging Folklore in Evaluation Research in Crime and Justice." *Journal of Experimental Criminology* 6: 209–227.

Weisburd, David, and Joshua C. Hinkle. 2012. "The Importance of Randomized Experiments in Evaluating Crime Prevention." In *The Oxford Handbook of Crime Prevention,* edited by Brandon C. Welsh and David P. Farrington, 446–465. New York: Oxford University Press.

Welsh, Brandon C., and David P. Farrington. 2000. "Monetary Costs and Benefits of Crime Prevention Programs." *Crime and Justice* 27: 305–361.

Welsh, Brandon C., David P. Farrington, and B. Raffan Gowar. 2015. "Benefit-Cost Analysis of Crime Prevention Programs." *Crime and Justice* 44(1): 447–516.

Welsh, Brandon C., and David P. Farrington. 2007. "Scientific Support for Early Prevention and Delinquency and Later Offending." *Victims and Offenders* 2: 125–140.

Welsh, Brandon C., and David P. Farrington. 2012. *The Oxford Handbook of Crime Prevention.* New York: Oxford University Press.

Welsh, Brandon C., David P. Farrington, and Lawrence W. Sherman. 2001. *Costs and Benefits of Preventing Crime.* Boulder, CO: Westview.

Welsh, Brandon C., Michael Rocque, and Peter W. Greenwood. 2014. "Translating Research into Evidence-Based Practice in Juvenile Justice: Brand-Name Programs, Meta-Analysis, and Key Issues." *Journal of Experimental Criminology* 10: 207–225.

Zhang, Ting. 2011. *Costs of Crime in Canada, 2008.* Ottawa, ON: Department of Justice Canada.

SECTION VII

CONCLUSIONS

....

CHAPTER 35

CONCLUSIONS AND IMPLICATIONS FOR DEVELOPMENTAL AND LIFE-COURSE CRIMINOLOGY

....

DAVID P. FARRINGTON, LILA KAZEMIAN, AND ALEX R. PIQUERO

In this concluding chapter, Section I summarizes some things that we know about developmental and life-course criminology, Section II reviews some things that we need to know, and Section III makes some recommendations about how future research can obtain answers to these questions.

I. WHAT DO WE KNOW?

....

This book shows that knowledge about developmental and life-course criminology has increased enormously in recent years. Section II of the book summarized the current state of knowledge about criminal careers: age and crime (Chapter 2, by Chester Britt), age of onset (Chapter 3, by Elaine Doherty and Sarah Bacon), specialization and versatility (Chapter 4, by Paul Mazerolle and Samara McPhedran), acceleration, deceleration, escalation, and de-escalation (Chapter 5, by Wesley Jennings and Bryanna Fox), persistence and desistance (Chapter 6, by Siyu Liu and Shawn Bushway), offending trajectories (Chapter 7, by Julien Morizot), and co-offending (Chapter 8, by Sarah van Mastrigt and Peter Carrington).

Many of the findings are well established. For example, it is clear that individual age–crime curves are often different from the aggregate age–crime curve and that the latter curve conceals specific categories of offending trajectories, such as life-course–persistent offenders, adolescence-limited offenders, and late-onset offenders. The typical age–crime curve is driven by prevalence rather than by the frequency of offending. It is also well known that an early age of onset predicts many subsequent offenses and a long criminal career duration. Most frequent offenders are versatile, tending to commit many different types of crimes and indeed many different types of antisocial behavior, but there is a small amount of specialization superimposed on a large amount of versatility. Specialization increases with age, and most violent offenders tend to be those who commit frequent offenses. Acceleration and deceleration in the frequency of offending, and escalation and de-escalation in the seriousness of offending, occur during different periods of the life course. The likelihood that desistance has occurred increases with the time since the last offense; after about 7 to 10 crime-free years, former offenders do not differ significantly from non-offenders in their probability of reoffending.

There has been surprisingly little research on the very important topic of co-offending, but some findings are quite well established. First, the well-known age–crime curve is a curve of offender-offense combinations. If two offenders are convicted for committing the same offense, this adds two cases to the curve. If the age–crime curve is corrected for co-offending and estimated for offenses alone, it has a later peak than the typical age–crime curve, because of the greater prevalence of co-offending in the teenage years. Second, the prevalence of co-offending decreases steadily with age and is more common in certain types of offenses, such as burglary and robbery, that also vary in their prevalence with age. Third, co-offending groups tend to be transitory, and the average size of co-offending groups decreases with age. Fourth, at older ages, mixed-sex groups become more common and the average age difference between co-offenders increases. Fifth, it is very important to study recruiters—offenders who continually offend with other people who are younger and/or are committing their first offense. These recruiters seem to persist in dragging new offenders into the net of offending.

Section III of this book provided an overview of the current state of knowledge about important developmental and life-course criminology theories: the developmental taxonomy (Chapter 9, by Tara McGee and Terrie Moffitt), developmental pathways (Chapter 10, by Rolf Loeber), the integrated cognitive antisocial potential theory (Chapter 11, by David Farrington and Tara McGee), the personal control theory (Chapter 12, by Marc Le Blanc), the social development model (Chapter 13, by Christopher Cambron, Richard Catalano, and David Hawkins), interactional theory (Chapter 14, by Terence Thornberry and Marvin Krohn), the situational action theory (Chapter 15, by Per-Olof Wikström and Kyle Treiber), and the age-graded theory of informal social control (Chapter 16, by John Laub, Zachary Rowan, and Robert Sampson). Each of these theorists summarizes the results of empirical tests of their theories, usually based on their own longitudinal studies. Most theories try to explain the development of offenders, but some (e.g., the integrated cognitive antisocial potential theory and the situational action theory) also try to explain the occurrence of offenses. A particularly interesting feature of interactional theory is that it has been applied to explain the intergenerational transmission of offending.

Section IV of this book summarized the current state of knowledge about risk factors and developmental correlates of offending: biosocial influences (Chapter 17, by Olivia Choy, Jill Portnoy, Adrian Raine, and colleagues), individual factors (Chapter 18, by Darrick Jolliffe and David Farrington), family influences (Chapter 19, by Abigail Fagan and Kristen Benedini), peer influences (Chapter 20, by Christopher Sullivan, Kristina Childs, and Shawn Gann), school factors (Chapter 21, by Debra Pepler), and substance use (Chapter 22, by Helene White). Many factors are well established as predictors and correlates of offending, including biological factors such as a low resting heart rate, individual factors such as high impulsiveness, family factors such as poor parental supervision, peer influences such as delinquent peers, and school factors such as relationships within the school. Importantly, research on changes within individuals shows that people commit more crimes during time periods when they are using alcohol or drugs than during other time periods. However, some important factors, such as empathy and psychopathy, tend to have been neglected in developmental and longitudinal research (see Fox, Jennings, and Farrington 2015).

Section V of this book focused on life transitions and turning points in offending careers: effects of marriage, cohabitation, parenthood, separation, and divorce (Chapter 23, by Delphine Theobald, David Farrington, and Alex Piquero), effects of employment and unemployment (Chapter 24, by Jukka Savolainen, Mikko Aaltonen, and Torbjorn Skardhamar), effects of neighborhood and residential mobility (Chapter 25, by David Kirk), effects of religion and the military (Chapter 26, by Leana Bouffard and Hae Rim Jin), effects of juvenile justice system processing (Chapter 27, by Anthony Petrosino, Carolyn Petrosino, Sarah Guckenburg, and colleagues), effects of incarceration (Chapter 28, by Lila Kazemian and Allyson Walker), and the role of cognitive transformations in desistance (Chapter 29, by Sarah Anderson and Fergus McNeill). This section also contains a special chapter on developmental and life-course criminology findings on women and girls (Chapter 30, by Lisa Broidy and Carleen Thompson).

Many results are well established. For example, offending generally decreases after marriage and generally increases after separation or divorce. Offending (especially property offending) is generally greater during periods of unemployment than during periods of employment, although a lot depends on the quality of the job. It is generally beneficial for ex-offenders to move away from their previous residential locations, but this poses a significant challenge for individuals who are returning from prison because of their limited resources. Becoming religious seems to have a protective effect against offending, but the effects of military service are more variable. Juvenile justice processing and incarceration generally have undesirable effects on offending. Cognitive transformations are important in the desistance process, including changes in identity, attitudes, beliefs, cognitive skills, motivation, and emotions. Many of the biopsychosocial risk factors correlated with male offending patterns are also correlated with female offending patterns, although there is some evidence that the salience of some factors (i.e., the strength of relationships), such as child maltreatment, may be greater for females.

Section VI of this book summarized knowledge about developmental interventions: family-based programs (Chapter 31, by Brandon Welsh and Steven Zane), preschool and school programs (Chapter 32, by Izabela Zych and David Farrington), cognitive-behavioral treatment (Chapter 33, by Georgia Zara), and cost-benefit analysis (Chapter 34, by Jobina Li and Cameron McIntosh). The good news is that systematic reviews and meta-analyses show that many programs are effective in reducing offending. Furthermore, in many cases the financial benefits of these programs greatly exceed their financial costs. Many specific programs are reviewed in detail in these chapters.

II. What Do We Need to Know?

A great deal is known about risk factors for offending in general (especially for the prevalence of offending), but less is known about risk factors for specific criminal career features, such as the age of onset, the frequency of offending per year, the age of desistance, the duration of criminal careers, specialization, versatility, acceleration, deceleration, escalation, de-escalation, and co-offending. Interestingly, the chapters in this book focus on explaining offending and rarely address the question of how accurately it is possible to predict criminal career features. Prediction questions have important practical implications for risk assessment.

It is particularly surprising that so little is known about the duration of criminal careers, in light of the many studies of life-course–persistent offenders. This is partly because many longitudinal surveys have not yet followed up their participants throughout their complete lives. As Liu and Bushway point out in Chapter 6, it is important in studying desistance to follow people up at least to age 70 and to take account of death and incapacitation. Jolliffe, Farrington, and Piquero (2016) defined life-course–persistent offenders in the Cambridge Study in Delinquent Development according to career duration (a first offense up to age 20 and a last offense at age 40 or later) and compared them with categories of offenders derived from trajectory analysis. Of the 37 life-course–persistent offenders, 18 were categorized in trajectory analysis as high-rate chronic (out of 20), 13 were categorized as low-rate chronic (out of 38), and 6 were in other categories (low adolescence peak and high adolescence peak). This analysis shows that life-course–persistent offenders identified by trajectory analysis do not overlap perfectly with life-course–persistent offenders defined according to the duration of criminal careers.

Surprisingly, the chapters in this book rarely mention protective factors. Ttofi and her colleagues (2016) identified several different types of protective factors. A direct protective factor (sometimes called a promotive factor) predicts a low probability of offending. It is not necessarily the reverse of a risk factor, since variables may be nonlinearly related to offending. A risk-based protective factor predicts a low probability of offending among a risk category. An interactive protective factor predicts a low probability of offending among a risk category but not among a non-risk category. For example, in the Cambridge Study in Delinquent Development, Farrington and Ttofi (2011) found that 57 percent of boys who were living in poor (dilapidated or slum) housing at age 8 to 10 were convicted up to age 50, compared with 32 percent of boys who were living in better housing. However, only 33 percent of boys who were living in poor housing and had good child-rearing at age 8 to 10 were convicted, compared with 66 percent of boys who were living in poor housing and did not have good child-rearing. Good child-rearing was an interactive protective factor that nullified the impact of the risk factor of poor housing. This result has important policy implications in suggesting that targeted interventions to improve child-rearing could improve the life chances of children who are living in poor housing.

A challenge to researchers is that many explanatory variables are intercorrelated, and it seems that a syndrome of intercorrelated risk factors leads to a syndrome of intercorrelated life outcomes within and between generations, including offending, violence, drug abuse, heavy drinking, drunk and reckless driving, heavy smoking, heavy gambling, promiscuous sex, physical and mental health problems, relationship problems, accommodation problems, employment problems, and so on. It is important to investigate the independent, additive, interactive, and sequential effects of explanatory variables in predicting offending. Several studies of biosocial interactions are reviewed in Chapter 17 by Olivia Choy and colleagues. It is also important to investigate reciprocal effects, which are emphasized in interactional theory (see Chapter 14, by Terence Thornberry and Marvin Krohn) and also in the chapter on family influences (Chapter 19, by Abigail Fagan and Kristen Benedini).

Another challenge to researchers relates to the problem of selection effects in drawing conclusions about the impact of explanatory variables. This is discussed in a number of chapters, sometimes in connection with the problem of disentangling state dependence and persistent heterogeneity explanations (e.g., Chapter 3 by Elaine Doherty and Sarah Bacon; Chapter 4 by Paul Mazerolle and Samara McPhedran). In Chapter 20, Christopher Sullivan and colleagues discuss whether peer influences involve selection or socialization. One way of addressing the problem of selection effects is to use propensity score matching. For example, people who get married tend to be different from people who do not get married, but married and unmarried people can be matched on their prior probability of getting married (see Chapter 23 by Delphine Theobald and colleagues). Another method is to focus on experiments in which the explanatory variable of interest is targeted. For example, in Chapter 24 Jukka Savolainen and colleagues review experiments that tried to improve employment. There should be more efforts to study explanatory variables experimentally where this is possible (Robins 1992).

In addition to the chapters on interventions in Section VI of this book, a number of other chapters point out the implications of their results for interventions. For example, in Chapter 13 Christopher Cambron and colleagues review implications of the social development model for interventions and tests of the social development model in intervention research. In Chapter 19, Abigail Fagan and Kristen Benedini review both longitudinal and experimental studies in trying to draw conclusions about family influences. It is important that developmental research should inform intervention research and vice versa (see, e.g., Farrington and Welsh 2007). However, a major problem is that there are rarely long-term follow-ups in intervention research (see, e.g., Farrington and Welsh 2013). It is clear that there should be more efforts to combine longitudinal and intervention studies.

Finally, as mentioned in Chapter 1 by Lila Kazemian, David Farrington, and Alex Piquero, there seems to be some disjunction between the research on onset, early risk factors, and criminal careers and the research on desistance. Whereas the research on criminal careers is highly quantitative, many researchers on desistance carry out more qualitative research and emphasize the role of human agency. There should be more attempts to bridge the gap between the type of desistance research reviewed in Chapter 6 by Siyu Liu and Shawn Bushway and the type of desistance research reviewed in Chapter 29 by Sarah Anderson and Fergus McNeill.

III. How Can We Find Out?

In many of the chapters of this book, the authors recommend the need to investigate the replicability of results: for males and females, at different ages, for different ethnic groups, in different times and places, for different generations, for different types of crimes, and even for other types of social problems or antisocial behavior. However, apart from Chapter 30 by Lisa Broidy and Carleen Thompson, which specifically addresses male–female differences, not many of these issues are studied in this book. Since many of the results presented are based on official records of offending, there is also a clear need to investigate criminal careers, risk factors, and the effects of life events according to research on self-reported offending (see, e g., Farrington et al. 2014). Also, there is a great need for more research on intergenerational transmission, protective factors, co-offending and recruiters, criminal career duration, and adult-onset offenders, for more biological variables in longitudinal studies, for more analyses of changes within individuals, and for more testable predictions and empirical tests of developmental and life-course theories. It would be desirable to build on simple criminal career models to derive exact quantitative predictions from theories (see, e.g., Farrington, MacLeod, and Piquero 2016). There is also a need for more systematic reviews and meta-analyses of risk factors and life events, in addition to the many systematic reviews and meta-analyses of interventions (see, e.g., Farrington, Gaffney, and Ttofi 2017).

It may be possible to answer some questions using administrative data. In Chapter 24, Jukka Savolainen and colleagues discuss results obtained from population registries, and Stewart and colleagues (2015) have reviewed the use of administrative data in developmental and life-course criminology research. However, most questions can be answered most effectively using prospective longitudinal surveys. The most useful surveys include repeated personal contacts with hundreds of people and measure self-reported and official offending and a wide range of risk factors and life events from childhood to adulthood. Surprisingly few of these kinds of surveys have ever been carried out anywhere in the world. Farrington and Welsh (2007) found that only 35 surveys of this kind had ever been published up to that time. It is desirable to follow up individuals in the community so that the offenders emerge naturally from the population and prospective probabilities can be calculated. However, for some purposes it is useful to follow up both community and offender samples, as Le Blanc and Frechette (1989) did in Montreal.

As mentioned before, it is desirable to combine longitudinal and intervention studies. However, very few of these combined studies have ever been carried out. Farrington (2013) could only find eight longitudinal-experimental studies with large samples and a follow-up period of at least 10 years involving interviews or questionnaires. It would also be useful to implement accelerated longitudinal designs, following up several cohorts simultaneously, in order to produce quicker results than in the typical single-cohort longitudinal studies. More than 30 years ago, Farrington, Ohlin, and Wilson (1986) proposed that four cohorts should be followed up in several large cities, from birth to age 6, age 6 to age 12, age 12 to age 18, and age 18 to age 24, with yearly assessments. By linking up the cohorts, it should be possible to draw conclusions about development from birth to age 24 in about six years. The nearest approach to this design has been the Causes and Correlates studies in Pittsburgh, Denver, and Rochester (see, e.g., Thornberry, Huizinga, and Loeber 1995). Farrington and his colleagues (1986) further proposed that the effects of four interventions should be tested experimentally in the middle of each follow-up period: a preschool program at age 3, a parent-training program at age 9, a peer/school program at age 15, and an employment/drug program at age 21. If some version of this design could be implemented, it might lead to great advances in our knowledge of developmental and life-course criminology.

References

Farrington, David P. 2013 "Longitudinal and Experimental Research in Criminology." In *Crime and Justice in America 1975–2025*, edited by Michael Tonry, 453–527. Chicago: University of Chicago Press.

Farrington, David P., Hannah Gaffney, and Maria M. Ttofi. 2017. "Systematic Reviews of Explanatory Risk Factors for Violence, Offending, and Delinquency." *Aggression and Violent Behavior* 33: 24–36.

Farrington, David P., John F. MacLeod, and Alex R. Piquero. 2016. "Mathematical Models of Criminal Careers: Deriving and Testing Quantitative Predictions." *Journal of Research in Crime and Delinquency* 53: 336–355.

Farrington, David P., Lloyd E. Ohlin, and James Q. Wilson. 1986. *Understanding and Controlling Crime: Toward a New Research Strategy.* New York: Springer-Verlag.

Farrington, David P., and Maria M. Ttofi. 2011. "Protective and Promotive Factors in the Development of Offending." In *Antisocial Behavior and Crime: Contributions of Developmental and Evaluation Research to Prevention and Intervention,* edited by Thomas Bliesener, Andreas Beelman, and Mark Stemmler, 71–88. Cambridge, MA: Hogrefe.

Farrington, David P., Maria M. Ttofi, Rebecca V. Crago, and Jeremy W. Coid. 2014. "Prevalence, Frequency, Onset, Desistance and Criminal Career Duration in Self-Reports Compared with Official Records." *Criminal Behaviour and Mental Health* 24: 241–253.

Farrington, David. P., and Brandon C. Welsh. 2007. *Saving Children from a Life of Crime: Early Risk Factors and Effective Interventions.* Oxford: Oxford University Press.

Farrington, David P., and Brandon C. Welsh. 2013. "Randomized Experiments in Criminology: What Has Been Learned from Long-Term Follow-ups?" In *Experimental Criminology: Prospects for Advancing Science and Public Policy,* edited by Brandon C. Welsh, Anthony A. Braga, and Gerben J. N. Bruinsma, 111–140. New York: Cambridge University Press.

Fox, Bryanna H., Wesley G. Jennings, and David P. Farrington. 2015. "Bringing Psychopathy into Developmental and Life-Course Criminology Theories and Research." *Journal of Criminal Justice* 43: 274–289.

Jolliffe, Darrick, David P. Farrington, and Alex R. Piquero. 2016. "More Research Is Needed on Life-Course-Persistent Offenders!" *The DLC Criminologist* 4(2): 15–19.

Le Blanc, Marc, and Marcel Frechette. 1989. *Male Criminal Activity from Childhood Through Youth: Multilevel and Developmental Perspectives.* New York: Springer-Verlag.

Robins, Lee N. 1992. "The Role of Prevention Experiments in Discovering Causes of Children's Antisocial Behavior." In *Preventing Antisocial Behavior: Interventions from Birth Through Adolescence,* edited by Joan McCord and Richard E. Tremblay, 3–20. New York: Guilford.

Stewart, Anna, Susan Dennison, Troy Allard, Carleen Thompson, Lisa Broidy, and April Chrzanowski. 2015. "Administrative Data Linkage as a Tool for Developmental and Life-Course Criminology: The Queensland Linkage Project." *Australian and New Zealand Journal of Criminology* 48: 409–428.

Thornberry, Terence P., David Huizinga, and Rolf Loeber. 1995. "The Prevention of Serious Delinquency and Violence: Implications from the Program of Research on the Causes and Correlates of Delinquency." In *Sourcebook on Serious, Violent, and Chronic Juvenile Offenders,* edited by James C. Howell, Barry Krisberg, J. David Hawkins, and John J. Wilson, 213–237. Thousand Oaks, CA: Sage.

Ttofi, Maria M., David P. Farrington, Alex R. Piquero, and Matthew DeLisi. 2016. "Protective Factors Against Offending and Violence: Results from Prospective Longitudinal Studies." *Journal of Criminal Justice* 45: 1–3.

INDEX

The letter *f* following a page number denotes a figure.

Printed in the USA/Agawam, MA
November 24, 2020

764615.021